West's Law School Advisory Board

CURTIS J. BERGER
Professor of Law, Columbia University

JESSE H. CHOPER
Professor of Law,
University of California, Berkeley

DAVID P. CURRIE
Professor of Law, University of Chicago

YALE KAMISAR
Professor of Law, University of Michigan

MARY KAY KANE
Dean and Professor of Law, University of California,
Hastings College of the Law

WAYNE R. LaFAVE
Professor of Law, University of Illinois

ARTHUR R. MILLER
Professor of Law, Harvard University

GRANT S. NELSON
Professor of Law,
University of California, Los Angeles

JAMES J. WHITE
Professor of Law, University of Michigan

CHARLES ALAN WRIGHT
Professor of Law, University of Texas

CASES AND MATERIALS ON
BANKRUPTCY

Third Edition

By

James J. White
Professor of Law
University of Michigan

Raymond T. Nimmer
Professor of Law
University of Houston

AMERICAN CASEBOOK SERIES®

WEST PUBLISHING CO.
ST. PAUL, MINN., 1996

American Casebook Series, the key symbol appearing on the front cover and the WP symbol are registered trademarks of West Publishing Co. Registered in the U.S. Patent and Trademark Office.

COPYRIGHT © 1985, 1992 WEST PUBLISHING CO.

COPYRIGHT © 1996 By WEST PUBLISHING CO.
                610 Opperman Drive
                P.O. Box 64526
                St. Paul, MN 55164-0526
                1-800-328-9352

All rights reserved
Printed in the United States of America
Library of Congress Cataloging-in-Publication Data

ISBN 0-314-09731-7

To
Nancy and Trish

For
guidance, advice and encouragement

*

Preface

The Preface to the first edition of this book, published in 1984, contained a somewhat apologetic explanation for the subordination of state law creditors' rights to the federal law of bankruptcy. That edition had six chapters devoted mostly to state law questions; this book has none. This is a bankruptcy book, pure and simple. One who wants to learn state creditors' rights law will learn it here only in the interstices of federal decisions decided almost exclusively in the bankruptcy and other federal courts. We find no reason to retreat from the assertions concerning the supremacy of bankruptcy law made in 1984, for today bankruptcy law is appropriating an even larger share of all of the conflicts between debtors and creditors. The scope of the state law of creditors' rights continues to shrink.

The book is aimed principally at questions that arise in and are associated with business bankruptcy. Most of these come up in Chapter 11 cases, large and small. Issues such as those having to do with the stay, lifting of the stay, may also be important for consumer bankruptcy, but they are most frequently litigated in business cases. If one's principal focus is on consumer bankruptcy, that person should probably look elsewhere for a book. We devote only Chapter 10 of this book to the Chapter 7 and Chapter 13 proceedings and Section 4 of Chapter 10 to exemptions. The most interesting and significant legal issues that confront the consumer lawyer are dealt with in those chapters, but that is not our focus. By using the example of a medium sized Chapter 11 case that was filed in Flint, Michigan in 1990 (the Action Auto case), and by setting out many of the documents that were actually filed in that case and following it through the chapters, we hope to lead the student through the various stages of a relatively straightforward Chapter 11 proceeding.

One who has been through this book from beginning to end should understand the function and the issues associated with the administrative powers in Chapter 3, the stay, lifting the stay, postpetition loans, executory contracts as well as the avoidance powers. That person should understand the significance of claims, how they are filed, what is secured and what is not. There is a taste of jurisdiction and venue, and much is made of the Chapter 11 plan and the issues associated with section 1129 and the other sections in Chapter 11.

Our goal is twofold. First, we hope to introduce the student to the basics of business bankruptcy and to the interpretive difficulties that are presented by the Code. Second we hope to stimulate the student's thought about the goals of bankruptcy and how those goals should be modified or met. Like the earlier editions, this one does not emphasize the grand issues of bankruptcy, but as in those, there is plenty here for the teacher who wants to raise such issues.

For one who seeks to build a sound foundation in business bankruptcy and wants a taste of the important problems in consumer bankruptcy, the text should do well. We hope others will find it as good a tool as we have.

J.J.W.
R.T.N.

July '96

Acknowledgements to Third Edition

Both authors wish to thank Stephanie Dement at the University of Houston for her fine work. Michael Barron, '95, Cass Buscher, '96, and Stephen Blanchard and Kathryn West deserve considerable credit for the Michigan branch of the project.

*

Acknowledgements to Second Edition

As in any book, many hands contributed to the final product presented here.

In the Texas branch of the project, deepest gratitude goes to Trish Krauthaus, a lawyer and a friend. As in all of our other projects, Trish provided a solid base of professional insight reviewing content and direction in this project throughout and giving the Texas member of this team invaluable guidance about content, direction and tone for the eventual completion of the product you are now reading. Without her advice, this project would not have been completed.

In the Michigan branch of the project, several students have contributed: Julie Goatley, '91; David Kravitz and Russell Brein, '93; David Gasky, '92; and Tom Pasternak, '91. Robert Fogler, '93, constructed the index. Kathryn West performed in her usual extraordinary way.

J.J.W
R.T.N.

*

Summary of Contents

	Page
PREFACE	v
ACKNOWLEDGEMENTS TO THIRD EDITION	vii
ACKNOWLEGEMENTS TO SECOND EDITION	ix
TABLE OF CASES	xxiii
TABLE OF STATUTES	xxvii

Chapter One. An Introduction to Creditors' Rights Under State Law — 1

Sec.
1. Introduction — 1
2. The Nature of Liability — 2
3. Default, the Onset of Liability — 10
4. Formal Debt Collection of Unsecured Debt — 13
5. Formal Debt Collection of Secured Debt — 22
6. Priority Among Creditor Claims — 24
7. Informal Debt Collection of Business Debts, Workouts, and Lender Liability — 26
8. Informal Debt Collection; Formal Collection of Consumer Debt, Fair Debt Collection and the Like — 35

Chapter Two. An Introduction to American Bankruptcy Law, Its Purpose and History — 51
1. The Goals of American Bankruptcy Law — 51
2. The History of American Bankruptcy Law — 53
3. A Guide to the Chapters in the Bankruptcy Code — 58
4. The Players, Their Rights and Obligations — 61
5. Interpreting the Bankruptcy Code, Terms and Definitions — 66
6. Life of a Typical Bankruptcy Case — 69

Chapter Three. Bankruptcy Jurisdiction and Venue — 93
1. Jurisdiction of the Bankruptcy Court — 93
2. Venue — 106
3. Jury Trials in Bankruptcy — 112

Chapter Four. Administrative Powers and the Debtor's Estate: Sections 362 and 361, the Automatic Stay and Adequate Protection — 122
1. The Scope of Section 362 — 122
2. The Reach of the Automatic Stay and Property of the Estate, Sections 362 and 541 — 126
3. Which Debtor Is Protected? — 136
4. Lifting the Stay — 149

Sec.	Page
5. Valuing the Secured Creditor's Collateral	166

Chapter Five. Administrative Powers and the Debtor's Estate: the Power to Use, Buy, Sell, Contract, and Borrow, Sections 363 and 364 — 176
1. Introduction — 176
2. Sales Out of Ordinary Course — 179
3. Use of Cash Collateral — 190
4. Paying Creditors and Suppliers — 199
5. Obtaining Credit After the Petition — 206

Chapter Six. Executory Contract: Section 365 — 219
1. Introduction — 219
2. Characterizing the Contract — 223
3. Balancing Interests: Lease and Franchise Agreements — 244
4. Collective Bargaining Agreements — 264

Chapter Seven. Avoidance Powers — 285
1. Introduction — 285
2. Trustee as a Lien Creditor and Purchaser, Section 544 — 286
3. Voidable Preferences, Section 547 — 300
4. Setoff — 347
5. Subordination — 357
6. Fraudulent Conveyances, Section 548 — 365
7. Avoidance of Postpetition Transactions — 419

Chapter Eight. Claims and Priorities — 423
1. Introduction — 423
2. Priority Claims — 428
3. General Unsecured Claims — 457
4. Environmental Claims — 464
5. When Is a Claim Born and How Is It Estimated? — 488
6. Estimating Claims for the Purpose of Distribution — 503

Chapter Nine. Reorganization Plans — 510
1. Introduction — 510
2. Postpetition to Pre-plan — 528
3. Impairment of Claims — 536
4. Classification of Claims — 544
5. Requirements for Confirmation, the Heart of Section 1129 — 562
6. New Value — 575
7. Disclosure, Voting and Pre-packaged Plans — 601
8. Post Confirmation — 635
9. Bankruptcy and the Wealthy Individual Debtor — 637

Chapter Ten. Chapters 7 & 13 — 656
1. Introduction — 656
2. Chapter 7 Liquidation — 663
3. Chapter 13 — 702
4. Exemptions — 732

	Page
INDEX	767

Table of Contents

	Page
Preface	v
Acknowledgements to Third Edition	vii
Acknowledgements to Second Edition	ix
Table of Cases	xxiii
Table of Statutes	xxvii

Chapter One. An Introduction to Creditors' Rights Under State Law — 1

Sec.
1. Introduction — 1
2. The Nature of Liability — 2
    A. Who May Be Sued? — 2
    B. Which Assets May Be Reached? — 5
        Problem 1–1 — 9
        Problem 1–2 — 9
3. Default, the Onset of Liability — 10
4. Formal Debt Collection of Unsecured Debt — 13
    Other (Mostly Obsolete) Formal Modes of Unsecured Debt Collection — 16
    A. Confession of Judgment — 17
    B. Imprisonment and Criminal Prosecution — 18
    C. Receivership — 19
    D. Assignments for the Benefit of Creditors — 20
    E. Wage Assignment — 21
5. Formal Debt Collection of Secured Debt — 22
6. Priority Among Creditor Claims — 24
7. Informal Debt Collection of Business Debts, Workouts, and Lender Liability — 26
    K.M.C. Co. v. Irving Trust Company — 28
    Questions — 34
8. Informal Debt Collection; Formal Collection of Consumer Debt, Fair Debt Collection and the Like — 35
    Bingham v. Collection Bureau, Inc. — 36
    Problem 1–3 — 49

Chapter Two. An Introduction to American Bankruptcy Law, Its Purpose and History — 51

1. The Goals of American Bankruptcy Law — 51
2. The History of American Bankruptcy Law — 53
3. A Guide to the Chapters in the Bankruptcy Code — 58
4. The Players, Their Rights and Obligations — 61
    A. The Bankruptcy Judge — 61
    B. The Trustee — 61

Sec.		Page
4.	The Players, Their Rights and Obligations—Continued	
	C. The "U.S. Trustee"	63
	D. Debtor in Possession	64
	E. Creditors' Committees	65
5.	Interpreting the Bankruptcy Code, Terms and Definitions	66
6.	Life of a Typical Bankruptcy Case	69
	A. Life of a Typical Consumer Chapter 7 or Chapter 13 Case	69
	B. Life of a Typical Chapter 11 Case	70
	Problem 2–1	72
	Problem 2–2	91
	Problem 2–3	91

Chapter Three. Bankruptcy Jurisdiction and Venue — 93

1. Jurisdiction of the Bankruptcy Court — 93
   Problem 3–1 — 99
   In Re Arnold Print Works, Inc. — 99
   Notes and Questions — 105
   Problem 3–2 — 106
2. Venue — 106
   A. Venue of Cases — 106
   B. Venue of Proceedings — 108
   C. Transfer of Venue — 110
      Problem 3–3 — 111
      Problem 3–4 — 111
      Problem 3–5 — 112
3. Jury Trials in Bankruptcy — 112
   Granfinanciera, S.A., Et Al. v. Nordberg, Creditor Trustee of Estate of Chase & Sanborn Corp., f/k/a General Coffee Corp. — 113
   Problem 3–6 — 121
   Problem 3–7 — 121

Chapter Four. Administrative Powers and the Debtor's Estate: Sections 362 and 361, the Automatic Stay and Adequate Protection — 122

1. The Scope of Section 362 — 122
2. The Reach of the Automatic Stay and Property of the Estate, Sections 362 and 541 — 126
   United States v. Whiting Pools, Inc. — 127
   Statutory Exceptions to the Stay — 131
   Problem 4–1 — 131
   In Re Price Chopper Supermarkets, Inc. v. Alpha Beta Company — 132
   Problem 4–2 — 135
   Problem 4–3 — 135
   Problem 4–4 — 136
3. Which Debtor Is Protected? — 136
   In the Matter of Minton Group, Inc. — 137
   Notes and Questions — 140
   Problem 4–5 — 141
   In Re Third Eighty–Ninth Associates — 142
   Notes and Questions — 146
   Note: Ownership and Protection — 148
   Problem 4–6 — 148
   Problem 4–7 — 148

TABLE OF CONTENTS

Sec.	Page
4. Lifting the Stay	149
In Re Jack Yanks and Ruth Yanks, Debtors	150
Notes and Questions	156
Problem 4–8	157
Lifting the Stay, Lack of Adequate Protection, Section 361	157
In Re Alyucan Interstate Corp.	159
Questions	161
Note: Reduction of Equity Cushion	161
Problem 4–9	162
In Re O'Connor	162
Question	166
5. Valuing the Secured Creditor's Collateral	166
In Re Castle Ranch of Ramona, Inc.	167
Notes and Questions	170
Problem 4–10	175

Chapter Five. Administrative Powers and the Debtor's Estate: the Power to Use, Buy, Sell, Contract, and Borrow, Sections 363 and 364 — **176**

Sec.	Page
1. Introduction	176
Problem 5–1	178
Problem 5–2	178
Problem 5–3	178
2. Sales Out of Ordinary Course	179
In Re Naron & Wagner, Chartered	180
Notes and Questions	185
In Re Braniff Airways, Inc., Pension Benefit Guaranty Corporation, Continental Air Lines, Inc. v. Braniff Airways, Inc.	186
Notes and Questions	189
Problem 5–4	189
Problem 5–5	190
3. Use of Cash Collateral	190
Questions	197
Rights of the Secured Creditor in Cash Collateral Absent Agreement.	197
4. Paying Creditors and Suppliers	199
In Re James A. Phillips, Inc.	200
Questions	205
Problem 5–6	206
5. Obtaining Credit After the Petition	206
In Re Roblin Industries, Inc.	209
Problem 5–7	217
Notes	217

Chapter Six. Executory Contract: Section 365 — **219**

Sec.	Page
1. Introduction	219
Problem 6–1	222
Problem 6–2	222
2. Characterizing the Contract	223
In Re Booth	223
Note: Security Interest vs. Lease	229
Lubrizol Enterprises, Inc. v. Richmond Metal Finishers, Inc.	230
Notes and Questions	235
Notes and Questions	237
Problem 6–3	238
In the Matter of James Taylor	238

Sec.		Page
2.	Characterizing the Contract—Continued	
	Questions	244
3.	Balancing Interests: Lease and Franchise Agreements	244
	In Re Lafayette Radio Electronics Corp.	245
	Problem 6–4	256
	Problem 6–5	256
	A Note on Bankruptcy of a Lessor or Seller	257
	In Re Pioneer Ford Sales, Inc.	257
	Note	263
	Problem 6–6	263
	Problem 6–7	263
4.	Collective Bargaining Agreements	264
	Truck Drivers Local 807 v. Carey Transp., Inc.	269
	Questions	280
	Problem 6–8	280
	Problem 6–9	280
	Question	284

Chapter Seven. Avoidance Powers — 285

Sec.		Page
1.	Introduction	285
2.	Trustee as a Lien Creditor and Purchaser, Section 544	286
	Problem 7–1	287
	Note: Article 9 Perfection	287
	Probasco v. Eads	288
	Questions	292
	In Re General Coffee Corp.	292
	Note	298
	Problem 7–2	298
	Problem 7–3	298
	Problem 7–4	299
	Moore v. Bay	299
	Notes and Questions	300
	Problem 7–5	300
3.	Voidable Preferences, Section 547	300
	In Re Union Meeting Partners	303
	Questions	310
	In Re Bohlen Enterprises, Ltd.	311
	Notes and Questions	318
	Problem 7–6	318
	Indirect Preferences and Recovery of Preferences from Persons Who Are Not Themselves Preferred	319
	In the Matter of Compton Corporation	320
	Notes and Questions	330
	Problem 7–7	330
	Problem 7–8	330
	Problem 7–9	330
	Problem 7–10	330
	Problem 7–11	331
	Problem 7–12	331
	Problem 7–13	331
	Problem 7–14	331
	Problem 7–15	332
	Union Bank v. Wolas	332
	Security Interests and Liens	338
	Note: Time of Transfer and Security Transactions	339
	Problem 7–16	339

Sec.	Page
3. Voidable Preferences, Section 547—Continued	
Note: Substantially Contemporaneous	340
Note: Time of Transfer and the Judicial Lien	340
Problem 7–17	341
Problem 7–18	341
In the Matter of Lackow Brothers, Inc.	342
Note on the Section 547(c)(5) Formulae	345
Problem 7–19	346
4. Setoff	347
Smith v. Mark Twain National Bank	349
Problem 7–20	356
Problem 7–21	356
Problem 7–22	357
5. Subordination	357
In Re N & D Properties, Inc.	358
Problem 7–23	363
Problem 7–24	364
Problem 7–25	365
6. Fraudulent Conveyances, Section 548	365
A. Introduction and Background	365
First National Bank of Fairbanks v. Enzler	368
Notes and Questions	373
Problem 7–26	373
Problem 7–27	374
In Re Newman	374
Note	378
B. Intercompany Guaranty Agreements	379
Telefest, Inc. v. VU–TV, Inc.	379
Note: Intercompany Guarantees	387
Problem 7–28	388
Problem 7–29	388
C. Leveraged Buyouts	389
Wieboldt Stores, Inc. v. Schottenstein	390
In Re the Ohio Corrugating Company	405
Note	416
Question	417
Problem 7–30	418
7. Avoidance of Postpetition Transactions	419
Problem 7–31	421
Note	421
Chapter Eight. Claims and Priorities	**423**
1. Introduction	423
Problem 8–1	424
Note	425
2. Priority Claims	428
Secured Creditors	428
Problem 8–2	428
Problem 8–3	429
Dewsnup v. Timm	429
Questions	443
Administrative Expenses and Priority Claims	443
In Re Colortex Industries, Inc.	444
Notes and Questions	456

Sec.	Page
3. General Unsecured Claims	457
In Re Chateaugay Corporation	457
Questions	463
Problem 8–4	463
4. Environmental Claims	464
Midlantic National Bank v. New Jersey Department of Environmental Protection	464
In Re Chateaugay Corp.	472
Notes and Questions	485
Problem 8–5	487
Problem 8–6	487
5. When Is a Claim Born and How Is It Estimated?	488
Kane v. Johns–Manville Corp.	488
Notes and Questions	500
Problem 8–7	501
6. Estimating Claims for the Purpose of Distribution	503
Bittner v. Borne Chemical Co., Inc.	504
Questions	508
Problem 8–8	508
Problem 8–9	508
Chapter Nine. Reorganization Plans	**510**
1. Introduction	510
Questions	523
The Basic Substantive and Procedural Rules in Chapter 11 Proceedings	523
Problem 9–1	526
Note: Plan Negotiation and Leverage	527
2. Postpetition to Pre–plan	528
The Exclusivity Period	528
Notes and Questions	535
Problem 9–2	536
3. Impairment of Claims	536
In Re Rolling Green Country Club	537
Notes and Questions	543
4. Classification of Claims	544
In Re United States Truck Co.	546
In Re Boston Post Road Limited Partnership	550
Problem 9–3	559
Problem 9–4	559
Problem 9–5	560
Problem 9–6	560
Note: Present Value	561
5. Requirements for Confirmation, the Heart of Section 1129	562
In Re Monnier Bros.	564
Questions	569
Matter of D & F Construction Inc.	569
Questions	572
Problem 9–7	572
Note: The 1111(b)(2) Election To Be Treated as a Fully Secured Creditor	573
Problem 9–8	574
Problem 9–9	575
6. New Value	575
In Re Bonner Mall Partnership	576

Sec.		Page
6.	New Value—Continued	
	Kham & Nate's Shoes No. 2, Inc. v. First Bank	593
	Notes and Questions	599
	Problem 9–10	600
	Problem 9–11	600
	Problem 9–12	600
7.	Disclosure, Voting and Pre-packaged Plans	601
	Century Glove, Inc. v. First American Bank of New York	603
	Problem 9–13	609
	Problem 9–14	610
	Questions	611
	In Re Allegheny International, Inc.	612
	Notes and Questions	634
8.	Post Confirmation	635
9.	Bankruptcy and the Wealthy Individual Debtor	637
	Questions	639
	In Re Herberman	640
	Questions	655

Chapter Ten. Chapters 7 & 13 — **656**

Sec.		Page
1.	Introduction	656
	Chapter 13 Consumer Plans	661
	Chapter 7 Compared	661
2.	Chapter 7 Liquidation	663
	In Re Kreps	665
	Problem 10–1	669
	In Re Touchard	669
	Problem 10–2	675
	Note: Discharge from Criminal Restitution Liability	676
	The Discharge, State Restrictions on the Discharge, Sections 524 and 525	676
	Florida Board of Bar Examiners v. G.W.L.	679
	Questions	685
	Duffey v. Dollison	685
	Note	694
	Problem 10–3	695
	Redemption and Reaffirmation, the Consumer Bankrupt and His Automobile, Section 722 and 524(c)	695
	In Re Bell	696
	Notes and Questions	701
	Problem 10–4	701
3.	Chapter 13	702
	A. Eligibility	702
	Confirmation Hearing; Form of Creditor Objections	704
	The Chapter 13 Trustee Appointment, Duties, and Payment	705
	Payment to Trustee	706
	Eastland Mortgage Co. v. Hart	706
	Notes and Questions	714
	Problem 10–5	715
	Note: Johnson v. Home State Bank, Herein of "Chapter 19" and "Chapter 20" Cases	715
	Co–debtor Stay	716
	Priorities and Payment	717
	Secured Creditors	718
	General Creditor, Discrimination and the Floor	719
	Determining the Amount of Payments to Be Made Under the Plan	720

Sec.	Page
3. Chapter 13—Continued	
Requirements for a Confirmable Plan	721
Fidelity & Casualty Company of New York v. Warren	722
Problem 10–6	731
4. Exemptions	732
Introduction	732
Problem 10–7	733
State Exemption Statutes	733
Exemptions in Bankruptcy	743
Exemptions, Liens, and Security Interests	745
Problem 10–8	747
Problem 10–9	747
Exemption of Retirement Benefits, a Special Case	748
Patterson v. Shumate	749
Notes and Questions	756
The Intersection of Fraudulent Conveyance and Exemption Rules	757
Smiley v. First National Bank of Belleville	757
Notes and Questions	765
INDEX	767

Table of Cases

The principal cases are in bold type. Cases cited or discussed in the text are roman type. References are to pages. Cases cited in principal cases and within other quoted materials are not included.

A.H. Robins Co., Inc., In re, 501
A.H. Robins Co., Inc. v. Piccinin, 147
Alan Wood Steel Co., Matter of, 265
Allegheny Intern., Inc., In re, 612, 635
Alyucan Interstate Corp., In re, 159
American Kitchen Foods, Inc., In re, 172
Arnett, In re, 340
Arnold Print Works, Inc., In re, 99
Aulick v. Largent, 326

Bank of Marin v. England, 420
Bell, In re, 696, 701
Berlin, In re, 141
BFP v. Resolution Trust Corp., 378
Bingham v. Collection Bureau, Inc., 36
Bittner v. Borne Chemical Co., Inc., 504, 508
Blackwelder Furniture Co., Inc., In re, 694
Bohlen Enterprises, Ltd., In re, 311, 318
Bonner Mall Partnership, In re, 576, 599
Booth, In re, 223, 229
Boston Post Road Ltd. Partnership, In re, 550
Braniff Airways, Inc., In re, 180, **186**
Brotherhood of Ry., Airline and S. S. Clerks, Freight Handlers, Exp. and Station Emp., AFL–CIO v. REA Exp., Inc., 264, 265
Brown v. Pennsylvania State Employees Credit Union, 677

Cafe Partners/Washington 1983, A New York Ltd. Partnership, In re, 283
Castle Ranch of Ramona, Inc., In re, 167
Celotex Corp. v. Edwards, 105, 106
Century Glove, Inc. v. First American Bank of New York, 603
Chateaugay Corp., In re, 961 F.2d 378, p. **457**

Chateaugay Corp., In re, 944 F.2d 997, p. **472**
Citizens Bank of Maryland v. Strumpf, 125
Coachlight Dinner Theatre of Nanuet, Inc., In re, 694
Coby Glass Products Co., Torigian Laboratories, Inc., 98
Colortex Industries, Inc., In re, 444
Commonwealth Oil Refining Co., Inc., Matter of, 110
Compton Corp., Matter of, 320
Continental Air Lines, Inc., In re, 185
Cooley, In re, 638
Cunningham v. Cunningham, 95

Dewsnup v. Timm, 429
D & F Const. Inc., Matter of, 569
D. H. Overmyer Co. Inc., of Ohio v. Frick Co., 18
Dock of the Bay, Inc., In re, 107
Duffey v. Dollison, 685
Durrett v. Washington Nat. Ins. Co., 378

Eastland Mortgage Co. v. Hart (In re Hart), 706, 714, 715

Farrey v. Sanderfoot, 746
Federal Press Co., Matter of, 503
Fidelity & Casualty Company of New York v. Warren (In re Warren), 722
First Nat. Bank of Fairbanks v. Enzler, 368
Fitzsimmons, In re, 643
Fleet Factors Corp., United States v., 486
Florida Bd. of Bar Examiners v. G. W. L., 679

Gafco, Inc. v. H.D.S. Mercantile Corp., 366
General Coffee Corp., In re, 292, 298
General Motors Acceptance Corp. v. Lum (In re Lum), 562
Granfinanciera, S.A. v. Nordberg, 112, 113

xxiii

xxiv   TABLE OF CASES

Herberman, In re, 640

Industrial Valley Refrigeration and Air Conditioning Supplies, Inc., In re, 185
In re (see name of party)

James A. Phillips, Inc., In re, 199, **200,** 206, 420, 420, 545
Johnson v. Home State Bank, 715

Kaiser Steel Corp. v. Charles Schwab & Co., Inc., 416
Kaiser Steel Corp. v. Jacobs, 417
Kane v. Johns–Manville Corp., 97, 424, **488,** 500, 501
Kelly v. Robinson, 676
Kham & Nate's Shoes No. 2, Inc. v. First Bank of Whiting, 593
K.M.C. Co., Inc. v. Irving Trust Co., 27, **28,** 34
Koch Refining v. Farmers Union Cent. Exchange, Inc., 147
Kreps, In re, 665, 669

Lackow Bros., Inc., Matter of, 310, **342**
Lafayette Radio Electronics Corp., In re, 245
Lawyers Title Insurance Co. v. Madrid (In re Madrid), 378
Levit v. Ingersoll Rand Financial Corp., 320
L.H. & A. Realty Co., Inc., In re, 123
Liberal Market, Inc. v. Malone & Hyde, Inc., 66
Lionel Corp., In re, 179, 185
Lubrizol Enterprises, Inc. v. Richmond Metal Finishers, Inc., 230, 235, 236, 237
Lynch v. Johns–Manville Sales Corp., 148

Martin's Point Ltd. Partnership, Matter of, 524
Matter of (see name of party)
Memphis Bank & Trust Co. v. Whitman, 562
Midlantic Nat. Bank v. New Jersey Dept. of Environmental Protection, 464, 486
Minton Group, Inc., Matter of, 137
Monnier Bros., In re, 564
Moore v. Bay, 299
Murel Holding Corp., In re, 158
Musikahn Corp., In re, 281

Naron & Wagner, Chartered, In re, 180
N & D Properties, Inc., In re, 358
Newman, In re, 374
N.L.R.B. v. Bildisco and Bildisco, 264, 265, 266, 267, 268, 280
Northern Pipeline Const. Co. v. Marathon Pipe Line Co., 56, 95, 96, 97, 98, 99, 106, 112, 266

Norwest Bank Worthington v. Ahlers, 575

O'Connor, In re, 162
Ohio Corrugating Co., In re, 405, 418
O–Jay Foods, Inc., In re, 283

Pacor, Inc. v. Higgins, 105
Patterson v. Shumate, 749
Pennsylvania Dept. of Public Welfare v. Davenport, 676
Perez v. Campbell, 677, 685
Pickens v. Pickens, 732
Pioneer Ford Sales, Inc., In re, 257
Portex Oil Co., In re, 107
Price Chopper Supermarkets, Inc., In re, 132
Probasco v. Eads, 288

Reliable Elec. Co., Inc. v. Olson Const. Co., 704
Roblin Industries, Inc., In re, 199, **209,** 217, 218
Rolling Green Country Club, In re, 537

Saybrook Mfg. Co., Inc., Matter of, 218
Schack Glass Industries Co., Inc., In re, 98
Schweitzer v. Consolidated Rail Corp., 500
Securities and Exchange Commission v. Canandaigua Enterprises Corp., 511
Shopmen's Local Union No. 455, Intern. Ass'n of Bridge, Structural and Ornamental Iron Workers, AFL–CIO v. Kevin Steel Products, Inc., 264, 265
S.I. Acquisition, Inc., Matter of, 147
Smiley v. First National Bank of Belleville, 757
Smith v. Mark Twain Nat. Bank, 349
Strumpf, In re, 125
Sweetwater, In re, 282, 283

Taylor, Matter of, 238
Telefest, Inc. v. VU–TV, Inc., 379
Texlon Corp., In re, 199
Third Eighty–Ninth Associates, In re, 142, 147
Toibb v. Radloff, 637
Touchard, In re, 669
Troy Indus. Catering Service, Matter of, 283
Truck Drivers Local 807, Intern. Broth. of Teamsters, Chauffeurs, Warehousemen & Helpers of America v. Carey Transp. Inc., 269

Union Bank v. Wolas, 332
Union Meeting Partners, In re, 303
United Sav. Ass'n of Texas v. Timbers of Inwood Forest Associates, Ltd., 157, 158, 159, 161
United States v. _____ (see opposing party)
United States Truck Co., Inc., In re, 546

TABLE OF CASES

Vero Cooling & Heating, Inc. v. Doebeck (In re Vero Cooling & Heating), 341

Walat Farms, Inc., In re, 282
Wetmore v. Markoe, 51
Whiting Pools, Inc., United States v., 122, **127**

Wieboldt Stores, Inc. v. Schottenstein, 390, 418
World Financial Services Center, Inc., In re, 98

Yanks, In re, 150, 156

Table of Statutes

UNITED STATES

UNITED STATES CONSTITUTION

Art.	This Work Page
I	95
	97
I, § 8, cl. 4	53
III	95

Amend.	
5	157
7	112

UNITED STATES CODE ANNOTATED
11 U.S.C.A.—Bankruptcy

Sec.	This Work Page
101	58
	66
101 et seq.	256
101(2)	107
101(5)	9
	67
	423
	487
101(8)	716
101(10)	58
101(13)	58
101(24)	661
101(29)	702
101(36)	9
	68
101(37)	9
	68
101(50)	68
101(51)	9
	68
101(51)(c)	91
101(51)(d)	149
101(53)	9
	68
102	67
	193
102(1)	124
105	147
	148
	148
107	486
109	58
	659

UNITED STATES CODE ANNOTATED
11 U.S.C.A.—Bankruptcy

Sec.	This Work Page
109(e)	661
	702
	703
157(e)	121
158(a)(2)	528
Ch. 3	58
Ch. 3, subch. I	58
Ch. 3, subch. II	58
Ch. 3, subch. III	58
Ch. 3, subch. IV	58
301	67
303	67
303(h)	67
303(h)(2)	20
305	58
321—324	61
327	58
329	58
330	216
341	664
341(a)	426
	601
343	601
	664
361	58
	71
	157
	158
	280
	428
361(1)	158
361(2)	158
361(3)	166
362	57
	58
	69
	71
	122
	124
	125
	126
	136
	148
	157
	158
	192
	280
	349
	428

xxvii

xxviii   TABLE OF STATUTES

UNITED STATES CODE ANNOTATED
11 U.S.C.A.—Bankruptcy

Sec.	This Work Page
362 (Cont'd)	657
	664
	677
	678
	744
362(a)	122
	125
	126
	167
362(a)(1)	126
362(a)(2)	126
362(a)(3)	126
362(a)(4)	126
362(a)(5)	126
362(a)(6)	126
362(a)(7)	126
	347
362(b)	123
	125
	126
362(b)(2)	640
362(c)(2)	123
	636
362(c)(2)(C)	123
362(d)	123
	124
	141
	149
362(d)(1)	149
	156
	157
	158
	283
362(d)(1)(A)	124
362(d)(2)	149
	156
	283
362(d)(3)	124
	149
362(e)	124
362(f)	124
362(g)	124
362(h)	124
363	58
	67
	70
	71
	176
	177
	179
	185
	190
	193
	198
	199
	420
363(a)	177
363(b)	177
	179
	180

UNITED STATES CODE ANNOTATED
11 U.S.C.A.—Bankruptcy

Sec.	This Work Page
363(c)(2)	178
	190
363(c)(2)(A)	347
363(c)(2)(B)	347
363(c)(4)	190
	193
363(e)	190
	283
363(h)	640
364	71
	173
	176
	177
	179
	206
	207
	207
	208
	209
	218
364(a)	177
	208
364(b)	177
	208
	209
364(c)	177
	208
	209
	210
	216
	455
364(d)	177
	208
365	58
	71
	219
	220
	221
	222
	236
	237
	244
	245
	263
	266
	268
	280
	282
	283
	677
365(b)	245
365(b)(1)(C)	245
365(b)(3)	245
	256
365(c)(3)	245
365(d)	263
365(d)(1)	219
365(d)(3)	281
365(d)(4)	220
	281

TABLE OF STATUTES

UNITED STATES CODE ANNOTATED
11 U.S.C.A.—Bankruptcy

Sec.	This Work Page
365(d)(10)	220
	257
365(g)	237
365(h)	257
365(i)	257
365(j)	257
365(n)	237
	263
Ch. 5	59
	194
501	676
501—507	67
501(c)	121
502	67
	423
	425
502(a)	423
502(b)	423
502(b)(2)	207
	463
502(b)(7)	245
502(e)	464
503	67
	443
503(b)	216
	456
503(b)(1)	208
503(b)(1)(A)	456
	485
503(b)(1)(B)	456
506	22
	58
	67
	428
	429
	486
	715
506(a)	161
	171
	428
	573
506(b)	161
	428
506(c)	429
	487
506(d)	428
507	67
	218
	425
	443
	657
507(a)	443
507(a)(1)	199
	513
	657
507(a)(3)	443
	514
507(a)(4)	514
507(a)(7)	514
	718

UNITED STATES CODE ANNOTATED
11 U.S.C.A.—Bankruptcy

Sec.	This Work Page
507(a)(8)	443
507(b)	194
	216
509	68
	423
	464
510	357
	364
510(a)	357
510(c)	357
	358
	364
521	701
521(1)	425
521(2)	701
522	59
	70
	633
	656
	657
	658
	665
	732
	743
	744
	748
522(b)	744
	745
522(c)	744
522(c)(1)—(c)(9)	744
522(c)(2)	745
522(d)	743
	744
	745
	749
522(d)(10)	744
522(d)(11)	744
522(e)	745
522(f)	745
	746
	747
	748
522(f)(1)	746
522(f)(1)(A)	746
522(f)(2)	748
522(g)	745
	746
	747
522(h)	745
	746
	747
522(i)	745
	746
523	59
	70
	121
	425
	443
	657
	658

xxix

TABLE OF STATUTES

UNITED STATES CODE ANNOTATED
11 U.S.C.A.—Bankruptcy

Sec.	This Work Page
523 (Cont'd)	665
	695
523(a)	658
523(a)(2)	657
	658
523(a)(3)	658
523(a)(4)	658
523(a)(5)	501
	657
523(a)(6)	657
	658
523(a)(7)	657
	676
523(a)(8)	657
	658
523(a)(9)	658
523(a)(10)	676
523(c)(1)	669
523(d)	657
524	59
	136
	657
	665
	676
	677
	678
	695
	696
524(a)(2)	676
524(a)(3)	676
524(c)	695
	696
524(d)	664
	701
525	658
	665
	676
	677
	678
	685
	694
	695
525(a)	677
	678
	685
525(b)	678
525(c)	678
	695
541	59
	67
	109
	122
	126
	127
	744
	749
541 to 554	59
541(a)	126
541(a)(1)	126

UNITED STATES CODE ANNOTATED
11 U.S.C.A.—Bankruptcy

Sec.	This Work Page
541(a)(5)	126
541(a)(6)	126
	244
	640
541(a)(7)	126
	640
541(b)	127
	744
541(c)	744
541(c)(2)	749
541(d)	744
542	421
542(c)	420
	421
544	59
	64
	69
	229
	286
	287
	298
544 et seq.	63
	71
544(a)	286
	286
	287
	288
	299
544(a)(3)	287
544(b)	109
	286
	300
545	59
	286
546	286
	417
546(e)	417
546(h)	206
547	59
	64
	69
	71
	111
	199
	286
	300
	320
	330
	339
	340
	341
	347
	348
	523
547(b)	286
	302
	339
	345
547(b)(1)	319
547(b)(1)—(b)(5)	301

TABLE OF STATUTES

UNITED STATES CODE ANNOTATED
11 U.S.C.A.—Bankruptcy

Sec.	This Work Page
547(b)(1)–(b)(5) (Cont'd)	302
547(b)(4)	320
547(b)(5)	302
	310
	311
547(c)	286
	302
	303
	339
547(c)(1)	302
	340
547(c)(2)	302
547(c)(3)	340
547(c)(5)	310
	345
	346
	348
547(e)	302
	341
547(e)(1)(A)	339
547(e)(1)(B)	339
	341
547(e)(2)	339
	340
	341
547(e)(3)	310
548	286
	300
	365
	367
	383
	418
548(a)(2)	365
	367
	373
548(a)(2)(A)	366
	367
548(a)(2)(B)	366
549	199
	420
	421
549(b)	421
549(c)	421
550	320
	420
550(a)	417
550(a)(1)	319
	320
	330
550(c)	320
551	365
552	158
	420
	422
552(a)	197
552(b)	422
552(b)(1)	197
	198
	199
552(b)(2)	198

UNITED STATES CODE ANNOTATED
11 U.S.C.A.—Bankruptcy

Sec.	This Work Page
552(b)(2) (Cont'd)	199
	310
553	285
	339
	347
	348
	356
553(a)(2)	348
553(a)(3)	348
	349
553(b)	348
	349
554	464
	656
554(c)	656
Ch. 7	55
	58
	59
	60
	61
	62
	63
	64
	69
	70
	72
	219
	244
	341
	365
	374
	423
	424
	425
	426
	429
	456
	501
	524
	527
	537
	562
	616
	635
	637
	638
	639
	655
	656
	657
	658
	659
	660
	661
	662
	663
	664
	665
	675
	676

TABLE OF STATUTES

UNITED STATES CODE ANNOTATED
11 U.S.C.A.—Bankruptcy

Sec.	This Work Page
Ch. 7 (Cont'd)	696
	701
	715
	716
	718
	719
	720
	721
	722
	732
	748
Ch. 7, subch. III	59
Ch. 7, subch. IV	59
701	61
	663
701—704	61
701—728	663
702	61
	663
704	62
	63
	663
705	663
707(b)	638
722	665
	695
	696
723	9
726	429
	443
	664
726(a)(1)	199
	218
726(a)(2)	218
726(a)(4)	501
727	59
	67
727(b)	67
727(d)	701
741	67
741(8)	417
Ch. 9	58
	59
	60
Ch. 11	2
	9
	52
	53
	55
	57
	58
	59
	60
	63
	64
	65
	69
	70
	71
	72

UNITED STATES CODE ANNOTATED
11 U.S.C.A.—Bankruptcy

Sec.	This Work Page
Ch. 11 (Cont'd)	91
	97
	99
	109
	111
	121
	135
	136
	141
	146
	149
	157
	167
	171
	172
	176
	179
	185
	189
	190
	191
	193
	206
	207
	209
	219
	220
	222
	229
	236
	244
	263
	280
	281
	282
	283
	298
	339
	340
	346
	370
	420
	421
	423
	424
	425
	426
	429
	443
	456
	463
	464
	508
	510
	511
	512
	513
	521
	523
	526

TABLE OF STATUTES

UNITED STATES CODE ANNOTATED
11 U.S.C.A.—Bankruptcy

Sec.	This Work Page
Ch. 11 (Cont'd)	527
	529
	530
	531
	532
	533
	534
	535
	536
	537
	573
	574
	586
	600
	601
	610
	611
	636
	637
	638
	639
	640
	655
	656
	664
	701
	703
	704
	718
	719
	720
	722
Ch. 11, subch. II	60
1101	67
1101(1)	64
1102	65
	193
1102(a)	92
1102(a)(1)	65
1102(a)(2)	65
1103	65
1103(c)	282
1104	63
1107	64
	193
1108	193
1111(b)	551
	574
	599
	600
	719
1111(b)(1)(B)	574
1111(b)(2)	567
	572
	574
1112	175
1113	220
	264
	267
	268

UNITED STATES CODE ANNOTATED
11 U.S.C.A.—Bankruptcy

Sec.	This Work Page
1113 (Cont'd)	269
	280
1114	280
1121	528
	529
	530
	533
1121(d)	532
	533
1121(e)	92
1122	60
	428
	523
	523
	524
	544
	545
	549
	718
	719
1122(a)	544
	560
1122(b)	545
	560
1123	60
	523
1123(a)(3)	536
1123(a)(4)	635
1124	523
	536
	537
	543
1124(3)	537
1125	524
	602
	635
1125(b)	524
	528
	529
1125(c)	602
1125(f)	92
1126	60
	523
1126(b)	611
1126(c)	524
1126(e)	635
1126(f)	523
	536
	541
1126(g)	523
1127	60
	526
	636
1127(b)	636
1127(c)	636
1127(d)	636
1128	526
1129	60
	65
	71

xxxiv   TABLE OF STATUTES

UNITED STATES CODE ANNOTATED
11 U.S.C.A.—Bankruptcy

Sec.	This Work Page
1129 (Cont'd)	72
	166
	185
	280
	428
	429
	512
	523
	524
	525
	541
	545
	553
	561
	562
	573
	722
1129(a)	229
	527
1129(a)(3)	560
1129(a)(7)	423
	424
	501
	524
	525
	537
	560
	562
1129(a)(8)	524
	525
	563
1129(a)(9)	443
	525
1129(a)(9)(A)	717
1129(a)(10)	525
1129(a)(11)	525
	563
1129(b)	229
	525
	527
	544
	560
	563
	572
	635
1129(b)(1)	560
	563
1129(b)(2)	428
	525
	561
	718
1129(b)(2)(A)	525
	563
1129(b)(2)(A)(i)(II)	544
1129(b)(2)(A)(iii)	525
1129(b)(2)(B)	429
	525
	563
1129(b)(2)(C)	525
1141	136

UNITED STATES CODE ANNOTATED
11 U.S.C.A.—Bankruptcy

Sec.	This Work Page
1141 (Cont'd)	508
	526
	637
	704
1141(c)	637
1141(d)	637
1141(d)(1)(A)	636
1142	636
1144	637
1167	264
Ch. 12	60
	563
	705
	706
	716
Ch. 13	2
	52
	55
	58
	59
	60
	63
	64
	69
	70
	207
	219
	425
	426
	537
	563
	638
	639
	656
	659
	660
	661
	662
	663
	664
	665
	676
	696
	701
	702
	703
	704
	705
	706
	715
	716
	717
	718
	719
	720
	721
	722
	732
1301	68
	716

TABLE OF STATUTES

UNITED STATES CODE ANNOTATED
11 U.S.C.A.—Bankruptcy

Sec.	This Work Page
1301 (Cont'd)	717
1301(c)(1)	717
1301(c)(2)	717
1302	63
1302(a)	63
1302(b)	705
1322	60
	705
	717
	721
1322(a)(2)	717
	722
1322(b)	719
	720
1322(b)(1)	718
	719
	720
1322(b)(2)	715
	722
1322(b)(5)	715
1322(c)	714
	715
	722
1322(c)(1)	714
1322(c)(2)	714
1324	704
1325	60
	561
	705
	718
	721
	722
1325(a)(3)	719
	721
	722
1325(a)(4)	719
	720
	721
	722
1325(a)(5)	714
	718
1325(a)(5)(A)	718
1325(a)(5)(B)(ii)	561
1325(b)	719
	722
1325(b)(1)(B)	655
	721
1326	703
1326(b)(1)	717
1326(c)	706
1328	60
	663
	704
1328(a)	691
	704
1328(a)(1)	715
1328(a)(3)	663
	676
1328(h)	663
3411(a)	64

UNITED STATES CODE ANNOTATED
15 U.S.C.A.—Commerce and Trade

Sec.	This Work Page
1692 et seq.	35

18 U.S.C.A.—Crimes and Criminal Procedure

Sec.	This Work Page
1471(b)	94

28 U.S.C.A.—Judiciary and Judicial Procedure

Sec.	This Work Page
157	95
	96
	99
157(a)	96
157(b)(2)(B)	97
157(b)(5)	112
157(c)	96
586	705
586(e)	706
1334	96
	98
1334(c)	97
1334(c)(1)	99
1334(c)(2)	97
	98
	105
1334(d)	99
1408	106
1408(1)	106
	107
1408(2)	107
	110
1409	99
	106
	108
	110
1409(a)	108
	109
1409(b)	108
	109
1409(b)—(e)	108
1409(c)	109
1409(d)	108
	109
1409(e)	109
1411	97
	112
1411(a)	112
1412	110
	111
1473(b)	108
1477	111
1477(a)	110
	111

UNITED STATES CODE ANNOTATED

42 U.S.C.A.—The Public Health and Welfare

Sec.	This Work Page
9601(20)(A)	486

POPULAR NAME ACTS

BANKRUPTCY ACT OF 1898

Sec.	This Work Page
60	300
60(d)	93
67(a)(4)	93
70(c)	286
70(e)	286

BANKRUPTCY REFORM ACT

Sec.	This Work Page
Ch. X	54
	55
	172
	176
	510
	511
	512
	636
Ch. XI	54
	55
	149
	510
	510
	511
	512
Ch. XII	54
	55
	510
	511
Ch. XIII	54
	60
	661

FAIR DEBT COLLECTION PRACTICES ACT

Sec.	This Work Page
803(6)	36
805	36
806	36
807	36
809	36
813	36
814	36

NATIONAL LABOR RELATIONS ACT

Sec.	This Work Page
8(a)(1)	264
8(d)	264

UNIFORM COMMERCIAL CODE

Sec.	This Work Page
1–201(19)	12
1–201(37)	219
	230
1–208	12
2–310(a)	10
Art. 2A	230
3–116(a)	3
Art. 4	356
4–210	319
4–303	421
Art. 6	300
Art. 9	24
	197
	229
	230
	287
	298
	301
	339
9–103	288
	299
9–115	288
9–201	288
	300
9–203	22
	287
	288
Art. 9, pt. 3	339
9–301	24
	287
	288
	300
9–306	190
	197
	198
9–307	339
9–310	24
9–401	288
9–402	288
Art. 9, pt. 5	22
9–504	22
9–505	22
9–506	696

FEDERAL TAX CODE

Sec.	This Work Page
401—408	748

UNIFORM FRAUDULENT CONVEYANCE ACT

Sec.	This Work Page
4	365

TABLE OF STATUTES

UNIFORM FRAUDULENT CONVEYANCE ACT

Sec.	This Work Page
5	365
	367
6	367
7	365
8	367
9(1)(a)	365

UNIFORM FRAUDULENT TRANSFER ACT

Sec.	This Work Page
3(b)	378
4	367
5	367

UNIFORM PARTNERSHIP ACT

Sec.	This Work Page
40	9

FEDERAL RULES OF BANKRUPTCY PROCEDURE

Rule	This Work Page
810	61

FEDERAL RULES OF BANKRUPTCY PROCEDURE

Rule	This Work Page
1007	601
1007(d)	193
	196
1014	110
	111
1014(a)(1)	110
1014(a)(2)	111
2002	193
2002(i)	192
2004	601
3002	425
	703
3002(c)	425
3003	425
3003(b)	425
3003(c)(3)	426
3004	704
3006	121
3014	573
3015	703
3016	602
3017	602
3018	524
	611
3020	704
3020(b)(2)	705
3022	636
4001	193
6007	193
9014	704
	705

CASES AND MATERIALS ON
BANKRUPTCY

Third Edition

*

Chapter One

AN INTRODUCTION TO CREDITORS' RIGHTS UNDER STATE LAW

§ 1. INTRODUCTION

According to Professor Durfee, the American Course in Creditors' Rights originated with the publication of Glenn's Lectures on Creditors' Rights and on "Rights and Remedies of Creditors" that were delivered at the Columbia Law School. Published in 1915, those lectures embodied not only much that we would now call Creditors' Rights, but also much that would be included in courses on Commercial Transactions, Article Nine or Real Property Security, as well as a large block of Bankruptcy.

Until 1970 almost every law school had a course called Creditors' Rights and that course would have dealt primarily with state law of creditors' remedies. With the rise of the consumer movement early in the 1970s, these courses became known as courses in Creditors' Rights and Debtors' Remedies. By increments between 1970 and 1985 bankruptcy law took a larger percentage of such courses year by year. With the passage of the new Bankruptcy Code in 1978 and with changes that had occurred in the practice between World War II and 1978, that encroachment upon state law creditors' rights courses by the federal bankruptcy law and the encroachment upon the creditors' rights practice by the bankruptcy law became more rapid. Today, for the first time since 1920, it is easy for a student to go through law school without any significant introduction to state law creditors' remedies. What had been staples of the curriculum in the 1930s and 1940s are now thought to be so insignificant that little or no time is devoted to them in the curricula of many law schools.

If there were more time, one could justify a careful examination of state law creditors' rights. A knowledge of state law creditors' rights is not likely to be critical for any practicing lawyer for its own sake. But that law and the rights that theoretically belong to the creditor—even if they are never exercised—are the foundation upon which negotiations between debtors and creditors proceed and upon which the bankruptcy law itself is built. With the explosive increase in bankruptcy filing and with the resort to bankruptcy at an earlier stage in a proceeding than would have occurred in earlier times, bankruptcy seems to be swallowing up state law collection actions. Today, an attempt to foreclose on a consumer debtor's mortgage is likely to be met by a filing of a Chapter 13 petition. The pursuit of a business debtor's assets on a judgment that has been received on a contract action is likely to result in a Chapter 11 filing. It is our impression that this pervasive use of bankruptcy has led to a corresponding decline in the use of state law collection devices. There are, of course, exceptions, but on balance we believe that a thorough knowledge of bankruptcy law is more important than the knowledge of state law creditors' rights.

With that justification we limit our treatment of state law creditors' rights to the expository discussion—problems and two cases in this chapter. One should not infer from the brevity of the coverage that state law creditors' rights can be ignored. For the few students who will practice creditors' rights in the areas where bankruptcy has not appropriated the field, those rights will be critical. For all students of bankruptcy law, they are important because bankruptcy law cannot be understood without some knowledge of state creditors' rights.

§ 2. THE NATURE OF LIABILITY

Because the beginning of all wisdom in creditors' rights is an understanding of a debtor's liability, we offer a word on the nature of liability. Defining liability requires knowledge of two things: (1) who a creditor may sue to recover a judgment in satisfaction of the debt owed to it, and (2) what assets a creditor may reach in satisfaction of its claim.

A. *Who May Be Sued?*

The answer depends upon the obligation. In the simplest obligation a single debtor signs a note promising to pay a creditor a sum of money on demand. In modern consumer transactions, that note is likely to be transformed into some form of retail installment sales contract, possibly an installment note that provides for periodic monthly payments. If the debtor defaults, the creditor may pursue only those assets owned by the debtor and may not look to assets of others connected with the debtor.

More complex are questions involving multiple parties to a debt liability. Let us look more closely at multiple party situations, starting with a hypothetical from a familiar area. Suppose Lessor A leases an apartment to college students B and C for one year. C drops out of school and leaves town. The scope of B and C's liability is not obvious from the fact that both have signed a lease. One might construe their obligation to require that either pay the full amount. The second possibility is that each is liable only for one half of the rent. Yet a third possibility is that neither is liable unless both can be brought to court in the same suit.

If B and C are held to be "jointly liable," neither B nor C would have liability unless each could be joined by personal service in the same suit. The practical effect of joint liability (given a compulsory joinder rule with personal service of process required) is that B can safely refuse to pay the rent if C leaves the jurisdiction.

On the other hand, if B and C are held to be "severally liable," A can recover the entire amount from either. Such liability is the most common. Since many statutes have eliminated the common law compulsory joinder rule and have converted joint duties into joint and several duties, creditors are generally free to sue either party in a joint obligation and to obtain a full recovery from either. It would be unusual, but not unheard of, for B and C each to owe only half the rent. In that case they would have neither several nor joint liability.

Since joint promisors are bound only by their common duty, the discharge of one promisor normally means the discharge of all promissors. However, in a severally-liable obligation, or in a joint and several obligation, any one debtor can be discharged without necessarily affecting the status of the others. Once again, we see that the conversion by statute of many joint obligations into joint and several obligations has provided the creditor with more flexibility. At the same time, the changes have made the subject of joint and several liability a confusing one. Remember that a joint and several obligation is similar to the old several obligation. Since most joint obligations have been converted by statute to joint and several duties, the old common law distinctions have largely vanished.

Under the Uniform Commercial Code, a party signing a note is liable in the capacity in which he signs. When two or more persons sign as makers, one maker might argue that he is obliged to pay only a pro rata share rather than the entire amount of the note. The UCC deals with this challenge in section 3–116(a):

> Except as otherwise provided in the instrument, two or more persons who have the same liability on an instrument as makers, drawers, acceptors, indorsers who indorse as joint payees, or anomalous indorsers are jointly and severally liable in the capacity in which they sign.

Consequently, a creditor will be able to recover the entire amount of the note from one comaker. The comaker who pays the instrument is, of course, entitled to contribution from the other comakers subject to a rebuttable presumption that, among themselves, each comaker is liable for an equal proportion of the debt.

A partnership, an association of two or more persons to carry on as co-owners of a business for profit, presents liability questions like those discussed above. General partners have joint and several liability for any non-criminal act that occurs in the scope of their partnership. Part of the basis for this liability is the fact that a partnership is not regarded as a completely separate legal entity in the same way as a person or a corporation might be. Each partner is seen as an agent of every other partner. He or she and the other partners are liable for the debts and obligations of the partnership and for the acts of all co-partners—so long as those acts fall within the scope of the partner's responsibility.

In a limited partnership, the liability of some members of the partnership is not joint and several. Usually such individuals have contributed a specified sum to the partnership in return for lessened liability for any obligations that might arise. Limited partners must comply with certain requirements, however, and courts watch closely to assure that partners do not obtain the advantages of a general partner without incurring exposure for liability. For instance, limited partners cannot exercise management control over the partnership.

A corporation is quite different. Its stockholders are merged into its identity and are not liable personally for the obligations of the corporation. In effect, a corporation is treated as separate from its owners and employees. Although the corporate veil is occasionally pierced, stockholders are seldom liable for any corporate debts or obligations. On the other hand, a corporation's directors and officers operate under obligations of trust and confidence to the organization. As such, they are required to act in good faith, and intentional deviations may give rise to liability.

A corporation's stockholders can be routinely subjected to liability as partners only if a corporation has been defectively incorporated. Cases distinguish between organizations whose corporate status fails because of some technical defect and those where an important step in the process of incorporation has been omitted. Parties in the first instance will not be held liable, whereas in the second instance, stockholders may have personal liability for corporate debts.

Business organization law affects credit law by limiting an investor's liability for debts incurred by a separately incorporated business. Even when a corporation is properly created under state law, however, the debts of the subsidiary can be imposed against the parent or owner in some cases by "piercing the corporate veil."

This is not the place to learn the mysteries of piercing the corporate veil. But the student should realize that the power of incorporation to protect shareholders' individual assets has suffered some recent decline in both state and federal law. That is particularly true for corporations which are part of a network of wholly owned subsidiaries of a common parent corporation or that are entirely owned and operated by a single shareholder. For example, federal pension law imposes direct liability on all corporate members of a common control group for certain debts associated with withdrawal from multi-employer pension plans. Another example occurs in bankruptcy where groups of related corporations are often jointly administered and may be "substantively consolidated."

Moreover, the idea that separate legal entities have liability only for their own actions has been under attack in tort and environmental law where some liability "runs with the property." For example, products liability law sometimes imposes "successor liability" on corporate buyers, and federal environmental law puts some clean-up obligations even on subsequent property owners who did no polluting.

Sometimes a creditor may have doubts about the prospective debtor's ability to pay. As a way to reduce its risk, this creditor may require the debtor to find another party willing to act as a guarantor or surety for the debtor's obligation. In effect, the guarantor or surety agrees to satisfy the outstanding debt if the debtor does not. This promise to serve as a "back-up" for the debtor's performance is made, however, with the expectation that the debtor will fulfill its commitment to the creditor. If a guarantor or surety is forced to satisfy the debtor's obligation, the guarantor has the right to recover from the debtor. Consequently, if a creditor unreasonably increases the risk that a guarantor or surety will be called upon to perform or diminishes the rights of the guarantor or surety against the debtor, the surety or guarantor will be discharged. Thus, if a creditor releases a debtor (thereby depriving the surety or guarantor of the right to recovery from the debtor by being subrogated to the creditor's rights) or if the creditor fails to perfect a security interest in the debtor's collateral (so rendering himself unable to recover the debt out of the collateral), the creditor may not be allowed to proceed against the surety or guarantor. Similarly, if the creditor and debtor agreed to extend the time in which payment was required to be made without informing the surety or guarantor, the surety or guarantor may be discharged.

B. Which Assets May Be Reached?

If a creditor has a valid claim against a debtor, it is superficially simple to determine its rights: seize the property, sell it and satisfy the debt from the proceeds, not so? In practice it is not so simple. First, the debtor's interests in various assets may be ill-defined or unclear. If the debtor is a partner, he has certain interests in the partnership assets; if he is the shareholder of a corporation, he has different interests. Once the creditor determines what the debtor's interests are, the creditor may still not be entitled to seize the assets because others have a prior right to those assets—a prior perfected security interest, for example. A creditor's right to seizure could also be frustrated by a law that prohibits the creditor of one joint owner from disrupting the enjoyment of the other non-debtor joint owner. Furthermore, the exemption laws, laws dealing with spendthrift trusts and the like, may withdraw certain of the debtor's assets from the creditor's reach, preserving them instead for the debtor's consumption.

Which assets a creditor may reach depends upon a number of factors. Some assets are simply thought to be inappropriate targets for the creditor. Thus both state and federal law "exempt" a variety of assets from the creditor's reach, thereby ensuring that the debtor will not be left completely destitute. The purpose and effect of these exemption laws is to prevent a creditor from pursuing such remedies as foreclosure, execution, or garnishment with respect to the exempted property. If a debtor possesses only assets that are encumbered by either mortgages or security interests or that may be exempted under state or federal law, an unsecured creditor is out of luck. The creditor will be unable to recover the amount it is owed. Where the debtor possesses some nonexempt unencumbered assets of insufficient value fully to satisfy the creditor's claim, the creditor may proceed against those assets; it is barred, however, from recovering the deficiency out of the remaining exempt assets.

Generally, exemption laws allow debtors to keep such necessities of life as clothing, household furnishings and appliances, tools of the trade, medical aids and the like up to a certain dollar value. Automobiles are often exempted up to a certain dollar value. Debtors are also typically allowed to exempt their unencumbered interest in their residence, at least up to a certain dollar value; in some jurisdictions, the unencumbered interest may be completely exempted.

State exemption laws vary considerably in the sorts of assets covered and the scope of the exemption provided. Some bear vestiges of an earlier era in their explicit exemptions for specific quantities of livestock, church pews, or wagons. Others reflect the more modern exemptions provided in the Bankruptcy Reform Act of 1978. Each gives some idea of the value placed on particular types of property by citizens of a particular state. Several federal statutes exempt such assets as Social Security payments and other disability and pension benefits.

In addition, federal bankruptcy law allows the debtor to choose either the exemptions provided under state law or the federal exemptions specified in the Bankruptcy Code, unless the debtor's state has limited the debtor to state exemptions by "opting out" of the federal exemptions. In Chapter 10 we will study exemptions in bankruptcy.

Exemptions have limits. Initially, one should understand that exemptions apply only to property not subject to a mortgage or other security interest; a creditor holding a mortgage or other consensual security interest on an article of exempt property may usually enforce it despite the exemption law. In addition, nonexempt assets cannot always be converted into exempt assets by one on the verge of bankruptcy for the sole purpose of taking advantage of the exemption laws. Finally, property bought when exempt assets are converted to cash will not normally remain beyond the creditor's reach.

Analogous to the restrictions placed upon a creditor's reach by exemption laws are the limitations on the ability of creditors to satisfy the obligation owed them by seizing a debtor's interest in a spendthrift trust or other restricted asset. Theoretically, a spendthrift trust is created to provide funds for the maintenance of the beneficiary while preserving those funds from his improvidence or incapacity; generally, neither actual improvidence nor incapacity of the beneficiary is required. As such, it may be thought of as ensuring that the debtor has some means of support in much the same way that exemptions are designed to leave the debtor with at least the bare essentials. Examples of restricted assets include employee plans such as pension, stock bonus, disability benefits, death benefits, or profit-sharing plans. Some state statutes expressly provide that a debtor's interest in assets of this nature is not subject to creditors' claims. Others place a limit on the amount that can be exempted.

The extent to which a spendthrift trust is beyond creditors' claims varies widely from state to state. At one extreme are states such as Delaware, Nevada and West Virginia which place both the income and the principal beyond the reach of the creditor if the terms of the trust expressly so provide. See, e.g., Nev.Rev.Stat. 166.110. Some states limit the value of the trust principal to which creditors are denied access; Virginia, for instance, provides an exemption for a spendthrift trust principal up to $500,000. Va.Code Section 55–19. Other states place limits on the amount of income which can be exempted. Oklahoma restricts exempt trust income to $5000 a year while Louisiana sets a maximum of $10,000 a year. 60 Okla.Stat. Section 175.25; La.Ann.-Rev.Stat. 9:2004. New York completely exempts the principal of the trust from creditor claims, but at most exempts only ninety percent of the trust income. Even less of the trust income will be exempted if it is unnecessary for the "reasonable requirements of the judgment debtor and his dependents." N.Y.—McKinney's Civ.Prac.Law & Rules Section 5205(d). In New York and in some of the other states with similar statutes, the effect of the statute has been substantially eviscerated by construing needs as being related to the beneficiary's "station in life."

Ultimately the creditor may be able to reach the fruit of the exempt or spendthrift trust tree. When exempt veterans' benefits are paid and invested in an interest bearing account, or when the proceeds of a spendthrift trust are spent to purchase goods, creditors will be able to reach the assets. Exactly when such assets lose their exempt status is a fruitful source of controversy between debtors and creditors.

Other assets normally considered appropriate targets for creditors may be unavailable to satisfy creditors' claims because of a discrepancy between the type of obligation and the type of ownership interest held by the debtor in the assets. For example, an individual creditor may not be able to reach property that the debtor owns concurrently with another party. One illustration of this restriction is the law concerning entireties property. Entireties property is property held jointly by husband and wife in states that recognize tenancies by the entirety. Traditionally, a tenancy by the entirety was applicable only to real property; some states now recognize it in personal property as well. Each spouse is deemed to be seized of the entire estate rather than the undivided fractional interest held by a joint tenant. Like a joint tenancy, each spouse has a "right of survivorship" whereby the surviving spouse succeeds to the ownership of the property free of any encumbrances incurred by the deceased spouse.

All states recognizing the entireties estate allow a creditor holding the joint obligation of husband and wife to proceed against entireties property. Considerable divergence exists, however, concerning the rights of individual creditors to proceed against entireties property. In most entireties states, a creditor of only one spouse cannot satisfy its claim out of entireties property. In other entireties states, an individual creditor can reach only the debtor spouse's expectancy interest in the right of survivorship. This is not likely to be much use unless the other (nondebtor) spouse is quite sick and soon to die. Only then could a purchaser be certain of succeeding to sole ownership of the property; if the debtor spouse died first, the nondebtor spouse would become the sole owner of the property and the purchaser would have spent money for nothing.

In several entireties states, an individual creditor can reach the debtor's present and expectancy interest. In these states the tenancy by the entirety is severed and a creditor of one spouse would be entitled to receive half of the rents and profits generated by the entireties property. Moreover, at least theoretically, the individual creditor has the right of possession and could even move in with the nondebtor spouse. More likely, the property would be sold at an execution sale and the proceeds would be divided between the creditor and nondebtor spouse.

Finally, a few entireties states retain the common law rule allowing a husband's individual creditors to levy on entireties property but prohibiting satisfaction of the wife's creditors' claims out of entireties property. This common law rule is more frequently followed with respect to satisfaction of joint obligations out of separate property; the husband's separate property is generally held to be subject to the claims of joint creditors while the wife's separate property may or may not be subject to joint claims, depending upon the state.

Even in states not recognizing the tenancy by the entirety, the "what asset" problem arises in the slightly different context of a joint bank account. When a bank is served with a garnishment notice for or wishes to setoff a debt owed by only one of the depositors, the issue of what portion of the account is garnishable or may be setoff arises. There is a rebuttable presumption in many states that a bank account is owned in equal percentages by each of the joint depositors and thus no more than half of the account can be reached by an individual creditor.

As a general rule, property owned jointly is subject to the claims of individual creditors, but the judgment lien will attach only to the interest of the debtor owner. Thus the creditor must be certain to get judgment within the lifetime of both owners; if its debtor dies before it gets a judgment, the co-owner will succeed to sole ownership of the property unencumbered by any obligations incurred by the deceased co-owner.

Similar restrictions exist in the partnership context. The Uniform Partnership Act, enacted in all but one state, seals partnership assets from the individual creditors of debtor partners. U.P.A. section 25 (1969). The individual creditor's exclusive remedy against partnership assets is a sort of lien known as a "charging order." Upon due application of a judgment creditor, a charging order is imposed by court order against the debtor partner's "interest" in the partnership, defined elsewhere as "his share of the profits and surplus." The individual creditor thus receives all payments from the partnership that otherwise would have gone to the debtor partner. The creditor may then foreclose on the charging order and, if he purchases the debtor-partner's interest, the creditor may ultimately terminate the partnership, thus forcing distribution of partnership assets.

Creditors of the partnership, on the other hand, may proceed against the assets of the partnership or of the individual partners.

Where partnership creditors and individual creditors seek the same assets, states follow the "jingle rule" codified in U.P.A. section 40 (1969). Under that rule, partnership creditors have priority with respect to partnership assets while individual creditors are granted priority with regard to individually owned assets. The old Bankruptcy Act also followed this rule because of its administrative ease. Section 723 of the Code changes this rule. It allows partnership creditors to retain priority with respect to partnership assets, but also to share equally with individual creditors when it comes to distribution of a partner's personal assets.

Problem 1-1

Chaliapin is a small business filing for bankruptcy under Chapter 11. Flagstad Hydraulics makes parts for Chaliapin. Flagstad recently shipped $20,000 of parts to Chaliapin but did not receive payment prior to the bankruptcy filing. Anderson Construction Company did extensive construction work on Chaliapin's warehouse. Anderson never received its final payment of $15,000. Finally, Sutherland Distribution Inc. prepaid for seven machines produced by Chaliapin. These machines had just been completed when Chaliapin filed. Sutherland had a perfected security interest in the completed machines.

Which of the above creditors has a lien in property of the debtor? (Sections 101(36), (37), (51), (53)).

Which has a claim to property of the debtor? (Section 101(5)).

Problem 1-2

Ponselle owns a steel mill in Reading, Pennsylvania. The company's liabilities are $1,000,000. Its assets could be liquidated for $500,000.

Assume that Ponselle and her husband have total assets of $1,500,000 and liabilities of $750,000.

Assess the ability of the steel mill's creditors to reach the personal assets of Ponselle in each of the following cases.

a. Ponselle operates the company as a sole proprietorship.

b. The company is a corporation; Ponselle owns 99 percent of the stock and manages the company.

c. The company is a partnership; Ponselle is one of two general partners.

d. The company is a partnership; Ponselle is one of two general partners and all of her property is held by the entirety with her husband in a state that recognizes entireties property.

In each case you should be able to determine the dollar amount that could be recovered.

§ 3. DEFAULT, THE ONSET OF LIABILITY

When does liability arise? Here again one must distinguish between two quite distinct issues. One issue deals with what events create an obligation to pay (e.g., money loaned, goods delivered). The other concerns when the payment is due or, failing that, when the creditor can resort to its rights against the debtor's property. Obviously, liability arises and payment is due in a contract whenever the contract so specifies. The creditor in such a case can resort to rights against the debtor when the debtor is "in default", but "default" has no clearly defined meaning. Subject to the contractual requirements of good faith and the limitations imposed by the unconscionability doctrine, liability will arise in the sense of becoming due whenever the agreement between debtor and creditor specifies.

Nonpayment of the indebtedness is the clearest and most universal ground for default. The basic demand note either specifies no particular time for payment or explicitly gives the creditor the right "to demand payment in full at any time." It is immediately "due" as soon as it has been executed and payment is required whenever the creditor demands it. Because the creditor can demand complete payment at any time after the note has been executed—within minutes if it so chooses—the statute of limitations also begins to run from the time of execution.

A time note, on the other hand, is payable only at the specified future time. The statute of limitations does not begin running until that time and default on grounds of non-payment cannot occur before then. In contracts for the sale of goods that are silent on time of payment, it is due "at the time and place at which the buyer is to receive the goods." UCC § 2–310(a). A similar rule requiring payment when the services have been rendered is often applied to service contracts that are silent on the matter of payment.

Many events besides nonpayment may be grounds of default. Some relate to the health of the debtor. Thus the death of an individual debtor or the termination of a business, whether as a result of business reverses or otherwise, could trigger liability. A bankruptcy filing by the debtor or other obligors such as sureties or guarantors could qualify. Other less severe changes in the condition or affairs of the obligors are also likely grounds of default. These might include loss of or damage to property of the obligors by theft or accident, levy or other legal process against such property and entry of any judgment against any of the obligors.

Another ground of default might be uncooperative behavior of the debtor. For instance, refusing to furnish the creditor with requested financial information or to permit inspection of books and records might put the debtor in default. Likewise, misrepresentations willfully made to the creditor could be a default.

The following is a typical default clause:

> **Section 7.** Events of Default; Acceleration. Any or all liabilities shall, at the option of Creditor and notwithstanding any time or credit allowed by any instrument evidencing any Liability, become immediately due and payable without notice or demand upon the occurrence of any of the following events of default: (a) default in the payment, when due and payable, of any amount due and payable hereunder or default in the payment or performances of any of the Liabilities; (b) default in the performance of any obligation or covenant contained or referred to herein; (c) any warranty, representation or statement made or furnished to Creditor by or on behalf of Debtor proves to have been false in any material respect when made or furnished; (d) failure of Debtor, after request by Creditor, to furnish financial information or to permit the inspection of its books and records; (e) any event which results in the acceleration of the maturity of the indebtedness of Debtor to others under any indenture, agreement or undertaking; (f) loss, theft, damage, destruction, sale or encumbrance to or of any of the Inventory, or the making of any levy, seizure or attachment thereof or thereon, or the entry of any judgment against Debtor; (g) death, dissolution, termination of existence, insolvency, business failure, appointment of a receiver of any part of the property of, assignment for the benefit of creditors by, or the commencement of any proceeding under any bankruptcy or insolvency laws by or against, Debtor or any guarantor or surety for Debtor; (h) any change in the condition or affairs, financial or otherwise, of Debtor or of any endorser, guarantor or surety for any of the Liabilities of which, in the good faith opinion of Creditor, impairs Creditor's security or increases its risk.

Upon default, most debt agreements give the creditor the right to "accelerate" the maturity of an installment obligation. Creditors usually insist upon such clauses to avoid an expensive series of lawsuits to collect each installment payment as *it* comes due. The acceleration clause is necessary to allow the creditor to sue for the entire balance in one lawsuit. Absent such a term, the creditor would theoretically have to bring a suit for each installment.

Sometimes no traditional default has yet occurred, but the creditor has reason to believe that such an occurrence is merely a matter of time. For this reason, default clauses are frequently drafted to allow the creditor to accelerate the maturity of the entire debt whenever it "deems itself insecure."

Section 1–208 of the UCC authorizes the use of such insecurity clauses so long as the creditor exercises its rights in "good faith." It provides:

> A term providing that one party or his successor in interest may accelerate payment or performance or require collateral or additional collateral "at will" or "when he deems himself insecure" or in words of similar import shall be construed to mean that he shall have power to do so only if he in good faith believes that the prospect of payment or performance is impaired. The burden of establishing lack of good faith is on the party against whom the power has been exercised.

Good faith is defined in section 1–201(19) as "honesty in fact." While section 1–208 does not require an objective basis for the creditor's actions, it clearly requires more than the creditor's whim to justify action.

Once default has occurred and liability has arisen, the creditor may still lose its right to payment if it waives the debtor's default. The clearest instance of such a waiver is discharge of a debt by accord and satisfaction. A contractual obligation is discharged by accord and satisfaction where a performance different from that claimed as due is rendered and accepted as full satisfaction of the original claim. Thus if a debtor obligated to allow the creditor to inspect its financial records refuses, but does allow the records to be audited from time to time by a third party and the creditor finds the substituted behavior acceptable, accord and satisfaction of a cause of action arising from the debtor's default has occurred and the creditor is barred from recovery. Similarly, suppose a debtor tenders a check to his creditor in a compromise amount between what it acknowledges its debt to be and what the creditor has demanded, clearly indicating that the check is intended to be "in full satisfaction" of the obligation. If the creditor indorses the check without indicating that it intends to preserve its rights to the balance allegedly owed or that it is cashing the check "under protest," it will be bound by accord and satisfaction and will forfeit all rights to recover any additional amount.

Many modern financing arrangements go far beyond traditional ideas of a single loan subject to fixed terms of repayment. Lenders with "revolving" loans secured by inventory, receivables or both may control the debtor's entire cash flow. They may demand continuing information about the debtor's business and their loan agreements may specify anticipated profit or net worth margins. Sometimes the agreement even gives the creditor a right to veto any major business decisions by the debtor. What are defaults and what rights are conferred by a default are quite complicated questions in such cases.

§ 4. FORMAL DEBT COLLECTION OF UNSECURED DEBT

The formal process—from demand for payment through suit to judgment to ultimate sale and collection against an unwilling debtor—can be long and arduous. In most law school classes the inquiry about a plaintiff's rights ends with the judgment. Yet against a clever and recalcitrant defendant, the judgment is only the beginning.

Perhaps we should start with an understanding about the rights that a general creditor does not possess. In the words of Professor Glenn:

> The debt itself confers upon the creditor no title in the debtor's property, nor does it raise any trust or equity therein. All other things being equal, the debtor holds his property free from any right of his creditors to specifically claim it or give directions with regard to its application; they have no title thereto, nor any equity therein.

G. Glenn, *The Rights and Remedies of Creditors Respecting Their Debtor's Property* 1 (1915). What then can an unsecured creditor do to obtain payment from a recalcitrant debtor?

The most ancient remedy for the creditor was to seek a money judgment through the action of debt. An action for debt could be maintained whenever the creditor sought recovery of a certain specific sum of money or of a sum that could readily be reduced to a certainty. A modern instance where this remedy might be used is the open account. An open account exists where individual transactions between the parties are lumped together to give rise to a single ground of liability. Thus where mechanics who are repeat customers of an auto supply store tell the proprietor to put each purchase on their account and then periodically pay the total purchases, an open account has been created.

Originally, an action for debt could be maintained when a creditor sought payment in the form of specific identifiable property as well as in the form of money. By the fifteenth century, however, debt was the appropriate action only where the defendant had promised a specific sum of money or a fixed quantity of fungible goods. Where the defendant had promised a specific chattel as payment, the correct action was detinue. Eventually detinue came to be regarded as a tort rather than contract remedy because it became available against any party wrongfully detaining a chattel belonging to a plaintiff, regardless of the manner in which the defendant came into possession of the chattel. In time its use as a means of enforcing an existing obligation was absorbed by the action of replevin.

The writ of replevin was available only to parties with a right of possession of or a lien on the property to be recovered; only creditors with security could replevy. It was also the only remedy available to creditors at common law that could be employed prior to judgment. The writ of replevin ordered the sheriff to seize the debtor's property and give it to the creditor pending the outcome of the trial. Later statutory modifications in some jurisdictions allowed the debtor to retain possession of the property if he posted a bond sufficient to cover the value of the disputed property. Once widely practiced, replevin is now sharply circumscribed by statutes and Supreme Court decisions.

Technical forms of action have now disappeared. Today's creditors simply file a civil action for the balance owed on the obligation. Frequently the defendant debtor will fail to respond to the suit and the creditor will be able to apply for a default judgment. Once the creditor has filed the default papers, the debtor cannot proceed with the case unless the court is willing to set aside the default.

Upon obtaining judgment, the creditor must find a method to collect. A variety of strategies is available. The classic judgment creditor's remedy is to procure a writ of execution that directs the sheriff to seize the debtor's property and to sell the property to satisfy the judgment and costs.

Perhaps a hypothetical example will help clarify the process. Suppose A owes B $10,000 for the purchase of some farm equipment and has refused to pay the debt. B commences suit with a prayer for the money owed. While the suit is pending, A may dispose of the assets in order to frustrate B's collection. To protect against that, formerly B could have routinely obtained a writ of attachment on A's property to secure the debt in the event he is able to get a judgment. (If B fails to win a judgment, the attachment dissolves.)

Once issued, the attachment order is sent to the sheriff in the county where A's property is located. The sheriff assures that the attached property is not removed from the county. He is also required to make a report to the court's clerk regarding the status of the attached property. These actions by the sheriff, generally referred to as "levy," involve the giving of notice of the encumbrance to both A and the public at large. Such an encumbrance gives creditor B many advantages. He is assured that A will not dispose of the assets through sale. He attains a priority position should A have other creditors, and B's consequent bargaining leverage may speed up a settlement. Finally, attachment provides the court with a basis for jurisdiction over non-residents who own attached property.

Creditors must be cautious in their use of attachment. Since the process makes it virtually impossible for the debtor to sell its property, wrongful attachment may lead to the debtor's recovering damages, either compensatory damages arising directly from the attachment or punitive damages stemming from maliciousness.

Typical state law limitations on the writ of attachment include restrictions on the type of actions in which attachment is available and the grounds on which a writ will be issued. Also there are requirements of notice and hearing before a debtor's goods or property can be seized. The right of attachment is narrow. For example, in Michigan an unsecured creditor will rarely have the right to attach its debtor's goods.

B might also resort to garnishment, a remedy similar to attachment but directed at a third party who holds property belonging to A. Frequent garnishees include the debtor's employer or a bank where the debtor holds an account. Unlike pure attachment, garnishment leaves the property in the care of the garnishee and at common law was used as both a pre- and post-judgment remedy. If used pre-judgment, though, garnishment is subject to many of the same limitations as attachment. Rare indeed is the case where the law permits garnishment of a debtor's wages before judgment.

Once B gets a judgment, either by default or through trial, collection is not automatic. In many states, a judgment is said to have lien status; that is, at the moment it is rendered—or in some states docketed—a judgment creates a lien on the real property of the debtor. This is the classic judicial lien; it is called a "judgment lien."

At this stage, the best remedy for the creditor is the statutory writ of execution issued by the court clerk which gives the creditor the right to have the debtor's real or personal property seized and sold in order to satisfy its claim. The judgment gives B the right to have a writ of execution delivered to the sheriff who then executes it by levying on the property, i.e., actually or constructively taking possession of it. This levy creates the second classic judicial lien; it is called an "execution lien".

After a waiting period in which the debtor can satisfy the judgment and retrieve its property, the sheriff will conduct a public sale of the property. Unlike attachment, which only allows property to be held pending litigation in order to ensure that there will be some means of satisfying any judgment obtained by the creditor, execution is the means by which a judgment may be satisfied.

Suppose, though, B's writ of execution is unable to produce enough property to satisfy the judgment because A has assigned his interests in the property to another person. In this event, B might obtain a creditor's bill to reach such property. Such bills are usually unnecessary, as writs of execution have been extended by statute to cover interests in property that were previously unreachable. B might also obtain a writ of garnishment, which is also available.

Finally, supplemental proceedings may achieve the same results as a creditor's bill through a simple and more summary process. Available only after a writ of execution is returned unsatisfied, supplemental proceedings provide for discovery of a debtor's assets, facilitate an injunction to prevent further disposition of property, create the power to appoint receivers, and render orders for the sale of property.

Most of the foregoing relates in one way or another to the idea of "judicial liens." A lien constitutes a property interest in some particular property of the debtor. For example, in most states a properly recorded judgment is a lien upon the debtor's real estate within the jurisdiction of the court. That is to say, a lien gives a creditor a property interest in the property which, if correctly recorded, will be superior to the rights of a subsequent purchaser of that property, a subsequent mortgagee, or a subsequent lien holder.

The word "lien" has more than one meaning. Ancient courts routinely, and modern courts occasionally, use the word to refer to security interests or claims under mortgages. We use the term to refer not only to "judicial liens" (i.e., those that arise in some cases upon judgment and in other cases upon the sheriff's seizure under a writ of execution, attachment, or garnishment, as described above), but also to other liens commonly known as "statutory liens." Statutory liens are those given by statute to artisans, mechanics, and others who do work on particular property and are not paid. Unlike judicial liens, they arise without the commencement of suit.

One of the issues to which creditors' rights books traditionally devoted many pages is the question of the priority of liens. The rules are many, complex, and of decreasing importance. We will devote some time to the question of judicial lien priority. However, debtors' willingness to declare bankruptcy as soon as the first clouds appear on the horizon and before anyone has acquired a lien has minimized the importance of judicial liens generally and has rendered arcane the study of lien priority.

When bankruptcy was less frequent and taking security was more complicated, the classical means of debt collection by judicial process were undoubtedly more important and more widely used. One who reads the appellate cases and observes an occasional court docket will conclude that only a small minority of all debts are now ever collected by that method.

OTHER (MOSTLY OBSOLETE) FORMAL MODES OF UNSECURED DEBT COLLECTION

In the days before the rise of political power of debtors, creditors were king and everyone knew it. In those days creditors had many rights that have now been taken from them by statute, by constitutional decision, or that have fallen into disuse for other reasons. Even though most of these formal collection devices are completely gone from the laws of most states and are rarely used in others, the student should not assume this is merely a history lesson. Because the abolition of these devices was piecemeal, often by statute or by constitutional mandate necessarily dependent upon a particular set of facts, some of these collection devices doubtless have continued vitality in some areas of practice in some of the states. Even where that is not so, one needs to understand these devices to understand some of the limitations that exist in state consumer credit law and in the Bankruptcy Code. Here we consider five modes of debt collection: confession of judgment, imprisonment and criminal prosecution, receivership, assignments for the benefit of creditors, and wage assignments.

A. Confession of Judgment

A confession of judgment clause in a debt instrument was a powerful tool for shortening the usual collection process. A typical clause which was used in Philadelphia in the early 1950s is as follows:

> The undersigned do hereby authorize and empower the Prothonotary or Clerk, or any attorney, of any court of record of Pennsylvania or elsewhere, now or at any time hereafter, to appear for and to enter judgment against the undersigned for the above sums, with or without declaration filed, with costs of suit, release or errors, without stay of execution and with fifteen percent (15%) of the amount of the principal due added for attorney's fees; and the undersigned also waive the right of inquisition on any real estate that may be levied on to collect this note, and do hereby voluntarily condemn the same and authorize the Prothonotary or Clerk to enter upon fi. fa. said voluntary condemnation, and the undersigned further agree that said real estate may be sold on a fi. fa. and the undersigned hereby waive and release all relief from any and all appraisement, stay or exemption laws of any State, or, of the United States, now in force or hereafter to be passed.

Note, *Confessions of Judgment,* 102 U.Pa.L.Rev. 524, fn. 3 (1954). The above clause is very broad in that it empowers any attorney to act for the debtor at any time (even prior to default), and it waives all right of review of appeal of the judgment or execution and even purports to waive statutory exemptions.

By eliminating the risk of a contested suit and by dispensing with a formal complaint and summons, such a clause obviously makes acquisition of a judgment much easier. It is also a form of security device, because in many states a recorded judgment automatically becomes a lien on the debtor's real property. When the judgment and lien may be created immediately after execution of the debt instrument, as above, the creditor also has the threat of a judicial sale as an informal inducement for the debtor to keep payments current.

The use of such clauses was common in early English debt collection practices and may date as far back as the Greeks in 200 B.C. The common law procedure whereby the defendant acknowledges the plaintiff's demands to be just, *cognovit actionem relecta verificatione*, resulted in common reference to confession of judgment provisions as "cognovit clauses" and instruments containing them as cognovit notes. In essence such clauses are similar to a power of attorney, with both specific and general powers delegated. The special aspects of cognovit clauses are that they appoint a debtor's agent and that they are executed prior to suit.

Although confession of judgment clauses were wonderful devices for shortening the collection process of just debt, their potential for abuse is obvious. Because the debtor would receive no notice of the action against him, he might have his property seized and even sold or his wages garnished without ever having an opportunity to present defenses to the debt action he might have. Because of that, most states greatly restricted the use of confession of judgment clauses and ultimately outlawed them. Where they were not outlawed, such clauses were often held to be unconstitutional because they violated the due process rights of the debtor. See, e.g., *D.H. Overmyer Co. v. Frick Co.*, 405 U.S. 174, 92 S.Ct. 775, 31 L.Ed.2d 124 (1972). Somewhere, someplace in the backwoods of a single state, recognition might still be given to confession of judgment clauses, but we doubt it. We believe that the day of the confession of judgment is over completely; it presents only historical interest.

B. *Imprisonment and Criminal Prosecution*

One of the classic debt collection techniques now infrequently used (but more frequently than we might imagine) is to hold the debtor hostage by threatening him with criminal prosecution or even putting him in jail. At common law and into the early nineteenth century in the United States, imprisonment for debt was accepted and frequently used. For instance, in the states of Massachusetts, Maryland, New York and Pennsylvania there were three to five times as many individuals imprisoned for debt as for crime in 1830. Ford, *Imprisonment for Debt*, 25 Mich.L.Rev. 24, 29 (1926). Reform led to the adoption of constitutional provisions forbidding imprisonment for debt in virtually every state and statutory proscription in several states where the constitution was silent.

Today, only particularly favored creditors can cause their debtors to be imprisoned for nonpayment. Under American law, the right is largely limited to wives to whom alimony and child support have not been paid and who can convince judges to hold their ex-husbands in jail for contempt. Generally, support payments can be enforced as a violation of criminal statutes making it illegal to default on such obligations or through the civil or criminal contempt power of the court. Regardless of the path taken, imprisonment can be the ultimate result although jail may be suspended on condition that support payments are made. In Michigan, for instance, a man in arrears on his support payments may be jailed for up to 90 days, subject to immediate release as a matter of right upon full payment of the arrearage or to release upon the discretion of the court on any terms acceptable to the court. Alternatively, the judge could place the man on probation, give him a suspended sentence or place him under a wage assignment. Because support obligations are imposed by court order in conjunction with divorce proceedings rather than arise out of a private agreement, courts find them easily distinguishable from the usual debt recovery case. Without the ability to enforce orders of support through the use of imprisonment as necessary, the reasoning goes, the court order would be without force or effect and would be unable to command obedience or respect, thereby seriously impairing the integrity of the judicial system.

C. Receivership

Two sorts of formal collection activities may be pursued in conjunction with execution. A judgment creditor unsure as to the value of the judgment debtor's assets may want to exercise its right to an examination of the debtor under oath. Although the precise method of examination varies among jurisdictions, the creditor is generally given the opportunity for a thorough questioning of the debtor and also of any other party alleged to have possession of assets belonging to the debtor. When the court orders an examination of the judgment debtor, the debtor must appear at the specified time and place before a judge or referee and respond under oath to various questions focusing on means of satisfying the judgment. In addition to being questioned about property which could be applied in payment of the judgment, the judgment debtor may also be asked about his income, financial interests and business affairs.

If the judgment creditor knows the judgment debtor has sufficient assets to satisfy the judgment, but is having practical difficulties in getting the judgment debtor to apply the specified property to the judgment or turn it over to the court, appointment of a receiver in aid of execution is appropriate. Essentially a receivership is the judicial appointment of a third party to preserve and ensure proper disposition of property owned by the debtor. Upon appointment, the receiver succeeds to whatever rights of title or possession the debtor had in the property placed in receivership. It may be authorized for personal as well as real property, corporate or individual.

Receivership had its heyday in the early part of the last century during the growth of railroads, financial institutions and other corporate enterprises. Because federal bankruptcy law operated only intermittently in the first part of the nineteenth century and did not apply to corporations in any case, creditors used receiverships as a means of reaching and distributing the assets of corporate debtors. As a result of the addition of corporate reorganization provisions to federal bankruptcy law, receiverships became much less important.

The use of receiverships today is mostly limited to real estate mortgages where it allows the receiver to take possession of the property, to repair or preserve it and to collect rents. In that arena, receivership still offers some advantages over other available remedies. It is generally faster and more convenient than pursuing an ejectment action. It may also allow a mortgagee to avoid some of the strict accounting duties and perhaps to insulate himself from certain tort and related landowner liabilities associated with being a mortgagee.

Nevertheless, even in the real estate context, receivership is not always feasible. Standards for the appointment of a receiver vary widely among the states. In some states appointment of a receiver as a practical matter may be almost impossible due to legislation enacted during the Depression to protect homeowners and farmers; in others, it can be done whenever the mortgagee requests. In several states a receiver will not be appointed unless the mortgagee can show that his security is impaired and perhaps also that the mortgagor is now insolvent; what constitutes impairment is, of course, the subject of much controversy.

D. *Assignments for the Benefit of Creditors*

A similar but broader collection device is the general assignment for the benefit of creditors. This involves the voluntary transfer of all of the debtor's assets to another party in trust to liquidate the assets and distribute the proceeds among the debtor's creditors. Although it resembles a fraudulent conveyance in that legal title passes with the assignment to the assignee and places the property beyond the reach of the debtor's individual creditors, courts have long upheld such assignments as long as they really were for the benefit of creditors.

In most states, assignments for the benefit of creditors are regulated by statute. These statutes usually require recording of the assignment, filing schedules of assets and liabilities and giving notice to the creditors as well as subjecting the debtor-assignor to the supervision of the court. Virtually all states prohibit preferential treatment of creditors except for those with liens or statutorily created priorities. Several states allow the assignee to set aside prior fraudulent conveyances and some permit the assignee to avoid preferential transfers.

The extent to which the assignment for the benefit of creditors remains a useful tool is unclear; regional variations in use seem to exist and reliable data are not available. Some observers have seen assignment for the benefit of creditors as a useful alternative to bankruptcy because of its greater simplicity and economy in reaching the same objective—namely the equitable distribution of a debtor's assets among its creditors. However, even in those states granting the assignee some avoidance powers, a trustee in bankruptcy would have important additional rights to recover property improperly disposed of by the debtor. From the debtor's standpoint too, bankruptcy offers advantages not available in the assignment for the benefit of creditors. Most importantly, bankruptcy discharges the debtor from liability for any deficiency remaining after his assets are liquidated and the proceeds distributed—an assignment for the benefit of creditors does not. In addition, federal exemptions provided by the Bankruptcy Code may be more generous than those allowed by state law.

In most cases both debtor and creditor will prefer bankruptcy to an assignment for the benefit of creditors. If the debtor for some reason prefers the assignment for the benefit of creditors, the creditors can still force the debtor into bankruptcy if they do not think the assignment will best serve their interests. Assuming that the required number of creditors willing to file can be found, section 303(h)(2) of the Bankruptcy

Code makes a general assignment for the benefit of creditors occurring within the previous 120 days a basis for an involuntary petition.

E. *Wage Assignment*

A wage assignment is another potentially powerful and abusive creditor's device, the use of which is now in decline. At first glance it might appear to be no more than a security interest in the "typical" consumer's prime asset, his future earning power. It is somewhat like a general assignment of accounts receivable with an after-acquired clause. Often this analogy holds true in that the creditor's action against the collateral is contingent on default; the creditor proceeds by notifying the employer of the assignment and requesting payment. However, the similarity to garnishment has led consumers and commentators to distrust wage assignments.

Wage assignments were prohibited by early English common law as violating the rules against assigning a chose in action. The rule was gradually relaxed as credit assumed a larger role in the economy, and the first specific American exception allowed seamen to assign their wages for necessaries before a voyage. The permissible scope of wage assignments was gradually expanded, especially in equity courts, to protect other tradesmen and creditors, but was often restricted where there was no employment contract or vested right at the time of the assignment. The use of wage assignments grew with industrialization in the late nineteenth century and by the early 1900's became a common security device in the retail installment loan industry. Abuses and association of the device with loan sharks also progressed in the early 1900's; those abuses prompted state legislatures and courts to regulate the device.

The main policy argument against wage assignments—as with most exemption arguments—is that the debtor and his dependents should not be deprived of a minimal means of support. Otherwise they will become a burden on the public treasury. If all or a significant portion of a debtor's future wages could be diverted to creditors, the debtor could become no more than an indentured servant, lose his incentive to work, and be unable to support his family.

Proponents of the device often argue that since consumers typically have no significant tangible assets, prohibition of wage assignments will eliminate the one viable form of collateral they have and deny them access to credit or greatly increase the cost of available credit. The empirical evidence concerning that argument is generally inconclusive, but one creditors' spokesman concluded that prohibition of wage assignments should produce no significant effects so long as access to wages through post-judgment garnishment is preserved. See Kripke, *Consumer Credit Regulation: A Creditor–Oriented Viewpoint,* 68 Colum.L.Rev. 445, 475 (1968). Some states, however, prohibit both wage assignments and wage garnishment. Creditors in such jurisdictions are left solely with rights to collect from an individual's non-exempt tangible assets.

When this leaves the unsecured creditor with no assets against which to enforce its claim, the term "debtor's liability" begins to lose all meaning.

§ 5. FORMAL DEBT COLLECTION OF SECURED DEBT

Thus far we have focused on the remedies available to unsecured creditors when a debtor defaults. The secured creditor has important additional rights.

Who is a secured creditor? In the preceding section we have already encountered secured creditors, namely, the unsecured creditor who procures a judgment and ultimately a lien. By acquiring that lien he has acquired the status, both under state law and under section 506 of the Bankruptcy Code, of a secured creditor. Here we are not concerned with that form of secured creditor, but rather with the person who becomes a secured creditor by voluntary agreement with the debtor. Such a creditor has complied either with the rules in Article Nine of the Uniform Commercial Code and so acquired a security interest in the personal property of the debtor, or with the applicable state rule concerning mortgages, deeds of trust, land-sale contracts, and the like, to acquire an interest in the debtor's real estate.

If the security is in the debtor's real estate, the creditor's road to recovery may be longer and less smooth than if the security is in the debtor's personal property and the road leads through part 5 of Article Nine of the Uniform Commercial Code. In either case, the state law (real estate law on the one hand and Article Nine on the other) will give the creditor rights not enjoyed by unsecured creditors. Speed, priority, and probability of recovery will always be enhanced and the cost of receiving payment reduced when the creditor is a secured as opposed to an unsecured creditor. The rights that the creditor enjoys arise only partly out of state law. They also arise out of the agreement, i.e., the mortgage or security agreement executed by the debtor.

If the secured creditor and debtor have complied with section 9–203 of Article Nine and so granted an effective security interest to the creditor in certain of the debtor's personal property, the creditor will have the right on default to take possession of the collateral and to dispose of it in satisfaction of its claim so long as it complies with the procedure in sections 9–504 and 9–505. If the creditor can obtain the collateral without breach of the peace, he does not have to go to court at all.

A creditor may also wish to secure an obligation with real estate. One method by which this may be done is the basic mortgage transaction. A real estate mortgage involves a transfer by a debtor-mortgagor to a creditor-mortgagee of real estate interest to be held as security for the payment of a debt evidenced by the mortgagor's promissory note. Initially the mortgage was actually conceived as a conveyance of a piece of property by the debtor to the creditor together with a promise on the part of the creditor to reconvey the property when and if the debtor paid.

As our ideas about security have become more sophisticated, the conveyance by the debtor to the creditor has come to be regarded merely as a conveyance of interest in the property, not as a conveyance of the entire title subject to reconveyance. If the debtor defaults, the creditor-mortgagee may foreclose on the mortgaged property and thereby cause the property to be sold in satisfaction of its claim. Some states permit only judicial foreclosure that requires the creditor-mortgagee to go to court; about half the states permit nonjudicial foreclosure under a power of sale. Many states place restrictions on the ability of the creditor to recover a deficiency judgment where the proceeds from the foreclosure sale are insufficient to satisfy the creditor's claim.

The most common substitute for a mortgage as a land financing device is the land sale contract. It is often used in states permitting judicial foreclosure as the only means of foreclosing a mortgage because it usually does not require court proceeding for foreclosure. Under an installment land contract, the vendee typically goes into possession and agrees to pay the purchase price in monthly installment payments of principal and interest over a period of several years. Legal title to the property is retained by the vendor until final payment is made. If a vendee defaults under such an arrangement, the vendor may pursue the traditional creditor remedies, sue for specific performance of the contract or for damages resulting from the breach, sue to quiet title, or may simply rescind the contract. Because most of these remedies are frequently slow and expensive as well as dependent upon the ability of a vendee to satisfy a money judgment, vendors usually rely on a forfeiture clause that is included in most land contracts. Typically such a clause will provide that "time is of the essence" and will grant the vendor upon the vendee's default the option to declare the contract terminated, to retake the premises and to retain all payments made thus far under the contract as liquidated damages. The forfeiture clause will also relieve the vendor from all further obligations under the contract.

Some states have laws to relieve some of the harshness inherent in the forfeiture remedy. Not surprisingly, these laws vary considerably from state to state. Several states have statutory grace periods during which the vendee may correct his default. Many courts refuse to enforce forfeiture clauses that they view as particularly inequitable. In addition, if a vendor has accepted late payments without taking any action, some courts will find that the vendor has waived his forfeiture rights. The vendee will then be given a redemption period within which the balance of the purchase price may be tendered. In some cases, the vendee will even be allowed simply to cure any arrearage and resume the original payment schedule.

One should understand how significantly secured status magnifies the creditor's rights against the debtor. Because the secured creditor normally commences a procedure directly against the property (by seizure under Article Nine and by replevin or foreclosure), there is no need in most cases to file an elaborate complaint, await an answer and face the prospect that the debtor will cause delay by asking for a jury or by imposing a series of defenses to its liability on an underlying debt claim. Where personal property can be seized without breach of the peace, the seizure, notice and liquidation of the property could all occur within two weeks. For an unsecured creditor to achieve the same result by court process would take no less than several months; it might take several years.

The secured creditor occupies a favored position not only with respect to a recalcitrant debtor but also with respect to other creditors. Assuming the security interest has been properly perfected, the secured creditor's rights are superior to those of an unsecured creditor and of a judicial lien holder (including a trustee in bankruptcy, UCC § 9–301). The secured creditor is not quite so well placed with respect to the statutory lien holder. Statutory lien holders are often given priority over secured creditors unless the law expressly subordinates them to the secured creditor. See section 9–310.

§ 6. PRIORITY AMONG CREDITOR CLAIMS

Invariably in bankruptcy and routinely outside of bankruptcy, the total value of claims against a debtor exceeds the value of the debtor's assets. When that is true, there must be a rule to determine who is paid and who goes wanting. This allocation could be done in many ways. One might treat all creditors equally and distribute the value of the assets pro rata. Or one might give priority to creditors who act faster (and get first to court or to judgment) than their competitors. Or one might give priority to lenders who protect themselves by taking security interests.

In general, Anglo–American law recognizes the right of secured creditors to achieve priority over other creditors. Thus, if the first creditor lends unsecured and a later creditor takes a security interest in an asset of the common debtor, the latter will enjoy priority over the first to the extent of the collateral's value. Among secured creditors, priority is generally determined under a rule of "first in time, first in right." Since multiple events cause the security interest to arise (making the loan, signing the loan documents, filing public notice), the law must determine which act establishes priority. Normally it is the act of giving public notice through a filing or taking possession of the collateral.

Although we will not deal at length with the methods of perfection of either security interests in Article 9 or mortgages under real property rules, our study of the rights of the trustee in bankruptcy to avoid liens and security interests will lead us to some consideration of perfection methods and priority of claims. However, most of the study of the perfection of such interests will be left to courses on Commercial Transactions or Real Estate Finance.

Among unsecured creditors who procure liens, Anglo–American rules of priority can also be summarized generally by "first in time, first in right." Note too that there are some significant exceptions to the "first in time" rule, and that the flat statement "first in time, first in right" is itself quite ambiguous here. For example, in the case of judicial liens, one might argue that the event establishing priority should be any one of a number of occurrences: the date a complaint is filed, the date judgment is rendered, the date the judgment is recorded, the date the sheriff goes on the property and levies, or perhaps even the date the related term of the court commences.

Which of the dates determines priority among judicial lien creditors varies from state to state. Most frequently a judgment lien takes priority from the time of docketing the judgment. An execution lien usually takes priority from the time of the sheriff's levy on the property.

Statutory liens create special priorities among otherwise unsecured creditors. Statutory liens may date from the time of some public notice, from the time labor is provided, or perhaps even from the time the first laborer employed by a contractor appears on the job. In some states, the material supplier, singled out from the great unwashed and favored by the legislature, is first in right though second in time.

Once one has learned the complicated set of rules in Article Nine for personal property and in other state law for real property, the student must then contend with a series of exceptions to these first in time rules. The most pervasive exception to the first in time rule is the rule that says the purchase money lender—one who finances the debtor's purchase of a new asset—will usually be entitled to priority *as to that asset* even over earlier perfected secured creditors. In addition to the purchase money lender, priority is often given to bona fide purchasers or those who have some of the same characteristics as bona fide purchasers, whether they are labelled as holders in due course, buyers in the ordinary course, or purchasers of chattel paper. The student has already met one variant of these in the course on property.

All of these priority rules can be altered by agreement among creditors. In commercial lending, such agreements are common. If a senior creditor cedes its position to a junior creditor, it will have "subordinated" its claim to the junior creditor in a contract called a "subordination agreement." Some subordination agreements provide for subordination of payment, others subordinate a creditor's security interest to another creditor's interest, others subordinate the creditor's rights in bankruptcy. Subordination agreements can be as intricate and detailed as the parties wish to make them.

There are other contractual terms that may have effects like subordination or security agreements. For example, a debtor might enter into a "negative pledge clause." Under such a clause the debtor promises not to grant a security interest to a third party in certain assets, thus, the "negative pledge."

Priorities are also sometimes established by laws that have no apparent relation to creditors' rights or explicit concern for them. For example, priority with respect to corporation assets is indirectly established by the fact that some people take stock and are classified as "shareholders" and others take debt and are classified as "creditors." Their rights are spelled out not in the creditor-debtor law but in corporation law. Individual debtors often have "priority" in certain assets against certain creditors because of state-law exemptions for individuals and families. A common example is the homestead exemption that would keep some or all of the homestead free from the claims of unsecured creditors.

Except to the extent that the trustee is given power to avoid certain security interests and other transfers, the Bankruptcy Code honors state law priorities. We will see that a creditor with a perfected security interest enjoys many rights and protections that are not granted to an unsecured general creditor. To the extent that there are competing secured creditors, one of whom would have priority over another under state law, that priority too is respected in bankruptcy. Although some of the most interesting and challenging questions in bankruptcy have to do with the trustee's avoidance of otherwise effective state law security interests, it is a mistake to regard those avoidance powers as the norm. They are the exception to the general rule of recognition of state law priorities in bankruptcy.

§ 7. INFORMAL DEBT COLLECTION OF BUSINESS DEBTS, WORKOUTS, AND LENDER LIABILITY

There is nothing new about negotiated debt settlement. Such negotiations between debtors and creditors have existed since the first debtor had difficulty in repaying his loan. Because of the large transaction costs—economists might call it dead weight loss—associated with the use of formal debt collection, not the least of which is the lost opportunity cost because of the time involved in transforming a claim against a debtor into money, it is almost always in the creditor's short-run economic interest to accept an immediate payment in cash of less than the full amount due rather than to pursue formal debt collection activity against a recalcitrant or failing debtor. Because a creditor's behavior with one debtor may influence the expectations and therefore the behavior of another, it is sometimes in the creditor's long-run interest to pursue a debtor even when such pursuit in that case will produce a lower return than acceptance of an offered settlement. Of course, if the debtor is not merely recalcitrant, but is in fact failing, and if therefore even the most aggressive formal debt collection will not produce full satisfaction, it is clearly in the creditor's interest to attempt to work out a mutual accommodation.

With the rise of debt as a percentage of assets in large areas of American commerce between 1970 and 1990, and with the growth of debtors' protection law against some of the creditor's most effective remedies—particularly the enactment of the Bankruptcy Code of 1978—it has become necessary for every creditor who does substantial business lending to engage in "workouts." Large lenders even have workout departments. The debtors' power in this negotiation comes from the ability to reduce a creditor's return by going into bankruptcy and so diverting a substantial part of its assets into the hands of lawyers and other creditors. Creditors' leverage in such negotiation arises not only from its legal rights, but also from the promise, explicit or implicit, of future loans and other cooperative behavior with which it tantalizes the debtor.

Of course, the creditor is unlikely merely to use the carrot; it will use the stick too. While offering new loans and a better future out of one side of its mouth, the creditor may be threatening foreclosure, repossession and ruin out of the other side. Worse, the creditor may be promising a glorious future while silently planning a campaign to cut off the debtor's credit and to seize its assets. Whether this behavior amounts to the legitimate assertion of the creditor's rights or to overreaching will depend to some extent upon one's point of view. In other areas creditor overreaching has been regulated by tort law, sometimes by bankruptcy statute, and particularly in consumer cases, by state and federal statute. In the last decade many American courts have handed down decisions based upon ancient common law principles but now organized under the rubric of "lender liability." Most of these cases arise out of creditor behavior upon debtor's threatened or actual default. Many of these cases are the product of a failed workout.

In many of the cases the debtor's claim is based upon the argument that the creditor failed to perform its obligation "in good faith." Debtors and creditors are not likely to share the same definition of good faith. Claims of lender liability may also include allegations of duress, fraud, racketeering (*RICO*), conversion, and most fundamentally, breach of contract. Many courts and juries have awarded large punitive damages in these cases.

Many contemporary allegations of lender liability fall within two categories. In the first, exemplified by the *KMC* case below, the debtor argues the creditor has made a "preemptive strike" and has, for example, closed down the debtor by shutting off the line of credit, by seizure of property, or by setting off against the debtor's bank accounts. Sometimes the debtor will argue that it was not in default. But even if the debtor was in default, some courts have found that particular creditor's acts exceeded those justified by the default. A second and less frequent group of cases involve creditors who take control of debtors' businesses. If a creditor holds a position on the debtor's board of directors, or exercises control over the business decisions of the debtor by threat or otherwise, it runs some risk of liability if those decisions prove to be unsuccessful.

The exact boundaries of "lender liability" are vague. It is not surprising that the initial response of creditors' lawyers to these cases has been to strengthen the wording in loan documents. However, even strongly worded clauses will be no defense against a clever debtor and no impediment to a judge who is sympathetic to a debtor's interests.

As this is written in 1991 the courts have begun to show skepticism about the debtor's injury claims when the creditor is alleged to have taken Draconian but unauthorized steps upon the debtor's default. With rare exceptions, such acts are taken only when things have gone badly because of debtor's earlier miscues. No rational creditor willingly puts a debtor out of business or impairs the debtor's power to pay the debt. This trend against lender liability is represented by a case from the Court of Appeals from the District of Columbia.

> There is no question that the actions of the Bank in this case appear somewhat unseemly. Indeed, we share [the] sentiment * * * that the Bank's 'heavy-handed treatment of its customer without prior notification is cause for dismay.' But, heavy-handed treatment and legally invalid conduct are two separate questions [and the exercise of acceleration and setoff here was not wrongful].[1]

One of the seminal lender liability cases was decided in 1985 by the Court of Appeals for the Sixth Circuit. It is set out below. As you read the case, ask not only whether it is a wise decision, but also how it could have been avoided by the managers or the lawyers for the bank.

K.M.C. CO. v. IRVING TRUST COMPANY
United States Court of Appeals, Sixth Circuit, 1985.
757 F.2d 752.

CORNELIA G. KENNEDY, CIRCUIT JUDGE.

Irving Trust Company (Irving) appeals from a judgment entered against it in this diversity action for breach of a financing agreement. K.M.C. is a Tennessee corporation headquartered in Knoxville and engaged in the wholesale and retail grocery business. In 1979, Irving and K.M.C. entered into a financing agreement, whereby Irving held a security interest in all of K.M.C.'s accounts receivable and inventory and provided K.M.C. a line of credit to a maximum of $3.0 million, increased one year later to $3.5 million at a lower rate of interest, subject to a formula based on a percentage of the value of the inventory plus eligible receivables. On March 1, 1982, Irving refused to advance $800,000 requested by K.M.C. This amount would have increased the loan balance to just under the $3.5 million limit. K.M.C. contends that Irving's refusal without prior notice to advance the requested funds breached a duty of good faith performance implied in the agreement and ultimately resulted in the collapse of the company as a viable business entity. Irving's defense is that on March 1, 1982, K.M.C. was already collapsing, and that Irving's decision not to advance funds was made in good faith and in the reasonable exercise of its discretion under the agreement.

Trial was conducted by a Magistrate on consent of the parties pursuant to 28 U.S.C. § 636(c). Although the financing agreement

---

1. *Boyle v. American Security Bank*, 531 A.2d 1258, 5 UCC2d 896, 900 (D.C.App. 1987).

contained a jury trial waiver clause, the Magistrate ordered a jury trial over defendant's objection. He based his decision upon the statement of plaintiff's president Leonard Butler, that Butler was told by a representative of Irving prior to signing the agreement that absent fraud, which was not present in the instant case, the waiver provision would not be enforced. The jury found Irving liable for breach of contract and fixed damages at $7,500,000 plus pre-judgment interest. Defendant's motions to dismiss and for a directed verdict and post-trial motions for judgment n.o.v., a new trial or a remittitur were denied.

Irving has raised several issues on appeal. First, it suggests that 28 U.S.C. § 636(c) permitting a Magistrate to conduct civil trials with the consent of the parties is unconstitutional. Second, it contends that the Magistrate erred in denying Irving's motion to strike plaintiff's demand for a jury trial. Third, it argues that it did not in fact breach the financing agreement with K.M.C., and that the jury's verdict is not supportable in law and is contrary to the weight of the evidence. Finally, it asserts that the Magistrate erred in admitting incompetent expert testimony on the question of damages.

* * *

[The court found Irving's first two contentions without merit.]

III. LIABILITY

Irving contends that the Magistrate erred in instructing the jury with respect to its obligations under the financing agreement, that K.M.C. failed to sustain its burden of showing that Irving acted in bad faith and that the jury's verdict was against the weight of the evidence. We conclude that the jury instructions were not in error and that the jury's verdict was supported by substantial evidence.

A. *Instructions*

The essence of the Magistrate's instruction to the jury was that there is implied in every contract an obligation of good faith; that this obligation may have imposed on Irving a duty to give notice to K.M.C. before refusing to advance funds under the agreement up to the $3.5 million limit; and that such notice would be required if necessary to the proper execution of the contract, unless Irving's decision to refuse to advance funds without prior notice was made in good faith and in the reasonable exercise of its discretion. Irving contends that the instruction with respect to notice gave undue emphasis to K.M.C.'s theory of the case and was an erroneous explanation of its contractual obligations, in that the decision whether to advance funds under the financing agreement was solely within the bank's prerogative. It reasons further that an implied requirement that the bank provide a period of notice before discontinuing financing up to the maximum credit limit would be inconsistent with the provision in the agreement that all monies loaned are repayable on demand.

As part of the procedure established for the operation of the financing agreement, the parties agreed in a supplementary letter that all receipts of K.M.C. would be deposited into a "blocked account" to which Irving would have sole access. Consequently, unless K.M.C. obtained alternative financing, a refusal by Irving to advance funds would leave K.M.C. without operating capital until it had paid down its loan. The record clearly established that a medium-sized company in the wholesale grocery business, such as K.M.C., could not operate without outside financing. Thus, the literal interpretation of the financing agreement urged upon us by Irving, as supplemented by the "blocked account" mechanism, would leave K.M.C.'s continued existence entirely at the whim or mercy of Irving, absent an obligation of good faith performance. Logically, at such time as Irving might wish to curtail financing K.M.C., as was its right under the agreement, this obligation to act in good faith would require a period of notice to K.M.C. to allow it a reasonable opportunity to seek alternate financing, absent valid business reasons precluding Irving from doing so. Hence, we find that the Magistrate's instructions were an accurate statement of the applicable law. *See Wells v. Alexandre*, 130 N.Y. 642, 29 N.E. 142, 143 (1891)("[I]f a notice was requisite to its proper execution, a covenant to give such notice will be inferred, for any other construction would make the contract unreasonable, and place one of the parties entirely at the mercy of the other." (citations omitted)); *cf.* U.C.C. § 2–309 comment 8 ("[T]he application of principles of good faith and sound commercial practice normally call for such notification of the termination of a going contract relationship as will give the other party reasonable time to seek a substitute arrangement.").

* * *

We [are not] persuaded by Irving's reasoning with respect to the effect of the demand provision in the agreement. We agree with the Magistrate that just as Irving's discretion whether or not to advance funds is limited by an obligation of good faith performance, so too would be its power to demand repayment. The demand provision is a kind of acceleration clause, upon which the Uniform Commercial Code and the courts have imposed limitations of reasonableness and fairness. * * * The Magistrate did not err in refusing the requested charge on the demand provision.

Irving did not object to the good faith portion of the Magistrate's instruction. Nevertheless, on appeal it suggests for the first time that before liability can be imposed, the proof must establish not only abuse of discretion but also bad faith, which it defines as synonymous with dishonesty. Even if such an argument were timely at this stage in the proceedings, which it is not, none of the cases cited by Irving are on point. * * * We conclude that the abuse of discretion standard under which the issue of liability was decided in the trial below was the correct one to apply in this instance.

B. *Sufficiency of the Evidence*

In diversity cases we look to the law of the state whose substantive law governs the action in determining whether there is sufficient evidence to support the jury's verdict. Under New York law, we may not set aside the jury's verdict unless the evidence so preponderates in favor of Irving that it is clear that the jury did not reach its conclusion on a fair interpretation of the evidence, or a contrary conclusion is the only reasonable one inferable from the proven facts. * * *

Irving contends that the sole factor determinative of whether it acted in good faith is whether it, through its loan officer Sarokin, *believed* that there existed valid reasons for not advancing funds to K.M.C. on March 1, 1982. It quotes *Blaine v. G.M.A.C.,* 82 Misc.2d 653, 655, 370 N.Y.S.2d 323, 327 (1975), for the proposition that under applicable New York law, it is the bank's "actual mental state" that is decisive. The Magistrate observed that there was competent evidence that a personality conflict had developed between Sarokin and Butler of K.M.C. He suggested that the jury may have concluded that Sarokin abused his discretion in refusing without notice to advance funds despite knowing that he was fully secured because of his disapproval of Butler's management philosophy.

Were the outcome of this case solely dependent upon Sarokin's *subjective* state of mind, we might feel constrained, despite the conclusions of the Magistrate above, to hold that the evidence was insufficient to support the verdict. However, to a certain extent the conduct of Irving must be measured by objective standards. While it is not necessary that Sarokin have been correct in his understanding of the facts and circumstances pertinent to his decision not to advance funds for this court to find that he made a valid business judgment in doing so, there must at least be *some* objective basis upon which a reasonable loan officer in the exercise of his discretion would have acted in that manner. The court in *Blaine* did state that

> [t]he test as to the *good faith* of the creditor in accelerating under an insecurity clause is a matter of the creditor's actual mental state and this is not negatived by showing there was no basis for the creditor's belief, and it is immaterial whether the information upon which the creditor based his determination was in fact not true or the creditor was negligent in not examining to determine whether it was true.

370 N.Y.S.2d at 327 (emphasis added). However, this definition followed the court's statement that "[t]he criterion for permissible acceleration * * * has the *dual* elements of (1) *whether a reasonable man would have accelerated the debt under the circumstances,* and (2) whether the creditor acted in good faith." *Id.* (emphasis added)(citation omitted). There is ample evidence in the record to support a jury finding that no reasonable loan officer in the same situation would have refused to advance funds to K.M.C. without notice as Sarokin did on March 1, 1982.

James Kuharski was executive vice president and manager of secured lending activities for Irving, and two levels above Sarokin in Irving's management hierarchy. Kuharski acknowledged that Irving owed its clients a duty of good faith, that it was not a policy of Irving to terminate financing without notice, and that if Sarokin believed that Irving was adequately secured he would not have been acting in accordance with that duty of good faith to have refused without notice to advance funds to K.M.C.

William Calloway was president of the Park National Bank in Knoxville, which was the depository bank for K.M.C.'s "blocked account" and a 20% participant with Irving in the financing agreement. He also acknowledged that he believed that there is a duty of good faith from a banker to his client that would require a period of notice prior to termination of financing if a loan was well secured. He testified further that on March 1, he believed that the loan to K.M.C. was fully secured as to both interest and principal, and *that any reasonable banker looking at the loan would agree that it was fully secured.*

Gerald Connolly was an attorney in Milwaukee, Wisconsin, one of whose clients was a large wholesaler named Gateway Foods. In response to a call from Butler on March 1, Gateway's president requested that Connolly assist K.M.C. in any way he could. Connolly testified that pursuant to that request he called Sarokin, who acknowledged in their conversation that Irving was adequately secured and that terminating financing would destroy K.M.C., and that Sarokin ultimately agreed to advance the funds requested by K.M.C., in part to give Connolly the opportunity to come to Knoxville and evaluate K.M.C. for the purpose of acquisition by Gateway Foods. Connolly testified that he called Irving the next day en route to Knoxville and was told by a subordinate that Sarokin had changed his mind about advancing funds, and that in a telephone conversation that night Sarokin stated that he had changed his mind and decided to "proceed with his game plan."

In fact, counsel for Irving conceded in his summation to the jury that the bank was adequately secured on March 1, 1982. He argued, however, that what is important is not the amount of security, but the capacity of the debtor to pay back the loan. The jury was entitled to find that a reasonable notice period would not change the ability of K.M.C. to pay the loan. The nature of the security was such that the loan would rapidly be paid down on demand. Irving's quarterly audits and other memoranda regarding K.M.C. consistently stated that the strength of its position was in the inventory, which was readily marketable. As late as two months before the events in question, the quarterly audit had concluded that even in the event of a liquidation of the company no loss would be sustained by Irving.

Generally, there was ample evidence in the record from which the jury could have concluded that March 1 simply was not that unusual a day in the history of the relationship between Irving and K.M.C. Such factors as payables and receivables, cited by Sarokin as the basis for his conclusion that K.M.C. was in a state of financial collapse, were closely monitored by Irving. Moreover, three days later, on March 4, Sarokin agreed to advance $700,000 to K.M.C., increasing its outstanding balance to $3.3 million. While the evidence was in conflict whether K.M.C.'s overall financial condition was deteriorating or improving, there is ample evidence belying Irving's characterization that on March 1, Sarokin was faced with a sudden crisis of unprecedented proportions. On this basis alone, the jury could have found that Irving did not fulfill its obligation of good faith performance to K.M.C. when it cut off financing without prior notice.

Irving also argues that it was entitled to a directed verdict on the ground that Sarokin reasonably believed that even if he advanced the $800,000 requested on March 1, K.M.C.'s checks to its suppliers would bounce in significant number and amount and K.M.C. would fold anyway. The events of March 1 were triggered by K.M.C.'s request the previous Friday for an extension of its line of credit to $4 million. Sarokin testified that he believed that K.M.C. would have required this extension, in addition to its request for $800,000 up to its $3.5 million line, to cover all of its outstanding checks. The evidence was substantially in conflict on whether with the $800,000 all of K.M.C.'s checks would have been honored when presented. The jury, by its verdict, resolved this fact issue in favor of K.M.C. In awarding damages to K.M.C. it found that Irving's breach caused K.M.C.'s injury. Irving does not object that the jury was improperly charged on causation. It necessarily follows from the jury's award of damages to the plaintiff that it found that checks would not have bounced. There was ample evidence in the record from which the jury could have so found. However, the question of whether checks in fact would have bounced is distinct from the question of whether Sarokin reasonably could have believed that they would bounce. On the record before us we do not think that the jury could find that Sarokin could not reasonably have held such a belief. Therefore, the question that we must address is whether such a belief in itself would constitute a valid business reason for Irving to refuse to advance the funds requested by K.M.C. without prior notice. We hold, on the particular facts before us, that it would not.

Whether or not the $800,000 requested would have been sufficient to cover all of K.M.C.'s outstanding checks, Sarokin's abrupt refusal to advance funds to K.M.C. on March 1 amounted to a unilateral decision on his part to wind up the company. If Sarokin had agreed to advance the $800,000 but no more, and checks still had bounced, we would have a different case. But, given that Sarokin knew or should have known that the bank was adequately secured, and that if adequately secured it was Irving's policy that some period of notice would be due before financing was denied, Sarokin's action could only be justified if in some way he reasonably believed that it was necessary to protect the bank's interests. There was ample evidence—in particular, the conclusion of Irving's auditors that no losses would be sustained by the bank in the event of liquidation, and Sarokin's decision on March 4 to advance almost the full amount requested just three days earlier, despite the fact the K.M.C. was in much worse condition because of the intervening damage to its credit standing—from which the jury could have concluded that Sarokin had no such reason in mind and hence that his action was arbitrary and capricious.

Finally, Irving contends that even if a period of notice were required, it would be unreasonable to impose upon it an obligation to continue financing K.M.C. for the length of time that would have been necessary to arrange alternative financing or a sale of the company. If Irving had given K.M.C. 30 days, 7 days, even 48 hours notice, we would be facing a different case. However, no notice was given. Until Sarokin told Butler on the phone the afternoon of March 1 that the $800,000 requested would not be advanced, not even Calloway of the Park Bank or Lipson, who had been sent down to Knoxville by Sarokin the previous Friday to gather information, both of whom lunched with Butler immediately before the call to New York, had any inkling that Sarokin might act as he did. Based upon the reasoning above, whether alternative financing could have been found or a sale arranged is pertinent to causation rather than whether Sarokin acted reasonably and in good faith, and there was ample evidence in the record from which the jury could find that either would have been possible.

IV. Damages

Irving contends that the Magistrate erred in admitting incompetent and nonprobative expert evidence pertaining to K.M.C.'s going concern value. In particular, it objects to the testimony of witnesses Ronnenberg and Wampler.

[The court found that the Magistrate acted properly.]

The judgment is affirmed.

Questions

1. Why did the bank refuse to make an advance to the debtor on March 1, 1982?

2. How much did the bank ultimately lend after the debtor's default?

3. Assume that you had been called to the table on behalf of the bank and asked for your advice. What would you have suggested?

4. One of your colleagues has suggested that *KMC v. Irving Trust* stands for the proposition that a creditor can never enforce a term in a revolving loan agreement that gives it the right to refuse to make new loans without giving the debtor a grace period of at least 30 and probably 90 days. In effect, she maintains that all creditors should regard all revolving loan arrangements, whatever their terms, as requiring 90 days notice before cut off. Do you agree?

Surely we have not seen the end of workouts, failed workouts, or of lawsuits associated with them. Whether lender liability will remain as a recognized rubric in debtor-creditor law is uncertain. We may have seen the highwater mark in such suits; fifteen years from now such cases may have receded back into the law of contracts and tort.

§ 8. INFORMAL DEBT COLLECTION; FORMAL COLLECTION OF CONSUMER DEBT, FAIR DEBT COLLECTION AND THE LIKE

Business workouts, lender liability suits and the like are the grand battles of state creditors' rights; the collection of consumer debt is the guerilla warfare fought on a smaller scale but with equal ferocity in the cities and backwoods. At its worst such debt collection includes various forms of harassment that even rise to the level of explicit threat or infliction of physical injury. Ironically the restrictions on formal debt collection that have been enacted in the last thirty years increase the significance of and enhance the relative payoffs associated with informal debt collection—including even illegal, informal debt collection.

The Congress, and to a lesser extent the state legislatures, have passed a hodgepodge of laws to control the collection of consumer debt. The largest and most comprehensive statute is the Fair Debt Collection Practices Act;[2] that Act contains a number of rules to restrict what were thought to be some of the most odious of the creditors' threats and other behavior, such as communicating with the debtor's employer, using notices that falsely showed commencement of legal action, and harassing telephone calls late at night. These statutes need not deal with the least subtle and the most aggressive of the creditors' acts because those acts (rearranging the debtor's face, poisoning his dog, shooting an occasional shot through his front window at night) would at least be torts, and sometimes, criminal acts.

One should not be fooled into thinking that the rough acts of debt collectors that offend the middle class sense of propriety can be abolished without cost. Doubtless there are consumer debtors who deserve to have their noses rearranged on their faces and many others who procure loans that later appear to be improvidently given. If consumer loans were restricted to those who could have procured them from middle class lenders, the problems of debt collection with which the federal and state statutes are concerned would disappear. Marginal and highly leveraged consumer debtors are no different from highly leveraged commercial organizations. They have no cushion, and when things turn against them, they default. If the creditor's collection devices against such debtors are eliminated, presumably the creditor will stop lending to that class of debtor—including those who could pay, but who are indistinguishable at the outset from those who could not. Those cut off will suffer a decline in their standard of living.

The Fair Debt Collection Practices Act was passed by Congress in 1978. Upon first reading, it appears to be a sweeping regulation of debt collection practices. However, its narrow definition of "debt collector"

---

2. 15 U.S.C. § 1692 et seq. (1988).

greatly limits its scope. Section 803(6) of the Act defines "debt collector"—the only actor covered by the Act—as "any person who uses any instrumentality of interstate commerce or the mail in any business, the *principal purpose* of which is the collection of any debts, or regularly collects or attempts to collect * * * debts * * * due *another*." (emphasis added) Thus, a creditor attempting to collect its own debts is not covered (unless the creditor is itself a collection agency), and presumably may use any methods that were available to it before the Act was passed.

Those collectors covered by the Act are significantly restricted in the actions they may take. For example, they may not call at "inconvenient times" (presumed to be other than 8 a.m. to 9 p.m.), they may not call at all without the attorney's consent if the consumer is represented by an attorney, they may not contact third parties about the debt (including the debtor's employer), and they may not communicate at all with the debtor, other than to advise the debtor of the cessation of collection activities or of further action being taken, if the debtor requests an end to communication or refuses in writing to pay the debt (section 805). In addition, of course, harassment and false or misleading representations are prohibited, and the debtor has a right to written validation of the debt within five days upon demand (sections 806, 807, 809).

A debt collector found to be in violation of the Act faces a civil action from any person aggrieved by the violation, whether the debtor or a third party. In addition, the Act may be enforced administratively, primarily by the Federal Trade Commission. However, if the debt collector can show that the violation was unintentional and the result of a bona fide error despite procedures designed to avoid such errors, or that the actions were taken in conformity with an FTC advisory opinion, the debt collector will escape liability. The debt collector has the burden of proof for these affirmative defenses (sections 813, 814). The following case demonstrates how these regulations play out.

BINGHAM v. COLLECTION BUREAU, INC.

United States District Court, District of North Dakota, 1981.
505 F.Supp. 864.

* * *

VAN SICKLE, DISTRICT JUDGE. This is an action by consumers, Michael and Peggy Bingham, against two related collection agencies, Collection Bureau, Inc. (CBInc), and Collection Bureau of North Dakota, Ltd. (CBLtd) for violations of the Fair Debt Collection Practices Act, 15 U.S.C. Section 1692 *et seq.*

Plaintiffs allege that the defendant CBInc violated the act in the following particulars:

a. Failure to give the written notice required by 15 U.S.C. Section 1692g.

b. The making of an unconscionable interest claim in violation of 15 U.S.C. Section 1692f(1).

c. Harassment by annoying telephone calls in violation of 15 U.S.C. Section 1692d(5).

d. Extortion by threat of imprisonment in violation of 15 U.S.C. Section 1692e(4).

e. Harassment by false threats of intent to take legal action in violation of 15 U.S.C. Section 1692e(5).

f. Slanderous representations that debtors were committing a crime in violation of 15 U.S.C. Section 1692e(7).

g. Falsely threatening nonjudicial attachment and garnishment in violation of 15 U.S.C. Section 1692f(6).

h. False and deceptive means to collect a debt by using two corporations with deceptively similar names in violation of 15 U.S.C. Section 1692e(10).

They alleged that the defendant CBLtd violated the act in the following particulars:

a. That the notice system used by CBLtd used false, deceptive and misleading language in violation of 15 U.S.C. Section 1692e.

b. That CBLtd, by its notice procedure, was guilty of "flat rating" in violation of 15 U.S.C. Section 1692j.

The defendants generally deny all allegations of wrongdoing. They deny that CBLtd is a "flat rater," and allege conscientious efforts to obey the spirit and language of 15 U.S.C. Section 1692, et seq. (Fair Debt Collection Practices Act), while still performing their economic obligation of liquidating bad debts.

FACTS

Mr. Broeckel is the controlling officer of both corporations. He immediately began plans for automation. He completed his automation, to computer, by June 18, 1979. As is developed later, the collection activities herein complained of occurred during and immediately after completion of the automation.

Mr. Broeckel was active in collector's associations, and so was cognizant of the passage of the Fair Debt Collection Practices Act. As a member of such associations he attended seminars regarding the Act, and prepared his employees for the restrictions imposed by the Act prior to its effective date (March 20, 1978). As the material became available, he required his collector personnel to review the current "Manual on Fair Debt Collection Practices Act" published by the American Collectors Association, Inc. This study, coupled with on-the-job training, and a telephone monitoring system, constitute his program intended to assure that any violation would be unintentional, and would occur despite procedures designed to avoid such violations.

Michael and Peggy Bingham are a young married couple who must rely on the unskilled labor market for their livelihood. They have two children, Rebecca, born in 1977, and Robert, born in 1978. Peggy

Bingham, who claims substantial damages to her personality by virtue of the conduct of the collectors, is 22 years old, obese, doll like, described by a psychologist witness as unsophisticated, immature, with limited ability to act without a leader, having an inadequate dependent personality. In 1977 they were living in Brinsmade, North Dakota. Rebecca was born in Mercy Hospital, Devils Lake. The Binghams had made several payments on current services but the 1977 bill and several subsequent accounts had been written off by the creditor hospital, and set over for collection.

March 23, 1979, Mercy Hospital sent to CBLtd a list of accounts for collection. The accounts, due by the Binghams, as transferred showed a balance of $958.65 due, included no loading for interest, and were computed from the hospital records by the hospital finance officer, Mr. Lindell (see exhibits 6 and 47). Since, at that time, the computer operation was not installed, it was set up on a control card (see exhibit 38). Both parties have agreed that the first notice of a five notice system was sent and received sometime between March 23, 1979 and April 24, 1979.

First was the "Urgent" notice (exhibit 46).

April 24, 1979 the "Past Due" notice was sent (exhibit 2).

April 24, 1979 the "Please Take Notice" notice was sent (exhibit 3). (Why they were sent out the same day was never satisfactorily explained except for the suggestion this occurred during the changeover from manual to computer record keeping.)

May 5, 1979 the "Avoid Further Action" notice was sent (exhibit 4).

May 14, 1979 the "Notice of Further Action" notice was sent (exhibit 5).[1]

The five notices elicited no response from either plaintiff. Mr. Bingham explained that:

I had heard from other guys it was hard to talk to the management at Devils Lake so I didn't try.

Mrs. Bingham asserted that she had no recollection of receiving the first notice. She received the second and third cards at the same time. And from the language of the fourth card she perceived a threat to put her in jail. She interpreted the fifth notice as a threat to bring a civil action to collect, carrying it to judgment if necessary. The first payment

---

1. The forms of the five notices used are attached as Appendix 1, 2, 3, 4, and 5. These five notices had in common:
   a. They showed CBLtd as mailer.
   b. They directed payment to Mercy Hospital.
   c. They showed the balance due as $958.65.

CBLtd sent these notices out for a fee of $4.95. They were sent with an understanding between the hospital and the collector that upon completion of the five notice series, the hospital, if it assigned the account for more aggressive collection, would assign it only to CBInc. CBInc took such assignment on a fee schedule which was computed at one-third for collection prior to authorization to sue, and fifty percent if the creditor did in fact authorize suit.

made in 1979 was made on June 1, 1979. It was received by the hospital and credited to a more recent account which had not been written off as a bad debt and set over for collection.

At the conclusion of the five notice program, CBLtd, then partially automated, ran a printout report on the results of the five notice system (see exhibits 16 and 55). One copy of the printout (exhibit 55) was returned about June 20, 1979 with directions to go forward with the next collection stage, that is, the telephone collector stage.

This stage called for skip tracing the debtor to determine whether telephone contacts were possible, and to gather information which would assist in a recommendation to sue or not to sue out the account, while exerting telephonic pressure to effect collection. This stage and the litigation stage were both handled under the name of CBInc.

Upon the return by Mercy Hospital of the Bingham account, with directions to proceed, a control card was made (see exhibit 38). The manual control system and the computer were jointly used, at least until August 1, 1979, in order to assure everyone that the computer system worked. The card was delivered to Vickie Eichbaum, a skip tracer, who traced the Binghams to Maddock, North Dakota. Michael Bingham answered the call to the Maddock number.

In keeping with well established policy the skip tracer, immediately upon learning that she was talking to the debtor, transferred the call to Jerry Huseby whose telephone alias[2] was "Mr. Mattson." The call should normally have gone to Clyde Hardesty whose telephone alias was "Mr. Hager," because Mr. Hardesty was handling the debtors' names from A to F.

Mrs. Bingham testified precisely and consistently as to the time, circumstance, and language of each telephone call. In fact, on cross examination she was unable to discuss the calls except in the order of her recital thus communicating the suggestion of rote rather than recollection testimony. Mrs. Bingham testified:

That all calls except the call-back of June 19, made at 10:30 to 1:00 p.m., were made at 10:30 to 11:00 a.m., and she knew this because they all came while she was preparing potatoes for lunch. That the caller always gave his name (alias), the name of his employer (CBInc.), and the name of the account (Mercy Hospital).

She testified to a total of 14 calls as follows:

> 1. June 11, 1979, Monday. First call a woman may have asked her to hold. Then Mr. Mattson stated he was calling for Mr. Hager. Stated it was about the hospital bill, amount $958.65, inquired about deposits, land, stock, inheritance, jewelry, "do you have a

---

2. The Department of Banks and Financial Institutions of North Dakota administers the Collection Agency Statutes, 13-04-02, et seq., N.D.C.C. Neither this statute nor the regulations issued pursuant to it provide for aliases. It seems that defendants are the only known agency which uses aliases, and for that reason counsel for the Department required the defendants to list the aliases used and the persons using those aliases.

wedding ring?" Told her unless she paid her bills she could go to jail. Asked to have her husband call back.

2. June 18, 1979, Monday. Mr. Hager called. Inquired where Michael worked, she told him but told him not to call the place of work. How much he made. She told him $120.00 a week. Asked for one whole check. She said she could not. Asked for $70.00 from each check. She offered $10.00 per week. He stated that was not enough.

3. June 19, 1979, Tuesday. Mr. Hager called. Said $10.00 was not enough. Said she shouldn't have children if she couldn't afford them. She told him that she, a Catholic, couldn't break her marriage vows.

4. June 20, 1979, Wednesday. Mr. Hager called. Wanted them to borrow the money.

5. June 21, 1979, Thursday. Mr. Hager called. Wanted to be paid right now.

6. June 25, 1979, Monday. Mr. Hager called. Told her to borrow from her parents. Unless paid he would garnish their wages and would have papers served on them.

7. June 26, 1979, Tuesday. Mr. Hager called. Urged them to borrow. Threatened garnishment.

8. June 27, 1979, Wednesday. Mr. Hager called. Said pay by July or else we will serve papers and garnish.

9. June 28, 1979, Thursday. Mr. Hager called and asked if she had the money. She said no.

10. June 29, 1979, Friday. Mr. Hager called.

11. June 29, 1979, Friday. Mr. Hager called in the evening.

12. & 13. July 6, 1979, Friday (long 4th of July weekend). Mr. Hager called. Michael Bingham answered. Hung up. Hager called back in a few minutes. Peggy's mother answered. Told Hager she was paying the phone bill and he was not to call on her phone again.

14. July 11, 1979, Wednesday. Mr. Hager called. She told him "anything further, call my lawyer."

Jerry Huseby (Mattson) testified that he spoke to Peggy on June 11. That despite the policy to record all debtor contacts, he did not record on either the account card (exhibit 38), or the computer (exhibit 45), this call. He denied he has ever threatened any debtor, including Peggy, with "going to jail." He denied any reference to a wedding ring. He knew his call occurred before June 20, 1979, because he had no computer picture to work from. He knew that he was subject to being monitored on the phones, and he had studied the manual.

Clyde Hardesty (Hager) stated that he was on vacation June 2 through 18, 1979. That he knew he was subject to telephone monitoring; that he called at the most on any account every other day. That he realized the danger of a claim of harassment, and as a business man he knew that given the work load of a collector, in excess of 100 calls a day, even an account this size could not be worked more often than every second or third day. He recalled two contacts on the 28th of June, and two contacts on the 11th of July. One was the call-back when he talked to Peggy's mother and one was a late call as authorized by Peggy. He did not always record no-answer calls. He denied using profanity. He denied calling to harass.

As part of the investigation addressed to finally deciding whether to recommend assignment for purposes of suit a collector must inquire into:

Assets, land, savings, investments, including jewelry, employment, wages, capacity to borrow, etc.

He denied making any call on June 19, 1979. He claimed he never has and never would have told a woman she should not have children unless she could afford them. He denies he called on June 20, 1979. He would tell a debtor that legal action to enforce a claim was a possibility and such an action could result in judgment and garnishment in aid of execution. He does ask if a young debtor can get help from parents. He did not and would not tell a debtor that it was illegal to refuse to pay a debt and he or she could go to jail.

On July 2, 1979 he recommended an assignment of the Bingham account and when it was returned to him, in the usual manner referred the claim to the legal department for suit. Return of the assignment began the third stage, reduction of the claim to judgment. In the course of this stage, Binghams received a notice of referral for action (see exhibit 1).

Plaintiffs claim a fraudulent loading of the interest because the original interest was computed from May, 1977 instead of being computed at reduced balances as certain payments were made. However the defendants did compute the interest at the legal rate from the date of last entry as reported by the hospital. And the hospital admission form called for the imposition of interest. I find no substantial error on the part of the defendants.

The following payments were made in the course of the collection efforts:

June 20, 1979	$10.00 paid to hospital
June 26, 1979	$10.00 paid to hospital
July 03, 1979	$10.00 paid to hospital
July 19, 1979	$10.00 paid to hospital
July 25, 1979	$10.00 paid to hospital

This extended recital of the facts is made because of the numerous issues raised as to the application of a statute that has heretofore received little judicial interpretation.

General Principles

In 1977 a new title was added to the Consumer Credit Protection Act. It was the Fair Debt Collection Practices Act, 15 U.S.C. Section

1692, which is in the tradition of "social legislation" so dear to the heart of William O. Douglas.

I also conclude that the standard of ability and conduct to which the debtor is held is on the low end of the spectrum of the "reasonable person."

However the framers of the statute recognized that the vast majority of the collectors are ethical persons and a purpose of the act was not to impose unnecessary restrictions on ethical debt collectors. *U.S.Code Cong. & Admin.News*, 1977, Vol. 2, pp. 1695, 1696.

The drafters recognized that:

Unlike creditors, who generally are restrained by the desire to protect their good will when collecting past due accounts, independent collectors are likely to have no future contact with the consumer and often are unconcerned with the consumer's opinion of them. *U.S.Code Cong. & Admin.News, supra,* p. 1696.

But, nevertheless, the abrasive persuasive collector is the adverse side of the coin of the unctuous persuasive credit extender, and the statute must be considered with that fact in mind.

Finally, in evaluating whether a given language choice tended to deceive, I will apply the principle that actual consumer testimony is not necessary in evaluating the tendency of language to deceive. *Exposition Press, Inc., supra,* p. 872.

This is the approach used by Judge McMillen in Rutyna v. Collection Accounts Terminal, Inc., 478 F.Supp. 980 (N.D.Ill.1979), *see* page 982, paragraph 3.

But I must work from some standard. While I appreciate the truth in Chief Justice Hughes' comment regarding judicial reasoning, unless some standards for determination are developed, rulings at the trial level will be little more than separate mirrorings of personal bias. I feel a proper standard is whether it is more likely so than not so that debtors on the low side of reasonable capacity who read a given notice or hear a given statement read into the message oppressiveness, falsehood or threat.

FINDINGS AND CONCLUSIONS

15 U.S.C. Section 1692k, Civil Liability provides:

(c) A debt collector may not be held liable under this subchapter if the debt collector shows by a preponderance of evidence that the violation was not intentional and resulted from bona fide error notwithstanding the maintenance of procedures reasonably adapted to avoid any such error.

I find, generally, that a program of constant on-the-job training, coupled with telephonic monitoring, supervision, and reference to a standardized manual is a procedure reasonably adapted to avoiding violations of the act.

I find as a fact that CBLtd and CBInc operated in the collection business as one "debt collector" within the meaning of 15 U.S.C. Section 1692a(6).

Turning to the specific mailed notices, and the specific claim that the five notice system communicated false, deceptive and misleading representation: All such conduct is in violation of 15 U.S.C. Section 1692d. Relevant portions of 15 U.S.C. Section 1692e provide:

> A debt collector may not use any false, deceptive, or misleading representation or means in connection with the collection of any debt. Without limiting the general application of the foregoing, the following conduct is a violation of this section: * * *

(2) The false representation of—

(A) the character, amount, or legal status of any debt; or

(B) any services rendered or compensation which may be lawfully received by any debt collector for the collection of a debt. * * *

(4) The representation or implication that nonpayment of any debt will result in the arrest or imprisonment of any person or the seizure, garnishment, attachment or sale of any property or wages of any person unless such action is lawful and the debt collector or creditor intends to take such action. * * *

(13) The false representation or implication that documents are legal process.

Form No. 1, as mailed in the Bingham case, does violate 15 U.S.C. Section 1692e in that it asserts that the creditor is a member of CBLtd, which carries with it an implication of wholesale distribution of credit information and generalized assistance in credit matters.

Form No. 2 contains the same false assertion that the creditor is a member of the collection organization. Otherwise I find no violation of the statute as to it.

Form No. 3 contains the same false assertion of membership. The warning that failure to pay would place the account in "jeopardy" is self-evidently true; and since no adverse consequences of the "jeopardy" were articulated, the form does not make a false representation.

Form No. 4 recites "Avoid Further Action." Plaintiffs claim this language is a violation of 15 U.S.C. Section 1692e(5) in that it is a threat of civil action that is not intended to be taken. In Trans World Accounts, Inc. v. F.T.C., 594 F.2d 212 (9th Cir.1979), cited by the plaintiffs, the collector sent a notice which said in part:

> Failure to appear * * * may result in immediate litigation by our client with ultimate seizure of property, auto, bank accounts * * * if judgment is obtained.

This message was sent by a flat-rater on a format which closely resembled a telegram and was one of a series which specifically talked about litigation, seizure, judgment, employment of counsel, and liability.

I find that the *Trans World Accounts* notices exceeded by far the language pattern of these notices and particularly the language of Form No. 4. "Action" is a positive, emphatic, word. But its use cannot be completely denied to a collector because others have used it with specific reference to the judicial process.

Form No. 5 inquires if recourse to a collection bureau will be the only alternative, and advises that the notice is final. The meaning may be either the last notice, or the debtor's last chance to stop the collection process before some more stringent step is taken. This language invites the conclusion that suit will be considered. It neither says nor invites the conclusion that suit has been decided upon. Plaintiffs raise the same claim of violation of law as was raised to exhibit 4. Again, the CBLtd program contemplated going forward to an aggressive telephone collection effort if the notice procedure failed. Thus I find the notice was not fraudulent.

Before evaluating the lawfulness of the telephone contact program, a few general observations are in order:

The telephone collectors who testified had certain characteristics in common. They were all young, competent verbalizers, with resonate voices and an authoritative manner of speech. They had better than average intelligence and had a touch of arrogance and of ruthlessness.

Telephone contacts as distinguished from personal contacts, while more efficient in terms of number of contacts made, and increased gross collections, are less efficient in terms of excellence of each contact, and extent to which an accurate evaluation of the debtor's situation, capacity, state of mind, etc., can be made.

Statements made and language used in a telephone contact can be and often are more oppressive than the same communication made in a face to face situation.

Plaintiffs claimed a total of fourteen calls. Defendant stated that the policy, subject to judgment decisions of the collector, was to average not more than one call every other day. "Hager" also claimed that aside from the opening call taken by "Mattson" he was on vacation and unable to make that many calls. "Mattson" took the call of June 11. "Hager" was absent until June 18. "Hager" stated he must have been absent until June 24 because he bought gas in North Sioux City, South Dakota, on June 22, and in Fargo on June 23. But the calls were logged on June 21 and June 25. "Hager" could easily have driven to North Sioux City, South Dakota, on the week end of June 21, leaving after work on Thursday. The Binghams made their first remittance generated by the collection effort on June 20. This payment was more likely caused by calls on June 18 and June 19, than the week old call of June 11. And while all telephone contacts are supposed to be logged, admittedly the call records on the computer printouts are not accurate (see exhibits 13 and 45).

Finally, fourteen calls between June 18 and July 11 is about one call every other day. So I conclude that it is more likely so than not so that the schedule of calls reported by Peggy is accurate.

Plaintiffs claim harassment was evidenced by the number of calls and the time of day of the calls. 15 U.S.C. Section 1692d(5) describes the violation of:

> Causing a telephone to ring or engaging any person in telephone conversation repeatedly or continuously with intent to annoy, abuse, or harass any person at the called number.

The calls came in a pattern of four days of calls, then four days of no calls. The calls produced results in terms of payments, and neither Peggy nor Michael told the caller to stop calling until July 11, when he did stop.

So I find no harassment in the number of calls.

As to the time of day of the calls, 15 U.S.C. Section 1692c(a)(1) provides that generally a debt collector may not communicate with the debtor:

> at any unusual time or place or a time or place known or which should be known to be inconvenient to the consumer. In the absence of knowledge of circumstances to the contrary, a debt collector shall assume that the convenient time for communicating with a consumer is after 8 o'clock antimeridian and before 9 o'clock postmeridian, local time at the consumer's location.

I interpret this statute to apply to telephonic communications.

The June 29 evening call was at the suggestion of Peggy. It was not harassment. It was not at an unreasonable time.

The July 6 call was terminated when Michael hung up after both parties were identified to each other. The recall came immediately. That was harassment.

As to the contents of the calls: My conclusion that the calls were made does not include a finding as to the contents of the calls.

As to the call of June 11, and the reference to the wedding ring. Inquiry as to the assets of the debtor is a necessary step for a collector to take. Inquiry as to jewelry, including rings, is not surprising in light of the current news coverage of the liquidation of jewelry because of the inflationary price of gold. I conclude that an inquiry as to assets including jewelry, for example, wedding rings, was made. But the inquiry was not interpreted as the inquirer intended. This is an example of the risk of telephonic communications with the less sophisticated. The applicable statute to this situation is the general prohibition against harassment, 15 U.S.C. Section 1692d.

I conclude that a telephonic inquiry by the collector about personal jewelry, which includes references to highly personal items like wedding rings, does have a natural consequence to harass, and therefore find it was harassment.

As to the threat of "going to jail." Peggy first claimed the threat was embodied in Form No. 4, then she found it again in the call of June 11. I conclude that her testimony as to this threat is not reliable.

As to the call of June 19, and the claimed statement by "Hager" that Peggy should not have children if she could not afford them. This call was one covered by Peggy's testimony from notes. This remark is not the kind which would have been pulled out of thin air by the witness. Her claimed response that she protested she could not violate her marriage vows shows she may be coloring the original remark by her recollection of the response. I conclude that some remark to that sense was made. I also conclude that any remark of that tenor in a telephonic collection contact is egregious and that the remark was harassment.

As to the claim of repeated threats of garnishment not in aid of execution. Peggy admitted she kept no notes of what was said after the first few calls, and her recollections ran together. Cross examination of the collectors demonstrated that they were sensitive to the risk of oppression by inaccurate and repeated threats of judgment, garnishment, attachment, etc., all of which can only follow a decision to sue, a successful suit, and proper procedures in aid of execution of a judgment.

But a discussion of the ramifications of suit does have its place in collection dialogues. I conclude that the plaintiffs have failed to establish that they suffered harassment and abuse because of improper discussions by the collector, of the possibility, and foreseeable consequences of civil action to collect.

There remains the problem of the use of aliases by telephonic collectors. As pointed out before, a telephone contact is an impersonal contact, and is a frustrating and disruptive experience for the unprepared recipient of the call.

Further, the lack of visible contact shields the caller and invites an aggressive caller to overreach. The risk of this sort of overreach is not so great where the conferees meet face to face. But it is greatly increased when the telephonic caller uses the additional shield of an alias.

The telephonic collector justifies the use of an alias to protect himself from abusive return calls to his office, home, etc. But a telephonic collecting technique which produced a substantial body of such reaction would be, for that reason, suspect.

I conclude that the use of an alias by a telephonic collector is conduct the natural consequence of which is to harass, oppress or abuse the debtor in connection with the collection of the debt.

LIABILITY

As to all of those findings adverse to the defendant except that dealing with the use of aliases, I find that the debt collector, specifically the management of the corporation, has shown by a preponderance of the evidence that the violation was not intentional on the part of the corporate collector, but has not shown that it resulted from bona fide errors of its agents. Therefore, liability attaches.

As to the use of aliases, I find that the management of the defendants did show by a preponderance of the evidence that the violation was not intentional and did result from bona fide error, namely, that it assumed it was in compliance with the law in the use and reporting of aliases, therefore, liability for past use of aliases does not attach.

DAMAGES

15 U.S.C. Section 1692k provides in relevant part:

(a) Except as otherwise provided in this section, any debt collector who fails to comply with any provision of this subchapter with respect to any person is liable to such person in an amount equal to the sum of—

(1) any actual damage sustained by such person as a result of such failure;

(2)(A) in the case of any action by an individual, such additional damages as the court may allow, but not exceeding $1,000; * * *

(3) in the case of any successful action to enforce the foregoing liability, the costs of the action, together with a reasonable attorney's fee as determined by the court. On a finding by the court that an action under this section was brought in bad faith and for the purpose of harassment, the court may award to the defendant attorney's fees reasonable in relation to the work expended and costs.

(b) In determining the amount of liability in any action under subsection (a) of this section, the court shall consider, among other relevant factors—

(1) in any individual action under subsection (a)(2)(A) of this section, the frequency and persistence of noncompliance by the debt collector, the nature of such noncompliance, and the extent to which such noncompliance was intentional; * * *.

ACTUAL DAMAGE

The psychologist who testified as to damages based his findings on two hours of observation, including some psychological testing, which occurred a substantial interval after the collection efforts stopped.

He concluded the period of the damage was about a year, that during the year she was no longer childlike in her happiness, that she had lost her interest in housework, that she was not paranoid, but distrustful of telephones. That her sleep was disturbed, she had nightmares, headaches, a sensitive stomach, and was prone to cry. He accepted her statements at face value and despite her obvious physical problems, concluded without further investigation that all her physical problems were psychosomatic, and caused by the wrongful acts of the telephone collectors. The proof of that claim is much too weak to accept.

Peggy herself testified that after the first call she "cried and cried and cried and cried." Her husband said she was still crying when he came home at noon on June 11, 1979.

But the impression that Peggy the witness communicated was that her crying was an habitual response to any difficult situation, and that it continued interminably until something occurred to divert her attention. Nor did the witness demonstrate any excessive depression or unstable personality traits during the several days of trial. She gave instead the impression of one who had always been over protected and had learned how to demand attention and protection from those around her.

I conclude that she suffered no permanent ill effects from the experience of the calls, and that most of her crying was habitual or cosmetic. However, she is of the group to be protected and she has suffered injury.

I find Peggy Bingham has suffered actual injury in the amount of $1000.00. I find Michael Bingham has suffered loss of consortium and therefore actual injury in the amount of $100.00.

Pursuant to 15 U.S.C. Section 1692k(a)(2) and (b)(1), I find that the false statements in the notices and the harassment and abuse in the telephone calls were not frequent and persistent, but were intentional acts by the agents of the defendant, therefore, I assess additional damages in the amount of $400.00.

Pursuant to 15 U.S.C. Section 1692k(a)(3), costs and attorney's fees will be allowed to the plaintiffs. Plaintiffs will prepare, serve and file an affidavit of costs and attorney's fees with a motion for allowance under the local rules.

It Is So Ordered

This Memorandum and Order is deemed to satisfy the requisites of Rule 52 and of the Federal Rules of Civil Procedure:

APPENDIX

App. 1

COLLECTION BUREAU OF NORTH DAKOTA, LTD.

URGENT
This is to confirm your PAST DUE balance as shown by records of our member IS THERE ANY REASON FOR YOUR DELAY IN PAYMENT? Please mail payment at once to our MEMBER or advise today! Kindly do it NOW.

TO THE ATTENTION OF	MAKE PAYMENT DIRECTLY TO	ACCOUNT NO.
XXXXXXXXX XXXXXXXXX XXYYYYYYYY	XXXXXXXXX XXXXXXXXX XY XXYYYYYYYYY	YYYYY PAY THIS AMOUNT XY XXXYYYYYXXXX

ALWAYS USE ENCLOSED RETURN ENVELOPE WITH MEMBERS ADDRESS SHOWING THROUGH WINDOW

App. 2

COLLECTION BUREAU OF NORTH DAKOTA, LTD.

THIS ACCOUNT IS LONG PAST DUE
We expect and INSIST on IMMEDIATE PAYMENT. We intend to be courteous, but collection is our purpose REMIT the balance to our MEMBER NOW.

TO THE ATTENTION OF	MAKE PAYMENT DIRECTLY TO	ACCOUNT NO.
BINGHAM, MICHAEL LEEDS, ND 58346	MERCY HOSPITAL E 7TH ST DEVILS LAKE, ND 58301	104970 PAY THIS AMOUNT 928.65

ALWAYS USE ENCLOSED RETURN ENVELOPE WITH MEMBERS ADDRESS SHOWING THROUGH WINDOW

App. 3

COLLECTION BUREAU OF NORTH DAKOTA, LTD.

PLEASE TAKE NOTICE!
Your account is still reported as DUE! It is IMPORTANT that you pay our MEMBER at once! Do not place your ACCOUNT IN JEOPARDY.

TO THE ATTENTION OF	MAKE PAYMENT DIRECTLY TO	ACCOUNT NO.
BINGHAM, MICHAEL LEEDS, ND 58346	MERCY HOSPITAL E 7TH ST DEVILS LAKE, ND 58301	104970 PAY THIS AMOUNT 928.65

App. 4

COLLECTION BUREAU OF NORTH DAKOTA, LTD.

AVOID FURTHER ACTION!
The decision is now yours.
DELAY CANNOT BE TOLERATED
ACT NOW TO PROTECT YOUR CREDIT AND AVOID POSSIBLE ADDITIONAL EXPENSES.

TO THE ATTENTION OF	MAKE PAYMENT DIRECTLY TO	ACCOUNT NO.
BINGHAM, MICHAEL LEEDS, ND 58346	MERCY HOSPITAL E 7TH ST DEVILS LAKE, ND 58301	104970 PAY THIS AMOUNT 928.65

ALWAYS USE ENCLOSED RETURN ENVELOPE WITH MEMBERS ADDRESS SHOWING THROUGH WINDOW

App. 5

COLLECTION BUREAU OF NORTH DAKOTA, LTD.

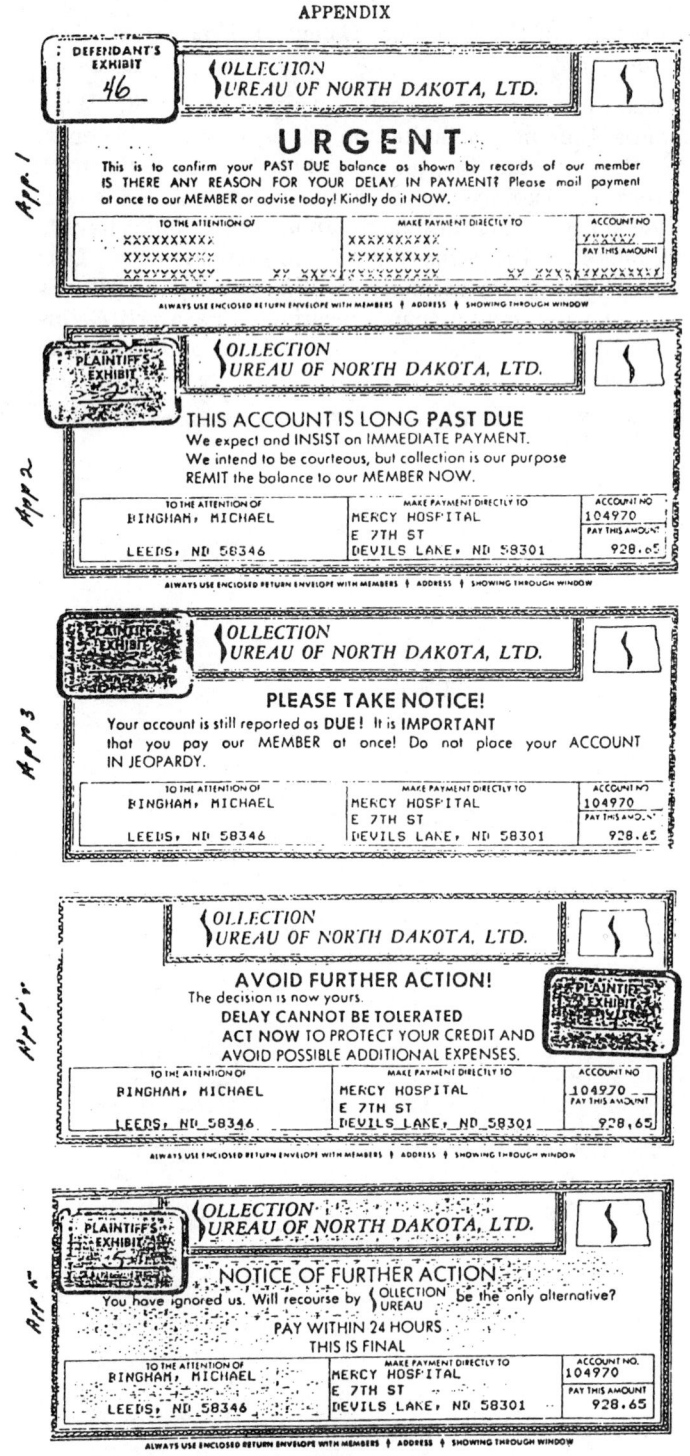

NOTICE OF FURTHER ACTION
You have ignored us. Will recourse by COLLECTION BUREAU be the only alternative?
PAY WITHIN 24 HOURS
THIS IS FINAL

TO THE ATTENTION OF	MAKE PAYMENT DIRECTLY TO	ACCOUNT NO.
BINGHAM, MICHAEL LEEDS, ND 58346	MERCY HOSPITAL E 7TH ST DEVILS LAKE, ND 58301	104970 PAY THIS AMOUNT 928.65

ALWAYS USE ENCLOSED RETURN ENVELOPE WITH MEMBERS ADDRESS SHOWING THROUGH WINDOW

Problem 1–3

It is not uncommon for creditors to employ lawyers to aid in the collection of debts. Must a lawyer engaged in consumer debt collection abide by the restrictions of the Fair Debt Collection Practices Act? Consider the following example:

Price Furniture Supply sells furniture on credit. When one of its customers, Domingo, defaulted on his payments, Price engaged the law firm of Pavarotti and Carreras to collect the debt. Pavarotti sent all of his letters to Domingo on his firm's letterhead, but never specifically threatened legal action (although a non-lawyer might have believed that the "legalese" in the letters did contain such a threat). Domingo filed a complaint against Pavarotti under the Fair Debt Collection Practices Act, alleging misleading communications. Pavarotti claims that he is not a "debt collector" as defined by the Act, and that in any event his actions were proper.

What result? Would it matter if Pavarotti were in-house counsel to Price?

Chapter Two

AN INTRODUCTION TO AMERICAN BANKRUPTCY LAW, ITS PURPOSE AND HISTORY

§ 1. THE GOALS OF AMERICAN BANKRUPTCY LAW

Although there are several types of bankruptcy proceedings that we will discuss in this course, each deals in a different way with a fundamentally similar factual pattern. Bankruptcy laws deal with cases in which a debtor's assets are inadequate to pay all of its debts. Someone will inevitably suffer a financial loss. The federal bankruptcy system provides a forum that distributes and allocates that loss. Ideally, bankruptcy proceedings also reduce the net loss.

In dealing with financially bleak circumstances, the various provisions of modern American bankruptcy law serve three fundamental purposes. One goal is commonly called the "fresh start." This principle says an individual debtor should have an opportunity to be freed from his or her obligations and to start over, at least if that person is willing to give up his or her current assets to creditors, even if those assets fall far short of paying all of the debts.

The idea of the fresh start made its appearance in American law at the beginning of the twentieth century. In *Wetmore v. Markoe,* 196 U.S. 68, 77, 25 S.Ct. 172, 176, 49 L.Ed. 390 (1904), the Supreme Court said, "systems of bankruptcy are designed to relieve the honest debtor from the weight of indebtedness which has become oppressive and to permit him to have a fresh start in business or commercial life, freed from the obligation and responsibilities which may have resulted from business misfortunes."

The discharge was an integral part of the 1898 Bankruptcy Act, and both Congress and the judiciary had consistently read the Act as including the "fresh start" as one of its primary goals. Townsend, *"Fresh Cash"—Another Element of a Bankrupt's "Fresh Start"?,* 31 U.Miami L.Rev. 275, 281 (1977). The development of the "fresh start" goes along with the view of the debtor as unfortunate rather than criminal. It contrasts with a creditors' rights view which holds that a debtor's primary obligation is to pay all debts validly incurred and the primary role of law is to encourage this to occur. In addition, the fresh start gives the debtor an incentive to continue to support himself and contribute to society.

The second goal of the bankruptcy law is to provide a set of equitable rules for the division of the debtor's property among various creditors. These rules determine the treatment of a perfected secured creditor and a creditor who is secured but unperfected, as well as regulating the rights of various parties who have received payments or other transfers of the debtor's assets in the days preceding the bankruptcy.

The third grand purpose of the bankruptcy law is to provide a mechanism for the rehabilitation of a business debtor who has the capacity to stay in business and to pay most or all of its debt. These are the rules in Chapter 11 which will form the backdrop for the negotiation among various business creditors and their debtors for a plan to lead the parties out of the wilderness. Although these rules grant the court the power to impose a plan on many unwilling creditors, in reality an imposed plan is properly regarded as a less desirable alternative to a negotiated settlement. The filing of a Chapter 11 holds the wolves at bay and gives opportunity for negotiation among the wolves and between the wolves and the sheep.

All three major goals of bankruptcy law are unlikely to be served in the same bankruptcy case. For example, if a corporate debtor is totally uninterested in a fresh start, it is better to allow the corporation to die and to start again with a new corporation. Likewise the "no asset" consumer case has little concern for equity among the various creditors because none of them will receive anything from the bankruptcy. Nor is the consumer case concerned with the rehabilitation mechanisms of the kind found in Chapter 11 or Chapter 13.

After more than fifteen years of experience with the new Chapter 11 proceedings, discussed below, some scholars are expressing considerable skepticism about the capacity of the current law to achieve the goals of rehabilitation or equitable distribution for failing corporations. The protracted bankruptcy proceedings of large American corporations such as Eastern Airlines, LTV Corporation, Johns–Manville, and REVCO Drug have shown that such proceedings are enormously expensive. This expense arises in part from lawyers' fees and the fees of accountants and investment bankers, but more importantly, the expense is associated with the continued operation of a business in a crippled form, where each business decision may be second-guessed by creditors' committees and by the court and where management's attention is repeatedly diverted by the need to satisfy such third parties. A cynic might claim that a fourth goal of the bankruptcy law is to enrich investment bankers, accountants, and bankruptcy lawyers. In any event, academic writers are now suggesting the unmentionable—that Chapter 11 is a failure and should be repealed or radically modified. Some have even argued for the repeal of Chapter 11 and for the substitution of law that would facilitate the sale of a successful company and the speedy dissolution of those that cannot be saved. See, e.g., Michael H. Bradley & Michael Rosenzweig, The Untenable Case of Chapter 11, 101 Yale L.J. 1043 (1992); Lucian A. Bebchuk, A New Approach to Corporate Reorganizations, 101 Harv. L.Rev. 775 (1988). There is also evidence that Chapter 11 has become a business strategy rather than a last ditch effort to avoid liquidation. "Filing for protection from creditors under the Bankruptcy Code used to be akin to contracting a social disease. Not any more * * *. Chapter 11 is no longer an embarrassment. People have watched mega-companies like Texaco and Manville go in, clean up their balance sheets creatively, and come out whole."[1]

§ 2. THE HISTORY OF AMERICAN BANKRUPTCY LAW

The Constitution gives Congress the right to establish "Uniform Laws on the subject of Bankruptcies throughout the United States." U.S. Const. Art. I, Section 8, cl. 4. Not surprisingly, however, the earliest American bankruptcy procedures were mere extensions of the older English practices of debt slavery and imprisonment, which in turn had evolved from the more barbaric Roman practices, some of which included dissection.

English law never sanctioned the last method, but the earliest English bankruptcy acts from the thirteenth century permitted creditors to levy on and sell a debtor's chattels, with the remedy of imprisonment also available. Litigation of the next four centuries brought little relief for the debtor. All bankruptcy proceedings were involuntary or creditor initiated. Seizure of property, imprisonment, and strict punishment for the concealment or fraudulent conveyance of property were the order of the day. Concessions to the debtor came slowly to English law. A bankruptcy law of 1705 allowed the debtor to retain a few necessary clothes. Another act of some 30 years later established the creation of an assignee elected by the creditors and responsible for the distribution of the debtor's estate. Still later acts during the eighteenth century permitted release from jail for debtors with debts of less than 100 pounds, provided that the debtor gave up his estate and took a debtor's oath. Even so, creditors could block such a release by paying a weekly fee for the debtor's prison food and maintenance.

The English systems of debtor imprisonment took root in the American colonies, nourished by both slavery and the indenture practice that brought many poor Englishmen and Europeans to this country. Countryman, *A History of American Bankruptcy Law,* 81 Com.L.J. 226, 228 (1976). Few states had insolvency laws giving a debtor release from

---

1. Ballen, *Strategy for the 1990's: Bankruptcy,* Fortune, Feb. 11, 1991, at 13. See also N.Y. Times, Jan. 27, 1991, § 3, at 2, col. 2 ("Used to be that a bankruptcy filing was a company's last exit. But these days it's more like a highway tollbooth.").

jail or a discharge of his debt. The first American bankruptcy act (1800) largely followed the eighteenth century English model described above. The years following were marked by experimentation on both sides of the Atlantic. One American development has special significance: several states in the 1830's enacted constitutional provisions that prohibited imprisonment for debt.

The spirit of this change soon led to the American Bankruptcy Act of 1841, which featured voluntary proceedings for both merchants and non-merchants whose debts totaled less than $2000. Lengthy imprisonment for bankruptcy ended, except for cases of willfulness or fraud. Bankruptcy assignees were authorized to reclaim property that had been fraudulently conveyed, and the common practice of transferring property to a preferred creditor was also sharply curtailed. More exemptions were extended to debtors; they were now permitted furniture and other items, as well as clothes. Discharge was permitted unless a majority of creditors filed written dissents. Probably because of the great number of discharges granted, this act was repealed after one year of operation.

America's third bankruptcy act, in 1867, provided for both voluntary and involuntary proceedings for merchants, non-merchants, and corporate debtors. Assignees continued to watch over fraudulent conveyances and preferences, and the debtor was allowed to exempt more of his personal goods from the creditor payments. Discharge could be denied if the debtor had committed any of a number of illegal, dishonest, or unpleasant acts. The consent of a majority of creditors was still required for discharge in most cases. Once again, creditor opposition and administrative problems led to the repeal of the act in 1878.

The next legislative effort, the Bankruptcy Act of 1898 was, with various amendments, in effect until 1978. It more closely resembled earlier American legislation than the many recent British enactments which had given control of bankruptcies to the Board of Trade. Exemptions were to be based on state law, and creditor consent was no longer required for discharge. On the assumption that the bankrupt's property was a trust for his creditors, those creditors were authorized to elect trustees, as in prior acts. The federal district courts remained the courts of bankruptcy. One particular innovation of the Act of 1898 was the creation of bankruptcy referees to replace the commissioners and registers of earlier acts. Responsible for both judicial and administrative functions, these referees were to be appointed by district judges and to be paid out of the filing fees and from a portion of the funds distributed.

Frequent amendments modified the Act. The Chandler Act of 1938 added Chapter X (Corporate Reorganization), Chapter XI (Arrangements), Chapter XII (Real Property Arrangements), and Chapter XIII (Wage Earners' Plans). In the mid 1970's new Bankruptcy Rules substantially modifying the Act of 1898 were promulgated by the Supreme Court. During this period Congress also appointed the Federal Commission on Bankruptcy Laws of the United States under the direction of Professor Frank Kennedy of the University of Michigan Law

School. The commission, comprising professors, legislators, and congressmen, prepared and presented a proposed draft of a new bankruptcy act to Congress in 1973. Report of the Commission on the Bankruptcy Laws of the United States, H.R.Doc. No. 93–137, Parts I and II, 93d Cong., 1st Sess. (1973). The Senate and the House of Representatives worked with the draft for a number of years, and each issued lengthy reports. See H.Rep. No. 595, 95th Cong., 1st Sess., reprinted in 1978 U.S.Code Cong. & Ad.News 5963; S.Rep. No. 598, 95th Cong., 2d Sess., reprinted in 1978 U.S.Code Cong. & Ad.News 5787. An amalgam of the Commission's proposals as well as House and Senate versions, the Bankruptcy Reform Act of 1978 was enacted on November 6, 1978. Most of its provisions took effect on October 1, 1979.

The Code represented the first complete revision of the bankruptcy law since 1898 and the first major revision since 1938. As we will see in succeeding chapters, the Code substantially expanded the rights of the consumer debtor, made Chapter 13 a more desirable alternative for those in debt, and expanded the number and variety of assets exempt from the creditors' reach. In the business area, the Code collapsed the old Chapters X, XI and XII into a "Chapter 11" proceeding. It significantly altered the avoidance provisions and, most important of all, it expanded the power of the trustee in bankruptcy to use and inhibit the creditors' control of property that was subject to a perfected security interest. History may tell us that the Code subtly but significantly shifted power from secured creditors to others in bankruptcy proceedings.

The Code's enactment coincided with a sharp increase in the number of business and individual bankruptcy filings. From 1977 to 1981 the total number of bankruptcies increased from 214,000 to more than 500,000. The annual rate has since risen to more than 800,000 in the year ending June 30, 1991. Of these, the vast majority—about 75 percent—are Chapter 7 cases; less than 2,000 are involuntary bankruptcies, i.e., initiated by creditors against debtors. The rate of Chapter 11 cases doubled from 1977 to 1981 and doubled again in 1982 to over 16,000. In 1989 there were 17,447 Chapter 11 filings. By 1994 the total number of cases annually had grown to 832,829. Of those 567,240 were Chapter 7, 249,877 were Chapter 13, and 14,773 were Chapter 11. For the moment at least, the number of filings appears to have leveled off.

NATIONAL TOTALS
BANKRUPTCY CASE FILINGS FOR CALENDAR YEARS 1980–1994

CALENDAR YEAR	TOTAL FILINGS	CHAPTER 7	CHAPTER 11	CHAPTER 12	CHAPTER 13	OTHER* CASES
1980	331,098	249,136	6,398	N/A	75,584	30
1981	363,847	260,664	10,041	N/A	93,139	3
1982	380,212	257,644	18,821	N/A	103,738	9
1983	348,881	234,551	20,284	N/A	94,038	8
1984	348,521	234,861	20,325	N/A	93,315	20
1985	412,510	281,053	23,376	N/A	108,069	12
1986	530,438	374,786	24,773	607	130,257	15
1987	577,999	409,595	20,078	6,125	142,161	40
1988	613,465	437,769	17,684	2,037	155,945	30
1989	679,461	476,470	18,281	1,445	183,214	51

CALENDAR YEAR	TOTAL FILINGS	CHAPTER 7	CHAPTER 11	CHAPTER 12	CHAPTER 13	OTHER* CASES
1990	782,960	543,334	20,783	1,346	217,468	29
1991	943,987	656,430	23,989	1,495	262,006	37
1992	971,517	681,663	22,634	1,608	265,577	35
1993	875,202	602,980	19,174	1,243	251,773	32
1994	832,829	567,240	14,773	900	249,877	39
TOTAL	8,992,927	6,268,206	281,364	16,808	2,426,161	388

*—Includes Chapter 7 stockbroker, Chapter 9, Chapter 11 railroads, and section 304 cases.

NOTE: The figures for 1983–1989 have been revised slightly from previous versions of this report.

BANKRUPTCY FILINGS BY DECADE: Bankruptcy case filings were far higher during the 1980's than in any other decade. On a per capita basis, filings during the 1980's were about double the level of the 1970's, and nearly ten times as high as during the 1940's. Further, bankruptcy case filings between 1990 and 1994 have been nearly twice the annual average for the 1980's.

U.S. POPULATION FILINGS PER:

DECADE	TOTAL FILINGS	U.S. POPULATION (AT END OF DECADE)	FILINGS PER 1,000 POP.
1900–1909	173,298	92,228,496	1.88
1910–1919	215,296	106,021,537	2.03
1920–1929	410,475	123,202,624	3.33
1930–1939	614,938	132,164,569	4.65
1940–1949	296,021	151,325,798	1.96
1950–1959	584,272	179,323,175	3.26
1960–1969	1,695,416	203,302,031	8.34
1970–1979	2,086,189	226,545,805	9.21
1980–1989	4,586,432	252,904,881	18.14
1990–1994	4,406,495		32.0 (EST.)

—Case filings through 1979 are for statistical years ended June 30th; filings since 1980 reflect calendar years. Population figures reflect census totals as of April 1 of each decade.

To what extent such increase in filing is attributable to the generosity of the new Code, to a change in society's notions about the morality of avoiding one's debt, and to the wider and more obvious availability of lawyers is greatly disputed and quite unclear.

In the summer of 1984 Congress undertook the first significant amendment of the 1978 Code. Students will find traces of those amendments throughout the book. The most significant purpose of the new law was to resolve the conflict about the status of bankruptcy judges that had arisen after the *Marathon* case held that judges serving under less than lifetime appointment could not have the type of jurisdiction that was intended by the 1978 Code. In addition, the 1984 amendments modestly restricted the rights of consumer debtors, established a special rule for governing a company's right to reject collective bargaining agreements in bankruptcy, and added a series of technical and special interest amendments.

Since 1984 the Bankruptcy Code has been revised almost annually. Seriatim Congress has addressed the interests of various special groups such as family farmers, technology licensees, and even Mothers Against Drunk Driving.

In 1994, Congress adopted more amendments to the Bankruptcy Code. These amendments were a hodgepodge that included a variety of small modifications to "improve administration." Among these were authority for bankruptcy judges to conduct jury trials in certain cases, a change in the eligibility to serve on Chapter 11 committees and a provision allowing interlocutory appeal on orders that increase or reduce certain time periods for the filing of plans under Chapter 11. These administrative changes may be critical to a lawyer in a particular case, but most involve the kind of detail that can be safely ignored by a student first confronting bankruptcy.

In the commercial bankruptcy arena, the 1994 amendments are designed to enhance speed and reduce abuse. Among the changes were provisions for small businesses (those with aggregated non-contingent debts of less than $2,000,000) to accelerate the time for filing claims and to make some modest disclosures in connection with a plan. In "single asset real estate" cases the new amendments make it easier and quicker for secured creditors to have the stay lifted.

The 1994 amendments show that Congress is awakening to the substantial costs that attend delay in bankruptcy and to the economies that can be gained by accelerating a bankruptcy case. With the election in 1994 of a Congress that is presumably more responsive to creditors' interests and less concerned about debtors', one might predict even more extensive modifications of Chapter 11 and perhaps of Chapter 7 in the years to come if the Republicans remain in control.

Bankruptcy law, as we will deal with it, stems not only from the Code, but also from the rich history that forms the backdrop for this comprehensive act. Many of the Code's sections are derived from analogous sections of the Act of 1898. References to these sections, the cases, and various commentaries illuminate Congress' intent in the Code. We can learn even more about the drafters' intent by consulting the Commission's report or the House and Senate reports. Federal and state consumer credit legislation also contributes significantly to bankruptcy law.

Another important source of bankruptcy law is the Bankruptcy Rules. In theory, these rules deal only with procedural and not substantive matters. However, only a legal neophyte or a layman would believe the two to be neatly divisible. In fact, the Bankruptcy Rules existing prior to the Bankruptcy Reform Act of 1978 contained many substantive provisions. Some of these have been incorporated into the Code. One such provision, long a fundamental debtor protection, is the automatic stay; it is now embodied in section 362 of the Code. Doubtless there will be cases under the Code in which the Bankruptcy Rules will make significant changes in or additions to the substantive law under the guise of procedural adjustments.

Bankruptcy law is also derived from state common law and statutory law. For example, the law pertaining to priority of garnishments, attachments, and executions tends to be state common law. Similarly, issues related to setoff, the rights to joint bank accounts, suretyship, and other traditional creditors' rights matters are found primarily in state case law and, to a lesser extent, in state statutory law.

§ 3. A GUIDE TO THE CHAPTERS IN THE BANKRUPTCY CODE

At the outset, the student should note several details about the Bankruptcy Reform Act of 1978. Chapters 1–15 are designated by Arabic numerals. Thus when one sees "Chapter 11" one knows the court is speaking about a case under the Code; a "Chapter XI" proceeding is a case under the Act of 1898. Second, note that there is only one even-numbered chapter; one finds Chapters 1, 3, 5, 7 and so on, but no 2, 4, or 6. The even numerals have been reserved for additions to the Code; Chapter 12 was added in 1986 for family farmers.

The drafters of the Code attempted to group into the first three chapters sections that have general applicability to the following chapters. For example, section 101(10) defines "creditor" and section 101(13) defines "debtor"; both terms appear in the following sections. Although section 101 is not as extensive as the definitional sections in the Uniform Commercial Code, it is much more extensive than anything in the Act of 1898. The student should turn there first for the answers to any definitional questions. Among other important matters found in Chapter 1 is section 109 which clarifies who can appear as a debtor in the chapters to follow. Thus, subsection b states the limitations on a Chapter 7 debtor, while subsections c, d, and e clarify who can appear as a debtor in actions involving Chapters 9, 11, and 13 respectively.

Chapter 3 (Case Administration) contains some of the most significant administrative and procedural sections in the entire Code. Subchapter I of Chapter 3 deals with the commencement of a case and tells how a voluntary or involuntary case is begun. Section 305 grants the court the power to "abstain" and thus dismiss a case where the interests of the creditors and debtors "would be better served by such dismissal." Subchapter II deals with "officers." It defines the people who may serve as trustees and provides for a variety of other administrative details. Sections 327 and 329 deal with the employment of professionals, with Section 329 addressing itself to the debtor's dealings with lawyers. In certain circumstances the court can order the return of fees paid prior to the bankruptcy. A variety of procedural rules will also be found in subchapter III; they will seldom be of importance to a lawyer representing the typical creditor in bankruptcy, but one should recognize their existence.

One of the most significant parts of the entire Code, subchapter IV of Chapter 3 contains provisions on adequate protection, the automatic stay, the use and sale of property in the estate, executory contracts, and unexpired leases. Meaty, novel, radical, and frequently litigated, such provisions as sections 361, 362, 363 and 365 may well cause legal historians fifty years from now to conclude that subchapter IV fundamentally altered the rights of secured creditors in ways not perceived at the time of the Code's passage. Because their intricacies will be crucial to bankruptcy practice for creditors' lawyers, we will dig into the mysteries of these sections in great detail in Chapters 3, 4 and 5 of this book.

Chapter 5 is titled "Creditors, the Debtor, and the Estate." Among its important sections is section 506 which defines the extent to which a party is treated as a "secured" or "unsecured" creditor. Other provisions deal with the amount of claims, their priority status, and the payment of administrative expenses. We deal with this section in Chapter 7.

Section 522, a critical section to which we will devote a large part of Chapter 10, represents a radical departure from both the American tradition and the Bankruptcy Act of 1898 in its establishment of a set of federal exemptions which the debtor may choose in lieu of any state exemptions available. As we have seen above, before the Code a debtor was limited to his state exemptions; no federal set of exemptions existed. In addition to their novelty, the exemptions under section 522 are substantially more generous than those accorded a debtor under the laws of most states. Moreover, section 522 has a provision for the avoidance of certain security interests.

Sections 523 and 524, dealing with discharge, are also significant and will occupy a major portion of Chapter 10. Many issues in this area deal with the reaffirmation of a particular debt and whether it can or should be excepted from the discharge. Some of the most critical substantive rules for business bankruptcy cases may be found in sections 541 to 554, which define the property of the estate (section 541), the trustee's avoiding power as a lien creditor (section 544), the status of statutory liens (section 545), and most important of all, the trustee's right to strike down preferences (section 547).

Chapter 7 is the first of the chapters that deals with a specific form of bankruptcy proceeding. Entitled "Liquidation," it governs what used to be known as "straight bankruptcy." The trustee simply collects the assets of the debtor, sells them, and distributes the proceeds to the creditors. Thus the Chapter 7 action may be distinguished from a Chapter 11 plan of reorganization under which a business may be kept in operation, and from a Chapter 13 wage earners' plan in which an individual might propose certain periodic payments to various creditors. Most bankruptcy proceedings are commenced under Chapter 7, and a large percentage of proceedings begun under Chapters 11 or 13 eventually wind up as Chapter 7 proceedings. Even so, one finds only a limited number of important provisions under Chapter 7. Section 727, which should be read together with sections 523 and 524, sets out rules denying the debtor any right to a discharge in certain circumstances. Subchapter III of Chapter 7 contains special provisions for stockbroker liquidations, while subchapter IV deals with commodity broker liquidations. These are matters about which the student will need to know either nothing or everything. In this book we ignore them both.

Chapter 9 is titled "Adjustment of Debts of a Municipality." We devote no space to it. Its inclusion in the Bankruptcy Reform Act of

1978 stems from the threat to default on many of its debts by New York City in the mid–1970's. The chapter doubtless contains a variety of delightful questions which one suspects might remain unanswered until well into the next century.

Chapter 11 is central to business bankruptcies. Although only a limited number of businesses successfully complete a Chapter 11 proceeding, many failing businesses start there in an attempt to remain in operation and work out their difficulties. Subchapter II, "The Plan," contains most of the provisions that will concern us: the classification of claims or interests (section 1122), the contents of the plan (section 1123), acceptance and modification (sections 1126 and 1127), and the confirmation of the plan (section 1129). These sections contain rules about the proposal and acceptance of the plan, and form the framework upon which a negotiated settlement among the creditors and between the creditors and the debtor can be built. Much of Chapter 11 will be of importance only to the bankruptcy lawyer, but certain provisions are critical even to the lawyer who represents only a single creditor in a Chapter 11 proceeding. Only by knowing a creditor's rights and those of the debtor can a lawyer take part in the negotiation about the plan, the treatment of the various parties, and the accommodation which must be worked out. We devote Chapter 9 to the provisions of Chapter 11.

Chapter 12, "Adjustment of Debts of a Family Farmer With Regular Annual Income," was enacted by Congress in 1986. Chapter 12 was modeled after Chapter 13, but is exclusively for farmers. Most farm families have too much debt to be eligible for Chapter 13 relief, and farmers were often adversely affected by the rules of Chapter 11. Among other things, Chapter 12 enables the farmer to keep his farm after reorganization even where the farm family probably could not keep it in a Chapter 11 proceeding because of the "absolute priority" rule, a rule we will discuss in Chapter 9.

Chapter 13, "Adjustment of Debts of an Individual With Regular Income," is a new development in the Code. Under the Act of 1898, wage earner plans were permitted but seldom used except in a few areas of the country. When they were used, such plans differed greatly from what we see under today's Chapter 13. The classic Chapter XIII plan under the Act provided for full payment to every creditor over a period of time while the typical plan under the Code provides only for partial payment to the typical creditor, in some cases for as little as ten cents on the dollar. Among Chapter 13's most important sections are Contents of Plan (section 1322), Confirmation of Plan (section 1325), and Discharge (section 1328). Whether the drafters foresaw the wide use of Chapter 13 under the Code and fully appreciated the reasons which might cause the consumer debtor to elect a Chapter 13 action over a Chapter 7 proceeding is unclear. In any event, a far larger share of consumer debtors have chosen Chapter 13 than could have been foreseen in 1978.

§ 4. THE PLAYERS, THEIR RIGHTS AND OBLIGATIONS

A. *The Bankruptcy Judge*

Center stage in the bankruptcy court is held by a person now known as a "bankruptcy judge." Traditionally such judges served terms of six years and were known as bankruptcy "referees." Under the 1898 Bankruptcy Act, the federal district judges in the various districts appointed and removed referees and reviewed their decisions. For many years the referee's determinations became effective only upon the approval of a district judge and district judges could review decisions of the referees de novo. In time the referees assumed most of the administrative and eventually most of the judicial burden. Under the 1973 rules the bankruptcy judge's order was final unless a timely appeal was taken. Rule 810 provided that the referee's findings of fact must be accepted unless they were "clearly erroneous."

The status and tenure of the bankruptcy judges have been among the thorniest of the bankruptcy issues considered by Congress and the courts. The good bankruptcy judges became learned students of the bankruptcy law, but they also had a low status in the federal court caste system. The dependence of bankruptcy judges upon district judges for personnel, equipment, and library budgets as well as their very appointments contributed to misgivings about the integrity of the system, especially when the district judge responsible for the appointment of a given bankruptcy judge then acted as an appellate judge reviewing his appointee's performance. Bankruptcy judges repeatedly emphasized the demands of their work, and the need to increase the prestige of their position in order to attract qualified people. Perhaps fearful of a dilution of their prestige, some district judges did not welcome the elevation of bankruptcy judges to the district judge level. Anderson, *A Digest of Broader Perspectives for Bankruptcy Court Reforms*, 81 Com. L.J. 240 (1976).

Under the 1984 amendments bankruptcy judges are appointed by the United States Court of Appeals for each circuit. The appointment is for fourteen years. This system of appointment is the outcome of several years of negotiations. Some suggested that bankruptcy judges should be appointed for life by the President. Presumably the appointment by the circuit courts was a compromise—to allow appointment by persons not intimately involved in the day-to-day operations of the court, but to withhold that patronage from the President.

B. *The Trustee*

If the bankruptcy judge is the king, the trustee in bankruptcy is the chief courtier in the bankruptcy court for cases brought under Chapter 7. Sections 321–324 deal with the trustee's qualifications and powers in general. Sections 701–704 give a fuller explanation. In Chapter 7 proceedings (liquidations), there is always a trustee. Initially under section 701 the U.S. Trustee appoints an interim trustee. Under section

702 the creditors may elect a regular trustee; failing that, the interim trustee continues to serve. In a liquidation case that involves substantial assets theoretically it would be in the interest of the creditors to elect a person known to be particularly competent in dealing with and liquidating such a business. In practice the real stimulus for election of a trustee might be a lawyer who knows that a particular trustee will hire that lawyer. In the typical consumer case however, it will not be in the creditors' interest to devote the time and effort necessary to elect a person known to them in order to supervise the liquidating of an estate that will include no assets for the creditors in any event. Section 704 specifies the duties of the trustee. It reads in full as follows:

Section 704. Duties of trustee

The trustee shall—

(1) collect and reduce to money the property of the estate for which such trustee serves, and close such estate as expeditiously as is compatible with the best interests of parties in interest;

(2) be accountable for all property received;

(3) ensure that the debtor shall perform his intention as specified in section 521(2)(B) of this title;

(4) investigate the financial affairs of the debtor;

(5) if a purpose would be served, examine proofs of claims and object to the allowance of any claim that is improper;

(6) if advisable, oppose the discharge of the debtor;

(7) unless the court orders otherwise, furnish such information concerning the estate and the estate's administration as is requested by a party in interest;

(8) if the business of the debtor is authorized to be operated, file with the court, with the United States trustee, and with any governmental unit charged with responsibility for collection or determination of any tax arising out of such operation, periodic reports and summaries of the operation of such business, including a statement of receipts and disbursements, and such other information as the United States trustee or court requires; and

(9) make a final report and file a final account of the administration of the estate with the court and with the United States trustee.

The typical Chapter 7 trustee in a consumer liquidation is likely to be appointed from a panel of "private trustees established under section 604(f) of Title 28." Persons on that panel may or may not be lawyers, but they are likely to be quasi professional trustees experienced in the ways of bankruptcies in which they are appointed and known both to the bankruptcy judge and to the lawyers who frequent the bankruptcy court. In theory, if the bankruptcy involves a business with considerable assets, the U.S. Trustee could appoint a person who is a lawyer experienced in such liquidation or who is a person with business experience of the kind that would be useful for such a liquidation. In practice the trustee may just be the one at the top of the list.

While there will always be a trustee in Chapter 7 proceedings, section 1104 contemplates the appointment of a trustee in Chapter 11 proceedings only in relatively unusual cases. In the typical Chapter 11 case the management of the company going into Chapter 11 will continue to operate the business as a "debtor in possession"; commonly there will be no trustee. However, if the court finds that there is fraud, dishonesty or incompetence on the part of the company's management or if an appointment is in the "interest of creditors," shareholders or others, the court has the duty to direct the U.S. Trustee to appoint a trustee. Appointments under 1104 either of trustees, or of persons known as "examiners" with more limited powers, come only "on the request of a party in interest."

Section 1302 presents yet a different scheme for Chapter 13. In many jurisdictions the U.S. Trustee has appointed a "standing trustee" for Chapter 13 cases under the provisions of 1302(d). Under the terms of 1302(a) that person will serve as the trustee in all Chapter 13 cases and will exercise the powers specified in 1302.

What are the powers of the trustee? Examine section 704 set out above. The Chapter 7 trustee must collect and reduce to money the property of the estate; he is accountable for all the property of the estate and must investigate the financial affairs of the debtor; he must also make appropriate reports and accounting. In many cases he is cast in the role of the opponent of secured creditors, and in his role as the supporter of the estate (i.e., the unsecured creditors) he attacks security interests under the terms of section 544 *et seq.* to bring that property into the estate and to keep it from going to the secured creditors or others. The Chapter 13 trustee, on the other hand, is more of a mother hen to the debtor. He not only must do the things specified in other parts of section 704, but must also advise and assist the debtor in performance of his Chapter 13 plan.

Thus the trustee is a central player in the bankruptcy drama. In some cases that person will be a sophisticated and powerful person who exercises great influence in the outcome of the case. In other bankruptcies the trustee will be no more than a functionary who fills out a form or two for a modest fee.

C. *The "U.S. Trustee"*

The student has now met Chapter 7 and 13 trustees, and trustees and examiners in Chapter 11. If that is not confusing enough, there is yet another animal: the "U.S. trustee."

The House of Representatives wanted to create a system of U.S. trustees to relieve bankruptcy judges of their administrative and supervisory duties. Under the Act, bankruptcy judges often worked closely with the trustees they appointed. A judge might suggest a schedule or cause of action to the trustee, and later decide on its validity in the bankruptcy court. In order to remove the appearance of impropriety arising from this coziness between the administering judge and the trustee, H.R. 8200 created the U.S. trustee.

The Senate felt that the U.S. trustee system would create a costly and unnecessary bureaucracy, and that the private rather than the public trustee should continue to predominate. After an experimental period, the U.S. Trustee system was adopted. The United States Trustee establishes and supervises the panel of private trustees for Chapter 7 cases, and appoints or serves as a Chapter 13 standing trustee. The U.S. trustee also appoints Chapter 11 trustees, creditor's committees and examiners, and conducts investigations to ensure that participants in bankruptcy cases are not avoiding the requirements of the Code. The House hoped that the creation of U.S. trustees would regularize the appointments process, assure a minimum standard of competence, and most important, eliminate "cronyism," and "the uncomfortably close relationship that exists between judges and 'their' trustees." H.R.Rep. 595, 95th Cong. 1st Sess. 107, reprinted in U.S.Code Cong. & Ad.News 1978, 5963, 6069. At this writing the U.S. Trustee system is still evolving. The role and effect of the U.S. Trustee have yet to be finally determined. For example, the 1994 amendment specifically designated the U.S. trustee as the person who "shall convene and preside at a meeting of creditors," section 341(a).

D. *Debtor in Possession*

A final important person in bankruptcy is the "debtor in possession." Under section 1101(1) that is the debtor. Under section 1107 the debtor in possession "shall have all the rights * * * and powers and shall perform all the functions and duties * * * of a trustee serving under this chapter." Thus, *mirabile dictu,* upon filing a petition in Chapter 11, the debtor is transformed into another person, a debtor in possession. This is a person capable of wielding the power of sections 544 and 547 and exerting the other powers of a trustee in bankruptcy. When we discuss a Chapter 11 case, it is likely that the person who has the trustee's powers is none other than the same person who was sitting in the executive chair the day before the petition was filed, then characterized as the president of the debtor and now called the "DIP."

In a typical Chapter 11 case the debtor in possession is the central figure in the proceeding. In theory this debtor in possession is neither a trustee nor the preexisting debtor, but a new legal construct of the Bankruptcy Code. In practice, of course, those who ran the debtor run the debtor in possession. While they have the rights and powers of a trustee and are subject to the obligations imposed on the trustee, they bring to the bankruptcy court their old allegiances and antagonisms, as well as their business judgment and experience. To the extent they retain their loyalty to the shareholders—most explicitly when they are the shareholders—these managers who are now the debtor in possession may show less interest in the rights of the creditors than the creditors think they should. In other cases the managers may be criticized for showing too little deference to the interests of shareholders. In any event, the rights and interests of the creditors and those of the shareholders are sure to come into direct and intense conflict when a Chapter 11 petition is filed. The "debtor in possession" may be the best available compromise on the operation of the bankrupt business, but it is not without its faults.

E. Creditors' Committees

In Chapter 11, sections 1102 and 1103, contemplate the appointment and service of creditors' committees. Under section 1102(a)(1) the U.S. trustee is directed to appoint a committee of creditors holding unsecured claims and is authorized under (a)(2) to appoint additional committees of creditors or shareholders. Normally the creditors' committees under (a)(1) consist of the persons willing to serve who hold the seven largest claims against the debtor. The various and somewhat vague rights of these committees are set out in section 1103. In fact the function of these committees is to negotiate with one another and with representatives of the debtor in order to operate the business on an interim basis and to arrive at a plan that can be confirmed under section 1129. Without some mechanism such as a creditors' committee to speak for identifiable groups, negotiations would be chaotic, and agreement would be impossible to reach. Because the true function of these committees is to negotiate, to engage mostly in private behavior, the student will see little reference in the cases or in the materials that follow to their service or appropriate function. One should not be misled by the absence of such references in the cases. Surely effective negotiation by and on behalf of the various creditors is one of the most important prerequisites to arriving at a successful and workable plan—at least in a large case.

In limiting the duties of the bankruptcy judges, the Code has shifted the responsibility for monitoring Chapter 11 debtors to the creditors' committees. "Thus while committees were relatively unused in certain judicial districts just a few years ago, they now play an integral part in reorganization proceedings in virtually all districts, and active, aggressive and vigilant committees have had a significant impact on the course of most Chapter 11 cases." Meir and Brown, *Representing Unsecured Creditors' Committees Under Chapter 11 of the Bankruptcy Code*, 56 Am.Bankr.L.J. 217 (1982). Contrary to the suggestions of Meir and Brown, there are no committees in many cases, and, even when committees are appointed, they are often moribund. See LoPucki, *The Debtor in Full Control—Systems Failure under Chapter 11 of the Bankruptcy Code?* 57 Am.Bankr.L.J., Part I–II, at 99, 247 (1983).

The creditors' committees can intervene in adversary proceedings initiated by the trustee, and sometimes can even initiate adversary proceedings in the name of the debtor in possession. See *Liberal Market, Inc. v. Malone & Hyde, Inc. (In re Liberal Market, Inc.)*, 14 B.R. 685 (Bankr.S.D.Ohio 1981). The power to initiate proceedings could be a significant committee weapon because it means that committees no longer have to rely on asking the court to appoint a trustee in place of the debtor in possession.

The lawyers who serve in bankruptcy court, the judges who preside over it and the trustees and other functionaries who make their living by serving in various roles at the court make up what some have called the "bankruptcy ring." In many jurisdictions there are limited numbers of persons who routinely work in the bankruptcy court. These persons become well known to one another and obviously they develop working accommodations. How those accommodations affect the ultimate outcome of cases is unclear. On the one hand, one might argue that the camaraderie and accommodations that develop inhibit appropriate challenges to indiscreet or improper behavior. On the other hand, the recurring contacts with one another doubtless eliminate the need for inefficient mating dances and allow an early and appropriate amount of disclosure. In one sense the close relations among the actors properly controls behavior; presumably one who deals in an unethical or inappropriate way with his peers in such a limited group pays for that activity (even conceivably with exclusion from the group) in a way that he would not pay if he were dealing *seriatim* with every member of the bar in a large metropolitan district.

However, even if the behavior of members of the bankruptcy ring is perfectly ethical, outsiders sometimes are skeptical. Harold Marsh, Chairman of the Bankruptcy Commission, testified in the hearings that "there exists a relationship between the Bankruptcy Judges, the trustees and the counsel for the trustees which many people, including many involved in the system, consider unhealthy from the point of view of proper judicial and governmental administration." Hearings on H.R. 31 and 32 before the Subcommittee on Civil and Constitutional Rights of the House Committee on the Judiciary, 94th Cong., 1st and 2nd Sess., pt. 1, 538 (1976). Marsh went on to say that historically, "a relatively small group of lawyers controlled the bankruptcy field. Those not within this group tended to regard them with suspicion and distrust." Id. Since 1978, the number of lawyers who work in bankruptcy has expanded exponentially. Much more than before 1978, today's bankruptcy lawyer is likely to have migrated from other business practice, not from collection work.

§ 5. INTERPRETING THE BANKRUPTCY CODE, TERMS AND DEFINITIONS

Students of the Bankruptcy Code who are uncertain of the definition of a word found in the Code should turn first to section 101. That

§ 5 INTERPRETING THE BANKRUPTCY CODE

section contains nearly sixty subsections, each of which contains one or more definitions. Some of those (such as the definition of debt) are short and simple. A few of the definitions are too abstract to be of use, but for the most part the definitions are concrete and helpful. Other sections dealing with specific topics such as section 741 on stockbroker liquidations or section 1101 on business reorganizations contain definitions that are applicable only to portions of the Code. A second important aid to interpretation is section 102, "Rules of Construction." That section contains the usual kind of information about construction, e.g., "the singular including the plural."

At the outset it may be helpful for the student to give explicit consideration to some of the most important definitions. Several sections of the Bankruptcy Code speak of the "order for relief." For example, section 727(b) says that the discharge in bankruptcy speaks as of the time of the order for relief. Debts incurred prior to the order for relief are discharged; those incurred later are not discharged. Section 301 states that commencement of a voluntary case under any of the chapters constitutes an "order for relief." Thus debts incurred before the filing of the petition will be discharged, those incurred later will not be discharged. In involuntary cases under section 303 the Code gives the debtor an opportunity to prove it should not be in bankruptcy. Accordingly the "order for relief" is not granted until there has been a trial to determine whether the debtor should be in involuntary bankruptcy. Section 303(h). Thus in an involuntary case some debts incurred after the petition is filed but before the "order" will be discharged under section 727.

Two of the most basic ideas that run throughout the Code are the definitions of a "claim" and "debtor." Section 101(5) states that a claim means a "right to payment" whether liquidated, unliquidated, etc., or a "right to an equitable remedy." Treatment of various claims is specified by sections 501–507. Claims are there divided into garden variety claims (presented under section 502), administrative expenses (dealt with under section 503), and expenses that are entitled to priority over general unsecured claims (section 507). Section 506 provides for a determination whether and to what extent a particular creditor is secured. In the common case in which the value of the collateral is less than the amount of the debt, the creditor will have two claims, one as a secured creditor to the extent of the value of the collateral and one as an unsecured creditor under section 502.

Another basic concept is the broad scope encompassed by the "property of the estate." Section 541 provides that the estate is comprised of all legal or equitable interests of the debtor in property, wherever located as of the commencement of the case. This includes intangible as well as tangible property, causes of action, and various more mundane types of property interests. It is often important to know what constitutes property of the estate because many sections of the Bankruptcy Code—such as section 363 dealing with the use, sale or lease of property—apply only to property of the estate.

The recurring references to liens, security interests, statutory liens, and judicial liens throughout the Bankruptcy Code will leave the student who has not already confronted these ideas in Commercial Transactions in considerable confusion. First the student should read section 101(36), (37), (50), and (53). These subsections define respectively:

(36) "judicial lien" means lien obtained by judgment, levy, sequestration, or other legal or equitable process or proceeding;

(37) "lien" means charge against or interest in property to secure payment of a debt or performance of an obligation;

(50) "security agreement" means agreement that creates or provides for a security interest;

(53) "statutory lien" means lien arising solely by force of a statute on specified circumstances or conditions, or lien of distress for rent, whether or not statutory, but does not include security interest or judicial lien, whether or not such interest or lien is provided by or is dependent on a statute and whether or not such interest or lien is made fully effective by statute[.]

Section 101(51) defines security interest as a subset of "lien." Most Uniform Commercial Code lawyers would regard a security interest as something different from a lien and would use the word lien to describe only statutory and judicial liens. The typical statutory lien is the so-called mechanic's lien which arises when someone does work on another's personal or real property. Under the law of all states such a workman may have a claim against the property that benefited from his work. The classical judicial lien is a judgment lien which normally attaches to the real property of the defendant upon the rendering of a judgment and the docketing or entry of that judgment in the appropriate records. Other judicial liens can arise upon the seizure of property by the sheriff either at the conclusion of a case (execution lien) or in certain circumstances during the pendency of the case (attachment lien). The common characteristic of judicial liens is that they arise only out of court action.

In several places the Code makes references to "co-debtors." Sections 509 and 1301. For most purposes in this book one need attach no particular significance to the fact that someone is defined as a guarantor as opposed to a surety or a co-debtor. Although those words may carry important distinctions in the law of particular states in certain circumstances, here we treat them as synonymous; none has a consistently different meaning from any of the others in bankruptcy law.

Finally are a series of words that may be unfamiliar to the student that we will not define here. These are words such as discharge, exemption and preference—terms of such great importance that each will occupy many pages within this book. For those words we attempt no definition here and ask only that the student await with patience the exposition of their meaning.

§ 6. LIFE OF A TYPICAL BANKRUPTCY CASE

Although each bankruptcy case is different from every other, there are certainly stereotypical forms of bankruptcy. In observing a year's filings of consumer Chapter 7's, Chapter 13's or Chapter 11's, one would quickly identify certain stereotypes. Here we hope to orient the student by identifying certain types of recurring behavior associated with specific kinds of cases and by setting out the initial forms that would be filed on the commencement of a consumer Chapter 7 and Chapter 13.

A. *Life of a Typical Consumer Chapter 7 or Chapter 13 Case*

The typical consumer Chapter 7 or Chapter 13 would be begun by filing a petition and paying the filing fee. A Chapter 13 might be stimulated by a foreclosure action by the mortgagee holding the mortgage on the debtor's house or possibly by the actions of some other creditor. The same might be true, although it is less likely, in the case of a consumer Chapter 7.

If the bankruptcy was stimulated by the acts of a particular secured creditor, the initial action after the filing is likely to involve the stay (staying the action of that particular creditor) and possibly a request by that creditor for lifting the stay under section 362. As we will see, any such request will bring into issue the idea of adequate protection and procedural provisions set out in section 362. The typical consumer case does not involve any litigation over the stay. Because the typical consumer has few assets, it is simply not sensible for the creditor (even if it thinks it has been wronged) to litigate at length with the consumer about the stay, lifting the stay or any other matter.

Shortly after the filing there will be a "first meeting of the creditors." This meeting is likely to be attended by the debtor, his lawyer, and a person appointed by the court as the trustee. Except in rare cases (and aside from the trustee as a representative of the creditors), there will be no members of the class after whom such meeting is named; no creditors will come to the meeting of the creditors. Knowing that the typical consumer has no assets that are not exempt or already encumbered, most creditors can better spend their time elsewhere and will not find it productive to attend any such meeting. However, certain recurring creditors (banks with large portfolios of consumer debt and credit card issuers) may send lawyer representatives to *every* meeting in every case.

After the meeting of the creditors, in an unusual consumer case the trustee might seek to invoke section 544 or 547. By doing so the trustee seeks to bring assets that have been conveyed to others or that nominally belong to others into the estate for the benefit of the general creditors. One suspects that it is a rare case in which the trustee in a consumer Chapter 7 or 13 invokes these sections. The trustee too has other business and appreciates the inefficiency of chasing small preferential payments or voidable transfers of assets with marginal value.

In a minority of the consumer cases, an individual creditor might find it in its interest to challenge the discharge or alternatively to assert that its particular debt was to be excepted from the discharge under section 523 or perhaps to challenge the exemption that the debtor has claimed under section 522. Such challenge will be most likely made only when the creditor has a realistic prospect of collecting out of future income if its debt is excepted from the discharge. By the same token, challenges to exemptions are most likely to be made when the item at issue has real value, such as the debtor's homestead. The typical consumer case will be concluded by a discharge months after the petition is filed and our debtor will be turned back on the street, clean of most debts.

Chapter 13 consumer cases involve different questions than those usually found in Chapter 7 cases. Here the debtor must not only file a petition but also must propose a plan for the payment of his creditors. Since by hypothesis the Chapter 13 debtor has regular earnings, the Chapter 13 debtor is likely to be somewhat more affluent, to have more possessions and to be more worthy of the critical interest of his creditors than a typical no asset Chapter 7 debtor. Because of this need for negotiation and for the proposal of a plan, the trustee may be called upon to be more active, and the creditors may be more significantly involved. Here more often than in the Chapter 7 case, a creditor will seek to have the stay lifted. Because of the need for a plan and periodic payments, creditors sometimes challenge the interest rate, the form and time of payments under the plan. Yet even in the classic Chapter 13 case, the payoffs are so low to the typical creditor that most creditors are completely passive.

B. Life of a Typical Chapter 11 Case

Most significant business bankruptcies are filed under Chapter 11 of the Code. While many Chapter 11 business cases eventually result in a liquidation of the business assets, the goal of Chapter 11 reorganization proceedings is to develop and obtain confirmation of a plan that restructures the debt and ownership of the debtor while continuing the use of the business assets as a going concern. In Chapter 11 the terms of the plan are usually determined by negotiation among the interested parties. A wide range of alternative reorganizations is possible.

Most Chapter 11 cases can be broken down into three overlapping phases. The first might be described as the "survival" stage. This typically involves a flurry of activity shortly after the case is filed. Unless the debtor has been able to accumulate some cash prior to filing bankruptcy, there will be negotiation over and the entry of an order under section 363 to enable the debtor in possession to use cash collateral in the operation of its business.

§ 6   LIFE OF A TYPICAL BANKRUPTCY CASE   71

The debtor in possession will have particular interest in using its checking account to pay employees and post-bankruptcy suppliers of services or goods. If the debtor cannot keep its employees on the job, it may soon lose all hope of a successful Chapter 11. These and other issues concerning the use of property of the estate are governed by section 363. That section is likely to be the ground on which the initial skirmishes are fought in a Chapter 11 proceeding.

Shortly after or during negotiation and litigation under section 363, one can expect that the debtor in possession will negotiate temporary agreements with its secured creditors for use of their collateral. Failing such an agreement, certain of the creditors will request the court to grant them relief from the automatic stay to enable them to seize and sell their collateral. These requests often involve a decision about whether the debtor in possession has provided the secured creditor with "adequate protection" of its interest under section 361.

The second, often overlapping phase involves a more permanent adjustment of the business. There are likely to be a series of legal actions, hearings and compromises related to issues arising out of sections 364, 365, and 544 et seq. The debtor in possession's goals are to maintain business operations and to enhance the value of the assets available to it. At this stage in the proceeding the debtor in possession may propose to abrogate labor contracts, leases and other executory contracts and may attempt to recapture assets transferred and payments made in the days before the filing. Here a successful debtor must also make business adjustments if the legal and financial adjustments are to work.

The third phase routinely overlaps the prior two and involves an effort to negotiate and obtain judicial confirmation of a reorganization plan. Chapter 11 confirmation standards are complex and are made even more so by the fact that the Chapter 11 reorganization need not be limited to debt restructuring. Chapter 11 plans routinely alter a debtor corporation's equity ownership.

Occasionally plans are imposed (in the crude bankruptcy term, a "cramdown") on mostly unwilling creditors by a debtor. While the "cramdown" is a constant negotiating threat, a real cramdown is a rare exception. Among successful plans the norm is a negotiated agreement in which all of the affected parties exert some influence and, presumably, are offered something better than what they would receive on liquidation. Throughout any hostile exchanges over sections 362, 365, and 547, the debtor in possession will have been negotiating with various creditors. The creditors will have been negotiating among themselves to determine whether they can agree on a plan that will satisfy section 1129. Although the Chapter 11 debtor has the exclusive right to file a plan of reorganization for the first 120 days of the case, this "exclusivity" period is often extended by the court (at least in the biggest cases). One can anticipate that there will be protracted negotiation among the various creditors and between them and the debtor in possession in any large reorganization case. Often these negotiations bear fruit, yielding a "consensual" plan for the reorganization. In some cases they produce only partial agreement and the debtor will ask the court to impose the resulting plan upon the dissenting creditors. At that point the parties will get out section 1129 and argue about its meaning and application in their case.

Problem 2-1

Robeson, a manufacturer of computer disk drives, has 1,000 shareholders and 150 employees. Robeson is in the process of developing a new line of disk drives; its present line has become outmoded. It owes $700,000 to Metropolitan Bank. This debt is secured by all of Robeson's inventory and other personal property and is six months in default. In addition Robeson owes $1,000,000 to Caruso Savings & Loan, secured by a mortgage on its manufacturing plant. It is one year in arrears on the mortgage ($100,000 in interest and principal). Robeson also owes $400,000 to its suppliers and most of these loans are in various stages of default.

If Robeson's personal property were liquidated, it would bring a net of $800,000 to $850,000. Its real estate would bring between $900,000 and $1,100,000. If the new line of disk drives were successful, the company would probably be worth $5,000,000 to $6,000,000 in three years. Robeson currently has $100,000 of cash in a bank account at First Federal Bank.

To understand how bankruptcy might affect the various parties, consider how an extended bankruptcy might change the relative status of the parties. Consider three possibilities:

1. Assume that Robeson files a Chapter 7. Who gets what?

2. Assume that Robeson files in Chapter 11 and that the new line of disk drives is successful. How should the company's value be apportioned?

3. Assume that Robeson files in Chapter 11, but the new line is as unsuccessful as the existing drives and the company is forced to liquidate one and one-half years from now. In one and one-half years the inventory and other personal property could be liquidated for $400,000 and that the unencumbered cash would be $4,500. Assume that the operations during one and one-half years in Chapter 11 produce net losses of $600,000 and that upon liquidation there will be $400,000 of unpaid debt owed to lawyers and postpetition suppliers that will be treated as administrative expenses. Except as stated in this paragraph, assume that the assets and liability remain as represented above. Who gets what now?

By reviewing the three scenarios you should be able to see how the interests of various creditors and of the shareholders are deeply in conflict. Out of these conflicts arise the disputes that we will consider in later Chapters.

Examine the attached petition, schedules (a selected sample), motion for appointment of a committee of unsecured creditors, and pleadings index. Then try to answer the questions in the problem that follows. These will give a taste of the events that occur in the early part of a Chapter 11 and of the steps that the lawyers for the debtor and the various creditors must take early in a Chapter 11 case.

§ 6 LIFE OF A TYPICAL BANKRUPTCY CASE 73

FOR COURT USE ONLY
Date Petition Filed 6-15-90
Case Number 90-11710
Bankruptcy Judge _____

UNITED STATES BANKRUPTCY COURT FOR THE ____stern DISTRICT OF Michigan

In re: Action Auto Stores, Inc.,
a/k/a Action Auto, Inc.; a/k/a Sabo, Corp.;
Lansing-Lewis Services, Inc; a/k/a JED Co. Debtor*

Soc. Sec. No. ____ Debtor's Employer's Tax Id. No. 38-1901597

CHAPTER 11
VOLUNTARY PETITION

1. Petitioner's mailing address, including county, is
2128 S. Dort Hwy.
Flint, Michigan 48507-5202
Genesee County

90-11710

2. ☐ Petitioner has resided within this district for the preceding 180 days, or for a longer portion of the preceding 180 days than in any other district.

2. ☐ Petitioner has been domiciled within this district for the preceding 180 days, or for a longer portion of the preceding 180 days than in any other district.

2. ☒ Petitioner's principal place of business has been within this district for the preceding 180 days, or for a longer portion of the preceding 180 days than in any other district.

2. ☐ The principal assets of the petitioner have been within this district for the preceding 180 days, or for a longer portion of the preceding 180 days than in any other district.

3. Petitioner is qualified to file this petition and is entitled to the benefits of title 11, United States Code as a voluntary debtor.
4. ☐ A copy of petitioner's proposed plan, dated _____ 19 _____ is attached.
   ☒ Petitioner intends to file a plan pursuant to chapter 11 of title 11, United States Code.
5. Exhibit A is attached to and made a part of this Petition. †

Wherefore, petitioner prays for relief in accordance with chapter 11 of title 11, United States Code.
WARNER, NORCROSS & JUDD

Signed: _____
Attorney for Petitioner Robert H. Skilton

Address: 900 Old Kent Building
111 Lyon Street, N.W.
Grand Rapids, Michigan 49503-2489

Petitioner(s) sign(s) if not represented by attorney

_____
Petitioner

_____
Petitioner

DECLARATION

INDIVIDUAL(S): I _____ and I, _____ the petitioner(s) named in the foregoing petition, declare under penalty of perjury that the foregoing is true and correct.

CORPORATION: I, C. James Sabo the Chairman of the corporation named as petitioner in the foregoing petition, declare under penalty of perjury that the foregoing is true and correct, and that the filing of this petition on behalf of the corporation has been authorized.

PARTNERSHIP: I, _____ a member—an authorized agent— of the partnership named as petitioner in the foregoing petition, declare under penalty of perjury that the foregoing is true and correct, and that the filing of this petition on behalf of the partnership has been authorized.

Executed on 6·15 19 90 _____
Signature of Petitioner

_____
Signature of Petitioner

6-15-90
Executed on

_____
Signature of Attorney for Petitioner

© 1987 JULIUS BLUMBERG, INC. NYC 10013

UNITED STATES BANKRUPTCY COURT FOR THE _____ DISTRICT OF _____

In re Action Auto Stores, Inc.; a/k/a Action Auto, Inc.; a/k/a Sabo Corp.; a/k/a JED Co.; Lansing-Lewis Services, Inc.
                                                                    Debtor

Soc. Sec. No. _____   Debtor's Employer's Tax Id. No. 38-1901597

FOR COURT USE ONLY
Date Petition Filed 6-15-90
Case Number 90-11710
Bankruptcy Judge
EXHIBIT "A"

1. Petitioner's employer's identification number is   38-1901597

2. If any of petitioner's securities are registered under section 12 of the Securities and Exchange Act of 1934, SEC file number is
   0-15887

3. The following financial data is the latest available information and refers to petitioners condition on
   March 31, 19 90, or as stated

		Approximate Number of Holders
a. Total assets:	$ 64,025,643	
b. Total liabilities:	$ 57,032,668 - 3/31/90	
Secured debt, excluding that listed below	$ 19,206,050	----
Debt securities held by more than 100 holders	$ ----	----
Secured	$ ----	----
Unsecured	$ ----	----
Other liabilities, excluding contingent or unliquidated claims	$ 37,826,618	
Number of shares of common stock	$ 2,967,500	605 as of 6/30/89

Comments, if any:

4. Brief description of petitioner's business: Retail auto parts, accessories and gasoline stores.

5. [If presently available, supply the following information.] The name of any person who directly or indirectly owns, controls, or holds, with power to vote, 20% or more of the voting securities of petitioner is   C. James Sabo

6. [If presently available, supply the following information.] The names of all corporations 20% or more of the outstanding voting securities of which are dirctly or indirectly owned, controlled, or held, with power to vote, by petitioner are
   Action Development Corporation
   Auto Star Wholesale, Inc.
   Action Pride, Inc.
   Action FEA Environmental Group

UNITED STATES BANKRUPTCY COURT
EASTERN DISTRICT OF MICHIGAN
SOUTHERN DIVISION - FLINT

In re:)
ACTION AUTO STORES, INC.) HON. ARTHUR J. SPECTOR
  a/k/a Action Auto, Inc.)
  a/k/a Jed Automotive,) STATEMENT OF PURPOSE
  a/k/a Sabor Corp.,)
  a/k/a Jed Co.,)
  a/k/a Lansing-Lewis Services, Inc.,) Case No. 90-11719
    Debtor.) (Chapter 11)
E.I.D. No. 38-1901597)

The Debtor states that it has amended its Schedule A-3 for one of three reasons:

1. to add a creditor;
2. to correct an address;
3. to correct the amount of the claim.

The Debtor shall submit more detailed information regarding the purpose for each amendment. The undersigned party hereby certifies and affirms that this Amendment Statement and the First Amendment to Schedule A-3 are true, accurate and correct to the best of his knowledge, information and belief.

Dated: July 23, 1990

ACTION AUTO STORES, INC.
By _____
Its Chairman

WINEGARDEN, SHEDD, HALEY,
LINDHOLM & ROBERTSON

_____
Dennis M. Haley
501 Citizens Bank Building
Flint, Michigan 48243
(313) 767-3600

Co-counsel for the Debtor

CASE NO. 90–11710
ACTION AUTO STORES, INC.
SCHEDULE A–3—Creditors Having Unsecured Claims Without Priority

(1) Name of Creditor and Mailing Address	(2) When Claim was Incurred and Consideration Therefor; Etc.			(3) C/U/D	(5) Claim Amount
Action Plumbing and Heating 310 North Dunbar Street Potterville, MI 48876					
	040290	040290 041790	55.00		
	3/26–3/29	032690 041090	165.00		
	031290	031290 032790	220.00		
	3/19–3/23	031990 040390	220.00		
	030590	030590 032090	275.00		
					$935.00
Action/FEA Environmental Group 1450 E. South Owosso, MI 48867					
	90–439	050290 060190	56.70		
	90–441	042890 052890	396.90		
	90–451	061490 071490	11251.50		
					$11,705.10
AT&T Consumer Sales & Service 4660 S. Hagadorn East Lansing, MI 48823					
	6/90 10103	061290 061390	–1991.38		
	66625–6/90	061690 061790	2.50		
	29526–6/90	052890 052990	9.00		
	95391–6/90	060290 060390	14.50		
	69010–6/90	061090 061190	37.60		
	34 MUSIC	060690 060790	50.00		
	10103–6/90	051290 051390	3131.02		
	5–90 10103	051290 051390	3643.14		
					$4,896.38
Coca Cola Bottling Co. of MI 808 South Adams Mt. Pleasant, MI 48858					
	9/89–10/89	060190 070190	998.28		
					$998.28
Coca Cola Bottling Co. of MI 216 Peekstock Road P.O. BOX 2680 Kalamazoo, MI 49001					
	CORRECT 02	030190 040190	1190.49		
					$1,190.49
Coca Cola Bottling Co. of MI 1031 Hasting Street Traverse City, MI 49684					
	8/89–9/89	060190 070190	1846.28		
Michigan Bell Telephone P.O. BOX 5030 Saginaw, MI 48663–0001					
	57 FINAL	061590 061690	–179.94		
	39 FINAL	061590 061690	–179.24		
	55 FINAL	061590 061690	–178.47		
	44 FINAL	061590 061690	–163.06		
	20–FINAL	061590 061690	–161.54		
	46–FINAL	061590 061690	–149.87		
	FINAL 26	061590 061690	–148.53		
	JUNE SERV.	061590 061690	–146.98		
	53 FINAL	061590 061690	–144.86		
		* * *			
	7–6/90	060790 063090	689.89		
	8026064	062190 062290	740.04		
	950 7/90	061590 061690	786.23		
	16–0690	062490 062590	1462.78		
	950–0690	062490 062590	2089.06		
	900JNSERV	061590 061690	5335.88		
					$33,351.57
Mr. Glenn Miller Consulting Geologist 6236 West Grand River Brighton, MI					
	23487–1	060990 070990	1995.00		
Parkside Cleaners 22645 Pontiac Trail South Lyon, MI 48178					
	8449	052390 062390	47.40		

§ 6   LIFE OF A TYPICAL BANKRUPTCY CASE   77

(1) Name of Creditor and Mailing Address	(2) When Claim was Incurred and Consideration Therefor; Etc.			(3) C/U/D	(5) Claim Amount
	8334	051690 061690	51.18		
	8227	050990 060990	54.35		
	8110	050290 060290	66.55		
					$219.48
Nationwide P.O. Box 60876 Charlotte, NC 28260					
	DN–62919–1	091989 061090	– 1399.64		
	12630–1	020689 061090	– 1253.96		
	330764–1	111589 061090	– 1188.00		
	13891–1	062689 001090	– 399.64		
	375736–1	021990 061090	– 166.03		
	330665–1	072589 061090	– 147.19		
	375735–1	021990 061090	– 36.36		
	329883–1	021990 061090	– 30.43		
	64103–1	030389 061090	422.26		
	62894–1	011289 061090	554.44		
	66555–1	062989 061090	2446.33		
	CK6611–1	060189 061090	2884.44		
	68655–1	103189 061090	3108.90		
	67925–1	092189 061090	3177.48		
	67256–1	081189 061090	3220.25		
					$11,192.83
GMAC P.O. BOX 867 Southfield, MI 48037					
	5-90 51181	050190 051590	374.95		
	51181 6/90	060190 061590	374.95		
					$749.90
Rose Goss 5058 Stanley Rd. Mt. Morris, MI 48458					
	P/E 6-16	061890 063090	840.00		
	052290–1	052290 060190	920.00		
					$1,760.00
First of Amer Bank–Frankenmuth PAYMENT PROCESSING CENTER P.O. BOX 24007 Lansing, MI 48909					
	5-90 1	050190 051090	500.00		
	6/90	060590 061090	500.00		
					$1,000.00
Livingston County					
	21490–1	030190 030290	499.67		
	21490	030190 030290	637.62		
					$1,137.29
M & N Lawn Care 8940 Tyre Rd. Ubly, MI 48475					
	5/90 CUT'S	060190 070190	88.00		
					$88.00
Mack's Fire Equipment 8364 W. "B" Avenue Otsego, MI 49078					
	2163	060190 070190	37.20		
	2166	060490 070490	48.90		
					$86.10
Marathon Petroleum Company P.O. Box 67–170A Detroit, MI 48267					
	566711	061190 062390	2435.28		
	578573	061490 062690	2713.00		
	551583	060690 061890	2859.00		
		* * *			
	585902	061790 062990	23644.61		
	562708	061090 062290	24655.55		
					$219,925.44
USA Fashion Magic P.O. Box 6000 San Francisco, CA 94160					
	Mar'90–1	030190 070190	– 179.17		
	13828–1	041690 061690	666.60		
	14134	051890 061790	808.20		
					$1,295.63
Sunoco P.O. Box 77098 Detroit, MI 48277					
	CORRECT–1	030190 043090	– 35623.28		
	6020–A	042490 061790	5572.80		
	6020–B	042490 071790	5572.80		

(1) Name of Creditor and Mailing Address	(2) When Claim was Incurred and Consideration Therefor; Etc.			(3) C/U/D	(5) Claim Amount
	6020–C	042490 061790	5572.80		
	DM62856–1	030190 043090	17811.64		
					($1,093.24)
Ryder Truck Rental Inc. P.O. Box 99088 Troy, MI 48099					
	448	042890 050890	114.00		
	1002545	053190 061190	143.00		
	1002197	052390 060490	172.15		
	01001570	051590 052590	246.75		
	01003448	061190 062190	286.00		
	435	042890 050890	592.00		
	01001062	050890 051890	1465.32		
	1003200	061190 062190	1618.46		
	01001689	051290 052290	2022.96		
	01001043	050890 051890	12160.48		
	1003180	061190 062190	14004.45		
					$32,825.57
Security Mutual Life Insurance P.O. Box 1625 Binghampton, NY 013902					
	SCH# 1 6/90	060190 060990	26000.00		
	0590–1	050190 053190	26000.00		
					$52,000.00
Thomas and Marge 319 Petrie Rd. Cadillac, MI 49601					
	0690	060190 060290	1300.00		
					$1,300.00
Weller Plastics Division P.O. Box 437 Des Moines, IA 50302					
	MAR	033190 060190	9000.00		
					$9,000.00
Whirley Industries 618 Fourth Ave. Warren, PA 16365					
	4072	042390 052390	3067.89		
					$3,067.89
Dawn Donuts 4124 West Saginaw Lansing, MI 48917					
	060590	060590 070590	14.04		
	W/E 61590	061590 071590	19.17		
	W/E 6990	060990 070990	44.81		
	6/10–15/90	061090 071090	90.16		
	5/31–6/9	053190 063090	187.37		
					$355.55
Dawn Donuts 6–4300 West Pierson Road Flint, MI 48507					
	11667	051490 061490	−1302.72		
	1259	041590 043090	−124.01		
	70667	051490 061490	−94.24		
	2323	042290 050790	−81.60		
	2339	040190 041190	−74.67		
	3616	052390 062390	−72.00		
	3635	052690 062690	−71.20		
	91842	031790 040190	−68.28		
	3218	060490 070490	−67.20		
	88669	042890 052890	−67.20		
		* * *			
	88639	042890 052890	152.48		
	2308	033090 041490	152.70		
	1198	040790 042290	155.68		
	3878	051390 061390	157.44		
	2278	032590 040990	157.66		
	3187	060990 070990	158.88		
	3601	052090 062090	158.88		
	3609	051990 061990	158.88		
	3642	052890 062890	158.88		
	88585	050590 060590	161.20		
	88586	050690 060690	161.20		
	3637	052790 062790	162.08		
	2312	033190 041590	164.94		
	2344	040190 041690	164.94		
	79139	031090 032590	165.50		
	3626	052590 062590	168.48		
	3239	060290 070290	171.68		
	91837	031790 040190	171.70		
	3856	051290 061290	178.08		

(1) Name of Creditor and Mailing Address	(2) When Claim was Incurred and Consideration Therefor; Etc.		(3) C/U/D	(5) Claim Amount
91827	031190 032690	184.70		
3665	052690 062690	189.12		
1256	041590 043090	218.14		
				$11,667.30

JUL 0 6 1990

UNITED STATES BANKRUPTCY COURT
FOR THE EASTERN DISTRICT OF MICHIGAN

In Re:

ACTION AUTO STORES, INC.
a/k/a ET AL

                                      Case No. 90-11710-AJS
                                      Chapter 11
                                      Hon. Arthur J. Spector

_____ Debtor(s)/

APPOINTMENT OF COMMITTEE OF UNSECURED CREDITORS

    Pursuant to Sections 1102(a) and 1102(b) of the Bankruptcy Code. the following creditors of the above-named debtor being among those holding the largest unsecured claims (or who are members of a committe organized by creditors before the order for relief under Chapter 11 of the Bankruptcy Code which are fairly chosen and is representative of the different kinds of claims to be represented) are willing to serve:

The Travelers Insurance Co.
Frederick A. Sabetta, Chairperson
One Tower Sq./ Tenth Floor Plaza BLDG.
Securities Dept.
Hartford, CT 06183
(203) 277-6269

Quaker State Corporation
Larry A. Drelick
255 Elm Street
Oil City, PA 16301
(814) 676-7932

The Kelley-Springfield Tire Co.
David E. Dohnal or Selby Highland
Willowbrook Road
Cumberland, MD 21502
(301) 777-6491/777-6552

BASF Corporation
Robert M. Spolar
100 Cherry Hill Road
Parsippany, NJ 07054
(201) 316-4512

[G9028]

Great American Insurance Co.
Stuart J. Rice, Esq.
3466 Penobscot Building
Detroit, MI 48226
(313) 962-7770

Standard Motor Products
a/k/a Sorensen Industries
Chester B. Edwards
31-78 Northern Boulevard
Long Island City, NY
(718) 392-0200

Exide Corporation
Tom Kocher or Alan Gauthier
645 Penn Street
Reading, PA 19612-4205
(215) 378-0627

Wagner Brake
Donald P. Burquin
930 Roosevelt Parkway
Chesterfield, MO 63017
(314) 532-8541

Blue Chip Products Inc.
Tony Cino
One Newbold Road
Fairless Hills, PA 19030
(215) 736-0901

Monroe Auto Equipment Co.
Jean F. Gustus
One International Drive
Monroe, MI 48161
(313) 243-8352

Rally Manufacturing
Tom Kruszewski
5255 N.W. 159th Street
Miami, FL 33014
(305) 628-2886

The above named individuals are therefore appointed to the Committee of Unsecured Creditors.

Respectfully Submitted,

CONRAD J. MORGENSTERN
UNITED STATES TRUSTEE

By: *Claretta Evans*
Claretta Evans
Office of the U.S. Trustee
477 Michigan Ave., Suite 1760
Detroit, MI 48226

[G9029]

July 3, 1990

* * * * * * * * * * * * * * * *

CERTIFICATE OF SERVICE

The undersigned employee of the Office of the United States Trustee hereby certifies taht a copy of this document was on this date mailed to:

_X_ Members of the Creditors' Committee	_X_ Debtor
____ Attorney for the Creditors' Committee	_X_ Counsel for Debtor
____ Trustee	____ Counsel for Trustee

Office of the United States Trustee

July 3, 1990

By _[signature]_
James A. Bordonaro   [G9030]

**UNITED STATES BANKRUPTCY COURT
EASTERN DISTRICT OF MICHIGAN
SOUTHERN DIVISION – FLINT**

In the Matter of:

ACTION AUTO STORES, INC.,
a/k/a Action Auto, Inc.,
a/k/a Sabo Corp., a/k/a
JED Co., Lansing Lewis
Services, Inc.,

    Debtor.

_____/

Chapter 11
Case No. 90-11710-S

Judge Arthur J. Spector

PLEADINGS INDEX NO. 1 – PAGE 1

1.	Chapter 11 Voluntary Petition: Petition Cover Sheet Statement Pursuant to Bankruptcy Rule 2016(b) List of Equity Security Holders	6/15/90
2.	Debtor's Application to Retain PaineWebber Inc. As Investment Bankers with Affidavit of Elizabeth K. Lambert and Supplemental Affidavit of Elizabeth K. Lambert and Memorandum in Support of Application	06/16/90
3.	Debtor's Application To Retain Winegarden, Shedd Haley, Lindholm and Robertson as Co-Counsel	6/16/90
4	Debtor's Application To Retain Warner, Norcross & Judd as Co-Counsel	6/16/90
5.	Debtor's Application To Retain James V. McTevia & Associates, Inc. as Business Consultants	6/16/90
6.	Debtor's Application (and Amended Application) to Retain Coopers & Lybrand as Accountants and (proposed) **Order Authorizing The Debtor To Employ Coopers & Lybrand as Accountants**	6/16/90 07/17/90
7.	Debtor's Application To Retain Michael Fox Auctioneers, Inc. and (proposed) Order Authorizing the Debtor To Retain Michael Fox Auctineers, Inc.	6/16/90 8/15/90
8.	Debtor's Motion For Permission To Use Cash Collateral	6/18/90

[G9031]

9.	Debtor's Motion For An Expedited Preliminary Hearing On Debtor's Motion For Authority To Use Cash Collateral and Ex-Parte Order Setting An Expedited Hearing On Debtor's Motion For An Expedited Preliminary Hearing For Authority To Use Cash Collateral	06/18/90 06/19/90
9.A.	Consent Order Authorizing Debtor's Use of Cash Collateral and Other Relief Pending Final Hearing AND	6/22/90
9.B.	**2nd Order**: Consent Order Authorizing Debtor's Use of Cash Collateral and Other Relief AND	7/06/90
9.C.	**3rd Order**: Consent Order Supplementing Consent Order Authorizing Debtor's Use of Cash Collateral And Other Relief	
9.D.	**4th Order**: Consent Order Extending Order Authorizing Debtor's Use of Cash Collateral and Other Relief	09/24/90
10.	Objection of Michigan National Bank To Debtor's Application To Retain PaineWebber, Inc. as Investment Bankers; Proof of Service	6/29/90
11.	Combined Motion of OLP To: (1) Compel Payment of Administrative Expenses (2) Compel Debtor to Assume or Reject Its Executory Lease; and (3) Lift the Automatic Stay and/or (4) for Adequate Protection and Brief In Support of Combined Motion; and Certificate of Service	6/29/90
12.	Michigan National Bank's Response to Debtor's Motion For Permission To Use Cash Collateral; and Memorandum	7/03/90
13.	Application For Order Authorizing Appointment of Secretary to Official Creditors' Committee	07/02/90
14.	Application Authorizing Retention of Accountants For Creditors'	07/03/90
15.	Application By Committee of Unsecured Creditors' Committee To Employ Legal Counsel and Affidavit and Proof of Service	07/06/90
16.	Debtor's Motion For Authority To Enter Into Post-Petition Financing Arrangement With Transamerica Insurance Finance Corporation and For Other Relief	07/09/90
17.	Order Granting Debtor's Motion For Authority To Enter Into Post-Petition Financing Arrangement With Transamerica Insurance Finance Corporation	07/20/90

18.	**Notice For Meeting of Creditors Combined With Notice of Automatic Stay and Appointment of Creditors' Committee**(Matrix List Attached)	07/03/90
19.	Debtor's Motion For An Extension of Time To Assume or Reject Unexpired Leases and Extension of Time to Pay Rent	07/13/90
20.	Creditors' Committee Objection to OLP Combined Motion and Brief to: (1) Compel Payment of Adminis. Expenses; (2) Compel Debtor To Assume or Reject its Executory Lease; and/or (3) Lift the Automatic Stay and/or (4) For Adequate Protection	07/13/90
21.	Debtor's Motion to Grant Adequate Assurance To Indiana Michigan Power Company and Other Relief; Notice of Time To File Response; Notice of Hearing; and (proposed) Order Granting Debtor's Motion For Adequate Assurance Under 11 U.S.C. §366(b)	07/16/90
22.	Debtor's Response To OLP's Combined Motion	07/90
23.	Debtor's Motion To Approve Self-Insurance of Workers Compensation Liability; and Notice of Time to File Response to Motion	07/16/90
24.	MNB's Answer To Debtor's Motion To Approve Self-Insurance of Workers' Compensation Liability; Proof of Service	07/24/90
25.	Debtor's Motion For Authority To Employ Special Counsel	07/90
26.	Objection to Debtor's Motion For Authority To Employ Dykema Gossett as Special Counsel; Proof of Service (Filed by Jaffe, Snider, on behalf of MNB)	07/25/90
27.	(Midlantic National Bank) Motion To Compel Debtor To Assume or Reject Executory Contracts Within Specified Time; Notice and Opportunity For Hearing	07/26/90
28.	Notice of Hearing on U.S. Trustee's Objection to (1) Debtor's Application to Employ James McTevia, et al.	07/30
29.	Motion For an Order (1) Authorizing Sale of Property of the Estate By Public Auction Free and Clear of Liens and Interests; (ii) Transferring Liens and Claims to Auction Proceeds; (iii) Authorizing Payment of Auction Sale Proceeds; and (iv) Granting Other Relief	07/30/90

30.	Objection of The United States Trustee Concerning Debtor's Application To Employ Co-Counsel; and Brief In Support of Objection to Debtor's Application To Employ Co-Counsel	07/13/90
31.	Objection of the United States Trustee To Application of the Unsecured Creditors' Committee For Authority to Employ Two Law Firms; Certificate of Service	07/19/90
32.	Debtor's Memorandum In Support of its Application To Retain PaineWebber, Inc. as Investment Banker	07/30/90
33.	Debtor's Application to Retain Real Estate Broker	07/13/90
34.	Combined Stipulated Order To Adjourn Hearing; Certificate of Service	07/31/90
35.	Motion To Lift Stay (filed by LeaseFirst)	07/05/90
36.	Creditors' Committee Objection To Motion For Relief From the Automatic Stay	07/26/90
37.	Appointment of Committee of Unsecured Creditors	07/06/90
38.	Motion To Compel Debtor To Reject or Assume Lease, to Perform Its Obligations Under the Lease, or in the Alternative, Motion To Modify or Lift The Automatic Stay; Notice of Hearing (filed by Ford Motor Credit)	07/13/90
39.	Debtor's Application To Retain Williams And Lipton Company As A Professional Appraiser	08/90
40.	Debtor's Brief In support of Motion to Continue Self-Insurance Program For Workers Compensation Liability	
41.	Debtor's Motion For Authority To Employ Special Counsel; Affidavit of Disinterestedness; Notice of Time For Filing Responses; Proof of Service and Notice of Hearing	07/30/90
42.	Response of Creditors' Committee To Debtor's Motion For Authority To Employ Special Counsel	08/10/90
43.	Notice of Hearing on Motion To Lift Stay To Permit Sun Refining & Marketing Company to Serve Notices of Termination of Franchise Agreements, to Terminate Franchise Agreements, to Recover Property held By the Estate, Or in the Alternative, To Compel Debtor to Reject Franchise Agreements; and Motion Re same; Proof of Service	08/07/90

44.	Reply to Debtor's Response to OLP's Combined Motion; Certificate of Service	08/09/90
45.	Response to Debtor's Motion For An Extension of Time To Assume or Reject Unexpired Leases and Extension of Time To Pay Rent; Certificate of Service	08/10/90
46.	Response of Michigan National Bank To Midlantic National Bank's Motion To Compel Debtor to Assume or Reject Executory Contract	08/17/90
47.	Debtor's Application To Retain Kleiman As a Professional Appraiser	08/15/90
48.	Joint Motion For Entry of Order Pursuant to 11 U.S.C. Section 546(c)(2)	08/17/90
49.	Order Allowing Unsecured Creditors' Committee to Employ Bodman, Longley & Dahling as Counsel	08/15/90
50.	Sun Refining & Marketing Company's Response To Debtor's Motion For An Order Authorizing Sale of Property of the Estate by Public Auction, and Objection To Proposed Distribution of Proceeds from Auction Sale	08/21/90
51.	Debtor's Objection To Motion For Order Authorizing Sale of Property of the Estate by Public Auction Free and Clear of any Interest in Such Property, Transferring Liens and Claims to Proceeds of Sale, Authorizing Payment of Auction Sale Proceeds and Granting Other Relief; Proof of Service	08/22/90
76.	Response of McDonnell Douglas Finance Corporation To Midlantic National Bank's Motion To Compel Debtor to Assume or Reject Executory Contract	08/22/90
77.	Response of McDonnell Douglas Finance Corporation To Motion For Order Granting Relief From Stay, Or in the Alternative, For Order Providing Adequate Protection on Behalf of Textron Capital Corporation	08/22/90
78.	State of Michigan's Response To Action Auto Store Inc's Notice of Proposed Public Auction	08/22/90
79.	Objection to Debtor's Motion For an Order Authorizing Sale of Property of the Estate By Public Auction Free and Clear of Liens and Interests; Transferring Liens and Claims to Auction Proceeds; Authorizing Payment of Auction Sale Proceeds; and Granting Other Relief (filed by Oakland County Treasurer's Office)	08/22/90

§ 6   LIFE OF A TYPICAL BANKRUPTCY CASE   87

80.	Ford Equipment Leasing Company's Objection to Debtor's Motion For Order (i) Authorizing Sale of Property of the Estate by Public Auction Free and Clear of Liens and Interests; (ii) Transferring Liens and Claims to Auction Proceeds; (iii) Authorizing Payment of Auction Sale Proceeds; and (iv) Granting Other Relief	08/22/90
81.	Objection of Ray Winnie Enterprises, Inc., Elray Winnie and Joyce Winnie to Debtor's Motion For Order Authorizing Sale of Property of the Estate	08/23/90
82.	Objection To Motion For an Order Authorizing Sale of Property (filed by Creditors: John R. Meyer, Jane T. Meyer, Thomas B. Meyer and Margaret Meyer)	08/24/90
59.	Debtor's Application To Retain Gardner, Carton & Douglas As Special Counsel (w/ attached Affidavit and	9/4/90
	Order Authorizing The Debtor to Retain Gardner, Carton & Douglas as Special Counsel	9/24/90
60.	Debtor's Motion For Order Authorizing Procedures For Interim Compensation And Reimbursement of Professionals; Brief In Support of Same; and Notice of Hearing	08/22/90
61.	CIT Group/Equipment Financing's Objection To Debtor's Proposed Public Auction Sale	08/22/90
62.	Objections of Textron Financial Corporation and Textron Capital Corporation To Debtor's Motion For an Order (i) Authorizing Sale of Property of the Estate by Public Auction Free and Clear of Liens and Interests; (ii) Transferring Liens and Claims to Auction Proceeds; (iii) Authorizing Payment of Auction Sale Proceeds; and (iv) Granting Other Relief	08/23/90
63.	Notice of Taking 2004 Examination of Donald Nance	08/29/90
64.	Notice of Taking 2004 Examination of Matthew Gould	08/31/90
65.	Creditors' Committee's Response to Debtor's Motion For Order Authorizing Procedures For Interim Compensation and Reimbursement of Expenses of Professionals	08/30/90

66.	Debtor's Objection to Motion For Lift of Stay to Permit Sun Refining & Marketing Company To Serve Notices of Termination of Franchise Agreements, To Terminate Franchise Agreements, To Recover Property Held by the Estate or, In the Alternative, to Compel Debtor to Reject Franchise Agreements and Brief In Support thereof	08/22/90 08/22/90
67.	Response of Creditors' Committee to Debtor's Motion For Approval To Assume Lease Agreement With The SABO Investment Partnership	08/24/90
67.	Motion of Whirlpool Financial Corp. to Compel Payment of Administrative Expense; and To Compel Debtor To Assume or Reject its Unexpired Leases and For Adequate Protection; Or to Lift the Automatic Stay; Brief in Support of Motion; and Notice of Opportunity For Hearing	08/24/90
68.	Ottawa Leasing Company, Inc.'s Motion To Modify Stay and/or Time to Assume or Reject Leases; and Notice of Time to File Objection to Motion	08/27/90
69.	Notice of Taking 2004 Examination of William Eglin	08/30/90
70.	Response of Michigan National Bank to Motion of Whirlpool Financial Corporation To Compel Payment of Administrative Expense, et al.	09/04/90
71.	Michigan National Bank's Objection To Debtor's Motion For Order Authorizing Procedures For Interim Compensation And Reimbursement of Professionals and Memorandum In Support of Objection to Debtor's Motion For Order Authorizing Procedures For Interim Compensation and Reimbursement of Professionals; and Certificate of Service	09/04/90 09/04/90
72.	Motion To Compel Debtor to Reject or Assume Lease, To Perform Its Obligations Under the Lease, or In the Alternative, Motion to Modify or Lift the Automatic Stay; and Motion For Expedited Hearing on above Motion; and Notice of Hearing	07/13/90
73.	Debtor's Response to (Ford Equipment Leasing) Motion For Expedited Hearing, To Motion To Compel Debtor To Reject or Assume Leases, To Perform Its Obligations Under the Lease, Or in the Alternative, Motion To Modify or Lift the Automatic Stay; and Brief In Support	07/23/90

74.	Motion For Order Directing Debtor In Possession To Assume or Reject Unexpired Lease and For Adequate Protection; Exhibits attached (filed by Textron Financial Corporation)	08/03/90
75.	Debtor's Motion For Approval To Assume Lease Agreement (Total of 8)	07/27/90
76.	Response of Creditors' Committee To Debtor's Motion For Approval To Assume Lease Agreement With: (Total of 7 people) (Filed by Official Unsecured Creditors' Committee)	08/24/90
77.	Response and Objection of Michigan National Bank to Motion For Approval to Assume Lease Agreement (Filed by Jaffe, Snider)	08/27/90
78.	Stipulated Order Adjourning Hearings On: (1) Textron Capital Corporation's Motion For Order Granting Relief From the Stay, or, In the Alternative, For Order Providing Adequate Protection; and (2) Textron Financial Corp.'s Motion For ORder Directing DIP to Assume or Reject Unexpired Lease and For Adequate Protection (filed by Textron Capital Corp.)	08/28/90
79.	Joint Motion For Entry of Order Pursuant to 11 U.S.C. §546(C)(2) (filed by Action Auto Stores & Quaker State Corp) Notice of Opportunity For Hearing;	09/04/90
80.	Application For Authority To Sell Real Estate (filed by Action Auto) and Notice of Sale Free and Clear of Liens; Affidavit of Service	09/04/90
81.	Order Granting Relief From Automatic Stay	09/06/90
82.	Michigan National Bank's Response To Textron Capital Corporation's Motion For Order Granting Relief From The Stay, or, In the Alternative, For Order Providing Adequate Protection	09/10/90
83.	Michigan National Bank's Response To Textron Financial Corporation's Motion For Order Directing DIP To Assume or Reject Unexpired Lease and For Adequate Protection; Certificate of Service	09/10/90
84.	OLP's Objection to Debtor's Motion For Order Authorizing Procedures for Interim Compensation and Reimbursement of Professionals;	09/17/90
85.	Notice of Intent to Present Order Authorizing Debtor To Retain Investment Banker For Signature and Entry;	09/17/90

86.	Notice of Intent To Present Order Authorizing Debtors To Retain Dykema Gossett As Special Counsel	09/18/90
87.	Objection to Proposed Order Authorizing Debtor To Retain Special Counsel (filed by The Creditors' Committee) and Notice of Hearing on Objection to Proposed Order Retaining Dykema Gossett	09/24/90 10/1/90
88.	Objection of Unsecured Creditors' Committee to Joint Motion For Entry of Order Pursuant to 11 U.S.C. §546(c)2	09/24/90
89.	Motion For Approval to Reject Unexpired Lease	9/19/90
90.	Debtor's Motion to Extend Exclusive Period	09/24/90
91.	Motion To Assume Truck Lease and Service Agreement; Notice of Time to File Response To Motion To Assume Truck Lease and Service Agreement	09/28/90
92.	Motion For Authority To Sell Real Property Free and Clear of Liens; **PROPOSED** Order Authorizing Sale of Property of the Estate Free and Clear of Liens and Interest and Transferring Liens and Claims to Proceeds (prepared by Zillgitt)	10/11/90 Not Entered
93.	**PROPOSED** Stipulation Resolving Ford Equipment Leasing Company's Motion To Compel Debtor to Reject or Assume Lease, to Perform its Obligations Under the Lease or in the Alternative, Motion to Modify or Lift the Automatic Stay (filed by Ford Equipment Leasing Company and Action Auto)	Not Entered
94.	Debtor's Motion For Permission to Sublease Realty To Premiere Packaging, Inc; Notice of Opportunity to File and Serve Response or Request For Hearing; and Notice of Hearing on said Motion	10/12/90
95.	Debtor's Motion For Authority To Pay Real Estate Taxes At Sale Closings; Notice of Opportunity For Hearing; and Notice of Hearing re said Motion	10/09/90
96.	Order Denying, In part, Quaker State Corporation's Demand For Reclamation of Goods	10/18/90
97.	MNB's Motion For Entry of Order Authorizing and Directing Debtor's Turnover of Net Real Estate Proceeds; Notice of Opportunity To File; and Notice of Hearing re said Motion;	10/15/90

1270C

Problem 2-2

Answer the following questions by examining the bankruptcy petition, the cover sheet, and the schedule.

1. What is the debtor's business?

2. Was the debtor insolvent on the date the petition was filed?

3. Why do you imagine debtor owes money to The Payment Processing Center at First of America of Livingston County and to Marathon Petroleum?

4. Can you imagine ways in which the representatives of various creditors who will serve on the committee of unsecured creditors may differ and disagree about what should be done in this bankruptcy?

5. Examine the pleadings index above. Can you guess about the lawyers' fees associated with the preparation, filing, and appearances associated with the 97 entries on that index?

6. At the time of the 97th entry, how long had bankruptcy been open?

7. Which of the documents in the index were the most important and stirred the most controversy in the early days of the bankruptcy?

8. Why would somebody such as Transamerica Insurance Finance Corporation (No. 17) agree to extend credit to somebody already in Chapter 11?

9. Why must the debtor grant "adequate assurance" to Indiana/Michigan Power Company? (No. 21.)

10. Why does the U.S. Trustee not want the debtor to employ co-counsel (No. 30)? And why (No. 31) is he objecting to the unsecured creditor's committee's employment of a law firm?

11. The parties are already beginning to quarrel over executory contracts and franchises. (Nos. 43 and 46.) What is going on there?

12. Are the lawyers going to be paid up front or do they have to wait to the end of the case? (No. 65.)

13. Michigan National Bank seems to be a big player in this game even in circumstances when it does not appear to be directly involved. Why is that? (Nos. 70, 71, 77, 82, 83).

Problem 2-3

You have been engaged to represent a client who plans to file a petition in Chapter 11. The client operates three retail stores with annual sales of $5,000,000. The client is insolvent and owes the bank $1,000,000 on a loan secured by inventory and equipment. The debtor owes between $500,000 and $800,000 in trade and miscellaneous unsecured credit. In addition, the client was recently sued by a group of customers who claim to have suffered an allergic reaction to a particular line of apparel that was sold by the client. These parties claim damages of at least $6,000,000.

The person who initially worked up the case in your office has suggested that the client could file as a small business under section 101(51)(c) and that the benefits of filing as a small business under sections 1102(a), 1121(e) and 1125(f) would outweigh the costs. Do you concur? (This problem illustrates the maxim that substantive law is secreted in interstices between procedural provisions. Almost everything in the quoted sections that relates to small businesses is nominally "procedural." But as the maxim suggests, these provisions may be more important than any of the substantive provisions that will apply to your client in its reorganization.)

Chapter Three

BANKRUPTCY JURISDICTION AND VENUE

§ 1. JURISDICTION OF THE BANKRUPTCY COURT

Under the Bankruptcy Act of 1898, the bankruptcy courts had only limited *in rem* jurisdiction known as "summary jurisdiction." This jurisdiction extended to all matters regarding the administration of the debtor's estate, but only to some disputes between the estate and adverse claimants involving rights to money or property in which the estate asserted an interest. Matters of administration included such things as selection of the officers administering the estate, conduct of creditors' meetings, sale of assets, and distribution of proceeds of the estate. Jurisdiction over "controversies arising in proceedings in bankruptcy" between the estate and adverse claimants existed only if summary jurisdiction was expressly provided as in a few special instances specified in Section 60(d) or 67(a)(4), the adverse claimant consented to the bankruptcy court's jurisdiction, or the bankruptcy court had possession of the disputed property. (Over time, summary jurisdiction in the rehabilitation chapter cases came to be based on title as well as possession.) Both consent and possession could be actual or constructive.

If an adverse claimant "consented" to the bankruptcy court's jurisdiction, almost any suit could be heard. Actual consent needs no explanation. However, an adverse claimant could also be said to have given his "constructive consent" to the bankruptcy court's jurisdiction by so minor an action as filing a proof of claim or failing to file a timely objection to jurisdiction.

Assuming neither actual nor constructive consent was given by the adverse claimant, the bankruptcy court's jurisdiction turned upon whether the disputed property was in the actual or constructive possession of the bankruptcy court. Property in the actual possession of the bankruptcy court included any property in the debtor's possession at the time the petition for bankruptcy was filed. Constructive possession existed if the bankruptcy court determined that the claim of the adverse party was merely "colorable"; the bankruptcy court had no jurisdiction if the adverse party was determined to have a *bona fide* claim to the property.

Where the bankruptcy court's summary jurisdiction could not be properly invoked, a plenary suit was required. This meant suit had to be instituted in a nonbankruptcy court. Thus, a considerable amount of a trustee's action to recover assets of the estate had to be instituted in a court other than the bankruptcy court.

Parties litigated jurisdictional issues frequently because no matter how the issue was decided, delay enhanced the power of one party or the other. Referees had to decide partial issues and postpone others until they could be determined by another court. Substantial delays, especially detrimental in rehabilitation cases, resulted because the dockets in state and federal courts were often more crowded than those of the bankruptcy courts. This delay inevitably increased the expenses of bankruptcy proceedings and sometimes deterred the trustee from seeking to enforce rights of recovery.

The Kennedy Commission and Congress sought to eliminate the basis for litigation of the jurisdictional issues which had consumed so much of the bankruptcy system's time, money and energy. They also hoped to foster development of a more uniform and coherent bankruptcy law. There would be no more fragmented cases heard partly by misinformed judges; everything was to stay under one roof—the bankruptcy court.

The 1978 Code explicitly granted jurisdiction to the federal district court over "all civil proceedings arising under title 11 or arising and related to cases under title 11." 18 U.S.C. § 1471(b). The law specified that the bankruptcy court for the district in which the case was commenced "shall exercise all of the jurisdiction conferred by this section * * *." Unless the court chose to abstain, virtually all litigation in which the debtor or the bankruptcy estate would be expected to have an interest would have been in the bankruptcy court's jurisdiction under the Code. "The idea of possession or consent as the sole basis for jurisdiction is eliminated. The Bankruptcy Court is given *in personam* jurisdiction as well as *in rem* jurisdiction to handle everything that arises in the Bankruptcy case." H.R.Rep. 595, 95th Cong., 1st Sess. 445 (1977), reprinted in 1978 U.S.Code Cong. & Ad.News, 5963, 6400. Under the theory of the 1978 Code, the bankruptcy court would have been able not only to exercise jurisdiction over suits against the debtor, but also over actions by trustees to recover amounts owed to the debtor or property set aside as exempt, and over a variety of other claims by the debtor against third parties. Formerly, most of these suits would have had to have been heard elsewhere. See, 1 Collier on Bankruptcy, ¶ 3.01(1)(b)[iv] (L. King, 15th ed., 1991). Indeed, in 1978 one was hard put to think of a case that might be of interest to the bankruptcy estate that could not have been heard in bankruptcy court. (One court drew the line at granting a divorce between husband and wife debtors in the bankruptcy court. See *Cunningham v. Cunningham,* 9 B.R. 70 (Bankr. D.N.M.1981).)

At the time of the Bankruptcy Code's enactment in 1978, some members of Congress had doubts about the constitutionality of the bankruptcy court described above. Clearly the court did not fit under Article III of the Constitution because the judges did not have lifetime tenure and there was no assurance that their salaries could not be reduced. On the other hand, it was unclear whether "legislative courts" of the kind contemplated by Article I of the Constitution could constitutionally assert the kind of jurisdiction contemplated in the Bankruptcy Code. Prior to 1978 the Supreme Court had handed down a series of Delphic opinions on the rights of Article I courts, and scholars were divided on the question whether the court established in the Code was constitutional. See *Bankruptcy Reform Act of 1978: Hearings on H.R. 31 and H.R. 32 Before the Subcomm. on Civil and Constitutional Rights of the House Comm. on the Judiciary,* 94th Cong. 1st and 2d Sess., 2682–2706 (1975–76). In response to those concerns, the House originally proposed an Article III court under which the judges would have had lifetime tenure. The Senate proposed 12 year terms.

The worst fears of those who doubted the constitutionality of the new court were realized in the decision of *Northern Pipeline Construction Co. v. Marathon Pipe* Line Co., 458 U.S. 50, 102 S.Ct. 2858, 73 L.Ed.2d 598 (1982). In effect, *Marathon* destroyed the bankruptcy court's jurisdictional basis.

In *Marathon,* the debtor in possession sought to sue Marathon Pipe Line for breach of a prepetition contract. Thus, the debtor in possession was the plaintiff and a third party the defendant. The debtor in possession brought the action in bankruptcy court. The defendant maintained the bankruptcy court lacked jurisdiction and furthermore that Congress lacked the power to authorize the bankruptcy court to hear such a case. The Supreme Court, in a plurality opinion, agreed with the defendant and held that Congress lacked the authority to grant jurisdiction to an Article I court to hear a proceeding as remote from the bankruptcy case as this one. Note, this was not a case in which the defendant had itself asserted a claim against the bankruptcy estate (so that the debtor in possession's suit might be regarded as a counterclaim) nor was it a case in any way directly related to the bankruptcy case, such as a claim about preferences, a challenge to a security interest, or a question concerning the administration of the assets of the debtor in possession.

As we have indicated above, the *Marathon* decision left the courts in chaos and the Congress in a state of indecision. After two years Congress sought to solve the problem first by granting jurisdiction generally to an Article III court, namely the district court, and then authorizing (by section 157) the delegation of jurisdiction to the bankruptcy court. Congress apparently recognized that under *Marathon* some cases should not be handled even by a federal district judge.

Accordingly it enacted 28 U.S.C. § 1334. The section provides that the district court, and *a fortiori* the bankruptcy court, must abstain from exercising jurisdiction in a proceeding based upon a state law cause of action:

> "related to * * * but not arising under * * * or arising in title 11 with respect to which an action could not have been commenced in a court of the United States absent jurisdiction under this section, * * * if an action is commenced, and can be timely adjudicated in a state forum or appropriate jurisdiction."

The conditions under which the district courts are required to abstain are so narrow that it is doubtful many such cases exist. Indeed, it is unclear what would happen if the *Marathon* case were reincarnated. In this respect, however, one must also consider the provisions on discretionary abstention.

Section 1334 was originally adopted as an interim rule. The interim rule was strongly criticized by several commentators as constitutionally invalid and unworkable. They argued that it attempted to do what the Supreme Court said Congress could not do. See Countryman, *Emergency Rule Compounds Emergency,* 57 Am.Bankr.L.J. 1 (1983); Kind, *The Unmaking of a Bankruptcy Court: Aftermath of Northern Pipeline v. Marathon,* 50 Wm. & Mary L.Rev. 99, 116–19 (1983). See also Lavien, *Comments on the Rule We Live By,* 88 Com.L.J. 130 (1983); Vihon, *Delegation of Authority and the Model Rule: The Continuing Saga of Northern Pipeline,* 88 Com.L.J. 64 (1983).

Congress was more circumspect in granting section 1334 jurisdiction to the bankruptcy courts than it had been in 1978. The relevant delegation provision is titled "Procedures" and is found in section 28 U.S.C. § 157. Using language that first appeared in the *Marathon* case, Congress defined cases within the bankruptcy court jurisdiction as "core proceedings arising in a case under title 11" and defined others as non-core proceedings. Core is roughly equivalent to arising in or arising under in the old vernacular, and non-core to those *not* arising in or arising under but "related." Please read section 157 of 28 U.S.C.

With the enactment of section 157, one needs to classify various proceedings as "core proceedings," "not core, but otherwise related," "neither core nor related," and, possibly, "other." Proceedings described as core proceedings in section 157 are more or less those characterized in section 1334 with the participle "arising." Assuming that the district court refers the cases under section 157(a), the bankruptcy judge will hear core proceedings as a judge, make findings, and hand down a judgment. This procedure occurs despite the opposition of one of the parties. The bankruptcy judge's authority over non-core, but otherwise related matters is limited by section 157(c) to making proposed findings of fact and conclusions of law to the district court. The district court has authority to review the findings and conclusions "de novo" if any party objects. In practice one suspects de novo review will be pro forma. Matters that are neither related nor core (such as the divorce between husband and wife debtors) presumably can be heard neither by the federal district court (absent some other jurisdictional basis) nor by the bankruptcy judge. Matters falling in the "other" category are the liquidation or estimation of contingent or unliquidated personal injury, tort or wrongful death claims identified in section 157(b)(2)(B). That section apparently made its way into the law to meet the concerns of plaintiff lawyers in the *Manville* case. It, together with section 1411 on jury trials, is designed to preserve the jury trial of a personal injury tort claim against a corporation in bankruptcy.

One final section that needs to be considered is the provision in section 1334(c) for mandatory abstention. It reads in full as follows:

> Upon timely motion of a party in a proceeding based upon a State law claim or State law cause of action, related to a case under title 11 but not arising under title 11 or arising in a case under title 11, with respect to which an action could not have been commenced in a court of the United States absent jurisdiction under this section, the district court shall abstain from hearing such proceeding if an action is commenced, and can be timely adjudicated in a State forum of appropriate jurisdiction. Any decision to abstain made under this subsection is not reviewable by appeal or otherwise. This subsection shall not be construed to limit the applicability of the stay provided for by section 362 of title 11, United States Code, as such section applies to an action affecting the property of the estate in bankruptcy.

The overlapping jurisdiction of state and federal courts raises the question when the district court, and therefore the bankruptcy court, must abstain from hearing a proceeding. By hypothesis all related and some core claims could and likely would have arisen and been heard outside the bankruptcy court even if the bankruptcy had not been filed. These are often disputes that arise out of the business operations of a Chapter 11 debtor, the kind that every business suffers whether it is in Chapter 11 or not. In many circumstances such claims might thus be heard in state court. As *Marathon* showed, some of these claims cannot constitutionally be heard by a federal judge who only possesses Article I powers.

Thus, on the one hand, there is the large and continuing question: when *should* the bankruptcy court in its discretion abstain from hearing the proceeding and allow it to be heard in the state court or possibly in another federal court. Secondly there is the more intricate, but ultimately less significant question: when *must* the bankruptcy and federal district court abstain because of the mandatory abstention provisions under section 1334(c)(2)? The latter question seems mostly an artifact of the *Marathon* decision.

The clumsy attempt in section 1334(c)(2) to deprive the federal district court of certain jurisdiction (the kind of jurisdiction that *Marathon* said a bankruptcy court could not have) raises many issues. Note, first, that it applies only to cases related but not core. Second, it applies only with respect to actions for which there is no independent federal jurisdiction. Third, it applies only "if an action is commenced" and can be "timely adjudicated." One way to read the section is that it does not apply at all unless the related suit (almost invariably a suit by the debtor in possession against a third party) had been commenced prior to the bankruptcy in state court. *In re World Financial Services Center, Inc.,* 64 B.R. 980 (Bankr.S.D.Cal.1986), aff'd, 860 F.2d 1090 (9th Cir.1988).

The statute itself speaks to the district court, not to the bankruptcy court. The cases addressed by the statute are presumably those which the bankruptcy court could not hear except by consent of the parties, but *Marathon* would not appear to require their withdrawal from the district court as opposed to the bankruptcy court. Nevertheless, if abstention is required of the district court, *a fortiori* it would be required of the bankruptcy court. Section (c)(2), which has aroused the fury of the law scholars, will soon become a dead letter. The section is so full of vague wording, and so obviously subject to narrow interpretation by a court that wishes to retain jurisdiction, that we doubt it will be frequently applied.

In summary, if the issue to be litigated is not core, courts faced with the claim that they should mandatorily abstain have generally applied a six or seven point test.

Whether the court in fact abstains on the grounds of section 1334 usually turns on the following four factors: (1) backlog of the state courts' calendars; (2) status of the bankruptcy proceeding; (3) complexity of the issues; and (4) whether the state court proceeding would prolong the administration of the estate. As indicated in (c)(2), any decision to abstain is not reviewable by appeal or otherwise.

Finally, neither the *Marathon* brouhaha nor the 1984 amendments deal specifically with the *in personam* jurisdiction question. Under the Act of 1898 bankruptcy courts used the standard minimum contacts criteria for determining the reach of *in personam* jurisdiction. Many cases have now held that the minimum contacts standard no longer applies in bankruptcy proceedings under the Code. See, e.g., *In re Schack Glass Industries Co.,* 20 B.R. 967 (Bankr.S.D.N.Y.1982); *Coby Glass Products v. Torigian Laboratories, Inc.,* 22 B.R. 961 (Bankr.D.R.I. 1982). Those cases remain good law and mean, for example, that a Florida creditor can be brought into the bankruptcy court in Detroit and be made to pay an account owing to the debtor in possession or to defend his right to the asset of the bankruptcy estate even though the asset is located in Florida.

Assuming that the 1984 amendments withstand constitutional challenge, how do they reshape the world that existed after 1978 but before *Marathon*? Clearly they reduce the authority of the bankruptcy judge, for that judge can no longer hand down judgments in non-core matters. Yet the bankruptcy judge's "findings of fact and conclusions of law" that are to be submitted to the district court may operate very much like binding judgment. If one represented a creditor called to a distant hearing on a non-core matter, should one be willing to tell the client to ignore the call and simply reply upon a de novo hearing by the district judge? A careful reading of (c)(1) shows that to be foolish. To earn the de novo hearing one must "timely and specifically" object to the bankruptcy judge's findings. Thus *Marathon* ultimately may be much ado about nothing; it is too soon to say for certain how non-core matters will be treated, whether they will wind up frequently in the state court or the federal district court or whether they will simply be handled in the bankruptcy court as the drafters of the 1978 Code always intended.

Problem 3–1

Assume Mays, who lived on a farm in southeastern Indiana near the Ohio border, moved to a farm in southern Ohio two weeks prior to filing a Chapter 11 petition. Mays filed in the bankruptcy court in Cincinnati, Ohio. Which of the following statements is accurate?

1. Jurisdiction is not proper.
2. Jurisdiction is not proper because of 28 U.S.C. § 1334(d).
3. Jurisdiction is proper because of § 157 and § 1409.
4. None of the above.

IN RE ARNOLD PRINT WORKS, INC.
United States Court of Appeals, First Circuit, 1987.
815 F.2d 165.

BREYER, CIRCUIT JUDGE.

Assume that B, a bankrupt company in the midst of federal bankruptcy proceedings, brings an ordinary state law contract claim against D, a private party, seeking money that D allegedly owed B before B went bankrupt. In *Northern Pipeline Construction Co. v. Marathon Pipe Line Co.*, 458 U.S. 50, 102 S.Ct. 2858, 73 L.Ed.2d 598 (1982), the Supreme Court held that federal bankruptcy judges lacked the constitutional power to adjudicate this controversy because they "do not enjoy the protections constitutionally afforded to Art. III judges." *Id.* at 60, 102 S.Ct. at 2866. This appeal raises a related question under Article III. It asks whether a federal bankruptcy court that is statutorily authorized to hear and determine "core" bankruptcy proceedings, 28 U.S.C. § 157(b) (1982 ed., Supp. III), may adjudicate a state law claim arising from a contract that 1) was made *after* B went bankrupt and 2) was made as part of B's efforts to liquidate estate assets. In our view, the matter of timing and the relation to judicial administration of the bankrupt's estate make a critical constitutional difference between *Marathon* and the present case. *Marathon* notwithstanding, the bankrupt company's legal action to collect a "post-petition" debt, brought as part of efforts to liquidate the estate, is a "core" proceeding that the bankruptcy court has the constitutional power to decide.

I

* * *

The Bankruptcy Amendments and Federal Judgeship Act of 1984. After the *Marathon* decision, Congress amended the Bankruptcy Act of 1978 in an effort to cure the constitutional defect in its jurisdictional provision. The new jurisdictional provisions distinguish between "core" bankruptcy proceedings and those that are merely "related to" title 11 cases. *See* Appendix. Upon referral from the district court, the bankruptcy judge has full statutory authority to "hear and determine * * * all core proceedings * * * " 28 U.S.C. § 157(b)(1). Representative Kastenmeier, one of the new law's co-sponsors, explained that core proceedings are "integral to the core bankruptcy function of restructuring debtor-creditor rights," 130 Cong.Rec. E1109 (daily ed. March 20, 1984), and that they include "all necessary aspects of a bankruptcy case," *id.* at E1108. The new law sets forth a nonexhaustive list of "core proceedings," including such obvious matters as "allowance[s] or disallowance[s] of claims," 28 U.S.C. § 157(b)(2)(B), as well as matters more relevant to this case, namely: "matters concerning the administration of the estate" and "other proceedings affecting the liquidation of the assets of the estate," 28 U.S.C. § 157(b)(2)(A), (O).

Non-core proceedings, those that the statute calls "related to" bankruptcy cases, concern aspects of the bankruptcy case that *Marathon* barred non-Article III judges from determining on their own. The sponsors of the 1984 Amendments that later became § 157 referred to this category of proceedings as "Marathon-type suits," by which they meant claims "concerned only with State law issues that did not arise in the core bankruptcy function of adjusting debtor-creditor rights." 130 Cong.Rec. H1848 (daily ed. March 21, 1984)(statement of Representative Kindness). In non-core proceedings, unless the parties consent to the bankruptcy court's jurisdiction, the bankruptcy judge has the power only to "submit proposed findings of fact and conclusions of law to the district court," and the parties are entitled to de novo review of any matter to which they "timely and specifically" object. 28 U.S.C. § 157(c)(1). Moreover, the bankruptcy court may (and sometimes must) abstain from hearing non-core matters, leaving the parties to sue in state court. *See* 28 U.S.C. § 1334(c)(1982 ed., Supp. III).

In the view of § 157's sponsors, the distinction between core and non-core proceedings cured the constitutional defect in § 1471. Bankruptcy judges would "decide all core bankruptcy proceedings, subject only to traditional appellate review," 130 Cong.Rec. E1108 (daily ed. March 20, 1984)(prepared statement of Representative Kastenmeier), as *Marathon* permitted. *See Marathon*, 458 U.S. at 71, 102 S.Ct. at 2871. Article III courts would retain ultimate control over "Marathon-type suits." The new structure would make it possible to the extent constitutionally permissible to hear matters relating to a single bankruptcy in a single forum. *See* 130 Cong.Rec. E1108 (daily ed. March 20, 1984)(prepared statement of Representative Kastenmeier).

The Present Litigation. The appellant in this case, Arnold Print Works, Inc. (Arnold), filed a petition in bankruptcy in 1981. It continued to manage its property under the provisions of the Bankruptcy Act as a "debtor-in-possession." 11 U.S.C. § 1107 (1982). As part of an effort to liquidate its assets, it sold printing rollers to George Apkin and Sons (Apkin), the appellee. Apkin, believing that Arnold had misrepresented the quality of the rollers, refused to pay about $9000 of the $20,000 purchase price. In April 1985, Arnold sued Apkin in the federal bankruptcy court for the $9000. Apkin told the court that Arnold was in the wrong forum because Arnold's claim was basically a state law contract claim, which made the proceeding non-core. Apkin also pointed to the new Act's abstention provisions, asking the court to abstain pursuant to 28 U.S.C. § 1334(c)(1), and thereby to force Arnold to sue in state court, where Apkin could insist on a jury trial.

* * *

II

Arnold asks us to determine whether the bankruptcy proceeding to consider its claim for payment of a post-petition debt is a core proceeding that the Constitution permits the bankruptcy court to adjudicate. We conclude that it is, and that neither justice nor comity with State courts requires that the bankruptcy court abstain from hearing the case. The bankruptcy court may therefore hear and decide it.

Core Proceedings. Assuming for the moment that the Constitution permits the bankruptcy court to adjudicate the claim, we believe that the statute's term "core" covers this proceeding. The action of a debtor-in-possession to collect a post-petition debt arising from the sale of the estate's assets, unlike a suit to recover a pre-petition debt, falls within the literal wording of 28 U.S.C. § 157(b)(2)(A), "matters concerning the administration of the estate," because it involves a claim that arose out of the administrative activities of a debtor-in-possession. *See In re L.A. Clarke & Son, Inc.,* 51 B.R. 31, 33 (Bankr.D.D.C.1985). It falls within the literal wording of 28 U.S.C. 157(b)(2)(O), "other proceedings affecting the liquidation of the assets of the estate," because the claim arose out of the debtor's efforts to liquidate estate assets. *Cf. In re Franklin Computer Corp.,* 50 B.R. 620, 625–26 (Bankr.E.D.Pa.1985)(noting that § 157(b)(2)(O) "supports a finding that an action on an account receivable is a core proceeding"). One can imagine arguments suggesting that it falls within other provisions as well. *See, e.g.,* 28 U.S.C. § 157(b)(2)(E)("orders to turn over property of the estate").

Moreover, the vast majority of courts that have considered the status of similar post-petition claims have held that they were core proceedings. The leading treatise on bankruptcy law agrees that in these post-petition cases, the "better result is that the proceeding is core." 1 King, Collier on Bankruptcy ¶ 3.01, at 3–41 (15th ed. 1986). The precedent in this circuit upon which the district court and bankruptcy court relied, *Mohawk Industries,* does not in fact present a direct holding to the contrary, for it involved a *pre*-petition, not a *post*-petition debt; thus the *Mohawk Industries* claim did not arise out of the "administration of the estate."

Further, the legislative history of the new statute indicates that Congress intended that "core proceedings" would be interpreted broadly, close to or congruent with constitutional limits. The sponsors repeatedly said that 95 percent of the proceedings brought before bankruptcy judges would be core proceedings. See 130 Cong.Rec. E1108–E1110 (daily ed. March 20, 1984)(statement of Representative Kastenmeier); *id.* at H1848, H1850 (daily ed. March 21, 1984)(statement of Representative Kindness). They used arguments strongly suggesting that they were pressing the notion to its constitutional bounds. They referred to the suits in the non-core category as "Marathon-type" cases, *see, e.g., id.* at E1108, E1109 (daily ed. March 20, 1984)(prepared statement of Representative Kastenmeier; *id.* at H1848 (daily ed. March 21, 1984) (statement of Representative Kindness), which they understood to be proceedings of "a very limited kind," *id.* at H1848 (daily ed. March 21, 1984)(statement of Representative Kindness). Representative Kastenmeier said that "jurisdiction in core bankruptcy proceedings is broader than the summary jurisdiction under pre–1978 law," 130 Cong.Rec. E1108 (daily ed. March 20, 1984), and summary jurisdiction covered post-petition claims. *See infra* pp. 169–70. We recognize that the authors of the section also spoke of "core" proceedings as those "integral to the core bankruptcy function of *restructuring debtor-creditor rights,*" 130 Cong.Rec. E1109, but the statutory list of core proceedings, and the discussion on the floor of Congress, make clear that this last italicized phrase was not meant to restrict core proceedings to competing claims directly against the estate. Rather, it referred generally to all proceedings that are *"non-Marathon"* bankruptcy matters.

Finally, the fact that a claim in a bankruptcy matter raises issues of state, rather than federal, law does not by itself determine that it is non-core, rather than core. A claim by a creditor for money owed by the debtor, a trustee's effort to set aside a preference, or a trustee's decision as to who has a better claim might depend entirely upon such matters of state law as the validity of a lien or an interpretation of a state recording statute. For this reason, Congress specifically provided that the "determination that a proceeding is not a core proceeding shall not be made solely on the basis that its resolution may be affected by State law." 28 U.S.C. § 157(b)(3). It is the nature of the proceeding—its relation to the basic function of the bankruptcy court—not the state or federal basis for the claim, that makes the difference here.

Article III. We now consider whether the determination that Arnold's action is a core proceeding creates an unconstitutional interpretation of § 157(b). We believe that it does not. The Constitution permits a non-Article III bankruptcy court to adjudicate post-petition claims related to administration or liquidation of a debtor's estate because the claims are both historically and functionally distinguishable from those at issue in *Marathon.*

The Supreme Court has repeatedly turned to history and tradition to help define the type of adjudicatory proceeding that the Constitution reserves exclusively for Article III courts. In *Thomas,* for example, the majority explicitly stated that *Marathon*'s holding applied to "a *traditional* contract action arising under the state law." *Thomas,* 105 S.Ct. at 3335 (emphasis added); *see also Marathon,* 458 U.S. at 64, 102 S.Ct. at 2867–68 (describing the history of the Article III exception for territorial courts). The Court has indicated that it will examine closely congressional attempts to control the adjudication of "rights [that] were *historically* ... subject to resolution by Article III courts." *See Schor,* 106 S.Ct. at 3259 (emphasis added).

If one examines the jurisdictional history of post-petition claims of the sort in issue here, one finds that they are not "traditional contract actions"; nor are they matters that "historically" have been decided only in the equivalent of Article III courts. To the contrary, bankruptcy courts have adjudicated claims like this one at least since the enactment of the Bankruptcy Act of 1898. Indeed, they have done so in exercise of "summary jurisdiction"—a jurisdiction permitting the bankruptcy court to sit as a court in equity, deciding without a jury matters that a jury might have decided had a party pressed the same claim in a state court. *See Katchen v. Landy,* 382 U.S. 323, 337, 86 S.Ct. 467, 477, 15 L.Ed.2d 391 (1966). Thus, *Collier* noted that under the 1898 Act, a

> court of bankruptcy has summary power over a delinquent purchaser at a sale in the bankruptcy proceedings. He may be ordered to pay the stipulated price or to pay the deficiency resulting from a resale. The jurisdiction of the court to act summarily in such a matter is the same as that of a court of equity in any judicial sale.

4B King, Collier on Bankruptcy ¶ 70.98, at 1202–03 (14th ed. 1978).

Similarly, in *In re Alan Wood Steel Co.,* 1 B.R. 167, 169 (Bankr. E.D.Pa.1979), a bankruptcy case that thoroughly explains the treatment of this jurisdictional issue under the 1898 Act, the court commented that its power to hear and adjudicate summarily a receiver's action to collect a post-petition account receivable was "crystal clear." The court characterized the action as one arising out of a contract "with officers of [the] court and as such the contracts [were] treated as contracts with the court itself." *Id.* at 168. The court added:

> With respect to contracts made by trustees, debtors in possession and other officers of the bankruptcy court, the necessity of the court retaining exclusive jurisdiction over matters arising out of such contracts is even more pronounced than in the case of other matters arising during the administration of a bankrupt estate. The courts have therefore adopted an extreme position with respect to this and have ruled that a party contracting with an officer of the court in fact contracts with the court itself, and by such act *subjects himself for the purposes of the contract to the summary jurisdiction of the court* * * *.

Id. (quoting *In re California Eastern Airways,* 95 F.Supp. 348, 351 (D.Del.1951)). Given potential court supervision of estate administration, the legal fiction that the debtor-in-possession is a court official and that the contract is with the court itself is a fiction that borders on the truth. It helps to distinguish the claim at issue here even on the view of *Marathon*'s plurality: Arnold makes the kind of claim that, historically speaking, might be characterized as raising matters of "public rights," defined as those arising between the government and others. *See Marathon,* 458 U.S. at 67, 102 S.Ct. at 2869. *Marathon* found no constitutional objection to a bankruptcy court deciding this sort of claim. Quite apart from the force of the fiction, the history of bankruptcy court jurisdiction means that a post-petition contract made with a debtor-in-possession cannot be called a "traditional" state contract action.

To the extent that Article III reflects a concern for procedural fairness, *see Crowell v. Benson,* 285 U.S. at 87, 52 S.Ct. at 306 (Brandeis, J., dissenting), this case again differs from *Marathon*. A party who contracts with an apparently healthy company—a company that has not filed a petition in bankruptcy—may find it unpleasantly surprising to have to defend its *pre*-petition contract in a bankruptcy court, without a jury or Article III protections. But it is difficult to see any unfair surprise in bringing a post-petition contract action before a bankruptcy court. Parties who contract with a bankrupt company's trustee or with a debtor-in-possession know that they are dealing with an agent responsible to a bankruptcy court; that the bankruptcy court would resolve subsequent disputes should therefore come as no surprise. *Cf.* 41 U.S.C. §§ 601 et seq. (1982)(establishing that parties who enter into contracts with the government subject themselves to a set of administrative procedures for resolving disputes growing out of those contracts). The risk of unfairness is therefore smaller here than in *Marathon*.

The resolution of separation of powers questions may also prove sensitive to practical considerations, such as the need to place in a single set of hands the various functions that Articles I, II, and III would otherwise keep separate. *See Chadha v. Immigration & Naturalization Service,* 634 F.2d 408, 425 (9th Cir.1980)("[C]ourts interpret separation of powers questions pragmatically, in order to preserve the essential design of the Constitution without imposing unworkable limitations."), *aff'd,* 462 U.S. 919, 103 S.Ct. 2764, 77 L.Ed.2d 317 (1983); *cf. Schor,* 106 S.Ct. at 3258 (considering whether there were practical reasons to find the CEA defective under Article III). If so, one might distinguish between a trustee in bankruptcy who *marshals* assets, as in *Marathon,* and a trustee in bankruptcy who *manages* and *disposes of* assets under bankruptcy court supervision, as in this case. One might reasonably believe that the risk of litigation in multiple forums would prove more disruptive in the latter instances than in the former. And to that extent, the need for orderly estate management, administration, and distribution would argue more strongly here than in *Marathon* for allowing adjudication by the bankruptcy court, despite its non-Article III characteristics.

The narrow interpretation that the Supreme Court has given to *Marathon,* the history of bankruptcy court jurisdiction over actions like these, and the differences between this case and *Marathon* with respect to fairness and practicality, together convince us that Arnold's claim may be heard by a non-Article III court. For the reasons we reviewed earlier, this case falls within the statutory category of core proceedings, so the case may be decided by a bankruptcy judge. We recognize that the bankruptcy court retains the power to abstain from deciding a case for reasons of justice, comity with State courts, or respect for State law, 28 U.S.C. § 1334(c)(1), but no such reason applies here. *Cf. In re Franklin*, 50 B.R. at 626 n. 8 (noting that "a finding that a matter is a core proceeding weighs heavily in favor of a denial of abstention"); *In re Pioneer Development Corp.*, 47 B.R. 624, 628 (Bankr.N.D.Ill.1985)(commenting that "abstention would be totally unwarranted" when there has been a determination that a proceeding is core).

The judgment of dismissal is vacated and the case is remanded to the bankruptcy court for proceedings not inconsistent with this opinion.

Notes and Questions

1. How can you tell that Steve Breyer is a former law professor and possibly a frustrated economist? (Answer: He starts his opinion with the verb "assume.")

2. How does this case escape section 1334(c)(2)?

3. How would the court deal with an insurance contract that had been written prior to the petition in bankruptcy to insure the party who is now the debtor in possession? (Assume that the debtor's claim against the insurance company arises out of postpetition events.)

In *Celotex Corporation v. Edwards*, ___ U.S. ___, 115 S.Ct. 1493, 131 L.Ed.2d 403 (1995) the Supreme Court found that a suit by an individual against a bonding company to enforce a judgement that he had previously recovered against a bankrupt debtor was a case related to "the debtor's bankruptcy." The court so found despite the fact that the suit was not technically against debtor but against a bonding company. In *Celotex*, the Supreme Court put considerable weight on the fact that a number of other asbestos plaintiffs had recovered bonded judgments against Celotex and that execution on these bonds would have a "direct and substantial adverse effect" on Celotex' ability successfully to reorganize.

The court cites and appears to endorse the general statement from *Pacor, Inc. v. Higgins*, 743 F.2d 984 (3d Cir.1984):

> The usual articulation of the test for determining whether a civil proceeding is related to bankruptcy is whether *the outcome of that proceeding could conceivably have any effect on the estate being administered in bankruptcy.* * * * Thus, the proceeding need not necessarily be against the debtor or against the debtor's property. An action is related to bankruptcy if the outcome could alter the debtor's rights, liabilities, options, or freedom of action (either positively or negatively) and which in any way impacts upon the handling or administration of the bankruptcy estate.

> If one includes everything that "could conceivably have any effect," what is excluded? It is hard to imagine a lawsuit to which the debtor is a party that would be excluded. It is hard to imagine exclusion of any suit

that would have a remote impact upon the debtor's property. And it is hard to imagine one against a related person, such as a partner, partnership, guarantor, or bonding company that would be excluded.

In *Celotex* the ultimate question was whether a bankruptcy court in Florida could enjoin a third party's proceeding against an Illinois bonding company on a judgment received in Texas. The Court held yes. Is the Court rebuilding what it tore down in *Marathon*?

Problem 3–2

Wagner was the buyer on a land sale contract of certain land in central Indiana for a price of $350,000. Wagner properly filed a bankruptcy petition in the bankruptcy court in central Illinois. At the time of the petition the property was worth more than $400,000 and Wagner was understandably anxious to get a judicial confirmation that he had a right to continue to pay and purchase the land. Wagner was in arrears on the land sale contract approximately $6,000, but sought to pay off that arrearage and to assume and pay the contract. Wagner commenced an adversary proceeding in the bankruptcy court in Illinois against the seller, seeking a finding that Wagner had a right to assume the contract and for an order permitting such assumption and for the approval of his payment of the arrearages over two years in installments. The defendant seller argues that the bankruptcy court has no jurisdiction to decide this question. What do you think?

§ 2. VENUE

To determine whether venue is proper in bankruptcy requires one again to distinguish between "cases" on the one hand and "proceedings" on the other. The "case" is the entire bankruptcy; to ask what is proper venue of the case is to ask in which bankruptcy court the petition should be filed. Once that petition has been filed, most, but not all, of the "proceedings" will have the same venue. Some proceedings that are no more than lawsuits that arise between a going concern and a third party will properly find venue in other courts or outside the bankruptcy system entirely. Section 1408 of 28 U.S.C. defines the proper venue of "cases." Section 1409 defines venue of proceedings.

A. Venue of Cases

The basic venue rule under section 1408(1) for cases is as follows:

"In the district * * * in which the domicile, residence, principal place of business in the United States, or principal assets in the United States * * * have been located for the longer portion of * * * the 180 day period preceding the filing."

Most venue issues are fairly straightforward. A typical case may have proper venue in several different districts. It is conceivable, for example, that a person could have a domicile in Ohio, be residing in Florida, operating a sole proprietorship whose principal place of business is in Georgia, and whose principal assets are an apartment complex in Mississippi. In that case venue would be proper in any one of the four jurisdictions.

It should also be apparent that some of the words fit more comfortably with some entities than with others. For example, we know that an individual can be domiciled in one place and reside in another; the same is true of a corporation. A corporation clearly could be domiciled in one place and have a principal place of business or its principal assets in another. Where does the place of incorporation fit in this classification scheme?

To understand the operation of 1408(1), consider first a corporation. One can imagine arguments on the question whether a Delaware corporation that has plants in several states has its principal place of business in one or another of those plants. For most purposes the Uniform Commercial Code defines the principal place of business as the place of the corporation's chief executive office. That definition might also work in many cases presented to the bankruptcy court. Some cases addressing that question have said that the principal place of business is the "nerve center." *In re Dock of the Bay, Inc.*, 24 B.R. 811, 814–15 (Bankr.E.D.N.Y.1982). One court defined "nerve center" to be "where those interested in [the corporation] choose primarily to conduct its business." *In re Portex Oil Co.*, 30 F.Supp. 138 (D.Or.1939), *aff'd sub nom. Clark Bros. Co. v. Portex Oil Co.*, 113 F.2d 45 (9th Cir.1940). Presumably this place will usually be the place of the chief executive offices or at least where most of the administration of the corporation is done. To say that venue is proper at the principal place of business does not deny the proposition that it might also be proper where the principal assets are located. Indeed it might be appropriate in certain circumstances to transfer the case, despite proper venue where filed, to another place where venue is even more appropriate.

Partnerships present somewhat more difficult venue questions. Partnerships are distinct entities from their general partners, yet the general partners, who bear the ultimate partnership liability, represent the partnership entity in a much more fundamental way than shareholders represent the corporate entity. However, at least one court has found "it is difficult to see how a partnership can be said to have a residence or domicile. * * * Therefore the only meaningful test for venue with respect to a partnership is the district in which it has its principal place of business or its principal assets."

Section 1408(2) deals not merely with the partners discussed above, but also provides that venue is proper in any case where a "person's affiliate has a case pending." Affiliate is quite broadly defined by section 101(2). It includes subsidiary, parent, and sibling corporations. Moreover, it includes a series of parent and subsidiary corporations which own as little as 20 percent of one another's stock. In addition, it includes certain entities which are related because the debtor leases "substantially all" of the debtor's property, and vice versa. Consider for a moment the consequences of this section. It means that LTV, a multibillion dollar corporation, headquartered in Dallas, finds proper venue in New York City because of an insignificant and formerly unknown subsidiary that owns a couple of ships. The purpose of the provision should be obvious. If the bankruptcy court is to supervise a reorganization of a complex economic organization that is composed of a series of related corporations, it is desirable that the administration take place in only one place and not be done piecemeal in a series of courts. Yet, cases such as LTV show that a large corporation will find venue in any of a large number of districts.

B. *Venue of Proceedings*

Section 1409 of title 28 covers venue of proceedings. Subsection (a) of section 1409 sets out the general provisions for venue of a proceeding in a bankruptcy case, while subsections (b) through (e) offer alternatives and exceptions. Subsection (a) provides:

> (a) Except as otherwise provided in subsection (b) and (d), a proceeding arising under title 11 or arising in or related to a case under title 11 may be commenced in the district court in which such case is pending.

This section provides that a proceeding "may" be commenced where the case is filed, not that it "must" be commenced there. Apparently the "may" of section 1409(a) distinguishes it from its exceptions in subsections (b) and (d) which use the mandate "only." However, the exhortation of section 1409(a) is stronger than it first appears, particularly in circumstances in which a litigant cannot find any other subsection of 1409 that grants venue. In that case, the "may" becomes "must." Thus, one might wish to think of section 1409(a) as stating the proposition that all proceedings "arising under," "in," or "related to" should presumptively be held before the bankruptcy court where the petition is filed. Having said that, consider the alternatives where other venue is possible or required.

As we have already pointed out, subsection (b) differs from subsection (a) in that it is mandatory. Where the trustee or debtor in possession seeks to recover a money judgment or property worth less than $1,000 or a consumer debt of less than $5,000, proper venue exists only in the district in which the defendant resides. Subsection (b) governs only those proceedings initiated by the DIP or the trustee. If a similar claim of less than $1,000 (or $5,000 in the case of a consumer debt) were commenced by a third party against the trustee, venue could be proper in the bankruptcy court where the case was filed.

The intent of the drafters in adopting section 1409(b) is clear. The House Report on section 1473(b)(which preceded section 1409(b) and had identical language) stated that the "section prevents unfairness to distant debtors of the estate, when the cost of defending would be greater than the cost of paying the debt owed." H.Rep. No. 595, 95th Cong., 1st Sess. 446 (1977). A similar unfairness would occur if, for reasons of venue, the trustee were forced to travel great distances, at an expense beyond the estate's capacity, in order to litigate a small claim brought by a third party.

Subsection (c) provides an alternative venue for a proceeding based upon the trustee's avoidance power under section 544(b), or power to claim specific property of the estate. It authorizes the debtor in possession to seek assets claimed under section 541 or 544(b) in any district where a case could have commenced had a title 11 case not been filed. Thus, in many cases in which the debtor in possession is seeking the return of assets that allegedly belong to the estate under section 541 or assets that were improperly conveyed and can be recovered under 544(b), the trustee will have the alternative of bringing the case where the petition is filed, or at the place of residence of the one possessing the property, or, conceivably, where the property is located. It is an alternative section, but it applies only to proceedings brought by the trustee or the debtor in possession, not to those where the trustee or debtor in possession is the defendant.

Subsections (d) and (e) respond to a unique problem of operating the continuing business under Chapter 11. It is familiar but ironic that one's capacity to do business is enhanced by one's ability to be sued. If parties are amenable to suit in the local court, locals are more likely to deal with them than if they must go to a distant place to sue. If all disputes between a Chapter 11 business and third parties had to be resolved in the bankruptcy court where the case is filed, that might deter merchants and others from dealing with Chapter 11 debtors who have far-flung business interests. Accordingly subsections (d) and (e) say that claims arising "after the commencement of such case" require that the trustee as plaintiff go to the district court where the case could have been brought absent bankruptcy in order to pursue its suit and permit the third party as plaintiff either to sue the debtor in possession in the district court where there would have been non-bankruptcy jurisdiction or in the district court where the case is pending. That means, in the case of LTV which filed its petition in New York and has continuing business operations in Pennsylvania, Ohio, and Texas, among other states, that as to any dispute that arose after the commencement of the case, the LTV debtor in possession must pursue third parties in the district court in Pennsylvania, Ohio, or Texas respectively, but that those wishing to sue LTV on transactions arising after the case, have the choice of proceeding in Texas, Ohio, or Pennsylvania, or in the main bankruptcy case in New York City.

Note that in all these cases, venue is in "the district court." Under local rules that usually means in "the bankruptcy court." Thus, the bankruptcy at least forecloses a state court action unless the bankruptcy court chooses to abstain. In effect, (d) and (e) prohibit the debtor in possession from using its section 1409(a) hometown venue for claims that arise after the petition was filed unless there would have been venue in that district absent the bankruptcy.

The general policies and rules in section 1409 seem fairly straightforward and unexceptional. One would expect most proceedings to be heard in the same court where the petition is filed, yet one can easily see why certain cases such as those in (b) or occasionally in (d) or (e) should be heard elsewhere.

C. Transfer of Venue

Perhaps the most important provision in the collection of venue statutes and rules is section 1412 which provides for transfer of venue:

> A district court may transfer a case or proceeding under title 11 to a district court for another district, in the interest of justice or for the convenience of the parties.

Disputes over change of venue are generally held to be core.

Section 1412 covers both cases and proceedings. Rule 1014 implements its provisions concerning cases and Rule 1014(a)(1) deals with transfer of cases where original venue is proper:

> If a petition is filed in a proper district, on timely motion of a party in interest, and after hearing on notice to the petitioners and other entities as directed by the court, the case may be transferred to any other district if the court determines that the transfer is in the interest of justice or for the convenience of the parties.

When venue is proper as it stands, the burden is on the moving party to demonstrate with a preponderance of the evidence that transfer is "in the interest of justice or the convenience of the parties." As one might expect, the courts have developed a set of criteria for balancing interests in decisions on transfer. This list varies in content from case to case, but six factors recur: (1) the relative economic harm to debtors and creditors if transfer is granted; (2) the location of the assets; (3) the economic administration of the estate; (4) the necessity for ancillary administration if liquidation should result; (5) the effect on parties' (including witnesses') willingness or ability to participate in the case or proceeding; (6) the existence of any intertwined relationship with another bankruptcy case under section 1408(2). *In re Commonwealth Oil Refining Co.,* 596 F.2d 1239 (5th Cir.1979).

As originally enacted, the Bankruptcy Reform Act of 1978 explicitly authorized a court to retain or transfer a case or proceeding even though it had been filed in a court where venue was improper:

> The bankruptcy court of a district in which is filed a case or proceeding laying venue in the wrong division or district may, in the interests of justice and for the convenience of the parties, retain such case or proceeding, or may transfer, * * * such case or proceeding to another district or division. 28 U.S.C. 1477(a).

Under 1477(a), the court lacked authority to dismiss a case or proceeding. In 1984 the quoted section was repealed and replaced by section 1412. Section 1412 refers to a transfer or change of venue in the interest of justice or for the convenience of the parties, but it makes no reference to improper venue. Although it is not clear whether transfer is mandatory under 1412, the section does not authorize dismissal. Moreover, Bankruptcy Rule 1014(a)(2) implicitly authorized the retention of jurisdiction in an improper venue until 1987 when the rule was changed in response to the repeal of section 1477(a). Now the rule reads:

> (2) *Cases Filed in Improper District.* If a petition is filed in an improper district, on timely motion of a party in interest and after hearing or notice to the petitioners and other entities as directed by the courts, the case may be dismissed or transferred to any other district if the court determines that transfer is in the interest of justice or for the convenience of the parties.

Where does this leave us? Under the laws that existed between 1978 and 1984, it was clear that a court could retain jurisdiction even though venue was improper if that was found to be in the interest of justice and the parties.

Under the current law it is unclear whether a court can retain a case or proceeding in an improper venue absent waiver by the parties. This lack of clarity arises partly because it is uncertain whether Congress' replacement of 1477 with 1412 was intended to withdraw the power that had previously been exercised by the courts to hear cases in improper venues.

Note finally that parties may waive their right to challenge proper venue, a topic with which rule 1014 deals. Exactly what acts constitute waiver are too detailed to consider here, but lawyers should be aware of that possibility and should examine rule 1014 and the cases with care if they hope to challenge venue.

Problem 3–3

Debtor properly files its Chapter 11 petition in New York. Subsequently debtor has two claims against a creditor located in Atlanta.

    a. The first claim arises out of a payment made to the Atlanta creditor 50 days before the petition was filed. The debtor in possession would like to recover this payment as a preference under section 547. May the debtor in possession recover that amount by a proceeding initiated in the New York bankruptcy court?

    b. The second claim against the same Atlanta creditor arose out of a dispute in connection with certain goods sold after the petition was filed. Again the debtor in possession would like to bring this warranty dispute before the bankruptcy court in New York. If the Atlanta creditor resists, can the debtor in possession force the court to require the hearing to be held in New York?

Problem 3–4

Paige Company manufactured a drug from 1971–1974. Due to mounting complaints and suits from users of the drug, Paige discontinued the product. By 1985 however the number of suits had grown to 5,000, including one filed by Ruth. In the face of the suits, the company filed bankruptcy in the Eastern District of Kentucky. The company then requested the transfer of all suits to the Eastern District of Kentucky for trial. Can the bankruptcy court transfer the suits? What advantages does Paige gain from the transfer of the personal injury cases? What arguments can Ruth make against the transfer?

Problem 3–5

Assume that Paige, in the foregoing case, was a Delaware corporation whose principal place of business was Louisville and whose manufacturing facilities were in Alabama and California. What alternatives would it have had with respect to the filing of its Chapter 11 case?

§ 3. JURY TRIALS IN BANKRUPTCY

The extent of the role of the jury under section 1411 is unclear. As part of the 1984 act solving the *Marathon* conundrum, Congress passed section 28 U.S.C. § 1411, titled "Jury Trials." Subsection (a) of section 1411 reads as follows:

> * * * This chapter and title 11 do not affect any right to trial by jury that an individual has under applicable non-bankruptcy law with regard to a personal injury or wrongful death tort claim.

Some argue that the right to jury trial in bankruptcy proceedings is limited (to the extent permitted by the Seventh Amendment) to cases heard by the district court (as mandated by section 157(b)(5)) involving personal injury or wrongful death tort claims. All would concede that there must be some other cases or proceedings in a bankruptcy case where the Seventh Amendment would demand a jury trial, but prior to *Granfinanciera, S.A. v. Nordberg*, 492 U.S. 33, 109 S.Ct. 2782, 106 L.Ed.2d 26 (1989), there was very little agreement on the scope of the Seventh Amendment's demands. *Granfinanciera, S.A. v. Nordberg* exceeded the wildest dreams of jury advocates. Apart from a few subtleties, the Court adopted a traditional Seventh Amendment analysis for determining when jury trials are appropriate in bankruptcy.

Granfinanciera arose out of the bankruptcy of the Chase & Sanborn Corporation ("C & S") which filed a petition on May 18, 1983. In 1985, Nordberg, the trustee for C & S estate, commenced an action in the district court to void three allegedly fraudulent transfers made to Granfinanciera, S.A. and Medex, Ltd. The district court referred the case to the bankruptcy court where it was first heard. The complaint alleged that at the time of the transfers, C & S was insolvent and that C & S received no consideration or less than a reasonably equivalent value in exchange for the transfers. Therefore, Nordberg alleged, the transfers were fraudulent conveyances which could be avoided under section 548(a)(2) and recovered for the benefit of the estate pursuant to section 550(a). In answer to the complaint, Granfinanciera and Medex requested a jury trial. Neither Granfinanciera nor Medex submitted a proof of claim against the estate.

GRANFINANCIERA, S.A., ET AL. v. NORDBERG, CREDITOR TRUSTEE OF ESTATE OF CHASE & SANBORN CORP., F/K/A GENERAL COFFEE CORP.

Supreme Court of the United States, 1989.
492 U.S. 33, 109 S.Ct. 2782, 106 L.Ed.2d 26.

JUSTICE BRENNAN delivered the opinion of the Court.

The question presented is whether a person who has not submitted a claim against a bankruptcy estate has a right to a jury trial when sued by the trustee in bankruptcy to recover an allegedly fraudulent monetary transfer. We hold that the Seventh Amendment entitles such a person to a trial by jury, notwithstanding Congress' designation of fraudulent conveyance actions as "core proceedings" in 28 U.S.C. § 157(b)(2)(H) (1982 ed., Supp. V).

* * *

III

Petitioners rest their claim to a jury trial on the Seventh Amendment alone. The Seventh Amendment provides: "In Suits at common law, where the value in controversy shall exceed twenty dollars, the right of trial by jury shall be preserved * * *." We have consistently interpreted the phrase "Suits at common law" to refer to "suits in which *legal* rights were to be ascertained and determined, in contradistinction to those where equitable rights alone were recognized, and equitable remedies were administered." *Parsons v. Bedford*, [28 U.S. 433], 3 Pet. 433, 447, 7 L.Ed. 732 (1830). Although "the thrust of the Amendment was to preserve the right to jury trial as it existed in 1791," the Seventh Amendment also applies to actions brought to enforce statutory rights that are analogous to common-law causes of action ordinarily decided in English law courts in the late 18th century, as opposed to those customarily heard by courts of equity or admiralty. *Curtis v. Loether*, 415 U.S. 189, 193, 94 S.Ct. 1005, 1007, 39 L.Ed.2d 260 (1974).

The form of our analysis is familiar. "First, we compare the statutory action to 18th–century actions brought in the courts of England prior to the merger of the courts of law and equity. Second, we examine the remedy sought and determine whether it is legal or equitable in nature." *Tull v. United States*, 481 U.S. 412, 417–418, 107 S.Ct. 1831, 1835, 95 L.Ed.2d 365 (1987)(citations omitted). The second stage of this analysis is more important than the first. * * * If, on balance, these two factors indicate that a party is entitled to a jury trial under the Seventh Amendment, we must decide whether Congress may assign and has assigned resolution of the relevant claim to a non-Article III adjudicative body that does not use a jury as factfinder.

A

There is no dispute that actions to recover preferential or fraudulent transfers were often brought at law in late 18th-century England. As we noted in *Schoenthal v. Irving Trust Co.,* 287 U.S. 92, 94, 53 S.Ct. 50, 51, 77 L.Ed. 185 (1932)(footnote omitted): "In England, long prior to the enactment of our first Judiciary Act, common law actions of trover and money had and received were resorted to for the recovery of preferential payments by bankrupts." * * * These actions, like all suits at law, were conducted before juries.

Respondent does not challenge this proposition or even contend that actions to recover fraudulent conveyances or preferential transfers were more than occasionally tried in courts of equity. He asserts only that courts of equity had concurrent jurisdiction with courts of law over fraudulent conveyance actions. * * * While respondent's assertion that courts of equity sometimes provided relief in fraudulent conveyance actions is true, however, it hardly suffices to undermine petitioners' submission that the present action for *monetary* relief would not have sounded in equity 200 years ago in England. In *Parsons v. Bedford, supra,* 3 Pet., at 447 (emphasis added), we contrasted suits at law with "those where equitable rights *alone* were recognized" in holding that the Seventh Amendment right to a jury trial applies to all but the latter actions. Respondent adduces no authority to buttress the claim that suits to recover an allegedly fraudulent transfer of money, of the sort that he has brought, were typically or indeed ever entertained by English courts of equity when the Seventh Amendment was adopted. In fact, prior decisions of this Court, * * * and scholarly authority compel the contrary conclusion:

> "[W]hether the trustee's suit should be at law or in equity is to be judged by the same standards that are applied to any other owner of property which is wrongfully withheld. If the subject matter is a chattel, and is still in the grantee's possession, an action in trover or replevin would be the trustee's remedy; and if the fraudulent transfer was of cash, the trustee's action would be for money had and received. Such actions at law are as available to the trustee today as they were in the English courts of long ago. If, on the other hand, the subject matter is land or an intangible, or the trustee needs equitable aid for an accounting or the like, he may invoke the equitable process, and that also is beyond dispute." 1 G. Glenn, Fraudulent Conveyances and Preferences § 98, pp. 183–184 (rev. ed. 1940).

* * *

We therefore conclude that respondent would have had to bring his action to recover an alleged fraudulent conveyance of a determinate sum of money at law in 18th-century England, and that a court of equity would not have adjudicated it.

B

The nature of the relief respondent seeks strongly supports our preliminary finding that the right he invokes should be denominated legal rather than equitable. Our decisions establish beyond peradventure that "[i]n cases of fraud or mistake, as under any other head of chancery jurisdiction, a court of the United States will not sustain a bill in equity to obtain only a decree for the payment of money by way of damages, when the like amount can be recovered at law in an action sounding in tort or for money had and received." *Buzard v. Houston,* 119 U.S., at 352, 7 S.Ct. at 252, citing *Parkersburg v. Brown,* 106 U.S. 487, 500, 1 S.Ct. 442, 452, 27 L.Ed. 238 (1883); *Ambler v. Choteau,* 107 U.S. 586, 1 S.Ct. 556, 27 L.Ed. 322 (1883); *Litchfield v. Ballou,* 114 U.S. 190, 5 S.Ct. 820, 29 L.Ed. 132 (1885).

* * *

Indeed, in our view *Schoenthal v. Irving Trust Co.,* 287 U.S. 92, 53 S.Ct. 50, 77 L.Ed. 185 (1932), removes all doubt that respondent's cause of action should be characterized as legal rather than as equitable. In *Schoenthal,* the trustee in bankruptcy sued in equity to recover alleged preferential payments, claiming that it had no adequate remedy at law. As in this case, the recipients of the payments apparently did not file claims against the bankruptcy estate. The Court held that the suit had to proceed at law instead, because the long-settled rule that suits in equity will not be sustained where a complete remedy exists at law, then codified at 28 U.S.C. § 384, "serves to guard the right of trial by jury preserved by the Seventh Amendment and to that end it should be liberally construed." * * * The Court found that the trustee's suit—indistinguishable from respondent's suit in all relevant respects—could not go forward in equity because an adequate remedy was available at law. There, as here, "[t]he preferences sued for were money payments of ascertained and definite amounts," and "[t]he bill discloses no facts that call for an accounting or other equitable relief." * * * Respondent's fraudulent conveyance action plainly seeks relief traditionally provided by law courts or on the law side of courts having both legal and equitable dockets.[7] Unless Congress may and has permissibly with-

---

7. Respondent claims to seek "avoidance" of the allegedly fraudulent transfers and restitution of the funds that were actually transferred, but maintains that petitioners have made restitution impossible because the transferred funds cannot be distinguished from the other dollars in petitioners' bank accounts. See Brief for Respondent 39–44. Because avoidance and restitution are classical equitable remedies, he says, petitioners are not entitled to a trial by jury. We find this strained attempt to circumvent precedent unpersuasive. Because dollars are fungible, and respondent has not requested an accounting or other specifically equitable form of relief, a complete remedy is available at law, and equity will not countenance an action when complete relief may be obtained at law. See, *e.g., Schoenthal v. Irving Trust Co.,* 287 U.S., at 94–95, 53 S.Ct., at 51–52. Moreover, because a plaintiff is entitled to return of any funds transferred in violation of 11 U.S.C. § 548 (1982 ed., Supp. V), and because a judge lacks equitable discretion to refuse to enter an award for less than the amount of the transfer, any distinction that might exist between "damages" and monetary relief under a different label is purely semantic, with no relevance to the adjudication of petitioners' Seventh Amendment claim. Indeed, even if the checks respon-

drawn jurisdiction over that action by courts of law and assigned it exclusively to non-Article III tribunals sitting without juries, the Seventh Amendment guarantees petitioners a jury trial upon request.

IV

Prior to passage of the Bankruptcy Reform Act of 1978, * * * "[s]uits to recover preferences constitute[d] no part of the proceedings in bankruptcy." *Schoenthal v. Irving Trust Co., supra,* at 94–95, 53 S.Ct., at 51. Although related to bankruptcy proceedings, fraudulent conveyance and preference actions brought by a trustee in bankruptcy were deemed separate, plenary suits to which the Seventh Amendment applied. While the 1978 Act brought those actions within the jurisdiction of the bankruptcy courts, it preserved parties' rights to trial by jury as they existed prior to the effective date of the 1978 Act. 28 U.S.C. § 1480(a) (repealed). The 1984 Amendments, however, designated fraudulent conveyance actions "core proceedings," 28 U.S.C. § 157(b)(2)(H)(1982 ed., Supp. V), which bankruptcy judges may adjudicate and in which they may issue final judgments, § 157(b)(1), if a district court has referred the matter to them, § 157(a). We are not obliged to decide today whether bankruptcy courts may conduct jury trials in fraudulent conveyance suits brought by a trustee against a person who has not entered a claim against the estate, either in the rare procedural posture of this case, * * * or under the current statutory scheme, see 28 U.S.C. § 1411 (1982 ed., Supp. V). Nor need we decide whether, if Congress has authorized bankruptcy courts to hold jury trials in such actions, that authorization comports with Article III when non-Article III judges preside over the actions subject to review in, or withdrawal by, the district courts. We also need not consider whether jury trials conducted by a bankruptcy court would satisfy the Seventh Amendment's command that "no fact tried by a jury, shall be otherwise reexamined in any Court of the United States, than according to the rules of the common law," given that district courts may presently set aside clearly erroneous factual findings by bankruptcy courts. Bkrtcy. Rule 8013. The sole issue before us is whether the Seventh Amendment confers on petitioners a right to a jury trial in the face of Congress' decision to allow a non-Article III tribunal to adjudicate the claims against them.

A

In *Atlas Roofing,* we noted that "when Congress creates new statutory 'public rights,' it may assign their adjudication to an administrative agency with which a jury trial would be incompatible, without violating the Seventh Amendment's injunction that jury trial is to be 'preserved' in 'suits at common law.'" 430 U.S., at 455, 97 S.Ct., at 1269 (footnote omitted). We emphasized, however, that Congress' power to block

---

dent seeks to recover lay untouched in petitioners' offices, legal remedies would apparently have sufficed. See, *e.g., Adams v. Champion,* 294 U.S. 231, 234, 55 S.Ct. 399, 400, 79 L.Ed. 880 (1935); *Whitehead v. Shattuck, supra,* 138 U.S., at 151, 11 S.Ct., at 277.

application of the Seventh Amendment to a cause of action has limits. Congress may only deny trials by jury in actions at law, we said, in cases where "public rights" are litigated: "Our prior cases support administrative factfinding in only those situations involving 'public rights,' *e.g.*, where the Government is involved in its sovereign capacity under an otherwise valid statute creating enforceable public rights. Wholly private tort, contract, and property cases, as well as a vast range of other cases, are not at all implicated."

We adhere to that general teaching. As we said in *Atlas Roofing:* " 'On the common law side of the federal courts, the aid of juries is not only deemed appropriate but is required by the Constitution itself.' " * * * Congress may devise novel causes of action involving public rights free from the strictures of the Seventh Amendment if it assigns their adjudication to tribunals without statutory authority to employ juries as factfinders. But it lacks the power to strip parties contesting matters of private right of their constitutional right to a trial by jury. As we recognized in *Atlas Roofing,* to hold otherwise would be to permit Congress to eviscerate the Seventh Amendment's guarantee by assigning to administrative agencies or courts of equity all causes of action not grounded in state law, whether they originate in a newly fashioned regulatory scheme or possess a long line of common-law forebears. * * * The Constitution nowhere grants Congress such puissant authority. "[L]egal claims are not magically converted into equitable issues by their presentation to a court of equity," * * * nor can Congress conjure away the Seventh Amendment by mandating that traditional legal claims be brought there or taken to an administrative tribunal.

In certain situations, of course, Congress may fashion causes of action that are closely *analogous* to common-law claims and place them beyond the ambit of the Seventh Amendment by assigning their resolution to a forum in which jury trials are unavailable. * * * Congress' power to do so is limited, however, just as its power to place adjudicative authority in non-Article III tribunals is circumscribed. * * * Unless a legal cause of action involves "public rights," Congress may not deprive parties litigating over such a right of the Seventh Amendment's guarantee to a jury trial.

In *Atlas Roofing, supra,* * * * we noted that Congress may effectively supplant a common-law cause of action carrying with it a right to a jury trial with a statutory cause of action shorn of a jury trial right if that statutory cause of action inheres, in or lies against, the Federal Government in its sovereign capacity. Our case law makes plain, however, that the class of "public rights" whose adjudication Congress may assign to administrative agencies or courts of equity sitting without juries is more expansive than *Atlas Roofing*'s discussion suggests. Indeed, our decisions point to the conclusion that, if a statutory cause of action is legal in nature, the question whether the Seventh Amendment permits Congress to assign its adjudication to a tribunal that does not employ juries as factfinders requires the same answer as the question whether Article III allows Congress to assign adjudication of that cause of action to a non-Article III tribunal. For if a statutory cause of action, such as respondent's right to recover a fraudulent conveyance under 11 U.S.C. § 548(a)(2), is not a "public right" for Article III purposes, then Congress may not assign its adjudication to a specialized non-Article III court lacking "the essential attributes of the judicial power." * * * And if the action must be tried under the auspices of an Article III court, then the Seventh Amendment affords the parties a right to a jury trial whenever the cause of action is legal in nature. Conversely, if Congress may assign the adjudication of a statutory cause of action to a non-Article III tribunal, then the Seventh Amendment poses no independent bar to the adjudication of that action by a nonjury factfinder. * * * In addition to our Seventh Amendment precedents, we therefore rely on our decisions exploring the restrictions Article III places on Congress' choice of adjudicative bodies to resolve disputes over statutory rights to determine whether petitioners are entitled to a jury trial.

In our most recent discussion of the "public rights" doctrine as it bears on Congress' power to commit adjudication of a statutory cause of action to a non-Article III tribunal, we rejected the view that "a matter of public rights must at a minimum arise 'between the government and others.'" * * * We held, instead, that the Federal Government need not be a party for a case to revolve around "public rights." * * * The crucial question, in cases not involving the Federal Government, is whether "Congress, acting for a valid legislative purpose pursuant to its constitutional powers under Article I, [has] create[d] a seemingly 'private' right that is so closely integrated into a public regulatory scheme as to be a matter appropriate for agency resolution with limited involvement by the Article III judiciary." * * * If a statutory right is not closely intertwined with a federal regulatory program Congress has power to enact, and if that right neither belongs to nor exists against the Federal Government, then it must be adjudicated by an Article III court. If the right is legal in nature, then it carries with it the Seventh Amendment's guarantee of a jury trial.

B

Although the issue admits of some debate, a bankruptcy trustee's right to recover a fraudulent conveyance under 11 U.S.C. § 548(a)(2) seems to us more accurately characterized as a private rather than a public right as we have used those terms in our Article III decisions. In *Northern Pipeline Construction Co.,* * * * the plurality noted that the restructuring of debtor-creditor relations in bankruptcy "may well be a 'public right.'" But the plurality also emphasized that state-law causes of action for breach of contract or warranty are paradigmatic private rights, even when asserted by an insolvent corporation in the midst of Chapter 11 reorganization proceedings. The plurality further said that "matters from their nature subject to 'a suit at common law or in equity or admiralty'" lie at the "protected core" of Article III judicial power * * *. There can be little doubt that fraudulent conveyance actions by bankruptcy trustees—suits which, we said in *Schoenthal v. Irving Trust Co.,* * * * "constitute no part of the proceedings in bankruptcy but concern controversies arising out of it"—are quintessentially suits at common law that more nearly resemble state-law contract claims brought by a bankrupt corporation to augment the bankruptcy estate than they do creditors' hierarchically ordered claims to a pro rata share of the bankruptcy res. See Gibson 1022–1025. They therefore appear matters of private rather than public right.

* * *

The 1978 Act abolished the statutory distinction between plenary and summary bankruptcy proceedings, on which the Court relied in *Schoenthal* and *Katchen*. Although the 1978 Act preserved parties' rights to jury trials as they existed prior to the day it took effect, 28 U.S.C. § 1480(a)(repealed), in the 1984 Amendments Congress drew a new distinction between "core" and "non-core" proceedings and classified fraudulent conveyance actions as core proceedings triable by bankruptcy judges. 28 U.S.C. § 157(b)(2)(H)(1982 ed., Supp. V). Whether 28 U.S.C. § 1411 (1982 ed., Supp. V) purports to abolish jury trial rights in what were formerly plenary actions is unclear, and at any rate is not a question we need decide here. See *supra,* at 2789, n. 3. The decisive point is that in neither the 1978 Act nor the 1984 Amendments did Congress "creat[e] a new cause of action, and remedies therefor, unknown to the common law," because traditional rights and remedies were inadequate to cope with a manifest public problem. * * * Rather, Congress simply reclassified a preexisting, common-law cause of action that was not integrally related to the reformation of debtor-creditor relations and that apparently did not suffer from any grave deficiencies. This purely taxonomic change cannot alter our Seventh Amendment analysis. Congress cannot eliminate a party's Seventh Amendment right to a jury trial merely by relabeling the cause of action to which it attaches and placing exclusive jurisdiction in an administrative agency or a specialized court of equity. * * *

Nor can Congress' assignment be justified on the ground that jury trials of fraudulent conveyance actions would "go far to dismantle the statutory scheme," * * * or that bankruptcy proceedings have been placed in "an administrative forum with which the jury would be incompatible." * * * To be sure, we owe some deference to Congress' judgment after it has given careful consideration to the constitutionality of a legislative provision. * * * But respondent has adduced no evidence that Congress considered the constitutional implications of its designation of all fraudulent conveyance actions as core proceedings. Nor can it seriously be argued that permitting jury trials in fraudulent conveyance actions brought by a trustee against a person who has not entered a claim against the estate would "go far to dismantle the statutory scheme," as we used that phrase in *Atlas Roofing,* when our opinion in that case, following *Schoenthal,* plainly assumed that such claims carried with them a right to a jury trial. In addition, one cannot easily say that "the jury would be incompatible" with bankruptcy proceedings, in view of Congress' express provision for jury trials in certain actions arising out of bankruptcy litigation. * * * And Justice White's claim that juries may serve usefully as checks only on the decisions of judges who enjoy life tenure, see *post,* at 82–83, overlooks the extent to which judges who are appointed for fixed terms may be beholden to Congress or Executive officials, and thus ignores the potential for juries to exercise beneficial restraint on their decisions.

It may be that providing jury trials in some fraudulent conveyance actions—if not in this particular case, because respondent's suit was commenced after the Bankruptcy Court approved the debtor's plan of reorganization—would impede swift resolution of bankruptcy proceedings and increase the expense of Chapter 11 reorganizations.[17] But "these considerations are insufficient to overcome the clear command of the Seventh Amendment." * * *

V

We do not decide today whether the current jury trial provision—28 U.S.C. § 1411 (1982 ed., Supp. V)—permits bankruptcy courts to conduct jury trials in fraudulent conveyance actions like the one respondent initiated. Nor do we express any view as to whether the Seventh Amendment or Article III allows jury trials in such actions to be held before non-Article III bankruptcy judges subject to the oversight provided by the district courts pursuant to the 1984 Amendments. We leave those issues for future decisions.[19] We do hold, however, that whatever the answers to these questions, the Seventh Amendment entitles petitioners to the jury trial they requested. Accordingly, the judgment of the Court of Appeals is reversed, and the case is remanded for further proceedings consistent with this opinion. (citations and most footnotes omitted)

It is so ordered.

17. Respondent argues, for example, that the prompt resolution of fraudulent transfer claims brought by bankruptcy trustees is often crucial to the reorganization process and that if, by demanding a jury trial, a party could delay those proceedings, it could alter the negotiating framework and unfairly extract more favorable terms for itself. Brief for Respondent 35. It warrants notice, however, that the provision of jury trials in fraudulent conveyance actions has apparently not been attended by substantial difficulties under previous bankruptcy statutes; that respondent has not pointed to any discussion of this allegedly serious problem in the legislative history of the 1978 Act or the 1984 Amendments; that in many cases defendants would likely not request jury trials; that causes of action to recover preferences may be assigned pursuant to the plan of reorganization rather than pursued prior to the plan's approval, as was done in this very case; and that Congress itself, in enacting 28 U.S.C. § 1411 (1982 ed., Supp. V), explicitly provided for jury trials of personal injury and wrongful death claims, which would likely take much longer to try than most preference actions and which often involve large sums of money.

19. Justice White accuses us of being "rather coy" about which statute we are invalidating, *post,* at 2806, n. 2, and of "preferring to be obtuse" about which court must preside over the jury trial to which petitioners are entitled. *Post,* at 2811. But however helpful it might be for us to adjudge every pertinent statutory and constitutional issue presented by the 1978 Act and the 1984 Amendments, we cannot properly reach out and decide matters not before us. The only question we have been called upon to answer in this case is whether the Seventh Amendment grants petitioners a right to a jury trial. We hold unequivocally that it does.

[The concurring opinion of JUSTICE SCALIA and the dissenting opinions of JUSTICES WHITE and BLACKMUN are omitted.]

Problem 3–6

Robinson files a Chapter 11 case. In due course Greenberg Oil files a $2,700 claim for fuel oil delivered shortly before bankruptcy. Robinson has a $5,000,000 breach of contract claim against Greenberg arising out of an unrelated transaction in which Robinson claimed that certain important pieces of its equipment were destroyed because of defective oil delivered by Greenberg. Robinson asks three questions:

1. May it bring this suit in the bankruptcy court?

2. Will Greenberg be entitled to a jury trial?

3. If a jury trial is to be conducted, must the case be heard by the district judge or can the bankruptcy judge sit at the bench during a jury trial? Prior to 1994 there was no explicit statutory authority for a bankruptcy judge to hear a jury trial. The bankruptcy judge's limited jury authority is stated in section 157(e).

Problem 3–7

1. In which of the following cases will the party be able to get a jury trial?

   a. Request by the debtor in possession on a preference claim.

   b. Request by the creditor on a preference claim.

   c. Request by a creditor on a preference claim who has a claim against the estate that has not been made in circumstances in which the debtor in possession has himself filed a proof of claim under section 501(c) on behalf of the creditor.

   d. Request by a creditor in a preference action. The creditor has made a claim against the estate but has withdrawn its claim under rule 3006.

   e. Suit in bankruptcy court by the debtor in possession against a debtor to collect a receivable. Assume that the debtor asks for a jury trial.

   f. An adversary proceeding in which a creditor claims that a debt is not dischargeable under section 523.

2. To what extent can a lawyer influence a court's judgment by asking or not asking for equitable relief? Does the request for an injunction mean that no jury trial is permitted? Alternatively, does the request only for damages (on the claim that the cause of action is for breach of contract) mean that a jury must be allowed?

3. What if a defendant in an adversary proceeding in a bankruptcy court brought by the debtor in possession had not filed a claim, but had joined in a request for relief from a stay with parties who had claims, and then filed a brief in that proceeding asking the bankruptcy court to determine the parties' rights? Would that, in and of itself, make sufficient concession to the equitable court's jurisdiction to deny a jury trial?

Chapter Four

ADMINISTRATIVE POWERS AND THE DEBTOR'S ESTATE: SECTIONS 362 AND 361, THE AUTOMATIC STAY AND ADEQUATE PROTECTION

§ 1. THE SCOPE OF SECTION 362

Filing a bankruptcy petition places the debtor's assets under the protection of the "automatic stay" of section 362. Section 362 stays nearly every creditor collection activity as of the filing of the bankruptcy petition. The debtor's filing interposes section 362 as an immediate barrier against further creditor action and creates breathing room for the debtor. A simple road map to the various provisions serves as a starting point to understanding the section. Section 362(a) lists the stayed activities; it stays the creditor not only from pursuing legal and administrative actions against the debtor but also from taking any action to repossess property or to enforce or perfect any lien. *United States v. Whiting Pools, Inc.*, 462 U.S. 198, 103 S.Ct. 2309, 76 L.Ed.2d 515 (1983), teaches that even the powerful IRS bows before the stay.

Obviously, section 362(a) stops lawsuits against the debtor in their tracks—tort, contract and otherwise. It bars demand for payment and forecloses repossession and setoff. Read the section carefully. See if you can imagine any act that a creditor would like to take against a debtor that might stimulate payment but that would not be barred. Note that the stay prohibits not only acts by or actions of the creditor against the debtor, but also acts and actions taken against "property of the estate." The latter provision makes it important to determine what assets remain "property of the estate" and what assets do not. If an action is taken directly against property (such as repossession) and the property is no longer the property of the estate, the stay does not apply. For these reasons, one seeking to apply the stay must also consult section 541 which defines the property of the estate.

There are exceptions to the stay. Section 362(b) describes acts that are not prohibited, such as continuing a criminal action against the debtor, collection of alimony and child support, and actions taken pursuant to the police power of the state.

In some states a foreclosing mortgagor must record a copy of the applicable judgment in the local real estate office within thirty days after the expiration of the redemption period to obtain full legal title. In such states, where an affirmative act is required, the automatic stay may prohibit that act and so extend the period of redemption. See *In re L.H. & A. Realty Co., Inc.*, 57 B.R. 265 (Bankr.D.Vt.1986).

Of course, the stay is not indeterminate. At the request of a secured creditor, it may be "lifted." Moreover, the stay ends under section 362(c)(2) when the case is "closed" or "dismissed." Finally, under section 362(c)(2)(C), the stay ends for most purposes when the discharge is granted. Unfortunately the times and terms in section 362(c)(2) do not always have a precise definition. Some bankruptcies that might be regarded as "closed" have continuing vitality for some purposes. Thus, it is not always clear when one of the events listed in section 362(c)(2) has occurred and so ended the stay.

In hundreds of cases each year secured creditors ask for the stay to be lifted. Typically they make this request under the terms of section 362(d) which reads as follows:

(d) On request of a party in interest and after notice and a hearing, the court shall grant relief from the stay provided under subsection (a) of this section, such as by terminating, annulling, modifying, or conditioning such stay—

(1) for cause, including the lack of adequate protection of an interest in property under subsection (a) of this section of such party in interest; or

(2) with respect to a stay of an act against property if,

(A) the debtor does not have an equity in such property; and

(B) such property is not necessary to an effective reorganization.

(3) with respect to a stay of an act against single asset real estate under subsection (a), by a creditor whose claim is secured by an interest in such real estate, unless, not later than the date that is 90 days after the entry of the order for relief (or such later date as the court may determine for cause by order entered within that 90–day period)—

(A) the debtor has filed a plan of reorganization that has a reasonable possibility of being confirmed within a reasonable time; or

(B) the debtor has commenced monthly payments to each creditor whose claim is secured by such real estate (other than a claim secured by a judgment lien or by an unmatured statutory lien), which payments are in an amount equal to interest at a current fair market rate on the value of the creditor's interest in the real estate.

This relief can be granted only after "notice and a hearing," a term defined in section 102(1). An actual hearing is not always required.

Section 362(e) fleshes out the procedures for preliminary and final hearings used in requesting relief from the stay. That section appears to offer the creditor a judicial decision denying the stay or, in the case of court inaction, the lifting of the stay. Reading the cases under section 362(e) tells one that the game is substantially more complicated than the provision indicates. In fact courts and debtors have found many ways of keeping the stay in existence for a long period of time, even after the request and despite the absence of final determination by the court.

Section 362(f) provides for relief from the stay without notice or a hearing if necessary to prevent irreparable harm to a movant. If a "party in interest" will suffer irreparable damage before there is an opportunity for notice and a hearing, the court "shall" grant relief from the stay upon request of that party.

Section 362(g) assigns burdens of proof. The party opposing relief has the burden on all issues except for the issue of the debtor's equity in property, an element of section 362(d)(1)(A). Section 362(h) provides for costs, attorneys' fees, and in certain circumstances, punitive damages for willful violations of the stay.

A person reading the cases under section 362 might conclude that the debtors have turned the tables on the creditors. The usual state legislative battle between creditors and debtors is for debtors to devise a "consumer protection" or debtor protection statute and for the creditors to find clever ways to escape the grips of that law. To a considerable extent, section 362 and the various amendments to it work the other way. Creditors have found it is difficult, expensive, and time consuming to escape the stay by use of sections 362(d) and 362(e). Here, creditors, not debtors, seek legislative help to cause the stay to be lifted or require the courts to lift the stay where they have proven unwilling to do so.

The most recent of these legislative responses to creditors are part of the 1994 amendments. Those amendments added subsection (d)(3)—to limit the stay to 90 days in certain real estate cases. The last sentence in 362(e) was modified by replacing "commenced" with "concluded."

The combination of bankruptcy judges' lack of interest in motions to lift the stay and of debtors' cleverness and guile in using the law in stalling has negated many of the "creditor protection" terms in 362. We suspect that the creditors' lot will not be greatly improved even by the new amendments until bankruptcy judges become persuaded of the serious injury done to secured creditors by continuing the stay in cases where successful reorganization is unlikely.

Since failure to hear or to decide a motion to lift the stay is not likely to be terminal to either party and will cause only incremental damage to a creditor who deserves to have the stay lifted, we suspect that these motions to lift are seldom high on the list of things to be done by a typical bankruptcy judge. Yet the collective injury to all secured creditors by the courts' failure promptly to hear and decide motions for the stay to be lifted may be greater than the total loss in other cases that seem individually to be much more important. Until creditors convince the bankruptcy courts of this, we suspect that they will meet the fate they have suffered for the past 15 years—namely continuation of stays in many circumstances where they should be lifted.

Beyond the basic provisions of section 362, more complicated questions arise as debtors and creditors manipulate pre-filing transactions to seek an advantage post-filing. Can property be sufficiently separated from the debtor through the structuring of the original transaction so that the property is not part of the estate and is free from the stay? Does the stay apply to actions taken by creditors against debtors other than the debtor in bankruptcy, but closely tied to him, such as a limited partner in a partnership in which the debtor is a general partner? We explore those questions below.

Many acts quite remote from the collection of a debt have been read by the courts to be prohibited by section 362. Examples are the delisting of a stock on the stock exchange or the revocation of accreditation of an educational institution. Of course these actions could have a powerfully deleterious impact on the finances of the affected institutions even though they are not related to the bankruptcy or to an attempt to collect a debt.

The lucky and the powerful are excluded from the stay by section 362(b); others are left to argue in front of the bankruptcy court that the acts they wish to perform are not prohibited by the letter or spirit of section 362(a). An example of a recurring dispute of this kind is found *In re David Strumpf,* 37 F.3d 155 (4th Cir.1994). In that case, Strumpf had a bank account at Citizens Bank of Maryland. When the petition was filed, Strumpf had more than $11,000 in the account and he owed the bank more than $5,000. Because of section 506(f) the bank should have been treated as a fully secured creditor by virtue of its right of setoff. Apparently Strumpf did not treat the bank as a secured creditor in his Chapter 13 plan and, after the plan was approved, the bank imposed an "administrative freeze" on his account and petitioned the court to lift the stay. Strumpf argued that the use of the administrative hold itself violated the stay and the bankruptcy court agreed. Ultimately the district court reversed and, even later, the Court of Appeals for the Fourth Circuit agreed with the bankruptcy court. The Supreme Court then held that the "freeze" was not a setoff and did not violate the automatic stay. *Citizens Bank of Maryland v. Strumpf,* ___ U.S. ___, 116 S.Ct. 286, 133 L.Ed.2d 258 (1995).

§ 2. THE REACH OF THE AUTOMATIC STAY AND PROPERTY OF THE ESTATE, SECTIONS 362 AND 541

Because three of the subsections of 362(a) apply only to actions against "property of the estate," what is "property of the estate" must be known before the reach of section 362 can be understood. First the student should read section 362(a) with care. Not only does the term "property of the estate" limit the stay, but terms such as "debtor" and "claim" are also important in determining which acts the stay prevents and what conduct it allows. Then the student must consider the definition of estate property found in section 541.

Section 362(a)(1) stays virtually all judicial and quasi-judicial activity against the debtor that was or could have been commenced before the case began or that is based on a claim that existed prior to the filing of the petition. Subsection (a)(2) bars enforcement of a judgment against the debtor or against property of the estate. Subsections (a)(3), (4) and (5) prohibit any act to get possession of or to exercise control over property of the estate, to create or perfect a lien against property of the debtor or of the estate, or to perfect or create a lien against property of the debtor to the extent the lien secures a claim that existed before the bankruptcy case began. Subsection (a)(6) prohibits any "act" to collect a debt from the debtor, and subsection (a)(7) prohibits setoff.

The provisions in subsection (a) are comprehensive and most actions that a creditor might wish to take with respect to a debtor are prohibited. For example, a demand letter mailed by a bank to an individual debtor clearly violates section 362(a). A combination of (a)(5) and (6) forecloses almost every conceivable act that a secured creditor might want to undertake against its collateral. The section 362(b) exceptions cut but little into the reach of section 362(a).

On its face (and at least with respect to a debtor's property and rights existing at the time a bankruptcy petition is filed) section 541(a) seems at least as inclusive as section 362(a). Note that section 541(a) covers property "wherever located and by whomever held" and includes under (a)(1) "all legal and equitable interests of the debtor in property as of the commencement of the case." Moreover, section 541(a)(5) brings into the estate certain property acquired within 180 days after the case was commenced. Sections 541(a)(6) and (7) include all proceeds, products, rent or profits of property of the estate and all property "that the estate acquires" after filing.

The section "includes all kinds of property, including tangible or intangible property, choses in action * * * and [property] merely out of the possession of the debtor [which] remained 'property of the debtor.' The debtor's interest in property also includes 'title to property.' * * *" S.Rep. No. 95–989, 95th Cong., 2d Sess. 82 (1978).

What "property" might not be property of the estate?

In subsection 541(b) ("Property not Included in the Estate") one can see the hand of special interests at work. Why, for example, would Congress single out "eligibility of the debtor to participate in programs authorized under the Higher Education Act of 1965?" Or why a transfer of interest of the debtor in "liquid or gaseous hydrocarbons?" Finally, is the provision of 541 added in 1994 that serves the peculiar interests of sellers of money orders. The point by now should be clear. Congress lacks the will to stand up to particular persons who ask for particular treatment, at least when the pleader's request is so narrow that it will not substantially upset the arrangement among creditors and debtors in general. These concessions make for an ugly and unprincipled statute.

UNITED STATES v. WHITING POOLS, INC.

Supreme Court of the United States, 1983.
462 U.S. 198, 103 S.Ct. 2309, 76 L.Ed.2d 515.

JUSTICE BLACKMUN delivered the opinion of the Court.

I

A

Respondent Whiting Pools, Inc., a corporation, sells, installs, and services swimming pools and related equipment and supplies. As of January 1981, Whiting owed approximately $92,000 in Federal Insurance Contribution Act taxes and federal taxes withheld from its employees, but had failed to respond to assessments and demands for payment by the IRS. As a consequence, a tax lien in that amount attached to all of Whiting's property.

On January 14, 1981, the Service seized Whiting's tangible personal property—equipment, vehicles, inventory, and office supplies—pursuant to the levy and distraint provision of the Internal Revenue Code of 1954. According to uncontroverted findings, the estimated liquidation value of the property seized was, at most, $35,000, but its estimated going-concern value in Whiting's hands was $162,876. The very next day, January 15, Whiting filed a petition for reorganization, under the Bankruptcy Code's Chapter 11. Whiting was continued as debtor-in-possession.

The United States, intending to proceed with a tax sale of the property, moved in the Bankruptcy Court for a declaration that the automatic stay provision of the Bankruptcy Code, § 362(a), is inapplicable to the IRS or, in the alternative, for relief from the stay. Whiting counterclaimed for an order requiring the Service to turn the seized property over to the bankruptcy estate pursuant to § 542(a) of the Bankruptcy Code. Whiting intended to use the property in its reorganized business.

B

The Bankruptcy Court determined that the IRS was bound by the automatic stay provision. Because it found that the seized property was essential to Whiting's reorganization effort, it refused to lift the stay. Acting under § 543(b)(1) of the Bankruptcy Code, rather than under § 542(a), the court directed the IRS to turn the property over to Whiting on the condition that Whiting provide the Service with specified protection for its interests.

The United States District Court reversed, holding that a turnover order against the Service was not authorized by either § 542(a) or § 543(b)(1). The United States Court of Appeals for the Second Circuit, in turn, reversed the District Court. It held that a turnover order could issue against the Service under § 542(a), and it remanded the case for reconsideration of the adequacy of the Bankruptcy Court's protection conditions. The Court of Appeals acknowledged that its ruling was contrary to that reached by the United States Court of Appeals for the Fourth Circuit in *Cross Electric Co. v. United States,* 664 F.2d 1218 (1981), and noted confusion on the issue among bankruptcy and district courts. 674 F.2d, at 145, and n. 1. We granted certiorari to resolve this conflict in an important area of the law under the new Bankruptcy Code.

II

By virtue of its tax lien, the Service holds a secured interest in Whiting's property. We first examine whether § 542(a) of the Bankruptcy Code generally authorizes the turnover of a debtor's property seized by a secured creditor prior to the commencement of reorganization proceedings. Section 542(a) requires an entity in possession of "property that the trustee may use, sell, or lease under section 363" to deliver that property to the trustee. Subsections (b) and (c) of § 363 authorize the trustee to use, sell, or lease any "property of the estate," subject to certain conditions for the protection of creditors with an interest in the property. Section 541(a)(1) defines the "estate" as "comprised of all the following property, wherever located: * * * all legal or equitable interests of the debtor in property as of the commencement of the case." Although these statutes could be read to limit the estate to those "interests of the debtor in property" at the time of the filing of the petition, we view them as a definition of what is included in the estate, rather than as a limitation.

A

In proceedings under the reorganization provisions of the Bankruptcy Code, a troubled enterprise may be restructured to enable it to operate successfully in the future. Until the business can be reorganized pursuant to a plan under 11 U.S.C. §§ 1121–1129 (1976 ed., Supp. V), the trustee or debtor-in-possession is authorized to manage the property of the estate and to continue the operation of the business. See § 1108. By permitting reorganization, Congress anticipated that the business would continue to provide jobs, to satisfy creditors' claims, and to produce a return for its owners. H.R.Rep. No. 95–595, p. 220 (1977). Congress presumed that the assets of the debtor would be more valuable if used in a rehabilitated business than if "sold for scrap." The reorganization effort would have small chance of success, however, if property essential to running the business were excluded from the estate. Thus, to facilitate the rehabilitation of the debtor's business, all the debtor's property must be included in the reorganization estate.

This authorization extends even to property of the estate in which a creditor has a secured interest. Although Congress might have safeguarded the interests of secured creditors outright by excluding from the estate any property subject to a secured interest, it chose instead to include such property in the estate and to provide secured creditors with "adequate protection" for their interests. At the secured creditor's insistence, the bankruptcy court must place such limits or conditions on the trustee's power to sell, use, or lease property as are necessary to protect the creditor. The creditor with a secured interest in property included in the estate must look to this provision for protection, rather than to the nonbankruptcy remedy of possession.

Both the congressional goal of encouraging reorganizations and Congress' choice of methods to protect secured creditors suggest that Congress intended a broad range of property to be included in the estate.

B

The statutory language reflects this view of the scope of the estate. As noted above, § 541(a)(1) provides that the "estate is comprised of all the following property, wherever located: * * * all legal or equitable interests of the debtor in property as of the commencement of the case." 11 U.S.C. § 541(a)(1) (1976 ed., Supp. V). The House and Senate Reports on the Bankruptcy Code indicate that § 541(a)(1)'s scope is broad. Most important, in the context of this case, § 541(a)(1) is intended to include in the estate any property made available to the estate by other provisions of the Bankruptcy Code. See H.R.Rep. No. 95-595, p. 367 (1977). Several of these provisions bring into the estate property in which the debtor did not have a possessory interest at the time the bankruptcy proceedings commenced.

Section 542(a) is such a provision. It requires an entity (other than a custodian) holding any property of the debtor that the trustee can use under § 363 to turn that property over to the trustee. Given the broad scope of the reorganization estate, property of the debtor repossessed by a secured creditor falls within this rule, and therefore may be drawn into the estate. While there are explicit limitations on the reach of § 542(a), none requires that the debtor hold a possessory interest in the property at the commencement of the reorganization proceedings.

As does all bankruptcy law, § 542(a) modifies the procedural rights available to creditors to protect and satisfy their liens. In effect, § 542(a) grants to the estate a possessory interest in certain property of the debtor that was not held by the debtor at the commencement of reorganization proceedings. The Bankruptcy Code provides secured creditors various rights, including the right to adequate protection, and these rights replace the protection afforded by possession.

C

This interpretation of § 542(a) is supported by the section's legislative history. Although the legislative Reports are silent on the precise issue before us, the House and Senate hearings from which § 542(a) emerged provide guidance. Several witnesses at those hearings noted, without contradiction, the need for a provision authorizing the turnover of property of the debtor in the possession of secured creditors.

We conclude that the reorganization estate includes property of the debtor that has been seized by a creditor prior to the filing of a petition for reorganization.

III

A

We see no reason why a different result should obtain when the IRS is the creditor. The Service is bound by § 542(a) to the same extent as any other secured creditor. The Bankruptcy Code expressly states that the term "entity," used in § 542(a), includes a governmental unit. § 101(14). Moreover, Congress carefully considered the effect of the new Bankruptcy Code on tax collection, see generally S.Rep. No. 95–1106 (1978) (Report of Senate Finance Committee), and decided to provide protection to tax collectors, such as the IRS, through grants of enhanced priorities for unsecured tax claims, § 507(a)(6), and by the nondischarge of tax liabilities, § 523(a)(1). S.Rep. No. 95–989, pp. 14–15 (1978). Tax collectors also enjoy the generally applicable right under § 363(e) to adequate protection for property subject to their liens. Nothing in the Bankruptcy Code or its legislative history indicates that Congress intended a special exception for the tax collector in the form of an exclusion from the estate of property seized to satisfy a tax lien.

B

Of course, if a tax levy or seizure transfers to the IRS ownership of the property seized, § 542(a) may not apply. The enforcement provisions of the Internal Revenue Code of 1954, 26 U.S.C. §§ 6321–6326 (1976 ed. and Supp. V), do grant to the Service powers to enforce its tax liens that are greater than those possessed by private secured creditors under state law. But those provisions do not transfer ownership of the property to the IRS.

The Service's interest in seized property is its lien on that property. The Internal Revenue Code's levy and seizure provisions, 26 U.S.C. §§ 6331 and 6332, are special procedural devices available to the IRS to protect and satisfy its liens, *United States v. Sullivan*, 333 F.2d 100, 116 (3d Cir.1964), and are analogous to the remedies available to private secured creditors. They are provisional remedies that do not determine the Service's rights to the seized property, but merely bring the property into the Service's legal custody. See 4 B. Bittker, Federal Taxation of Income, Estates and Gifts ¶ 111.5.5, p. 111–108 (1981). At no point does the Service's interest in the property exceed the value of the lien. The IRS is obligated to return to the debtor any surplus from a sale. 26

U.S.C. § 6342(b). Ownership of the property is transferred only when the property is sold to a bona fide purchaser at a tax sale. See *Bennett v. Hunter,* [76 U.S. 326], 9 Wall. 326, 336, 19 L.Ed. 672 (1870); 26 U.S.C. § 6339(a)(2); Plumb, 13 Tax L.Rev., at 274–275. In fact, the tax sale provision itself refers to the debtor as the owner of the property after the seizure but prior to the sale. Until such a sale takes place, the property remains the debtor's and thus is subject to the turnover requirement of § 542(a).

IV

When property seized prior to the filing of a petition is drawn into the Chapter 11 reorganization estate, the Service's tax lien is not dissolved; nor is its status as a secured creditor destroyed. The IRS, under § 363(e), remains entitled to adequate protection for its interests, to other rights enjoyed by secured creditors, and to the specific privileges accorded tax collectors. Section 542(a) simply requires the Service to seek protection of its interest according to the congressionally established bankruptcy procedures, rather than by withholding the seized property from the debtor's efforts to reorganize.

The judgment of the Court of Appeals is affirmed.

It is so ordered.

STATUTORY EXCEPTIONS TO THE STAY

In 1995 subsection (b) of section 362 contains 18 acts to which the stay does not apply. These run the gamut from a criminal action against the debtor (it would hardly be right for a murderer to escape trial and conviction by filing Chapter 7) to the presentment of a negotiable instrument or acts of various taxing authorities. When section 362(b) was first enacted in 1978 it contained only eight numbered paragraphs. With each revision of the Bankruptcy Code additional exceptions have been added, thus, willy nilly, the reach of the stay has been cut back in various specific areas. Most of these areas relate to particularly powerful or sympathetic creditors.

Problem 4–1

Juno Electronics operates factories in three states that produce components for health care equipment. One of the factories, located in Maine, is subject to a multimillion dollar mortgage held by Athena Bank. Juno faces two distinct, but pressing problems. The first is that the mortgage on the Maine factory has been in default for several months with Athena posting the property for foreclosure each month, but withdrawing the sale. Each month, Juno receives a demand letter from Athena claiming that it will actually sell the property at foreclosure at 10:00 a.m. on the first Tuesday of the next month unless it is paid in full. The second problem is that Juno and its officers are being investigated by the federal office that controls import and export activity for an alleged violation of export control laws by selling equipment to China. An adverse result on this investigation could result in a large fine against the company and the officers, as well as an order closing one segment of Juno's business (its export division).

a. Can Juno prevent either the foreclosure or the investigation and anticipated fine by filing bankruptcy?

b. If Juno does not file bankruptcy until noon on the first Tuesday of the month and Athena purchases at the foreclosure auction at 10:15, does Juno have any right or action against Athena?

IN RE PRICE CHOPPER SUPERMARKETS, INC. v. ALPHA BETA COMPANY

United States District Court, Southern District of California, 1984.
40 B.R. 816.

Opinion on: Motion for Summary Judgment

Louise DeCarl Malugen; Bankruptcy Judge.

Price Chopper Supermarkets, Inc. ("Price Chopper" or "Debtor"), a discount retail grocer, purchased certain grocery inventory from Alpha Beta Company ("Alpha Beta"), executing a $125,000 promissory note in favor of Alpha Beta on February 19, 1981. To assure payment of this promissory note, Alpha Beta requested and received a $125,000 standby Letter of Credit from the Bank of America ("Bank") on February 28, 1981. The Letter of Credit provided that at any time up to May 15, 1981 the Bank had an irrevocable obligation to pay Alpha Beta $125,000 upon presentation of a sight draft, the February 19 promissory note from the Debtor, and a statement from Alpha Beta that the Debtor's note was in default.

To assure the Bank's reimbursement in the event it was called upon to perform under the Letter of Credit, on March 3, 1981, Debtor authorized the Bank to debit its checking account in the amount of $2,000 per day.

Commencing March 5, 1981, the Bank deducted $2,000 per day from Debtor's account and transferred the debited sums to its "Bancontrol/Price Chopper" account. These deductions continued until April 13, 1981, with a total of $78,000 having accumulated in the Bancontrol account by that date.

On April 14, 1981, a substitute arrangement for assuring the Bank's repayment was entered into between Debtor and the Bank. The Debtor's president's wife, Marion Jacobs, lent the Debtor 1,012 shares of AT & T common stock to be pledged as collateral for the Debtor's obligation to the Bank. Ms. Jacobs executed a "Security Agreement: Lent Collateral" ("Lent Collateral Agreement") which authorized the borrower (the Debtor) to deliver the stock to the Bank and grant the Bank a security interest in the stock for "any present or future indebtedness" of debtor to the Bank. On the same date, Ms. Jacobs and the debtor executed a "Security Agreement: Secured Party In Possession" ("Security Agreement"), granting the Bank a security interest in the stock.

On April 15, 1981, the Bank sent Alpha Beta a $78,000 cashier's check, together with a letter that stated:

"These funds are to be applied toward the note that you hold drawn by Price Chopper Supermarkets, Inc. If you are in agreement, *the negotiation of this check will reduce the exposure of Bank of America under the Letter of Credit issued to you* as the beneficiary in the original amount of $125,000 to $47,000. If you are not in agreement with the above, please return the cashier's check." (*emphasis added*)

On April 15, 1981, the Bancontrol/Price Chopper account was debited for $78,000. On May 15, 1981, an amendment to the Letter of Credit was executed between the Bank and the Debtor, reducing the Letter of Credit from $125,000 to $47,000, and extending the expiration date of the Letter of Credit to September 15, 1981. By telegram dated May 29, 1981, the Bank informed Alpha Beta of the amendment to the Letter of Credit.

On June 16, 1981, the debtor filed a petition for reorganization under Chapter 11. On August 6, 1981, Alpha Beta wrote to the Bank, declaring a default under the promissory note of February 19, 1981, and demanding payment on the Letter of Credit. Subsequent to the demand, the Bank sold the AT & T stock, and sometime between the period of August 17 and 20, 1981, realized $57,818.86 for the shares. Thereafter, the Bank remitted $47,000 to Alpha Beta and the balance to Ms. Jacobs.

ISSUES

The Trustee has moved for summary judgment on his complaint against Alpha Beta and the Bank, and cross-motions have been made by Alpha Beta for summary judgment in its favor on the Trustee's complaint or, in the alternative, on its cross-claim for indemnity against the Bank. Likewise, the Bank has made a cross-motion for summary judgment. The following issues are presented by the Trustee's summary judgment motion and the cross-motions of Alpha Beta and the Bank:

* * *

2. Was the AT & T stock property of the estate,

   a. the proceeds of which should be turned over by the Bank to the Trustee under Section 542; or,

   b. the proceeds of which are recoverable from Alpha Beta as a post-petition transfer under Section 549?

II. *Post–Petition Transfer*

The Trustee has moved to set aside the post-petition sale of the AT & T stock by the Bank. Contending that the stock was the property of the estate, he has asked for summary judgment against the Bank for turnover of the proceeds under Section 542 and/or recovery of the proceeds paid to Alpha Beta and Jacobs as a post-petition transfer under Section 549.

Pivotal to the Trustee's ability to recover from any of the above defendants is the determination of whether AT & T stock was property of the estate. The Court finds that it was not and accordingly denies the Trustee's motions for summary judgment and grants the cross-motions of Alpha Beta and the Bank.

Section 541(a)(1) defines property of the estate as "* * * all legal or equitable interests of [the] debtor in property as of the commencement of the case." The Trustee contends that the Debtor had a legal interest in the stock by virtue of the Lent Collateral Agreement. Further, he contends that the Debtor had an equitable interest in the stock because the Lent Collateral Agreement and the "Collateral Receipt: Non–Negotiable" documents (both bank forms) required the Bank to deliver the stock to Price Chopper upon payment of the debt.

The Bank argues that the stock did not become property of the estate because it was lent to the Debtor and "earmarked" for use in satisfaction of the obligation of a specific creditor of the Debtor. The Bank cites 4 *Collier on Bankruptcy* (15th ed.), Para. 547.25, pp. 547–94 which states:

> "In cases when a third person makes a loan to a debtor specifically to enable him to satisfy the claim of a designated creditor, the proceeds never become part of the debtor's assets and therefore no preference is created. The rule is the same regardless of whether the proceeds of the loan are transferred directly by the lender to the creditor or are paid to the debtor with the understanding that they will be paid to the creditor in satisfaction of his claim, so long as such proceeds are clearly 'earmarked'."

The Trustee takes great pains to distinguish the "earmarking" cases claiming that the cited cases involved preferences and not post-petition transfers. However, the Trustee's argument misses the point that in both preference cases (where the issue is depletion of the Debtor's estate by a preferential payment) and in post-petition transfer cases (where the issue is removal of an asset from the Debtor's estate) the critical question is whether there was a transfer of property which could have been a part of the estate available for distribution to all creditors. Although there are no post-petition transfer cases addressing this issue, we find the rationale of the *Grubb v. General Contract Purchase Corp.*, 18 F.Supp. 680 (S.D.N.Y.1937) and *[In re] Sun Railings, Inc.*, 5 B.R. 538 (Bankr.S.D.Fla.1980) cases equally applicable to post-petition transfer cases.

Finally, the Trustee argues that even if the earmarking cases are applicable to post-petition transfers, the stock was not earmarked because the Debtor could have used the collateral to pay or secure other debts. It does not appear from the facts before this Court that the Debtor had that choice.

The AT & T stock was never transferred to the Debtor; it remained in the name of its true owner until sold. The Lent Collateral Agreement signed by Jacobs, indicates that the property lent to Price Chopper was 1,012 shares of AT & T stock "* * * registered in the name of Mrs. Marion Jacobs, Cust., Michele Jacobs Unif. Gift Min. Act. N.Y. * * * " Deductions from the Bancontrol/Price Chopper account were discontinued only when Jacobs pledged her shares of AT & T stock to secure the remainder of the obligation to the Bank. The delivery of the stock to the Bank was made contemporaneously with Jacobs' execution of the Lent Collateral Agreement. When the "Offer To Sell Securities" (another bank form) dated August 7, 1981, was signed by Jacobs shortly before the shares were sold to satisfy the Letter of Credit, she signed in her capacity as custodian for the minors.

The uncontroverted fact that the stock remained registered in Jacobs' name at all times prevented the Debtor from doing anything with the stock other than what Jacobs directed. It remained her property. Accordingly, the stock never entered the Debtor's estate and the post-petition sale of the stock is not in violation of the Section 362 stay, giving rise to a Section 542 recovery, nor a Section 549 postpetition transfer.

This Opinion shall constitute findings of fact and conclusions of law in accordance with Bankruptcy Rule 7052. The attorney for Alpha Beta shall submit an appropriate order within ten (10) days of the filing of this Opinion.

Problem 4–2

Diana sells an apartment building to Artemis for $16 million. Artemis pays cash, but reserves $3 million of the purchase price to apply against any unforeseen defects or liabilities associated with the property. The money is given to an escrow agent with instructions to turn it over to Diana if, after six months, no defects or claims have been discovered. If claims are discovered, the escrow agent is instructed to turn over sufficient money to Artemis to cover Artemis' sworn written estimate of the amount of the claim.

Artemis files in Chapter 11 before the end of the six-month period. When Diana asks for the $3 million at the end of the six-month period, the escrow agent asks your opinion whether it can hand over the money without violating the stay. The debtor in possession has asserted that the money in escrow is "property of the estate" and so subject to the stay.

Problem 4–3

Artemis is a small company that specialized in manufacture of submunitions to go into cluster bombs (of the kind that were so effectively used in Desert Storm). With the cutback in the defense business after 1991, the bomb business became highly competitive. Artemis was able to procure only a small part of the contracts it had formerly enjoyed and even those offered a lower return. In 1993, Juno, the president of Artemis, was thrown out by the creditors. His successor was even less successful and the company filed Chapter 11 at the end of 1993.

A series of events have occurred since the filing. Which does section 362 bar?

a. May the New York Stock Exchange de-list the securities of Artemis because it filed in bankruptcy?

b. Assuming that they meet state law standards for doing so, may several Artemis shareholders now file a derivative action against Juno for mismanagement of the company?

c. Aphrodite is an employee of Artemis. On December 15, 1993, the first hearing on the merits of her worker's compensation claim occurred. Does the Chapter 11 petition stay any further proceedings?

d. May Artemis's union go on strike against the company?

e. In its efforts to regain a share of the defense department's bomb contracts, Artemis constructed a very fancy new retarded bomb. It turned out that some of these were defective and when they were dropped from the aircraft the retarding device failed to activate. As a consequence, the aircraft that dropped them was destroyed in the blast. The government and some of the survivors of the pilots who were killed in the explosion have sued Artemis. May the plaintiffs continue these lawsuits?

Problem 4–4

Athena Bookstore filed for bankruptcy on October 13. At the time of the petition Athena owned a van. Diana Bank held a note and security lien on the van; Athena was two months delinquent on the note at the time of filing. After several amendments and hearings, the final version of the debtor's plan was confirmed on May 15 of the year after filing. The plan requires Athena to cure all delinquencies and to continue paying the monthly installments to Diana. The plan contains the clause:

> "The automatic stay provided in 11 U.S.C. § 362 staying certain acts against the Debtors and Debtors' property shall remain in full force and effect after confirmation."

a. Can Diana repossess the van on May 16?

b. Can Diana repossess the van on July 16 after Athena has missed two monthly installments?

c. Consider Diana's actions if the clause extending the stay did not exist.

Consider sections 362, 1141, and 524.

§ 3. WHICH DEBTOR IS PROTECTED?

Although the stay applies only against the debtor and the debtor's property, third parties who are associated with the debtor or whose assets may back up the debtor's liability sometimes seek protection of the stay. Where the person making that claim is an insurance company, or possibly a well capitalized guarantor, the offer to extend the stay and applying the discharge to such third parties may entice those parties into making substantial contributions to the bankruptcy estate. That is apparently what happened in A.H. Robins, where insurance companies made a large contribution of cash—in part as a quid pro quo for being protected by *Robins'* own discharge. Consider the following case.

IN THE MATTER OF MINTON GROUP, INC.
United States District Court, Southern District of New York, 1985.
46 B.R. 222.

MEMORANDUM OPINION AND ORDER

HAIGHT, DISTRICT JUDGE.

This is an appeal from a February 14, 1983 order of Bankruptcy Judge Howard Schwartzberg, entered pursuant to a February 7, 1983 decision, which dismissed an adversary action brought by the trustee in bankruptcy of Minton Group, Inc. against David M. Lee and Paul Barrett. 27 B.R. 385. The action sought to avoid the perfection by Lee and Barrett of a mortgage on real property owned by a limited partnership called Rochelle Terrace Associates.

The facts are related in detail in Judge Schwartzberg's February 7 decision. Briefly, Minton Group, debtor in the bankruptcy proceedings, was the general partner in Rochelle Terrace Associates, owning a 25% equity interest. In late 1981, prior to Minton Group's bankruptcy, Rochelle Terrace acquired real property. As part of the purchase price Rochelle Terrace gave a mortgage to Lee and Barrett, who were principals of the corporate seller of the property. For reasons unexplained, neither Rochelle Terrace's deed to the property nor its mortgage to Lee and Barrett was recorded until late 1982, approximately one month after the initiation of these bankruptcy proceedings. Minton Group's trustee brought this adversary action to avoid perfection of the tardily recorded mortgage.

* * *

The initial question—which I find dispositive—is whether a debtor's interest in real property owned by a limited partnership of which the debtor is the general partner is sufficient to qualify the property as "property of the debtor" for purposes of § 544 or "property of the estate" for purposes of § 362(a)(4). Analysis of this question reveals two separate issues: 1) the nature of the property interest of a general partner in the property of the partnership, and 2) whether this type of interest qualifies the property as "property of the debtor."

The trustee notes that the general partner's bankruptcy caused the dissolution of the partnership and argues that upon dissolution ownership of the partnership's property vested pro rata in the hands of the partners. Appellees do not disagree as to the fact of dissolution but do dispute its consequences. They argue that before and after dissolution the property was owned solely by the partnership. The partners, it is argued, had no interest in the property but only an interest in the partnership. Both views are incorrect.

New York partnership law dictates that upon the bankruptcy of any partner, a partnership dissolves. N.Y. Partnership L. § 62(5). However, dissolution does not terminate the partnership; dissolution must be distinguished from "winding up," which, by settling the equities among partners, does extinguish the entity. N.Y. Partnership L. §§ 60, 61; *Kraus v. Kraus,* 250 N.Y. 63, 67, 164 N.E. 743 (1928). Therefore, dissolution does not immediately change the nature of the property interest of the partners in partnership property.

The interest of partners in "specific property" of the partnership, * * *, is a statutorily-defined interest referred to as a tenancy in partnership. N.Y. Partnership L. § 51(1). Contrary to appellees' assertion, this is not equivalent to a tenancy in common, although the tenancy in partnership is converted to a tenancy in common once the partnership winds up. In contrast to the full possessory rights of a tenant in common, the rights of a tenant in partnership are quite limited. Without the consent of all partners, a partner has no right to possess partnership property for any purpose other than those of the partnership. Perhaps more important in this context, a partner's interest in partnership property is not subject to attachment or execution except to satisfy a claim against the partnership. Creditors of the partner cannot reach it. Further, the interest may not be assigned by the partner individually. * * * In other words, the interest grants no individually exercisable rights to the partner. Thus it is said that "a partner has no personal right in any specific partnership property * * * and any real estate which the partnership owns is considered personalty." *La Russo v. Paladino,* 109 N.Y.S.2d 627, 630 (Sup.Ct.1951), aff'd, 280 App.Div. 988, 116 N.Y.S.2d 617 (1952).

Thus it cannot be said that Minton Group had no property interest in the real estate of Rochelle Terrace. The issue on appeal, however, is whether this limited property interest is sufficient to qualify the property as "property of the debtor" or its "estate" for purposes of §§ 544 and 362. Under § 70(a)(5) of the former Bankruptcy Act, whether an interest in land was within the debtor's estate was determined by whether it was alienable and subject to levy by the debtor's creditors. * * * The new Code, however, has thrown out these restrictions. *See, In re Goff,* 706 F.2d 574, 578 (5th Cir.1983); *In re Ryerson,* 739 F.2d 1423, 1425 (9th Cir.1984). The debtor's estate now includes "all legal and equitable interests of the debtor in property." 11 U.S.C. § 541(a)(1). The interest in property at issue here would thus seem to be clearly within the estate of the debtor, for, however circumscribed, it is a legal interest in property.

This does not yet answer the question posed above. The determination that this particular interest in property is within the debtor's estate does not necessarily bring the real property itself within the estate. There is a distinction between owning an interest in land and owning the land itself. Useful in this regard is the distinction drawn in the Restatement of Property between an "interest" and "complete property." An "interest" is defined as a right, privilege, or power, or a group of such rights, privileges or powers, regarding land. Restatement of Property § 5 (1936). Plainly there are a large number of interests which may simultaneously be possessed with regard to any piece of land. "Complete property" is the *totality* of interests which it is legally possible to have in a given piece of land. Restatement, § 5e. "Ownership" of a thing is possession of complete property in it. Restatement, § 10b. With these concepts in mind, it can be seen that while Minton Group "owned" a particular, circumscribed interest in Rochelle Terrace's property, it did not own the property. Only the partnership as a whole exercised complete control over the property; only it "owned" the property. Because Minton Group exercised too few rights in regard to the land to qualify it as Minton Group's property, the trustee has no power to reach transactions involving the land, nor does the automatic stay reach it. In order to bring the land itself within the reach of either § 362 or § 544, the debtor must be able to exercise a greater degree of control over the land than is given by the limited power granted by a tenancy in partnership—sufficient control so that the land itself is "of" the debtor or its estate.

In support of his contrary position, the trustee cites *In re Imperial "400" National, Inc.,* 429 F.2d 671 (3d Cir.1970) and *In re Elemar Associates,* 3 B.D.C. 958 (Bankr.S.D.N.Y.1977). In *"400"*, the Third Circuit considered whether a debtor partner's interest in the partnership (as opposed to the partnership's property) was "property" under § 70(a)(5), holding that it was. There are significant differences between that case and this. First, as indicated, the court was concerned with the whole of the partner's interest in the partnership, not just its interest in the partnership's property. The debtor, of course, exercised complete control over its share in the partnership. Its interest was not limited. This is underscored by the fact that under the partnership agreement the partners held their interests in the partnership as tenants in common. 429 F.2d at 674. Thus, the debtor had "an unrestricted right to transfer its interest." 429 F.2d at 678. In contrast, a tenancy in partnership is not freely alienable. Unlike a tenant in common, a tenant in partnership may not call for partition and sale. *Altman v. Altman,* 271 App.Div. 884, 67 N.Y.S.2d 119, 121 (1946), *aff'd.,* 297 N.Y. 973, 80 N.E.2d 359 (1948). Because the property interest involved in *"400"* is significantly different from the one at issue here, *"400"* is not controlling.

In *Elemar Associates,* Judge Babitt considered whether the assets of a partner in a debtor partnership were so closely allied with the assets of the partnership as to prevent a joint creditor of the partner and the partnership from proceeding against assets of the partner to satisfy the joint debt. This case, too, is readily distinguishable. In *Elemar,* it was the partnership, not the partner, which was bankrupt. Because of the unlimited liability of the partner, his assets were potentially available to satisfy the partnership's debt. To permit a joint creditor of the partner and partnership to move against the partner's assets would in effect have permitted the creditor to circumvent the distribution of the debtor's assets undertaken in Bankruptcy Court, for that creditor would have unrestricted access to assets which were potentially available for distribution to all of the partnership's creditors. Here no such problem arises. Appellees are not creditors of the debtor but of Rochelle Terrace. Creditors of the debtor have no claim on the assets of Rochelle Terrace beyond their claim on Minton Group's partnership interest—which is by definition calculated only after Rochelle Terrace has satisfied its debt to appellees. N.Y. Partnership L. § 52. Because appellees' claims to assets of Rochelle Terrace are necessarily "superior" to any claims of Minton Group's creditors, to permit them to record their mortgage against Rochelle Terrace's asset will give them no unfair advantage over creditors of the bankrupt. The concerns of *Elemar* do not arise.

The limited case law available supports Judge Schwartzberg's decision. Almost on point is *In re Panitz & Co.*, 270 F.Supp. 448 (D.Md. 1967), *aff'd. sub nom. Hammerman v. Arlington Federal Savings & Loan Assoc.*, 385 F.2d 835 (4th Cir.1967). The district court there declared that the interest of a limited partner in property owned by the limited partnership is not "property" for purposes of § 70a(5) of the old Bankruptcy Act. In so holding the court noted that under Maryland law the limited partner could not transfer the underlying property. Nor was the property subject to seizure by the partner's creditors. * * * More recently, in *In re Venture Properties, Inc.*, 37 B.R. 175 (Bankr.D.N.H. 1984), it was held that a debtor general partner's interest in real property owned by the partnership was not "property of the estate" for purposes of § 541. The court noted that the debtor's general partner status gave it "reason to be concerned" about the property's disposition, "but this 'interest' does not amount to a 'legal or equitable interest in property' within the meaning of § 541 * * *." 37 B.R. at 176. My reasoning leads me to a conclusion similar to those reached in *Panitz* and *Venture Properties*. The interest under New York law of a general partner in property of the partnership is not sufficient to cause the property to be classified as property of the debtor or its estate for purposes of 11 U.S.C. §§ 544 and 362. Thus the trustee had no power to avoid perfection of liens affecting the property under § 544, nor would the automatic stay of § 362 have affected the perfection.

Judge Schwartzberg's order is affirmed. The appeal is dismissed.

It is SO ORDERED.

Notes and Questions

Judge Haight distinguishes between the case in which a partner of a partnership is bankrupt and a case in which the partnership itself but not the partner is bankrupt. In either case the trustee is seeking to extend the stay to the other party. What justifies a distinction?

Problem 4-5

Sometimes assets are transferred between related parties on the eve of bankruptcy of one of those parties. In the two cases discussed below, why did the parties behave as they did? How would their behavior affect the automatic stay?

1. Mascone and Berlin are general partners in a partnership that operates two Burger Kings. The partnership owns the real estate on which the Burger Kings are operated; Western Financial holds a mortgage from the partnership on both pieces of property. There is $1,000,000 outstanding on each of the two mortgages. The partnership defaults on both mortgages and the mortgagee commences foreclosure proceedings. Mascone and Berlin make an agreement to dissolve the partnership and Mascone transfers all of his interest in the partnership to Berlin, who in consideration of that transfer, agrees to assume all of the debts of the partnership and to indemnify Mascone against any liability. Nine months after that agreement is signed and on the eve of foreclosure, Berlin files in Chapter 11 individually. Notwithstanding the filing, Western Financial pursues its foreclosure; it claims the foreclosure is not stayed because it is against the partnership, not against Berlin individually.

   a. What did the parties hope to accomplish by dissolving the partnership?

   b. Does Berlin's bankruptcy stay the foreclosure against the real estate that originally (and perhaps still) belonged to the partnership?

   In *In re Berlin*, 151 B.R. 719 (Bankr.W.D.Pa.1993), the court, reading the Pennsylvania law in a novel way, concluded that the real estate was not "property of the bankruptcy estate." How can you justify that outcome?

2. Assume alternatively that Berlin was a wealthy investor who owned many pieces of property in his individual name and the name of himself and his wife. One project in Cleveland had been losing money for several years. There is a $2,500,000 mortgage outstanding on that property. Because he has so many assets and it would be troublesome—and embarrassing as well—Berlin does not want to file bankruptcy individually. Accordingly, one of the lawyers in your office has suggested that Berlin transfer the Cleveland property to a corporation and have the corporation file a Chapter 11 petition. Of course, Berlin is personally liable on the $2,500,000 mortgage. Others in your office have raised several questions.

   a. Will the stay protect Berlin against a suit by the mortgagee?

   b. If the property is transferred to a corporation which promptly files a Chapter 11 petition, will the case be dismissed as not in good faith?

   c. Will the bankruptcy of the corporation be treated as a "single asset bankruptcy" and, if so, how will the provisions of 362(d) affect or restrict the stay?

IN RE THIRD EIGHTY-NINTH ASSOCIATES
United States District Court, Southern District of New York, 1992.
138 B.R. 144.

The Debtor is a New York limited partnership which constructed and owns a 263-unit condominium apartment building in Manhattan (the "Monarch"). It is also the sponsor of fifty-three residential and three commercial units in the Monarch which presently remain unsold (the "Unsold Units").

LaSala 89th Street Development Company ("LDSC") and Sopher are the Debtor's managing general partners. Thomas and Kenneth are the managing general partners of LSDC, though neither is, individually, a partner of the Debtor. Sopher, the Debtor's other partner, heads the J.I. Sopher company, which he proclaims to be the "premiere renting and selling" real estate agency in New York. Sopher orchestrated the sales of the sold units in the Monarch and is responsible for obtaining lessors for the Unsold Units. Thomas and Kenneth are also the sole officers of LaSala Management, Inc. ("LSM"), the managing agent of the Monarch. It is undisputed that LSM is responsible for the day-to-day operation of the Monarch.

From August 1985 through November 1987, Chase made a series of loans to the Debtor, secured by certain mortgages on the Monarch, to finance the construction of the building. In respect to a loan of $5,050,000 made in November 1987, Thomas, Kenneth and Sopher executed a guaranty in an amount limited to $1,093,000 (the "Guaranty").

The Debtor defaulted on the loans to Chase, the remaining principal amount of which is somewhere between $9.3 and $10.6 million. On July 26, 1991, Chase commenced an action in New York State Supreme Court seeking to foreclose on the Monarch in satisfaction of the outstanding amounts. Chase also commenced a state court action against Thomas, Kenneth and Sopher seeking judgment on the Guaranty in the sum of $1,093,000 (the "Guaranty Action").

On November 5, 1991, the Debtor commenced an adversary proceeding in the Bankruptcy Court seeking an injunction pursuant to 11 U.S.C. § 105 staying Chase from proceeding against the Guarantors in the Guaranty Action until the consummation of a plan of reorganization. Chase opposed this motion and simultaneously moved to lift stay pursuant to 11 U.S.C. § 362(d) and to dismiss the Debtor's Chapter 11 petition.

Following a hearing on November 25, 1991 (the "Hearing"), Chief Judge Lifland denied Chase's lift stay and dismissal motions and granted the Debtor's motion under 11 U.S.C. § 105, entering an order "permanent[ly]" enjoining Chase from proceeding against the Guarantors in the Guaranty Action until February 9, 1992. Chief Judge Lifland concluded that the estate would be adversely affected in the absence of the stay because the Guaranty Action would impair the Guarantors' ability to infuse capital in the reorganization, and would detract from their "key" roles in maintaining, operating and protecting the Debtor's principal asset. He also concluded that "without [Sopher's], perhaps heavy handed manipulation of the rental market, * * * the building would not even be as fully rented as it is." *Id.*

Chief Judge Lifland stayed Chase's action against the Guarantors pursuant to his authority under 11 U.S.C. § 105(a). Section 105(a) gives a bankruptcy court the power to issue "any order, process or judgment that is necessary or appropriate to carry out the provisions of [the Bankruptcy Code]." This section bestows authority on the bankruptcy court to "use its equitable powers to assure the orderly conduct of the reorganization proceedings." *In re Neuman*, 71 B.R. 567, 571 (S.D.N.Y. 1987).

It is commonly recognized that this authority includes the power to enjoin a party from proceeding against non-debtor third parties, but only under "limited circumstances." *See, e.g., Costa & Head* 68 B.R. at 298 (action against partners of debtor; stay denied); *In re Lahman Manufacturing Co.*, 33 B.R. 681, 682 (Bankr.D.S.D.1983) (action against officers/guarantors of debtor; stay granted) *In re Otero Mills, Inc.*, 21 B.R. 777, 778 (Bankr.D.N.M.1982) (action against officers/guarantors of the debtor; stay granted); *aff'd,* 25 B.R. 1018 (D.C.N.M.1982). Because the practical effect of such an injunction is to broaden the scope of the automatic stay beyond the terms of the 11 U.S.C. § 362(a), this is a power that must be used "sparingly." The debtor bears the burden of proof in obtaining the "extraordinary and drastic remedy" of an injunction.

The Debtor makes much ado over Chase's suggestion that a stay under § 105(a) is available only upon a showing of irreparable harm and the other traditional criteria for a preliminary injunction. The Debtor argues that, inconsistencies notwithstanding, under the standard within this district for the issuance of an injunction pursuant to § 105, a creditor's state court action against a non-debtor third party may be stayed if the action would " 'embarrass, burden, delay, or otherwise impede the reorganization proceedings,' " if the proceeding would "defeat or impair" the bankruptcy court's jurisdiction or if the stay is necessary "to preserve or protect the debtor's estate and reorganization prospects."

This opinion need not contribute to this debate in view of my prior expression on the subject, *see Neuman,* 71 B.R. at 571–72. More importantly, the record demonstrates that it was not clearly erroneous to enter the stay of the Guaranty Action against Thomas and the Debtor has not satisfied its burden under even the lower standard with respect to Kenneth and Sopher.

Pursuant to their authority under § 105, courts have stayed creditor actions against non-debtor third parties where they have found that the estate will be adversely affected because the action will impede the nondebtor third party from injecting funds into the reorganization, because the action would detract from the invaluable time and attention the non-debtor third party would otherwise devote to the continued operation of the debtor's business or the reorganization effort, or because the claims against the non-debtor third parties are really claims against the debtor and therefore impair the automatic stay. The Bankruptcy Court found that the existence of the first two of these conditions warranted imposition of the stay.

Chief Judge Lifland concluded that the Guarantors were "key" to the Debtor's reorganization. Indeed, if it was established that the estate would suffer if the Guarantors' services and attention were compromised by the distraction of defending against the Guaranty Action, this factor could justify a stay. Courts have stayed creditor actions against non-debtor third parties under this rationale where, for example, an officer devoted over 50% of his time to and was "irreplaceable" in the reorganization effort, where an officer was a "key staff member" of the reorganization task force, where the principals/guarantors performed all or most of the debtor's business, and where the general partner was "intimately connected" with the management of the debtor's business. On the other hand, where a general partner testified about his duties for the debtor "largely in generalities," the court found the evidence that the estate would be burdened if malpractice actions were allowed to proceed against him insufficient to justify a stay under § 105.

Chief Judge Lifland's second conclusion in support of the stay was that the Guaranty Action would impair the funding of the reorganization because the Guarantors were willing to infuse $1.4 million. Indeed, where present and substantial, this factor may justify relief under § 105. For instance, courts have stayed creditor actions against non-debtor third parties where the only source of adequate financing for the reorganization was the personal real estate of the principals/guarantors which the creditor sought to foreclose, and where it was uncontested that an officer/guarantor intended to sell the property upon which the creditor would foreclose and contribute the proceeds to the debtor to pay corporate debts. In contrast, this factor did not justify a stay under § 105 where general partners "were extremely vague on their projected personal financial commitments to the Debtor's rehabilitation" and "the degree of the showing that such commitments will be likely to be required and to be made" was not substantial, or where there was no evidence that securities pledged by general partners were actually available to the debtor or could be used realistically in the organization.

Based on Thomas's affidavit and Hearing testimony, it was not clearly erroneous to find that Thomas's involvement in the Debtor's business and reorganization would be sufficiently impeded by the Guaranty Action to constitute a burden on the estate.

Thomas testified that he and Kenneth are responsible for collecting rent and common charges, paying bills, making repairs, assuring that the building is rented to its highest capacity, conducting tenant relations, supervising building staff and acting as liaison with the board of the Monarch. Although the cross-examination established that many of these functions are actually performed by LSM's staff, including clerks and a superintendent, it was also uncontested that these activities take place under his direct supervision. Thomas testified that he devotes up to fifty percent of his time to the Monarch and "managing the Debtor." While the "key" nature of Thomas's role in the Debtor's business and reorganization may not have been established to the degree shown in some of the cases cited above, it was not clearly erroneous to conclude that the estate would be adversely affected if deprived of his services.

With respect to Kenneth and Sopher, however, the record does not establish that either of the factors cited by the Chief Judge Lifland is present in this case. In this regard, the conclusions of the court in *University Medical Center*, 82 B.R. 754 (Bankr.E.D.Pa.1988), are particularly apt. There the court stated that although the debtor's counsel

> asked their witnesses the right questions * * * , focusing upon their time and financial commitments to reorganization which might be adversely impacted by the bankruptcy * * *, [t]heir difficulty was that their witnesses provided answers to their questions which simply failed to satisfy the demanding criteria imposed upon them.

Id. at 757.

Kenneth did not even testify or submit an affidavit to permit an assessment of the depth of his commitment to the Debtor's reorganization efforts. In his testimony, Thomas did claim that both he and Kenneth perform the various management functions he described. Nevertheless, with one insignificant exception, the record is devoid of any evidence of the extent of Kenneth's responsibilities in particular, the extent of his ability and/or willingness to fund the reorganization, or the extent to which either or both would be impacted by having to defend against the Guaranty Action.

On the record, it was also clearly erroneous to find that Sopher performs functions for the Debtor and the reorganization effort that would be impeded by the State Court Action. Although Sopher's vigorous policies with respect to selling and renting units in the Monarch are said to be invaluable to the Debtor, the record demonstrates that Sopher's role at this point does not extend beyond policy making. He testified, for instance, that he personally does not show apartments, but rather delegates this task to his 150 sales agents. There is no evidence that defending against the Guaranty Action would in any way impair Sopher's ability to sustain and implement his policies.

The record also does not support the finding that the Guaranty Actions would burden the estate by impairing an infusion of capital. The Guarantors have proposed, and purportedly remain willing, collectively to inject $1.4 million into the reorganization. Nevertheless, except for Thomas's testimony that defending the Guaranty Action would impair *his* ability to make capital contributions, the record contains no evidence that a joint judgment against the Guarantors would affect their collective ability to make such an infusion. Perhaps more importantly, the Guarantors have until now conditioned this infusion of capital on Chase's release of the Guaranty and some of its security interests in the Monarch, a proposal decisively rejected by Chase. The conditional nature of the infusion casts serious doubt on whether any funds actually are available to the Debtor for use in the reorganization.

A third justification articulated by courts in entering stays pursuant to § 105 is that the claims against the non-debtor third parties are really claims against the debtor and therefore attempts at an "end run" around the automatic stay. *See, e.g., Lomas,* 117 B.R. at 67–68 (suit against officers for making misrepresentation upon which creditor relied in making loan to debtor corporation; adverse judgment could collaterally estop debtor's defenses); *In re Comark,* 53 B.R. 945 (Bankr.C.D.Cal. 1985) (suit against partners on partnership debt); *In re Old Orchard Inv. Co.,* 31 B.R. 599 (W.D.Mich.1983) (same). Chief Judge Lifland made no finding as to this factor, and it therefore need not be addressed here. Suffice it to say, however, that upon this record, this rationale would not support imposition of a stay under § 105. This is not a backdoor attempt to acquire assets of the Debtor, but rather an action on independent obligations of Guarantors, two of whom are not even general partners of the Debtor in their own right. Nor does there appear to be any realistic threat that any issues determined in the Guaranty Action could be used to collaterally estop the Debtor in defending against Chase's claim.

Conclusion

For the foregoing reasons, the findings of the Bankruptcy Court in support of its November 25, 1991 order staying the Guaranty Action by Chase against Kenneth and Sopher are clearly erroneous, and therefore the order is reversed as to these Guarantors and the matter is remanded to the Bankruptcy Court for further proceedings consistent with this proceeding. The order is affirmed as to Thomas.

It is so ordered.

Notes and Questions

1. What is the basis in the Bankruptcy Code for depriving a creditor of an individual bargain with a person who is not in bankruptcy—namely a guarantor officer of a bankrupt company? If that guarantor will put new funds into the company if he need not pay his guarantee, other creditors will welcome an injunction against a suit on the guarantee. But what authorizes the court to reallocate the wealth among various creditors in such a way?

2. Since Thomas LaSala, Kenneth LaSala, and Jacob Sopher are presumably jointly and severally liable, Chase should be able to recover the entire amount of its guarantee from Kenneth and Sopher. How does the stay (or the ultimate discharge in Chapter 11) affect their rights of contribution against their co-guarantor Thomas? If the injunction becomes "permanent," and if it also enjoins the right of contribution between guarantors, there may be angry words during the LaSala family dinner at Thanksgiving,

not so? Were you the Congress or the Supreme Court, what stays against guarantors of bankrupts' debts would you authorize and how would you justify them?

3. In *A.H. Robins Co., Inc. v. Piccinin*, 788 F.2d 994 (4th Cir.1986), the Court of Appeals for the Fourth Circuit held that actions against the companies who insured against the tort liability of the bankrupt company (A.H. Robins) were properly barred under both the automatic stay and an injunction under section 105. *Piccinin* regarded the insurance company's liability as different from the liability of a codebtor.

> Under the weight of authority, insurance contracts have been said to be embraced in this statutory definition of "property." * * * Any action in which the judgment may diminish this "important asset" is unquestionably subject to a stay under this subsection. Accordingly, action * * * against the insurer or against officers of employees of the debtor who may be entitled to indemnification under such policy or who qualify as additional insureds under the policy are to be stayed under section 362(a)(3).

Piccinin at 1001–1002. The reorganization plan eventually adopted in *Robins* used the proceeds of insurance policies as a large part of the fund made available for tort claimants.

Surely a court should be slow to extend the stay to third parties or to assets not within the bankruptcy estate. On the other hand, certain derivative claims ought to be asserted if, and only if, there is a successful claim against the underlying debtor. Such derivative claims cannot be pursued until that underlying claim is established. On that ground one might distinguish cases like *Third Eighty-Ninth Associates*, where the whole idea of the guarantee is that the guarantor will be liable in the case of this very eventuality, namely, failure of the underlying debtor, from cases like *Piccinin*, where the insurance company's liability is particularly dependent upon an earlier establishment of the claims against the insured.

In effect, one might argue that the pre-bankruptcy expectation of creditors who have a claim against the guarantor and of creditors who have a claim against the insurance company are different. The expectation of the creditor in the former case is that the bankruptcy would not foreclose a suit against the guarantor, but that would not necessarily be the expectation in the insurance case. Is that wrong?

In *In re S.I. Acquisition, Inc.*, 817 F.2d 1142 (5th Cir.1987), the court held that a creditor's action against the parent of a bankruptcy company was barred by the automatic stay. The lawsuit was based on a debt owed by the bankrupt to the creditor. The creditor alleged that the parent was liable for this debt as an alter ego of the bankrupt. Based on its conclusion that Texas alter ego law would make the parent responsible for the debts of the subsidiary (if the facts to support the allegation existed) without requiring any particular creditor to prove reliance, the alter ego claim was treated as property of the estate. See also *Koch Refining v. Farmers Union Central Exchange, Inc.*, 831 F.2d 1339 (7th Cir.1987).

Note: Ownership and Protection

The revised Uniform Limited Partnership Act expressly states that partners hold no interest in partnership property. This rule reflects the close parallel between "partnership" investment and investment through corporate business structures. The Act's provision invites the conclusion that a bankruptcy by a *partner* does not prevent action against *partnership* assets.

Section 362 directly protects only the assets of the entity that filed bankruptcy. This so-called "entity theory" permeates bankruptcy law and is evident in other situations concerning the scope of bankruptcy protection. A common application occurs in reference to claims against joint tortfeasors or codebtors when only one codebtor files bankruptcy. The courts are virtually unanimous in holding that (absent special circumstances justifying equitable relief under section 105) one codebtor is not protected by the bankruptcy of the other. See, e.g., *Lynch v. Johns–Manville Sales Corp.*, 710 F.2d 1194 (6th Cir.1983). A number of these decisions arose from the Manville and A.H. Robins bankruptcies in the early 1980s; these cases held that actions against joint tortfeasors are not stayed by the bankruptcy of a codebtor.

Problem 4–6

Diana is the sole owner of Juno Incorporated, a real estate management firm. Juno is the general partner in two partnerships, each of which are 99 percent owned by groups of limited partners. Aphrodite Bank holds separate mortgages on all of the property of each partnership. Diana has guaranteed the debt of the first partnership, but not of the second. Aphrodite is threatening to foreclose on both properties and expects the foreclosure sale to produce a large deficiency claim. It has also filed suit on the Diana guaranty.

   a. If Diana and Juno cause the first partnership to file bankruptcy, can Aphrodite proceed with either its foreclosure or its guaranty litigation?

   b. If the second partnership files bankruptcy, can Aphrodite or any other creditor sue Juno on its liability under state law for the unpaid debts of the partnership?

   c. Assuming that a basis to do so exists under state law, can the limited partners file and prosecute a lawsuit against Juno or Diana for breach of fiduciary duty in operating the partnership or for fraud in wrongfully inducing the partners to invest?

Problem 4–7

Jupiter is a general partner of the Styx Partnership. The partnership owns a 100 unit apartment complex. Its total debt is $3,500,000. Almost all of that debt is secured by a mortgage to Zephyr insurance company. Facing some difficult times, Jupiter causes the Styx Partnership to convey the property to a newly formed Styx Corporation. Consideration is a promise by Styx Corporation to assume the partnership's debt of $3,500,000 and to pay $200,000 in addition. Styx Corporation is controlled by Jupiter's friend Mars. Sixty days after the transfer, and before Styx Corporation has paid anything to Styx Partnership or Zephyr, the corporation files in Chapter 11. You are counsel for Zephyr, who asks the following questions:

1. Will Styx Corporation's filing stay any suit on my mortgage against Jupiter personally and against the Styx Partnership?

2. Assuming that the stay or something like it will apply not only to the Styx Corporation but also to the Styx Partnership and possibly to Jupiter, how soon can the stay be lifted? Consider here sections 101(51)(d) and 362(d)(3), both added in 1994.

3. If the court under section 105 enjoins collection activity against Jupiter and against the Styx Partnership, is the injunction affected by section 362(d)(3)?

4. Any better ideas for Zephyr?

§ 4. LIFTING THE STAY

In practice, the effects of the stay fall into an initial stage (halting pre-bankruptcy creditor collection activity) and a secondary stage (protecting the debtor's possession of business assets during the bankruptcy). During the secondary stage, the section becomes a lens through which the court observes the debtor's use of assets, particularly when creditors seek the return or sale of those assets.

Automatic stay litigation *during* the bankruptcy case focuses on section 362(d); it usually arises from demands by a secured creditor for possession of its collateral or, at least, for protection of the value of its interest in the collateral.

Prior to the 1978 Code, the debtor's ability to modify the rights of secured lenders under Chapter XI was limited and uncertain. Chapter 11 and the rest of the 1978 Code changed that by giving the debtor in possession significant power to offset secured creditors' rights. What policy is served by putting the secured lender at the mercy of the bankruptcy court? When the creditor may lose significant value through delay alone, who benefits? These questions lie behind decisions on lifting the stay.

Sections 362(d)(1) and (2) contain two independent grounds for granting relief from the stay. Section 362(d)(1) requires that the court lift or modify the stay "for cause, including a lack of adequate protection" of the creditor's interest in property. Section 362(d)(2) requires relief from the stay if the debtor has no equity in the property *and* the property is not "necessary" to an effective reorganization. Before we turn to the heart of section 362 litigation, namely the question of when the stay may be lifted for lack adequate protection under subsection (d)(1), let us examine subsection (d)(2).

IN RE JACK YANKS AND RUTH YANKS, DEBTORS

United States Bankruptcy Court, Southern District of Florida, 1984.
37 B.R. 394

ORDER ON MOTION FOR RELIEF

SIDNEY M. WEAVER, BANKRUPTCY JUDGE.

This matter is before the Court upon the Motion of MIRIAM SARNOFF and FLAGSHIP NATIONAL BANK OF MIAMI, as Co-Trustees under the WILL OF ALEX MANSION, DECEASED ("Sarnoff/Flagship"), pursuant to Bankruptcy Rule 4001 et seq., seeking relief from the automatic stay imposed by Section 362 of the Bankruptcy Code, to permit Movants to foreclose their liens against certain real and personal property belonging to the Debtors' estate, which foreclosure suit is now pending in the Circuit Court in and for Dade County, Florida, Case No. 80–15720 CA (23).

FACTS

The Debtors Jack Yanks and Ruth Yanks, filed a petition for relief under Chapter 11 of the Bankruptcy Code on October 20, 1983. The Movants, Sarnoff/Flagship, are one of several secured creditors listed in the schedules.

Hearings were held before the Court on January 10, 1984, and January 12, 1984.

The Court, having heard the testimony of witnesses, argument of counsel, reviewed the pleadings and documentary evidence, and being otherwise fully advised in the premises, finds as follows:

1. The real and personal property upon which Movants, Sarnoff/Flagship, hold a valid first mortgage and liens are:

Parcel # 1—Debtors' interest in a leasehold estate, with the right of Debtors to use and occupy the real property in accordance with the terms of an existing lease, together with the utilization of the liquor license and personal property located thereon.

Located on said site is a one-story restaurant, known as Hurricane Harbor North.

Parcel # 2—Unimproved parcel of land held in fee simple title.

2. The restaurant, located at 12415 Biscayne Boulevard, North Miami, Florida, was operated until July 2, 1981, at which time a fire destroyed the operation. The fire damage remains unimproved, with the business inoperative and without any production of income.

3. The total sum due from the Debtors to the Movants under the real estate mortgage and security interest in personal property, together with other costs advanced for insurance premiums, real property taxes, advance for rent on ground lease, and costs incurred in the State Court foreclosure, excluding any allowance of reasonable attorneys' fee, as of January 10, 1984, is the sum of $358,348.46.

§ 4   **LIFTING THE STAY**   151

4. The property of the Debtors is further subject to a valid perfected second lien held by Great American Bank of Dade County, formerly The Second National Bank of North Miami ("GAB"), in the sum of $308,786.60 as of January 10, 1984.

5. The Debtors have not made any payments to the Movants, none to GAB, and none to other lien holders since the date of the filing of the petition for relief on October 20, 1983. The outstanding 1983 real and personal property taxes have not been paid. There further remains unpaid the following judgments or liens:

	Movants' Exhibits	Hearing 1/10/84
(a)	Final Judgment (Miami Purveyors, Inc. vs. Hurricane Corp., a Florida corporation, d/b/a Hurricane Harbor), $1,958.22, plus interest in the amount of $97.90, costs of $32.00, attorney fees $500.00. County Court, Dade County # 80–0341–CC–24 Entered: April 8, 1980 Interest: 6% per year Recorded: April 16, 1980 OR Book 10718/1596	Ex. # 27
(b)	Federal Tax Lien Under Internal Revenue Laws— Taxpayer: Hurricane Corp., a corporation t/a Hurricane Harbor Restaurant 12415 Biscayne Boulevard North Miami, Florida 33181 $814.01 Filed: April 23, 1980 ORB 10728/1413	Ex. # 26
(c)	Federal Tax Lien Under Internal Revenue Laws— Taxpayer: Hurricane Corp., a corporation t/a Hurricane Harbor Restaurant 12415 Biscayne Boulevard North Miami, Florida 33181 $7,769.40 Filed: June 25, 1980 ORB 10790/159	Ex. # 25
(d)	Notice of Tax Lien, State of Fla., Dept. of Labor and Employment Security— Against: Hurricane Corp., a corporation t/a Hurricane Harbor Restaurant 12415 Biscayne Boulevard North Miami, FL 33181 $2,428.25 Filed: July 2, 1980 ORB 10797/1398	Ex. # 24
(e)	Federal Tax Lien Under Internal Revenue Laws— Taxpayer: Hurricane Corp., a corporation t/a Hurricane Harbor Restaurant 12415 Biscayne Boulevard North Miami, FL 33181 $1,970.99 Filed: August 4, 1980 ORB 10830/73	Ex. # 23
(f)	Federal Tax Lien Under Internal Revenue Laws— Taxpayer: Hurricane Corp., a corporation t/a Hurricane Harbor Restaurant 12415 Biscayne Boulevard North Miami, FL 33181	Ex. # 22

		Movants' Exhibits	Hearing 1/10/84
	Filed:	$5,184.03 October 23, 1980 ORB 10907/2104	
(g)	State of Florida, Department of Revenue (Warrant for Collection of Delinquent Sales and Use Tax)—		Ex. # 21
	Taxpayer:	(Gallery Restaurant & Lounge Corp.) 12415 Biscayne Boulevard North Miami, FL 33181 $59,352.85	
	Filed:	November 24, 1981 ORB 11279/273	
(h)	Federal Tax Lien Under Internal Revenue Laws—		Ex. # 20
	Taxpayer:	Hurricane Corp., a corporation t/a Hurricane Harbor Restaurant 12415 Biscayne Boulevard North Miami, FL 33181 $13,720.56	
	Filed:	February 11, 1980 ORB 10653/1812	
(i)	Final Judgment (City National Bank of Miami, etc., vs. Eric N. Starr)—		Ex. # 18
		Circuit Court, 11th Judicial Circuit In and For Dade County, Florida # 79–13942 CA 20	
	Entered:	February 22, 1980 $55,684.78	
	Filed:	March 4, 1980 ORB 10677/212	

---

6. Dennis G. Wilson, the expert witness of Movants, Sarnoff/Flagship, testified that the purpose of his appraisal was to estimate the market value of the lease advantage in Parcel # 1 and the fee value for Parcel # 2. Parcel # 2, being owned in fee, has a limited use, as parking facilities for the restaurant located in Parcel # 1. No figures were available for an income approach since the business has been inoperative since the fire in July 1981. Wilson's valuation being that the lot was valued in the sum of $270,000.00, with a value placed on the leasehold interest of $185,000.00, for a grand total value of $455,000.00.

7. The Debtor, Jack Yanks, testified that in his opinion the lot was valued at $350,000.00, with a value of between $450,000.00 and $500,-000.00 for the leasehold interest, making a total of between $800,000.00 and $850,000.00.

8. Mr. Joe T. DePrimo was called by the Debtors as their expert witness; however, after preliminary questions were asked of the witness regarding his expertise as an appraiser, the Court learned that the witness was a real estate broker and had an interest in the outcome of the proceedings, having a listing for the sale of the property. The Court rejected the witness as a real estate appraiser, however allowing the witness to testify and give his opinion of the value of the property as a real estate broker.

9. The Debtors' witness, Mr. J.T. DePrimo, testified that in his opinion the estimated value of the Debtors' leasehold interest in Parcel # 1 (including the business personalty) was valued in the sum of $375,000.00. The value placed on the fee simple interest of the Debtors (Parcel # 2) being $330,000.00, for a grand total of $705,000.00.

Conclusions of Law

The Court has before it for determination the question of whether it should grant relief from the automatic stay imposed by Section 362(a) of the Bankruptcy Code to permit Movants (Sarnoff/Flagship) to continue their now pending foreclosure action against the real and personal property of the Debtors, Jack Yanks and Ruth Yanks, in the Circuit Court of the 11th Judicial Circuit In and For Dade County, Florida.

1. Relief from stay is governed by 11 U.S.C., Section 362, which states in pertinent part:

"Section 362. Automatic Stay.

* * *

"(d) On request of a party in interest and after notice and a hearing, the court shall grant relief from the stay provided under subsection (a) of this section, such as by terminating, annulling, modifying, or conditioning such stay—

"(1) for cause, including the lack of adequate protection of an interest in property of such party in interest; or

"(2) with respect to a stay of an act against property, if—

"(A) the debtor does not have an equity in such property; and

"(B) such property is not necessary to an effective reorganization.

* * *

"(g) In any hearing under subsection (d) or (e) of this section concerning relief from the stay of any act under subsection (a) of this section—

"(1) the party requesting such relief has the burden of proof on the issue of the debtor's equity in property; and

"(2) the party opposing such relief has the burden of proof on all other issues."

2. The first question which the Court must concern itself with being whether the Debtors have any equity in the subject properties. The burden of proof in this regard resides in the party requesting relief. 11 U.S.C., Sec. 362(g). *See In re Bialac,* 15 B.R. 901, 903 (9th Cir. Bkrtcy.App. 1981).

The Court has considered the testimony of the witnesses, including the professionals, reviewed the documentary evidence, and so finds that the outstanding balance due to the Movants (Sarnoff/Flagship), as reflected in Movants' (Sarnoff/Flagship) Ex. # 16, hearing 1/10/84, of the sum of $358,346.46, must be revised to the sum of $229,375.52, excluding the sum of $128,972.94, which relates to sums due on the promissory note relating to the personal property under the security agreement.

The Court further finds that the Debtors' interest is further encumbered by the following liens:

(a) Great American Bank of Dade County, formerly The Second National Bank of North Miami (GAB), in the sum of $308,786.12.

(b) Federal Tax Lien, Internal Revenue Service, filed April 23, 1980, in the sum of $814.01.

(c) Final Judgment, Miami Purveyors, Inc., entered April 8, 1980, recorded April 16, 1980, in the principal amount of $1,958.22, plus interest in the amount of $97.90, costs of $32.00, attorneys' fees of $500.00, plus accrued interest.

(d) Federal Tax Lien, Internal Revenue Service, filed June 25, 1980, in the sum of $7,769.40.

(e) State of Florida, Dept. of Labor & Employment Security, filed July 2, 1980, in the sum of $12,428.25.

(f) Federal Tax Lien, Internal Revenue Service, filed August 4, 1980, in the sum of $1,970.99.

(g) Federal Tax Lien, Internal Revenue Service, filed Oct. 23, 1980, in the sum of $5,184.03.

(h) State of Florida, Dept. of Revenue, filed Nov. 24, 1981, in the sum of $59,352.85.

(i) Federal Tax Lien, Internal Revenue Service, filed Feb. 11, 1980, in the sum of $13,720.56.

(j) Final Judgment, City National Bank of Miami, filed March 4, 1980, in the sum of $55,684.78.

The Court has considered the expert testimony of the professional real estate appraiser of the Movants (Sarnoff/Flagship), Dennis G. Wilson, the testimony of the Debtor, Jack Yanks, and his witness, real estate broker, Joe T. DePrimo, regarding the valuation of the subject property, and the Court finds that the value of the property as set by the Movants' appraiser, Dennis G. Wilson, is low. Further consideration should have been given to the present zoning, as also the benefit from the street improvements and existing utilities. On the other hand, the Court finds that the value set by the Debtor, Jack Yanks, is not completely reliable. This is borne out by the Debtors' own witness, Mr. DePrimo, whose value is approximately $100,000.00 less. The Court further recognizes and finds the Debtors' witness, Mr. DePrimo, not to be a disinterested party, in that he, as a real estate broker, has the listing of the property for sale. The Court rejects the value placed by Mr. DePrimo as being too high. The Court has taken into consideration the present condition of the restaurant, which has been inoperative and without any production of income since the fire in July 1981, plus the time and unknown costs required to restore the restaurant building to operation, and accordingly finds the fair market value to be $600,000.00.

It is the judgment of the Court that the Movants (Sarnoff/Flagship) have sustained their burden of proof on the issue that the Debtors do not have any equity in the property, as required under Sec. 362(d)(2)(A) of the Bankruptcy Code, taking into consideration the value of the property and all encumbrances against it. See *In re Faires,* 34 B.R. 549 (Bankr. W.D.Wash.1983).

3. Pursuant to 11 U.S.C., Sec. 362(g)(2) of the Bankruptcy Code, the burden of proof in showing that the property is necessary to an effective reorganization is on the Debtors. The Debtors have not convinced the Court that the subject property is in any way necessary to the operation of the Debtors' business.

The property involved herein is one of eight pieces of non-exempt real estate listed in Schedule B–1 of the Debtors' schedules.

The only testimony offered by the Debtors in regard to the necessity of said property for an effective reorganization was by the Debtor, Jack Yanks. The Debtor, Jack Yanks, testified that in addition to the subject property, the Debtors had between $7 and $8 million dollars worth of other properties. The testimony of Jack Yanks failed to reflect how or why the subject property would be utilized to a successful reorganization. *Barclays Bank of New York, N.A. v. Saypol (In re Saypol),* 10 BCD (CRR) 1057, 1061, 31 B.R. 796 (Bkrtcy.S.D.N.Y.1983).

A "mere financial pipe dream" is insufficient to meet the criterion of Sec. 362(d)(2), *Frankford Trust Co. v. Dublin Properties (In re Dublin Properties),* 12 B.R. 77, 81 (Bkrtcy.E.D.Pa.1981).

The Debtors have failed to meet their burden of proof under Sec. 362(g) that the subject property is necessary to an *effective* Chapter 11 reorganization. *In re Fortin,* 5 B.C.D. 90 (B.D.Conn.12/6/79). * * *

4. It is further apparent to the Court, from the testimony and documentary evidence, that relief from the automatic stay must be granted to the Movants (Sarnoff/Flagship) in that said Movants are not adequately protected. 11 U.S.C., Sec. 362(d) provides:

> "On request of a party in interest and after notice and hearing, the Court shall grant relief from the stay * * *, such as by terminating, annulling, modifying, or conditioning such stay—(1) for cause, including lack of adequate protection in property of such party in interest * * *"

In re Paradise Boat Leasing Co., 5 B.R. 822, 824, 2 C.B.C.2d 1153 (U.S.D.C.V.I.1980).

The evidence before the Court does not reflect sufficient cash flow from the Debtors' business operation to pay for the continuous accrual of interest on the various outstanding promissory notes held by the secured creditors, payment of the accruing real property taxes for the year 1983, and payment of the delinquent ground lease payments, wherein the owner of the ground lease has advised the Court of its termination of the ground lease. The Court has considered the benefits and harms to each party and concludes that just cause exists under Sec. 362(d)(1) for the modification requested by the Movants (Sarnoff/Flagship). See *In re Trident Corp.,* 19 B.R. 956, 958, CCH Sec. 68686 (Bkrtcy.E.D.Pa.1982), aff'd 22 B.R. 491 (U.S.C.E.D.Pa.1982).

Accordingly, it is

ORDERED, ADJUDGED and DECREED that the Motion for Relief from Stay filed by Miriam Sarnoff and Flagship National Bank of Miami, as Co-Trustees under the Will of Alex Mansion, Deceased, be and the same hereby is granted for the purpose of continuing that action pending in the Circuit Court of the 11th Judicial Circuit In and For Dade County, Florida, Case # 80-15720 CA (23), including all counterclaims and crossclaims which the Debtors, Jack Yanks and Ruth Yanks, may have against the Movants (Sarnoff/Flagship).

Notes and Questions

The "no equity" standard in section 362(d)(2) does not require that the creditor show harm to any specific economic interest. The justification for relief from the stay is somewhat different from that commonly put forward for section 362(d)(1). In section 362(d)(2) Congress is telling us that the creditor should be allowed to take its collateral because there is no reason not to recognize the creditor's rights in property as superior to those of the debtor.

One reason why property might not be needed for reorganization is that the property is only tangential to the business (for example, hunting acreage owned by an industrial corporation). A similar conclusion about need could be reached in reference to an abandoned and dilapidated factory the debtor has no plans to reopen.

As in *In re Yanks,* many courts have used section 362(d)(2) in a quite different circumstance. Some creditors have successfully argued that an asset is "not needed" for a reorganization—irrespective of its relation to the business—if no "effective" reorganization is possible. The legislative history of this subsection apparently confirms that it was intended to apply more broadly than in the case of an abandoned factory, but does not clarify when or how.

How would you respond to the following argument in the *Yanks* case?

In his request for lifting of the stay, creditor argues that the asset is not necessary for an effective reorganization because none is possible. It calls upon the court to make a judgment too early in the proceeding about the possibility of reorganization. Therefore the court should not allow the lifting of the stay simply because the debtor cannot bring forward a detailed plan of reorganization at this early point, only a few months after the petition was filed.

Would your response change if the property in question was an apartment complex which in the six months following the bankruptcy petition had never shown a positive cash flow?

Problem 4-8

Venus has recently filed under Chapter 11. Venus's desert laboratory is mortgaged to Sappho and Aries. Sappho has the superior mortgage. The land and lab are worth $1,000,000; Sappho's mortgage is for $700,000 and Aries's is for $500,000.

Sappho asks the court to lift the stay due to a lack of equity. Venus argues that the presence of Aries gives equity to Sappho, and that the stay should not be lifted. Is this a good argument? Is there a different outcome if Aries asks for the stay to be lifted? Should Venus be allowed to keep the property if it is Venus's only asset and there is no deterioration in the property value?

LIFTING THE STAY, LACK OF ADEQUATE PROTECTION, SECTION 361

We come now to one of the recurring questions in bankruptcy cases: when is there an absence of adequate protection as defined in section 361? Here we focus on adequate protection as it relates to obtaining relief from the automatic stay. Adequate protection tests recur in the Code and are a restraint on the DIP's business control in several settings.

Examine section 362(d)(1). It provides that the stay should be lifted or modified for "cause, including the lack of adequate protection of an interest in property. * * *" Relief under this provision for lack of adequate protection runs only to parties holding an "interest in property" that is inadequately safeguarded by the debtor in possession. Under conventional analysis, an unsecured creditor cannot demand adequate protection since it holds no interest in property.

The idea of adequate protection stems in part from Fifth Amendment prohibitions on taking property without just compensation, but a more important policy source is a belief that the bargain reached by a secured lender should be recognized in bankruptcy to the extent possible. While in bankruptcy "giving a secured creditor an absolute right to his bargain may be impossible or severely detrimental * * *, the purpose of [section 362] is to ensure that the secured creditor receive in value essentially what he bargains for." Weintraub & Resnick, *Puncturing the Equity Cushion—Adequate Protection for Secured Creditors in Reorganization Cases,* 14 UCC L.J. 284, 285 (1982).

Section 362(d)(1) requires adequate protection of the value of the creditor's interest in the property. How is value defined? Is it merely a number of dollars equivalent to the amount for which the collateral could be sold? Does it also include value lost because the creditor cannot sell promptly and reinvest? Whether section 361 value includes the right to be compensated for "lost opportunity cost" was a raging controversy until 1988 when *United Savings Association of Texas v. Timbers of Inwood Forest Associates, Ltd.,* 484 U.S. 365, 108 S.Ct. 626, 98 L.Ed.2d 740 (1988) was decided.

Assume, for example, a creditor with a mortgage of $1,000,000, secured by an asset worth $800,000. Under state law, the creditor would have been able to complete its foreclosure and sell the property on January 1, 1987. If the debtor filed a petition in bankruptcy in December of 1986 and no plan was confirmed until the end of 1989, the creditor will have been deprived of interest on the value of the collateral ($800,000) for two years by comparison to results under state law. In effect, the creditor has lost the opportunity to reinvest the $800,000 and earn a return on it. Some courts regarded this lost income as part of the value to be protected under sections 362 and 361; others did not.

In *Timbers,* the Supreme Court held that this lost opportunity cost was not covered as part of the 362(d)(1) and 361 value. Therefore the debtor is not required to pay or to protect the creditor's right to interest on the $800,000 in our hypothetical case. The full protection that the creditor will receive is protection of its right to receive value equivalent to $800,000 on the eventual resolution of the bankruptcy. (Compare section 506(b) regarding interest for creditors whose collateral is worth more than their debt.)

Decisions such as *Timbers* show which interests of a creditor are protected, but they leave open the issue how that protection will be provided. Section 361 spells out three examples how adequate protection might be provided to a creditor. These three illustrations are not exhaustive and the possibilities are limitless.

Section 361 suggests first that adequate protection may be provided by requiring the debtor in possession to make a cash payment or periodic cash payments. This method outlined in subsection (1) is occasionally used to provide payments that offset depreciation in the value of collateral. It is no surprise that cash payments are not the debtor's favored method of giving adequate protection. Some debtors will not have sufficient cash to make payments. Even if cash is available, every debtor would prefer to have the discretion to use whatever cash is available in other continuing business operations.

Subsection (2) authorizes the debtor in possession to grant security in other property in the form of a replacement lien to the extent that the stay "results in a decrease in the value of [the creditor's] interest" in the collateral. This too seems a plausible method of giving adequate protection, but in practice it also has its drawbacks. The typical debtor in bankruptcy may have long since granted a security interest in everything it owns. One source of potentially free assets usable for this purpose, however, comes from application of section 552 which bars application of a prepetition security interest against postpetition property that does not constitute proceeds of original collateral.

The third subsection of 361 is taken from an opinion of Judge Learned Hand, *In re Murel Holding Corp.,* 75 F.2d 941 (2d Cir.1935). It provides for adequate protection through any other relief that will result "in the realization by such entity of the *indubitable equivalent* of such entity's interest in such property." Despite its first use in 1935, the term "indubitable equivalent" was seldom used in judicial opinions or legislation until the adoption of the 1978 Code and its meaning continues to be a matter of some mystery.

The various provisions for adequate protection have one thing in common; they balance the interests of the bankrupt estate and the debtor in possession in continuing to use important property with the financial interests of the secured creditor. After the *Timbers* decision, the secured creditor will suffer some uncompensated economic loss due to the delay in retaking its collateral. Adequate protection recognizes that the creditor has a protected interest in being adequately (if not completely) protected in the remainder of its financial position.

To understand the options actually used by debtors, one needs to make a basic distinction in treatment between an undersecured creditor and an oversecured creditor who holds an equity cushion. The equity cushion exists because the collateral's appraised value exceeds the creditor's claim.

Does the following case correctly apply the law? The outcome violates the bargain between the debtors and the secured creditor. Not so? (So what?)

IN RE ALYUCAN INTERSTATE CORP.

United States Bankruptcy Court, District of Utah, 1981.
12 B.R. 803.

* * *

RALPH R. MABEY, BANKRUPTCY JUDGE. This case raises the question whether an "equity cushion" is necessary to provide adequate protection under 11 U.S.C. Section 362(d)(1). This Court concludes that it is not.

On January 14, 1981, Alyucan Interstate Corporation (debtor), a construction and real estate development firm, filed a petition under Chapter 11 of the Code. On May 4, Bankers Life Insurance Company of Nebraska (Bankers Life), holder of a trust deed on realty owned by debtor, brought this action for relief from the automatic stay under Section 362(d). The complaint alleges that the realty secures a debt in the principal amount of $1,220,000 and that Bankers Life is not adequately protected. On May 20, the preliminary hearing contemplated by Section 362(e) was held. After receiving evidence, the Court fixed the value of the realty on the date of the petition at $1,425,000 and found that there had been no erosion in that value as of the hearing. The debt owing was $1,297,226 as of the petition, and with interest accruing at roughly $8,000 per month, had increased to $1,330,761 as of the hearing. Thus, there was an "equity cushion" of $127,774 or approximately nine percent of the value of the collateral, as of the petition, which had decreased to $94,239, or approximately six and one half percent of the value of the collateral, as of the hearing. As interest accumulates, and if no payments are made, this cushion will dissipate within a year.

* * *

The Equity Cushion Analysis

[T]here is a trend toward defining adequate protection in terms of an "equity cushion": the difference between outstanding debt and the value of the property against which the creditor desires to act. Where the difference is substantial, a cushion is said to exist, adequately protecting the creditor. As interest accrues, or depreciation advances, and the margin declines, the cushion weakens and the stay may be lifted. Naturally, courts disagree on what is an acceptable margin. The emerging view, however, may be that the stay should be terminated when the cushion will be absorbed through interest, commissions, and other costs of resale. The cushion analysis enjoys practical appeal and ease of application.

This Court rejects a cushion analysis upon four grounds: (1) It is inconsistent with the purpose of adequate protection. (2) It is inconsistent with the illustrations of adequate protection found in Section 361. (3) It is inconsistent with the statutory scheme of Section 362(d). (4) It has no basis in the historical development of relief from stay proceedings.

(1) The cushion analysis, by focusing on the ratio of debt to collateral, obscures the purpose of adequate protection, viz., to guard against impairment of a lien. This blurring of objectives may produce improper results. If Bankers Life had been undersecured at the petition, for example, the absence of cushion would have dictated relief from the stay, even though the stay did not impair its lien and notwithstanding the usual appreciation in the value of realty.

(2) Since the thrust of adequate protection is to assure maintenance of the value of the lien, it is largely compensatory. Sections 361(1) and (2) therefore speak not in terms of preserving equity but in terms of compensating for any "decrease in the value of [an] interest in property." Moreover, the cushion analysis, because it is confined to the relationship between debt and collateral in a specific property, ignores the recoverability of value, not only from the property at stake but also from other sources. Sections 361(1) and (2), which provide for interim payments and replacement liens, contemplate that value from other assets held by debtors may be appropriated to supply any needed protection. Indeed, the legislative history to Section 361 suggests the use of sureties or guarantors for this purpose * * *. Even if the debtor has no other assets, it is nevertheless conceivable that an enterprise valuation, which approaches value in terms of capitalized earnings, could show an income potential sufficient to meet the adequate protection standard.

(3) Under Section 362(d)(2) a lack of equity, absent a further showing that the property is unnecessary to an effective reorganization, does not warrant relief from the stay. This statutory provision expresses a legislative judgment, first, that it is the absence of equity rather than any particular cushion which is the criterion for relief from stay, and second, that the absence of equity is not alone dispositive—the court

must still weigh the necessity of the property to an effective reorganization. The cushion analysis is inconsistent with this judgment. It makes surplusage out of Section 362(d)(2) which speaks in terms of equity and reorganization. Indeed, this dual requirement emphasizes the role of equity, when present, not as a cushion, but to underwrite, through sale or credit, the rehabilitation of debtors.

(4) The cushion analysis is alien to the development of stay litigation. The stay provisions in Chapter proceedings in the Act, former 11 U.S.C. Sections 714, 814, and 828, as implemented through Bankruptcy Rules 10–601, 11–44, and 12–43, allowed relief "for cause shown." This was interpreted to require consideration of a number of factors, including the presence of equity, the likelihood of harm to the creditor, prospects for reorganization, and essentiality of the property in the operation of the estate * * *.

Although the "idea of equity" became "something of a totem for courts," * * * it was equity in the sense contemplated under Section 362(d)(2), not an equity cushion. Thus, it was acknowledged that "deciding whether to continue or vacate the stay solely on the ground of the debtor's equity in the property may produce an unjust result," for example where "the encumbered property is so vital to the operation of debtor's business that foreclosure will simply not be allowed." * * *

Questions

1. Judge Mabey correctly foresaw the outcome in *Timbers,* not so?

2. As a matter of policy are Judge Mabey and the Supreme Court correct? If they are reading the statute correctly, should it be changed to recognize the secured creditor's lost opportunity cost?

Note: Reduction of Equity Cushion

Many events might reduce an equity cushion. Among the various possibilities are the risks that the real estate may depreciate, unpaid taxes (with a priority greater than the creditor's) may accumulate against the property, or interest on the debt (accruing under section 506(b)) may eat up the cushion. Not all of these sources of lost value are compensable under an adequate protection analysis.

The equity cushion analysis also depends upon the court's appraisal of the value of the property under section 506(a). Particularly where the asset is unique (such as a piece of real estate) there can be a wide range of reasonable opinions about its value, and none of these opinions can be tested without an actual sale of the property. Sometimes the parties will reach an agreement about the value in certain markets or under certain sale conditions, but disagree about the appropriate market. For example, some would argue that real estate should be valued on the basis of an auction sale. Others could argue that it should be valued based on a hypothetical market sale in which the seller has a reasonable time to market the property to willing buyers. No real guidance is provided by section 506(a).

If the court makes an incorrect estimate of value and allows the debtor to use an imaginary equity cushion to protect the secured lender, who pays when it is later determined that the value of the property was far less than originally estimated? Does the judge pay? The appraiser?

Although real estate varies in value from time to time and place to place, it is less subject to sudden depreciation or transformation and disappearance than are other forms of collateral. Consider inventory or accounts receivable that will be sold or collected during the reorganization. If the debtor in possession does anything but hold the proceeds or pay them to the creditor, the value of the security will be diminished.

In most cases no equity cushion exists or long survives. Protection often requires that the creditor's lien be extended to new property whose value will replenish or replace the value lost when proceeds are spent.

Problem 4–9

A limited partnership established by a real estate developer owns the Apollo Arms, a hotel in Lansing, Michigan. The developer is the only general partner; twenty physicians are limited partners. The hotel has been losing money and was forced to file bankruptcy. The hotel currently averages about $120,000 per month in room rental receipts and has monthly operating expenses of $89,000. Hermes Bank has a first mortgage of $13 million, while Dionysus Bank has a second mortgage of $5 million. Both mortgages also purport to create a perfected lien on the hotel room receipts. The partnership has $100,000 in unsecured debts. One appraisal indicates that the hotel is worth $12 million. The partnership's appraisers claim that the value is $19 million.

1. If Hermes asks for relief from the stay, what must the partnership offer or prove to keep the hotel?

2. If Dionysus Bank asks?

3. What result if both banks demand relief from the stay?

4. If the value of the collateral is found to be $13,200,000, does either Hermes or Dionysus accrue or collect interest? (Compare sections 502 and 506.)

IN RE O'CONNOR

United States Court of Appeals, Tenth Circuit, 1987.
808 F.2d 1393.

JOHN P. MOORE, CIRCUIT JUDGE.

This is an appeal from a judgment of a district court sitting as an appellate court in bankruptcy. The district court reversed an order which granted the Debtors' motion to use cash collateral pursuant to 11 U.S.C. § 363 based upon a finding that the subject creditors were adequately protected. We hold that whether the Debtors have provided adequate protection is a question of fact which must be judged on the clearly erroneous standard. Since the district court failed to apply the correct standard of review, we reverse its judgment.

The controversy under consideration evolves from a voluntary petition for reorganization filed by Mr. William Joseph O'Connor and Mrs.

Jane Elizabeth O'Connor, husband and wife, (Debtors) pursuant to Chapter 11 of the Bankruptcy Reform Act of 1978 (Code). During administration of the case, the Debtors sought leave from the bankruptcy court to use certain cash on deposit in a court-controlled bank account to drill 3 gas wells in areas previously leased by a limited partnership in which Mr. O'Connor was the general partner. To protect creditors claiming interests in the subject cash, Debtors offered replacement liens on the well proceeds and on other unencumbered regular monthly income received by Mr. O'Connor. MBank Dallas, N.A., (Bank) asserted a security interest in the cash and objected to the Debtors' proposal.

After notice and a hearing * * * the court made findings of fact and concluded it would be in the best interest of the estate to grant the leave requested. The court further concluded that the Bank would be adequately protected by the replacement liens offered by the Debtors.

The Bank appealed this decision to the district court which set bond and stayed the use of the cash. The district court ultimately reversed the bankruptcy court, concluding the bankruptcy court erred in finding the Bank would be adequately protected. Relying upon *Rader v. Boyd*, 267 F.2d 911 (10th Cir.1959), the district court concluded that the replacement liens were too speculative to provide the adequate protection required by 11 U.S.C. § 363(e).

The record indicates the Debtors had cash available from operations in the amount of $721,600. Since that cash represented proceeds from property on which the Bank claimed a security interest, it asserted the funds were subject to a proceeds lien and were "cash collateral" within the meaning of 11 U.S.C. § 363. The record, however, discloses the Bank's exclusive claim to that collateral has been contested by another secured creditor in a companion proceeding. That creditor claims a mechanic's lien filed before perfection of the Bank's lien gives it priority over the Bank. Yet, for the sake of an expedient determination of the issue of adequate protection in the instant proceeding, neither the Debtors nor the other secured creditor have contested the nature and extent of the Bank's claim to the cash collateral. Notwithstanding, there is no question that the value of the lien held by the Bank for which adequate protection was sought could not exceed the amount of the money on deposit in the controlled account at the time the Debtors sought leave to use the cash collateral.

At the hearing before the bankruptcy court, the Debtors offered evidence that in the area in which Debtors proposed to drill, Mr. O'Connor's limited partnership had 150 proven wells, 148 of which were still producing. Mr. O'Connor testified that the 3 proposed wells would be drilled "on the inside of what we have already established as producing wells, therefore putting the risk down to a very nominal level." He also testified that purchasers of the gas to be produced were already available and that there was presently a ready market for that gas which would extend well into the future. The Debtors' expert testified that future cash flow could be expected from the project in the sum of

$6,774,862 and that the O'Connor share of that expectation was $5,284,392. In the opinion of the expert, the Debtors' interest, discounted to present value, was worth $3,674,071 at the time of the hearing. Although the Bank offered contrary evidence, the bankruptcy court rejected the Bank's assertions.

On the basis of the disputed evidence, the bankruptcy court found that "future net revenues attributable to Debtors' interest in the wells will be $5.2 million and that the present value of those revenues is in excess of $2.8 million." The court further found that Debtors had additional unencumbered property with "a present value of $10,000 per month." The bankruptcy court concluded that the Bank was adequately protected by the replacement liens in the properties having these values and, as a consequence, "granting the motion would be in the best interest of the estate and its creditors."

In its appeal to the district court and in its brief here, the Bank has advanced many reasons why the bankruptcy court reached the wrong decision but gives only passing treatment to the issue of consequence; that is, whether the bankruptcy court's findings are clearly erroneous. We have not considered the issue before, but we are convinced that whether a creditor is adequately protected is a question of fact.

The whole purpose in providing adequate protection for a creditor is to insure that the creditor receives the value for which the creditor bargained prebankruptcy. House Rep. No. 95–595, 95th Cong., 2d Sess. 53, *reprinted in* 1978 U.S. Code Cong. & Admin.News 5787, 5963, 6295. In determining these values, the courts have considered "adequate protection" a concept which is to be decided flexibly on the proverbial "case-by-case" basis. *In re Martin,* 761 F.2d 472 (8th Cir.1985); *In re Monroe Park,* 17 B.R. 934 (D.C.Del.1982). Since "value" is the linchpin of adequate protection, and since value is a function of many factual variables, it logically follows that adequate protection is a question of fact. We have said that a clearly erroneous finding is one that leaves the reviewing court with the distinct and firm conviction that a mistake was made. We are left with no such conviction here.

The question of adequacy was examined and decided by the bankruptcy court on disputed but sufficient evidence. Mr. O'Connor testified that the wells were going to be drilled in a proven area in which all his previous attempts had been successful. He explained that he had drilled 150 wells and all were still producing except for 2 which had experienced mechanical failure. In addition, Debtors' expert witness testified that ready buyers existed to buy the product of the proposed wells in a quantity to provide a cash flow more than sufficient to protect the Bank's proceeds lien. Not only does this evidence support the bankruptcy court's conclusion that there was adequate protection, but it points out the very reason why *Rader* is inapposite here.

It must be remembered that the question of adequate protection is no longer confined to the conditions that exist at the time of confirmation as found in *Rader.* The use and definition of the concept of adequate protection has advanced beyond the scope of the term in the context of pre-Code bankruptcy laws in existence when *Rader* was decided. That change makes reliance upon older case law a treacherous adventure under the Code. 2 *Collier on Bankruptcy* ¶ 361.01 (15th ed. 1979).

Rader dealt with the final treatment of the secured claim of a creditor in a Chapter XII arrangement proceeding under the Bankruptcy Act of 1898. That circumstance and its bearing upon the property rights and expectations of creditors are unlike the conditions presented in this case.

In this case, Debtors, in the midst of a Chapter 11 proceeding, have proposed to deal with cash collateral for the purpose of enhancing the prospects of reorganization. This quest is the ultimate goal of Chapter 11. Hence, the Debtors' efforts are not only to be encouraged, but also their efforts during the administration of the proceeding are to be measured in light of that quest. Because the ultimate benefit to be achieved by a successful reorganization inures to all the creditors of the estate, a fair opportunity must be given to the Debtors to achieve that end. Thus, while interests of the secured creditor whose property rights are of concern to the court, the interests of all other creditors also have bearing upon the question of whether use of cash collateral shall be permitted during the early stages of administration.

The first effort of the court must be to insure the value of the collateral will be preserved. Yet, prior to confirmation of a plan of reorganization, the test of that protection is not by the same measurements applied to the treatment of a secured creditor in a proposed plan. In order to encourage the Debtors' efforts in the formative period prior to the proposal of a reorganization, the court must be flexible in applying the adequate protection standard. In doing so, however, care must be exercised to insure that the vested property rights of the secured creditor and the values and risks bargained for by that creditor prior to bankruptcy are not detrimentally affected.

Here, the creditor had a proceeds lien in cash worth $721,600. The Debtors proposed to use the cash thereby reducing the *value* of the creditor's security interest by $721,600, but in exchange, the Debtors proposed to give the creditor a *new* proceeds lien in property presently worth over five times that sum. The only distinction between the security interest the Bank had in the cash and the substitute security interest in the new wells is the risk inherent in drilling a dry hole. Yet, the flexibility in judging whether that risk was significant or insignificant is what distinguishes this case from *Rader*.

The bankruptcy court found, in effect, that because the wells were to be drilled in proven areas, the risk to the Bank was not significant. That determination is supported by substantial evidence, and it is critical to the issue of adequate protection that exists in this case.

The Bank argued and continues to argue strenuously that granting the Debtors' motion was improper because the effect was contrary to the "reorganizational effect" of the plan it had proposed. The bankruptcy court found that the Bank's plan was nothing more than a program for liquidation of the Debtors' assets and concluded it was more appropriate at that stage of the proceedings to allow the Debtors an opportunity to reorganize. We agree with that conclusion.

The judgment of the district court is REVERSED.

Question

Is the test of adequacy "subjective" or "objective"? Assume two creditors. The first is a risk adverse, conservative banker who lends only on mortgages against residential and income producing real estate. He never lends more than 70% of the value of the mortgaged property even though others lend 90–95% in similar circumstances. The second lends against such problematic assets as oil and gas wells not yet drilled. Assume that each has a $1,000,000 loan against an $800,000 asset; the debtor proposes to allow the asset to decline in value by use while replacing it by granting a lien on another asset with an $800,000 value.

Assume that all appraisers agree that the new asset has an $800,000 present value but that that value is achieved not by standard deviations in predicted value between $850,000 and $750,000 but between $200,000 and $1,400,000. Can the conservative banker reject that asset even though he admits it has a present value of $800,000 because the asset's value is so variable that he will not sleep at night? Is the other creditor—accustomed to such fluctuations—required to take the risk? Put another way, can one force a secured creditor seeking adequate protection to take risks or accept collateral of the kind that he would not accept if he were doing the transaction voluntarily? Can you see how the risk adverse creditor might find some support for his subjective argument in section 361(3)? Does "indubitable" mean "having equivalent value even to the most risk adverse?"

§ 5. VALUING THE SECURED CREDITOR'S COLLATERAL

Too often the neophyte believes that the law is everything; the veteran knows that the law is nothing, the facts are everything. The entire face of a bankruptcy case can be changed by a judicial finding that a particular asset has value X, not value Y. Unlikely to be overturned on appeal, that finding determines whether the stay is to be lifted, whether interest is to be paid, and whether the creditor receives much or little on reorganization under section 1129. Inherent in the judicial discretion to determine the value of various assets in the bankruptcy estate is at least as great a power as the court has in interpretation of the law in a hundred different ways. In reading the case that follows, the student should generalize to other circumstances where value may be even more indeterminate (for example, the value of Pan American Airways' routes between JFK and Heathrow or of its many gates at La Guardia).

In the bankruptcy court, valuation will be determined by appraisal and expert testimony, not by sale. Only a party completely without imagination or resources will fail to find an expert to affirm its position on valuation. Thus, one can expect that each party will be able to provide plausible valuation testimony.

The *Castle Ranch* case, then, is here as a warning to students. Understand that the things we routinely assume away in law school, namely, that X has value Y, and Z has value A, are the hard things in practice, and by comparison, what we find to be hard in law school—finding the law—is easy in practice.

IN RE CASTLE RANCH OF RAMONA, INC.

United States Bankruptcy Court, Southern District of California, 1980.
3 B.R. 45.

HERBERT KATZ, BANKRUPTCY JUDGE. This is an action seeking relief from the automatic stay provisions of Section 362(a) of the Bankruptcy Code [11 U.S.C. Section 362(a)], brought by two limited partnerships who are the beneficiaries of an all inclusive deed of trust on property owned by the debtor which secures a promissory note in the original principal amount of $1,396,109.00.

The debtor acquired the property here in question, a 338 acre ranch called the Castle Ranch, by a grant deed from one Bob Witmondt on December 19, 1979. Witmondt had acquired the property one year earlier, on December 29, 1978, from the plaintiffs.

Witmondt, pursuant to the terms of his purchase, was obligated to make a deferred down payment of $289,963.00 on or about June 15, 1979, and another payment of $82,284.54 on or about June 29, 1979. When these payments were not made, plaintiffs commenced foreclosure proceedings under the aforementioned deed of trust.

The foreclosure sale was scheduled to be conducted on December 19, 1979, the date upon which Witmondt transferred the property to the debtor, and the date the debtor filed for relief under Chapter 11 of Title 11 U.S.C., the Bankruptcy Code.

The hearing on plaintiff's request for relief, which was duly requested by the debtor pursuant to the procedures adopted in this district, commenced on February 8, 1980, within the 30 day requirement of Section 362(e), and concluded on February 14, 1980.

At the commencement of the trial, it was determined by this court that the matter would be treated as a preliminary hearing under Section 362(e). This ruling was necessitated by the fact that the time for filing an answer to the six count complaint seeking relief from the stay had not yet expired.

Plaintiffs in their complaint, not only sought relief from the automatic stay, but in the alternative sought adequate protection by way of an order that payments be made as provided in the note and deed of trust if the stay were continued, a shortening of the 120 day exclusive period the debtor has for filing a plan of arrangement under Section

1121(b) of the Code, or a dismissal of the proceedings because they were a sham and fraud on the court and creditors.

At the trial, neither side produced the types of appraisals courts have come to rely upon when determining values of properties, that is neither side produced an M.A.I. appraisal.

Plaintiffs, who had the burden of proof on the issue of equity, [Section 362(g)(1)], produced a Mr. McWhorter who has been a realtor in the area where the property is located, for well over 25 years. McWhorter testified at great length about his familiarity with the general area, sale and offers on various properties, zoning, sub-division problems, water problems, etc.

Defendant presented a Mr. Rodolff, who also had been a realtor in the area for a number of years and testified about his familiarity with the property, as well as others in the general vicinity, and some of the other matters McWhorter testified to.

It should be pointed out that the property here in question is, by the testimony of every witness called, a unique property. It consists of 338 acres containing a house, called the Castle, which was built between 1916 and 1921, out of stone and block with walls about 4 feet thick, open beams, walls painted by Indians and containing about 12,000 square feet of space. In addition to the main house, the property contains four smaller living units and a number of out buildings. The property has a lake, stocked with fish, is just east and in front of a water reservoir and has sources of water and other utilities. It is very close to, and a corner of it, fronts on, State Highway 76.

The property is located in the Santa Maria Valley of San Diego County, approximately six miles east of the community of Ramona, on Highway 67.

After listening to the prime witnesses on the issue of value, I have concluded that defendant's witness Rodolff, who estimated the value of the property at $5,300.00 per acre, cannot be relied upon.

His knowledge of the valley and his experience with property therein coupled with the comparables he relied upon in arriving at that stated value simply was not credible.

He testified that 75% of his valuation was derived by using basically two comparables which sold for much more than $5,300.00 per acre. But these were small parcels on buildable sites and, according to his own testimony, small parcels in that valley always demand prices several thousand dollars per acre higher than large parcels such as the subject property.

His other main comparable consisted of two 119 acre parcels which sold in 1979 for $2,500.00 per acre. His explanation as to why those parcels were worth so much less than his value for the subject property, simply was not plausible.

I have concluded that Rodolff's testimony of value for the land cannot be relied upon.

McWhorter discussed many of the properties in the valley, both as to recent sales, offers and old sales. In particular he took into account a property just to the northeast of the subject property consisting of 700 plus acres which sold in March of 1979 for about $2,992.00 per acre, as well as other properties of substantial size in the general area.

He explained the problem of subdividing and obtaining maps in the valley, the water and sewer problem and the tree planting moratorium which limits the use of property as avocado or citrus groves.

After being on the stand for the better part of two days, he finally concluded that the property was worth $2,500 per acre on a *cash sale* (emphasis added). He did, however, state that if this property were subdivided, he felt the lots would "sell like hot cakes." I should also point out that his valuation does not include the house.

Several other witnesses testified as to value as well.

* * *

Based on all of the evidence I have heard, I have concluded that this property has a value, given sufficient time to properly market it, of about $3,500 per acre or $1,183,000, and that the main house has a value of about $500,000, for a total value of $1,683,000.

There is presently owing on the deed of trust held by the plaintiffs the sum of approximately $1,537,503.00, exclusive of taxes and attorneys fees. Interest accrues at the rate of approximately $9,753.00 per month.

It is therefore apparent that the debtor has little or no equity in the property.

It is also apparent that the property, which is the debtor's only asset, other than some personal property of nominal value, is necessary to an effective reorganization.

* * *

What we have here in the form of a Chapter 11 proceeding under the Code is nothing more nor less than a Chapter XII proceeding under the Bankruptcy Act, with the exception that the debtor is a corporation. It is simply a one asset case in which the debtor either has to sell his property, refinance it, or seek new capital to solve its problems.

In order to accomplish those ends, the debtor must have equity in the property, which is nonexistent here.

In order to continue the stay in effect as a result of this preliminary hearing, under Section 362(e), I must find that there is a reasonable likelihood that the debtor will prevail at any final hearing held pursuant to Section 362(d).

Section 362(d) speaks of granting relief from the Section 362(a) stay, either by modifying, terminating, annulling or conditioning it. Any of those latter can be done for cause, which is not defined, including the lack of adequate protection, or if the debtor does not have an equity and the property is not necessary for effective reorganization.

I have concluded that there is not a reasonable likelihood that the debtor will prevail at a final hearing because although the property is clearly needed for reorganization, the debtor has no equity in the property.

The value of the secured parties' interest in that property is being eroded at the rate of $9,753.00 per month, which is the amount of interest running on the debt, without any concomitant increase in value. In order to be adequately protected, as that term is used in Section 361, at a minimum the debtor would have to be able to pay those sums on a monthly basis. It cannot do so. It has no assets other than the property here involved.

Since the debtor will not be able to adequately protect the plaintiff's interest in the property it is unlikely that it could prevail in a Section 362(d) hearing.

As I indicated earlier, this case is a typical Bankruptcy Act Chapter XII proceeding. The debtor's predecessor here gambled on the hopes that he would be able to sell this property for a quick profit. In fact he entered into a contract to advertise this property for sale before he closed escrow in December 1978. His hopes did not come to fruition. There is no equity and no method of adequately protecting plaintiffs.

Under the Code, this type of case can be solved, as it could be under the Act, by a sale, refinance, or infusion of new capital.

The debtor and its predecessor in interest have already had 14 months in which to sell or refinance without any success.

With no equity, it is unlikely that new capital can be attracted to solve its economic problem.

Since these solutions seem highly unlikely, it would appear that the debtor's ability to prevail at any final hearing under Section 362(d) is also unlikely.

Since I cannot find that the debtor is likely to prevail at that hearing, I believe the stay must be annulled.

The whole purpose of the statutory scheme of Section 362, as I understand it, was to relieve a creditor from the stay imposed upon him in a relatively expeditious manner where no good reason for continuing the stay exists. This is one of those cases.

The stay is to vacate.

Counsel for plaintiff shall prepare Findings of Fact, Conclusions of Law and a Judgment in conformity with this Opinion.

Notes and Questions

The amount of adequate protection that must be paid to a secured creditor may be directly related to the value of its collateral and to the changes in that value over the course of the bankruptcy. If the collateral is worthless, no adequate protection is required. If the collateral has great value, large requirements for adequate protection may be created. If the value of the collateral exceeds the creditor's claim, however, the excess value in itself may adequately protect the creditor without further action by the debtor.

In bankruptcy, the Code protects secured claims rather than secured creditors. Section 506(a) provides that a claim will be treated as a secured claim "to the extent of the value of [the] creditor's interest * * * in such property [and as] an unsecured claim to the extent that the value of such creditor's interest * * * is less than the amount of [its] allowed claim." Thus, a creditor with a $1 million claim whose collateral is valued at $750,000 will have a $750,000 secured claim and a $250,000 unsecured claim. The secured creditor's payment from the reorganization plan is also directly related to the value of its collateral. If the collateral is worthless, the creditor is unsecured and eats at the unsecured creditors' trough. If the collateral has value, the creditor must receive payments with a present value equal to the value of the collateral.

In the negotiations over and the litigation concerning the Chapter 11 plan, the value of various assets and of a certain creditor's collateral will be critical. Not only the debtor and secured creditors but also various unsecured creditors will be arguing for different valuations while the plan is being negotiated. Although the parties may take different sides at different times, the issues will remain the same, namely, how does one measure the value of these particular assets?

Even to the inexperienced student, it will come as no surprise that the debtor in possession and the creditor are likely vigorously to dispute issues concerning valuation of the collateral and of the business as it emerges from bankruptcy.

Consider just a few of the problems that might develop. First, it is likely that the parties will disagree on the method of valuation. The standard will ultimately depend on the assumptions made regarding the use or disposition of the property. One party is likely to argue that liquidation value is appropriate. The other will maintain that the property's going concern value should be used. Even if a standard can be agreed upon, it is unlikely that the debtor in possession and the creditor will agree upon the result of its application to particular property.

Unfortunately, the Bankruptcy Code provides little assistance to the judge who is trying to determine which standard to apply. "The draftsmen of the Code apparently took to heart the Supreme Court's admonition that 'value is a word of many meanings, [which] gathers its meanings in a particular situation from the purpose for which a valuation is being made,' because the Code does not prescribe the method or methods of valuation to be used." Pachulski, *The Cram Down and Valuation Under Chapter 11 of the Bankruptcy Code,* 58 N.C.L.Rev. 925, 951–52 (1980). Instead, section 506 directs the court to determine the value of collateral "in light of the purpose of the valuation and of the proposed disposition or use of such property, and in conjunction with any hearing on such disposition or use or on a plan affecting such creditor's interest." While this provides the courts with a great deal of flexibility, it also results in much confusion.

In *In the Matter of American Kitchen Foods, Inc.,* 1976 WL 23699, 9 Collier Bankr.Cas.2d (MB) 537 (Bankr.D.Maine 1976), Bankruptcy Judge Cyr held that the standard of valuation in every case should be based on "the most commercially reasonable disposition practicable." But this articulation only restates the question. When the petition is filed, the creditor will argue that the most reasonable action would be liquidation of debtor's assets. Conversely, the debtor will claim that a rehabilitation is possible and that he should be permitted to keep and use his property. The judge is thus left in the same position, namely having to choose between two acceptable methods of valuation.

Despite this ambiguity, certain generalizations can be made. The tradition of bankruptcy cases under Chapter X, the forerunner of Chapter 11, suggest that liquidation value is the appropriate standard when a valuation based on liquidation is higher than one based on projected future income, thus making liquidation the only economically justifiable course of action. At the threshold of a case, however, a successful reorganization frequently appears to be a reasonable prospect and the going concern value of the creditor's collateral or of the business as a whole will often be calculated as substantially higher than the liquidation value. In these circumstances, "the court is likely to avoid making and relying on a stark determination of the liquidation value." Kennedy, *The Automatic Stay in Bankruptcy,* 11 U.Mich.J.L.Ref. 177, 246 (1978).

Adoption of the going concern value at the outset of a case has been attractive to courts for two reasons. First, courts have felt that this standard was in keeping with the spirit of reorganization.

> The very purpose of a reorganization proceeding is to avoid a forced sale of assets and to preserve the going concern value of the business by continuing its operations. It is incongruous to value a business that is being reorganized on the basis of the price its assets could fetch on a piecemeal liquidation when the entire theory of the reorganization is that the debtor is being preserved as a going concern. Accordingly, the business was properly valued as an integrated unit, not a discrete piece of property to be sold.

Pachulski, *The Cram Down and Valuation Under Chapter 11 of the Bankruptcy Code,* 58 N.C.L.Rev. 925, 939 (1980). Similarly, the valuing of a secured creditor's interest in the debtor's inventory or other asset on the basis of the price likely to be received upon liquidation at a foreclosure sale would be inconsistent with the underlying premise of reorganization that the debtor will continue its operations.

Second, courts have known that their decision as to the valuation of the debtor's property could be revised. The Bankruptcy Code provides that valuation determined for one purpose is not necessarily binding for any other purpose. As a result, the bankruptcy judge could avoid the premature termination of the case which would result from the use of the liquidation value. Instead, she could adopt the going concern value with the knowledge that, if any information surfaced casting doubt upon the possibility of a successful rehabilitation, she could then apply a different standard of valuation to reach a different value.

Once a standard has been agreed upon, it is unlikely that the parties will agree upon the rule's application. To take a simple case, consider the value of a used car. Looking first at one of the recognized authorities, such as the Blue Book, one finds that three values are listed for a car: average wholesale, average retail, and average loan value. In addition, these values must be raised or lowered depending upon whether the car has air-conditioning or a stereo, upon the number of miles on the odometer, and upon other quantifiable attributes. All of these ambiguities crop up in the valuation process before one has even come to the question whether the Blue Book is relevant for a particular market, and before one has considered the idiosyncratic qualities of this particular automobile (i.e., that it has a beautiful mermaid painted on the back or that its right rear fender is crumpled). If these problems are present in computing the value of a simple, almost fungible commodity such as an automobile, consider the problems inherent in valuing a business, or the equipment and inventory of a business, or raw land in Florida.

Liquidation value is typically derived from expert testimony about the probable net proceeds upon the sale of the assets in question.

If a court decides to use going concern value, it will be necessary to select one among several techniques to measure such value. One mode of evaluating going concern value of an asset such as a hotel is to determine the amount of revenue that asset will produce and then to "capitalize" that income. A similar approach for valuing the reorganized business is known as the capitalized earnings approach.

Unless the parties agree on a value, valuation hearings will be conducted that consist of proofs of valuation by various expert appraisers. Liquidation value is an expert's idea of the net proceeds that might be realized on the sale of assets. The conditions of the assumed sale, of course, influence the estimated value because they define the market in which the hypothetical sale occurs. Thus, for example, an assumed immediate auction of equipment will yield a "liquidation value," while an assumed sale at a more leisurely pace may yield a "fair market value."

While the process of valuing a business on the basis of a capitalization of earnings is difficult, the theory is simple. Initially, the business's stream of income for the future is projected. To account for the time value of money as well as the risk that the projected stream of income may never be realized, the projected stream of future income must be discounted to reflect the present value of the anticipated earnings. The discounted present value for the projected stream of future income is determined by multiplying the average annual projected income by a multiplier which is the inverse of the appropriate capitalization rate. The capitalization rate is basically "the rate of return that a potential investor, familiar with all the risks involved, would require to invest in the business. The greater the risk, the higher the required rate of return." Haynsworth, *Valuation of Business Interests*, 33 Mercer L.Rev. 457, 475–76 (1982). The higher the required rate of return, the lower the multiplier and consequently, the lower the going concern value of the business. Thus if the capitalization rate (the expected rate of return necessary before an investor would invest) were 20 percent, the multiplier would be 5 and such a business would have a lower going concern value than a business with a capitalization rate of 10 percent.

It goes without saying that mathematical precision in the projecting of a business's future income is neither possible nor required. However, accuracy is important. The obvious starting place for determining a firm's prospective income is to look at its past and present earnings. Some courts simply average the earnings of the debtor's business over the last five years. Other courts employ a weighted average which focuses on the income received during the most recent years.

The student should consider the appropriateness of this approach. Since the debtor has filed bankruptcy, it is likely that its most recent earnings will have been small. If these earnings are not representative, basing future income projections solely on such past income earned will result in a projection that is too low. Most agree that the projected future income "must be based not on present earnings alone, but on factors that may influence income in the future." Pachulski, *The Cram Down and Valuation Under Chapter 11 of the Bankruptcy Code,* 58 N.C.L.Rev. 925, 940 (1980). Among other things, the court should examine the experience of other firms in the same industry. However, it is frequently impossible to find comparable companies. As one commentator noted, "just try to find a truly comparable business (similar in size, type, financial statistics, age, plant, management, prospects, etc.) to the business being appraised. Better yet, try to find such a comparable business which was sold [and therefore evaluated] recently." McCarter & Greenley, *Business Valuations,* 16 U.Tulsa L.J. 41, 61–62 (1980). In addition to examining comparable firms, the court should also take into account the anticipated trends in the debtor's industry and in the economy. Clearly, easier to say than to do.

Even if future income can be accurately projected, the use of earnings as the primary determinant of the value of a business can be deceptive. For instance, non-cash charges such as depletion as well as large exploration and development costs incurred by smaller oil companies result in only nominal reported net earnings by these businesses; such companies frequently report book losses. However, because such companies may depend on a few large finds, an aggressive exploration program may be more important than steady growth in income. Thus, for these and other businesses, such as partnership real estate ventures, valuation on the basis of projected "cash flow" rather than probable "earnings" may be more appropriate. Cash flow is found by adding depletion or depreciation back to net income and further adjusting income by taking into account the full cost of amortizing the company's debt.

Assuming the court has determined the business's future income, the value of that income is found by multiplying the earnings by the appropriate capitalization rate. Even a slight change in the capitalization rate can significantly affect the valuation of a business and consequently, the size slice of the estate each creditor will receive in satisfaction of its claim. As with the projection of future earnings, information about comparable firms is helpful, but difficult to find.

Problem 4–10

George Restaurant files bankruptcy. It owes $1,500,000 to unsecured creditors. It also owes $2,900,000 to Bank One. Bank One has a mortgage on George's building. If sold at auction today, the building and land would bring $2,200,000 because of economic weakness in the real estate market. The estimated fair market value of the property (disregarding the auction as a way of measuring that value) has declined to $3,100,000 from $3,300,000 last year. The remaining useful life of the building is approximately ten years. Annual real estate taxes are $50,000. George's other assets include $100,000 cash and $75,000 of inventory and equipment. Without paying creditors, real estate tax, or building repairs, George's current income is $500 per week net of other operating expenses.

    a. Two months after the bankruptcy petition is filed, Bank One requests relief from the stay. What position should the unsecured creditors take? What result if George argues that the restaurant will be profitable over the next few months because of a new chef and better advertising, but it offers no payments to Bank One?

    b. Six months after relief from the stay is denied, Bank One demands that its attorney get its asset back. George has not filed a reorganization plan and the restaurant's income is now hovering at a negative $2,000 per month. What action can Bank One take? See section 1112.

Chapter Five

ADMINISTRATIVE POWERS AND THE DEBTOR'S ESTATE: THE POWER TO USE, BUY, SELL, CONTRACT, AND BORROW, SECTIONS 363 AND 364

§ 1. INTRODUCTION

Chapter 11 transforms the owners and managers of a bankrupt business into debtors in possession (DIP). This permits the people who are most familiar with the business to continue operating it without trustee supervision. Although Congress believed this system would offer the debtor a better chance to reorganize, it recognized that giving a DIP unfettered discretion was troubling since it presented an opportunity to make decisions damaging to the business and creditors. Or to take a more jaundiced view, it left the fools and knaves in charge who had brought the business to this sorry state. The alternative, to bring in an outsider, proved expensive and not particularly successful in Chapter X cases prior to 1978.

To meet the short-term concerns of the estate, sections 363 and 364 authorize a variety of activities, some of which may be taken without court approval (if they are in the ordinary course), and others allowed only with court approval. Section 363 authorizes sale, lease and other "uses" of the debtor's assets. These uses would include acts such as flying the aircraft of a bankrupt airline on a revenue producing route, operating the machinery subject to a security interest, and selling goods out of inventory and free of the security interest of the floor-planner. Ultimately the uses will also include making payments on debt incurred after the petition is filed and, perhaps, more extensive transactions such as the sale of all assets of the company, or signing long-term leases.

Section 364 authorizes the debtor in possession to borrow. The most simple borrowing is trade credit—unsecured, open-term credit routinely granted by sellers of goods and services. Typically this debt can be incurred without court intervention. It also contemplates the possibility, with court approval, for large-scale borrowing to facilitate extraordinary transactions undertaken to preserve assets and to make the reorganization possible.

Rather than placing postpetition ordinary course unsecured creditors in the same position as the prepetition unsecured creditors, section 364(a) grants them administrative expense status. This puts postpetition trade creditors, the most likely postpetition lenders, at the front of the unsecured payment line along with lawyers, accountants and other "administrative expense" claimants. This priority status encourages the trade creditor to continue to supply goods (which are to be used according to section 363) during the bankruptcy period. The continued lending by postpetition creditors makes reorganization possible. Section 364(b) grants administrative expense status also to nonordinary course unsecured creditors, provided there is notice and a hearing.

If subsections (a) and (b) do not get the debtor all of the credit it needs, section 364(c) allows the grant of "super priority" to a creditor to encourage a loan. "Super priority" elevates a creditor above other creditors with administrative expense claims. Another option provided by (c) is to give a creditor a security interest in unencumbered property or a junior security interest in encumbered property.

Subsection (d) is the best possible option for a creditor and can be used only if the other sections will not induce the creditor to lend. This section allows a creditor to take a senior security interest in property which is already encumbered, provided the first creditor is given adequate protection. These secured loans for postpetition operating expenses that are authorized under section 364(c) or (d) are sometimes called "DIP financing."

Sections 363 and 364 protect creditors by limiting the DIP's discretion. Before a debtor is able to sell all of its property under section 363, the creditors understandably want some guarantee they will be paid. One way section 363 counteracts creditor fears is by requiring "adequate protection" of collateral. The other is through the "notice and a hearing" provisions of section 363(b) for nonordinary course transactions. This second requirement prevents a store from selling all of its inventory at once without notifying its creditors. Creditors with interests in cash collateral (defined in section 363(a)) are also given the protection of notice and a hearing due to the special nature and liquidity of the collateral.

What happens at the hearing and how does a court decide whether to approve or disapprove the proposed transaction? The transactions are typically supported by the debtor in possession and, if resisted at all, are resisted by creditors with a financial stake in the estate. Occasionally courts justify deference to the debtor's judgment and base that conclusion on a loose "business judgment" test. In other cases courts impose their own judgments on whether the transaction should proceed.

Here a court might demand proof of "necessity" or a "sound business reason" for the transfer. Even less often than the debtor or its creditors is a court equipped by training or experience to operate a business. This courtroom is a poor substitute for sensible management decisions made in the board room.

Problem 5–1

Kahn Craft, a manufacturer of commemorative plates that failed to sell on late night TV, is contemplating bankruptcy. They come to you for advice. Kahn wonders whether section 363(c)(2) will bar use of its cash.

1. Kahn owed Bollinger Bank $2 million borrowed for operating expenses. Kahn's account at Bollinger Bank has a balance of $500,000. Is this cash collateral? Could Kahn avoid the restrictions of section 363(c)(2) by moving its account to another bank prior to the filing?

2. Bollinger Bank has a security interest in proceeds from the sale of plate inventory. Is this cash collateral? Even if it were deposited in another bank?

Problem 5–2

Payton is a domestic auto manufacturer who has recently filed for bankruptcy. In an attempt to streamline operations, Payton would like to sell one of its manufacturing facilities to Toyota. The plant is located in Flint, Michigan. Kauper Bank has a lien on the Flint plant. Payton also plans to institute a 25 percent additional discount on new autos sold to its dealers.

1. Are these ordinary course sales that do not require court approval?

2. Assuming the sale is subject to 363(b), how could either the bank or general unsecured creditors prevent the debtor's actions? What if good business purpose arguments could be made on behalf of both Payton and the creditors' positions?

Problem 5–3

Mr. Syverud owns a farm in Iowa. The farm was profitable until 1981. From 1982 to 1991 it has lost money. Syverud contends that the farm is being run as efficiently as possible. He claims that the recent losses were the result of bad weather, the dismal economy and a defective batch of seed. Given time, he is convinced that he can make the farm profitable again. However, on May 1, 1991 he decided that it was necessary to file a petition in bankruptcy under Chapter 11.

At the time the petition was filed, it was estimated that the value of the farm, equipment, livestock and crops was $475,000.

This property secured a total indebtedness of approximately $550,000. Syverud owed $300,000 to Eisenberg Savings and Loan for this mortgage on his farm. The remaining $250,000 represent the accumulation of loans and credit transactions with various suppliers.

Syverud, as debtor in possession, has come to you to determine exactly what he may do with the property of the estate. He tells you that Eisenberg and his other creditors are likely to oppose any proposal that he makes. Specifically he wants to know:

1. May he continue to use his tractors to plant and cultivate the crops?

2. May he harvest crops already planted and sell them?

3. If he can sell the crops, may he use the proceeds to (a) buy more seed or repair worn equipment; (b) buy food for his family?

4. Can Syverud use cash to (a) pay postpetition debt; (b) pay prepetition debt; (c) buy fertilizer?

§ 2. SALES OUT OF ORDINARY COURSE

Most businesses in Chapter 11 need major adjustments to survive. Failing to make such adjustments, many leave Chapter 11 through liquidation. Of those that do survive Chapter 11, most leave through the exit marked Reorganization Plan Approved by Creditors. It would be a mistake, however, to focus merely upon the negotiation of a reorganization plan as the only factor determining the outcome of a successful reorganization. The negotiation of the ultimate plan, on the one hand, and the day-to-day operation, on the other, proceed in parallel, sometimes overlap and occasionally compete for importance. Sometimes the operation of the business and the purchase and sale of assets truly determines the nature and status of the reorganized business.

In fact, many decisions made by the debtor in possession and contested by the parties prior to the proposal and approval of the plan have a dramatic impact on the ultimate reorganization. For example, if the DIP fails to resist a request for a relief from the stay, a critical asset may be taken by a secured creditor. Such a loss to the estate, in and of itself, may determine the kind of reorganization possible with the remaining assets. By the same token, the skill with which the debtor in possession runs the business and manipulates sections 363 and 364 will have an impact on which assets are available for reorganization when a plan is proposed. The most dramatic of these pre-plan acts of the debtor in possession is the sale of all or of a critical asset of the business.

Section 363 does not limit how much of a business can be sold prior to an approved plan. The courts have searched for a standard to define when such sales are appropriate and when not. One case, *In re Lionel Corp.*, 722 F.2d 1063 (2d Cir.1983), involved a toy train manufacturer that wanted to sell its most valuable asset, its interest in a corporation which manufactured electronic components. The company held the stock purely for investment purposes. The creditors' committee urged the sale over the objections of the chief executive officer and shareholders of Lionel. The Second Circuit solved the problem by following a middle path between Lionel's argument that section 363(b) allowed only emergency sales, and the creditors' desire to give the judge total discretion.

The rule we adopt requires that a judge determining a section 363(b) application expressly find from the evidence presented before him at the hearing a good business reason to grant such an application. Id. at 1070.

The case that follows, *In re Naron & Wagner, Chartered*, 88 B.R. 85 (Bankr.D.Md.1988) tests the application of the *Lionel* principle in a situation where the debtor proposes selling all of the business's assets. The next case, *In re Braniff Airways, Inc.*, 700 F.2d 935 (5th Cir.1983), presents an unusual agreement between the debtor and one of its competitors. These cases represent only a sample of the unique arrangements for which debtors attempt to get court approval under section 363.

IN RE NARON & WAGNER, CHARTERED

United States Bankruptcy Court, District of Maryland, 1988.
88 B.R. 85.

E. STEPHEN DERBY, BANKRUPTCY JUDGE.

In this Chapter 11 case the Debtor has sought to sell all of its operating assets before it has had a plan of reorganization confirmed, and in fact before it has even filed a plan. The Debtor has advised the Court that it intends to file a plan of liquidation within the exclusive period provided to the Debtor by 11 U.S.C. Section 1121.

The Debtor, Naron & Wagner, Chartered, is a local accounting firm. Its principal operating assets were an accounting practice, associated office leases and equipment, and a wholly owned subsidiary known as Business Computer Group ("BCG"), which is engaged in the business of distributing computer hardware and software and providing various related services.

This Court previously approved the sale of Debtor's accounting practice and related assets, including the amendment, assumption and assignment of certain leases, on motion and after notice to all creditors and parties in interest pursuant to 11 U.S.C. Sections 363(b)(1) and 365 and Bankruptcy Rules 6004 and 6006. The Court concluded, based on the evidence proffered without objection at the hearing, that there were "good business reason[s]" for granting Debtor's motions. *In re Lionel Corp.*, 722 F.2d 1063, 1071 (2 Cir.1983). The Debtor was unable to continue its accounting practice profitably or with adequate personnel; the accounting practice was an intangible asset dependent on client good will and, if not timely sold, would quickly lose all of its realizable value for the bankruptcy estate because clients whom Debtor could not service would retain new accountants; preservation of the accounting practice by its sale to another accounting firm would facilitate Debtor's collection of over $600,000 of accounts receivable which it retained, because clients would continue to receive uninterrupted accounting services; and the amendment, assumption and assignment of leases which were an integral part of the sale transaction would avoid or minimize additional claims against the bankruptcy estate.

Presently before the Court is Debtor's motion for approval of the private sale of all the assets of BCG free and clear of liens, encumbrances, claims and interests. BCG is the Debtor's last operating asset. The purchaser is ProVAR, Inc., a Maryland corporation. The principals of ProVAR are the current management of BCG, namely, the president and a vice president. There is no creditors' committee in this case, no objections have been filed, and the United States Trustee has not taken any position, although the Section 341 first meeting of creditors has been held.

This matter raises several issues. First, under what circumstances, if any, should the Court approve a Chapter 11 debtor's sale of substantially all its operating assets prior to confirmation of a plan of reorganization. Second, what protections must be afforded to creditors and other parties in interest before such a sale may be approved by the Court. Third, have the necessary protections been afforded here to creditors and other parties in interest. Finally, do circumstances exist in this case which justify approval of the sale of Debtor's last major operating asset. It is appropriate for the Court to consider these issues because the Court's approval has been sought by the Debtor and because sale of all assets of BCG, a non-debtor but wholly-owned subsidiary corporation of the Debtor, will directly govern the realizable value of Debtor's 100% ownership interest. *Cf. In Re Equity Funding Corporation of America,* 492 F.2d 793 (9th Cir.1974), *cert. denied, Herman Invest. Co. v. Loeffler,* 419 U.S. 964, 95 S.Ct. 224, 42 L.Ed.2d 178 (1974). Further, Debtor's approval of this sale appears required under Maryland law because Debtor is the sole shareholder of BCG, and substantially all of the assets of BCG are being sold. Md.Corps. & Ass'ns Code Ann. § 3-105 (1985 Repl.Vol.).

As to the first question, the Court concludes that a Chapter 11 debtor may in certain circumstances sell all or substantially all of its assets, or a substantial asset, pursuant to 11 U.S.C. Section 363(b) prior to confirmation of a plan of reorganization. Such a sale may even be made, as here, prior to filing a plan of reorganization. However, before such a sale can be approved, the court must "* * * expressly find from the evidence presented before [it] at the hearing a good business reason to grant such an application." *In re Lionel Corp., supra,* 722 F.2d at 1071. In other words, the court should not approve such a sale unless it is able, based on the evidence, "* * * to articulate sound business justifications for [its] decisions." *Id.* at 1066. In *Lionel* the Court of Appeals reversed approval of a Chapter 11 debtor's preconfirmation sale of an 82% common stock interest in a profitable subsidiary because the objector's evidence demonstrated there was not a good business reason for the sale. The subsidiary was less subject than other companies to wide market fluctuations; there was no reason why those interested in purchasing the stock would not be just as interested in six months; and the stock was being sold only because the unsecured creditors' committee insisted, although debtor preferred to retain its ownership interest.

This court adopts the rationale of the *Lionel* case. It will not follow *White Motor Credit Corporation,* 14 B.R. 584 (Bkrtcy.N.D.Ohio 1981). There is no requirement that only an emergency will permit a Chapter 11 debtor's preconfirmation use of Section 363(b), but a Chapter 11 debtor may not use Section 363(b) without establishing a good business reason for such use. *See also Stephens Industries, Inc. v. McClung,* 789 F.2d 386 (6th Cir.1986). The Chapter 11 plan confirmation process provides numerous protections to parties in interest, and a debtor should not be allowed to "* * * use § 363(b) to sidestep the protection creditors have when it comes time to confirm a plan of reorganization," or inappropriately to establish the terms of a plan *sub rosa* through use of Section 363(b). *In re Continental Air Lines, Inc.,* 780 F.2d 1223, 1227 (5th Cir.1986). *See also In re Braniff Airways, Inc.,* 700 F.2d 935 (5th Cir.1983). The sale proposed here is not a *sub rosa* plan because it seeks only to liquidate assets, and the sale will not restructure rights of creditors, as in the *Braniff* case, *supra.*

As to the second question of what protections must be afforded creditors and other parties in interest when a Section 363(b) preconfirmation sale of important assets is proposed, this court concludes that a Chapter 11 debtor which proposes to sell all or substantially all its assets pursuant to Section 363(b), prior to confirmation or filing its plan, must provide notice to all parties in interest. This notice should be sufficient to inform all interested parties of the anticipated impact of the sale on debtor's business and/or anticipated plan. For example, in the instant case the notice should contain enough information to alert interested parties that this is their last chance to be heard prior to the Debtor filing a plan to distribute the proceeds of liquidation in accordance with the priority of each creditor.

Basic to the structure of the Bankruptcy Code is that debtors are provided a fresh start through liquidation, adjustment of debts, or reorganization, while creditors and other parties in interest are protected by the requirement they receive notice and an opportunity to be heard on matters which affect their positions. The concept of "after notice and a hearing" is defined flexibly in 11 U.S.C. Section 102(1)(A) as "* * * such notice as is appropriate in the particular circumstances, * * *." The requirement of "after notice and a hearing" is the predicate of many actions authorized under the Bankruptcy Code, such as the sale of property of the estate outside the ordinary course of business under 11 U.S.C. Section 363(b)(1). If notice which is appropriate under the circumstances to allow creditors and other parties in interest to protect their rights is not provided, the structural tension inherent in the Bankruptcy Code which balances the rights of all parties is subverted.

The Court has a responsibility to review this proposed sale carefully because of the circumstances of the sale. The sale is private; it is to a corporation controlled by insiders of the seller, which is Debtor's subsidiary; the sale will liquidate a substantial asset of Debtor; and the sale is a preconfirmation sale controlled by the Debtor in Chapter 11, rather than a sale within a Chapter 7 case where a disinterested trustee controls the proposed liquidation of assets. The Chapter 11 Debtor is here liquidating all or substantially all its assets without providing creditors and equity holders with adequate information through a written disclosure statement approved by the court after notice and a hearing pursuant to 11 U.S.C. Section 1125. Creditors are not offered an opportunity to protect their interests through the Chapter 11 voting and confirmation process.

It is important that the court be satisfied with the notice provided by the debtor-in-possession, even where no party in interest has objected to the proposed sale of estate property outside the ordinary course of business. The absence of objections is without meaning if notice adequate to invite objections by interests adversely affected was not provided. Assuming adequate notice, the process is more likely to be self-policing, with parties in interest objecting when they believe their rights have been violated. When there has not been an objection, the court should review the adequacy of the notice to ensure that inadequate notice was not the cause of the failure of a party in interest to object.

The primary function of Chapter 11 is for the reorganization of a business, although liquidation plans are authorized. 11 U.S.C. § 1123(b)(4). Consequently, if the purpose of a debtor in proposing the sale of assets within a Chapter 11 proceeding is to dispose of all or a substantial portion of debtor's business and thus prevent reorganization, parties in interest are entitled to notice of that result from the proposed action so they may know to protect any interests they may have in the continuation of the business. If parties in interest are provided copies of a liquidation plan under Chapter 11 with the right to object to confirmation, or if they receive a disclosure statement describing a liquidation because votes are being solicited from an impaired class (11 U.S.C. § 1125(b)), then this protection is provided. By contrast, under Chapter 7 such additional disclosure might not be expected because an express purpose and function of Chapter 7 is liquidation of the bankruptcy estate, and such liquidation is sponsored by a disinterested trustee.

For a Chapter 11 preconfirmation sale of all or substantially all of a debtor's assets, appropriate notice should be a functional substitute for the adequate information which would be contained in a disclosure statement concerning the proposed transaction. *See In re Santec Corp.*, 49 B.R. 59, 60 (Bkrtcy.D.N.H.1985) and *In re Bertholet Enterprises, Inc.*, 66 B.R. 566, 567 (Bkrtcy.D.N.H.1986). Where a plan has not been circulated or even filed, the court must assume a class will be impaired and a disclosure statement will be required for a Chapter 11 plan. *Cf. In re Forrest Hills Associates, Ltd.*, 18 B.R. 104 (Bkrtcy.D.Del.1982); *In re Transload and Transport, Inc.*, 61 B.R. 379 (Bkrtcy.M.D.La.1986). *See In re Jeppson*, 66 B.R. 269 (Bkrtcy.D.Utah 1986). A somewhat different rationale is set forth in *In re Conroe Forge & Mfg. Corp.*, 82 B.R. 781

(Bkrtcy.W.D.Pa.1988), where an undersecured lienholder was denied preconfirmation distribution of the proceeds of sale of its collateral in a liquidating Chapter 11 because, in part, the disclosure statement requirement should not be short-circuited. In order for notice to provide appropriate, and thus adequate, information in the instant situation, the notice should: 1) place all parties in interest on notice that Debtor is liquidating its business under Chapter 11; 2) disclose accurately the full terms of the sale, including the identity of the purchaser; 3) explain the effect of the sale as terminating Debtor's ability to continue in business, and 4) explain why the proposed price is reasonable and why the sale before confirmation is in the best interests of the estate.

The Court earlier refused to authorize this proposed sale of the assets of BCG without a second notice of the proposed sale to all creditors which adequately advised them of what was happening. The original notice failed to disclose that the proposed sale was of the last major operating asset of Debtor, that Debtor was liquidating all of its assets, and that a portion of the described consideration to be paid by the purchaser would not be passed through to the Debtor but would be used to satisfy a claim against BCG by Debtor's joint venturer.

Consequently, in considering the third question whether the required protections have now been afforded by Debtor to parties in interest, the issue is whether Debtor's second notice provided information which was appropriate under the circumstances. The Court concludes the second notice is minimally adequate. The second, Supplemental Notice, discloses that the sale is of substantially all of the assets of BCG, that BCG is a wholly-owned subsidiary of Debtor, and that BCG is one of Debtor's last remaining major assets. Further, the second notice corrects and describes in greater detail the amount and manner of payment of the purchase price and resolution of the joint venturer's claim. The fact of Debtor's liquidation is reasonably apparent in the context of this case from this notice and prior notices sent by Debtor to all interested parties.

As to the final issue, the Court concludes that the Debtor has proffered and provided sufficient evidence and reasons that the proposed Section 363(b) sale of its last operating asset prior to confirmation is supported by "good business reason[s]". *Lionel, supra,* at 1071.

First, BCG is not currently a viable business. The Debtor underwrote BCG's operations to the extent of $750,000 in the two years BCG has operated, and Debtor has been unable to provide additional working capital to BCG after filing its bankruptcy petition. BCG is currently only able to service its trade debt, and it cannot service its financial obligations to Debtor.

Second, failure to close the sale quickly will likely result in a halt of BCG's continuous operations. If BCG cannot be sold as a going concern, there will be a substantial decrease in its value to the Debtor's estate.

Third, the net purchase price to be realized by Debtor after the purchaser's assumption of certain liabilities of BCG is $390,713.08—

$43,000 in cash at closing and the balance in notes at 9% interest. This price substantially exceeds the $246,721.00 estimated liquidation value of BCG's assets.

Fourth, BCG's key personnel have suggested they will seek other employment if the future viability of the business and their jobs is not promptly resolved by the proposed sale.

Finally, Debtor has proffered that the proceeds from the proposed sale, when combined with other assets being liquidated, will be sufficient to pay non-insider creditors in full, so that only insider creditors are likely to be at risk of being adversely affected if the price was insufficient.

For these reasons, the Court believes it is in the best interests of all parties in interest to authorize this sale, and an order has been separately entered.

Notes and Questions

Suppose that a purchaser wishes to buy all the assets of a Chapter 11 debtor. The purchase can be made under section 363 or as part of a reorganization plan that meets the various standards for confirmation. When may a court approve a sale of all or substantially all the assets of a debtor under section 363 where such a sale forecloses any possibility of reorganization under section 1129?

Courts commonly say there must be a "business justification" for a nonordinary course sale. *In re Continental Air Lines, Inc.,* 780 F.2d 1223 (5th Cir.1986); *In re Lionel Corp.,* 722 F.2d 1063 (2d Cir.1983). These courts also require that the sale be "in good faith" or "in the best interests" of the creditors. *In re Industrial Valley Refrigeration and Air Conditioning Supplies, Inc.,* 77 B.R. 15 (Bankr.E.D.Pa.1987).

Do all of these tests come to only one question: "Will the sale generate the best price?" If the present value of the business's earnings is higher than the proposed sale price or, alternatively, if other buyers can be found who will pay a higher price, the sale should not normally be approved. If the contrary is true, it should be approved. A court's failure to approve a sale at the best price allows lawyers, accountants, investment bankers and others to deplete the estate and further diminish the prospects of successful reorganization.

Some commentators argue that a broader analysis is appropriate to recognize the differences between sections 363 and 1129. In a section 363 sale, the debtor in possession makes the decision with court approval but without a formal vote of creditors of the kind contemplated by 1129. A section 1129 plan, on the other hand, requires substantial disclosure to creditors. In addition, at least one class of creditors impaired by the plan must accept it. A section 363 sale entails formal disclosure only when the court orders it. Are "some commentators" right?

IN RE BRANIFF AIRWAYS, INC., PENSION BENEFIT GUARANTY CORPORATION, CONTINENTAL AIR LINES, INC. v. BRANIFF AIRWAYS, INC.

United States Court of Appeals, Fifth Circuit, 1983.
700 F.2d 935.

GEE, CIRCUIT JUDGE:

The facts and procedural history of this case are exceedingly complex. However, the succinct summary by the district court below is sufficient to afford an understanding of our decision today:

On May 13, 1982, Braniff and Braniff International Corporation ("International") filed petitions for reorganization under Chapter 11 of the Bankruptcy Code (the "Code") and were continued in the management and operation of their businesses and properties as debtors-in-possession pursuant to Sections 1107 and 1108 of the Code. No trustee or examiner was appointed. Shortly thereafter, to minimize the effect of Braniff's termination of service, the Department of Transportation and Federal Aviation Administration (DOT/FAA) distributed to other carriers, on an emergency basis, approximately 100 of the over 400 [landing] slots allocated to Braniff. [For safety reasons, the FAA allocates hourly landing slots at airports among the various airlines. *See* Part II, *infra*.] On May 24, 1982, DOT/FAA issued Special Federal Aviation Regulation ("SFAR") 44–4, 47 Fed.Reg. 22,492 (1982) providing for allocation of the remaining slots formerly used by Braniff through participation by air carriers in a random draw.

Thereafter, on May 27, 1982, the Unsecured Creditors' Committee filed an Application seeking a declaration of whether the FAA allocation of former Braniff slots constituted a violation of the automatic stay under 11 U.S.C. § 362 or of a temporary restraining order entered earlier by the Bankruptcy Court proscribing interference with Braniff's property. On June 24, 1982, the Bankruptcy Court approved a stipulation among the United States, Braniff, and the Unsecured Creditors' Committee, stating that the slots would be recalled and made available "[s]hould Braniff or an air carrier succeeding to the rights, duties and obligations of Braniff begin operations."

On December 23, 1982, Braniff filed an application for approval of a proposed agreement between Braniff and PSA. On December 30, 1982, Braniff filed with the Bankruptcy Court a "Memorandum of Understanding" as a basis for a proposed settlement and compromise of all claims, counterclaims, and potential litigations by and among Braniff, certain unsecured creditors, and certain secured creditors.

Between December 30, 1982, and January 3, 1983, various notices of hearings on the proposed agreements were mailed or published. These documents gave notice of a hearing to be held on January 14, 1983, to consider the matters set forth in the PSA Agreement and the Memorandum of Understanding. As stated in these notices, a hearing commenced before United States Bankruptcy Judge John Flowers on January 14, 1983, in the United States Bankruptcy Court for the Northern District of Texas, Fort Worth Bankruptcy Division.

From January 14, 1983, through January 26, 1983, all interested parties were afforded an opportunity to present evidence on their behalf. The Bankruptcy Court heard oral arguments on January 28, 1983, and announced its opinion in this matter on Monday, January 31, 1983. The Bankruptcy Court entered its "Order Regarding the PSA Agreement and Agreement and Stipulation" and its "Findings of Fact and Conclusions of Law Approving the PSA Agreement and Agreement and Stipulation" on February 1, 1983. On that same date, the Bankruptcy Court entered an order pursuant to Sections (e)(2)(A)(i) and (e)(3) of the Local Rule, certifying its order and findings for immediate review to the United States District Court for the Northern District of Texas.

In re Braniff Airways, Inc., No. CA4–83–57–E (N.D.Tex. Feb. 18, 1983) (unpublished memorandum opinion).

The Bankruptcy Court approved both the PSA Agreement and the Memorandum of Understanding between Braniff and its creditors (both agreements hereinafter jointly referred to as the "PSA transaction"). Pursuant to a Local Rule,[1] the district court conducted a *de novo* review of the Bankruptcy Court's findings. In three days of hearings, the district court heard testimony, received evidence and heard oral argument. Thereafter, the district court, as had the Bankruptcy Court, approved the PSA transaction. Because business exigencies required that the PSA transaction be consummated soon if it was to happen at all, we granted this expedited appeal.

Three principal issues are presented. First, was the district court's approval of the PSA transaction authorized under Section 363(b) of the Bankruptcy Code, 11 U.S.C. § 363(b)? Second, did the district court have the power to order the FAA to allocate certain landing "slots" at various airports to Braniff so that Braniff could transfer them in the PSA transaction? Third, did the district court have the power to order Braniff's assumption of its defaulted lease on terminal facilities at Washington National Airport and its subsequent assignment in the PSA transaction without FAA approval?

1. *See In re Braniff Airways, Incorporated, et al.,* 700 F.2d 214 (5th Cir.1983)(district court and bankruptcy court constitutionally exercised jurisdiction pursuant to Local Rule).

I.

The courts below approved the PSA transaction pursuant to Section 363(b) of the Bankruptcy Code, which provides:

> The trustee, after notice and a hearing, may use, sell, or lease, other than in the ordinary course of business, property of the estate.

11 U.S.C. § 363(b).

The appellants contend that § 363(b) is not applicable to sales or other dispositions of all the assets of a debtor, and that such a transaction must be effected pursuant to the voting, disclosure and confirmation requirements of the Code. *See In re White Motor Credit Corp.*, 14 B.R. 584 (Bkrtcy.N.D.Ohio 1981). Braniff responds that cases decided before and after promulgation of the Code authorize a § 363(b) sale of all of a debtor's assets. *See In re Dania Corp.*, 400 F.2d 833 (5th Cir.1968); *In re WHET, Inc.*, 12 B.R. 743, 750–51 (Bkrtcy.D.Mass.1981).

We need not express an opinion on this controversy because we are convinced that the PSA transaction is much more than the "use, sale or lease" of Braniff's property authorized by § 363(b). Reduced to its barest bones, the PSA transaction would provide for Braniff's transfer of cash, airplanes and equipment, terminal leases and landing slots to PSA in return for travel scrip, unsecured notes, and a profit participation in PSA's proposed operation. The PSA transaction would also require significant restructuring of the rights of Braniff creditors. Appellants raise a blizzard of objections to each of these elements of the deal. It is not necessary, however, to decide whether each individual component of the PSA transaction is or is not authorized by § 363 because the entire transaction was treated by both courts below as an integrated whole. Since certain portions of the transaction are clearly outside the scope of § 363, the district court was without power under that section to approve it. Its order must be reversed.

Three examples will illustrate our rationale. The PSA Agreement provided that Braniff would pay $2.5 million to PSA in exchange for $7.5 million of scrip entitling the holder to travel on PSA. It further required that the scrip be used only in a future Braniff reorganization and that it be issued only to former Braniff employees or shareholders or, in a limited amount, to unsecured creditors. This provision not only changed the composition of Braniff's assets, the contemplated result under § 363(b), it also had the practical effect of dictating some of the terms of any future reorganization plan. The reorganization plan would have to allocate the scrip according to the terms of the PSA agreement or forfeit a valuable asset. The debtor and the Bankruptcy Court should not be able to short circuit the requirements of Chapter 11 for confirmation of a reorganization plan by establishing the terms of the plan *sub rosa* in connection with a sale of assets.

Second, under the agreement between Braniff and its creditors, the secured creditors were required to vote a portion of their deficiency claim in favor of any future reorganization plan approved by a majority of the unsecured creditors' committee. Again, such an action is not comprised by the term "use, sell, or lease," and it thwarts the Code's carefully crafted scheme for creditor enfranchisement where plans of reorganization are concerned. See 11 U.S.C. § 1126.[2]

Third, the PSA transaction also provided for the release of claims by all parties against Braniff, its secured creditors and its officers and directors. On its face, this requirement is not a "use, sale or lease" and is not authorized by § 363(b).

For these reasons, we hold that the district court was not authorized by § 363(b) to approve the PSA transaction and that its order is reversed. In any future attempts to specify the terms whereby a reorganization plan is to be adopted, the parties and the district court must scale the hurdles erected in Chapter 11. See e.g. 11 U.S.C. § 1125 (disclosure requirements); id. § 1126 (voting); id. § 1129(a)(7)(best interest of creditors test); id. § 1129(b)(2)(B)(absolute priority rule). Were this transaction approved, and considering the properties proposed to be transferred, little would remain save fixed based equipment and little prospect or occasion for further reorganization. These considerations reinforce our view that this is in fact a reorganization.

Notes and Questions

Has history proved the court wrong? Once a proud name in American commercial aviation, "Braniff" now appears only as faded spots on walls where abandoned signs formerly proclaimed its existence at Newark, Dallas, and many other airports. Ultimately Braniff was reorganized, failed; was reorganized a second time, failed a second time. Then the name was purchased by a charter airline that went into bankruptcy in 1991. Had the PSA transaction been approved, it is possible that some of the Braniff employees who found themselves working on light planes, flying commuters, and drawing unemployment, would have been working for PSA. Does this case suggest something wrong with Chapter 11 proceedings?

Problem 5–4

Sallyanne owns several manufacturing plants at which she produces semiconductor chips for personal computers. Five months after filing Chapter 11 bankruptcy, Sallyanne decided to close her plant in Toledo and sell the plant in Newark since both were losing money. Lehman Bank holds the mortgage on the Toledo factory, while there is no lien on the Newark plant.

---

2. We are aware that the Code provides for certain adjustments in the rights of creditors pursuant to a valid § 363 transaction in order to provide "adequate protection" to secured creditors. 11 U.S.C. § 363(e) (condition use, sale or lease so as to assure "adequate protection" of secured creditors' interest); 11 U.S.C. § 361 (periodic payments, additional liens, or other relief may be used to provide adequate protection). However, nothing has been brought to our attention that would indicate that this particular provision of the PSA transaction was adopted to assure adequate protection and we do not see how it could have been. More important, the other provisions discussed in the text affect only unsecured creditors and are wholly unrelated to any issue of adequate protection. Accordingly, although some actions that technically are not "uses, sales or leases" may be authorized by § 363 and § 361 to assure "adequate protection," the offending portions of the PSA transaction are not within that rubric.

Will Sallyanne require court approval for either proposed action? If so, under what standard should the court rule?

Assume that the Toledo factory will be sold for $3 million and that the secured lender agrees to the sale because it and Sallyanne believe that this is a fair price. The unsecured creditors object because they believe it is too soon to sell. They believe that the company stands a better chance of eventual success if all of the plants are kept in operation. If both sides offer proof that their judgment is correct, how should the court rule?

Problem 5-5

You represent Kahn Cleanser Corp., which has been in bankruptcy for six months. The debtor's major asset is a manufacturing plant located in the outer suburbs of Chicago, directly in the path of suburban growth. The factory is losing money. One week ago, the bank that holds the lien on this factory notified you of a potential buyer who will pay a price that exceeds the secured debt by $100,000. The buyer will close the plant and use the property for residential development. This will leave 1,000 employees with no jobs. After several days on the telephone, you learn that most of Kahn's 500 unsecured creditors will reject a reorganization plan that proposes the sale since it would give them only 5 cents on the dollar. Since management believes this is still the best deal available, you file papers requesting approval of the sale under section 363. What result? What action can shareholders take if they desire to prevent management's action?

§ 3. USE OF CASH COLLATERAL

The Code distinguishes between the use of cash collateral and the use of other types of property. To be "cash collateral" an asset must have certain qualities (i.e., cash, negotiable instruments, etc.) and some party besides the debtor must have an interest in it. Typically the "other party" is a secured creditor such as a bank who has lent money to the debtor and who therefore has a potential right of setoff against the bank account. Another secured creditor might be a person who claims that cash or money in an account is "proceeds" arising from the sale of that creditor's collateral and subject to a security interest under section 9-306 of the Uniform Commercial Code. Almost always, therefore, cash collateral negotiation and cash collateral claims are between the debtor and a secured creditor. Most commonly the secured creditor is the debtor's principal bank. This bank will not only be the place where the debtor maintains his deposit account, but will most likely be a principal secured creditor as well.

Section 363(c)(4) requires that the DIP segregate an account for cash collateral. Section 363(e) entitles any party with an interest in the cash collateral to adequate protection. Finally, section 363(c)(2) authorizes the use of the cash collateral only if there is an agreement with all of the parties with an interest in the collateral or, upon the court's authority after a "notice and a hearing".

With exceptions that are hard to imagine, a debtor entering Chapter 11 will have substantial need for cash. Almost always there will be payrolls to be met, suppliers to be paid and many other new purchases necessary for the continued operation of the business. Without cash the debtor will be stymied and may be forced into liquidation. Accordingly the first order of business in a typical Chapter 11 is to present the court with a negotiated "cash collateral" order or to seek a court order in the face of a lender's refusal to agree to such an order. Clever secured creditors will make the best of a bad thing and will use the debtor's need for cash as an opportunity to negotiate issues that may come later in the Chapter 11 and to incorporate those agreements into the cash collateral order.

A Cash Collateral Order is set out below.

UNITED STATES BANKRUPTCY COURT
FOR THE EASTERN DISTRICT OF MICHIGAN
SOUTHERN DIVISION—FLINT

In re: ACTION AUTO STORES, INC.
    a/k/a Action Auto, Inc.
    a/k/a Sabo Corp., a/k/a JED Co.
    a/k/a Lansing–Lewis Services, Inc.

Case No. 90–11710
Identification # 38–1901597
Date of Filing: 06/15/90
Atty. for Debtor:

Debtor.

Warner, Norcross & Judd
900 Old Kent Blg.
111 Lyon St., N.W.
Grand Rapids, MI 49503–2489

NOTICE FOR MEETING OF CREDITORS COMBINED
WITH NOTICE OF AUTOMATIC STAY AND APPOINTMENT
OF CREDITORS' COMMITTEE

TO: The Debtor, Creditors and other parties in interest

An order for relief under 11 U.S.C., Chapter 11 having been entered on a petition filed by the above-named Debtor, YOU ARE HEREBY NOTIFIED that:

1. A *meeting of creditors* shall be held on July 23, 1990 at 10:00 a.m. in the Courtroom of the Bankruptcy Judge, Room 114, Federal Building, 600 Church Street, Flint, Michigan 48502. The Debtor shall appear through its president or other executive officer for the purpose of being examined by creditors and other interested parties. The Debtor has been retained in possession and is authorized to continue the operation of its business and manage its property.

2. The Debtor will file a list of creditors and equity security holders scheduling the amounts due. It is not necessary for a creditor who desires to participate in the case or share in any distribution to file a proof of claim unless the claim is not listed, listed incorrectly, or listed as disputed, contingent or unliquidated as to amount. Such proofs of claim

are to be filed on or before a date to be later fixed by the Court of which you will be notified.

3. Creditors may not commence or continue acts or proceedings against the Debtor or property of the Debtor, the same having been *stayed automatically* upon the commencement of this case as provided in 11 U.S.C. § 362.

4. Rule 2002(i) of the Bankruptcy Rules allows the Court to send notices of certain proceedings only to creditors' committees and to creditors that request in writing receipt of such notices. The notices affected by this rule are with respect to (1) proposed use, sale or lease of property other than in the ordinary course of business; (2) hearings on approval of a compromise or settlement of controversy; and (3) hearings on all applications for compensation or reimbursement of expenses. If a creditor wishes to receive the aforementioned notices, it must send a written request to be placed on the special mailing matrix. Such request shall be filed with the Clerk of the Bankruptcy Court, 600 Church Street, Flint, Michigan 48502. If you do not specifically request such notices, you will not receive them.

Dated: July 3, 1990.

ARTHUR J. SPECTOR
U.S. Bankruptcy Judge

UNITED STATES BANKRUPTCY COURT
EASTERN DISTRICT OF MICHIGAN
SOUTHERN DIVISION—FLINT

In the Matter of:

ACTION AUTO STORES, INC.,
a/k/a Action Auto, Inc.,
a/k/a Sabo Corp., a/k/a
JED Co., Lansing Lewis
Services, Inc.,

    Debtor.
_____/

Chapter 11
Case No. 90–11710–S

Judge Arthur J. Spector

CONSENT ORDER AUTHORIZING DEBTOR'S USE
OF CASH COLLATERAL AND OTHER RELIEF
PENDING FINAL HEARING

At a session of said Court held in the Federal Building, Bay City, Michigan on June 22, 1990
PRESENT: Honorable Arthur J. Spector

United States Bankruptcy Judge

Action Auto Stores, Inc. ("Debtor"), having filed a motion (the "Motion") for authority to use the cash collateral of Michigan National Bank (hereinafter the "Bank") and Travelers Insurance Company ("Travelers"), the Court having examined the Motion, and upon completion of a preliminary hearing as provided for under Bankruptcy Rule 4001(b);

THE COURT FINDS AS FOLLOWS:

A. On June 15, 1990 (the "Filing Date"), Debtor filed a petition under Chapter 11 of the Bankruptcy Code ("Code"). Since that time, Debtor has remained in possession of its assets and has continued to operate and manage its business as a debtor in possession pursuant to 11 U.S.C. §§ 1107 and 1108.

B. No committee of creditors holding unsecured claims (the "Committee") or any other committee has been appointed, as provided by Section 1102 of the Code.

C. Prior to the Filing Date, the Bank entered into certain financing arrangements with Debtor, evidenced by, among other things, notes, loan agreements, security agreements, mortgages and other documents and writings (collectively hereinafter referred to as the "Prepetition Loan Documents").

D. According to the Bank's books as of the Filing Date, the Debtor was indebted to the Bank in the approximate amount of $24,800,000 plus interest, costs and expenses (the "Indebtedness").

E. The Bank maintains that the Prepetition Debt is secured by cash collateral pursuant to the Prepetition Loan Documents.

F. All cash, checks, refunds (including tax refunds), negotiable instruments, documents of title, deposit accounts, securities, and other cash equivalents which are now or may hereafter come into the possession, custody or control of the Debtor, constitute and will continue to constitute cash collateral of the Bank, must be segregated and accounted for, pursuant to Section 363(c)(4) of the Code, and cannot be used by the Debtor in operating its business or managing its affairs, necessitating the immediate authorization of its use of cash collateral to avoid immediate and irreparable harm to the estate pending the final hearing provided for in this Order (the "Final Hearing").

G. Debtor has provided notice of this preliminary hearing and the terms of the Motion to all creditors holding secured claims of record, creditors holding the twenty largest unsecured claims (according to Debtor's Bankruptcy Rule 1007(d) filing), and the United States Trustee as set forth in a proof of service filed herein and such notice, together with the Notice procedure set forth in paragraph 9 hereof, constitutes sufficient "notice and a hearing" under 11 U.S.C. § 363, 11 U.S.C. § 102, Bankruptcy Rules 2002, 4001, and 6007.

H. The entry of this Order is in the best interest of the estate and its creditors.

I. Until the Final Hearing, these findings of fact shall be binding upon the Debtor only and shall not bind any other creditor or other party in interest.

Accordingly, IT IS HEREBY ORDERED as follows:

1. Debtor is hereby authorized to use cash collateral only as described herein.

2. Debtor may use cash collateral only to the extent that the same is necessary to avoid immediate and irreparable harm. The use of cash collateral shall be limited to those categories of items and in the amounts set forth in Schedule A. Cash collateral may not be used to pay or cure any prepetition obligations of the Debtor, including any arrearages under any lease, equipment or executory contract.

3. To secure the Debtor's use of the Bank's cash collateral, the Debtor is, by entry of this Order, authorized to, and by virtue hereof does hereby, grant Bank a lien in all of the Debtor's right, title and interest in all of the Debtor's property acquired on or after the Filing Date to the same extent that the same is a substitution for that existing prior to the Filing Date as set forth in the Prepetition Loan Documents.

4. To the extent that the Debtor has provided the Bank with adequate protection of the Bank's interest in the Debtor's property and the Bank's interest, notwithstanding such adequate protection, in such property is diminished, then to the extent that the same is diminished, the Bank shall be and is given by virtue of this Order an 11 USC § 507(b) BR claim to all of the property of the estate and the proceeds thereof including but not limited to, all causes of action and proceeds of causes of action of the Debtor granted to the Debtor under Chapter 5 of the Code, from which the amount of diminution shall be paid.

5. Upon entry of this Order, Bank shall receive copies of all insurance policies presently in effect showing Debtor's coverage of the Bank's interest in all of the Debtor's property.

6. Until repayment of all Indebtedness, Debtor will:

(a) Deliver to the Bank, Travelers, and Sun Refining copies of all reports and other financial information filed with the Bankruptcy Court concurrently with the filing thereof, permit the Bank to audit the books and records of Debtor at all times reasonably requested by the Bank and to make copies thereof or extracts therefrom, and permit the Bank access to the Debtor's premises at any time during normal business hours.

(b) Promptly give to the Bank, Travelers, and Sun Refining prior written notice of:

(i) the sale or execution of a contract for sale of any property other than in the ordinary course of business as presently being conducted, which notice shall be sufficient advance notice to permit the Bank reasonable inquiry concerning the transaction; and

(ii) the occurrence of any event or any matter which has resulted or will result in a material adverse change in its business, assets, operations or financial condition.

(c) Deliver to the Bank and counsel for the Bank and Travelers and counsel and Sun Refining and its counsel concurrently with their filing copies of each pleading or report heretofore or hereafter filed with the Bankruptcy Court by the Debtor, and shall notify counsel for the Bank of any pleading received, save and except for proofs of claim, including, but not limited to, any application or motion to the Bankruptcy Court by any party in interest for the appointment of a trustee or dismissal of the Bankruptcy Case, or for a change of venue.

(d) Provide the Bank (to the attention of John June) and counsel, Travelers and counsel, Sun and its counsel with: (i) weekly statements of actual cash receipts and disbursements by the Tuesday of each week for the prior week and weekly copies of Debtor's check register by Tuesday of each week for the prior week; (ii) a profit and loss statement for the proceeding week by the Tuesday of the subsequent week (beginning June 26); (iii) inventory reports required by the Bank on a weekly basis commencing Tuesday, June 26 and by the next Tuesday for each subsequent week thereafter, (if the report is not satisfactory to the Bank, Debtor shall provide such additional information as the Bank shall reasonably request); (iv) all other documentation reasonably required by the Bank; and (v) a weekly status report in writing on efforts to sell the Debtor and its property and the prospects for any sale.

(e) Debtor shall immediately obtain and maintain during the term hereof insurance covering all property subject to the Bank's liens to its full replacement value without deduction for depreciation. All insurance policies required pursuant to this paragraph shall be written on forms which provide no less coverage than the so called all risk property form and shall be carried in sufficient amount so as to avoid the imposition of any co-insurance penalty in the event of a loss. All such policies of insurance shall be further endorsed to name the Bank as an additional named insured and provide a mortgagee clause in favor of the Bank.

(f) At all times comply with all laws, statutes, rules, regulations, order and directions of any governmental authority having jurisdiction over the Debtor or its business, the violation of which would have a material adverse effect upon the Debtor.

7. Upon entry of this Order, the liens granted to the Bank by virtue of this Order shall be valid and perfected as against all third parties, without regard to applicable federal, state or local filing and recording statutes, provided, that the Bank may, but need not, take such

steps as it deems appropriate to comply with such federal, state or local statutes.

8. If any or all of the provisions of this Order are hereafter modified, vacated or stayed by subsequent order of this or any other Court, such stay, modification or vacation shall not affect the validity of this Order or the validity and enforceability of any lien or priority authorized and granted hereby to the Bank, and notwithstanding such stay, modification or vacation, any authorized use of cash collateral pursuant to this Order prior to the effective date of any modification, stay or vacation, to or for the benefit of the Debtor shall be governed in all respects by the original provisions of this Order and the Bank shall be entitled to all the rights and benefits granted herein.

9. Within two (2) business days from the date of the entry of this Order, Debtor shall serve (or cause to be served)(a) a copy of this Order on each creditor holding a secured claim of record, (b) creditors identified on the lists filed pursuant to Bankruptcy Rule 1007(d). A final hearing shall be held in Bankruptcy Court, 102A Federal Building, 600 Church Street, Flint, Michigan 48502, on July 3, 1990 at 2:30 p.m. (the "Final Hearing") to determine whether this Order shall become a final order.

10. It is further ordered that the Debtor shall immediately supply to the Bank copies of all records and/or materials necessary to establish the amount and cost of all inventory of the Debtor as of the Filing Date which shall be completed, to the extent possible, prior to the Final Hearing.

11. Absent an earlier termination, the Debtor is authorized to use the Bank's cash collateral, subject to the terms and conditions set forth herein, until the Final Hearing.

_____
United States Bankruptcy Judge

Counsel for Action Auto Stores, Inc.:

Robert H. Skilton

Warner, Norcross & Judd
900 Old Kent Building
111 Lyon Street, N.W.
Grand Rapids, Michigan 49503–2489

Counsel for Michigan National Bank:

Lawrence K. Snider

Jeffrey Chimovitz

Jaffe, Snider, Raitt & Heuer
Professional Corporation
One Woodward Avenue
Suite 2400
Detroit, Michigan 48226

Questions

1. The order is on the paper of "Jaffe, Snider, Raitt & Heuer." Who do they represent in Action Auto?

2. What is included by the language "which are now or may hereafter come into the possession" in Finding of Fact F?

3. May the cash collateral be used to pay postpetition debts?

4. What rights does paragraph 3 of the order give to the Bank?

5. Does the bank have to be notified of ordinary course sales? Non-ordinary course sales?

6. What did the Bank get out of agreeing to the order in addition to notices and reports?

7. Can the debtor in possession later modify the order and release itself from the order?

RIGHTS OF THE SECURED CREDITOR IN CASH COLLATERAL ABSENT AGREEMENT.

A typical secured creditor with a perfected interest in personal property will have a direct claim on accounts receivable, negotiable instruments, cash and other items of after-acquired personal property under the after-acquired property clause and security agreement. That clause may be broad or narrow, but it usually claims all the kinds of after-acquired property that are like or related to the original collateral.

Section 552(a) invalidates the after-acquired property clause as to the collateral acquired after the commencement of the case. It flatly states that the property acquired by the debtor "after the commencement of the case is not subject to any lien resulting from any security agreement entered into * * * before the commencement of the case." So the creditor's most direct claim in after-acquired assets is cut off by section 552(a).

Section 552(b)(1) gives back some of what 552(a) takes. It recognizes the right of the secured creditor to "proceeds, product, offspring or profit to the extent provided by * * * [the] security agreement and by applicable non-bankruptcy law * * * ." In effect subsection (b)(1) grants to a properly secured Article 9 creditor what section 9–306 would grant—mainly identifiable proceeds—to the extent the security agreement covers those proceeds. For example, in the typical revolving loan against inventory much chattel paper, many negotiable instruments, and a good deal of the cash received by the debtor will constitute identifiable proceeds under 9–306. The combination of that section and the security agreement will give the secured creditor an automatically perfected security interest in many of those assets, at least for a limited period of time. The upshot of 552(b)(1) is that a debtor who has granted a security interest in personal property that produces proceeds will be forced to negotiate with its secured creditor to get the right to use cash collateral. Failing that, the debtor violates section 363 if it uses the cash collateral.

If the collateral is real estate and not personal property, the rules have been different. Many mortgages against commercial real estate claim the right to rents and other profits derived from the use of the real estate. In some cases these profits have been hard to classify; particularly troublesome for the courts have been payments for room rentals at hotels. Some courts have described these as rent, others as fees from a license to use property. Whether these are classified as rent or in some other way, they have often escaped the reach of the mortgage holder under 552(b)(1). That is because (b)(1) authorizes the claim by a creditor only to the extent provided by the security agreement and "by applicable non-bankruptcy law." Under the law of many states the mortgage holder's right to rent (or at least the perfection of that right) is dependent upon the mortgage holder taking some action such as seizure of the property, or appointment of a receiver to collect the rents. In the real estate law of many states there is no provision analogous to 9-306 to grant an automatic perfected security interest in rents and the like. Litigation over claims to hotel room rentals, other rentals and the like has been widespread and the results—in part because they depend upon varied state law—have not been consistent.

In response to that case law—and presumably to the pleas of mortgage holders—Congress enacted 552(b)(2) in 1994. Note how different (b)(2) is from (b)(1). The new subsection explicitly authorizes the "security interests [to] extend to such rents and such fees * * * to the extent provided in such security agreements." Unlike (b)(1), which is limited to the terms of "applicable non-bankruptcy law," (b)(2) is limited only by the terms of the security agreement. While (b)(1) merely recognizes an existing right granted by 9-306, (b)(2) grants a security interest as a matter of federal law. To reiterate, unlike (b)(1) the rule in (b)(2) does not merely recognize rights that would otherwise exist under state law, but grants the secured creditor additional rights that the secured creditor may not have had outside of bankruptcy.

Consider the practical consequences of 552(b)(1) and (b)(2). Assume that the secured creditor holds a mortgage on the debtor's hotel and that the secured creditor is fed up with the debtor's behavior. Accordingly the mortgagee refuses to enter into a cash collateral agreement and insists instead under 552(b)(2) that all rents be handed over to it to satisfy its $5,000,000 claim. That will leave the debtor without cash flow to pay taxes or the wages of the various clerical and service employees at the hotel. Reorganization without an infusion of other capital will be impossible. The adoption of 552(b)(2) may substantially alter the balance of power between real estate mortgagees and mortgagors. Under the terms of (b)(1) and (b)(2), of course, the court can "order otherwise" based on "equities of the case." If you represented the debtor in our case how would you argue the "equities?" And what would you advise your client about the probable outcome?

§ 4. PAYING CREDITORS AND SUPPLIERS

One important use of property under section 363 is paying suppliers for goods necessary to the business. Suppose that the DIP holds $100,000 of unencumbered cash. As the case progresses, two possible uses of this cash arise. One option is to pay suppliers or employees who deliver products and services to the debtor after the bankruptcy petition. Although suppliers often demand cash on delivery, they hold "administrative claims" against the estate if they deliver on credit. Such claims are entitled to be paid in full prior to any payment to unsecured prepetition creditors. *See* sections 507(a)(1) and 726(a)(1). Section 363 contemplates the DIP's use of these funds to pay suppliers.

A second use of the cash is to pay creditors who hold claims for prepetition services, loans or deliveries. Much in the Bankruptcy Code, including the policy of section 547, the terms of section 549, and the general policy of equity in distribution of assets, suggests that a bankruptcy petition freezes the rights of the prepetition creditors. Their right to recover from the estate is placed behind that of creditors who make loans after the petition. Normally one would expect that the prepetition claimants will be paid only in a reorganization plan or in a distribution upon liquidation.

Nevertheless there is much evidence that debtors make payments to certain prepetition creditors. The power of some creditors (e.g., the employees or a supplier of a critical substance) may be irresistible. In *In re James A. Phillips, Inc.*, 29 B.R. 391 (Bankr.S.D.N.Y.1983), we see Judge Sofaer struggling in such a case to find a basis under section 363 or elsewhere to permit such a payment. *In re Roblin Industries,* infra page 209, confronts this problem with respect to a secured creditor.

Buried in the fine print of a cash collateral or some other arrangement that is clearly permissible under section 363 will sometimes be a "cross collateralization" provision or other term that may have the economic effect of paying or more adequately securing a prepetition debt. When such rights are asserted by the secured creditor, they come under the rubric of *In re Texlon Corp.*, 596 F.2d 1092 (2d Cir.1979), a case decided by Judge Friendly in the Court of Appeals for the Second Circuit.

Consider the debtor's incentives here. They do not necessarily encourage compliance with section 549. It will often clearly be in the economic interest of the debtor to violate the rules of 549 by making direct and generous payments to the most powerful of its prepetition claimants. Note that the DIP is likely to be spending *other people's money,* i.e., money that would go to *other* creditors if the business liquidated without the payment having been made.

IN RE JAMES A. PHILLIPS, INC.
United States District Court, Southern District of New York, 1983.
29 B.R. 391.

ABRAHAM D. SOFAER, DISTRICT JUDGE. Armstrong World Industries, Inc. ("Armstrong") appeals from orders entered by former Bankruptcy Judge Roy Babitt authorizing certain payments by the debtor in possession James A. Phillips, Inc. ("Phillips"). For the reasons that follow, Armstrong's appeal is denied and the Bankruptcy Judge's orders are affirmed.

Phillips is an acoustical ceilings and walls contractor, and Armstrong is a supplier of construction materials. On December 14, 1981 Armstrong obtained a $74,101.91 judgment against Phillips for goods sold and delivered. On June 11, 1982, having suffered major losses on a large construction project and in anticipation of an execution to justify Armstrong's judgment, Phillips filed a petition under chapter 11 of the Bankruptcy Code, 11 U.S.C. Section 101, et seq. Armstrong has not moved for conversion or dismissal of that filing, see 11 U.S.C. Section 1112(b), or for relief from the stay of execution of its judgment, see 11 U.S.C. Section 362(d)(1). On June 16, 1982, Phillips applied to the Bankruptcy Court for authority to pay a number of construction suppliers other than Armstrong. That same day Judge Babitt signed orders authorizing the payments without a hearing and without notice to Armstrong or to any of Phillips' other creditors. Armstrong's counsel learned of these orders a few days after June 16, during a check of Phillips' file in the Bankruptcy Court. On June 25, 1982 Judge Babitt heard argument on and denied Armstrong's application to vacate his orders.

Phillips maintains that the payments authorized by the Bankruptcy Court were essential to its hopes for survival. The suppliers to whom the payments were authorized had provided materials to Phillips at three construction sites. Phillips had substantially completed its work at two of those sites, but in response to one supplier's threat to file a mechanics' lien on the buildings involved, the contractors at the sites, Regal Construction Corp. and O & Y Construction Corp., stopped payment on checks delivered to Phillips and indicated that further payments due Phillips would not be forthcoming until all suppliers with potential liens were paid. The amounts due Phillips from Regal and O & Y (respectively $27,279 and $104,206) were substantially greater than the amounts authorized by the Bankruptcy Court to be paid the suppliers on each site ($10,065 and $36,665). At the third site Phillips had not substantially completed its work, and had not been contacted by the contractor, George A. Fuller Co., or by any of the suppliers who had the right to file liens on the real property involved. Moreover, the amount then due Phillips from Fuller ($42,261) was substantially less than the amount authorized to be paid the suppliers on the site ($69,421). Phillips maintains, however, that the potential liens of the unpaid suppliers posed a real threat to its eventual realization of a substantial profit on its contract with Fuller.

Armstrong objects to the payment of over $117,000 to other suppliers of Phillips, while Armstrong's judgment against Phillips for over $74,000 remains unsatisfied, with execution frozen by Phillips' chapter 11 petition. As a result of the payments authorized by Judge Babitt, Armstrong's share of the monies owed Phillips' top fourteen creditors jumped from 35% to 61%. Relying upon various provisions of the Bankruptcy Code as well as the decisions in *In re* Texlon Corp., 596 F.2d 1092 (2d Cir.1979), and *In re* Sullivan Ford Sales, 2 B.R. 350 (Bkrtcy. D.Me.1980), Armstrong challenges the Bankruptcy Court's orders as improper, ex parte authorizations of preferential payment.

At the root of the many difficulties posed by this appeal is the nature of the potential liens available to the "preferred" supplier-creditors. The suppliers' right to assert liens under state law is not stayed by the debtor's chapter 11 petition. Rather, Section 362(b)(3) and Section 546(b) of the Bankruptcy Code, permit such liens to "relate back" to the time of the underlying debt's creation as provided by New York Lien Law Section 13(5)(McKinney's 1982). *See In re* C. H. Stuart, Inc., 17 B.R. 400 (Bkrtcy.W.D.N.Y.1982); *In re* Fiorillo & Co., 19 B.R. 21, 8 B.C.D. (CRR) 1169 (Bkrtcy.S.D.N.Y.1982); King, et al., 4 *Collier on Bankruptcy* ¶ 546.03 (1979). Armstrong's lien rights apparently were never exercised within the 120 days after furnishing materials allowed by New York Lien Law Section 10 (McKinney's 1982), and, in any event, in June 1982 the construction projects to which Armstrong had delivered supplies for Phillips no longer figured in Phillips' business operations. Thus, despite its judgment against Phillips, Armstrong was in a substantially inferior position to that of the suppliers with potential lien rights involving projects where Phillips either was owed money or had ongoing contractual obligations. The only remedy available to Armstrong, execution on its state-court judgment, was stayed; the remedy available to the other suppliers, placing liens on the construction sites to which they had delivered materials for Phillips, was not stayed. Due to the interaction of state and federal law which gives such suppliers potential remedies unaffected by Section 362's automatic stay, the suppliers were effectively in a separate class from Phillips' other unsecured creditors.

The Code provides no clear answer to the question whether Armstrong was entitled to notice of the applications to pay the suppliers. Indeed, one cannot fault the Bankruptcy Court's equivocal conclusion at the June 25, 1982 hearing that "maybe it [the application for payments] should have been on notice and hearing because it's out of the ordinary, although I am not even sure it's so." On this appeal Armstrong initially relied on Section 1109(b) of the Code, which provides that a party in interest "may raise and appear and be heard on any issue in a case under [chapter 11]." The notice requirement in this section is implicit at best. As the leading treatise has observed, the question of notice under Section 1109(b) "undoubtedly will be a source of litigation," but any rule requiring "a right to notice of all steps taken in the reorganization * * * would result in much unwarranted difficulty and expense." 5 *Collier on Bankruptcy,* p. 1109.02[3] (1979).

Unlike the implicit notice requirement of Section 1109(b), provisions elsewhere in the Code explicitly deal with the issue of notice. Section 363(b) and Section 363(c)(1), provide that a trustee may use, sell or lease the bankrupt's property without notice and a hearing only so long as the transactions are conducted "in the ordinary course of business." These provisions apply to a debtor in possession under 11 U.S.C. Section 1107(a). Thus, if the payments in this case were transactions "in the ordinary course of business," there was no need for notice or hearing under the Bankruptcy Code; indeed, payments in the ordinary course need not be authorized by a Bankruptcy Court at all, since Section 1107(a) and Section 1108, automatically permit the debtor in possession to operate its business. *See In re* Hanline, 8 B.R. 449 (Bkrtcy.N.D.Ohio 1981) (transaction outside ordinary course does not require court authorization where no creditor objects following proper notice). In its reply papers, Armstrong shifted the focus of its arguments to Section 363, implicitly assuming that the payments authorized by the Bankruptcy Court were not in the ordinary course of business. At oral argument and in correspondence to the Court, Phillips has challenged this assumption by pointing out that an acoustical subcontractor would, in the ordinary course of its business, generally pay creditors with potential mechanics' lien law rights before creditors without such rights.

The legislative history of Section 363 provides no test or guideline concerning the scope of the "ordinary course of business" standard. Nonetheless, the apparent purpose of requiring notice only where the use of property is extraordinary is to assure interested persons of an opportunity to be heard concerning transactions different from those that might be expected to take place so long as the debtor in possession is allowed to continue normal business operations under 11 U.S.C. Section 1107(a) and Section 1108. The touchstone of "ordinariness" is thus the interested parties' reasonable expectations of what transactions the debtor in possession is likely to enter in the course of its business. So long as the transactions conducted are consistent with these expectations, creditors have no right to notice and hearing, because their objections to such transactions are likely to relate to the bankrupt's chapter 11 status, not the particular transactions themselves. Where the debtor in possession is merely exercising the privilege of its chapter 11 status, which include the right to operate the bankrupt business, there is no general right to notice and hearing concerning particular transactions. To preclude such transactions, interested parties must apply to the Bankruptcy Court for relief from the stay, 11 U.S.C. Section 362(d)(1), or for conversion or dismissal of the chapter 11 petition, 11 U.S.C. Section 1112(b).

Under this analysis, payments of the sort involved here might well have been "in the ordinary course of business." Given the special status of suppliers whose unstayed lien rights have not expired under state law, payment to such suppliers following a contractor's chapter 11 filing would appear a reasonable response to business exigencies. But for the accelerated nature of the payments precipitated by Phillips' Chapter 11 filing, the payment of suppliers with potential lien rights seems within the ordinary course of Phillips' business activities. *Cf. In re* Listle/Shreeves Corp., 20 B.R. 421, 423 (Bkrtcy.M.D.Fla.1982)("It is an accepted practice of the construction industry to pay subcontractors and to bond off mechanics' liens against real property * * * by posting either a bond or placing funds in the registry of the court.") This appears to be what Judge Babitt meant when he stated at the July 25 hearing, "I don't think [the payments] are out of the ordinary if you weren't in Chapter 11."

In its post-argument brief, however, Phillips acknowledges that the payments in this case were made under exigent circumstances and at an accelerated rate. Although payment of suppliers with potential lien rights may be ordinary, Phillips implicitly recognizes that payment of such suppliers in advance of payment from the main contractor is extraordinary. Indeed, Phillips' counsel admitted at the June 25, 1982 hearing that the payments "were out of the ordinary." One might argue that the filing of a chapter 11 petition can reasonably be expected to require accelerated payments of creditors with potential lien rights. But this is a factual matter, turning on the particular circumstances presented, including whether the creditor involved had filed or had threatened to file a lien, and whether payment delayed until the general contractor had paid the debtor would jeopardize the relationship between the contractor and debtor. These are the sorts of issues on which creditors in the Chapter 11 proceeding should have an opportunity to be heard, however summarily, before the accelerated payments are formally authorized by a Bankruptcy Court. Such an opportunity would ensure that the facts alleged by the debtor in possession are at least colorably supported, and would avoid preferential payments that may be commercially unsupportable or downright fraudulent. The safe course under the statute therefore appears to be, as Judge Babitt ultimately concluded, to require that notice of some sort be given to creditors of the estate before accelerated payments to potential lienors are authorized.

The notice required, however, should not be permitted to undermine the capacity of the debtor in possession to accomplish the legitimate ends sought by the transactions at issue.

* * *

A final consideration weighing against reversal of the Bankruptcy Court's order is Section 363(m)'s specific provision that "reversal or modification on appeal of an authorization under subsection (b) or (c) of this section of a sale or lease of property does not affect the validity of a sale or lease under such authorization to an entity that purchased or leased such property in good faith * * *." If this provision were applicable to the Bankruptcy Court orders in this case, then a reversal of those orders would have no practical significance, since the relief Armstrong seeks in this case is reversal of the order permitting the payments. Armstrong argues that Section 363(m) is inapplicable because payments to suppliers are not sales or leases of property. The definition sections of the Code do not define "sale" or "lease", and an analysis of Section 363's use of the terms provides no clear answer to their scope in Section 363(m). A reasonable argument could be made, however, that Section 363(m)'s failure to mention the term "use" should be considered significant, and that by implication the reference in Section 363(m) to "sale or lease" should be construed to exclude a purchase of supplies with cash. Regardless of whether Section 363(m) should be deemed to apply here, however, the policy behind Section 363(m) is evidently to protect third parties that rely on Bankruptcy Court authorizations in their dealings with the trustee or debtor. That policy is particularly implicated in potential mechanics' liens which, under state law, have now expired. Regardless of whether those suppliers would have filed liens in the absence of the Bankruptcy Court order, they likely would have done so if Phillips had failed to pay them even after being paid by its contractors. If the payments to them are invalidated now, however, the suppliers will be left without payment from Phillips and without the state-law lien rights that were previously available to secure payment for the goods and services they provided at the construction sites. Such a result would unfairly prejudice the suppliers who relied upon the Bankruptcy Court's authorization of payments by not filing liens once payments were received from Phillips.

On the other hand, Section 363(b) simply states that "[t]he trustee, after notice and a hearing, may use, sell, or lease, other than in the ordinary course of business, property of the estate." Here, despite the absence of any reference to "transactions", the words "use, sell, or lease" seem intended to include the entire range of transactions the trustee or debtor might enter; were it otherwise, the statute would not authorize transactions, other than "use", "sale", or "lease", which were not in the ordinary course despite the fact that notice was given. Similarly, Section 363(c)(2) provides that the "trustee may not use, sell or lease cash collateral", unless all parties with an interest in the collateral consent or a court authorizes such use, sale or lease after notice of a hearing. Here, the words "use, sell or lease" were intended to cover a broad range of transactions; otherwise numerous transactions involving cash collateral, such as purchasing supplies with proceeds in which a secured creditor has an interest, would be exempt from the requirements of Section 362(c)(2), when in fact those requirements are plainly designed to protect creditors with security interests in cash.

Appellant's reliance on *In re* Texlon Corp., 596 F.2d 1092 (2d Cir.1979), is misplaced. That case was decided under the old Bankruptcy Act and involved the ex parte authorization of a financing scheme whereby one creditor obtained security for prepetition unsecured debt in exchange for advancing secured credit to the bankrupt. The Second Circuit affirmed a reversal of the Bankruptcy Court's authorization, because the financing scheme was too preferential to have been approved solely on representations of the debtor in possession as to the unavailability of other sources of credit. 596 F.2d at 1098. The preferential nature of the payments authorized in this case, however, is not nearly as pronounced. Whereas the "preferred" creditor in Texlon received a security interest on prepetition debt in exchange for extending additional secured debt, the suppliers in this case received accelerated payment on prepetition debt that could effectively have been secured by potential lien rights not stayed by Phillips' Chapter 11 petition. These rights are in themselves exceptions to the accepted bankruptcy principle of equal distribution among creditors, ... and as such they cannot be ignored in evaluating the propriety of the orders in this case.

* * *

Appellant's reliance on *In re* Sullivan Ford Sales, 2 B.R. 350 (Bkrtcy. D.Maine 1980), is similarly misplaced. In that case, Bankruptcy Judge Cyr refused to authorize without sufficient notice a financing scheme involving the use of "cash collateral" and the creation of new debt with a special priority over administrative expenses. Under Section 364(c)(1) and Section 363(c)(2)(B), the special priority and the use of "cash collateral" unquestionably could not have been authorized without appropriate notice. Unlike the payments in this case, those transactions were by their nature out of the ordinary course of the debtor's business and they created potential prejudice to the debtor's creditors wholly unrelated to the prejudice inherent in allowing a debtor to attempt rehabilitation while the claims of its creditors are stayed. Moreover, the Bankruptcy Court in *Sullivan* emphasized the possibility that, given the twelve-day interval between filing of the petition and the request for ex parte relief, the allegedly emergency nature of the debtor's requests may have been intentionally created by the debtor. 2 Bankr. at 354. In this case, despite Armstrong's assertions to the contrary, there is nothing to suggest that Phillips waited five days before submitting its applications to the Bankruptcy Court in order to create an emergency situation to induce a Bankruptcy Judge to grant ex parte relief. The threat to Phillips' business was unexpectedly created when one of its creditors threatened to file liens on its jobs, causing two of its contractors to stop or withhold payments due to Phillips for work it had performed.

In conclusion, despite the improper lack of any notice, the Bankruptcy Court orders in this case must be affirmed. The error in not affording notice was harmless, and Armstrong has failed to question the essential facts supporting the ex parte orders. Invalidating the payments made would also unfairly prejudice the suppliers who acted in apparent good faith. The orders of the Bankruptcy Court are affirmed.

So Ordered.

Questions

1. What is the best defense of a debtor's payment of a prepetition liability

(a) under the statute?

(b) as a policy matter?

2. How, as a practical matter, did the situation presented to Judge Sofaer in *Phillips* arise?

3. Do you think Judge Babitt has kindly feelings toward the lawyer that got him to sign the *ex parte* order? There is surely a lesson here for trial lawyers, not so?

Problem 5–6

Durfee operates a manufacturing business. Shortly before filing bankruptcy, its accounts receivable had a face value of $2.5 million. Durfee owned inventory, real estate and equipment worth $10.5 million. Durfee's debts exceed $20 million. Shortly after filing bankruptcy, Durfee conducts the following transactions without requesting court approval. It collects $300,000 cash from accounts receivable that are not subject to a security interest, and

(1) Uses $100,000 of cash to pay salaried employees for the month's work immediately preceding the filing;

(2) pays $50,000 to a major supplier for a three-month old debt (would it matter that this was an installment on a long-term contract to be assumed under § 365 or that supplier sold on a series of separate contracts?);

(3) pays a postpetition supplier $10,000 for goods received;

(4) pays $15,000, a postpetition installment, on a secured lien against equipment.

As counsel for the unsecured creditors' committee, what action do you suggest?

What result if, prior to taking these actions, Durfee requested court approval?

In 1994 Congress added section 546(h). Assume its application to two cases. In one case Seller sells $500,000 of steel to Debtor 60 days prior to Debtor's bankruptcy on open credit. In the other case Seller sells the same amount of steel at the same time but receives payment in cash. Do you see why Debtor will not be able to return the steel and receive a repayment of its money in the second case under the terms of 546(h)? If, in the first case, the Debtor has no use for the steel (assume that its manufacturing facility has been closed), can the steel be returned? Why would the Seller take it back and how would the accounts of the Seller and the Debtor be adjusted?

§ 5. OBTAINING CREDIT AFTER THE PETITION

The very presence of a business in Chapter 11 suggests that it is in need of money, or at minimum, of liquidity. Thus, most businesses that are going to continue in Chapter 11 will need continued sources of credit. These may come in the form of conventional bank financing or in open credit on sales.

Section 364 outlines the standards under which borrowing by a DIP will be permitted in bankruptcy. If a DIP must turn to formal financing under section 364, it occasionally seeks credit from lenders from whom it has never borrowed before or, at least, to whom it owes no current debt. However, a moment's reflection indicates why that will be an unusual event, especially at early stages of a bankruptcy. Creditors who do not have some powerful reason to do so are unlikely to regard debtors in bankruptcy as valued customers. What might a DIP offer to change this viewpoint?

The same is not necessarily true of a creditor who has already lent a large amount of money to the debtor prior to Chapter 11. In the economist's jargon, this creditor has large "sunk costs". The DIP can plausibly argue as follows: "If we liquidate the company today, you will receive far less than half of your loan. If, on the other hand, we overcome our present problems, we will not only be able to pay you 100 cents on the dollar, but interest at the prime rate plus. However, in order to get us through the stormy seas, we will need additional credit." Many creditors are persuaded by that argument or at least are unwilling to opt for the 50 cents per dollar today while they can instead hope for fuller recovery in the future.

Finally, in our examination of section 364, we should not overlook other sources of cash or credit that may be available to the lucky or clever debtor. In this and the past chapter we have seen a number of instances in which the debtor in effect forced the creditor to make a loan against the creditor's will. This is true in all cases in which the secured creditor is unable to have the stay lifted yet the court authorizes the use of cash collateral. When we consider Chapter 11 plans and Chapter 13 plans, we will see other instances in which the debtor is in effect able to force a creditor to make or continue a loan against its will.

Other sections of the Bankruptcy Code have the same consequence, though they may not be obvious to the student. Assume a debtor with a large unsecured debt on which it is obliged to pay $1,000,000 in interest per month. Upon filing a petition in bankruptcy the obligation to pay interest on unsecured debt is stayed. The funds previously used to pay the interest liability will be free cash available for use in the business. Do you see how section 502(b)(2) may free the debtor entirely from its interest liability?

A particularly perspicacious debtor may squirrel away some money in expectation of bankruptcy. This money is kept in a bank to which the debtor owes no debt, otherwise it would become cash collateral and subject to setoff.

Section 364 establishes a hierarchy of postpetition credit. Together with the case law, it makes possible at least six different levels of credit.

The most junior form of postpetition credit is one that no creditor seeks, but some creditors receive. This is postpetition credit sharing parity with the prepetition general creditors. Only a fool or a good friend would willingly extend credit to someone in bankruptcy with the understanding that he would share equally with the preexisting general creditors. Creditors in this position are mostly those who have extended credit believing it to be covered by section 364(a)(and so entitled to administrative expense treatment) only to find that it is not so. They may also have loaned under section 364(b)(nonordinary course) without giving the required notice. As we will see, these creditors are sometimes rudely sent to the purgatory of general creditors to punish them for their failure to comply with section 364.

The first level of credit explicitly contemplated by section 364 is that credit entitled to "priority" under section 503(b)(1) as an administrative expense. That is to say, the typical ordinary course credit in section 364(a) and the typical nonordinary course credit authorized after notice and a hearing under section 364(b) enjoys administrative expense priority; in any liquidation or in a confirmed plan it will be paid before the general creditors.

If the debtor is unable to obtain unsecured credit under (b), it can apply for credit under (c). Credit given under (c)(1) may be entitled to administrative expense "super" priority (i.e., administrative expense with a status higher than that of other administrative expenses). Alternatively, the creditor may receive a security interest in property that is unencumbered, or a junior security interest on property that is encumbered. Thus (c) provides two new levels of credit.

The most senior level of credit contemplated by section 364 is found in subsection (d). It may be granted only if no lenders are willing to lend under subsections (a), (b) or (c), and if adequate protection is given to other creditors whose interests will be subordinated by the new security. Under (d) the new credit can have a lien "senior or equal" to existing liens. This new credit truly enjoys "superpriority." As one might expect, the battles in (d) tend to be fought over the question whether there is adequate protection for the existing secured creditors whose interest will be subordinated to the new loan.

Section 364 does not specifically contemplate the final level of credit, the apotheosis of postpetition credit. This credit carries with it "cross-collateralization." In these cases the creditor bargains not only to have security for its new postpetition loan, but also to have its prepetition unsecured debt secured by the new collateral. This credit is different from all others under section 364 because it grants security not merely for new dollars put into the estate after the petition, but also for dollars loaned prior to the petition. Section 364 does not cover cross-collateralization and its status in the law is still uncertain.

Several general problems face the courts in deciding section 364 issues. Commonly a postpetition creditor with the debtor in possession in tow will argue for the most senior form of credit for which any case can be made under section 364. It will be up to the other creditors to show that the credit could have been obtained elsewhere at lesser cost. It is up to the judge to determine who speaks the truth. For example, secured credit may be granted under (c) only if the trustee is "unable to obtain unsecured credit" allowable under (b). How does one determine that the particular creditor who is now willing to lend under (c) or (d) would not have lent under (b)? How does one determine that there are others who will lend under (b) who are not in court? Usually, the creditor gives testimony and the debtor testifies about the many places it has applied for credit and has been rejected.

The trouble with the testimony of the creditor is that it is self-serving. If one were a creditor and were told by her lawyer that she could get security if she refused to lend without security and was then asked what she would wish to do, could she truthfully say that she would not lend without security? Indeed, she would be a fool to lend without security if merely by refusing to do so she could get such security. Thus, one should be suspicious of the creditor who is quite willing to lend under (d), but who is offended at the suggestion that it might become a lender unsecured under (b) or with only a junior lien under (c).

One might also be suspicious of the debtor's testimony that it sought credit in many places and was rejected. This brings to mind the motorist who dutifully procures three bids for accident repair from body shops, but manipulates them in such a way to insure that the body shop he wishes to use will be the one that is authorized by his insurance company. It will not be difficult for a debtor in possession to procure a handful of loan rejections. By hypothesis, as a debtor in Chapter 11, he is a pariah already and a whispered aside to the loan officer ("just turn me down, this is only pro forma anyway") may be enough to procure a denial.

One fears that the only way a judge is likely to get to the bottom of the question is by playing "chicken." Only by denying the motion for super-priority and observing the creditor will one test the truth of the parties' assertions. These are tough decisions for the courts to make, but given the structure of section 364, we think they are unavoidable.

IN RE ROBLIN INDUSTRIES, INC.

United States Bankruptcy Court, Western District of New York, 1985.
52 B.R. 241.

JOHN W. CREAHAN, BANKRUPTCY JUDGE.

On July 1, 1985, Roblin Industries, Inc., filed its petition for relief under Chapter 11 of the Bankruptcy Code. 11 U.S.C. Chapter 11. At the same time, applications were filed and orders entered with respect to several matters, mostly of a routine nature. Among these were orders approving the employment of attorneys and accountants and the payment of pre-petition wages to some four hundred employees. Also filed at that time was a motion for court approval of a stipulation entered into between the debtor and Marine Midland Bank, N.A., and Chemical Bank (Banks). The stipulation sets forth the terms and conditions under which the Banks will loan the debtor up to twelve million dollars ($12,000,000) during the reorganization proceedings.

Roblin Industries, Inc., is engaged in the production of specialty steel and related products. At the time it filed its Chapter 11 petition it was without funds to pay salaries and wages, to purchase inventory, and to cover other daily operating expenses. Papers in support of the motion for an interim financing order demonstrate Roblin's pressing need for immediate borrowing to obviate a disruption of its manufacturing operations. Counsel for the debtor submitted a proposed financing order in connection with its motion. After a hearing conducted on shortened telephone notice to the debtor's twenty largest creditors, an order was entered on July 2, 1985, authorizing the requested financing on an interim basis. The order provided that a further hearing would be conducted on August 6, 1985, on notice to all creditors and other parties in interest. It provided further that certain provisions of the stipulation would not be effective should the Court not continue the order following the final hearing on August 6, 1985. The order authorized the debtor to borrow from the Banks up to a maximum of $12,000,000 secured by a lien on all of the debtor's pre-petition and post-petition property subject to certain enumerated security interests which were acknowledged to be senior. Provisions also were made for super-priority status under section 364(c) of the Code [11 U.S.C. § 364(c)] and for cross-collateralization of pre-petition indebtedness.

For some years pre-petition Roblin has financed its operations not only with Marine and Chemical but also with Chase Manhattan Bank, N.A. Pursuant to that joint financing conducted under a series of agreements, the debtor's obligations as of June 24, 1985, amounted to $23,724,224.50. Under one of the agreements, the debtor had incurred debt of $7,371,912 for revolving credit. These obligations were secured by liens on all of the debtor's real and personal property, subject to certain senior interests mentioned in the order. Chase is not participating in the post-petition financing.

On August 6, 1985, the Court conducted the final hearing mandated by the order of July 2, 1985. Objections to the existence and continuation of the order of July 2, 1985, and to the stipulation dated July 1, 1985, were served and filed by United States Trust Company of New York (U.S. Trust). U.S. Trust is the indenture trustee of subordinated debentures held by approximately 400 persons. The objections were vigorously supported by counsel representing other unsecured creditors who appeared and actively participated in the hearing.

Specific objections are addressed to certain provisions of not only the order but also the stipulation. To the extent that the order approves the stipulation, its provisions are certainly relevant. To the extent that the objectionable provisions of the stipulation are not authorized by the Bankruptcy Code or by the Court, they do not bind the debtor's estate. *Compare* 11 U.S.C. § 549. (The section deals with transfers, not transactions in general.) The Court's duty here is not to dictate the terms of post-petition financing arrangements between the debtor and its lenders, but to deny its blessing of any transactions that are not appropriate.

WAIVER OF RIGHTS

Most repugnant to the objecting parties is provision numbered "2" of the stipulation which they characterize as a settlement of any and all controversies that may exist by virtue of pre-petition transactions between the debtor and its lenders, the Banks. Provision 2 states:

> 2. The Pre–Petition obligations are properly accelerated and demanded, the debtor waives any notice in connection therewith, and all such obligations are now due and payable and are not subject to any offset, claim, counterclaim or defense.

The Court is satisfied that the objection is well founded. While provision 2 is not effective under the terms of the July 2, 1985, interim financing order, it will become effective if the Court continues that order. The Banks argue that no sane financier will lend into a lawsuit and that such terms are common and are a part of the existing loan agreement. The Court cannot argue with the Banks' logic.

The commencement of the Chapter 11 case, however, in providing the debtor with an opportunity for financial relief, has also interdicted the rights of all those who have dealt with it in the past. We no longer have only the interests of the parties to a pre-petition credit agreement to consider. We now have a new entity "armed cap-a-pie with every right and power which is conferred by the law of the state upon its most favored creditor." *In re Waynesboro Motor Co.*, 60 F.2d 668, 669 (S.D.Miss.1932); cited in 4 Collier on Bankruptcy, ¶ 544.02 at 544–4, 544–5 (15th ed. 1985). See also, 11 U.S.C. § 1106. There are new intervening rights also provided for in the Code which are part of the quid pro quo. These legislatively created rights, available to a trustee or Code debtor, are intended to benefit all creditors. While U.S. Trust argues that approval of the stipulation would read section 510 out of Title 11, in the Court's view it would render useless any of the debtor's powers of avoidance. Furthermore, in the Court's view, if authorized it would bind any trustee who was appointed in the case.

As argued by counsel for U.S. Trust, the provision is in the nature of a settlement, which can only be approved on a proper showing. *In re Lion Capital Group*, 49 B.R. 163, 175 (Bankr.S.D.N.Y.1985). Additionally, a debtor in possession, like a trustee, is a fiduciary of each creditor of the estate. As such, it must exercise that measure of care that an ordinarily prudent person would exercise under similar circumstances. *In re Cochise College Park, Inc.*, 703 F.2d 1339, 1357 (9th Cir.1983); *Wolf v. Weinstein*, 372 U.S. 633, 650, 83 S.Ct. 969, 979, 10 L.Ed.2d 33, 47 (1963); *Ford Motor Credit Co. v. Weaver*, 680 F.2d 451, 461 (6th Cir.1982). A blanket waiver of unspecified rights in the early stages of a complex corporate reorganization would not appear to manifest prudent judgment.

Also objectionable to U.S. Trust is that provision which stipulates that "[t]he Banks hold a valid, duly perfected security interest in the Pre–Petition Collateral to secure the payment of the Pre–Petition Obligations." (Provision numbered "1".) Such a finding, whether by virtue of the stipulation or by reference to the multitude of voluminous documents submitted at the hearing, would be in the same nature as the waiver of defenses. To the extent that this is the purpose of the provision, it is inappropriate at this point without an opportunity for more comprehensive scrutiny by interested parties. It would be improper for the Court to make such a finding in the face of creditor objections. To adjudicate the validity, priority, or extent of a lien requires the commencement of an adversary proceeding. Rule 7001, Rules of Bankruptcy Procedure. On the basis of these two objections alone, the Court cannot give final approval to the stipulation.

CROSS-COLLATERALIZATION

Further provisions of the stipulation and/or order that U.S. Trust finds objectionable are those relating to cross-collateralization, the super-priority provided for in section 364(c), and the adequacy of the Banks' pre-petition collateral. U.S. Trust argues that before authorizing cross-collateralization, the Court must find inter alia that the proposed financing is in the best interest of creditors generally. In support, the creditor cites *In re Texlon Corp.*, 596 F.2d 1092 (2d Cir.1979) and *In re Vanguard Diversified, Inc.*, 31 B.R. 364, 366 (Bankr.E.D.N.Y.1983). At first blush, *Texlon* appears to stand for a more limited proposition. As the court states at 1098:

> In order to decide this case we are not obliged, however, to say that under no conceivable circumstances could "cross-collateralization" be authorized. Here it suffices to hold that, despite the absence from § 344 of the specific requirement of notice contained in § 116(2), see note 3 *supra*, a financing scheme so contrary to the spirit of the Bankruptcy Act should not have been granted by an *ex parte* order, where the bankruptcy court relies solely on representations by a debtor in possession that credit essential to the maintenance of operations is not otherwise obtainable.

The opinion goes on to state that a hearing may determine that other sources of financing are available, that other creditors might wish to share in the financing on similarly favorable terms, or that creditors would rather the case not continue at the price of preferring a particular lender. In *Vanguard,* Judge Parente extracts from *Texlon* and other sources some considerations useful in addressing the cross-collateralization issue. Judge Parente's suggestions make good sense. He suggests that if the debtor wishes to engage in this disfavored means of financing, it must demonstrate that:

(1) Absent the proposed financing, its business operations will not survive, see Weintraub & Resnick, *supra* at 90–91;

(2) It is unable to obtain alternative financing on acceptable terms, Weintraub & Resnick, *supra* at 90, see *In re Texlon, supra* at 1098;

(3) The proposed lender will not accede to less preferential terms; and

(4) The proposed financing is in the best interests of the general creditor body, see *In re Texlon Corp., supra* at 1098–99.

Vanguard at 366.

With respect to the first element, Mr. Roncalato, the debtor's vice-president and chief financial officer, testified that, absent the interim borrowing authorized by the July 2, 1985, order, the debtor would have to suspend operations. It was further evident from Mr. Roncalato's testimony and from papers filed in connection with the present motion that the debtor has for several years financed its daily operations in substantially the same manner now in effect under the interim order. While able to continue in business, it has not been able to meet all its obligations. Despite this ongoing financing, the debtor is in default for several years past of payments due under a pension plan arrangement for the benefit of some former employees. The Court is satisfied that, absent the proposed financing, the debtor will be unable to purchase inventory, meet its payroll, maintain its property, and continue in operation.

As to whether the debtor is able to obtain alternative financing, the state of the evidence is less than satisfactory. Over objection by counsel, the Court permitted hearsay testimony with respect to efforts by the debtor's principal to obtain alternative financing. In effect, the debtor was denied the opportunity to offer admissible evidence. However, the Court addresses the cross-collateralization objection, not because it is necessary to its decision, but because the parties are entitled to be apprised of the Court's viewpoint in the event they should hereafter modify the terms of their agreement. For present purposes, the Court is satisfied that admissible evidence is available to support this element should it be necessary in the future. It should be noted that no eager financier has rushed to succor the debtor, one of the prospects opined in *Texlon*, 596 F.2d at 1098.

Dennis Dombek, an officer of Chemical Bank, testified that he was involved in negotiating the terms of the financing in question. While he was not asked his reasons, he made the unadorned statement that the Banks were not willing to lend on any terms other than those proposed. Mr. Roncalato exhibited a sound knowledge of the debtor's financial condition. His inability to wax eloquent concerning "equitable subordination" and "domination and control" upon cross-examination has little bearing on his expertise in his own field. The Court is satisfied that he negotiated the best terms he could under the circumstances.

With respect to the final element of Judge Parente's test, that the financing be in the best interest of creditors, the Court has never been sure that creditors ever have all the information necessary to determine with certainty where their best interest lies. The general consensus to be drawn from the arguments of the several creditors' counsel present and supporting the objections of U.S. Trust is, as to be expected at this point, in support of the lending. It is the terms they object to. They seem to feel that the present arrangement will be continued on terms more favorable to the debtor and to themselves. Whether that assumption is warranted or not remains to be seen. The Court can only approve or disapprove the proposed arrangement. It cannot require the Banks to put additional funds at risk against their better judgment.

The Banks and debtor "believe" the pre-petition obligations are oversecured. U.S. Trust claims that in reality they are undersecured. If in fact they are undersecured, absent financing the debtor would in all likelihood shut down, liquidation would follow, and unsecured creditors would receive no distribution from the debtor's estate. As pointed out in the objections filed by U.S. Trust, the debtor is engaged in an industry convulsed by rising costs and declining markets. The liquidation value of a moribund steel plant is highly speculative. Western New York already has several such facilities. Bethlehem Steel's Lackawanna plant alone had at one time 21,000 employees. With the exception of two mills employing 1,500 people, the plant has remained idle for some years with no viable prospect for sale or reopening. Roblin's reorganization or its sale as a going concern is speculative at this point. An ongoing operation which maintains the value of plant and equipment at a level in excess of liquidation is in the best interest not only of the Banks but of all creditors. The provisions for cross-collateralization to permit that operation are not contrary to the spirit or intent of the Code.

SUPER-PRIORITY

The financing order provides that as part of their loan package the Banks shall be given a priority expense over any and all other expenses of the debtor that are provided for in sections 503(b) or 507(b) of the Code. 11 U.S.C. §§ 503(b), 507(b). This "super-priority" is provided for in section 364(c)(1) of the Code. However, creditors argue that to grant such a priority in effect would deny the creditors' committee the ability to retain quality professionals to carry forward an energetic review of the debtor's affairs because of the uncertainty of reimbursement from the debtor's estate. This very argument failed to impress the United States Court of Appeals for the Second Circuit in *In re Flagstaff Foodservice Corporation,* 739 F.2d 73 (2d Cir.1984). The bankruptcy court in *Flagstaff* had awarded to professionals who had served in the case interim compensation from post-petition assets subject to a lender's lien provided for in a financing order similar to that proposed here. The order also provided for the section 364(c)(1) super-priority. In reversing the award of compensation, the court recognized the problem which is raised here. It recognized the interplay between sections 364(c)(1), 503(b), 507(b), and 330, and stated:

> Looking to the plain language of these sections, as we are bound to do, *Caminetti v. United States,* 242 U.S. 470, 485, 37 S.Ct. 192, 194, 61 L.Ed. 442 (1917), we conclude that GECC's security interest has priority over appellees' claims for professional services, *In re Malaspina,* 30 B.R. 267, 270 (Bkrtcy.W.D.Pa.1983); 3 *Collier on Bankruptcy* ¶ 507.05, at 507–44 (15th ed. 1984). To the extent that *In re Callister,* 15 B.R. 521 (Bkrtcy.D.Utah 1981), *appeal dismissed,* 673 F.2d 305 (10th Cir.1982), relied upon by appellees, is to the contrary, we decline to follow it. Where, as here, the statutory language clearly expresses the congressional intent, a court may not read another meaning into the statute in order to arrive at a result which the court deems preferable. *Central Trust Co. v. Official*

Creditors' Committee of Geiger Enterprises, Inc., 454 U.S. 354, 359–60, 102 S.Ct. 695, 697–98, 70 L.Ed.2d 542 (1982); *In re Fidelity Mortgage Investors,* 690 F.2d 35, 39–40 (2d Cir.1982). Attorneys may, as Levin & Weintraub did here, secure a portion of their fee in advance. *See Matter of Arlan's Dep't. Stores, Inc.,* 615 F.2d 925, 935–37 (2d Cir.1979). If attorneys need more encouragement than this to participate in chapter 11 proceedings, *Congress, not the courts, must provide it.* Under the law as it presently exists, knowledgeable bankruptcy attorneys must be aware that the priority ordinarily given to administration expenses may "prove illusive in light of the various provisions in the Code for competing or super-priorities." 2 *Collier on Bankruptcy* ¶ 364.02, at 364–6 (15th ed. 1984). Section 364(c)(1) is such a provision. *Emphasis supplied.*

Id. at 75. Because counsel here comprehend the scenario in advance is no reason to deny to a proposed lender those safeguards provided by the legislature.

Indeed, in *Flagstaff* the court appears more concerned with the chilling effect a denial of those safeguards might have on potential reorganization financiers.

> Saddling unconsenting secured creditors with professional fees, such as are sought by appellees, would discourage those creditors from supporting debtors' reorganization efforts * * *. The Financing Order granting GECC a super-priority position was intended to give GECC protection against the very awards made herein. The lack of sufficient unencumbered assets to pay appellees' fees is not an adequate basis for denying GECC its super-priority status. *See Seaboard Nat. Bank v. Rogers Milk Products Co., supra,* 21 F.2d [414] at 417 [1927]. Although it has been well said that "professionals should not be expected to finance the administration of liquidation or reorganization cases," 2 *Collier on Bankruptcy* ¶ 331.01, at 331–3 (15th ed. 1984), "it does not follow that in the event the estate has no unencumbered funds from which to pay such expenses, the secured creditor becomes obligated to satisfy these obligations." *In re S & S Indus., Inc., supra,* 30 B.R. [395] at 399 [Bankr.E.D.Mich.1983].

Flagstaff, supra, 739 F.2d at 77.

More recently the Circuit has reiterated those concerns in another decision involving the same debtor. *See, In re Flagstaff Foodservice Corporation,* 762 F.2d 10, 13 (2d Cir.1985).

Lien Under Section 363(e)

The objection to the super-priority, to the value of the debtor's prepetition collateral, and to that provision of the order granting the Banks a lien on post-petition assets pursuant to section 363(e) as adequate protection for the debtor's use of certain pre-petition collateral, are all inextricably bound up with the issue of cross-collateralization. Also involved are those aforementioned substantive provisions of the Code.

[11 U.S.C. §§ 503(b), 507(b), 364(c), 330]. Although provided by Congress, they reflect competing considerations. Because they sometimes collide, it does not follow that they are offensive.

Specific provisions of the Code provide for each facet of the cross-collateralization issue. Post-petition advances may be secured not only by post-petition assets but by pre-petition assets as well as by a super-priority grant against otherwise unencumbered assets. 11 U.S.C. § 364(c)(1), (2), (3). Secured parties can be given a security position on post-petition assets as adequate protection for the use of collateral which secures pre-petition obligations. 11 U.S.C. §§ 361, 363(e). The harm to be perceived arises from the concern that the reorganization opportunity provided by the Code is not intended solely for the benefit of pre-petition secured lenders but for all creditors. If the effort is successful and a plan of reorganization is confirmed, no harm should result. If it fails, the result to be avoided is an improvement in the Banks' position such as was evident in *Texlon.* 596 F.2d at 1095. There liquidation of the post-petition assets fully satisfied the post-petition secured obligations and yielded an excess. The lender sought to have the excess applied to its pre-petition obligation. Although not in issue nor discussed in the opinion, the lender apparently sought to do so solely on the basis of the cross-collateralization provision. Evidently, no substantive showing was made in support of the lender's request. There was no claim that the lender had suffered a diminution in the value of its pre-petition collateral during the attempt to reorganize. In short, without a basis for entitlement, it was a windfall. That is the harm to be perceived. It creates an issue only if the reorganization effort fails. It will not arise if the effort is successful. It is an issue which is needless to attempt to resolve at this juncture. While the preamble of the stipulation (p. 3) does indicate that the parties believe the Banks are oversecured, it is not so stipulated, nor will the Court make that finding.

The Court does not seek to ignore the fact that with a continuation of the debtor's operation under the proposed arrangement, the Banks may well realize on pre-petition obligations to the extent of the value of the existing inventory and accounts valued by Mr. Roncalato at $6,899,-678 and $5,787,981 respectively. Presumably the initial inventory would be used up in the debtor's manufacturing operation. The ensuing product would convert to accounts. Under the credit agreement, the proceeds of this collateral would be collected by the debtor as agent for the Banks and credited to the pre-petition secured debt.

Other than to question the collectibility of all of these accounts, the creditors do not raise objection to this provision of the financing arrangement. New advances based on a formula percentage of inventory and receivables will be secured by all existing and future assets, one side of the cross-collateralization coin. The adequate protection lien under section 363(e), the reverse side of the cross-collateralization coin, is only necessary to protect the Banks to the extent that a diminution in value results from the debtor's use of (as the order recites at page 4) "certain of the Pre–Petition collateral." Presumably this includes all collateral other than inventory and accounts which under the proposal require no protection. Records may be maintained with respect to the inventory used and accounts collected post-petition. Such records and competent testimony with respect to the value of other collateral will establish the extent of the Banks' damages, if any, suffered during the course of the reorganization effort should it fail. There is no useful purpose to be served by a present adjudication of the over/undersecured position of the Banks' pre-petition loans at this time. To the extent indicated, the lien pursuant to section 363(e) would be appropriate and in accord with the substantive provisions of section 361.

* * *

Problem 5–7

Assume that Krier holds a $50,000 unsecured claim against Weiler Corp., a debtor in bankruptcy. As a condition for granting new credit of $100,000 at the prime rate of interest plus one percent, Krier demands (and Weiler agrees to) a lien on the Weiler factory securing the entire $150,000 debt. The funds provided by Krier will be used to pay employees for three months and to continue operations. Weiler has been losing money at a rate of $5,000 per month. Weiler has other secured and unsecured creditors. Weiler requests approval for the transaction.

1. Who will object, with what result? What result if the factory already secures a $55,000 debt of another creditor?

2. Instead of the foregoing proposal, Weiler proposed that Kamisar Bank will provide $150,000 cash to the company on condition that the funds will be secured by the factory. What result?

Notes

The cross-collateralization argument made in *Roblin* is merely another version of the argument, "I am so powerful that you must give me what I want even though it violates the spirit of the act." Is that so?

It is necessary to understand when cross collateralization occurs and when not. If the secured creditor who seeks "cross collateralization" was fully secured at the date of the petition, no issue exists. In this case the creditor is merely taking assets owned by the debtor at the time of the petition to secure subsequent loans, an event clearly permitted by section 364 and contemplated by the Code.

Assume, however, that a creditor has a $10,000,000 debt and $8,000,000 of collateral. The agreement provides merely that the security will continue so that a new loan of $2,000,000 and the existing loan of $10,000,000 will be commingled and that all of the collateral (assume it is inventory and accounts) will also be commingled. Can you see how over a period of time (and even though the company is not doing well) the relative priority of the parties will shift? Assume, for example, that our debtor, who would have suffered a $2,000,000 loss on liquidation, causes the business to be operated in such a way that the inventory and accounts are maximized at the expense of other assets or expenditures. Assume that the company goes into liquidation a year later at a time when the accounts and inventory are

$14,000,000 and the loans outstanding against them are $13,900,000. By virtue of a series of discrete transactions, none of which obviously violates the Code, a creditor, by his cross collateralization order, will have been paid his $2,000,000 prepetition debt or have received security for it.

In *Matter of Saybrook Mfg. Co.*, 963 F.2d 1490 (11th Cir.1992) the court explicitly rejected cross-collateralization. It held that cross-collateralization is not permitted under the Code. The principal creditor was owed $34,000,-000 secured by collateral worth approximately $10,000,000. It proposed a postpetition loan of $3,000,000 and the use of both prepetition and postpetition collateral to secure all of its loans.

Noting that no other court of appeals had explicitly ruled on the legitimacy of cross-collateralization, the court rested its rejection of cross-collateralization principally on two points. First, section 364, which deals extensively with postpetition credit, does not authorize cross-collateralization. The court seems to be saying that the silence of 364 should be construed as a congressional rejection of cross-collateralization. Second, the court concluded that granting cross-collateralization would violate the explicit priority rules set out in section 507. In effect, cross-collateralization could have lifted some or all of the creditor's $24,000,000 of prepetition unsecured debt from 726(a)(2) over the top of apparently prior claims described in 507 and given priority by 726(a)(1). Is *Saybrook* or *Roblin* better law?

Chapter Six

EXECUTORY CONTRACT: SECTION 365

§ 1. INTRODUCTION

What is an executory contract? Although the answer to that question is central to section 365, the Code does not define the term. The most frequently cited definition, that of Professor Countryman, defines an executory contract as one "that is so far unperformed on both sides that the failure of either party to complete his performance would be a material breach excusing future performance from the other party." Countryman, *Executory Contracts in Bankruptcy,* 57 Minn.L.Rev. 439 (1973). Even this definition is subject to debate.

Section 365 defines the debtor's rights concerning unexpired leases and executory contracts. In this chapter, we examine the large and undifferentiated body of problems that fall under section 365. Under this section, a trustee or DIP can either reject, assume and retain, or assume and assign a lease or executory contract.

The initial problem is deciding whether a contract is executory or not. Sometimes the problem is straightforward, as in distinguishing a secured sale from a lease, a problem familiar to students of commercial transactions. Section 1–201(37) of the Uniform Commercial Code tells how to distinguish a lease from a security agreement. At the other end of the definitional spectrum are issues involving licensing and franchising, where distinctions are much less clear. Here, the difficult issues have led to congressional amendments to section 365 which limit the debtor's right to reject licenses.

The next problem is deciding what to do once it is determined section 365 applies. In Chapter 7 cases there is a 60 day rule; leases and executory contracts not assumed within 60 days after the petition are deemed rejected (section 365(d)(1)). In Chapter 11 and Chapter 13, the same time limit applies for leases of non-residential property, but no time limit exists for other executory contracts, such as residential leases and personal property leases. These can be assumed or rejected at any time prior to the formulation of the plan. In a typical Chapter 11 bankruptcy, the creditor may be left in limbo for a considerable period. Congress created the exception for non-residential real property leases (section 365(d)(4)) in response to complaints from the commercial real estate industry.

The addition of section 365(d)(10) in 1994 mitigates the problem of personal property lessors. Under that provision, a trustee or a lessee debtor must perform the lessee's obligations that arise more than 60 days after the petition until it assumes or rejects. That requirement will doubtless hasten decisions to assume or reject by the trustee or debtor; in any case it may leave the lessor indifferent since the trustee will have to pay rent while he ponders his decision.

Rejection of an executory contract or lease under section 365 is a breach of that contract and entitles the creditor to a claim for damages. If the contract is not assumed, the time of the breach is deemed to be *prior* to the date of filing. This means that the claimant is treated as a prepetition general creditor and not as a postpetition administrative expense claimant.

Section 365 gives the trustee or DIP certain substantive rights not enjoyed outside of bankruptcy. Assumption represents a decision by the trustee to undertake both the rights and obligations of the contract. He may either perform, and receive reciprocal performance, or assign the contract. The trustee may even assume a contract or a lease on which the debtor defaulted prior to the bankruptcy, but the trustee must cure the default or give adequate assurances that it will be cured prior to the assumption. Note too that "ipso facto" clauses—clauses which say that a contract terminates ipso facto on bankruptcy—are rendered ineffective by section 365.

On the other hand, the trustee's substantive rights are limited in some respects. He may not evict tenants if the property involved is rental real property. The same limitation exists on timeshare property, land sales contracts, and intellectual property contracts. Collective bargaining agreements are subject to the special treatment provided in section 1113.

Certain executory contracts may not be assumed or assigned at all. Agreements terminating before the bankruptcy, loan commitments and other financing agreements are not assumable. Contracts not assignable under state law, such as personal service contracts, are not assignable in bankruptcy.

The cases under section 365 come in many different forms. In times of inflation debtors will seek to assume long-term leases and assign them to a third party in return for a substantial payment, and the landlords attempt to foreclose such an assignment in the hope of capturing the now inflated rental value for themselves. These recurring cases may involve a variety of the intricacies of section 365 as the landlord argues alternatively that his lease is not assignable either because it is not transferable under state law, because his variation of the ipso facto clause is not barred by section 365, because the lease in fact terminated before the bankruptcy, or because the debtor has failed to follow one of the rules contained in section 365 itself.

Quite different cases arise when the debtor is the lessor or is the licensor of a product. Here the debtor will attempt to reject the lease and thus recapture the benefits in order to sell the rights yet another time to a third party who will pay more. Some of this activity is explicitly prohibited by section 365. Analogous, but slightly different, are cases in which the debtor has bound himself to perform a personal service contract he now wishes to cancel (to sing for a rock band, for example, or not to compete with his former partners in the practice of medicine). One commentator, Mr. Andrew, would argue that these cases are like those discussed above and are beyond the reach of section 365.

Sometimes a creditor argues that his agreement is a lease under section 365 and not a security agreement to be dealt with elsewhere. A creditor makes this argument because the debtor will not be able to enjoy the benefit of the "lease" unless the debtor conforms to the letter of the lease contract. If, on the other hand, the lease turns out to be a security agreement, the debtor may be able to "cramdown" and so use the asset at a cost that is lower than agreed upon originally.

As we explore section 365, consider Mr. Andrew's contention that much of current case law and commentary on executory contracts is confused:

> I suggest that much of the jurisprudence of "rejection" is profoundly confused, and that the strikingly simple concept embodied in that term has been all but lost in the confusion * * * [R]ejection is not the revocation or repudiation or cancellation of a contract or lease, nor does it affect contract or lease liabilities. It is simply a bankruptcy estate's decision not to assume, because the contract or lease does not represent a favorable or appropriate investment of the estate's resources. Rejection does not change the substantive rights of the parties to the contract or lease, but merely means that the bankruptcy estate itself will not become a party to it. Simply put, the election to "assume or reject" is the election to assume or not to assume; "rejection" is the name for the latter alternative.

> Far from benign, the confusion over rejection has yielded wasteful litigation, absurd results, and dramatic distortions in bankruptcy law. Understanding that rejection does not affect contract liabilities demonstrates, for example, that litigation over whether rejection will be permitted is largely a pointless exercise. That understanding also makes clear that terminating rights in or to property arising under contracts that happen to be "executory" is fundamentally contrary to general bankruptcy principles, to the history and purpose of executory contracts doctrine itself, and to common sense. The most serious consequence of the confusion over rejection is that it has diverted attention away from important questions of bank-

ruptcy policy, focusing it instead on the generally meaningless question of what constitutes an "executory" contract.

Andrew, *Executory Contracts in Bankruptcy: Understanding "Rejection"*, 59 Colo.L.R. 845, 848–49 (1988).

Before we examine some of the more esoteric issues in section 365, consider the two following problems as a way of testing your knowledge of the basic role and operation of that section.

Problem 6–1

Pound Manufacturing produces health foods for the over-forty market. As part of its ordinary business, Pound maintains "all-risks" insurance with Jane Salisbury Assurance Corp. The insurance agreement calls for quarterly premiums of $95,000 and Salisbury agrees to reimburse Pound for any losses arising out of damages caused by Pound's products. Pound handles the defense of lawsuits, but has strict obligations to make Salisbury aware of all litigation and settlements. Various states prohibit companies like Pound from doing business unless they have insurance coverage. Pound is contemplating a Chapter 11 filing.

Pound consults you about the status of its insurance coverage in bankruptcy. Its recent claims have been very high and it suspects that Salisbury may be looking for a way to avoid the contract.

1. Can Pound continue to do business without the insurance in bankruptcy?

2. If Pound files bankruptcy but cannot pay the first quarterly payment due, what will happen?

Problem 6–2

Hesse Cab operates its taxicab company with an innovative computer system designed by Kant Corp. and leased to Hesse for six years at a rate of $480,000 per year. It has an option to purchase at the end of the term. Despite its superior technology, Kant has been losing money because it entered into contracts like that with Hesse before it realized that the cost of performing contracts like that with Hesse is much higher than it estimated. Kant files Chapter 11.

1. If Kant sends Hesse a letter stating that it plans to reject its lease, what can Hesse do to prevent this? Losing the computer will put it out of business. What rights would Hesse have if the lease were rejected?

2. Assume that Kant has no serious financial problems, but that Hesse files bankruptcy. It desires to retain the lease, but has no cash. When it filed, Hesse was two months in arrears on the $40,000 per month rent. How long can Hesse wait to assume the lease? If it waits two months and, having accumulated some cash, then seeks to assume the lease, what is Kant's best argument for denial of a right to assume? Does your answer change if the lease provided that it terminates automatically whenever a payment is not made?

§ 2. CHARACTERIZING THE CONTRACT

IN RE BOOTH

United States Bankruptcy Court, District of Utah, 1982.
19 B.R. 53.

Introduction and Factual Background

Ralph R. Mabey, Bankruptcy Judge. This case asks whether debtor, who is vendee under a contract for deed, has rights in an "executory contract" within the meaning of 11 U.S.C. Section 365.

Debtor is a debtor in possession under Chapter 11. He is a broker and dealer in real property. His schedules show land worth $2,641,550, most of which has been bought or sold on contracts for deed.

Lewis and Edris Calvert (sellers) made a contract to sell land to debtor at a price of $97,200, with $1,100 down, and the balance payable over time with interest. Sellers must convey title when debtor completes performance. They may forfeit his interest if he defaults. Debtor has resold the property, again using a contract, to a third party, John Collett.

Sellers moved for an order, pursuant to Section 365(d)(2), directing debtor to assume or reject their contract. Debtor demurred, arguing that the contract is not executory and that Section 365 is inapplicable. After denying the motion orally on the record, the court files this explanatory memorandum.

Executory Contracts and Bankruptcy Policy

Sellers point to the definition of executory contract formulated by Professor Countryman: "a contract under which the obligations of both the bankrupt and the other party to the contract are so far unperformed that the failure of either to complete performance would constitute a material breach excusing the performance of the other." Countryman, *Executory Contracts in Bankruptcy: Part I*, 57 Minn.L.Rev. 439, 460 (1973). This definition embraces the contract for deed, they maintain, because both sides have unperformed obligations, viz. payment by debtor and delivery of title by sellers. Failure of either to complete performance would constitute a material breach excusing the performance of the other.

Countryman propounded a definition of executory contract which was "functional," that is, "defined in the light of the purpose for which the trustee is given the option to assume or reject. Similar to his general power to abandon or accept other property, this is an option to be exercised when it will benefit the estate." Countryman, *supra* at 450. From this premise, he framed his test of performance due on both sides. If the creditor has performed, rejection would be meaningless, since "the estate has whatever benefit it can obtain * * * and * * * rejection would neither add to nor detract from the creditor's claim or the estate's liability." *Id.* at 451. Assumption likewise would be meaningless, and further, would transform the obligation of debtor into a cost of administration, "a prerogative which the Bankruptcy Act has never been supposed to have vested in either the trustee or the court." *Id.* at 452. If the debtor has performed, assumption adds nothing to his right to performance. Rejection, on the other hand, would not constitute a breach. In short, the Countryman test is an index to when assumption or rejection of a contract will "benefit the estate" and therefore of when a contract is executory.

Section 365, however, reflects a number of policies, including not only benefit to the estate but also protection of creditors. The Countryman test may often define the benefit to the estate, but does it always? And does it speak to the protection of creditors? *See* Julis, "Classifying Rights and Interests Under the Bankruptcy Code," 55 *Am.Bank.L.J.* 223 (1981). These questions underlie the refusal of the Commission to define executory contract, Report of the Commission on the Bankruptcy Laws of the United States, H.Doc. No. 93–137, Part I at 199 (1973)("any succinct statutory language risks an unintended omission or inclusion"), especially in relation to the contract for deed.

Sections 365(i) and 365(j), for example, give special treatment to nondebtor vendees of land sale contracts. They were passed in response to the plight of nondebtor vendees under former law. In *In re* New York Investors Mutual Group, 143 F.Supp. 51 (S.D.N.Y.1956); the debtor had contracted to sell land to a buyer for $105,000. There was a down payment of $15,000 with the balance due at closing in 18 months. Prior to closing, debtor was adjudicated bankrupt. The trustee sought and the referee ordered rejection of the contract with buyer. This order was affirmed on appeal. The court ruled that the interest of buyer was subject to rejection by the trustee and that the remedy of buyer "is a claim for damages for breach of the agreement." *Id.* at 54. Thus buyer, who under state law may have owned the land, was relegated to the status of an unsecured creditor. *New York Investors* was followed. E.g., Gulf Petroleum, S.A. v. Collazo, 316 F.2d 257 (1st Cir.1963); Matter of Philadelphia Penn Worsted Company, 278 F.2d 661 (3d Cir.1960). But there was uneasiness over its result, and some courts moved to soften its impact. E.g., *In re* Mercury Homes Development Co., 4 B.C.D. 837 (N.D.Cal.1978)(trustee may reject contract but cannot deprive vendee of interest in land).

Meanwhile, reformers sought change. The Commission spearheaded this movement and Sections 365(i) and 365(j) evolved from its report, *see* Report of the Commission on the Bankruptcy Laws of the United States, *supra* at Sections 4 602(d) and 4 602(f)(1), which in turn, was derived from a working paper, *see id.* at Part I, at 199 n. 114, at 206 n. 160, Part II, at 158 n. 17, at 172 173 n. 21, later published as Lacy, *Land Sale Contracts in Bankruptcy*, 21 U.C.L.A.L.Rev. 477 (1973).

The method for apportioning the benefits and burdens of insolvency, Lacy wrote, cannot be found through "definitions of 'executory' * * *. Instead, the search should be for a policy which defines those interests of present or potential value which may properly be taken from others for the benefit of the bankrupt or his estate." *Id.* at 482. Nondebtor vendees deserve special treatment, not because their contract is executory in the sense the performance remains due on both sides, but because "the purchaser in this kind of contract is likely to be the buyer of a home or farm or small business who has adjusted to a new location. Very often, especially in the case of a residential buyer, he will be poor. Certainly, modern American bankruptcy policy places as high a value on relieving the poor from the consequences of their own and others' improvidence as in doing perfect justice between creditors." *Id.* at 484.

He criticized the assumption that the purchaser whose contract is rejected after he has paid a part of the price will have only an unsecured "claim" but that "he may get the land if he has paid the entire price on the ground that the contract is no longer 'executory.' * * * The suggested distinction between paid-in-part and paid-in-full seems utterly capricious. Instead, one should not speculate about the meaning of 'executory' but rather should consider what ought to be thrown into the pot for general creditors and when it is fair to recognize special claims to certain assets." Lacy, *supra* at 487.

Others echoed Lacy. One, emphasizing the "economic consequences" of rejection, argued that the nondebtor vendee should not be "used as a resource by the trustee to increase the bankrupt's estate and the cost of the bankruptcy [should] be completely borne by commercial creditors. This would increase the creditors' incentive to deal only with sound vendors and would entirely remove this 'policing' function from the vendees, who occupy the poorest position to exercise such control. Moreover, the commercial creditors are capable of distributing the risks of a vendor's bankruptcy, but the vendees are not. The creditors can simply pass on the increased costs of vendor bankruptcy by raising the cost of credit. Most likely, the vendees would ultimately pay for most of this increase in the cost of credit. But they would be paying as a group, and therefore the risks of bankruptcy would be distributed evenly and rationally—rather than falling completely on a small and arbitrary group of vendees." Note, *Bankruptcy and the Land Sale Contract*, 23 Case Wes.Res.L.Rev. 393, 410–411 (1972).

Thus, Sections 365(i) and 365(j), far from representing the Countryman test, are a tonic for the consequence of its application. This suggests that in the final analysis, executory contracts are measured not by a mutuality of commitments but by the nature of the parties and the goals of reorganization. A debtor as vendee is free from the constraints of Section 365, and is thereby afforded flexibility in proposing a plan, but meanwhile must provide, upon request, adequate protection to vendors. A debtor, as vendor, may use Section 365 as a springboard to rehabilitation but not at the expense of vendees. *Cf. In re* Summit Land Co., 13 B.R. 310 (Bankr.D.Utah 1981). Thus, it is the consequences of applying Section 365 to a party, especially in terms of benefit to the estate and the protection of creditors, not the form of contract between vendor and vendee, which controls. This conclusion is supported by many statutory provisions and much judicial gloss.

EXECUTORY CONTRACTS AND THE POLICIES OF BENEFIT TO
THE ESTATE AND THE PROTECTION OF CREDITORS

The contract for deed, where debtor is vendee, benefits the estate more when viewed as a lien than as an executory contract. This is because treatment of the contract for deed as a lien enlarges the value of the estate and furthers the rehabilitation of the debtor. This treatment likewise makes adequate protection available to creditors.

1. Enlarging the Value of the Estate

The assumption or rejection of executory contracts, like the strong-arm and other avoiding powers, "is a valuable weapon ... in the armory of the trustee," meant to free "his estate to pay a larger dividend to general creditors." If the contract for deed is viewed as an executory contract, it may be assumed or rejected, but if assumed, it must be taken *cum onere,* that is, debtor must take the contract as written, with its benefits and burdens.

In practical terms this means that, absent assumption of the contract, vendor may enforce his remedy of forfeiture. Vendor, although in substance a mortgagee, may receive an advantage over other lienors, and the estate may be deprived of whatever equity exists in the property. The bankruptcy court, as a court of equity, regards substance over form, demands equality of treatment among creditors, and loathes a forfeiture. The contract should be treated as a lien; the vendor is thereby placed on a par with other lienors; forfeiture and the loss of equity are prevented.

This result is analogous to the treatment of security interest disguised as leases. The lessor is entitled to assumption and performance of the lease or rejection and return of the property, with any equity lost to the estate. The security interest disguised as a lease, however, is treated as a lien, with any equity available to the estate. *Cf.* Countryman, *supra* at 484–491; *In re* Scrap Disposal, Inc., 15 B.R. 296, 8 B.C.D. 504, 506 (9th Cir.BAP, 1981); *In re* Rojas, 10 B.R. 353 (9th Cir.BAP, 1981).

2. Furthering the Rehabilitation of the Debtor

Executory contracts should be handled to "assist in the debtor's rehabilitation." H.R.Rep. No. 95–595, 95th Cong., 1st Sess. 348 (1977), U.S.Code Cong. & Admin.News, p. 6304. If the contract is executory, and if it is assumed during the interim between petition and plan, defaults must be cured, damages must be paid, and adequate assurance of performance must be given, all as costs of administration. If the contract is assumed in a plan, the same conditions must be satisfied with the accumulated costs of administration payable on the effective date of the plan. The same burdens are imposed if the contract is assigned, in or without a plan. Indeed, one court has held that the stay does not prevent suits for payments which accrue postpetition as administrative claims. *See In re* Kors, Inc., 13 B.R. 683 (Bankr.D.Vt.1981).

If the contract is a lien, assumption is irrelevant, and no administrative costs are incurred. Instead of taking the contract *cum onere,* the lien may be "dealt with" in a plan, viz., by scaling down the debt, reducing the interest rate, and extending maturities. With or without a plan, the property may be sold free of the lien.

Debtor, like most dealers in the contract for deed, uses that instrument because other financing is unavailable. He can afford little down, and hopes to subdivide and resell in order to meet payments. Chapter 11 has not improved his cash flow. *Cf.* Countryman, *supra* at 484–491; *In re* Yale Express System, Inc., 384 F.2d 990, 992 (2d Cir.1967). Treating the contract as a lien thus allows more latitude in proposing a plan and thereby furthers the rehabilitation of the debtor * * *.

* * *

The Basis for Distinguishing Between Debtors as Vendors and as Vendees

Sellers contend that Sections 365(i) and 365(j) mean that contracts for deed are executory contracts. They argue that because Sections 365(i) and 365(j) treat some contracts for deed as executory contracts, all contracts for deed must be executory contracts. Put differently, it would be anomalous if contracts where the debtor sells realty are executory but contracts where the debtor buys realty are not. This would result in the contract between debtor and Collett being executory and the contract between debtor and sellers being nonexecutory although both are identical in form. Consistency in the treatment of contracts for deed, whether debtor is vendor or vendee, is necessary for a sensible construction of the Code.

Seller's argument founders, however, on at least two shoals. First, treatment of the contract for deed as an executory contract, where debtor is vendee, ignores the reasons for enacting Sections 365(i) and 365(j). They were passed to give nondebtor vendees the protection of mortgagors. Viewing the contract for deed as a lien, where debtor is vendee, therefore is consistent with the spirit of these provisions. Second, consistency in terminology, that is treating contracts for deed as executory contracts under Section 365 in every instance, favors nondebtor vendees over debtor vendees and debtor vendors over debtor vendees in bankruptcy. Particularized treatment of the contract for deed is necessary to avoid these consequences.

First. Sections 365(i) and 365(j), as discussed above, were enacted to prevent harm which had occurred under prior law to nondebtor vendees. They accomplish this purpose, where the vendee is in possession, by allowing him to stay, continue payments, and receive title. In short, he is treated as a mortgagor, an analogy frequently drawn by proponents of Sections 365(i) and 365(j). *See, e.g.,* Nambar, *Contracts in Bankruptcy* 152 (1977); Lacy, *supra* at 480 and 485; Note, *supra* at 397 and 410.

Countryman notes that mortgages are not executory contracts and "where the vendor of land is himself the purchase money mortgagee, including those cases where applicable nonbankruptcy law will treat the land sale contract as a mortgage, the situation seems no different." Countryman, *supra* at 472. Then what of a debtor as vendor in California where contracts for deed are deemed mortgages? Under the Countryman test this would not be an executory contract. But this interpretation would deprive homeowners of the protection either by sacrificing the symmetry of sellers' argument or by recognizing that vendees are seen as mortgagors under Section 365(i). What about the debtor as vendee? We can take Countryman at face value and call the contract a lien, bypassing Section 365, but it will still be the same piece of paper, which under different circumstances, mandates special treatment to nondebtor vendees under Section 365(i).

Second. Consistency in the characterization of the contract leads to disparity in the treatment of the parties for other reasons. Where debtor is vendor, vendees are protected at least with a lien for the amount paid on the contract under Section 365(j). But where debtor is vendee, he has no protection under Section 365(j). Absent cure and adequate assurance of performance, he stands to lose, through forfeiture, his equity in the property. Likewise, debtor as vendor, under some circumstances, may sell the property free of liens. Thus, unencumbered proceeds, or encumbered proceeds for which adequate protection is provided, may underwrite operations pending workout of a plan, or fund a plan. But debtor as vendee may have no similar option. He must find cash to cure and supply adequate assurance of performance before he may assume the contract. And assumption is a condition to assignment of the contract.

The upshot is that nondebtor vendees, by virtue of Sections 365(i) and 365(j), may receive more favorable treatment in bankruptcy than debtor vendees. And debtor vendors, because of other policies and provisions in the Code, may fare better than debtor vendees. It may be argued that this disparity in treatment is warranted because of the risk of default when debtor is vendor, or because the nondebtor, in each instance, is an innocent victim. But this argument admits that the reasons for calling a contract "executory" may have less to do with the terms of the "paper" than with the status of the parties and their interests in light of bankruptcy policies.

CONCLUSION

The court is reluctant to depart from a rule as workable as the Countryman test. But application of the rule in this case contradicts the reason for its existence. Classifying the contract for deed, where debtor is vendee, as a lien rather than an executory contract benefits the estate by enlarging the value of the estate and furthering the rehabilitation of the debtor. Sellers, as lienors, enjoy adequate protection. This is in harmony with the rationale for Sections 365(i) and 365(j). The blessings and burdens of reorganization are fairly distributed between creditors and the estate.

* * *

Note: Security Interest vs. Lease

Booth teaches the significance of achieving a particular characterization of a contract. The characterization battle, a prevalent theme throughout bankruptcy law, is well displayed in the interaction between the Bankruptcy Code and Article 9 of the Uniform Commercial Code (UCC). The characterization of a property interest as a security interest or a lease is often a critical issue outside bankruptcy as well.

If the claim against the debtor's property is determined to be a lease, the trustee may either assume or reject it. If it is rejected, the "lessor" gets its property back and has a claim for damages resulting from the rejection. If the trustee chooses to assume the lease, courts must "insure that the trustee's performance under the contract or lease gives the other contracting party the full benefit of his bargain." H.Rep. No. 595, 95th Cong. 1st Session 348, *reprinted in* 1978 U.S.Code Cong. & Ad.News 5963, 6304–05. Thus any default must be cured and any damages resulting from default must be paid. Once the lease has been assumed, all rental payments thereafter must be paid at the time and in the amount specified in the original agreement. See 365(d). Any default subsequent to assumption is treated as an administrative expense.

When the claim against the debtor's property is a security interest, the other contracting party's interest may be affected in very significant ways. If the creditor (lessor) has not filed or otherwise perfected its security interest, the trustee can avoid it under section 544, leaving the creditor (lessor) with nothing but an unsecured claim. Even if the lessor has been cautious and filed just in case its "lease" was ruled a security interest, the lessor (creditor) is vulnerable to modifications in its contractual terms that would not be permitted in a true lease. If the lease is truly a security agreement, the DIP may retain and use the collateral by giving the creditor adequate protection without ever being required to "assume" the "lease."

With the exception of a failure to perfect, the chief differences between the two classifications often manifest themselves in the terms of a reorganization plan confirmed pursuant to section 1129(a) and (b). A true lessor can demand full compliance with its lease or return of the property in a reorganization. In contrast, the creditor holding a security interest can demand only deferred payments with a present value equal to its secured claim plus treatment as an unsecured creditor for any deficiency.

The economic differences can be huge, but if the lease is actually a security agreement, sometimes the debtor and sometimes the creditor benefits. Suppose, for example, that IBM leases a computer to Microcode for five years for monthly payments of $25,000 under a lease which allows Microcode to purchase the computer at the end of the lease for $5,000. Microcode files under Chapter 11 after the first year of the lease.

Assume that Microcode desires to keep the computer. If the contract is a true lease, Microcode must assume the lease, cure any default and pay the full rent of $25,000 for the remainder of the lease ($1.2 million over four years). The value of the computer is irrelevant in deciding the monthly payments.

If the contract grants a security interest, on the other hand, the future rent is a debt owed to IBM and secured by the computer. In a reorganization plan Microcode must pay IBM deferred cash payments with a present value equal to the IBM secured claim (e.g., the lesser of the debt or the value of the collateral). For example, if the computer's value is $400,000, Microcode might pay sixty equal installments with a total of $400,000 plus interest at the current rate and deal with the remaining unsecured debt in the same way it will deal with other unsecured creditors. The monthly obligation is less than one-half the payment required by the lease. If, however, the computer is worth $1.2 million, IBM has a $900,000 secured claim and must receive no less than $900,000 plus interest over the sixty months. Of course, the debtor owns the computer.

For personal property leases, the classification issue usually depends on an application of state law. Versions of the Uniform Commercial Code prior to 1988 draw the difference largely in terms of whether the purported lease gives the lessee an option to purchase the property for nominal consideration or whether it requires payment of a greater purchase option price. See Boss, *"Leases and Sales Ne'er or Where Shall the Twain Meet?"* 1983 Ariz.St.L.J. 357.

Together with the new Article 2A of the UCC dealing with true leases the drafters proposed a new definition of security interest. The new section 1–201(37) directs one's attention to the basic question, did the "lessor" really retain any reversionary interest? If the answer to that question is no (either because the goods will be worn out during the lease term, because the lessee has an option at a very low price to acquire the asset, or for other reasons) then the contract is a security agreement and not a lease and is governed by Article 9, not by Article 2A. If, on the other hand, the lessor retains a significant economic stake in the asset, the opposite is true.

While litigation about classifying personal property leases is common in bankruptcy court, even more intriguing questions about what constitutes an executory contract arise in connection with other valuable contract rights. The following cases illustrate two of the most common sources of controversy over this classification issue. Consider how the court goes about determining the type of agreement and the consequences that flow from that determination.

LUBRIZOL ENTERPRISES, INC. v. RICHMOND METAL FINISHERS, INC.

United States Court of Appeals, Fourth Circuit, 1985.
756 F.2d 1043.

JAMES DICKSON PHILLIPS, CIRCUIT JUDGE:

I

In July of 1982, RMF entered into the contract with Lubrizol that granted Lubrizol a nonexclusive license to utilize a metal coating process technology owned by RMF. RMF owed the following duties to Lubrizol under the agreement: (1) to notify Lubrizol of any patent infringement suit and to defend in such suit; (2) to notify Lubrizol of any other use or licensing of the process, and to reduce royalty payments if a lower royalty rate agreement was reached with another licensee; and (3) to indemnify Lubrizol for losses arising out of any misrepresentation or breach of warranty by RMF. Lubrizol owed RMF reciprocal duties of accounting for and paying royalties for use of the process and of cancelling certain existing indebtedness. The contract provided that Lubrizol would defer use of the process until May 1, 1983, and in fact, Lubrizol has never used the RMF technology.

RMF filed a petition for bankruptcy pursuant to Chapter 11 of the Bankruptcy Code on August 16, 1983. As part of its plan to emerge from bankruptcy, RMF sought, pursuant to § 365(a), to reject the contract with Lubrizol in order to facilitate sale or licensing of the technology unhindered by restrictive provisions in the Lubrizol agreement. On RMF's motion for approval of the rejection, the bankruptcy court properly interpreted § 365 as requiring it to undertake a two-step inquiry to determine the propriety of rejection: first, whether the contract is executory; next, if so, whether its rejection would be advantageous to the bankrupt.

Making that inquiry, the bankruptcy court determined that both tests were satisfied and approved the rejection. But, as indicated, the district court then reversed that determination on the basis that neither test was satisfied and disallowed the rejection. This appeal followed.

II

We conclude initially that, as the bankruptcy court ruled, the technology licensing agreement in this case was an executory contract, within contemplation of 11 U.S.C. § 365(a). Under that provision a contract is executory if performance is due to some extent on both sides. *NLRB v. Bildisco and Bildisco,* 465 U.S. 513, 104 S.Ct. 1188, 1194 n. 6, 79 L.Ed.2d 482 (1984). This court has recently adopted Professor Countryman's more specific test for determining whether a contract is "executory" in the required sense. By that test, a contract is executory if the "'obligations of both the bankrupt and the other party to the contract are so far unperformed that the failure of either to complete the performance would constitute a material breach excusing the performance of the other.'" *Gloria Manufacturing Corp. v. International Ladies' Garment Workers' Union,* 734 F.2d 1020, 1022 (4th Cir.1984)(quoting Countryman, *Executory Contracts in Bankruptcy: Part I,* 57 Minn.L.Rev. 439, 460 (1973)). This issue is one of law that may be freely reviewed by successive courts.

Applying that test here, we conclude that the licensing agreement was at the critical time executory. RMF owed Lubrizol the continuing duties of notifying Lubrizol of further licensing of the process and of reducing Lubrizol's royalty rate to meet any more favorable rates granted to subsequent licensees. By their terms, RMF's obligations to give notice and to restrict its right to license its process at royalty rates it desired without lowering Lubrizol's royalty rate extended over the life of the agreement, and remained unperformed. Moreover, RMF owed Lubrizol additional contingent duties of notifying it of suits, defending suits and indemnifying it for certain losses.

The unperformed, continuing core obligations of notice and forbearance in licensing made the contract executory as to RMF. In *Fenix Cattle Co. v. Silver (In re Select–A–Seat Corp.)*, 625 F.2d 290, 292 (9th Cir.1980), the court found that an obligation of a debtor to refrain from selling software packages under an exclusive licensing agreement made a contract executory as to the debtor notwithstanding the continuing obligation was only one of forbearance. Although the license to Lubrizol was not exclusive, RMF owed the same type of unperformed continuing duty of forbearance arising out of the most favored licensee clause running in favor of Lubrizol. Breach of that duty would clearly constitute a material breach of the agreement.

Moreover, the contract was further executory as to RMF because of the contingent duties that RMF owed of giving notice of and defending infringement suits and of indemnifying Lubrizol for certain losses arising out of the use of the technology. Contingency of an obligation does not prevent its being executory under § 365. *See In re Smith Jones, Inc.*, 26 B.R. 289, 292 (Bankr.D.Minn.1982)(warranty obligations executory as to promisor); *In re O.P.M. Leasing Services, Inc.*, 23 B.R. 104, 117 (Bankr.S.D.N.Y.1982)(obligation to defend infringement suits makes contract executory as to promisor). Until the time has expired during which an event triggering a contingent duty may occur, the contingent obligation represents a continuing duty to stand ready to perform if the contingency occurs. A breach of that duty once it was triggered by the contingency (or presumably, by anticipatory repudiation) would have been material.

Because a contract is not executory within the meaning of § 365(a) unless it is executory as to both parties, it is also necessary to determine whether the licensing agreement was executory as to Lubrizol. *See Bildisco*, 465 U.S. at 517 n. 6, 104 S.Ct. at 1194 n. 6. We conclude that it was.

Lubrizol owed RMF the unperformed and continuing duty of accounting for and paying royalties for the life of the agreement. It is true that a contract is not executory as to a party simply because the party is obligated to make payments of money to the other party. *See Smith Jones*, 26 B.R. at 292; H.Rep. No. 95–595, 95th Cong., 2d Sess. 347, *reprinted in* 1978 U.S.Code Cong. & Ad.News 5787, 5963, 6303–04. Therefore, if Lubrizol had owed RMF nothing more than a duty to make fixed payments or cancel specified indebtedness under the agreement, the agreement would not be executory as to Lubrizol. However, the promise to account for and pay royalties required that Lubrizol deliver written quarterly sales reports and keep books of account subject to inspection by an independent Certified Public Accountant. This promise goes beyond a mere debt, or promise to pay money, and was at the critical time executory. *See Fenix Cattle,* 625 F.2d at 292. Additionally, subject to certain exceptions, Lubrizol was obligated to keep all license technology in confidence for a number of years.

Since the licensing agreement is executory as to each party, it is executory within the meaning of § 365(a), and the district court erred as a matter of law in reaching a contrary conclusion.*

III

There remains the question whether rejection of the executory contract would be advantageous to the bankrupt. *See Borman's, Inc. v. Allied Supermarkets, Inc.,* 706 F.2d 187, 189 (6th Cir.1983). Courts addressing that question must start with the proposition that the bankrupt's decision upon it is to be accorded the deference mandated by the sound business judgment rule as generally applied by courts to discretionary actions or decisions of corporate directors. *See Bildisco,* 465 U.S. at 518, 104 S.Ct. at 1195 (noting that the business judgment rule is the "traditional" test); *Group of Institutional Investors v. Chicago, Milwaukee, St. Paul & Pacific Railroad,* 318 U.S. 523, 550, 63 S.Ct. 727, 742, 87 L.Ed. 959 (1943)(applying business judgment rule to bankrupt's decision whether to affirm or reject lease); *Control Data Corp. v. Zelman (In re Minges),* 602 F.2d 38, 43 (2d Cir.1979)(applying *Institutional Investors* outside of railroad reorganizations); *Carey v. Mobil Oil Corp. (In re Tilco, Inc.),* 558 F.2d 1369, 1372–73 (10th Cir.1977)(applying *Institutional Investors* to rejection of gas contracts).

As generally formulated and applied in corporate litigation the rule is that courts should defer to—should not interfere with—decisions of corporate directors upon matters entrusted to their business judgment except upon a finding of bad faith or gross abuse of their "business discretion." *See, e.g., Lewis v. Anderson,* 615 F.2d 778, 782 (9th Cir.1979); *Polin v. Conductron Corp.,* 552 F.2d 797, 809 (8th Cir.1977). Transposed to the bankruptcy context, the rule as applied to a bankrupt's decision to reject an executory contract because of perceived business advantage requires that the decision be accepted by courts unless it is shown that the bankrupt's decision was one taken in bad faith or in gross abuse of the bankrupt's retained business discretion.

In bankruptcy litigation the issue is of course first presented for judicial determination when a debtor, having decided that rejection will be beneficial within contemplation of § 365(a), moves for approval of the rejection. The issue thereby presented for first instance judicial determination by the bankruptcy court is whether the decision of the debtor that rejection will be advantageous is so manifestly unreasonable that it could not be based on sound business judgment, but only on bad faith, or

---

*We disagree with the district court's characterization of the transaction as effectively a completed sale of property. If an analogy is to be made, licensing agreements are more similar to leases than to sales of property because of the limited nature of the interest conveyed. Congress expressly made leases subject to rejection under § 365 in order to "preclude any uncertainty as to whether a lease is an executory contract" under § 365. 2 *Collier on Bankruptcy* ¶ 365.02 (L. King 15th ed. 1984).

whim or caprice. That issue is one of fact to be decided as such by the bankruptcy court by the normal processes of fact adjudication. And the resulting fact determination by the bankruptcy court is perforce then reviewable up the line under the clearly erroneous standard. *See Minges*, 602 F.2d at 43; *see generally 1 Collier on Bankruptcy* ¶ 3.03(8)(b)(L. King 15th ed. 1984).

Here, the bankruptcy judge had before him evidence not rebutted by Lubrizol that the metal coating process subject to the licensing agreement is RMF's principal asset and that sale or licensing of the technology represented the primary potential source of funds by which RMF might emerge from bankruptcy. The testimony of RMF's president, also factually uncontested by Lubrizol, indicated that sale or further licensing of the technology would be facilitated by stripping Lubrizol of its rights in the process and that, correspondingly, continued obligation to Lubrizol under the agreement would hinder RMF's capability to sell or license the technology on more advantageous terms to other potential licensees. On the basis of this evidence the bankruptcy court determined that the debtor's decision to reject was based upon sound business judgment and approved it.

On appeal the district court simply found to the contrary that the debtor's decision to reject did not represent a sound business judgment. The district court's determination rested essentially on two grounds: that RMF's purely contingent obligations under the agreement were not sufficiently onerous that relief from them would constitute a substantial benefit to RMF; and that because rejection could not deprive Lubrizol of all its rights to the technology, rejection could not reasonably be found beneficial. We conclude that in both of these respects the district court's factual findings, at odds with those of the bankruptcy court, were clearly erroneous and cannot stand.

A

In finding that the debtor's contingent obligations were not sufficiently onerous that relief from them would be beneficial, the district court could only have been substituting its business judgment for that of the debtor. There is nothing in the record from which it could be concluded that the debtor's decision on that point could not have been reached by the exercise of sound (though possibly faulty) business judgment in the normal process of evaluating alternative courses of action. If that could not be concluded, then the business judgment rule required that the debtor's factual evaluation be accepted by the court, as it had been by the bankruptcy court. *See Schein v. Caesar's World, Inc.*, 491 F.2d 17, 20 (5th Cir.1974).

B

On the second point, we can only conclude that the district court was under a misapprehension of controlling law in thinking that by rejecting the agreement the debtor could not deprive Lubrizol of all rights to the process. Under 11 U.S.C. § 365(g), Lubrizol would be entitled to treat rejection as a breach and seek a money damages remedy; however, it could not seek to retain its contract rights in the technology by specific performance even if that remedy would ordinarily be available upon breach of this type of contract. *See In re Waldron,* 36 B.R. 633, 642 n. 4 (Bankr.S.D.Fla.1984). Even though § 365(g) treats rejection as a breach, the legislative history of § 365(g) makes clear that the purpose of the provision is to provide only a damages remedy for the non-bankrupt party. H.Rep. No. 95–595, 95th Cong., 2d Sess. 349, *reprinted in* 1978 U.S.Code Cong. & Ad.News 5963, 6305. For the same reason, Lubrizol cannot rely on provisions within its agreement with RMF for continued use of the technology by Lubrizol upon breach by RMF. Here again, the statutory "breach" contemplated by § 365(g) controls, and provides only a money damages remedy for the non-bankrupt party. Allowing specific performance would obviously undercut the core purpose of rejection under § 365(a), and that consequence cannot therefore be read into congressional intent.

IV

Lubrizol strongly urges upon us policy concerns in support of the district court's refusal to defer to the debtor's decision to reject or, preliminarily, to treat the contract as executory for § 365(a) purposes. We understand the concerns, but think they cannot control decision here.

It cannot be gainsaid that allowing rejection of such contracts as executory imposes serious burdens upon contracting parties such as Lubrizol. Nor can it be doubted that allowing rejection in this and comparable cases could have a general chilling effect upon the willingness of such parties to contract at all with businesses in possible financial difficulty. But under bankruptcy law such equitable considerations may not be indulged by courts in respect of the type of contract here in issue. Congress has plainly provided for the rejection of executory contracts, notwithstanding the obvious adverse consequences for contracting parties thereby made inevitable. Awareness by Congress of those consequences is indeed specifically reflected in the special treatment accorded to union members under collective bargaining contracts, *see Bildisco,* 465 U.S. at 517–520, 104 S.Ct. at 1193–96, and to lessees of real property, *see* 11 U.S.C. § 365(h). But no comparable special treatment is provided for technology licensees such as Lubrizol. They share the general hazards created by § 365 for all business entities dealing with potential bankrupts in the respects at issue here.

The judgment of the district court is reversed and the case is remanded for entry of judgment in conformity with that entered by the bankruptcy court.

REVERSED AND REMANDED.

Notes and Questions

Consider Mr. Andrew's view of *Lubrizol.*

The use of avoiding-power rejection has not been limited to the termination of rights to real property. Recently, its most notorious use has been the cancellation of interests of licensees and franchisees of intangible personal property, such as patents, copyrights, trade secrets and the like, in bankruptcy cases of licensors or franchisors. Precisely the same two-asset issue arises here as in the case of leases and sales contracts: The debtor-licensor or debtor-franchisor has rights in the license or franchise agreement, and also has residual rights in the underlying asset, the intangible property.

Does rejection of the agreement terminate the non-debtor party's right to the licensed or franchised use of the underlying asset? Because the estate succeeds only to the debtor's rights in that asset, the answer should be no. Rejection is not a rescission of the license or franchise, but merely the estate's determination not to assume it. Thus, so long as the license or franchise is not otherwise avoidable, the estate should be in the same position as any other non-assuming transferee of the debtor's rights in the asset.

The case that illustrates perhaps better than any other what is wrong with avoiding-power rejection, and how the Countryman test of an "executory" contract fuels it, is the Fourth Circuit's decision in *Lubrizol Enterprises Inc. v. Richmond Metal Finishers, Inc.* There the debtor had licensed certain technology to Lubrizol non-exclusively, and sought in its chapter 11 case to reject the license and terminate Lubrizol's rights to the technology. The key issue, thought the court, was the hunt for mutual "executoriness."

Addressing first the debtor-licensor's side of the agreement, the court found executory aspects in the "continuing duties of notifying Lubrizol of further licensing of the process and of reducing Lubrizol's royalty rate to meet any more favorable rates granted to subsequent licensees." In addition, the debtor had the "additional contingent duties of notifying [Lubrizol] of suits, defending suits and indemnifying it for certain losses."

The "executoriness" of Lubrizol's side of the arrangement was more difficult, because the court thought the mutual performance test required remaining duties other than merely the payment of money. But the necessary "executory" obligations were found, as the court explained in this remarkable passage:

> [I]f Lubrizol had owed [the debtor] nothing more than a duty to make fixed payments or cancel specified indebtedness under the agreement, the agreement would not be executory as to Lubrizol. However, the promise to account for and pay royalties *required that Lubrizol deliver written quarterly sales reports and keep books of account subject to inspection by an independent Certified Public Accountant.* This promise goes beyond a mere debt, or promise to pay money, and was at the critical time executory.

The court went on to approve rejection of the license and termination of the licensee's interest, relying in part on the absence of any special protection for licensees in section 365.

The passage just quoted is one of the most noteworthy in the annals of avoiding-power rejection. Lubrizol had what everyone apparently believed was a perfectly valid license. Nothing suggests that the license was in any way subject to termination by any creditor of, or purchaser from, the debtor under non-bankruptcy law, or that it was in any other way avoidable under bankruptcy law. It also seems quite clear that if the license had been found to have been non-"executory," the court would have enforced it. *Lubrizol lost its right to the technology because it had the duty to "deliver written quarterly sales reports and keep books of account subject to inspection."*

The court did not pause to ask why the happenstance of "executoriness" should control an issue so important as the licensee's continued ability to use the technology. Its only real attempt at an explanation of the result was to observe that the "clear" purpose of section 365(g), the rejection-as-breach rule, "is to provide only a damages remedy for the non-bankrupt party," a point to which I return below. Other courts similarly have applied avoiding-power rejection in this context, although uneasiness with the result again has suggested to some the need for "balancing" or "good faith" tests.

Concern with the *Lubrizol* result also led in 1987 to the introduction in Congress of the "Intellectual Property Bankruptcy Protection Act" by Senator Dennis DeConcini. He criticized the "technical dissection of intellectual property licensing agreements" which led to "situations where a completed transaction involving intellectual property is really nothing more than a promise that can be broken." He thus proposed to "deny bankrupt licensors the ability to deprive licensees of irreplaceable intellectual property" by providing "protections similar to those offered in real estate sales agreements and leases." Andrew, *Executory Contracts in Bankruptcy: Understanding "Rejection"*, 59 Colo.L.R. 845, 916–919 (1988).

1. See section 365(n).

2. Is Andrew right?

Notes and Questions

Many of the ways in which debtors use section 365 are not merely to escape onerous and unprofitable obligations, but rather to divert assets to other, arguably more efficient, ends and, most important, to keep the entire efficiency gain for themselves and to deprive the prior contracting party of it.

Within this group would be at least the following cases:

1. Debtor has agreed to sell oil at $15 a barrel; it can now be sold at $25 a barrel. Can the seller abandon the contract, resell at the higher price and satisfy the original party's damage claim at less than one hundred cents on the dollar?

2. What about a singer who has made an improvident contract and can now sell his voice and work at a much higher price than that for which he previously contracted? What of an incorporated rock band that seeks to achieve the same result?

In a sense all of those are engaging in "avoidance behavior." Would Mr. Andrew argue that none of them be permitted to use section 365? If he would not argue that, how does one draw the line between those cases and the ones that he does contemplate?

Problem 6–3

You are a bankruptcy practitioner in Beverly Hills. J.J. Rousseau, a newly recognized rock star, comes to you with his problem. He tells you that the commercial success of a rock star is generally short lived and that the income of rock stars is likely to rise meteorically and descend with equal speed. Last year, before his newfound popularity, he signed a contract with Locke Recording Studio. For $40,000 per year Rousseau granted L.R.S. the right to all the royalties on his records and to the revenues from a variety of public appearances he plans to make. Due to an unforeseen improvement in his status among rock fans, Rousseau estimates that annually for the next two years he will be able to earn in excess of one million dollars in royalties and appearance fees which will now go to L.R.S. under the contract. He has sought to renegotiate his contract with the studio but it has declined all his requests. The contract runs for three years but Rousseau is fearful that the bloom will be off his success by the end of three years and he wishes to enjoy the fruits of his current success. His total assets amount to less than one hundred thousand dollars and consist of a car, some musical instruments, and a few small pieces of real estate. What do you suggest?

Consider the case that follows.

IN THE MATTER OF JAMES TAYLOR

United States Court of Appeals, Third Circuit, 1990.
913 F.2d 102.

FULLAM, DISTRICT JUDGE.

James Taylor, as debtor-in-possession in this Chapter 11 bankruptcy proceeding, sought the bankruptcy court's approval of his decision to reject certain executory contracts, including a music-publishing agreement dated November 13, 1985, between the debtor and the appellant, Delightful Music, Ltd. The latter objected, moved to dismiss the bankruptcy petition, and requested the court to abstain from ruling on the rejection request.

The Bankruptcy Court granted permission to reject the executory contract, and refused to dismiss the bankruptcy petition or abstain. The district court upheld these rulings, *In re Taylor,* 103 B.R. 511 (D.N.J. 1989), and Delightful now appeals.

Under 28 U.S.C. § 158(d), this court has jurisdiction to review "final" orders. In the bankruptcy context, finality is accorded a somewhat flexible, pragmatic definition, *see, In re Comer,* 716 F.2d 168, 171 (3d Cir.1983). The order approving rejection of appellant's contracts fully and finally resolved a discrete set of issues, leaving no related issues for later determination; we conclude that that order is final and appealable for purposes of § 158(d) and 28 U.S.C. § 1291. *See generally, Century Glove v. First Amer. Bank of N.Y.,* 860 F.2d 94, 97–99 (3d Cir.1988). The order refusing to dismiss the bankruptcy petition is likewise appealable, *In the Matter of Christian,* 804 F.2d 46 (3d Cir.

1986).[1]

This appeal presents an issue which has not previously been addressed in any reported appellate decision, namely, whether executory contracts for the personal services of the debtor may be rejected under § 365 of the Bankruptcy Code. Appellant argues that personal-service contracts are not, and cannot become, part of the estate being dealt with in the bankruptcy court, and therefore cannot be rejected or otherwise affected in a Chapter 11 proceeding. Alternatively, appellant argues that rejection should not have been permitted in this case because it was not sought in good faith and would not benefit the estate. A final argument is that the bankruptcy petition should have been dismissed because the debtor was not insolvent at the time the petition was filed, and lacked a genuine reorganization purpose, and because the petition was not filed in good faith.

I. FACTUAL BACKGROUND

James Taylor is a well-known professional musician and entertainer. From 1979 until mid-February 1988, he served as the lead singer and principal songwriter in a group known as "Kool and the Gang" ("The Group").

The services of The Group were furnished pursuant to various contracts arranged through "furnishing companies"—corporate entities in which various members of The Group held ownership interests. Thus, Quintet Associates, Ltd. was a corporation formed by the members of The Group to handle its recording contracts. Fresh Start Music, Inc. handled The Group's musical publishing business. A third corporation, variously known as Road Gang Enterprises, Inc. and/or Road Gang Associates, Ltd., arranged The Group's concerts and tours.

Until 1985, Quintet contracted to provide The Group's exclusive recording services to DeLite Recorded Sound Corp., and the individual members of The Group were required to furnish their recording services to Quintet so that Quintet could fulfill its contractual obligations to DeLite. In 1985, DeLite assigned its rights to Polygram Records, Inc., which entered into a new agreement with Quintet. Mr. Taylor and the other individual members of The Group executed "inducement letters" assenting to these arrangements. Concomitantly, Quintet entered into a music-publishing agreement with the appellant, Delightful Music, Ltd., which was a corporate affiliate of DeLite. This arrangement, too, was sanctioned by "inducement letters" executed by Mr. Taylor and other members of The Group.

In November 1986, similar arrangements were concluded between Fresh Start and Polygram for the services of Group members as songwriters; by this agreement, Polygram was required to pay royalties for songs written by Group members but not recorded by The Group.

---

1. But the order denying the motion to abstain is, by the express terms of the statute, not appealable. 11 U.S.C. § 305(c). Insofar as the appellant challenges the abstention decision, the appeal will be dismissed.

In consequence of these contractual arrangements, appellant obtained the exclusive worldwide copyrights in all of the musical compositions of The Group, and of Mr. Taylor as a principal writer for The Group. Appellant was obliged to secure and protect copyrights, make master recordings and other audio-visual reproductions of The Group's compositions, print, publish and sell sheet music of The Group's compositions, market these products and issue licenses, and collect performance fees. And Mr. Taylor was contractually obligated to compose and perform, as a principal member of The Group, musical compositions sufficient to produce at least eight record albums (subject to various options). In the event Mr. Taylor should terminate his membership in The Group, he would remain personally liable to fulfill his remaining obligations as a solo artist—*i.e.*, to compose and perform enough musical compositions to produce the required minimum number of albums—under a "leaving member clause" in the pertinent agreements.

Upon completion of a February 1988 tour of The Group, Mr. Taylor left The Group to pursue a solo career. The bankruptcy petition was filed on May 23, 1988. At that time, only one album had been released.

Beginning at least as early as 1985, The Group and its various related corporate entities experienced financial difficulties, apparently due in large part to life-styles involving unduly lavish expenditures, in excess of the substantial income generated by their performances. They borrowed money, from banks, their agent, and their pension funds, and these advances were secured by assignments of future revenues under the recording agreements, as well as by the personal guarantees of The Group members, including Mr. Taylor.

When the bankruptcy petition was filed, Mr. Taylor was in the following unenviable position: he was owed substantial amounts by Group entities, but with virtually no prospect of payment; he was contractually obliged to write and perform enough musical compositions to provide at least seven additional albums, but any revenues these efforts might generate would be retained by The Group's creditors; and he had personally guaranteed the obligations of The Group and its related entities in amounts greatly in excess of the remaining equity in his home, which was his only significant asset.

II. Dismissal of the Bankruptcy Petition

If the bankruptcy court and district court erred in refusing to dismiss the bankruptcy proceeding in its entirety, the issue of contract-rejection would be moot. We therefore first address the dismissal question.

In affirming the bankruptcy court's refusal to dismiss the petition, the district court found that the "debtor's current financial condition justifies the filing of a voluntary petition in bankruptcy". *Taylor,* 103 B.R. at 521. The court noted that the bankruptcy petition lists liabilities totaling $4,518,701.50 ($2,530,730 secured, $1,987,969.50 unsecured), and assets totaling only $734,215. The court further concluded that appellant had not established that the petition was filed in bad faith.

We review the factual component of these findings under the clearly erroneous standard, and the legal component *de novo*.

Appellant contends that, if the personal liabilities of the debtor had not been improperly confused with the debts of the various Group entities, and if the debtor's personal liabilities had been properly evaluated to reflect their contingent nature, the debtor's financial picture would not be nearly bleak enough to warrant filing for bankruptcy; in addition, appellant argues, *inter alia,* that many of the listed liabilities are not enforceable against the debtor for various reasons; that the debtor was merely an accommodation-maker, whose liability was extinguished by the acts of the other parties; and that the debtor's obligations had been canceled by virtue of novations or settlement agreements. We reject these arguments.

Even if debtor's contingent liabilities (approximately $1.2 million in amount) were disregarded, his debts would greatly exceed his assets.[2] Moreover, appellant's argument rests upon an unduly optimistic view as to the remoteness of the contingency. The district court expressly found that the debtor was not a mere accommodation party—he was, after all, personally guaranteeing repayment of loans to Group entities (owned by The Group members) for the direct benefit of the members of The Group, himself included. Whether a novation occurred as to certain of these guaranty transactions depends upon the intent of the parties. This is a factual question, and the findings set forth in the record are not clearly erroneous.[3]

In short, we conclude that the order appealed from, to the extent appellant's motion to dismiss the bankruptcy proceeding was denied, must be affirmed.

III. REJECTION OF EXECUTORY CONTRACTS FOR PERSONAL SERVICES

As set forth in § 1107, a debtor-in-possession in a Chapter 11 proceeding has the same powers with respect to executory contracts as a trustee. And 11 U.S.C. § 365 provides as follows:

> "(a) Except as provided [in subsection (c) of this section], the trustee, subject to the court's approval, may assume or reject any executory contract or unexpired lease of the debtor.
>
> "* * *
>
> "(c) The trustee may not assume or assign any executory contract or unexpired lease of the debtor * * * if—
>
> "(1)(A) applicable law excuses a party, other than the Debtor, to such contract or lease from accepting performance from or rendering

---

2. Of course, if later facts adduced before the bankruptcy court present a different financial picture, the statute permits the court to reconsider the appropriateness of dismissal. *See* 11 U.S.C. § 305(a).

3. The assertion that the debtor lacked a true intent to reorganize is not borne out by the record. Presumably a proposed plan of reorganization will emerge in due course, or the alternatives of dismissal or conversion resorted to. No issue of undue delay is presented at this stage.

performance to an entity other than the debtor or the debtor in possession * * * and

"(B) such party does not consent to such assumption or assignment."

It is clear that contracts for personal services fall within (c)(1)(A), since "applicable law" excuses the parties from accepting performance from, or rendering performance to, non-signatories.

Thus, § 365(a) permits a trustee to *assume or reject* any executory contract, but § 365(c) adds the limitation that a trustee may not *assume or assign* an executory contract for personal services unless the parties consent.

On its face, the statute places no restrictions on a trustee's right to reject a personal services contract. This is not in the least surprising, since, as we read the statute, it implicitly provides that any executory contract which is not assumed—either in the course of the proceedings, or in the reorganization plan approved by the court—is automatically rejected. See 11 U.S.C. § 365(g)(1).

Appellant argues that this straightforward reading of the plain language of § 365 is inappropriate, because it does not take into account other provisions of the Bankruptcy Code, most notably § 541(a)(6) which, in defining "property of the estate," makes clear that the proceeds of the debtor's post-petition personal services are excluded from the estate. Since an executory contract for the debtor's personal services is not part of the estate, the argument continues, such a contract is not within the "jurisdiction" of the trustee, and the trustee simply has no power to deal with such a contract. This line of argument rests upon some fundamental misconceptions.

To the extent that money is due the debtor for pre-petition services under a personal services contract, the debtor's claim for those sums is undoubtedly an asset of the estate which passes to the trustee/debtor-in-possession. And this is so regardless of whether the trustee later affirms or rejects the contract. Stated otherwise, the issue of affirmance or rejection relates only to those aspects of the contract which remained unfulfilled as of the date the petition was filed. It serves no useful purpose to speak generally about whether "the contract" becomes part of "the estate". The real question is the status of the reciprocal rights and obligations of the contracting parties arising after the petition was filed. As to these, the "assume or reject" dichotomy means simply that if the trustee wishes to obtain for the estate the future benefits of the executory portion of the contract, the trustee must also assume the burdens of that contract, as an expense of bankruptcy administration (*i.e.,* having priority over all pre-bankruptcy claims of creditors).

It is simply a *non sequitur* to suggest that a trustee may not reject an executory contract because it is not property of the estate. It is the trustee's decision (whether to assume or reject) that determines whether the benefits of an executory contract will or will not become property of the estate. And that decision is obviously within the power ("jurisdiction") of the trustee.

Personal services contracts differ from other executory contracts only in that the consent of the parties is required before the trustee has authority to assume them—a qualification which reflects the peculiar nature of such contracts and the widespread distaste for involuntary servitude. On the other hand, the trustee's authority to reject extends to all executory contracts—including personal-services contracts.

When an executory contract is not assumed (is rejected), 11 U.S.C. § 365(g) provides:

> "(g) * * * The rejection of an executory contract * * * constitutes a breach of such contract * * *

> "(1) if such contract or lease has not been assumed under this section or under a plan confirmed under Chapter 9, 11 or 13 of this title, immediately before the date of the filing of the petition * * *."

Appellant has a claim against the debtor's estate for whatever damages the rejection/breach has occasioned. This claim, like the claims of other creditors, will have to be dealt with in the reorganization plan.

The parties' research has uncovered only two reported decisions directly pertinent to this appeal. In *In re Noonan,* 17 B.R. 793 (Bankr. S.D.N.Y.1982), the court permitted the trustee to reject an executory personal-services contract in a Chapter 11 proceeding which had been voluntarily converted to a Chapter 7. In *In re Carrere,* 64 B.R. 156 (Bankr.C.D.Cal.1986), the court ruled that a debtor in possession or trustee has no "standing" to reject a personal services executory contract (since the "trustee has no interest in the contract, he has no standing to act at all under § 365", 64 B.R. at 159). In *Carrere,* a TV actress contractually committed to perform in a daytime serial program was offered a more lucrative role on another program, and the court found that the sole purpose in filing for bankruptcy was to enable her to reject her existing contract and accept the new offer, in order to improve her financial position—a purpose not compatible with the true aim of the bankruptcy law. It seems probable that the principal basis for the court's decision was its conclusion that the bankruptcy proceeding itself might well have been dismissed. At any rate, for the reasons already discussed, we reject the notion that a trustee lacks power to deal with personal-service contracts.

The remaining issue is whether this particular executory contract was properly rejected. Since we are dealing with a personal-services contract which could not be assumed without the parties' consent, and which would therefore, sooner or later, be deemed rejected in the absence of such consent, the debtor-in-possession was confronted with an extremely limited choice: he could reject the contract, or he could defer decision pending formulation of a plan of reorganization—in case the parties might change their minds and consent to assumption of the contract in the plan itself. In these circumstances, the traditional "business judgment" test of benefit to the estate, *see, Sharon Steel Corp. v. National Fuel Gas Distrib. Corp.*, 872 F.2d 36, 39–40 (3d Cir.1989) has only limited application. We have no hesitation in concluding that no useful purpose would have been served by delaying the rejection decision. Indeed, the task of formulating a successful reorganization plan is undoubtedly aided by promptly clarifying the potential availability of some or all of the revenues from the debtor's post-petition creative efforts.

IV. CONCLUSION

The district court properly decided that the Bankruptcy Code permits a debtor-in-possession to reject an executory contract for personal services, with court approval; that rejection of appellant's contract was appropriate; and that the bankruptcy proceeding should not be dismissed. We affirm those rulings. To the extent the appeal challenges the refusal to abstain, the appeal is dismissed.

Questions

1. As a matter of contract law, how should Delightful Music's damages be measured?

2. What assets, aside from Taylor's home, will be included in the estate? Suppose Taylor signs new recording and publishing contracts after he files. Do proceeds from these agreements enter the estate? What about proceeds from pre-filing contracts that are based on post-filing compositions and performances? Proceeds from pre-filing recordings (in the form of royalties for others' use of such recordings on radio and TV before and after the filing)? See 11 U.S.C. § 541(a)(6). Do the answers to these questions explain why Mr. Taylor chose to file under Chapter 11 rather than under Chapter 7? What other reasons might he have had?

3. What would Mr. Andrew say about Taylor's case?

§ 3. BALANCING INTERESTS: LEASE AND FRANCHISE AGREEMENTS

One primary application of section 365 involves balancing the right of the lessor of real estate against the right of the tenant, its trustee or DIP. Historically, the most common application of this conflict involved a lessor who desired to terminate the lease and a lessee who hoped to assume and continue to perform the lease or to assume and assign the lease.

The particular conflict is acute in times of economic change with increasing rental value for commercial real estate. Especially if the lease contains a fixed rental rate, in inflationary periods a tenant's right to use (or to transfer the right to use) the property at a fixed rent over a long period of time may have substantial value. Assume for example that business leases in 1965 were at $3.00 per square foot per year and J.S. Mill signed a 20–year lease. Mill goes bankrupt ten years later when the fair market value of such leases has risen to $15.00 per square foot. The right to use the premises for the continuing ten years at the fixed rent is obviously worth fighting over.

Formerly, lessors sought to protect such increments of value for themselves by including "ipso facto" clauses in their leases. As we have seen, the Bankruptcy Code outlaws such clauses, but the large increments of value available in such leases has stimulated lessors to find alternative routes to the same destination. Subsection 365(c)(3) enacted in 1984 strengthens the landlord's hand somewhat. The cases and problems that follow will give the student the opportunity to examine those questions. The student should also consider what questions are paramount in times of deflation as rental rates decline.

Section 365 contains a variety of rules that establish certain responsibilities for the trustee in bankruptcy if he wishes to assume and then to assign a lease. Section 502(b)(7) states rules for the damages that the lessor may assert as a result of the termination of the lease. Note that there may be a variety of different claims to be asserted in the bankruptcy depending upon the time of rejection of the lease and upon whether or not it is rejected. For example, there may be rental payments due but unpaid at the time the petition is filed, rental payments for the period of use after the petition but before rejection or acceptance, and liabilities arising from other failures on the part of the lessee.

Section 365(b) contains a series of provisions with which a trustee who wishes to assume a lease must comply. These are designed to prohibit the trustee from simply making the lessor a continued involuntary creditor and exposing him to continued risk. Note that section 365(b)(3) has a special provision included apparently to mollify a specific pressure group. Where no default is found, the lessor is not entitled to adequate assurance of future performance under section 365(b)(1)(C).

IN RE LAFAYETTE RADIO ELECTRONICS CORP.
United States Bankruptcy Court, Eastern District of New York, 1981.
12 B.R. 302.

C. Albert Parente, Bankruptcy Judge.

Lafayette Radio Electronics Corporation (hereinafter "debtor") filed an order to show cause on July 24, 1980, seeking permission pursuant to 11 U.S.C. § 365(a) to assume a real estate lease (hereinafter "prime lease") entered into with Jonnet Development Corporation (hereinafter "landlord"), and to sublease the premises to Roaman's Stores of Pennsylvania, Inc. (hereinafter "Roaman's").

* * *

Subsequently, the landlord changed the locks on the leasehold premises in violation of the automatic stay provisions of § 362 of the Bankruptcy Code. The landlord was found in contempt of this Court, and the Court levied a fine on the landlord for failure to turn over to the debtor a key to the new lock. The order of contempt is presently on appeal to the District Court for the Eastern District of New York.

The landlord timely filed an answer in opposition to the debtor's order to show cause, intromitting the following affirmative defenses: (1) improper venue; (2) failure to join an indispensable party; to wit, the Municipality of Monroeville, Pennsylvania; (3) that as a result of certain post-petition defaults the debtor has no standing to move to assume the prime lease; (4) that the agreement between the debtor and Roaman's is an assignment, not a sublease, and must therefore comply with certain provisions of the prime lease; and (5) failure to provide adequate assurance of future performance pursuant to § 365(b)(1) and (3) of the Bankruptcy Code.

The hearing was concluded February 25, 1981.

The Court makes the following findings of fact:

(1) Debtor entered into the prime lease with Jonnell Enterprises, Inc. on March 21, 1967, for the premises in the Monroe Plaza Shopping Center, Monroeville, Pennsylvania, known as Lafayette Location Number 28. The term of the prime lease is ten years with two options to renew for an additional five years each.

* * *

(4) Prior to the filing of the petition in bankruptcy, the debtor was current in all of its obligations under the prime lease. Since the filing, the debtor has defaulted in its rent payments for the months of November and December 1980, and January 1981. Robert Crimmins, Director of Real Estate for the debtor, testified that he has in his possession checks to cover the rent arrears.

(5) Crimmins testified that the debtor had failed to pay a real estate tax escalation for 1980 due to the fact that the debtor was never billed for said tax.

(6) The roof over the leasehold premises leaks when it rains, which has resulted in extensive damage to the premises, including the floor, walls and electrical system. Repairs are estimated at approximately $38,000. The cause of the damage to the roof is in dispute.

(7) In furtherance of its efforts to reorganize, the debtor commenced a program of subleasing those retail outlets which had been closed, at rentals in excess of the lease rentals set forth in the prime leases between the various landlords and the debtor.

(8) At present, the debtor's sublease program is generating an annual income stream of $650,000. Crimmins testified that upon completion of the sublease program, the debtor expects the annual income generated to be approximately $900,000.

(9) As part of the sublease program, the debtor commenced this action seeking the Court's permission to assume the prime lease, and to sublease the premises to Roaman's. Predicated upon the sublease agreement, the debtor will realize a net income of at least $19,652 per year, the difference between the debtor's rent obligation under the prime lease and Roaman's obligation under the sublease. The total income to

the debtor over the full term of the sublease will be in excess of $130,000.

(10) Roaman's Stores, Inc., a parent company of the sublessee, is the guarantor of the sublease. The guarantor oversees Roaman's operation of about a dozen stores in Pennsylvania, as well as similar operations in other states. The net worth of the guarantor is approximately $2.1 million.

(11) Roaman's intends to operate a retail clothing store known as Sizes Unlimited in the leasehold premises. Said store specializes in large size women's wear.

(12) Monroe Plaza Shopping Center is a "strip" center, not an enclosed mall. There are approximately twenty stores in the center, including three clothing stores. Of the three, Arturn offers a full line of women's clothing and children's clothes; the second store sells primarily women's sportswear and jeans; and the third is a large retail clothing store, selling a complete line of men's and women's clothing.

(13) Arturn has an exclusivity clause in its lease with the landlord, purportedly prohibiting any new retail clothing stores from doing business in the shopping center during the term of the Arturn lease.

Based on the foregoing findings of fact, the following issues are before the Court:

* * *

(3) Has the debtor provided the requisite probative measure of adequate assurances pursuant to § 365(b) permitting it to assume the prime lease; and

(4) Is the proposed sublease in the best interests of the debtor and its creditors?

* * *

III.

The next issue which must be resolved is whether or not the debtor has met his burden of proof by offering adequate assurances pursuant to § 365(b), such that this Court should permit the debtor to assume the prime lease.

As previously noted, "If the court determines that assumption would substantially further the debtor's reorganization effort and that the rights of other parties to the contract or lease are receiving their due recognition and protection, the court is obliged to grant the necessary approval." *In re Lafayette Radio Electronics Corp.*, 7 B.R. 189, 191 (Bankr.E.D.N.Y.1980)(hereinafter cited as "*Lafayette I* ").

* * *

The landlord alleges three defaults by the debtor with respect to § 365(b)(1)(A); to wit, failure to pay rent obligations incurred for the months of November, December 1980 and January 1981; failure to pay a real estate tax escalation; and failure to repair damages resulting from leaks in the roof of the leasehold premises.

As all three of these defaults occurred after the filing of the Chapter 11 petition, the landlord sets forth as an affirmative defense that the debtor has no standing to move to assume the prime lease. The clear language of § 365(b)(1)(A) states "If there has been a default * * *" without any differentiation between pre-petition and post-petition defaults. The landlord does not cite any authority for his novel reading of this section. Therefore, the Court finds that the debtor does have standing to move to assume the prime lease.

With respect to the default in the payment of the rent, Crimmins testified that the debtor is prepared to cure all rent defaults. The landlord did not controvert this testimony.

Crimmins admitted that the debtor did not pay any real estate tax escalation for 1980, and concedes that the payment of said tax escalation is the duty of the debtor under the terms of the prime lease. However, the debtor contends that the duty does not arise until the debtor is billed by the landlord for the tax escalation.

Neither party introduced evidence as to whether past tax escalations have been paid by the debtor before or after billing.

Rider 44 to the prime lease provides, in relevant part:

If the Tenant's share of the real estate taxes upon the Shopping Center for any tax year commencing after the base year shall exceed Tenant's share of the real estate tax upon the Shopping Center for the base year, Tenant will pay the amount of such excess to Landlord as additional *rent*. (Emphasis added).

Paragraph three of the prime lease states, in part, that the "Landlord agrees to submit monthly bills for the *rent* to the Tenant." (Emphasis added). As Rider 44 provides that the tax escalation is additional rent, the Court finds that no duty exists for the debtor to pay said tax escalation until the debtor is billed pursuant to paragraph three of the prime lease. Therefore, the Court holds that, although the debtor breached the lease in not paying the tax escalation, failure of the landlord to give proper notice of the money owing prevents that breach from becoming a default. *See Lafayette I, supra* at 192–93.

The third default alleged by the landlord is the failure of the debtor to repair damage to the leasehold premises caused by leaks in the roof.

Since the landlord is contending that the debtor has not cured this default, nor provided adequate assurance that the default will be promptly cured, the landlord has the burden of proving the existence of the default. The Court finds that the landlord has failed to meet this burden.

Joseph Jonnet, an officer of the landlord, testified that on several occasions he had observed mechanics and agents of the debtor on the roof of the premises, working on the antennas and air conditioning units.

Elmer Jonnet, another officer of the landlord, testified that he observed the manager of the debtor's store running across the roof of the premises with several other people. Afterward, he found holes in the roof and tools which, in his opinion, could have been used to cause these holes.

Assuming, *arguendo,* that agents for the debtor were on the roof, there is no evidence to indicate that the tools were owned or used by these agents. Thus, the landlord has failed to establish probatively that the debtor willfully caused any damage to the roof.

This is particularly true in the instant case in light of the testimony of Robert Mitchell, a roofing contractor who examined the roof on behalf of Roaman's. Mitchell testified that, in his opinion, the damage to the roof was caused by normal wear and tear, and that he had not seen any indication that the damage was the result of willful or negligent acts.

Paragraph nine of the prime lease provides, in relevant part, that:

> in no event shall the Tenant be required to make any repairs * * * which may be necessary as a result of damage or destruction by fire, the elements or casualty, by reason of any structural default or failure * * * except that Tenant and not Landlord shall be exclusively liable therefor to the extent that Tenant is covered by insurance therefor.

Pursuant to this clause, and based upon a finding that the damage to the roof was the result of normal wear and tear, the Court holds that the landlord is responsible for making repairs to the roof and the premises for all damages caused by the leaking roof, to the extent that such repairs are not covered by the debtor's insurance.

Therefore, the Court concludes that the debtor is not in default with respect to repairing the roof or the resulting damages to the premises.

As the landlord has not alleged any pecuniary loss arising out of the aforementioned rent default, § 365(b)(1)(B) does not apply in the instant case.

IV.

A.

The final requirement of § 365(b)(1) is that the debtor provide adequate assurance of future performance under the prime lease.

Both parties agree that the leasehold premises is located in a shopping center. Therefore, the special considerations of § 365(b)(3) must be complied with if adequate assurance is to be given.

* * *

The landlord contends that the lease arrangement between the debtor and Roaman's is an assignment, while the debtor alleges that said arrangement is a sublease. At issue is whether the debtor or Roaman's is to be the primary focus of the Court's inquiry into adequate assurance of future source of rent payments to the landlord. *In re Lafayette Radio*

Electronics Corp., 9 B.R. 993 (Bankr.E.D.N.Y.1981)(hereinafter cited as "*Lafayette II* ").

Case law in Pennsylvania clearly holds that "where the lessee of land transfers all of his interest therein, it is an assignment, and not a sublease thereof. A lease or a sublease must, in legal contemplation, leave in the lessor or sublessor some estate in reversion." *In re Bayley,* 177 F. 522, 524 (W.D.Pa.1909); *Morrisville Shopping Center v. Sun Ray Drug Co.,* 381 Pa. 576, 112 A.2d 183 (1955); *Ottman v. Albert Co.,* 327 Pa. 49, 192 A. 897 (1937).

The intention of the parties in making the lease arrangement is not controlling, as "it is a cardinal rule in the construction of papers that it is the paper itself which determines its character, and not what the parties may have chosen to designate as its character." *Bayley, supra* at 524.

The debtor alleges two reversions which make the lease arrangement between it and Roaman's a sublease. The first is that the debtor will receive approximately $2,793 per month from Roaman's, while it will pay a rent of only $1,041.67 per month to the landlord under the prime lease.

However, the Supreme Court of Pennsylvania has stated that a reversion in rent is insufficient of itself to support a finding that a sublease exists. *Morrisville Shopping Center, supra* 381 Pa. 576, 112 A.2d at 187–88. *See also Thomas v. U.S.,* 505 F.2d 1282 (Ct.Cl.1974).

The second reversion alleged by the debtor is that the sublease terminates one day prior to the termination of the prime lease.

> Rider A to the prime lease provides that: Landlord shall give Tenant at least 30 days written notice of the date upon which the demised premises shall be ready for initial occupancy by the Tenant, and shall deliver the said premises for such occupancy to the Tenant on such date. The term of this lease shall commence on such date and shall terminate on a date ten years thereafter unless sooner terminated as provided in this lease. Landlord agrees to deliver said premises to Tenant pursuant to forgoing (sic) provisions not later than October 1, 1967.

The debtor contends that the premises were not turned over to it until November 15, 1967. Thus, the debtor asserts that upon proper exercise of the two options to renew, the prime lease terminates on November 15, 1987. As the sublease terminates on November 14, 1987, the debtor alleges that a reversion has been retained.

The landlord asserts that, as Rider A uses the date of October 1, 1967, as the last day on which the landlord could deliver the premises, October 1, 1967, is the starting date for the prime lease. Therefore, the landlord asserts that the debtor has not retained a reversionary interest in the prime lease.

Crimmins testified that he has in his possession a document which was signed by the landlord, agreeing that the starting date of the prime lease was November 15, 1967. The landlord disputed the interpretation placed on said document by Crimmins. Neither party introduced said document into evidence.

The landlord indicated that the debtor moved into the premises on October 1, 1967, but that "certain things that had to be done" were not finished until after that date.

Although the starting date of the prime lease was the subject of a state court action in Pennsylvania, as well as subsequent arbitration proceedings, neither party introduced the results of these actions into evidence.

The debtor did, however, read from a part of the decision rendered by the Court of Common Pleas of Allegheny County in the aforementioned state court action. In that decision, Judge Hester stated, in part, that "Defendant-lessor agreed to deliver the demised premises to the Plaintiff not later than October 1, 1967. He was unable to deliver that premises by the aforementioned date, but did by November 15, 1967."

Although the Court would prefer that the entire decision by Judge Hester were before it in evidence, based on that portion of the decision cited above, the Court finds that the debtor has sustained his burden of proof that the starting date of the prime lease was November 15, 1967.

Predicated upon the above finding and the failure of the landlord to introduce the entire decision rendered by Judge Hester to support its position, or to allege that the above cite was taken out of context, this Court is constrained to find that the prime lease began on November 15, 1967. Thus, the prime lease will terminate on November 15, 1987, and the debtor has retained a reversionary interest in the prime lease of one day.

In light of this reversion, particularly when taken in conjunction with the reversion in rent, the Court holds that the lease arrangement between the debtor and Roaman's is a sublease.

Based upon the finding that the lease arrangement is a sublease, the primary focus of the inquiry into the adequate assurance of a source of rent and other consideration pursuant to § 365(b)(3)(A) is on the debtor.

Three assurances have been offered by the debtor as proof that it can meet its financial obligations under the prime lease. First, that the income stream generated by the sublease program is sufficient to satisfy the rent obligations under the prime lease. Second, the proposed merger between the debtor and Wards Company, Inc. Third, the viability of Roaman's.

This Court has, in two previous proceedings, held that the stream of income generated by the sublease program, and the proposed merger with Wards, form sufficient adequate assurance of future performance by the debtor. *Lafayette I, supra; Lafayette II, supra.*

The testimony adduced at the hearing revealed that Roaman's is currently operating about a dozen stores in Pennsylvania similar to the one which they proposed to open in the leasehold premises. In addition, the sublease provides for a guarantor, Roaman's Stores, Inc., which has a net worth of approximately $2.1 million.

The landlord did not controvert this evidence. Furthermore, the landlord introduced no evidence of its own to suggest that Roaman's or its guarantor might have any financial difficulties in the future, based on their present operations.

Therefore, the Court finds that adequate assurance of future performance has been provided, in compliance with § 365(b)(3)(A).

There is no provision in either the prime lease or the sublease for percentage rent. Thus, § 365(b)(3)(B) does not apply to the case at bar.

B.

The landlord contends that an exclusivity clause in the lease of one of the clothing stores currently operating in the shopping center, Arturn, prohibits a store of the type proposed by Roaman's from moving into the shopping center. Said exclusivity clause provides, in full, that "The Tenant [Arturn] is hereby guaranteed that no other stores other than existing stores shall be permitted to engage in retail clothing and related items sales in the Shopping Center for the duration of this lease agreement." Said lease agreement is in operation until April 15, 1985.

The debtor alleges, and the Court so finds, that the landlord has waived his right to seek enforcement of the exclusivity clause against the debtor.

* * *

As developed in Pennsylvania, the elements which must be established to support a finding of equitable estoppel are (1) silence by the complaining party in the face of a duty to speak; (2) lack of knowledge and a means of knowledge of the truth by the party seeking estoppel; (3) reliance upon the silence; and (4) detriment. * * *

In the case at bar, the debtor introduced into evidence a letter requesting notice from the landlord of any exclusivity clauses which had been granted to other tenants in the shopping center. Said letter was dated April 10, 1980. A return receipt, signed by one Laurie Sproul for the landlord on April 14, 1980, was also introduced into evidence.

According to undisputed testimony adduced at the hearing, the landlord never responded to said letter. Thus, the debtor was not made aware of the existence of the exclusivity clause until the hearing on February 5, 1981, and was not provided with a copy of said clause until the subsequent hearing on February 25, 1981.

Paragraph 5(c) of the prime lease provides, in relevant part, that "Landlord will, upon receiving request therefor from the Tenant, supply Tenant with *reasonable promptness* with a then current list of all restrictions granted to other tenants in the Shopping Center."

Clearly, the debtor has met his burden of proof with respect to equitable estoppel. The landlord, despite his affirmative duty to respond to the debtor's inquiry, remained silent for ten months. Furthermore, this silence was maintained throughout six months of this proceeding, until the purported existence of the exclusivity clause was first announced at the February 5, 1981, hearing. Even then, the landlord failed to provide the debtor with a copy of the Arturn lease until the beginning of the subsequent hearing on February 25.

The debtor complied with its duties under the prime lease by its written inquiry to the landlord, and had every right to rely, as it did, on the landlord's silence to proceed with the negotiations with Roaman's for a sublease.

The costs incurred by the debtor and Roaman's in pursuing the sublease in this action constitute a detriment to the debtor and to Roaman's which would not have occurred but for the silence of the landlord. This is true not only on the financial costs to the debtor, but also as to the cost of the lost opportunity to make arrangements with a different sublessee.

Predicated upon the landlord's failure to provide prompt notice of the existence of the exclusivity clause, and in reliance upon the laws of Pennsylvania as cited above, the Court finds that the landlord is equitably estopped from seeking to enforce the exclusivity clause in the Arturn lease against either the debtor or Roaman's, with respect to the sublease in the case at bar.

C.

The final consideration which must be made in determining whether or not adequate assurance has been provided pursuant to § 365(b)(1) and (3) is that the tenant mix or balance of the shopping center will not be substantially disrupted by the presence of Roaman's in the leasehold premises.

The Court has found no cases which have directly considered the question of tenant mix as set forth in § 365(b)(3)(D).

The legislative history with respect to § 365(b)(3) in general states that:

> A shopping center is often a carefully planned enterprise, and though it consists of numerous individual tenants, the center is planned as a single unit, often subject to a master lease or financing agreement. Under these agreements, the tenant mix in the shopping center may be as important to the lessor as the actual promised rental payments, because certain mixes will attract higher patronage of the stores in the center, and thus a higher rental for the landlord from those stores that are subject to a percentage of gross receipts rental agreement. Thus, in order to assure a landlord of his bargained for exchange, the court would have to consider such factors as the nature of the business to be conducted by the trustee or his assignee, whether that business complies with the require-

ments of any master agreement, whether the kind of business will generate gross sales in an amount such that the percentage rent specified in the lease is substantially the same as that would have been provided by the debtor, and whether the business proposed to be conducted would result in a breach of other clauses in master agreements relating, for example, to tenant mix and location.

House Report No. 95–595, 95 Cong., 1st Sess. (1977) 348–49, U.S.Code Cong. & Admin.News 1978, 5963, 6305.

No evidence of any master agreement or percentage rent arrangement was introduced in the case at bar. Nor was any suggestion made that a master plan exists for the shopping center in question which would have a bearing on the issue of tenant mix.

However, the Court recognizes that the level of competition between stores is an important factor which must be considered in the instant inquiry. The success or failure of the individual tenants as a result of a change in the tenancy of the leasehold premises will not only affect the other tenants of the shopping center, but also the amount of rent which the landlord will be able to charge in the future.

The Court concludes that the issue of tenant mix is a question of fact which must be resolved on a case by case basis. The primary consideration before the Court is to balance the interests of the landlord and the current tenants in maintaining a competitive level of business, as well as offering a diversity of merchandise, against the interests of the debtor and sublessee in using the leasehold premises to operate a business.

The Court finds that the burden of proof is on the debtor to provide adequate assurances that the tenant mix will not be substantially disrupted by the presence of Roaman's in the shopping center.

The debtor contends that Sizes Unlimited, the store to be operated by Roaman's in the shopping center, offers clothing which is not sold by the other tenants of the center. Louis Rich, executive vice-president and chief financial officer of Roaman's Inc., the parent corporation of the sublessee, Roaman's, testified that Sizes Unlimited has a special clientele, large women. He further testified that, while a large retail department store would carry clothing for large women, stores selling only women's clothing usually do not sell the large sizes offered by the Roaman's store.

Rich stated that he had gone "carefully through every store that might represent some competitive position, and [in] this particular center, Monroe Plaza, there isn't a single store that has a significant—I would say to the most extent they hardly have any degree of merchandise in our particular fashion specialty."

In juxtaposition to this opinion, Elmer Jonnet testified for the landlord that, with the inclusion of Sizes Unlimited, the footage in the shopping center devoted to retail clothing stores would increase from

35,000 to 40,000 square feet, out of a total footage for the entire center of 110,000.

However, the landlord failed to controvert Rich's testimony that the present clothing stores do not offer the same general merchandise as that sold by Sizes Unlimited.

The Court recognizes that a significant portion of this shopping center will be used for retail clothing stores if the debtor is permitted to assume the prime lease and sublease the premises to Roaman's. The Court is also cognizant of the fact that, as long as the clothing stores offer different types of merchandise and cater to different clientele, the tenant mix will remain balanced. The level of competition within the shopping center will not be unduly burdensome to any of the current stores through direct competition with Sizes Unlimited.

It must be stressed that, while the exclusivity clause has been found to have been waived by the landlord, the fact that one of the existing clothing stores felt it necessary to attempt to prohibit new clothing stores is an important factor which the Court has not overlooked in its examination of the tenant mix.

However, as the foregoing inquiry exhibits, the landlord has failed to offer any evidence to dispute the testimony of Rich that the holder of the exclusivity clause, Arturn, will not be directly affected by the presence of Sizes Unlimited in the Monroe Plaza Shopping Center. It is evidentially significant that no representative of Arturn appeared or sought to testify on the exclusivity or tenant mix issues before the Court.

Therefore, the Court finds that the debtor has provided adequate assurance that the tenant mix will not be substantially disrupted if Roaman's subleases the premises.

Predicated upon the foregoing analysis, the Court holds that the debtor has complied with § 365(b)(1)(C) and (b)(3) by providing adequate assurances of future performance under the prime lease.

V.

The final issue before the Court in the instant case is whether or not the proposed sublease with Roaman's should be approved. This Court has previously stated that the issue of approval of a sublease turns on whether or not the sublease is in the best interests of the creditors and the estate. *Lafayette II, supra.*

Crimmins testified that this sublease will give the debtor a net income in excess of $130,000 over the term of the sublease.

On two previous occasions, the Court has held that the proposed merger between the debtor and Wards Company, Inc. is "a vital step toward the debtor proffering a plan of arrangement to its creditors." *Lafayette I, supra; Lafayette II, supra.* This Court has also previously noted that there is a condition precedent to the proposed merger, requiring that the income stream from the debtor's sublease program reach $825,000 annually, *Lafayette II, supra.* Thus, the sublease with

Roaman's is a significant factor in the debtor's attempt to offer a plan for confirmation.

The Court finds that the proposed sublease is in the best interests of the creditors and estate, and should be approved.

Conclusion

Premised upon the foregoing findings of fact and conclusions of law, the Court holds that: (1) the debtor has provided the adequate assurances necessary pursuant to § 365(b)(1) and (3) and is, therefore, permitted to assume the prime lease; (2) the landlord's affirmative defenses are hereby dismissed, as the landlord has failed to sustain its burden of proof with respect to said defenses; (3) the landlord has a duty under the terms of the prime lease to promptly repair the roof and all resulting damages to the leasehold premises; (4) the agreement between the debtor and Roaman's is a sublease; and (5) the proposed sublease is in the best interests of the creditors and estate, and is hereby approved.

SETTLE ORDER.

Problem 6–4

How might a lessor draft a lease so as to make it unassignable under section 365? What would be the effect of the following lease provision?

1. *Lessor preserves economic gain*

If Lessee assumes this lease and proposes to assign the same pursuant to the provisions of the Bankruptcy Code, 11 U.S.C. section 101 *et seq.* (the "Bankruptcy Code") to any person or entity who shall have made a bona fide offer to accept an assignment of this lease on terms acceptable to the Lessee, then notice of such proposed assignment, setting forth (i) the name and address of such person, (ii) all of the terms and conditions of such offer, and (iii) the adequate assurance to be provided Lessor to assure such person's future performance under the lease, including, without limitation, the assurance referred to in section 365(b)(3) of the Bankruptcy Code, shall be given to Lessor by the Lessee no later than twenty (20) days after receipt by the Lessee, but in any event no later than ten (10) days prior to the date that the Lessee shall make application to a court of competent jurisdiction for authority and approval to enter into such assignment and assumption, and Lessor shall thereupon have the prior right and option, to be exercised by notice to the Lessee given at any time prior to the effective date of such proposed assignment, to accept an assignment of this lease upon the same terms and conditions and for the same consideration, if any, as the bona fide offer made by such person, less any brokerage commissions which may be payable out of the consideration to be paid by such.

Problem 6–5

The accounting firm of Hegel and Aquinas has occupied space in the First Bank Office Tower for the past 15 years. Five years ago, it signed a 30–year lease at a fixed rental rate per month plus annual increments of 10 percent. The rate today is $35,000 per month, which is $5,000 per month less than market value for comparable office space. Hegel and Aquinas files bankruptcy.

1. They hope to remain in the Bank building during their reorganization, but they are two months behind in rent. Their lease contains standard provisions for automatic termination if the firm files bankruptcy and for termination on 20 days notice for failure to pay rent when due. What action must Hegel and Aquinas take to preserve the lease? How much must they pay the Bank after filing?

2. Based on your advice, Hegel and Aquinas decide that relocating their offices is the better course of action. They find a potential sublessee, ComSens Corporation, that is willing to pay for an assignment of the lease. ComSens operates a telephone pornography business. The Bank demands that the court prevent the proposed assignment because it will destroy the character of the building and because ComSens' financial condition is uncertain and it may be unable to perform the financial terms of the lease. Bank cites a clause in the lease which prevents assignment without the consent of the lessor. What result?

A Note on Bankruptcy of a Lessor or Seller

We have seen that the Code allows the tenant or lessee to capture the economic benefits of a lease by assuming it or to avoid the burdens of an onerous lease by rejecting it. This protects the interests of the bankruptcy estate at a cost to the lessor. Should a similar balance occur if the lessor or a contract seller of real property is the bankrupt party?

Section 365(h) governs the rejection of leases where the debtor is the lessor. It gives the lessee the option either to treat the lease as terminated or to remain in possession for the balance of the lease period along with any renewal or extension enforceable against the lessor under applicable nonbankruptcy law. No similar provision exists regarding bankruptcy of lessors of personal property. (Even recently enacted 365(d)(10) does not help, does it?)

Section 365(i) contains provisions similar to those of (h) for situations in which a trustee rejects an executory contract for the sale of real estate under which the purchaser is in possession. Section 365(j) goes even further to protect the purchaser. It grants a lien on the debtor's interest in the property to the purchaser who chooses to treat the land contract as terminated or who is not in possession, but only for that portion of the purchase price actually paid.

Which contract should not be assignable?

IN RE PIONEER FORD SALES, INC.

United States Court of Appeals, First Circuit, 1984.
729 F.2d 27.

BREYER, CIRCUIT JUDGE.

The Ford Motor Company appeals a federal district court decision, 30 B.R. 458, allowing a bankrupt Ford dealer (Pioneer Ford Sales, Inc.) to assign its Ford franchise over Ford's objection to a Toyota dealer

(Toyota Village, Inc.). The district court decided the case on the basis of a record developed in the bankruptcy court. The bankruptcy court, 26 B.R. 116, had approved the transfer, which ran from Pioneer to Fleet National Bank (Pioneer's principal secured creditor) and then to Toyota Village. Fleet sought authorization for the assignment because Toyota Village will pay $10,000 for the franchise and buy all parts and accessories in Pioneer's inventory at fair market value (about $75,000); if the franchise is not assigned, Ford will buy only some of the parts for between $45,000 and $55,000. Thus, the assignment will increase the value of the estate. Fleet is the appellee here.

The issue that the case raises is the proper application of 11 U.S.C. § 365(c)(1)(A), an exception to a more general provision, 11 U.S.C. § 365(f)(1), that allows a trustee in bankruptcy (or a debtor in possession) to assign many of the debtor's executory contracts even if the contract itself says that it forbids assignment. The exception at issue reads as follows:

> (c) The trustee [or debtor in possession] may not assume or assign an executory contract * * * of the debtor, whether or not such contract * * * prohibits assignment if—
>
> (1)(A) applicable law excuses [the other party to the contract] from accepting performance from * * * an assignee * * * whether or not [the] * * * contract * * * prohibits * * * assignment.

The words "applicable law" in this section mean "applicable nonbankruptcy law." See H.R.Rep. No. 95–595, 95th Cong., 1st Sess. 348 (1977), *reprinted in* [1978] U.S.Code Cong. & Ad.News 5787, 5963, 6304; S.Rep. No. 95–989, 95th Cong.2d Sess. 59 (1978), *reprinted in* [1978] U.S.Code Cong. & Ad.News 5787, 5845. Evidently, the theory of this section is to prevent the trustee from assigning (over objection) contracts of the sort that contract law ordinarily makes nonassignable, *i.e.* contracts that cannot be assigned when the contract itself is silent about assignment. At the same time, by using the words in (1)(A) "whether *or not* the contract prohibits assignment," the section prevents parties from using contractual language to prevent the trustee from assigning contracts that (when the contract is silent) contract law typically makes assignable. *Id.* Thus, we must look to see whether relevant nonbankruptcy law would allow Ford to veto the assignment of its basic franchise contract "whether or not" that basic franchise contract itself specifically "prohibits assignment."

The nonbankruptcy law to which both sides point us is contained in Rhode Island's "Regulation of Business Practices Among Motor Vehicle Manufacturers, Distributors and Dealers" Act, R.I.Gen.Laws § 31–5.1–4(C)(7). It states that

> [N]o dealer * * * shall have the right to * * * assign the franchise * * * without the consent of the manufacturer, except that such consent shall not be unreasonably withheld.

The statute by its terms, allows a manufacturer to veto an assignment where the veto is reasonable but not otherwise. The statute's language also indicates that it applies "whether or not" the franchise contract itself restricts assignment. Thus, the basic question that the case presents is whether Ford's veto was reasonable in terms of the Rhode Island law.

Neither the district court nor the bankruptcy court specifically addressed this question. Their failure apparently arose out of their belief that 11 U.S.C. § 365(c)(1)(A) refers only to traditional personal service contracts. But in our view they were mistaken. The language of the section does not limit its effect to personal service contracts. It refers *generally* to contracts that are not assignable under nonbankruptcy law. State laws typically make contracts for personal services nonassignable (where the contract itself is silent); but they make other sorts of contracts nonassignable as well. *See, e.g.,* N.Y.State Finance Law § 138 (1974)(making certain government contracts unassignable); N.Y.General Municipal Law § 109 (1977)(same); N.C.Gen.Stat. § 147–62 (1978)(same). The legislative history of § 365(c) says nothing about "personal services." To the contrary, it speaks of letters of credit, personal loans, and leases—instances in which assigning a contract may place the other party at a significant disadvantage. The history thereby suggests that (c)(1)(A) has a broader reach.

The source of the "personal services" limitation apparently is a bankruptcy court case, *In re Taylor Manufacturing, Inc.,* 6 B.R. 370 (Bankr.N.D.Ga.1980), which other bankruptcy courts have followed. The *Taylor* court wrote that (c)(1)(A) should be interpreted narrowly, in part because it believed that (c)(1)(A) conflicted with another section, (f)(1), which states in relevant part:

> Except as provided in subsection (c) * * *, notwithstanding a provision * * * in applicable law that prohibits * * * the assignment of [an executory] contract * * * the trustee may assign [it] * * *.

As a matter of logic, however, we see no conflict, for (c)(1)(A) refers to state laws that prohibit assignment "whether or not" the contract is silent, while (f)(1) contains no such limitation. Apparently (f)(1) includes state laws that prohibit assignment only when the contract is *not* silent about assignment; that is to say, state laws that enforce contract provisions prohibiting assignment. *See* 1 Norton, *Bankruptcy Law and Practice* § 23.14. These state laws are to be ignored. The section specifically excepts (c)(1)(A)'s state laws that forbid assignment even when the contract *is* silent; they are to be heeded. Regardless, we fail to see why a "conflict" suggests that (c)(1)(A) is limited to "personal services."

The *Taylor* court cites 2 *Collier on Bankruptcy* § 365.05 and the Commission Report, H.R.Doc. No. 93–137, 93rd Cong., 1st Sess. 199 (1973), in support. Both of these sources speak of personal services. However, they do not say that (c)(1)(A), was intended to be *limited* to personal services. Indeed, since it often is difficult to decide whether or not a particular duty can be characterized by the label "personal service," it makes sense to avoid this question and simply look to see whether state law would, or would not, make the duty assignable where the contract is silent. Thus, the Fifth Circuit has found no reason for limiting the scope of (c)(1)(A) to personal service contracts. *In re Braniff Airways, Inc.*, 700 F.2d 935, 943 (5th Cir.1983). Fleet concedes in its brief that "the exception to assignment [of § 365(c)(1)(A)]is not limited to personal services contracts." We therefore reject the district court's conclusion in this respect.

Although the district court did not explicitly decide whether Ford's veto was reasonable, it decided a closely related question. Under other provisions of § 365 a bankruptcy court cannot authorize assignment of an executory contract if 1) the debtor is in default, unless 2) there is "adequate assurance of future performance." § 365(b)(1)(C). Pioneer is in default, but the bankruptcy and district courts found "adequate assurance." For the sake of argument, we shall assume that this finding is equivalent to a finding that Ford's veto of the assignment was unreasonable. And, we shall apply a "clearly erroneous" standard in reviewing the factual element in this lower court finding. Fed.R.Civ.P. 52. On these assumptions, favorable to Fleet, we nonetheless must reverse the district court, for, in our view, any finding of unreasonableness, based on this record, is clearly erroneous.

Our review of the record reveals the following critical facts. First, in accordance with its ordinary business practice and dealer guidelines incorporated into the franchise agreement, Ford would have required Toyota Village, as a dealer, to have a working capital of at least $172,000, of which no more than half could be debt. Toyota Village, however, had a working capital at the end of 1981 of $37,610; and its net worth was $31,747. Although the attorney for Fleet at one point in the bankruptcy proceedings said Toyota Village could borrow some of the necessary capital from a bank, he made no later reference to the point, nor did he ever specifically state how much Toyota Village could borrow. Since the tax returns of Toyota Village's owner showed gross income of $27,500 for 1981, there is no reason to believe that the owner could readily find the necessary equity capital.

Second, at a time when Japanese cars have sold well throughout the United States, Toyota Village has consistently lost money. The financial statements in the record show the following operating losses:

	1977	1978	1979	1980	1981
Loss	($7,522)	($7,552)	($13,938)	($12,684)	($21,317)

At the same time, the record contains no significant evidence tending to refute the natural inference arising from these facts. The bankruptcy court mentioned five factors that it said showed that Toyota Village gave "adequate assurance" that it could do the job.

1) Toyota Village was an established dealership.

2) Toyota Village was "located within 500 yards of the present Ford dealership."

3) Toyota Village had a proven track record for selling cars.

4) Toyota Village was willing and able to pay $15,000 that Pioneer still owed Ford.

5) The owner and sole stockholder of Toyota Village testified that he was willing and able to fulfill the franchise agreement.

The first of these factors (dealer experience), while favoring Toyota Village, is weak, given the record of continuous dealership losses. The second (location) proves little, considering that Pioneer went bankrupt at the very spot. The third (track record) cuts against Toyota Village, not in its favor, for its track record is one of financial loss. The fourth (willingness to pay a $15,000 debt that Pioneer owed Ford) is relevant, but it shows, at most, that Toyota Village *believed* it could make a success of the franchise. The fifth (ability to act as franchisee) is supported by no more than a simple statement by the owner of Toyota Village that he could do the job.

We do not see how the few positive features about Toyota Village that the record reveals can overcome the problem of a history of losses and failure to meet Ford's capital requirements. In these circumstances, Ford would seem perfectly reasonable in withholding its consent to the transfer. Thus, Rhode Island law would make the franchise unassignable.

The Rhode Island authority we have found supports this conclusion. In *Dunne Leases Cars & Trucks v. Kenworth Truck Co.*, 466 A.2d 1153 (R.I.1983) the Supreme Court of Rhode Island held that failure to meet a condition in the franchise agreement requiring a leasing business to be removed from the dealership site, provided due cause for the manufacturer's decision to *terminate* the dealership agreement. In *Scuncio Motors, Inc. v. Subaru of New England, Inc.*, 555 F.Supp. 1121 (D.R.I. 1982), *aff'd,* 715 F.2d 10 (1st Cir.1983), the federal district court for the District of Rhode Island wrote that failure to meet a franchise requirement to provide additional selling space provided cause to terminate a dealer contract. Inability to meet capital requirements, as revealed here, would seem to provide reasonable grounds for objecting to a franchise transfer *a fortiori*. If not, a manufacturer would have to allow the transfer of its franchise to virtually any auto dealer.

One might still argue that under Rhode Island law the only "reasonable" course of action for Ford is to allow the transfer and then simply terminate Toyota Village if it fails to perform adequately. This suggestion, however, overlooks the legal difficulties that Ford would have in proving cause for termination under the Rhode Island "Regulation of Business Practices Among Motor Vehicle Manufacturers, Distributors and Dealers" Act. R.I.Gen.Laws § 31–5.1–4(D)(2). The very purpose of the statute—protecting dealer reliance—suggests that it ought to be more difficult for a manufacturer to terminate a dealer who has invested in a franchise than to oppose the grant of a franchise to one who has not. In any event, the law does not suggest a manufacturer is "unreasonable" in objecting to a transfer unless he would have "good cause" to terminate the transferee. And, to equate the two standards would tend to make the "unreasonable" provision superfluous. Thus, we conclude that the Rhode Island law would make the franchise unassignable on the facts here revealed. Therefore, neither the bankruptcy court nor the district court had the power to authorize the transfer.

We shall briefly consider three additional points. First, Ford notes that the franchise contract says that Michigan law governs. We thus cannot be certain that Rhode Island provides the relevant nonbankruptcy law without deciding whether its "dealer protection" policies are sufficiently strong to overcome the contract's "choice of law" provision as applied in a diversity case brought in a Rhode Island federal court. *See Restatement (Second) of Conflict of Laws* § 187 (1971); *D'Antuono v. CCH Computax Systems, Inc.,* 570 F.Supp. 708, 812–13 (D.R.I.1983). We avoid this "conflicts" question, however. For one thing, we have no reason to believe that Michigan law differs in any relevant respect. *See* Mich.Stat.Ann. § 19.856(34)(1)(i) [M.C.L.A. § 445.1574(1)(i)]. For another, Fleet, standing in Pioneer's shoes, asks us to decide the matter as one of Rhode Island law. It has not briefed Michigan law. Thus, we take Fleet to have waived the point.

Second, the district court and bankruptcy court noted that Ford did not object when the two people who run Pioneer, Messrs. Perron and Rosenthal, assigned the franchise to Mr. Arthur Manchester, the former retired owner of Pioneer Ford. Ford explains that it did not formally object to this assignment—which took place the day before bankruptcy was declared—because it believed Manchester intended to resign the dealership, not assign it via Fleet to Toyota. Regardless, no one suggests that Ford failed to object to the Fleet or Toyota assignments. Nor does anyone argue that a manufacturer who consents to one assignment must thereafter consent to all assignments. Moreover, Arthur Manchester had previously run the Pioneer franchise successfully. We do not see how Ford's consent to Perron and Rosenthal's transfer to their former employer, Manchester, could show that a failure to consent to a subsequent transfer to Toyota Village was unreasonable.

Third, Ford argues that the bankruptcy court lacked jurisdiction over the proceeding for the reasons set forth in *Northern Pipeline Construction Co. v. Marathon Pipe Line Co.,* 458 U.S. 50, 102 S.Ct. 2858, 73 L.Ed.2d 598 (1982). It adds that the district court lacked jurisdiction to enter its order authorizing the assignment of the franchise because the court rules allowing district courts to decide bankruptcy matters are unlawful. We need not consider these questions. Technically speaking, if Ford is correct on these contentions, the proper action for this court is to order that the district court's judgment be vacated. We take that same action because we accept Ford's arguments on the merits. We shall consider these "bankruptcy jurisdiction" matters in other cases, the facts of which bring the legal issues more clearly into focus. And, even though they are labelled "jurisdictional," we need not decide them now. *Secretary of the Navy v. Avrech,* 418 U.S. 676, 677–78, 94 S.Ct. 3039, 3039–40, 41 L.Ed.2d 1033 (1974)(court can avoid answering a "difficult jurisdictional issue" when decision on the merits renders it moot.).

For these reasons, the judgment of the district court is

Reversed.

Note

The licensee protections in section 365(n) do not deal with the more common case in franchise transactions where the franchisee files bankruptcy. Establishing and retaining trademark rights requires that the owner of trademark exercise the right to protect the quality of business that is done under the mark. Thus, as a matter of general law, trademark licenses cannot be assigned without the consent of the mark's owner. Should a different rule apply in bankruptcy? If not, how can section 365 be used to protect the franchiser?

Problem 6–6

Assume that International Motors offers a franchise in a completely new line of automobiles. Under the terms of the franchise, each dealer is assigned a territory that might include as much as a one or two county area. The dealer is free to operate in that area out of one place of business or from several. Franchiser agrees not to authorize others to operate in that area. While the franchisee would be permitted to operate out of one or many areas, it is obliged to erect a particular kind of showroom and a particular kind of maintenance and parts store to comply with the overall International Motors plan. Assume that one dealer goes into bankruptcy and proposes to assign his franchise to your client. Your client already operates a Toyota dealership in the same area and would like to combine the operation to sell some of the International Motors cars out of those locations and also to operate other locations devoted exclusively to the International Motors cars. However, your client does not wish to be bound to build showrooms of a particular shape and style as the original franchise requires. If the bankruptcy court will approve, can your client make an assignment without becoming obliged to comply with the building and separation terms? Are there any specific terms that International could add to its franchise agreement to reduce its risks? If, instead of a dealer filing bankruptcy, International files. Can it cancel some dealer contracts and assume others?

Problem 6–7

On May 2, Aquinas, owner of a Burger King franchise, filed under Chapter 11. Since then, Aquinas has continued in possession of its property and in operation. The Burger King Corporation asked the court to compel Aquinas to adopt or reject the franchise agreement under 365(d). Aquinas rejected. Burger King Corporation then sought to enforce a non-compete covenant that was part of the original franchise agreement. Aquinas argues that since the franchise agreement has been rejected, the covenant not to compete had no further effect. How would you rule?

§ 4. COLLECTIVE BARGAINING AGREEMENTS

Collective bargaining agreements are executory; they ordinarily involve a duty on the part of both employees and the employer to continue to perform throughout the term of the agreement. In its original form, however, the Bankruptcy Code did not place any restrictions on rejection of collective bargaining agreements except for those agreements subject to the Railway Labor Act. (See section 1167 of the Bankruptcy Code.) The 1984 adoption of section 1113 changed this.

The treatment of collective bargaining agreements in bankruptcy produces a conflict between the debtor's power to reject executory contracts (to benefit the estate as a whole) and the obligations of employers to unionized labor in the National Labor Relations Act (NLRA) prohibiting unilateral modifications of collective bargaining contracts by employers (NLRA section 8(a)(1)) and establishing procedures for their termination (section 8(d)).

The history of collective bargaining agreements in bankruptcy—leading to the enactment of section 1113—is stormy and controversial. The leading court decisions prior to a Supreme Court ruling in *NLRB v. Bildisco & Bildisco,* permitted the debtor in possession to reject collective bargaining contracts without complying with NLRA procedures, but arguably imposed higher standards for the rejection than would apply in other executory contracts.

In *Shopmen's Local Union No. 455 v. Kevin Steel Products, Inc.,* 519 F.2d 698 (2d Cir.1975), the court held that the debtor in possession as a new entity is not a party to any existing labor agreement and is not subject to the contract termination provisions of the NLRA. The court in that case did not apply the business judgment standard used for other contracts because it believed that approach ignored the policies of the NLRA. The impact of rejection of a collective bargaining agreement on the rights of workers and the favored status those rights have been accorded by Congress require a more stringent examination of the evidence presented to justify rejection of such a contract. In the rejection of a collective bargaining agreement the standard is not simply whether rejection would improve the financial status of the debtor. Instead, rejection of a collective bargaining agreement requires "thorough scrutiny" and the court should carefully balance the equities on both sides, keeping in mind that rejection may serve to deprive employees of their seniority, welfare and pension rights. The court did not specifically set out what other factors should be considered. It appeared to approve the union's suggestion that the bankruptcy judge should consider the employer's motivation to ensure the employer does not simply desire to rid himself of the union, proof of the debtor's financial condition, the source of the debtor's difficulties, and the benefit to be gained by rejection.

In *Brotherhood of Railway, Airline and Steamship Clerks v. REA Express, Inc.,* 523 F.2d 164 (2d Cir.1975), this standard was modified.

This case involved a request for permission to reject a contract governed by the R.L.A., but did not involve railway employees. Despite the difference between the R.L.A. and the N.L.R.A. the court held that *Kevin Steel* was applicable and the contract could be rejected. It went on to say that "in view of the serious effects which rejection has on the carrier's employees it should be authorized only where it clearly appears to be the lesser of two evils and that unless the agreement is rejected, the carrier will collapse and the employees will no longer have jobs." Id. at 172.

These two cases taken together established a two-pronged standard for allowing rejection. A good example of this is provided by *In re Alan Wood Steel Co.*, 449 F.Supp. 165 (E.D.Pa.1978). The court set out a two-step analysis to be used in deciding whether to permit rejection of a collective bargaining agreement:

> First, the court should determine that the agreement is onerous and burdensome to the estate, so that failure to reject will make a successful arrangement impossible. Second, the equities must be balanced and found to favor the debtor. Then, and only then, may rejection of a collective bargaining agreement be permitted.

449 F.Supp. at 169.

In balancing the equities two factors were crucial in this case. First, the debtor and receivers had, since the beginning of the bankruptcy proceeding, negotiated and bargained with the union in good faith and out of a desire to reach agreement. Thus, there was no suggestion that the receivers were improperly motivated. Second, the debtor's steel-making activities had been completely terminated with no possibility of recovery or recall of workers. Thus the workers had less of an equitable claim against rejection than where the debtor's business is ongoing.

Both *REA* and *Alan Wood* set strict standards for a trustee desiring to reject a collective bargaining agreement, although in each case rejection was permitted on the facts. However, these cases and *Kevin Steel* were pre-Code. In *NLRB v. Bildisco & Bildisco,* the Supreme Court rejected the more stringent tests of *REA* and *Alan Wood* in favor of the *Kevin Steel* test.

The *Bildisco* court, in an opinion written by Justice Rehnquist, held that "executory contracts" include collective bargaining agreements and that the bankruptcy court could approve the rejection of such agreements "upon an appropriate showing." The Court further held that the debtor in possession does not commit an unfair labor practice when it unilaterally terminates or modifies the agreement prior to the court's rejection.

First, the Supreme Court found the appropriate showing necessary for a bankruptcy court to reject a collective bargaining agreement included evidence that the "agreement burdens the estate and that after careful scrutiny the equities balance in favor of rejecting the labor contract." Justice Rehnquist also stated that the bankruptcy court had to be sure reasonable efforts had been made to negotiate a voluntary modification. Specifically,

> * * * The Bankruptcy Court must make a reasoned finding on the record why it has determined that rejection should be permitted. Determining what would constitute a successful rehabilitation involves balancing the interests of the affected parties—the debtor, creditors and employees. The Bankruptcy Court must consider the likelihood and consequences of liquidation for the debtor absent rejection, the reduced value of the creditors' claims that would follow from affirmance and the hardship that would impose on them, and the impact of rejection on the employees. In striking the balance, the Bankruptcy Court must consider not only the degree of hardship faced by each party, but also any qualitative differences between the types of hardship each may face.

Next, the Court found that neither the National Labor Relations Act nor section 365 prohibited the unilateral rejection of modification of a collective bargaining agreement prior to formal rejection by the bankruptcy court. Enforcement of such an unfair labor practice claim would "run directly counter to * * * the Bankruptcy Code and to the Code's overall effort to give a [DIP] some flexibility and breathing space." This acceptance of unilateral rejection did not, however excuse the DIP's obligation to negotiate in good faith.

What do you think of the following analysis of the post *Bildisco* events in Congress?

The Supreme Court issued its decision in *Bildisco* less than two months before the jurisdiction of the bankruptcy courts would expire under the interim legislation. During the two years since the *Marathon Pipeline Co. v. Northern Pipeline Co.* decision, Congress has tried unsuccessfully to agree upon a permanent solution to the jurisdictional conundrum caused by the Supreme Court's holding that an important part of the jurisdiction of the bankruptcy court was unconstitutional. Incapable of arriving at a consensus on the fundamental political issues, Congress extended the bankruptcy court's jurisdiction for a limited time on four occasions. At the end of each extension various parties seized the opportunity to get their particular bankruptcy project enacted into law in return for a vote for the continuance of the bankruptcy court.

Union representatives sought to use the March 31, 1984 deadline as a device to get Congress to reverse *Bildisco*. In effect the unions made the reversal of that decision the price of their vote, and they were successful in the House. House Bill 5174, continuing the bankruptcy court beyond March 31, would have reversed *Bildisco*. Desiring to appear resolute, the Senate refused to adopt such a rule, and the parties resolved the immediate impasse on four occasions by merely extending the bankruptcy court's jurisdiction to May 1, then to May 26, June 20 and finally, to June 26, 1984.

Approaching the May 26th deadline, the *Bildisco* issue was again presented: this time it took the form of a Senate proposal. Senator

Packwood introduced a bill that borrowed the balancing of the equities test from *Bildisco,* some procedural requirements from the House bill, and inserted some additional tests.

On June 29th, after a two-day hiatus in which there was no bankruptcy court, Congress passed the new section 1113. That section traces its lineage first to House Bill 5174, which passed the House of Representatives on March 21, 1984. Its immediate predecessor is the Packwood Amendment, which was introduced in the Senate on May 22, 1984. Section 1113 contains many of the features of each of its predecessors, but is measurably more favorable to management interests than either of the original proposals.

The House bill was a square attempt to overturn nearly every aspect of *Bildisco* and to adopt the union position. Like section 1113 and all other proposed amendments, it barred unilateral rejection. It contained a form of the REA test—to approve a rejection of a collective bargaining agreement, a court would have had to find that "the jobs covered by such agreement will be lost and any financial reorganization of the debtor will fail." Prior to any rejection, it would also have required the trustee in bankruptcy to propose a modification of the collective bargaining agreement that was "deemed necessary by the trustee for such successful financial reorganization of the debtor and preservation of the jobs * * *." Because the proposal authorized the court to put off a hearing on a request for rejection for an indefinite period for "cause," it offered substantially greater opportunity for delay than the bill which ultimately passed.

The Packwood Amendment substituted the balance of the equities test, for the REA test; it tightened up the time-lines somewhat, and it modified the proposal that had to be made by the trustee from one merely "deemed necessary by the trustee for successful financial reorganization" to one that would permit "the reorganization, taking into account the best estimate of the sacrifices expected to be made by all classes of creditors and other affected parties * * *."

Section 1113 carries forward the balancing of the equities test, but, like Packwood, requires that the equities "clearly" favor rejection. It modifies the management proposal to require not simply that the management consider the union's needs or the sacrifices of all classes, as in Packwood, but that "all of the affected parties are treated fairly and equitably." It contains a fairly rigid timetable that should normally produce a decision on rejection no later than fifty-one days after the filing of an application for rejection.

Finally, section 1113 contains two provisions not found in either of the other versions, which may be of significance. First, it authorizes unilateral rejection of the collective bargaining agreement if the court does not rule on the application for rejection within thirty days after the commencement of the hearing. Second, it authorizes the court to permit interim modification of a collective bargaining agreement on behalf of a management that has not complied with the other conditions of section

1113 if it is "essential to the continuation of the debtor's business or necessary to avoid irreparable damage to the estate."

What will be the consequence of the enactment of section 1113? Because the language is purposefully ambiguous and because it plays upon a vast and varied landscape, one cannot be sure. Surely it makes the law measurably less certain; it will make the trial judge's decision more discretionary and speculative; it will introduce greater guesswork into the lives of those who must advise management and unions about their rights.

Consider some of the important but undefined terms in section 1113. The court may approve a rejection only if it finds that the union representative has refused to accept management's proposal for modification of the contract "without good cause."

Good cause is not defined in this section. Presumably this requires that the court not only make its own determination whether the management proposal was fair and equitable, but also whether the union decision was itself justified on factors that may be unrelated to the merits of the modification proposal. By what standard is the court to measure these things? Is the union's refusal "with good cause" if nonunionized workers of competing businesses are accepting terms similar to those offered? Are all refusals "for a good cause" if the management proposal was too niggardly? The legislation provides no answer to these questions.

Thus the most certain consequence of the new enactment is that the already loose jointed law will be made even more so. We have turned the bankruptcy judges loose in the garden to do what they please. Only after many cases have made their way through the federal court system will we know what modifications are "fair and equitable," which refusals are "with good cause," and how one tests the equities to find which "clearly" favor rejection.

Yet the standards for rejection may not be the important matter. Unless the very act of Congressional enactment signals that labor unions are to be treated more generously than they have been previously, we believe that the courts will continue routinely to reject collective bargaining agreements. The standards, however uncertain, will not make a critical difference.

The majority in *Bildisco* held explicitly that the National Labor Relations Act, and implicitly that section 365, did not prohibit a unilateral rejection of a collective bargaining agreement. Section 1113 of the new bankruptcy amendment specifically reverses that rule; it bars unilateral rejection except in very limited circumstances. Inability to reject unilaterally will be significant only if prompt and final judicial determination cannot be had. At least superficially it appears that section 1113 has dealt with the problem of judicial delay. It provides specifically that a hearing on a proposed rejection must be commenced not later than twenty-one days after the application for rejection and by requiring the court to rule within thirty days after the commencement of the hearing. The section puts teeth in this requirement by authorizing unilateral rejection if the court fails to rule within thirty days.

There are at least two potential difficulties with the superficial reading suggested above. First, the application for rejection apparently cannot be made until the trustee has made a proposal for modification of the contract, and possibly, until the union has had an opportunity to pass on that proposed modification. Moreover it is possible that the union will be able to procure a stay pending an appeal of an unfavorable ruling by the bankruptcy judge. One can appeal an order as of right "if it is a final order" and, as a matter of discretion, under [28 U.S.C.] section 1334(b) if it is not final. The rules grant considerable discretion to the courts to stay an order, to require a bond, or to make other appropriate disposition. If the rejection is stayed pending appeal, and particularly if the union is not made to put up a large bond, the apparently short timelines in section 1113 go for naught.

By authorizing a right unilaterally to reject a collective bargaining agreement, the Supreme Court gave management something that many management lawyers never expected to receive. It freed them not just from the clutches of the NLRB, but also from the requirements of getting a bankruptcy judge's approval. Section 1113 will now require the bankruptcy court's approval, but it displays a Congressional intent that this approval be granted or withheld promptly.

When legislation springs from Congress' brow at the end of the session and under the heat of intense lobbying, it is difficult to predict the ultimate consequences. If the bankruptcy courts are skeptical of union claims and, deep down, believe that unionized employees should not be treated better than others, the new law will have no significant impact. If a new and different group of judges have different views, there is more than enough leeway in the legislation to favor the union position by a favorable finding on any number of determinations that must be made in the legislation.

TRUCK DRIVERS LOCAL 807 v. CAREY TRANSP., INC.

United States Court of Appeals, Second Circuit, 1987.
816 F.2d 82.

ALTIMARI, Circuit Judge:

This appeal involves the showing a debtor-employer must make in order to obtain Bankruptcy Court approval of the employer's application to reject a collective bargaining agreement in accordance with 11 U.S.C. § 1113. [We affirm] Carey Transportation's right to reject two collective bargaining agreements with Truck Drivers Local 807.

FACTS AND PROCEEDINGS BELOW

Carey, a wholly owned subsidiary of Schiavone Carrier Corporation, commenced this litigation by filing a voluntary reorganization petition under Chapter 11 of the Bankruptcy Code in April 1985. Carey, both prior to and since that filing, has been engaged in the business of providing commuter bus service between New York City and Kennedy and LaGuardia Airports.

Local 807 has been the exclusive bargaining representative of Carey's bus drivers and station employees. Local 807 and Carey entered into collective bargaining agreements covering these two groups of employees on August 20, 1982, thereby settling a sixty-four day strike by union members. These two agreements were scheduled to expire on February 28, 1986.

Carey officials have blamed the strike for a subsequent 30% drop in ridership and the yearly revenue losses that preceded its filing for reorganization. Carey has operated at a loss since at least December 31, 1981, reporting annual losses of $750,000 for fiscal year 1983, $1,500,000 for fiscal year 1984, and $2,500,000 for fiscal year 1985.

In September 1983, Carey terminated fifty Local 807 members employed as station workers, although an arbitrator later directed that ten of them be rehired with back pay. The net result of these forty layoffs, according to Carey officials, has been an annual cost savings of approximately $1 million.

In 1984 and 1985, Carey sought and obtained concessions from a union representing Carey's mechanics and repair-shop workers. Those concession led to layoffs of approximately eight workers and annual cost savings estimated at $144,000.

In June 1984, Carey proposed several modifications in its agreements with Local 807. After negotiations, Local 807 and Carey agreed on certain supplemental provisions applicable only to drivers hired after July 1, 1984. These "second-tier" drivers would not get any paid sick days, and they would receive significantly reduced wages, overtime pay, and benefits. These changes, according to Carey, yielded savings of only $100,000 prior to Carey's filing for bankruptcy. The reason given for the relatively small savings was that seasonal variation in industry business resulted in few drivers being hired after the effective date of the Supplement.

On January 31, 1985, counsel for Carey wrote to Local 807 representatives, requesting additional modifications of the two agreements. A series of meetings took place during February and March of 1985, with Carey warning that a failure to reach agreement could force the company to file a Chapter 11 petition and, most likely, apply for permission to reject the existing agreements. Near the end of these sessions, union negotiators agreed to present to union members a set of modifications affecting lunch periods, booking and check-out time, driver rotation rules, holidays, vacation days, sick days, fringe benefit contributions, supplemental unemployment compensation, and supplemental disability insurance. Those concessions, if approved and implemented, would have yielded approximately $750,000 in yearly savings.

On March 27th, however, management added to this proposed modification several additional terms, and described the resultant package as its final offer. In essence, this last set of modifications would have extended the expiration date of the contract for an additional two years, with wages and fringe benefits frozen at the proposed levels until April 1, 1987. At that time, a "reopener" provision would permit the union to bargain for increased wages and benefits during the final year of the extended contract. The union requested that there be binding arbitration if reopener negotiations proved unsuccessful, but management rejected this demand.

This final offer was submitted to the bargaining unit employees on March 29, 1985 and rejected by an 82–7 vote. According to Local 807's business agent, the union members were particularly adamant about not accepting the two-year contract extension and the freeze on wages and benefits.

Carey filed its Chapter 11 petition with the Bankruptcy Court on April 4, 1985, and one day later, delivered to Local 807 a proposal to modify its collective bargaining agreements pursuant to 11 U.S.C. § 1113(b)(1)(A). This post-petition proposal was designed to achieve annual savings of $1.8 million for each of the next three fiscal years.

Carey planned to achieve savings of this magnitude by (1) freezing all wages for second-tier drivers and reducing wages for first-tier drivers (those on the payroll prior to July 1, 1984) by $1.00 per hour; (2) reducing health and pension benefit contributions by approximately $1.50 per hour; (3) replacing daily overtime with weekly overtime; (4) eliminating all sick days and reducing the number of paid holidays; (5) eliminating supplemental workers' compensation and supplemental disability payments; (6) eliminating premium payments and reducing commissions paid to charter drivers; and (7) changing numerous scheduling and assignment rules. All terms were to be frozen for three years under this post-petition proposal.

When Carey presented this proposal to Local 807, company officers were projecting fiscal year 1986 losses of approximately $950,000. (Carey revised this estimate shortly thereafter, projecting losses of $746,000.) In a cover letter accompanying this proposal, Carey asserted that it needed to slash cost by considerably more than its projected losses in order to improve its long-term financial health by updating and expanding its bus fleet, operations, and maintenance facilities. Without savings of this magnitude, Carey explained, it would be unable to propose a feasible reorganization plan to creditors and resolve its indebtedness to them. Carey requested a meeting with Local 807 representatives "to discuss the proposals and to attempt to reach mutually satisfactory modifications of the agreement[s]."

Shortly after the Company submitted its post-petition proposal, dissension within Local 807 became obvious; in fact, virtually all union members formed a "Drivers Committee" and hired an attorney to represent them separately from Local 807 officials. The Drivers Committee then refused to participate in most post-petition negotiations, despite union officials' pleas that they reconsider that decision to "stonewall" these sessions.

In the meantime, Carey filed its section 1113 application to reject its bargaining agreements. The Bankruptcy Court scheduled and conducted five days of hearings on Carey's application, urging the parties to continue negotiations at the same time. After the third day of hearings, a Local 807 officer presented to Carey a counter-proposal designed to achieve annual cost savings of $776,000. The counter-proposal would have extended the expiration date of the existing agreements by fifteen months, and frozen wages and benefits except for a reopener, with binding arbitration, scheduled for June 24, 1986. Carey found the counter-proposal unacceptable, and the hearing continued.

The central issues at the hearing, as on this appeal, were whether the post-petition proposal contained only necessary modifications of the existing agreements, see 11 U.S.C. § 1113(b)(1)(A), whether that proposal treated all parties fairly and equitably, see id., whether Local 807 lacked good cause for rejecting that proposal, see § 1113(c)(2), and whether the balancing of the equities clearly favored rejection of the bargaining agreements, see § 1113(c)(3).

On June 14, 1985, the bankruptcy court issued its decision approving Carey's application to reject the collective bargaining agreements. Bankruptcy Judge Lifland adopted, with certain modifications, a nine-step analysis of § 1113 first used in *In re American Provision Co.*, 44 B.R. 907 (Bankr.D.Minn.1984). Applying this analysis, he held that Carey had met its burden of proving compliance with the procedural and substantive standards set forth in the statute. *See In re Carey Transportation, Inc.*, 50 B.R. 203 (Bankr.S.D.N.Y.1985).

On appeal, the United States District Court for the Southern District of New York affirmed.

Discussion

Congress enacted section 1113 of the Bankruptcy Code, 11 U.S.C. § 1113, in response to *NLRB v. Bildisco & Bildisco*, 465 U.S. 513, 104 S.Ct. 1188, 79 L.Ed.2d 482 (1984), where the Court concluded that a debtor-in-possession could reject a collective bargaining agreement, subject to certain constraints.

Bildisco involved two key holdings. The first involved the proper substantive standard to be used by bankruptcy courts asked to approve rejections of collective bargaining agreements, while the second involved the procedural prerequisites to rejection. In defining the substantive standard, the Supreme Court declined to adopt this court's previous rule that rejection could be approved only after a finding that adherence to the agreement would "thwart efforts to save a failing [company] in bankruptcy from collapse." *Brotherhood of Railway, Airline & Steamship Clerks v. REA Express, Inc.*, 523 F.2d 164, 167–69 (2d Cir.), cert. denied, 423 U.S. 1073, 96 S.Ct. 855, 47 L.Ed.2d 82 (1975). The Court instead endorsed the equitable standard set forth in *In re Brada Miller Freight System, Inc.,* 702 F.2d 890 (11th Cir.1983), and held that the debtor need only prove "that the collective-bargaining agreement burdens the estate, and that after careful scrutiny, the equities balance in favor of rejecting the labor contract." 465 U.S. at 526, 104 S.Ct. at 1196.

On the procedural question, the *Bildisco* Court held that a reorganizing debtor did not have to engage in collective bargaining before modifying or rejecting provisions of the agreement, and such unilateral alterations by a debtor would not violate either section 8(a)(5) or section 8(d) of the National Labor Relations Act, 29 U.S.C. §§ 158(a)(5), (d). *See* 465 U.S. at 534, 104 S.Ct. at 1200. This procedural ruling intensified existing congressional concerns over reports that some companies were misusing the bankruptcy law in collective bargaining. *See Wheeling–Pittsburgh Steel Corp. v. United Steelworkers,* 791 F.2d 1074, 1082 (3d Cir.1986). Congressional response to *Bildisco* was swift, culminating within a few short months in the passage of section 1113.

Merits of the Decision Below

In *Century Brass,* 795 F.2d at 272, this court observed that Congress undeniably overturned the procedural prong of *Bildisco* when it enacted section 1113. Although *Century Brass* turned on the debtor's failure to satisfy these new procedural requirements, the court briefly outlined the substantive showings a debtor must make before its application to reject a collective bargaining agreement may receive judicial approval. These substantive standards are at issue on this appeal.

Briefly stated, the statute permits the bankruptcy court to approve a rejection application only if the debtor, besides following the procedures set forth by Congress, makes three substantive showings. The first is that its post-petition proposal for modifications satisfies § 1113(b)(1), which in turn limits the debtor to proposing only "those necessary modifications in * * * benefits and protections that are necessary to permit the reorganization of the debtor," and obliges the debtor to assure the court that "all creditors, the debtor and all affected parties are treated fairly and equitably." Second, the debtor must show that the union has rejected this proposal without good cause. Bankr.Code § 1113(c)(2). Third, the debtor must prove that "the balance of the equities clearly favors rejection of [the bargaining] agreement." Code § 1113(c)(3). The first two statutory requirements go beyond the substantive test adopted by the *Bildisco* Court, but the requirement represents a codification of the equitable test adopted in *Bildisco.*

We reaffirm and, where necessary, explicate the *Century Brass* panel's discussion of section 1113's substantive requirements. We affirm the decision below because it substantially comports with our reading of the statute, and because Judge Lifland's factual findings are not clearly erroneous.

1. Compliance with § 1113(b)(1)

(a) Necessity of the modifications

As the *Century Brass* panel noted, this provision "emphasizes the requirement of the debtor's good faith in seeking to modify its existing labor contract." 795 F.2d at 273. Although all courts appear to agree on that basic principle, a judicial controversy has arisen over two additional, related questions raised by this provision: (1) how necessary must the proposed modifications be, and (2) to what goal must those alterations be necessary?

In answer to the first of these questions, the Third Circuit concluded that "necessary" as used in subsection (b)(1)(A) is synonymous with "essential" in subsection (e), which authorizes the court to approve certain non-negotiated interim changes while the rejection application is pending. Thus, the court held, necessity must "be construed strictly to signify only modifications that the trustee is constrained to accept." *Wheeling-Pittsburgh Steel*, 791 F.2d at 1088. As to the second question, the Third Circuit concluded that the statute requires the bankruptcy court to focus its attention on "the somewhat shorter term goal of preventing * * * liquidation * * * rather than the longer term issue of the debtor's ultimate future." *Id.* at 1089.

Local 807 asks us to adopt the Third Circuit's reasoning, arguing that the post-petition proposal must fail because it sought more than break-even cost reductions, because the proposed three year term was too long in relation to the eight months remaining under the existing agreement, and because it did not provide for wages and benefits to "snap-back" in the event that Carey's financial performance improved. *See Wheeling–Pittsburgh Steel*, 791 F.2d at 1089–90. We decline to do so.

First of all, the legislative history strongly suggests that "necessary" should not be equated with "essential" or bare minimum. Although the Third Circuit may be correct that the "necessary" language was viewed as a victory for organized labor because it approximated the "minimum modifications" language urged by Senator Packwood, *see id.* at 1088, Congress obviously did not adopt Senator Packwood's proposal. Instead, as the *Wheeling-Pittsburgh Steel* panel acknowledged, Congress settled on "a substitute for this clause." Congress' ultimate choice of this substitute clause suggests that it was uncomfortable with language suggesting that debtor must prove that its initial post-petition proposal contained only bare-minimum changes.

Judge Lifland, in the decision below, properly pointed out a second reason for not reading "necessary" as the equivalent of "essential" or bare minimum. Because the statute requires the debtor to negotiate in good faith over the proposed modifications, any employer who initially proposed truly minimal changes would have no room for good faith negotiating, while one who agreed to any substantive changes would be unable to prove that its initial proposals were minimal. Thus, requiring the debtor to propose bare-minimum modifications at the outset would make it virtually impossible for the debtor to meet its other statutory obligations.

The Third Circuit's answer to the "necessary to what" question is also troubling. In our view, the *Wheeling-Pittsburgh* court did not adequately consider the significant differences between interim relief requests and post-petition modification proposals. Interim relief is available only until the hearing process is completed—normally within two months, *see* § 1113(d)(1), (2)—and only upon showing that adherence to the agreement during that time could imperil "continuation of the debtor's business" or cause "irreparable damage to the estate." *Id.* § 1113(e). In the interim relief context, therefore, it is only proper that the court focus on the bare minimum requirements for short-term survival. In making the decision whether to permit the debtor to reject its bargaining agreement, however, the court must consider whether rejection would increase the likelihood of successful reorganization. A final reorganization plan, in turn, can be confirmed only if the court determines that neither liquidation nor the need for further reorganization is likely to follow. *Id.* at 417 (quoting Bankr.Code § 1129(a)(11)). Thus, in virtually every case, it becomes impossible to weigh necessity as to reorganization without looking into the debtor's ultimate future and estimating what the debtor needs to attain financial health. As the *Royal Composing Room* court phrased it, "A debtor can live on water alone for a short time but over the long haul it needs food to sustain itself and retain its vigor." *Id.* at 418.

Moreover, the length of Carey's proposal and the absence of a snapback provision likewise did not require rejection of the proposal. While the Third Circuit relied on a similar argument in finding a proposed modification not "necessary" for purposes of section 1113, this argument was not raised in either court below and may not be raised here for the first time. The only exception to this rule, avoidance of manifest injustice, *id.*, is inapplicable here because Local 807 wholly failed to demonstrate that Carey's proposed three year term was unnecessary or exceeded either the prevailing industry practice or the parties' past experience.

In sum, we conclude that the necessity requirement places on the debtor the burden of proving that its proposal is made in good faith, and it contains necessary, but not absolutely minimal, changes that will enable the debtor to complete the reorganization process successfully. [W]e cannot conclude that the lower court either misread or misapplied the "necessary modifications" requirement as a matter of law.

Each of the findings pertinent to this inquiry, moreover, is supported by substantial evidence in the record. For instance, record evidence indicates that Carey was losing large sums of money, that its Local 807 labor costs (in contrast to other employees' salaries and benefits) were well above industry averages, and that Carey lacked sufficient assets to meet its current expenses. This well-documented testimony from Carey officials supports the court's finding that Carey had good faith reasons for seeking modifications in its Local 807 agreements. Moreover, record evidence also supports the view that Carey needed to upgrade its facilities and its vehicles in order to complete reorganization successfully. Therefore the bankruptcy court's conclusion that Carey needed to obtain modifications of the magnitude requested, and not merely break-even cost reductions as Local 807 argues, is not clearly erroneous.

(b) Fairness as to all parties.

The requirement that the debtor assure the court that "all creditors, the debtor and all affected parties are treated fairly and equitably," Code § 1113(b)(1)(A), is a relatively straightforward one. The purpose of this provision, according to *Century Brass,* 795 F.2d at 273, "is to spread the burden of saving the company to every constituency while ensuring that all sacrifice to a similar degree." Local 807 argues that the bankruptcy court erred as a matter of both law and fact in assessing the burdens imposed on management, non-union employees, the parent company, and Carey's creditors. We disagree.

The debtor is not required to prove, in all instances, that managers and non-union employees will have their salaries and benefits cut to the same degree that union workers' benefits are to be reduced. To be sure, such a showing would assure the court that these affected parties are being asked to shoulder a proportionate share of the burden, but we decline to hold that this showing must be made in every case.

Rather, a debtor can rely on proof that managers and non-union employees are assuming increased responsibilities as a result of staff reductions without receiving commensurate salary increases; this is surely a sacrifice for these individuals. Particularly where, as here, the court finds that only the employees covered by the pertinent bargaining agreements are receiving pay and benefits above industry standards, it is not unfair or inequitable to exempt the other employees from pay and benefit reductions.

Local 807 has consistently argued that Carey's managers and supervisors are more than adequately compensated, that Local 807 members are not paid substantially more than their counterparts working for Carey's competitors, and that non-union staffing levels have increased rather than decreased since Schiavone purchased Carey. But substantial record evidence supports each of the bankruptcy court's contrary conclusions. For instance, the record contains unrebutted testimony that Carey drivers' hourly wages and benefits exceeded those paid by other private carriers by several dollars per hour, while managers' and supervisors' compensation packages were described as "barely competitive." Carey also offered evidence of pre-petition reductions in its managerial staff (from twenty-four to fifteen people) and its non-union supervisory staff (from fifteen to twelve), achieved by increasing the remaining officials' responsibilities. In light of this record evidence, we cannot disturb the bankruptcy court's findings on this score.

The lower court also correctly looked to pre-petition concessions obtained from the mechanic's union and two of Carey's principal creditors—the MTA and the Port Authority—as proof that these parties were contributing fairly and equitably to the effort to keep Carey afloat. Because a section 1113 application will almost always be filed before an overall reorganization plan can be prepared, the debtor cannot be expected to identify future alterations in its debt structure. Local 807 argues that the lower court overlooked Schiavone's status as a substantial creditor of its subsidiary and Carey's failure to show that Schiavone would write off part of this debt. We reject the suggestion that the statutory requirement that "all creditors" be treated fairly and equitably, see § 1113(b)(1)(A), means that a creditor who is also an owner of the debtor must ordinarily take a smaller percentage dividend than other creditors on its bona fide claims. The mere fact that there have been intercompany transactions between a debtor and its owner is not a source of unfairness to other creditors unless the transactions themselves were financially unfair to the debtor. Local 807 has not called to our attention, nor has our own review of the record disclosed, any evidence to indicate that Schiavone's claims against Carey arise from transactions that were financially unfair to Carey. And were there an indication of such unfair dealing, it would not necessarily support the Union's argument that Carey's rejection of its labor contract should be disapproved. The more appropriate response would seem to be to seek the equitable subordination of claims by the owner, see 11 U.S.C. § 510(c), or the appointment of a trustee who could seek recovery of any fraudulent conveyance, see 11 U.S.C. §§ 544, 548, 1140(a); these remedies would more fairly and equitably benefit all interested parties, not just the union members.

Finally, we note that even if a greater sacrifice is required of an owner-creditor than of other creditors, a write-off of outstanding debts is not the only way a creditor can assist its debtor. Here the record shows that Schiavone did not charge any interest on its loans to Carey, and that Schiavone otherwise subsidized Carey's day-to-day operations. By doing so, Schiavone made sacrifices that contributed significantly to Carey's survival.

In light of this evidence, we affirm the bankruptcy court's ruling that all parties were participating "fairly and equitably" in the attempt to save Carey from liquidation.

2. *Good Cause*

The debtor's obligation to prove that the union lacked good cause for refusing the post-petition proposal, like the necessity question, has been the subject of some debate among commentators and the courts. The bankruptcy court here reasoned that because the proposed modifications were necessary, fair, and equitable, the union's refusal to accept them was without good cause. This reasoning, of course, suggests that the good cause provision adds nothing to the other substantive requirements of the statute.

We conclude, nonetheless, that this analysis is proper where, as here, the union has neither participated meaningfully in post-petition negotiations nor offered any reason for rejecting the proposal other than its view that the proposed modifications were excessive. At least one commentator has noted that the statute appears to authorize conduct similar to what the Drivers Committee did here: "stonewalling" post-petition negotiations and hoping that the courts will find that the proposal does not comply with subsection (b)(1). This tactic is unacceptable and inconsistent with Congressional intent, as the *Royal Composing Room* opinion makes clear. This good cause requirement was "intended to ensure that a continuing process of good faith negotiations will take place before court involvement."

Thus, even though the debtor retains the ultimate burden of persuading the court that the union lacked good cause for refusing proposed modifications, the union must come forward with evidence of "its reason for declining to accept the debtor's proposal in whole or in part. If prehearing, a union has assigned no reason for its refusal to accept a debtor's proposal, it has perforce refused to accept the proposal without good cause under Code § 1113(e)(2)." We agree with the bankruptcy court that because the union engaged in such prehearing stonewalling here, it now cannot claim that it had good cause for refusing the proposal.

Local 807 insists that because it later counter-proposed modifications that would have yielded significant cost savings, it had good cause for rejecting the debtor's proposal. We find, however, that ample record evidence supports the bankruptcy court's conclusion that this counter-proposal did not have the backing of union members. In fact, the counter-proposal was virtually identical to a pre-petition request that the union members had rejected overwhelmingly. A union's presentation of a counter-offer that its members do not support does not satisfy the good cause requirement. Moreover, we have already upheld the lower court's finding that greater than break-even cost savings were necessary. Therefore, this is not a situation where a union's counter-proposal of an equally effective set of modifications might justify its refusal to accept management's proposal. The union's manifest failure to participate meaningfully in the post-petition negotiations confirms its lack of justification for rejecting Carey's proposed modifications.

3. *Balancing the Equities*

This requirement, as we noted in *Century Brass*, is a codification of the *Bildisco* standard. Therefore, the factors identified in *Bildisco* and other cases preceding section 1113's enactment remain applicable today. And although we do not seek to set outer limits on what courts may consider under this broad, flexible test, we note the *Bildisco* Court's reminder that bankruptcy courts "must focus on the ultimate goal of Chapter 11 when considering these equities. The Bankruptcy Code does not authorize freewheeling consideration of every conceivable equity, but rather only how the equities relate to the success of the reorganization." 465 U.S. at 527, 104 S.Ct. at 1197.

The lower court's decision, for the most part, is consistent with still-vital case law applying this equitable balancing test. From *Bildisco* and the cases consistent with its analysis, we glean at least six permissible equitable considerations, many of which also factor into the other substantive requirements imposed by section 1113. Those are (1) the likelihood and consequences of liquidation if rejection is not permitted; (2) the likely reduction in the value of creditors' claims if the bargaining agreement remains in force; (3) the likelihood and consequences of a strike if the bargaining agreement is voided; (4) the possibility and likely effect of any employee claims for breach of contract if rejection is approved; (5) the cost-spreading abilities of the various parties, taking into account the number of employees covered by the bargaining agreement and how various employees' wages and benefits compare to those of others in the industry; and (6) the good or bad faith of the parties in dealing with the debtor's financial dilemma. The only analytical error we find in the lower court's balancing of the equities in this case was its insistence that an allegation of bad faith in initiating the chapter 11 proceeding may not be raised in an objection to a section 1113 application. *See* 50 B.R. at 212–13. We agree with the *Brada Miller* court, 702 F.2d at 900, that equity would preclude a court from approving rejection if the debtor were misusing the entire chapter 11 process. But the lower court's suggestion that this contention would better be raised in a motion to dismiss the entire proceeding or to have a receiver appointed is of no moment. This is because Judge Lifland alternatively found, with ample support in the record, that Carey had a good faith need for seeking protection under chapter 11.

Substantial record evidence supports the lower court's other findings pertinent to this inquiry, despite the union's continued insistence that such support is lacking. For instance, documentary evidence in the record is consistent with the district court's findings that unionized labor costs were approximately 60% above the industry average, that 66% of Carey's employees are unionized, that managers, supervisors, and non-union workers were receiving less than average compensation while taking on increased workloads, and that Local 807, therefore, could fairly be expected to bear a substantial proportion of the needed cost-cutting measures. Record evidence also clearly shows that increasing losses in previous years, and continued but decreasing projected losses in the then-current year, made liquidation a very real threat. The Union has not attempted to refute the evidence that the company's low asset value, the secured creditors' existing claims, and the anticipated costs of administration and liquidation, would leave little or nothing for unsecured creditors and shareholders if the liquidation threat materialized. In view of this substantial and largely unrebutted evidence, we concur in the bankruptcy court's conclusion that the equities favored rejection of the Local 807 agreements.

CONCLUSION

For these reasons, we affirm the judgment of the district court upholding the bankruptcy court's approval of Carey's section 1113 application to reject its bargaining agreements with Local 807.

Questions

What should be the status of workers' claims in a Chapter 11? Should workers covered by a collective bargaining agreement have the same, greater or fewer rights than other contracting parties under section 365? Starting from the position that even workers under contract are no more than future creditors who may have contract claims, the Congress has taken several steps down the road toward recognition of some greater worker claims. In response to the *Bildisco* case, Congress first enacted section 1113, discussed above. Subsequently it passed section 1114 to protect the payment of insurance benefits to retired employees.

Even in reorganization cases, one hears an occasional theme of the workers' interest: will potential buyer A do more for the employees than potential buyer B? Seldom are the prospects of the employees explicitly placed in the equation and evaluated as a numerical addition where it might cause a corresponding numerical subtraction in the equation of the amounts that would otherwise go to the shareholders. Should the equation in Chapter 11 (particularly in section 1129) recognize the rights of the employees as somehow different from and superior to the rights of other future creditors? The unions would say yes. Conservative economists might say no. They might argue that society is served by reallocation of labor to new projects and is injured by maintenance of failing companies in the forlorn hope of saving its employees.

What do you think?

Problem 6–8

1. In Chapter 11, Locke announces a unilateral reduction of wages by 20 percent. As counsel for the union, what action would you advise?

2. Instead of filing, what if Locke waits until the current agreement expires? What rights does the union have in negotiating the new agreement?

3. Suppose the Locke Airways seeks to change the collective bargaining agreement before filing and as a means of forestalling bankruptcy. How should the union respond? Should it stonewall and so force bankruptcy?

Problem 6–9

In our model case, Action Auto, Inc. moved for relief on various grounds in connection with its lease. The Creditor Committee's reply brief is set out below. Consider how sections 361, 362 and 365 intersect here.

UNITED STATES BANKRUPTCY COURT
EASTERN DISTRICT OF MICHIGAN
SOUTHERN DIVISION—FLINT

IN RE:
ACTION AUTO STORES, INC.,
a/k/a Action Auto, Inc.,   Case No. 90–11710–S
a/k/a Sabo Corp.,   (Chapter 11)
a/k/a JED Co.,
Lansing Lewis Services, Inc.,   HON. ARTHUR J. SPECTOR
_____/

CREDITORS' COMMITTEE'S OBJECTION TO OLP—ACTION, INC.'S COMBINED MOTION AND BRIEF TO: (1) COMPEL PAYMENT OF ADMINISTRATIVE EXPENSES; AND (2) TO COMPEL DEBTOR TO ASSUME OR REJECT ITS EXECUTORY LEASE; AND/OR (3) LIFT THE AUTOMATIC STAY; AND/OR (4) FOR ADEQUATE PROTECTION

* * *

II. THE DEBTOR SHOULD BE ALLOWED TO HAVE AT LEAST SIXTY DAYS AFTER FILING TO ASSUME OR REJECT THE LEASE UNDER 11 U.S.C. § 365(d)(4).

Section 365(d)(4) of the Bankruptcy Code provides that nonresidential real property leases must be assumed or rejected within sixty days after the filing of a bankruptcy petition, unless the court extends that period for cause. A lease is deemed rejected if it is not assumed or rejected within this period. 11 U.S.C. § 365(d)(4).

In *In re Musikahn Corp.,* 57 B.R. 942 (Bankr.E.D.N.Y.1986), the landlord moved to compel the Chapter 11 debtor-in-possession to assume or reject a nonresidential real property lease. The Court denied the landlord's motion, finding that §§ 365(d)(3) and (d)(4) did not provide the landlord with the power to compel the debtor-in-possession to assume or reject a lease before the expiration of the sixty-day period. Id. at 944. The Court stated:

> Through the establishment of the 60–day period, Congress sought to expedite the trustee's decision to assume or reject; however, there is no indication that Congress intended to endow a lessor with a mechanism for harassing the trustee into making a hasty and ill-advised determination prior to the expiration of the statutory period. *See,* Statement by the Honorable Orrin G. Hatch, P.L. 98–353, 130 Cong.R. S8891, 3 U.S.Code Cong. & Ad.News 576, 598–601 (1984). Accordingly, this court finds the landlord's motion to compel incongruous with existing bankruptcy law and, as such, denies the motion.

> The landlord can attempt to quicken the assumption process through its opposition to the debtor's motion to extend the statutory 60–day period. This court may grant such an extension for cause where the trustee has demonstrated that it cannot accurately assess the value of the lease to the estate within the prescribed 60–day period. *Unit Portions,* 53 B.R. at 85. In the present case, the debtor asserts two grounds upon which such relief is required: (1) the debtor requires additional time to assess

the profitability of this location during the "busy season" between Christmas and the end of March; and (2) the debtor is in the midst of negotiations with third parties to obtain loans which will be used to provide working capital and satisfy postpetition rent obligation.

The landlord has not sufficiently refuted this showing of cause through its assertions that it has incurred the burdens of upkeep as well as the loss of a prospective lessee for the premises. The Code provides the landlord with an avenue for relief should the debtor reject the lease, see generally 11 U.S.C. § 365(g). Additional safeguards within the Code dictate that prior to the trustee's assumption of the lease, the landlord be made whole for damages due to debtor's default. See generally, 11 U.S.C. § 365(b). Furthermore, the landlord's claim that the debtor's chances of obtaining financing are "slim at best" is mere speculation and hardly an invalidation of the debtor's showing of cause. Accordingly, this court grants the debtor's cross motion to extend the statutory period in which it can assume or reject the lease * * *

OLP emphasizes that the Debtor knows what it will do with the lease and should therefore be compelled to assume or reject the lease now. However, as this Court held in *In re Walat Farms, Inc.,* 69 B.R. 529, 534 (Bankr.E.D.Mich.1987), a Chapter 11 debtor-in-possession must first obtain court approval before there is any assumption or rejection. The Debtor should not be forced to make a hasty decision without fully considering the consequences of assumption or rejection.

In addition, the Creditors' Committee has not had sufficient time to intelligently assess the Debtor's financial situation and make a recommendation as to which leases should be assumed or rejected. In fact, as of the date of this objection, counsel for the Creditors' Committee have not received a copy of the underlying sale agreement, nor had the opportunity to investigate the transaction. In addition, the Creditors' Committee has not had any reasonable opportunity to perform its duties under § 1103(c), including without limitation its investigation of the desirability of the continuation of the Debtor's business.

The Debtor should be allowed at least sixty days after filing to carefully evaluate the benefits and burdens of the lease. It is especially important to the unsecured creditors that the Debtor make an informed, deliberate decision. In fact, if the Debtor assumes any leases, administrative expenses are created which obviously have priority over the claims of the unsecured creditors. It is essential that the Debtor not assume any leases until the Creditors' Committee has had sufficient time to review the desirability of the Debtor's continued business operations generally or at a particular site.

Alternatively, if leases are rejected without sufficient time for investigation, the rejection may be detrimental to the estate. In any event, OLP's motion to compel assumption or rejection of the lease should be denied as premature.

III. OLP IS NOT ENTITLED TO ADEQUATE PROTECTION.

Lessors are not entitled to adequate protection pending the lessee's decision to assume or reject. *In re Sweetwater,* 40 B.R. 733, 745 (Bankr. D.Utah 1984). Instead, a lessor's exclusive remedies are found in § 365. Id.

In *Sweetwater,* the lessor was the assignee of leases with the debtor-lessee. After filing its Chapter 11 petition, the debtor-lessee retained possession of the property, but made no lease payments. The lessor filed motions requesting that the court (1) set a date by which the debtor must assume or reject leases; (2) compel the debtor to adequately protect the lessor's interest in the leased property for the period between the filing of the petition and the date of the debtor's assumption or rejection of the leases; and (3) grant relief from the automatic stay if adequate protection was not provided. Id. at 734.

The court in *Sweetwater* exhaustively analyzed the legislative history regarding adequate protection and noted that "nowhere in the legislative history have lessors been mentioned as being entitled to adequate protection." *Id.* at 742. The court concluded that Congress intended to provide adequate protection to secured creditors only, not lessors. Id. at 745. The court also concluded that requiring debtors to provide lessors with adequate protection pursuant to § 363(e) would defeat the policy in § 365 of allowing the debtor to make a careful and informed decision whether to assume or reject an unexpired lease. Id. Therefore, the court held that a lessor is not "an entity that has an interest in property" for the purposes of § 363(e) and that a lessor's exclusive remedies are found in § 365. Id.

Although the lease in *Sweetwater* involved personal property, the *Sweetwater* analysis applies where there is a lease of nonresidential real property. *In re Cafe Partners/Washington 1983,* 81 B.R. 175, 180 (Bankr.D.D.C.1988).

The court's decision in *In re Troy Industrial Catering Service,* 2 B.R. 521 (Bankr.E.D.Mich.1980), may support the proposition that lessors are entitled to adequate protection under § 363(e) pending a decision to assume or reject a lease. However, as the court in *Sweetwater* noted, the legislative history or the structure of the Bankruptcy Code as a whole was not considered in the *Troy Industrial* case. *Sweetwater,* 40 B.R. at 743.

IV. THE AUTOMATIC STAY SHOULD NOT BE LIFTED.

As discussed above, a lessor's exclusive remedy is found in §. 365. A lessor may not move for relief from stay under § 362(d)(1) because it cannot complain of a lack of adequate protection in the first place. *In re O–Jay Foods, Inc.,* 110 B.R. 895, 897 (Bankr.D.Minn.1989).

OLP may also not rely on § 362(d)(2) for relief from the stay because § 365 provides its sole remedy. However, assuming that OLP could seek relief from the stay pursuant to § 362(d)(2), such relief should not be granted because it is not certain yet which store locations will be necessary for a successful reorganization.

CONCLUSION

For the reasons set forth above, OLP's Motion to (1) Compel Payment of Administrative Expenses; and (2) Compel Debtor to Assume or Reject Its Executory Lease; and/or (3) Lift the Automatic Stay; and/or (4) For Adequate Protection should be denied.

Respectfully submitted,
MILLER, JOHNSON, SNELL & CUMMISKEY

Local Counsel for Official
Unsecured Creditors' Committee

Dated: July 13, 1990 By _____
Thomas P. Sarb

And _____
Joseph M. Ammar

Business Address:
800 Calder Plaza Building
Grand Rapids, MI 49503

Question

If you represented Action Auto, how would you respond to the Creditor Committee's arguments?

Chapter Seven

AVOIDANCE POWERS

§ 1. INTRODUCTION

In the dark days prior to a bankruptcy filing, desperate debtors and creditors are tempted to find ways to improve their situations. A debtor whose partnership is going under could "give" "his" yacht to his wife to remove it from the grasp of partnership creditors. A creditor might choose to perfect a security interest properly or to pressure the debtor into granting a security interest for the first time. This behavior might be compared to that of the crew of a passenger ship who know the ship is sinking and who choose to flee in the only lifeboats available rather than notify the passengers.

The Bankruptcy Code requires equitable distribution of the seats in the lifeboats. The avoidance powers provided in the Code are designed to enforce the rule by allowing the trustee to avoid or undo certain pre-filing transactions that have impaired the other claims.

This Chapter deals with the trustee's avoidance powers. Section 548 of the Bankruptcy Code covers fraudulent conveyances. Classical fraudulent conveyances are crude attempts by debtors to transfer their property to others, usually relatives or friends, in an effort to deprive creditors of that property. The newest fraudulent conveyances have arisen out of leveraged buyouts (LBOs).

Another important section of the Code, section 553, deals with setoff. Setoff means quite different things to different people. To a student of civil procedure it is the right of a defendant to reduce the plaintiff's recovery by "setting off" a claim that the defendant has against the plaintiff. To others it means simply the netting of an account, and to some it may be regarded as akin to a security interest. However one characterizes the right of setoff, it is an important creditor's right that is used extensively by financial institutions, particularly banks. A setoff that one might meet in a bankruptcy proceeding would go as follows: Construction Corp. has a $100,000 bank account at Bank and Trust. It has also borrowed $500,000 from Bank and Trust, and it is in default on that loan. When Bank's patience wears thin, it decides to "set off". By the act of setting off it will reduce Construction's bank account to zero and correspondingly reduce the obligation that it owes to the bank to $400,000. The mutual debts (the deposit owed by the bank to the depositor and the debt owed by the depositor to the bank) are netted against one another.

Section 547 governs voidable preferences. Unlike section 548, section 547 is a considerable refinement of their shared common law antecedent—fraudulent conveyance law. The trustee can use section 547 to challenge transfers to creditors made on the eve of bankruptcy. Section 547(b) is a broad net that catches many payments which would otherwise alter the relationship of the creditors. By creating many exceptions to the rule, section 547(c) narrows section 547(b) considerably.

Section 544 is probably more important than all of the other avoidance provisions combined. It implements state law and policy in two ways. First, section 544(a) (the "strong arm" clause), avoids improperly perfected security transfers. Here the trustee is a hypothetical creditor. This section aids in the enforcement of state law statutes regulating the recording of security interests.

Second, 544(b) allows the trustee to step into the shoes of an actual unsecured creditor to pursue its state law claims. This section has recently been used as an alternative means of attacking fraudulent conveyances. Such claims arise under laws such as the Uniform Fraudulent Conveyances Act (UFCA) and the Uniform Fraudulent Transfers Act (UFTA). The UFCA is the earlier statute, written in 1918, codifying the long-standing common law rules and adding an objective test which presumed fraudulent intent in certain situations if fair consideration was lacking. In 1984 the UFTA revision was promulgated. Approximately one-third of the states have adopted the UFTA.

Finally, sections 545 and 546 apply to statutory liens. Section 545 allows the trustee to avoid certain statutory liens; section 546 limits this authority.

Avoidance powers can increase the size and alter the distribution of a debtor's estate. They police the behavior of creditors and other parties in dealing with a debtor in financial trouble who has not yet filed bankruptcy. The threat of their use may sometimes inhibit creditors' most aggressive instincts even in cases where no bankruptcy occurs.

§ 2. TRUSTEE AS A LIEN CREDITOR AND PURCHASER, SECTION 544

Section 544 is the child of sections 70(c) and 70(e) of the Bankruptcy Act of 1898. Section 544(a) makes the trustee (as of the date of the petition) into a judgment lien creditor, a judicial lien creditor and a purchaser of real estate. Because section 544(a) merely grants the trustee a state law status, the strength of that status depends on state law. Section 544 gives the trustee rights equivalent to a judgment lien creditor, but state law determines what powers a judgment lien creditor holds. Not to worry, however; state laws with respect to judicial liens tend to be quite consistent.

Section 544(a) is often asserted against security interests in personal property. When so, the applicable state law is almost always UCC 9-301. Read it and see how it fits. Do you see how it elevates the trustee over unperfected or improperly perfected secured creditors?

UCC Article 9 applies only to personal property. The law relating to real estate security interests is less uniform. Section 544(a)(3) allows the trustee to upset unperfected mortgages in states where a bona fide purchaser could do so but a lien creditor could not. (Do you see why the trustee is not treated as a bona fide purchaser with respect to personal property?) The adequacy of perfection of a real estate lien is frequently tested by reference to the rights of "purchasers," not "lien creditors," and often depends in part on concepts of actual or constructive notice, not merely on filing priority.

Problem 7–1

Assume that debtor files a petition in bankruptcy on 4/15/99. At the date of the petition the trustee seeks to set aside each of the following transactions under 544(a). What would you advise?

(1) A transaction in which the debtor is the lessee of an expensive industrial machine. Under the terms of the lease the lessee pays $700 per month for 8.5 years. At the end of that time the debtor has the right to purchase the machine for its fair market value or to return it to the lessor. The lessor has not filed a financing statement. Would it matter that the projected useful life of the machine was nine years as opposed to eighteen?

(2) Debtor, a company incorporated in Illinois with its headquarters in Chicago, borrowed money from an Ohio bank and granted the Ohio bank a security interest in the inventory of and proceeds from the inventory of its Ohio retail store, located in Cincinnati. The Ohio bank filed a financing statement covering the inventory and proceeds in the county in which Cincinnati is located and in Columbus, Ohio. At the date the bankruptcy petition is filed, there is $200,000 of inventory and $400,000 of accounts receivable. Can the trustee successfully challenge the secured creditor's claims to either of these assets?

(3) Long before bankruptcy, the Chicago Debtor gave a bank in Springfield, Illinois a security interest in the inventory in its downstate plant. Twenty days before the bankruptcy was filed, the bank discovered that it had not filed a financing statement. Fifteen days before the bankruptcy, the bank filed a proper financing statement in Springfield.

Note: Article 9 Perfection

Daunting at first, Article 9 is really quite simple. First, a security agreement must "attach"—which is to say, it must satisfy 9–203. The term "attachment" means that the security agreement is valid between the creditor and the debtor, but does not tell whether it is effective against third parties. Section 9–201 gives a presumption of effectiveness, but section 9–301 (visited above in Problem 7–1) radically restricts the effect of 9–201. Usually 9–203 requires that there be a written agreement, that the agreement grant a security interest to the debtor, that the creditor give value (by lending or promising to make a loan), and that the debtor have rights in the collateral (i.e., usually be its owner). These requirements are quite simple and no particular form is necessary. A security agreement could be written in one sentence on the back of an old envelope.

The trick comes in "perfecting" the security interest. Usually perfection requires that the parties give public notice of the secured creditor's interest. The most common mode of notice is by filing a financing statement, sometimes called a "UCC–1". In most cases the filing is done at the Secretary of State's office in the state where the goods are located. In other cases the filing is done locally (at the county Register of Deeds office) or in the state of the debtor's chief place of business. Section 9–401 tells where filing is to be done within the state; section 9–103 tells which state. Section 9–402 tells what the UCC–1 must say.

In addition to filing there is the possibility of "automatic perfection" and the possibility of perfection by taking possession; section 9–115 introduces yet another mode of perfection for some assets, "control." The former, automatic perfection, applies only in limited cases where it was thought that others would not be misled by the absence of public notice. Read again sections 544(a) and 9–301. In effect, UCC 9–301 states that lien creditors have priority over unperfected security interests. The combination of 9–301 and 544(a) makes it clear that a trustee in bankruptcy or the debtor in possession is a lien creditor on the date the petition is filed. The upshot of this is that any security interest that is not perfected on the date the petition is filed can be set aside under 544(a) by the trustee or debtor in possession.

PROBASCO v. EADS

United States Court of Appeals, Ninth Circuit, 1988.
839 F.2d 1352.

BOOCHEVER, CIRCUIT JUDGE:

Appellant William R. Probasco (Probasco) appeals from the Bankruptcy Appellate Panel's order, 69 B.R. 730, affirming the bankruptcy court's judgment that Bill J. Eads (Eads), as debtor in possession, could assert 11 U.S.C. § 544(a)(3)(Supp. IV 1986) to avoid Probasco's unrecorded one-half interest in Parcel 1 of the Quail Meadows development. The controlling issue on appeal is whether a debtor in possession holding record title to property had constructive notice of an interest in that property, which, because of a secretarial mistake, did not appear on record.

* * *

Background

The facts are undisputed. In 1978, Eads purchased Quail Meadows, consisting of 76.61 acres of undeveloped land. Approximately seventy-five percent of the acreage is in Parcel 1 and the remaining twenty-five percent is in Parcels 2 and 3.

In 1981, Eads agreed to make Probasco a one-half owner of Quail Meadows in exchange for Probasco's agreement to execute jointly with the Eads, a $600,000 note secured by a trust deed encumbering Quail Meadows. In addition, Probasco agreed to make payments on the note. A deed was to have been recorded conveying a fifty percent undivided interest in Quail Meadows from the Eads to Probasco concurrently with the recordation of the trust deed securing the $600,000 note.

The documents were executed and recorded in August 1981. The escrow company that prepared the deed and the deed of trust failed to attach a legal description of Parcel 1 to either the deed or the deed of trust. Both documents contained descriptions of Parcels 2 and 3. The escrow company has since gone out of business.

After August 1981, Eads and Probasco proceeded with their plans to subdivide the Quail Meadows property. Engineers, surveyors, and attorneys were employed to secure a tentative subdivision map which was approved by the Madera County Board of Supervisors. In connection with securing the subdivision plans, Probasco paid $25,000 for a sewer easement through neighboring property.

In July 1982, Eads filed a voluntary petition for reorganization under Chapter 11 of the Bankruptcy Code, 11 U.S.C. §§ 1101–74 (1982 & Supp. IV 1986). In August 1982, Probasco also filed a voluntary petition for reorganization under Chapter 11. The omission of a description of Parcel 1 from the deed and the deed of trust was not discovered until after the filing of both petitions.

The underlying adversary proceedings were commenced by Eads in his capacity as debtor in possession. The parties seek a determination of the nature, extent, and validity of all liens and other interests in the Quail Meadows property.

* * *

Analysis

1. The Strong Arm Clause

Title 11 U.S.C. § 544(a)(Supp. IV 1986), "the strong arm clause," gives a bankruptcy trustee power to avoid certain transfers or liens against property in the bankruptcy estate.

Section 544(a)(3) allows the trustee to avoid all obligations and transfers that would be avoidable by "a bona fide purchaser of real property * * * that obtains the status of a bona fide purchaser * * * at the time of the commencement of the [bankruptcy] case, whether or not such a purchaser exists." Section 544(a) grants the bankruptcy trustee this power "without regard to any knowledge of the trustee or of any creditor." The powers of a bona fide purchaser for purposes of section 544(a) are defined by state law.

* * *

Placer Savings & Loan Ass'n v. Walsh (In re Marino), 813 F.2d 1562, 1565 (9th Cir.1987). A debtor in possession has the same rights, powers, functions, and duties, except the right to compensation, as a bankruptcy trustee. 11 U.S.C. § 1107 (1982 & Supp. IV 1986).

II. Constructive Notice

Probasco argues that under California law Eads could not take title to Quail Meadows as a bona fide purchaser because he had constructive notice of Probasco's ownership in the property. The law of California requires every conveyance of real property to be recorded in order to be valid against a subsequent purchaser or mortgagee of the same property, who in good faith and for valuable consideration records first. Thus, under California law a bona fide purchaser who records prevails over a prior transferee who failed to record.

Actual or constructive notice of a prior unrecorded transfer removes a subsequent purchaser from the protection of the recording acts. Clear and open possession of real property constitutes constructive notice of the rights of the party in possession to subsequent purchasers. Such a prospective purchaser must inquire into the possessor's claimed interests, whether equitable or legal. * * * Therefore, a bona fide purchaser who records does not take priority over one in clear and open possession of real property.

Eads, by virtue of section 544(a)(3), has the rights of a hypothetical bona fide purchaser. The language of the section renders the trustee's or any creditor's knowledge irrelevant. It does not, however, make irrelevant notice constructively given by open possession any more than it would make irrelevant the constructive notice given by recorded instruments that might evidence a competing claim of title to the real property in question.

* * *

Probasco argues that in July 1982, when Eads filed his bankruptcy petition, the undisputed evidence of the physical condition of the Quail Meadows property as well as the subdivision activity on the property was more than sufficient to give constructive notice of Probasco's interest in Parcel 1. The evidence consisted of (1) surveyor's stakes criss-crossing all three parcels, (2) a fence around the perimeter with no intervening fences dividing parcels, (3) roadways across the three parcels which were not fenced at parcel lines, (4) proximity of the parcels to freeways, shopping centers and other subdivisions indicating that the parcels were part of a subdivision, and (5) a tentative subdivision map filed with the Clerk of Madera County.

Constructive notice is defined by California Civil Code § 19 (West 1982) as follows:

Every person who has actual notice of circumstances sufficient to put a prudent man upon inquiry as to a particular fact, has constructive notice of the fact itself in all cases in which, by prosecuting such inquiry, he might have learned such fact.

Whether the circumstances are sufficient to put one on inquiry of another's interest in property is a question of fact.

* * *

At issue is whether a prudent purchaser would have actual notice of circumstances giving rise to inquiry about the unity of ownership of all three parcels. The fact that Eads had an interest in all three parcels does not dispose of that issue. The question is whether a prudent person, observing the indicia of unity of ownership of all three parcels, and knowing that Probasco had a one-half interest in Parcels 2 and 3, would be placed on inquiry about his interest in the remainder of Quail Meadows. It is almost inconceivable that such a prudent person, knowing that Parcels 2 and 3 were jointly owned, and seeing a perimeter fence around all three parcels, no fence between the parcels, the staking of all three parcels, and roads traversing the entire property, would not inquire whether a one-half owner of Parcels 2 and 3 had an interest in Parcel 1.

The California Code applies the standard of a "prudent" person. "Prudent" is defined as "a: marked by wisdom or judiciousness, b: shrewd in the management of practical affairs, c: marked by circumspection." *Webster's Ninth New Collegiate Dictionary* (1984). A prudent purchaser inquiring as to the unity of ownership of all three parcels "might have learned" of Probasco's interest in Parcel 1. Cal.Civ.Code § 19.

The bankruptcy court concluded that none of the conditions of the property at the commencement of the case or the fact of the filing of the subdivision map with the Clerk of Madera County were acts inconsistent with the record title to the property so as to raise a duty of inquiry in a prospective purchaser. The Eads in their brief to this court amplified that terse conclusion, stating:

> Appellants' brief noted the presence of a road across Parcel 1 to Parcels 2 and 3, of a fence around Parcels 1, 2 and 3 and of certain survey stakes as items which would have given a bona fide purchaser constructive notice of the Probascos' interest in Parcel 1. Even if these items constituted "possession, use or occupancy" of which a bona fide purchaser would be deemed to have knowledge, such possession, use and occupancy was joint between Probascos and Eads and, thus, not inconsistent with the record title.

The error in their argument and the bankruptcy court's conclusions is that the physical evidence indicated a unity of ownership of all three parcels and the record revealed that two of those parcels were owned jointly by Eads and Probasco. The indications of unity of ownership were such as to put a prudent person on inquiry as to whether Probasco also had an interest in Parcel 1. Such an interest in Parcel 1 was inconsistent with the record title indicating that the Eads were its sole owners. We are left with the definite and firm conviction that the bankruptcy court made a mistake in finding that there was no constructive notice and voiding Probasco's interest in Parcel 1. Upon remand the court should reform the deed from Eads to Probasco to include Parcel 1 in accordance with the undisputed intention of the parties. *See Higgs v. United States,* 546 F.2d 373, 375–76, 212 Ct.Cl. 146 (1976)(where parties intended that land involved in sales contract include two parcels and draftsmanship error excluded one parcel, reformation appropriate to reflect parties' true intent).

* * *

CONCLUSION

Eads, acting as debtor in possession under the strong arm powers of 11 U.S.C. § 544(a)(3), had constructive notice placing him on inquiry which might have revealed Probasco's interest in Parcel 1. Eads therefore did not take Parcel 1 free of Probasco's interest. * * *

AFFIRMED in part, REVERSED in part, and REMANDED.

Questions

1. Would the court have held that Probasco's unrecorded deed was protected if there was no open and notorious possession, but the debtor (and *a fortiori* debtor in possession) had actual knowledge of the interest? If not, what is the significance of use and possession of the property?

2. If there was no possession of the property by Probasco, but all of the creditors and the debtor knew of Probasco's claim, this court would have held the interest to be invalid, true?

IN RE GENERAL COFFEE CORP.

United States Court of Appeals, Eleventh Circuit, 1987.
828 F.2d 699.

GODBOLD, CIRCUIT JUDGE:

This is an appeal by debtor General Coffee and intervenor Shawmut Boston International Banking Corporation from an adverse bankruptcy decision by the district court that General Coffee, as debtor-in-possession, could not bring into its estate over $6 million it held in constructive trust for City National Bank of Miami ("CNB"). We affirm.

[The underlying transaction was part of a fraud committed by Camilio Bautista. Bautista was an officer of the plaintiff bank and also an officer of the parent of the debtor. The funds that are claimed to be part of the constructive trust were originally represented by an $8,000,000 CD that was owned by City National Bank. In effect Bautista stole the $8,000,000 CD. Using it as collateral, he borrowed $8,000,000 from a Panamanian bank on behalf of the debtor's parent. He then put at least $6,400,000 of that amount into the debtor's account and withdrew the $6,400,000 in a check to pay one of the debtor's legitimate obligations arising out of its purchase of Chase & Sanborn. The net effect of the transaction was to take an asset of the bank (the CD) and by a series of transactions to use the value represented by that CD to pay a debt owed by the debtor, General Coffee. Recognizing that the $8,000,000 CD belonged to it, City National argued that $8,000,000 CD turned into the $6,400,000 balance in the account which was paid out to General Coffee, who paid it to Chase & Sanborn. It claims that these assets became and remain the corpus of a constructive trust that arose under Florida law when its asset, the $8,000,000 CD, was converted.]

The court explained that under Florida law "a constructive trust comes into existence on the date of the order or judgment of a court of competent jurisdiction declaring that a series of events has given rise to a constructive trust." *In re General Coffee Corp.*, 41 B.R. 781, 783 (Bankr.S.D.Fla.1984)(*In re General Coffee I*)(quoting *Palmland Villas I Condominium Assoc. v. Taylor,* 390 So.2d 123, 124 (Fla. 4th DCA 1980)). Thus, the court concluded, CNB's constructive trust arose after General Coffee has filed for bankruptcy, and General Coffee could bring the trust assets into the bankruptcy estate through its strong-arm powers under 11 U.S.C. § 544:

* * *

On appeal the district court reversed. It held that the bankruptcy court's exclusive reliance on *Palmland Villas* was misplaced. The holding in *Palmland Villas* that a constructive trust does not arise until decreed by a court was, according to the district court, contrary to Florida law. The court explained that the Florida Supreme Court has long accepted the majority view that a constructive trust arises as a matter of law when the facts giving rise to the fraud occur. The district court concluded, therefore, that the constructive trust in favor of CNB arose prior to the filing of General Coffee's bankruptcy petition.

* * *

II. Constructive Trust

The bankruptcy court relied exclusively on *Palmland Villas* to conclude that a constructive trust does not exist until the date of judgment declaring that a series of events has given rise to a constructive trust. General Coffee contends that the bankruptcy court properly applied Florida law and that the district court erred in refusing to follow controlling Florida precedent.

"A federal court applying state law is bound to adhere to decisions of the state's intermediate courts absent some persuasive indication that the state's highest court would decide the issue otherwise." *Silverberg v. Paine, Webber, Jackson & Curtis, Inc.,* 710 F.2d 678, 690 (11th Cir.1983). We believe, however, that *Palmland Villas* does not accurately reflect Florida law. With the exception of *Palmland Villas* Florida courts have consistently applied the majority view on when constructive trusts arise. We are convinced that, if presented with this issue, the

Florida Supreme Court would reaffirm the majority approach that a constructive trust arises when the facts giving rise to the fraud occur.

* * *

Although these decisions did not expressly adopt the majority rule, they applied that rule to the facts of each case. Subsequent Florida appellate court decisions have similarly applied, without expressly adopting, the majority rule that a constructive trust exists from the time the facts giving rise to it occur.

* * *

The only Florida appellate decision to reject the majority approach was *Palmland Villas*. The court relied exclusively on *Wadlington v. Edwards*, 92 So.2d 629 (Fla.1957) and *Yawn v. Blackwell*, 343 So.2d 906 (Fla. 3d DCA 1977). The court's entire reasoning was as follows:

> An action for the declaration of a constructive trust may be barred if the events giving rise to the necessity for the imposition of this equitable remedy transpired beyond the period permitted by the applicable statute of limitations, usually expressed in terms of laches. See *Yawn v. Blackwell*, 343 So.2d 906 (Fla. 3d DCA 1977). This leads inevitably to the conclusion that a constructive trust is not created by the facts themselves since no trust is found where the operable facts occur beyond the statutory period. The facts simply form the basis upon which a court may presently impose a trust if the statute of limitations has not barred this remedy. *Wadlington v. Edwards*, 92 So.2d 629 (Fla.1957).

Palmland Villas, 390 So.2d at 125.

Wadlington and *Yawn* hold only that a beneficiary of a constructive trust will be precluded from obtaining equitable relief if he has sat on his rights. Because a constructive trust beneficiary may be denied equitable relief because he has sat on his rights does not "inevitably" lead to the conclusion that a constructive trust does not exist until so decreed by a court of equity.

* * *

We hold that under the Florida law that we are convinced the Supreme Court of that state would find controlling, a constructive trust in favor of CNB came into existence before General Coffee filed its petition in bankruptcy.

III. Property of the Estate

Because we agree with the district court that the constructive trust in favor of CNB came into existence before the bankruptcy proceedings began, we must decide whether General Coffee can nevertheless bring the trust assets into the estate for distribution to its creditors under 11 U.S.C. § 544(a). Section 544(a), the "strong-arm" provision of the Bankruptcy Code, permits a trustee to avoid secret liens against property in the debtor's possession. It grants a trustee the rights of an essentially ideal lienholder against property in which the debtor does not possess complete title.

The district court held that General Coffee could not use § 544(a) to defeat CNB's rights as beneficiary of the constructive trust. The court explained that under 11 U.S.C. § 541(d), the estate took only legal title to the trust assets, subject to the equitable interests of CNB. The court concluded, relying exclusively on *In re Quality Holstein Leasing,* 752 F.2d 1009 (5th Cir.1985), that the provisions defining property of the estate in § 541(d) prevail over a trustee's strong-arm powers under § 544.

The drafters of the Bankruptcy Code appear not to have anticipated the potential for tension between sections 541(d) and 544(a). Since the enactment of § 541(d), however, many courts have recognized that these sections are not always easily reconciled because § 541(d) excludes certain equitable interests from the estate of a bankrupt while § 544(a) permits the trustee to bring certain tainted property into the control of the estate. For example, where the debtor holds certain real property in constructive trust for another because of fraud, § 541(d) excludes from the estate the constructive trust beneficiary's equitable interest in the property. *See, e.g., Quality Holstein Leasing,* 752 F.2d at 1012; *In re Elin,* 20 B.R. 1012, 1015–16 (D.N.J.1982), aff'd mem., 707 F.2d 1400 (3d Cir.1983). It appears, however, that § 544(a) would bring the trust property into the estate in spite of § 541(d). Section 544(a) would permit the bankruptcy trustee to bring the constructive trust property into the estate through his strong-arm powers as a hypothetical bona fide purchaser because a constructive trust beneficiary's interest in real property is, by definition, an unrecorded interest, which is inferior to the interest of a bona fide purchaser of the real property.

Courts have responded to the tension between these sections in two ways. Some courts, like the district court here, have held that § 541(d) prevails over the trustee's strong-arm powers under § 544(a). *See, e.g., Quality Holstein Leasing,* 752 F.2d at 1013; *In re Triple A Coal Co.,* 55 B.R. 806, 813 (Bankr.S.D.Ohio 1985); *In re Earl Roggenbuck Farms, Inc.,* 51 B.R. 913, 917 (Bankr.E.D.Mich.1985). These courts have reasoned that "[a]lthough [§ 544(a)'s strong-arm] powers allow a trustee to assert rights that the debtor itself could not claim to property, Congress did not mean to authorize a bankruptcy estate to benefit from property that the debtor did not own." Any other interpretation would, according to these courts, render § 541(d) meaningless.

A majority of courts have rejected this approach. They have held that sections 541(d) and 544(a) operate independently. Thus, property not part of the estate under § 541(d) may come into the estate under § 544(a). These courts have reasoned as follows:

> [A] reading and comparison of § 541(d) and § 544 leads to the inescapable conclusion that § 541(d) does not represent a general limitation on the trustee's avoidance powers under § 544. Section 541(d) qualifies the trustee's right under § 541(a) to succeed to

certain property interests possessed by the debtor at the time of the filing of his bankruptcy petition. In contrast, § 544(a) arms the trustee at the time of the filing of the debtor's bankruptcy petition with all the rights and powers of various creditors and transferees of the debtor so as to avoid incomplete or improperly perfected transfers of the debtor and thereby insure an equality of distribution among the debtor's general unsecured creditors. *See, e.g.,* 4 L. King, Collier on Bankruptcy ¶ 541.01, 541–5 to 541–9 and ¶ 544.01, 544–2 to 544–4 (15th ed. 1982); 2 W. Norton, Bankruptcy Law and Practice §§ 29.01 and 30.01 (1982). Section 544(a) in fact contemplates that the debtor has no remaining interest in the property which is the subject of the avoided transaction. The trustee is thus given the ability to bring into the estate, in addition to the debtor's property as defined by § 541(a) and limited by § 541(d), any property which he can obtain through his avoidance powers under the Bankruptcy Code, including his ability to invalidate certain transfers by the debtor under § 544(a).

Anderson, 30 B.R. at 1009–10. Although this result seems to contradict the language of § 541(d), these courts have explained that it is consistent "with the letter and with the spirit of the Bankruptcy Code."

This circuit has never resolved the tension between sections 541(d) and 544(a). Nor do we need to do so here. The result in this case is the same under either approach.

Under the minority approach, CNB's interest in the trust assets as beneficiary of the constructive trust does not come into General Coffee's bankruptcy estate. Where a debtor holds property in a constructive trust for another, "[t]he rule is elementary that the estate succeeds only to the title and rights in the property that the debtor possessed * * *. Therefore * * *, the estate will generally hold such property subject to the outstanding interest of the beneficiaries." *Georgia Pacific Corp. v. Sigma Serv. Corp.,* 712 F.2d 962, 968 (5th Cir.1983)(quoting 4 *Collier on Bankruptcy* ¶ 541.13 (L.King 15th ed. 1987)); *see also Quality Holstein Leasing,* 752 F.2d at 1012. Thus, because § 541(d) prevails over a trustee's strong-arm powers under § 544(a), CNB has a right to recover the assets of the constructive trust.

CNB has the same rights under the majority approach. Section 544(a) confers on the bankruptcy trustee the rights of a hypothetical "ideal creditor" under state law. 4 *Collier on Bankruptcy* ¶ 544.02. General Coffee contends that because a constructive trust is essentially an equitable lien, it is defeated by a subsequent lienholder without notice. General Coffee is correct that under Florida law "an equitable lien is superior to the right of all persons except bona fide purchasers, or subsequent valid lienholders, without notice," but General Coffee goes too far. Although it is difficult to define a constructive trust precisely, it is not an equitable lien under Florida law.

Florida law defines an equitable lien as follows:

An equitable lien is not an estate of property in the thing itself nor a right to recover the thing, that is, a right which may be the basis of a possessory action. It is simply a right of a special nature over a thing, which constitutes a charge or encumbrance upon it, so that the very thing itself may be proceeded against in an equitable action * * *.

Tucker v. Prevatt Builders, Inc., 116 So.2d 437, 439–40 (Fla.1959); *see also Hullum v. Bre–Lew Corp.,* 93 So.2d 727, 730 (Fla.1957). A constructive trust, on the other hand, is a trust relationship created "by equity to prevent the unjust enrichment of one person at the expense of another as the result of fraud, undue influence, abuse of confidence or mistake in the transaction that originates the problem." *Wadlington v. Edwards,* 92 So.2d 629, 631 (Fla.1957); *see also Steinhardt v. Steinhardt,* 445 So.2d 352, 356 (Fla. 3d DCA 1984). In a trust relationship the trust beneficiary possesses an equitable ownership interest in the trust property, while the trustee possesses legal title to the property. *See Axtell v. Coons,* 82 Fla. 158, 89 So. 419, 420 (1921). A constructive trust beneficiary therefore possesses an equitable ownership interest in the trust property, which is substantively different than an equitable lien against the property. *See generally* A. Scott, *The Law of Trusts* § 463 (3d ed. 1967). The question before us is thus whether an ideal creditor would prevail over a constructive trust beneficiary under Florida law.

We have found no Florida cases on this question. We believe, however, that for purposes of priority in bankruptcy a constructive trust beneficiary should have the same rights to the trust assets that a beneficiary of an express trust would have. An express trust beneficiary clearly has priority to trust assets over a judicial lienholder or execution creditor. CNB's rights as beneficiary of the constructive trust therefore would prevail over a hypothetical ideal lienholder.

Professor Scott would reach a similar conclusion. As he discussed in his treatise on trusts, a constructive trust beneficiary prevails over all subsequent takers of the trust property except bona fide purchasers. A. Scott, *The Law of Trusts* § 462.4, at 3621. He explained his reasoning with the following example:

> [W]here A's money is wrongfully taken by B and is used by B to purchase land, A is entitled to enforce a constructive trust of the land. In this case A has such an interest in the land as to enable him to reach it in satisfaction of his claim. He can reach the land even though B is insolvent, since B's creditors are not in the position of bona fide purchasers.

Id. § 462.5, at 3423; *cf. In re Storage Technology Corp.,* 55 B.R. 479, 484 (Bankr.D.Colo.1985)(beneficiary of a constructive trust prevails over a judicial lien creditor under Colorado law).

We hold that because General Coffee cannot bring the trust assets into its bankruptcy estate under either approach, CNB is entitled to recover the traced assets of $6,488,011.

AFFIRMED.

Note

Extended too far, the doctrine of constructive trust could play havoc with quite strict and rather rigid rules of perfection and priority in Article 9 and in the real estate law. In thinking about *General Coffee* and about the three problems that follow this note, ask yourself how far the theory of constructive trust should be permitted to wander into the bailiwick of Article 9 and of real estate law.

What do you think of the following argument: Constructive trust laws should rarely if ever be permitted to overturn the priorities that would otherwise apply in bankruptcy. Constructive trust law may make sense when the beneficiary of a trust pursues an evil trustor, but in bankruptcy the competition is not between the evil trustor and the well-intentioned beneficiary but between the beneficiary (one creditor) and other creditors—all of whom in one way or another have been misled by the debtor. How do you balance the equities among these creditors?

Problem 7–2

Ruth is a novelist. Based on reviewing the first five completed chapters, Mark Publishing contracts with Ruth for a book on the Russian revolution. Mark gives Ruth a $200,000 advance against royalties. The written contract requires that Ruth deliver a manuscript "acceptable" to Mark and provides that Mark owns the copyright and all rights to the book in return for a 15 percent royalty. Ruth completes the manuscript several months later, but never delivers any part of it to Mark. Instead, Ruth files Chapter 11 bankruptcy. Ruth has been offered $1 million for the book from Herod Films. Mark files a motion in bankruptcy court requesting that Ruth hand over the book which Mark claims to own. Mark alleges that (1) the contract gives it ownership of the book and (2) if that is not true, then the court should find that Ruth holds the manuscript in constructive trust for Mark because Ruth fraudulently induced Mark to pay $200,000 for the manuscript, always intending to sell it to someone else. What result if Ruth responds that there is no valid title claim by Mark because that claim is cut off under section 544?

Problem 7–3

Noah sells its West Virginia factory to Canaan Foundry Inc. Because of difficulties in obtaining signatures from the various parties needed to record the real estate deed, no recording occurs even though Canaan takes possession of the facility and begins to operate the plant. Noah files bankruptcy. The trustee, seeing an opportunity for a quick profit, sues Canaan under section 544 to set aside the sale. State law invalidates any unrecorded transfer of real estate as against a bona fide purchaser without notice of the transaction. What result? If Canaan can prove that Noah acted fraudulently in preventing a valid recording of the deed, can it effectively assert a constructive trust to defeat the claim of Noah?

Problem 7–4

Seller, Satan, sells electrical appliances and finances their sale. Assume that Satan sold a variety of appliances to Herod Appliance Corporation, a New York retailer. The items were stored in New York and Satan properly perfected a security interest by a filing both locally and in Albany. Unbeknownst to Satan, Herod moved a large share of its inventory that was not held actually on the shelves in stores to a warehouse across the Hudson in New Jersey. Much of the inventory remained in New Jersey for more than four months. Because Satan's security interest was never perfected in New Jersey, it so became unperfected under the terms of 9–103.

When Herod went into bankruptcy, Satan argued that it had a constructive trust on the assets under New Jersey law and thus that its rights were superior to the trustee's rights under 544(a). The security agreement between Satan and Herod provided that Herod could not move any collateral outside of New York without the permission of Satan. The movement in question occurred without Satan's knowledge or permission. Will Satan defeat the trustee? Should it?

MOORE v. BAY

Supreme Court of the United States, 1931.
284 U.S. 4, 52 S.Ct. 3, 76 L.Ed. 133.

Certiorari, 283 U.S. 814, to review an affirmance of an order of the District Court holding a chattel mortgage to be valid as to creditors whose claims came into existence subsequently to its recordation.

Mr. Justice Holmes delivered the opinion of the Court.

The bankrupt executed a mortgage of automobiles, furniture, show room and shop equipment that is admitted to be bad as against creditors who were such at the date of the mortgage and those who became such between the date of the mortgage and that on which it was recorded, there having been a failure to observe the requirements of the Civil Code of California, § 3440. The question raised is whether the mortgage is void also as against those who gave the bankrupt credit at a later date, after the mortgage was on record. The Circuit Court of Appeals affirmed an order of the District Judge giving the mortgage priority over the last creditors. Whether the Court was right must be decided by the Bankruptcy Act since it is superior to all state laws upon the subject.

The trustee in bankruptcy gets the title to all property which has been transferred by the bankrupt in fraud of creditors, or which prior to the petition he could by any means have transferred, or which might have been levied upon and sold under judicial process against him. Act of July 1, 1898, c. 541, § 70; U.S. Code, Title 11, § 110. By § 67, Code, Title 11, § 107(a), claims which for want of record or for other reasons would not have been valid liens as against the claims of the creditors of the bankrupt shall not be liens against his estate. The rights of the trustee by subrogation are to be enforced for the benefit of the estate. The Circuit Courts of Appeals seem generally to agree, as the language of the Bankruptcy Act appears to us to imply very plainly, that what thus is recovered for the benefit of the estate is to be distributed in "dividends of an equal percentum on all allowed claims, except such as have priority or are secured." Bankruptcy Act, § 65, Code, Title 11, § 105.

Decree reversed.

Notes and Questions

1. What are the rights of a creditor who lends money in the "gap" between another creditor's taking a security interest and that creditor's later perfection? See UCC sections 9–201, 9–301 and section 544(b).

2. Because section 544(b) permits subrogation only to the rights of actual unsecured creditors, the effect of the section on perfected security interests and recorded mortgages is minimal. The major application of 544(b) in current law is to enable the trustee to use state fraudulent conveyances law in the event that state law rules are more favorable than the federal fraudulent conveyance provisions outlined in section 548.

Problem 7–5

In which of the following cases can the trustee use 544(b) to upset the secured creditor's claim?

1. On January 1 Ezra takes a security interest in Boaz's inventory but does not perfect it. On February 1 Zachariah loans money without security to Boaz; on March 1 Ezra perfects his security interest by filing; six months later the debtor goes bankrupt.

2. Seeing the storm clouds of bankruptcy on the horizon, Boaz conveys his new $60,000 Mercedes to his wife, Ruth. More than a year later he files in bankruptcy. You may assume that the only consideration for the transfer was the love and affection which Ruth showed to the debtor.

3. Boaz was in the retail shoe business. Early in 1984 he sold his entire inventory and business to a third party and disappeared with the money to parts unknown. Several months later Boaz returned, declared bankruptcy, and the events described above were discovered. You may assume that neither party complied with the provisions of the bulk sales law (UCC Article 6).

§ 3. VOIDABLE PREFERENCES, SECTION 547

Section 547 is one of the most interesting sections in the Bankruptcy Code. It is filled with fascinating intricacies and it has potential application to a wide variety of complex and intriguing fact patterns.

The goals of the Bankruptcy Code coincide with those of Section 60 of the Act of 1898. The Kennedy Commission recognized the desirability of invalidating secret transfers and avoiding certain transfers of property made within limited periods of time prior to filing. However, the Commission also believed that certain aspects of the Act impeded progress toward those goals. Specifically, the Commission was most concerned about the burden of proving insolvency, and the relationship between the Act and the Uniform Commercial Code.

Under the Act, the trustee had to prove that the transfer was made while the debtor was insolvent, and that the creditor had "reasonable cause to believe that the debtor was insolvent." While the Commission recognized the value of invalidating only those transfers made while the debtor was insolvent, it believed that common sense indicates that a business is usually insolvent for a number of months before it files a petition for bankruptcy. Report of the Commission on Bankruptcy Laws of the United States, H.R.Doc. No. 93-137, 93rd Cong., 1st Sess. 19 (1973). Notwithstanding this fact, it was difficult to prove insolvency. Therefore the Commission introduced the presumption of insolvency during the 90 days preceding the filing of the petition.

Except for "insider" cases, the Commission also dispensed with the "reasonable cause to believe" standard on the grounds that a creditor's state of mind has no rational connection to the equitable distribution of the debtor's assets, and that the massive amount of litigation on the subject had minimized the effectiveness of the preferences section. (In 1984 Congress abolished the "reasonable cause to believe" condition for insider preferences as well.)

The Commission's other major concern was with the relationship between the Act and the UCC. The terminology of the UCC deviated considerably from that of the Bankruptcy Act and so created problems of statutory construction. The Commission wanted the new Code to track the UCC. One of the biggest problems was a line of cases which said that no Article 9 security interest perfected before the four-month preference term could be defeated even as to property acquired by the debtor on the eve of bankruptcy.

The Commission recognized the validity of an after-acquired property clause as to inventory and receivables financing, but limited its effect by saying that creditors could not improve their positions at the expense of the estate during the 90-day preference period. Basically, the Commission's aim was not to redesign the goals of the original preference section, but to streamline it, and remove some of the "encrustations" which were reducing its effectiveness. Its principal concession to creditors was to shorten the preference period from the Act's four months to the Code's 90 days.

The student should first note the five conditions listed in 547(b)(1)–(5) that must be met in order for there to be a voidable preference.

(b) Except as provided in subsection (c) of this section, the trustee may avoid any transfer of an interest of the debtor in property—

(1) to or for the benefit of a creditor;

(2) for or on account of an antecedent debt owed by the debtor before such transfer was made;

(3) made while the debtor was insolvent;

(4) made—

(A) on or within 90 days before the date of the filing of the petition; or

(B) between ninety days and one year before the date of the filing of the petition, if such creditor at the time of such transfer was an insider; and

(5) that enables such creditor to receive more than such creditor would receive if—

(A) the case were a case under Chapter 7 of this title;

(B) the transfer had not been made; and

(C) such creditor received payment of such debt to the extent provided by the provisions of this title.

Several aspects of section 547(b) deserve special mention. First, no explicit definition of "antecedent debt" is provided; Congress left the courts for the most part free to make this determination. The student should compare some of the limitations found in subsection (c) particularly section 547(c)(1). Second, unless made to an insider, the transfer must occur within ninety days of the petition. This requirement is particularly important in the case of perfection on the eve of bankruptcy of a security interest granted long previously. Analyzing the fact situation requires determination about when the "transfer" was made, for if it was made at the time that the security agreement was signed (before the 90 day period), there is no preference; conversely, if the "transfer" occurred upon perfection, it may well be a voidable preference. Note that 547(e) provides a detailed set of rules to determine when a transfer has occurred. Note also that the test for a transfer is different depending on whether the property is real or personal. Third, a provision whose significance is easy to overlook is the term in subsection (b)(5) that provides the transfer must enable the creditor to receive more than he would have received if the transfer had not been made and the case were "under Chapter 7" (i.e. in liquidation). Without this requirement, any payment by a debtor to a secured creditor within ninety days of the petition not offset by a contemporaneous loan would be a voidable preference.

Even if 547(b)(1)–(5) is satisfied, certain transfers cannot be avoided by the trustee because they are excepted from the reach of 547(b) by one of the subsections of 547(c). The student should read 547(c) with care and again should ask what kinds of transactions might fall within it. Consider the case in which the debtor makes a payment to a utility company a week prior to filing a petition in bankruptcy. While the facts of this case make it a likely candidate for treatment under 547(b), the case may be excepted from (b)'s reach by (c)(2). What policy supports the exceptions of 547(c)?

A classic preference is a payment in cash by a debtor to an unsecured creditor within 90 days prior to the bankruptcy filing. This payment violates the Code because it permits one creditor to be treated better than the others. But not all payments to unsecured creditors constitute preferences. Some are protected by Section 547(c). Others are protected by the manner in which they are made and, most importantly, by the source of the funds for the transfer.

IN RE UNION MEETING PARTNERS

United States Bankruptcy Court, Eastern District of Pennsylvania, 1994.
163 B.R. 229.

DAVID A. SCHOLL, BANKRUPTCY JUDGE

[The debtor was a Pennsylvania partnership that owned two office buildings. Lincoln National, a secured creditor holding mortgages on both properties, had taken whatever action was necessary under Pennsylvania Law to perfect its interests in rents prior to the petition. During the ninety days before the petition was filed, it sent a letter to the tenants in the debtor's buildings, demanding they pay the rents directly to Lincoln. Apparently the tenants commenced payments directly to Lincoln, but it is unclear how much money was paid after the demand and before the petition was filed.

Lincoln challenged the trustee's claim of a preference on several grounds. First, it argued that sending the demand letter was not a transfer. Second, it maintained it did not receive more than it would have received on liquidation (it was a secured creditor) and third, it argued that the debtor was not insolvent.]

* * *

C. DISCUSSION

1. Lincoln's Dispatch of the Rent Demand Letters to the Debtor's Tenants Effected a "Transfer" of a "Property Interest of the Debtor"

The preference provision of the Bankruptcy Code invoked by the Debtor as to Counts I and II of the Complaint provide in pertinent part, at 11 U.S.C. § 547(b), as follows:

> (b) Except as provided in subsection (c) of this section, the trustee may avoid any transfer of an interest of the debtor in property—
>
> (1) to or for the benefit of a creditor;
>
> (2) for or on account of an antecedent debt owed by the debtor before such transfer was made;
>
> (3) made while the debtor was insolvent;
>
> (4) made—
>
> (A) on or within 90 days before the date of the filing of the petition; * * *
>
> (5) that enables such creditor to receive more than such creditor would receive if—
>
> (A) the case were a case under chapter 7 of this title;

(B) the transfer had not been made; and

(C) such creditor received payment of such debt to the extent provided by the provisions of this title.

We must first determine whether the delivery of Lincoln's rent demands constituted a "transfer" of an "interest of the debtor in property" as required by the preamble of 11 U.S.C. § 547(b). *See In re Vogue Coach Co.*, 132 B.R. 454, 457 (Bankr.N.D.Okla.1991). The definition of transfer contained in the Bankruptcy Code, at 11 U.S.C. § 101(58)[54], is very broad and includes "every mode, direct or indirect, absolute or conditional, voluntary or involuntary, of disposing of or parting with property or with an interest in property, including retention of title as a security interest. * * * "

Unfortunately, the Bankruptcy Code does not provide a definition of the phrase "interest of the debtor in property," although this phrase is used several times in the Bankruptcy Code. *See, e.g.*, 11 U.S.C. §§ 547(b), 548(a). We must, therefore, turn to applicable state law, e.g., the law of Pennsylvania, to determine whether the Debtor had an interest in property which was transferred as a result of the sending of the rent demand letters. * * *

The bankruptcy judges of this district held in the past that a mortgagee which took assignment of rents in the mortgage documents must additionally take actual or constructive possession of rents in order to "perfect" its security interests in those rents. *See In re Wynnewood House Associates* 121 B.R. 716, 721–26 (Bankr.E.D.Pa.1990)(FOX, J.). Under this analysis, it is easy to conceive that a mortgagee would have received an avoidable preference when it took constructive possession of rents by sending demand or attornment letters to its debtor-mortgagor's tenants within the ninety (90) days preceding the debtor's bankruptcy. There is no question that perfecting a security interest during the ninety (90) day period prior to the filing of a bankruptcy petition can be a preference in accordance with 11 U.S.C. § 547(b) and 11 U.S.C. § 547(e). *See, e.g., In re Camp Rockhill, Inc.*, 12 B.R. 829, 832-33 (Bankr.E.D.Pa. 1981); and 4 COLLIER ON BANKRUPTCY, 1547.16[4], at 547–71 (15th ed. 1993).

As we noted in *Union Meeting I*, 160 B.R. at 766, however, *Mountain View* is a controlling precedent which has ruled that a mortgagee's lien on rents arises when a mortgage containing an assignment of rents clause or another documents of like effect are duly recorded, and that any subsequent lien, including, presumably, the lien of a bankruptcy trustee as a bona fide purchaser pursuant to 11 U.S.C. § 544, would be junior to the lien of the mortgagee. 5 F.3d at 38–39. This decision is consistent with the recent trend of both bankruptcy and appellate courts, including courts in this district, expanding the rights of mortgagees taking rent assignments. * * *

Although we have some misgivings regarding the soundness of *Mountain View* holdings and we are not convinced that the repercussions it will have on single asset bankruptcies-debtors are, on balance, fair to all players in the bankruptcy system, we are nonetheless bound by its dictates. It is thus clear that Lincoln had a senior lien on the rents at the time it recorded its mortgage and its assignment of rents and profits, which the parties, in the Stipulation of Facts, agree was duly accomplished on May 24, 1988. Therefore, the sending of the rent demands did not "perfect" Lincoln's interest in the rents, which had been perfected on May 24, 1988, and did not constitute a preference for that reason.

We now turn to the Pennsylvania state law, as we are required to do, in order to determine if the sending of the rent demands resulted in some other parting of an interest of the Debtor in its property. It is obvious that once the Debtor's tenants started paying the rents to Lincoln as a result of the demands, the Debtor, at a minimum, was deprived of its right to possess and use the rents. State law bears this out. In the case *Colbassani v. Society of Christopher Columbus*, 159 Pa.Super. 414, 48 A.2d 106 (1946), a mortgagee, having obtained a judgment against its mortgagor, issued a writ of attachment execution against both the mortgagor and the tenant of the mortgaged property as garnishee. The mortgagee then sought to obtain all rents due and to become due from the tenant. 159 Pa.Super. at 416, 48 A.2d at 106. The mortgagor and the intervening tenant petitioned to have the writ stayed. *Id.* The trial court stayed the writ and the mortgagee appealed. *Id.* In resolving the appeal, the court noted that

> [t]he mortgage in this case contained a clause: "Together with * * * the rents * * * thereof." This is but a pledge and under such a clause where there is no default in the mortgage, *the mortgagor, and not the mortgagee, is entitled to the rents*. If the mortgage becomes in default, the mortgagee can destroy the mortgagor's right to the rents by suing out the mortgage, by bringing ejectment, by entering into possession of the premises, *or by giving the tenant formal notice to pay the mortgagee*. Any of these steps results in the pledge being reduced to possession by the pledgee-mortgagee and entitles the latter to the rents.

159 Pa.Super. at 416, 48 A.2d at 107 (emphasis added). * * *

From the foregoing, we can conclude only that the Debtor's right to use the rents prior to Lincoln's enforcement of its lien is "an interest of the debtor in property." *Cf. M & L Business, supra*, 160 B.R. at 856, ("It is elemental property law that one of the 'interests in property' included in the total bundle of property rights is the right of possession"); *In re Bell & Beckwith*, 64 B.R. 620, 630 (Bankr.N.D.Ohio 1986)("The right to possession is a proprietary interest in property which can, if transferred, serve as the basis of an action under 11 U.S.C. Section 548(a)"); H.R.REP. NO. 595, 95th Cong., 1st Sess. 314 (1977), U.S.Code Cong. & Admin.News 1978 pp. 5787, 6271 ("House Report")("The definition of transfer is as broad as possible.... Under this definition, any transfer of an interest in property is a transfer, including a transfer of possession, custody or control even if there is no transfer of

title, because possession, custody, and control are interests in property.")
* * *

2. *The Debtor, Who Has the Burden of Proving All of the Elements of Section 547(b), Failed to Establish That the Sending of the Rent Demand Letters Allowed Lincoln to Receive More Than It Would Have in a Hypothetical Chapter 7 Case, as Required by Section 547(b)(5)*

In light of our conclusion that an interest of the Debtor in property was transferred at the time Lincoln sent the rent demands to the Debtor's tenants, we must now determine if the remaining requirements of 11 U.S.C. § 547(b) are met. The plaintiff in a § 547 proceeding bears the burden of proving all of the elements of 11 U.S.C. § 547(b). See 11 U.S.C. § 547(g)("For the purposes of this section, the trustee has the burden of proving the avoidability of a transfer under subsection (b) of this section. ..."). * * * Because we do not believe that the Debtor met this burden, we will examine this subsection first.

Section 547(b)(5) requires the bankruptcy court to "undo" the transfers in question and then construct a hypothetical liquidation of the debtor as of the petition date to determine whether the defendant-creditor received more as a result of the transfers than it would have received in a Chapter 7 liquidation case. The plaintiff, to satisfy § 547(b)(5), must show that the creditor was preferred in some amount, and it cannot succeed if it is proven that (1) the creditor was fully secured; (2) the transfer was nothing more than a seizure of the secured creditor's collateral; or (3) the unsecured creditors would be paid in full in a Chapter 7 case. * * *

Lincoln's debt is not fully secured. The parties have stipulated that, as of the Petition Date, the amount of Lincoln's loan was at least $9,364,186.65. The parties have also stipulated that the value of the Property at the time Lincoln sent the rent demands, which was less than one month before the Petition Date, was no more than $6,762,000. Thus, if Lincoln received pre-petition rents as a result of its sending the rent demand letters, it might be shown that it reduced the amount of the unsecured portion of its claim thereby. (* * * a payment to an undersecured creditor during the preference period may constitute a preference if the payment does not result in a corresponding reduction of that creditors' lien, or a corresponding increase in the debtor's equity in that creditor's collateral). This situation would be analogous to an accounts receivable lender improving its collateral position within the ninety (90) days before its borrower's bankruptcy. See 11 U.S.C. § 547(c)(5). Although the Debtor suggests this very scenario in its Supplemental Brief, the record is devoid of any evidence regarding the amount of rents which might have been collected by Lincoln pre-petition. Given the close proximity between the date that the rent demands were sent to the Debtor's tenants and the Petition Date, it is certainly possible that all rents collected by Lincoln after it sent the demand letters were post-petition rents. The Debtor has not proven to the contrary.

As noted above, in light of the *Mountain View* holding that a mortgagee's security interest in rents is perfected upon the recording of a document containing a rent assignment, Lincoln's interests in the rents has been perfected, for bankruptcy purposes, since May 24, 1988. Thus, in a hypothetical liquidation of the Debtor on the Petition Date, which is the date as of which the hypothetical liquidation must be constructed, * * * Lincoln would be entitled to the entire value of the Property, including any value attributable to the rental income stream, whether it had sent the rent demand letters or not.

The Debtor, as might be expected, argues that, while *Mountain View* supports Lincoln's position on the § 547(b)(5) issue in establishing that its security interest in the rents was perfected long before the 90–day preference period commenced, the very presence of the paragraph from that Opinion quoted at page 232 *supra* suggests that the fact that notices to tenants were provided in the 90–day preference period may well be significant. In fact, there appears to be no reason for the *Mountain View* court to have even mentioned this factor unless it believed that it *was* significant.

There is some logical force to this argument. However, the *Mountain View* language in issue does not state that the preference provisions of the Code *would* be implicated if the rent demand letters had been dispatched within the 90–day period, but only that they are *not* implicated if the demands were made prior to the 90–day period.

The few cases which have discussed the preference issue have reached their conclusions on whether the requirements of § 547(b)(5) have been satisfied solely on the basis of whether the respective mortgagees' security interests in rents were deemed perfected prior to the dispatches of demands for rents from tenants.

Thus, in the one decision in which the result favors the debtor, and a preference regarding certain rent payments, was found, * * * the result is driven by the district court's acceptance of the bankruptcy court's conclusion that, under the applicable state law of Colorado, the secured lender "did not perfect its interests in the rents until the post-petition filing of its notices [to the tenants] pursuant to 11 U.S.C. § 546(b)." *Id.*

However, in two cases in which the perfections of the security interests of the respective mortgagees were found to have occurred, under applicable state laws of Utah and New York, respectively, at the times of the recordings of the documents providing for an assignment of rents, the debtors were found incapable of avoiding the respective mortgagees' interests in the rents. * * *

There is no question that *Mountain View* determined that, under Pennsylvania law, a mortgagee's security interest in rents is perfected upon recordation of the pertinent security documents. Therefore, we cannot follow *Meridith Millard* under its own reasoning, and we are obliged to reach a conclusion consistent with that attained in *SLC* and *Financial Center*.

Thus, we are constrained, by the reasoning of *Mountain View*, to conclude that the Debtor has not proven that Lincoln would receive more in a Chapter 7 liquidation on account of its claim as a result of the dispatch of the rent demand letters. Therefore, we must conclude that the Debtor has failed to meet its burden necessary to establish a preference arising under 11 U.S.C. § 547(b)(5).

3. *The Debtor Has Also Not Proven That It Was Insolvent at the Time the Rent Demand Letters Were Sent to Its Tenants by Lincoln, Notwithstanding the Initial Presumption of Insolvency in Its Favor*

In addition to concluding that the Debtor has not met its burden of proving the element required by 11 U.S.C. § 547(b)(5), we find that the Debtor has also not proven that it was insolvent at the time of the transfers, as required by 11 U.S.C. § 547(b)(3).

The Bankruptcy Code, at 11 U.S.C. § 101(32)(B), defines the insolvency of a partnership as the

> financial condition such that the sum of such partnership's debts is greater than the aggregate of, at a fair valuation—
>
> (i) all of such partnership's property * * * ; and
>
> (ii) the sum of the excess of the value of each general partner's nonpartnership property * * * over such partner's non-partnership debts. * * *

The Debtor has the ultimate burden of proof on this issue as well, it is aided by a statutorily-created presumption of insolvency in its favor within the 90-day preference period. 11 U.S.C. § 547(f). However, if the party opposing the claim of a preference produces evidence to meet or rebut the presumption, then the presumption disappears completely and the burden of proving insolvency reverts to the Debtor. *See In re Old World Cone Co.*, 119 B.R. 473, 476–78 (Bankr.E.D.Pa.1990). *See also, e.g., In re Taxman Clothing Co.*, 905 F.2d 166, 168 (7th Cir.1990); *In re Koubourlis*, 869 F.2d 1319, 1322 (9th Cir.1989); and *In re Emerald Oil Co.*, 695 F.2d 833, 837–38 (5th Cir.1983).

The parties have agreed, in the Stipulation of Facts, that, at the time Lincoln sent the rent demands, the Debtor's assets totaled no more than $6,762,000, and the Debtor's liabilities totaled approximately $10 million. These facts would indicate that the Debtor, standing alone, was insolvent on the crucial date of the transfer.

However, the parties have also attached to the Stipulation of Facts certain financial statements of the Debtor's five general partners, identified by their names and respective holdings in *Union Meeting I, supra*, 160 B.R. at 763, ("the General Partners"). These financial statements declare that each of the General Partners has a substantial net worth. Specifically, the parties have stipulated that, at the time that the rent demands were sent, the General Partners' nonpartnership assets exceeded their nonpartnership debts by approximately $44 million.

It is also to be noted that the Stipulation of Facts provides that, if the General Partners were called to testify, they would each state that they have contingent guaranty liabilities totaling, in the aggregate, approximately $23 million. It is also stipulated that the General Partners would testify to their belief that they would experience adverse tax consequences if they were forced to liquidate their assets.

We conclude from these Stipulations, for the purposes of our analysis, that the General Partners have additional nonpartnership debts which, though contingent, can be valued at $23 million. Since we are accepting the $23 million debt figure, notwithstanding the contingent nature of these liabilities, we are unwilling to deduct anything more from this figure in consideration of the General Partners' "belief" that they would incur tax liabilities if forced to liquidate their assets. Thus, the remaining nonpartnership assets of the General Partners totals approximately $21 million. When added to the Debtor's assets of over $6.7 million, the total assets exceed the Debtor's liabilities of about $10 million by $17.7 million.

The Debtor argues that the General Partners' nonpartnership assets should not be included in the insolvency calculation because Lincoln's debt is nonrecourse and Lincoln would not have access to the General Partners' assets to ensure repayment of its debt. In other words, the Debtor would have us recognize a condition in application of 11 U.S.C. § 101(32)(B)(ii) which would prevent us from considering a general partner's nonpartnership assets when determining insolvency unless nonbankruptcy partnership law would otherwise permit the creditor to resort to such assets. In support of this argument, the Debtor cites to legislative history of the insolvency definition wherein it is stated that "for a partnership, the definition is modified to account for the liability of a general partner for the partnership's debts." House Report, *supra*, at 312, U.S.Code Cong. & Admin.News 1478 at 6264. Thus, the Debtor reasons, if a general partner has no individual liability for a particular partnership debt, then the partner's nonpartnership assets should not be added to the mix of the Debtor's assets in the calculation of the Debtor's insolvency.

Although the Debtor's argument is not without logical and equitable appeal, 11 U.S.C. § 101(32)(B) is not ambiguous, and we are thus not at liberty to create conditions which do not appear in the text of the statute. The few cases construing this Code section do not indicate a willingness to append any such conditions to the Code, *see In re Davis*, 120 B.R. 823, 825 (Bankr.W.D.Pa.1990); and *In re Writing Sales, L.P.*, 96 B.R 175, 177 (Bankr.E.D.Wis.1989). Also, the currently-in-vogue "plain language" theory of Bankruptcy Code interpretation, without resort to legislative history, would allow no such reading. *See Patterson v. Shumate*, 504 U.S. 753–, 112 S.Ct. 2242, 2246–48, 119 L.Ed.2d 519 (1992); *Taylor v. Freeland & Kronz*, 503 U.S. 638, __ __, 112 S.Ct. 1644, 1648, 118 L.Ed.2d 280 (1992); and *Union Bank v, Wolas*, 502 U.S. 151, __, __, 112 S.Ct. 527, 532, 534, 116 L.Ed.2d 514 (1991).

Thus, in light of the "plain language" of § 101(32)(B), we must conclude that the Debtor has failed to meet its burden of proving that, at the time the rent demands were sent to its tenants, the Debtor was insolvent, as that term is defined in the Bankruptcy Code. Therefore, the Debtor has failed to meet its burden under 11 U.S.C. § 547(b)(3) and could not avoid the effect of those demand letters even if we held in its favor on the more controversial § 547(b)(5) issue.

* * *

1. Judgment is entered in favor of the Defendant, LINCOLN NATIONAL LIFE INSURANCE CO., and against Plaintiff–Debtor, UNION MEETING PARTNERS.

2. The Complaint in this Proceeding is DISMISSED in its entirety.

Questions

1. How does a landlord's right to rent differ from a secured creditor's right to the payments on accounts receivable? In the latter case the Bankruptcy Code makes clear there is no "transfer" of an account until the account has come into existence. See section 547(e)(3). Does the debtor landlord have "rights in the property transferred," i.e., in the rents prior to the time they have been earned? If not, surely Judge Scholl is right that no transfer has occurred, true? But if no transfer has occurred, how can one add the present value of the stream of rent payments to the secured creditor's claim for the purpose of measuring the impact of the transfer under 547(b)(5)?

2. Now change two things. Assume the debtor was insolvent. Assume the jurisdiction where the debtor was located did not have the Pennsylvania rule, i.e., as a matter of state law that there is no perfection as to future rent until a receiver had been appointed. Assume finally that the transaction occurs after 1994 so that it is subject to the new 552(b)(2) enacted in 1994 that reads in part as follows:

> Except as provided in sections 363, 506(c), 522, 544, 545, 547, and 548 of this title, and notwithstanding section 546(b) of this title, if the debtor and an entity entered into a security agreement before the commencement of the case and if the security interest created by such security agreement extends to property of the debtor acquired before the commencement of the case and to amounts paid as rents of such property or the fees, charges, accounts, or other payments for the use or occupancy of rooms and other public facilities in hotels, motels, or other lodging properties, then such security interest extends to such rents and such fees, charges, accounts, or other payments acquired by the estate after the commencement of the case to the extent provided in such security agreement, except to any extent that the court, after notice and a hearing and based on the equities of the case, orders otherwise.

Now what? Has the addition of 552(b)(2) converted our hypothetical state into a Pennsylvania? All of these questions should be revisited when you read the *Lackow* case and consider 547(c)(5).

3. Do you see how 547(b)(5) saves a payment to a fully secured creditor within the preference period from a preference claim? Do you see why a similar payment to an "undersecured" creditor almost always flunks 547(b)(5)?

4. Is the payment of a rent or the payment of an amount collected on an account receivable the same as the transfer of the collateral to the creditor? Or rather should such a payment be treated as no different from any other payment to an undersecured secured creditor?

IN RE BOHLEN ENTERPRISES, LTD.

United States Court of Appeals, Eighth Circuit, 1988..
859 F.2d 561..

IRVING HILL, SENIOR DISTRICT JUDGE.

In this opinion we reverse a judgment of the district court in a bankruptcy case because it erroneously applied the doctrine of "earmarking" to justify rejection of a claim that a transfer of funds to a pre-existing creditor was a voidable preference.

FACTS

Bohlen Enterprises Ltd. ("debtor") was a retail office equipment business in Waterloo, Iowa. Mr. William F. Bohlen was its president. In late April 1986 the debtor owed two separate obligations to the National Bank of Waterloo, Iowa ("bank"). One obligation was a short-term inventory loan dating from November, 1985, in the principal amount of $189,000. The other obligation was a long-standing arrangement for an open line of credit in the principal amount of $125,000. Both obligations were secured by a single security agreement.

In late April, 1986 the bank was insisting that the $189,000 obligation, which was overdue, be repaid by the end of that month. Mr. Bohlen went to the John Deere Community Credit Union ("credit union") in Waterloo and applied for a $200,000 loan. He disclosed to the credit union the debtor's $125,000 obligation to the bank but failed to disclose its $189,000 obligation. Mr. Bohlen told the credit union that if it provided the $200,000 loan, $125,000 of the proceeds would be used to repay the $125,000 obligation to the bank and the rest would be used for miscellaneous purposes. The credit union agreed to those arrangements.

Although the credit union's formal approval of the loan did not occur until May 1, 1986, it apparently determined on April 30, 1986 that the loan would be granted. On that date the credit union opened a share draft account in the debtor's name and gave Mr. Bohlen some blank share drafts to use in drawing on the share draft account.

The opening of the share draft account on April 30, the day before the approval and funding of the loan, is a critical fact in the rather bizarre series of transactions which followed that event. The transcript does not disclose why the share draft account was opened in advance of the loan's being approved and funded, or why the borrower was given the blank share drafts before there was any money in the account.

In any event, Mr. Bohlen on April 30, 1986, purported to utilize and draw upon the share draft account despite the fact that on that date it had nothing in it. That day he issued a share draft on that account in the sum of $192,000 payable to the bank, which he then deposited in the debtor's checking account at the bank. He then immediately wrote three checks on the debtor's checking account at the bank totalling $191,777.27. All three checks were payable to the bank.

The three checks collectively constitute the transfer which is alleged to be the voidable preference. One was for $189,000 to repay the entire principal of the debtor's larger loan obligation. The second was for $1,708.77 which paid the interest on that obligation to date. The third check was for $1,068.50 which paid the interest on the debtor's $125,000 obligation to date. The principal of the $125,000 loan obligation remained unpaid.

The conclusion is inescapable that Mr. Bohlen on his own had decided to pay off the $189,000 obligation to the bank, which he was being pressured to retire at once, and to leave the $125,000 obligation unpaid. The conclusion is likewise inescapable that Mr. Bohlen expected his $192,000 share draft to be made good by the credit union's depositing the entire $200,000 of loan proceeds in the share draft account so that he could freely draw upon the account as he saw fit. But the credit union did not put the entire proceeds of the loan at Mr. Bohlen's disposal. Instead it deposited only $74,931.50 of the loan proceeds in the share draft account. It funded the rest of the loan on May 1, 1986 by issuing a check for $125,068.50 jointly payable to the debtor and the bank.

The credit union obviously intended the joint payee check to be endorsed to the bank to pay off the $125,000 obligation as Mr. Bohlen had promised. If Mr. Bohlen endorsed that check and turned it over to the bank, the bank would clearly use it as repayment of the $125,000 loan and this would leave Mr. Bohlen without funds to cover the unauthorized payment already made of the $189,000 obligation. Mr. Bohlen was apparently unable to solve that dilemma and the joint payee check was never negotiated.

So on the morning of May 2, 1986, Mr. Bohlen realized that his attempt to pay off the $189,000 obligation to the bank without ever disclosing that obligation to the credit union would fail because the full $200,000 had not been put at his disposal. Only $75,000 was available to him to pay the $192,000 share draft he had written. The remaining $125,000 of new proceeds were embodied in the joint payee check and not available to him. He needed another $125,000 to cover. So on May 2, 1986, at 8:05 A.M., utilizing a drive-thru window at the credit union, Mr. Bohlen purported to deposit into the debtor's share draft account at the credit union, a check for $125,000 which he wrote on the debtor's checking account at the bank. That check, having been written on an account with no funds in it, was eventually dishonored. It seems clear that that check was written in a desperate check-kiting scheme in which Mr. Bohlen was playing for time.

In the meantime, during the night of May 1, 1986, the share draft of $192,000 was presented to the credit union for payment by the normal electronic process. It cleared electronically, i.e., it was honored and paid. The next morning, May 2, 1986, a clerk in the operations department of the credit union noted the electronic clearance but took no action because of Mr. Bohlen's deposit in the share draft account that morning of the debtor's $125,000 check drawn on the bank account. The clerk was also apparently relying on the approximately $75,000 of the loan proceeds which the credit union was transferring into the share draft account that day. The two sums together would cover the $192,000 share draft.

* * *

The debtor filed a Chapter 11 bankruptcy petition on July 21, 1986. On August 19, 1986, the bankruptcy trustee commenced this adversary proceeding against the bank. The trustee asserted that the three checks written by Mr. Bohlen on April 30, 1986, totalling $191,777.27 in favor of the bank, constituted a voidable preference and that the said sum should be disgorged by the bank and made a part of the debtor's estate.

* * *

Following a trial, the bankruptcy judge in a lengthy written opinion, held that $125,068.50 of the $191,777.27 was not a voidable preference because of earmarking. He rejected all of the bank's other claims and theories and ordered the bank to disgorge the remainder, $66,708.77.

Both sides appealed the bankruptcy court's decision, 78 B.R. 556, to the district judge, who affirmed the bankruptcy court in all respects. 91 B.R. 486.

Both sides have appealed to us from the judgment below. The trustee argues that the application of the earmarking doctrine to any of the funds in issue is an error of law. The bank contends that the lower court's application of the earmarking doctrine was legally correct but did not go far enough. The bank argues that the doctrine should be extended to protect the entire $191,777.27. Alternatively, if the doctrine is held not to protect some or all of the transfer, the bank maintains that it nonetheless has a right to retain the entire sum under Section 547(b)(5) because it would have received at least an equal sum in a Chapter 7 distribution. In making this latter assertion, the bank on appeal no longer presses its claim of lien. The assertion is solely premised on the alleged right of setoff.

THE MERITS

The prerequisites for a voidable preference are set forth in 11 U.S.C. § 547(b). Section 547(b) begins with a threshold requirement that a voidable preference must involve a "transfer of an interest of the debtor in property * * * " If such a transfer is involved, the transfer must also be:

(1) to or for the benefit of the creditor,

(2) for or on account of an antecedent debt,

(3) made while the debtor was insolvent,

(4) made on or within 90 days before the date of the filing of the petition, and

(5) one that enables the creditor to receive more than such creditor would receive in a Chapter 7 liquidation of the estate.

The trustee has the right to set aside as a voidable preference any transaction satisfying all of the above requirements.

It is undisputed that requirements (1) through (4) above are met in the instant case. Requirement (5) is in dispute and we deal with that dispute *infra*. The major dispute in the case centers around the threshold requirement that the transfer being attacked be a transfer of an interest of the debtor in property.

A. *The Earmarking Doctrine*

We first turn to the question of whether the earmarking doctrine was properly applied to any of the funds in this case. In so doing, it is appropriate for us to consider the origins and rationale of the doctrine and its various applications.

The earmarking doctrine is entirely a court-made interpretation of the statutory requirement that a voidable preference must involve a "transfer of an interest of the debtor in property". Equivalent language has existed in the Bankruptcy Act for many decades. However, neither the Act, nor the present Code, have apparently ever defined when a transfer involves "property of the debtor", leaving definition of the term entirely to the courts.

In every earmarking situation there are three necessary dramatis personae. They are the "old creditor", (the pre-existing creditor who is paid off within the 90–day period prior to bankruptcy), the "new creditor" or "new lender" who supplies the funds to pay off the old creditor, and the debtor.

When new funds are provided by the new creditor to or for the benefit of the debtor for the purpose of paying the obligation owed to the old creditor, the funds are said to be "earmarked" and the payment is held not to be a voidable preference.

The earliest enunciation of the doctrine occurred in cases where the new creditor providing new funds to pay off the old creditor, was himself also obligated to pay that prior debt. In other words, the new creditor was a guarantor of the debtor's obligation, such as a surety, a subsequent endorser or a straight contractual guarantor. Where such a guarantor paid the debtor's obligation directly to the old creditor, the courts rejected the claim that such payment was a voidable preference.

See e.g. National Bank of Newport v. National Herkimer County Bank, 225 U.S. 178, 32 S.Ct. 633, 56 L.Ed. 1042 (1912). The holding rested on a finding that the new creditor's payment to the old creditor did not constitute a transfer of the debtor's property. The courts buttressed this conclusion with the rationale that no diminution of the debtor's estate had occurred since the new funds and new debt were equal to the preexisting debt and the amount available for general creditors thus remained the same as it was before the payment was made. A possible additional rationale may have been the view that such a result was needed to avoid unfairness and inequity to the new creditor. If his direct payment to the old creditor was voided, and the money was ordered placed in the bankruptcy estate, the new creditor, as guarantor, would have to pay a second time.

Where the guarantor, instead of paying the old creditor directly, entrusted the new funds to the debtor with instructions to use them to pay the debtor's obligation to the old creditor, the courts quite logically reached the same result. *See e.g., First National Bank of Danville v. Phalen,* 62 F.2d 21 (7th Cir.1932)(check made out to debtor with instructions to endorse the check to old creditor); *In Re Reusch & Co.* 44 F.Supp. 677, 680 (D.N.J.1942)(guarantor's funds placed in debtor's possession prior to debtor writing check for payment to old creditor).

In this latter type of case, the courts have been willing to overlook the fact that the method chosen by the guarantor to pay off the old creditor was one in which the debtor was given some control of the new funds. The courts have said that even when the guarantor's new funds are placed in the debtor's possession before payment to the old creditor, they are not within the debtor's "control". *See e.g. Matter of Howdeshell of Fort Myers,* 55 B.R. 470, 474 (Bankr.M.D.Fla.1985); *In Re Jaggers,* 48 B.R. 33, 36 (Bankr.W.D.Texas 1985). In some instances the language used has been that the debtor was holding the new funds "in trust" or in a "fiduciary capacity". In other cases the courts have said they would not let form control over substance. *See e.g. Brown v. First National Bank of Little Rock,* 748 F.2d 490, 492 n. 6 (8th Cir.1984). Finally, as in the direct payment situations, almost every opinion emphasizes that the result involves "no diminution" in the debtor's estate.

The courts have extended the doctrine beyond the guarantor situations and have applied it to situations where the new creditor is not a guarantor but merely loans funds to the debtor for the purpose of enabling the debtor to pay the old creditor. The same rationales have been used to justify the results where the doctrine has been so extended, i.e., that the debtor held the new money "in trust", that the debtor did not have "control" of the new money and that the transaction did not diminish the debtor's estate. Earmarking has been held to exist where the new lender himself directly pays the old creditor, *see e.g. Grubb v. General Contract Purchase Corporation,* 94 F.2d 70 (2d.Cir.1938), and even in cases where the new lender entrusts the funds to the debtor with instructions to use them to pay the old creditor. *See e.g. In Re Sun*

Railings Inc., 5 B.R. 538 (Bankr.S.D.Fla.1980); 4 Collier on Bankruptcy § 547.03 at 547.25 (15 ed. 1987).

As a matter of first impression, it would seem that the doctrine should not have been so extended. The equities in favor of a guarantor or surety, the risk of his having to pay twice if the first payment is held to be a voidable preference, are not present where the new lender is not a guarantor himself. Yet the courts, without much detailed analysis of the differences, have routinely made the extension to non-guarantors.

Where there is no guarantor, the earmarking doctrine does not help either the new creditor or the debtor. In fact the new creditor is harmed. He is a general creditor whose recovery must come from a debtor's estate which is diminished to the extent that the payment made to the old creditor cannot be recovered as a preference. The only person aided by the doctrine is the old creditor, who had nothing to do with earmarking the funds, and who, in equity, deserves no such benefit. We can see no basis for preferring this old creditor to another who was paid with non-earmarked funds.

It is not necessary for us to decide whether the earmarking doctrine, as thus far enunciated in non-guarantor situations, should be preserved, limited, or even rejected entirely. The instant case involves an extension of the doctrine beyond situations in which it has heretofore been applied. Recognizing the important public policy behind the entire scheme of voidable preferences, and recognizing that the earmarking doctrine is an exclusion from the general applicability of voidable preferences, we see no basis for extending the doctrine at all and particularly to the instant facts.

In our view, the transaction should meet the following requirements to qualify for the earmarking doctrine:

(1) the existence of an agreement between the new lender and the debtor that the new funds will be used to pay a specified antecedent debt,

(2) performance of that agreement according to its terms, and

(3) the transaction viewed as a whole (including the transfer in of the new funds and the transfer out to the old creditor) does not result in any diminution of the estate.

In the instant case it is crystal clear that the second requirement is not met. The agreement was not performed according to its terms and we therefore deem the decision below to be an unjustified extension of the earmarking doctrine beyond its previous boundaries. It cannot be disputed that the agreement between the parties was that part of the proceeds of the credit union's new loan would be used to pay the $125,000 obligation. For reasons of its own, the debtor did not perform that agreement. It used the funds to pay a different antecedent debt which happened to be owed to the same creditor, and of which the new lender was completely unaware. The joint payee check for $125,068.50, which could be characterized as evidence of an attempted or contemplated earmarking, was never negotiated.

To be sure, the instant case involves a very unusual situation, i.e., two separate debts being owed to the same old creditor and the new funds being used to discharge a debt to that very creditor but a debt other than the one the parties agreed would be discharged. Suppose that the debtor in the instant case had violated the agreement by using the new loan proceeds to pay an antecedent debt owed to an outsider, someone other than the bank. There is no doubt that that payment would be held to be a voidable preference despite the attempted earmarking. We see no rational basis for reaching a different result in the instant case where the debtor likewise violated his agreement with the new lender and failed to pay off the designated debt as promised.

Even if we apply the frequently invoked test of whether the debtor had "control" over the funds provided by the new lender, the instant facts nevertheless require a holding that a voidable preference has occurred. One cannot conceive of greater or more telling "control" of the new funds by the debtor than to have the debtor use them for its own purposes and in violation of its agreement with the new lender.

The bankruptcy judge apparently recognized that his decision involved an extension of the earmarking doctrine as previously applied. He invoked general equitable principles to justify the extension. As he put it, a court of equity should "look through form to substance" and should "act to achieve the intended result [of the parties]". Failure to do so, he argued, would "result in unjust enrichment to the estate and the general creditors."

We disagree. In our view, extending the doctrine to the instant facts is not required by equitable principles. We fail to see how holding this transfer to be a voidable preference could produce "unjust enrichment" to the debtor's estate or to anyone else. The recovery of voidable preferences has not been viewed as unjustly enriching the debtor's estate or the general creditors in any sense. We also fail to see how bringing the instant facts within the earmarking doctrine can be said to achieve the parties' "intended result". The general equitable concept of carrying out the parties' intent is of dubious applicability in this context, where none of the parties contemplated the debtor's bankruptcy, the unwinding of transactions, and the division of the estate. Moreover, the bank's only intention was that its $189,000 loan would somehow be repaid, regardless of the source of the funds. Finally, the transaction as consummated by the debtor, i.e., the failure to pay the $125,000 obligation and using the loan proceeds to pay off a $189,000 debt which had not been revealed to the new lender, is certainly not the result which the new lender intended. Equity does not require a court to construct a hypothetical transaction which did not occur in order to allow what is really a preference to remain in the old creditor's hands.

* * *

For the reasons above stated the judgment below is reversed. The case is remanded to the district court for further proceedings in conformity with this opinion.

McMillian, Circuit Judge, dissenting.

I respectfully dissent. I would affirm the judgment of the district court.

* * *

Here, the credit union clearly "earmarked" the funds by making its check payable to the debtor and the bank jointly. Consequently, these funds were never the property of the debtor. To disregard the clear intention of the new creditor is to unjustly enrich the debtor's estate as a result of the debtor's own breach of its obligation. This is the kind of injustice that the "earmarked funds" doctrine was created to avoid. For this reason, I would affirm the judgment of the district court.

Notes and Questions

1. What was the statutory justification for the decision in *Bohlen?* In representing a prospective creditor of an insolvent debtor, would you advise that it make an unsecured "earmarked" loan or that it obtain a security interest?

2. A business bankruptcy often comes after a failed effort at debt restructuring. The debtor does not simply wake up one morning and file bankruptcy. It reaches that judgment after having sought every other possible avenue of escape.

Assume that you represent one of the existing creditors whose claim will be bought out for 80 cents on the dollar. How should you arrange for the payment to be made from the sister corporation that will be providing the money for the workout?

Problem 7-6

Debtor Bethlehem Lewiston has maintained a cash management account at Third National Bank for several years. About six months prior to Bethlehem's bankruptcy, Third began to monitor the account closely and determined that Bethlehem was probably running a kite. Its average uncollected daily balances were in excess of $2,000,000 90 days prior to bankruptcy. At approximately that time the officers of Third called the representatives of Bethlehem into the bank and told them they would have to close the account. In the following three months Bethlehem apparently continued to run the kite but in fact incorporated another bank into the kite so that the kite gradually shifted away from Third to other banks. On the date the involuntary petition was filed Third had a positive balance of approximately $1700, but there were almost $4,000,000 of liabilities outstanding at two other banks. Examination of the activity in the account in the 90 days prior to bankruptcy shows there were many deposits payable to the order of Third drawn on First and upon other participants in the kite.

The trustee makes the following arguments: (1) Allowing a depositor to draw on uncollected funds (and thus to have "ledger balances" which are in fact made up of uncollected amounts) is making a loan to the depositor equal to the amount of the uncollected funds. The trustee notes that Third charged the debtor "transaction fees" that were computed at ten percent annual rate on the amount of the uncollected average balances. (2) The gradual reductions of those negative balances over the 90 day period were repayment of the loan; they constitute preferences of approximately $2,000,000.

Third responds as follows: (1) There was no loan; it was simply a "courtesy" to allow the depositor to draw on uncollected funds. (2) Even if there was a loan, we gave new and contemporaneous value by allowing repeated draws on the account. (3) Even if there was a loan that was paid down within 90 days, those payments in the form of checks drawn on other banks and payable to the order of Third were earmarked funds. (4) Our loans were secured, see UCC 4–210.

How would you respond to the bank's arguments?

Indirect Preferences and Recovery of Preferences from Persons Who Are Not Themselves Preferred

Section 547(b)(1) covers not merely transfers to a creditor but also transfers "for the benefit of" a creditor. The transfer of the debtor's property might be to one person but if it benefited another it might be a preference as to the latter and so recoverable from it. First consider an unlikely case, but one commonly cited to illustrate (b)(1). Debtor owes creditor $1,000,000. Creditor in turn owes third party $1,000,000. Creditor agrees to forgive his loan to debtor provided debtor agrees to pay $1,000,000 to third party. The practical effect of this transaction is to prefer creditor, for it is as though his debt had been repaid. In the absence of the "for the benefit of" language in (b)(1) the trustee could not recover this preference from creditor.

A more common preference that falls within (b)(1) is a payment made on a debt that is guaranteed or that is backed up by a standby letter of credit. Assume that debtor owes creditor $1,000,000 and that the $1,000,000 loan is backed up by a standby letter of credit or by the guarantee of a sister corporation. When the $1,000,000 is paid to creditor, the potential liability of the issuer of the letter of credit or of the guarantor is discharged. So the benefit is to the issuer of the letter of credit or the guarantor. Note that the issuer and the guarantor are themselves "creditors" in the sense that they have contingent or potential claims against the debtor. These arise from their right to be subrogated to the creditor's claim against the debtor when they pay off the original creditor's claim on the debtor's default.

A related but different problem arises under section 550(a)(1) when the trustee seeks to recover an indirect preference from the "initial transferee" and there are three parties involved. The most obvious case for the application of 550(a)(1) would be a case when debtor transfers $1 million to Creditor #1 in satisfaction of a liability and Creditor #1 in turn transfers it to Creditor #2. Creditor #1 is the initial transferee, and the preference could be recovered from him. Alternatively the trustee could recover the $1 million from the second transferee (at least if there was not a transfer for value and in good faith).

But 550(a)(1) might also apply in our three-party transaction to provide that the amount can be recovered from the creditor as the "initial transferee" even though the transfer was "for the benefit" of the issuer of the letter of credit or the guarantor. This latter problem—that of recovery from the initial transferee who was not himself guilty of a preference, a case where it benefited a third party—reached its high point in a celebrated 7th Circuit decision commonly known as the "Deprizio case", but styled *Levit v. Ingersoll Rand*, 874 F.2d 1186 (7th Cir.1989).

In that case several insiders, the Deprizios, had guaranteed a loan to Ingersoll Rand. Within one year of bankruptcy but more than 90 days before bankruptcy the debtor paid off the loan. The trustee successfully argued that the payment was a preference to an insider (the Deprizios) under 547(b)(4) and secondly that it could be recovered from Ingersoll Rand (the initial transferee) because of section 550(a)(1). The decision threatened one year of payments on many guaranteed loans. Banks argued that it was unfair and ironic to punish those careful enough to get an insider's guarantee.

In 1994 Congress adopted section 550(c) to prohibit the recovery of such a preference from "a transferee that is not an insider." Although some have argued the amendment does not actually prohibit the finding of a preference under section 547 since it applies only in 550 as to the person from whom it can be recovered, we believe that the 1994 amendment will end the *Deprizio* issue.

Even assuming that *Deprizio* is gone, recovery from third parties who may or may not themselves be guilty of preferences remains for transactions that occur within 90 days of bankruptcy. Even where the law is clear, it is complex and sometimes hard to understand. We suspect there are more than a few cases where the operation of section 550 and perhaps of 547 is not clear.

To wrestle with these problems, consider the following case and the problems that follow it.

IN THE MATTER OF COMPTON CORPORATION

United States Court of Appeals, Fifth Circuit, 1987.
831 F.2d 586.

JERRE S. WILLIAMS, CIRCUIT JUDGE:

This is a bankruptcy preference case in which a bankruptcy trustee seeks to recover a transfer made via a letter of credit for the benefit of one of the debtor's unsecured creditors on the eve of bankruptcy. The bankruptcy court and the district court found there to be no voidable preference. We reverse.

I. FACTUAL BACKGROUND

In March 1982, Blue Quail Energy, Inc., delivered a shipment of oil to debtor Compton Corporation. Payment of $585,443.85 for this shipment of oil was due on or about April 20, 1982. Compton failed to make timely payment. Compton induced Abilene National Bank (now

MBank–Abilene) to issue an irrevocable standby letter of credit in Blue Quail's favor on May 6, 1982. Under the terms of the letter of credit, payment of up to $585,443.85 was due Blue Quail if Compton failed to pay Blue Quail this amount by June 22, 1982. Compton paid MBank $1,463.61 to issue the letter of credit. MBank also received a promissory note payable on demand for $585,443.85. MBank did not need a security agreement to cover the letter of credit transaction because a prior 1980 security agreement between the bank and Compton had a future advances provision. This 1980 security agreement had been perfected as to a variety of Compton's assets through the filing of several financing statements. The most recent financing statement had been filed a year before, May 7, 1981. The letter of credit on its face noted that it was for an antecedent debt due Blue Quail.

On May 7, 1982, the day after MBank issued the letter of credit in Blue Quail's favor, several of Compton's creditors filed an involuntary bankruptcy petition against Compton. On June 22, 1982, MBank paid Blue Quail $569,932.03 on the letter of credit after Compton failed to pay Blue Quail.

In the ensuing bankruptcy proceeding, MBank's aggregate secured claims against Compton, including the letter of credit payment to Blue Quail, were paid in full from the liquidation of Compton's assets which served as the bank's collateral. Walter Kellogg, bankruptcy trustee for Compton, did not contest the validity of MBank's secured claim against Compton's assets for the amount drawn under the letter of credit by Blue Quail. Instead, on June 14, 1983, trustee Kellogg filed a complaint in the bankruptcy court against Blue Quail asserting that Blue Quail had received a preferential transfer under 11 U.S.C. § 547 through the letter of credit transaction. The trustee sought to recover $585,443.85 from Blue Quail pursuant to 11 U.S.C. § 550.

Blue Quail answered and filed a third party complaint against MBank. On June 16, 1986, Blue Quail filed a motion for summary judgment asserting that the trustee could not recover any preference from Blue Quail because Blue Quail had been paid from MBank's funds under the letter of credit and therefore had not received any of Compton's property. On August 17, 1986, the bankruptcy court granted Blue Quail's motion, agreeing that the payment under the letter of credit did not constitute a transfer of debtor Compton's property but rather was a transfer of the bank's property. The bankruptcy court entered judgment on the motion on September 10, 1986. Trustee Kellogg appealed this decision to the district court. On December 11, 1986, the district court affirmed the bankruptcy court ruling, holding that the trustee did not establish two necessary elements of a voidable transfer under 11 U.S.C. § 547. The district court agreed that the trustee could not establish that the funds transferred to Blue Quail were ever property of Compton. Furthermore, the district court held that the transfer of the increased security interest to MBank was a transfer of the debtor's property for the sole benefit of the bank and in no way benefited Blue

Quail. The district court therefore found no voidable preference as to Blue Quail. The trustee is appealing the decision to this Court.

II. THE LETTER OF CREDIT

It is well established that a letter of credit and the proceeds therefrom are not property of the debtor's estate under 11 U.S.C. § 541. * * * When the issuer honors a proper draft under a letter of credit, it does so from its own assets and not from the assets of its customer who caused the letter of credit to be issued. * * * As a result, a bankruptcy trustee is not entitled to enjoin a post petition payment of funds under a letter of credit from the issuer to the beneficiary, because such a payment is not a transfer of debtor's property (a threshold requirement under 11 U.S.C. § 547(b)). A case apparently holding otherwise, *In re Twist Cap., Inc.*, 1 B.R. 284 (Bankr.M.D.Fla.1979), has been roundly criticized and otherwise ignored by courts and commentators alike.

Recognizing these characteristics of a letter of credit in a bankruptcy case is necessary in order to maintain the independence principle, the cornerstone of letter of credit law. Under the independence principle, an issuer's obligation to the letter of credit's beneficiary is independent from any obligation between the beneficiary and the issuer's customer. All a beneficiary has to do to receive payment under a letter of credit is to show that it has performed all the duties required by the letter of credit. Any disputes between the beneficiary and the customer do not affect the issuer's obligation to the beneficiary to pay under the letter of credit.

Letters of credit are most commonly arranged by a party who benefits from provision for goods or services. The party will request a bank to issue a letter of credit which names the provider of the goods or services as the beneficiary. Under a standby letter of credit, the bank becomes primarily liable to the beneficiary upon the default of the bank's customer to pay for the goods or services. The bank charges a fee to issue a letter of credit and to undertake this liability. The shifting of liability to the bank rather than to the services or goods provider is the main purpose of the letter of credit. After all, the bank is in a much better position to assess the risk of its customer's insolvency than is the service or goods provider. It should be noted, however, that it is the risk of the debtor's insolvency and not the risk of a preference attack that a bank assumes under a letter of credit transaction. Overall the independence principle is necessary to insure "the certainty of payments for services or goods rendered regardless of any intervening misfortune which may befall the other contracting party." *In re North Shore,* 30 B.R. at 378.

The trustee in this case accepts this analysis and does not ask us to upset it. The trustee is not attempting to set aside the post petition payments by MBank to Blue Quail under the letter of credit as a preference; nor does the trustee claim the letter of credit itself constitutes debtor's property. The trustee is instead challenging the earlier transfer in which Compton granted MBank an increased security interest in its assets to obtain the letter of credit for the benefit of Blue Quail. Collateral which has been pledged by a debtor as security for a letter of credit is property of the debtor's estate. *In re W.L. Mead,* 42 B.R. at 59. The trustee claims that the direct transfer to MBank of the increased security interest on May 6, 1982, also constituted an indirect transfer to Blue Quail which occurred one day prior to the filing of the involuntary bankruptcy petition and is voidable as a preference under 11 U.S.C. § 547. This assertion of a preferential transfer is evaluated in Parts III and IV of this opinion.

It is important to note that the irrevocable standby letter of credit in the case at bar was not arranged in connection with Blue Quail's initial decision to sell oil to Compton on credit. Compton arranged for the letter of credit after Blue Quail had shipped the oil and after Compton had defaulted in payment. The letter of credit in this case did not serve its usual function of backing up a contemporaneous credit decision, but instead served as a back up payment guarantee on an extension of credit already in jeopardy. The letter of credit was issued to pay off an antecedent unsecured debt. This fact was clearly noted on the face of the letter of credit. Blue Quail, the beneficiary of the letter of credit, did not give new value for the issuance of the letter of credit by MBank on May 6, 1982, or for the resulting increased security interest held by MBank. MBank, however, did give new value for the increased security interest it obtained in Compton's collateral: the bank issued the letter of credit.

When a debtor pledges its assets to secure a letter of credit, a transfer of debtor's property has occurred under the provisions of 11 U.S.C. § 547. By subjecting its assets to MBank's reimbursement claim in the event MBank had to pay on the letter of credit, Compton made a transfer of its property. The broad definition of "transfer" under 11 U.S.C. § 101(50) is clearly designed to cover such a transfer. Overall, the letter of credit itself and the payments thereunder may not be property of debtor, but the collateral pledged as a security interest for the letter of credit is.

Furthermore, in a secured letter of credit transaction, the transfer of debtor's property takes place at the time the letter of credit is issued (when the security interest is granted) and received by the beneficiary, not at the time the issuer pays on the letter of credit. *In re Briggs Transportation Co.,* 37 B.R. 76, 79 (Bankr.D.Minn.1984). *In re M.J. Sales & Distributing Co.,* 25 B.R. 608 (Bankr.S.D.N.Y.1982)(transfer of pledged collateral occurs not when bank forecloses on it, but when it is pledged.)

The transfer to MBank of the increased security interest was a direct transfer which occurred on May 6, 1982, when the bank issued the letter of credit. Under 11 U.S.C. § 547(e)(2)(A), however, such a transfer is deemed to have taken place for purposes of 11 U.S.C. § 547 at the time such transfer "takes effect" between the transferor and transferee if such transfer is perfected within 10 days. The phrase "takes effect" is undefined in the Bankruptcy Code, but under Uniform Commercial Code Article 9 law, a transfer of a security interest "takes effect" when the security interest attaches. Because of the future advances clause in MBank's 1980 security agreement with Compton, the attachment of the MBank's security interest relates back to May 9, 1980, the date the security agreement went into effect. The bottom line is that the direct transfer of the increased security interest to MBank is artificially deemed to have occurred at least by May 7, 1981, the date MBank filed its final financing statement, for purposes of a preference attack against the bank. This date is well before the 90 day window of 11 U.S.C. § 547(b)(4)(A). This would protect the bank from a preference attack by the trustee even if the bank had not given new value at the time it received the increased security interest. MBank is therefore protected from a preference attack by the trustee for the increased security interest transfer under either of two theories: under 11 U.S.C. § 547(c)(1) because it gave new value and under the operation of the relation back provision of 11 U.S.C. § 547(e)(2)(A). The bank is also protected from any claims of reimbursement by Blue Quail because the bank received no voidable preference.

The relation back provision of 11 U.S.C. § 547(e)(2)(A), however, applies only to the direct transfer of the increased security interest to MBank. The indirect transfer to Blue Quail that allegedly resulted from the direct transfer to MBank occurred on May 6, 1982, the date of issuance of the letter of credit. The relation back principle of 11 U.S.C. § 5478(e)(2)(A) does not apply to this indirect transfer to Blue Quail. Blue Quail was not a party to the security agreement between MBank and Compton. So it will not be able to utilize the relation back provision if it is deemed to have received an indirect transfer resulting from the direct transfer of the increased security interest to MBank. Blue Quail, therefore cannot assert either of the two defenses to a preference attack which MBank can claim. Blue Quail did not give new value under § 547(c)(1) and it received a transfer within 90 days of the filing of Compton's bankruptcy petition.

III. Direct/Indirect Transfer Doctrine

The federal courts have long recognized that "[t]o constitute a preference, it is not necessary that the transfer be made directly to the creditor." *National Bank of Newport v. National Herkimer County Bank,* 225 U.S. 178, 184, 32 S.Ct. 633, 635, 56 L.Ed. 1042G (1912). "If the bankrupt has made a transfer of his property, the *effect* of which is to enable one of his creditors to obtain a greater percentage of his debt than another creditor of the same class, circuity of arrangement will not avail to save it." *Id.* (Emphasis added). To combat such circuity, the courts have broken down certain transfers into two transfers, one direct and one indirect. The direct transfer to the third party may be valid and not subject to a preference attack. The indirect transfer, arising from the same action by the debtor, however, may constitute a voidable preference as to the creditor who indirectly benefitted from the direct transfer to the third party.

This is the situation presented in the case before us. The term "transfer" as used in the various bankruptcy statutes through the years has always been broad enough to cover such indirect transfers and to catch various circuitous arrangements. * * * The new Bankruptcy Code implicitly adopts this doctrine through its broad definition of "transfer." Examining the case law that has developed since the *National Bank of Newport* case yields an understanding of what types of transfers the direct/indirect doctrine is meant to cover.

In *Palmer v. Radio Corporation of America*, 453 F.2d 1133 (5th Cir.1971), a third party purchased from the debtor a television station for $40,000 cash and the assumption of certain liabilities of the debtor, including unsecured claims by creditor RCA. This Court found the direct transfer from the debtor to the third party purchaser constituted an indirect preferential transfer to creditor RCA. We found that the assumption by the third party purchaser of the debt owed by the debtor to RCA and the subsequent payments made thereunder constituted a voidable transfer as to RCA. The court noted that such indirect transfers as this had long been held to constitute voidable preferences under bankruptcy laws. 453 F.2d at 1136.

Although the *Palmer* court did not elaborate its reasoning behind this holding, such reasoning is self evident. A secured creditor was essentially substituted for an unsecured creditor through the transfer of the television station to the third party purchaser and the assumption of the unsecured debt by the purchaser. The third party purchaser was in effect secured because it had the television station. Creditor RCA would receive payments directly from the solvent third part without having to worry about its original debtor's financial condition. The original debtor's other unsecured creditors were harmed because a valuable asset of the debtor, the television station, was removed from the debtor's estate. The end result of the *Palmer* case was that the third party's payments on the RCA debt were to be made to the debtor's estate instead of to RCA. RCA would then recover the same percentage of its unsecured claim from the estate as the other unsecured creditors.

In *In re Conard Corp.*, 806 F.2d 610 (5th Cir.1986), we found a voidable indirect transfer on facts similar to those of *Palmer v. Radio Corporation of America*. In the *Conard* case, the debtors bought several restaurants from the Burtons in exchange for an unsecured promissory note. A third party in turn purchased the restaurants from the debtors and assumed the payments to the Burtons on the promissory note. Relying on the analysis of the *Palmer* case, we held that the transfer of the restaurants by the debtors in exchange for a simultaneous assumption of the Burton debt by the third party benefitted the Burtons and constituted a voidable indirect transfer as to the Burtons.

We observed that as a result of executing the assumption of debt agreement, the debtors transferred to the Burtons the debtors' right to receive from the third party so much of the sales price for the restaurants as was needed to reimburse the Burtons on their unsecured note.

Once again a secured creditor, in effect, was substituted for an unsecured creditor by the transfer, and a depletion of the debtor's estate occurred. We held that the trustee of the debtor could recover from the Burtons the payments made by the third party to the Burtons and that the Burtons would recover only their proportionate share of the value of the unencumbered assets of the debtor along with the other unsecured creditors.

* * * The creditor in *Aulick* [*Aulick v. Largent*, 295 F.2d 41 (4th Cir.1961)] made the same argument that Blue Quail makes in the case at bar. The creditor claimed that the payment to it by the third party endorser came from the endorser's personal funds and thus the payment did not deplete the debtor's estate. Therefore one of the essential elements of a voidable preference was lacking.

The court rejected this argument relying on *National Bank of Newport*. The *Aulick* court found there to be two transfers arising from the pledge of stock to the third party, one direct and one indirect, and then collapsed them, in effect, into a single one for a preference attack against the indirect transferee creditor. The court noted that if the debtor had delivered the shares of stock directly to the unsecured creditor as security for the antecedent debt, the creditor would have clearly received a voidable preference. The court held that such a result could not be avoided by indirect arrangement. "[P]references obtained by indirect or circuitous arrangements are to be struck down just as quickly as those obtained by direct arrangements." 295 F.2d at 52.

In *Virginia National Bank v. Woodson*, 329 F.2d 836 (4th Cir.1964), the debtor had several overdrawn accounts with his bank. The debtor talked his sister into paying off $8,000 of the overdrafts in exchange for an $8,000 promissory note and an assignment of some collateral as security. The debtor's sister made the $8,000 payment directly to the bank. The $8,000 technically was never part of the debtor's estate. The court, however, held that the payment of the $8,000 by the sister to the bank was a preference as to the bank to the extent of the value of the collateral held by the sister. The court noted that the measure of the value of a voidable preference is diminution of the debtor's estate and not the value of the transfer to the creditor.

In the *Woodson* case the sister was secured only to the extent the pledged collateral had value; the remainder of her loan to her brother was unsecured. Swapping one unsecured creditor for another unsecured creditor does not create any kind of preference. The court held that a preference in such a transaction arises only when a secured creditor is swapped for an unsecured creditor. Only then is the pool of assets available for distribution to the general unsecured creditors depleted because the secured creditor has priority over the unsecured creditors. Furthermore, the court held that the bank and not the sister had received the voidable preference and had to pay back to the trustee an amount equal to the value of the collateral. * * *

IV. THE DIRECT/INDIRECT DOCTRINE IN THE CONTEXT OF A LETTER OF CREDIT TRANSACTION

The case at bar differs from the cases discussed in Part III *supra* only by the presence of the letter of credit as the mechanism for paying off the unsecured creditor. Blue Quail's attempt to otherwise distinguish the case from the direct/indirect transfer cases does not withstand scrutiny.

In the letter credit cases discussed in Part II *supra*, the letters of credit were issued contemporaneously with the initial extension of credit by the beneficiaries of the letters. In those cases the letters of credit effectively served as security devices for the benefit of the creditor beneficiaries and took the place of formal security interests. The courts in those cases properly found there had been no voidable transfers, direct or indirect, in the letter of credit transactions involved. New value was given contemporaneously with the issuance of the letters of credit in the form of the extensions of credit by the beneficiaries of the letters. As a result, the 11 U.S.C. § 547(c)(1) preference exception was applicable.

The case at bar differs from these other letter of credit cases by one very important fact: the letter of credit in this case was issued to secure an antecedent unsecured debt due the beneficiary of the letter of credit. The unsecured creditor beneficiary gave no new value upon the issuance of the letter of credit. When the issuer paid off the letter of credit and foreclosed on the collateral securing the letter of credit, a preferential transfer had occurred. An unsecured creditor was paid in full and a secured creditor was substituted in its place.

The district court upheld the bankruptcy court in maintaining the validity of the letter of credit issued to cover the antecedent debt. The district court held that MBank, the issuer of the letter of credit, could pay off the letter of credit and foreclose on the collateral securing it. We are in full agreement. But we also look to the impact of the transaction as if affects the situation of Blue Quail in the bankrupt estate. We hold that the bankruptcy trustee can recover from Blue Quail, the beneficiary of the letter of credit, because Blue Quail received an indirect preference. This result preserves the sanctity of letter of credit and carries out the purposes of the Bankruptcy Code by avoiding a preferential transfer. MBank, the issuer of the letter of credit, being just the intermediary through which the preferential transfer was accomplished, completely falls out of the picture and is not involved in this particular legal proceeding.

MBank did not receive any preferential transfer—it gave new value for the security interest. Furthermore, because the direct and indirect transfers are separate and independent, the trustee does not even need to challenge the direct transfer of the increased security interest to MBank, or seek any relief at all from MBank, in order to attack the indirect transfer and recover under 11 U.S.C. § 550 from the indirect transferee Blue Quail.

We hold that a creditor cannot secure payment of an unsecured antecedent debt through a letter of credit transaction when it could not do so through any other type of transaction. The purpose of the letter of credit transaction in this case was to secure payment of any unsecured antecedent debt for the benefit of an unsecured creditor. This is the only proper way to look at such letters of credit in the bankruptcy context. The promised transfer of pledged collateral induced the bank to issue the letter of credit in favor of the creditor. The increased security interest held by the bank clearly benefitted the creditor because the bank would not have issued the letter of credit without this security. A secured creditor was substituted for an unsecured creditor to the detriment of the other secured creditors.

We also hold, therefore, that the trustee can recover under 11 U.S.C. § 550(a)(1) the value of the transferred property from "the entity for whose benefit such transfer was made." In the case at bar, this entity was the creditor beneficiary, not the issuer, of the letter of credit even though the issuer received the direct transfer from the debtor. The entire purpose of the direct/indirect doctrine is to look through the form of a transaction and determine which entity actually benefitted from the transfer.

The fact that there was a prior security agreement between the issuing bank and the debtor containing the future advances clause does not alter this conclusion. As we pointed out in Part II *supra,* this prior security agreement gave MBank an additional shield from preferential attack because of the relation back mechanism of 11 U.S.C. § 547(e)(2)(A). 11 U.S.C. § 547(e)(2)(A), however, does not avail Blue Quail to shield it from a preferential attack for the indirect transfer. The indirect transfer to Blue Quail occurred on May 6, 1982, when the letter of credit was issued and the increased security interest was pledged. This was the day before the involuntary bankruptcy petition was filed. For purposes of 11 U.S.C. § 547, a transfer of Compton's property for the benefit of Blue Quail did occur within 90 days of the bankruptcy filing. The bankruptcy and district courts erred in failing to analyze properly the transfer of debtor's property that occurred when Compton pledged its assets to obtain the letter of credit. This transfer consisted of two aspects: the direct transfer to MBank which is not a voidable preference for various reasons and the indirect transfer to Blue Quail which is a voidable preference.

All of the requirements of 11 U.S.C. § 547(b) have been satisfied in the trustee's preferential attack against Blue Quail. There was (1) a transfer of Compton's property for the benefit of Blue Quail (2) for an antecedent debt owed by Compton (3) made while Compton was insolvent (4) within 90 days before the date of the filing of the petition (5) that enabled Blue Quail to receive more than it would receive under a Chapter 7 liquidation. The net effect of the indirect transfer to Blue Quail was to remove $585,433.85 from the pool of assets available to Compton's unsecured creditors and substitute in its place a secured claim for the same amount.

The precise holding in this case needs to be emphasized. We do not hold that payment under a letter of credit, or even a letter of credit itself, constitute preferential transfers under 11 U.S.C. § 547(b) or property under 11 U.S.C. § 541. The holding of this case fully allows the letter of credit to function. We preserve its sanctity and the underlying independence doctrine. We do not, however, allow an unsecured creditor to avoid a preference attack by utilizing a letter of credit to secure payment of an antecedent debt. Otherwise the unsecured creditor would receive an indirect preferential transfer from the granting of the security for the letter of credit to the extent of the value of that security. Our holding does not affect the strength of or the proper use of letters of credit. When a letter of credit is issued contemporaneously with a new extension of credit, the creditor beneficiary will not be subject to a preferential attack under the direct/indirect doctrine elaborated in this case because the creditor will have given new value in exchange for the indirect benefit of the secured letter of credit. Only when a creditor receives a secured letter of credit to cover an unsecured antecedent debt will it be subject to a preferential attack under 11 U.S.C. § 547(b).

V. Liability of MBank for the Preferential Transfer

Blue Quail has no valid claim against MBank for reimbursement for any amounts Blue Quail has to pay the trustee under the trustee's preference claim, just as the trustee has no preference challenge against MBank. Blue Quail received the preferential transfer, not MBank. MBank gave new value in exchange for the increased security interest in its favor. Thus, it is insulated from any assertion of a voidable preference. The bank in no way assumed the risk of a preference attack by issuing the letter of credit. For these reasons, we affirm the district court's dismissal of Blue Quail's request to proceed against MBank for reimbursement.

In addition, the trustee may not set aside the $1,4361.61 fee Compton paid MBank to issue the letter of credit. This payment is not a preferential transfer. MBank has fully performed its duties under the terms of the letter of credit and has earned this fee. The services MBank rendered in issuing and executing the letter of credit constitute new value under the 11 U.S.C. § 547(c)(1) preference exception.

VI. Conclusion

Blue Quail Energy received an indirect preferential transfer from Compton Corporation on May 6, 1982, one day prior to the filing of Compton's bankruptcy petition. We reverse the district court and render judgment in favor of Trustee Kellogg against Blue Quail Energy, Inc. in the amount of $585,433.85 plus interest to be fixed by the district court pursuant to 11 U.S.C. §§ 547, 550. The district court's dismissal of Blue Quail's claim against MBank for reimbursement is affirmed.

REVERSED IN PART, AFFIRMED IN PART, AND REMANDED.

Notes and Questions

Assume that Blue Quail is insolvent when the trustee tries to recover the preference. Can the trustee then turn to MBank and recover the amount of the preference from MBank under 550(a)(1) on the ground that MBank was the "the initial transferee" of the security interest?

Problem 7-7

Assume that MBank had issued a letter of credit to Blue Quail without security one year prior to the bankruptcy. Sixty days before the bankruptcy, the debtor pays Blue Quail's debt in full and the letter of credit is cancelled. Upon bankruptcy the trustee seeks the return of the payment from MBank on the ground that it was a payment to or for the benefit of MBank under section 547. What is your response? How could you forestall such a claim in the future?

Problem 7-8

Fifty days before its bankruptcy, Edwards, Inc. a printing concern, sold three of its presses and other assets to a buyer for a total consideration of $3,000,000. Buyer paid $1,000,000 in cash; the other $2,000,000 took the form of buyer's assumption of the liabilities of three creditors who had unsecured claims against Edwards that were associated in one way or another with the assets that were sold to the buyer. Assume that Edwards had been insolvent six months prior to bankruptcy. Do you see a preference here?

Problem 7-9

Six months prior to its bankruptcy, Edwards paid $500,000 in satisfaction of an unsecured loan to its bank. This loan was guaranteed individually by two of the Edwards brothers, who are principals in the business. The trustee has considered going after these transfers as a preference but is concerned about the 1994 amendments to 550. How do you advise the trustee?

Problem 7-10

Assume Edwards, Inc. had a longstanding obligation to Greenstreet Finance of $1,000,000. Several years ago Nations Bank issued a standby letter of credit for $1 million naming Greenstreet the beneficiary. Under the terms of this letter of credit, Greenstreet can draw on the letter under either of two conditions: (1) upon default by Edwards on the $1 million; (2) anytime within 60 days of notification by Nations Bank that the bank chooses not to renew the letter of credit. About four months before Edwards' bankruptcy, Nations Bank gives notice to Greenstreet that it does not intend to renew the letter of credit. Accordingly Greenstreet prepares a draft to draw on the letter of credit, but, in last minute negotiations, Edwards prevails upon Nations Bank to renew the letter of credit by agreeing to give collateral to the bank in the amount of $1,000,000.

Notwithstanding the renewal, Greenstreet draws on the letter of credit after Edwards' bankruptcy. The trustee would like to recover the $1,000,-000 from Greenstreet on the ground that the granting of security within three months of bankruptcy to Nations was an indirect preference to Greenstreet. What do you think? Do you have any better ideas?

Problem 7–11

John, a secured creditor, has a first mortgage securing a debt of $60,000. James, the second secured creditor, has a mortgage securing a $20,000 debt. Each of these mortgages is on Simon's real estate, which has a fair market value of $65,000. In the three months prior to the filing of the petition, Simon (the debtor) makes two payments of $20,000 each to the first mortgagee. Has Simon committed a preference?

Problem 7–12

Assume that a company, Chicago Construction, Inc. is controlled by the three Deprizio brothers. Like all construction companies, Chicago Construction has many creditors. One of the largest debts is a $3,000,000 unsecured line of credit owed to First Chicago Bank. All three of the Deprizio brothers are guarantors of this line of credit. As the financial problems of Chicago Construction increase, the Deprizio brothers decide to pay off First Chicago's debt. Eight months later, Chicago Construction declares bankruptcy. Arguing that the payment to First Chicago was a preference both to the Deprizio guarantors and to First Chicago, the trustee tries to recover the amount from each of them. Do you see how the argument could be made? Do you see why there can be no recovery from First Chicago under section 550 as amended in 1994?

Problem 7–13

A debtor, Gideon Transportation Co., leased two Red Sea tugboats from Joshua Towing Company. During the 90 days prior to the filing of its bankruptcy, Gideon paid $149,000 of past due fuel bills to Exxon of Tennessee. After these payments, Gideon continued to use both boats and ran up additional unpaid fuel bills of $170,000. Under applicable federal law, unpaid fuel bills automatically become a lien on boats that consume fuel for which there is no payment. These liens attach to the boats and are superior to the lessor's interest even though the lease provides that the lessor's interest is superior to the lien. Gideon was in arrears by $130,000 for its rental from Joshua at the time the bankruptcy petition was filed.

Advise the bankruptcy trustee on the possibility of recovering the $149,000.

Problem 7–14

Assume that the debtor files a petition in Chapter 11 on 9/1. Determine in each of the following cases whether there has been a preference that can be set aside. Except where otherwise provided assume that no one is an insider. Treat each numbered paragraph separately.

1. On 4/5 Bank issued a letter of credit payable to unsecured creditor on behalf of debtor and took a security interest in debtor's assets to secure its obligation to pay.

2. The letter in 1. was drawn on 8/25.

3. On 8/1 Bank issued a letter of credit payable to unsecured creditor on behalf of debtor and took a security interest in debtor's assets to secure its obligation to pay.

On 8/25 the letter was drawn upon and Bank paid creditor. Who received a preference, if anyone, Bank or creditor?

4. On 8/1 Bank issued a letter of credit to unsecured creditor on behalf of debtor, but took no security interest. On 8/25 the letter was drawn upon and Bank paid creditor.

5. On 4/5 Bank issued a letter of credit to unsecured creditor and took a security interest in debtor's assets to secure its obligation. The Bank, but not the creditor, is an insider of the debtor.

Problem 7–15

David Extermination Corporation receives a revolving line of unsecured credit from Goliath Financial. Goliath makes daily advances covering the operating expenses of David (averaging $84,000 per month) and is repaid in the middle of the following month when David receives payments on the service contracts that it has with numerous consumers. During the first two years of operation, David's payments always occurred by check between the 12th and the 19th of the month. This same pattern is present in the 30 other deals that Goliath has within the industry. During the past six months, however, the payments have begun to come to Goliath around the 22nd and 23rd of the month. Since it was always paid, Goliath made no complaint. In June David's payment did not arrive on the 23rd and Goliath called to find out why the payment has not been received. Five days later, David delivered a check for the month of June. David filed bankruptcy the next day.

Assume that the daily advances were $3,000 on each day up to the filing of bankruptcy. David's trustee examined the relationship and attempts to recover the payment from Goliath as a preference. Will Goliath's defense be successful?

UNION BANK v. WOLAS

United States Supreme Court, 1991.
502 U.S. 151, 112 S.Ct. 527, 116 L.Ed.2d 514.

JUSTICE STEVENS delivered the opinion of the Court.

On December 17, 1986, ZZZZ Best Co., Inc. (Debtor) borrowed seven million dollars from petitioner, Union Bank (Bank).[1] On July 8, 1987, the Debtor filed a voluntary petition under Chapter 7 of the Bankruptcy Code. During the preceding 90–day period, the Debtor had made two

---

1. The Bankruptcy Court found that the Bank and Debtor executed a revolving credit agreement on December 16, 1986, in which the Bank agreed to lend the Debtor $7 million in accordance with the terms of a promissory note to be executed and delivered by the Debtor. No. 87–13692 (Bkrtcy. Ct. CD Cal., Aug. 22, 1988), App. to Pet. for Cert. 12a. On December 17, 1987, the Debtor executed and delivered to the Bank a promissory note in the principal sum of $7 million. The promissory note provided that interest would be payable on a monthly basis and would accrue on the principal balance at a rate of .65% per annum in excess of the Bank's reference rate. *Ibid.*

interest payments totalling approximately $100,000 and had paid a loan commitment fee of about $2,500 to the Bank. After his appointment as trustee of the Debtor's estate, respondent filed a complaint against the Bank to recover those payments pursuant to § 547(b).

The Bankruptcy Court found that the loans had been made "in the ordinary course of business or financial affairs" of both the Debtor and the Bank, and that both interest payments as well as the payment of the loan commitment fee had been made according to ordinary business terms and in the ordinary course of business. As a matter of law, the Bankruptcy Court concluded that the payments satisfied the requirements of § 547(c)(2) and therefore were not avoidable by the trustee. The District Court affirmed the Bankruptcy Court's summary judgment in favor of the Bank.

Shortly thereafter, in another case, the Court of Appeals held that the ordinary course of business exception to avoidance of preferential transfers was not available to long-term creditors. *In re CHG International, Inc.*, 897 F.2d 1479 (C.A.9 1990). In reaching that conclusion, the Court of Appeals relied primarily on the policies underlying the voidable preference provisions and the state of the law prior to the enactment of the 1978 Bankruptcy Code and its amendment in 1984. Thus, the Ninth Circuit concluded, its holding in *CHG International, Inc.* dictated a reversal in this case. 921 F.2d 968, 969 (1990).[5] The importance of the question of law decided by the Ninth Circuit, coupled with the fact that the Sixth Circuit had interpreted § 547(c)(2) in a contrary manner, *In re Finn*, 909 F.2d 903 (6th Cir.1990), persuaded us to grant the Bank's petition for certiorari. 500 U.S. 915, 111 S.Ct. 2009, 114 L.Ed.2d 97 (1991).

I

We shall discuss the history and policy of § 547 after examining its text. In subsection (b), Congress broadly authorized bankruptcy trustees to "avoid any transfer of an interest of the debtor in property" *if* five conditions are satisfied and *unless* one of seven exceptions defined in subsection (c) is applicable. In brief, the five characteristics of a voidable preference are that it (1) benefit a creditor; (2) be on account of antecedent debt; (3) be made while the debtor was insolvent; (4) be within 90 days before bankruptcy; and (5) enable the creditor to receive a larger share of the estate than if the transfer had not been made. Section 547 also provides that the debtor is presumed to have been insolvent during the 90-day period preceding bankruptcy. 11 U.S.C. § 547(f). In this case, it is undisputed that all five of the foregoing conditions were satisfied and that the interest and loan commitment fee payments were voidable preferences unless excepted by subsection (c)(2).

---

5. In so holding, the Ninth Circuit rejected the Bank's argument that the revolving line of credit in this case was not "long-term" because it was for less than one year. 921 F.2d 968, 969 (1990). Because we hold that the ordinary course of business exception applies to payments on long-term as well as short-term debt, we need not decide whether the revolving line of credit was a "long-term" debt.

The most significant feature of subsection (c)(2) that is relevant to this case is the absence of any language distinguishing between long-term debt and short-term debt. That subsection provides:

"The trustee may not avoid under this section a transfer—

* * *

"(2) to the extent that such transfer was—

"(A) in payment of a debt incurred by the debtor in the ordinary course of business or financial affairs of the debtor and the transferee;

"(B) made in the ordinary course of business or financial affairs of the debtor and the transferee; and

"(C) made according to ordinary business terms."

Instead of focusing on the term of the debt for which the transfer was made, subsection (c)(2) focuses on whether the debt was incurred, and payment made, in the "ordinary course of business or financial affairs" of the debtor and transferee. Thus, the text provides no support for respondent's contention that § 547(c)(2)'s coverage is limited to short-term debt, such as commercial paper or trade debt. Given the clarity of the statutory text, respondent's burden of persuading us that Congress intended to create or to preserve a special rule for long-term debt is exceptionally heavy. *United States v. Ron Pair Enterprises, Inc.*, 489 U.S. 235, 241–242, 109 S.Ct. 1026, 1030–1031, 103 L.Ed.2d 290 (1989). As did the Ninth Circuit, respondent relies on the history and the policies underlying the preference provision.

II

The relevant history of § 547 contains two chapters, one of which clearly supports, and the second of which is not inconsistent with, the Bank's literal reading of the statute. Section 547 was enacted in 1978 when Congress overhauled the Nation's bankruptcy laws. The section was amended in 1984. For purposes of the question presented in this case, the original version of § 547 differed in one significant respect from the current version: it contained a provision that the ordinary course of business exception did not apply unless the payment was made within 45 days of the date the debt was incurred. That provision presumably excluded most payments on long-term debt from the exception.[9] In 1984 Congress repealed the 45-day limitation but did not substitute a comparable limitation. See Bankruptcy Amendments and Federal Judgeship Act of 1984, Pub.L. 98–353, § 462(c), 98 Stat. 333, 378.

---

9. We use the term "presumably" because it is not necessary in this case to decide whether monthly interest payments on long-term debt were protected by the initial version of § 547(c)(2). Cf. *In re Iowa Premium Service Co., Inc.*, 695 F.2d 1109 (C.A.8 1982)(en banc)(holding that interest obligations are "incurred" when they become due, rather than when the promissory note is signed). We refer to "most" instead of "all" long-term debt payments because of the possibility that a debtor's otherwise avoidable payment was made within 45 days of the date the long-term loan was made.

Respondent contends that this amendment was intended to satisfy complaints by issuers of commercial paper[10] and by trade creditors[11] that regularly extended credit for periods of more than 45 days. Furthermore, respondent continues, there is no evidence in the legislative history that Congress intended to make the ordinary course of business exception available to conventional long-term lenders. Therefore, respondent argues, we should follow the analysis of the Ninth Circuit and read § 547(c)(2) as protecting only short-term debt payments. Cf. *In re CHG International,* 897 F.2d, at 1484.

We need not dispute the accuracy of respondent's description of the legislative history of the 1984 amendment in order to reject his conclusion. For even if Congress adopted the 1984 amendment to redress particular problems of specific short-term creditors, it remains true that Congress redressed those problems by entirely deleting the time limitation in § 547(c)(2). The fact that Congress may not have foreseen all of the consequences of a statutory enactment is not a sufficient reason for refusing to give effect to its plain meaning. *Toibb v. Radloff,* 501 U.S. 157, 111 S.Ct. 2197, 115 L.Ed.2d 145 (1991).

Respondent also relies on the history of voidable preferences prior to the enactment of the 1978 Bankruptcy Code. The text of the preference provision in the earlier Bankruptcy Act did not specifically include an exception for payments made in the ordinary course of business. The courts had, however, developed what is sometimes described as the "current expense" rule to cover situations in which a debtor's payments on the eve of bankruptcy did not diminish the net estate because tangible assets were obtained in exchange for the payment. See *Marshall v. Florida National Bank of Jacksonville,* 112 F.2d 380–382 (C.A.5 1940); 3 Collier On Bankruptcy ¶ 60.23, p. 873 (14th ed. 1977). Without such an exception, trade creditors and other suppliers of necessary goods and services might have been reluctant to extend even short-term credit and might have required advance payment instead, thus making it difficult for many companies in temporary distress to have remained in business. Respondent argues that Congress enacted § 547(c)(2) in 1978 to codify that exception, and therefore the Court should construe § 547(c)(2) as limited to the confines of the current expense rule.

---

10. Because payments to a commercial paper purchaser within 90 days prior to bankruptcy may be preferential transfers under § 547(b), a purchaser could be assured that the payment would not be avoided under the prior version of § 547(c)(2) only if the commercial paper had a maturity of 45 days or less. Commercial issuers thus complained that the 45–day limitation lowered demand for commercial paper with a maturity in excess of 45 days. See Hearings before the Subcommittee on Judicial Machinery of the Senate Committee on the Judiciary, 96th Cong., 2d Sess., 8–27 (1980) (statements of George Van Cleave, partner, Goldman, Sachs & Co., and James Ledinsky, Senior Vice President, A.G. Becker & Co.).

11. Trade creditors stated that normal payment periods in many industries exceeded 45 days and complained that the arbitrary 45–day limitation in § 547(c)(2) deprived these trade creditors of the protection of the ordinary course of business exception to the trustee's power to avoid preferential transfers. See, *e.g.,* Hearings on Bankruptcy Reform Act of 1978, before the Subcommittee on Courts of the Senate Committee on the Judiciary, 97th Cong., 1st Sess., 259–260 (1981)(statement of Vyto Gestautas on behalf of the National Association of Credit Management).

This argument is not compelling for several reasons. First, it is by no means clear that § 547(c)(2) should be construed as the statutory analogue of the judicially crafted current expense rule because there are other exceptions in § 547(c) that explicitly cover contemporaneous exchanges for new value.[13] Those provisions occupy some (if not all) of the territory previously covered by the current expense rule. Nor has respondent directed our attention to any extrinsic evidence suggesting that Congress intended to codify the current expense rule in § 547(c)(2).[14]

The current expense rule developed when the statutory preference provision was significantly narrower than it is today. To establish a preference under the Bankruptcy Act, the trustee had to prove that the challenged payment was made at a time when the creditor had "reasonable cause to believe that the debtor [was] insolvent." 11 U.S.C. § 96(b)(1976 ed.). When Congress rewrote the preference provision in the 1978 Bankruptcy Code, it substantially enlarged the trustee's power to avoid preferential transfers by eliminating the reasonable cause to believe requirement for transfers made within 90 days of bankruptcy and creating a presumption of insolvency during that period. See 11 U.S.C. §§ 547(b), (c)(2), (f); H.R.Rep. No. 95–595, p. 178 (1977), U.S.Code Cong. & Admin.News 1978, pp. 5787, 6138. At the same time, Congress created a new exception for transfers made in the ordinary course of business, 11 U.S.C. § 547(c)(2). This exception was intended to "leave undisturbed normal financial relations, because it does not detract from the general policy of the preference section to discourage unusual action by either the debtor or his creditors during the debtor's slide into bankruptcy." H.R.Rep. No. 95–595, at 373.

In light of these substantial changes in the preference provision, there is no reason to assume that the justification for narrowly confining the "current expense" exception to trade creditors before 1978 should apply to the ordinary course of business exception under the 1978 Code. Instead, the fact that Congress carefully reexamined and entirely rewrote the preference provision in 1978 supports the conclusion that the text of § 547(c)(2) as enacted reflects the deliberate choice of Congress.[15]

---

13. Thus, for example, § 547(c)(1) exempts a transfer to the extent that it was a "contemporaneous exchange for new value given to the debtor," and § 547(c)(4) exempts a transfer to a creditor "to the extent that, after such transfer, such creditor gave new value to or for the benefit of the debtor * * *."

14. In fact, the legislative history apparently does not even mention the current expense rule. See Broome, Payments on Long–Term Debt as Voidable Preferences: The Impact of the 1984 Bankruptcy Amendments, 1987 Duke L.J. 78, 97.

15. Indeed, the House Committee Report concludes its discussion of the trustee's avoidance powers with the observation that the language in the preference section of the earlier Bankruptcy Act was "hopelessly complex" and had been "subject to varying interpretations. The bill undoes the numerous amendments that have been heaped on section 60 during the past 40 years, and proposes a unified and coherent section to deal with the problems created by prebankruptcy preferential transfers." H.R.Rep. No. 95–595, p. 179 (1977), U.S.Code Cong. & Admin.News 1978, p. 6139. Respondent's assumption that § 547(c)(2) was intended to preserve pre-existing law is at war with this legislative history.

III

The Bank and the trustee agree that § 547 is intended to serve two basic policies that are fairly described in the House Committee Report. The Committee explained:

> "A preference is a transfer that enables a creditor to receive payment of a greater percentage of his claim against the debtor than he would have received if the transfer had not been made and he had participated in the distribution of the assets of the bankrupt estate. The purpose of the preference section is twofold. First, by permitting the trustee to avoid prebankruptcy transfers that occur within a short period before bankruptcy, creditors are discouraged from racing to the courthouse to dismember the debtor during his slide into bankruptcy. The protection thus afforded the debtor often enables him to work his way out of a difficult financial situation through cooperation with all of his creditors. Second, and more important, the preference provisions facilitate the prime bankruptcy policy of equality of distribution among creditors of the debtor. Any creditor that received a greater payment than others of his class is required to disgorge so that all may share equally. The operation of the preference section to deter 'the race of diligence' of creditors to dismember the debtor before bankruptcy furthers the second goal of the preference section—that of equality of distribution." *Id.*, at 177–178, U.S.Code Cong. & Admin.News 1978, pp. 6137, 6138.

As this comment demonstrates, the two policies are not entirely independent. On the one hand, any exception for a payment on account of an antecedent debt tends to favor the payee over other creditors and therefore may conflict with the policy of equal treatment. On the other hand, the ordinary course of business exception may benefit all creditors by deterring the "race to the courthouse" and enabling the struggling debtor to continue operating its business.

Respondent places primary emphasis, as did the Court of Appeals, on the interest in equal distribution. See *In re CHG International*, 897 F.2d, at 1483–1485. When a debtor is insolvent, a transfer to one creditor necessarily impairs the claims of the debtor's other unsecured and undersecured creditors. By authorizing the avoidance of such preferential transfers, § 547(b) empowers the trustee to restore equal status to all creditors. Respondent thus contends that the ordinary course of business exception should be limited to short-term debt so the trustee may order that preferential long-term debt payments be returned to the estate to be distributed among all of the creditors.

But the statutory text—which makes no distinction between short-term debt and long-term debt—precludes an analysis that divorces the policy of favoring equal distribution from the policy of discouraging creditors from racing to the courthouse to dismember the debtor. Long-term creditors, as well as trade creditors, may seek a head start in that race. Thus, even if we accept the Court of Appeals' conclusion that the availability of the ordinary business exception to long-term creditors does not directly further the policy of equal treatment, we must recognize that it does further the policy of deterring the race to the courthouse and, as the House Report recognized, may indirectly further the goal of equal distribution as well. Whether Congress has wisely balanced the sometimes conflicting policies underlying § 547 is not a question that we are authorized to decide.

IV

In sum, we hold that payments on long-term debt, as well as payments on short-term debt, may qualify for the ordinary course of business exception to the trustee's power to avoid preferential transfers. We express no opinion, however, on the question whether the Bankruptcy Court correctly concluded that the Debtor's payments of interest and the loan commitment fee qualify for the ordinary course of business exception, § 547(c)(2). In particular, we do not decide whether the loan involved in this case was incurred in the ordinary course of the Debtor's business and of the Bank's business, whether the payments were made in the ordinary course of business, or whether the payments were made according to ordinary business terms. These questions remain open for the Court of Appeals on remand.

The judgment of the Court of Appeals is reversed and the case is remanded for further proceedings consistent with this opinion.

It is so ordered.

JUSTICE SCALIA, concurring.

I join the opinion of the Court, including Parts II and III, which respond persuasively to legislative-history and policy arguments made by respondent. It is regrettable that we have a legal culture in which such arguments have to be addressed (and are indeed credited by a Court of Appeals), with respect to a statute utterly devoid of language that could remotely be thought to distinguish between long-term and short-term debt. Since there was here no contention of a "scrivener's error" producing an absurd result, the plain text of the statute should have made this litigation unnecessary and unmaintainable.

SECURITY INTERESTS AND LIENS

All else being equal, granting a security interest to an existing, unsecured creditor within 90 days of bankruptcy creates a preference. The grant of a security interest is no different from a payment to a creditor because assets are "given" to one creditor and so made unavailable to others. A simple example will illustrate the problem. Assume that C Corporation has assets of $5 million and owes two equal unsecured debts totalling $10 million. In this case, both debtors will receive 50 percent of the assets on liquidation. But if one of the unsecured creditors secured its debt of $5 million with the assets of the company, it

§ 3   **VOIDABLE PREFERENCES**   339

will receive the entire $5 million on liquidation and the other creditor will receive nothing.

Whether security interests may be avoided depends on the answers to two questions under section 547. First, was there a transfer for an antecedent debt that fits the other characteristics of a preference? (Section 547(b)). Second, is the preference protected by any of the itemized exemptions applicable to security interests or other liens? (Section 547(c)).

Note: Time of Transfer and Security Transactions

In dealing with security interests under preference rules, it is often critically important to determine when the "transfer" occurred in the transaction. The Code defines a transfer as the granting of an interest on the debtor's property.

Conceivably one could select any one of three events to be the time a transfer occurs in a security transaction. The first might be the time at which the security transaction became effective between the debtor and creditor. In Article 9 this would usually occur upon the signing of the security agreement and the making of the loan. Second, one might select the time at which the transaction became perfected. In the typical case this would be the time of filing under Article 9. Third, one might delay the time of transfer with respect to any piece of collateral until the time when the collateral itself was transferred to the debtor from a third party and thus became subject to the after-acquired property clause. One could also overlay any variety of relation-back provisions on the three suggested above.

Generally, transfers under section 547(e)(1)(A) and (B) occur at the time of "perfection." For the purpose of personal property, that is deemed to be when security interest becomes so far perfected that the secured creditor will have rights superior to a lien creditor—in other words, when the test of part 3 of Article 9 has been met. In the case of real property the "perfection" demands that the secured creditor will have rights superior to those of a "bona fide purchaser." (By reading section 9–307, which elevates certain bona fide purchasers over even perfected security interests, one can see why it would not be feasible to use a bona fide purchaser test in the case of personal property. If such a test were used, no one taking a security interest in inventory would even pass the test.) Note that the drafters carefully classify fixtures together with personal property for the purpose of perfection. Note finally the relation back provisions in section 547(e)(2).

Problem 7–16

David lends Benjamin $1,000,000, secured by an interest in Benjamin's inventory of automobiles. If Benjamin files for bankruptcy, in which of the following situations can the trustee avoid the transfer?

1. The parties sign a security agreement on October 1; on October 9, David files a financing statement; on November 20, Benjamin files a petition in Chapter 11.

2. The parties sign a security agreement on October 1; David files a financing statement on October 15; on November 20, Benjamin files a

petition in Chapter 11. Assume alternatively that David's loan (a) is a purchase money loan for the inventory; (b) is not a purchase money loan for the inventory. Consider here the 1994 amendments to 547(c)(3).

3. On October 1, David files a financing statement; on October 9, the parties sign the security agreement, and the loan is made; on November 20, Benjamin files for bankruptcy.

4. The parties sign a security agreement on October 1; on October 15, David files a financing statement. David advances an additional $500,000, unsecured, on November 1. On November 20, Benjamin files a Chapter 11 petition.

Note: *Substantially Contemporaneous*

Section 547(c)(1) saves transfers that the parties intended to be contemporaneous and were, in fact, substantially contemporaneous. Like many subsections in the Code, section 547(c)(1) is ambiguous. Other parts of section 547 state a ten-day limitation, but (c)(1) gives no explicit limits. Security Mutual Bank attempted to use the loose language of section 547(c)(1) to save its security interest in an automobile in *In re Arnett*, 731 F.2d 358 (6th Cir.1984). The bank had not perfected its interest through the state's certificate of title laws until 33 days after lending to Arnett. In this case the court refused to adopt the bank's position, arguing that if section 547(c)(1) is read expansively, it would make 547(c)(3) and (e)(2) moot. The ten-day limit as to security interests stands firm, regardless of reasons for a longer delay. Does *Arnett* doom Benjamin's argument in the Sixth Circuit?

Note: *Time of Transfer and the Judicial Lien*

The typical judicial lien presents problems analogous to those faced by security interest holders: namely, when does the transfer occur? If the lien is deemed to have arisen more than 90 days prior to bankruptcy, there is no voidable preference. If, on the other hand, the lien is deemed to have arisen with the 90 days before the petition is filed, there is a preference.

Judicial liens can arise at a variety of different times, depending upon the applicable state law. In some states, the mere rendition of judgment is sufficient to give rise to a lien on real property or fixtures owned by the judgment debtor. More often the lien on real estate is deemed to have arisen only after some further step such as the docketing of judgment is taken; docketing of the judgment is taken to be the same sort of public notice to others as the recording of a deed might be. Typically a lien against personal property does not arise until there is an actual levy (i.e., seizure by the sheriff) on the property.

Taken alone, such variation among the states is not particularly troublesome in determining the time at which a particular judicial lien arises. In some circumstances, however, there may be a difference between the time at which the lien arises and the time when it is deemed effective. If, for instance, the lien does not become effective until docketed or levied, it may still "relate back" to some earlier event such as attachment or issuance of the writ to the sheriff. It is not immediately clear whether this relation back doctrine would allow the judgment creditor to beat an intervening lien creditor or a secured party perfecting his interest in the interim. If the judgment lien is not superior to the interest of the intervening lien creditor, then under section 547(e), transfer could only have occurred at the time the property was levied upon. However, even if state law sets the time of transfer as the time of the event to which the judgment relates back, it is not certain whether the Bankruptcy Code will recognize such a retroactive effect. For one case that does so see Vero Cooling & Heating v. Dobeck (*In re Vero Cooling & Heating*), 11 B.R. 359 (Bankr.S.D.Fla.1981).

Section 547(e)(2) specifies that a transfer is made at the time it is perfected if perfection occurs more than ten days after the time the transfer takes effect between the parties. One might argue that because an intervening lien creditor cannot obtain a lien that would be superior to that of the original lien creditor once docketing or levying occurs on the original lien, the time of perfection ought to "relate back" under the Bankruptcy Code just as it does under state law. On the other hand, one might argue that under section 547(e)(1)(B) perfection occurs only at the time levying triggers the relation back mechanism.

Problem 7–17

On May 1, Isaiah obtained a judgment against Ezekiel. On July 1, Isaiah filed a certificate of judgment to get a judgment lien on Ezekiel's farm. On September 1, Ezekiel filed a petition in Chapter 7.

1. Isaiah and Ezekiel live in Alabama. In Alabama, a judgment lien is established upon the filing of a certificate; the lien does not relate back. Ala.Code § 6–9–211 (1975). Can the judicial lien be set aside under section 547?

2. Isaiah and Ezekiel live in Connecticut. Connecticut law says that if one files a certificate of judgment within four months after the judgment, the lien relates back to the time of attachment. Conn.Gen.Stat.Ann. § 49–44 (West 1958). Can the trustee use section 547 to avoid the judicial lien?

Problem 7–18

Rachel Acceptance provides funds under pervasive security agreements for various equipment acquisitions by asbestos removal companies. Benjamin Cleaners is an asbestos removal company which has been growing rapidly as federal clean-up requirements increase. Rachel has provided the financing for the growth of Benjamin. It has a financing statement covering its equipment filed in all states where Benjamin works. Due to poor management, Benjamin experienced a sudden and severe cash shortage and lost two-thirds of its business to aggressive competitors. It asks for forbearance by Rachel in enforcing the security interest in the equipment, even though Benjamin has not made consistent payments for five months. Before responding, Rachel asks your advice about its preference risk in several transactions it funded over the past few months.

1. About six months ago, Rachel advanced $105,000 to Benjamin to purchase a new air cleaning system for use on dangerous sites. Benjamin ordered the equipment from Med Air when it received the money from Rachel. The equipment was not delivered until last week and Med has not been fully paid. Benjamin has no cash. Is there a preference and would

there be another preference if Rachel gives Benjamin additional cash with which to pay off Med Air?

2. Four weeks ago, Rachel consented to Benjamin's trading its air compressor for a new compressor received from John Baptist Tool Company. The new compressor has a value of $250,000 and John gave Benjamin credit for $95,000 on the old machine. The old compressor was left at John's factory three days before the new compressor was delivered. Benjamin paid the price difference from its own cash. Has Rachel achieved a preference? What result if Rachel had funded the difference?

IN THE MATTER OF LACKOW BROTHERS, INC.

United States Court of Appeals, Eleventh Circuit, 1985.
752 F.2d 1529.

HANCOCK, DISTRICT JUDGE:

This case involves an appeal by the Co–Trustees, William R. Roemelmeyer and Jeanette Tavormina (hereinafter referred to as Co–Trustees), of the bankrupt debtor, Lackow Brothers, Inc. (hereinafter referred to as Debtor), from a judgment entered by the bankruptcy court and affirmed by the district court in favor of Walter E. Heller & Company Southeast, Inc. (hereinafter referred to as Creditor). Co–Trustees brought an adversary proceeding in bankruptcy court to avoid a transfer of property made by Debtor to Creditor on the ground that the payments were preferential transfers voidable under 11 U.S.C. § 547(b). We affirm the lower court's determination that the payments were not preferential transfers pursuant to 11 U.S.C. § 547(b) and (c)(5).

Debtor was a manufacturer of moderately priced jewelry with inventory consisting primarily of gold jewelry. In September of 1980 Debtor and Creditor entered into an Inventory Loan Security Agreement and Accounts Financing Security Agreement under which Creditor received a promissory note and agreed to advance Debtor monies in exchange for a security interest in Debtor's inventory, goods, merchandise, accounts receivable, general intangibles and contract rights. On April 1, 1981, Debtor filed a voluntary petition under Chapter 11 of the Bankruptcy Code. After an unsuccessful attempt at reorganization, the case was converted to a Chapter 7 proceeding on August 4, 1981, at which time appellants were appointed Co–Trustees to liquidate Debtor's estate. On February 19, 1982, Co–Trustees filed a complaint alleging that Debtor had made preferential payments in the amount of $365,000 to Creditor within ninety days of the filing of the Chapter 11 petition. In order for the transfer to be avoided under section 547(b), the Co–Trustees had to prove that Creditor received more from these payments than it otherwise would have received in a Chapter 7 liquidation. The Creditor denied the allegations and affirmatively argued that the payments were specifically excluded from the Trustee's avoidance power under section 547(c)(5). In order to fall within this exception to preferential transfers, a creditor must prove that its financial position did not improve within the ninety days prior to bankruptcy.

In bankruptcy court, the Co–Trustees maintained that on the date of the filing of the petition Creditor was undersecured; therefore, according to *Barash v. Public Finance Corp.*, 658 F.2d 504 (7th Cir. 1981), the payments made within ninety days of bankruptcy applied first to the unsecured component of Creditor's debt. The Co–Trustees premised this argument on the bankruptcy court's previous determination that the value of the pledged collateral on April 1, 1981 was $922,000.[3] Undisputed evidence showed that on April 1, 1981, Debtor owed Creditor approximately 1.6 million dollars. If the Co–Trustees could get the bankruptcy court to readopt its April 1, 1981 determination of value then Creditor would have a secured claim in the amount of $922,000 and an unsecured claim in the amount of approximately $678,000. Under *Barash, supra,* the $365,000 payment would apply toward the $678,000 unsecured claim and the bankruptcy court would have to avoid the preferential transfer.

Creditor relied on uncontradicted evidence of the "computer value" of the collateral on both the ninetieth day prior to bankruptcy (January 1, 1981) and on the date of bankruptcy (April 1, 1981), both to rebut the allegation of a preferential transfer under section 547(b) and affirmatively to prove the section 547(c)(5) exception. The computer printouts were routine accounting reports sent from Debtor to Creditor, upon which Creditor relied to advance additional funds. These records established that: (1) on January 1, 1981, the pledged collateral was worth approximately 4.7 million dollars while Debtor's obligation was approximately 1.9 million dollars; and (2) on April 1, 1981, the pledged collateral was worth approximately 3.9 million dollars and Debtor's obligation was approximately 1.6 million dollars. These values clearly establish that Creditor was fully secured. Hence, Creditor argued that it received no more than it would have received under Chapter 7 liquidation. Furthermore, since Creditor was fully secured on January 1 and April 1, its position did not improve within the ninety days prior to bankruptcy. Thus, the payments fell within the section 547(c)(5) preferential transfer exception.

Maintaining that the valuation of collateral must be determined on a case-by-case basis, the bankruptcy court refused to adopt its earlier value on April 1, 1981 and held that the proper valuation standard was the "ongoing concern" value of the collateral, as reflected in the routine accounting reports. The bankruptcy court concluded that Creditor did not improve its position by accepting Debtor's payments and therefore the payment was specifically excepted from preference under 11 U.S.C. § 547(c)(5).

* * *

3. This previous determination of the value of the collateral by the bankruptcy court resulted from an action brought by the Creditor against the Co–Trustees to obtain relief under 11 U.S.C. § 362. This determination was made in October of 1981, six months after the filing of the Chapter 11 petition and subsequent to the conversion to Chapter 7 liquidation.

In this case the method used to value the collateral is crucial to determining whether the payments to Creditor in the ninety days prior to bankruptcy are subject to preference attack. Since Creditor had a "floating lien" on Debtor's inventory and accounts receivable, the section 547(c)(5) exception to preferential transfers applies and our inquiry should be whether Creditor's position "improved" relative to what it was preceding bankruptcy. To determine "improvement in position," Creditor's "position" is relevant on two different dates: January 1, 1981, ninety days before the filing of the Chapter 11 petition, and April 1, 1981, the date of the filing of the petition. Thus, the value of the accounts receivable and inventory must be calculated on these two dates. If the "ongoing concern" value is used, no "improvement in position" exists; however, if the liquidation value is used, improvement is apparent and the transfer should be avoided.

Section 506(a) of the Bankruptcy Code provides only general principles we should follow in determining what standard of valuation is proper in calculating the value of a creditor's secured claim: "* * * Such value shall be determined in light of the purpose of the valuation and of the proposed disposition or use of such property, and in conjunction with any hearing on such disposition or use or on a plan affecting such creditor's interest." 11 U.S.C. § 506(a). The legislative comments to this section do not give any further guidance except to reiterate that we are to determine value on a case-by-case basis, taking into account the facts of each case and the competing interests in the case. H.R.Rep. No. 545, 95th Cong., 1st Sess. 356 (1977) *reprinted in* 1978 U.S.Code Cong. & Ad.News 5787, 6312.

In an effort to provide some guidance to the courts in determining what value to use in calculating "improvement in position," Collier on Bankruptcy, a leading treatise in bankruptcy law, suggests that the liquidation value be used in a liquidation case under Chapter 7 and that the going concern value be used in a Chapter 9, 11, or 13 case. This advice is not set in cement, as Collier recognizes that other standards of value may be appropriate in certain cases. 4 Collier on Bankruptcy ¶ 547.41 at 129 (15th ed. 1984). Co–Trustees argue that Collier supports their position that the liquidation value should have been adopted in the bankruptcy and district courts as the value of the collateral on both January 1 and April 1, and therefore, that Creditor's position improved. We are convinced, however, that this case is one in which a standard of value other than the liquidation value is not only more appropriate, but even mandatory.

The *only* evidence before this court showing what the monetary value of the accounts receivable and inventory was on January 1, 1981, is the value as shown on the computerized accounting reports. Despite Co–Trustees' argument on this appeal that the "computer value" is not credible we have before us absolutely no evidence indicating that the accounting records were inaccurate or untrustworthy. The Co–Trustees did not challenge the accuracy of those records in the bankruptcy court. Moreover, the bankruptcy court specifically determined that these ongoing concern values were derived from Debtor's own routine accounting reports to Creditor in the regular course of business and that the values were properly admissible. The only evidence in the record of value for the ninetieth day prior to the filing of bankruptcy is the ongoing concern value; therefore, this is the *only* standard of valuation that can be applied to determine if Creditor's position improved between January 1 and April 1, 1981. The fact that Creditor sold Debtor's collateral for 1.2 million dollars *after* the Chapter 11 petition was filed does not shed much light on what the collateral was worth nine months earlier on the ninetieth day *before* filing of bankruptcy, especially taking into consideration the nature and type of the collateral. We agree with the district court's holding that the only standard of valuation that could be applied in this case to any degree of accuracy would be the "ongoing concern" standard. See *Matter of Lackow Bros., Inc.,* 19 B.R. 601 (Bankr.S.D.Fla.1982).

* * *

We conclude that the holdings of the bankruptcy court and the district court were not clearly erroneous in using the ongoing concern value to determine that pursuant to section 547(c)(5) Creditor had not improved his position between the ninetieth day prior to bankruptcy and the actual date the petition was filed. We therefore AFFIRM.

Note on the Section 547(c)(5) Formulae

Section 547(b) in effect challenges every acquisition of after-acquired property within ninety days and not accompanied by a contemporaneous advance where the amount of the debt exceeds the value of the collateral. Because under-collateralization seems likely to be the rule rather than the exception, the trustee and the secured creditor seeking after-acquired property will often be at odds with each other. The trustee's challenge to after-acquired property may be somewhat mitigated by the exemption set out in section 547(c)(5).

The formula adopted in section 547(c)(5) is often referred to as an "improvement of position" test. The formula purports to draw a compromise applicable to floating liens involving frequently changing collateral and avoiding the need to monitor and develop proof about many small transfers. The goal was to simplify the computation of preferences with regard to floating liens and to protect a creditor from unnecessary exposure to preference liability.

Can the formula be applied when the debtor makes payments during the 90 days prior to bankruptcy? While the originally proposed version of section 547(c)(5) referred to all transfers made by the debtor in the formula, the enacted version of (c)(5) protects only transfers of security interests to the extent that "such transfers" do not improve the position of the creditor. Suppose that an undersecured creditor obtained $3,000 of new security and $1,000 in payments during the 90 days prior to the debtor's bankruptcy. In addition, it made a $2,000 new advance during this period. Its net change during the 90 days was an improvement of $2,000 despite having received a total of $4,000 in potentially avoidable transfers. How should the formula be applied to protect the creditor?

One approach assumes that the trustee can recover only $1,000 in security and $1,000 for the payment. If you accept this as appropriate, test the result if the trustee is first required to recover the $1,000 voidable payment and only then to compute the (c)(5) formula. Also consider whether the trustee could first recover $2,000 of security and, after completing the formula recovery, go back and recover the $1,000 payment.

Problem 7–19

In which of the following situations may the trustee recover a transfer of property as a voidable preference under section 547(c)(5)'s "improvement in position" test?

1. Solomon has a livestock farming operation in which he raises hogs. To finance his farming operation he obtains a $50,000 loan from Bank which takes a security interest in his livestock, valued at $30,000. In April, many of Solomon's sows give birth, thereby increasing the value of the livestock to $45,000. In June, Solomon declares bankruptcy. Does it matter whether the trade creditors such as Solomon's provider of hog feed were fully paid?

2. Abraham owns an ailing bicycle factory. On June 7, he obtains a $100,000 loan from Isaac by giving him a security interest in components intended to be used in the production of a new line of frames. At that time the components are worth $75,000. During the summer Abraham's employees assemble the components into finished inventory worth $100,000. The response of bicycle enthusiasts to the new frame is disappointing and on September 7, Abraham files a Chapter 11 petition.

3. Samuel is a farmer who, in exchange for a loan, has granted David a security interest in his forthcoming crop from the year. The loan transaction occurred in March. Although Samuel has a good harvest, he finds it insufficient to pay his debts and, in November, decides to file for bankruptcy. May David retain the appreciation in the value of his collateral due to the maturation of crops? Suppose spring planting proceeds without incident but in late April a hail storm wipes out half of Samuel's crop. A government subsidy program provides Samuel with "disaster payments" which he gives to David. Can the trustee recover the transfer of the "disaster payments"?

4. Zacharias had a properly perfected security interest in Lazarus' inventory and accounts receivable. On March 1, 1995, Lazarus' inventory and accounts had a value of $1,500,000. On that date, the amount of the debt secured by the collateral was $2,000,000. On March 3, Lazarus paid $700,000 to Zacharias. On March 4, 1995, Zacharias extended an additional $400,000 of credit. Between March 6 and April 20, Lazarus sold or otherwise liquidated approximately $1,400,000 of collateral and acquired $1,200,000 of new collateral. On April 23, Zacharias loaned an additional $500,000 to Lazarus. On the date Lazarus' petition in bankruptcy was filed (April 29, 1995) the debt stood at $2,200,000 and the collateral had a value of $1,300,000.

The Trustee in bankruptcy has challenged the $700,000 payment on March 3 as a preference and has claimed that all of the new collateral acquired within the 90 days prior to filing constitutes a voidable transfer. How would you respond if you represented Zacharias?

§ 4. SETOFF

The scope of the creditor's right of setoff in the bankruptcy context with respect to prepetition debts is determined by section 553. Section 553 does not create any new right of setoff. It merely acknowledges the applicability, subject to a few restrictions discussed below, of any right to setoff existing independently of bankruptcy law. The section does state that only mutual debts may be setoff, but this is unlikely to be of much consequence given the universal requirement of mutuality in the law of setoff generally. Basically, the consequence of section 553 is that a bank may setoff deposits made in the ordinary course of business against matured obligations of its depositor at any time before the petition is filed. Deposits resembling preferential transfers proscribed by section 547 may not be setoff.

As we saw above, once the bankruptcy petition has been filed, the right of setoff is specifically subject to the automatic stay (section 362(a)(7)). Despite the stay of setoff, the creditor may be able to prevent the debtor in possession or trustee from using the property in which the creditor has a setoff interest. Some banks have "frozen" deposit accounts; courts have split on the question whether freezing an account violates the stay. The debtor in possession or trustee has two ways to obtain the property. The first is provided by section 363(c)(2)(A). Under that section the creditor and debtor or trustee can negotiate an agreement whereby the debtor will retain or regain use of the property and provision will be made to protect the creditor's setoff interest. Failing such an argument, under section 363(c)(2)(B), the trustee or debtor in possession, after notice and a hearing, can obtain use of the property without the creditor's consent if it is shown that the creditor's setoff interest is "adequately protected."

Setoff under section 553 is not deemed to be a preference. This construction can most simply be explained by reference to explicit legislative history to the effect that setoff was not to be considered a transfer but rather was to be governed by a special set of rules. See 124 Cong.Rec. 33993 (1978). However, the history behind setoff is long, the policy reasons supporting the doctrine are sound and, in general it is desirable that setoff not be considered a preference. Compelling a creditor to pay in full his indebtedness to the debtor's estate while paying him perhaps only a portion of the debtor's obligation to him may seem unjust. Allowing banks to setoff against deposit accounts provides a simple, efficient means for a bank to secure credit outstanding to a depositor. Moreover, because the right of setoff is so well established, other creditors have notice of that possibility without the necessity of filing.

However, a setoff may still have certain preferential aspects. If, for example, a depositor prior to bankruptcy intentionally builds up his account balance with a bank to increase the amount of the debt that may be setoff, other creditors can properly complain. To deal with the possible preferential aspects of setoff, section 553 contains its own provisions. These section 553 provisions include subsection (a)(2) on transferred claims, subsection (a)(3) on buildups and subsection (b) on improvements in position. As in section 547, there is a presumption of insolvency during the ninety days preceding bankruptcy.

Section 553(a)(2) provides that a claim will not be eligible for setoff if:

> such claim was transferred, by an entity other than the debtor, to such creditor—
>
> (A) after the commencement of the case; or
>
> (B)(i) after 90 days before the date of the filing of the petition; and
>
> (ii) while the debtor was insolvent;

When a debtor is insolvent and bankruptcy is imminent, claims against the debtor are of course worth less than their face value. However, to the person owing a debt to the insolvent debtor, the claim may be worth near its face value because of the right of setoff. This provision of section 553(a)(2) is designed to prevent the trafficking at a discount in claims against an insolvent debtor from those with no debt owed to the insolvent to those with debt owed.

Section 553(a)(3) provides that a creditor cannot setoff if:

> (3) the debt owed to the debtor by such creditor was incurred by such creditor—
>
> (A) after 90 days before the date of the filing of the petition;
>
> (B) while the debtor was insolvent; and
>
> (C) for the purpose of obtaining a right of setoff against the debtor.

This subsection prohibits the creation or increase in the deposit account (debt) if it is "for the purpose of obtaining a right to setoff." If such activity were not prohibited, a creditor could obtain a preference over other creditors. For example, without this provision a bank could possibly threaten to accelerate the balance of a loan to a debtor unless additional funds were deposited to provide a greater setoff and so more fully secure the loan. If bankruptcy later occurred, the additional deposited funds would no longer be available to other creditors.

Subsection (b) is a new and much more significant statutory provision that is aimed directly at the problem dealt with by section 553(a)(3). It resembles the problem dealt with in section 547(c)(5). It reads as follows:

> (b)(1) Except with respect to a setoff of a kind described in section 362(b)(6), 362(b)(7), 362(b)(14), 365(h)(2), or 365(i)(2) of this title, if a creditor offsets a mutual debt owing to the debtor against a claim

against the debtor on or within 90 days before the date of the filing of the petition. Then the trustee may recover from such creditor the amount so offset to the extent that any insufficiency on the date of such setoff is less than the insufficiency on the latter of—

(A) 90 days before the date of the filing of the petition; and

(B) the first date during the 90 days immediately preceding the date of the filing of the petition on which there is an insufficiency.

(2) In this subsection, "insufficiency" means amount, if any by which a claim against the debtor exceeds a mutual debt owing to the debtor by the holder of such claim.

Note some of the differences between subsections (b) and (a)(3). First, section 553(b) contains no requirement that an increase in the debt owed by the creditor to the debtor be for the "purpose" of obtaining setoff, or even that the improvement in the creditor's position be caused by a debt increase rather than a claim decrease. Second, section 553(b) contains no requirement that the debtor be insolvent when the improvement in the creditor's position occurs. Third, the language of section 553(b) refers only to setoffs actually occurring in the 90 day period before the petition filing and not to the creditor's right to setoff in general. Thus, if the creditor does not exercise setoff before bankruptcy, he may be able to setoff the entire amount after the petition filing (assuming the section 362 stay is lifted). This provision may have the effect of discouraging prepetition setoff. If prepetition setoff can effectively be checked, the debtor's bank account will remain available for continued operations.

SMITH v. MARK TWAIN NATIONAL BANK

United States Court of Appeals, Eighth Circuit, 1986.
805 F.2d 278.

MAGILL, CIRCUIT JUDGE.

Plaintiff Robert H. Smith ("Trustee"), as Trustee in Bankruptcy of Reidy Marketing, Inc. ("Debtor"), brought two separate suits based on recovery provisions of the Bankruptcy Code against defendant Mark Twain National Bank ("Bank"). Trustee sought recovery of the proceeds of certain assets liquidated by Bank, *Smith v. Mark Twain National Bank*, No. 84–0031–C(4)(E.D.Mo. filed Jan. 6, 1984)(the "set-off case"), and turnover of a post-petition certificate of deposit, *Smith v. Mark Twain National Bank*, No. 83–2541–C(4)(E.D.Mo. filed Nov. 7, 1983)(the "turn-over case"). The district court subsequently consolidated these actions and tried them in a bench trial. Bank appeals the district court's entry of judgment based on 11 U.S.C. § 553(b) for $616,154.03 and the award of prejudgment interest in favor of Trustee in the set-off case, and the granting of Trustee's motion for summary judgment based on 11 U.S.C. § 542 in the turnover case. Trustee cross-appeals for recovery of Bank's assessment of early withdrawal penalties on certain certificates of deposit in the set-off case and for Bank's allegedly wrongfully-earned profits in both cases. For the reasons discussed below, we affirm in part and reverse in part.

I. BACKGROUND

A. *Financial Dealings*

Bank is a nationally chartered banking association with its principal place of business in St. Louis County, Missouri. From 1976 through mid-1981, Bank and Debtor maintained a business relationship in which Bank provided financing for Debtor's petroleum products brokerage business. The financing consisted of letters of credit and of loans to Debtor to fund petroleum purchases. In constructing the financing arrangements, Bank "relied on various certificates of deposit and repurchase agreements it issued to [D]ebtor as collateral for the credit and loans extended to [D]ebtor." *Smith v. Mark Twain National Bank*, 57 B.R. 373, 374 (E.D.Mo.1986).

Initially, Bank and Debtor *orally* agreed that all certificates of deposit and repurchase agreements issued by Bank and in Bank's possession would be collateral for any credit extended. On March 20, 1979, however, Debtor and Bank executed the first of a series of written security and pledge agreements. The front of this agreement listed as collateral a certificate of deposit in Bank's possession on that day. The reverse side of the agreement contained a clause providing for a security interest in after-acquired collateral. The reverse side also contained a paragraph 7, which provided that the occurrence of certain events would constitute default, including "if Bank deem[ed] itself insecure." *Mark Twain*, 57 B.R. at 375.

By early 1981, Debtor had been granted a $2,500,000 line of credit from Bank, evidenced by a note from Debtor to Bank in the same amount. The note provided that "[t]he [Debtor] and all endorsers, sureties, accommodation parties, guarantors and other parties hereto waive presentment for payment, demand for payment, protest and notice of every kind and nature." On June 1, 1981, Bank increased the line of credit to $4,000,000, which was evidenced by Debtor's promissory note to Bank executed on the same day. This note contained the same language as the previous note. On June 5, 1981, Bank advanced $972,144 to Debtor on the line of credit.

On June 1, 1981, Bank had in its possession three certificates of deposit with a total face value of $2,025,000. Bank also had in its possession two repurchase agreements, together totalling $2,683,000, exclusive of interest.

On June 8, 1981, Debtor executed a second security and pledge agreement in favor of Bank, the front side of which provided:

> Pledgor does hereby give and grant unto Bank as security for [p]ledgor's liability and obligations hereunder, a lien, with full right of setoff, upon any deposit or other account of pledgor with Bank and all securities and property of any kind and of whatsoever nature

belonging to pledgor or in which pledgor has any right, title or interest and which, for any purpose have come into the possession, custody or control of Bank.

Mark Twain, 57 B.R. at 376. Debtor also executed an assignment to Bank on June 8, 1981.

On June 29, 1981, Debtor executed a third security and pledge agreement granting Bank a security interest in the three aforementioned certificates of deposit. The reverse side of the agreement contained language identical to the two previous agreements. All of the security and pledge agreements also contained a paragraph 9, which permitted Bank to "demand, sue for, collect and/or receive money, securities or other property at any time due, payable or receivable on account of or in exchange for any such part of the collateral." On June 29, Debtor also executed an assignment of the $1,500,000 certificate of deposit to Bank.

On June 30, 1981, Bank advanced Debtor $3,008,917 on Debtor's line of credit. Bank made this advance to enable Debtor to pay one of its creditors. This transaction was evidenced by Debtor's promissory note to Bank executed on June 30 for the same amount. The June 30 note contained the same language as the two previous notes. The June 29 security and pledge agreement was executed by Debtor in conjunction with the June 30 advance.

In early July of 1981, Bank and Debtor entered into two repurchase agreements in the amounts of $300,000 and $700,000. On July 13, 1981, they were rolled over into one agreement in the amount of $1,000,000. On July 27, 1981, Bank and Debtor entered into another repurchase agreement in the amount of $1,000,000, which was in Bank's possession on July 31, 1981.

In late July of 1981, Debtor orally requested the withdrawal of $1,350,000 of its funds held by Bank. Bank "informed [D]ebtor that if he made written demand for withdrawal of funds, his collateral would be liquidated." *Mark Twain,* 57 B.R. at 378. Nevertheless, on July 30, 1981, Debtor, by telegram, requested Bank to wire transfer $1,350,000 to Debtor's account at a Mobile, Alabama bank. Also on that date, Bank issued a $200,000 certificate of deposit to Debtor, and Debtor executed an assignment of the certificate to Bank.

B. Bank's Actions on July 31, 1981

On July 31, 1981, Bank sent Debtor a telex and a letter informing Debtor that its request of July 30, 1981, "was not within the terms of its agreement," and that Bank "deemed itself insecure" and "had applied all funds of [D]ebtor's deposit accounts and repurchase agreement proceeds to reduce [D]ebtor's loan balance." *Mark Twain,* 57 B.R. at 377. Further, in the telex and letter, Bank demanded full payment of the balance still due and owing after its collection action. As of this date, none of the security and pledge agreements had been cancelled or released.

In reducing Debtor's loan balance on July 31, 1981, Bank used a series of bookkeeping transactions. Bank credited certain amounts, corresponding to Debtor's various accounts and assets held by Bank, to Debtor's outstanding indebtedness.

On August 7 and 10, 1981, two checks totalling $225,130, which had been deposited for the same amount in Debtor's demand deposit account to produce the July 31 balance of $445,176, were returned marked "Stop Payment." These checks were charged back to Debtor's account, and the amount actually credited to Debtor's outstanding indebtedness on July 31, 1981 was adjusted to $228,158.

C. Debtor's Bankruptcy and Post–Bankruptcy Dealings

On August 31, 1981, an involuntary petition for relief under Chapter 7 of the Bankruptcy Code was filed in the Bankruptcy Court for the Southern District of Alabama against Debtor. The court entered an order for relief on November 11, 1981, and Smith was appointed as Trustee on January 19, 1982.

On November 6, 1981, post-bankruptcy petition and pre-order for relief, Debtor wire-transferred $250,000 to Bank which, on the same day, issued a certificate of deposit in Debtor's name. On or after November 6, Bank received from Debtor a security and pledge agreement, which listed the postpetition certificate of deposit as collateral, and an assignment of the certificate. The certificate was assigned to Bank "as security and collateral for a loan of even date herewith and for any other indebtedness or liabilities, present or future, absolute or contingent, direct or indirect * * *." Trustee, in a memorandum to Bank dated February 10, 1982, requested Bank to turn over the certificate of deposit. In a letter to Debtor dated February 12, 1982, Bank acknowledged receipt of Debtor's memorandum. Although Bank also indicated in its letter that turnover of the certificate would be forthcoming at some point in the future, Bank never gave the certificate to Trustee.

D. Trustee's Suits and the District Court's Decisions

1. The Set–Off Case

On January 6, 1984, Trustee filed a complaint against Bank in the set-off case. Trustee sought, under three different theories, to recover all or part of the approximately $3,600,000 allegedly transferred from Debtor to Bank on July 31, 1981. Count I of Trustee's complaint sought to avoid the transfer under Section 547 of the Bankruptcy Code, 11 U.S.C. § 547, relating to preferential transfers, and to recover the transfer under 11 U.S.C. § 550. Count II sought recovery under Section 553 of the Code, 11 U.S.C. § 553, relating to set-offs. Count III sought damages on a theory of common-law conversion.

On January 10, 1986, the district court issued a memorandum opinion and judgment in favor of Trustee, ordering Bank to pay Trustee $606,154.08 and prejudgment interest at nine percent per annum from

July 31, 1981. *Mark Twain,* 57 B.R. at 379. The court rejected Counts I and III, granting Trustee relief only on Count II. *See id.*

* * *

II. Discussion: The Set-off Case

A. Application of Section 553(b) to Foreclosure of Bank's Security Interest

Bank contends that the district court erred as a matter of law in applying 11 U.S.C. § 553(b) to Bank's liquidation of Debtor's collateral. Bank asserts that it had a valid security interest in Debtor's certificates of deposit and repurchase agreements which it held as collateral, and that it properly foreclosed its security interest in that collateral. Bank further contends that section 553(b) of the Code, 11 U.S.C. § 553(b), applies only to set-offs and not to valid foreclosures of security interests. Bank thus concludes that only the unsecured accounts—the checking, savings and demand deposit accounts—were subject to the insufficiency analysis under section 553(b). Accordingly, Bank maintains that the judgment award should be reduced to $228,158, the amount offset on the two checks returned marked "Stop Payment."

Under what is commonly known as the "strong-arm clause" of the Bankruptcy Code, the trustee is given the rights and powers of a judicial lien creditor as of the date of bankruptcy. 11 U.S.C. § 544(a)(1). The extent of these rights and powers, however, is measured by the substantive law of the jurisdiction governing the property in question. 4 Collier on Bankruptcy ¶ 544.02, at 544–8,–9 (15th ed. 1986)(citations omitted); *see, e.g., Angeles Real Estate Co. v. Kerxton,* 737 F.2d 416, 418 (4th Cir.1984). The property in this case is subject to the laws of Missouri.

Under Article 9 of the U.C.C. as adopted in Missouri, a trustee in bankruptcy becomes a lien creditor as of the date the bankruptcy petition is filed and has priority over all unperfected security interests. Mo.Ann.Stat. §§ 400.9–301(a)(b), (3)(Vernon 1965); *see In re Schalk,* 451 F.Supp. 268, 270 (E.D.Mo.1978), *aff'd,* 592 F.2d 993 (8th Cir.1979); *see also In re Keidel,* 613 F.2d 172, 173–74 (7th Cir.1980) (trustee in bankruptcy, as a lien creditor, is "defeated by the holder of a perfected interest."). Thus, although the district court did not address this issue, Bank's contention first requires us to determine whether it had a valid and perfected security interest in the certificates of deposit and repurchase agreement before August 31, 1981, the day the bankruptcy petition was filed.

* * *

Although the district court did not address whether Bank had a security interest in the certificates of deposit or repurchase agreements, it is clear from the foregoing analysis that Missouri law authorized Bank to take a security interest in Debtor's certificates, whether or not they were negotiable. The instruments were pledged, and the course of dealings between the parties indicated that they intended to create a security interest. *See* Mo.Ann.Stat. §§ 400.9–102(1)(a), (2)(Vernon 1965); *see also Montavon v. Alamo National Bank,* 554 S.W.2d 787, 791 (Tex.Civ.App.1977)(security interest found where certificates of deposit were delivered to bank to secure a line of credit, the bank relied on the certificates in advancing credit, and the applicable provisions of the Texas Business and Commerce Code were complied with by the parties). Moreover, simply because the proceeds of the certificates were held in the form of bank deposits does not mean that they were excluded from Article 9 coverage. *See Morris Plan,* 598 S.W.2d at 560.

Additionally, the differences between the certificates of deposit and the repurchase agreements in this case were minor; the repurchase agreements generally had a shorter term of maturity, a higher rate of interest, a larger principal and were backed by government securities. Both instruments, however, constituted an unconditional promise by Bank to repay Debtor, and were, in substance and legal effect, promissory notes from Bank to Debtor. *See Kaw Valley State Bank and Trust v. Commercial Bank of Liberty,* 567 S.W.2d 710, 712 (Mo.App.1978). Further, both parties treated the two instruments similarly in this case. For these reasons, and for the limited purposes of this case, we treat the repurchase agreements in the same manner as the certificates of deposit. We therefore find that both are instruments subject to security interests.

* * *

Based on the foregoing analysis, we hold that Bank's security interest in the certificates of deposit and repurchase agreements has priority over Trustee's section 544(a)(1) lien. *See In re Schalk,* 592 F.2d 993, 996 (8th Cir.1979). This determination, however, does not end our inquiry; we must next address Trustee's contentions that Bank's foreclosure of its security interest in this particular case was invalid.

* * *

C. *Inapplicability of Section 553 to Bank's Foreclosure*

Finally, having determined that Bank's actions on July 31, 1981 amounted to a valid foreclosure of its security interest in the collateral, we now address whether the district court erred in applying 11 U.S.C. § 553(b) to these actions.

In bankruptcy cases, section 553 of the Bankruptcy Code, 11 U.S.C. § 553, governs the set-off of mutual debts between a bankrupt debtor's estate and a creditor. Section 553(a) provides that the Bankruptcy Code is generally inapplicable to the right of a creditor to offset mutual debts that arise before the filing of the bankruptcy petition. *See* 11 U.S.C. § 553(a). This right of set-off, however, may be limited by the "improvement in position test" found in section 553(b). *See* 11 U.S.C. § 553(b).

Various authorities, cases and commentators have noted that the rules in section 553 "do not apply with respect to 'set-offs' that are in fact seizure of property subject to a security interest * * *."

* * *

One author states, with specific reference to banks:

> To afford themselves increased protection in the event that they must setoff prior to filing, banks should consider taking consensual security interests in their customers' accounts where possible under applicable state law. [Citation omitted]. *Since what was formerly a setoff could be converted into foreclosure and sale of collateral, the setoff provisions of the Code should not apply.* However, such a foreclosure and sale occurring during the 90 days * * * before the filing would be subject to avoidance as a preference.

Bank Setoff, supra, at 227 (emphasis added).

We believe the rationale behind this distinction is persuasive. The drafters of section 553 "regard the right to offset as the equivalent of a perfected security interest". *Id.* at 210 (citing H.R.Rep. No. 595, 95th Cong., 1st Sess. 185 (1977)), U.S.Code Cong. & Admin.News 1978, pp. 5787, 6145. If the right was unperfected, the trustee, in its role as a hypothetical judicial lien creditor, *see* 11 U.S.C. § 544(a)(1), could set it aside; thus, there would be no need to protect this interest. Apparently, the reason that the drafters treat set-off in this manner "is that the parties intend to create a perfected interest but either cannot or, as a matter of business practice, do not, do so." *Bank Setoff, supra,* at 210 (citing H.R.Rep. No. 595, 95th Cong., 1st Sess. 185–86 (1977); 11 U.S.C. § 506(a)). Moreover, where the interest *is* perfected, the trustee still is protected to the extent it can avoid the resulting foreclosure and sale as a preferential transfer under section 547 of the Bankruptcy Code, 11 U.S.C. § 547.

We therefore conclude that 11 U.S.C. § 553 is inapplicable to *valid foreclosures of security interests.* Moreover, although Trustee could again attempt to avoid Bank's foreclosure of its interest as a preference under 11 U.S.C. § 547, this issue has not been appealed. We note, however, that the district court specifically found that Trustee failed to meet its burden of proof on this claim. *See Smith v. Mark Twain National Bank,* 57 B.R. 373, 379 (W.D.Mo.1986). Because this finding does not appear to be clearly erroneous, neither a reversal nor a remand is required on this issue. *See* Fed.R.Civ.P. 52(a); *Anderson v. City of Bessemer City,* 470 U.S. 564, 574, 105 S.Ct. 1504, 1512, 84 L.Ed.2d 518 (1985).

In conclusion, we hold that on the facts of this case, Bank's actions on July 31, 1981 with respect to the certificates of deposit and the repurchase agreement constituted a valid foreclosure of its security interest in that collateral. Moreover, because we find that 11 U.S.C. § 553 does not apply to valid foreclosures of security interests, we hold that the district court erred in applying section 553(b) to Bank's foreclosure of the collateral.

* * *

V. CONCLUSION

We hold that the district court erred as a matter of law in applying 11 U.S.C. § 553(b) to Bank's valid foreclosure of its security interest in the collateral, and in awarding interest from the date of set-off. Accordingly, Trustee's award is reduced to $228,158, the amount offset on Debtor's unsecured accounts, and interest should accrue on this amount from January 6, 1984, the commencement date of the set-off case. We also hold that Bank is equitably estopped from asserting the 11 U.S.C. § 549(d) defense and that Trustee is entitled to recover the principal balance of the postpetition certificate of deposit plus all accrued interest thereon, based on 11 U.S.C. § 549 and 11 U.S.C. § 542. The decision of the district court is reversed in part and affirmed in part, and judgment should be awarded consistent with this opinion.

Problem 7-20

Moses has a perfected security interest in the accounts receivable of Jacob. As the business worsens Jacob liquidates the accounts according to the schedule set out below and builds the deposit account. The chairman of the loan committee now asks two questions:

1. If we set off now (July 15) and Jacob goes into bankruptcy, will any of the amount set off have to be returned to the bankruptcy estate?

2. If we put Jacob into bankruptcy now, will we ultimately receive or lose the amount in the deposit account?

SCHEDULE OF ACCOUNTS RECEIVABLE AND DEPOSIT BALANCES

	April 15	May 15	June 15	July 15
Accounts Receivable	$450,000	$340,000	$160,000	$ 50,000
Cash in	100,000	220,000	350,000	430,000

Problem 7-21

The bank president calls to tell you that Jacob surprised everyone by filing a petition in bankruptcy on the day after you discussed the possibility of putting them into bankruptcy. She tells you that the president of Jacob appeared this morning in the bank's lobby with a check drawn on the account and payable to a competing bank for $430,000 (the amount of collected funds in the account). For the moment the teller put off Jacob, but the president of the bank is very nervous. She points out that failure to honor a properly drawn check may cause the bank to have liability for wrongful dishonor under Article 4 of the Uniform Commercial Code. Secondly, she makes the obvious point that the bank ought not be deprived of its security in the form of the deposit account without having its $500,000 debt paid. What do you advise?

As an aside she says she understands since there was no setoff prior to the petition, any exposure under section 553 is now gone. Is the president of the bank correct in that judgment?

Problem 7-22

Rachel *owes* Eastern Airlines (that is on the verge of bankruptcy) $1,000,000 for services rendered by the airline to Rachel. Rachel proposes to purchase $1,000,000 of debts of the airline (for approximately 10 to 12 cents on the dollar). If those debts can be set off against the $1,000,000 that Rachel owes the airline, is there any problem with Rachel's proposal? Will it help things if the setoff occurred before the petition?

§ 5. SUBORDINATION

Section 510, specifically section 510(c), provides yet another way for the trustee to subordinate the claims of certain creditors. Any party may consent to the subordination of its claim, and this subordination is enforceable under section 510(a). Consensual subordination is likely to occur when, for example, a company needs an infusion of new money, and the creditors subordinate their claims to that of the lender as part of the loan agreement. This consent may be either explicit or implicit.

The more interesting cases come under 510(c). Section 510(c) allows courts to subordinate claims and interests as equity requires; essentially it is a statutory legitimation of the court's exercise of equitable power before 1978. Courts will subordinate a claim under 510(c) if it is a capital contribution rather than a loan, if the debtor is thought to be merely an "instrumentality" of the creditor and if there is some indication of fraud. The general pattern in a capital contribution case is that a major shareholder gives a sum of money to its corporation, and the corporation later files for bankruptcy. The bankruptcy court must then decide whether to treat this money as a loan or a capital contribution, that is, whether to treat the claimant as a creditor (possibly secured) or as a shareholder.

It will often be difficult to decide whether a given claim should be treated as a loan or as a capital contribution. A general rule subordinating all loans by insiders is not desirable because that would discourage officers, directors and shareholders from lending to closely held corporations in financial difficulty. Yet a failure to subordinate some such loans may force creditors to assume risks of loss usually associated only with the entrepreneurship interests of shareholders. In making a determination, courts will consider such factors as whether the party providing the money expected to be repaid and whether the company is "undercapitalized."

Undercapitalization—initial contribution of funds by shareholders which is inadequate to meet the foreseeable business needs of the corporation—is a highly subjective concept not easily reducible to formula. The acceptable debt-capital ratio will undoubtedly vary among industries and among individual enterprises in each industry. Determining the appropriate ratio even for a particular company is likely to be difficult. Some courts try to determine whether an outsider lender would have lent money to the company at the time the money in question was given to the company, but this inquiry is unlikely to meet with much greater success than the original inquiry regarding undercapitalization. In short, it will frequently be impossible for courts to know whether a given commercial operation can be said to be "undercapitalized" and thus a candidate for the application of section 510(c) to any funds transferred to it. In part because of the amorphous character of the undercapitalization concept courts are reluctant to grant subordination of claims on that basis alone.

When a court believes the debtor is the "alter ego" or "instrumentality" of the creditor and there is a history of foul play, mismanagement, or the use of the powers of an insider for personal advantage, it will use section 510(c) to subordinate claims of such creditors. For example, the court might subordinate the claims of a parent company which managed its subsidiary to the benefit of the parent and to the detriment of the subsidiary's other creditors. In general, domination and control of the debtor is not enough; the creditor must also unfairly disadvantage the debtor or reduce the amount other creditors will be able to recover.

Finally, courts will subordinate claims because of fraud. Fraud often crops up in instrumentality or capital contribution cases. In addition, fraud may prevent a party from raising a valid defense. If this precludes the disallowance of a claim, the court might nevertheless subordinate that claim.

IN RE N & D PROPERTIES, INC.
United States Court of Appeals, Eleventh Circuit, 1986.
799 F.2d 726.

CLARK, CIRCUIT JUDGE:

Appellant David Cranshaw, bankruptcy trustee for debtor N & D Properties, Inc. brings this appeal from the district court's denial of subordination or invalidation of appellee Julia Estes' secured claims against the estate of the debtor. Mrs. Estes, a minority shareholder of the debtor corporation, had filed a claim against the estate for loans to the debtor in the amount of $320,000. The bankruptcy court found verifiable loans in the amount of only $192,858 and deemed $60,000 of that sum to be a capital contribution. The remaining $132,858 was then subordinated to unsecured creditor's claims on grounds of appellee's inequitable conduct toward the debtor. The bankruptcy court refused to invalidate the claim as a fraudulent conveyance or a disguised capital contribution. Appellee sought review of the order to subordinate her claims in the district court. The district court overturned the bankruptcy court's conclusions regarding inequitable conduct and let the adjusted claim of $132,858 stand as a secured claim prior to those of unsecured creditors. Denial of invalidation on alternative grounds was affirmed. The trustee now appeals from the district court order, alleging error in the denial of subordination and invalidation. We reverse in part and affirm in part.

I. Facts

Appellee Julia Estes is a Marietta, Georgia housewife. Some years ago, she inherited several hundred thousand dollars. In February, 1980, her accountant and tax advisor, James Dowis, asked her to help him start a retail furniture business under the name N & D Properties, Inc. Estes lent N & D $40,000, with interest to be paid as a percentage of sales, and principal to be repaid "when the store got on its feet." Eight months later, appellee pledged bonds worth $100,000 to enable N & D, the debtor, to borrow money from First National Bank of Gwinnett ("FNBG"). In return, Estes received 450 shares, or 47.4 percent, of N & D. N & D then loaned appellee $25,000 of the bank loan proceeds. Appellee used the money to construct a swimming pool at her home, and repaid the loan a year later. In April, 1981, appellee pledged on behalf of N & D some American Brands Corporation stock to First National Bank of Cobb ("FNBC"). FNBC secured its loans to N & D not only with appellee's stock collateral, but also with a security interest in the debtor's inventory.

Over the course of the next two years, the debtor borrowed approximately $389,588 against appellee's stock collateral. Appellee was personally obligated on most of the debtor's borrowings from FNBC. In addition to pledging valuable assets in support of bank loans, appellee from time to time also made numerous small loans to the debtor.

From the debtor's inception, business affairs were directed by James Dowis rather than appellee. Dowis was the majority shareholder and president, as well as the bookkeeper and part-time store manager. Dowis' management of the debtor's affairs was inept. He failed to keep adequate records of sales and expenses, failed to maintain a trust account for consumer deposits, engaged in check kiting and used misleading and inaccurate financial statements to obtain financing from banks and trade creditors. Dowis also withdrew approximately $273,000 from the debtor for personal expenses, including the purchase of equipment for his soybean farm called "Teaselwood Farms."

Although appellee left management to Dowis and visited the debtor's store on only two or three occasions, she had several opportunities to learn of the debtor's financial problems. For example, appellee occasionally received the debtor's financial statements. Close inspection of these would have revealed that appellee's pledged collateral was erroneously listed as an asset of the corporation. This misrepresentation inflated the debtor's assets and thereby obscured the debtor's weak financial position. Appellee also could have learned about the debtor's problems by examining her own personal tax returns. During the years in which the debtor operated, Dowis prepared appellee's tax returns and included substantial tax deductions based on the debtor's repeated losses. Although appellee signed the returns, she never questioned why the debtor continued to lose money nor did she connect the losses with the debtor's constant need for additional loans. The bankruptcy court attributed appellee's failure to discover the debtor's problems to appellee's lack of business education, experience and judgment.

Appellee was eventually alerted to the debtor's true financial condition in April 1983, when she learned that FNBC was considering calling its loan of $189,588. Appellee then met with Dowis and the debtor's staff to determine whether appellee should put more money into the business. One month later, the debtor's fortunes slipped again as its principal supplier stopped further shipment of furniture.

On June 23, FNBC called its loans and appellee retained a business consultant to investigate the debtor's situation in detail. Appellee's consultant learned about Dowis' mismanagement, including his failure to keep adequate records and to create a trust account for customer deposits. Despite this knowledge, appellee took no steps to close the store. The debtor continued to advertise and sell furniture, offering substantial discounts to customers who paid 50 to 100 percent of the purchase price in advance. The debtor promised delivery in six to eight weeks, even though its suppliers still refused to make further shipments. On July 18, appellee's consultant recommended that appellee make no further investment in the debtor. Appellee liquidated her stock collateral to pay FNBC and took an assignment of FNBC's security interest in the debtor's inventory.

Sometime thereafter, appellee decided that the debtor should file for protection under the bankruptcy laws. On July 22, appellee loaned the debtor $1,200 for filing fees and expenses, taking a second security interest in the debtor's remaining assets. On July 29, appellee became an officer of the debtor in order to file a valid bankruptcy petition. Three days later, the debtor filed for bankruptcy and appellee immediately resigned as secretary. On August 25, appellee filed her claim against the debtor's estate.

* * *

III. Discussion of Issues on Appeal

The trustee here contends that appellee was anything but a passive victim of the majority shareholder's mismanagement. He argues that appellee and her co-shareholder devised a scheme whereby they would operate the debtor without any true capitalization, obtaining the benefits of ownership, including cash disbursements and tax losses, but not incurring any of the risks of capital investment. The trustee points to almost all of appellee's contacts with the debtor as evidence of inequitable conduct requiring subordination. Furthermore he contends that the debtor's lack of proper capitalization requires disallowance of any claim against the estate since the numerous loans should be considered capital investment. Lastly, the trustee seeks a finding of appellee's personal liability for certain payments received from the debtor. While we do not adopt the trustee's characterization of events in detail, we do agree that the district court erred in overturning the decision to equitably subordinate appellee's claim. We decline, however, to invalidate the claim as a capital contribution or to find personal liability.

A. Equitable Subordination

Section 510(c) of the Bankruptcy Code provides that claims against the debtor's estate may be accorded a priority inferior to those of secured or unsecured creditors where "the principles of equitable subordination" so dictate. This section's legislative history indicates that such principles are to be found in case law on the subject. *See* S.Rep. No. 989, 95th Cong., 2nd Sess. 74 (1978); U.S.Code Cong. & Admin.News 1978, pp. 5787, 5860. Binding precedent in this circuit holds that equitable subordination is proper where three elements are established:

(1) that the claimant has engaged in inequitable conduct;

(2) that the conduct has injured creditors or given unfair advantage to the claimant; and

(3) that subordination of the claim is not inconsistent with the Bankruptcy Code.

See In re Mobile Steel, 563 F.2d 692 (5th Cir.1977).

The burden and sufficiency of proof required are not uniform in all cases. Where the claimant is an insider or a fiduciary, the trustee bears the burden of presenting material evidence of unfair conduct. *See In re Multiponics,* 622 F.2d 709, 714 (5th Cir.1980). Once the trustee meets his burden, the claimant then must prove the fairness of his transactions with the debtor or his claim will be subordinated. *See id.* If the claimant is not an insider or fiduciary, however, the trustee must prove more egregious conduct such as fraud, spoilation or overreaching, and prove it with particularity. *See In re Ludwig Honold Mfg. Co.,* 46 B.R. 125 (Bkrtcy.E.D.Pa.1985)(citing *In re W.T. Grant,* 699 F.2d 599 (2d Cir.1983)).

In light of these distinctions, the trustee's claim of error on equitable subordination cannot be properly evaluated until the appropriate standard and burden of proof are determined. The correct standard, of course, depends upon if and when appellee became an insider or fiduciary of the debtor. The Bankruptcy Code defines an insider as an officer, director, or "person in control of the debtor" corporation. *See* § 101(28)(B). A fiduciary, under general corporate theory, includes an officer, director, agent, majority shareholder or a minority shareholder exercising actual control over the corporation. *See* 12B Fletcher, *Cyclopedia Corporations* § 5811 at 156–57 (1984). A shareholder has control when she determines corporate policy, whether by personally assuming management responsibility or by selecting management personnel. *See* Berle, *"Control" in Corporate Law,* 58 Colum.L.Rev. 1212 (1958).

In this case, appellee clearly was an insider and fiduciary as of July 29, 1983, when she became secretary of the debtor. According to the bankruptcy court's findings, however, appellee actually became an insider well before this date because she controlled the debtor throughout the month of July, 1983. Indeed, the record indicates that appellee took control of the debtor shortly after FNBC called its loans on June 23. For example, appellee immediately retained legal counsel to evaluate the debtor's options and to negotiate an extension of the debtor's loans. A business consultant was also hired to review the debtor's operations. The consultant made initial recommendations with respect to changes needed in management personnel, pricing policy, cost control and capital investment. As appellee's agent, the consultant also attempted to negotiate a new lease for the debtor and new supply agreements with trade creditors. He even sought to arrange additional security to protect debtor's premises from irate consumer creditors. Although appellee never made any of the recommended changes in the debtor's operations, that was not because the majority shareholder thwarted her efforts. Rather, appellee was ultimately advised to abandon the debtor to bankruptcy proceedings, and she followed that advice without consulting the majority shareholder.

Thus, appellee was a controlling shareholder and insider at least from July 1, 1983. She owed a fiduciary duty toward the debtor and its creditors from that date forward, and she bears the burden of proving the fairness of her actions while in control. We find that appellee has not met her burden and therefore the district court erred in not subordinating her claim. Appellee's behavior while in control indicates that she was acting solely for her own benefit, to minimize her risk of loss without any consideration for other creditors. Such pursuit of personal gain at the expense of other creditors has been recognized as a breach of fiduciary duty justifying equitable subordination. *See In re American Lumber Co.,* 7 B.R. 519 (Bankr.D.Minn.1979); *see also In re W.T. Grant Co., supra* at 610–11.

In this case, the unfairness of appellee's actions is best demonstrated by a comparison of the steps appellee took on behalf of creditors and the steps she took on her own behalf. At the time appellee took control, she knew that the debtor's suppliers had cut off further shipments and that the debtor was still soliciting business with large advertised discounts. Shortly thereafter, appellee also learned, through her agent, that the debtor was taking cash deposits up to 100 percent without maintaining a trust account. Customers were also being deceived as to the time of delivery and the reason for delay. Despite this knowledge, appellee took no steps to stop advertising, to segregate deposits, to reduce the percentage of deposits accepted or to simply close the store. Appellee instead made every effort to encumber all assets and obtain a priority in the impending bankruptcy proceedings.

In determining that appellee acted inequitably, we note that most of her actions (or rather inaction) disadvantaged only a portion of the creditors, specifically the consumer creditors. Trade creditors were not harmed by appellee's tolerance of shoddy business practices or by her effort to obtain FNBC's security interest by subrogation and assignment. The latter creditors could easily have learned that appellee was the debtor's surety and therefore entitled under state law to assume FNBC's secured position. Since equitable subordination operates only to redress the amount of actual harm done, see In re Westgate–California Corp., 642 F.2d 1174, 1176 (9th Cir.1981), the portion of appellee's claim based upon FNBC's secured status is subordinated only to the claims of consumer creditors. Appellee's second secured claim of $1,200 should, however, be subordinated to the claims of both consumer and trade creditors. Appellee obtained this second secured claim on the eve of bankruptcy, when she not only knew of Dowis' misrepresentations to the trade creditors but also knew that the debtor was insolvent and about to file a petition. Clearly, this was a breach of fiduciary duty toward all creditors and the claim must be fully subordinated.

B. Invalidation of Claims for the Capitalization

In addition to equitable subordination, the trustee seeks complete invalidation of appellee's claims against the debtor. The trustee argues that all of appellee's loans to the debtor should be deemed capital contributions because appellee and her fellow-shareholder engaged in "a scheme and device" to avoid the risks of business ownership. According to the trustee, appellee repeatedly made loans to the debtor to avoid properly capitalizing the business with her inheritance.

Shareholder loans may be deemed capital contributions in one of two circumstances: where the trustee proves initial under-capitalization or where the trustee proves that the loans were made when no other disinterested lender would have extended credit. See In re Multiponics, Inc., 622 F.2d 709 (5th Cir.1980). The trustee has proven neither circumstance in this case. The bankruptcy court never found that the debtor was under-capitalized at the outset. In fact, the trustee's expert testified that capitalization was adequate for the limited scope of the debtor's business at that time. Furthermore, the trustee never showed that at the time of appellee's subsequent loans the debtor was ineligible for loans from unaffiliated lenders. Without proof of either set of facts, invalidation of appellee's claim would be improper.

* * *

The order of the district court is therefore AFFIRMED in part and REVERSED in part.

Problem 7–23

E.F. Saul Investment Co. promoted a limited partnership investment to the general public involving a proposed acquisition of five apartment buildings in Chicago. A total of 400 limited partners agreed to invest $80,000 each, paying the first $20,000 and agreeing to pay the remaining $60,000 two years later. Saul took the funds, paid itself a 25 percent commission and used the remaining money to purchase five buildings from Rebekah Capital Co. Rebekah was owned by two former Saul executives. It acquired the properties only after the Saul partnership was created and with the expectation of immediate resale. Rebekah received 20 percent more than it paid to purchase the properties. Saul did little or no investigation of the viability of the apartment projects. The general partner of the partnership was Saul I, a wholly owned affiliate of Saul Investment.

Another subsidiary of Saul managed the apartments for $5,600 per month. After one year, it became clear that the income from the apartments would not be sufficient to pay fees, maintenance costs and the mortgage payments to the bank because of the steep decline in the rental market and real estate values in Chicago. Knowing that it would take an additional $5 million to operate for the next year, Saul "loaned" that amount to the partnership. This kept the business going for one year. At this time, 90 percent of the limited partners made their final payment. Even so, the partnership was insolvent.

Saul I caused the partnership to file bankruptcy, proposing to liquidate all assets. If creditors (including Saul) are paid before the ownership (i.e., limited partners), all of the creditors will be paid in full, but nothing will be left for the limited partners. Can the limited partners use section 510 to change this result?

Problem 7-24

Rebekah Bank, which had been the primary lender for the Esau Lumber Company (ELC), financed the acquisition of the operating assets of ELC by Jacob's Lumber, Inc. In January, 1981 the bank loaned Jacob's Lumber $1.5 million directly and $1 million indirectly in the form of a loan to Jacob's Lumber's Employees Stock Ownership Plan and Trust Agreement (ESOT). Jacob's Lumber guaranteed the second loan.

Poor business climate forced Jacob's in December, 1981 to borrow an additional $100,000 to supplement a cash shortage. Jacob's paid the first two installments, but defaulted on the third. At about the same time, ESOT defaulted on its payments. ESOT's only assets were 10,000 shares of common stock in Jacob's Lumber, which had no value. Rebekah Bank sent a letter to Jacob's Lumber reciting all existing defaults. In response Jacob's Lumber gave to Rebekah Bank a perfected security interest in all of its inventory, equipment and accounts receivable. This transaction occurred in June, 1982. At the time, Jacob's other creditors had unsecured claims of $400,000.

Rebekah Bank then began reviewing ELC checks that had not been sent, and decided which ones would be sent based on whether payment was likely to enhance the value of Jacob's accounts receivable. Many general unsecured creditors were not paid. The bank made several advances to ELC to finance a project the bank thought might be profitable and in which the bank had a security interest. It also "suggested" Jacob's Lumber replace Esau with Saul as president.

Thereafter, Rebekah Bank foreclosed its security interest in Jacob's inventory, and began to sell the inventory and apply the proceeds to ELC's debt. Finally, an involuntary petition for bankruptcy was filed in February of 1983.

1. Was the transfer of security interest in inventory and equipment a voidable preference?

2. Can the trustee challenge it under 510(c)?

Problem 7–25

Esau Bank was the lender in Paul Acquisition Corporation's LBO of Job Sailboats, Inc. The surviving entity, Job Corporation, ceased operations within two years due to its inability to carry its large debt burden. The shutdown was immediately followed by an involuntary petition for Chapter 7 relief filed by three other creditors. Eventually, the bankruptcy court found that the Trustee would succeed in avoiding most of Esau Bank's liens as fraudulent conveyances under sections 4 and 5 of the UFCA and under section 548(a)(2).

Esau Bank contended that it should retain a general unsecured claim and participate in a *pro rata* distribution of the estate. Not surprisingly, the Trustee did not agree. Rather, the Trustee argued that any creditor successfully relying on the UFCA or on section 548 was entitled to full satisfaction before the fraudulent transferee shared in any recovery.

What, if any, are the policy justifications for subordinating the bank in these circumstances? Who should prevail? In reaching your decision, consider UFCA section 9(1)(a) and Bankruptcy Code sections 548 and 551.

§ 6. FRAUDULENT CONVEYANCES, SECTION 548

A. Introduction and Background

Fraudulent conveyances are commonly divided into two categories, those involving actual intent and those evidencing certain objective criteria from which the court is directed to draw the conclusion that the transfer was fraudulent. In the student's mind and often in the practitioner's, these transactions are likely to run together. From the practitioner's standpoint, the distinction between actual intent cases and others will be blurred because the evidence which the practitioner must submit in order to prove even actual intent will often contain some of the same elements demanded by the objective standard. Perhaps, however, it is useful to distinguish between the cases in which the creditor is asking the finder of fact to draw inferences about the debtor's actual intention based on certain events and cases in which the proof of certain events upsets the transaction regardless of the actual intention of the debtor. To put it another way, if the creditor stipulates in the first case that the debtor had no actual intention to defraud, the creditor is out of court; in the second case he could enter into such a stipulation and yet prove a fraudulent conveyance.

The Bankruptcy Code, the UFTA, and the UFCA have similar provisions concerning "actual" fraudulent intent of the debtor:

> UFCA, Section 7, *Conveyance Made With Intent to Defraud*. Every conveyance made and every obligation incurred with actual intent, as distinguished from intent presumed in law, to hinder, delay, or defraud either present or future creditors, is fraudulent as to both present and future creditors.

Bankruptcy Code, Chapter 11 Section 548 (11 U.S.C. § 548).

(a) The trustee may avoid any transfer of an interest of the debtor in property, or any obligation incurred by the debtor, that was made or incurred on or within one year before the date of the filing of the petition, if the debtor—

> (1) made such transfer or incurred such obligation with actual intent to hinder, delay or defraud any entity to which the debtor was or became, on or after the date that such transfer occurred or such obligation was incurred, indebted; or * * *.

The major question under these provisions deals with proof of intent. Typically there is no direct proof of fraudulent intent. Rather plaintiff must submit circumstantial evidence from which one can infer actual intent. In *Gafco, Inc. v. H.D.S. Mercantile Corp.*, 47 Misc.2d 661, 263 N.Y.S.2d 109, 114 (1965); the court put it as follows:

> * * * Since it is impossible to look into [the debtor's] mind for the purpose of ascertaining his intent, it is necessary to consider the circumstances surrounding the [conveyance] and determine the intent from what he did or failed to do. And, by reason of its nature, fraud is usually very difficult to prove by direct evidence, and such proof is unnecessary. * * * The issue of fraud is commonly determined by certain recognized indicia, denominated "badges of fraud," which are circumstances so frequently attending fraudulent transfers that an inference of fraud arises from them. * * * Inadequacy of consideration, secret or hurried transactions not in the usual mode of doing business, and the use of dummies or fictitious parties are common examples of "badges of fraud." * * * Although "badges of fraud" are not conclusive and are more or less strong or weak according to their nature and the number occurring in the same case, "a concurrence of several badges will always make out a strong case." * * *
>
> So that, mere adroitness of technique should not be permitted to obscure the real facts. Whether a transaction constitutes a fraudulent transfer must be determined from its intent and effect and not from its form; a court will look at the results and not at the devious ways by which they were accomplished. * * *

The Bankruptcy Code and both uniform acts have provisions that rely on certain circumstances surrounding a conveyance to find a conclusive presumption of a fraudulent conveyance despite lack of actual intent. Section 548(a)(2)(A) allows the trustee to avoid a transfer made within one year of the petition filing if the debtor "received less than a reasonably equivalent value in exchange for such transfer or obligation," and if one of the three requirements of section 548(a)(2)(B) is met. Under the requirements of section 548(a)(2)(B) the debtor must:

> i) be insolvent at the time of transfer or be made insolvent by the transfer,

ii) be engaged in business, or about to engage in business or a transaction for which any property remaining would be an unreasonably small capital, or

iii) intend to incur or believe he will incur debts beyond his ability to timely pay.

The UFTA provisions are modeled on the language of section 548 and enable a creditor to invalidate transfers made or obligations incurred by a debtor for less than reasonably equivalent value. The debtor's financial condition at the time of the transfer must also fit within one of three insolvency-related conditions in UFTA sections 4 and 5. The UFTA, however, limits the right to invalidate such transfers made by an insolvent debtor to creditors whose claims existed at the time of the transfer itself.

The UFCA language relating to "objective" fraud is older and, perhaps, less precise. Sections 4, 5, 6 and 8 of the UFCA roughly parallel the foregoing "objective" fraud provisions. Section 4 provides:

Conveyances by Insolvent. Every conveyance made and every obligation incurred by a person who is or will be thereby rendered insolvent is fraudulent as to creditors without regard to his actual intent if the conveyance is made or the obligation is incurred without a fair consideration.

Sections 5, 6, and 8 also require the conveyance to be made without "fair consideration." Section 5 concerns a person in business where property left after the conveyance is an unreasonably small capital. Section 6 concerns a debtor who intends to incur, or believes he will incur, debts beyond his ability to timely pay. Lastly, section 8 concerns conveyances of partnership property.

Section 548(a)(2) and the UFTA use the term "reasonably equivalent value" while the UFCA uses the term "fair consideration." The UFCA defines fair consideration to require that property conveyed must be "a fair equivalent" or not "disproportionately small" and that it must be transferred in good faith. Section 548 contains no explicit good faith requirement.

For several reasons, plaintiffs are likely to regard proof of the objective standard as preferable to proof of actual intent. Even with the help of the "badges of fraud" and presumptions to be drawn from them, it is often difficult to prove the debtor's actual intent. Conversely, it will often be easy to prove the debtor's insolvency and to show the exact value received from a transfer. Moreover, these objective standards may provide relief where a conveyance is unfair even if there was no actual intent to defraud. In reading the cases and notes that follow, the student should appreciate the extent to which section 548(a)(2)(A) has been applied to protect creditors in circumstances well beyond traditional fraudulent conveyance cases.

FIRST NATIONAL BANK OF FAIRBANKS v. ENZLER

Supreme Court of Alaska, 1975.
537 P.2d 517, rehearing denied 539 P.2d 80 (1975).

BOOCHEVER, JUSTICE.

On this appeal, we are presented with the question of whether Mr. Enzler's transfer of all his property to his wife should be set aside as a fraudulent conveyance. This case has its origins in an ill-fated business venture entered into between appellee Mr. Enzler and Mr. Gordon Frye in which Mr. Enzler agreed to demonstrate a certain model of Bellanca aircraft in return for a five percent commission on any sales generated by his demonstration. In furtherance of this plan, Mr. Enzler purchased a Bellanca airplane for the sum of $34,720.00, $27,517.90 of which he borrowed from the First National Bank of Fairbanks on a six-month note due November 16, 1969. The Bank entered into a security agreement with Mr. Enzler for the loan with the airplane as collateral.

During the six months that he had possession of the airplane, Mr. Enzler demonstrated it to 30 or 40 people, but no sales resulted. When the note came due, Mr. Enzler was unable to meet his obligation under it. The Bank directed him to return the airplane by flying it to Anchorage International Airport and leaving it, which he did sometime in late November or early December 1969. At the time the plane was returned, it was thought to be worth more than the debt owed. Mr. Carpenter, the Bank's loan officer who was involved in this loan and who had financed in excess of 100 airplanes during the course of his career, testified that after one year of use, the market value of the plane would be about $29,000.00. Mr. Carpenter further testified that a plane with less than 120 hours on the engine, as was the case with this particular plane, would be classified as nearly new. After returning the plane, Enzler continued to negotiate with the Bank in an attempt to regain the plane, but no feasible agreement could be reached.

On February 11, 1970, Mr. Enzler executed two warranty deeds and an assignment by virtue of which he transferred his interest in any property, real or personal, to Mrs. Enzler. The deeds were properly recorded in the Kenai Recorder's Office. Testimony by both Mr. and Mrs. Enzler was to the effect that significant marital discord had evolved out of Mr. Enzler's recurring business failures through which he had managed to reduce a $17,000.00 savings account to $3,000.00 in the course of a year. As a result of Mr. Enzler's financial ineptitude, Mrs. Enzler became concerned for her own and her family's welfare and insisted that Mr. Enzler would either have to leave the family by way of divorce or sign over all his interest in their assets to her so that she would have complete control of the family's remaining property. Following this transfer of assets, Mr. Enzler continued to live with the family and operate the family sawmill as he had before.

In early May 1970, Mr. Enzler received notice that the plane would be sold to the highest bidder at a sale to take place on May 18, 1970 at

Safeway Airways. Mr. Enzler tried to attend the sale, but it was not held at the place specified. However, the plane was sold on the 18th to the Bank for $26,000.00. The plane was then subsequently sold by the Bank for the sum of $22,500.00. The Bank claimed a deficiency of $12,307.06 and commenced a lawsuit against Mr. Enzler for that amount. The Bank's action for the deficiency was later dismissed on the Bank's motion.

After consulting an attorney, Mr. Enzler filed a petition in bankruptcy on September 24, 1971. The trustee in bankruptcy thereafter filed a complaint in superior court seeking to have the February 11, 1970 conveyance between Mr. and Mrs. Enzler set aside as fraudulent. Because of the Bank's status as a creditor, it was joined as a nominal defendant in the suit. On June 8, 1973, Judge Hanson filed his memorandum opinion in the case finding the transfer not to have been fraudulent for the reasons that there was no debt owing at the time of the conveyance, that the conveyance was for sufficient consideration and that there was no intent to defraud creditors. Costs and attorney's fees were awarded to Enzler.

The trustee in bankruptcy and the Bank appeal from this decision contending that the Bank was in fact a creditor of Mr. Enzler at the time of the challenged transfer, that the transfer was not supported by adequate consideration and that the evidence presented below proved an intent on the part of the Enzlers to defraud the Bank by means of the transfer. The Bank also protests the award of costs and attorney's fees against it as inequitable since it did not initiate the action, but rather was joined as a defendant by plaintiff D'Spain.

The primary question confronting us on this appeal is whether the transfer challenged here is to be rendered void as in violation of AS 34.40.010 which provides:

> A conveyance or assignment, in writing or otherwise, of an estate or interest in lands, or in goods, or things in action, or of rents or profits issuing from them or a charge upon lands, goods, or things in action, or upon the rents or profits from them, made with the intent to hinder, delay, or defraud creditors or other persons of their lawful suits, damages, forfeitures, debts, or demands, or a bond or other evidence of debt given, action commenced, decree or judgment suffered, with the like intent, as against the persons so hindered, delayed, or defrauded is void.

Inasmuch as the acts condemned by AS 34.40.010 are, by the terms of the statute, dependent upon the existence of a debtor-creditor relationship, we must initially examine the facts of the present case to determine whether such a relationship existed. The Enzlers contend that at the time of the February 11, 1970 transfer, no debt was owing the Bank. The trial court agreed with the Enzlers' contention in this regard.

On this aspect of the appeal, the Enzlers argue that, since the plane was worth more than the debt owed the Bank at the time the plane was returned, the return of the plane satisfied Mr. Enzler's obligation to the

Bank. Such an argument is flawed by the fact that the estimated value of collateral when returned does not determine whether the debt thereby secured is satisfied. Rather, it is the amount for which the collateral may be sold at a subsequent execution sale that determines whether the obligation is extinguished. Until such time as this latter amount is determined, one in the position of Mr. Enzler remains potentially liable on the debt to the extent that the amount owed exceeds the sale price. Although the liability in the interim period is contingent in that it will only arise should the collateral sell for less than the amount owing, this fact does not preclude the present existence of a debt owed by the contingently liable party to the secured creditor. The Uniform Fraudulent Conveyance Act defines a debt as including "any legal liability, whether matured or unmatured, liquidated or unliquidated, absolute, fixed or contingent."

That a contingent debt may be the basis of a debtor-creditor relationship under our fraudulent conveyance statute is apparent from the holding of the Oregon Supreme Court in *Hillsboro Nat. Bank v. Garbarino*. Interpreting a statute virtually identical to AS 34.40.010, the Oregon court stated:

> We observe that the term "creditors" is not restricted to those whose demands are overdue. The statute is in favor of all creditors, and not any particular class of them. It is quite as culpable for the debtor to alienate his property with intent to defraud one whose claim is not yet due as thus to seek to injure one whose demand has matured. To distinguish between the two wrongs is not consonant with sound logic.

Consequently, we find that at the time of the February 11, 1970 transfer, a debt was owed the Bank, which therefore was a creditor of Mr. Enzler.

We now turn to the question of whether Mr. Enzler's transfer of all his assets to his wife was fraudulent with regard to his then creditor, the Bank. The law in Alaska is that in cases such as this, the intent to defraud will not be presumed. Rather, it is a question of fact usually to be proved by circumstantial evidence. Appellants refer the court to *Evans v. Trude* as a case in which many of the circumstantial facts which may be combined to prove the ultimate fact of intent to defraud are enumerated.

> The badges of fraud here are as clearly apparent as they are multitudinous. The compelling ones in terms of long-recognized indicia of fraud are: (1) The consideration * * * is inadequate. * * * (2) The transfer of the property was in anticipation of a pending suit * * *. (3) The transferor-debtor was insolvent * * *. (4) There was a failure to record the instrument within a reasonable length of time * * *. (5) The conveyance was a transfer of all or substantially all the debtor's property * * *. (6) The retention of possession of the premises by the grantor from the date of the execution of the deed * * * stands unexplained * * *. (7) The transfer so completely depleted the assets of Dale Trude that his

creditor, the plaintiff, has thereby been hindered and delayed in recovering any part of his judgment. * * * (8) The relationship of the parties becomes an additional badge of fraud when there also appear other circumstances which of themselves incite distrust and suspicion * * *.

While such facts as these are to be considered in determining whether a transfer will be found fraudulent, we have indicated that the weight to be accorded these facts will vary depending on the case.

> Badges of fraud must be viewed within the context of each particular case, and where their presence is satisfactorily accounted for, or where their existence is not inconsistent with a construction of the transaction as a valid one, they deserve to be accorded little weight.

Said to be badges of fraud in this case are the lack of consideration for the transfer of all of Mr. Enzler's assets, Mr. Enzler's continued use and employment of the property much as he had prior to the transfer and Mr. Enzler's awareness at the time of the transfer of the possibility that the Bank would seek a deficiency judgment against him.

The Enzlers argue that the transfer was supported by consideration from any of three sources. They place greatest emphasis on the fact that the transfer was in exchange for Mrs. Enzler's forbearance in a divorce action against Mr. Enzler. However, they refer the court to no authority supporting this position. However, appellants cite several cases to the contrary, the most apposite being *Oppenheimer v. Collins*. In that case, as here, a creditor attacked as fraudulent a conveyance from Mr. Collins to Mrs. Collins of the former's interest in an inheritance for the sole consideration of the withdrawal by Mrs. Collins of her action for divorce and her consent to continue marital relations. While recognizing that the wife had valid grounds for her divorce action, the court stated with reference to her relinquishment of this meritorious action:

> Another most cogent reason [for not recognizing forbearance from divorce suit as valuable consideration] is the utter inability to protect the rights of creditors in the property of a husband if such contracts can be deemed a valid consideration.

Our independent survey of the authority in this area indicates that in those cases which held one spouse's forbearance in pursuing a meritorious divorce action to be valid consideration for a transfer of property from the other spouse only the two spouses were involved. We are not called upon here to decide whether such consideration is valid as between the husband and wife alone, but rather whether such consideration is valid as against a third party creditor. For the reason expressed by the Wisconsin Supreme Court, we think not.

Also urged by the Enzlers as consideration for the transfer is Mrs. Enzler's assumption of some of her husband's debts. Specifically, reference is made to a $5,000.00 loan to Mr. Enzler from the National Bank of Alaska to consolidate previous debts amassed as a result of purchases of sawmill equipment. While there was some question as to whether Mrs. Enzler was a co-obligor on this loan, the trial court apparently found that she was not when it stated: "Testimony at the trial was to the effect that the wife had paid off other debts of the husband. * * *" But even if Mrs. Enzler was not obligated on the note, we do not think that her payment of the $5,000.00 loan can serve as consideration for the transfer to her of all her husband's assets. The financing statement which Mr. Enzler filled out for the Bank listed his total assets as being in excess of $128,000.00 with total liabilities of less than $4,000.00. Assuming that Mrs. Enzler held an equal interest in these assets, she still received in excess of $60,000.00 worth of assets in exchange for the assumption of a $5,000.00 obligation. In *Blumenstein v. Phillips Ins. Center, Inc., supra,* we adopted the proposition that inadequate consideration will be found where

> the disparity between the true value * * * and the price paid is so great as to shock the conscience and strike the understanding at once with the conviction that such transfer never could have been made in good faith.

Under this standard, we find the assumption of a $5,000.00 obligation to be inadequate consideration for the transfer of more than $60,000.00 worth of assets.

Finally, the Enzlers point to certain recitations of consideration contained in the instruments of transfer[19] as proof that the transfer was supported by sufficient consideration. Appellants point out, however, that "[t]he recitals in [these instruments] are not alone sufficient to establish the fact of consideration". If these recitations are to be the basis of a finding of sufficient consideration, the facts recited must find independent verification in the record. A careful review of the record reveals no such corroboration of the recitations in the deed, and we therefore find that these recitations do not establish consideration for the transfer.

Our finding that the transfer of assets by Mr. Enzler to his wife was not supported by adequate consideration does not alone necessitate a conclusion that the transfer was made with a fraudulent intent. The other "badges of fraud" mentioned by the Bank and D'Spain must first

---

19. By warranty deeds, Mr. Enzler conveyed to his wife his interest in the remaining acreage of their homestead and his interest in the property upon which they now live. With regard to the first interest, the deed stated that the transfer was for one dollar and other good and valuable consideration and further:

> This conveyance is made for the reason that Grantor has been operating his personal business at a loss and the Grantee has been primarily responsible for keeping taxes paid and general maintenance of property.

As to the second deed, after the recitation of one dollar and other good and valuable consideration, the deed stated:

> This conveyance is made for the reason that the Grantee has actually contributed the major share of the purchase price and cost of acquisition and this merely clarifies the status of the title which, for all practical purposes, should be in Grantee regardless of the manner in which it was originally acquired * * *.

The assignment of personalty merely recited that it was made for good and valuable consideration.

be considered. With regard to the fact that Mr. Enzler was left insolvent following the transfer, there is quite obviously a satisfactory explanation since the purpose of the entire transaction was expressly to place Mr. Enzler in such a state that he could no further dissipate the remaining family assets. Similarly, concerning Mr. Enzler's unchanged lifestyle, this also was a purpose of the transaction, at least insofar as Mr. Enzler was concerned, since in exchange for his transfer of all his assets to his wife, she allowed him to remain with the family and continue on as he had before the transfer. Finally, the possibility that the Bank might have sought a deficiency judgment against Mr. Enzler does not by itself place Mr. Enzler in the posture of a debtor who transfers property in anticipation of a pending suit as perhaps appellants seek to suggest. In the context of proving an intent to defraud creditors, there must be a distinction made between the transfer of property by a contingent debtor who, while aware of the possibility of owing a debt at some future time, reasonably concludes that that possibility will not arise, and the debtor who believes a suit is in the offing and who, in anticipation thereof, conveys property. The bona fide nature of the transfer in the former case is significantly less subject to suspicion than in the latter.

A perusal of the other "badges of fraud" not specifically mentioned by the appellants but enumerated in *Evans* indicates that in the present case, they are either not present or there exists an adequate explanation for their presence. The deeds by which Mr. Enzler conveyed his real property to his wife were promptly recorded. As noted, the fact that the transfer involved all of Mr. Enzler's assets is satisfactorily explained. At the time of the transfer, there was no judgment outstanding against Mr. Enzler. While the relationship between the Enzlers is generally considered one which would excite suspicion in this context, there do not appear to be such other circumstances existing in the present case as would "of themselves incite distrust and suspicion."

On the whole, while there are facts in the instant case which tend to cast suspicion on the bona fide nature of the transfer, they are not such as to allow us to say that the trial court's finding was clearly erroneous. We thus affirm the lower court's decision that the transfer by Mr. Enzler of all his assets to his wife was not done with the intent to defraud the Bank and, therefore, is not void under AS 34.40.010.

* * *

Notes and Questions

1. Was the foregoing case tried as one of actual fraud or proof of objective standards?

2. How would the court have decided this case had it been brought under 548(a)(2)?

Problem 7-26

Ruth is an eccentric but highly successful neurosurgeon. Her gross revenues from surgery are seldom less than $700,000 a year and occasionally exceed the one million dollar mark. Because of the large risks involved in neurosurgery, her malpractice premium has recently reached $125,000 per year. Ruth is quite confident of her ability and is convinced that almost all medical malpractice cases are really cases in which the doctors did not commit malpractice but in which there was an unavoidably bad outcome. Accordingly, she decided to cancel her malpractice insurance. Several months after she cancelled her insurance she transferred all her property to an irrevocable trust. Cars and all other personal belongings of Ruth and her husband are held in his name. Under the terms of the trust, income goes only to Ruth's husband. The trustee is a local bank and the beneficiaries of the trust upon the death of the doctor and her husband are their children. The only condition upon which the trust can be dissolved is the death of both husband and wife.

Four years later, at a time when the corpus of the trust stands at $2.5 million, the heirs of a supremely disappointed patient procure a $2 million malpractice judgment against Ruth. They come to you to ask whether they can reach the assets that are held in the trust and if not, whether they can reach the doctor's income. Assume that the assets would be free from the reach of creditors in a state court action if they had not been fraudulently conveyed. (Note that the doctor has entered into an agreement with her hospital and with each of her patients that they will make payment directly to the trust.)

Is the doctor's threat of bankruptcy to avoid the judgment creditor's claim against her future income credible?

Problem 7–27

On the first of February, Benjamin files a petition in Chapter 7. Early in March his wife, Sarah is killed in an auto accident and he inherits approximately $500,000 of real property from her. He however renounces the inheritance under the state intestacy law and the property then passes to debtor's two children, Jacob and Esther.

Can Benjamin's trustee reach any of that property for the bankruptcy estate?

IN RE NEWMAN

United States Bankruptcy Court, Southern District of New York, 1981.
11 B.R. 628.

[The facts may be summarized as follows: On September 11, 1979, Chrysler Credit Corp. received a judgment of $86,704 against the debtor, Joseph Newman. Six days after the judgment and two days before judgment was docketed, Newman assigned to his father-in-law, Andrew Charla, promissory notes due from the New Rochelle Manufacturing Corp. (NRM) on which payments due totalled $97,000. In exchange for these notes, Charla paid the debtor $54,500 in cash. Approximately one month later, the debtor transferred $40,000 of the $54,500 he had received from Charla to J.E.S. Equities, Inc.—a corporation owned solely by the debtor's children—in return for which J.E.S. gave to the debtor a promissory note for $40,000. The balance on this note would be paid in monthly installments of $100 with an annual interest rate of 7%.

The Bankruptcy Court found that on the date Newman transferred the NRM promissory notes to his father-in-law, he was rendered insolvent within the definition of Section 101(26) of the Bankruptcy Code and Section 271 of the New York Debtor and Creditor Law. The debtor was also insolvent at the time he transferred the $40,000 in cash to J.E.S. Equities, Inc.]

* * *

Second Cause of Action

The second cause of action in the trustee's complaint alleges a fraudulent transfer by the debtor in violation of Code Section 548(a)(2) under circumstances where the debtor's actual intent to hinder, delay or defraud creditors is irrelevant because constructive intent is presumed as a result of a transfer by the debtor for less than a reasonably equivalent value made at a time when the debtor was insolvent and within one year before the date of the filing of the petition. The governing language in Code Section 548(a)(2) is as follows:

> (a) The trustee may avoid any transfer of an interest of the debtor in property * * * that was made * * * within one year before the date of the filing of the petition, if the debtor—
>
> * * *
>
> (2)(A) received less than a reasonably equivalent value in exchange for such transfer or obligation; and
>
> (B)(i) was insolvent on the date that such transfer was made * * * or became insolvent as a result of such transfer * * *.

The term "insolvent" is defined in Code Section 101[(32)]as follows:

> (A) with reference to an entity other than a partnership, financial condition such that the sum of such entity's debts is greater than all of such entity's property, at the fair valuation, exclusive of—
>
> (i) property transferred, concealed, or removed with intent to hinder, delay or defraud such entity's creditors; and
>
> (ii) property that may be exempted from property of the estate under Section 522 of this title; * * *

Having admitted the facts set forth in paragraphs 18 through 21 of the Trustee's Request for Admissions, the debtor has admitted insolvency within the meaning of Code Section 106[(32)]on November 15, 1979, before and after the debtor's transfer of $40,000 to J.E.S. in exchange for the J.E.S. promissory note. Since the transfer was within one year before the filing of the involuntary petition against him (it was made within 15 days before the filing of the involuntary petition), the only issue remaining is whether or not such transfer was for less than a reasonably equivalent value.

The defendants have admitted in response to the trustee's Request for Admissions that on November 15, 1979, when the debtor transferred $40,000 in cash to J.E.S. in exchange for a promissory note in the amount of $40,000, with a pay-out period of 36 years and 11 months, commencing November 15, 1982, at an interest rate of 7% per annum, the discounted value of such note at a lending institution was less than $40,000. The trustee submitted an affidavit in support of his motion and in connection with his Requests for Admissions from an official at Financial Publishing Company, engaged in the business of computing mathematical tables, to the effect that the discounted value of the J.E.S. note was less than $12,500. (Assuming that J.E.S. had existed during the nearly 37 year period and had the capacity to pay). It does not require the services of an expert on mathematical computations to conclude that a $40,000 note from J.E.S. (controlled by the debtor's children), payable to the debtor over a period of nearly 37 years at 7% interest is not the reasonable equivalent of $40,000 in cash on hand now. Surely, the creditors of this estate should not be directed to accept $40,000 over a period of 37 years with interest at 7% per annum as the reasonable equivalent of $40,000 in cash today, especially since the defendants have admitted that the discounted value of the note was less than $40,000 when the exchange was made.

Thus, there is no genuine disputable question of fact that the debtor transferred $40,000 to the defendant, J.E.S., on November 15, 1979, within one year before the filing of the involuntary petition on November 24, 1979, and received less than a reasonably equivalent value in exchange for such transfer at a time when the debtor was insolvent. Accordingly, the trustee is entitled to recover the fraudulent conveyance of $40,000 from J.E.S. pursuant to Code Section 548(a)(2).

* * *

Twelfth Cause of Action

Section 273–a of the New York Debtor and Creditor Law forms the basis for the trustee's claim in the twelfth cause of action to recover the debtor's transfer of $40,000 to J.E.S. on November 15, 1979. This Section reads as follows:

> Every conveyance made without fair consideration when the person making it is a defendant in an action for money damages or a judgment in such an action has been docketed against him, is fraudulent as to the plaintiff in that action without regard to the actual intent of the defendant if, after final judgment for the plaintiff, the defendant fails to satisfy the judgment.

Neither actual intent to defraud nor insolvency at the time of the transfer need be shown. A transfer without fair consideration is fraudulent as to an existing unpaid creditor whose judgment was docketed against the debtor at the time of the transfer. *In re* Russo, 1 B.R. 369

(Bankr.E.D.N.Y.1979), affirmed September 11, 1980, (E.D.N.Y., Nickerson, D.J.).

In this case, Chrysler held a docketed judgment for $96,241.44 when the debtor transferred $40,000 to J.E.S. on November 15, 1979, which judgment has not been satisfied. It has also been found that the J.E.S. note for $40,000 with a pay-out period of 36 years and 11 months at 7% interest per annum and with the first payment to be made on November 15, 1982, was disproportionately small as compared with $40,000 in cash so as not to constitute fair consideration.

Accordingly there is no genuinely disputable question of fact for determination in the twelfth cause of action. The trustee is entitled, as a matter of law, to recover the fraudulent conveyance of $40,000 from J.E.S. pursuant to Section 273–a of the New York Debtor and Creditor Law.

First, Third and Eleventh Causes of Action

These causes of action relate to the debtor's transfer on September 17, 1979, six days after the jury verdict in favor of Chrysler, of a series of promissory notes payable to NRM, totalling approximately $97,000, to his father-in-law, the defendant, Andrew Charla, for $54,500 in cash. The first cause of action invokes Code Section 548, the third cause of action is based on Section 273 of the New York Debtor and Creditor Law, and the eleventh cause of action relies upon Section 273–a of the New York Debtor and Creditor Law. Central to all three causes of action is the crucial issue as to whether or not the debtor's receipt of $54,500 in cash from the defendant, Andrew Charla, is a reasonably equivalent value and fair consideration for the debtor's transfer of the NRM notes totalling approximately $97,000. The debtor has admitted that this transfer rendered him insolvent and that it was made within one year of the filing of the involuntary bankruptcy petition. He has also admitted the existence of the Chrysler judgment docketed against him which has not been satisfied.

Unlike the second, seventh and twelfth causes of action, where the debtor admitted that the discounted value of the $40,000 J.E.S. note he received in exchange for his transfer of $40,000 in cash to J.E.S. was less than $40,000 when the exchange was made, there is no such admission as to the discounted value of the NRM notes. Therefore, there exists a question of fact that must be established by the evidence as to whether or not the debtor's receipt of $54,500 from the defendant, Andrew Charla, in exchange for the notes, totalling approximately $97,000, constitutes a reasonably equivalent value within the meaning of Code Section 548, or fair consideration as defined in Section 272 of the New York Debtor and Creditor Law. Therefore, the trustee's motion for summary judgment must be denied as to these causes of action.

* * *

Mercantile Fraudulent Conveyances

Originally fraudulent conveyance laws were low profile non-controversial elements of creditors' rights law. Today, however, fraudulent conveyance rules broadly affect many high stakes commercial transactions. In the following sections we explore some of these transactions. As we survey this more modern case law, the student should consider how far the law has been transformed. Are the policies at work here equivalent to those found in the traditional forms of fraudulent conveyance?

RESCISSION OF FORECLOSURE SALES

The question when a foreclosure sale may be rescinded as fraudulent was a minor tempest of the 1980s. One approach, taken in *Lawyers Title Insurance Co. v. Madrid (In re Madrid)*, 21 B.R. 424 (9th Cir.BAP 1982), stands for the proposition that the sale price obtained at a regularly conducted, noncollusive foreclosure sale is conclusively presumed to represent "reasonably equivalent value" as required by section 548(a)(2)(A). On the other hand, *Durrett v. Washington National Insurance Co.*, 621 F.2d 201 (5th Cir.1980) held that an apparently noncollusive foreclosure sale that resulted in a price of 57.7 percent of the fair market value of the property could nonetheless be rescinded as not providing "reasonably equivalent value." *Durrett* also suggested that any sale for less than 70 percent of fair market value could be rescinded. Some courts have followed *Durrett;* others have followed *Madrid,* and a few have refused to adopt a conclusive presumption of reasonable equivalence at a noncollusive foreclosure sale but have not chosen a rigid cutoff like the *Durrett* 70 percent rule. See *Matter of Bundles,* 856 F.2d 815 (7th Cir.1988).

* * *

Note

In the 1994 case, *BFP v. Resolution Trust Corporation*, 114 S.Ct. 1757, 128 L.Ed.2d 556, the Supreme Court resolved the dispute by siding with the decision in *Madrid*. Noting that *Durrett* was a considerable and unwarranted interference with state law on foreclosure, the Court concluded "[w]e deem, as the law has always deemed, that a fair and proper price, or a 'reasonably equivalent value,' for foreclosed property, is the price in fact received at the foreclosure sale, so long as all the requirements of the State's foreclosure law have been complied with" [at 1765].

Of course, it would still be possible for a court to conclude that a foreclosure produced too low a price, was so a fraudulent conveyance under state law and thus voidable by use of the state fraudulent conveyance law and 544(b). For two reasons state law is unlikely to serve the trustee's purpose. First, section 3(b) of UFTA explicitly rejects the idea that a foreclosure sale can be measured against some fair market value. It provides that "a person gives reasonable equivalent value if the person acquires * * * an asset pursuant to a regularly conducted, non-collusive foreclosure sale * * *." Where UFTA has been adopted state law is the same as the federal law after BFP. But even state law without UFTA presents a problem for the trustee. Now deprived of the argument that the foreclosure complying with state law violates 548, the trustee must argue that a general state law (namely, the state law on fraudulent conveyances) conflicts with and overcomes a more specific state law (namely the state law governing foreclosure, often a state law that is filled with exquisite detail). It will take a hardy lawyer to convince a court that a creditor who has complied with fanatical detail on a real estate foreclosure proceeding (giving notice for 52 consecutive weeks in a local newspaper, bowing toward the east four times a day on alternate Sundays, etc.) should have its foreclosure set aside because it somehow fails to satisfy a very general requirement in UFCA or in the state common law because the transfer was incurred "without a fair consideration."

B. Intercompany Guaranty Agreements

TELEFEST, INC. v. VU–TV, INC.

United States District Court, District of New Jersey, 1984.
591 F.Supp. 1368.

BARRY, DISTRICT JUDGE.

The question before the court is whether a security agreement executed on May 6, 1983 for the benefit of intervenor Manufacturers Hanover Trust ("MHT") by defendant VU–TV, Inc. ("VU–TV") and by the company of which VU–TV is a wholly-owned subsidiary, CATV Products, Inc. ("CATV"), constituted a fraudulent conveyance within the meaning of the Uniform Fraudulent Conveyance Act ("UFCA"), as adopted by New Jersey, 25 N.J.S.A. 2–7 through 2–19 ("NJFCA"). If that conveyance was fraudulent, MHT will be impaired to the extent of the fraud in asserting what is otherwise a priority security interest in funds being held by Graphic Scanning, Inc. ("Graphics") for the benefit of VU–TV.

Plaintiff TeleFest, Inc. ("TeleFest") seeks to recover a portion of those funds to recompense the violations of a licensing agreement that it had with defendant VU–TV. Barton Press, Inc. ("Barton"), is a judgment lien creditor, seeking to recover on a contract breached by VU–TV. For the reasons set forth below, I conclude that TeleFest and Barton have failed to prove that the security agreement between MHT and VU–TV amounted to a fraudulent conveyance.

TeleFest entered into a licensing agreement with VU–TV on March 22, 1982. TeleFest licensed to VU–TV the world-wide distribution rights of videotapes of musical performances given at the ChicagoFest Blues Series in 1981. VU–TV agreed to pay TeleFest seventy percent of the gross proceeds of world-wide sales, with a minimum payment of fifty thousand dollars. Simultaneously, the two parties agreed that, in consideration of $7500, VU–TV would distribute another videotape, "Cheap Trick Live at ChicagoFest".

Alleging that VU–TV failed to pay the specified guaranteed amounts and to perform other contractual obligations, TeleFest brought this action on March 4, 1983. VU–TV failed to answer or otherwise appear and, on April 8, 1983, TeleFest was granted an Order of Final Judgment against VU–TV for $57,500, plus costs.

Barton obtained a default judgment against VU–TV on April 19, 1984 in the Superior Court of New Jersey in the amount of $85,323.86. It attempted to levy on that judgment on June 11, 1984, but found that the VU–TV account receivable held by Graphics was affected by restraints imposed by this court on November 22, 1983. Barton sought permission to intervene under Fed.R.Civ.P. 24(b). Notwithstanding the fact that Barton is not indispensable, the motion to intervene was granted because Barton's claim and the main action involve common questions of law and fact.

MHT claims that its security agreement has priority over the judgments of both TeleFest and Barton. The basis for its claim is set forth in the affidavit of MHT Senior Vice-President Joseph Adamko, dated June 4, 1984. According to that affidavit, CATV's predecessor, Gamco Industries, Inc., opened an account and obtained a secured loan from MHT on May 15, 1980. In November, 1980, Gamco sold its assets and changed its name to CATV. The Gamco loan was repaid by January, 1981. In July, 1981, MHT, a New York banking association, agreed to extend a $100,000 unsecured line of credit to VU–TV at two percent over the prime rate of interest in exchange for the personal guarantees of VU–TV's Treasurer, Martin Horak, and its Secretary, Leon Poitrais, and the cross-corporate guarantee of CATV.

An MHT "Credit Facility Review" was conducted in March and April, 1982 in connection with a plan of Horak and Poitrais and a VU–TV and CATV stockholder, Ted Leder, to obtain a $300,000 loan to purchase San Antonio Home Entertainment, Inc. ("San Antonio"). A statement entitled "Credit Department Review", dated March 12, 1982, was issued as part of that effort. The statement described VU–TV's business, its financial condition, and the results obtained through the end of September, 1981 by the company. It concluded that VU–TV was a "company which has recorded strong sales growth and sizeable profit margins, and earnings have been reinvested to increase its equity base." The reviewer also noted that the corporate officers were highly expert and experienced and that the company was positioning itself for expansion to European markets.

MHT agreed to provide the requested loan, but cross-corporate guarantees were to be executed by VU–TV, CATV and San Antonio with each company cross-collateralizing with all assets, including receivables, the loans of the other companies. The collateralization was to cover all outstanding loans, including those that had previously been unsecured. A general security agreement was to be executed and filings on the companies' assets made. In May, 1982, the cross-guarantees of the companies and related documents, prepared by MHT's legal department, were supposedly sent to Horak. Loans were also extended in April and May, 1982 to CATV, which received $300,000, and to San Antonio, which received $20,000.

VU–TV and CATV's cross-guarantees and the UCC filing statements were not executed with the other documents in May and June, 1982.

MHT is unable to account for this lapse, but believes that it either failed to prepare those documents, did not receive them back from Horak, or received the documents executed, but "misplaced" them. MHT discovered "sometime in early 1983" that it did not have the desired guarantees. An MHT "Interoffice Letter", dated January 20, 1983, requested the MHT Legal Department to prepare guarantees and UCC filings for VU–TV, CATV and San Antonio.

The loans that had been made to the related companies were renewed by MHT at each maturity date and further loans extended. As of January, 1983, CATV owed MHT $450,000, VU–TV owed $50,000 and San Antonio owed $17,000. By June, 1983, the loan balances had been reduced, and CATV owed $385,000, VU–TV owed $50,000, and San Antonio owed $15,000. Although MHT filed financing statements for VU–TV accounts receivable on April 15, 1983 with the Clerk of Middlesex County, New Jersey, and on April 18, 1983 with the Secretary of State of New Jersey, it was not until May 6, 1983 that CATV executed a "Guarantee of all Liability and Security Agreement" ("Guarantee"). VU–TV executed a similar agreement, thereby cross-collateralizing the loans extended to the related entities.

* * *

TeleFest contests the priority of security interest on a number of grounds, one of which is TeleFest's assertion that because MHT obtained the security agreement from VU–TV after the entry of TeleFest's default judgment against VU–TV without fair consideration and at a time when the latter was already insolvent, MHT was the grantee of a fraudulent conveyance within the meaning of the UFCA, as adopted in New Jersey.

* * *

TeleFest argues that to the extent that VU–TV's security agreement guaranteed debts incurred by CATV and San Antonio, the agreement was a conveyance or obligation incurred without fair consideration. However, separate and apart from the issue of fair consideration, TeleFest is obliged to show that VU–TV was insolvent at the time of the conveyance to MHT because, in actions to set aside a conveyance as fraudulent to the creditors of the grantor, the burden of proving fraud rests upon the plaintiff.

* * *

It is readily apparent then that TeleFest has a heavy burden to show insolvency as the first step in proving a fraudulent conveyance. It has gone some distance in meeting that burden, but hardly far enough to warrant the conclusion that no reasonable jury could find other than that VU–TV was insolvent on May 6, 1983. MHT's characterization of many of the statements in the affidavits presented by TeleFest as hearsay is an accurate one, and it is far from obvious that the material obtained "is more probative on the point for which it is offered than any other evidence which the proponent can procure through reasonable efforts." Fed.R.Evid. 803(24)(B).

There is simply not the abundant clarity, provided through a balancing of available assets and expected liabilities, that on the date of the transfer the grantor of the conveyance was unable to pay its debts as they became due. The most that can be said is that there is evidence that VU–TV may have been paying some debts, e.g. those to the bank, but not others, e.g. rent and wages, as they became due. I cannot say that, as a matter of law, that the state of VU–TV's finances amounted to insolvency for the purpose of determining that there was a fraudulent conveyance.

Not only is the question of insolvency one of fact, but whether "fair consideration" inhered in a conveyance is also generally a question of fact, *In re Roco Corp., supra* at 981–982; *Klein v. Tabatchnick, supra* at 1047–1048; 4 *Collier on Bankruptcy* (15th Ed.1982) ¶ 548.09 at 548–96 to 97. Since insolvency has not been established, the court need not reach the question of fair consideration, but because the parties have forcefully argued their respective views in regard thereto, it will be discussed.

Where a conveyance is supported by an antecedent debt, a grantee of that conveyance may support it when it is attacked as fraudulent by merely pointing to the antecedent debt as the consideration, provided the grantee acted in good faith in accepting it. *Johnson v. Lentini,* 66 N.J.Super. 398, 406, 169 A.2d 208 (Ch.1961); *Hersh v. Levinson Bros., Inc., supra,* 117 N.J.Eq. at 133, 174 A. 736; *Riverside Trust Co. v. Dietrich,* 112 N.J.Eq. 43, 45, 163 A. 275 (1932). It is a different case, however, where there is an antecedent debt owed by someone other than the grantor. *See* Annotation, *Transaction in consideration of discharge of antecedent debt owed by one other than grantor as based on "fair consideration" under Uniform Fraudulent Conveyance Act,* 30 A.L.R.2d 1209. It is there stated, at 1210, that

> No case within the scope of this annotation has been discovered wherein the court has upheld a transaction, the consideration for which was the discharge of an antecedent debt owed by one other than the grantor, as based on 'fair consideration' under the Uniform Fraudulent Conveyance Act.

This principle applies not only with regard to a spouse's "conveyance" in consideration of the release of another spouse's debt, *see,* for example, *Hollander v. Gautier,* 114 N.J.Eq. 485, 489, 168 A. 860, 862 (Ch.1933), and the mortgage of partnership property to pay a partner's debts; 30 A.L.R.2d at 1212, but also with regard to a corporation paying the debt of another corporation. Although the case law in this area is sparse, it is more plentiful than the one case cited in the Annotation, *supra,* i.e. *Bennett v. Rodman & English,* 2 F.Supp. 355 (S.D.N.Y.) *aff'd* without opinion, 62 F.2d 1064 (2d Cir.1932). There have been at least three more recent cases that stand for the proposition that a transaction, the consideration for which was an antecedent debt of a corporation owed by one other than the corporate grantor, was not supported by "fair consideration" under the Uniform Fraudulent Conveyance Act.

In *In Re B–F Building Corporation,* 312 F.2d 691 (6th Cir.1963), an insolvent company named B–F owned certain real property, which it leased to Baird–Foerst, also bankrupt and a distributor of General Electric appliances. An individual named Baird was president of and held a controlling interest in both corporations. B–F owned premises occupied by Baird Foerst, but purchased a new site. Its checks in payment for the land were returned for insufficient funds. Baird–Foerst borrowed money from the Central National Bank and B–F defaulted on the land contract. Both companies became financially strapped and B–F decided to assist Baird Foerst by giving the bank from which the latter had borrowed a demand cognovit note for the sum borrowed. The note was endorsed by Baird and indicated that it was secured by the sale of B–F property. The District Court found, after both companies petitioned for bankruptcy, that the execution of the demand cognovit note was fraudulent because unsupported by consideration. B–F was found to owe a considerable sum to General Electric, which argued that payment of another's debt is a transfer without fair consideration. The Sixth Circuit agreed, citing, among other cases, *Davis v. Hudson Trust Co.,* 28 F.2d 740 (3d Cir.1928), a case involving a husband-wife fraudulent conveyance.

In Re B–F Building Corporation, Bennett, Davis, and *Edward Hines W. Pine Co. v. First National Bank,* 61 F.2d 503 (7th Cir.1932), represent a line of cases that support the proposition that, while the agreement of a creditor to extend a debtors time for payment or forbear suing on a claim constitutes a "valuable" consideration for the promise of a third party to pay a debt, such valuable consideration is not synonymous with "fair" consideration under the statute. Rosenberg, *supra* at 256. It might well be argued that the case at bar is similar to *In Re B–F Building Corporation, supra,* in that here VU–TV has attempted to affect a conveyance, consideration for which is not primarily a debt that it already owed MHT but, rather, debts owed by two related companies. The rule in *In Re B–F Building Corporation* and the other cases cited is a useful one in that it prevents insolvent corporations from preferring one creditor over another to an extent greater than their actual debt to the creditor preferred. This results in a more equitable distribution of the insolvent corporation's assets when creditors knock at the door of the troubled entity and militates against the insolvent corporation using its remaining assets for the benefit of related entities.

MHT distinguishes *In Re B–F Building Corporation* on two grounds: (1) that the debtor company was demonstrably insolvent at the time of the conveyance and (2) that the court's conclusion that fair consideration had not passed was premised on its finding that "the only thing the bank gave for [the debtor's] demand note * * * was an unsecured and probably worthless note of [debtor's related company]," while here a guarantee was given that cross-collateralized the loan with the corporation's assets. MHT relies upon what it calls the "identity of interest" rule found in *In Re Royal Crown Bottlers of North Alabama,* 23 B.R. 28 (Bankr.N.D.Ala.1982). There, the court held that an insolvent debtor receives "less than a reasonably equivalent value" when it transfers property for a consideration to a third party, but that

> A clear distinction from this rule exists, however, if the debtor and the third party are so related or situated that they share an 'identity of interests', because what benefits one, will in such case, benefit the other to some degree.

Id. at 30 (footnote omitted).

MHT asserts that the June 4, 1984 Adamko affidavit shows the "close and intertwined relationship" between the parent company and its subsidiaries and that the loans to CATV were based on that close relationship and benefited VU–TV. TeleFest retorts that MHT has the burden of specifically showing how such a benefit accrued to VU–TV from the loans to its parent. It quotes a passage from *Royal Crown Bottlers, supra* which sets out the "identity of interest" rule:

> The ultimate question then becomes one of determining the value of this vicarious benefit and testing it by the measure of 'reasonably equivalent' for the property transferred by the insolvent debtor.
>
> When the consideration for a transfer passes to the parent corporation of a debtor/subsidiary making the transfer * * * the benefit to the debtor may be presumed to be nominal, in the absence of proof of a specific benefit to it.

I am satisfied that it was intended that a benefit would flow to VU–TV through the loans to CATV and San Antonio ultimately guaranteed by VU–TV. In April, 1982, when MHT was considering whether or not to extend a $300,000 loan to CATV for the purchase of San Antonio, MHT certainly regarded CATV and VU–TV as having an identity of interest. An internal memo from MHT Assistant Vice–President Fasano, dated April 12, 1982, in which that loan is discussed is, in fact, entitled "VU–TV, Inc. CATV Products, Inc." This memo evidences what MHT has consistently argued, i.e. that it always regarded VU–TV and its parent in tandem in its dealing with these companies. Such an outlook is relevant in considering whether the transferee of a conveyance acted in good faith. *See generally Good Faith and Fraudulent Conveyances,* 97 Harvard Law Review 495 (December 1983). It should also be noted that here the loan transactions were obviously at arm's length, another indicia of the transferee's good faith. Rosenberg, *supra* at 249.

Even more important than good faith in considering whether fair consideration passed is the nature of the transferor's business and its relationship with its parent. It is clear from the "Credit Department Review" and the Harris memo discussed above that VU–TV was devoted to providing programming for cable television companies, e.g. the ChicagoFest Blues Series. Monies loaned to VU–TV's parent to purchase a cable television system or for other moves directed toward expansion would most probably provide an additional and obviously secure market for VU–TV. The consideration for VU–TV's guarantee of the loans of its parent and sister companies may not have been a direct benefit, but it was a specific enough benefit for a reasonable trier of fact to conclude that fair consideration inhered in the conveyance.

In any event, the notion that a benefit accrues to a subsidiary only when there is a direct flow of capital to that entity the result of its guarantee of a loan to its parent is inhibitory of contemporary financing practices, which recognize that cross-guarantees are often needed because of the unequal abilities of interrelated corporate entities to collateralize loans. As one commentator has noted

> * * * (C)ourts often require a benefit to the guarantor corporation so that the transaction ostensibly fulfills a corporate purpose of the guarantor and is therefore not ultra vires. The concept of 'benefit' cannot, however, be defined precisely. For example, securing a future sale might constitute a benefit. Consummating a transaction which will improve a corporation's public image might also be said to benefit that company. Since the concept of benefit involves the potential for such a wide range of results, courts have often required that the benefit be 'direct'. It is questionable whether this requirement has helped, however, since courts also vary considerably in their interpretation of the term 'direct.'

Note, *Upstream Financing and the Use of the Corporate Guarantee,* 53 Notre Dame Lawyer 840, 842 (1978).

Where there are indicia of a bona fide financing arrangement, not designed as a shield against other creditors, the lack of perceptible "direct" benefit to a subsidiary guaranteeing the loan of its parent should not be viewed as tantamount to a lack of "fair consideration" under the UFCA. Indirect benefit provides the necessary "fair consideration".

> [Some courts have] rationalized upholding various transfers against fraudulent conveyance challenges by finding that sufficient consideration passed to the transferor because an opportunity had been given to it to escape bankruptcy through the strengthening of an affiliated corporation that received the benefit of the transfer. Such an approach seems indisputably proper when a weak but still solvent entity is rendered insolvent only because of the inclusion of the guaranty on the liability side of the balance sheet. This permits the analysis to focus upon economic reality in the appropriate factual context without rewarding legal laxity or inflexibly ignoring real benefits merely because they have no place on the company's balance sheet.

Such an approach would lead to a finding of fair consideration for a guaranty in a variety of other appropriate contexts. If an alter ego situation presents sufficient consideration, then so should the guaranty of a loan to a third party that is not the alter ego of the guarantor but whose continued health and existence is vitally important to the guarantor—a vital supplier or customer, for example. Under this approach, fair consideration to the guarantor could be found without much difficulty when the loan to the affiliated corporation strengthens its operation sufficiently so that the health of the guarantor is maintained or improved, even though bankruptcy was not imminent.

Rosenberg, supra at 245–246 (footnotes omitted).

The author cites, among other cases, *Williams v. Twin City Company,* 251 F.2d 678, 681 (9th Cir.1958), in which it is stated that direct consideration running from the creditor to the debtor need not be present for there to be fair consideration. Instead, consideration can run to a third party, so long as it is given in exchange for the promise sought to be enforced. Contemporary corporate practices of vertically and horizontally dividing the integrated operations of what is essentially one enterprise among a number of legally distinct entities, making it necessary for financial institutions to frequently obtain "upstream" and "cross-stream" collateralizations, demand that a broad view of "fair consideration" be taken.

One commentator on the law affecting "upstream" guarantees, in which a subsidiary guarantees the repayment of a loan to a parent corporation, and "cross-stream" guarantees, in which a subsidiary guarantees the repayment by another subsidiary of a common parent corporation, see Coquillette, *Guaranty of and Security for the Debt of a Parent Corporation by a Subsidiary Corporation,* 30 Case Western L.Rev. 433, 434 & n. 4 (1980), has opined that

> Because Parent and Subsidiary are part of a single economic unit, it is both logical and desirable that Parent be able to borrow based on the value of its subsidiaries' property and assets and that lenders be able to enjoy the full amount of protection which the borrower can make available. Clear legal treatment of these transactions would enable borrowers and lenders to enjoy commercially required confidence in the effectiveness of their arrangements, but the law relating to upstream guaranties and associated grants of security interests is at present difficult to determine and apply.

Id. at 436–437 (footnote omitted). Coquillette also has concluded that it is desirable for indirect benefits to a subsidiary to suffice as "fair consideration":

* * *

The following hypothetical with "facts" very like those in the instant matter has been posited by yet another commentator in support of the proposition that fair consideration may inhere in a conveyance even though that consideration results only in indirect benefit to the guarantor. A parent corporation, P, which owns two subsidiaries, A and B, asks a bank for a $2 million loan to be used to acquire C, a company that will be integrated into P's manufacturing and marketing system. A and B are required to guarantee the loan to P with equipment, inventory and accounts receivable. Eventually, P, A and B file for reorganization under Chapter XI and then for liquidation.

The 'fair equivalent' received by A and B may also be sought in benefits which they expected to receive from P's acquisition of C, or other benefits resulting from the over-all corporate relationship. For instance, in our hypothetical case it was believed that the acquisition of C was desirable because its product line complemented that of A. Bank could argue that A at least expected to benefit by the affiliation with C. In other fact situations the indirect benefits may be even clearer and more substantial. The transaction of which the guaranty is a part may safeguard an important source of supply, or an important customer for the guarantor. Or substantial indirect benefits may result from the general relationship between the parent corporation and its subsidiaries, rather than the particular transaction giving rise to the guaranty.

* * *

Normandin, "Intercorporate Guaranties and Fraudulent Conveyances" in *Personal Property Security Interests Under the Revised UCC* 361, 370–371 (1977).

Here, I find that there was "fair consideration" and reject the claim that the guarantee constituted a fraudulent conveyance.

* * *

The motion to declare a fraudulent conveyance is denied. MHT is declared to have a priority of security interest in so much of the fund that is being held by Graphics as will satisfy VU–TV's debt to MHT.
* * *

Note: Intercompany Guarantees

Guarantee agreements in commercial loan transactions among related companies are commonplace. They are also often used to save a debtor with financial problems. These guarantees may consist of "downstream guarantees" (the parent guarantees the subsidiary's liability), "upstream guarantees" (the subsidiary guarantees the parent's debt), or "cross stream" (where one subsidiary guarantees the debt of another). In theory the downstream guarantee does not harm the creditors of the parent corporation because any value derived from a guarantee of the subsidiary's debt redounds to the benefit of the parent in the form of added value to the stock of the subsidiary that is held by the parent. The converse is not true. A creditor of a subsidiary that guarantees the parent's debt might claim that the subsidiary has taken on additional liabilities without gaining any additional assets or other benefit—hence, the argument for a fraudulent conveyance. The same argument can of course be made by the brother or sister corporation.

One response to this argument is that seen in the *ATV* case above, namely, that the benefit from the loan proceeds itself somehow came to the one granting the guarantee and thus that fair value is given. A second argument is that the one granting the guarantee in fact gets back a bundle of equitable rights that offset the liability. These are the rights to be subrogated to the claim of the person whose debt is guaranteed, the right of contribution, reimbursement, etc. If these rights are held to be valuable, then there is fair value for the guarantee because they are received in exchange. There has been very little development of this argument in the cases and, of course, the argument is weakest when it is needed most. That is to say, cases in which the guarantee is most desperately needed by the parent are the very cases when a claim against the parent by way of reimbursement and contribution are worth the least.

Note, too, that the treatment of the liabilities associated with the guarantees and of the equitable right may have an impact on the solvency of the guarantor and thus upon the question whether the guarantee was a fraudulent conveyance because it was made by an insolvent guarantor. In general, guarantees are not shown as liabilities on the balance sheet. Good accounting practice says that contingent liabilities that are exceedingly remote need not be shown on the financial statements at all, that those with greater probability of producing an actual liability must be footnoted and that only those that can both be estimated and are probable sources of liability need to be shown on the balance sheet itself. In that setting it is likely that no proof of guarantee need ever be shown in the financial statement until the entire amount needs to be shown on the balance sheet. That is, a guarantee is likely to remain so contingent that it need not be shown until the very day that someone shows up from the bank with a demand for payment; at which point presumably it becomes a full fledged liability, entitled to appear on the balance sheet at the full amount of the guarantee.

Problem 7–28

Assume that Parent holding company is going to borrow $5,000,000. Two million of that amount will go to Subsidiary Adam and three million will go to Subsidiary Eve. Both Subsidiaries Adam and Eve will guarantee the debt, but each guarantee will be written such that the total amount of the guarantees will be capped at $10 less than the net worth of the Subsidiary. Thus, in no case could the signing of the guarantee and addition of that liability to its balance sheet render it insolvent (in the balance sheet sense). Assume that Subsidiary Adam has an approximate net worth of $2,000,000 and Subsidiary Eve has a net worth of approximately $1,000,000. Will you give Client your opinion that such guarantees will be immune from attack as fraudulent conveyances?

Problem 7–29

Carson is putting together a reorganization plan and is concerned about what treatment it should give to several claims in the file. It contemplates a single class of unsecured claims and a separate class for each secured claim. In each of the following, assume that Carson filed bankruptcy on June 20, but became insolvent before December 10 of the previous year.

    a. A secured claim by Bank One based on a mortgage given to it by Carson on December 19 on land owned by Carson in Utah. The land secures a $900,000 loan that Bank made on June 22.

    b. A $500,000 unsecured claim by Bank Two for a deficiency resulting from a foreclosure sale of land owned by Carson that Bank Two conducted on March 11. The land sold for $10 per acre to Levit Company for a total price of $700,000. Evidence suggests that the value of land in that area ranges from $9 per acre to $18 per acre.

c. A claim filed by Primary on a guarantee of Carson. The guarantee was given in favor of Bosum, a company that is owned by the same group of individuals that owns Carson. The guaranty was given on February 11.

C. *Leveraged Buyouts*

The term "leveraged buyout" has been used to describe a variety of transactions. Practically all corporate acquisitions today are leveraged to some extent. They may be conducted by management, corporate affiliates, or third parties. They may be hostile or friendly. They may be conducted by tender offer or negotiated merger. They may involve the sale of assets or securities. [All] of these leveraged transactions have a common characteristic: assets of the subject company are used as collateral for a loan that is obtained to pay all or part of the purchase price of the company * * *

Statement of David Ruder, Chairman of S.E.C., to Senate Committee on Finance, January 25, 1989.

"Leveraged buyouts" include the most complex of contemporary commercial deals and many of the most controversial. In addition to various concerns arising under corporate law, securities rules and other fields of commercial law, a leveraged buyout also raises difficult questions under fraudulent conveyance law. Fraudulent conveyance law, the student will recall, originally was designed to invalidate transfers from debtors to their spouses. It is difficult to compare this situation to transactions conducted by giant corporate entities such as A.H. Robins and Campeau.

Assume that we intend to acquire Dinah Cotton Company. We reach an agreement with Dinah's shareholders agreeing to pay $100 per share for stock presently valued at $45 per share. Dinah has $300 million in assets and $200 million in mostly unsecured debt. The purchase will cost $250 million. Based on current projections, the business operations of Dinah can provide $45 to $60 million in net income (after tax and operational costs). We promise to pay the shareholders $100 per share because we have obtained a commitment from Israel Bank to lend $250 million secured by the assets of Dinah. This creates the leveraged acquisition. No one loses if the assets perform as projected or exceed expectations. The fraudulent conveyance issue will arise in the event that Dinah fails to produce enough income to service both the old debt and the new debt created by the acquisition. Who should bear the loss in such event? That is *the* question in the following cases.

WIEBOLDT STORES, INC. v. SCHOTTENSTEIN
United States District Court, Northern District of Illinois, 1988.
94 B.R. 488.

HOLDERMAN, DISTRICT JUDGE:

* * *

I. INTRODUCTION

Wieboldt's complaint against the defendants concerns the events and transactions surrounding a leveraged buyout ("LBO") of Wieboldt by WSI Acquisition Corporation ("WSI"). WSI, a corporation formed solely for the purpose of acquiring Wieboldt, borrowed funds from third-party lenders and delivered the proceeds to the shareholders in return for their shares. Wieboldt thereafter pledged certain of its assets to the LBO lenders to secure repayment of the loan.

The LBO reduced the assets available to Wieboldt's creditors. Wieboldt contends that, after the buyout was complete, Wieboldt's debt had increased by millions of dollars, and the proceeds made available by the LBO lenders were paid out to Wieboldt's then existing shareholders and did not accrue to the benefit of the corporation. Wieboldt's alleged insolvency after the LBO left Wieboldt with insufficient unencumbered assets to sustain its business and ensure payment to its unsecured creditors. Wieboldt therefore commenced this action on behalf of itself and its unsecured creditors, seeking to avoid the transactions constituting the LBO on the grounds that they are fraudulent under federal and state fraudulent conveyance laws.

II. FACTS

A. Parties

1. Wieboldt

William A. Wieboldt began operating Wieboldt in Chicago as a dry goods store in 1883. Mr. Wieboldt's business prospered and diversified. In 1907 Wieboldt was incorporated under Illinois law. Wieboldt's business continued to expand. In 1982 Wieboldt's business was operated out of twelve stores and one distribution center in the Chicago metropolitan area. At that time, Wieboldt employed approximately 4,000 persons and had annual sales of approximately $190 million. Its stock was publicly traded on the New York Stock Exchange.

During the 1970's, demographic changes in Wieboldt's markets, increased competition from discount operations, and poor management caused Wieboldt's business to decline. Wieboldt showed no profit after 1979 and was able to continue its operations only by periodically selling its assets to generate working capital. These assets included its store in Evanston, Illinois and some undeveloped land.

2. Defendants

Wieboldt brings this action against 119 defendants. These defendants can be grouped into three non-exclusive categories: (1) controlling shareholders, officers and directors; (2) other shareholders of Wieboldt's common stock who owned and tendered more than 1,000 shares in response to the tender offer ("Schedule A shareholders"); and (3) entities which loaned money to fund the tender offer.

a. Controlling Shareholders, Officers and Directors

The individuals and entities who controlled Wieboldt in 1982 became controlling shareholders as a direct or indirect result of a 1982 takeover effort. At some time prior to or during 1982, Julius and Edmond Trump, each citizens of the Republic of South Africa and permanent residents of New York, purchased 30% of Wieboldt's outstanding shares by launching a takeover. After the takeover, the Trump brothers conveyed approximately one-half of these shares to Jerome Schottenstein and, directly or indirectly, to certain persons and entities affiliated with Mr. Schottenstein (collectively referred to as the "Schottenstein interests"). As a result of these transactions, the Schottenstein interests and the Trump brothers (through its agent, MBT Corporation) (collectively referred to as the "Trump interests") each owned approximately 15% of Wieboldt's then outstanding shares and became Wieboldt's controlling shareholders.[3]

Wieboldt's Board of Directors consisted of nine individuals. In late 1982, Mr. Schottenstein became the Chairman of the Board. He nominated Irving Harris, George Kolber, and Myron Kaplan to serve as directors. William W. Darrow, Robert A. Podesta, and David C. Keller also began serving in 1982. In 1984, MBT Corporation nominated James Jacobson and Albert Roth to the Wieboldt Board of Directors. These nine individuals served on the Board until December 19, 1985.

b. Schedule A Shareholders

In addition to the Schottenstein and Trump interests, Wieboldt had a number of shareholders as of December 20, 1985 who owned more than 1,000 shares of Wieboldt's common stock. Wieboldt has listed these shareholders and the number of shares that they held on that date on a schedule which they have appended to their complaint ("Schedule A").[4] Directors Keller, Podesta and Darrow (the "insider shareholders") also owned more than 1,000 shares each.[5]

c. The LBO Lenders and Related Entities

On November 20, 1985 WSI commenced a tender offer for all outstanding shares of Wieboldt's common stock, for all of Wieboldt's outstanding shares of preferred stock, and for all outstanding options to purchase Wieboldt's stock. The tender offer was financed through three

---

[3]. The Trump brothers, MBT Corporation, Mr. Schottenstein and the Schottenstein affiliates are collectively referred to in this opinion as "controlling shareholders."

[4]. The following Schedule A shareholders have already been dismissed in this action: Tessie Brown, Herbert E. Harper, William Jarvis, Alan J. Levine, Louis R. Pearlman, Ruby E. Prince, Morton Simpson, Carole G. Simpson, Robert P. Wieboldt, and West Orange Orthopedic Association.

[5]. Keller owned 3,500 shares; Podesta owned 4,816 shares, and Darrow owned 2,078 shares.

related financial transactions between Wieboldt and certain lenders and affiliated parties. These three transactions effected the LBO of Wieboldt.

Wieboldt has included as defendants in this action four of the entities which were involved in these financial transactions: One North State Street Limited Partnership ("ONSSLP"), State Street Venture ("SSV"), Boulevard Bank National Association ("Boulevard Bank"), BA Mortgage and International Realty Corporation ("BAMIRCO"), and General Electric Credit Corporation ("GECC").[6] The roles these entities played in the tender offer and subsequent buyout are described below.

B. *The Tender Offer and Related Transactions*

By January, 1985 Wieboldt's financial health had declined to the point at which the company was no longer able to meet its obligations as they came due. On January 23, 1985 WSI sent a letter to Mr. Schottenstein in which WSI proposed a possible tender offer for Wieboldt common stock at $13.50 per share. The following day, Mr. Schottenstein informed Wieboldt's Board of Directors of the WSI proposal and the Board agreed to cooperate with WSI in evaluating the financial and operating records of the company. WSI proceeded to seek financing from several lenders, including Household Commercial Financial Services ("HCFS").

During 1985 it became apparent to Wieboldt's Board that WSI would accomplish its tender offer by means of an LBO through which WSI would pledge substantially all of Wieboldt's assets, including the company's fee and leasehold real estate assets, as collateral. Many of these real estate assets already served as collateral for $35 million in secured loan obligations from Continental Illinois National Bank ("CINB") and other bank creditors. Wieboldt was at least partially in default on these obligations at the time of the LBO.

In order to free these assets for use as collateral in obtaining tender offer financing, WSI intended to sell the One North State Street property and pay off the CINB loan obligations. In furtherance of these efforts, WSI entered into a joint venture with Bennett & Kahnweiler Associates ("BKA"), a real estate broker. WSI and BKA intended to sell the One North State Street property to a partnership for $30,000,000. The partnership would then mortgage the property to a funding source. Accordingly, BKA applied for and BAMIRCO accepted a first mortgage term loan on the property.

The sale of the One North State Street property did not generate sufficient funds to pay off the CINB loan obligations. Consequently, WSI sought additional funds from GECC through the sale of Wieboldt's customer charge card accounts. GECC agreed to enter into an accounts purchase agreement after WSI acquired Wieboldt through the tender

---

6. These entities are collectively referred to in this opinion as "State Street defendants."

offer. One term of the accounts purchase agreement required Wieboldt to pledge all of its accounts receivable to GECC as additional security for Wieboldt's obligations under the agreement.

Thus, by October, 1985 HCFS, BAMIRCO, and GECC had each agreed to fund WSI's tender offer, and each knew of the other's loan or credit commitments.[7] These lenders were aware that WSI intended to use the proceeds of the financing commitments to (1) purchase tendered shares of Wieboldt stock; (2) pay surrender prices for Wieboldt stock options; or (3) eliminate CINB loan obligations.

The Board of Directors was fully aware of the progress of WSI's negotiations. The Board understood that WSI intended to finance the tender offer by pledging a substantial portion of Wieboldt's assets to its lenders, and that WSI did not intend to use any of its own funds or the funds of its shareholders to finance the acquisition. Moreover, although the Board initially believed that the tender offer would produce $10 million in working capital for the company, the members knew that the proceeds from the LBO lenders would not result in this additional working capital.

Nevertheless, in October, 1985 the Board directed Mr. Darrow and Wieboldt's lawyers to work with WSI to effect the acquisition. During these negotiations, the Board learned that HCFS would provide financing for the tender offer only if Wieboldt would provide a statement from a nationally recognized accounting firm stating that Wieboldt was solvent and a going concern prior to the planned acquisition and would be solvent and a going concern after the acquisition. Mr. Darrow informed WSI that Wieboldt would only continue cooperating in the LBO if HCFS agreed not to require this solvency certificate. HCFS acceded to Wieboldt's demand and no solvency certificate was ever provided to HCFS on Wieboldt's behalf.

On November 18, 1985 Wieboldt's Board of Directors voted to approve WSI's tender offer, and on November 20, 1985 WSI announced its offer to purchase Wieboldt stock for $13.50 per share.[8] By December 20, 1985 the tender offer was complete and WSI had acquired ownership of Wieboldt through its purchase of 99% of Wieboldt's stock at a total price of $38,462,164.00. All of the funds WSI used to purchase the tendered shares were provided by HCFS and were secured by the assets which BAMIRCO and GECC loan proceeds had freed from CINB obligations. After the LBO,

---

7. HCFS committed an amount sufficient to fund the offer; BAMIRCO committed $28 million; and GECC extended WSI a line of credit which was not to exceed $35 million.

8. Approximately 1,900 shareholders held the 2,765,574 shares of Wieboldt common stock that were outstanding on that date. As a result of the offer, Mr. Schottenstein and his affiliates tendered at least 416,958 shares and received $5,628,933.00 from WSI. MBT Corporation tendered the Trump brothers' 480,072 shares and received $6,480,972.00 from WSI. The Schedule A shareholders, Mr. Keller, Mr. Darrow and his wife, and Mr. Podesta also tendered their shares at the offer price.

1. Wieboldt's One North State Street property was conveyed to ONSSLP as beneficiary of a land trust established with Boulevard Bank as trustee;

2. Substantially all of Wieboldt's remaining real estate holdings were subject to first or second mortgages to secure the HCFS loans; and

3. Wieboldt's customer credit card accounts were conveyed to GECC and Wieboldt's accounts receivable were pledged to GECC as security under the GECC accounts purchase agreement.

In addition, Wieboldt became liable to HCFS on an amended note in the amount of approximately $32.5 million.[9] Wieboldt did not receive any amount of working capital as a direct result of the LBO.

On September 24, 1986 certain of Wieboldt's creditors commenced an involuntary liquidation proceeding against Wieboldt under Chapter 7 of the United States Bankruptcy Code ("the Code"). On the same day, Wieboldt filed a voluntary reorganization proceeding pursuant to Chapter 11 of the Code. Wieboldt's Chapter 11 proceeding is entitled *In re Wieboldt Stores, Inc.,* 68 B.R. 578 (Bankr.N.D.Ill.1986) and is pending on the docket of Bankruptcy Judge Susan Pierson DeWitt of the United States Bankruptcy Court for the Northern District of Illinois.

C. *The Complaint*

In its complaint, Wieboldt alleges that WSI's tender offer and the resulting LBO was a fraudulent conveyance under the federal bankruptcy statute and the Illinois fraudulent conveyance laws. Counts I, III, and V are based on Section 548(a)(1) of the Code, 11 U.S.C. § 548(a)(1). The essence of Count I is that the controlling and insider shareholders tendered their shares to WSI in response to WSI's offer with the actual intent to hinder, delay or defraud Wieboldt's unsecured creditors. Count III brings a similar claim against the State Street defendants for their role in the sale of the One North State Street property. Likewise, Count V, which names GECC as defendant, claims that the pledging of Wieboldt's customer charge card accounts and other accounts receivable violated Section 548(a)(1).

Counts II, IV, VI, and VII are based on Section 548(a)(2) of the Code, 11 U.S.C. § 548(a)(2). Counts II and VII allege that the tender offer to Wieboldt shareholders (including the Schedule A shareholders) was a fraudulent conveyance because it and the resulting LBO "rendered Wieboldt insolvent or too thinly capitalized to continue in the business in which it was engaged * * *." (Complaint ¶¶ 113, 139). Count IV claims that the sale of the One North State Street property violated Section 548(a)(2); Count VI claims that the pledging of Wieboldt's accounts receivable violated Section 548(a)(2).

---

9. The amount of WSI's note to HCFS represents the $38 million that WSI paid to Wieboldt shareholders less an immediate payment on that amount from the proceeds of the One North State Street sale.

Count VIII alleges that each of the three transactions (the tender offer, the sale of One North State Street property, and the pledging of the Wieboldt accounts receivable) violated the Illinois fraudulent conveyance law, Ill.Rev.Stat. ch. 59, § 4. The essence of the claim in Count VIII is that Wieboldt did not receive fair consideration for the property it conveyed and was insolvent at the time of the conveyances. (Complaint ¶ 144). In each of Counts I through VIII, Wieboldt seeks to avoid the transfer of assets made to the named defendants as a result of the LBO.

Finally, Counts IX, X and XI allege that the Board of Directors breached its fiduciary duty and violated Section 9.10(c)(1) of the Illinois Business Corporation Act ("IBCA") by cooperating in and approving the LBO notwithstanding its practical effect on Wieboldt's solvency and future as a going concern. Counts IX, X and XI seek $100 million in compensatory damages and the costs of bringing this lawsuit. In addition, Count X seeks $500 million in punitive damages from the directors.

III. Discussion

* * *

1. Applicability of Fraudulent Conveyance Law

Both the federal Bankruptcy Code and Illinois law protect creditors from transfers of property that are intended to impair a creditor's ability to enforce its rights to payment or that deplete a debtor's assets at a time when its financial condition is precarious. Modern fraudulent conveyance law derives from the English Statute of Elizabeth enacted in 1570, the substance of which has been either enacted in American statutes prohibiting such transactions or has been incorporated into American law as a part of the English common law heritage. *See* Sherwin, "Creditors' Rights Against Participants in a Leveraged Buyout," 72 Minn.L.Rev. 449, 465–66 (1988).

The controlling shareholders, insider shareholders, and some of the Schedule A shareholders argue that fraudulent conveyance laws do not apply to leveraged buyouts. These defendants argue (1) that applying fraudulent conveyance laws to public tender offers effectively allows creditors to insure themselves against subsequent mismanagement of the company; (2) that applying fraudulent conveyance laws to LBO transactions and thereby rendering them void severely restricts the usefulness of LBOs and results in great unfairness; and (3) that fraudulent conveyance laws were never intended to be used to prohibit or restrict public tender offers.

Although some support exists for defendants' arguments, this court cannot hold at this stage in this litigation that the LBO in question here is entirely exempt from fraudulent conveyance laws. Neither Section 548 of the Code nor the Illinois statute exempt such transactions from their statutory coverage. Section 548 invalidates fraudulent "transfers" of a debtor's property. Section 101(50) defines such a transfer very broadly to include "every mode, direct or indirect, absolute or conditional, voluntary or involuntary, of disposing of or parting with property or with an interest in property, including retention of title as a security interest." 11 U.S.C. § 101(50). Likewise, the Illinois statute applies to gifts, grants, conveyances, assignments and transfers. Ill.Rev.Stat. ch. 59, ¶ 4. The language of these statutes in no way limits their application so as to exclude LBOs.

In addition, those courts which have addressed this issue have concluded that LBOs in some circumstances may constitute a fraudulent conveyance. *See e.g., Kupetz v. Continental Illinois National Bank and Trust,* 77 B.R. 754 (Bankr.C.D.Cal.1987), *aff'd Kupetz v. Wolf,* 845 F.2d 842 (9th Cir.1988)(applying Section 548 and the California statute, West's Ann.Cal.Civ.Code ¶¶ 3439–3439.12); *In re Ohio Corrugating Company,* 70 B.R. 920 (Bankr.N.D.Ohio 1987)(applying Section 548 and the Ohio statute, Ohio Rev.Code, Sect. 1336.01 *et seq.*); *In re Anderson Industries, Inc.,* 55 B.R. 922 (Bankr.W.D.Mich.1985)(applying Michigan law, M.C.L.A. § 566.11); and *United States v. Gleneagles Investment Co., Inc.,* 565 F.Supp. 556 (M.D.Pa.1983), *aff'd in part and remanded in part United States v. Tabor Court Realty,* 803 F.2d 1288 (3d Cir.1986), *cert. denied, McClellan Realty Co. v. United States,* 483 U.S. 1005, 107 S.Ct. 3229, 97 L.Ed.2d 735 (1987)(applying the Pennsylvania Uniform Fraudulent Conveyances Act, 39 P.S. § 351). *See also* Sherwin, "Creditor's Rights Against Participants in a Leveraged Buyout," 72 Minn.L.Rev. 449 (1988). Defendants have presented no case law which holds to the contrary.

The court is aware that permitting debtors to avoid all LBO transfers through the fraudulent conveyance laws could have the effect of insuring against a corporation's subsequent insolvency and failure. *Anderson Industries, Inc.,* 55 B.R. at 926; *see also* Baird & Jackson, *supra* n. 11 at 839. In light of the case law and the broad statutory language, however, this court sees no reason to hold as a general rule that LBOs are exempt from the fraudulent conveyance laws. As the court stated in *Anderson,* "[i]f this holding is too broad in the light of the present marketplace, it is the legislature, not the courts, that must narrow the statute." 55 B.R. at 926.

2. *The Structure of the Transaction*

Although the court finds that the fraudulent conveyance laws generally are applicable to LBO transactions, a debtor cannot use these laws to avoid any and all LBO transfers. In this case, certain defendants argue that they are entitled to dismissal because the LBO transfers at issue do not fall within the parameters of the laws. These defendants argue that they are protected by the literal language of Section 548 of the Code and the "good faith transferee for value" rule in Section 550. They contend, initially, that they did not receive Wieboldt property during the tender offer and, secondarily, that, even if they received Wieboldt property, they tendered their shares in good faith, for value, and without the requisite knowledge and therefore cannot be held liable under Section 550.

The merit of this assertion turns on the court's interpretation of the tender offer and LBO transactions. Defendants contend that the tender offer and LBO were composed of a series of interrelated but independent transactions. They assert, for example, that the transfer of property from HCFS to WSI and ultimately to the shareholders constituted one series of several transactions while the pledge of Wieboldt assets to HCFS to secure the financing constituted a second series of transactions. Under this view, defendants did not receive the *debtor*'s property during the tender offer but rather received *WSI*'s property in exchange for their shares.

Wieboldt, on the other hand, urges the court to "collapse" the interrelated transactions into one aggregate transaction which had the overall effect of conveying Wieboldt property to the tendering shareholders and LBO lenders. This approach requires the court to find that the persons and entities receiving the conveyance were direct transferrees who received "an interest of the debtor in property" during the tender offer/buyout, and that WSI and any other parties to the transactions were "mere conduits" of Wieboldt's property. If the court finds that all the transfers constituted one transaction, then defendants received property from Wieboldt and Wieboldt has stated a claim against them.

Few courts have considered whether complicated LBO transfers should be evaluated separately or collapsed into one integrated transaction. However, two United States Courts of Appeals opinions provide some illumination on this issue. *See Kupetz v. Wolf,* 845 F.2d 842 (9th Cir.1988); *United States v. Tabor Court Realty,* 803 F.2d 1288 (3d Cir.1986), *cert. denied McClellan Realty Co. v. United States,* 483 U.S. 1005, 107 S.Ct. 3229, 97 L.Ed.2d 735 (1987).

In *Kupetz,* the debtor corporation (Wolf & Vine) was owned in equal shares by an individual, Morris Wolf, and the Marmon Group. When Mr. Wolf retired, Marmon decided to sell the company and concluded that David Adashek was a suitable buyer. Mr. Adashek subsequently obtained control of the company through a series of transactions which constituted an LBO. Thereafter, Wolf & Vine could not service the additional debt that resulted from the buyout. The company eventually filed for bankruptcy under Chapter 11 of the Code.

The dispute before the district court resulted when the trustee in bankruptcy sought to avoid the LBO transfers on the grounds that the manner in which the sale was financed constituted a fraudulent conveyance to Mr. Wolf and the Marmon Group. After the case proceeded to a jury trial, the district court directed a verdict in favor of the selling shareholders on the fraudulent conveyance claims. 845 F.2d at 844–45. The trustees appealed.

The Ninth Circuit affirmed the district court's decision and declined to strike down the LBO on fraudulent conveyance grounds. The court concluded that the trustee could not avoid the transfer to the shareholders because (1) they did not sell their shares in order to defraud Wolf & Vine's creditors; (2) they did not know that Mr. Adashek intended to leverage the company's assets to finance the purchase of shares; and (3) the LBO had the indicia of a straight sale of shares and was not Wolf & Vine's attempt to redeem its own shares. 845 F.2d at 848–50. However, the Ninth Circuit in its opinion in *Kupetz* stated:

> In an LBO, the lender, by taking a security interest in the company's assets, reduces the assets available to creditors in the event of failure of the business. The form of the LBO, while not unimportant, does not alter this reality. Thus, where the parties in an LBO fully intend to hinder the general creditors and benefit the selling shareholders the conveyance is fraudulent under [the fraudulent conveyance laws].

845 F.2d at 846.

In *Kupetz* the Ninth Circuit discussed shareholder liability under the fraudulent conveyance laws. The Third Circuit in *United States v. Tabor Court*, 803 F.2d 1288 (3d Cir.1986), *cert. denied McClellan Realty Co. v. United States,* 483 U.S. 1005, 107 S.Ct. 3229, 97 L.Ed.2d 735 (1987), addressed the liability of an LBO lender. In *Tabor Court,* the controlling shareholders of the debtor corporation (Raymond Group) solicited a purchaser for the company. The purchaser formed a holding company (Great American) to purchase Raymond Group's outstanding shares. Great American acquired Raymond Group by borrowing funds from a third party lender (IIT) and securing the loan with both first and second mortgages on Raymond Group's assets. After the company failed and many of its assets had been sold to various investment groups, the United States government sought to reduce to judgment certain tax liens on Raymond Group's property and satisfy the judgments out of assets which the company owned before it mortgaged those assets to secure the LBO funds. 803 F.2d at 1291–94.

The Third Circuit affirmed the district court's conclusion that the mortgages that the Raymond Group gave to IIT were fraudulent conveyances within the meaning of the constructive and intentional fraud sections of the Pennsylvania UFCA. 803 F.2d at 1296. In affirming the district court, the Third Circuit noted that all three parties—the lender, the debtor, and the purchaser—participated in the loan negotiations, and that IIT therefore knew of the purpose to which Great American intended to put the loan proceeds. *Id.* The court held that the district court, in interpreting the LBO, correctly integrated the series of transactions because the Raymond Group merely served as a conduit for the transfer between IIT and Great American (and ultimately to the shareholders), and did not receive the funds as any form of consideration. 803 F.2d at 1302.

Neither of these cases involved transactions which were identical to the WSI–Wieboldt buyout. However, the *Kupetz* and *Tabor Court* opinions are nonetheless significant because the courts in both cases expressed the view that an LBO transfer—in whatever form—was a fraudulent conveyance if the circumstances of the transfer were not "above board." *Kupetz,* 845 F.2d at 847. Thus, even though the court in *Kupetz* declined to hold the selling shareholders liable, there was no showing in *Kupetz* that the shareholders intended to defraud Wolf & Vine's creditors nor even knew that the purchaser intended to finance the takeover by leveraging the company's assets. On the other hand, the court in *Tabor Court* found the LBO lender liable because it participated in the negotiations surrounding the LBO transactions and knew that the proceeds of its loan to Great American would deplete the debtor's assets to the point at which it was functionally insolvent under the fraudulent conveyance and bankruptcy laws. These cases indicate that a court should focus not on the formal structure of the transaction but rather on the knowledge or intent of the parties involved in the transaction.

Applying this principle to defendants' assertions, it is clear that, at least as regards the liability of the controlling shareholders, the LBO lenders, and the insider shareholders, the LBO transfers must be collapsed into one transaction. The complaint alleges clearly that these participants in the LBO negotiations attempted to structure the LBO with the requisite knowledge and contemplation that the full transaction, tender offer and LBO, be completed. The Board and the insider shareholders knew that WSI intended to finance its acquisition of Wieboldt through an LBO (Complaint ¶¶ 51, 72) and not with any of its own funds (Complaint ¶ 69). They knew that Wieboldt was insolvent before the LBO and that the LBO would result in further encumbrance of Wieboldt's already encumbered assets. (Complaint ¶¶ 44, 53, 54, 73, 75–78, 88). Attorneys for Schottenstein Stores apprised the Board of the fraudulent conveyance laws and suggested that they structure the LBO so as to avoid liability. (Complaint ¶¶ 81, 82). Nonetheless, these shareholders recommended that Wieboldt accept the tender offer and themselves tendered their shares to WSI. (Complaint ¶¶ 91, 95, 97, 99, 100, 101).

Wieboldt's complaint also alleges sufficient facts to implicate the LBO lenders in the scheme. HCFS, BAMIRCO and GECC were well aware of each other's loan or credit commitments to WSI and knew that WSI intended to use the proceeds of their financing commitments to purchase Wieboldt shares or options and to release certain Wieboldt assets from prior encumbrances. (Complaint ¶¶ 66, 67). Representatives of the lenders received the same information concerning the fraudulent conveyance laws as did the Board of Directors. (Complaint ¶ 80). These LBO lenders agreed with WSI and the Board of Directors to structure the LBO so as to avoid fraudulent conveyance liability. (Complaint ¶ 82).

The court, however, is not willing to "collapse" the transaction in order to find that the Schedule A shareholders also received the debtor's property in the transfer. While Wieboldt directs specific allegations of fraud against the controlling and insider shareholders and LBO lenders, Wieboldt does not allege that the Schedule A shareholders were aware that WSI's acquisition encumbered virtually all of Wieboldt's assets. Nor is there an allegation that these shareholders were aware that the consideration they received for their tendered shares was Wieboldt property. In fact, the complaint does not suggest that the Schedule A shareholders had any part in the LBO except as innocent pawns in the scheme. They were aware only that WSI made a public tender offer for shares of Wieboldt stock. (Complaint ¶ 98). Viewing the transactions from the perspective of the Schedule A shareholders and considering their knowledge and intent, therefore, the asset transfers to the LBO lenders were indeed independent of the tender offer to the Schedule A shareholders.

This conclusion is in accord with the purpose of the fraudulent conveyance laws. The drafters of the Code, while attempting to protect parties harmed by fraudulent conveyances, also intended to shield innocent recipients of fraudulently conveyed property from liability. Thus, although Subsection (a) of Section 550 permits a trustee to avoid a transfer to an initial transferee or its subsequent transferee, Subsection (b) of that Section limits recovery from a subsequent transferee by providing that a trustee may not recover fraudulently conveyed property from a subsequent transferee who takes the property in good faith, for value, and without knowledge that the original transfer was voidable.[22] Subsection (b) applies, however, only to subsequent transferees.

Similarly, the LBO lenders and the controlling and insider shareholders of Wieboldt are direct transferees of Wieboldt property. Although WSI participated in effecting the transactions, Wieboldt's complaint alleges that WSI was a corporation formed solely for the purpose of acquiring Wieboldt stock. The court can reasonably infer from the complaint, therefore, that WSI served mainly as a conduit for the exchange of assets and loan proceeds between LBO lenders and Wieboldt and for the exchange of loan proceeds and shares of stock between the LBO lenders and the insider and controlling shareholders. On the other hand, the Schedule A shareholders are not direct transferees of Wieboldt property. From their perspective, WSI was the direct transferee of Wieboldt property and the shareholders were merely indirect transferees because WSI was an independent entity in the transaction.

In sum, the formal structure of the transaction alone cannot shield the LBO lenders or the controlling and insider shareholders from Wieboldt's fraudulent conveyance claims. These parties were aware that the consideration they received for their financing commitments or in exchange for their shares consisted of Wieboldt assets and not the assets of WSI or any other financial intermediary. The Schedule A shareholders, on the other hand, apparently unaware of the financing transactions, participated only to the extent that they exchanged their shares for funds from WSI. Therefore, based on the allegations in the complaint, the court concludes that:

---

22. Section 550(b) also prohibits a trustee from recovering such property from a good faith transferee of such a transferee.

1. the motions to dismiss filed by the LBO lenders, insider shareholders, and controlling shareholders are denied at this point because these parties received Wieboldt property through a series of integrated LBO transactions; and

2. the Schedule A shareholders' motions to dismiss are granted because these defendants did not receive Wieboldt property through the separate exchange of shares for cash.

3. *The Elements of a Fraudulent Conveyance*

As discussed above, the transfers to and between the debtor and the LBO lenders, controlling shareholders, and insider shareholders are subject to the provisions in Section 548(a) of the Code and Section 4 of the Illinois statute. The court now must determine whether Wieboldt's complaint states sufficient facts to allege the elements of these causes of action.

a. Section 548(a)(1)

In order to state a claim for relief under Section 548(a)(1) of the Code, a debtor or trustee must allege (1) that the transfer was made within one year before the debtor filed a petition in bankruptcy, and (2) that the transfer was made with the actual intent to hinder, delay or defraud the debtor's creditors. 11 U.S.C. § 548(a)(1). *See In re F & C Services, Inc.*, 44 B.R. 863, 871–72 (Bankr.S.D.Fla.1984). Although defendants do not dispute that the LBO transfers occurred within a year of the date on which Wieboldt filed for bankruptcy, they vigorously assert that Wieboldt has failed to properly allege "intent to defraud" as required by Section 548(a)(1).

"Actual intent" in the context of fraudulent transfers of property is rarely susceptible to proof and "must be gleaned from inferences drawn from a course of conduct." *In re Vecchione,* 407 F.Supp. 609, 615 (E.D.N.Y.1976). A general scheme or plan to strip the debtor of its assets without regard to the needs of its creditors can support a finding of actual intent. *In re F & C Services,* 44 B.R. at 872. In addition, certain "badges of fraud" can form the basis for a finding of actual intent to hinder, delay or defraud. 4 *Collier on Bankruptcy* ¶ 548.02[5] (15th ed. 1987).

Counts I and III of Wieboldt's complaint state a claim under Section 548(a)(1). Count I, which Wieboldt brings against the controlling and insider shareholders, states that these defendants exchanged their shares with the actual intent to hinder, delay or defraud Wieboldt's unsecured creditors. (Complaint, ¶ 109). Count III states that the State Street defendants received Wieboldt's interest in One North State Street property with the actual intent to defraud Wieboldt's unsecured creditors. (Complaint ¶ 118). The complaint also states generally that the LBO Lenders and the controlling and insider shareholders structured the LBO transfers in such a way as to attempt to evade fraudulent conveyance liability. (Complaint ¶¶ 80–83). These allegations are a sufficient assertion of actual fraud. Defendants' motions to dismiss Counts I and III are therefore denied.

b. Section 548(a)(2)

Unlike Section 548(a)(1), which requires a plaintiff to allege "actual fraud," Section 548(a)(2) requires a plaintiff to allege only constructive fraud. A plaintiff states a claim under Section 548(a)(2) by alleging that the debtor (1) transferred property within a year of filing a petition in bankruptcy; (2) received less than the reasonably equivalent value for the property transferred; and (3) either (a) was insolvent or became insolvent as a result of the transfer, (b) retained unreasonably small capital after the transfer, or (c) made the transfer with the intent to incur debts beyond its ability to pay. 11 U.S.C. § 548(a)(2).

Defendants argue that Wieboldt's allegation of insolvency is insufficient as a matter of law to satisfy the insolvency requirement in Section 548(a)(2)(B)(i). Section 101(31)(A) of the Code defines "insolvency" as a condition which occurs when the sum of an entity's debts exceeds the sum of its property "at a fair valuation." 11 U.S.C. § 101(31)(A). Wieboldt's complaint alleges that the corporation was insolvent in November, 1985 "in that the fair saleable value of its assets was exceeded by its liabilities when the illiquidity of those assets is taken into account." (Complaint, ¶¶ 112, 121).

Wieboldt's allegations satisfy the "insolvency" requirement of Section 548(a)(2)(B)(i). Defendants' attempt to distinguish Wieboldt's phrase "fair saleable value" from Section 101(31)(A)'s "fair valuation" is, as Wieboldt suggests, "hypertechnical." (Mem. in Opp. at 66). "Fair valuation" is near enough in meaning to "fair value of saleable assets" to defeat defendants' motion to dismiss. *See In re A. Fassnacht & Sons, Inc.*, 45 B.R. 209, 217 (Bkrtcy.E.D.Tenn.1984). In addition, Wieboldt did not destroy its claim of insolvency by characterizing its assets as "illiquid" at the time of the transfer. In determining "fair valuation," a court must consider the property's intrinsic value, selling value, and the earning power of the property. *Black's Law Dictionary*, 538 (5th Ed.1979). Assets may be reduced by the value of the assets that cannot be readily liquidated. *Briden v. Foley*, 776 F.2d 379, 382 (1st Cir.1985). The complaint meets the financial condition test of Section 548(a)(2)(B)(i).

Finally, defendants claim that Wieboldt cannot state a claim under Section 548(a)(2) because it received "reasonably equivalent value" in the transfer to the shareholders and the conveyance of the One North State Street property. Wieboldt granted a security interest in substantially all of its real estate assets to HCFS and received from the shareholders in return 99% of its outstanding shares of stock.[25] (Com-

---

25. Defendants argue that WSI (and not Wieboldt) received the outstanding shares of Wieboldt stock. However, a court analyzing an allegedly fraudulent transfer must direct its attention to "what the Debtor surrendered and what the Debtor received, irrespective of what any third party may have gained or lost." *In re Ohio Corrugating Co.*, 70 B.R. 920, 927 (Bkrtcy.N.D.Ohio 1987). As discussed in Section C.2. of this

plaint ¶¶ 102, 103(b)). This stock was virtually worthless to Wieboldt. *In re Roco Corp.,* 701 F.2d 978, 982 (1st Cir.1983); *In re Ipswich Bituminous Concrete Products, Inc.,* 79 B.R. 511, 517 (Bkrtcy.D.Mass. 1987); *In re Corporate Jet Aviation, Inc.,* 45 B.R. 629, 634 (Bkrtcy. N.D.Ga.1985). *See also Hyde Properties v. McCoy,* 507 F.2d 301, 307 (6th Cir.1974)(decided under the Tennessee fraudulent conveyance statute, T.C.A. § 64–311, 64–312). Wieboldt received less than a reasonably equivalent value in exchange for an encumbrance on virtually all of its non-inventory assets, and therefore has stated a claim against the controlling and insider shareholders.

Likewise, the court need not dismiss Wieboldt's Section 548(a)(2) claim against the State Street defendants on the grounds that Wieboldt received reasonably equivalent value in exchange for its One North State Street property. The effect and intention of the parties to the One North State Street conveyance was to generate funds to purchase outstanding shares of Wieboldt stock. Although Wieboldt sold the property to ONSSLP for $30 million, and used the proceeds to pay off part of the $35 million it owed CINB, Wieboldt did not receive a benefit from this transfer. (Complaint ¶¶ 56, 58). *See Tabor Court,* 803 F.2d at 1300. Defendants knew that the conveyance would neither increase Wieboldt's assets nor result in a net reduction of its liabilities. In fact, all parties to the conveyance were aware that the newly unencumbered assets would be immediately remortgaged to HCFS to finance the acquisition. (Complaint ¶ 104). According to the complaint, therefore, Wieboldt received less than reasonably equivalent value for the conveyance of the One North State Street property and has stated a claim against the State Street defendants under Section 548(a)(2).

In sum, Counts II and IV of Wieboldt's complaint state a claim under Section 548(a)(2). Defendants' motions to dismiss these counts are denied.

c. *Illinois Fraudulent Conveyance Law*

Under Section 544(b) of the Code, a trustee may avoid transfers that are avoidable under state law if there is at least one creditor at the time who has standing under state law to challenge the transfer. 11 U.S.C. § 544(b).[27] Wieboldt utilizes this section to pursue a claim under the Illinois fraudulent conveyance statute, Ill.Rev.Stat. ch. 59, § 4.

The Illinois fraudulent conveyance statute is similar to Section 548 of the Code. The statute provides that:

opinion, the court considers the tender offer and buyout transfers as one transaction for the purposes of this motion.

27. Defendants challenge Wieboldt's standing to assert a claim under Section 544(b) because it has failed to identify a single creditor who could have challenged the transactions at the time they occurred. Again, defendants' reading of the complaint is hypertechnical. By January, 1985 Wieboldt was without sufficient working capital to pay at least $7 million in company obligations. (Complaint ¶ 43). Moreover, it was in default on its obligations to CINB at the time of the LBO. (Complaint ¶ 55). The court can fairly infer from these facts that a creditor existed who could have challenged the LBO transfers at the time they occurred.

> Every gift, grant, conveyance, assignment or transfer of, or charge upon any estate, real or personal, * * * made with the intent to disturb, delay, hinder or defraud creditors or other person, * * * shall be void as against the creditors, purchasers and other persons.

Ill.Rev.Stat. ch. 59, § 4 (1976). Illinois courts divide fraudulent conveyances into two categories: fraud in law and fraud in fact. *Tcherepnin v. Franz,* 475 F.Supp. 92, 96 (N.D.Ill.1979). In fraud in fact cases, a court must find a specific intent to defraud creditors; in fraud in law cases, fraud is presumed from the circumstances. *Id.*

Count VIII of Wieboldt's complaint purports to state a claim against the insider and controlling shareholders, Schedule A shareholders, and State Street defendants for fraud in law. Fraud in law occurs when a debtor makes a voluntary transfer without consideration, and the transfer impairs the rights of creditors. *Tcherepnin v. Franz,* 457 F.Supp. 832, 836 (N.D.Ill.1978). To state a claim for fraud in law, a plaintiff must allege: (1) a voluntary gift; (2) an existing or contemplated indebtedness against the debtor; and (3) the failure of the debtor to retain sufficient property to pay the indebtedness. *United States ex rel. Hartigan v. Alaska,* 661 F.Supp. 727, 729 (N.D.Ill.1987); *Tcherepnin,* 457 F.Supp. at 836. Wieboldt's complaint alleges that the LBO transfers were fraudulent because "Wieboldt did not receive fair consideration for the property it conveyed and was insolvent at the time of the conveyance because it was then unable to meet its obligations as they became due." (Complaint ¶ 144).

Wieboldt's complaint clearly alleges the elements of fraud in law. Although Wieboldt's complaint does not specifically allege that it made a "voluntary gift," a transfer for grossly inadequate consideration is deemed to be a "voluntary gift" under Illinois law. *Indiana National Bank v. Gamble,* 612 F.Supp. 1272, 1276 (N.D.Ill.1984). As previously discussed, Wieboldt did not receive a benefit from these transfers. *See* Section 111.C.a(2) of this opinion. Second, Wieboldt clearly was obligated to a number of entities at the time of the transfers and in fact had defaulted on its obligations to CINB. (Complaint ¶¶ 43, 55). Finally, Wieboldt alleges that the LBO transfers rendered it insolvent. (Complaint ¶ 44). An insolvent corporation does not have sufficient assets to repay its obligations. The complaint therefore satisfies the elements of fraud in law under Section 4.

Defendants nevertheless assert that Wieboldt cannot state a claim under the Illinois statute because the "bona fide purchaser" rule in Section 5 protects them from liability. Section 5 of Chapter 59 provides:

> [Section 4] shall not affect the title of a purchaser for a valuable consideration, unless it appears that he had notice of the fraudulent intent of his immediate grantor, or of the fraud rendering void the title of such grantor.

Ill.Rev.Stat. ch. 59, ¶ 5 (1976).

The court need not dismiss the complaint on the ground that Wieboldt failed to negate the elements of Section 5. Section 5 provides an affirmative defense to charges that an entity received a fraudulent conveyance. *See Tcherepnin v. Franz,* 485 F.2d 1251, 1259 (7th Cir. 1973), *cert. denied McGurren v. Ettelson,* 415 U.S. 918, 94 S.Ct. 1416, 39 L.Ed.2d 472 (1974). A plaintiff is not required to plead facts showing that the defendants are *not* bona fide purchasers of the property. *Cf. Reagan v. Baird,* 94 Ill.Dec. 151, 158, 487 N.E.2d 1028, 140 Ill.App.3d 58 (1985), where the court held that a plaintiff need not establish that the transferee knew of or participated in the fraud in order to set aside a fraudulent conveyance.

In sum, the court cannot dismiss Wieboldt's claim under Section 4 of the Illinois statute. Defendants' motion to dismiss Count VIII is denied.

* * *

IN RE THE OHIO CORRUGATING COMPANY

United States Bankruptcy Court, Northern District of Ohio, 1988.
91 B.R. 430.

WILLIAM T. BODOH, BANKRUPTCY JUDGE.

This cause comes before the Court on the Amended Complaint filed by the Official Creditors Committee ("OCC") on April 13, 1987. The Complaint seeks a determination that the transfer and obligations incurred by the Debtor in connection with a leveraged buyout ("LBO")[1] should be avoided pursuant to both applicable federal and state law. This is a core proceeding as set forth in 28 U.S.C. Sec. 157(b)(2)(H).

BACKGROUND

In 1983, MALCOLM SHEPPARD began exploring the possibility of acquiring a manufacturing company through a fully leveraged buyout. In 1984, Mr. Sheppard was introduced to the Debtor as a potential acquisition. The Debtor was a manufacturer of steel containers for the chemical and agricultural industries. Mr. Sheppard visited the Debtor's operations on July 17, 1984, and subsequently commenced an investigation into the feasibility of acquiring and operating the Debtor. The Debtor had sustained a net loss in 1982 of approximately Three Hundred Five Thousand & 00/100 Dollars ($305,000.00) while experiencing net income of approximately Eighty–Two Thousand & 00/100 Dollars ($82,000.00) in 1983. Financial forecasts prepared in August 1984 projected losses for September, October, and November 1984, with a projected profit expected in December 1984. In anticipation of a purchase, Mr. Sheppard formed DPAC, INC. ("DPAC I") in August 1984. He was at all times its sole shareholder and director.

---

1. An LBO, or leveraged buyout, is a business transaction in which a company is sold under a financial arrangement whereby the purchasers borrow all, or substantially all, of the purchase price which is secured by mortgages on the assets of the selling company.

On November 14, 1984, DPAC, INC. ("DPAC I"), and the Debtor entered into a loan agreement with SECURITY PACIFIC BUSINESS CREDIT, INC. ("SP"), whereby SP agreed to loan DPAC I One Million, Four Hundred Seventy-Five Thousand & 00/100 Dollars ($1,475,000.00) so that DPAC I could acquire the Debtor's stock from the shareholders of the Debtor. SP also agreed to finance the Debtor's working capital needs by allowing the Debtor to borrow against certain of its accounts receivable, thereby creating a revolving line of credit. In return, SP was to be granted a first-position security interest in all of the unencumbered assets of the Debtor.

After the loan transaction was completed, a new company called GEOROMAC, INC., was formed. As a result of numerous transactions, DPAC I was merged into the Debtor with the Debtor assuming part of the DPAC I obligation to SP of One Million, Three Hundred Thousand, Two Hundred & 00/100 Dollars ($1,300,200.00), secured by a lien on all of the assets of the Debtor. GEOROMAC also became sole shareholder of the Debtor and changed its name to DPAC, INC. ("DPAC II").

After the acquisition, it appears that the new management team effected various changes in the Debtor's operations to minimize expenses. The Debtor's operations apparently were successful during the first four months of operation. Beginning in April 1985, however, a significant price deterioration in the market occurred, resulting in a sizeable loss of sales volume because of the Debtor's inability to reduce its prices and stay competitive. At the same time, SP substantially reduced the number of accounts against which the Debtor could borrow, thereby curtailing the Debtor's revolving line of credit.

The Debtor filed its Voluntary Petition under Chapter 11 of Title 11 September 30, 1985. The Debtor's commission agent, who was responsible for approximately half of the Debtor's sales volume, terminated his services when the Petition was filed. As a result, reorganization became impossible and a liquidation of the business was planned. At the time of the filing of the Petition, all creditors' claims against the Company on November 14, 1984, had been fully paid. In fact, trade creditors' accounts turned over six or seven times during the Company's ten months of operation after the buyout.

When creditors realized that there would be insufficient funds for distribution to them upon liquidation, the OCC demanded that the Debtor-in-Possession take the necessary actions to avoid the transactions involved in the LBO on the grounds that it was fraudulent as to creditors of the Debtor. The Debtor took no action in response to this demand. By Order dated January 13, 1986, the Court authorized the OCC to initiate the present adversary action. As a result, the OCC originally filed this adversary action on January 13, 1986. The Amended Complaint filed on April 13, 1987, contains three (3) counts. The First Count charges that SP's loan and resultant collateralization in substantially all of the Debtor's property was a fraudulent transfer pursuant to 11 U.S.C. Sec. 548. The Second Count alleges that the same transactions constitute a fraudulent conveyance pursuant to Chapter 1336 of the Ohio Revised Code. The final count avers that the purchase of capital stock constituted an impermissible redemption of stock by reason of Ohio Rev.Code Sec. 1701.35. A trial on this matter was commenced on February 29, 1988, and concluded on March 2, 1988.

I. *Preliminary Matters*

Before considering the testimony and evidence adduced at trial, the Court wishes to address, in a preliminary fashion, three threshold issues which arise in connection with this proceeding. The Defendants urge that fraudulent conveyance law (1) is generally inapplicable to LBOs, (2) is specifically inapplicable to acquirers in an LBO, and (3) does not protect creditors whose claim matured subsequent to the transfer. We will deal with each seriatim.

A. *Applicability of Fraudulent Conveyance Law to LBOs*

In a previous Opinion, this Court determined that federal and state statutes governing fraudulent conveyances generally could be applied to avoid LBOs. *In re Ohio Corrugating Co.,* 70 B.R. 920 (Bankr.N.D.Ohio 1987). In their Post–Trial Brief, the Defendants challenge that finding by referring the Court to the holding in *Credit Managers Ass'n. v. Federal Co.,* 629 F.Supp. 175 (C.D.Cal.1985), in which the court questioned the applicability of fraudulent conveyance law to LBOs. Contrary to defendant's assertion, the court in *Credit Managers* did not decide that fraudulent conveyance law was inapplicable to LBOs. In fact, the court reserved its decision on this issue when it wrote:

> As this 'important conceptual question' [whether an LBO presents fraudulent conveyance problems] was not briefed by the parties, and as there are other grounds for its decision, the court does not answer the question.

Id. at 179. Moreover, this Court does not find the questions raised in *Credit Managers* to be decisive. The fact that fraudulent conveyance law originally did not envision its use to avoid LBOs is not important. The very essence of common law is its adaptability to unique situations and changing fact patterns. If the rights of creditors have been impaired, we see no reason to except LBOs from the operation of fraudulent conveyance law if the transfers otherwise fit within the statutory framework. Furthermore, the suggestion in *Credit Managers* that LBOs ought to be exempted from fraudulent conveyance law because of the occasional benefit which might inure to creditors is not persuasive. In addition to the District Court's heavy reliance on an arguably incorrect reading of a commentary, that suggestion is largely a policy matter which is most appropriately left to the consideration of Congress and state legislatures. Additionally, this Court believes that whatever merit that argument may have in partially leveraged buyouts, the argument is meritless in fully leveraged buyouts such as this.

B. Applicability of Fraudulent Conveyance Law to Acquirers

The Defendants also contend that no authority exists for the proposition that transfers to a purchaser in an LBO constitute a fraudulent conveyance. It is true that the reported decisions thus far have focused on the avoidability of LBO transactions based on fraudulent conveyance actions involving lenders, * * *.

However, the Court believes there is as much reason to scrutinize the equivalency of the exchange between the purchaser and the selling company as between the lender or selling shareholders and the target company. Indeed, one writer has suggested:

> In the context of an LBO, the implicit transaction between the target and the acquirer must be examined in order to determine whether a fraudulent conveyance has occurred. The target conveys value to the acquirer when the target becomes bound under the terms of the lending agreement. The acquirer gains by incurring a lower rate of interest, or by even procuring credit at all. The lender, in contrast, has not been enriched; the value of the target's guarantee is offset by the proceeds of the loan * * *. It is the acquirer, not the lender, who receives the benefit of the target's guarantee. Thus, the existence *vel non* of arms-length bargaining between the target and the lender is largely irrelevant to the question of whether or to what extent the target received fair consideration.

Note, Fraudulent Conveyance Law and Leveraged Buyouts, supra note 3, at 1503–04. The Court is persuaded that transfers between a purchaser and the target company in an LBO may be avoided as a fraudulent transfer.

C. Applicability of Fraudulent Conveyance Law to Subsequent Creditors

The Defendants also suggest that fraudulent conveyance law may only be used to protect creditors who had a claim at the time the transfer was made. In support of this position, the Defendants cite *Credit Managers,* 629 F.Supp. at 180.

Section 548 of the Bankruptcy Code specifies the circumstances under which a conveyance may be considered fraudulent and, thus, avoidable. Sec. 548(a)(1) requires actual fraudulent intent while Sec. 548(a)(2) is a constructive fraud provision. Under this latter Section, a transfer is conclusively presumed to be fraudulent when certain conditions are met. This is the Section under which the OCC is proceeding in the present case.

It is this Court's considered opinion that the constructive fraud provisions of the Bankruptcy Code may only be invoked to protect creditors whose claims existed at the time the conveyance was made or the obligation was incurred. We reach this conclusion for several reasons. Initially, it must be recognized that fraudulent conveyance laws were intended to protect creditors who were otherwise unable to protect their interests when faced with impairment of those interests by debtors' actions. It appears to the Court that subsequent creditors are in a substantially different position from existing creditors. In this case, creditors appear to have willingly extended credit to the Debtor after the buyout in reliance on the performance of the "new" company. There is no suggestion that creditors were unaware of the change in either the management or the financial position of the Debtor. In fact, there was testimony that many creditors were given a current financial statement. We see no basis here for holding that the constructive fraud provisions of 11 U.S.C. Sec. 548 may be utilized as a form of insurance for creditors whose claims matured after the buyout. As the court wrote in *Credit Managers:*

> Credit could liberally be extended to such companies regardless of their assets or cash flow with the knowledge that the buyout could always be attacked later if the company folded.

Id. at 181. Our interpretation of 11 U.S.C. Sec. 548(a)(2) is consistent with the recent decision by the Ninth Circuit in *Kupetz v. Wolf,* 845 F.2d 842 (9th Cir.1988). Our finding here effectively disposes of the OCC's complaint as it relates to liability under the Bankruptcy Code because it was undisputed that the creditors' claims involved in this action arose after the buyout. We wish to point out, however, that even if our view of Sec. 548(a)(2) is incorrect, the OCC still would not be entitled to judgment under the Bankruptcy Code. The Court makes this alternative finding in order to expedite administration of this estate if a reviewing court should determine that the constructive fraud provisions in 11 U.S.C. Sec. 548(a)(2) may be utilized to protect creditors whose claims mature subsequent to the buyout.

II. Fraudulent Conveyances Under the Bankruptcy Code

11 U.S.C. Sec. 548(a)(2) provides:

* * *

The burden of proof rests on the party alleging the presence of an avoidable transfer. Thus, in order to prevail under Sec. 548(a)(2), the OCC must establish four (4) elements:

(1) A debtor's interest in property was transferred;

(2) The transfer occurred within one (1) year preceding the Petition date;

(3) An exchange for less than a reasonably equivalent value occurred;

(4) The debtor was either insolvent or severely undercapitalized on the date of transfer or was rendered insolvent or undercapitalized as a result of the transfer.

In re Duque Rodriquez, 77 B.R. 939, 940 (Bankr.S.D.Fla.1987); *In re Butcher,* 72 B.R. 447, 449 (Bankr.E.D.Tenn.1987).

The Defendants do not contest the first two elements. Indeed, it appears that the Debtor transferred a security interest in substantially all of its property to SP for the loan obligation, the proceeds of which was received by DPAC I. Similarly, it is also beyond dispute that the questionable transfer occurred within one (1) year of September 30, 1985, the date of filing the Petition. Therefore, the Court need only address the latter two elements.

A. *Reasonably Equivalent Value*

The OCC contends that the Debtor did not receive a reasonably equivalent value in exchange for its incurring of the loan obligation and transferring of the security interest. The standard requires the Debtor to have received either a direct or indirect economic benefit in order to constitute reasonably equivalent value. *In re Ohio Corrugating Co.,* 70 B.R. at 927. In this proceeding, the Debtor incurred an obligation whereby it encumbered virtually all of its assets to SP for the benefit of DPAC I, which received the loan proceeds used to purchase the Debtor's outstanding stock. DPAC I then conveyed the Debtor's stock to DPAC II, of which Mr. Sheppard was the sole shareholder. Thus, DPAC I received a controlling equity interest in the Debtor without any transfer of consideration to the Debtor in exchange for the Debtor's incurrence of a security interest in virtually all of its assets. As a result, the Debtor did not receive a reasonably equivalent value in exchange for the obligation it incurred. DPAC II, as the successor in interest to DPAC I, expressly assumed most of the liabilities of DPAC I, including the liability resulting from the fraudulent transfer.[6] As a result, the liability of DPAC I and DPAC II is coterminous.

B. *Financial Condition of the Debtor*

The other element which the OCC must prove in this proceeding is that the Debtor's financial condition fulfilled the statutory provisions. The Code specifies three (3) alternative showings which may establish this element. Plaintiff must show that the debtor (1) was insolvent either before or as a result of the transfer; or (2) was undercapitalized; or (3) intended or believed debts would be incurred beyond its ability to pay as such debts matured. We need not deal with the latter two elements because the OCC elected to proceed on the basis of the Debtor's insolvency alone.

A debtor is deemed to be insolvent when "the sum of such entity's debts is greater than * * * [a fair valuation] of such entity's property." 11 U.S.C. Sec. 101(31)(A). Fair valuation has been construed to refer to the fair market value of the Debtor's assets and liabilities within a reasonable time of the transfer. *Briden v. Foley,* 776 F.2d 379, 382 (1st

---

6. Even if there had been no express assumption, it appears that the transferee of an acquirer would not be insulated from the right of avoidance by reason of that transfer. 11 U.S.C. Sec. 550(a). Accordingly, the Court believes that when an original purchaser in an LBO conveys property (which was acquired in a transaction subject to avoidance as a fraudulent conveyance), the transferee takes the property subject to a right of avoidance unless the transferee is a bona fide purchaser for value without notice. 11 U.S.C. Sec. 550(b).

Cir.1985). This explanation was expanded upon by the court in *In re Joe Flynn Rare Coins, Inc.,* 81 B.R. 1009 (Bankr.D.Kan.1988), where it wrote:

> [F]air value does not mean the amount the property would bring in the worst circumstances or in the best * * *. For example, a forced sale price is not fair value though it may be used as evidence on the question of fair value * * *. The general idea of fair value is the amount of money the debtor could raise from its property in a short period of time, but not so short as to approximate a forced sale, if the debtor operated as a reasonably prudent and diligent businessman with his interests in mind, especially a proper concern for the payment of his debts.

Id. at 1017. We will shortly consider the merits of several differing valuations in analyzing the Debtor's solvency.[7] A plethora of financial information was introduced in an attempt to prove the insolvency of the Debtor after the transfer date of November 14, 1984. We will use the Debtor's November 30, 1984 balance sheet ("NBS") as a basis upon which to determine the Debtor's solvency. If the Court finds the Debtor was insolvent as of November 30, 1984, the Court can presume that the Debtor was also insolvent sixteen (16) days earlier, in the presence of evidence indicating the Debtor's financial situation had not changed materially during the intervening period.

The Debtor's NBS recites total liabilities of about 1.5 million dollars against total assets of approximately 3.8 million. However, the OCC contends that the Debtor's balance sheets must be modified in several important respects in order to produce a balance sheet which more nearly reflects the actual financial condition of the Debtor.

1. Valuation of Assets

The Plaintiff first maintains that the value of land, machinery and equipment ought to be recalculated. The Defendants support a valuation of One Million, Four Hundred Twenty-Six Thousand, Six Hundred Four & 00/100 Dollars ($1,426,604.00) for the property, plant and equipment. The Court believes that such a valuation would be excessive. The Court will accept the Andrako and Associates appraisal of Four Hundred Fifty Thousand & 00/100 Dollars ($450,000.00) as the base value for the land, buildings and two cranes. However, the appraisal evidently did not make adjustment for the needed repair and replacement of the roof covering the plant building. Documentary evidence indicates that a cost of Two Hundred Eighty-Six Thousand & 00/100 Dollars ($286,000.00) had been quoted for such a replacement. Testimony also indicated that required roof repairs in excess of Forty Thousand

---

7. We reject the OCC's contention that going-concern valuations are unreasonable. As *Collier on Bankruptcy* suggests:

There is overwhelming authority to the effect that normally * * * [fair] valuation must be made from the vantage of a going concern and that subsequent dismemberment or impossibility to dispose of plant, equipment, inventory, etc., as an entirety should not enter into the picture.

2 *Collier on Bankruptcy,* Sec. 101.31[4] (15th ed. 1988).

& 00/100 Dollars ($40,000.00) would have to be deducted dollar for dollar from the appraisal. Thus, if Two Hundred Forty–Six Thousand & 00/100 Dollars ($246,000.00) is subtracted from the Andrako appraisal, a remainder of Two Hundred Four Thousand & 00/100 Dollars ($204,-000.00) is left. Accordingly, the Court assigns this value to the property and buildings.

The value assigned to the machinery and equipment has shown considerable variance. A walk-through appraisal ("wta") of Six Hundred Fifty Thousand & 00/100 Dollars ($650,000.00) was rendered on October 8, 1984. On November 5, 1984, a "going concern" value ("gcv") of the machinery was set at One Million & 00/100 Dollars ($1,000,000.00). Finally, a "nuts and bolts" appraisal ("nba") of Four Hundred Eighty–Two Thousand, Nine Hundred Twenty–Five & 00/100 Dollars ($482,925.00) was given on August 23, 1985. A "wta" is generally considered to be an approximation based upon visual inspection. On the other hand, an "nba" involves the identification and listing of each item of machinery and equipment to which values are assigned. The Court finds the "nba" to be more reliable than the "wta" based upon the character of the two appraisals. We also credit the "nba" over the "gcv" because the "nba" more nearly reflects a proportional amount of the eventual sale price of Four Hundred Sixty Thousand & 00/100 Dollars ($460,000.00) for all assets of the estate conducted in May, 1986. Accordingly, for purposes of determining insolvency, the Court will credit the "nba" of Four Hundred Eighty–Two Thousand, Nine Hundred Twenty–Five & 00/100 Dollars ($482,925.00).

The OCC also suggests that the inventory should be discounted by percentages which would reflect the amount one could realize from a public auction. However, the Court believes this would unfairly assign a liquidation value to the inventory rather than a going concern value. Indeed, it appears to the Court that the inventory ought to be valued on a cost basis rather than the LIFO adjusted basis which was utilized. We feel the cost basis more accurately reflects a going concern value than the LIFO adjusted basis. Therefore, the Court's reconstituted balance sheet will show inventory valued at cost.

2. *Undisclosed Liabilities*

The Plaintiff also contends that the Debtor failed to record a number of liabilities on its balance sheet. First, the Plaintiff charges unfunded benefits arising under the Pension Plan amounted to a minimum of Five Hundred Sixty–Two Thousand, Eighteen & 00/100 Dollars ($562,018.00), which amount should have been noted as a liability on the Debtor's balance sheet. In response, the Defendants introduced testimony by Mr. Robert Grace, a managing partner in Ernst & Whinney. Mr. Grace indicated that

> [T]he disclosure of vested benefits or past-service kinds of liabilities are * * * future liabilities and * * * appropriate accounting * * * would not require those kinds of liabilities to be recorded [before the benefits actually accrue].

The Court recognizes that generally accepted accounting principles ("GAAP") do not control a court's decision regarding the solvency of an entity. However, the Court is inclined to assign presumptive validity to the treatment of assets and liabilities according to GAAP. To do otherwise would unfairly penalize the LBO participants who reasonably relied on GAAP in assessing the solvency of the Debtor prior to the buyout. In this case, the Plaintiff failed to show the unreasonableness of treating the liability for unfunded Plan benefits as a future liability justifying its exclusion from the balance sheet.

Furthermore, Announcement 36 from the Financial Accounting Services Board (FASB 36) only requires footnote disclosure of unfunded defined benefit plan obligations; it requires inclusion neither on the balance sheet nor in a court's solvency analysis. The Plaintiff's contention that off-balance sheet liabilities should be considered in a solvency analysis are not well-taken. The Court feels that participants in an LBO must be protected from the perfect hindsight often evidenced in creditors' subsequent attacks on the corporate buyout. GAAP is a reasonable measure of what liabilities ought to be included in a balance sheet and, therefore, in the solvency analysis.

None of the cases cited by the OCC to support the inclusion of contingent liabilities in a solvency analysis interpret Section 548 of the Bankruptcy Code. Finally, the Court is unconvinced that valuing the Plan's bond portfolio at maturity value was patently unreasonable given the fact that the Debtor intended to hold the bonds until maturity.

The only other significant unrecorded liability appears to be approximately Four Hundred Seventy-Two Thousand & 00/100 Dollars ($472,000.00) in steel invoices. The absence of such entries would materially affect the accuracy of liabilities noted on a balance sheet. As a result, this amount will have to be recognized on the Court's reconstituted balance sheet. The Court considers the undisclosed liability of Two Thousand, Two Hundred Two & 00/100 Dollars ($2,202.00) attributable to a 1983 automobile lease to be insignificant and of minimal impact. Finally, speculation concerning uncertain and indeterminate liability resulting from possible environmental violations must be discounted.

The Defendants contend that the Debtor was solvent because it was able to pay its debts as such obligations matured. This argument will be considered below. However, it should be noted that if insolvency is clearly demonstrated according to a balance sheet determination, the Debtor's ability to pay its debts as they mature is irrelevant. On the other hand, the Debtor's ability to pay its debts as they mature may be relevant where evidence of balance sheet insolvency appears to be either speculative or inconclusive.

Based on the foregoing, the Court believes that the most accurate balance sheet which can be compiled to determine the Debtor's solvency would reveal the following financial condition as of November 30, 1984:

ASSETS
Cash/Accounts Receivable/Securities	$ 760,712
Inventories	700,464
Prepaid Expenses/Miscellaneous	86,962
Machine & Equipment	482,925
Property & Buildings	204,000
Total Assets	$2,235,063

LIABILITIES
Accounts Payable	$1,343,123
Accrued Expenses	290,023
SP Loan	1,300,000
Total Liabilities	$2,933,146.

While the reconstituted balance sheet would indicate that the Debtor was insolvent by almost Seven Hundred Thousand & 00/100 Dollars ($700,000.00), we are not confident that this balance sheet is entirely accurate. We view the reconstituted balance sheet to be important evidence tending to show the Debtor's insolvency. But, our lack of faith in the numbers precludes us from according a conclusive presumption of insolvency of the Debtor based on the reconstituted balance sheet alone. As a result, the Court feels the need to canvass other factors in order to determine whether or not they would support a finding of insolvency.

  3. *Other Factors*

There is no evidence that DPAC I, DPAC II, or MALCOLM SHEPPARD ever intended to defraud the Debtor's creditors. Indeed, this Court rejected such a claim when it ruled on the Defendant's Motions for Summary Judgment. *In re Ohio Corrugating Company,* 70 B.R. at 928. While a fraudulent conveyance claim may be established by constructive intent, the OCC has not upheld its burden of proof to support a finding of constructive fraud. Furthermore, there appears to be a requirement of a small degree of scienter or awareness of fraud in cases brought under Sec. 548(a)(2) for the purpose of avoiding LBOs. This was the approach taken in *Kupetz v. Wolf,* 845 F.2d at 842. While the Court believes that the constructive fraud provisions ought to be construed as requiring some degree of scienter, it is unnecessary to so hold. It is enough to find that Defendant's intent would not contribute anything to buttress a finding of insolvency.

The Debtor's history of operating losses is cited by the Plaintiff as evidence of insolvency. However, the Court is reluctant to rely on these reports because it appears that the profit/loss figures are skewed in both 1982 and 1983. In 1982, the Debtor elected to discontinue the steel pail line and wrote it down to its estimated realizable value, resulting in a sizeable loss. In 1983, the line was sold at a profit, which contributed to the profit that Debtor reported that year. In addition, the Court does not feel that any helpful inferences can be drawn regarding the Debtor's solvency in 1984 from the Debtor's profitability in the years preceding 1982.

The most important factor which tends to support the Debtor's solvency after the buyout was its ability and practice of paying its debts as they matured. Testimony showed that during the Debtor's normal operating cycles, trade creditors were paid off at least six or seven times over the ten-month period of operation after the buyout. This may have been due, in large part, to the revolving line of credit provided by SP which allowed the Debtor to borrow against its accounts receivable. In any event, this factor tends to belie the contention that this was a company which was in the throes of insolvency.

Finally, the Court is not convinced that Debtor's insolvency resulted from the buyout. The Court is persuaded that industry-wide price reductions, declining sales volumes, and an inability to borrow fully against its accounts receivable were primarily responsible for the Debtor's eventual insolvency.

In summation, the Court must find that there is insufficient evidence to buttress the inference of insolvency drawn from the admittedly doubtful reconstituted balance sheet. Thus, we must find that the OCC failed to sustain its burden of proving insolvency which is necessary if we are to find liability under Sec. 548 of the Bankruptcy Code.

III. Fraudulent Conveyances Under Ohio Law

Ohio Revised Code Ann. Sec. 1336.04 (Anderson, 1979) provides:

> Every conveyance made and every obligation incurred by a person who is or will be thereby rendered insolvent is fraudulent as to creditors without regard to his actual intent if the conveyance is made or the obligation is incurred without a fair consideration.

As in our consideration under 11 U.S.C. Sec. 548(a)(2), the threshold issue that must be addressed is whether subsequent creditors may assert a cause of action based on the constructive fraud provision found in Ohio Rev.Code Sec. 1336.04. This Court finds that Ohio law does not permit a creditor whose claim matured subsequent to the allegedly fraudulent transfer to set aside the transfer pursuant to Ohio Rev.Code Sec. 1336.04. An early Ohio Supreme Court case held that a conveyance was not avoidable for merely constructive fraud at the instance of a subsequent creditor. *MacQueen v. Dollar Sav. Bank Co.*, 133 Ohio St. 579, 15 N.E.2d 529 (1938). Although Ohio Rev.Code Secs. 1336.05 and 1336.06 now speak explicitly in terms of authorizing certain constructive fraud actions against future creditors, Sec. 1336.04 is silent as to its applicability to future creditors. By including subsequent creditors in the constructive fraud provisions found in Ohio Rev.Code Secs. 1336.05 and 1336.06, we are compelled to presume that the Ohio legislature purposely excluded subsequent creditors from the ambit of the constructive fraud provision found in Ohio Rev.Code Sec. 1336.04. Thus, the *MacQueen* decision continues to be valid as it pertains to that provision.

The Court has already outlined how all creditors who existed at the time of the buyout have been paid, and all present claims were created after the transaction. Therefore, we find no obligation of the Defendants on the basis of Ohio Rev.Code Sec. 1336.04.

IV. *Improper Stock Redemption*

The OCC's final argument is that the LBO constituted an impermissible redemption of stock under state law. Ohio Rev.Code Ann. Sec. 1701.35 (Anderson 1985) reads, in part:

> (B) A corporation shall not purchase its own shares, except as provided in this Section, nor shall a corporation purchase or redeem its own shares if immediately thereafter its assets would be less than its liabilities plus its stated capital, if any, or if the corporation is insolvent, or if there is reasonable ground to believe that by such purchase or redemption it would be rendered insolvent.

As used in this Section, "insolvent" means that "the corporation is unable to pay its obligations as they become due in the usual course of affairs." Ohio Rev.Code Ann. Sec. 1701.01(O)(Anderson 1985 & Supp. 1987).

The Court does not view the payments to the Debtor's former shareholders as a distribution *by the Debtor* to its former shareholders. They received the payments to which they were entitled under the agreement with DPAC I. Furthermore, even if these payments were deemed to be distributions within the meaning of Ohio Rev.Code Ann. Sec. 1701.35(B), the Court has already outlined how the Debtor paid its obligations as they matured over after the buyout. Thus, the Debtor would not be "insolvent" as that term is defined for purposes of Ohio corporate law in Ohio Rev.Code Ann. Sec. 1701.01(O)(Anderson 1985 & Supp.1987). Accordingly, the OCC's final argument is not well-taken.

Conclusion

While transfers between a purchaser and the target company in an LBO ought to be subject to avoidance as a fraudulent transfer, a purchaser in an LBO transaction should not be required to be an insurer of the ultimate success of the purchased enterprise, except by legislative action determining public economic policy. Our extensive consideration of the evidence and applicable law in this action convinces us that, as regards the remaining Defendants, DPAC II and MALCOLM K. SHEPPARD, there is an insufficient basis shown for avoiding this LBO transaction. Judgment shall be entered for Defendants DPAC II and MALCOLM K. SHEPPARD.

This Memorandum Opinion shall constitute the Court's findings and conclusions pursuant to Bankruptcy Rule 7052. An appropriate Order shall enter.

Note

In *Kaiser Steel Corp. v. Charles Schwab & Co., Inc.*, 913 F.2d 846 (10th Cir.1990), an outside group agreed to purchase all outstanding Kaiser Steel common stock and to merge with Kaiser Steel. Under the LBO agreement, a tendered share would be converted into $22.00 and two shares of preferred stock in the new entity.

Some of Schwab's customers were beneficial owners of Kaiser Steel common stock. Most of the actual certificates were held by a securities clearinghouse called the Depository Trust Company ("DTC"). DTC tendered and received the cash and preferred stock. The money was transferred to Schwab, which in turn credited the customers' accounts.

Kaiser Steel filed for bankruptcy three years later. The DIP then brought a fraudulent conveyance action against several defendants involved in the LBO, including Schwab. Schwab then moved for summary judgment on two separate grounds. First, Schwab argued that it was not liable because it was a "mere conduit" instead of a transferee. See 11 U.S.C. § 550(a). Second, the brokerage contended that the LBO payments were exempt from avoidance as settlement payments under section 546(e). Judge Anderson of the Tenth Circuit affirmed the district court's grant of summary judgment on the settlement issue without reaching the conduit question.

The ultimate holding in the case was that Schwab's LBO payments were settlement payments within the meaning of sections 546(e) and 741(8). The court initially found that section 741(8)'s definition of "settlement payment" was extremely broad in scope. It then found that this interpretation was consistent with the legislative intent underlying section 546. This intent was "to protect the nation's financial markets from the instability caused by the reversal of settled securities transactions." 913 F.2d at 848 (quoting *Kaiser Steel Resources, Inc. v. Jacobs,* 110 B.R. 514, 522 (D.Colo.1990)). Finally, the court concluded that this interpretation of "settlement payment" was consistent with the way the securities industry defined "settlement," e.g., the "completion of a securities transaction." 913 F.2d at 849 (quoting A. Pessin & J. Ross, *Words of Wall Street: 2000 Investment Terms Defined* 227 (1983)).

Kaiser Steel took the position that, because none of the legislative history discussed LBOs or other exceptional transactions, section 546(e) was meant to apply only to routine securities transactions. While conceding that this position was not entirely invalid, the court nonetheless refused to read this limitation into the Code due to the absence of any restrictions in sections 546(e) or 741(8). Otherwise, the court said that it would be engaging in "an act of judicial legislation." 913 F.2d at 850.

Question

If *Kaiser Steel* is correct, section 546(e) protects not only intermediaries such as Schwab, but also shareholders, and if other cases holding secured creditors liable are allowed to stand, the law will be exactly backwards, not so? To the extent someone gets an undeserved benefit in the LBO, it must be the shareholders of the target company, who by virtue of the LBO are lifted over those who are nominally superior to them, namely, the creditors. Yet, if *Kaiser Steel* stands, those people will be immunized (at least in many LBO cases), while the bank that actually put new and good funds into the LBO will itself be punished. What is the solution?

Problem 7–30

In the Dinah acquisition described at the outset of this Section, assume that the preexisting debt owed by Dinah Cotton was in the form of public bonds issued several years prior to the leveraged acquisition. At the time the bonds were issued, Dinah was an established company of blue chip character, analogous to IBM, AT & T and similar companies. Because these companies never default on their debts, the Dinah bonds were issued at a 7 percent interest rate. They traded on the public markets at about 90 percent of face value. The acquisition changed the entire picture of the company, increasing its debt-equity ratio and greatly increasing the risk that Dinah might not pay its debts. The bond prices dropped immediately to 50 percent of face value.

1. Can the unsecured bondholders take any action to recover their "loss" before any actual default occurs?

2. If Dinah defaults on its bonds and on its secured debts three years after the acquisition and immediately files bankruptcy, what action should the bondholders seek from the trustee in bankruptcy? Will they be successful?

It is quite unclear whether other courts, and particularly the Supreme Court, will go down the path marked by *Ohio Corrugating* or that of *Wieboldt*. Apart from the general difficulty of applying an ancient statute to a new legal procedure, those challenging LBOs have had some difficulty in identifying the villain. On the one hand is the shareholder who has theoretically injured his creditor by bootstrapping himself over those creditors and "cashing out" at a time when the creditors are left unpaid. Yet in a public LBO, many, perhaps a large majority, of those shareholders are entirely passive. They are widows and orphans living in Council Bluffs, who, *mirabile dictu,* receive a large check in the mail for their RJR Nabisco shares one day. They have never been to Wall Street; they harbor not a single evil thought against the corporate creditors and they have taken no part whatsoever in the LBO.

Second are the banks. The banks in these cases have merely done what they routinely do, lend money and take security. Clearly the bank financing an LBO knows what is going on. Are they co-conspirators? Most of the early cases (and some of the recent) have difficulty finding any fault with the bank. Unless the transaction is "collapsed" (i.e., unless the court indulges in the fiction that the bank's money went directly to the shareholders, whereas the security came out of the target company), those challenging the banks have an insurmountable argument—that the debtor received reasonably equivalent value in the form of the loan that the bank made to the target company.

There are other problems as well. Among those are the questions raised in *Ohio Corrugating.* Although all of the relevant laws (UFCA, UFTA, and section 548) contemplate that "future creditors" can challenge a conveyance that occurred well before they were creditors, the theory upon which such challenge is apparently premised is a secret undercapitalization. That theory, of course, will not justify a fraudulent conveyance challenge to a publicly disclosed LBO. Consider a representative of Procter and Gamble who has continued to extend trade credit to Revco in the hundreds of thousands or even millions of dollars and who has received payments on that credit over a two year period. Procter and Gamble would hardly be ignorant of the LBO and would be hard-pressed to show that it had not made a conscious business decision to continue to lend despite the buyer's low capital and high leverage. If one is looking for a plaintiff to attack an LBO, surely such sophisticated short term lenders are among the least deserving.

An economist might look at this question in yet another way. He might also challenge the common LBO fraudulent conveyance analysis. The economist might argue that all debtors will adjust to the possibility of an LBO and that all creditors henceforth will build in a small LBO premium.

In some cases the premium is explicitly negotiated. Consider a case like *Revco* where the existing bondholders were given the option at the time of the LBO either to receive an increased interest payment or to become fully secured (along with the banks that were financing the LBO). Surely any argument out of the mouths of such bondholders is unpersuasive. Both those who took security and those who took higher interest knowingly confronted the modest capitalization and explicitly bargained for a particular kind of treatment with that knowledge. Why should they be permitted now to challenge the LBO two years later?

Anticipating the possibility of the bankruptcy of any LBO, all good bond lawyers will have negotiated for a term in the bond indenture that protects their creditors against such an eventuality. The agreement could take many forms. For example, it might make an LBO a default on the bonds so giving the creditors a right to proceed at once. Or it might require the debtor to grant security, to subordinate the LBO debt, or to increase the interest rate. Having gone through such a negotiation and having agreed to lend in the face of the LBO prospect, the complaint that the contemplated LBO now constitutes a fraudulent conveyance is weak.

Finally is the question whether the LBO is an evil that should be stamped out by the covert tool of fraudulent conveyance law. Some who are eager to attack LBOs as fraudulent conveyances probably harbor the belief that LBOs are antisocial behavior designed to make undeserving people rich and destined to throw deserving employees out of work. For such people it is mere happenstance that the tool at hand is fraudulent conveyance law. What is the courts' proper role?

§ 7. AVOIDANCE OF POSTPETITION TRANSACTIONS

Transactions involving the debtor's property that occur after the filing of a voluntary or involuntary petition present a series of issues related to those discussed above. First, one should consider the sort of situation presented in *In re Phillips* [set forth at pp. 200 to 205] where the debtor has a strong motivation to pay certain creditors immediately. In that case, Phillips was an acoustical ceilings and walls contractor facing stoppage of all further payments due to it as a result of a threatened filing of a mechanics' lien by one of its unpaid suppliers. Thus, to ensure an uninterrupted flow of payments, Phillips needed to pay all suppliers with potential liens immediately. A similar situation exists where a company in Chapter 11 intends to rely upon certain creditors, perhaps those geographically closer, after reorganization but has no further use for others. In the absence of authorization by the court such as that obtained in *In re Phillips,* postpetition payments to such creditors may be avoided by the trustee under section 549.

One must also consider the rights of one who buys something from the debtor or sells something to the debtor after the petition and in ignorance of its filing. Analogous problems are presented when bailees and quasi-bailees follow the debtor's instructions, instructions sometimes issued prior to the filing of the petition and thus deliver property of the debtor not to the debtor's estate or trustee but to third parties. A classical case of this sort is the "Bank of Marin" problem, in which a bank, owing a debt in the form of a deposit to the debtor, pays a check drawn against that deposit after the petition is filed. *Bank of Marin v. England,* 385 U.S. 99, 87 S.Ct. 274, 17 L.Ed.2d 197 (1966). In *Marin* the trustee challenged that distribution and argued that the bank had misappropriated the funds of the bankruptcy estate. No less appealing is the case of the buyer of real estate who conducts a closing and pays his money in ignorance of the petition that has been filed immediately preceding that closing.

Finally are two other problems. The first involves the title of a person, who through a series of transfers, receives an asset which the debtor initially transferred in a voidable transaction. The second is the case of the secured creditor who claims proceeds and after-acquired property. That creditor may look to and be relying on assets acquired by the debtor's estate in postpetition transactions. Here the difficulty does not arise because of the continuing apparent authority of the debtor to deal in his own proceeds, but the converse: they raise the issue of the true title of the debtor in possession or trustee.

These problems are addressed in four sections of the Bankruptcy Code: section 549 (dealing with the general problem of transfers by the debtor after the filing of the petition), section 542(c)(dealing with the Bank of Marin problem), section 550 (dealing with the liability of the transferee of an avoided transfer, a transfer that may or may not have occurred after the petition had been filed), and section 552 (on the postpetition effect of a security interest). One can state the general principles set out in those sections as follows:

The general rule is that transfers out of the estate (except as authorized by section 363 to that trustee) after the petition are invalid and can be avoided under section 549. Transfers into the estate after the petition are generally not subject to the creditor's security interest and thus will be shared by all the creditors and will not be given directly to the secured creditor.

There are important exceptions to both of those rules. Initially one might take a look at section 549 and ask why there is a special rule in 549(b) for involuntary cases and another yet different special rule in 549(c) for transfers of real estate in counties outside that in which the case is filed. To test one's understanding of sections 549 and 542, consider the following problem.

Problem 7–31

1. Assume that the debtor, Micah, writes a check to payee, Jeremiah, for $10,000 on April 25. On April 27, Micah files a petition in bankruptcy and the check is presented for payment at the payor bank, Uriah National Bank and Trust, on May 2, and paid. The trustee now seeks to recover the $10,000 alternatively from Uriah National and Jeremiah. Compare section 542(c), section 549 and section 4–303 of the Uniform Commercial Code. The Bankruptcy Code states a clear rule about the payor's liability. The rule concerning the liability of the payee is less clear.

2. Assume the same facts, except instead of giving a check, Micah entered into an agreement to sell his new Mercedes to buyer for $35,000. On April 25, the two met and the buyer took possession of the car on May 1. Jeremiah paid Micah by certified check and obtained certificate of title. Assume that Jeremiah gave up the check in ignorance of the fact that Micah had filed a petition in bankruptcy two days previously.

   (a) Suppose Micah deposited Jeremiah's check in his bank account and upon the filing of the petition the account became property of the estate. May the trustee get the Mercedes back from Jeremiah? If so, could Jeremiah insist on the return of his $35,000?

   (b) Suppose Micah immediately spent the $35,000. What may the trustee recover from Jeremiah in this case?

3. Assume that the cashier's check had not been presented for payment at the time the trustee makes a claim on the Mercedes and that the buyer causes his bank to stop payment on the cashier's check. Can the trustee now sue on the check and also insist upon the return of the Mercedes under section 549?

Note

Consider now a typical floor plan or floating lien covering a merchandiser's inventory, present and after-acquired, accounts present and after-acquired, and proceeds. Such security interests abound. Without fail they claim proceeds and after-acquired collateral.

Assume, for example, that Solomon Bank had lent $2 million against $3 million worth of inventory at the time debtor, Delilah, declared bankruptcy. If it were a Chapter 11 case and the business continued in operation, Solomon Bank would be totally unsecured unless it were able to maintain a claim on the proceeds that arose from the sale of that collateral. If we assume further that the entire collateral would turn over within 30 days, then we find from section 552 that the security would not attach to after-acquired collateral, surely the secured creditor will have to have some right in the proceeds or he will have no effective collateral. It is in response to just that argument that section 552 grants the secured creditor an interest in "proceeds, product, offspring, rents or profits." Note the ominous statement that follows in section 552(b): "Except to the extent that the court, after notice and a hearing and based on the equities of the case, orders otherwise." What are the equities that would justify a decision otherwise? The quoted language was inserted from the Senate bill in lieu of the following language from the House bill, "Except to the extent that the estate acquired such proceeds, product, offspring, rents, or profits to the prejudice of other creditors holding unsecured claims." The language in Senate Report 95–989 that is reported in many versions of the Bankruptcy Code (including the widely distributed 1981 edition of the West Publishing Company) is written to go with the earlier Senate version that was not enacted. Is one to conclude that the exceptions governed by the "equities of the case" are more limited than those set out in that report that refers to "raw materials ... converted into inventory, inventory into accounts at some expense to the estate thus depleting the fund available for general unsecured creditors * * * "?

Chapter Eight

CLAIMS AND PRIORITIES

§ 1. INTRODUCTION

Claims practice in bankruptcy affects both how much a creditor obtains from the bankruptcy estate and whether a particular obligation owed by a debtor will be discharged at completion of the bankruptcy. Section 101(5) of the Code defines "claim" broadly. It contemplates that the bankruptcy case will deal with and resolve all of the legal obligations of the debtor. A claim is any "right to payment" or any "right to an equitable remedy * * * if breach [of such right] gives rise to a right to payment" regardless of whether these rights have been reduced to judgment or whether they are liquidated or unliquidated, matured or unmatured, contingent or fixed, undisputed or disputed.

Distribution from the bankruptcy estate to the holder of a claim does not occur unless the claim has been "allowed." Standards for claim allowance are contained in sections 502 and 509 of the Code. In most cases allowance is routine and most claims in bankruptcy are handled with little or no dispute. A proof of claim filed by a creditor is deemed allowed unless an objection to that claim occurs. 11 U.S.C. § 502(a). Where an objection is made, section 502(b) establishes the standards of allowability. Generally, claims enforceable under nonbankruptcy law are allowed; they are allowed in the amount established "as of the date of the filing of the petition."

But allowance does not equal payment. The Code makes a hierarchy of claims and generally provides that higher priority claims must be paid in full before lower priority claims receive anything from the estate. But even within the group of nonpriority general unsecured claims, there may not be a direct relationship between the amount allowed for various claims and their recovery from the estate. In a Chapter 7 case, the distribution among creditors of equal rank is pro rata. In Chapter 11, the reorganization plan determines distribution. The plan places creditors into classes and specifies the amount to be received by each class. Because of section 1129(a)(7) no creditor may receive less than that creditor would have received upon liquidation unless the creditor *individually* agrees. Even then creditors who would have received identical distributions on liquidation may receive different amounts in Chapter 11. That is because different creditors may be put in different classes and receive different assets (e.g. stock for one and cash for another). While these assets may be of nominally equal value, one may be worth more than another.

In addition to determining the amount that is likely to be distributed to a particular creditor, the existence and amount of a creditor's claim also determines the size of that creditor's vote and, in some cases, whether the creditor's right will be "discharged" at the end of the Chapter 7, Chapter 11, or other proceeding. Essentially every dollar of an allowed claim equals one vote within a class for the purpose of confirmation of a plan. The number of votes one holds in a Chapter 11 case may determine whose plan is confirmed, whose plan is rejected, and whose voice is the strongest in the negotiations.

Creditors' rights that have not yet risen to the level of claims cannot be allowed and are generally not discharged (although the latter statement is still controversial, at least in cases like *Manville* where there has been an attempt to limit the rights of tort claimants who technically do not hold "claims"). In the case of individual bankrupts some claims can be exempted from the discharge and will carry over against the debtor after the bankruptcy. Thus the nature and amount of the claim will sometimes have to be determined in order to know the effect of the discharge.

Problem 8–1

Havisham Lumber filed a petition in Chapter 11 on June 11, 1992. At that time it had assets of $2,200,000. The lumber yard was worth $1,500,000 and the personal property was worth $700,000.

What would be the least each of the following claimants could be forced to accept in Chapter 11 under section 1129(a)(7), i.e., what would each receive in a distribution in Chapter 7?

1. A mortgage loan secured by the lumberyard. The current principal balance on the mortgage loan is $2,100,000. The debtor is currently in default on fourteen monthly interest payments totalling $24,500. Two of the default months occurred before the petition; twelve are after the petition.

2. Unsecured notes with a face amount of $2,000,000. These notes bear interest at 15 percent payable monthly; the principal is payable in a lump sum in the year 2010. They are currently trading at 10 on the New York Stock Exchange. Interest payments were current when the petition was filed; no interest has been paid since.

3. $175,000 for lawyers' fees, employees' wages, and other business expenses, all incurred after the petition was filed.

4. $30,000 in prepetition wages owed to three corporate executives who have since been discharged.

5. Income tax for the years 1987 and 1989 of $306,000 and $26,000 respectively. You may assume that returns were timely filed, but that the amounts in question were not shown to be due. There is also a claim for withholding taxes that should have been paid in 1985 of $50,000.

Assume that Havisham makes the following proposals with respect to each of the claims. How would the creditors be expected to react?

1. Mortgage loan ($2,100,000 principal, $24,500 interest) $1,500,000 of principal will be paid in full with interest over ten years. The remaining $600,000 will be treated as an unsecured loan and paid pro rata with the other unsecured creditors. There will be no payment on the $24,500 interest claim because that is not an allowable claim under 502.

2. $2,000,000 of notes will be included in the estate as a $200,000 unsecured claim (the current value at which they are trading on the New York Stock Exchange) and will receive a pro rata payment based on that $200,000.

3. Postpetition wages and operating expenses will be paid in full upon confirmation. Postpetition lawyers' and accountants' fees will be paid over a five-year period without any interest payment.

4. The prepetition wages will be treated as unsecured debt and receive a pro rata payment.

5. Because they fall outside the three-year period in section 507, the income and withholding taxes will be treated as general unsecured debt.

You should be suspicious of the debtor's proposals; almost all of them are erroneous. To see why, dig around in sections 507, 502 and 523.

Note

Above we saw a partial list of creditors that was filed in the Action Auto case. In Chapter 11, Rule 3003 provides that the filing of such a schedule of liabilities pursuant to section 521(1) of the Code constitutes prima facie evidence of the validity of the amount of claims of the creditor. Rule 3003(b) goes on "it shall not be necessary for a creditor or equity security holder to file a proof of claim or interest except as provided * * * " Thus in Chapter 11—at least with respect to claims that are not disputed but are revealed on the debtor's schedule—the creditor need take no particular action in order to have its claim recognized in bankruptcy. However, if the claim is omitted from the schedule or if it is listed for a different amount than the creditor thinks is appropriate, then even in Chapter 11 the creditor must file its own proof of claim.

The normal rule in Chapters 7 and 13 (stated in Rule 3002) is that the creditor must itself file a proof of claim. Presumably it is the drafter's assumption that individuals who are the most frequent filers under Chapters 7 and 13 may not keep accurate books and that neither the court nor the creditors should rely upon filings that may be based upon fragmentary records. Under Rule 3002(c) the proof of claim must be filed normally under

Chapters 7 or 13 within ninety days after the first date set for the meeting of creditors, all pursuant to section 341(a) of the Code. In Chapter 11 the date after which filings are barred is left to the discretion of the court; Rule 3003(c)(3) instructs the court to "fix" such a date.

In some cases the debtor may be in such disarray (as because of a dissolution of a law firm) that no adequate schedule will be filed. In other cases the parties may be moved by certain strategic ideas in inviting (or not inviting) claims. Consider the notice of the bar date in the case of Gaston and Snow that was published December 23, 1991 in the *Wall Street Journal*. The case involved a law firm that was in a liquidating Chapter 11.

§ 1 INTRODUCTION

UNITED STATES BANKRUPTCY COURT
SOUTHERN DISTRICT OF NEW YORK
--x
In Re: :   Chapter 11
                                                  :   Case No. 91 B 14594 (CB)
GASTON & SNOW,   :
                                                  :
Debtor.   :
--x

NOTICE OF LAST DATE FOR FILING PROOFS OF CLAIMS AGAINST THE DEBTOR

NOTICE IS HEREBY GIVEN THAT the Honorable Cornelius Blackshear, United States Bankruptcy Judge, has made **JANUARY 23, 1992, AT 5:00 P.M. EASTERN STANDARD TIME AS THE LAST DATE AND TIME (THE "CLAIMS DATE") WHEN PERSONS MAY FILE CLAIMS AGAINST GASTON & SNOW, THE ABOVE-CAPTIONED DEBTOR (THE "DEBTOR")**. Only claims **received** on or before the Claims Date will be considered by the Debtor in accordance with the provisions of the Federal Rules of Bankruptcy Procedure Rule 3003.

"CLAIMS" means any and all claims against the Debtor of whatever character arising prior to or on October 25, 1991, that qualifies as a claim pursuant to section 101(4) of title 11, United States Code (the "Bankruptcy Code"), whether secured or unsecured, fixed or contingent, liquidated or unliquidated, including, but not limited to, all claims arising out of any act, error or omission of the Debtor (including, its members, associates and other persons for whose acts, errors or omissions the Debtor is legally responsible) in rendering or failing to render professional services for others in the Debtor's capacity as a lawyer, fiduciary, or notary public ("MALPRACTICE CLAIMS").

NORMALLY, A DEBTOR WILL FILE A SCHEDULE LISTING CLAIMS THAT ARE LIQUIDATED, UNDISPUTED AND NON-CONTINGENT PRIOR TO SETTING A CLAIMS DATE (THE "SCHEDULE OF LIABILITIES"). NO SCHEDULE OF LIABILITIES HAS YET BEEN FILED IN THIS CASE. THEREFORE, **EVERY CLAIMANT MUST** FILE A PROOF OF CLAIM BY THE CLAIMS DATE. IF YOU HAVE A CLAIM AND FAIL TO FILE A PROOF OF CLAIM IN THE MANNER PRESCRIBED BELOW ON OR BEFORE THE CLAIMS DATE STATED ABOVE, YOUR CLAIM WILL BE FOREVER BARRED, YOU WILL NOT BE ENTITLED TO ANY DISTRIBUTION ON THAT CLAIM AND YOU WILL RECEIVE NO FURTHER NOTICES REGARDING YOUR CLAIM. IF YOU **DO NOT** HOLD A CLAIM AGAINST THE DEBTOR YOU NEED NOT FILE A CLAIM BY THE CLAIMS DATE.

TO ALL FORMER CLIENTS OF THE DEBTOR: THIS IS NOT AN INVITATION TO ASSERT A MALPRACTICE CLAIM UNLESS YOU HAVE A **TRUE CLAIM**. IF YOU **DO NOT** HAVE A LEGITIMATE MALPRACTICE CLAIM, AND YOU FILE A FALSE PROOF OF CLAIM, YOU MAY BE SUBJECT TO FINES OF NOT MORE THAN $5,000 OR IMPRISONMENT OF NOT MORE THAN FIVE YEARS, OR BOTH, PURSUANT TO TITLE 18, UNITED STATES CODE, 18 U.S.C. § 152.

All proofs of claim must be **filed** so as to be **actually received** by the below-listed party, on or before **5:00 P.M. EASTERN STANDARD TIME ON JANUARY 23, 1992** at the following address:
GASTON & SNOW CLAIMS PROCESSING
Bowling Green Station
P.O. Box 42
New York, New York 10274-0042

If mailed, a proof of claim must be **filed** and **received** by the above-listed party on or before January 23, 1992 at 5:00 p.m. Eastern Standard Time.

If hand-delivered or by courier (but NOT by U.S. Mail) between the hours of 8:30 a.m. and 5:00 p.m., Eastern Standard Time, on business days, on or before January 23, 1992, then to: Gaston & Snow Claims Processing, Clerk of the Bankruptcy Court, Southern District of New York, Alexander Hamilton United States Customs House, One Bowling Green, Room 614, New York, New York 10004-1408.

If you have further questions about this notice, you may contact O'Melveny & Myers at (800) 446-9853, ext. 2248, or Poorman Douglas at (503) 293-5082 or, the Clerk of the Court, United States Bankruptcy Court, during the hours of 9:30 a.m. to 12 noon, or 1:30 p.m. to 4:00 p.m., Monday through Friday. ALL OTHER QUESTIONS, SUCH AS WHETHER YOU SHOULD FILE A PROOF OF CLAIM OR TAKE ANY OTHER ACTION WITH RESPECT TO YOUR CLAIM, SHOULD BE DIRECTED TO YOUR ATTORNEY.

Dated: New York, New York
            December 19, 1991

By Order of the Court

/s/ Cornelius Blackshear
United States Bankruptcy Judge

O'MELVENY & MYERS
Attorneys for
Harrison J. Goldin, Trustee
for the estate of Gaston & Snow
153 East 53rd Street
New York, New York 10022

[G9040]

§ 2. PRIORITY CLAIMS

SECURED CREDITORS

The bankruptcy distribution system established by the Code makes important distinctions among allowed claims. Some of these distinctions are the result of state or other non-bankruptcy law. One example of such a distinction is between "secured" and "unsecured" creditors. Secured creditors occupy the top position in the priority hierarchy. The provisions of sections 361, 362, and 1129 ensure that the secured creditors retain "the benefit of their bargain" as envisioned by Congress. House Report No. 595, 95th Congress, 2d Sess. 339. Sections 361 and 362 provide for adequate protection of a secured creditor's interest to guarantee that the value of the collateral will not depreciate subsequent to the bankruptcy petition. Section 1129 ensures that the secured creditor receives at least as much as it would at liquidation—the value of the collateral (up to the amount of the debt).

The determination of secured status is made pursuant to section 506. Under section 506(a) a creditor has a secured claim only to the extent of the value of the collateral. The remainder of the claim is unsecured. An "oversecured" creditor (one whose collateral value exceeds its debt), however, is entitled to fees, charges, and costs under subsection (b). Section 506(d) addresses liens which secure a claim that is not "allowed."

Problem 8–2

To understand how the calculation of the value of a secured claim is done and to see its consequences, consider the following problem.

1. Assume at the outset of Problem 8–1 that the secured creditor had argued the value of the lumberyard was $2,500,000. Recall that the creditor's loan was only $2,100,000. Section 506(b) tells you why the creditor might want to argue that.

2. Alternatively the creditor might argue that the value of the real estate was only $1,800,000. To see why the creditor might argue that consider sections 362 and 361.

3. Finally, consider how section 506 and the court's determination of the value of the underlying collateral will influence decisions under sections 1122 and 1129 on the kind of plan that can be proposed.

Assume first that the creditor's claim is $2,100,000 and that the value of the collateral is $1,700,000. Consequently the court will divide the claim into two parts, a $400,000 unsecured claim and a $1,700,000 secured claim. These will be included in separate classes under section 1122. Each will receive different treatment under section 1129. Unless the creditor agrees to the proposal made by the debtor, the debtor will have to give the creditor fair and equitable treatment under section 1129(b)(2) and that, for the secured portion, is likely to mean that the creditor will retain its lien on the real estate (or possibly receive it in satisfaction of that claim). If it does not receive the real estate or cash payment, the secured creditor will receive a promise of payment with a present value equal to $1,700,000. The remainder of the claim, for $400,000, needs to be protected only under section 1129(b)(2)(B). That subsection promises no more than a pro rata share of the remaining assets (assuming the debtor itself or the other equity holders who are subordinate do not take anything).

If the court had concluded that the lumberyard had a value of $2,100,000, then no plan could have been approved over the objection of the creditor that did not give it present value of $2,100,000. Section 506 and the valuation process that underlies it have a dramatic impact on the kind of plan that can be approved.

Problem 8–3

Assume a Chapter 7 case with total assets of $170,000 and the following claims:

1. $200,000 note held by bank, secured by debtor's $120,000 office building (included in the $170,000 of assets).

2. Law firm's claim for the return of its $20,000 deposit on a lease that it held in the bankrupt's building. The proposed lease was rejected by the debtor in possession during the case.

3. Income tax of $35,000 owed by the debtor for the immediately preceding year.

4. Trustee's fees of $19,000 for administering the estate.

5. Other unsecured claims of $100,000.

If the total assets consisted not of $170,000, but only of the $120,000 office building, would everything go to the bank (assuming it has a valid mortgage)? Consider section 506(c).

Application of section 506 affects the distribution in a Chapter 7 proceeding under section 726 in exactly the same way as it affects a Chapter 11 under section 1129. Under section 726, the secured creditor will have a right to the collateral itself or to the value of the collateral. The unsecured portion will share pro rata with other unsecured creditors in the assets. In the case that follows, *Dewsnup v. Timm,* the debtors attempted to use section 506 in a more clever way to enable them to purchase the collateral for the court-established value even in circumstances in which the creditor opposed that.

DEWSNUP v. TIMM

Supreme Court of the United States, 1992..
502 U.S. 410, 112 S.Ct. 773, 116 L.Ed.2d 903..

JUSTICE BLACKMUN delivered the opinion of the Court

We are confronted in this case with an issue concerning § 506(d) of the Bankruptcy Code, 11 U.S.C. § 506(d). May a debtor "strip down" a creditor's lien on real property to the value of the collateral, as judicially determined, when that value is less than the amount of the claim secured by the lien?

I

On June 1, 1978, respondents loaned $119,000 to petitioner Aletha Dewsnup and her husband, T. LaMar Dewsnup, since deceased. The loan was accompanied by a Deed of Trust granting a lien on two parcels of Utah farmland owned by the Dewsnups.

Petitioner defaulted the following year. Under the terms of the Deed of Trust, respondents at that point could have proceeded against the real property collateral by accelerating the maturity of the loan, issuing a notice of default, and selling the land at a public foreclosure sale to satisfy the debt.

Respondents did issue a notice of default in 1981. Before the foreclosure sale took place, however, petitioner sought reorganization under Chapter 11 of the Bankruptcy Code, 11 U.S.C. § 1101 *et seq.* That bankruptcy petition was dismissed, as was a subsequent Chapter 11 petition. In June 1984, petitioner filed a petition seeking liquidation under Chapter 7 of the Code, 11 U.S.C. § 701 *et seq.* Because of the pendency of these bankruptcy proceedings, respondents were not able to proceed to the foreclosure sale. See 11 U.S.C. § 362.

In 1987, petitioner filed the present adversary proceeding in the Bankruptcy Court for the District of Utah seeking, pursuant to § 506, to "avoid" a portion of respondents' lien. * * * Petitioner represented that the debt of approximately $120,000 then owed to respondents exceeded the fair market value of the land and that, therefore, the Bankruptcy Court should reduce the lien to that value. According to petitioner, this was compelled by the interrelationship of the security-reducing provision of § 506(a) and the lien-voiding provision of § 506(d). Under § 506(a) ("An allowed claim of a creditor secured by a lien on property in which the estate has an interest * * * is a secured claim to the extent of the value of such creditor's interest in the estate's interest in such property"), respondents would have an "allowed secured claim" only to the extent of the judicially determined value of their collateral. And under § 506(d)("To the extent that a lien secures a claim against the debtor that is not an allowed secured claim, such lien is void"), the court would be required to void the lien as to the remaining portion of respondents' claim, because the remaining portion was not an "allowed secured claim" within the meaning of § 506(a).

The Bankruptcy Court refused to grant this relief. *In re Dewsnup*, 87 B.R. 676 (Bankr.D.Utah 1988). After a trial, it determined that the then value of the land subject to the Deed of Trust was $39,000. It indulged in the assumption that the property had been abandoned by the trustee pursuant to § 554, and reasoned that once property was abandoned it no longer fell within the reach of § 506(a), which applies only to "property in which the estate has an interest," and therefore was not covered by § 506(d).

The United States District Court, without a supporting opinion, summarily affirmed the Bankruptcy Court's judgment of dismissal with prejudice. * * *

The Court of Appeals for the Tenth Circuit, in its turn, also affirmed. *In re Dewsnup,* 908 F.2d 588 (10th Cir.1990). Starting from the "fundamental premise" of § 506(a) that a claim is subject to reduction in security only when the estate has an interest in the property, the court reasoned that because the estate had no interest in abandoned property, § 506(a) did not apply (nor, by implication, did § 506(d)). The court then noted that a contrary result would be inconsistent with § 722 under which a debtor has a limited right to redeem certain personal property.

* * *

II

As we read their several submissions, the parties and their *amici* are not in agreement in their respective approaches to the problem of statutory interpretation that confronts us. Petitioner-debtor takes the position that § 506(a) and § 506(d) are complementary and to be read together. Because, under § 506(a), a claim is secured only to the extent of the judicially determined value of the real property on which the lien is fixed, a debtor can void a lien on the property pursuant to § 506(d) to the extent the claim is no longer secured and thus is not "an allowed secured claim." In other words, § 506(a) bifurcates classes of claims allowed under § 502 into secured claims and unsecured claims; any portion of an allowed claim deemed to be unsecured under § 506(a) is not an "allowed secured claim" within the lien-voiding scope of § 506(d). Petitioner argues that there is no exception for unsecured property abandoned by the trustee.

Petitioner's *amicus* argues that the plain language of § 506(d) dictates that the proper portion of an undersecured lien on property in a Chapter 7 case is void whether or not the property is abandoned by the trustee. It further argues that the rationale of the Court of Appeals would lead to evisceration of the debtor's right of redemption and the elimination of an undersecured creditor's ability to participate in the distribution of the estate's assets.

Respondents primarily assert that § 506(d) is not, as petitioner would have it, "rigidly tied" to § 506(a), Brief for Respondents 7. They argue that § 506(a) performs the function of classifying claims by true secured status at the time of distribution of the estate to ensure fairness to unsecured claimants. In contrast, the lien-voiding § 506(d) is directed to the time at which foreclosure is to take place, and, where the trustee has abandoned the property, no bankruptcy distributional purpose is served by voiding the lien.

In the alternative, respondents, joined by the United States as *amicus curiae,* argue more broadly that the words "allowed secured claim" in § 506(d) need not be read as an indivisible term of art defined by reference to § 506(a), which by its terms is not a definitional provision. Rather, the words should be read term-by-term to refer to any claim that is, first, allowed, and, second, secured. Because there is no question that the claim at issue here has been "allowed" pursuant to § 502 of the Code and is secured by a lien with recourse to the underlying collateral, it does not come within the scope of § 506(d), which voids only liens corresponding to claims that have *not* been allowed and secured. This reading of § 506(d), according to respondents and the United States, gives the provision the simple and sensible function of voiding a lien whenever a claim secured by the lien itself has not been allowed. It ensures that the Code's determination not to allow the underlying claim against the debtor personally is given full effect by preventing its assertion against the debtor's property.

Respondents point out that pre-Code bankruptcy law preserved liens like respondents' and that there is nothing in the Code's legislative history that reflects any intent to alter that law. Moreover, according to respondents, the "fresh-start" policy cannot justify an impairment of respondents' property rights, for the fresh start does not extend to an *in rem* claim against property but is limited to a discharge of personal liability.

III

The foregoing recital of the contrasting positions of the respective parties and their *amici* demonstrates that § 506 of the Bankruptcy Code and its relationship to other provisions of that Code do embrace some ambiguities. * * *

We conclude that respondents' alternative position, espoused also by the United States, although not without its difficulty, generally is the better of the several approaches. Therefore, we hold that § 506(d) does not allow petitioner to "strip down" respondents' lien, because respondents' claim is secured by a lien and has been fully allowed pursuant to § 502. Were we writing on a clean slate, we might be inclined to agree with petitioner that the words "allowed secured claim" must take the same meaning in § 506(d) as in § 506(a). But, given the ambiguity in the text, we are not convinced that Congress intended to depart from the pre-Code rule that liens pass through bankruptcy unaffected.

1. The practical effect of petitioner's argument is to freeze the creditor's secured interest at the judicially determined valuation. By this approach, the creditor would lose the benefit of any increase in the value of the property by the time of the foreclosure sale. The increase would accrue to the benefit of the debtor, a result some of the parties describe as a "windfall."

We think, however, that the creditor's lien stays with the real property until the foreclosure. That is what was bargained for by the mortgagor and the mortgagee. The voidness language sensibly applies only to the security aspect of the lien and then only to the real deficiency in the security. Any increase over the judicially determined valuation during bankruptcy rightly accrues to the benefit of the creditor, not to the benefit of the debtor and not to the benefit of other unsecured creditors whose claims have been allowed and who had nothing to do with the mortgagor-mortgagee bargain.

Such surely would be the result had the lienholder stayed aloof from the bankruptcy proceeding (subject, of course, to the power of other persons or entities to pull him into the proceeding pursuant to § 501), and we see no reason why his acquiescence in that proceeding should cause him to experience a forfeiture of the kind the debtor proposes. It is true that his participation in the bankruptcy results in his having the benefit of an allowed unsecured claim as well as his allowed secured claim, but that does not strike us as proper recompense for what petitioner proposes by way of the elimination of the remainder of the lien.

2. This result appears to have been clearly established before the passage of the 1978 Act. Under the Bankruptcy Act of 1898, a lien on real property passed through bankruptcy unaffected. This Court recently acknowledged that this was so. See *Farrey v. Sanderfoot,* 500 U.S. 291, ___, 111 S.Ct. 1825, 1829, 114 L.Ed.2d 337 (1991)(slip op. 6) ("Ordinarily, liens and other secured interests survive bankruptcy"); *Johnson v. Home State Bank,* 501 U.S. 78, ___, 111 S.Ct. 2150, 2154, 115 L.Ed.2d 66 (1991)(slip op. 5)("Rather, a bankruptcy discharge extinguishes only one mode of enforcing a claim—namely, an action against the debtor *in personam*—while leaving intact another—namely, an action against the debtor *in rem.*").

3. Apart from reorganization proceedings, see 11 U.S.C. §§ 616(1) and (10) (1976 ed.), no provision of the pre-Code statute permitted involuntary reduction of the amount of a creditor's lien for any reason other than payment on the debt. Our cases reveal the Court's concern about this. In *Long v. Bullard,* 117 U.S. 617, 620–621, 6 S.Ct. 917, 918, 29 L.Ed. 1004 (1886), the Court held that a discharge in bankruptcy does not release real estate of the debtor from the lien of a mortgage created by him before the bankruptcy. And in *Louisville Joint Stock Land Bank v. Radford,* 295 U.S. 555, 55 S.Ct. 854, 79 L.Ed. 1593 (1935), the Court considered additions to the Bankruptcy Act effected by the Frazier–Lemke Act, 48 Stat. 1289 (1934). There the Court noted that the latter Act's "avowed object is to take from the mortgagee rights in the specific property held as security; and to that end 'to scale down the indebtedness' to the present value of the property." The Court invalidated that statute under the Takings Clause. It further observed: "No instance has been found, except under the Frazier–Lemke Act, of either a statute or decision compelling the mortgagee to relinquish the property to the mortgagor free of the lien unless the debt was paid in full."

Congress must have enacted the Code with a full understanding of this practice. See H.R.Rep. No. 95–595, p. 357 (1977)("Subsection (d) permits liens to pass through the bankruptcy case unaffected").

4. When Congress amends the bankruptcy laws, it does not write "on a clean slate." Furthermore, this Court has been reluctant to

accept arguments that would interpret the Code, however vague the particular language under consideration might be, to effect a major change in pre-Code practice that is not the subject of at least some discussion in the legislative history. * * * Of course, where the language is unambiguous, silence in the legislative history cannot be controlling. But, given the ambiguity here, to attribute to Congress the intention to grant a debtor the broad new remedy against allowed claims to the extent that they become "unsecured" for purposes of § 506(a) without the new remedy's being mentioned somewhere in the Code itself or in the annals of Congress is not plausible, in our view, and is contrary to basic bankruptcy principles.

The judgment of the Court of Appeals is affirmed.

Justice Scalia, with whom Justice Souter joins, dissenting.

With exceptions not pertinent here, § 506(d) of the Bankruptcy Code provides: "To the extent that a lien secures a claim against the debtor that is not an allowed secured claim, such lien is void * * *." Read naturally and in accordance with other provisions of the statute, this automatically voids a lien to the extent the claim it secures is not both an "allowed claim" and a "secured claim" under the Code. In holding otherwise, the Court replaces what Congress said with what it thinks Congress ought to have said—and in the process disregards, and hence impairs for future use, well-established principles of statutory construction. I respectfully dissent.

I

This case turns solely on the meaning of a single phrase found throughout the Bankruptcy Code: "allowed secured claim." Section 506(d) unambiguously provides that to the extent a lien does not secure such a claim it is (with certain exceptions) rendered void. See 11 U.S.C. § 506(d)(emphasis added). Congress did not leave the meaning of "allowed secured claim" to speculation. Section 506(a) says that an "allowed claim" (the meaning of which is obvious) is also a "secured claim" "to the extent of *the value of [the] creditor's interest in the estate's interest in [the securing] property.*" (This means, generally speaking, that an allowed claim "is secured only to the extent of the value of the property on which the lien is fixed; the remainder of that claim is considered unsecured." *United States v. Ron Pair Enterprises, Inc.*, 489 U.S. 235, 239, 109 S.Ct. 1026, 1029, 103 L.Ed.2d 290 (1989).) When § 506(d) refers to an "allowed secured claim," it can only be referring to that allowed "secured claim" so carefully described two brief subsections earlier.

The phrase obviously bears the meaning set forth in § 506(a) when it is used in the subsections of § 506 other than § 506(d)—for example, in § 506(b), which addresses "allowed secured claim[s]" that are oversecured. Indeed, as respondents apparently concede, even when the phrase appears outside of § 506, it invariably means what § 506(a) describes: the portion of a creditor's allowed claim that is secured after the calculations required by that provision have been performed. * * * The statute is similarly consistent in its use of the companion phrase *"allowed unsecured claim"* to describe (with respect to a claim supported by a lien) that portion of the claim that is treated as "unsecured" under § 506(a). * * * When, on the other hand, the Bankruptcy Code means to refer to a secured party's entire allowed claim, *i.e.,* to both the "secured" and "unsecured" portions under § 506(a), it uses the term *"allowed claim"*—as in 11 U.S.C. § 363(k), which refers to "a lien that secures an allowed claim." Given this clear and unmistakable pattern of usage, it seems to me impossible to hold, as the Court does, that "the words 'allowed secured claim' in § 506(d) need not be read as an indivisible term of art defined by reference to § 506(a)." We have often invoked the " 'normal rule of statutory construction that "identical words used in different parts of the same act are intended to have the same meaning." ' " * * * That rule must surely apply, *a fortiori,* to use of identical words *in the same section of the same enactment.*

The Court makes no attempt to establish a textual or structural basis for overriding the plain meaning of § 506(d), but rests its decision upon policy intuitions of a legislative character,[1] and upon the principle that a text which is "ambiguous" (a status apparently achieved by being the subject of disagreement between self-interested litigants) cannot change pre-Code law without the imprimatur of "legislative history." Thus abandoning the normal and sensible principle that a term (and especially an artfully defined term such as "allowed secured claim") bears the same meaning throughout the statute, the Court adopts instead what might be called the one-subsection-at-a-time approach to statutory exegesis. "[W]e express no opinion," the Court amazingly

---

1. For example: "That is what was bargained for by the mortgagor and the mortgagee. * * * Any increase over the judicially determined valuation during bankruptcy rightly accrues to the benefit of the creditor.... [W]e see no reason why [the lienholder's] acquiescence in [the bankruptcy] proceeding should cause him to experience a forfeiture of the kind the debtor proposes * * * [T]he benefit of an allowed unsecured claim does not strike us as proper recompense for what petitioner proposes by way of the elimination of the remainder of the lien." *Ante,* at 7–8.

Apart from the fact that these policy judgments are inappropriate, it is not at all clear that evisceration of § 506(d) is even necessary to effectuate them. The feared "windfall" to the debtor may be prevented by 11 U.S.C. § 551, which preserves liens avoided under § 506(d) and other provisions of the Code "for the benefit of the estate," *i.e.,* for the benefit of the general unsecured creditors. See Note, An Individual Debtor's Right to Avoid Liens Under Section 506(d) of the Bankruptcy Code, 12 Cardozo L.Rev. 263, 280–281 (1990). See also *In re Ward,* 42 B.R. 946, 952–953 (Bankr.M.D.Tenn.1984). And the creditor whose lien has been stripped may even prevail over the other unsecured creditors by reason of 11 U.S.C. § 363(k), which permits such an undersecured creditor to apply the entire amount of his allowed claim (secured and unsecured) against the purchase price of the collateral at the trustee's foreclosure sale. This appears to enable the lien-stripped creditor (at least in the context of a trustee-managed foreclosure sale) to use his "unsecured claim" to capture any post-evaluation appreciation in the collateral. See Carlson, Undersecured Claims Under Bankruptcy Code Sections 506(a) and 1111(b): Second Looks at Judicial Valuations of Collateral, 6 Bankr.Devs.J. 253, 272–279 (1989). I would leave these questions for resolution on remand.

says, "as to whether the words 'allowed secured claim' have different meaning in other provisions of the Bankruptcy Code." "We * * * focus upon the case before us and allow other facts to await their legal resolution on another day."

II

As to the meaning of this single subsection (considered, of course, in a vacuum), the Court claims to be embracing "respondents' alternative position," which is "that the words 'allowed secured claim' in § 506(d) need not be read as an indivisible term of art defined by reference to § 506(a)," and that "secured claim" (for purposes of § 506(d) alone) simply connotes an allowed claim that is "secured" in the ordinary sense, *i.e.*, that is backed up by a security interest in property, whether or not the value of the property suffices to cover the claim. The Court attributes this position to the United States as well, but the Government's position is in fact different—and significantly so, since it *does* (as proper statutory interpretation ought to do) give the phrase "allowed secured claim" a uniform meaning. I must describe the Government's theory, and explain why it does not work.

The distinctive feature of the United States' approach is that it seeks to avoid invalidation of the so-called "underwater" portion of the lien by focusing, *not* upon the phrase "allowed secured claim" in § 506(d), but upon the prior phrase "secures a claim." ("To the extent that a lien *secures a claim* against the debtor that is not an allowed secured claim, such lien is void" (Emphasis added.)) Under the Government's textual theory, this phrase can be read to refer not merely to the *object* of the security, but to its *adequacy*. That is to say, a lien only "secures" the claim in question up to the value of the security that is the object of the lien—and only up to *that* value is the lien subject to avoidance under § 506(d). This interpretation succeeds in giving the phrase "allowed secured claim," which appears later in § 506(d), a meaning compatible with that compelled by § 506(a). But that is its only virtue.

To begin with, the interpretation renders some of the language in § 506(d) surplusage. If the phrase "[t]o the extent that a lien *secures* a claim" describes only that portion of a claim that is secured by actual economic value, then the later phrase "is not an allowed *secured* claim" should instead have read simply "is not allowed." For the phrase "allowed secured claim" *itself* describes a claim that is *actually* secured in light of § 506(a)'s calculations. Another reading of § 506(d)'s opening passage is available, one that does not assume such clumsy draftsmanship—and that employs, to boot, a much more natural reading of the phrase "lien secures a claim." The latter ordinarily describes the relationship between a lien and a claim, not the relationship between the value of the property subject to the lien and the amount of the claim. One would say that a "mortgage secures the claim" for the purchase price of a house, even if the value of the house was inadequate to satisfy the full amount of the claim. In other words, "[t]o the extent that a lien *secures* a claim" means in § 506(d) what it ordinarily means: "to the extent a lien provides its holder with a right to retain property in full or partial satisfaction of a claim." It means that in § 506(d) just as it means that in § 506(a), see 11 U.S.C. § 506(a)("An allowed claim of a creditor *secured* by a lien * * * is a secured claim to the extent * * *")(emphasis added), and just as it means that elsewhere in the Bankruptcy Code, see, *e.g.*, § 362(a)(5) ("to the extent that such lien *secures* a claim"); 11 U.S.C. § 363(k)("lien that *secures* an allowed claim"). An unnatural meaning should be disfavored at any time, but particularly when it produces a redundancy. See *Montclair v. Ramsdell*, 107 U.S. 147, 152, 27 L.Ed. 431 (1883).

Of course *respondents'* interpretation also creates a redundancy in § 506(d). If a "secured claim" means only a claim for which a lien has been given as security (whether or not the security is adequate), then the prologue of § 506(d) can be reformulated as follows: "To the extent that a lien secures a claim against the debtor that is not an allowed claim secured by a lien, such lien is void * * *." Quite obviously, the phrase "secured by a lien" in that reformulation is utterly redundant and absurd—as is (on respondents' interpretation) the word "secured," which bears the same meaning. In other words, both the United States' interpretation and respondents' interpretation create a redundancy: the former by making both parts of the § 506(d) prologue refer to *adequate* security, and the latter by making both parts refer to *security plain-and-simple*. Only when one gives the words in the first part of the prologue ("[t]o the extent that a lien secures a claim") their natural meaning (as the Government does not) *and* gives the words in the second part of the prologue ("allowed secured claim") their previously established statutory meaning (as the respondents do not) does the provision make a *point* instead of a *redundancy*.

Moreover, the practical consequences of the United States' interpretation would be absurd. A secured creditor holding a lien on property that is completely worthless would not face lien avoidance under § 506(d), *even if the claim secured by that lien were disallowed entirely*. The same would be true of a lien on property that has *some* value but is obviously inadequate to cover all of the disallowed claim: the lien would be voided only to the extent of the property's value at the time of the bankruptcy court's evaluation, and could be asserted against any increase in the value of the property that might later occur, in order to satisfy the disallowed claim. Unavoided liens (or more accurately, potentials of unavoided liens, since no one knows whether or when future evaluations of the relevant property will exceed that of the bankruptcy court) would impede the trustee's management and settlement of the estate. It would be difficult, for example, to sell overencumbered property subject to outstanding liens pursuant to 11 U.S.C. § 363(b) or (c), since any post-sale appreciation in the property could be levied upon by holders of disallowed secured claims. And in a sale of debtor property "free and clear" of the liens attached to it, see 11 U.S.C. § 363(f)(3), the undisturbed portion of the disallowed claimant's lien might attach to the proceeds of that sale to the extent of the collateral's post-petition appreciation, preventing the trustee from distributing some or all of the sale proceeds to creditors holding allowed claims. If possible, we should avoid construing the statute in a way that produces such absurd results.

III

Although the Court makes no effort to explain why petitioner's straightforward reading of § 506(d) is textually or structurally incompatible with other portions of the statute, respondents and the United States do so. They point out, to begin with, that the two exceptions to § 506(d)'s nullifying effect both pertain to *the disallowance of claims,* and not to *the inadequacy of security,* see 11 U.S.C. §§ 506(d)(1) and (2)—from which they conclude that the applicability of § 506(d) turns only on the allowability of the underlying claim, and not on the extent to which the claim is a "secured claim" within the meaning of § 506(a). But the fact that the statute makes no exceptions to invalidation by reason of inadequate security in no way establishes that such (plainly expressed) invalidation does not exist. The premise of the argument—that if a statute qualifies a noun with two adjectives ("allowed" and "secured"), and provides exceptions with respect to only one of the adjectives, then the other can be disregarded—is simply false. The most that can be said is that the two exceptions in § 506(d) do not *contradict* the United States' and respondents' interpretation; but they in no way suggest or support it.

Respondents and the United States also identify supposed inconsistencies between petitioner's construction of § 506(d) and other sections of the Bankruptcy Code; they are largely illusory. The principal source of concern is § 722, which enables a Chapter 7 debtor to "redeem" narrow classes of exempt or abandoned personal property from "a lien securing a dischargeable consumer debt." The price of redemption is fixed as "the amount of the *allowed secured claim* of [the lienholder] that is secured by such lien" (emphasis added). This provision, we are told, would be largely superfluous if § 506(d) automatically stripped liens securing undersecured claims to the value of the collateral, *i.e.,* to the value of the allowed secured claims.

This argument is greatly overstated. Section 722 is necessary, and not superfluous, because § 506(d) is not a *redemption* provision. It reduces the value of a lienholder's equitable interest in a debtor's property to the property's liquidation value, but it does not insure the debtor an opportunity to "redeem" the property at that price, *i.e.,* to "free [the] property * * * from [the] mortgage or pledge by paying the debt for which it stood as security." Black's Law Dictionary 1278 (6th ed. 1990). Congress had good reason to be solicitous of the debtor's right to redeem personal property (the exclusive subject of § 722), since state redemption laws are typically less generous for personalty than for real property. Compare, *e.g.,* Utah Code Ann. § 57–1–31 (1990) with Uniform Commercial Code § 9–506, 3A U.L.A. 370 (1981). The most that can be said regarding § 722 is that petitioner's construction of § 506(d) would permit a more concise formulation: Instead of describing the redemption price as "the amount of the allowed secured claim * * * that is secured by such lien" it would have been *possible* to say simply "the amount of the claim * * * that is secured by such lien"—since § 506(d) would automatically have cut back the lien to the amount of the allowed secured claim. I would hardly call the more expansive formulation a redundancy—not when it is so far removed from the section that did the "cutting back" that the reader has likely forgotten it.

Respondents and their *amicus* also make much of the need to avoid giving Chapter 7 debtors a better deal than they can receive under the other Chapters of the Bankruptcy Code. They assert that, by enabling a Chapter 7 debtor to strip down a secured creditor's liens and pocket any post-petition appreciation in the property, petitioner's construction of § 506(d) will discourage debtors from using the preferred mechanisms of reorganization under Chapters 11, 12, and 13. This evaluation of the "finely reticulated" incentives affecting a debtor's behavior rests upon critical—and perhaps erroneous—assumptions about the meaning of provisions in the reorganization chapters. Respondents assume, for example, that a debtor in Chapter 13 cannot strip down a mortgage placed on the debtor's home; but that assumption may beg the very question the Court answers today. True, § 1322(b)(2) provides that Chapter 13 filers may not "modify the rights of holders of secured claims" that are "*secured only by a security interest in real property that is the debtor's principal residence,*" 11 U.S.C. § 1322(b)(2)(emphasis added). But this can be (and has been) read, in light of § 506(a), to prohibit modification of the mortgagee's rights only with respect to the portion of his claim that is deemed secured under the Code, see, *e.g., In re Hart,* 923 F.2d 1410, 1415 (C.A.10 1991); *Wilson v. Commonwealth Mortgage Corp.,* 895 F.2d 123, 127 (C.A.3 1990). If petitioner's construction of § 506(d) were applied consistently in this fashion to the Code's various chapters, see 11 U.S.C. § 103(a)(providing that "chapters 1, 3, and 5 * * * [shall] apply in a case under chapter 7, 11, 12, or 13"), Chapter 7 would not appear unduly attractive. In any event, reorganization contains other enticements to lure a debtor away from Chapter 7. It not only permits him to maintain control over his personal and business assets, but affords a broader discharge from prepetition *in personam* liabilities. Compare, *e.g.,* 11 U.S.C. § 523 (listing numerous exceptions to Chapter 7 discharge) with 11 U.S.C. § 1328(a) (listing two exceptions to Chapter 13 discharge). * * *

Finally, respondents and the United States find it incongruous that Congress would so carefully protect secured creditors in the context of reorganization while allowing them to be fleeced in a Chapter 7 liquidation by operation of § 506(d). This view mistakes the generosity of treatment that creditors can count upon in reorganization. There, no more than under Chapter 7, can they demand the benefit of post-evaluation increases in the value of property given as security. See 11 U.S.C. §§ 1129(b)(2)(A) and 1325(a)(5)(permitting "cram-down" of reorganization plan over objections of secured creditors if creditors are to receive payments equal in present value to the cash value of the collateral, and if creditors retain liens securing such payments).

IV

I must also address the Tenth Circuit's basis for the decision affirmed today (alluded to by the Court, but not discussed), that § 506 does not apply to property abandoned by the bankruptcy trustee under § 554, see 11 U.S.C. § 554. Respondents' principal argument before us was a modified (and less logical) version of the same basic point—*viz.,* that although § 506(*a*)applies to abandoned property, § 506(*d*)does not. I can address the point briefly, since the plain-language obstacles to its validity are even more pronounced than those raised by the Court's approach.

The Court of Appeals' reasoning was as follows: § 506(d) effects lien-stripping only with respect to property subject to § 506(a); but by its terms § 506(a) applies only to property "in which the estate has an interest"; since "[t]he estate has no interest in, and does not administer, abandoned property," § 506(a), and hence § 506(d), does not apply to it. *In re Dewsnup,* 908 F.2d 588, 590–591 (C.A.10 1990). The fallacy in this is the assumption that the application of § 506(a)(and hence § 506(d)) can be undone if and when the estate ceases to "have an interest" in property in which it "had an interest" at the outset of the bankruptcy proceeding. The text does not read that way. Section 506 automatically operates upon all property in which the estate has an interest at the time the bankruptcy petition is filed. Once § 506(a)'s grant of secured-creditor rights, and § 506(d)'s elimination of the right to "underwater" liens and liens securing unallowed claims have occurred, they cannot be undone by later abandonment of the property. Nothing in the statute expressly permits such an unraveling, and it would be absurd to imagine it. If, upon the collateral's abandonment, the claim bifurcation accomplished by § 506(a) were nullified, the status of the creditor's allowed claim—*i.e.,* whether (and to what extent) it is "secured" or "unsecured" for purposes of the bankruptcy distribution—would be impossible to determine. Instead, the claim would have to be treated as either completely "secured" or completely "unsecured," neither of which disposition would accord with the Code's distribution principles. The former would deprive the secured claimant of a share in the distribution to general creditors altogether. See 11 U.S.C. § 726 (providing for distribution of property of the estate to unsecured claimants). The latter (treating the claim as completely unsecured) would permit the lienholder to share in the pro rata distribution to general creditors *to the full amount of his allowed claim* (rather than simply to the amount of § 506(a)-defined "unsecured claim") while reserving his *in rem* claim against the security. Respondents' variation on the Tenth Circuit's holding avoids these alternative absurdities only by embracing yet another textual irrationality—asserting that, even though the language that is the *basis* for the "abandonment" theory (the phrase "in which the estate has an interest") is contained in § 506(a), and only applies to § 506(d) *through* § 506(a), nonetheless only the effects of § 506(d) and *not* the effects of § 506(a) are undone by abandonment. This hardly deserves the name of a theory.

V

As I have said, the Court does not trouble to make or evaluate the foregoing arguments. Rather, in Part II of its opinion it merely describes (uncritically) "the contrasting positions of the respective parties and their *amici* "concerning the meaning of § 506(d), and concludes, because the positions are contrasting, that there is "ambiguity in the text." (This mode of analysis makes every litigated statute ambiguous.) Having thus established "ambiguity," the Court is able to summon down its *deus ex machina:* "the pre-Code rule that liens pass through bankruptcy unaffected"—which cannot be eliminated by an ambiguous provision, at least where the "legislative history" does not mention its demise.

We have, of course, often consulted pre-Code behavior in the course of interpreting gaps in the express coverage of the Code, or genuinely ambiguous provisions. And we have often said in such cases that, absent a textual footing, we will not presume a departure from longstanding pre-Code practice. * * * But we have *never* held pre-Code practice to be determinative in the face of what we have here: contradictory statutory text. To the contrary, where "the statutory language plainly reveals Congress' intent" to alter pre-Code regimes, *Pennsylvania Dept. of Public Welfare v. Davenport, supra,* at 563, we have simply enforced the new Code according to its terms, without insisting upon "at least some discussion [of the change from prior law] in the legislative history."

For an illustration of just how plainly today's opinion is at odds with our jurisprudence, one need only examine our most recent bankruptcy decision, *Union Bank v. Wolas,* 502 U.S. 151, 112 S.Ct. 527, 116 L.Ed.2d 514 (1991). There also the parties took "contrasting positions" as to the meaning of the statutory text, but we did not shrink from finding, on the basis of our own analysis, that no ambiguity existed. There also it was urged upon us that the interpretation we adopted would overturn pre-Code practice with "no evidence in the legislative history that Congress intended to make" such a change, *Wolas, supra,* 112 S.Ct., at 531. We found it unnecessary to "dispute the accuracy of [that] description of the legislative history * * * in order to reject [the] conclusion" that no change had been effected. "The fact," we said, "that Congress may not have foreseen all of the consequences of a statutory enactment is not a sufficient reason for refusing to give effect to its plain meaning." And "the fact that Congress carefully reexamined and entirely rewrote the preference provision in 1978 supports the conclusion that the text of § 547(c)(2) as enacted reflects the deliberate choice of Congress." What was true of the preference provision in *Wolas* is also true of the secured claims provisions at issue in the present case: Congress's careful reexamination *and entire rewriting* of those provisions supports the conclusion that, regardless of whether pre-Code practice is retained or abandoned, the text means precisely what it says. Indeed, the rewriting here is so complete that, no matter how deeply one admires and venerates "pre-Code law," it is impossible to interpret § 506(d) in a manner that entirely preserves it—and the Court itself, for all its protestation of fealty, does not do so. No provision of the former Bankruptcy Act, nor any pre-Code doctrine, purported to invalidate—across the board—liens securing claims disallowed in bankruptcy, see 11 U.S.C. § 107 (1976 ed.); see also 4 Collier on Bankruptcy § 67 (14th ed. 1978), yet that is precisely what § 506(d), as interpreted by the Court today, accomplishes.

It is even more instructive to compare today's opinion with our decision a few years ago in *United States v. Ron Pair Enterprises, Inc.*, 489 U.S. 235, 109 S.Ct. 1026, 103 L.Ed.2d 290 (1989), which involved another subsection of § 506 itself. The issue was whether § 506(b) made post-petition interest available even to those oversecured creditors whose liens were nonconsensual. The Court of Appeals had held that it did not, because such a disposition would alter the pre-Code rule and there was no "legislative history" to support the change. We disagreed. The opinion for the Court began "where all such inquiries must begin: with the language of the statute itself." We did not recite the contentions of the parties and declare "ambiguity," but entered into our own careful consideration of "[t]he natural reading of the [relevant] phrase," the "grammatical structure of the statute," and the "terminology used throughout the Code." Having found a "natural interpretation of the statutory language [that] does not conflict with any significant state or federal interest, nor with any other aspect of the Code," we deemed the pre-Code practice to be irrelevant. And whereas today's opinion announces the policy judgment that "[a]ny increase over the judicially determined valuation during bankruptcy rightly accrues to the benefit of the creditor," in *Ron Pair* we were undeterred by the fact that our result was "arguably somewhat in tension with the desirability of paying all creditors as uniformly as practicable," 489 U.S., at 245–246, 109 S.Ct., at 1033. "Congress," we said, "expressly chose to create that alleged tension." Almost point for point, today's opinion is the methodological antithesis of *Ron Pair*—and I have the greatest sympathy for the Courts of Appeals who must predict which manner of statutory construction we shall use for the next Bankruptcy Code case.

* * *

The principal harm caused by today's decision is not the misinterpretation of § 506(d) of the Bankruptcy Code. The disposition that misinterpretation produces brings the Code closer to prior practice and is, as the Court irrelevantly observes, probably fairer from the standpoint of natural justice. (I say irrelevantly, because a bankruptcy law has little to do with natural justice.) The greater and more enduring damage of today's opinion consists in its destruction of predictability, in the Bankruptcy Code and elsewhere. By disregarding well-established and oft-repeated principles of statutory construction, it renders those principles less secure and the certainty they are designed to achieve less attainable. When a seemingly clear provision can be pronounced "ambiguous" *sans* textual and structural analysis, and when the assumption of uniform meaning is replaced by "one-subsection-at-a-time" interpretation, innumerable statutory texts become worth litigating. In the bankruptcy field alone, for example, unfortunate future litigants will have to pay the price for our expressed neutrality "as to whether the words 'allowed secured claim' have different meaning in other provisions of the Bankruptcy Code." Having taken this case to resolve uncertainty regarding one provision, we end by spawning confusion regarding scores of others. I respectfully dissent. (citations omitted).

Questions

1. If the law were amended to permit what Dewsnup proposed to do, how would mortgage lenders respond?

2. Justice Scalia is exactly right but totally wrong, not so?

ADMINISTRATIVE EXPENSES AND PRIORITY CLAIMS

After secured claims come priority claims, as defined by section 507. The system provides for class-based distribution. The various provisions on claims, distributions, priority and discharge (507, 726, 523, etc.) harbor many inarticulated conclusions and assumptions about the just deserts of particular claimants and particular debtors. For example, the $4,000 priority in 507(a)(3) arises out of an inarticulated assumption that unpaid employees are more deserving than unpaid trade creditors. The priorities in section 507(a)(8) for taxes may reflect a similar judgment about claims of the federal, state and local government or—to a more cynical person—a reflection of the power of the king in representing his own interests in his own legislation. The 1994 amendments doubled the wage priority from $2,000 to $4,000; they also increased the amount of certain other priorities. After 1994 there will be adjustments of the dollar amounts in section 507(a) at three year intervals to reflect changes in the Consumer Price Index. Within a class, all claimants participate pro rata. If the estate is insufficient to pay an entire class, lower classes receive nothing.

The confirmed reorganization plan establishes the Chapter 11 distribution system. Although the overall distribution is defined by the plan, section 1129(a)(9) gives section 507 priority claims and secured creditors the ability to demand preferential treatment.

Under section 507, first priority is reserved for "administrative expenses." Section 503 defines administrative expenses, including all actual or necessary expenses of operating the estate, as well as attorneys' and professional fees. Note that this in effect elevates most postpetition claims over prepetition unsecured claims. In Chapter 11, administrative expenses will often be large. Since many of the postpetition operating expenses that would otherwise be administrative claims will be paid before confirmation, a disproportionate share of administrative expenses will be lawyers' and other professional fees. These fees, often in the millions of dollars, must be paid before any unsecured creditor is paid.

In Re Colortex, the case that follows, deals with the question whether interest on a postpetition administrative expense is also an administrative expense. This case is an artifact of the slow pace of reorganization. If a company were routinely reorganized in two months or even six months, the parties might not find it worth their while to quarrel over postpetition interest. When cases drag on for years, interest can become a large number well worth fighting over.

IN RE COLORTEX INDUSTRIES, INC.

United States Court of Appeals, Eleventh Circuit, 1994.
19 F.3d 1371.

ANDERSON, CIRCUIT JUDGE:

This appeal presents two issues—an issue of first impression with respect to the appropriate priority in bankruptcy for interest on trade debts accruing during a Chapter 11 reorganization; and also an issue involving a claim for immediate payment. We affirm the district court with respect to both issues.

FACTS AND PROCEDURAL HISTORY

This case arises from the filing of a Chapter 11 petition in the United States Bankruptcy Court for the Northern District of Georgia, Rome Division by Colortex Industries, Inc. ("Debtor") on October 24, 1989. Subsequent to filing, Debtor sought the extension of postpetition credit from Varsity Carpet Services, Inc., Textile Coating, Ltd., and Chem–Tech Finishers, Inc. (collectively "Varsity" or "appellants"). Varsity performed the requested carpet finishing services on a credit basis between October 26, 1989 and February 1, 1990 while the Debtor operated under Chapter 11.

On April 17, 1990, the bankruptcy court approved conversion of Debtor's Chapter 11 case to a case under Chapter 7. Subsequently, on March 2, 1992, Varsity filed a motion pursuant to 11 U.S.C. § 503(b)(1)(A) seeking immediate payment and administrative expense priority on the principal indebtedness incurred postpetition and interest accruing thereon to date. The trustee in bankruptcy for Debtor, Thomas D. Richardson, ("Trustee" or "appellee") filed a response and objection to Varsity's motion.

The bankruptcy court held hearings on Varsity's claims on April 14, 1992. The parties stipulated that the estate at the time of the hearing had $723,738.00 on deposit. Varsity argued that its claim should be paid immediately because the estate was solvent, stating that the Trustee's final report at the time of conversion to Chapter 7 reflected only $153,742.93 in unpaid debts. The Trustee argued that a number of outstanding Chapter 7 administrative expense claims, superpriority claims, and other Chapter 11 administrative expense claims against the estate precluded immediate payment. The bankruptcy court entered an order allowing the claim of Varsity as Chapter 11 administrative claims, representing principal indebtedness only. Varsity's requests for interest and immediate payment were denied.

Upon appeal, the district court reversed the bankruptcy court's determination regarding interest, holding that the interest accruing during the Chapter 11 period on Varsity's postpetition trade debt should be accorded flat administrative expense priority under § 503(b)(1)(A), but that upon conversion to Chapter 7, interest accruing thereafter should be accorded only fifth priority under § 726(a)(5). *Varsity Carpet Services, Inc. v. Richardson*, 146 B.R. 881, 887 (N.D.Ga.1992). The district court affirmed the bankruptcy court's denial of Varsity's motion for immediate payment, concluding that the bankruptcy court had not abused its discretion in denying immediate payment where the record did not adequately reflect the total amount of claims against the estate. *Id.* at 888.

The Trustee cross-appeals the district court's determination that interest is entitled to first priority as an administrative expense. The Trustee urges this Court to adopt the bankruptcy court's position—i.e., that only the principal debt is entitled to administrative expense priority. Varsity appeals the district court's denial of its motion for immediate payment. Varsity also argues that, in addition to administrative expense priority for interest *during the Chapter 11 period*, it should also be entitled to the same priority for interest accruing after the conversion to Chapter 7. For the reasons set out below, we affirm the district court; we hold that Varsity is entitled to administrative expense priority for interest accrued during the Chapter 11 period, but not for interest accruing after conversion; we also hold that the district court did not abuse its discretion in denying Varsity's claims for immediate payment.
* * *

DISCUSSION

I. Administrative Expense Priority for Interest

The Trustee argues that the district court erred in granting first administrative expense priority for interest on Varsity's postpetition trade claims. According to the Trustee, the plain language of the Code does not accord administrative expense priority (or first priority) for interest on postpetition administrative expense claims. The Trustee relies upon the general rule in bankruptcy that accrual of interest is suspended upon the filing of a bankruptcy petition, with any exception to this general rule narrowly construed to maximize the value of the estate preserved for the benefit of all creditors. Although the Trustee concedes that some courts have accorded interest on postpetition tax liabilities priority as an administrative expense, the Trustee urges that those decisions be circumscribed to the tax area, due to specific legislative history. Specifically, the Trustee notes that prior law dictated that administrative expense priority be accorded interest on tax claims based upon the Supreme Court decision of *Nicholas v. United States*, 384 U.S. 678, 86 S.Ct. 1674, 16 L.Ed.2d 853 (1966). The Trustee argues that prior law would dictate that interest on trade debts, as opposed to tax liabilities, would receive a lower priority than the attendant administrative expense claim.

Varsity rejects the Trustee's construction of the Code, urging that 11 U.S.C. §§ 503(b) and 507 should be read broadly to permit interest as an administrative expense priority, relying upon the Code's definition of the term "including" to suggest that the list in § 503(b)(1)(A) enumerating allowed administrative expenses is non-exhaustive. Varsity urges that failure to accord priority for interest on credit extended to a debtor in Chapter 11 would discourage creditors from extending credit because according interest a lower priority would in essence constitute an interest-free loan to the debtor. Such a result is inimical to Chapter 11's goal of reorganization of the debtor, according to Varsity. Varsity relies upon this Court's decision in *In re Allied Mechanical Services, Inc.*, 885 F.2d 837 (11th Cir.1989), in which this Court, concluding that the Supreme Court's decision in *Nicholas* had continuing vitality, accorded administrative expense priority (or first priority) for interest on postpetition tax claims.

A. *Statutory Scheme of Distribution*

In determining this question of priority, we turn first to the Bankruptcy Code itself. Rules of statutory construction dictate that the plain meaning is conclusive, "except in the 'rare cases [in which] the literal application of a statute will produce a result demonstrably at odds with the intentions of its drafters.'" *United States v. Ron Pair Enterprises, Inc.* * * * Finally, where a statute is ambiguous, we must analyze whether our interpretation accords with established precedent prior to the enactment of the Code, mindful that "'no changes in law or policy are to be presumed from changes in language in [a statute's] revision unless an intent to make such changes is clearly expressed.'" *Finley v. United States*, 490 U.S. 545, 554, 109 S.Ct. 2003, 2009, 104 L.Ed.2d 593 (1989). * * * Silent abrogation of judicially created concepts is particularly disfavored when construing the Bankruptcy Code. * * *

In determining the priority of administrative expenses, a series of sections are applicable. Section 726 instructs that in a Chapter 7 liquidation the corpus of the estate is distributed according to the priorities of section 507. Section 507 in turn directs that first priority is given to administrative expenses:

(a) The following expenses and claims have priority in the following order:

(1) First, administrative expenses allowed under section 503(b) of this title, and any fees and charges assessed against the estate under chapter 123 of title 28. * * *

11 U.S.C. § 507. Section 503 defines administrative expenses as including "the actual, necessary costs and expenses of preserving the estate" as well as postpetition taxes and penalties associated with those taxes:

(a) An entity may file a request for payment of an administrative expense.

(b) After notice and a hearing, there shall be allowed administrative expenses, other than claims allowed under section 502(f) of this title, including—

(1)(A) the actual, necessary costs and expenses of preserving the estate, including wages, salaries, or commissions for services rendered after the commencement or the case;

(B) any tax—

(i) incurred by the estate, except a tax of a kind specified in section 507(a)(7) of this title; or

(ii) attributable to an excessive allowance of a tentative carryback adjustment that the estate received, whether the taxable year to which such adjustment relates ended before or after the commencement of the case; and

(C) any fine, penalty, or reduction in credit relating to a tax of a kind specified in subparagraph (B) of this paragraph; * * *

11 U.S.C. § 503.

No provision of the Code specifically provides for the payment of interest on administrative expenses. Section 726 is the only provision which expressly provides for interest:

(a) Except as provided in section 510 of this title, property of the estate shall be distributed—

* * *

(5) fifth, in payment of interest at the legal rate from the date of the filing of the petition, on any claim paid under paragraph (1), (2), (3), or (4) of this subsection; * * *

11 U.S.C. § 726.

Section 726(a)(5), the fifth priority, apparently codifies the "solvency exception" developed by case law prior to the enactment of the Bankruptcy Code. * * * Under this exception, where the debtor ultimately proves solvent, a balance of the equities dictates that creditors may receive any surplus, including claims for interest arising postpetition, ahead of payment to the debtor. * * * The legislative history states that section 726(a)(5) "provides that postpetition interest on prepetition claims is ... to be paid to the creditor." S.Rep. No. 95–989, 95th Cong., 2d Sess. 5, *reprinted in* 1978 U.S.Code Cong. & Admin.News, 5787, 5883. Whether section 726(a)(5) may be applied to claims for postpetition interest on claims arising postpetition is arguably ambiguous. The legislative history is barren of any mention of according interest priority on trade claims pursuant to section 726(a)(5).

It is noteworthy that the right of an administrative claimant to interest is not specifically provided for in 11 U.S.C. § 503(b)(1). Rather, if a right to such postpetition interest is to be found, it must be derived from a broad interpretation of that section's use of the term "including." As is evident from the Code's "Rules of Construction," the use of the word "including" is not intended to be limiting. 11 U.S.C. § 102(3). Thus, by implication, Congress did not intend section 726 to be exhaustive, suggesting that the enumerated category for administrative expenses does not necessarily preclude judicial construction to permit other claims reasonably demonstrated to be "actual, necessary" costs of administration, including interest. * * *

Despite the expansiveness with which the administrative expense category may be treated, such judicial construction is limited by the countervailing doctrine that section 503 priorities should be narrowly construed in order to maximize the value of the estate preserved for the benefit of all creditors. *Otte v. United States*, 419 U.S. 43, 53, 95 S.Ct. 247, 254, 42 L.Ed.2d 212 (1974). In determining how to best preserve the estate, two factors must be balanced: "maintaining the estate in as healthy a form as possible for the benefit of creditors while allowing essential costs of administering an ongoing business venture to be paid up front, thereby giving the debtor its best shot at emerging as a vital concern." *In re Dant & Russell, Inc.*, 853 F.2d 700, 707 (9th Cir.1988). Thus, a balance must be struck between the goal of maximizing the estate and the goal of encouraging on-going business with third parties to facilitate the continued operations of the business, and thus the reorganization. *Id.* at 706–07. That balance may never be struck to denigrate the clear intent of section 503(b)(1)(A) which is to satisfy the actual and necessary costs of preserving the estate. Although section 503(b) should be read narrowly to preserve the debtor's scarce resources, the ultimate goal of Chapter 11 is to marshall those resources to provide the best possible opportunity for a successful rehabilitation which will ultimately redound to the benefit of all creditors.

B. *Case law*

A survey of cases construing the Bankruptcy Code offers little guidance; the diversity of approaches indicates the complexity of the issue. One line of decisions has denied claims for interest on administrative expense claims. *See In re Fred Swain, Inc.*, 97 B.R. 660, 661–62 (Bankr.S.D.Fla.1989)(denying administrative claim status to postpetition interest, liquidated damages and attorneys' fees on an administrative expense claim premised on the lack of Congressional intent to award such interest); *In re Goldblatt Bros., Inc.*, 61 B.R. 459, 463 (Bankr. N.D.Ill.1986)(while indicating that as a rule postpetition interest is prohibited found that creditor was entitled to interest on implied trust theory); *In re John Clay*, 43 B.R. 797, 812 (Bankr.D.Utah 1984)(denying interest on postpetition deliveries of sheep accorded administrative expense priority premised on absence of language in the Code permitting such interest). One decision has indicated that, barring an express contract, interest is not ordinarily entitled to administrative expense priority, absent extraordinary equities favoring its award. *In re American International Airways, Inc.*, 77 B.R. 490, 494–95 (Bankr.E.D.Pa. 1987).

Another line of cases has allowed interest to accrue on allowed administrative claims where authorized by express statutory or contractual authority. * * * At least one decision has held that because interest is an integral part of the underlying administrative expense, it should be accorded administrative expense priority and awarded at the statutory rate. *In re Mesa Refining, Inc.*, 66 B.R. 36, 38–39 (Bankr.D.Colo.1986). * * *

C. *The Tax Cases*

Varsity urges that the reasoning of this Court in *In re Allied Mechanical Serv., Inc.*, 885 F.2d 837 (11th Cir.1989) controls. This Court in *In re Allied Mechanical* held that the government was entitled to administrative expense priority on its claim for interest on postpetition tax liability, relying primarily on the Supreme Court's decision in *Nicholas v. United States*, 384 U.S. 678, 86 S.Ct. 1674, 16 L.Ed.2d 853 (1966). *Id.* at 839. Key to the decision was that under prior law, as articulated in *Nicholas*, interest on postpetition tax liability was accorded administrative expense priority, although the Bankruptcy Act, like the Code, did not explicitly so provide. *Id.* Thus, *In re Allied Mechanical* rested upon the principle that guides our decision today: absent affirmative Congressional intent to the contrary, judicially created doctrines under prior law remain viable, with silent abrogation particularly disfavored. * * *

Other courts examining the issue have divided over the treatment of interest on tax liability. A majority of the cases accord administrative expense priority. * * *

In light of the ambiguity of the legislative history surrounding interest on tax liabilities, these cases rely upon the articulation of prior law in *Nicholas*. Fueling these cases is the belief that Congress, despite striking the Senate version of the Code which expressly would have authorized the collection of interest, meant to implicitly retain such an allowance, either as part of the tax itself or as a natural concomitant of a "fine, penalty, or reduction in credit" per § 503(b)(1)(C). These cases have thus refused to interpret Congressional inaction, or silence as constituting a repudiation of prior law. * * *

We continue to embrace the result and reasoning in *In re Allied Mechanical* as representing the better approach in light of prior law as articulated in *Nicholas*. We now examine *Nicholas* as well as other prior law to determine whether the rationale of *Nicholas* may be fairly read to favor administrative expense priority for interest attendant to trade debts.

D. *Prior Law*

The Bankruptcy Act, like the Code, had no provision specifically permitting post-bankruptcy interest on claims in general or on tax claims in particular. Under the Act, the courts adhered to the equitable principle that the accrual of interest was suspended with the filing of the petition. *Sexton v. Dreyfus*, 219 U.S. 339, 344, 31 S.Ct. 256, 257, 55

L.Ed.244 (1911). As explained by Justice Holmes in *Sexton*, this equitable principle, derived from a well-established tenet of English law, operates to fix the moment when the affairs of the debtor are concluded. *Id.* at 344, 31 S.Ct. at 257. Given that all claims do not bear the same rate of interest, the rule suspends accrual at filing under the rationale that "[a]s this delay was the act of law, no one should thereby gain an advantage or suffer a loss." *American Iron & Steel Mfg. Co. v. Seaboard Air Line Ry.*, 233 U.S. 261, 266, 34 S.Ct. 502, 504, 58 L.Ed. 949 (1914). In addition to avoiding unfairness as between competing creditors, the denial of postpetition interest on prepetition claims also avoided the administrative inconvenience of recomputation of interest. * * *

Denial of postpetition interest on prepetition claims was not an ironclad rule, and over time, exceptions arose. The first, the "solvency exception" discussed *supra*, provided that where an estate had sufficient assets to pay all claims in full, creditors would receive postpetition interest before any surplus would be returned to the bankrupt. * * * A second exception allowed dividends and interest earned by securities held by the creditor as collateral to be applied to postpetition interest. A third exception of more doubtful provenance provided interest for oversecured claims. *See United States v. Ron Pair Enterprises*, 489 U.S. 235, 246, 109 S.Ct. 1026, 1033, 103 L.Ed.2d 290 (1989). Far from being rigid categories, each of these exceptions represented the development by courts of flexible guidelines for the exercise of their equitable powers. *Id.* at 248, 109 S.Ct. at 1034. Animating the development of such guidelines was the underlying equitable principle first articulated by the Supreme Court in *Vanston*:

> It is manifest that the touchstone of each decision on allowance of interest in bankruptcy, receivership and reorganization has been a balance of equities between creditor and creditor or between creditors and the debtor.

Vanston Bondholders Protective Committee v. Green, 329 U.S. 156, 165, 67 S.Ct. 237, 241, 91 L.Ed. 162 (1946).

The Trustee urges that this articulation of prior law governing interest on prepetition claims should govern the outcome of the decision today. Were it not for the Supreme Court's decision in *Nicholas*, we would be inclined to agree. Nevertheless, because that decision expressly addresses the award of interest on claims arising *postpetition* and during a reorganization or arrangement, as opposed to other prior law which addresses the propriety of postpetition interest on *prepetition claims*, *Nicholas* guides our analysis.

The Supreme Court in *Nicholas* addressed the question of whether to permit interest on taxes incurred during a corporate arrangement under Chapter XI of the Bankruptcy Act which was superseded by a bankruptcy proceeding. The context of *Nicholas* is analogous to the instant context—i.e., a debt incurred during a Chapter 11 reorganization, which is superseded by a conversion to Chapter 7. Tracing the prior law, the *Nicholas* Court concluded that prior decisions concerning the suspension of interest on prepetition claims "reflect[ed] the broad equitable principle that creditors should not be disadvantaged vis-a-vis one another by legal delays attributable solely to the time-consuming procedures inherent in the administration of the bankruptcy laws." 384 U.S. at 683, 86 S.Ct. at 1679. The Court, nevertheless, while recognizing the strong considerations of equity and administrative convenience underpinning this rule, declined to treat identically interest on claims arising prepetition and those arising postpetition during a period of arrangement:

> To be sure, the amount of interest that accumulates on a debt incurred during a Chapter XI arrangement depends upon the duration of a proceeding that takes place under the direction and authority of the bankruptcy court. But interest claimed on such a debt does not arise through a "delay" of the law in any meaningful sense. The underlying obligation of the debtor in possession is incurred as part of a judicial process of rehabilitation of the debtor that the procedures of Chapter XI are designed to facilitate. Interest on a current Chapter XI obligation is therefore different in kind from interest claimed during the arrangement period on a debt incurred before the Chapter XI petition was filed.

Id. at 684–85, 86 S.Ct. at 1680 (internal citation omitted).

The Court also determined that where the arrangement period is interrupted by the subsequent filing of a bankruptcy petition, the equitable rationale fueling the Court's earlier decisions would apply to suspend the accrual of interest. *Id.* at 685, 86 S.Ct. at 1680. Thus, the Court held that "the accumulation of interest on a debt must be suspended once an enterprise enters a period of bankruptcy administration beyond that in which the underlying interest-bearing obligation was incurred." *Id.* Thus, the treatment of interest would correspond to which of the three relevant periods of bankruptcy in which the claim arose.

The Court found support for this division from the threefold hierarchy of priorities for tax claims under the Bankruptcy Act. First, § 63a(4) provided that taxes incurred in the pre-arrangement period received fourth priority in distribution. Second, taxes incurred during the arrangement period received first priority under § 64a(1). Finally, the last sentence of § 64a(1) subordinated arrangement expenses within that priority to expenses of the superseding bankruptcy administration.

With substantial refinements, the current Code parallels the threefold hierarchy of priorities for tax claim under the Bankruptcy Act. Section 507(a)(7), analogous to § 63a(4), accords seventh priority to claims for taxes not entitled to administrative expense priority pursuant to § 503(b)(1)(B). Section 507(a)(1) in turn parallels § 64a(1) by according administrative expense priority to those taxes incurred by the estate as defined in § 503(b)(1)(B). See § 726(a)(1). Section 726(b) duplicates § 64a(1)'s subordination of arrangement expenses by providing that administrative expenses incurred during liquidation take precedence over reorganization expenses accorded administrative expense priority pursuant to § 503(b).

In examining the applicability of the threefold hierarchy rationale to trade claims, the Code supports an analogy. Prepetition trade debts would generally be unsecured and under § 726(a)(2) would be paid after distribution of § 507 claims (which includes taxes distributed pursuant to § 507(a)(7)). Trade debts incurred during Chapter 11 and accorded administrative expense priority, as are tax claims, would be distributed, pursuant to § 726(a)(1), as first priority claims under § 507(a)(1) as defined in § 503(b)(1)(A). Finally, § 726(b) subordinates administrative expenses, whether such expenses are trade debts satisfying the criteria of § 503(b)(1)(A) or taxes as defined in § 503(b)(1)(B), incurred during reorganization to those administrative expenses attendant to a Chapter 7 liquidation. Accordingly, the structure of the Code supports the thesis that the *Nicholas* rationale embraces trade debts as well as taxes.

The next question that arises is whether the policy rationale of *Nicholas* offers any explanation of whether taxes and trade debts should be treated differently. The Supreme Court articulated the policy rationale as follows:

> The allowance of interest on Chapter XI debts until the filing of a petition in bankruptcy promotes the availability of capital to a debtor in possession and enhances the likelihood of achieving the goal of the proceeding the ultimate rehabilitation of the debtor. Disallowance of interest on Chapter XI debts might seriously hinder the availability of such funds and might in many cases foreclose the prospect of the debtor's recovery.

Nicholas, 384 U.S. at 687, 86 S.Ct. at 1681.

This Policy applies with equal, if not greater, force in the context of trade debts. Whereas tax obligations accrue as a matter of law, the debtor and creditor voluntarily create trade debts to continue the business as a going concern. The taxing authority as an involuntary creditor does not choose its debtors; the presence or absence of interest is irrelevant to the governments "choice" to become a creditor. However, disallowance of interest may properly be viewed as a disincentive to voluntary creditors. Thus, the *Nicholas* rationale—that disallowance of interest may "hinder the availability" of funds—operates with greater force in the instant context involving voluntary creditors than in the *Nicholas* context itself. Further, there is no reason why postpetition creditors, whether involuntary or voluntary, should fund the debtor's rehabilitation with interest-free loans. As noted by the Supreme Court, "[i]n most situations, interest is considered to be the cost of the use of the amounts owing a creditor and an incentive to prompt repayment and, thus, an integral part of a continuing debt." *Bruning v. United States*, 376 U.S. 358, 360, 84 S.Ct. 906, 908, 11 L.Ed.2d 772 (1964). A business unable to meet the current costs of doing business, costs which include the time value of money, will be unable ultimately to successfully reorganize and to continue as a going concern. Although reorganization may afford the debtor certain accommodations, such accommodations are not without limit:

> 'Although the fundamental goal of Chapter 11 is the ultimate rehabilitation of the debtor, the treatment of administrative expenses as debts entitled to first priority status suggests an overriding policy that a debtor's efforts to reorganize shall be financed by the debtor, not the debtor's post-petition creditors. * * * '

In re Allied Mechanical Serv. Inc., 885 F.2d 837, 839 (11th Cir.1989) (quoting *In re Gould & Eberhardt Gear Machinery Corp.*, 80 B.R. 614, 617 (D.Mass.1987)).

The structure of the Code also supports treating the interest on trade debts accorded administrative expense priority similarly to interest on tax claims accorded such priority. The *Nicholas* Court alluded to the principle that the Bankruptcy Act placed administrative expenses on a parity, including claims for taxes. 384 U.S. at 691, 86 S.Ct. at 1683. * * * The Code similarly provides that claims allowable pursuant to § 503(b) as administrative expenses share equally without sub-priorities. * * * The concept of parity for administrative expenses flows from the premise underlying the category. The threshold requirement for an administrative expense is that it be actual and necessary to the preservation of the estate; the benefit must run to the debtor and be fundamental to the conduct of its business. *In re Continental Airlines*, 146 B.R. 520, 526 (Bankr.D.Del.1992). Administrative expense priority prevents unjust enrichment from this benefit:

> The principal purpose of according administrative priority to claims for benefit to the estate is to prevent unjust enrichment of the debtor's estate, rather than simply to compensate the claimant. Conceptually, the costs of administration are a kind of priority afforded to those who either help preserve and administer the estate or who assist with the rehabilitation of the debtor so that all creditors will benefit.

In re Coal–X Ltd. 76, 60 B.R. 907, 912 (Bankr.D.Utah 1986). To the extent that creditors otherwise on a parity are treated differently with respect to interest, the debtor is unjustly enriched. Thus, if one claimant is to be preferred over others, "the purpose should be clear from the statute." * * *

Thus, our analysis concludes that the language of the Code gives no guidance as to the priority of interest on administrative expense trade debts, that neither the statute nor the legislative history indicate[s] a clear intent to abrogate the prior law, and thus that it is appropriate for us to look for guidance to the prior law. For the reasons discussed above, we conclude that the *Nicholas* rationale provides an appropriate analogy in the prior law.

However, the Trustee argues that the Seventh Circuit's decision in *In re Brooks and Woodington, Inc.*, 505 F.2d 794 (7th Cir.1974), not *Nicholas*, represents prior law. *Brooks* held that accountants employed by the bankruptcy trustee were not entitled to an administrative expense claim for interest on their underlying claim for accountant's fees rendered on behalf of the estate. The court's discussion of the interest issue was very cursory, with no reference to *Nicholas,* although denying interest accrued on claims incurred during the reorganization proceeding would directly contradict the Supreme Court's decision. *Id.* at 799. It is noteworthy that the argument for interest was not even raised until the reply brief, *id.,* and that this fact was one of the grounds of the decision disallowing interest:

> In the light of the generally prevailing bankruptcy rule applicable to interest bearing claims *and particularly in view of the manner in which the claim for interest has been asserted in this particular appeal,* we hold that appellants are not to be allowed interest on the amount of their claim.

Id. (emphasis supplied). Further, the court's reference to the prevailing bankruptcy rule was obviously to the *Sexton* rule, although the court offered no explanation of why this rule represented a suitable analogy. Interest on postpetition administrative claims incurred during a period of reorganization implicates different policy considerations from the award of postpetition interest on prepetition claims. As articulated by the court in *In re Far West Corp.,* 120 B.R. 551 (Bankr.E.D.Cal.1990):

> The rationale for according certain postpetition claims priority status was to prevent the reorganization or administration of the estate from being jeopardized by a creditor's refusal to deal with the debtor postpetition while the policy considerations behind the general rule suspending the accrual of interest on prepetition claims were premised upon notions of equity and administrative convenience.

Id. at 554 (internal citations omitted). For the foregoing reasons, we decline to accord precedential value to the *Brooks* decision.

The Trustee also argues that the analogy to interest on postpetition taxes, and the analogy to *Nicholas,* is misplaced because first priority for such interest flows from § 503(b)(1)(C)(specifically providing that penalties relating to an administrative expense claim for taxes carry the same priority as the tax). The Trustee observes that if Congress intended penalties attendant to taxes to carry the same priority as the tax, Congress must also have intended that interest attendant to taxes should carry the same priority. Finally, the Trustee notes that there is no provision similar to § 503(b)(1)(C) from which we might infer a Congressional intent that interest on an administrative expense trade debt should carry the same priority as the trade debt. Although we acknowledge the inference from § 503(b)(1)(C), and the absence of a similar provision with respect to administrative expense trade debts, we nevertheless conclude that the *Nicholas* rationale is applicable. At the time *Nicholas* was decided, there was no statutory provision similar to § 503(b)(1)(C). Thus, the instant context, in which there is also no such similar statutory provision, is similar to the context addressed by the Supreme Court in *Nicholas.* We find that it is appropriate to employ the

Nicholas rationale. Also, the *Nicholas* opinion uses language suggesting that the rationale applies generally to administrative expense "debts" and not merely to administrative expense "taxes". 384 U.S. at 687, 689, 86 S.Ct. at 1681, 1683. Finally, as discussed above, the similar structure of the relevant statutes and the similarity of policy concerns indicate that the analogy to *Nicholas* is appropriate.

In summary, because the language of the Code is silent, and the statute and legislative history indicate no clear intent to abrogate prior law, we look to the prior law. As indicated in the foregoing discussion, we conclude that the most reasonable reading of the prior law is that the priority accorded to interest on trade debts incurred as administrative expenses during Chapter 11 should be determined pursuant to the *Nicholas* rationale. Accordingly, we hold that interest on trade debts incurred as administrative expenses during Chapter 11 enjoys the same priority as the administrative expense itself, but that upon conversion to Chapter 7, the interest accruing thereafter enjoys only the fifth priority pursuant to § 726(a)(5).

II. *The Right to Immediate Payment*

Varsity argues that the district court erred in affirming the bankruptcy court's denial of its motion for immediate payment. The determination of the timing of payment of administrative expenses is a matter within the discretion of the bankruptcy court. Because the bankruptcy court was aware of significant claims that held a potentially higher priority than those of Varsity, we readily conclude that the bankruptcy court did not abuse its discretion.

Conclusion

Based on the foregoing, we affirm the district court's award of administrative expense priority for interest accruing during the Chapter 11 proceeding on Varsity's trade claims arising during that proceeding, with interest accruing after conversion entitled to fifth priority pursuant to § 726(a)(5). We affirm the district court's denial of Varsity's motion for immediate payment of its administrative expense claims. Accordingly, the judgment of the district court is

AFFIRMED.

---

1. Assume that Trade Creditor A and Trade Creditor B each perform services to the tune of $200,000 for Debtor in bankruptcy. Assume that A has a term in its agreement that Debtor will pay ten percent compounded per year. B has no such term. As part of the reorganization does A but not B get interest for the period after the service has been performed and before payment?

2. The court does not rely on section 364(c) but it might have. Do you see how section 364(c) and the policy that supports 364(c) might have helped?

Notes and Questions

1. Only a few cases interpret section 503(b)(1)(A). The section defines administrative expenses to include "the actual, necessary costs and expenses of preserving the estate, including wages, salaries, or commissions for services rendered after the commencement of the case * * * " But why are the cases so rare? As this is written, one of the largest retail chains in the United States, one of the largest steel manufacturers, and several of the large airlines are operating in Chapter 11. Presumably each of those business organizations will ultimately treat almost every single dollar spent and every single obligation incurred after the petition as an administrative expense. Why is there so little controversy?

Which of the following expenses might be challenged as not "actual" and "necessary"?

   a. That portion of the salary of the CEO of the retail chain that exceeded the greater of $1,000,000 per year or the average in the industry?

   b. Money spent by an airline in Chapter 11 for hiring a lobbyist in connection with modification of the federal law concerning the operation of airlines?

   c. A payment by a large oil company while it is in Chapter 11 to support an opera program on public radio and television?

2. Sometimes the unsecured creditors seek a bite or two from the mortgagee's apple. Assume the following case: the corporate debtor's sole asset is an apartment complex. During its 12 months in bankruptcy the DIP spends $100,000 in legal fees, and more than one million dollars in maintenance, advertising and administration of the apartment complex. When the debtor gives up and converts from a Chapter 11 to a Chapter 7, $500,000 of these expenses are still unpaid. There is no money in the estate.

The Chapter 7 trustee proposes that the $500,000 be taken from the mortgagee (whose perfected mortgage debt is conceded to attach to and exceed the value of the apartment complex) and paid to the various creditors. The trustee argues such claims must be paid under the terms of section 506(c).

(c) The trustee may recover from property securing an allowed secured claim the reasonable, necessary costs and expenses of preserving, or disposing of, such property to the extent of any benefit to the holder of such claim.

You represent the mortgagee; how would you respond?

3. Returning to the apartment complex described above, assume the mortgagee pays real estate tax that would otherwise become an assessment against the property and would have priority over the mortgage. If a reorganization plan is proposed that does not treat that payment as an administrative expense, can the mortgagee submit it as such and insist upon reimbursement of the tax paid under the terms of section 503(b), particularly 503(b)(1)(B)? What if the mortgagee had not paid a tax, but had rather

paid a $200,000 bill for replacing the roofs on most of the apartment buildings?

§ 3. GENERAL UNSECURED CLAIMS

IN RE CHATEAUGAY CORPORATION

United States Court of Appeals, Second Circuit, 1992.
961 F.2d 378.

OAKES, CHIEF JUDGE:

Valley Fidelity Bank & Trust Co. ("Valley") and intervenors appeal from a judgment of the United States District Court for the Southern District of New York, Shirley Wohl Kram, *Judge*, affirming a judgment of the United States Bankruptcy Court for the Southern District of New York, Burton R. Lifland, *Chief Judge*. The bankruptcy court granted partial summary judgment in favor of the debtor, the LTV Corporation ("LTV"), disallowing Valley's claims to the extent they included unamortized original issue discount ("OID"). On this appeal, Valley argues that the bankruptcy court and district court erred by holding (1) that new OID arose on an exchange of debt securities performed as part of LTV's failed attempt to avoid bankruptcy through a consensual workout, and (2) that amortization of OID should be calculated by the constant interest method, rather than by the straight line method. For the reasons set forth below, we reverse in part and affirm in part. We hold first that while claims must be disallowed to the extent of unamortized OID, no new OID arose on LTV's debt-for-debt exchange, and second, that OID amortization should be calculated by the constant interest method.

FACTS

In July 1986, LTV, a steel company that makes defense and industrial products, filed for Chapter 11 reorganization along with sixty-six of its subsidiaries. LTV filed objections in September 1989 to two proofs of claim, numbers 20,069 and 20,067, filed in November 1987 by Valley on behalf of the holders of two securities, the "Old Debentures" and the "New Notes." Valley is the trustee for both the Old Debentures and the New Notes.

The Old Debentures are 13⅞% Sinking Fund Debentures due December 1, 2002, of which LTV had by December 1, 1982 issued a total face amount of $150,000,000. Of that face amount, $125,000,000 had been issued to the public, for which LTV received $110,935,000 in cash. The remaining $25,000,000 had been issued to subsidiary pension funds, in lieu of cash contributions of $22,167,000. The proceeds received for the Old Debentures thus amounted to 88.67% of their face value.

The New Notes are LTV 15% Senior Notes due January 15, 2000. In May 1986, LTV offered to exchange $1,000 face amount of New Notes and 15 shares of LTV common stock for each $1,000 face amount of Old Debentures. As of June 1, 1986, $116,035,000 face amount of Old

Debentures had been exchanged for the same face amount of New Notes and LTV Common Stock.

In its proofs of claim, Valley did not deduct any amount for unamortized OID. LTV objected to the claims and moved for partial summary judgment, seeking an order disallowing unamortized OID. LTV argued that unamortized OID is unmatured interest which is not allowable by virtue of section 502(b)(2) of the Bankruptcy Code, 11 U.S.C. § 502(b)(2)(1988), and that therefore the claims must be reduced by the amount of unamortized OID. A number of other creditors intervened to address questions of law that they believe may affect their own claims against LTV.

The bankruptcy court granted partial summary judgment for LTV. *In re Chateaugay Corp.*, 109 B.R. 51, 58 (Bankr.S.D.N.Y.1990). The court held that unamortized OID is not allowable under section 502(b)(2), and that the proper method for calculating unamortized OID is the constant interest method. *Id.* The court also held that as indenture trustee, Valley was the proper party in interest to receive notice of LTV's objections. *Id.* Concluding that the amount of unamortized OID on the Old Debentures could be calculated using uncontroverted evidence, but that the amount on the New Notes could not be calculated until a disputed fact—the fair market value of the Old Debentures at the time of the exchange—was resolved, the court granted LTV's motion except as to the amount of unamortized OID on the New Notes. *Id.*

LTV and Valley thereafter stipulated to $3,554,609 and $8,174,134 as the amount of unamortized OID on the Old Debentures and the New Notes, respectively, calculated in accordance with the bankruptcy court's opinion. After that stipulation, Judge Lifland on March 27, 1990 entered a judgment partially disallowing, in the above amounts, Valley's proofs of claim. The district court affirmed the bankruptcy court's decision in its entirety. *In re Chateaugay Corp.*, 130 B.R. 403, 405 (S.D.N.Y.1991).

DISCUSSION

I. Original Issue Discount and Section 502(b)(2)

A

Original issue discount results when a bond is issued for less than its face value. The discount, which compensates for a stated interest rate that the market deems too low, equals the difference between a bond's face amount (stated principal amount) and the proceeds, prior to issuance expenses, received by the issuer. OID is amortized, for accounting and tax purposes, over the life of the bond, with the face value generally paid back to the bondholders on the maturity date. If the debtor meets with financial trouble and turns to the bankruptcy court for protection, as in the present case, then OID comes into play as one of the factors determining the amount of the bondholder's allowable claim in bankruptcy.

Section 502 of the Bankruptcy Code, the framework for Chapter 11 claim allowance, provides that a claim shall be allowed "except to the extent that ... such claim is for unmatured interest." 11 U.S.C. § 502(b)(2)(1988). The first question we face is whether unamortized OID is "unmatured interest" within the meaning of section 502(b)(2). We conclude that it is. As a matter of economic definition, OID constitutes interest. *United States v. Midland–Ross Corp.*, 381 U.S. 54, 57, 85 S.Ct. 1308, 1310, 14 L.Ed.2d 214 (1965)(treating OID for tax purposes as income, not capital); *see also* Frank J. Slagle, Accounting for Interest: An Analysis of Original Issue Discount in the Sale of Property, 32 S.D.L. Rev. 1, 21 n. 108 (1987)("The amount of the discount represents compensation to the Lender for the use and forbearance of money, i.e., interest."). Moreover, the Bankruptcy Code's legislative history makes inescapable the conclusion that OID is interest within the meaning of section 502(b)(2). The House committee report on that section explains:

> Interest disallowed under this paragraph includes postpetition interest that is not yet due and payable, and any portion of prepaid interest that represents an original discounting of the claim, yet that would not have been earned on the date of bankruptcy. For example, a claim on a $1,000 note issued the day before bankruptcy would only be allowed to the extent of the cash actually advanced. If the original issue discount was 10% so that the cash advanced was only $900, then notwithstanding the face amount of [the] note, only $900 would be allowed. If $900 was advanced under the note some time before bankruptcy, the interest component of the note would have to be prorated and disallowed to the extent it was for interest after the commencement of the case.

H.Rep. No. 595, 95th Cong., 1st Sess. 352–53 (1977), *reprinted in* 1978 U.S.C.C.A.N. 5787, 5963, 6308–09.

The courts that have considered the issue under section 502(b)(2) have held that unamortized OID is unmatured interest and therefore unallowable as part of a bankruptcy claim. * * * The *Public Service* court stated it plainly: "The word 'interest' in the statute is clearly sufficient to encompass the OID variation in the method of providing for and collecting what in economic fact is interest to be paid to compensate for the delay and risk involved in the ultimate repayment of monies loaned." 114 B.R. at 803.

Applying this reasoning to the case at hand, we conclude, as did the bankruptcy and district courts, that OID on the Old Debentures, to the extent it was unamortized when the bankruptcy petition was filed, should be disallowed. We now turn to the main issue in dispute: the applicability of section 502(b)(2) to the New Notes, which were issued in a debt-for-debt exchange offer as part of a consensual workout.

B

A debtor in financial trouble may seek to avoid bankruptcy through a consensual out-of-court workout. Such a recapitalization, when it involves publicly traded debt, often takes the form of a debt-for-debt exchange, whereby bondholders exchange their old bonds for new bonds. The debtor hopes that the exchange, by changing the terms of the debt, will enable the debtor to avoid default. The bondholders hope that by increasing the likelihood of payment on their bonds, the exchange will benefit them as well. The debtor and its creditors share an interest in achieving a successful restructuring of the debtor's financial obligations in order to avoid the uncertainties and daunting transaction costs of bankruptcy.

An exchange offer made by a financially troubled company can be either a "fair market value exchange" or a "face value exchange." * * * In a fair market value exchange, an existing debt instrument is exchanged for a new one with a reduced principal amount, determined by the market value at which the existing instrument is trading. By offering a fair market value exchange, an issuer seeks to reduce its overall debt obligations. Usually, this is sought only by companies in severe financial distress. A face value exchange, by contrast, involves the substitution of new indebtedness for an existing debenture, modifying terms or conditions but not reducing the principal amount of the debt. A relatively healthy company faced with liquidity problems may offer a face value exchange to obtain short-term relief while remaining fully liable for the original funds borrowed.

The question is whether a face value exchange generates new OID. The bankruptcy court, in an opinion endorsed by the district court, held that it does. The court reasoned that, by definition, OID arises whenever a bond is issued for less than its face amount, and that in LTV's debt-for-debt exchange, the issue price of the New Notes was the fair market value of the Old Debentures. The court therefore concluded that the New Notes were issued at a discount equaling the difference between their face value and the fair market value of the Old Debentures. *In re Chateaugay Corp.*, 109 B.R. at 56–57.

The bankruptcy court's reasoning leaves us unpersuaded. While its application of the definition of OID to exchange offers may seem irrefutable at first glance, we believe the bankruptcy court's logic ignores the importance of context, and does not make sense if one takes into account the strong bankruptcy policy in favor of the speedy, inexpensive, negotiated resolution of disputes, that is an out-of-court or common law composition. *See* H.R.Rep. No. 95–595, 95th Cong., 1st Sess. 220 (1977), *reprinted in* 1978 U.S.S.C.A.N. 5963, 6179–80; *see also In re Colonial Ford, Inc.*, 24 B.R. 1014, 1015–17 (Bankr.D.Utah 1982)("Congress designed the Code, in large measure, to encourage workouts in the first instance, with refuge in bankruptcy as a last resort."). If unamortized OID is unallowable in bankruptcy, and if exchanging debt increases the amount of OID, then creditors will be disinclined to cooperate in a consensual workout that might otherwise have rescued a borrower from the precipice of bankruptcy. We must consider the ramifications of a rule that places a creditor in the position of choosing whether to cooperate with a struggling debtor, when such cooperation might make the creditor's claims in the event of bankruptcy smaller than they would have been had the creditor refused to cooperate. The bankruptcy court's ruling places creditors in just such a position, and unreversed would likely result in fewer out-of-court debt exchanges and more Chapter 11 filings. Just as that ruling creates a disincentive for creditors to cooperate with a troubled debtor, it grants a corresponding windfall both to holdouts who refuse to cooperate and to an issuer that files for bankruptcy subsequent to a debt exchange. * * *

The bankruptcy court's decision might make sense in the context of a fair market value exchange, where the corporation's overall debt obligations are reduced. In a face value exchange such as LTV's, however, it is unsupportable. LTV's liability to the holders of the New Notes was no less than its liability to them had been when they held the Old Debentures. The bankruptcy court, by finding that the exchange created new OID, reduced LTV's liabilities based on an exchange which, because it was a face value exchange, caused no such reduction on LTV's balance sheet.

We hold that a face value exchange of debt obligations in a consensual workout does not, for purposes of section 502(b)(2), generate new OID. Such an exchange does not change the character of the underlying debt, but reaffirms and modifies it. *Cf. In re Red Way Cartage Co.*, 84 B.R. 459, 461 (Bankr.E.D.Mich.1988)(in context of preferential transfers, settlement agreement did not create new debt, but only reaffirmed the antecedent debt); *In re Magic Circle Energy Corp.*, 64 B.R. 269, 273 (Bankr.W.D.Okla.1986)(same, explaining, "We do not accept the proposition that the consolidation of [debt] into a long-term promissory note wrought a metamorphosis wherein the nature of the debt was altered."); *In re Busman*, 5 B.R. 332, 336 (Bankr.E.D.N.Y.1980) ("the rule [of 502(b)(2)] is clearly not entrenched as an absolute").

In the absence of unambiguous statutory guidance, we will not attribute to Congress an intent to place a stumbling block in front of debtors seeking to avoid bankruptcy with the cooperation of their creditors. Rather, given Congress's intent to encourage consensual workouts and the obvious desirability of minimizing bankruptcy filings, we conclude that for purposes of section 502(b)(2), no new OID is created in a face value debt-for-debt exchange in the context of a consensual workout. Thus, OID on the new debt consists only of the discount carried over from the old debt, that is, the unamortized OID remaining on the old debt at the time of the exchange.

The cases upon which the bankruptcy court relied in reaching a contrary conclusion are distinguishable. The court found support for its conclusion by looking to tax cases, because under the Internal Revenue Code, for purposes of determining taxable income, an exchange offer generates new OID. * * * The tax treatment of a transaction, however, need not determine the bankruptcy treatment. * * * The tax treatment of debt-for-debt exchanges derives from the tax laws' focus on realization events, and suggests that an exchange offer may represent a sensible time to tax the parties. The same reasoning simply does not apply in the bankruptcy context. See Kirschner, supra, 21 Seton Hall L.Rev. at 655–56.

Similarly distinguishable is *In re Allegheny Int'l, Inc.*, 100 B.R. 247 (Bankr.W.D.Pa.1989), upon which the bankruptcy court relied heavily in determining that new OID was created by LTV's debt exchange. In *Allegheny*, the court considered and rejected the argument "that section 502(b)(2) does not apply * * * to debentures created in the context of an exchange offer." Id. at 250. That case, however, involved a debt-for-equity exchange, not a debt-for-debt exchange. The debtor in *Allegheny* offered to exchange debt instruments for previously issued preferred stock. Id. at 248. Thus, the stockholders had no claim against the debtor prior to the exchange, and the debtor's balance sheet reflected an increase in overall liabilities from the exchange. We need not decide whether *Allegheny* was correct. Whether or not its reasoning is sound in the context of a debt-for-equity exchange, it is inapplicable to a debt-for-debt exchange such as LTV's.

II. *Calculating OID Amortization*

We now turn to the methodology for calculating OID amortization. Valley argues that the proper method for calculating unamortized OID under the Bankruptcy Code is the straight line method, by which the amount of the discount is spread equally over the duration of the maturation of the note. Under the straight line method, the same amount of interest accrues during each day of the instrument's term. LTV argues, in contrast, that the constant interest method—which also goes by the names yield-to-maturity, effective interest, or economic accrual—should be used. The constant interest method calculates OID amortization on the assumption that interest is compounded over time. Under the constant interest method, the amount of interest that accrues each day increases over time.

The bankruptcy court and district court opted for the constant interest method, and we agree. The constant interest method comports more closely than the straight line method with economic reality. * * *

One bankruptcy court has held that OID should be calculated by the straight line method for purposes of Bankruptcy Code section 502(b)(2), *Allegheny*, 100 B.R. at 254, but its reasoning is unconvincing. That court simply noted that the legislative history of section 502(b)(2) provides that unmatured interest should be "pro-rated," and assumed without analysis that the prorating must be done so that the increases are constant through time, rather than so that the rate of increase is constant through time. To say that interest must be pro-rated is only to restate the question, which is what method should be used for that prorating.

One further point must be addressed regarding the calculation of OID amortization. Our holding today that, for purposes of section 502(b)(2), no new OID is created by a face value debt-for-debt exchange in a consensual workout, means that the old OID is carried over to the new debt. In other words, when the Old Debentures were exchanged for the New Notes, the New Notes carried a discount equaling the amount of OID remaining on the Old Debentures after amortization by the constant interest method. The amount of OID remaining must then be amortized, again employing the constant interest method, over the life of the New Notes. Thus, a creditor's claim in bankruptcy may differ depending on whether the creditor participated in a workout; that difference, however, derives not from any new OID created by the exchange, but from the logical necessity of an amortization schedule that concludes on the maturity date. In the present case, because the New Notes carried an earlier maturity date than the Old Debentures, those bondholders who cooperated with the debtor find themselves with a slightly larger claim in bankruptcy, after the disallowance of unamortized OID, than those who did not.

Accordingly, the judgment of the district court is affirmed in part and reversed in part, and the matter remanded to the district court for remand to the bankruptcy court for further proceedings consistent with this opinion.

Questions

1. You represent a creditor in a workout who holds a single debenture with a face amount of $1.1 million bearing interest at 10% per year. There is no original issue discount and no interest in default. In the workout the debtor proposes to exchange the debenture for a new debenture that bears a face amount of $900,000 together with a 15% rate of interest or alternatively with a $1.1 million debenture. Would you have an interest in the holding in Chateaugay?

2. Why did the parties argue over the mode of calculation of the original issue discount? Are the interests of the DIP and the creditor in conflict?

3. What is the justification for the denial of unamortized interest as a claim under 502(b)(2)?

4. Do you see why the appellate court is right and Judge Lifland was wrong? Consider the status of the creditor who agrees to the workout versus the status of a creditor who refused the workout. If the value of the $1,000,000 debenture was only $200,000, the one who refused to turn in his debenture would nevertheless get a $1,000,000 claim—and assuming no original issue discount. That would be so even though the current value of the claim was only 20% of the face value. If, on the other hand, there was an exchange of old debt (1.0) for new debt (0.2) $800,000 would be turned into original issue discount under Judge Lifland's theory. Thus the agreeable person who had gone along with the workout would be put in a worse position than the recalcitrant one.

Problem 8–4

Wilderness Corporation is in a Chapter 11 bankruptcy proceeding. One of the claims asserted against the debtor is a $2 million note secured by the debtor's factory in Detroit. The factory has a current market value of only

$500,000. The bank that holds that mortgage also holds a guaranty issued by Scipio, the majority shareholder of Wilderness. In the Chapter 11 plan proposed by Wilderness, unsecured creditors will receive 20 cents per dollar on their claims. If Scipio has not paid anything on the guaranty at the time of distribution under the plan, will Scipio (an unsecured creditor holding a contingent claim) receive any distribution? Would the result change if Scipio had made a payment of $700,000 to the bank on account of the guaranty? See sections 502(e) and 509.

§ 4. ENVIRONMENTAL CLAIMS

In the past ten years two Supreme Court cases, a handful of appellate cases, and a larger number of bankruptcy cases have dealt with the priority of claims for environmental cleanup in bankruptcy. Many have characterized the issue as whether a trustee in bankruptcy can abandon property under section 554 that is rendered worthless because of the presence of hazardous or toxic waste. A smaller number of cases has focused directly on the priority of the environmental claim.

MIDLANTIC NATIONAL BANK v. NEW JERSEY DEPARTMENT OF ENVIRONMENTAL PROTECTION

Supreme Court of the United States, 1986.
474 U.S. 494, 106 S.Ct. 755, 88 L.Ed.2d 859.

JUSTICE POWELL delivered the opinion of the Court.

These petitions for certiorari, arising out of the same bankruptcy proceeding, present the question whether § 554(a) of the Bankruptcy Code, 11 U.S.C. § 554(a), authorizes a trustee in bankruptcy to abandon property in contravention of state laws or regulations that are reasonably designed to protect the public's health or safety.

I

Quanta Resources Corporation (Quanta) processed waste oil at two facilities, one in Long Island City, New York, and the other in Edgewater, New Jersey. At the Edgewater facility, Quanta handled the oil pursuant to a temporary operating permit issued by the New Jersey Department of Environmental Protection (NJDEP), respondent in No. 84–801. In June 1981, Midlantic National Bank, petitioner in No. 84–801, provided Quanta with a $600,000 loan secured by Quanta's inventory, accounts receivable, and certain equipment. The same month, NJDEP discovered that Quanta had violated a specific prohibition in its operating permit by accepting more than 400,000 gallons of oil contaminated with PCB, a highly toxic carcinogen. NJDEP ordered Quanta to cease operations at Edgewater, and the two began negotiations concerning the cleanup of the Edgewater site. But on October 6, 1981, before the conclusion of negotiations, Quanta filed a petition for reorganization under Chapter 11 of the Bankruptcy Code. The next day, NJDEP issued an administrative order requiring Quanta to clean up the site. Quanta's financial condition remained perilous, however, and the following month, it converted the action to a liquidation proceeding under Chapter 7. Thomas J. O'Neill, petitioner in No. 84–805, was appointed trustee in bankruptcy, and subsequently oversaw abandonment of both facilities.

After Quanta filed for bankruptcy, an investigation of the Long Island City facility revealed that Quanta had accepted and stored there over 70,000 gallons of toxic, PCB-contaminated oil in deteriorating and leaking containers. Since the mortgages on that facility's real property exceeded the property's value, the estimated cost of disposing of the waste oil plainly rendered the property a net burden to the estate. After trying without success to sell the Long Island City property for the benefit of Quanta's creditors, the trustee notified the creditors and the Bankruptcy Court for the District of New Jersey that he intended to abandon the property pursuant to § 554(a). No party to the bankruptcy proceeding disputed the trustee's allegation that the site was "burdensome" and of "inconsequential value to the estate" within the meaning of § 554.

The City and the State of New York (collectively New York), respondents in No. 84–805, nevertheless objected, contending that abandonment would threaten the public's health and safety, and would violate state and federal environmental law. New York rested its objection on "public policy" considerations reflected in applicable local laws, and on the requirement of 28 U.S.C. § 959(b), that a trustee "manage and operate" the property of the estate "according to the requirements of the valid laws of the State in which such property is situated." New York asked the Bankruptcy Court to order that the assets of the estate be used to bring the facility into compliance with applicable law. After briefing and argument, the court approved the abandonment, noting that "[t]he City and State are in a better position in every respect than either the Trustee or debtor's creditors to do what needs to be done to protect the public against the dangers posed by the PCB-contaminated facility." The District Court for the District of New Jersey affirmed, and New York appealed to the Court of Appeals for the Third Circuit.

Upon abandonment, the trustee removed the 24-hour guard service and shut down the fire-suppression system. It became necessary for New York to decontaminate the facility, with the exception of the polluted subsoil, at a cost of about $2.5 million.

On April 23, 1983, shortly after the District Court had approved abandonment of the New York site, the trustee gave notice of his intention to abandon the personal property at the Edgewater site, consisting principally of the contaminated oil. The Bankruptcy Court approved the abandonment on May 20, over NJDEP's objection that the estate had sufficient funds to protect the public from the dangers posed by the hazardous waste.

Because the abandonments of the New Jersey and New York facilities presented identical issues, the parties in the New Jersey litigation consented to NJDEP's taking a direct appeal from the Bankruptcy Court to the Court of Appeals pursuant to § 405(c)(1)(B) of the Bankruptcy Act of 1978.

A divided panel of the Court of Appeals for the Third Circuit reversed. *In re Quanta Resources Corp.,* 739 F.2d 912 (1984); *In re Quanta Resources Corp.,* 739 F.2d 927. Although the court found little guidance in the legislative history of § 554, it concluded that Congress had intended to codify the judge-made abandonment practice developed under the previous Bankruptcy Act. Under that law, where state law or general equitable principles protected certain public interests, those interests were not overridden by the judge-made abandonment power. The court also found evidence in other provisions of the Bankruptcy Code that Congress did not intend to pre-empt all state regulation, but only that grounded on policies outweighed by the relevant federal interests. Accordingly, the Court of Appeals held that the Bankruptcy Court erred in permitting abandonment, and remanded both cases for further proceedings.

We granted certiorari and consolidated these cases to determine whether the Court of Appeals properly construed § 554, 469 U.S. 1207, 105 S.Ct. 1168, 84 L.Ed.2d 319. We now affirm.

II

Before the 1978 revisions of the Bankruptcy Code, the trustee's abandonment power had been limited by a judicially developed doctrine intended to protect legitimate state or federal interests. This was made clear by the few relevant cases. In *Ottenheimer v. Whitaker,* 198 F.2d 289 (C.A.4 1952), the Court of Appeals concluded that a bankruptcy trustee, in liquidating the estate of a barge company, could not abandon several barges when the abandonment would have obstructed a navigable passage in violation of federal law. The court stated:

> "The judge-made [abandonment] rule must give way when it comes into conflict with a statute enacted in order to ensure the safety of navigation; for we are not dealing with a burden imposed upon the bankrupt or his property by contract, but a duty and a burden imposed upon an owner of vessels by an Act of Congress in the public interest." *Id.,* at 290.

In *In re Chicago Rapid Transit Co.,* 129 F.2d 1 (CA7), cert. denied, 317 U.S. 683, 63 S.Ct. 205, 87 L.Ed. 547 (1942), the Court of Appeals held that the trustee of a debtor transit company could not cease its operation of a branch railway line when local law required continued operation. While the court did not forbid the trustee to abandon property (*i.e.,* to reject an unexpired lease), it conditioned his actions to ensure compliance with state law. Similarly, in *In re Lewis Jones, Inc.,* 1 BCD 277 (Bankr.E.D.Pa.1974), the bankruptcy court invoked its equitable power to "safeguard the public interest" by requiring the debtor public utilities to seal underground steam lines before abandoning them.

Thus, when Congress enacted § 554, there were well-recognized restrictions on a trustee's abandonment power. In codifying the judicially developed rule of abandonment, Congress also presumably included the established corollary that a trustee could not exercise his abandonment power in violation of certain state and federal laws. The normal rule of statutory construction is that if Congress intends for legislation to change the interpretation of a judicially created concept, it makes that intent specific. *Edmonds v. Compagnie Generale Transatlantique,* 443 U.S. 256, 266–267, 99 S.Ct. 2753, 2759–60, 61 L.Ed.2d 521 (1979). The Court has followed this rule with particular care in construing the scope of bankruptcy codifications. If Congress wishes to grant the trustee an extraordinary exemption from non-bankruptcy law, "the intention would be clearly expressed, not left to be collected or inferred from disputable considerations of convenience in administering the estate of the bankrupt." *Swarts v. Hammer,* 194 U.S. 441, 444, 24 S.Ct. 695, 696, 48 L.Ed. 1060 (1904); see *Palmer v. Massachusetts,* 308 U.S. 79, 85, 60 S.Ct. 34, 37, 84 L.Ed. 93 (1939)("If this old and familiar power of the states [over local railroad service] was withdrawn when Congress gave district courts bankruptcy powers over railroads, we ought to find language fitting for so drastic a change"). Although these cases do not define for us the exact contours of the trustee's abandonment power, they do make clear that this power was subject to certain restrictions when Congress enacted § 554(a).

III

Neither the Court nor Congress has granted a trustee in bankruptcy powers that would lend support to a right to abandon property in contravention of state or local laws designed to protect public health or safety. As we held last Term when the State of Ohio sought compensation for cleaning the toxic waste site of a bankrupt corporation:

"Finally, we do not question that anyone in possession of the site—whether it is [the debtor] or another in the event the receivership is liquidated and the trustee abandons the property, or a vendee from the receiver *or the bankruptcy trustee*—must comply with the environmental laws of the State of Ohio. Plainly, that person or firm may not maintain a nuisance, pollute the waters of the State, or refuse to remove the source of such conditions." *Ohio v. Kovacs,* 469 U.S. 274, 105 S.Ct. 705, 711–12, 83 L.Ed.2d 649 (1985)(emphasis added).

Congress has repeatedly expressed its legislative determination that the trustee is not to have *carte blanche* to ignore non-bankruptcy law. Where the Bankruptcy Code has conferred special powers upon the trustee and where there was no common-law limitation on that power, Congress has expressly provided that the efforts of the trustee to marshal and distribute the assets of the estate must yield to governmental interest in public health and safety. *Post,* at 766–767. One cannot assume that Congress, having placed these limitations upon other aspects of trustees' operations, intended to discard a well-established judicial restriction on the abandonment power. As we held nearly two years ago in the context of the National Labor Relations Act, "[T]he debtor-in-possession is not relieved of all obligations under the [Act] simply by filing a petition for bankruptcy." *NLRB v. Bildisco & Bildisco,* 465 U.S. 513, 534, 104 S.Ct. 1188, 1201, 79 L.Ed.2d 482 (1984).

The automatic stay provision of the Bankruptcy Code, § 362(a), has been described as "one of the fundamental debtor protections provided by the bankruptcy laws." S.Rep. No. 95–989, p. 54 (1978); H.R.Rep. No. 95–595, p. 340 (1977), U.S.Code Cong. & Admin.News 1978, pp. 5787, 5840, 5963, 6296. Despite the importance of § 362(a) in preserving the debtor's estate, Congress has enacted several categories of exceptions to the stay that allow the Government to commence or continue legal proceedings. For example, § 362(b)(5) permits the Government to enforce "nonmonetary" judgments against a debtor's estate. It is clear from the legislative history that one of the purposes of this exception is to protect public health and safety:

"Thus, where a governmental unit is suing a debtor to prevent or stop violation of fraud, *environmental protection,* consumer protection, *safety, or similar police or regulatory laws,* or attempting to fix damages for violation of such a law, the action or proceeding is not stayed under the automatic stay." H.R.Rep. No. 95–595, *supra,* at 343 (emphasis added); S.Rep. No. 95–989, *supra,* at 52 (emphasis added), U.S.Code Cong. & Admin.News 1978, pp. 5838, 6299.

Petitioners have suggested that the existence of an express exception to the automatic stay undermines the inference of a similar exception to the abandonment power: had Congress sought to restrict similarly the scope of § 554, it would have enacted similar limiting provisions. This argument, however, fails to acknowledge the differences between the predecessors of §§ 554 and 362. As we have noted, the exceptions to the judicially created abandonment power were firmly established. But in enacting § 362 in 1978, Congress significantly broadened the scope of the automatic stay, see 1 W. Norton, Bankruptcy Law and Practice § 20.03, pp. 5–6 (1981), an expansion that had begun only five years earlier with the adoption of the Bankruptcy Rules in 1973, see *id.,* § 20.02, at 4–5. Between 1973 and 1978, some courts had stretched the expanded automatic stay to foreclose States' efforts to enforce their antipollution laws, and Congress wanted to overrule these interpretations in its 1978 revision. See H.R.Rep. 95–595, *supra,* at 174–175, U.S.Code Cong & Admin.News 1978, pp. 6134–6136. In the face of the greatly increased scope of § 362, it was necessary for Congress to limit this new power expressly.

* * *

IV

Although the reasons elaborated above suffice for us to conclude that Congress did not intend for the abandonment power to abrogate certain state and local laws, we find additional support for restricting that power in repeated congressional emphasis on its "goal of protecting the environment against toxic pollution." *Chemical Manufacturers Assn., Inc. v. Natural Resources Defense Council, Inc.,* 470 U.S. 116, ___, 105 S.Ct. 1102, 1117, 84 L.Ed.2d 90 (1985). Congress has enacted a Resource Conservation and Recovery Act, 42 U.S.C. §§ 6901–6987, to regulate the treatment, storage, and disposal of hazardous wastes by monitoring wastes from their creation until after their permanent disposal. That Act authorizes the United States to seek judicial or administrative restraint of activities involving hazardous wastes that "may present an imminent and substantial endangerment to health or the environment." 42 U.S.C. § 6973; see also S.Rep. No. 98–284, p. 58 (1983). Congress broadened the scope of the statute and tightened the regulatory restraints in 1984. In the Comprehensive Environmental Response, Compensation, and Liability Act, as amended by Pub.L. 98–80, § 2(c)(2)(B), Congress established a fund to finance cleanup of some sites and required certain responsible parties to reimburse either the fund or the parties who paid for the cleanup. The Act also empowers the Federal Government to secure such relief as may be necessary to avert "imminent and substantial endangerment to the public health or welfare or the environment because of an actual or threatened release of a hazardous substance." 42 U.S.C. § 9606. In the face of Congress' undisputed concern over the risks of the improper storage and disposal of hazardous and toxic substances, we are unwilling to presume that by enactment of § 554(a), Congress implicitly overturned long-standing restrictions on the common-law abandonment power.

V

In the light of the Bankruptcy trustee's restricted pre–1978 abandonment power and the limited scope of other Bankruptcy Code provisions, we conclude that Congress did not intend for § 554(a) to pre-empt all state and local laws. The Bankruptcy Court does not have the power to authorize an abandonment without formulating conditions that will adequately protect the public's health and safety. Accordingly, without reaching the question whether certain state laws imposing conditions on abandonment may be so onerous as to interfere with the bankruptcy adjudication itself, we hold that a trustee may not abandon property in contravention of a state statute or regulation that is reasonably designed to protect the public health or safety from identified hazards. Accordingly, we affirm the judgments of the Court of Appeals for the Third Circuit.

It is so ordered.

JUSTICE REHNQUIST, with whom THE CHIEF JUSTICE, JUSTICE WHITE and JUSTICE O'CONNOR join, dissenting.

The Court today concludes that Congress did not intend the abandonment provision of the Bankruptcy Code, 11 U.S.C. § 554(a), to preempt "certain state and local laws." In something of a surprise ending, the Court limits the class of laws that can prevent an otherwise authorized abandonment by a trustee to those "reasonably designed to protect the public health or safety from identified hazards." While this limitation reduces somewhat the scope of my disagreement with the result reached, it renders both the *ratio decidendi* and the import of the Court's opinion quite unclear. More important, I remain unconvinced by the Court's arguments supporting state power to bar abandonment. The principal and only independent ground offered—that Congress codified "well-recognized restrictions of a trustee's abandonment power"—is particularly unpersuasive. It rests on a misreading of three pre-Code cases, the elevation of that misreading into a "well-recognized" exception to the abandonment power, and the unsupported assertion that Congress must have meant to codify the exception (or something like it). These specific shortcomings in the Court's analysis, which are addressed in greater detail below, stem at least in part from the Court's failure to discuss even in passing either the nature of abandonment or its role in federal bankruptcy.

Abandonment is "the release from the debtor's estate of property previously included in that estate." 2 W. Norton, Bankruptcy Law and Practice § 39.01 (1984), citing *Brown v. O'Keefe,* 300 U.S. 598, 602–603, 57 S.Ct. 543, 546–47, 81 L.Ed. 827 (1937). Prior to enactment of the Bankruptcy Code in 1978, there was no statutory provision specifically authorizing abandonment in liquidation cases. By analogy to the trustee's statutory power to reject executory contracts, courts had developed a rule permitting the trustee to abandon property that was worthless or not expected to sell for a price sufficiently in excess of encumbrances to offset the costs of administration. 4 L. King, Collier on Bankruptcy ¶ 554.01 (15th ed. 1985)(hereinafter Collier). This judge-made rule served the overriding purpose of bankruptcy liquidation: the expeditious reduction of the debtor's property to money, for equitable distribution to creditors, *Kothe v. R.C. Taylor Trust,* 280 U.S. 224, 227, 50 S.Ct. 142, 143, 74 L.Ed. 382 (1930). 4 Collier ¶ 554.01. Forcing the trustee to administer burdensome property would contradict this purpose, slowing the administration of the estate and draining its assets.

The Bankruptcy Code expressly incorporates the power of abandonment into federal bankruptcy legislation for the first time. The relevant provision bears repeating:

> "(a) After notice and a hearing, the trustee may abandon any property of the estate that is burdensome to the estate or that is of inconsequential value to the estate." 11 U.S.C. § 554(a)(amended 1984).

This language, absolute in its terms, suggests that a trustee's power to abandon is limited only by considerations of the property's value to the estate. It makes no mention of other factors to be balanced or weighed and permits no easy inference that Congress was concerned about state environmental regulations. Indeed, as the Court notes, when Congress *was* so concerned it expressed itself clearly, specifically exempting some environmental injunctions from the automatic stay provisions of § 362 of the Code, 11 U.S.C. §§ 362(b)(4), (5)(1982 ed. and Supp. II). See *Ohio v. Kovacs,* 469 U.S. 274, 105 S.Ct. 705, 83 L.Ed.2d 649 (1985).

* * *

I fully appreciate the Court's concern that abandonment may "aggravat[e] already existing dangers by halting security measures that preven[t] public entry, vandalism, and fire." *Ante,* at 758, n. 3. But in almost all cases, requiring the trustee to notify the relevant authorities before abandoning will give those authorities adequate opportunity to step in and provide needed security. As the Bankruptcy Court noted in No. 84–805: "The City and State are in a better position in every respect than either the Trustee or debtor's creditors to do what needs to be done to protect the public against the dangers posed by the PCB-contaminated facility." App. to Pet. for Cert. 73a. And requiring notice before abandonment in appropriate cases is perfectly consistent with the Code. It advances the State's interest in protecting the public health and safety, and, unlike the rather uncertain exception to the abandonment power propounded by the Court, at the same time allows for the orderly liquidation and distribution of the estate's assets. Here, of course, the trustee provided such notice and the relevant authorities were afforded an opportunity to take appropriate preventative and remedial measures.

I likewise would not exclude the possibility that there may be a far narrower condition on the abandonment power than that announced by the Court today, such as where abandonment by the trustee itself might create a genuine emergency that the trustee would be uniquely able to guard against. The United States in its brief as *amicus curiae* suggests, for example, that there are limits on the authority of a trustee to abandon dynamite sitting on a furnace in the basement of a schoolhouse. Although I know of no situations in which trustees have sought to abandon dynamite under such circumstances, the narrow exception that I would reserve surely would embrace that situation.

What the Court fails to appreciate is that respondents' interest in these cases lies not just in protecting public health and safety but also in protecting the public fisc. In No. 84–805, before undertaking cleanup efforts, New York unsuccessfully sought from the Bankruptcy Court a first lien on the Long Island City property to the extent of any expenditures it might make to bring the site into compliance with state and local law. New York did not appeal the Court's denial of a first lien, and proceeded to clean up the site (except for the contaminated subsoil). It now presses a claim for reimbursement, maintaining that the trustee should not have been allowed to abandon the site. The New Jersey Department of Environmental Protection, in No. 84–801, apparently seeks to undo the abandonment and force the trustee to expend the estate's remaining assets cleaning up the site, thereby reducing the cleanup costs that must ultimately be borne by the State.

The Court states that the "abandonment power is not to be fettered by laws or regulations not reasonably calculated to protect the public health or safety from imminent and identifiable harm." *Ante,* at 763, n.

9. Because the Court declines to identify those laws that it deems so "reasonably calculated," I can only speculate about its view of respondents' claim that abandonment can be conditioned on a total cleanup. One might assume, however, that since it affirms the judgments below the Court means to adopt respondents' position. The Court of Appeals, as I read their opinions in these cases, apparently would require the trustee to expend all of Quanta's available assets to clean up the sites. But barring abandonment and forcing a cleanup would effectively place respondents' interest in protecting the public fisc ahead of the claims of other creditors. Congress simply did not intend that § 554 abandonment hearings would be used to establish the priority of particular claims in bankruptcy. While States retain considerable latitude to ensure that priority status is allotted to their cleanup claims, see *Ohio v. Kovacs,* 469 U.S., at 277, 105 S.Ct., at 707 (O'Connor, J., concurring), I believe that the Court errs by permitting them to impose conditions on the abandonment power that Congress never contemplated. Accordingly, in each of these cases I would reverse the judgment of the Court of Appeals.

IN RE CHATEAUGAY CORP.

United States Court of Appeals, Second Circuit, 1991.
944 F.2d 997.

JON O. NEWMAN, CIRCUIT JUDGE:

This appeal presents important issues at the intersection of bankruptcy law and environmental law. The issues arise on an appeal and a cross-appeal from the March 26, 1990, judgment of the District Court for the Southern District of New York (John E. Sprizzo, Judge) in connection with the Chapter 11 reorganization of the LTV Corporation and its related companies (collectively "LTV").

* * *

BACKGROUND

LTV is a diversified steel, aerospace, and energy corporation with operations in several states. LTV filed a bankruptcy petition under Chapter 11 on July 16, 1986. The debtor's schedule of liabilities included 24 pages of claims, labeled "contingent," that were held by EPA and the environmental enforcement officers of all fifty states and the District of Columbia. The schedule provided no details concerning these claims. EPA filed a proof of claim for approximately $32 million, representing response costs incurred pre-petition at 14 sites where LTV had been identified as a "potentially responsible party" ("PRP") under CERCLA. *See* 42 U.S.C. § 9607(a)(1988). EPA alleges that only one of these sites has reached the point where no further response costs are anticipated, and that the 14 sites are not necessarily all of the sites for which LTV might ultimately be determined to be a PRP. Thus, the $32 million in incurred response costs might be only a small fraction of the total CERCLA liability that EPA will ultimately assert against LTV.

Appreciating the distinction between the listed contingent claims and the claim for incurred response costs requires some understanding of the framework for recovery of CERCLA response costs. Section 104 of CERCLA authorizes EPA to take "any ... response measure consistent with the national contingency plan which [EPA] deems necessary to protect the public health or welfare or the environment" whenever "any hazardous substance is released or there is a substantial threat of such a release into the environment * * *." Upon identification of a release or threatened release, EPA makes an investigation to determine if the environmental risk is of sufficient severity to warrant inclusion of the site on the National Priorities List. Thereafter, EPA selects an appropriate remedy and can either order the potentially responsible party to take the remedial action under section 106(a), *id.* § 9606(a), or take the remedial action itself, using so-called Superfund money, and seek reimbursement for such response costs under section 107(a), after the costs have been incurred.

With respect to the listed contingent claims, *i.e.*, those for which response costs had not been incurred pre-petition, LTV informed the Government that it expected confirmation of a reorganization plan to discharge all obligations of LTV concerning environmental liabilities that are traceable to pre-petition conduct of LTV, including obligations for response costs that are incurred post-confirmation. In disagreement with that position, the Government brought an adversary proceeding for a declaratory judgment that response costs incurred post-confirmation are not dischargeable because they do not arise from pre-petition claims. In the Government's view, it does not have a "claim" within the meaning of the Bankruptcy Code, 11 U.S.C. § 101(4)(1988), for reimbursement of CERCLA response costs until those costs have been incurred.

On the primary issue between the parties, the District Court ruled substantially in favor of LTV. Judge Sprizzo did not go quite so far as to consider response cost claims to be dischargeable whenever based on LTV's pre-petition conduct, a position that would have included LTV's pre-petition conduct of placing hazardous substances in sealed containers, followed by release of the substances into the environment years after confirmation. However, he agreed with LTV to the extent of ruling that an obligation to reimburse EPA for response costs is a dischargeable claim whenever based upon a pre-petition release or threatened release of hazardous substances. This ruling covers releases that have occurred pre-petition, even though they have not then been discovered by EPA (or anyone else).

The Court then considered which environmental claims based on injunctions were dischargeable. Applying that portion of the Code definition of "claim" that includes a "right to an equitable remedy for breach of performance if such breach gives rise to a right to payment," *id.* § 101(4), Judge Sprizzo stated that claims for injunctive relief based on a pre-petition release or threatened release would be dischargeable if the injunctive relief was an option EPA was electing to use in lieu of incurring response costs itself and thereafter seeking reimbursement; on the other hand, he continued, "where there is no right to such payment for cleanup or other remedial costs, claims for injunctive relief do not fall within the Bankruptcy [Code] and are not dischargeable."

This deceptively simple statement perhaps obscures difficult questions of application because it is not clear which forms of injunctive relief Judge Sprizzo regards as being an option to EPA's right of response cost reimbursement and which entail "no right to such payment." As an example of the latter category, the District Judge cited section 106 of CERCLA, yet this is the provision the Government views as its alternative remedy to incurring and seeking reimbursement for response costs under section 107. In any event, it is clear that Judge Sprizzo intended to render nondischargeable some forms of injunctive relief that go far beyond merely ordering LTV to stop a release or threatened release of hazardous substances. He expressly rejected LTV's contention that an injunctive provision should be dischargeable "merely because the debtor would be required to expend money in order to comply with the injunction," and observed, "To accept that argument would render dischargeable any claims for injunctive relief other than those merely seeking the cessation of some unlawful activity." Plainly, the District Court has ruled not dischargeable some injunctive provisions requiring cleanup activity, but it is not entirely clear how the Court proposes to identify those that are dischargeable because they are an option to recovery of response costs. Moreover, we learn nothing about the scope of the judgment on this aspect of the case from its terms because it omits all precision as to what rights are being declared, reciting only that both the plaintiffs' and the defendants' motions for summary judgment "are granted in part and denied in part."

It may be that the Court sought to distinguish somewhat mechanically between those injunctive provisions that contain within their terms an option for payment and those that do not. The Court initially recognized that "an optional *right* to payment," such as EPA has under section 107, "is nonetheless a right to payment and the fact that EPA may not choose to exercise that option in no way negates the existence of that right. It follows that absent any congressional intent to preclude the dischargeability of such claims, these claims for injunctive relief fall within the broad language of Section 101(4)." That observation would seem to render dischargeable all injunctive provisions for cleanup activity since EPA always has the option to incur response costs and seek reimbursement. Yet the Court immediately thereafter ruled nondischargeable claims for injunctive relief "where there is no right to such payment for cleanup or other remedial costs," citing, among other provisions, section 106 of CERCLA. *Id.* at 523.

The parties appear to take differing views of the extent to which the judgment rules injunctive relief to be dischargeable. The Government views the judgment as holding "post-confirmation environmental obligations * * * not dischargeable." Brief for United States at 23 n. ___. Elaborating somewhat, the Government says that the District Court "properly recognized that injunctive relief requires the debtor to spend its own money to ensure that *its continuing operations* comply with law." *Id.* (emphasis added). Though that statement leaves it unclear whether the Government thinks that what survives confirmation are injunctive provisions concerning only post-confirmation pollution or all injunctive provisions requiring cleanup of pre-petition pollution, subsequent papers make clear that the Government understands the District Court to have left unaffected by discharge all injunctions ordering the estate "to clean up its property."

The cross-appellants understand the District Court to have ruled nondischargeable injunctive provisions requiring cleanup of pre-petition actual or threatened discharges, but they too do not distinguish between provisions that are an option to recovery of response costs and those that are not. In their view, all injunctive provisions should be dischargeable if they seek to remedy pre-petition discharges (because the option of seeking reimbursement for response costs is always available), and nondischargeable provisions are only those that require the debtor to cease conduct resulting in discharges. At least that appears to be the position of LTV. *See* Brief for LTV at 24–25. The Unsecured Creditors appear to go further, contending "that any injunctive relief which requires the expenditure of money creates a right to payment which gives rise to a dischargeable claim." *See* Brief for Unsecured Creditors at 8.

Finally, the District Court granted EPA's request for a declaratory judgment that cleanup costs assessed post-petition with respect to sites currently owned by LTV, where there has been a pre-petition release or threatened release, are entitled to an administrative priority, 11 U.S.C. § 503(b)(1)(A)(1988).

EPA, New York, and the Equity Holders appeal the ruling that pre-petition releases and threatened releases are dischargeable claims. LTV and the Unsecured Creditors cross-appeal to challenge the rulings concerning the non-dischargeability of injunctive remedies and the entitlement of cleanup costs on LTV-owned properties to an administrative priority.

Discussion

Before considering the separate issues, it will be useful to discuss the parties' disagreement as to the overall approach that should guide our resolution of the case. All the parties, to varying degrees, point to a conflict between the Bankruptcy Code and CERCLA and urge that one statute or the other be accorded primacy, depending on which statute supports the position they assert in this litigation.

We agree that the Bankruptcy Code and CERCLA point toward competing objectives. The Code aims to provide reorganized debtors with a fresh start, an objective made more feasible by maximizing the scope of a discharge. CERCLA aims to clean up environmental damage, an objective that the enforcement agencies in this litigation contend will be better served if their entitlement to be reimbursed for CERCLA response costs based on pre-petition pollution is not considered to be a "claim" and instead may be asserted at full value against the reorganized corporation. Preliminarily, we note that the conflict in objectives might not be quite as stark as the parties contend. Cleaning up the environment will not necessarily be aided by agreeing with the agencies that they do not yet have "claims." A determination that the CERCLA response costs ultimately to be incurred are not now claims might impair the prospects of achieving a viable reorganization, with the result that the debtor, instead of reorganizing, liquidates under Chapter 7 or dissolves under state law, and the assets of the corporation are either unavailable for environmental cleanup costs because such costs are not yet "claims" entitled to pro rata payment, or available only to the limited extent that such costs are considered unaccrued claims for which reserves must be established under state law.

But to whatever extent the Code and CERCLA point in different directions, we do not face in this context a conflict between two statutes, each designed to focus on a discrete problem, which happen to conflict in their application to a specific set of facts. Here, we encounter a bankruptcy statute that is intended to override many provisions of law that would apply in the absence of bankruptcy—especially laws otherwise providing creditors suing promptly with full payment of their claims. Of course, the comprehensive nature of the bankruptcy statute does not relieve us of the obligation to construe its terms, nor may we resolve all issues of statutory construction in favor of the "fresh start" objective, regardless of the terms Congress has chosen to express its will. Our point is the more limited one that in construing the Code, we need not be swayed by the arguments advanced by EPA that a narrow reading of the Code will better serve the environmental interests Congress wished to promote in enacting CERCLA. If the Code, fairly construed, creates limits on the extent of environmental cleanup efforts, the remedy is for Congress to make exceptions to the Code to achieve other objectives that Congress chooses to reach, rather than for courts to restrict the meaning of across-the-board legislation like a bankruptcy law in order to promote objectives evident in more focused statutes.

With these considerations in mind, we turn to the specific issues.

1. *Unincurred CERCLA response costs for pre-petition releases as "claims."* Section 101(4)[5] of the Bankruptcy Code defines a "claim" as a

> (A) right to payment, whether or not such right is reduced to judgment, liquidated, unliquidated, fixed, contingent, matured, unmatured, disputed, undisputed, legal, equitable, secured, or unsecured; or
>
> (B) right to an equitable remedy for breach of performance if such breach gives rise to a right to payment, whether or not such right to an equitable remedy is reduced to judgment, fixed, contingent, matured, unmatured, disputed, undisputed, secured, or unsecured.

Congress unquestionably expected this definition to have wide scope. "By this broadest possible definition * * * the bill contemplates that all legal obligations of the debtor, no matter how remote or contingent, will be able to be dealt with in the bankruptcy case." H.R.Rep. No. 595, 95th Cong., 2d Sess. 309 (1978). That language surely points us in a direction, but provides little indication of how far we should travel.

As a matter of bankruptcy theory, it has been persuasively argued that a "claim" should be deemed to exist whenever, in the absence of bankruptcy, a particular claimant has the right to reach the debtor's assets. *See* Thomas H. Jackson, *The Logic and Limits of Bankruptcy Law* 34–35 (1986); *see also Vanston Bondholders Protective Committee v. Green,* 329 U.S. 156, 170, 67 S.Ct. 237, 243, 91 L.Ed. 162 (1946) (Frankfurter, J., concurring)(non-bankruptcy law determines existence of a claim). That approach, Professor Jackson argues, maximizes bankruptcy law as a collective debt-collection device, thereby achieving its primary objective. But we are obliged to apply the bankruptcy law that Congress has enacted, not to reformulate it as theorists would prefer to see it. Thus, for example, we have declined to consider as a "claim" a civil service retirement agency's right to recoup an employee's loan from future retirement benefits because the agency has no right to reimbursement; it can never do more than offset the loan against future benefits. *See In re Villarie,* 648 F.2d 810, 812 (2d Cir.1981). The putative claimant in *Villarie* did not hold an unmatured claim on which it could one day sue; under the governing non-bankruptcy law that defined its rights, it could never sue. It thus had no "right to payment" within the meaning of the Code's definition of "claim." Though *Villarie* does not comport with Professor Jackson's theoretical model, it endeavors to faithfully apply the Bankruptcy Code as written.

Defining claims to include any ultimate right to payment arising from pre-petition conduct by the debtor comports with the theoretical model of assuring that all assets of the debtor are available to those seeking recovery for pre-petition conduct. But such an interpretation of "claim" yields questionable results. Consider, for example, a company that builds bridges around the world. It can estimate that of 10,000 bridges it builds, one will fail, causing 10 deaths. Having built 10,000 bridges, it becomes insolvent and files a petition in bankruptcy. Is there a "claim" on behalf of the 10 people who will be killed when they drive across the one bridge that will fail someday in the future? If the only test is whether the ultimate right to payment will arise out of the debtor's pre-petition conduct, the future victims have a "claim." Yet it must be obvious that enormous practical and perhaps constitutional problems would arise from recognition of such a claim. The potential victims are not only unidentified, but there is no way to identify them. Sheer fortuity will determine who will be on that one bridge when it crashes. What notice is to be given to these potential "claimants"? Or would it suffice to designate a representative for future victims and authorize the representative to negotiate terms of a binding reorganization plan?

To expect "claims" to be filed by those who have not yet had any contact whatever with the tort-feasor has been characterized as " 'absurd.' "

Even where a tort victim has had some pre-petition contact with the tort-feasor, such as purchasing a product or working in proximity to hazardous materials, some courts have declined to recognize a "claim" in advance of some manifestation of injury. Yet other courts, construing the broad definition of "claim" under the Bankruptcy Code, have ruled that those exposed to a hazardous product like asbestos do have claims, despite the absence of manifest injury. *Cf. Grady v. A.H. Robins Co.,* 839 F.2d 198, 203 (4th Cir.1988)(user of Dalkon shield had claim subject to automatic stay, but not necessarily dischargeable claim, though injury not apparent from use of shield), *cert. dismissed,* 487 U.S. 1260, 109 S.Ct. 201, 101 L.Ed.2d 972 (1988). In *In re UNR Industries, Inc.,* the Seventh Circuit, in dismissing the appeal, expressly noted the "difficult and far-reaching questions" concerning whether future asbestos victims have pre-petition claims. 725 F.2d at 1120.

Accepting as claimants those future tort victims whose injuries are caused by pre-petition conduct but do not become manifest until after confirmation, arguably puts considerable strain not only on the Code's definition of "claim," but also on the definition of "creditor"—an "entity that has a claim against the debtor that *arose* at the time of or before the order for relief concerning the debtor." 11 U.S.C. § 101(9)(A)(1988)(emphasis added). It has been suggested that the "arose" limitation is an inartfully drafted provision not intended to exclude tort victims injured by pre-petition conduct, but designed instead to make sure that those supplying goods and services to the debtor during reorganization do not fall within the category of claimants who have their claims reduced pro rata. *See* Mark Roe, *Bankruptcy and Mass Tort,* 84 Colum.L.Rev. 846, 895–96 (1984). Indeed, reading the "creditor" definition too narrowly risks undue limitation of the deliberately broad definition of "claim," especially the express inclusion of unmatured and contingent claims.

We need not decide how the definition of "claim" applies to tort victims injured by pre-petition conduct, especially as applied to the difficult case of pre-petition conduct that has not yet resulted in detectable injury, much less the extreme case of pre-petition conduct that has not yet resulted in any tortious consequence to a victim. We deal here with the far more manageable problem of sums ultimately to be owed to EPA at such time as it incurs CERCLA response costs. When such costs are incurred, EPA will unquestionably have what can fairly be called a "right to payment." That right is currently unmatured and will not mature until the response costs are incurred. In the context of contract claims, the Code's inclusion of "unmatured" and "contingent" claims is usually said to refer to obligations that will become due upon the happening of a future event that was "within the actual or presumed contemplation of the parties at the time the original relationship between the parties was created." *In re All Media Properties, Inc.,* 5 B.R. 126, 133 (Bankr.S.D.Tex.1980), *aff'd mem.,* 646 F.2d 193 (5th Cir.1981).

The concepts of "maturity" and "contingency" are not readily transferable from the context of contracts to that of tort and statutory claims.

Yet the evident intent of Congress to apply broadly the definition of "claim" counsels against the narrow reading urged by EPA, especially in the context of obligations arising out of public regulation. Though there does not yet exist between EPA and LTV the degree of relationship between claimant and debtor typical of an existing though unmatured contract claim, the relationship is far closer than that existing between future tort claimants totally unaware of injury and a tort-feasor. EPA is acutely aware of LTV and vice versa. The relationship between environmental regulating agencies and those subject to regulation provides sufficient "contemplation" of contingencies to bring most ultimately maturing payment obligations based on pre-petition conduct within the definition of "claims." True, EPA does not yet know the full extent of the hazardous waste removal costs that it may one day incur and seek to impose upon LTV, and it does not yet even know the location of all the sites at which such wastes may yet be found. But the location of these sites, the determination of their coverage by CERCLA, and the incurring of response costs by EPA are all steps that may fairly be viewed, in the regulatory context, as rendering EPA's claim "contingent," rather than as placing it outside the Code's definition of "claim."

Judge Sprizzo recognized that "before a contingent claim can be discharged, it must result from pre-petition conduct fairly giving rise to that contingent claim." Though relying on pre-petition conduct, the District Court did not go so far as to include CERCLA response costs attributable to any action of the debtor that occurred pre-petition, such as the construction of a storage facility. Instead, the Court carefully limited its ruling to pre-petition releases or threatened releases of hazardous substances.

We think the District Court properly applied the Bankruptcy Code's definition of "claim."

Moreover, we are not unmindful of the observations of Justice O'Connor concerning the disadvantage to environmental claimants if "claim" is interpreted to exclude items like unincurred CERCLA response costs. *See Ohio v. Kovacs*, 469 U.S. 274, 285–86, 105 S.Ct. 705, 711, 83 L.Ed.2d 649 (1985)(O'Connor, J., concurring). Accepting EPA's argument in this Chapter 11 reorganization case would leave EPA without any possibility of even partial recovery against a dissolving corporation in a Chapter 7 liquidation case. Indeed, while EPA obviously prefers in this case to keep its CERCLA claim outside of bankruptcy so that it may present it, without reduction, against the reorganized company that it anticipates will emerge from bankruptcy, one may well speculate whether, if unincurred CERCLA response costs are not claims, some corporations facing substantial environmental claims will be able to reorganize at all.

We see no merit in EPA's contention that holding unincurred CERCLA response costs to be "claims" so long as a release or threatened release of hazardous wastes has occurred pre-petition is precluded by CERCLA itself. Specifically, EPA points to the 1986 amendment to section 113 of CERCLA, prohibiting pre-enforcement judicial review. Pub.L. No. 99–499, § 113(c)(2), 100 Stat. 1613, 1649 (1986)(codified at 42 U.S.C. § 9613(h) (1988)); *see In re Combustion Equipment Associates, Inc.,* 838 F.2d 35, 37 (2d Cir.1988). In considering this contention, we note preliminarily that EPA is not asserting that the issue of whether it has dischargeable "claims" for the unincurred response costs is not ripe for adjudication in an action for a declaratory judgment. EPA took that position in *In re Combustion Equipment Associates, Inc., supra,* in which the debtor, after emerging from reorganization, sought a declaratory judgment that unincurred response costs based on pre-petition releases were claims that had been discharged. We considered that dispute unripe, leaving open the issue of whether a declaratory judgment would be appropriate *during* a reorganization proceeding, at a time when the bankruptcy court has the power to estimate contingent claims. *Id.,* 838 F.2d at 40. EPA, having brought this declaratory judgment action, is not disputing that the suit is ripe; it is contending that the ban on pre-enforcement judicial review requires that it receive a declaratory judgment upholding its contention that unincurred response costs are not dischargeable "claims." We disagree.

The assumption that appears to underlie EPA's concern that the bankruptcy proceeding amounts to pre-enforcement judicial review of CERCLA claims is that extensive factual inquiry will have to be undertaken. EPA contends that it "would be forced to litigate in the bankruptcy proceedings to liquidate and fix any claims it might conceivably have against [LTV] for post-confirmation response costs" at numerous sites. This is not necessarily so. Contingent claims may be estimated if their liquidation "would unduly delay the administration of the case." Though EPA fears that even an estimation process would "embroil the parties and the bankruptcy court in disputes over the wisdom and scope of possible remedies," Brief for United States at 42, nothing prevents the speedy and rough estimation of CERCLA claims for purposes of determining EPA's voice in the Chapter 11 proceedings, with ultimate liquidation of the claims to await the outcome of normal CERCLA enforcement proceedings in which EPA will be entitled to collect its allowable share (full or pro rata, depending on the reorganization plan) of incurred response costs.

We agree with Judge Sprizzo that CERCLA's prohibition of pre-enforcement review is simply inapplicable. The Court is not being called upon to "review any challenges to removal or remedial action selected under section 9604 of this title, or to review any order issued under section 9606(a) of this title." 42 U.S.C. § 9613(h)(1988). We therefore need not decide whether CERCLA's ban on pre-enforcement review, if applicable, would constitute an implied repeal of the authority otherwise conferred on federal courts by the Bankruptcy Code.

2. *Injunctive remedies as "claims."* As we have noted, the Code's definition of "claim" includes a

(B) right to an equitable remedy for breach of performance if such breach gives rise to a right to payment, whether or not such right to an equitable remedy is reduced to judgment, fixed, contingent, matured, unmatured, disputed, undisputed, secured, or unsecured.

11 U.S.C. § 101(4)(B)(1988). As with the portion of the "claim" definition concerning monetary obligations, thoughtful commentators have urged an interpretation of the "equitable remedy" language to carry out what they understand to be the appropriate objectives of bankruptcy law. *See* Douglas G. Baird & Thomas H. Jackson, *Kovacs and Toxic Wastes in Bankruptcy*, 36 Stan.L.Rev. 1199, 1204 (1984)(hereinafter "Baird"). We reckon with their argument not only because of its force but also because its consideration illuminates and helps resolve the difficulty we have encountered in understanding the scope of the District Court's ruling.

Professors Baird and Jackson advance the thesis that injunctions imposing an equitable obligation should be dischargeable claims whenever a non-bankrupt corporation could have effectively escaped from the burden of the obligation through dissolution under state law. In making the argument, they purport to divide the universe of environmental injunctions into (a) those that impose obligations "that arise because of the debtor's continued existence and that would disappear if the debtor were to cease operations" and (b) those that impose obligations "that result from activities engaged in before the filing of the petition and whose consequences *continue* to exist even if the debtor goes out of business." Baird, *supra,* at 1204 (emphasis in original). In their view, obligations in the first category are not dischargeable claims; those in the second category are. Their point is that this classification achieves the desirable result of mirroring non-bankruptcy consequences under prevailing substantive law (whether state or federal). If a corporation dissolves in the absence of bankruptcy, its obligations in the first category cease to have meaning; therefore, obligations of this sort should not be affected by bankruptcy and are properly considered non-dischargeable. On the other hand, obligations in the second category would be claims upon a debtor in dissolution; therefore, the governmental enforcers of the obligation should share in the assets of the corporation and this result is achieved if the obligations are recognized as claims.

An initial difficulty with the argument, before we even consider whether it squares with the Bankruptcy Code as written, is that the two categories are not as mutually exclusive as the argument suggests. For Baird and Jackson, the distinction is simply between an injunction "to cease polluting" (non-dischargeable) and an injunction "to clean up toxic wastes that already have been deposited" (dischargeable). For some injunctions, the distinction is clear. An order to stop burning high-sulphur fuel is clearly in the first category, and an order to remove containers of radioactive waste, feared to become insecure in the future, is clearly in the second category. But what of an order, typical of CERCLA orders, to clean up a toxic waste site from which hazardous substances are leaching into nearby water supplies? To some extent the order requires the defendant to "stop polluting," *i.e.*, to stop the run-off of hazardous substances from its property, and to some extent the order requires the defendant to "clean up toxic wastes that have already been deposited," *i.e.*, to pay for the removal of the hazardous substances.

We will return to the classification problem shortly, but for now, assuming that some orders can be divided as suggested, we consider whether the Bankruptcy Code makes the distinction that has been urged. Manifestly, the Code does not say expressly that dischargeable orders are those that impose mandatory obligations to remedy past misconduct and that non-dischargeable orders are those that impose prohibitions against future misconduct. Instead, the Code defines "claim" to include "an equitable remedy for breach of performance if such breach gives rise to a right to payment." 11 U.S.C. § 101(4)(B)(1988). That wording, Baird and Jackson argue, is merely an "inartful[ ]"way of capturing the distinction they endorse.

We think we must endeavor to apply the "claim" definition as written, mindful of the purposes of bankruptcy law but without the prerogative of rewriting it to maximize bankruptcy objectives that Congress might not have fully achieved. Thus, we must determine whether the injunctions, alleged to give rise to dischargeable "claims," impose a remedy for a performance breach that gives rise to a right of payment. A clear example of such an order may help to focus our inquiry. A seller of a unique property has an enforceable duty to convey the property to a buyer. For breach of that duty, a court may order the remedy of specific performance. In some states, however, the specific performance obligation may be satisfied by an alternative right to payment, in which event the specific performance creditor has a "claim" in bankruptcy. *See* 2 *Collier on Bankruptcy* ¶ 101.05, at 101–31 (15th ed. 1991). This was the example used in Congress in explaining the reach of section 101(4)(B).

While this example illustrates the type of injunction that gives rise to a dischargeable claim, its simplicity contrasts with the more typical injunctions encountered in environmental cases, and therein lies our problem. These injunctions, as we have noted, frequently combine an obligation as to which the enforcing agency has an alternative right to payment with an obligation as to which no such alternative exists. An injunction that does no more than impose an obligation entirely as an alternative to a payment right is dischargeable. Thus, if EPA directs LTV to remove some wastes that are not currently causing pollution, and if EPA could have itself incurred the costs of removing such wastes and then sued LTV to recover the response costs, such an order is a "claim" under the Code. On the other hand, if the order, no matter how phrased, requires LTV to take any action that ends or ameliorates current pollution, such an order is not a "claim."

We think that is precisely the distinction the District Court was endeavoring to achieve when it ruled that injunctions sought as an option to EPA's (or a state's) right to incur and sue for response costs are within section 101(4), but that "where there is no right to such payment for cleanup or other remedial costs, claims for injunctive relief" are not dischargeable. In any event, it is the distinction we believe is made by the "claim" definition of the Code. EPA is entitled to seek payment if it elects to incur cleanup costs itself, but it has no authority to accept a payment from a responsible party as an alternative to continued pollution. Thus, a cleanup order that accomplishes the dual objectives of removing accumulated wastes and stopping or ameliorating ongoing pollution emanating from such wastes is not a dischargeable claim. It is true that, if in lieu of such an order, EPA had undertaken the removal itself and sued for the response costs, its action would have both removed the accumulated waste and prevented continued pollution. But it is only the first attribute of the order that can be said to remedy a breach that gives rise to a right to payment. Since there is no option to accept payment in lieu of continued pollution, any order that to any extent ends or ameliorates continued pollution is not an order for breach of an obligation that gives rise to a right of payment and is for that reason not a "claim." But an order to clean up a site, to the extent that it imposes obligations distinct from any obligation to stop or ameliorate ongoing pollution, is a "claim" if the creditor obtaining the order had the option, which CERCLA confers, to do the cleanup work itself and sue for response costs, thereby converting the injunction into a monetary obligation. We recognize that most environmental injunctions will fall on the non-"claim" side of the line. On this understanding, we affirm the District Court's ruling concerning injunctions.

In reaching this conclusion, we have reckoned with the Supreme Court's decision in *Ohio v. Kovacs,* 469 U.S. 274, 105 S.Ct. 705, 83 L.Ed.2d 649 (1985), and agree with Judge Sprizzo that it does not preclude the ruling he has made. *Kovacs* involves an individual debtor rather than a corporate debtor and a Chapter 7 liquidation rather than a Chapter 11 reorganization, but neither distinction appears to affect the Court's determination that the cleanup order obtained by Ohio was a dischargeable claim. What seems to have been decisive was the fact that Ohio obtained the appointment of a receiver, precluded Kovacs from taking any steps to comply with the injunction, and was seeking from Kovacs only the payment of money. The Court expressly noted that it was not deciding "what the legal consequences would have been had Kovacs taken bankruptcy before a receiver had been appointed and a trustee had been designated with the usual duties of a bankruptcy trustee." *Id.* at 284, 105 S.Ct. at 710 (footnote omitted). The Court also emphasized that it was "not question[ing] that anyone in possession of the site * * * must comply with the environmental laws of the State of Ohio."

To some extent *Kovacs* involves the same dilemma we face in determining what aspects of an environmental injunction give rise to a right of payment. The order in *Kovacs* enjoined the defendants "from causing further pollution of the air or public waters" and "required the defendants to remove specified wastes from the property." Like most environmental decrees, it thus contained "a negative order to cease polluting" and "an affirmative order to clean up the site." However, the Court was spared the need to determine precisely which obligations of the order, as entered, could be said to constitute a "claim" because, by virtue of Ohio's actions, "the cleanup order had been converted into an obligation to pay money." To the extent that CERCLA affords EPA and others a right to payment in lieu of an order directed solely at cleanup, *Kovacs* indicates that such an order is a "claim." And to the extent that an order is obtained under CERCLA or any other environmental statute that seeks to end or ameliorate pollution, we are satisfied that nothing in *Kovacs* permits a discharge of such obligation. As the Court concluded, a person or firm in possession of a site "may not maintain a nuisance, pollute the waters of the State, or refuse to remove the source of such conditions."

We recognize that in the context of environmental remedies the line between "claim" injunctions and non-"claim" injunctions could arguably be drawn somewhat differently, for example, by placing on the non-"claim" side only those injunctions ordering a defendant to stop current activities that add to pollution (*e.g.*, depositing new hazardous substances), while leaving on the "claim" side all other injunctions, including those that direct the cleanup of sites from which hazardous substances, previously deposited, are currently contributing to pollution. But we believe that placing on the non-"claim" side all injunctions that seek to remedy on-going pollution is more faithful to the Supreme Court's teachings in both *Kovacs* and *Midlantic National Bank v. N.J. Dep't of Environmental Protection*, 474 U.S. 494, 106 S.Ct. 755, 88 L.Ed.2d 859 (1986). It is difficult to understand how any injunction directing a property owner to remedy ongoing pollution could be a dischargeable "claim" if, as *Kovacs* instructs, the owner "may not maintain a nuisance, pollute the waters of the State, or refuse to remove the source of such conditions." Moreover, leaving such injunctions outside the category of dischargeable "claims" is entirely consistent with *Midlantic's* holding that the Bankruptcy Code does not entitle a debtor to abandon property in violation of an environmental regulation "that is reasonably designed to protect the public health or safety from identified hazards." 474 U.S. at 507, 106 S.Ct. at 762.

3. *Administrative priority.* The Bankruptcy Code accords an administrative priority to "actual, necessary costs and expenses of preserving the estate." 11 U.S.C. § 503(b)(1)(A)(1988). The District Court ruled that all clean-up costs assessed post-petition with respect to sites currently owned by LTV where there has been a pre-petition release or threatened release of hazardous wastes will be entitled to administrative priority. LTV and the unsecured creditors challenge this ruling, viewing it as an unwarranted attempt to convert pre-petition contingent claims into priority claims by the simple expedient of liquidating them, *i.e.*, incurring response costs and securing reimbursement. EPA contends that response costs paid during administration with respect to pre-

petition releases or threatened releases are necessary to preserve the estate in the sense that they enable the estate to maintain itself in compliance with applicable environmental laws. The Equity Holders urge that decision as to whether reimbursement for any response costs is entitled to administrative priority cannot be made until there has been a careful assessment of the facts peculiar to each payment.

The District Court drew support for its ruling from the Supreme Court's decision in *Midlantic,* which ruled that a bankruptcy trustee could not abandon property in contravention of state or local laws designed to protect public health or safety. If property on which toxic substances pose a significant hazard to public health cannot be abandoned, it must follow, the Court reasoned, that expenses to remove the threat posed by such substances are necessary to preserve the estate. We agree, as have other courts considering the same issue.

LTV's argument that EPA should not be able to obtain administrative priority for a contingent claim by liquidating it overlooks the fact that EPA is doing more than fixing the amount of its claim; it is acting, during administration of the estate, to remedy the ongoing effects of a release of hazardous substances. As the Government acknowledges in response to the contention of the Equity Holders, nothing in the District Court's ruling eliminates the obligation of notice and hearing before the allowance of a particular request for payment of an administrative expense. See 11 U.S.C. § 503(b)(1)(A)(1988). The District Court has ruled that response costs for post-petition remedial action qualify as administrative expenses; whether any particular item of cost is entitled to priority requires a particularized determination.

CONCLUSION

The judgment of the District Court is affirmed. No costs.

Notes and Questions

1. Justice Rehnquist is right, not so? The issue in all of these environmental cleanup cases is not really power to abandon but who bears the cost of the cleanup. Is the cost to be borne exclusively by the citizens of the state? Should the unsecured creditors share? Perhaps the unsecured creditors should be completely subordinated (by making the cleanup claim an administrative expense).

Most of the cases that have squarely faced the issue have held that environmental cleanup costs that were not paid prior to the filing of the petition are administrative expenses. In order for something to qualify as an administrative expense under section 503(b)(1)(A) it must constitute part of the "actual, necessary cost and expenses of preserving the estate * * *." There are two requirements buried in the quoted language. First, the claim must arise (and *a fortiori* an amount not already spent must be spent) after the petition has been filed. Second, even postpetition expenses must be the actual necessary costs of preserving the estate.

What arguments could be made by unsecured creditors that cleanup costs are not administrative expenses?

2. What if there is CERCLA liability under section 107 (i.e., where the bankruptcy estate as an owner has joint and several liability with prior owners for the cleanup)?

3. What arguments might be made by one doing environmental cleanup to support secured status in an ensuing bankruptcy? Consider the language of *Midlantic* and section 506. Could a state grant such a claim secured status with priority over existing perfected secured creditors?

4. Is the answer a statutory grant of priority? To grant priority to environmental cleanup would be foolish if such grant of priority would cause any significant number of lenders to decline to lend, at least if the cost of such refusals were greater than the cost to the state of bearing the cleanup expense itself. One cannot be certain what creditors would do in the face of a higher priority for such cleanup expenses. The creditors' own assertions about their future behavior in the face of such legislation should seldom be taken at face value. Thus, the economic calculation is a difficult one; it depends upon highly uncertain predictions about the behavior of the relevant actors in the face of such new legislation.

5. The imposition of joint and several liability on every potential owner of or operator on a site where waste has been disposed has already caused some significant dislocation and prompts bizarre behavior when the deepest pocket who owns the smallest share bears the greatest loss. Surely any subordination should not go beyond the subordination of the creditor who holds security in the very asset that is to be cleaned up. That subordination might be defended on the ground the secured creditor is a better, less expensive preventer of pollution than is a state agency or other party. Arguably the current cases that grant administrative expense priority place the monitoring cost on the parties least likely to do monitoring, namely, the trade and other unsecured creditors. (Hello, I'm your plumber, and I would like to do an EPA inspection of your property before I fix your leaking pipe.)

CERCLA excludes from the definition of "owner or operator" any "person who, without participating in the management of a * * * facility, holds indicia of ownership primarily to protect his security interest in the * * * facility." 42 U.S.C. § 9601(20)(A). Although at first glance this appears to exempt most secured creditors from liability, the Eleventh Circuit in *United States v. Fleet Factors Corp.*, 901 F.2d 1550 (11th Cir.1990), *cert. denied*, 498 U.S. 1046, 111 S.Ct. 752, 112 L.Ed.2d 772 (1991) construed the exemption narrowly, undoubtedly sending fear through the community of secured creditors. The court held that even if a secured creditor was not involved in day-to-day operation of a facility, it could be held liable under CERCLA "if its involvement with the management of the facility is sufficiently broad to support the inference that it could affect hazardous waste disposal decisions if it so chose." Id. at 1558. The court discounted concerns that its ruling would create disincentives to lend to businesses with potential hazardous waste disposal problems. Rather, it reasoned that its ruling "should encourage potential creditors to investigate thoroughly the waste treatment systems and policies of potential debtors * * * and debtors, aware that inadequate waste treatment will have a significant adverse impact on their loan terms, will have powerful incentives to improve their handling of hazardous wastes." Id. It remains to be seen if other courts will follow the lead of the Eleventh Circuit.

The Environmental Protection Agency has responded to that case and to the fear of the secured creditors with proposed regulations, which if enacted will help to alleviate creditors' concerns.

6. If environmentally damaged property cannot be abandoned even though no assets exist to pay for the cleanup, how does the reorganization case end?

Problem 8–5

Assume that your client holds a mortgage on debtor's property. The real estate subject to the mortgage would have a $10 million value if it were clean of the toxic waste that has been spilled on the land. The debtor estimates it will cost at least $8 million and possibly as much as $11 million to clean up the spill. Your client's mortgage secures a debt of $5 million. In addition to that liability, the debtor owes $40 million to various trade and other creditors and has $25 million of assets in addition to the property subject to the mortgage. Your client, the mortgagee, asks several questions:

1. Is there any chance that I have liability already under CERCLA as someone with a property interest (my mortgage) held while there has been a toxic disposal on the property?

2. What if the stay is lifted and I foreclose and purchase at the foreclosure sale and thus become owner of the property? Will that render me liable for cleanup of the toxic waste under the joint and several liability of CERCLA?

3. If the trustee can be persuaded (or forced) to spend the $8 million to cleanup the property, will I, as the mortgagee, then take the property as first claimant under my mortgage and get the first $5 million? In discussion the trustee has been claiming that section 506(c) gives her the right to take the first $8 million for the cleanup costs before I (the mortgagee) get anything. What do you think about that?

4. There is a vague state statute that gives a lien on property cleaned up to one who does an environmental cleanup. How will that lien interact with my mortgage?

5. Assume that the state has ordered the debtor to clean up the site. If, instead of cleaning up the site, the debtor simply files in bankruptcy and purports to be discharged of the liability to the state, how does the debtor deal with the argument under section 101(5), that the state's order is not a "claim" that can be discharged because it is merely the *request* for an equitable remedy, that is, it does not "give rise to a right to payment."

Problem 8–6

You represent a debtor corporation that faces a large toxic waste cleanup liability. No administrative action has yet occurred, nor has any clean up been conducted. The company has approximately $500,000 in unencumbered assets and a profitable factory worth $2 million, but subject to a $1.9 million mortgage. In addition, it owns the land on which the toxic waste has been dumped. That land was thought to be worth $1 million before the waste was discovered. The cleanup cost, however, will be no less than $5 million. The company has over 500 unsecured creditors with total debts of about $800,000. There are 200 shareholders. The company is in bankruptcy. In light of the case law that has evolved respecting CERCLA liability, what are the company's options for dealing with this liability? Is there any course of action that it might follow which would preserve any value for the unsecured creditors or the shareholders?

§ 5. WHEN IS A CLAIM BORN AND HOW IS IT ESTIMATED?

As we have seen, one might want to know when a claim is born and its value for several reasons. One needs to know the answer to these questions to determine who gets to vote and how many votes that person holds, who gets a distribution, and the priority of that distribution. And, of course, one needs to know which claims are discharged by the bankruptcy and which have not yet risen to the level of "claims" and so continue as potential claims against the assets of the reorganized company. In *Kane v. Johns–Manville Corp.*, 843 F.2d 636 (2d Cir.1988), Judge Newman deals with both of these questions in a fairly clever way. Although questions about the value of claims can often be finessed in determining how much each person gets to vote, a similar finesse is much harder to accomplish when one is determining the amount actually to be paid out upon liquidation of a bankrupt company. In the latter case, someone has to make a decision about who gets what dollars. Consider how cleverly the bankruptcy court dealt with the estimation question in *Kane:*

KANE v. JOHNS–MANVILLE CORP.
United States Court of Appeals, Second Circuit, 1988.
843 F.2d 636.

Before NEWMAN, WINTER, and MINER, CIRCUIT JUDGES.

JON O. NEWMAN, CIRCUIT JUDGE.

This appeal challenges the lawfulness of the reorganization plan of the Johns–Manville Corporation ("Manville"), a debtor in one of the nation's most significant Chapter 11 bankruptcy proceedings. Lawrence Kane, on behalf of himself and a group of other personal injury claimants, appeals from an order of the District Court for the Southern District of New York (Whitman Knapp, Judge) affirming an order of the Bankruptcy Court (Burton R. Lifland, Chief Judge) that confirmed a Second Amended Plan of Reorganization (the "Plan"). Kane and the group of 765 individuals he represents (collectively "Kane") are persons with asbestos-related disease who had filed personal injury suits against Manville prior to Manville's Chapter 11 petition. The suits were stayed, and Kane and other claimants presently afflicted with asbestos-related disease were designated as Class–4 creditors in the reorganization proceedings. Kane now objects to confirmation of the reorganization Plan on several grounds: it discharges the rights of future asbestos victims who do not have "claims" within the meaning of 11 U.S.C. § 101(4)(1982), it was adopted without constitutionally adequate notice to various interested parties, the voting procedures used in approving the Plan violated the Bankruptcy Code and due process requirements, and the Plan fails to conform with the requirements of 11 U.S.C. § 1129(a) and (b)(1982 & Supp. IV 1986). We determine that Kane lacks standing to challenge the Plan on the grounds that it violates the rights of future claimants and other third parties, and we reject on the merits his remaining claims that the Plan violates his rights regarding voting and fails to meet the requirements of section 1129(a) and (b). The order of the District Court affirming the Bankruptcy Court's confirmation of the Plan is affirmed.

BACKGROUND

Prior to its filing for reorganization in 1982, Manville was the world's largest miner of asbestos and a major manufacturer of insulating materials and other asbestos products. Beginning in the 1960's, scientific studies began to confirm that exposure to asbestos fibers over time could cause a variety of respiratory diseases, including certain forms of lung cancer. A significant characteristic of these asbestos-related diseases is their unusually long latency period. An individual might not become ill from an asbestos-related disease until as long as forty years after initial exposure. Hence, many asbestos victims remain unknown, most of whom were exposed in the 1950's and 1960's before the dangers of asbestos were widely recognized. These persons might not develop clinically observable symptoms until the 1990's or even later.

As a result of the studies linking respiratory disease with asbestos, Manville became the target in the 1960's and 1970's of a growing number of products liability lawsuits. By the early 1980's, Manville had been named in approximately 12,500 such suits brought on behalf of over 16,000 claimants. New suits were being filed at the rate of 425 per month. Epidemiological studies undertaken by Manville revealed that approximately 50,000 to 100,000 additional suits could be expected from persons who had already been exposed to Manville asbestos. On the basis of these studies and the costs Manville had already experienced in disposing of prior claims, Manville estimated its potential liability at approximately $2 billion. On August 26, 1982, Manville filed a voluntary petition in bankruptcy under Chapter 11. From the outset of the reorganization, all concerned recognized that the impetus for Manville's action was not a present inability to meet debts but rather the anticipation of massive personal injury liability in the future. *See In re Johns–Manville Corp.*, 36 B.R. 743, 745 (Bankr.S.D.N.Y.1984), *aff'd*, 52 B.R. 940 (S.D.N.Y.1985).

Because future asbestos-related liability was the *raison d'etre* of the Manville reorganization, an important question at the initial stages of the proceedings concerned the representation and treatment of what were termed "future asbestos health claimants" ("future claimants"). The future claimants were persons who had been exposed to Manville's asbestos prior to the August 1982 petition date but had not yet shown any signs of disease at that time. Since the future claimants were not yet ill at the time the Chapter 11 proceedings were commenced, none had filed claims against Manville, and their identities were unknown. An Asbestos Health Committee was appointed to represent all personal injury claimants, but the Committee took the position that it represented the interests only of "present claimants," persons who, prior to the petition date, had been exposed to Manville asbestos and had already developed an asbestos-related disease. The Committee declined to represent the future claimants. Other parties in the proceedings, recognizing that an effective reorganization would have to account for the future asbestos victims as well as the present ones, moved the Bankruptcy Court to appoint a legal guardian for the future claimants. The Bankruptcy Court granted the motion, reasoning that regardless of whether the future claimants technically had "claims" cognizable in bankruptcy proceedings, *see* 11 U.S.C. § 101(4), they were at least "parties in interest" under section 1109(b) of the Code and were therefore entitled to a voice in the proceedings. The Court appointed a Legal Representative to participate on behalf of the future claimants. *See In re Johns–Manville Corp.,* 36 B.R. 743 (Bankr.S.D.N.Y.1984), *aff'd,* 52 B.R. 940 (S.D.N.Y.1985). Additionally, the Court invited any person who had been exposed to Manville's asbestos but had not developed an illness to participate in the proceedings, and two such persons appeared.

The Second Amended Plan of Reorganization resulted from more than four years of negotiations among Manville, the Asbestos Health Committee, the Legal Representative, the Equity Security Holders' Committee, and other groups interested in the estate.[1] *See Manville Corp. v. Equity Security Holders Committee (In re Johns–Manville Corp.),* 66 B.R. 517, 518–33 (Bankr.S.D.N.Y.1986). The cornerstone of the Plan is the Asbestos Health Trust (the "Trust"), a mechanism designed to satisfy the claims of all asbestos health victims, both present and future. The Trust is funded with the proceeds from Manville's settlements with its insurers; certain cash, receivables, and stock of the reorganized Manville Corporation; long term notes; and the right to receive up to 20% of Manville's yearly profits for as long as it takes to satisfy all health claims. According to the terms of the Trust, individuals with asbestos-related disease must first try to settle their claims by a mandatory exchange of settlement offers with Trust representatives. If a settlement cannot be reached, the claimant may elect mediation, binding arbitration, or traditional tort litigation. The claimant may collect from the Trust the full amount of whatever compensatory damages he is

---

1. The Plan provides for nine classes of claims and interests: administrative expenses (Class 1), secured claims (Class 2), asbestos property damage claims (Class 3), present asbestos health claims (Class 4), employee and non-asbestos material claims (Class 5), other unsecured claims (Class 6), interests of preferred stockholders (Class 7), interests of common stockholders (Class 8), and interests of certain individual plaintiffs in pending lawsuits (Class 9). Future asbestos health claimants are not part of any class but are treated as "other asbestos obligations" under the Plan and are subject to the same claims handling facility as the present health claimants in Class 4.

awarded. The only restriction on recovery is that the claimant may not obtain punitive damages.

The purpose of the Trust is to provide a means of satisfying Manville's ongoing personal injury liability while allowing Manville to maximize its value by continuing as an ongoing concern. To fulfill this purpose, the Plan seeks to ensure that health claims can be asserted only against the Trust and that Manville's operating entities will be protected from an onslaught of crippling lawsuits that could jeopardize the entire reorganization effort. To this end, the parties agreed that as a condition precedent to confirmation of the Plan, the Bankruptcy Court would issue an injunction channeling all asbestos-related personal injury claims to the Trust (the "Injunction"). The Injunction provides that asbestos health claimants may proceed only against the Trust to satisfy their claims and may not sue Manville, its other operating entities, and certain other specified parties, including Manville's insurers. Significantly, the Injunction applies to all health claimants, both present and future, regardless of whether they technically have dischargeable "claims" under the Code. The Injunction applies to any suit to recover "on or with respect to any Claim, Interest or Other Asbestos Obligation." "Claim" covers the present claimants, who are categorized as Class–4 unsecured creditors under the Plan and who have dischargeable "claims" within the meaning of 11 U.S.C. § 101(4). The future claimants are subject to the Injunction under the rubric of "Other Asbestos Obligation," which is defined by the Plan as asbestos-related health liability caused by pre-petition exposure to Manville asbestos, regardless of when the individual develops clinically observable symptoms. Thus, while the future claimants are not given creditor status under the Plan, they are nevertheless treated identically to the present claimants by virtue of the Injunction, which channels all claims to the Trust.

The Plan was submitted to the Bankruptcy Court for voting in June of 1986. At that time relatively few present asbestos health claimants had appeared in the reorganization proceedings. Approximately 6,400 proofs of claims had been filed for personal injuries, which accounted for less than half of the more than 16,000 persons who had filed pre-petition personal injury suits against Manville. Moreover, Manville estimated that there were tens of thousands of additional present asbestos victims who had neither filed suits nor presented proofs of claims. Manville and the creditor constituencies agreed that as many present claimants as possible should be brought into the proceedings so that they could vote on the Plan. However, the parties were reluctant to embark on the standard Code procedure of establishing a bar date, soliciting proofs of claims, resolving all disputed claims on notice and hearing, and then weighting the votes by the amounts of the claims, as such a process could delay the reorganization for many years. To avoid this delay, the Bankruptcy Court adopted special voting procedures for Class 4. Manville was directed to undertake a comprehensive multi-media notice campaign to inform persons with present health claims of the pendency of the reorganization and their opportunity to participate. Potential health claimants who responded to the campaign were given a combined proof-of-claim-and-voting form in which each could present a medical diagnosis of his asbestos-related disease and vote to accept or reject the Plan. For voting purposes only, each claim was valued in the amount of one dollar. Claimants were informed that the proof-of-claim-and-voting form would be used only for voting and that to collect from the Trust, they would have to execute an additional proof of claim establishing the actual value of their damages.

The notice campaign produced a large number of present asbestos claimants. In all, 52,440 such claimants submitted proof-of-claim-and-voting forms. Of these, 50,275 or 95.8% approved the Plan, while 2,165 or 4.2% opposed it. In addition to these Class–4 claimants, all other classes of creditors also approved the Plan. Class 8, the common stockholders, opposed the Plan.

A confirmation hearing was held on December 16, 1986, at which Manville presented evidence regarding the feasibility and fairness of the Plan. Objections to confirmation were filed by several parties, including Kane. On December 18, 1986, the Bankruptcy Court issued a Determination of Confirmation Issues in which it rejected all objections to confirmation. *In re Johns–Manville Corp.*, 68 B.R. 618 (Bankr.S.D.N.Y. 1986). With respect to Kane's challenge to the Injunction and the voting procedures, the Court relied primarily on its broad equitable powers to achieve reorganizations. Furthermore, the Court found that, based on an extensive liquidation and feasibility analysis presented by Manville at the hearing, the Plan was workable, in the best interests of the creditors, and otherwise in conformity with the requirements of 11 U.S.C. § 1129(a) and (b). The Court entered an order confirming the Plan on December 22, 1986. Kane and others appealed. By order dated July 15, 1987, the District Court affirmed the Bankruptcy Court's confirmation order "for substantially the reasons set forth" in the Bankruptcy Judge's Determination of Confirmation Issues. This appeal followed.

DISCUSSION

A. Standing

The Legal Representative of the future claimants challenges Kane's standing to bring this appeal. The Legal Representative contends that Kane is not directly and adversely affected by the confirmation order and that his appeal improperly asserts the rights of third parties, namely the future claimants. * * *

We are satisfied that Kane is a "person aggrieved" by the Bankruptcy Court's order confirming the Plan. As a general rule, creditors have standing to appeal orders of the bankruptcy court disposing of property of the estate because such orders directly affect the creditors' ability to receive payment of their claims.

* * * In the present case, Kane, a creditor, has economic interests that are directly impaired by the Plan. His recourse to the courts to

pursue damages for his injuries is limited by the settlement procedures mandated by the Trust, he is not entitled to punitive damages, and, ultimately, his recovery is subject to the Trust's being sufficiently funded. Kane might receive more under this Plan than he would receive in a liquidation. However, he might do better still under alternative plans. Since the Second Amended Plan gives Kane less than what he might have received, he is directly and adversely affected pecuniarily by it, and he therefore has standing to challenge it on appeal.

Having determined that Kane may appeal the Bankruptcy Court's confirmation order, we must now decide whose rights Kane will be permitted to assert.

* * *

He asserts five claims:

(1) The Injunction violates the Bankruptcy Code because it affects the rights of future asbestos victims who do not have "claims" within the meaning of 11 U.S.C. § 101(4).

(2) The Injunction violates due process because future claimants were given inadequate notice of the discharge of their rights.

(3) The special voting procedures for Class 4 violate due process because present claimants were given inadequate notice of the hearing at which the voting procedures were adopted.

(4) The Class–4 voting procedures violate the Code because persons were permitted to vote before their claims were "allowed" pursuant to 11 U.S.C. § 502 (1982 & Supp. IV 1986), claims were arbitrarily assigned a value of one dollar each for voting purposes and creditors were denied the opportunity to object to claims.

(5) The Plan fails to meet the requirements of 11 U.S.C. § 1129(a) and (b) because it was not proposed in good faith, it is not in the best interests of all creditors, it is not feasible, and it is not fair and equitable with respect to dissenting classes.

Kane does not dispute that his challenges to the Injunction (claims (1) and (2)) assert the constitutional and statutory rights only of the future claimants. Additionally, we note that claim (3) regarding notice of the voting procedures asserts only third-party rights. Kane was present at the June 23, 1986, hearing at which the voting procedures were adopted and had an opportunity to object, which he concedes that he exercised. Kane's claim with respect to notice of voting procedures is that notice was inadequate only as to present health claimants (other than himself) who were not informed of the special voting procedures and might have wanted to object. The question we must consider is whether on this appeal of the confirmation order, Kane may assert claims of these third parties. We conclude that he may not.

Generally, litigants in federal court are barred from asserting the constitutional and statutory rights of others in an effort to obtain relief for injury to themselves. *Warth v. Seldin*, 422 U.S. 490, 499, 509, 95

S.Ct. 2197, 2205, 2210, 45 L.Ed.2d 343 (1975); *see Phillips Petroleum Co. v. Shutts,* 472 U.S. 797, 804–05, 105 S.Ct. 2965, 2971, 86 L.Ed.2d 628 (1985); *Singleton v. Wulff, supra,* 428 U.S. at 114, 96 S.Ct. at 2874. Though this limitation is not dictated by the Article III case or controversy requirement, the third-party standing doctrine has been considered a valuable prudential limitation, self-imposed by the federal courts. In *Singleton,* the Supreme Court articulated two important policies justifying such a limitation: "first, the courts should not adjudicate [third-party] rights unnecessarily, and it may be that in fact the holders of those rights either do not wish to assert them, or will be able to enjoy them regardless of whether the in-court litigant is successful or not. Second, third parties themselves usually will be the best proponents of their own rights." 428 U.S. at 113–14, 96 S.Ct. at 2874 (citations omitted). The Supreme Court has recognized that under some special circumstances these concerns are not present. Thus, where the litigant's interests are closely allied with those of the third parties, standing is permitted because the litigant is likely to be as effective a proponent of the third-party rights as the third parties themselves. *E.g., Singleton v. Wulff, supra,* 428 U.S. at 117–18, 96 S.Ct. at 2876 (plurality opinion)(physicians may assert patients' privacy rights); *Griswold v. Connecticut,* 381 U.S. 479, 481, 85 S.Ct. 1678, 1680, 14 L.Ed.2d 510 (1965)(same); *Pierce v. Society of Sisters,* 268 U.S. 510, 534–36, 45 S.Ct. 571, 573–74, 69 L.Ed. 1070 (1925)(owners of private school may assert rights of potential pupils and their parents). Furthermore, where third parties are unable to assert their own rights, current litigants are allowed to assert third-party claims that might otherwise remain unvindicated. *See Singleton v. Wulff, supra,* 428 U.S. at 115–16, 96 S.Ct. at 2875 (plurality opinion); *id.* at 125–26, 96 S.Ct. at 2879–80 (Powell, J., concurring in part and dissenting in part); *NAACP v. Alabama,* 357 U.S. 449, 459–60, 78 S.Ct. 1163, 1170, 2 L.Ed.2d 1488 (1958). However, where these special considerations are absent, a litigant is restricted to asserting his own constitutional and statutory rights. *See Warth v. Seldin, supra.*

The prudential concerns limiting third-party standing are particularly relevant in the bankruptcy context. Bankruptcy proceedings regularly involve numerous parties, each of whom might find it personally expedient to assert the rights of another party even though that other party is present in the proceedings and is capable of representing himself. Third-party standing is of special concern in the bankruptcy context where, as here, one constituency before the court seeks to disturb a plan of reorganization based on the rights of third parties who apparently favor the plan. In this context, the courts have been understandably skeptical of the litigant's motives and have often denied standing as to any claim that asserts only third-party rights. *E.g., Kremer v. Clarke (In re Frank Fehr Brewing Co.),* 268 F.2d 170, 179 (6th Cir.1959), *cert. denied,* 362 U.S. 963, 80 S.Ct. 880, 4 L.Ed.2d 878 (1960)("[i]f the creditors are willing to accept less than they might otherwise be entitled to, it is not for the common stockholders to insist that they not be permitted to do so"); *In re Evans Products Co.,* 65 B.R. 870, 875 (S.D.Fla.1986)(debtors lack standing to raise the rights of wrongly classified creditors as a means to attack the overall reorganization plan); *In re Snyder,* 56 B.R. 1007, 1010–11 (N.D.Ind.1986)(debtor may not challenge plan on ground that notice was inadequate to creditors); *see also Holywell Corp. v. Bank of New York,* 59 B.R. 340, 349 (S.D.Fla.1986); *Palm Springs Owners Association v. Sweetwater (In re Sweetwater), supra,* 57 B.R. at 746–47; *In re Adana Mortgage Bankers, Inc.,* 14 B.R. 29, 30 (Bankr.N.D.Ga.1981).

Prudential concerns weigh heavily against permitting Kane to assert the rights of the future claimants in attacking the Plan. First, Kane's interest in these proceedings is potentially opposed to that of the future claimants. Both Kane and the future claimants wish to recover from the debtor for personal injuries. To the extent that Kane is successful in obtaining more of the debtor's assets to satisfy his own claims, less will be available for other parties, with the distinct risk that the future claimants will suffer. Thus, we cannot depend on Kane sincerely to advance the interests of the future claimants. Second, the third parties whose rights Kane seeks to assert are already represented in the proceedings. Though it is true, as Kane points out, that the future claimants themselves are not before the Court, they are ably represented by the appointed Legal Representative. Therefore, it is not necessary to allow Kane to raise the future claimants' rights on the theory that these rights will be otherwise ignored. The Bankruptcy Court appointed the Legal Representative specifically for the purpose of ensuring that the rights of the future claimants would be asserted where necessary. Certainly as between Kane and the Legal Representative, there is no question that the latter is the more reliable advocate of the future claimants' rights, and we may confidently leave that task entirely to him.

* * *

We have so far determined that Kane does not have standing to challenge the Injunction nor to assert the rights of other Class–4 members in challenging the notice of voting procedures. In contrast, Kane does have standing to assert his remaining claims regarding the validity of the voting procedures and compliance with the requirements of section 1129(a) and (b); these claims allege violations of Kane's own rights under the Code.

B. *Voting Procedures*

* * *

Kane contends that the special Class–4 voting procedures adopted by the Bankruptcy Court violated his rights under the Code in several ways. First, since proofs of claims and votes were simultaneously solicited from present claimants in a combined mailing form, no creditor had an opportunity to object to the Class–4 members' claims before their votes were cast. Kane argues that this lack of opportunity to object prejudiced him because some of the claims might have been invalid and counting votes of those with invalid claims diluted his own vote. Second, Kane argues that the Bankruptcy Court improperly "allowed" claims for voting purposes in the arbitrary amount of one dollar, thereby depriving him of the opportunity to vote his claim weighted in the amount indicated in his proof of claim. By weighting all Class–4 votes equally, the Bankruptcy Court, in Kane's view, failed to adhere to the Code's voting scheme whereby a minority of class members with just over one third of the value of the total claims may reject a plan. Finally, Kane suggests that by assigning the one dollar value to all of the claims, the Bankruptcy Court might have discouraged Plan opponents with large claims from casting their votes since such opponents might have believed that, without the benefit of weighted voting, their opposition to the Plan would be futile.

* * *

We need not decide whether the special Class–4 voting procedures violate the Code because, in view of the outcome of the vote, the alleged irregularities were at most harmless error. * * * The harmless error rule has been invoked in the bankruptcy context where procedural irregularities, including alleged errors in voting procedures, would not have had an effect on the outcome of the case.

* * *

None of the procedures that Kane contends were required would have changed the outcome of the vote. With respect to denial of the opportunity to object to the Class–4 claims before they were voted, no substantial rights were impaired because Kane is unable to show that, had he been afforded a chance to object, any of the present health claims would have been excluded. The only objection Kane contends that he would have asserted is that the combined proof-of-claim-and-voting form approved by the Bankruptcy Court permitted a filing supported only by a written medical diagnosis of an asbestos-related condition without evidence that the claimant was exposed to Manville's product, as opposed to the product of some other company. However, it is clear from the record that this objection would have been unavailing. The combined proof-of-claim-and-voting form required anyone who had not already filed a lawsuit against Manville to submit a diagnosis of his disease *and* to represent that he had been exposed to Manville's product. Such a representation would have sufficed to warrant accepting the claim for voting purposes, especially in the absence of any particularized contrary evidence from Kane. In any event, since 95.8% of those Class–4 members who voted approved the Plan, the result would not have been different unless more than 90% of those who voted in favor had invalid claims, an improbable circumstance.

Similarly, Kane was not prejudiced by the assignment of a one dollar value to each claim. If we make the reasonable assumption that the percentage of claims that are valid is the same for "yes" votes and "no" votes, then the "no" votes would have to be at least ten times larger, on average, than the "yes" votes in order to change the result from what occurred with equal weighting of each vote. Nothing in the record gives any indication that such a large variation in claims existed, much less that the "no" votes were the larger claims. Indeed, it is safe to assume that if the procedures insisted upon by Kane had been used, all the votes would have still been weighted roughly the same since significant variations would not likely occur in the damages sustained by similar groups of people from similar kinds of injuries. Even if Kane is correct that some Plan opponents with larger claims were discouraged from voting, no prejudice occurred. Even if we make the unlikely assumption, favorable to Kane, that Plan opponents in Class 4, on average, had claims twice the size of the claims of Plan proponents, the number of "no" votes in this class would have had to increase nearly six times, from 2,165 to 12,569, in order to change the result. If there really were 12,569 Class–4 claimants opposed to the Plan, it is highly unlikely that 10,404 or 83% of them would have been discouraged from voting.

C. Section 1129 Requirements

* * *

Subsection 1129(a)(3) requires that the plan be proposed "in good faith and not by any means forbidden by law." The good-faith test means that "the plan was proposed with 'honesty and good intentions' and with 'a basis for expecting that a reorganization can be effected.'" *Koelbl v. Glessing (In re Koelbl),* 751 F.2d 137, 139 (2d Cir.1984)(quoting *Manati Sugar Co. v. Mock,* 75 F.2d 284, 285 (2d Cir.1935)); *see also Connell v. Coastal Cable T.V., Inc. (In re Coastal Cable T.V., Inc.),* 709 F.2d 762, 765 (1st Cir.1983)(to be proposed in good faith, plan "must bear some relation to the statutory objective of resuscitating a financially troubled corporation"). We are satisfied that Manville honestly believed that it was in need of reorganization and that the Plan was negotiated and proposed with the intention of accomplishing a successful reorganization. *See In re Johns–Manville Corp.,* 36 B.R. 727, 741 (Bankr. S.D.N.Y.), *leave to appeal denied,* 39 B.R. 234 (S.D.N.Y.), *reh'g denied,* 39 B.R. 998 (S.D.N.Y.), *mandamus denied,* 749 F.2d 3 (2d Cir.1984). The Bankruptcy Court found that "Johns–Manville was and remains 'a financially besieged enterprise in desperate need of reorganization of its crushing real debt, both present and future.'" 68 B.R. at 632 (quoting *In re Johns–Manville Corp., supra,* 36 B.R. at 741). This finding is not clearly erroneous. *See Koelbl v. Glessing (In re Koelbl), supra,* 751 F.2d at 139 (applying clearly erroneous standard to question of good-faith proposal of reorganization plan).

Subsection 1129(a)(7) incorporates the former "best interest of creditors" test and requires a finding that each holder of a claim or interest either has accepted the plan or has received no less under the plan than what he would have received in a Chapter 7 liquidation. At the confirmation hearing, Manville presented an extensive liquidation analysis based on documentary evidence and expert testimony. Kane submitted no evidence. The Bankruptcy Judge accepted Manville's proof that all creditors and equity holders would receive substantially more under the Plan than they would have received if Manville were liquidated. In particular, the Bankruptcy Court found that Class–4 present asbestos health claimants would receive 100% on their claims under the Plan but would have received only 56%–81% in a liquidation. These findings are not clearly erroneous. *See United Properties, Inc. v. Emporium Department Stores, Inc.,* 379 F.2d 55, 63–64 (8th Cir.1967)(applying clearly erroneous standard to former "best interests" test).

Subsection 1129(a)(11) requires that the plan is not likely to be followed by liquidation or the need for further financial reorganization. As the Bankruptcy Court correctly stated, the feasibility standard is whether the plan offers a reasonable assurance of success. Success need not be guaranteed. *See Prudential Insurance Co. v. Monnier (In re Monnier Bros.),* 755 F.2d 1336, 1341 (8th Cir.1985); *In re Wolf,* 61 B.R. 1010, 1011 (Bankr.N.D.Iowa 1986). As with the liquidation analysis, Manville presented extensive evidence on feasibility at the confirmation hearing, while Kane presented no evidence. The Bankruptcy Judge found that "the Debtor's reasonable and credible projections of future earnings have established that the reorganized corporation is unlikely to face future proceedings under this title." 68 B.R. at 635.

* * *

Kane argues that the Bankruptcy Court's finding of feasibility was incorrect because the Trust is inadequately funded and will not be able to satisfy the claims against it. He contends that accepting Manville's estimate of $26,000 as the average liquidation cost of present claimants' suits, the Trust will need $1.352 billion to pay the 52,000 present claimants who filed claims. Since the Trust, according to Kane, is funded through the first five years with only $1.104 billion, he argues that it will fall $248 million short of paying the present claimants. There are two major errors in Kane's analysis. First, his account of the Trust's short-term funding is incorrect because he omits the value of Manville stock, which Kane estimates to be worth from $80.8 million to $146.4 million and which Manville estimates to be worth from $323 million to $585 million. Second, and more importantly, Kane completely ignores the long-term funding of the Trust. Not all present asbestos claims must be paid immediately upon confirmation, and many will not be liquidated and presented for payment even within the first five years. More likely, payment of present health claims will be spread out over roughly a ten-year period. In years six through ten, the Trust will receive annual payments of $75 million as well as up to 20% of Manville's yearly profits. This additional funding will be more than sufficient to pay the few present claimants who might not recover from the Trust's assets accumulated over the first five years. Moreover, since the $75 million annual payments continue through year 27 and the 20% profit-sharing continues for as long as necessary to pay all claims, the

Trust will also be adequate to pay the claims of the future asbestos victims. The Bankruptcy Court's finding that the Plan offers reasonable assurance of success in this regard is not clearly erroneous. *See Prudential Insurance Co. v. Monnier (In re Monnier Bros.), supra,* 755 F.2d at 1341 (applying clearly erroneous standard to feasibility determination); *Pizza of Hawaii, Inc. v. Shakey's, Inc. (In re Pizza of Hawaii, Inc.),* 761 F.2d 1374, 1377 (9th Cir.1985)(same).

* * *

The order of the District Court affirming the Bankruptcy Court's confirmation order is affirmed.

MINER, CIRCUIT JUDGE, concurring:

Since the bankruptcy judge was empowered to estimate the claims of the Class–4 creditors, and did not abuse his discretion in doing so, I perceive no need to apply a harmless error analysis or to employ mathematical calculations to sustain the voting procedures adopted. * * *

By the time of the June 23, 1986 hearing held to consider the Disclosure Statement and the Second Amended and Restated Plan of Reorganization filed by the debtors, approximately 6,400 proofs of claim had been submitted by asbestos health claimants for personal injuries. It was apparent at that juncture in the proceedings that the administration of the case would be delayed unduly if each of those unliquidated claims were to be considered separately for allowance purposes. Referring to the number of actual lawsuits then pending on behalf of asbestos health claimants, the bankruptcy judge observed that more than 16,500 hearings would be necessary "to treat each individual claim discretely." Joint App. at 697. In the words of the debtors' attorney, "the practical effect of having to value each and every claim individually would * * * be delay[] beyond anybody's reasonable expectations and probably lifetime." *Id.* at 730. The problem of delay was even more apparent at the conclusion of the notice campaign, when proof-of-claim-and-voting forms had been received from 52,440 claimants.

Under the circumstances, the bankruptcy judge properly exercised his authority to estimate each of the claims at $1.00. The asbestos health claims were especially suited to estimation because of the uncertain nature of both liability and damages. Moreover, the very purpose of the reorganization would be defeated if each claim were to be considered separately for purposes of allowance and voting. Indeed, the delay entailed by such an approach would not only be fatal to the entire plan but might very well be fatal to any recovery for the claimants. Section 502(c)(1) is designed to forestall these types of consequences. * * *

In sum, I am of the opinion that the specific Code provisions referred to above are sufficient to support the voting procedures approved by the bankruptcy judge. Those procedures not only comply with the Code in all respects but also serve to further the overall purposes of Chapter 11 in cases of this nature. I concur with the reasoning of the majority opinion in all other respects, and, of course, with the conclusions reached therein.

Notes and Questions

1. The trust fund in *Manville* is funded by various sources of money and also received 24 million shares of stock in the "new" Manville Corporation. Shareholders of "old" Manville stock had all of their shares cancelled and received pro rata distribution of 3 million new shares. When all other shares and warrants are considered, the former shareholders held less than 10% of the new company.

While this settlement was being reached, but before confirmation of a plan, Manville shareholders attempted to call a stockholder meeting to oust management and to replace them with someone who would cut a better bargain for the owners. The bankruptcy court stayed this proposed meeting. Declining to adopt the bankruptcy court's analysis, the Court of Appeals found that stockholder meetings should normally be allowed but it agreed that a stay was appropriate if the proposed meeting was a substantial abuse of the bankruptcy process. On remand, the lower court made the requisite finding to deny a meeting and the plan was confirmed. On whose behalf were the managers of Manville negotiating the plan? For whom were they operating the company?

2. After the decision in *Kane,* what is the status of a potential tort plaintiff who may have been exposed to injurious substances long before but who shows no injury until long after the confirmation of the plan? *Kane* ducked the issue, not so? In contrast, the Court of Appeals for the Third Circuit in *Schweitzer v. Consolidated Rail Corp. (Conrail),* 758 F.2d 936 (3d Cir.1985), held that under the former Bankruptcy Act future causes of action for asbestos injury were not yet claims and therefore not dischargeable claims where there had been no manifestation of injury.

> [T]here is generally no cause of action in tort until a plaintiff has suffered identifiable, compensable injury. * * * It is true that the possible existence of subclinical asbestos-related injury prior to manifestation may be of interest to a histologist. Likewise, the existence of such injury may be of vital concern to insurers and their insureds who have bargained for liability coverage triggered by "bodily injury." We believe, however, that subclinical injury resulting from exposure to asbestos is insufficient to constitute the actual loss or damage to a plaintiff's interest required to sustain a cause of action under generally applicable principles of tort law.
>
> Moreover, we are persuaded that a contrary rule would be undesirable as applied in the asbestos-related tort context. If mere exposure to asbestos were sufficient to give rise to an F.E.L.A. cause of action * * * proof of damages in such cases would be highly speculative, likely resulting in windfalls for those who never take ill and insufficient compensation for those who do.

If the "future" claims are not discharged or bound to the terms of the plan, how will possible claimants collect their claims when they arise? The legal entity that injured them will surely be gone. What if the business is broken into parts and sold off as separate operating units?

3. In *In re A.H. Robins Co., Inc.*, 88 B.R. 742 (E.D.Va.1988) the plan established a trust for the payment of Dalkon Shield claims. The trust was funded with contributions of cash from the company, from major insurers of Robins, and from the proceeds of an acquisition of Robins by American Home Products Corporation (AHP). AHP paid in excess of $2.5 billion for Robins. Robins had earned pre-tax profits of over $170 million during its last year in bankruptcy. The *Robins* court placed a nominal estimated value on the tort claims for purposes of voting, stating that it was "intellectually and morally" satisfied that this was appropriate. The court estimated the total value of all pending claims at $2.475 billion.

4. The court thus made two separate estimates of the claims and then confirmed a procedure for their liquidation and payment out of a trust fund. Do either of the estimates determine the amount that a claimant will receive under the plan?

5. Finding that punitive damages would not have been recovered in any liquidation of Robins, the *Robins* court disallowed all claims for punitive damages. Under section 726(a)(4), in a liquidation all claims for penalties, punitive damages, exemplary damages or the like are subordinate in distribution to general unsecured claims. While this section applies only in a liquidation case, it certainly justifies a reorganization plan that separately classifies punitive damage claims apart from other unsecured claims. It also suggests that, for debtors unable to pay general unsecured claims in full, zero payment of punitive damage claims can be approved under section 1129(a)(7).

6. A final issue in *Robins* and *Manville* involves the effect of the confirmed plan on liability of third parties such as insurance companies. In *Robins* the confirmed plan protected both managers and insurers. This was done by a release of liability and an injunction against the filing of lawsuits. In return for that protection, the protected parties contributed substantial sums to the trust fund. What if, unlike *Robins,* where the creditors accepted the plan, a large majority of claimants had rejected the plan?

Problem 8–7

Alvin and Barbara Taylor filed a joint petition in Chapter 7. Cleda Bush, Alvin's former wife, has challenged Alvin's attempt to discharge his obligation to pay her one-half of his military pension. In the earlier divorce, Alvin had agreed to pay one-half of his pension to Cleda. (Assume for the purpose of this problem that any obligation Alvin would have to Cleda would not be in the nature of alimony and would therefore not be excepted from discharge under section 523(a)(5)).

Cleda has argued that Alvin's liability to her is not dischargeable. Her principal argument is that the liability arises as a series of "mini" liabilities each month when he receives the pension, and he in turn has an obligation to remit a portion of it to her. Thus, she argues, the liability did not arise prior to the petition and is therefore not dischargeable under Alvin's Chapter 7. How would you respond to that argument if you represented Alvin?

Judge Arnold responded to this argument as follows:

Taylor and his new wife, Barbara, then filed a chapter 7 bankruptcy petition, and that is where this lawsuit begins. The Taylors listed their obligation to Mrs. Bush as a debt, and sought to have it discharged. Mrs. Bush objected. She argued that this obligation couldn't be a debt because the property—the right to one-half of Mr. Taylor's pension— was already hers. The Bankruptcy Court, and the District Court on review, agreed with Mrs. Bush, and refused the Taylors' request for discharge. As this Court notes, both courts supported their decision with alternative holdings. First, both courts held that this obligation was not a pre-petition debt within the meaning of the Bankruptcy Code. Thus it could not be discharged. Alternatively, both courts held that the divorce decree created a constructive trust for Mrs. Bush's benefit, and further, that that trust relationship (between Mr. Taylor and Mrs. Bush) should not be disturbed in bankruptcy. Today our Court adopts both these grounds. I think it errs in doing so.

The Taylors' obligation to Mrs. Bush falls within the Bankruptcy Code's broad and flexible definition of a debt. Since it is a debt, it is dischargeable. The words of the statute leave no legitimate room for doubt. Under 11 U.S.C. § 101[(12)], a "debt" is simply a liability on a claim. A "claim," in turn, is:

> (A) [a] right to payment, whether or not such right is reduced to judgment, liquidated, unliquidated, fixed, contingent, matured, unmatured, disputed, undisputed, legal, equitable, secured, or unsecured * * *.

11 U.S.C. § 101[(5)]. Bush has a claim against the Taylors. She had, each month for as long as Mr. Taylor lived, a right to payment of a portion of his pension.

The Court suggests that there can be no discharge in this case because, instead of one debt, it involves a lot of mini-debts, each accruing on the fifteenth of every month. This reasoning ignores the Code's plain inclusion of unmatured debts within the definition of dischargeable debts. The fifteenth of each month brings partial maturity of *the* debt in this case, not a new debt. This "many-debts" understanding of the Taylors' obligation is further undermined by Mrs. Bush's theory of the case: part of the pension has been hers since the divorce. Whatever her interest in this property, it does not appear on the fifteenth of each month. Right reason and the plain meaning of the Code point unequivocally in one direction: there is only one debt in this case, and it is dischargeable.

A former spouse's obligations for alimony, maintenance, and child support are not debts under the Code, 11 U.S.C. § 523(a)(5), and therefore are not dischargeable. But Mrs. Bush stipulated below that the Taylors' obligation was for a property settlement, and was not in the nature of alimony, maintenance, or support. The Court seeks to avoid this characterization by labeling the Washington court's action a division of property rather than a property settlement, *ante* at 993. This however, is a distinction more subtle than real, given counsel's arguments in this case. Washington is a community-property state, and that may well affect the nature of Mrs. Bush's property rights under the divorce decree. Property is, after all, a creature of state law. But Mrs. Bush has not argued—not in this Court or in the District Court or the Bankruptcy Court—that the Taylors should be denied a discharge because of the special pre-divorce nature or origin of her property rights in the pension. That argument might be promising. It is, however, a matter of Washington state law, of which neither the Court nor I can be certain, because no one has argued the matter. This theory is foreclosed to Mrs. Bush at this late date in the suit. And it is likewise inappropriate for the Court to inject the issue into the case now.

The Court also places great weight on the fact that the divorce decree speaks of Mrs. Bush's interest in Mr. Taylor's pension as her "sole and separate property." But that language does not compel the result sought by the Court. Whenever a debt arising from the division of marital property is discharged, the non-debtor spouse is thereby deprived of his or her sole and separate property. That is the hard, but legislatively settled, fact of bankruptcy involving former spouses. Whatever the merits of that decision, Congress has not excepted marital property settlements from the reach of bankruptcy. And we are not at liberty to redefine "debt" in order to accomplish that result. The Taylors' obligation to make periodic payments to Mrs. Bush is a debt. It should, pursuant to their request and along with the rest of their debts, be discharged.

Do you think Mrs. Bush won or lost?

§ 6. ESTIMATING CLAIMS FOR THE PURPOSE OF DISTRIBUTION

When there is to be a distribution of money, irrevocable decisions face the bankruptcy judge. One court has described the options available to the bankruptcy court as follows:

> Options for the court in estimating claims include accepting the claimant's claim at face value, estimating the claim at zero and waiving discharge of the claim under section 1141(d), arriving at its independent estimation of the claim, or utilizing a jury trial to obtain an accurate estimation.[1]

The difficulties with allowing parties to pursue a lawsuit in state court so to determine the value of their claims are obvious. If such a claim is potentially large, the entire distribution from the estate will have to be held up pending its determination.

On the other hand, the evaluation in the bankruptcy court itself is not a perfect way of estimating such claims. Must the bankruptcy court itself hold a trial as though it were a state court? If not, is it merely to hold a mini-trial and then estimate the probability of success? Assume a claimant with a 49 percent probability of success against the bankrupt company for the full amount of its $2 million claim and a 51 percent chance that it will receive nothing. How does one "estimate" such a

---

1. *In re Federal Press Co.,* 116 B.R. 650, 653 (Bankr.N.D.Ind.1989).

claim? Does it have a value of $980,000 ($2,000,000 x .49) or a value of zero ("I find it more probable than not that your claim is invalid")?

BITTNER v. BORNE CHEMICAL CO., INC.

United States Court of Appeals, Third Circuit, 1982.
691 F.2d 134.

Opinion of the Court

Gibbons, Circuit Judge.

Stockholders of The Rolfite Company appeal from the judgment of the district court, affirming the decision of the bankruptcy court to assign a zero value to their claims in the reorganization proceedings of Borne Chemical Company, Inc. (Borne) under Chapter 11 of the Bankruptcy Code (Code), 11 U.S.C. §§ 1–151326 (Supp. IV 1981). Since the bankruptcy court neither abused its discretionary authority to estimate the value of the claims pursuant to 11 U.S.C. § 502(c)(1) nor relied on clearly erroneous findings of fact, we affirm.

I.

Prior to filing its voluntary petition under Chapter 11 of the Code, Borne commenced a state court action against Rolfite for the alleged pirating of trade secrets and proprietary information from Borne. The Rolfite Company filed a counterclaim, alleging, *inter alia,* that Borne had tortiously interfered with a proposed merger between Rolfite and the Quaker Chemical Corporation (Quaker) by unilaterally terminating a contract to manufacture Rolfite products and by bringing its suit. Sometime after Borne filed its Chapter 11 petition, the Rolfite stockholders sought relief from the automatic stay so that the state court proceedings might be continued.[1] Borne then filed a motion to disallow temporarily the Rolfite claims until they were finally liquidated in the state court. The bankruptcy court lifted the automatic stay but also granted Borne's motion to disallow temporarily the claims, extending the time within which such claims could be filed and allowed if they should be eventually liquidated.

Upon denial of their motion to stay the hearing on confirmation of Borne's reorganization plan, the Rolfite stockholders appealed to the district court, which vacated the temporary disallowance order and directed the bankruptcy court to hold an estimation hearing. The parties agreed to establish guidelines for the submission of evidence at the hearing, and, in accordance with this agreement, the bankruptcy court relied on the parties' choice of relevant pleadings and other documents related to the state court litigation, and on briefs and oral argument. After weighing the evidence, the court assigned a zero value to the Rolfite claims and reinstated its earlier order to disallow temporarily the claims until such time as they might be liquidated in the state

---

1. Since the standing of the Rolfite stockholders to pursue these claims under state law was apparently not challenged before the bankruptcy court, we take no position on that issue.

court, in effect requiring a waiver of discharge of the Rolfite claims from Borne. Upon appeal, the district court affirmed.

II.

Section 502(c) of the Code provides: There shall be estimated for purposes of allowance under this section—

(1) any contingent or unliquidated claim, fixing or liquidation of which, as the case may be, would unduly delay the closing of the case * * *.

The Code, the Rules of Bankruptcy Procedure, 11 U.S.C.App. (1977), and the Suggested Interim Bankruptcy Rules, 11 U.S.C.A. (1982), are silent as to the manner in which contingent or unliquidated claims are to be estimated. Despite the lack of express direction on the matter, we are persuaded that Congress intended the procedure to be undertaken initially by the bankruptcy judges, using whatever method is best suited to the particular contingencies at issue. The principal consideration must be an accommodation to the underlying purposes of the Code. It is conceivable that in rare and unusual cases arbitration or even a jury trial on all or some of the issues may be necessary to obtain a reasonably accurate evaluation of the claims. *See* 3 *Collier on Bankruptcy* ¶ 502.03 (15th ed. 1981). Such methods, however, usually will run counter to the efficient administration of the bankrupt's estate and where there is sufficient evidence on which to base a reasonable estimate of the claim, the bankruptcy judge should determine the value. In so doing, the court is bound by the legal rules which may govern the ultimate value of the claim. For example, when the claim is based on an alleged breach of contract, the court must estimate its worth in accordance with accepted contract law. *See, e.g.,* 3 *Collier on Bankruptcy* ¶ 57.15[3.2] (14th ed. 1977). However, there are no other limitations on the court's authority to evaluate the claim save those general principles which should inform all decisions made pursuant to the Code.

In reviewing the method[2] by which a bankruptcy court has ascertained the value of a claim under section 502(c)(1), an appellate court may only reverse if the bankruptcy court has abused its discretion.[3] That standard of review is narrow. The appellate court must defer to the congressional intent to accord wide latitude to the decisions of the tribunal in question. Section 502(c)(1) of the Code embodies Congress' determination that the bankruptcy courts are better equipped to evaluate the evidence supporting a particular claim within the context of a

---

2. The issue of whether a bankruptcy court used an appropriate method to estimate a claim is distinct from the issue of whether the bankruptcy court reached valid findings of fact. Appellate review of the former is governed by an abuse of discretion standard. Review of the latter is limited by the "clearly erroneous" standard. *See infra* Section III of this opinion.

3. An estimate made pursuant to section 57(d) of the Bankruptcy Act, the predecessor to section 502(c)(1) of the Code, was subject to the same standard of review. *See* 3 *Collier on Bankruptcy* ¶ 57.15[3.2] (14th ed. 1977) "The bankruptcy court ha[d] exclusive jurisdiction to direct the manner and the time in which such a claim is to be liquidated or estimated as to its amount, and its decision should be subject to review only on the ground of abuse of discretion."

particular bankruptcy proceeding. Thus, an appellate court can impose its own judgment only when "the factors considered [by the bankruptcy court] do not accord with those required by the policy underlying the substantive right or if the weight given to those factors is not consistent with that necessary to effectuate that policy * * *." *Gurmankin v. Costanzo,* 626 F.2d 1115, 1119–20 (3d Cir.1980).

According to the Rolfite stockholders, the estimate which section 502(c)(1) requires is the present value of the probability that appellants will be successful in their state court action. Thus, if the bankruptcy court should determine as of this date that the Rolfite stockholders' case is not supported by a preponderance or 51% of the evidence but merely by 40%, they apparently would be entitled to have 40% of their claims allowed during the reorganization proceedings, subject to modification if and when the claims are liquidated in state court. The Rolfite stockholders contend that instead of estimating their claims in this manner, the bankruptcy court assessed the ultimate merits and, believing that they could not establish their case by a preponderance of the evidence, valued the claims at zero.

We note first that the bankruptcy court did not explicitly draw the distinction that the Rolfite stockholders make. Assuming however that the bankruptcy court did estimate their claims according to their ultimate merits rather than the present value of the probability that they would succeed in their state court action,[4] we cannot find that such a valuation method is an abuse of the discretion conferred by section 502(c)(1).

The validity of this estimation must be determined in light of the policy underlying reorganization proceedings. In Chapter 11 of the Code, Congress addressed the complex issues which are raised when a corporation faces mounting financial problems.

> The modern corporation is a complex and multi-faceted entity. Most corporations do not have a significant market share of the lines of business in which they compete. The success, and even the survival, of a corporation in contemporary markets depends on three elements: First, the ability to attract and hold skilled management; second, the ability to obtain credit; and third, the corporation's ability to project to the public an image of vitality * * *.
>
> One cannot overemphasize the advantages of speed and simplicity to both creditors and debtors. Chapter XI allows a debtor to negotiate a plan outside of court and, having reached a settlement with a majority in number and amount of each class of creditors, permits the debtor to bind all unsecured creditors to the terms of the arrangement. From the perspective of creditors, early confirmation of a plan of arrangement: first, generally reduces administrative expenses which have priority over the claims of unsecured

---

4. The Rolfite stockholders have not convincingly established that the bankruptcy court would have assigned their claims a greater value using the estimation method which they propose. *See infra* Section III of this opinion.

creditors; second, permits creditors to receive prompt distributions on their claims with respect to which interest does not accrue after the filing date; and third, increases the ultimate recovery on creditor claims by minimizing the adverse effect on the business which often accompanies efforts to operate an enterprise under the protection of the Bankruptcy Act.

124 Cong.Rec. H 11101–H 11102 (daily ed. Sept. 28, 1978)(statement of Rep. D. Edwards of California, floor manager for bankruptcy legislation in the House of Representatives). Thus, in order to realize the goals of Chapter 11, a reorganization must be accomplished quickly and efficiently.

If the bankruptcy court estimated the value of the Rolfite stockholders' claims according to the ultimate merits of their state court action, such a valuation method is not inconsistent with the principles which imbue Chapter 11. Those claims are contingent[5] and unliquidated. According to the bankruptcy court's findings of fact, the Rolfite stockholders' chances of ultimately succeeding in the state court action are uncertain at best. Yet, if the court had valued the Rolfite stockholders' claims according to the present probability of success, the Rolfite stockholders might well have acquired a significant, if not controlling, voice in the reorganization proceedings. The interests of those creditors with liquidated claims would have been subject to the Rolfite interests, despite the fact that the state court might ultimately decide against those interests after the reorganization.[6] The bankruptcy court may well have decided that such a situation would at best unduly complicate the reorganization proceedings and at worst undermine Borne's attempts to rehabilitate its business and preserve its assets for the benefit of its creditors and employees.[7] By valuing the ultimate merits of the Rolfite stockholders' claims at zero, and temporarily disallowing them until the final resolution of the state action, the bankruptcy court avoided the possibility of a protracted and inequitable reorganization proceeding while ensuring that Borne will be responsible to pay a dividend on the claims in the event that the state court decides in the Rolfite stockholders' favor.[8] Such a solution is consistent with the

---

5. The Rolfite stockholders assert that the claims are not contingent since they are not dependent on some future event which may never occur. In as much as the very existence of the claims in the reorganization proceeding is dependent on a favorable decision by the state court, the Rolfite stockholders are clearly mistaken.

6. The Rolfite stockholders admitted as much in their first appeal to the district court. Brief for Appellants, Appendix at Pa. 1217–19.

7. Certainly this consideration played a role in the bankruptcy court's initial decision to disallow the claims. According to the court, "[T]o allow the hotly disputed claims, both present and prospective, herein referenced, would be for all practical purposes to doom Borne's rehabilitation efforts, now nearing their final stages, defeating the very purpose of reorganization * * *." Brief for Appellants, Appendix at Pa. 30.

8. While the "equitable considerations" referred to by the bankruptcy court could have properly influenced the method of evaluation of the claims chosen by the court, they would not have permitted the court to evaluate as zero claims which in fact have a higher value under the method of evaluation chosen by the bankruptcy court. But because we find that the bankruptcy court did not err in its evaluation of the claims, the error, if any, in the court's

Chapter 11 concerns of speed and simplicity but does not deprive the Rolfite stockholders of the right to recover on their contingent claims against Borne.

Questions

1. Because the court in *Bittner* required "a waiver of the discharge of the Rolfite claims from Borne," it did not have to face the hard question—what should be given to Rolfite upon liquidation. If the court were to face that question, what is to be said for the present value estimation compared with the "ultimate merits" estimation of a claim?

2. Which of the two are other courts following where those courts decide to have actual estimation hearings and allow the parties to present evidence to give the court a judgment about the kind of case that ultimately would be put on in a state court trial?

Problem 8–8

Debtor Manufacturing produces industrial chemicals. A major chemical accident at one of its plants forces Debtor to file Chapter 11. After a few months of operation, it is ready to propose a reorganization plan. It has $500,000 of unsecured trade debt held by twenty creditors. In addition, there are eight filed lawsuits pending based on the accident, each claiming $3 million in injury. Three of the cases involve personal injury claims, while the rest involve damage to property caused by the toxic discharge. Prior to bankruptcy, three lawsuits from the accident were tried in state court, each resulting in a verdict for Debtor.

If Debtor liquidated today, there would be $500,000 for unsecured creditors. If it continues in business under a plan, as much as $1 million additional value will be available. Unless each creditor agrees, Debtor cannot confirm a reorganization plan unless the plan gives each unsecured creditor value equal to what that creditor would receive in liquidation.

1. What should Debtor propose to do with the claims in its plan based on the lawsuits if it knows that trial of the cases would not occur for four years in state court? If it asks the court to estimate the claims, what procedure should the court use and what result if it finds that there is a 30 percent chance that the plaintiffs will win?

2. Can the lawsuit claimants be put in the same class as the trade creditors?

3. No environmental agency has filed a claim against Debtor for the lingering problems from the chemical spill. Should Debtor's plan make any provision for such claims? If not, are those claims discharged under section 1141 if a plan is confirmed?

Problem 8–9

Barclay is about to file a reorganization plan. It has support from its secured lender (Chase) for a plan that extends the $30 million Chase debt to

references to "equitable considerations" as buttressing its decision would not effect the outcome.

fourteen years with interest at market rate and treats the $2 million deficiency as it treats trade creditors. There are twenty unsecured trade creditors with a total debt of $179,000 whose committee supports a plan giving unsecured creditors .50 per dollar paid over four years with 10 percent interest. A liquidation would yield no more than .01 per dollar to these unsecured claims. Barclay needs advice about how to deal with several other creditors:

a. How should the plan deal with Barron, which is owed $150,000 unsecured, and with Garry, a company that has guaranteed payment of the Barron debt? Does your answer change if Garry has already repaid half of the Barclay's debt to Barron?

b. How should the plan deal with five individuals who bought expensive homes from Barclay two years ago and are currently asserting separate claims totalling $800,000 alleging that Barclay's sloppy workmanship in the construction of the homes left latent defects that are just now appearing. Those defects have caused serious damages to the homes in question. Although the sales occurred before bankruptcy, the lawsuits were filed after bankruptcy. It is likely that these claims will take several years to be resolved in state court. For at least one claim there is no more than a 30 percent chance of success at trial.

c. How should the plan deal with the possibility that some of the thirty other home buyers in the same area who purchased from Barclay may have claims that they have not yet asserted?

Chapter Nine

REORGANIZATION PLANS

§ 1. INTRODUCTION

Finally we consider reorganization plans themselves. These are the theoretical product of a Chapter 11 proceeding. Because many Chapter 11 cases end without a reorganization plan approved (confirmed) by the court, the real product of a Chapter 11 often is liquidation.

Most Chapter 11 plans are developed by a long and fitful negotiation. The plan can establish virtually any new debt and ownership terms on which the parties agree. Chapter 11 rules cast the shadow under which the negotiation takes place. In the negotiation, dissenters receive some protection but may be forced to comply with terms of the majority. Once confirmed by the bankruptcy court, the plan becomes effective and binding on creditors.

Chapter 11 covers the territory formerly included in Chapters X, XI, and XII. Originally Chapter X was designed for the reorganization for publicly held companies, Chapter XI was designed for the reorganization of privately held companies, and Chapter XII for real estate reorganizations. The drafters of this earlier framework contemplated significant involvement by the Securities and Exchange Commission in any Chapter X reorganization. In the absence of a watchdog to oversee a reorganization, Congress feared that the managers would take advantage of the public bondholders and shareholders who were thought to be ignorant and ill represented. On the other hand, the principal actors in Chapter XI were thought to be institutional lenders, such as banks, who could look out for their own interests and who needed no help from the SEC.

For a variety of reasons, in practice things did not operate in the way the drafters had contemplated. In the first place, Chapter X cases were enormously expensive and very time consuming. They always involved the appointment of a trustee to run the business and that trustee was invariably someone who was not familiar with it. They also required continued negotiation with the SEC and repeated court appearances. Other reasons for preferring Chapter XI to Chapter X also existed. If an outsider trustee came in to run a business in Chapter X, that outsider would select his own lawyer and it would often not be the lawyer who had previously represented the corporation. If, on the other hand, the corporation went into Chapter XI and existing management continued to operate it, that management could be relied upon to retain the same counsel. One need not be unduly cynical to imagine that the lawyer for and the management of the prospective bankrupt would have an interest in electing Chapter XI over Chapter X.

In any event, the practice that developed was quite inconsistent with the initial policy. Most publicly held corporations that went into bankruptcy ultimately went into Chapter XI, not Chapter X, and a fair amount of litigation over which chapter was appropriate ensued. Although Chapter XI was faster, simpler, and less expensive, the court had no authority under the chapter to affect the rights of secured creditors without the creditors' consent. Conversely, under Chapter X and Chapter XII the secured creditors could be compelled under certain circumstances to participate in a plan to which they had not consented. These differences contributed to the quantity of litigation and one court commented that the patient would probably die while the doctors argued about which operating table he should be on. (*Securities and Exchange Commission v. Canandaigua Enterprises Corp.*, 339 F.2d 14, 19 (2d Cir.1964)).

Against this background, Congress enacted Chapter 11. That chapter molds together some new ideas with parts of the old X, XI and XII. Under Chapter 11 the debtor will continue to operate the business unless the court makes a finding that a trustee should be appointed. The court may also appoint an "examiner," a person without the powers of a trustee but with the power to look into certain things and make reports. Normally, the debtor will take off its "debtor" hat and commence running the business as the "debtor in possession." As the debtor in possession, the old management will have the powers that are given under the Bankruptcy Code to the trustee in bankruptcy. Thus the management, as debtor in possession, will have authority to avoid liens, reject or adopt contracts, and propose a plan of reorganization.

In enacting Chapter 11 Congress explicitly rejected the SEC position that it should be made the protector of public investors in reorganization cases. (You have heard the joke about the three most common lies? Number three is: "I am from the federal government and I am here to help you.") The SEC has no formal role, no right to appeal; it is explicitly not "a party in interest." In short, Congress was ultimately persuaded by those who argued that the costs of SEC involvement outweighed the benefits to public investors.

Chapter 11 differs in many material respects from its predecessors. These differences create a contemporary bankruptcy practice that bears little direct resemblance to what occurred prior to 1978. Chapter 11 allows the parties a greater range of options in restructuring the company. Chapter X required strict compliance with the rule of absolute priority. This rule holds that senior lenders must be paid in full before less senior claimholders (or shareholders) receive anything. This priority system was "absolute" in that it could not be varied by agreement of the parties. By contrast, in Chapter 11 the parties may allocate values in any manner that they agree, so long as dissenters receive fair treatment. Ideas of absolute priority apply, but they can be waived by agreement of the classes in Chapter 11.

This emphasis on agreement in Chapter 11 more closely resembles former Chapter XI than former Chapter X. But Chapter 11 also has numerous important differences from Chapter XI. The most critical is the inclusion of secured creditors and provision for imposing a plan upon such creditors against their will. A crucial factor in establishing the rule under which a plan may be imposed upon an unwilling creditor is the test that must be met in order to protect the creditor's interest. Chapter XI required only that the "best interests" of the creditor be served. "Best interests" was construed to mean that a creditor must receive as much as it would have received on a liquidation. Under Chapter X a plan could be imposed upon a creditor only if the provisions for the creditor were "fair and equitable" or granted "absolute priority." Under the absolute priority rule, a senior debt had to be paid in full before any class junior to it could receive anything.

Section 1129 of Chapter 11 has adopted a variation of the absolute priority rule. A plan must grant the members of a dissenting class a "fair and equitable" portion. The imposition of a plan upon a class of dissenting creditors is described in the vernacular as a "cramdown." It will come as no surprise that some of the most interesting and challenging questions from Chapter 11 involve the cramdown in one way or another.

Perhaps the best way to understand reorganization plans is to see one. Set out below, then, is the plan of reorganization filed by Action Auto Stores on July 5, 1991 in the Bankruptcy Court of the Eastern District of Michigan.

Action Auto started out in 1976 as one store in Flint, Michigan, that sold automotive parts. The company expanded steadily until in 1989 there were 71 Action Auto stores. Although the company continued to be profitable, its aggressive expansion program necessitated acquisition of undeveloped real estate. Inventories increased and liquidity problems resulted. When the Michigan economy went into decline in 1989, Action Auto had to sell stores to meet mortgage and other obligations. These sales proved to be inadequate to meet the company's needs, and in March of 1990 the company obtained a $9 million secured line of credit from Michigan National Bank, for which Action Auto granted the Bank a security interest in substantially all of its assets. Sales continued to decline, however, and in June 1990 the company stopped making payments to its vendors. On June 15, 1990, Action Auto filed a petition in Chapter 11. Action Auto continued to operate in a limited fashion after its Chapter 11 filing.

The plan filed by Action Auto proposes a complete liquidation of all of the company's assets except its name, and a reorganization under the name Action Auto funded with new capital.

UNITED STATES BANKRUPTCY COURT
EASTERN DISTRICT OF MICHIGAN
SOUTHERN DIVISION

In re)	Hon. Arthur J. Spector
)	
ACTION AUTO STORES, INC.,)	Case No. 90–11710–AJS
a/k/a Action Auto, Inc.,)	
a/k/a Jed Automotive,)	Chapter 11
a/k/a Sabo Corp.,)	
a/k/a Jed Co.,)	
a/k/a Lansing–Lewis Services, Inc.,)	
Debtor.)	
_____/)	

DEBTOR'S PLAN OF REORGANIZATION

The Chapter 11 Debtor herein, Action Auto Stores, Inc., proposes the following Chapter 11 Plan to its creditors and shareholders:

Article I

Definitions

All capitalized terms used in this Plan and not otherwise defined have the meanings given to them in Exhibit A attached to this Plan, unless the context clearly requires otherwise. As used in this Plan, any terms defined in the Bankruptcy Code shall have the meanings given to them in the Bankruptcy Code, unless the context clearly requires otherwise.

Article II

Classification of Claims

1. *Class 1. Administrative Claims.* This class is composed of all proper expenses of administration of the Estate of Action Auto which have not been disallowed by the Court including, but not limited to, all fees and expenses of the attorneys for Action Auto and the attorneys for the Official Committee of Unsecured Creditors as the same may be allowed by the Bankruptcy Court. This class includes all such charges, expenses, fees and other sums due from Action Auto which are accorded priority under Section 507(a)(1) of the Bankruptcy Code. This class does not include any claims the State of Michigan, Department of Natural Resources (the "State") may have against Action Auto or the Estate on account of contamination or other environmental problems at any Action Auto store site.

2. *Class 2. Administrative and Other Claims of the State of Michigan.* This class is composed of any and all claims the State has

against Action Auto or the Estate arising from or relating to environmental or contamination conditions on real estate at any time owned or leased by Action Auto.

3. *Class 3. Wage Claims.* This class is composed of all allowed claims for wages, salaries, or commissions, including vacation, severance, and sick leave pay earned by the individual claimant within 90 days before the filing of this bankruptcy case on June 15, 1990. Claimants in this class must have earned the amount claimed within 90 days before June 15, 1990. As provided in Section 507(a)(3) of the Bankruptcy Code, the total claimed by any individual claimant in this category cannot exceed $2,000. Any claim for wages, commissions, and the like held by an individual earned outside of the 90-day period or in excess of $2,000 shall be treated as a general unsecured claim under classes 10, 11, and 12.

4. *Class 4. Employee Benefit Plans.* This class is composed of all allowed claims for contributions to employee benefit plans arising from services rendered within 180 days before the date of the filing of this bankruptcy case on June 15, 1990. As provided in Section 507(a)(4) of the Bankruptcy Code, the claim for any such plan cannot exceed a sum equal to the number of employees covered by such plan multiplied by $2,000 less (a) amounts paid to covered employees as a member of Class 3 and less (b) the aggregate amount paid on behalf of such employees to any other employee benefit plan.

5. *Class 5. Priority Tax Claims.* This class is composed of all allowed claims for unpaid taxes and other assessments entitled to priority under Section 507(a)(7) of the Bankruptcy Code.

6. *Class 6. Allowed Claim of Michigan National Bank Secured by Assets Being Sold to Total.* This class is composed of the claim of Michigan National Bank that is secured by assets of Action Auto that will be sold to Total.

7. *Class 7. Allowed Claim of Michigan National Bank Secured by Assets Not Being Sold to Total on Which Michigan National Bank Had a Lien Prior to March 19, 1990.* This class is composed of the claim(s) of Michigan National Bank that are secured by assets of Action Auto on which Michigan National Bank had a lien or security interest prior to the March 19, 1990 Transaction and which are not being sold to Total.

8. *Class 8. Allowed Claim of Michigan National Bank Secured by Assets Not Being Sold to Total on Which Michigan National Bank Obtained A Lien On Or After March 19, 1990.* This class is composed of the claim(s) of Michigan National Bank that are secured by assets of Action Auto on which Michigan National Bank obtained a lien or security interest on or after the March 19, 1990 Transaction and which are not being sold to Total.

9. *Class 9. Allowed Secured Claim of Sun Oil Company.* This class is composed of the allowed secured claim of Sun Oil Company.

10. *Class 10. General Unsecured Claims of Less Than $100.* This class is composed of all allowed general unsecured claims of less than $100. Any holder of a Class 11 claim may elect Class 10 treatment for its claim if the claimant agrees to reduce its claim to $100.

11. *Class 11. General Unsecured Claims of Between $100 and $1,000.* This class is composed of all allowed general unsecured claims of between $100 and $1,000. Any holder of a Class 12 claim may elect Class 11 treatment for its claim if the claimant agrees to reduce its claim to $1,000.

12. *Class 12. General Unsecured Claims of Greater Than $1,000.* This claim is composed of all allowed unsecured claims greater than $1,000 and includes the unsecured portion of the claims of Michigan National Bank, Sun Oil Company, and any other secured creditor.

13. *Class 13. Shareholder Interests.* This class is composed of all shareholders of Action Auto Stores, Inc.

Article III

Settlement and Payment of Claims

1. *Class 1 Claims. Administrative.* Allowed claims in Class 1 shall not be impaired and shall be paid in full from the Liquidation Fund on the Effective Date or as funds become available. Certain administrative expense claimants have agreed to reduce their claims, as described in the Disclosure Statement. THIS CLASS IS NOT IMPAIRED.

2. *Class 2 Claims. Administrative and Other Claims of the State of Michigan.* At the closing of the Total Sale, $5.391 million of the proceeds of the Total Sale will be reserved to pay for expenses incurred in remediating environmental problems at Action Auto store sites being purchased by Total. The State shall have no other Environmental claim against Action Auto or the Estate on account of an Environmental Issue.

3. *Class 3 Claims. Wage Claims.* Allowed claims in Class 3 shall not be impaired and shall be paid in full from the Liquidation Fund on the Effective Date or as funds become available. THIS CLASS IS NOT IMPAIRED.

4. *Class 4 Claims. Employee Benefit Plans.* Allowed claims in Class 4 shall not be impaired and shall be paid in full from the Liquidation Fund on the Effective Date or as funds become available. THIS CLASS IS NOT IMPAIRED.

5. *Class 5 Claims. Priority Tax Claims.* Allowed claims in Class 5 shall not be impaired and shall be paid in full from the Liquidation Fund on the Effective Date or as funds become available. THIS CLASS IS NOT IMPAIRED.

6. *Class 6 Claims. Allowed Claim of Michigan National Bank Secured by Assets Being Sold to Total.* At the closing of the Total Sale, Michigan National Bank shall be paid from the proceeds of the Total Sale Four Million Dollars ($4,000,000) plus an amount equal to that paid

by Total for any inventory purchased by it. In no event, however, shall Michigan National Bank receive from any source more than the New Value on account of assets of the Estate that first became subject to a lien in favor of Michigan National Bank as a result of the March 19, 1990 Transaction. THIS CLASS IS IMPAIRED.

7. *Class 7. Allowed Claim of Michigan National Bank Secured by Assets Not Being Sold to Total on Which Michigan National Bank Had A Lien Prior to March 19, 1990.* Michigan National Bank shall retain its lien in any assets of the Estate not sold to Total on which Michigan National Bank had a lien or security interest prior to the March 19, 1990 Transaction. Action Auto will abandon as of the Effective Date all assets on which Michigan National Bank had a lien, security interest, or mortgage prior to the March 19, 1990 Transaction.

8. *Class 8. Allowed Claim of Michigan National Bank Secured by Assets Not Being Sold to Total on Which Michigan National Bank Obtained A Lien On Or After March 19, 1990.* Michigan National Bank will retain its lien on all property of the Estate on which Michigan National Bank first obtained a lien on or after the March 19, 1990 Transaction, subject to any defenses Action Auto may have to such liens. All property on which Michigan National Bank first obtained a lien on or after the March 19, 1990 Transaction will be liquidated by the Liquidation Agent, with Michigan National Bank retaining a lien in the proceeds of such property to the same extent and with the same priority as its lien in the property, provided however that in no event shall Michigan National Bank receive an amount greater than the New Value afforded the Debtor by the March 19, 1990 Transaction.

9. *Class 9. Allowed Secured Claim of Sun Oil Company.* Sun Oil Company will receive payment of $325,000 from the proceeds of the Total Sale on account of its mortgages held on properties being sold to Total. In addition, the Debtor reserves the right to cause the recovery of any monies paid to Sun as a result of any liens placed on the Debtor's assets after the March 19, 1990 Transaction or to seek the application of such amounts against the New Value portion of the March 19, 1990 Transaction. Any remaining claim of Sun Oil Company shall be unsecured.

10. *Class 10. General Unsecured Claims of Less Than $100.* Allowed claims in Class 10 shall not be impaired and shall be paid in full on the Effective Date. THIS CLASS IS NOT IMPAIRED. This class is subject to Article VIII, Section 3 of this Plan.

11. *Class 11. General Unsecured Claims of Between $100 and $1,000.* Allowed claims in Class 11 shall be paid on the Effective Date an amount equal to fifty percent (50%) of the allowed amount of the claim. THIS CLASS IS IMPAIRED. This class is subject to Article VIII, Section 3 of this Plan.

12. *Class 12. General Unsecured Claims of Greater Than $1,000.* After the payment of Class 1, 3, 4, 5, 10 and 11 claims, the remaining funds in the Liquidation Fund, if any, shall be distributed *pro rata* to

holders of Allowed Class 12 Claims, the distribution to be made one hundred and twenty (120) days after the Effective Date and additional distributions as additional funds become available. This class is subject to Article VIII, Section 3 of this Plan.

In addition, subject to Article VIII, Section 3 of this Plan, by the Effective Date the Debtor shall issue preferred stock in the face amount of One Million Dollars ($1,000,000)(the "Preferred Stock") which shall be held by the Liquidation Agent for the benefit of Class 12 Claims. Annual payments on principal equal to 20% of Net Cash Flow of the Debtor shall be paid by the Debtor to the Liquidation Agent. The Debtor shall redeem the Preferred Stock on the sixth anniversary of the issuance of the Preferred Stock by paying to the Liquidation Agent the entire unpaid balance of the face amount of the Preferred Stock. Any funds the Liquidation Agent collects on account of the Preferred Stock shall be distributed *pro rata* to the holders of Class 12 Claims. THIS CLASS IS IMPAIRED. This class is subject to Article VIII, Section 3 of this Plan.

13. *Class 13. Shareholder Interests.* The holders of equity securities of Action Auto shall receive no distributions or dividends on those equity securities under the Plan. As of the Effective Date of the Plan, the Articles of Incorporation of Action Auto will be amended to provide that each outstanding share of Action Auto common stock will be converted into .1 shares of Action Auto common stock (the "Stock Conversion"). The Articles of Incorporation will also be amended to provide that the total number of authorized common stock shall equal the total number of shares outstanding after the Stock Conversion times 100.

Article IV

Means for Execution and Implementation of Plan

A. *Total Sale*

   1. *Background*

Shortly after the commencement of this case, Action Auto retained the investment banking firm of Paine Webber to locate prospective purchasers of Action Auto's business. After several months of contacting potential acquirers and investors, Paine Webber located Total, which expressed an interest in purchasing all or part of Action Auto's business. Total and Action Auto thereafter engaged in negotiations for a sale to Total of substantially all of Action Auto's assets. As of the date of this Plan, Total and Action had reached an agreement in principal on the terms of such a sale (the "Total Agreement"), subject to final comments by the State.

   2. *Terms of Total Sale.*

The Total Agreement provides that:

a. Total will acquire 30 of the Debtor's store sites and will take an assignment of the Debtor's interest in seven additional sites (the "Purchased Sites").

b. Total will acquire Action Auto's interest in fixtures and other personal property, and in government permits, warranties and service contracts associated with the Purchased Sites.

c. Total will acquire Action Auto's inventory of motor fuel, Quaker State Motor Oil and food and beverage items.

d. Total will not acquire the name "Action Auto", receivables or Action Auto's inventory of automotive parts.

e. Total will pay $13,582,682, subject to adjustments provided in the Total Agreement, for the Purchased Assets.

f. The closing will occur as soon as possible after satisfaction of the conditions set forth in the Total Agreement and upon confirmation of this Plan.

In conjunction with seeking confirmation of this Plan, Action Auto will ask that the Court approve the Total Sale. The proceeds, net of payments to parties holding liens on the Purchased Assets, closing costs, taxes, and the environmental reserve shall be deposited into the Liquidation Fund for distribution as provided in Article II of this Plan.

B. *Disposition of Other Assets of the Estate*

Excluding the assets to be sold to Total, the Action Auto Estate owns approximately twenty parcels of undeveloped real estate, an inventory of automotive parts, and miscellaneous other items of personal property. In addition, Action Auto has claims against third parties totalling approximately $2.4 million. On the Effective Date, Action Auto will abandon any real estate on which Michigan National Bank had a valid and perfected mortgage prior to the March 19, 1990 transaction. The right and power to dispose of the remaining assets and collect on the actions against third parties will be transferred as of the Effective Date to the Liquidation Agent, who will deposit the proceeds of the assets and actions (net of liens, taxes, and costs incurred in realizing on the amount collected) into the Liquidation Fund for distribution as provided in Article II of this Plan.

C. *Reorganization of Action Auto*

Action Auto has received a letter of intent from Somerset Holdings, Inc. ("Somerset") to invest new capital into the Company. Somerset will invest sufficient funds to pay Class 10 and Class 11 claims and additional money for development and working capital purposes. Somerset and other investors, which will include James Sabo, Richard Sabo, Robert Sabo and Donald Nance, all present principals of Action Auto (the "Sabo Group"), will invest a minimum of $1,000,000 into the Company. Somerset and the Sabo Group will share their investment in the reorganized Action Auto on a 3 to 1 ratio. In exchange for their investment, the investors shall receive sufficient shares of the common stock of Action Auto, which shall not be subject to the Stock Conversion described in Article II, Section 13, so that the investors will hold 99% of the outstanding shares of Action Auto common stock upon the complete funding of their investment.

The reorganization of Action Auto is premised on the Company securing long term leases from Total on terms acceptable to the Company for the service part areas of those current Action Auto stores that have dedicated space for the sale of automotive parts. As a reorganized Company, Action Auto will sell at retail automotive parts from those stores and possibly from other locations (including former Action Auto stores that have been surrendered to the lessors of those stores).

On the Effective Date, the reorganized Action Auto will issue preferred stock in the total face amount of $1,000,000 (the "Preferred Stock") to the Liquidation Agent, who will hold the Preferred Stock for the benefit (on a *pro rata* basis) of the holders of Class 12 claims. The Articles of Incorporation for Action Auto will be amended to provide for: one, the issuance of the Preferred Stock; two, the payment of annual distributions to holders of Preferred Stock, *pro rata,* equal to 20% of Net Cash Flow; and three, the retirement of the Preferred Stock on the sixth anniversary of the Effective Date for the face amount of the Preferred Stock less any payments made in earlier years.

In conjunction with seeking confirmation of this Plan, Action Auto will request an order of the Bankruptcy Court approving the amendments to the Articles of Incorporation described herein and approving the issuance of common stock and the Preferred Stock as described in this Section.

Article V

Debtor's Right to Object to Claims

The Debtor reserves its right to object to any and all claims filed against Action Auto and its estate for purposes of allowances and distribution and for purposes of voting on the Plan. In the event that an objection to a claim is filed by Action Auto or any other party in interest, including the Official Creditors Committee of Action Auto, no distributions will be made to the holder of that claim under the Plan until that objection is determined by the entry of a final and nonappealable order or judgment of the Bankruptcy Court.

Article VI

Property of the Estate

Upon confirmation of the Plan, all property of the estate shall be transferred as provided in this Plan and no property, other than the name "Action Auto Stores" and derivations of that name shall revest in Action Auto. All persons and entities are permanently enjoined from taking any action to obtain possession of property of the estate by means other than those set forth in this Plan.

Article VII

Modification of the Plan

Action Auto may propose amendments or modifications of this Plan at any time prior to confirmation. After confirmation of the Plan, Action Auto may, with the approval of the Bankruptcy Court, remedy any defect or omission, or reconcile any inconsistencies in the Plan or the Order of Confirmation, in such manner as may be necessary to carry out the purposes and intent of the Plan.

Article VIII

Confirmation and Consummation of the Plan

1. It shall be a condition precedent to the confirmation of this Plan that on or prior to the Confirmation Date, the Bankruptcy Court shall have entered:

    A. An order approving the Total Sale;

    B. An order establishing the Liquidation Fund and appointing the Liquidation Agent under terms as described in this Plan.

2. It shall be a condition precedent to the consummation of this Plan that the Total Sale shall have been closed on terms satisfactory to Action Auto and The State.

3. It shall be a condition precedent to the payment of Class 10 and Class 11 claims and the issuance of the Preferred Stock that:

    A. Action Auto shall have executed leases with Total for the automotive parts areas of those Purchased Sites that contain automotive parts areas;

    B. The Court shall have entered an order amending the Articles of Incorporation as provided in Articles III and IV of this Plan;

    C. The Court shall have entered an order authorizing the issuance of the Preferred Stock and authorizing the issuance of common stock to the Investors as provided in this Plan;

    D. The State shall have agreed to limit or eliminate any liability that the reorganized Action Auto would have on account of any Environmental Issue.

In the event that either or both conditions precedent to the payment of Class 10 and Class 11 claims and the issuance of the Preferred Stock do not occur, then the rest of this Plan shall remain in force except that Class 10, 11, and 12 claims shall be grouped into a single class and holders of those claims shall receive cash distributions on a *pro rata* basis from the Liquidation Fund after the payment of all senior classes as provided in this Plan.

Article IX

Rejection Of Executory Contracts and Unexpired Leases

On the date of the closing of the Total Sale, Action Auto will assume and assign to Total the unexpired leases for the following store sites:

Store No.	Store Address	City, State
1	2130 South Dort Highway	Flint, Michigan
4	G–5016 Chio Road at Carpenter	Flint, Michigan
6	4232 South Saginaw Road	Burton, Michigan
17	101 E. Flint	Davidson, Michigan
27	1943 S. Cedar Street	Holt, Michigan
36	2901 Gratiot	Detroit, Michigan
62	22540 Pontiac Trail	South Lyon, Michigan

Action Auto rejects any and all other executory contracts and unexpired leases still in existence.

Article X

Retention of Jurisdiction

The Bankruptcy Court will retain jurisdiction until the Plan is confirmed. Following confirmation of the Plan, the Bankruptcy Court will retain jurisdiction over this case for the following purposes:

1. The classification of the claims of any creditor, and reexamination of claims which have been allowed, and the determination of any objections as may be filed to creditors' claims.

2. The determination of all questions and disputes regarding title to the assets of the Estate, and determination of all causes of action, controversies, disputes, or conflicts, whether or not subject to action pending as of the date of confirmation relating to the Plan and including the power to determine all questions relating to the March 19, 1990 Transaction as well as the allocation and/or recovery of funds received by Michigan National Bank and Sun Oil Company arising from collateral relating thereto.

3. The correction of any defect, the curing of any omissions, or the reconciliation of any inconsistency in the Plan or Order of Confirmation as may be necessary to carry out the purposes and intent of this Plan.

4. To enforce and interpret the terms and conditions of this Plan, the Bankruptcy Code and rules promulgated thereunder, and all orders, judgments, injunctions and rulings entered in connection with this Chapter 11 case.

5. Entry of any order, including injunctions, necessary to enforce the title, rights, and powers of Action Auto and the Estate and to impose such limitations, restrictions, terms and conditions on such title, rights, and powers as the Bankruptcy Court may deem necessary.

6. To continue any litigation commenced by Action Auto or the Estate.

7. To enforce the terms of any agreements entered into by Action Auto with any third party.

8. To ensure that the intent of the Plan is carried out.

9. Entry of a final decree.

Dated: July 5, 1991   ACTION AUTO STORES, INC.

By _____
       Its Chairman

Exhibit A

Definitions

1. "Action Auto" shall mean Action Auto Stores, Inc., a Michigan corporation and the debtor herein.

2. "Confirmation Date" shall mean the day on which the Bankruptcy Court holds a hearing on the confirmation of this Plan.

3. "Court" means the United States Bankruptcy Court, Eastern District of Michigan.

4. "Effective Date" shall mean twenty-one (21) days after the date on which the Total Sale closes.

5. "Environmental Issue" shall mean any possible claim against Action Auto arising from any federal, state or local environmental law or regulation.

6. "Estate" shall mean the estate in bankruptcy of Action Auto Stores, Inc.

7. "Liquidation Agent" shall mean the person or entity designated by the Debtor and consented to by the Official Committee of Unsecured creditors who shall administer the Liquidation Fund.

8. "Liquidation Fund" shall mean a trust which shall hold the proceeds of the Total Sale (net of the $4,000,000 payment to Michigan National Bank) and any and all other sales of Action Auto's assets. Any assets of Action Auto, including all avoidance actions under the Bankruptcy Code, not reduced to cash as of the Effective Date shall be transferred to the Liquidation Fund for liquidation by the Liquidation Agent.

9. "March 19, 1990 Transaction" shall mean the transaction under the terms of which Michigan National Bank and the Travellers Insurance Company received liens in substantially all of the assets to secure all antecedent debt owed to them by the Debtor as well as to secure the New Value.

10. "Net Cash Flow" shall mean the quarterly cash flow of the reorganized Action Auto, net of debt service and expenditures for capital improvements.

11. "New Value" shall mean the consideration afforded the Debtor in the amount of approximately $6,175,000.00 in the March 19, 1990 Transaction.

12. "Total" shall mean the Total Petroleum Company.

13. "Total Sale" shall mean the sale of substantially all of the Debtor's assets to the Total Petroleum Company, as described in Article IV of this Plan.

Questions

1. Can the March 19, 1990, transaction be avoided (except to the extent of the new value) as a preference under section 547?

2. Would you advise Michigan National Bank to accept the plan? Why?

3. Who pays for the environmental damage caused by petroleum contamination at some of Action Auto's sites? What if more money is needed?

4. The debtor stated in its disclosure statement that even if the plan were rejected, it intended to proceed with the Total sale. Would you have any objection as counsel for Michigan National Bank? As counsel for a general unsecured (class 12) creditor?

THE BASIC SUBSTANTIVE AND PROCEDURAL RULES IN CHAPTER 11 PROCEEDINGS

If one ignores railroad reorganizations and post confirmation matters, only 21 sections in Chapter 11 remain. Several of these are short, perfunctory provisions; a handful of critical sections determine rights under Chapter 11. The central substantive section is 1129: confirmation of plan. One might regard 1129 as the core of Chapter 11. A variety of other substantive and procedural sections are related to and attached to this hub like spokes of a wheel—impairment of claims or interests (1124), acceptance of plan (1126), classification of claims or interests (1122).

While the provisions of section 1129 govern the standards for confirmation of a plan, the content of a plan is also shaped by the terms of section 1123. The plan divides up claims and interests into classes, and requires the debtor to specify whether each class is to be impaired or unimpaired. In the case of the impaired classes, the plan must describe how each class will be treated, for example, how much it will be paid. Finally, the plan must state the means for its execution—where the debtor will get the money to pay its creditors.

Section 1122 on classification must be read together with section 1124 on impairment and section 1126 on acceptance of a plan. It is critical to the debtor in possession that at least one class accept the plan. It is desirable that many of the classes accept the plan. Under section 1126(f) a class whose interests are not impaired is deemed to have accepted the plan; conversely, a class which is to receive nothing under the plan is deemed to have rejected it under section 1126(g). Between those extremes, a class has accepted a plan under section 1126(c) if at least two-thirds in amount and more than one-half in number of the allowed claims of such class accept the plan. The mechanics of acceptance or rejection of a plan are governed by Rule 3018.

Because the debtor in possession would like to procure as many acceptances as possible, the DIP may classify the various parties in such a way as to increase the total number of acceptances. Courts have held that section 1122 requires substantial similarity, but not homogeneity. For example, it is legitimate to place three holders of promissory notes secured by a single mortgage in the same class, even though two members are limited partners in the debtor. See *In re Martin's Point Limited Partnership,* 12 B.R. 721, 727 (Bankr.N.D.Ga.1981): It is the "nature" of the claims being classified together that is significant, not the nature of other claims or interests a creditor might have. The lack of specific classification guidelines may suggest that the debtor has a great deal of freedom in classification. However, any party in interest may challenge the classification as irrational or inequitable.

After the debtor in possession has proposed a plan and has classified the various claims and interests, it must solicit their acceptances. To do that the DIP must provide at or before the solicitation a "written disclosure statement approved after a notice and hearing by the court as containing adequate information" (1125(b)). Note the pointed exclusion of traditional SEC solicitation rules in 1125(b): the question whether the statement contains adequate information "is not governed by any otherwise applicable non bankruptcy law rule or regulation * * *." Even a cursory reading of section 1125 discloses that the court has a great deal of discretion in approving disclosure statements. Because such a statement cannot be transmitted prior to court approval and because an acceptance or rejection may not be solicited unless the holder receives a plan or a summary of the plan, there is obviously a complex interplay between the negotiation of the plan itself and the appropriate disclosures prior to the time of a formal solicitation of acceptance or rejection. Section 1125 contemplates solicitation by the debtor in possession. Does it contemplate the possibility of solicitation by others as well?

Section 1129 is long and complicated. For the moment we will pick out the most critical provisions. That is not to say that the provisions we do not discuss are unimportant. We will endeavor to deal with those which present the most important and frequently recurring questions. At the outset, one should know that certain provisions of an otherwise defective plan can be effective if the class that is affected votes for the plan notwithstanding the fact that there may be some dissenters within that class. Other defects may be asserted by individual dissenters even though they are outvoted by the other members of their class.

The first significant requirement is contained in section 1129(a)(7). That provision requires that *each* holder of a claim or interest either accept the plan or receive under it no less than it would have received upon liquidation under Chapter 7. Under section 1129(a)(8) each class must either accept the plan or find itself unimpaired. As an alternative to compliance with section 1129(a)(8)(but *not* to (a)(7)), the plan may provide each nonaccepting creditor with "fair and equitable treatment," i.e., a cramdown.

Subsection (a)(9) requires the payment of administrative expenses in cash and gives special treatment to certain other claims such as wages. Subsection (a)(11) requires that the plan be "feasible." A plan is feasible only if it is "not likely to be followed by the liquidation with the need for further financial reorganization * * *." Subsection (a)(10) requires that at least one class accept the plan.

The intellectual sport in section 1129 rises from the use of section 1129(b). That provision authorizes the court to confirm a plan despite the fact that one or more classes have not accepted it, provided only that 1) it does not "discriminate unfairly" and 2) it is "fair and equitable" with respect to each class of claims or interest that is impaired. The idea of "fair and equitable" does not come into play with respect to a class that has accepted the plan. A party who is a member of a class that has accepted may not individually raise his voice to challenge the plan on the grounds that it is not fair and equitable, or that it unfairly discriminates against him. He is bound by the vote of the other members of his class. Section 1129(b)(2) gives a complicated litany of factors that must be met for a plan to be "fair and equitable."

As a general proposition a secured creditor may have a plan crammed down upon it (i.e., a plan is "fair and equitable") if it allows the creditor to retain its security interest in the collateral, and the plan provides for payments with a present value equal to the value of the interest in the collateral. Because section 1129(b)(2)(A) provides three alternatives and specifies only that "fair and equitable" includes these three alternatives, one cannot speak categorically about the meaning of the words "fair and equitable". Moreover one should note the old menace, "indubitable equivalence," in section 1129(b)(2)(A)(iii).

Under section 1129(b)(2)(B) unsecured creditors must receive something under the plan with a present value equal to the allowed amount of their claims, or alternatively there must be provisions that no class junior to them will receive anything. Thus if an unsecured creditor has a $1000 note, he must receive the whole $1000 claim if the shareholders are to receive even one cent. Subsection (C) of 1129(b)(2) has an analogous provision for "interests" ("interests" are rights of shareholders, partners and others technically not creditors).

On a superficial reading, section 1129 is complicated but relatively easy to understand. When one begins to deal with concrete cases, it becomes much more difficult, especially when one allows for the range of possibilities that multi-party negotiations may create for reorganizing a debtor. The following problems are relatively simple; they challenge the student to exercise his or her understanding of the section.

Section 1127 provides for modification of a previously proposed plan. Section 1128 provides merely that there should be a confirmation hearing and that parties can oppose confirmation.

For the purpose of this book, the most important section of subchapter 3 on post confirmation matters, is section 1141, "Effect of Confirmation." This section provides, among other things, that parties are bound by a confirmed plan, the property of the estate is returned to the debtor after the confirmation, and the property "dealt with by the plan" is free and clear of all claims and interests except as provided in the plan. Moreover, with certain exceptions, the confirmation discharges the debtor from any debt that arose prior to the date of the confirmation. Thus, section 1141 is the discharge provision of Chapter 11, and one looks to it to see the legal effect of the various obligations owed by the debtor as a result of the confirmation of a particular plan.

Problem 9–1

Assume that a corporation is undergoing reorganization. Its balance sheet is as follows:

Mortgagee Debt	$1,000,000
Collateral	500,000
(real estate current value)	
Secured Creditor Debt	500,000
Collateral	400,000
(inventory current value)	
Trade Creditor	200,000
General Creditor	200,000
50 Common Stockholders	

The court has found the liquidation value of the corporate assets, exclusive of the collateral, to be $700,000.

1. Assume that a plan has been proposed as follows:

		Amt. of claim	Payment
Class 1:	Mortgagee as Secured Creditor	($500,000 pv)	$500,000
Class 2.	Secured creditor	($400,000 pv)	400,000
Class 3.	Mortgagee (as unsec.)	$500,000	250,000
	Secured creditor (as unsec.)	100,000	50,000
	Trade creditor	200,000	100,000
	General creditor	200,000	100,000

a. Assume that mortgagee, secured creditor and trade creditor vote for the plan, but that general creditor votes against it. Assume that the common stockholders retain no stock and that the stock is sold to a third party who pays the fair value of the stock into the corporation as working capital. Can the plan that would give the Class 1 and Class 2 creditors present value equal to their collateral and that would give the Class 3 creditors $.50 on the dollar be confirmed over the objection of general creditor? What would be the statutory basis for the general creditor's objection?

b. Could such a plan be challenged as not fair and equitable under 1129(b)?

2. Assume an alternative plan under which mortgagee, secured creditor, trade creditor and general creditor are all in separate classes. Mortgagee will receive present value of $500,000 together with a lien on the real estate. Secured creditor will receive $400,000 present value together with a continuing security interest in the inventory. Trade and general creditors will each receive cash payment on confirmation of $140,000.

a. If mortgagee and secured creditor vote for the plan, but trade and general creditors vote against it, can the general creditor upset the plan as not fair and equitable?

b. Could trade creditor upset the plan in those cases if the common shareholders were to keep their equity interest? How could one change the plan to satisfy general creditor's fair and equitable complaint under those circumstances?

Note: Plan Negotiation and Leverage

Chapter 11 both requires and encourages negotiation and compromise among parties affected by a plan of reorganization. Section 1129(a)'s acceptance requirements and the alternative section 1129(b), which allows confirmation despite a class's failure to accept, both set the stage and provide the tools for making a plan. Absent a cramdown, each class of claims or interests must either be unimpaired, or accept the plan if there is to be confirmation. Debtors rarely possess sufficient resources to leave all creditors unimpaired (e.g., by payment in full), and therefore debtors must negotiate for creditors' acceptance. Even where the debtor attempts a cramdown under section 1129(b), the Code requires acceptance by at least one impaired class.

Apart from the acceptance requirements, creditors' primary negotiating tools are delay and the threat of successful legal challenge to the priority or validity of a creditor's claim. Financing arrangements may require confirmation of a plan within a relatively short time, and protracted confirmation proceedings encourage customers to take their business elsewhere. Furthermore, the debtor may not want to risk losing the business if it loses in court. Conversely, the threat of cramdown gives the debtor the most effective tool in its belt. Section 1129(b) allows confirmation, despite a class's nonacceptance, so long as the plan provides certain minimal treatment for the dissenting class. The power of a class to bind all of its members prevents a few intractable creditors from blocking a plan. The debtor can also threaten to "give up", i.e., convert the case to Chapter 7 and deny all creditors a chance at increased reorganization value.

Whether the debtor (and creditors) settle or hold out and try their luck in court depends on estimates of the strengths and weaknesses of each side's case, the financial flexibility of the debtor, its willingness to risk losing, and the quality of counsel. Debtors sometimes compromise by offering creditors a piece of the hoped for profits in exchange for agreement (i.e., that distributions under the plan equal a percentage of post confirmation profits). A debtor might reject that alternative for several reasons. First, the company might be too thin; sharing profits with creditors might deprive any new investor of a return on its investment. Second, the debtor might believe it can beat the creditors in court. Finally, a debtor might be willing to risk losing its company. One can also speculate on the reasons behind a creditor committee's "no compromise" position in such a case. It might feel that by hanging tough, it could force the debtor to cave in and give it something extra.

§ 2. POSTPETITION TO PRE-PLAN
THE EXCLUSIVITY PERIOD

There are two limitations on those who wish to propose plans in competition with the debtor. First is the exclusivity period in section 1121. Normally only the debtor may file a plan within the 120 days after the date of the petition. If the debtor files a plan within the 120 days, the exclusivity period is extended an additional 60 days (to a total of 180). Thus in virtually all cases the debtor has an unencumbered period of 4 months. In reality, the exclusivity period is routinely extended for months, sometimes for years. During that period no competitor "may file a plan". The exclusive right to file a plan has great significance in the reorganization since it carries with it the ability to establish the negotiation framework.

Thus, for example, so long as it holds exclusivity, the debtor can adopt a negotiating position that insists that prior owners retain ownership of the company, even if creditors are not paid in full. The creditors can effectively prevent confirmation of this proposal by withholding their consent to it, but until the debtor's exclusive right to file a plan is terminated, the creditors cannot obtain a vote on any alternative reorganization. By limiting the period to 120 days, section 1121 was intended to put a certain amount of pressure on the debtor while it recognized the need for the debtor to remain in control of the reorganization process. Congress also recognized the creditors' interest in expediting the bankruptcy proceedings. A routine granting of extensions of the exclusivity period can destroy the balance that Congress intended.

In 1994 Congress recognized the problem of repeated extensions and adopted section 158(a)(2) which reads as follows: "The district court shall have jurisdiction to hear appeal from interlocutory orders and decrees issued under Section 1121(d) * * * increasing or reducing the time periods referred to in section 1121 * * * " This may seem pretty weak medicine for so virulent a disease, but only time will tell whether disappointed creditors will take appeals and whether district courts will overrule bankruptcy courts' extensions.

The second limitation is contained in section 1125(b). The author of a competing plan may not solicit a rejection of the debtor's plan until the debtor's written disclosure statement is approved and transmitted. Although section 1125(b) does not say that a creditor with a competing plan must send his own disclosure statement, that is a fair reading of the statute. Subsection (b) requires the distribution of only "the plan or a summary of the plan" and a written disclosure statement approved by the court containing "adequate information." Only by implication does one conclude that the adequate information refers to the particular plan under consideration. A creditor could argue that he could distribute his own plan and that he need not distribute a disclosure statement if one had already been distributed concerning the debtor's plan. That does not seem a sensible reading of section 1125(b).

Consider the restraints that these rules put on one who is seeking the rejection of the debtor's plan and who may or may not have a competing plan in his pocket. Conceivably one could read section 1121 to prohibit any solicitation for or consideration of a competing plan during the exclusivity period. Of course, that is not what section 1121 says. It merely prohibits the "filing" of a plan; it does not prohibit discussion or dissemination of a competing plan.

Consider how one might ask for an extension.

UNITED STATES BANKRUPTCY COURT
FOR THE EASTERN DISTRICT OF MICHIGAN

In re:)
)
ACTION AUTO STORES, INC.,) Honorable Arthur J. Spector
a/k/a Action Auto, Inc.,)
a/k/a Jed Automotive,) Case No. 90–11710–AJS
a/k/a Sabo Corp.,) (Chapter 11)
a/k/a Jed Co.,)
a/k/a Lansing–Lewis Services, Inc.,) DEBTOR'S MOTION TO EX–
) TEND EXCLUSIVE PERIOD
Debtor.) TO PROPOSE A CHAPTER
) 11 PLAN AND TO SOLICIT
E.I.D. No. 38–1901597) ACCEPTANCES
)

The Chapter 11 Debtor herein, Action Auto Stores, Inc. ("Debtor"), by and through its counsel, Warner, Norcross & Judd, for its motion to extend the Chapter 11 debtor's exclusive period in which to propose a Chapter 11 plan, states as follows:

1. The Chapter 11 debtor herein, Action Auto Stores, Inc. ("Debtor"), commenced this Chapter 11 case on June 15, 1990, by filing a voluntary petition with this Court. Since that date, it has been operating its business as debtor-in-possession.

2. Debtor is engaged in the business of selling gasoline, automotive parts and repair services on a retail basis through forty-five (45) stores located throughout the State of Michigan. Debtor is a company whose stock has been and continues to be publicly traded on recognized securities markets.

3. The Official Creditors Committee (the "Committee") was appointed by the United States Trustee on July 3, 1990. The Committee, however, has just recently been authorized by this Court to retain counsel.

4. Debtor has recently retained Paine Webber Incorporated ("PaineWebber") to assist it in marketing the Debtor's assets and/or attracting new investors.

5. Debtor has also recently obtained this Court's permission to conduct an auction sale of its surplus and unproductive real estate. This auction is scheduled to take place on September 27, 1990, in Flint. The parcels of realty to be offered at auction are located in 34 Michigan counties and are 51 in number. In the event these parcels are sold at auction, the closings of these sales will not occur until some time after the auction.

6. In its Business Plan filed with this Court, Debtor states that it intends to pare down the scope of its enterprise to what Debtor expects will be a profitable, core group of stores. This reduction of the scope of Debtor's enterprise should occur by means of the real estate auction described herein. Thereafter, Debtor hopes to either sell these core assets on a going concern basis or attract new investment which will enable Debtor to propose a reorganization plan.

7. From June 15, 1990 to the present, Debtor has been engaged in extensive negotiations and litigation with certain of its creditors who claim to be lessors of realty and equipment. Debtor has also devoted substantial efforts to arranging the real estate auction described herein.

8. PaineWebber has prepared a sale/investment memorandum for circulation to potential buyers and investors. This memorandum is in the process of being distributed to interested persons.

9. In order to propose a plan or to sell its assets, Debtor will be required, as a practical matter, to resolve most, if not all, of its disputes with its so-called "lessors." In addition, PaineWebber will require additional time to market the Debtor's assets and/or investment opportunities in a manner calculated to realize in the highest return to the Debtor, its creditors and shareholders.

10. The foregoing facts constitute sufficient "cause" to increase the 120–day and 180–day periods specified in 11 U.S.C. § 1121.

WHEREFORE, the Chapter 11 debtor herein requests that this Court enter an Order

>   (i) extending Debtor's initial 120–day exclusive period to file a Chapter 11 plan for another 120–day period;
>
>   (ii) extending Debtor's initial 180–day exclusive period to solicit acceptances of any such plan for another 180–day period; and
>
>   (iii) granting such other and further relief as may be just and proper under the circumstances.

Dated: September 5, 1990 WARNER, NORCROSS & JUDD

By _____
    Patrick E. Mears (P31316)
    Attorneys for Chapter 11 Debtor

Business Address:
    900 Old Kent Building
    111 Lyon Street, N.W.
    Grand Rapids, Michigan 49503
Telephone: (616) 459-6121

UNITED STATES BANKRUPTCY COURT
FOR THE EASTERN DISTRICT OF MICHIGAN

In re:	
ACTION AUTO STORES, INC.,	Honorable Arthur J. Spector
a/k/a Action Auto, Inc.,	
a/k/a Jed Automotive,	Case No. 90-11710-AJS
a/k/a Sabo Corp.,	(Chapter 11)
a/k/a Jed Co.,	
a/k/a Lansing-Lewis Services, Inc.,	
Debtor.	
E.I.D. No. 38-1901597	

DEBTORS' BRIEF IN SUPPORT OF
MOTION FOR EXTENSION OF EXCLUSIVITY PERIODS

The Chapter 11 debtor herein, Action Auto Stores, Inc. ("Debtor"), submits this Brief in support of its Motion to extend its exclusive periods in which to file a Chapter 11 plan and to solicit acceptances of that plan from creditors and equity security holders. Sufficient "cause" exists for this requested extension for the following reasons. First, the size and complexity of this Chapter 11 case and the delay in appointing professionals justify an extension of these periods. Second, there is a reasonable possibility that Debtor will propose a viable plan in the near future. Third, an extension of these exclusive periods will not prejudice creditors or equity security holders.

STATEMENT OF FACTS

Debtor is a Michigan business corporation that is headquartered in Flint, Michigan. Debtor sells gasoline and replacement automobile parts and provides automobile repair service at 45 stores located throughout the State of Michigan. Debtor's common stock is publicly traded.

Debtor commenced this Chapter 11 case by filing a voluntary petition on June 15, 1990. In its Schedules, Debtor lists $62 million in assets and $81 million in debts, making this Chapter 11 case one of the largest (if not the largest) currently pending in this state. Debtor is currently operating its business as a debtor in possession and is permitted to use cash collateral until October 15, 1990.

The United States Trustee formed an Official Creditors' Committee on July 3, 1990, but it was not until recently that the Committee has been able to retain counsel. Although the law firm of Warner, Norcross & Judd was retained at the beginning of this case, there have been significant delays in obtaining the appointment of other professionals to assist Debtor in its reorganization efforts, including Debtor's special counsel and investment banker.

In its Business Plan filed with this Court, Debtor reiterated its intent to pare down the scope of its business operations to a core group of profitable assets. Once this is accomplished, Debtor believes that it can sell this core group of assets as a going concern or attract new investment by third parties. To accomplish the goal of shedding excess assets, Debtor will auction a significant amount of its real estate on September 27, 1990.

Since this case was commenced, Debtor has been preoccupied with negotiating with its vendors for extension of trade credit, negotiating with "lessors" over new contract terms and litigating disputes with certain of those lessors in this Court. Also, since there was delay in appointing PaineWebber as Debtor's investment banker, PaineWebber has been unable until recently to begin its marketing efforts.

Debtor's exclusive period in which to file a plan terminates on or about October 13, 1990, which is a Saturday. Debtor's exclusive period in which to solicit acceptances of that plan terminates on December 12, 1990. In its Motion, Debtor requests that these periods be extended to February 9, 1991, and April 10, 1991, respectively.

ARGUMENT

I

SUFFICIENT CAUSE EXISTS TO EXTEND DEBTOR'S EXCLUSIVE PERIODS

Because of the size and complexity of this Chapter 11 case and the delays in obtaining the appointment of professionals, this Court should find that sufficient "cause" exists to extend Debtor's exclusive periods to file a plan and to solicit acceptances of that plan under 11 U.S.C. § 1121(d). In addition, Debtor is making substantial progress towards reorganizing its affairs and restructuring its business operations. Finally, an extension of these exclusive periods as requested in Debtor's Motion will not prejudice the rights of creditors or equity security holders.

A. *The Standards for Determining "Cause".*

This Court may, for cause, extend the original 120–day and 180–day exclusivity periods set forth in 11 U.S.C. § 1121. In determining what constitutes "cause" under § 1121(d), courts have focused on the following factors:

> (i) the size and complexity of the case;
>
> (ii) the extent to which the debtor has been diligent in preparing a reorganization plan;
>
> (iii) the probability that an extension will lead to successful rehabilitation;
>
> (iv) the passage of time since the debtor's Chapter 11 filing; and
>
> (v) whether the debtor is using the extension to prolong the reorganization process for impermissible purposes.

See, e.g., *In re Pine Run Trust, Inc.,* 67 B.R. 432 (Bankr.E.D.Pa.1986); *In re Perkins,* 71 B.R. 294 (W.D.Tenn.1987); *In re Public Service Co. of New Hampshire,* 88 B.R. 521 (Bankr.D.N.H.1988).

B. *The Unusual Size and Complexity of this Case Necessitate an Extension of the Exclusivity Period.*

The traditional ground for granting an extension of the exclusivity period is the large size of the Debtor and the concomitant difficulties in formulating a plan for reorganization. *In re Manville Forest Products Corp.,* 31 B.R. 991 (S.D.N.Y.1983); *In re Pine Run Trust,* supra, at 435. This bankruptcy case is one of the largest being administered in the State of Michigan. The Debtor's schedule lists debts in excess of $81 million and assets exceeding $62 million. Considerable time and effort has been dedicated to the tasks of evaluating assets and claims and negotiating with suppliers. Extensive negotiation and litigation with certain creditors who claim to be lessors of realty and equipment have further diverted attention and resources away from formulation of a reorganization plan. While litigation over rights in the estate property is not, of itself, a proper reason for extension, *In re Lake in the Woods,* supra, at 342, it should be considered as indicative of the overall complexity of the case. *In re Swatara Coal Co.,* 49 B.R. 898 (Bankr. E.D.Pa.1985). The Debtor has embarked on a comprehensive program to sell unprofitable assets, reallocate resources to profitable concerns, and solicit investments. Successful implementation of this program is a critical prerequisite to formation of an acceptable reorganization plan. The administrative burdens of implementation necessitate additional time to insure the maximum return to the Debtor, its creditors and shareholders. In short, the "sheer mass, weight, volume and complication" of the Debtor's filings "undoubtedly justify a shakedown period." *In re Manville Forest Products Corp.,* supra, at 995.[1]

---

1. The legislative history of 11 U.S.C. § 1121(d) reveals that Congress intended that courts give great weight to the size of the debtor and the complications of reorga-

C. *The Debtor's Progress to Date Reflects a Reasonable Possibility of Rehabilitation.*

Some courts have been reluctant to grant extensions solely because the Chapter 11 case is large and complex, unless the debtor demonstrates that it has made progress towards formulating a reorganization plan. *In re Sharon Steel Corp.,* 78 B.R. 762 (Bankr.W.D.Pa.1987); *In re Public Service Co. of New Hampshire,* supra, at 537. The Debtor in the instant case has made substantial progress towards preparing a Chapter 11 plan. In just over two months since the Chapter 11 filing on June 15, 1990, the Debtor has filed a Business Plan with this Court, retained PaineWebber, Inc. to assist in marketing its assets and has conducted extensive negotiations with creditors over various "lease" arrangements. Additionally, the Debtor has diligently sought, and received, permission from this Court to conduct an auction sale of surplus and unproductive real estate. This activity, in the face of the overall complexity of the case, establishes the requisite cause for extension of the exclusivity period. *In re Nicolet, Inc.,* 80 B.R. 733 (Bankr.E.D.Pa.1987). The fact that progress has been made in areas critical to a successful reorganization reflects a strong possibility that an acceptable plan can be formulated if an extension is granted. See *In re Pine Run Trust, Inc.,* supra, at 435 (some promise of probable success in formulating a plan of reorganization recognized as an element of cause for an extension). See also *In re Swatara Coal Co.,* supra, at 900 (debtor's progress reflects probability that successful rehabilitation will occur). This is not a case where the debtor has repeatedly sought extensions without making headway toward a viable solution. *In re Ravenna Industries, Inc.,* 20 B.R. 886 (Bankr.N.D.Ohio 1982)(White, B.J.).

D. *Granting the Extension Will Not Prejudice Creditors and Shareholders.*

A bankruptcy court may refuse to grant an extension of the exclusivity period where it would be used as a tactical device to pressure unwilling creditors to accept a plan they find objectionable. *In re Lake in the Woods,* supra, at 345. This is not the situation before this Court. The Debtor here is seeking the extension solely to permit it to formulate a plan for submission to its creditors.

Similarly, a motion for an extension may be denied where repeated extensions have been granted and the debtor has suffered financially during the extended exclusivity periods. *In re Ravenna Industries, Inc.,* supra; *In re Sharon Steel Corp.,* supra. Again, this is not applicable here. This is the Debtor's first motion for an extension and there has been no real deterioration of the Debtor's financial condition since June 15, 1990. The steps taken by the Debtor will likely enable it to file an acceptable plan and rehabilitate itself, thereby resulting in a benefit to the estate, its creditors and shareholders.

nization engendered by size. *In re Lake in the Woods,* supra, at 344, 345 (citing S.Rep. N. 989, 95th Cong., 2d Sess., 118 (1978)).

CONCLUSION

For the foregoing reasons, this Court should enter an Order granting Debtor's motion for an extension of the Debtor's exclusive periods to file a Chapter 11 plan and to solicit acceptances thereof.

Dated: September 6, 1990

WARNER, NORCROSS & JUDD

By _____
    Patrick E. Mears (P31316)
Attorneys for Chapter 11 Debtor

Business Address:
  900 Old Kent Building
  111 Lyon Street, N.W.
  Grand Rapids, Michigan
  49503-2489
Telephone: (616) 459-6121

Notes and Questions

1. Extensions are routinely granted in Chapter 11 cases, frequently for months, occasionally for years. Why do you suppose that is?

2. Some have suggested and at least one of your editors believes that the extended time now routinely involved in Chapter 11 and the leisurely pace at which they proceed is their principal defect and may ultimately cause repeal or, at minimum, radical change in Chapter 11. A cynic might ask: who is against delay? Surely not the management of the debtor company who are being paid their salaries. Not the lawyers for the debtor in possession who are being paid hourly fees, nor—one suspects—in their heart of hearts, even the lawyers for the creditors who are also being paid hourly fees. Nor the investment bankers or accountants. Who, then, is against extensions? Surely the creditors are against them to the extent the losses will fall on the backs of these creditors who might otherwise have been paid.

For example, at the outset of the Eastern Airlines bankruptcy, it was believed that the unsecured creditors would be paid in full, or nearly so. After several years of large losses in operation of the airline—losses which essentially diverted creditors' money into the hands of employees, trade creditors, and other suppliers—the unsecured creditors received only a small dividend on the ultimate liquidation. There is also a cost inherent in what we have discussed above, namely, in the restriction upon the activity of management and the necessity for management to devote a large share of its energy to the bankruptcy process itself and to dealing with various parties to that process.

In reading the Brief and the Motion (which was granted by Judge Spector) one can see that no great showing needs to be made in order to earn an extension.

3. Not all creditors lose by delay and it is often the case that the debtor's motion to extend exclusivity is joined by the unsecured creditors. Do you see why?

4. If no extensions were authorized or granted in any Chapter 11 in the bankruptcy law, what do you think would happen? It is far from clear that creditors or other competitors would come forward with competing plans the day after the exclusivity period ended. More likely, the threat of such plan and the saber rattling that the secured creditors in particular could do ("I have a plan in my pocket that calls for liquidation of the company and my taking the principal assets according to my security interest") might well stimulate the debtor in possession and stimulate his lawyer to act more quickly to negotiate more effectively and to produce a plan earlier on. Surely that would be desirable, even if the plan proposed were not quite as refined as one that might be posed six months or one year later.

Problem 9-2

The Cratchetts are joint general partners in XMAS–Past, whose sole asset is an office building in New York. Its primary creditor is Micawber Financial, which holds a $10 million note secured by the building. In addition, there are various unsecured creditors with about $2 million of debt. XMAS filed bankruptcy because it could not reach agreement with Micawber for modifying the loan terms. Within two weeks after filing under Chapter 11, XMAS filed a plan giving Micawber the appraised value of the building ($9 million) plus interest over twenty years. The interest rate is lower than that in the original note because market rates have fallen. The plan will give unsecured creditors payments based on "net profits" received during the five years after confirmation. This is the plan that Micawber rejected during the prebankruptcy negotiations.

Micawber is willing to propose a plan that will give the unsecured creditors more than the DIP's plan will (e.g., a cash payment of $600,000 on the date of confirmation). Can Micawber propose or discuss its plan? Should the court shorten exclusivity to allow it to do so? If the court retains exclusivity, how would you advise your unsecured creditor clients (who know of Micawber's idea) to vote on the XMAS plan?

§ 3. IMPAIRMENT OF CLAIMS

"Impairment" triggers important rights in Chapter 11. A plan must propose treatment for every class of "impaired" claims or interests (§ 1123(a)(3)). Only impaired creditors may vote on the plan. Code section 1126(f) establishes a conclusive presumption that classes of unimpaired claims accept the plan. The right to vote gives the class power to reject the plan and so to invoke the protections of cramdown.

Section 1124 of the Code defines a claim as "impaired" unless it fits within one of two narrow exceptions. The first exception applies if the plan does not alter the legal, equitable or contractual rights of the holder. Examples of alteration of the rights of a creditor are the changing of the amount of principal, changing the interest rate, altering the maturity, and changing the form or amount of collateral. In one sense a creditor's rights are like Humpty Dumpty: after a two or three year Chapter 11 proceeding there is no way to put them back together again. That is not the alteration spoken of in section 1124. Conceivably a plan could propose to put a creditor in the same position as the creditor was in at the time the petition was filed by granting a security interest with identical collateral. That would leave the creditor technically unimpaired, even though practically in a much worse position than if the Chapter 11 had never been filed. Even an alteration that enhances the value of the creditor's claim impairs it.

The second way to leave a creditor unimpaired is to cure a default and reinstate the maturity date under the original agreement. The most obvious application of this rule allows a debtor to undo an acceleration clause in a mortgage—possibly even after a judgment or foreclosure as long as state law has not merged the judgment and mortgage. Such cases are routine in Chapter 13. There the debtor continues to pay the unaccelerated amount and pays the missed installments with interest over the life of the plan, usually three years. By rendering the creditor unimpaired the debtor can retain the benefit of a favorable interest rate on a defaulted loan.

Before 1994 the plan left a creditor unimpaired if the plan provided for the full amount of the creditor's claim in cash on the effective date of the plan. In 1994 Congress removed subsection 1124(3) and so did away with the cash payment exception to impairment. Apparently it amended the section to make it clear that a solvent creditor would have to pay not only the full amount of an unsecured creditor's claim but also interest on that claim in order to leave the "impaired" creditor in as good a position as that creditor would have been upon liquidation under Chapter 7. As we will see, an unimpaired creditor does not get a vote and is not protected by 1129(a)(7)—the section that requires all impaired creditors to get at least as much as they would get on liquidation. Congress may have caused more trouble by its elimination of the cash payment exception than it would have caused by leaving it.

IN RE ROLLING GREEN COUNTRY CLUB

United States Bankruptcy Court, District of Minnesota, 1982.
26 B.R. 729.

KENNETH G. OWENS, BANKRUPTCY JUDGE. Hearing was held before the undersigned on August 11, 1982 to consider confirmation, or its refusal, of two competing plans of reorganization as submitted respectively by the debtor Rolling Green Country Club and First National Bank of Minneapolis, the holder of security interests in the nature of real estate mortgages on the premises of the debtor. The proponent of each plan has objected to confirmation of the other and the committee of unsecured creditors originally objecting to confirmation of each plan is now an objector only as to the plan of First National Bank of Minneapolis having at hearing withdrawn its objection to the plan of the debtor. The debtor's plan in brief proposes to borrow from one Bruce Hendry $467,444.00 of which $325,000.00 would be available to fund its proposed payment plan. The plan proposes to cure an existing default with respect to the interests of First National Bank of Minneapolis and to pay all other classes of interest in full, except leaving in place for payment on due date November 1, 2001 the holders of bonds, building certificates and transferable certificates. The plan of First National Bank contemplates liquidation of the properties of the debtor through the device of the appointment of a liquidating trustee and provides either for surrender of security, or payment of secured creditors and payment of all other interested parties out of the proceeds of liquidation on an effective date defined to be such date as the proceeds of liquidation in the hands of the trustee become sufficient to effect the required payments.

* * *

PERTINENT FINDINGS OF FACT

* * *

2.

The club's facility is encumbered by first and second real estate mortgages securing loans obtained from the First National Bank of Minneapolis. The club has had a long and troubled history of management of that debt. The original principal amount of the debt secured by the first mortgage was $800,000.00 and the second mortgage secures a debt in the original principal amount of $130,000.00.

3.

The mortgages were made at then prevalent interest rates far less than those now prevailing. The debtor nevertheless over the course of the years had substantial difficulty in maintaining its payments of principal and interest.

(a) The debtor in May 1971 requested First National Bank of Minneapolis (hereafter First Bank) to grant a two year moratorium on principal payments on both mortgages, and that request was granted.

(b) The debtor again in December 1971 requested that First Bank grant an additional 13 month moratorium on the payments of principal and interest as to both mortgages which request was granted.

(c) The debtor again in April 1975 requested that First Bank grant a moratorium on principal payments and in response the bank granted such a moratorium on principal payments for a period of six months as to both the first and second mortgages.

(d) In November 1976 and through February 1977, the debtor was unable to make its installment payment on either mortgage.

(e) The debtor again in February 1977 requested that principal payment for the period November 1976 through May 1977 be extended to the maturity dates of the first and second mortgages and that request was granted by First Bank.

(f) The second mortgage became due July 1, 1980 having a then principal balance of $65,116.32. The debtor failed to make the payment and requested an extension to July 1, 1984 to be payable in monthly installments of $1,812.24, and that extension was granted by First Bank.

(g) The debtor failed to make its monthly payments on the first and second mortgages beginning again on June 1, 1981 and has made no payments since.

4.

The principal balance due and owing on the first mortgage at the date of hearing is $605,412.15 and the principal balance owing on the second mortgage is $53,200.64. Interest accrues on the mortgages respectively at the rate of $126.13 per diem and $22.17 per diem.

5.

The present fair market value of the debtor's club premises including the golf course and subject to the mortgages to First Bank is in a range between $1,440,000.00 and $2,000,000.00. The value of the premises is in excess of the total present mortgage debt and the liquidation value of the premises and all other assets of the debtor is in excess of its total listed indebtedness, both secured and unsecured.

6.

First Bank commenced a foreclosure proceeding by advertisement, and a Sheriff's sale was scheduled to be held on January 13, 1982 with respect to the real estate premises subject to its mortgages. On the day prior to the scheduled sale, the debtor on January 12, 1982 filed its voluntary petition for reorganization under Chapter 11 of the Bankruptcy Code in this court and obtained the benefits of the automatic stay provided by Section 362 of the Bankruptcy Code, (11 U.S.C. Section 362).

7.

If First Bank had been permitted to continue its foreclosure proceeding, it would have, on the expiration of the period of redemption, January 13, 1983, a sum having by reason of increased and now prevailing interest rates representing a more valuable investment than the investment presently secured under its mortgages at a lesser rate if the debtor's plan is confirmed, defaults in payments on the mortgages are cured, the expenses of sale and cost of deferment paid and due dates reinstated. The difference in investment value to the bank is $164,651.64 using a discount rate based on opportunity cost of 17.68% with respect to the first mortgage and 17.8% with respect to the second mortgage.

* * *

DISCUSSION OBJECTIONS TO DEBTOR'S PLAN

* * *

The bank's principal contention is that the bank as a claimant separately classified is impaired in that it will not receive payment of the $164,651.64 which it would expect to be able to receive if permitted in effect to re-accelerate its mortgage investment, that it has not accepted the debtor's plan and, the value of its security exceeding its claimed debt, such acceptance is required and, accordingly, the requirements for confirmation found in Section 1129(a)(7), (8) and (10) have not been met. * * *

* * *

The bank contends it is impaired because it would be in a better position if permitted to proceed to foreclosure and thus obtain the accelerated fruits of its mortgage, and that the impairment has not been removed by the debtor through compliance in its plan with Section 1124 of the Bankruptcy Code (11 U.S.C. Section 1124).

* * *

If the failure of First Bank to realize the benefits of the acceleration and realization which would have occurred on the anticipated foreclosure of its mortgages constitutes "damages" within the meaning of Section 1124(2)(C) then First Bank as a claimant and as a separate class is impaired for the plan makes no provision for such payment to the bank as a claimant or as a class.

The word "damages" must be given a meaning consonant with the overall thrust and meaning of the section within which it is obtained.

* * *

The purpose of the section is to permit the financially embarrassed debtor to retain the security and enjoy the benefits of the original security arrangements. In that the purpose is to protect against the rights lost simply by reason of acceleration. It would seem fruitless indeed if the debtor is required in order to enjoy the benefit of this section to pay the total expected present economic cost of retaining or restoring the maturities provided in the instrument. I conclude accordingly that the term damages does not encompass that result. The damages have a lesser measure intended to protect the security holder from the expenses to which he has been put by reason of the denial of his right of acceleration. That is the extent to which he can reasonably rely on the instrument or on local law and suffer detriment by reason of the effect of this section on such right of acceleration. The security holder simply cannot expect to be held totally harmless from the effects of the application of Section 1124, and any such reliance on the security instrument or local law is not "reasonable" in the context of the title and in the context of the section. The security holder may only reasonably rely on the right of acceleration or foreclosure based on the instrument and local law to the extent of compensation for any expenses he may have incurred, in this case attorneys' fees incident to the foreclosure and reimbursement for the out-of-pocket loss occasioned by the fact that the payments in default have been deferred. That loss is adequately compensated by an appropriate interest allowance. The economic loss of expectation mentioned in the foregoing findings has a speculative basis assuming no decline in the cost of funds overtime, and is not "damage" of the type contemplated by this section and need not be compensated.

The plan as amended provides for the payment of such damages "as may be allowed pursuant to 11 U.S.C. Section 1124(2)(C)". I deem that to be a sufficient provision under Section 1124 as reflected in the succeeding findings.

Since the bank is not impaired, there is no necessity for its affirmative acceptance.

The claim of its impairment was the principal basis for the First Bank's additional contention that confirmation must be denied since no class of claims has accepted the plan which is said to be a deviation from the requirements of Section 1129(a).

* * *

11 U.S.C. Section 1126(f) provides that an unimpaired class is "deemed to have accepted the plan" and accordingly solicitation of acceptances with respect to such class is not required. The present problem as posed originally by the parties is whether a "deemed" acceptance by a class is the equivalent of the "acceptance" prescribed in Section 1129(a)(10). *See In Re Barrington Oaks General Partnership,* 15 B.R. 952 (Bankr.D.Utah 1981). I do not however think it necessary to reconcile the two provisions in that context. Subsection (10) seems to be pointed simply to prevent an improper insider effect and to prevent as had occurred under Chapter XII of the former Bankruptcy Act a situation where all impaired classes could be subjected to "cram down" based on existing values thus depriving impaired classes of appropriate expectations. *See In Re Pine Gate Associates,* 2 B.C.D. 1478 (N.D.Ga.1976). I believe the section has only that effect and was so intended, the intention being reflected and hopefully to be perfected on adoption of the technical amendments to the Bankruptcy Reform Act of 1978. There Section 1129(a)(10) is rewritten and clarified to read "if a class of claims is impaired under the plan, at least one class of claims is impaired under the plan must accept the plan, determined without including any acceptance of the plan by an insider". Whereas here no class of claims is impaired and accordingly no solicitation of claims is required, it would be a useless gesture to require a disclosure statement and solicitation of claims from creditors who are in reality being paid in full. [Editor's Note: The court is interpreting 1129 and 1126(f) as they existed prior to the 1984 amendments. The court correctly guesses the Congressional intent that was carried out in the 1984 amendments.]

First Bank further contends the debtor's plan is not confirmable because of an insufficient showing of the financial ability of Mr. Hendry to carry out his conditional commitment to advance funding for the plan, and that there has been an insufficient showing of the debtor's ability even with such funding to continue its operation over time so as to assure, as is required by Section 1129(a)(11), that confirmation of the debtor's plan is not likely to be followed by liquidation or a need for further financial reorganization. As to the financial worth of Mr. Hendry, the court observes that no issue was made in any formal objection questioning his financial worth. The court assumes that the word "confirmation" in the mentioned subsection contemplates as well an execution or consummation of the plan, the real intendment of the subsection being to avoid confirmation of plans which even if consummated are fruitless as an instrument to reorganization. In the present situation, there being no showing of his inability, it would be appropriate to confirm the plan and if there is an immediate failure of funding, appropriate remedies are available under the Bankruptcy Code.

While the proof offered to show a continued viability of operation after confirmation is not conclusive, it does demonstrate a reasonable probability that such will occur. While the immediate plan certainly considers an enhancement of membership, it obviously does not foreclose other adjustments by way of economics or of increased charges for the use of the club's facilities. The court is not prepared to say that the debtor has not shown accordingly the probability of a continued operation sufficient to fund the extended plan payments on the mortgage and to deal with other exigencies. The failure of the debtor to meet the requirements of its mortgage in prior years by maintaining a sufficient membership base or establishing adequate fees does not compel, in my view, any contrary conclusion.

Objections to the First Bank Plan

* * *

The bank's own claim, and its class, strangely is impaired in fact but not in law for the plan deprives the bank of the right of acceleration, an alteration of its legal and contractual rights, but since the planned cure complies with Section 1124(2)(A)–(D) by definition the deprivation does not constitute impairment. No other class of claims is impaired since the plan provides for payment in full with interest, the amount to which the holders would be entitled on a liquidation of this solvent estate.

The bank's acceptance as a separate class also conforms to the requirements of Section 1129(a)(10) even if facially construed.

The bank's plan is also confirmable.

Selection of a Plan

As previously indicated, the creditors' committee while adhering to its objections to the First Bank plan has withdrawn and does not object to the debtor's plan. In this situation, the court is bound to consider those expressed preferences of the creditors in its determination as to which plan to confirm such consideration being mandated by Section 1129(c). While the court is of course free to make its own determination having taken into account such preference there is nothing in the present situation which the court feels is compelling to the contrary. Accordingly the First Bank plan while confirmable should not be confirmed and the plan of the debtor being not only confirmable but meeting the preference of creditor should be confirmed. The following additional findings are intended to that end.

* * *

ACCORDINGLY, IT IS ORDERED that the debtor's motion to substitute its amendment plan of reorganization is granted, and it is further—

ORDERED that judgment enter:

1.

That the amended plan of reorganization filed by Rolling Green Country Club, a Minnesota corporation, debtor herein, is confirmed.

2.

That pursuant to the said plan of reorganization upon cure of the default in the mortgages between debtor and The First National Bank of Minneapolis, and upon payment to the said First National Bank of Minneapolis of its attorneys' fees and expenses incurred in and about the foreclosure proceeding together with interest at the rate of 17.5% per annum on the amount of mortgage payments due pursuant to the mortgages between the debtor and The First National Bank of Minneapolis dated March 12, 1969 and June 25, 1970 from the time that such payments were due to the effective date of the amended plan of reorganization as damages pursuant to Section 1124(2)(C) of the Bankruptcy Code that said mortgages are reinstated according to their terms and conditions as they existed prior to default by the debtor.

* * *

4.

This court shall retain jurisdiction of the debtor subsequent to entry hereof for the purpose of entering other and further orders relating to the consummation of the plan of reorganization, for the purpose of allowing claims and hearing objections if any thereto, for conducting and completing adversary proceedings heretofore filed for the purpose of determining or resolving any defaults, disputes or similar matters under the amended plan of reorganization. In all other respects, the court on the date of this order relinquishes jurisdiction over the debtor and its operations.

Notes and Questions

1. Did the court hold that the First National Bank is not impaired despite the opportunity cost that it suffered? This is an example of a case where a creditor would vote against the plan even if it were unimpaired. Compare the interest rates that the bank will receive on its mortgage as part of the confirmation and on unpaid amounts that now will be paid to cure. What is the test of "cure" with respect to back payment which satisfies section 1124?

2. If the court had concluded that the bank's claim was impaired, would the plan have been approved under section 1129(b)? Note that section 1129(b)(2)(A)(i)(II) requires that the claim in a dissenting class receive deferred cash payment with a value as of the date of the plan at least as great as the value of the interest in the property. Did this plan achieve that result?

3. How does a court choose which plan to confirm? This court seems simply to count creditors' noses, and rely on the fact that a larger number of creditors voted for the debtor's plan, rather than the bank's. Is this the correct approach? If not, what alternative method might be used?

§ 4. CLASSIFICATION OF CLAIMS

Section 1122(a) restricts a debtor's ability to lump dissimilar claims into the same class. "[A] plan may place a claim or an interest in a particular class only if such claim or interest is substantially similar to the other claims or interests of such class." (§ 1122(a)). This prevents the debtor from diluting voting rights of a creditor who holds greater rights than other creditors by including the creditor's claim in a much larger class of dissimilar claims.

Aside from dumping diverse claims into a single class, the debtor might also want to split similar claims of equal priority into smaller classes. Although section 1122 does not prohibit this, such splitting holds the potential for abuse. For example, a debtor might devise a friendly but theoretically impaired class by giving full payment but delaying it for 30 days, and then cramdown against all significant creditors of the estate.

Reading the cases and thinking about statutory rules on classification confronts one starkly with the question whether the debtor is ever permitted to treat one class of creditors better than another nonconsenting class despite the fact that both would be treated the same on liquidation. First consider a clear case: a debt carrying a below market rate of interest on which there has been a default. Assume, for example, that the debtor has defaulted on a mortgage that bears interest at 6 percent at a time when the current rate is 11 percent. The Code explicitly contemplates that the debtor can separately classify the mortgage, cure the default, and so leave the mortgagee unimpaired to carry merrily on for the next 20 years of the term at 6 percent. That particular creditor will be substantially worse off than other creditors who must receive *present value* equal to the allowed amount of their claims. In the case of our hypothetical mortgagee, the present value of its claim will substantially exceed the amount it is to be paid over the time because the contract interest rate (6%) is lower than would be used to compute the present value of an impaired, dissenting claim (here 11%).

Second is the possibility of manipulating the present value findings in such a way as to favor one set of creditors over another while apparently giving each of them the same thing. Consider the proposal to pay trade creditors in cash, paying others an identical "present value" over five years. As a matter of theory, this is not discrimination, for by hypothesis the promise to pay over five years has an identical value to the cash payment today. One suspects that the theory and the practice diverge here. Faced with the choice of $50,000 cash on the date of confirmation of the plan or of the possibility of receiving $50,000 with even a generous interest payment over five years, most creditors would elect the former.

A third case permitting distortion arises in section 1122 itself. Section 1122(b) explicitly authorizes establishing a separate set of claims that are below a certain amount. Implicitly this authorization invites separate treatment for that class, usually more favorable treatment.

The fourth way of favoring one set of creditors over another arises from the operation of the business. There is nothing to prevent the debtor from directing a larger share of its business to a creditor it wishes to favor than would otherwise be directed to that creditor. Likewise there is nothing that prohibits the debtor from negotiating higher prices for goods purchased from that creditor. To the extent that this creditor gets additional business at higher prices than it would receive if it were not a creditor, it is receiving a de facto premium payment on its preexisting debt. Although judicial references to such behavior are rare, surely it occurs frequently.

The fifth possibility is closely allied to the fourth. This would involve simply making payments to one prepetition creditor while declining to make similar payments to other creditors. This occurred in *In re James A. Phillips, Inc.,* 29 B.R. 391 (S.D.N.Y.1983), where the debtor made payments to a creditor who had a mechanics lien on an ongoing building project and who threatened to withhold future deliveries. With some difficulty the court in that case approved the payments.

The question remains whether the debtor can overtly treat one group of creditors not covered by any of the above exceptions better than another group by separate classification when both sets of creditors would receive the same percentage payment on liquidation. Except as discussed above, nothing in the Code explicitly authorizes such payment and much implies that such preference is improper. Yet there are strong utilitarian arguments for the more favorable treatment of one creditor compared with another. Where a particular financial or trade creditor is critical to the continuing existence of the business, and another creditor is completely unimportant because that creditor's loan dealt only with a division that is to be liquidated under the plan, debtor, shareholders, and employees will wish to favor the powerful creditor on purely utilitarian grounds. The real question is whether there is any room in 1122 and 1129 for the recognition of power.

IN RE UNITED STATES TRUCK CO.
United States Court of Appeals, Sixth Circuit, 1986.
800 F.2d 581.

CORNELIA G. KENNEDY, CIRCUIT JUDGE.

The Teamsters National Freight Industry Negotiating Committee (the Teamsters Committee), a creditor of U.S. Truck Company, Inc. (U.S. Truck)—the debtor-in-possession in this Chapter 11 bankruptcy proceeding—appeals the District Court's order confirming U.S. Truck's Fifth Amended Plan of Reorganization. The Teamsters Committee complains that the plan does not satisfy three of the requirements of 11 U.S.C. § 1129. The District Court, which presided over the matter after the resignation of Bankruptcy Judge Stanley B. Bernstein, held that the requirements of section 1129 had been satisfied. We agree.

I

Underlying this appeal is the Teamsters Committee's claim that U.S. Truck is liable to its employees for rejecting a collective bargaining agreement between the local union and U.S. Truck. After filing its petition for relief under Chapter 11 of the Bankruptcy Code on June 11, 1982, U.S. Truck, a trucking company primarily engaged in intrastate shipping of parts and supplies for the automotive industry, sought to reject the collective bargaining agreement. U.S. Truck rejected the agreement with the approval of then-Bankruptcy-Judge Woods, in December 1982. Judge Woods found that rejection of the agreement was "absolutely necessary to save the debtor from collapse." New agreements have been negotiated to the satisfaction of each participating local union. Such agreements have been implemented over the lone dissent of the Teamsters Joint Area Rider Committee. Under the most recently mentioned agreement in the record (due to have expired in March 1985), U.S. Truck was able to record monthly profits in the range of $125,000 to $250,000. These new agreements achieved such results by reducing wages and requiring employees to buy their own trucking equipment, which the employees then leased to the company.

The parties agreed to an estimate of the size of the Teamsters Committee claim against U.S. Truck so that the confirmation plan could be considered. The District Court held a hearing to consider the plan on January 23, 1985. The court considered three objections by the Teamsters Committee to the plan. Consideration of the objections, and the court's treatment of them, requires an understanding of the statutory scheme for approval of a Chapter 11 reorganization plan.

* * *

III

The Teamsters Committee's first objection is that the plan does not meet the requirement that at least one class of impaired claims accept the plan, because U.S. Truck impermissibly gerrymandered the classes in order to neutralize the Teamsters Committee's dissenting vote. The reorganization plan contains twelve classes. The plan purports to impair five of these classes—Class VI (the secured claim of Manufacturer's National Bank of Detroit based on a mortgage); Class VII (the secured claim of John Graham, Trustee of Transportation Services, Inc., based on a loan); Class IX (the Teamsters Committee's claim based on rejection of the collective bargaining agreement); Class XI (all secured claims in excess of $200.00 including those arising from the rejection of executory contracts); and Class XII (the equity interest of the stockholder of the debtor). As noted above, section 1129(a)(10), as incorporated into subsection (b)(1), requires at least one of these classes of impaired claims to approve the reorganization plan before it can be confirmed. The parties agree that approval by Class XII would not count because acceptance must be determined without including the acceptance of the plan by any insider. The Code's definition of "insider" clearly includes McKinlay Transport, Inc. Thus, compliance with subsection (a)(10) depends on whether either of the other three classes that approved the plan—Class VI, Class VII, or Class XI—was a properly constructed impaired class. The Teamsters Committee argues that Classes VI and VII were not truly impaired classes and that Class XI should have included Class IX, and hence was an improperly constructed class.[6] Because we find that Class XI was a properly constructed class of impaired claims, we hold that the plan complies with subsection (a)(10).

The issue raised by the Teamsters Committee's challenge is under what circumstances does the Bankruptcy Code permit a debtor to keep a creditor out of a class of impaired claims which are of a similar legal nature and are against the same property as those of the "isolated" creditor. The District Court held that the Code permits such action here because of the following circumstances: (1) the employees represented by the Teamsters Committee have a unique continued interest in the ongoing business of the debtor; (2) the mechanics of the Teamsters Committee's claim differ substantially from those of the Class XI claims; and (3) the Teamsters Committee's claim is likely to become part of the agenda of future collective bargaining sessions between the union and the reorganized company. Thus, according to the court, the interests of the Teamsters Committee are substantially dissimilar from those of the creditors in Class XI. We must decide whether the Code permits separate classification under such circumstances.

Congress has sent mixed signals on the issue that we must decide. Our starting point is 11 U.S.C. § 1122.

§ 1122. Classification of claims or interests

(a) Except as provided in subsection (b) of this section, a plan may place a claim or an interest in a particular class only if such

---

6. Had the debtor included the Teamsters Committee's claim in Class XI, the Committee's vote to reject the plan would have swung the results of the Class XI vote from an acceptance to a rejection. *See* 11 U.S.C. § 1126(c)(setting forth the requirement that creditors holding at least two-thirds in amount of allowed claims of a class accept).

claim or interest is substantially similar to the other claims or interests of such class.

(b) A plan may designate a separate class of claims consisting only of every unsecured claim that is less than or reduced to an amount that the court approves as reasonable and necessary for administrative convenience.

The statute, by its express language, only addresses the problem of dissimilar claims being included in the same class. It does not address the correlative problem—the one we face here—of similar claims being put in different classes. Some courts have seized upon this omission, and have held that the Code does not require a debtor to put similar claims in the same class.

We think the courts erred in holding that section 1122(a) prohibits classification based on the presence of a co-debtor. Section 1122(a) specifies that only claims which are "substantially similar" may be placed in the same class. It does not require that similar claims *must* be grouped together, but merely that any group created must be homogeneous. Although some courts have held that section 1122(a) prohibits classification based on any criterion other than legal right to the debtor's assets, the plain language of the statute contradicts such a construction. Moreover, section 1122(a) so interpreted would conflict with section 1322(b)(1), which specifically authorizes designation of more than one class of unsecured creditor, each presumably with equal legal rights to the debtor's estate.

Further evidence that Congress intentionally failed to impose a requirement that similar claims be classified together is found by examining the "classification" sections of the former Bankruptcy Act. The applicable former provisions were 11 U.S.C., sections 597 (from former Chapter X) and 751 (from former Chapter XI).

§ 597. Classification of creditors and stockholders

For the purposes of the plan and its acceptance, the judge shall fix the division of creditors and stockholders into classes according to the nature of their respective claims and stock. For the purposes of such classification, the judge shall, if necessary, upon the application of the trustee, the debtor, any creditor, or an indenture trustee, fix a hearing upon notice to the holders of secured claims, the debtor, the trustee, and such other persons as the judge may designate, to determine summarily the value of the security and classify as unsecured the amount in excess of such value.

§ 751. Classification of creditors

For the purposes of the arrangement and its acceptance, the court may fix the division of creditors into classes and, in the event of controversy, the court shall after hearing upon notice summarily determine such controversy.

Section 597 was interpreted to require all creditors of equal rank with claims against the same property to be placed in the same class. Congress' switch to less restrictive language in section 1122 of the Code seems to warrant a conclusion that Congress no longer intended to impose the now-omitted requirement that similar claims be classified together. However, the legislative history indicates that Congress may not have intended to change the prior rule. The Notes of the Senate Committee on the Judiciary state:

> This section [1122] codifies current case law surrounding the classification of claims and equity securities. It requires classification based on the nature of the claims or interests classified, and permits inclusion of claims or interests in a particular class only if the claim or interest being included is substantially similar to the other claims or interests of the class.

It is difficult to follow Congress' instruction to apply the old case law to the new Code provision. The old case law comes from two different sources. Chapter X of the old Act was designed for thorough financial reorganizations of large corporations. It imposed a very formal and rigid structure to protect the investing public. Chapter XI was designed for small nonpublic businesses, did not permit the adjustment of a secured debt or of equity, and thus contained few investor-protection measures. The idea behind Chapter 11 of the Code was to combine the speed and flexibility of Chapter XI with some of the protection and remedial tools of Chapter X. Thus, Congress has incorporated, for purposes of interpreting section 1122, the case law from two provisions with different language, that were adopted for different purposes, and that have been interpreted to mean different things.

In this case, U.S. Truck is using its classification powers to segregate dissenting (impaired) creditors from assenting (impaired) creditors (by putting the dissenters into a class or classes by themselves) and, thus, it is assured that at least one class of impaired creditors will vote for the plan and make it eligible for cramdown consideration by the court. We agree with the Teamsters Committee that there must be some limit on a debtor's power to classify creditors in such a manner. The potential for abuse would be significant otherwise. Unless there is some requirement of keeping similar claims together, nothing would stand in the way of a debtor seeking out a few impaired creditors (or even one such creditor) who will vote for the plan and placing them in their own class.[8]

We are unaware of any cases that deal with this problem as it arises in this case. As we noted above, the legislative history of the Code provides little assistance in determining what limits there are to segregating similar claims. Nevertheless, we do find one common theme in

---

8. We need not speculate in this case whether the purpose of separate classification was to line up the votes in favor of the plan. The debtor admitted that to the District Court. *See* Debtor's Response to Objections to Confirmation Filed by the Teamsters National Freight Negotiating Committee, at 6 (Jan. 23, 1985).

the prior case law that Congress incorporated into section 1122. In those pre-Code cases, the lower courts were given broad discretion to determine proper classification according to the factual circumstances of each individual case.

* * * The District Court noted three important ways in which the interests of the Teamsters Committee differ substantially from those of the other impaired creditors. Because of these differences, the Teamsters Committee has a different stake in the future viability of the reorganized company and has alternative means at its disposal for protecting its claim. The Teamsters Committee's claim is connected with the collective bargaining process. In the words of the Committee's counsel, the union employees have a "virtually unique interest." These differences put the Teamsters Committee's claim in a different posture than the Class XI claims. The Teamsters Committee may choose to reject the plan not because the plan is less than optimal to it as a creditor, but because the Teamsters Committee has a noncreditor interest—*e.g.*, rejection will benefit its members in the ongoing employment relationship. Although the Teamsters Committee certainly is not intimately connected with the debtor, to allow the Committee to vote with the other impaired creditors would be to allow it to prevent a court from considering confirmation of a plan that a significant group of creditors with similar interests have accepted. Permitting separate classification of the Teamsters Committee's claim does not automatically result in adoption of the plan. The Teamsters Committee is still protected by the provisions of subsections (a) and (b), particularly the requirements of subsection (b) that the plan not discriminate unfairly and that it be fair and equitable with respect to the Teamsters Committee's claim. In fact, the Teamsters Committee invokes those requirements, but as we note in the following sections, the plan does not violate them. * * *

[The court further held that the former equity holders were entitled to retain their ownership of the company based on their contributions of $100,000 new value to the reorganization.]

IN RE BOSTON POST ROAD LIMITED PARTNERSHIP

United States Court of Appeals, Second Circuit, 1994.
21 F.3d 477.

MILTON POLLACK, SENIOR DISTRICT JUDGE.

Debtor seeks confirmation of a Plan of Reorganization filed under Chapter 11 of the Bankruptcy Code. The Bankruptcy Court denied confirmation, holding that the Plan impermissibly (i) separately classified similar claims solely to create an impaired assenting class; and (ii) classified as "impaired" a class of residential security depositors whose interests were in fact benefitted by the Plan. The District Court affirmed the Bankruptcy Court's rulings on both issues. Debtor challenges both holdings.

Background

Plaintiff–Appellant, Boston Post Road Limited Partnership ("BPR"), is a limited partnership formed pursuant to the Connecticut Uniform Limited Partnership Act, Conn.Gen.Stat. §§ 34–9 to–82 (1993), consisting of a single individual general partner, George Boyer, and a single limited partner, George Myers. BPR was formed in 1984 to acquire and manage a residential and office complex located in Waterford, Connecticut. In March of 1988, BPR mortgaged the complex to Connecticut Bank and Trust Company ("the Bank") to secure a loan of approximately $14 million. BPR thereafter defaulted on the mortgage payments, and on July 20, 1990, the Bank instituted a mortgage foreclosure action in Connecticut state court. In January 1991, the Bank became insolvent, its assets were seized by the U.S. Comptroller of Currency, and the Federal Deposit Insurance Corporation ("FDIC") became the holder of BPR's mortgage.

The FDIC continued to pursue foreclosure of the mortgaged property and on August 1, 1991, the Connecticut Superior Court entered a judgment of strict foreclosure against BPR and set October 28, 1991 as BPR's last day for redemption. On that date, BPR filed a voluntary *pro se* petition for relief under Chapter 11 of the Bankruptcy Code in the United States Bankruptcy Court for the District of Connecticut, thereby staying foreclosure. Approximately six months later, on March 16, 1992, the FDIC filed its proof of claim in BPR's bankruptcy.

On June 18, 1992, BPR filed its Second Amended Plan of Reorganization (the "Plan") in the Bankruptcy Court. The Plan proposed the following seven classes of creditors.

Class 1—unsecured claims of residential tenants to security deposits entitled to priority under Section 507(a)(7) of the Bankruptcy Code;

Class 2—secured claims held by creditors with liens and/or security interests on or in the real estate asset of the debtor (i.e., the secured portion of the FDIC's mortgage);

Class 3—secured interests of residential tenants whose security deposits are being held by the Debtor in interest-bearing bank accounts;

Class 4—unsecured claims of trade creditors;

Class 5—unsecured deficiency claims of creditors who have some security for their debt but not enough to cover the full amount owed (i.e., the unsecured portion of the FDIC's mortgage);

Class 6—interests of the limited partner; and

Class 7—interests of the general partner.

In relevant part, the Plan proposed to pay the FDIC's secured claim (Class 2), estimated at $1.445 million, over a fifteen-year term, utilizing negative amortization with a balloon payment at the end of the fifteenth year following confirmation of the Plan; to pay the trade creditors' unsecured claims (Class 4), totalling approximately $5000, over a six-year term without interest; to pay the FDIC's unsecured mortgage deficiency claim (Class 5), estimated at $500,000, without interest following the earlier of a sale of the property or the fifteenth year following Plan confirmation; and to pay the residential security deposit holders (Class 3) a rate of interest on their residential security deposits *higher* than that statutorily mandated. In essence, the Plan was fashioned to permit a possible "cramdown" under 11 U.S.C. § 1129(b), over the anticipated objection of the FDIC, by far the BPR's largest unsecured creditor. Ultimately, Class 1 turned out to be non-existent; Classes 2 and 5 voted to reject the Plan; and Classes 3, 4, 6 and 7 voted to accept the Plan.

On August 12, 1992, the Bankruptcy Court (Robert L. Krechevsky, Chief B.J.) held a hearing on the Plan's confirmation. At the hearing, the FDIC challenged the Plan on several grounds. In particular, it faulted the Plan for (i) segregating the Class 4 unsecured trade debts from the unsecured mortgage deficiency claim of the FDIC solely to gerrymander an impaired class which would approve the Plan; and (ii) classifying as "impaired" the Class 3 residential tenants with security deposits who would receive a *higher* interest rate on their security deposits than the statutorily mandated rate.

After hearing initial arguments, the Bankruptcy Court requested briefs and thereafter rendered a decision denying confirmation of the Plan on October 2, 1992. In its decision, the Bankruptcy Court held that (i) the FDIC's unsecured claim should have been placed in the same class with other unsecured creditors; and (ii) the residential security deposits were not "impaired" within the meaning of Bankruptcy Code § 1124(1). In light of these two rulings, the Code requirements for Plan confirmation were not satisfied because the Plan failed to obtain an affirmative vote of a legitimately impaired class of non-insider creditors. The District Court affirmed on June 23, 1993, and the Debtor has appealed to this Court.

Discussion

A plan of reorganization under the Bankruptcy Code may be confirmed if either of two voting requirements is met: (i) each class of impaired claims has accepted the Plan, 11 U.S.C. § 1129(a)(8); or (ii) "at least one class of claims that is impaired under the plan has accepted the plan, determined without including any acceptance of the plan by any insider." 11 U.S.C. § 1129(a)(10). The latter makes available a "cramdown" procedure. If the debtor chooses to utilize the cramdown procedure (having failed to secure the vote of all the impaired classes), the plan must meet all of the statutory requirements enumerated in § 1129(b)(essentially that the plan is fair and equitable and does not discriminate unfairly against any impaired claims), in addition to the prerequisites of § 1129(a) which are imposed on every plan.

The voting structure set forth in the Bankruptcy Code for approval of a reorganization plan mandates that claims be placed in classes and that votes be counted on a class basis. Acceptance by a particular class of creditors occurs when "at least two-thirds in amount and more than one-half in number of allowed claims of such class ... have accepted ... such plan." 11 U.S.C. § 1126(c).

Cramdown of a plan of reorganization involving claims secured by real property owned by the debtor also often implicates Sections 506(a) and 1111(b) of the Bankruptcy Code. Section 506(a) provides that a claim secured by a lien on property is considered secured up to the value of such property and unsecured for the remainder. In this case, the FDIC's claim, totalling $1,945,000, is secured by the Debtor's sole asset, a residential and office complex. The value of the property, as agreed to by Debtor and the FDIC, is $1,445,000. Thus the FDIC has a secured claim in the amount of $1,445,000 and is entitled to an unsecured deficiency claim for the remaining $500,000. Under Section 1111(b)(2), a secured creditor may elect to have its entire mortgage claim treated as secured notwithstanding Section 506(a), thereby waiving its entitlement to an unsecured deficiency claim and increasing the amount of its secured claim. Here, however, the FDIC did not make such an election and the time to do so has expired.

In a typical single asset real estate case such as this, the mortgagee creditor often objects to the proposed plan, thereby requiring the debtor to seek cramdown of the Plan over the mortgagee creditor's objection. Here the Debtor took two approaches in an attempt to obtain a consenting class of "impaired" creditors. First, Debtor classified the FDIC's unsecured mortgage deficiency claim of $500,000 separately from unsecured trade claims, which total only $5,000. If the deficiency claim were classified together with the other unsecured claims, the FDIC's vote against the Plan would preclude acceptance by that class. This is so because the amount of the FDIC's deficiency claim is one hundred times the amount of all other unsecured claims, making it impossible for Debtor to obtain the affirmative vote of two-thirds in amount of such class as required by Section 1126(c) of the Bankruptcy Code. Debtor's second approach to obtaining a consenting class of "impaired" creditors was to create a purportedly impaired class of residential tenants who placed security deposits with Debtor (Class 3). The Plan provided that holders of such claims would receive interest on their security deposits at a rate of 8% rather than the 5¼ mandated by Connecticut state law. Debtor asserted that this "enhancement" of that class' claims constituted "impairment" within the meaning of Section 1124.

Debtor contended that the approval of each of classes 3 and 4 satisfied the requirement of consent of an impaired class. (The consent of classes 6 and 7, the general and limited partners, could not be counted because these were insider classes.) Both the Bankruptcy Court and the District Court held (i) classifying the FDIC's unsecured mortgage deficiency claim separately from the unsecured claims of trade creditors solely to create an assenting allegedly impaired class was impermissible; and (ii) the class of claims comprising residential tenants with security deposits was not properly classified as impaired, because the value of such claims was enhanced—not impaired—under Debtor's Plan. These rulings precluded Debtor from obtaining acceptance of its Plan by an impaired class of claims, and thereby precluded cramdown. Debtor challenges holdings on appeal.

A. Separate classification of the several unsecured claims was without a legitimate reason.

Section 1122 of the Bankruptcy Code generally governs classification of claims. Section 1122 provides:

§ 1122. Classification of claims or interests.

(a) Except as provided in subsection (b) of this section, a plan may place a claim or an interest in a particular class only if such claim or interest is substantially similar to the other claims or interests of such class.

(b) A plan may designate a separate class of claims consisting only of every unsecured claim that is less than or reduced to an amount that the court approves as reasonable and necessary for administrative convenience.

11 U.S.C. § 1122 (1993). While the section bars aggregating dissimilar claims in the same class, it does not explicitly address whether similar claims must be placed in the same class. This issue of the permissibility of separate classification of similar types of claim is one that has yet to be addressed by the Second Circuit, and it remains a "hot topic" both among practitioners and in the academic community. See Peter E. Meltzer, *Disenfranchising the Dissenting Creditor Through Artificial Classification or Artificial Impairment*, 66 Am. Bankr. L.J. 281 (1992).

In addressing this question, the Bankruptcy and District Courts in the instant action were guided by the holdings of several other circuits, in decisions cited *infra*, that similar claims could not be placed in different classes solely to gerrymander a class that will assent to the plan. See *In re Boston Post Road Ltd. Partnership*, 145 B.R. 745, 748 (Bankr.D.Conn.1992)("The courts ... have uniformly prohibited a debtor from classifying similar claims differently in order to gerrymander an affirmative vote in favor of a reorganization plan."); *In re Boston Post Road Ltd.Partnership*, 154 B.R. 617, 621 (D.Conn.1993)("classes may not be manipulated so as to gerrymander the voting process and circumvent the § 1129 requirements"). The other circuits have generally held that separate classification of similar claims is permissible only upon proof of a legitimate reason for separate classification, and that separate classification to gerrymander an affirmative vote is impermissible. *See, e.g., Phoenix Mut. Life Ins. Co. v. Greystone III Joint Venture (In re Greystone III)*, 995 F.2d 1274,1279 (5th Cir.1991), cert. denied, 506 U.S. 821, 113 S.Ct. 72, 121 L.Ed.2d 37 (1992) ("[T]hou shalt not classify similar claims differently in order to gerrymander an affirmative vote on a reorganization plan.").

Debtor contends that the Second Circuit should decline to follow the leads of the other circuits. It urges that Section 1122 be interpreted to permit far more liberal separate classification of similar claims. Debtor attempts to support its contentions with reference to recent judicial interpretations of Section 1122, legislative intent, and policy considerations.

Debtor first cites two recent opinions by bankruptcy judges holding that separate classification of similar claims is in fact mandated. *See In re D & W Realty Corp.*, 156 B.R. 140, 141 & n. 3 (Bankr.S.D.N.Y.1993) (holding that "separate classification is not only appropriate, it is in fact mandated by the Bankruptcy Code and Rules," but acknowledging that it "has not found [this opinion] articulated anywhere else"), *rev'd*, 165 B.R. 127 (S.D.N.Y.1994); *In re SM 104 Ltd.*, 160 B.R. 202, 218–19 (Bankr.S.D.Fla.1993)(holding that unsecured deficiency claims created by § 1111(b) are not substantially similar to other unsecured claims, while asserting that the "circuit courts and the majority of district and bankruptcy courts have missed the forests for the trees").

Debtor then notes that the wording of Section 1122 does not require that all unsecured claims be classified together, but merely states that only claims that are substantially similar *may* be placed together. Debtor contends that this wording, especially when compared with the less flexible wording of the Bankruptcy Act of 1898, reflects Congress' intent to dispense with the requirement that similar claims be classified together.

Finally, Debtor contends that prohibiting separate classification effectively bars the debtor in single-asset cases from utilizing the cramdown provisions of the Code. In single-asset bankruptcy cases, the creditor-mortgagee usually has an unsecured deficiency claim, which, if placed in the class containing other unsecured claims (usually trade debt), will often overwhelm the class. Consequently, the mortgagee will control the vote of the class and the debtor will be unable to present an impaired class to approve the plan. Debtor suggests that such an outcome creates a "conflict of interest": the mortgage creditor will vote its deficiency claim primarily to protect its interests as a secured creditor, whereas only those creditors who have truly unsecured claims should be the spokespeople of the unsecured class.

Debtor's arguments in support of its suggested interpretation of § 1122 are unavailing. First, the ruling in *In re D & W Realty Corp.*, 156 B.R. 140 (Bankr.S.D.N.Y.1993) was reversed on appeal. *In re D & W Realty Corp.*, 165 B.R. 127 (S.D.N.Y.1994). The ruling in *In re SM 104 Ltd.*, 160 B.R. 202 (Bankr.S.D.Fla.1993), runs counter to the overwhelming weight of judicial authority. All the circuit courts that have heretofore visited the question of when similar claims may be classified separately have held that similar claims may not be separately classified separately solely to engineer an assenting impaired class:

> [I]f § 1122(a) permits classification of "substantially similar" claims in different classes, such classification may only be undertaken for reasons independent of the debtor's motivation to secure the vote of an impaired, assenting class of claims. *Greystone III*, 995 F.2d 1274,

1279 (5th Cir.1991), cert. denied, 506 U.S. 821, 113 S.Ct. 72, 121 L.Ed.2d 37 (1992);

[A]lthough separate classification of similar claims may not be prohibited, it "may only be undertaken for reasons independent of the debtor's motivation to secure the vote of an impaired, assenting class of claims." *Travelers Ins. Co. v. Bryson Properties, XVIII (In re Bryson Properties XVIII)* 961 F.2d 496, 502 (4th Cir.)(quoting *Greystone III*, 995 F.2d at 1279), *cert. denied*, 506 U.S. 866, 113 S.Ct. 191, 121 L.Ed.2d 134 (1992);

[I]f the classifications are designed to manipulate class voting * * *, the plan cannot be confirmed. *Olympia & York Florida Equity Corp. v. Bank of New York (In re Holywell Corp.)*, 913 F.2d 873, 880 (11th Cir.1990);

The debtor's discretion to place similar claims in different classes is not unlimited, however. Classifications designed to manipulate class voting must be carefully scrutinized. There is potential for abuse when the debtor has the power to classify creditors in a manner to assure that at least one class of impaired creditors will vote for the plan, thereby making it eligible for the cram down provisions. *Hanson v. First Bank of South Dakota, N.A.*, 828 F.2d 1310, 1313 (8th Cir.1987);

Unless there is some requirement of keeping similar claims together, nothing would stand in the way of a debtor seeking out a few impaired creditors (or even one such creditor) who will vote for the plan and placing them in their own class. *Teamsters Nat. Freight Industry Negotiating Comm. v. U.S. Truck Co. (In re U.S. Truck Co.)*, 800 F.2d 581, 586 (6th Cir.1986).

Indeed, some courts have gone even further, holding that a plan must classify all substantially similar claims together, regardless of the debtor's intent. *See Granada Wines, Inc. v. New England Teamsters and Trucking Indus. Pension Fund*, 748 F.2d 42, 46 (1st Cir.1984).

The preeminent case on the question is *Greystone III*, a case whose facts are quite similar to those in the instant case before the court. In *Greystone III*, the Court of Appeals for the Fifth Circuit observed that although similar claims may be placed in different classes, a wholly permissive reading of the statute would render subsection (b) of § 1122, which specifically allows classification of small claims, superfluous. In widely quoted language, the Fifth Circuit concluded:

[There is] one clear rule that emerges from otherwise muddled case on § 1122 claims classification: thou shalt not classify similar claims differently in order to gerrymander an affirmative vote on a reorganization plan.

Greystone III, 995 F.2d at 1279.

Furthermore, contrary to Debtor's position, several courts have concluded that an analysis of legislative history in fact sheds little light onto the meaning of Section 1122. *See U.S. Truck*, 800 F.2d at 585–86 (concluding, after careful analysis of the classification sections of the former Bankruptcy Act and legislative history of Section 1122, that "Congress has sent mixed signals on the issue"); *In re Jersey City Medical Center*, 817 F.2d 1055, 1060 (3d Cir.1987)(noting that "the legislative history behind § 1122 is inconclusive" regarding the significance of the wording of the section). Moreover, a reading of Section 1122 in the context of the rest of the Code suggests that discretionary separate classification of similar claims would undermine the Section 1111(b) election. As explained above, Section 1111(b) of the Bankruptcy Code permits an undersecured creditor to choose whether (i) its claim should be divided into a secured claim equal to the court-determined value of the collateral and an unsecured claim for the deficiency, or (ii) its entire claim should be considered secured. The purpose of the Section 1111(b) election is to allow the undersecured creditor to weigh in its vote with the votes of the other unsecured creditors. Allowing the unsecured trade creditors to constitute their own class would effectively nullify the option that Congress provided to undersecured creditors to vote their deficiency as unsecured debt.

Finally, approving a plan that aims to disenfranchise the overwhelmingly largest creditor through artificial classification is simply inconsistent with the principles underlying the Bankruptcy Code. A key premise of the Code is that creditors holding greater debt should have a comparably greater voice in reorganization. Thus, although Debtor protests that prohibiting it from separating the unsecured claim of the FDIC from those of its trade creditors will effectively bar single asset debtors from utilizing the Code's cramdown provisions, Debtor fails to persuade that a single-asset debtor *should* be able to cramdown a plan that is designed to disadvantage its overwhelmingly largest creditor. Chapter 11 is far better served by allowing those creditors with the largest unsecured claims to have a significant degree of input and participation in the reorganization process, since they stand to gain or lose the most from the reorganization of the debtor. This Court thus holds that separate classification of unsecured claims solely to create an impaired assenting class will not be permitted; the debtor must adduce credible proof of a legitimate reason for separate classification of similar claims.

In the instant case, Debtor was unable and failed to adduce credible proof of any legitimate reason for segregating the FDIC's unsecured claim from the unsecured claims of BPR's trade creditors. Debtor's reasons for why it should have been permitted to separately classify the FDIC's unsecured claim were: (1) the FDIC's and the trade creditors' unsecured claims were created from different circumstances and arise under different Bankruptcy Code sections; and (2) BPR's future viability as a business depends on treating its trade creditors more favorably than the FDIC. Neither is availing. The different origins of the FDIC's unsecured deficiency claim and general unsecured trade claims, claims which enjoy similar rights and privileges within the Bankruptcy Code, do not alone justify separate segregation. *See* Meltzer, *supra* at 299. More importantly, BPR has failed to present any evidence of a legitimate business reason for the separate classification of similarly situated unsecured creditor claimants. The trade creditors in Class 4 were few and consisted of a landscaper, property appraisers, rubbish removers, and accountants. None were essential to BPR's future. Both lower courts accordingly found an absence of a valid justification for the isolation of the FDIC deficiency claim. No evidence to the contrary was adduced.

B. The residential security holders are not a class entitled to vote on the Plan.

Debtor classified the residential tenants whose security deposits it was holding as a separate and "impaired" class for the purposes of a cramdown under § 1129(a). In fact those interests were not harmed at all by the Plan, but are better off under the Plan. Under Connecticut law, residential security holders are entitled to interest on their security deposits at a rate of 5 and ¼%. Conn. Gen. Stat. § 47a–21 (1993). Under the proposed Plan, the interest payable on security deposits held by the landlord was increased beyond the statutory rate to 8%.

Debtor urges that the word "impaired" in § 1124 be interpreted merely as "altered" or "changed" and contends that the Class 3 creditors' rights were certainly altered by the Plan. In support of its interpretation of § 1124, Debtor points first to the language of the statute, legislative history, and a recent Ninth Circuit opinion, *In re L & J Anaheim Assoc.*, 995 F.2d 940 (9th Cir.1993), which allegedly adopted Debtor's interpretation of Section 1124.

This Court need not even reach the issue of whether an "altered" claim may qualify as "impaired." In this case, the Class 3 tenant security depositors could not constitute a voting class of creditors for purposes of effecting cramdown. Any claim for return of tenant security deposits would arise from the lease between the debtor and the tenant. Under the Bankruptcy Code, unexpired leases must be assumed or rejected by the Debtor. 11 U.S.C. § 365. When, as in the instant case, the Debtor does neither, the leases continue in effect and the lessees have no provable claim against the bankruptcy estate. *Greystone III*, 995 F.2d at 1281. The obligations assumed by the debtor under the continued leases constitute post-petition administrative claims. *See* 11 U.S.C. § 503(b)(1)(A). Such administrative claims are defined as priority claims under 11 U.S.C. § 507(a)(1), and must be paid in full in cash pursuant to 11 U.S.C. § 1129(a)(9)(A); their holders are not entitled to vote on a plan of reorganization. As the Fifth Circuit held in *Greystone III*:

> A debtor in Chapter 11 must either assume or reject its leases with third parties. 11 U.S.C. § 365. If the debtor does neither, the leases continue in effect and the lessees have no provable claim against the bankruptcy estate. *See Matter of Whitcomb & Keller Mortgage Co.*, 715 F.2d 375, 378–79 (7th Cir.1983); *In re Cochise College Park, Inc.*, 703 F.2d 1339, 1352 (9th Cir.1983). Under the

Code, only creditors are entitled to vote on a plan of reorganization. *See* 11 U.S.C. § 1126(c). A party to a lease is considered a "creditor" who is allowed to vote, 11 U.S.C. § 1126(c), only when the party has a claim against the estate that arises from rejection of a lease. *In re Perdido Motel Group, Inc.*, 101 B.R. 289, 293–94 (Bankr.N.D.Ala.1989). If, however, the debtor expressly assumes a lease, the lessee has no "claim" against the debtor under § 1126(a). See 11 U.S.C. §§ 365(g), 502(g). The rights created by assumption of the lease constitute a post petition administrative claim under section 503(b)(1)(A) of the Code. *LJC Corp. v. Boyle*, 768 F.2d 1489, 1494 n. 6 (D.C.Cir.1985). The holder of such a claim is not entitled to vote on a plan of reorganization. 11 U.S.C. § 1126(a); *In re Distrigas Corp.*, 66 B.R. 382, 385–86 (Bankr.D.Mass.1986); *Greystone III*, 995 F.2d at 1281. *See also In re Cantonwood Assocs. Ltd. Partnership*, 138 B.R. 648, 656 (Bankr.D.Mass.1992)(where Debtor neither assumes nor rejects leases, tenants' claims are post-petition administrative claims). Thus the Class 3 creditors' approval of the Plan was of no effect because its members were not entitled to vote on the Plan.

CONCLUSION

To summarize: Debtor's Plan of Reorganization was properly denied confirmation for lack of the assent of an impaired non-insider class of creditors. The unsecured trade creditors do not qualify as such a class; they were segregated without any demonstrated legitimate reason from like unsecured creditors, who rejected the Plan and whose claims predominated in amount over those of the trade creditors. Nor do residential security deposit holders qualify as such a class; as holders of administrative claims, they were not entitled to vote on the Plan of Reorganization.

Affirmed.

Problem 9–3

In the Action Auto plan presented at the outset of this chapter, could Sun Oil Company, which holds an unsecured claim in addition to its other claims, prevent confirmation of the plan by voting no and objecting to the classification of claims?

Problem 9–4

Expectations Ltd. owns a small hotel in Los Angeles. The value of the hotel is currently $7 million. London Bank holds a $10 million debt secured by the hotel. Expectation's only other creditors are various small trade creditors owed a total of $75,000 for goods delivered before the bankruptcy. Expectations designs a plan of reorganization with three classes of creditors. The first includes the London Bank's secured claim and provides for payment of the claim over six years at prime rate plus three percent. The second class consists of London Bank's unsecured deficiency. This will be paid in full with the same interest rate over a period of ten years, mostly in a balloon payment of $2 million at the end of the tenth year. The trade creditors are class three and receive payment in full without interest during the six months after confirmation. All prior shareholders of Expectations retain their shares of stock. Class three votes yes. London Bank votes no. What are London's best arguments for preventing confirmation of the plan? Will it succeed in doing so?

Problem 9–5

In a plan of a small steel company that is otherwise confirmable, Class 1, Trade Creditors with $5,000,000 of claims, will receive total payments of $5,000,000 without interest, payable over three years. Class 2, Other General Creditors, including certain note holders, will receive 50 percent of their claims payable plus 10 percent interest over five years.

Unhappy with their lot, the general creditors vote against the plan and argue that it cannot be approved for several reasons. First, they maintain they must be included in the same class with the trade creditors on the ground that each would share equally upon liquidation. Second, they maintain the plan is not fair and equitable because under 1129(b)(1) it "discriminates unfairly." Third, they argue the discrimination means the plan is not proposed in good faith and thus violates 1129(a)(3).

If you represented these creditors, how would you reply to the debtor's responses? Debtor's responses are as follows:

1. The present value of 90 percent over three years without interest is no different than 50 percent over five years with 10 percent.

2. Even if the present value of the two numbers were different, each exceeds liquidation value and therefore satisfies (a)(7). All 1129(b) prohibits is unfair discrimination. This discrimination is "fair" because continued success of the debtor depends upon having good relations with the continuing trade creditors, but not upon continuing good relations with the bondholders and other general creditors with whom it has no need or intention of dealing.

3. All section 1122(a) requires is that dissimilar claims be put in separate classes. It does not require that similar claims be put in the same class. The absence of such a requirement must mean that some discrimination is permissible.

Could the plan be justified under 1122(b) if a condition to be included in the trade creditor class was that each trade creditor accept a reduced amount?

Problem 9–6

James Corporation creditors include: Bank One, with a $750,000 debt secured by a lien on $610,000 in inventory; Bank Two, with a $55,000 unsecured debt representing the deficiency from a prior foreclosure; Supplier 1, with a $100,000 debt, consisting of $80,000 for supplies delivered prior to bankruptcy and $20,000 for supplies delivered after the bankruptcy; Supplier 2, with $100,000 prepetition supplies; IRS, with an income tax claim of $60,000 for income incurred in the year prior to the bankruptcy filing; J, who is a judgment creditor owed $400,000 based on a prebankruptcy fraud action; and Supplier 3, owed $800 for prebankruptcy delivery of goods. James Corporation has 1000 shareholders. It also owes $10,000 each to twelve creditors based on publicly traded bonds (promises by James Corporation to pay) that are "subordinate to all debt owed by James." You have been asked to devise the proper classifications for a plan to be proposed by James Corporation. Assume that the company would distribute .10 per dollar to unsecured creditors in a liquidation case. James has several questions:

a. If I wish to give a different percentage payment to Supplier 2 than to Bank Two, what rule would apply if they are in the same class? Would the rule be different if they were in different classes?

b. If at least one unsecured class of creditors must accept the plan, how many affirmative votes do I need by the creditors of that class in order to have a confirmable plan?

c. What is the minimum I can give to Supplier 1's postpetition claim in the plan? What about the IRS claim?

d. Having answered all of that, what classifications do you propose?

Note: Present Value

Sections 1129(b)(2) and 1325(a)(5)(B)(ii) require that the present value of the property to be distributed under the plan be not less than the allowed amount of the claim. The reason is clear—a dollar today is worth more than a dollar in a year or in five years. The formula for calculating present value is also relatively simple and straightforward.

$$PV = \frac{x}{(1 + i)^t}$$

where "PV" is present value, "i" is the interest or "discount" rate, and "t" is the number of years hence that the amount "x" will be paid.

For example, Madame LaFarge has a secured claim of $500,000, and the plan proposes to pay her $200,000 a year for 3 years, starting one year after confirmation. Assume a discount rate of 15%. Then the present value of what Madame LaFarge is to receive is calculated as follows:

$$PV = \frac{200{,}000}{(1 + .15)}.1 + \frac{200{,}000}{(1 + .15)}.2 + \frac{200{,}000}{(1 + .15)}.3 = 456{,}645$$

$$173{,}913 \qquad 151{,}229 \qquad 131{,}503$$

The present value is less than $500,000, the amount of Madame LaFarge's allowed claim, so the plan does not meet the standards of section 1129 or section 1325.

However, if the court used a different discount rate, say 8 or 9 percent, the present value would be greater than $500,000. Clearly a great deal depends on which discount rate is used. The court determines the discount rate, and various cases have used a number of different approaches, including the stated contract rate, the prime rate, the legal rate of interest, and the rate for three month Treasury notes.

Collier takes the position that deferred payment amounts to a coerced loan, and therefore that the discount rate ought to correspond to the "market interest rate," that is, the rate which the creditor would charge on a loan to a third party with similar terms, duration, collateral and risk. One case which has used this approach is *Memphis Bank and Trust v. Whitman*, 692 F.2d 427 (6th Cir.1982): "The most appropriate current interest rate is the current market rate for similar loans at the time the new loan is made, not some other unrelated, arbitrary rate" (at 431). The court said that a bankruptcy court can deviate from the market rate, but only if it has good reason. Often courts add one or two interest rate points to the "market" rate to compensate a creditor for its "greater" risk.

Other courts have used considerably lower discount rates on the grounds that "the court is not aiming to produce a lender's profit but only to protect the creditor from loss caused by its being paid over a period of time." *General Motors Acceptance Corp. v. Lum, (In re Lum)*, 1 B.R. 186, 188 (Bankr.E.D.Tenn.1979). The court used the legal rate of interest (the rate allowed on judgments), which was 8%, and adjusted it upward to 10% because of economic conditions.

An interest rate can be divided into two components: 1) the "riskless rate," which is set by the rate for U.S. Treasury bills or similar obligations and merely compensates the lender for the delay in receipt of the principal and 2) the risk rate, which compensates for the risk that the lender will not get his money back. One of the problems with using the legal rate of interest is that it is often lower even than the "riskless rate."

However, there are also difficulties associated with trying to define the risk component of the interest rate. It is easy to say that one ought to use a market rate, but is a loan to the debtor riskier or less risky than a loan to someone else? The debtor is insolvent, it is true; on the other hand, it has a plan for regaining solvency.

A fear of driving the debtor to liquidation may accompany the court's concern about overcompensating the creditor, and these factors sometimes lead the court to decide on low discount rates as well.

§ 5. REQUIREMENTS FOR CONFIRMATION, THE HEART OF SECTION 1129

If all classes and individuals accept the reorganization plan or are unimpaired by the plan, section 1129 proposes few restraints on the terms of any plan. If one or more *individual claimholders* do not accept, however, the "best interest" test of 1129 must be met as to those claimholders. If one or more *classes* of claims do not accept, a "cramdown" requires that the plan not discriminate unfairly and that it be "fair and equitable". In addition, of course, every plan must be "feasible." The three requirements, feasibility, equity, and best interest, are the most significant limitations. The other sections of 1129 contain provisions that will occasionally be critical, but much less frequently the subject of debate than the three we list here.

Section 1129(a)(7)'s best interest test protects individual dissenting claimants by requiring that each claimholder receive property equal in value to the amount that creditor would receive in a Chapter 7 liquidation of the debtor. There is a similar rule in Chapter 12 and Chapter 13. One demonstrates compliance with the best interest test through a liquidation analysis that shows the value of the debtor's assets, secured claims against those assets, the priority claims against those assets, and a calculation of the percent distribution to each type of claim including the general creditors. Necessarily, liquidation analysis involves judgment and even speculation about the liquidation value of various assets. To reiterate, the best interest test applies to individual creditors and is the principal protection of an individual dissenter who is included in a class with others and outvoted by his class members.

If a class, as opposed to an individual, rejects a plan, section 1129(a)(8) is not met, and the plan can be approved over the objection of that class only by satisfying the fair and equitable requirements contained in section 1129(b). That section allows confirmation, despite the rejection of one or more classes:

> If the plan does not discriminate unfairly, and it is fair and equitable, with respect to each class of claims or interest that is impaired under, and has not accepted, the plan.

Section 1129(b)(1). The Code defines what is "fair and equitable" differently for secured creditors than for others.

Section 1129(b)(2)(A) provides three alternative standards for the cramdown of a plan over the objection of a class of secured creditors. The most common way to meet that test is for the plan to allow the secured creditors to retain their liens on the secured property and to receive cash payments with the face amount of at least the allowed amount of the claim and a present value equal to the value of their collateral.

Unsecured creditors look for protection in section 1129(b)(2)(B). The provisions of that subsection require that the unsecured creditor be paid in full or that "the holder of any claim or interest that is junior to [the critical class] * * * not receive or retain under the plan on account of such unit, claim or interest, any property." In effect, this says that the shareholders can take nothing from a plan if a class of unsecured creditors votes against it or it is not paid in full. This is a powerful weapon in the negotiation of a plan, and one that no debtor dares ignore.

Section 1129(a)(11) requires that the plan be "not likely to be followed by liquidation or the need for further financial reorganization". This is the feasibility requirement. It requires the court to conclude, at least if the plan is challenged, that the debtor has the financial resources to carry out the plan and that the projections and other assumptions made by the debtor in constructing this plan are plausible and will permit the events predicted in the plan to come to pass. Needless to say, the bankruptcy court has enormous discretion in determining what is and what is not feasible. We suspect that one judge's feasibility is another's impossible dream. Thus, this requirement might have a great deal of bite in certain jurisdictions and very little in others. Those certain to benefit from feasibility litigation are expert witnesses on business finance.

IN RE MONNIER BROS.

United States Court of Appeals, Eighth Circuit, 1985.
755 F.2d 1336.

HENLEY, SENIOR CIRCUIT JUDGE.

These appeals are from a decision of the District Court for the District of South Dakota modifying and affirming the bankruptcy court's confirmation of a chapter 11 reorganization plan. Debtors (Monnier Brothers, a partnership consisting of Alan Dale Monnier and Thomas Richard Monnier; and Alan Dale Monnier and Thomas Richard Monnier and their wives, as individuals) appeal from the district court's decision to increase the rate at which interest on debtors' secured indebtedness to Prudential Insurance Company would accrue during operation of the plan. Prudential contends in a cross appeal that the plan ought not to have been confirmed, urging that (1) the plan does not give "adequate protection" to Prudential's secured interest; (2) the plan is not feasible; and (3) the plan is unfair and inequitable, and discriminates against Prudential. For reasons to be stated, we affirm.

Debtors are farmers. Prudential loaned debtors $800,000 on May 16, 1981. The loan was evidenced by a note, and secured by a mortgage upon farmland debtors own in Deuel County, South Dakota. By the terms of the note and mortgage, interest on the Prudential loan would accrue at a rate of thirteen percent per annum, and at a rate of fifteen percent per annum on overdue installments. The term of the loan was fifteen years, although Prudential could shorten this term after giving notice to the borrowers. The first installment of principal was due on June 1, 1983. Debtors failed to make this principal payment, having filed their original chapter 11 petitions in the United States Bankruptcy Court for the District of South Dakota on January 3, 1983.

Prudential then requested the bankruptcy court to modify the automatic stay of 11 U.S.C. § 362, so that Prudential might begin state foreclosure proceedings. After a hearing, the bankruptcy court denied Prudential's request for modification of the stay. The bankruptcy court determined that the fair market value of the Deuel County property was $1,356,000; that as of March 1, 1983, debtors' total indebtedness to Prudential, including accrued interest, had been $1,012,209.63; that continued use of the property by debtors was essential to successful reorganization; and that the "equity cushion of approximately $300,000.00" would provide adequate protection for Prudential during the preconfirmation period.

Subsequently, the bankruptcy court confirmed the plan over Prudential's objections. (Ten other classes of creditors, most of them holding fully secured claims, had accepted the plan.) The confirmed plan described how and when each claim would be repaid, and made predictions as to 1983 crop yields, crop prices, and expenses. The plan provided for an initial payment by debtors of $75,000 toward accrued interest then owing on the Prudential debt. The plan also called for the remaining indebtedness to Prudential to be repaid in level amortized installments over a fifteen year period. Under the confirmed plan, interest was to accrue on the Prudential claim for periods prior to the confirmation date at the default rate set by the note and mortgage, and thereafter at a 10.5 percent rate (the December, 1983 United States treasury bill annual investment yield discount factor). Because the plan did not provide for immediate payment in cash of Prudential's claim, and because Prudential opposed the plan, the district court, at debtors' request, invoked the "cram down" provisions of chapter 11 to confirm the plan. 11 U.S.C. § 1129(b).

Prudential then sought review in the district court. The district court affirmed confirmation of the plan, but reversed the bankruptcy court's order of confirmation "insofar as the order fixes the interest rate that is paid The Prudential Insurance Company of America to be 10.5% rather than the 13% rate set out in the mortgage." The present appeals followed.

1. INTEREST RATE

* * *

Under § 1129(b)(2)(A)(i)(II), deferred cash payments due Prudential must total "a value, as of the effective date of the plan, of at least the value of [Prudential's] interest in the estate's interest in" the collateral. Since the Prudential loan was accelerated and oversecured, Prudential had a right at the date the plan became effective to the unpaid principal plus any contract rate interest that had accrued up until that time. The task of the bankruptcy court was to determine what rate of interest would insure Prudential ultimately receive the full value of that amount, given that the plan provided for level amortized payments over a fifteen year period.

One of the Code's few clues about what factors to take into account in selecting an appropriate interest rate appears in § 1129(b)(2)(A)(iii); that section states that a plan may be confirmed over the objections of a secured creditor if the plan affords the creditor the "indubitable equivalent" of his claim. 11 U.S.C. § 1129(b)(2)(A)(iii). Legislative history indicates Congress intended for this phrase to take on the meaning given it by Judge Learned Hand in *In re Murel Holding Corp.*, 75 F.2d 941, 942 (2d Cir.1935). *See In re American Mariner Industries*, 734 F.2d 426, 433 (9th Cir.1984). As the Ninth Circuit has noted, *Murel* emphasized two factors in determining whether a reorganization plan provided a secured creditor adequate protection for the full value of his claim:

> Judge Hand concluded that the creditor's right to "get his money or at least the property" may be denied under a plan for reorganization only if the debtor provides a "substitute of the most indubitable

equivalence." Such *a substitute clearly must both compensate for present value and insure the safety of the principal.*

In re American Mariner Industries, 734 F.2d at 433 (emphasis added). Although § 1129(b)(2)(A)(iii), with its "indubitable equivalent" standard, is stated as an alternative to deferred repayment of the secured debt under § 1129(b)(2)(A)(i)(II), we are satisfied from a reading of *Murel* that the congressional reference to the case expresses threshold requirements applicable to selection of an appropriate interest rate. *Cf. In re American Mariner Industries,* 734 F.2d at 432 ("indubitable equivalent" provision of 11 U.S.C. § 361 is a "catch-all alternative").

In the present case, neither Prudential nor debtors provided the bankruptcy court with much assistance in determining what interest rate would compensate Prudential for the time value of its money and the risks to its principal. Prudential provided no evidence on the issue, other than the rate set by the contract. Debtors, relying on 5 *Collier on Bankruptcy* ¶ 1129.03, at 1129–63 n. 45, provided the bankruptcy court with the prime rate, federal fund rate, discount rate, call money rate, commercial paper rate, certificates of deposit rate, and treasury bill rate, that had been reported in the December 9, 1983 *Wall Street Journal.* The debtors ignored, however, a subsequent passage from the *Collier* discussion:

> The appropriate discount rate must be determined on the basis of the rate of interest which is reasonable in light of the risks involved. Thus, in determining the discount rate, the court must consider the prevailing market rate for a loan of a term equal to the payout period, with due consideration for the quality of the security and the risk of subsequent default.

5 *Collier on Bankruptcy* ¶ 1129, at 1129–65. We note that the treasury bill rate, which the bankruptcy court ultimately applied, reflected one rate of return available on a short term, low risk investment. *See In re Loveridge Machine & Tool Co.,* 36 B.R. 159 (Bankr.D.Utah 1983).

According to the "market value" appraisal of the Deuel County property, Prudential was, at the time the plan became effective oversecured, both with respect to principal and with respect to interest that had accrued under the contract. In these circumstances, we cannot say the district court erred in requiring interest to be paid under the plan at the contract rate. Only some twenty months had elapsed between the time the contract was made and the time the plan was confirmed; the contract, like the plan, contemplated a fifteen year payment term; and identical security was involved, since under the plan, Prudential retains a lien on the Deuel County property. In other words, the contract rate, which was a rate agreed upon in an arms length bargain between businessmen, presumably reflected the prevailing cost of money (at least as of May, 1981), the prospects for appreciation or depreciation of the value of the security, and the risks inherent in a long-term agricultural loan. Lacking any evidence correlating other rates with the "coerced loan" contemplated by the plan, the district court did not err in reinstating the contract rate of interest. *Cf. In re Southern States Motor Inns, Inc.,* 709 F.2d 647, 651–53 (11th Cir.1983)(error, in selecting interest rate applicable to deferred repayment under chapter 11 of tax claim, to ignore variations between the length of the payment period, quality of security, and the risk of subsequent default), *cert. denied,* 465 U.S. 1022, 104 S.Ct. 1275, 79 L.Ed.2d 680 (1984); *In re Loveridge Machine & Tool Co.,* 36 B.R. 159 (Bankr.D.Utah 1983)(in chapter 11 cram down, interest rate should consist of risk-free rate, plus additional interest to compensate creditor for risks posed by the plan).

2. Adequate Protection

Prudential argues that its interests were not adequately protected during the preconfirmation period, and will not be adequately protected during operation of the plan. In support of this argument, Prudential contends that the bankruptcy court erred in using the market value, rather than the liquidation value, of the Deuel County property in assessing the extent of the "equity cushion" available to protect Prudential. Prudential further argues that an equity cushion is not, in itself, sufficient protection for a secured creditor's interest; and that in any event the equity cushion in this case is too small to assure protection of Prudential over the life of the plan.

We note that "adequate protection" is not a standard the Bankruptcy Code uses in connection with confirmation decisions. Instead, the adequate protection requirements apply primarily in the context of preconfirmation proceedings. *See, e.g.,* 11 U.S.C. § 362(d). Insofar as Prudential now contends the plan is too risky, such concerns must be addressed in terms of the cram down standards of 11 U.S.C. § 1129(b), or the feasibility requirement of 11 U.S.C. § 1129(a)(11).

* * *

3. Feasibility

Section 1129(a)(11) provides that the court shall confirm a plan only if "[c]onfirmation * * * is not likely to be followed by liquidation, or the need for further financial reorganization, of the debtor * * * unless such further * * * reorganization is proposed in the plan." 11 U.S.C. § 1129(a)(11). Prudential argues that debtors' plan does not meet the § 1129(a)(11) feasibility requirement. Specifically, Prudential alleges that debtors' projected earnings and yields are overly optimistic; that the plan fails to take into account income taxes which will become due upon sale of crops; and that the district court's upward adjustment of the interest rate on the deferred repayment of the Prudential loan made the plan unworkable. Prudential also argues that debtors' disclosure statement showed projected expenses and plan payments for 1983 would exceed 1983 earnings by $100,000.

Construing feasibility requirements in the context of a plan of arrangement proposed under the Bankruptcy Act, this court stated: "[i]n determining whether [a plan] is feasible, the bankruptcy court has an obligation to scrutinize the plan carefully to determine whether it offers a reasonable prospect of success and is workable." *United Properties, Inc. v. Emporium Department Stores, Inc.*, 379 F.2d 55, 64 (8th Cir.1967). Success need not be guaranteed.

* * *

The bankruptcy court found that debtors' plan was feasible; and the district court, after considering briefs and hearing oral argument on the feasibility issue, affirmed the finding. We have carefully reviewed the record, and cannot say that the feasibility finding, as affirmed by the district court, was clearly erroneous. Projecting future income of, and expenses of, an extensive farming operation such as debtors' cannot be an exact science. The bankruptcy court heard evidence about the accuracy of debtors' crop yield and earnings projections, and reasonably resolved the conflicts in that evidence in debtors' favor. The plan states that "all taxes of any kind whatsoever will be paid at or before the same become due;" Prudential did not inquire into this matter during the many hearings on the plan, nor did Prudential present evidence of its own about the effect taxes might have. Similarly, aside from conclusory statements, Prudential has not attempted to show that the district court's adjustment of the interest rate on the Prudential claim made the plan unworkable. Prudential's predictions of a $100,000 shortfall in 1983 fail to take into account $225,000 from 1982 crop sales which the disclosure statement indicated would be applied toward 1983 expenses. It is true that during the first years the plan is in effect, the amount of such carry-over earnings will likely decrease, year by year; however, several debts will be discharged under the plan after five years, and payments due creditors under the plan will then decrease. It appears debtors operated within the bounds of their projections in 1983.

* * *

4. § 1129(b)(1)

Section 1129(b)(1) provides that before claims of a dissenting class of secured creditors may be "crammed down" by confirmation of a reorganization plan, the court must determine that the plan "does not discriminate unfairly, and is fair and equitable." 11 U.S.C. § 1129(b)(1). As Prudential notes, the "fair and equitable standard" includes, but is not limited to, the requirement under § 1129(b)(2) that the creditor receive the full value of his claim. Indeed, "fair and equitable" is a term of art, and means, among other things, that the plan must assure each creditor's claim is given appropriate priority. *See In re King Resources Co.*, 651 F.2d 1326, 1340 (10th Cir.1980). Prudential argues, essentially, that the fact that it is forced to wait longer than other creditors under the plan to receive full compensation for its claim makes the plan unfair, inequitable, and discriminatory.

We are not persuaded by this argument. When the proposed treatment of Prudential's claim is contrasted with treatment of other secured claims, no inequity or discrimination is apparent. The cram down provisions contemplate deferred repayment of secured loans. Prudential, like all other secured creditors under the plan, will receive repayment in level amortized payments over a fixed term of years. Prudential retains its lien; its original loan to debtors had a fifteen year term; and its collateral is not subject to rapid depreciation, unlike the machinery securing certain other debts the plan encompasses. When the proposed treatment of Prudential's claim is compared with treatment of unsecured claims, again no inequity or discrimination is apparent. The unsecured creditors will receive no interest, even though repayment of principal will be in level amortized payments over a ten year term; and the unsecured creditors retain no liens to protect them in the event of a default.

As indicated, the judgment of the district court is affirmed.

Questions

1. Do you think the debtor successfully completed the plan?

2. Would a reasonable and prudent lender have been indifferent between payment of cash in the principal amount at confirmation of the plan and receipt of the debtor's promise that was proposed under the plan? If not, the promise does not have present value equal to the principal value, correct?

MATTER OF D & F CONSTRUCTION INC.

United States Court of Appeals, Fifth Circuit, 1989.
865 F.2d 673.

CLARK, CHIEF JUDGE.

This is a Chapter 11 bankruptcy case. D & F Construction, Inc., ("the debtor"), proposed a Chapter 11 plan of reorganization to which only Mercury Savings Association of Texas and Ben Milam Savings and Loan Association ("Mercury/Milam") objected. The bankruptcy court confirmed the debtor's plan over Mercury/Milam's objection under the "cram-down" provisions of 11 U.S.C. § 1129(b). The district court affirmed. Mercury/Milam appeals. We reverse the judgment of the district court upholding the confirmation and remand with directions.

On August 29, 1984 Cimarron Properties Joint Venture ("Cimarron") obtained a $6.4 million construction loan from Mercury/Milam to purchase land and construct a 192–unit apartment complex in Fort Worth, Texas. The loan was evidenced by a one-year promissory note and was secured by a deed of trust, a financing statement, and an assignment of rents.

Cimarron purchased land and commenced construction, but was unable to complete the apartment complex. Richard Drummonds and David Ford agreed to complete the construction of the complex and formed the debtor corporation for that purpose. The debtor made an agreement with Mercury/Milam whereby it assumed the construction loan, acknowledged the security agreements, and received an additional $960,000 loan from Mercury/Milam. This loan was secured by a second lien on the complex. The debtor also executed a Net Profits Agreement with Mercury/Milam, which provided that Mercury/Milam and the debtor would split on a fifty-fifty basis (i) the net cash flow generated from the apartment complex, (ii) the net proceeds from significant events such as insurance awards and condemnation proceedings and (iii) any net proceeds received upon sale or refinancing of the apartment complex.

The debtor completed construction of the complex but failed to pay the construction loan upon expiration of its term. Mercury/Milam began foreclosure proceedings, and on October 6, 1986 the debtor filed a bankruptcy petition under Chapter 11 of the Bankruptcy Code. Mercury/Milam filed a proof of claim for approximately $7 million. The bankruptcy court valued the apartment complex at $5 million, and found that amortization of this amount at a ten percent (10%) annual interest rate would provide Mercury/Milam with the present value of its security. In December 1986, Mercury/Milam filed an election under 11 U.S.C. § 1111(b) to treat the entire amount of its claim as secured.

The debtor filed a plan of reorganization on February 23, 1987. The plan provided for Mercury/Milam's secured claim as follows: (i) Mercury/Milam's liens on the apartment complex would be evidenced by a new deed of trust; (ii) the Net Profits Agreement would be rejected and Mercury/Milam would instead receive one-half of any net proceeds from the sale of the complex for an amount in excess of its claim; (iii) Mercury/Milam would be paid the $5 million present value of its security over a fifteen-year period with interest at the rate of 10% per annum on the unpaid balance. The plan provided for increasing monthly payments during the fifteen-year period beginning at $30,000 and increasing to $47,500 for years six through fifteen. Initially the monthly payments would be insufficient to cover the interest accruing, so at the end of the fourth year the amount owed to Mercury/Milam would increase from $5 million to $5,350,875.39. Ensuing payments would begin then to reduce the principal, but not until the end of the twelfth year would the amount owed fall below $5 million. At the end of the fifteenth year more than $4.7 million would still be owed, and the plan provided for a balloon payment of $4,740,980.19 on April 15, 2002.

The plan specified that Mercury/Milam had no unsecured claim because of the § 1111(b) election. The plan also contained provisions for the payment of five other classes of claims totalling less than $100,000, and allowed Messrs. Drummonds and Ford to purchase 100% of the stock in the reorganized debtor for $10,000.

The bankruptcy court confirmed the debtor's plan over Mercury/Milam's objections. The district court upheld the confirmation, and Mercury/Milam appeals.

Section 1129(b)(1) of the bankruptcy code provides that a debtor may "cram down" its plan over the objection of a creditor "if the plan does not discriminate unfairly, and is fair and equitable with respect to each class of claims or interests that is impaired under, and has not accepted, the plan." 11 U.S.C. § 1129(b)(1). Section 1129(b)(2) then sets forth requirements which must be met for a plan to be "fair and equitable." A plan which does not meet the standards set forth in § 1129(b)(2) cannot be "fair and equitable." However, technical compliance with all the requirements in § 1129(b)(2) does not assure that the plan is "fair and equitable." 5 Collier on Bankruptcy ¶ 1129.03 at 1129–52 (15th ed. 1988). Section 1129(b)(2) merely states that "the condition that a plan be fair and equitable with respect to a class *includes* the following requirements * * *." 11 U.S.C. § 1129(b)(2)(emphasis added). Section 102(3) of the bankruptcy code states that the word "includes" is not limiting. 11 U.S.C. § 102(3). The sponsors of the Bankruptcy Reform Act of 1978 noted:

> Although many of the factors interpreting 'fair and equitable' are specified in paragraph (2), others, which were explicated in the description of section 1129(b) in the House report, were omitted from the House amendment to avoid statutory complexity and because they would undoubtedly be found by a court to be fundamental to 'fair and equitable' treatment of a dissenting class.

124 Cong.Rec. 32,407 (1978). Section 1129(b)(2) sets minimal standards plans must meet. However, it is not to be interpreted as requiring that every plan not prohibited be approved. A court must consider the entire plan in the context of the rights of the creditors under state law and the particular facts and circumstances when determining whether a plan is "fair and equitable." *See In re Spanish Lake Associates,* 92 B.R. 875, 878 (Bankr.E.D.Mo.1988); *In re Edgewater Motel, Inc.,* 85 B.R. 989, 998 (Bankr.E.D.Tenn.1988).

Assuming without deciding that the requirements set forth in § 1129(b)(2) are literally met, the debtor's plan is neither fair nor equitable. Mercury/Milam did not lend its credit to this project on the strength of Cimarron's fiscal integrity nor that of the debtor. It furnished the funds that paid for constructing the apartments on the basis that it be given a right under Texas law to recover its funds from the land and improvements if they could not be repaid as promised. The debtor and all other creditors are bound to have recognized this situation when they contributed their time and goods. Yet, under the plan, Mercury/Milam cannot exercise the foreclosure rights it reserved. In addition, the plan's negative amortization requires that for the first twelve years Mercury/Milam increase its financing of this project and thus assume a worse financial position than it was in at the time of confirmation. The net effect of negative amortization is to force Mercury/Milam to make a post-confirmation loan to the debtor for a period of twelve years.

We do not hold there can never be an occasion when negative amortization would be fair and equitable. We do say this plan is not fair and equitable. Negative amortization coupled with deferring substantially all repayment of principal for fifteen years can only be considered reasonable if one speculates that the present condition of the Fort Worth, Texas real estate market will improve substantially. While this speculation may be wholly acceptable from the standpoint of the debtor and the other classes of creditors, it is an altogether impermissible speculation from the standpoint of Mercury/Milam which is effectively denied access to the security it contracted for during the next fifteen years and must furnish further funding to the project.

A plan that is not fair and equitable with respect to an impaired secured creditor cannot be confirmed on the basis that such inequity is necessary to protect junior creditors. If market conditions are such that an effective plan of reorganization cannot be developed that is fair and equitable to dissenting creditors, Mercury/Milam is entitled to foreclose on its liens. *In re Timbers of Inwood Forest Associates, Ltd.*, 808 F.2d 363 (5th Cir.1987), *aff'd*, 484 U.S. 365, 108 S.Ct. 626, 98 L.Ed.2d 740 (1988).

Without deciding whether the debtor's plan might meet the literal requirements of § 1129(b)(2), we held that it is not fair and equitable as to Mercury/Milam. This holding makes it unnecessary to reach Mercury/Milam's other arguments.

The judgment of the district court is reversed with directions to vacate the order of the bankruptcy court confirming the debtor's plan and remand the estate to the bankruptcy court for further proceedings not inconsistent with this opinion.

REVERSED AND REMANDED WITH DIRECTIONS.

Questions

1. What is "negative amortization"?

2. Where dozens, perhaps even hundreds of plans could be proposed, how does one decide whether a particular judge will regard a particular plan as "fair and equitable"?

3. Once one gets beyond basic rules explicitly stated in 1129(b), what should be the touchstone? Risk? Security? Reasonable expectations?

Problem 9–7

Uriah Heep Company declared bankruptcy on June 12, 1990. The shareholders of the company are primarily the employees. Heep wanted to provide something for those shareholders and wanted to give as little as possible to one of the unsecured creditors, Scrooge, with a $150,000 claim. Scrooge was privately suing Heep as CEO on a separate matter. After consultation with local financial institutions, Heep proposes the following plan. You may assume that everyone will vote for the plan except for Scrooge.

Copperfield Bank: $1,000,000 claim, $1,000,000 collateral, plan $900,000 cash. Secured creditor No. 2: $500,000 claim, $450,000 collateral, $450,000 present value payable over two years. Local junior creditors (10 creditors) with unsecured claims totaling $500,000 will receive $500,000 present value payments over five years. Twelve other unsecured creditors with claims totaling $250,000 (including Scrooge's $150,000), receive $150,000 without interest over two years. Shareholders retain their shares.

If you represent Scrooge, how do you object? Which objections are likely to be successful?

Assume on liquidation the unsecured creditors would receive a 50 percent dividend.

Note: The 1111(b)(2) Election To Be Treated as a Fully Secured Creditor

Section 1111(b)(2) reads in full as follows, "If such an election is made, then notwithstanding section 506(a) of this title, such claim is a secured claim to the extent that such claim is allowed." Rule 3014 allows the eligible creditor to elect application of this section any time prior to the conclusion of the disclosure statement hearing unless the court decides to fix a later time. On first reading the subsection is incomprehensible. Unfortunately the section does not become much more comprehensible on successive readings. For one of the drafters' ideas on its meaning, *See,* Klee, *All You Ever Wanted to Know About Cramdown Under the New Bankruptcy Code,* 53 AM Bankr.L.J. 133 (1979).

In a sense the section is designed to allow an "undersecured" secured creditor to be treated as a fully secured creditor in a Chapter 11 proceeding. The section's workings can best be explained by an example. Assume a case in which the creditor has a claim of $2,000,000 and has a perfected security interest in real estate that the court has valued at $1,000,000 and would have a claim as an unsecured creditor to the extent of $1,000,000. If there was a payment of 10% to the unsecured creditors, our hypothetical creditor would receive $100,000 in liquidation of the $1,000,000 unsecured portion of his claim and continue to have a security interest in the land (and presumably ultimately be paid a $1,000,000) on his $1,000,000 secured claim. If the real estate appreciated radically in value in the year following the confirmation and was thereafter sold for $3,000,000 our hypothetical creditor would still receive only $1,000,000 on his secured claim because the remainder of his claim would have been discharged as an unsecured claim.

If, however, our undersecured creditor had exercised his section 1111(b)(2) election, he would in effect have waived any right to distribution on the unsecured portion of his claim. He would instead have been treated as a secured creditor to the full extent of his $2,000,000 claim. Under the provisions of section 1129, he would have to receive deferred cash payments totalling at least $2,000,000 with a present value of at least $1,000,000 (the value of his collateral) assuming the "indubitable equivalence" option is not taken.

Because the creditor surrenders any claim to a deficiency when he elects the 1111(b)(2) option, he is likely to make the election in circumstances in which he believes the court has undervalued the collateral or in which he believes the collateral will appreciate substantially in the period following the confirmation. The most likely case for such an election would involve real estate where the creditor might conclude that market factors of short duration have caused the court to impose the low value. Nevertheless even the creditor who correctly predicts the trend of the market faces the possibility that his deferred cash payments under the plan may be extended so far in the future that their present value is very little more than the $1,000,000 secured claim.

Two limitations on the creditor's right to elect application of 1111(b)(2) are specified in 1111(b)(1)(B). If a creditor's interest in his collateral is of "inconsequential value", he is not permitted to elect 1111(b)(2) treatment. A common example of this situation is where the creditor holds a third mortgage on property already securing first and second mortgages greater than the value of the property. In addition, if the creditor is a recourse creditor, he may not elect 1111(b)(2) treatment if the property will be sold during the proceedings or under the plan because in that instance he would be permitted to bid in the full amount of his claim at such a sale.

Problem 9–8

Pip Transportation has filed in Chapter 11. Chuzzlewit Bank has a $7,000,000 claim secured by several truck and warehouse facilities owned by the debtor with a present value of $5,000,000. Marley Bank and Trust has a secured loan against the freight company's trucks. The ten trucks are currently valued at $1,000,000. They secure a $2,000,000 debt owed to the bank. Various other creditors have claims that total $250,000.

1.(a) Suppose that Pip will pay the secured portion of everyone's claim in full ($5,000,000 to Chuzzlewit and $1,000,000 to Marley) and will pay only one percent of the unsecured claims (one percent represents the court's estimation of liquidation value). Should the secured creditors elect 1111(b)(2)? Do you see what they will give up if they make that election?

(b) What if the court valued Pip's liquidation value such that Pip could pay 70 percent of its unsecured claims?

2. Suppose Chuzzlewit Bank elects 1111(b) and Pip agrees to make payments to Chuzzlewit over a four year period with a present value of $5,000,000 consisting of total payments of $7,000,000 in 48 equal monthly installments. Chuzzlewit argues that the interest payment cannot be included in arriving at the $7,000,000 of total payment. Is it correct?

3. Assume that the plan proposed in 2 is approved. Pip makes total payments of $3,500,000 over two years to Chuzzlewit Bank and then, by a stroke of luck and because of change in the market, is able to sell the working facilities for $8,000,000 cash. How much of that cash goes to Chuzzlewit?

    a. $2,000,000?

    b. $1,500,000?

    c. $3,500,000?

    d. Some larger amount, because interest must be deducted from earlier payments?

4. Chuzzlewit believes that its collateral has been mostly undervalued and that should affect the 1111(b)(2) election, correct?

5. What if Pip sells the property one month after the deal has been made and allows the buyer to take "subject to" the existing mortgage of Chuzzlewit Bank. Can Chuzzlewit complain about that? Do you see why it might want to?

6. Can Pip include a term in the plan that would guarantee Chuzzlewit Bank a total of $7,000,000 plus interest if the land is sold any time within the next 10 years for more than $7,000,000?

Problem 9–9

Twist Refinery owns a refinery and associated real estate in Alabama. The refinery has an uncertain value which you estimate to be around $17 million, give or take $2 million. London Bank's first lien on the refinery is for $17 million. The second lien, held by Paris Savings is for $7 million. Twist also holds an inventory of oil, imported from Nigeria, several valuable oil purchase contracts, and several oil sales agreements with major corporations. While these assets all have value, if they were liquidated the total value of all assets today would be no more than $23 million. That is because the value in the contracts probably could not be saved by assignment. Twist has $1 million of unsecured debt spread among 150 creditors.

You represent one of the unsecured creditors. Twist's president gives you three options to support: (1) liquidate the company today, (2) cram down on the secured creditors, pay all unsecureds thirty cents per dollar, and leave the current shareholders as owners, or (3) cram down on the secured creditors and give 100 percent of ownership to the unsecured class on a pro rata basis, but no payment on their debt.

To compare the options, your client would have to make an estimate of the present value, if any, that would come to it as the owner of the company. To do that, it would have to make some assumptions about the earning capacity of the business. What would be the minimum earning capacity to cause your client to opt for number 3, as opposed to number 1 or number 2, among the alternatives?

§ 6. NEW VALUE

We have already met the absolute priority rule, the version of the fair and equitable doctrine that applies to unsecured creditors. We have learned that this rule prohibits the shareholders from keeping any of their shares if there is a dissenting class of unsecured creditors that is not paid in full. Both before and after the enactment of the Code in 1978, some courts recognized the right of shareholders to purchase equity interests for "new value" even though the absolute priority rule would have prohibited their retention of such interests. The continued vitality of that rule after the Code's adoption is in doubt.

The Supreme Court has held that an owner of a business cannot retain ownership under cramdown rules by merely promising to contribute "sweat equity" to the company, that is, by continuing to work in the business. The Court reserved ruling on whether the new value exception continues under the Bankruptcy Code. *Norwest Bank Worthington v. Ahlers,* 485 U.S. 197, 203 n. 3, 108 S.Ct. 963, 967 n. 3, 99 L.Ed.2d 169 (1988):

> The United States, as *amicus curiae,* urges us to reverse the Court of Appeals ruling and hold that codification of the absolute

priority rule has eliminated any "exception" to that rule suggested by *Los Angeles Lumber,* 308 U.S. 106 (1939). See Brief for United States as *Amicus Curiae* 17–23. Relying on the statutory language and the legislative history, the Solicitor General argues that the 1978 Bankruptcy Code "dropped the infusion-of-new-capital exception to the absolute priority rule." Id. at 22.

We need not reach this question to resolve the instant dispute. * * * [W]e think it clear that even if the *Los Angeles Lumber* exception to the absolute priority rule has survived enactment of the Bankruptcy Code, this exception does not encompass respondents' promise to contribute their "labor, experience, and expertise" to the reorganized enterprise.

Thus, our decision today should not be taken as any comment on the continuing vitality of the *Los Angeles Lumber* exception—a question which has divided the lower courts since passage of the Code in 1978. * * * Rather, we simply conclude that even if an "infusion-of-money or money's worth" exception to the absolute priority rule has survived the enactment of § 1129(b), respondents' proposed contribution to the reorganization plan is inadequate to gain the benefit of this exception. (citations omitted).

IN RE BONNER MALL PARTNERSHIP

United States Court of Appeals, Ninth Circuit, 1993.
2 F.3d 899.

REINHARDT, CIRCUIT JUDGE.

This case requires us to decide whether the new value "exception" to the absolute priority rule survives the enactment of the Bankruptcy Reform Act of 1978 (better known as the Bankruptcy Code), which replaced the Bankruptcy Act of 1898. The new value exception allows the shareholders of a corporation in bankruptcy to obtain an interest in the reorganized debtor in exchange for new capital contributions over the objections of a class of creditors that has not received full payment on its claims. Whether this doctrine is viable under the Bankruptcy Code has significant implications for the relative bargaining power of debtors and creditors in Chapter 11 cases. Although no circuit court has taken a definitive position on the question, *dicta* in several opinions demonstrate intra and inter-circuit disagreements. District and bankruptcy courts are sharply divided on the question, as are the commentators. The question will in all probability ultimately be decided by the Supreme Court. In the meantime, we conclude that the new value exception remains a vital principle of bankruptcy law.

I. BACKGROUND

In 1984–85, Northtown Investments built Bonner Mall. The project was financed by a $6.3 million loan, secured by the mall property, from First National Bank of North Idaho, which later sold the note and deed of trust to appellant U.S. Bancorp Mortgage Co. ("Bancorp"). In

October 1986 the mall was purchased by appellee Bonner Mall Partnership ("Bonner"), subject to the lien acquired by Bancorp. Bonner is composed of six partners, five trusts and one individual investor, and was formed for the express purpose of buying the mall. Unfortunately, the cash-flow from the mall was much smaller than Bonner expected. When Bonner failed to pay its real estate taxes to Bonner County, Idaho, Bancorp commenced a nonjudicial foreclosure action. After several unsuccessful attempts to renegotiate and restructure Bonner's debt, Bancorp set a trustee's sale for March 14, 1991.

On March 13, 1991, Bonner filed a Chapter 11 (reorganization) bankruptcy petition, which automatically stayed the foreclosure sale. 11 U.S.C. § 362(a). Bancorp moved for relief from the stay under section 362(d)(2). As a condition to obtaining relief under that provision, Bancorp was required to show that Bonner had no equity in the mall and that Bancorp's claim against Bonner was undersecured. *United Sav. Ass'n of Tex. v. Timbers of Inwood Forest Assoc., Ltd.*, 484 U.S. 365, 377, 108 S.Ct. 626, 633, 98 L.Ed.2d 740 (1988). Because Bancorp established these facts, the burden shifted to Bonner to prove 1) that its retention of the mall was necessary to an effective reorganization, and 2) that there was a reasonable possibility of a successful reorganization within a reasonable time. *See id.* After two hearings on Bancorp's motion, the bankruptcy court denied it without prejudice. In his order denying relief the bankruptcy judge assumed the continued existence of the new value exception, noted its strict requirements, and expressed doubts whether Bonner could satisfy them. Nevertheless, he allowed Bonner thirty days to propose a plan.

Bonner filed a reorganization plan relying on the new value doctrine. In response Bancorp renewed its motion to lift the stay. Bancorp argued 1) that the new value exception did not survive the enactment of the Bankruptcy Code; and 2) even if it did, Bonner's plan was still unconfirmable as a matter of law. The parties stipulated that the motion involved only legal questions, so no evidence was taken. The bankruptcy court accepted Bancorp's first argument but did not reach the second. The bankruptcy judge noted that after his original order the Fifth Circuit had concluded in its "convincing" decision in *Phoenix Mut. Life Ins. Co. v. Greystone III Joint Venture, (In re Greystone III Joint Venture)*, 995 F.2d 1274 (5th Cir.1991), *petition for rehearing granted in part and opinion withdrawn in part,* 995 F.2d at 1284 (per curiam), *cert. denied,* 506 U.S. 821, 113 S.Ct. 72, 121 L.Ed.2d 37 (1992), that there is no longer a new value exception. On that basis, the judge granted Bancorp's motion for relief from the automatic stay. After the bankruptcy judge stayed his order at Bonner's request, Bonner appealed to the district court.

On appeal, the district judge determined that the only issue before him was whether the Bankruptcy Code had eliminated the new value exception. He found that it had not. In doing so he relied on the Supreme Court's ruling in *Dewsnup v. Timm,* 502 U.S. 410, 112 S.Ct. 773, 116 L.Ed.2d. 903 (1992), which was handed down after the bankruptcy court's decision and which emphasized the Court's reluctance to overturn pre-Code practice (*see infra*). Moreover, by the time of the district court's opinion the relevant portion of the Fifth Circuit's *Greystone* opinion had been withdrawn. The district court reversed the judgment of the bankruptcy court and remanded for further proceedings consistent with its opinion. 142 B.R. 911. It refused to address Bancorp's alternative argument that Bonner's plan was unconfirmable as a matter of law even if the new value exception survived. Instead its order stated: "Confirmation of the plan proposed by the Debtor must be addressed by the bankruptcy court on remand." Bancorp filed a timely appeal to this court. Like the district court, we resolve only the question whether the new value exception survives. The issue is one of law. Accordingly, our review is *de novo*.

* * *

III. BONNERS PLAN, CONFIRMATION, AND THE NEW VALUE EXCEPTION

Bonner's proposed reorganization plan ("the Plan") provides for the transfer of all of Bonner Mall *Partnership*'s assets (the mall for all practical purposes) to a new corporation, Bonner Mall *Properties, Inc.,* created by the Plan to carry out its provisions. One of the most significant features of the Plan is the treatment of Bancorp's $6.6 million claim, for which the mall is collateral. In the course of his original order denying Bancorp's motion for relief from the stay, the bankruptcy judge valued the mall at $3.2 million. This meant that Bancorp's claim against Bonner was undersecured: it was secured as to $3.2 million and unsecured as to $3.4 million. *See* 11 U.S.C. § 506(a). The unsecured portion of Bancorp's claim represents the vast majority of Bonner's unsecured debt. Under the Plan, the $3.2 million debt to Bancorp secured by the mall would be paid 32 months after the Plan's confirmation, with interest payments payable monthly in the interim. Payment of all other secured debt would be deferred. All unsecured creditors of Bonner who are owed more than $1000 would be paid according to a pro-rata distribution of 300,000 shares of preferred stock in the new corporation. Each share would be valued at $1.00.[14] The preferred stock would be convertible to a maximum of 300,000 shares of common stock once Bonner paid off the secured part of Bancorp's claim.

Under the Plan the equity owners, *i.e.* the partners, would receive nothing on their claims. However, to raise additional capital for the new corporation, the partners would contribute a total of $200,000 in cash to Bonner Mall Properties in exchange for 2 million of the 4 million authorized shares of the new corporation's common stock. No other persons are designated to receive stock in exchange for such contributions. The Plan also states that the partners would subsidize any shortfall in working capital during the first 32 months after confirmation of the plan. Moreover, the trustee for the five trust-partners of Bonner

14. Thus, Bancorp would receive less than ten cents on the dollar in preferred stock for its unsecured claim.

Mall Partnership is to contribute a collateral trust mortgage on a 4500-acre property as a guarantee of payment of the debts assumed by Bonner Mall Properties.[16] In exchange, the new corporation is to service part of the trustee's debt on the property.

Section 1129(a) of Chapter 11 establishes thirteen requirements for confirmation of a reorganization plan, all of which must generally be satisfied. One such requirement is set forth in subsection (a)(8), which mandates that "[w]ith respect to each class [of claims], A) such class has voted to accept the plan or B) such class is not impaired under the plan." 11 U.S.C. § 1129(a)(8). Under Bonner's Plan all claim classes are impaired and, therefore, all must accept the plan for a consensual confirmation. It is a foregone conclusion that at least the unsecured class of which Bancorp is the principal member will vote not to confirm the plan in view of the minimal return Bancorp will receive on the unsecured fraction of its claim.

However, the Code provides that where all requirements for confirmation but section 1129(a)(8) are met, the bankruptcy court *shall* confirm a Chapter 11 reorganization plan over the objection of an impaired class or classes "if the plan does not discriminate unfairly, and is *fair and equitable,* with respect to each class of claims or interests that is impaired under, and has not accepted, the plan." 11 U.S.C. § 1129(b)(1) (emphasis added). This form of confirmation is commonly known in bankruptcy parlance as a "cramdown" because the plan is crammed down the throats of the objecting class(es) of creditors. The issue before the bankruptcy judge in deciding whether to grant Bancorp's motion for relief from the stay was whether Bonner's Plan had a reasonable possibility of confirmation in a cramdown, *i.e.,* whether the standards set forth in section 1129(b)(1) could feasibly be satisfied.

The resolution of this question turns on whether there is a reasonable possibility that a bankruptcy judge could find Bonner's Plan "fair and equitable." Section 1129(b)(2) of the Code defines "fair and equitable" as *including* several enumerated *requirements*. The section, which is at the heart of the controversy between the parties, states, *inter alia,* that a plan will be considered "fair and equitable" only if:

(B) With respect to a class of unsecured claims—

(i) the plan provides that each holder of a claim of such class receive or retain on account of such claim property of a value, as of the effective date of the plan, equal to the allowed amount of such claim; *or*

(ii) the holder of any claim or interest that is junior to claims of such class will not receive or retain under the plan on account of such junior claim or interest any property.

---

16. Bonner claims the property's fair market value is $4.5 million, with equity of approximately $2 million. These figures are disputed. Bancorp states that the property is the subject of a state court foreclosure proceeding.

(emphasis added). Section 1129(b)(2)(B) is a two-part codification of the judge-made absolute priority rule, compliance with which was a prerequisite to any determination that a plan was "fair and equitable" under the Bankruptcy Act.

Here, each of the unsecured claims against Bonner will not be paid in full on the effective date of the Plan. As a result, section 1129(b)(2)(B)(i) cannot be satisfied. Therefore, Bonner's Plan cannot be held to be "fair and equitable" unless it complies with the provisions of section 1129(b)(2)(B)(ii). If it fails to meet the requirements of that section it is unconfirmable as a matter of law. A critical area of dispute in this case is whether Bonner's Plan violates section 1129(b)(2)(B)(ii) and, in turn, the absolute priority rule and the "fair and equitable" principle.

Under pre-Code Bankruptcy Act practice, a plan that allowed stockholders in the business that had filed for bankruptcy protection (old equity) to receive stock in the reorganized debtor in exchange for contributions of added capital (new value) could under certain conditions satisfy the absolute priority rule and be considered "fair and equitable" even though a senior class was not paid in full. * * * That set of conditions became known collectively as the "new value exception" to the absolute priority rule; the terms of that "exception" will be discussed below.

Although the question we must ultimately answer is whether the new value exception survived the enactment of the Bankruptcy Code, we should note, preliminarily, that the term "exception" is misleading. The doctrine is not actually an exception to the absolute priority rule but is rather a corollary principle, or, more simply a description of the limitations of the rule itself. It is, as indicated above, the set of conditions under which former shareholders may lawfully obtain a priority interest in the reorganized venture. The Supreme Court appeared to recognize as much in *Case v. Los Angeles Lumber* when it stated that if a new capital contribution satisfies certain conditions "the creditor cannot complain that he is not accorded full right of priority against the corporate assets." 308 U.S. at 122, 60 S.Ct. at 10 (internal quotation omitted). More properly, the new value exception should be called something like the "new capital-infusion doctrine" or as one commentator has suggested, "the scrutinize old equity participation rule." Elizabeth Warren, *A Theory of Absolute Priority*, 1991 Annual Survey of American Law 9, 42.

The question whether the adoption of the Code served to eliminate the new value exception was before the Supreme Court in *Norwest Bank Worthington v. Ahlers*, 485 U.S. 197, 108 S.Ct. 963, 99 L.Ed.2d 169 (1988). While there is language in the opinion questioning the viability of the doctrine, the Court explicitly stated that it was not deciding the issue. Instead, the Court assumed that the doctrine existed but found that all of its requirements were not satisfied under the facts of the case.

Since *Ahlers,* several courts of appeals have avoided a direct holding on the viability of the "exception" by using the same stratagem.

Other appellate courts have given mixed signals on whether the principle survives. The Seventh Circuit seems internally divided on the question: In one case it analyzed a reorganization plan in light of the exception, while stating that the status of the doctrine is an open question after *Ahlers*; another panel criticized the exception and strongly hinted that it is moribund; and a third stopped just short of holding that the exception survives. The Fourth Circuit had suggested that if the new value exception exists it is narrow in scope. Our own Bankruptcy Appellate Panel has recognized the continued existence of the exception. *See Carson Nugget, Inc. v. Green (In re Green),* 98 B.R. 981, 982 (9th Cir.BAP 1989)(per curiam).

* * * [W]e hold that the Code permits the confirmation of a reorganization plan that provides for the infusion of capital by the shareholders of the bankrupt corporation in exchange for stock if the plan meets the conditions that plans were required to meet prior to the Code's adoption.

IV. THE NEW VALUE EXCEPTION AND THE CODE

Our explanation of why we hold that the new value exception survives will address several distinct but related issues. First, we determine that the Code provision codifying the absolute priority rule does not prohibit confirmation of a new value plan. Second, we decide that Congress' failure expressly to include the new value doctrine as a standard to be considered in applying the "fair and equitable" principle does not reflect an intent to eliminate the exception. Finally we conclude that the new value exception is fully consistent with the structure and underlying policies of Chapter 11.

A. *The Codification of the Absolute Priority Rule Does Not Serve to Eliminate the New Value Exception.*

The parties take diametrically opposed positions as to the consistency of the new value exception with 11 U.S.C. section 1129(b)(2)(B)(ii). Bancorp argues that: 1) Bonner's Plan violates the absolute priority rule because the old equity owners will have an ownership interest in the new company even though Bancorp's unsecured claim will not be paid in full and 2) the plain meaning of 11 U.S.C. section 1129(b)(2)(B)(ii) demonstrates that the new value exception did not survive the enactment of the Code. Bonner contends that: 1) the infusion of new capital from a source outside the bankruptcy estate, even if the source is a former equity holder, is an independent act that does not violate the absolute priority rule and 2) section 1129(b)(2)(B)(ii) does not forbid confirmation of plans that meet the requirements of the new value exception.

In determining whether section 129(b)(2)(B)(ii) abolishes the new value exception we apply the traditional tools of statutory construction. The interpretation of a statutory provision must begin with the plain meaning of its language. * * * Where statutory language is unambiguous the judicial inquiry is complete. It is a cardinal principle of statutory construction that a court must give effect if possible, to every clause and word of a statute. * * * When the statutory scheme is coherent and consistent, there generally is no need for a court to inquire beyond the plain language. * * * Applying these familiar rules, we concluded that the plain language of section 1129(b)(2)(B)(ii) demonstrates that Bonner's, and not Bancorp's reading of the provision is correct.

1. Because Qualifying New Value Plans Do Not Give Old Equity Holders Stock in the Reorganized Debtor "On Account Of" Their Prior Ownership Interests, They Do Not Violate 11 U.S.C. Section 1129(b)(2)(B)(ii).

Eleven U.S.C. section 1129(b)(2)(B)(ii) requires that a plan provide that with respect to a class of unsecured claims that has not received full payment—

> the holder of any claim or interest that is junior to the claims of such class will not receive or retain under the plan *on account of such junior claim or interest* any property. (emphasis added)

In plainer English the provision bars old equity from receiving any property via a reorganization plan *"on account of"* its prior equitable ownership when all senior claim cases are not paid in full. * * * The central inquiry in determining the reach of the prohibition is the meaning of the critical words "on account of."

We have no difficulty in reconciling the "on account of" language with new value exception. Under Bankruptcy Act practice, old equity was required to meet several requirements in order to take advantage of that doctrine. Former equity owners were required to offer value that was 1) new, 2) substantial, 3) money or money's worth, 4) necessary for a successful reorganization and 5) reasonably equivalent to the value or interest received. *Case v. Los Angeles Lumber,* 308 U.S. at 121–22 60 S.Ct. at 10–11; *[In re] Snyder,* 967 F.2d [1126], 1131. Several courts have concluded that if a proposed plan satisfied all of these requirements, *i.e.,* the new value exception, it will not violate section 129(b)(2)(B)(ii) of the Code and the absolute priority rule. Such a plan, they reason, will *not* give old equity property *"on account of"* prior interests, but instead will allow the former owners to participate in the reorganized debtor *on account of* a substantial, necessary, and fair new value contribution. * * * We agree with their analysis.

We recognize that in some larger sense the reason that former owners receive new equity interests in reorganized ventures is that they are former owners. But it is also true that in new value transactions old equity owners receive stock in exchange for the additional capital they invest. Causation for any event has many and varied levels. Here, the answer to the meaning of the phrase "on account of" lies in the level of causation Congress had in mind when it prohibited old equity owners from receiving property "on account of" their prior interests. A reading of the full text of section 1129(b)(2)(B)(ii) makes it clear that what Congress had in mind was direct or immediate causation rather than a more remote variety, and that it did not intend to prohibit persons who receive stock because they have provided new capital from becoming participants in the reorganized debtor simply because they were also owners of the original enterprise.[23]

Had Congress intended that old equity never receive any property under a reorganization plan where senior claim classes are not paid in full, it could simply have omitted the "on account of" language from section 1129(b)(2)(B)(ii). We would than be left with an absolute prohibition against former equity owners' receiving or retaining property in the reorganized debtor in such circumstances. The expansive reading of the phrase "on account of such junior claim or interest" suggested by Bancorp would lead to the identical result, thus rendering the disputed phrase superfluous. Under that interpretation any distribution to old equity would always be "on account of" its former interest in some sense. We decline Bancorp's invitation to nullify Congress' deliberate use of the term "on account of such junior claim or interest", particularly since nearly identical language can be found throughout the Code. Congress must have intended the "on account of" language to have some significant meaning as well as some particular limiting effect.

We believe that Congress intended the "on account of" phrase in section 1129(b)(2)(B)(ii) to require bankruptcy courts to determine whether a reorganization plan that gives stock to former equity holders does so primarily because of their old interests in the debtor or for legitimate business reasons. The new value doctrine provides the means by which a court can discover whether a particular new capital transaction is proposed "on account of" old equity's prior ownership or "on account of" its new contribution. In other words, in evaluating whether a reorganization plan satisfies the requirements of the new value exception a court is in fact determining whether old equity is unjustifiably attempting to retain its corporate ownership powers in violation of the absolute priority rule or whether there is genuine and fair exchange of new capital for an equity interest.

Contrary to Bancorp's contentions, section 1129(b)(2)(B)(ii) does not by its terms eliminate, or even refer to, the new value exception. Rather, the language of that section and the requirements of the new value principle complement each other. Consequently, the fact that a reorganization plan provided for a new value transaction does not in and of itself violate 11 U.S.C. section 1129(b)(2)(B)(ii) and the absolute priority rule.

---

23. Professor Warren has stated:
The Code does not prohibit old equity from becoming a post-petition financer of the business or a post-plan owner of the business. The Code leaves old equity in the same position as any other potential investor: it may offer to buy any of the assets of the estate on the same terms as any other buyer.

A Theory of Absolute Priority at 39. Accord Raymond T. Nimmer, *Negotiating Bankruptcy Reorganization Plans: Absolute Priority and New Value Contributions*, 36 Emory L.J. 1009, 1051 (1987); Bruce A. Markell, *Owners, Auctions and Absolute Priority in Bankruptcy Reorganizations*, 44 Stan.L.Rev. 69, 96–102 (1991).

2. The "On Account Of" Language of Section 1129(b)(2)(B)(ii) Does Not Bar Plans That Give Old Equity Alone the Opportunity to Acquire Stock for a New Capital Contribution.

As Bancorp notes, several courts have held that where a reorganization plan gives old equity *alone* the right to obtain an interest in the reorganized debtor in exchange for new value, as Bonner's Plan does, the old equity holders are given "property" *on account of their prior ownership interests* and the absolute priority rule is violated. The Fourth Circuit held that such plans violate section 1129(b)(2)(B)(ii), even assuming the new value exception still exists. * * * Under this analysis the "property" given to old equity in violation of the absolute priority rule is *not* the stock in the reorganized debtor received in exchange for a new value contribution. Rather "*[the] exclusive right* of [the] Debtor's existing partners to obtain equity interests in [the] Debtor itself constitutes property that the partners retain 'on account of' their existing interests." *Outlook/Century*, 127 B.R. at 654 (emphasis added).

We disagree with this analysis. Even assuming that an exclusive opportunity is "property,"[27] it does not follow that such an opportunity is property received or retained "on account of" old equity's prior ownership interests in the debtor. A proposed reorganization plan may give old equity the exclusive opportunity to purchase stock in exchange for new capital for other reasons. Exclusivity may be given because the plan proponent may believe that the participation of old equity in the new business will enhance the value of the business after reorganization. It is possible the debtor will conclude that additional funding will be easier to obtain if the old owners, the most likely investors, know in advance that their partners will all be familiar faces. Even more important, it may be apparent to the proponents of the plan that there will be no other legitimate investors who would be willing to put substantial capital into a business that is just emerging from Chapter 11 protection. As the Supreme Court has stated "[g]enerally, additional funds will be essential to the success of the undertaking, and it may be impossible to obtain them unless stockholders are permitted to contribute and retain an interest sufficiently valuable to move them." *Kansas City Terminal Ry. Co. v. Central Union Trust Co.*, 271 U.S. 445, 455, 46 S.Ct. 549, 552, 70 L.Ed. 1028 (1926); *accord Mason v. Paradise Irrigation Dist.*, 326 U.S. 536, 541–43, 66 S.Ct. 290, 292–93, 90 L.Ed. 287 (1946)(new money may not be available unless there is a "strong inducement"). The proponent of a plan may have good reason to believe that old equity would not participate without the incentive of an exclusive opportunity.

---

27. The definition of "property" under the Code is extremely broad and includes intangible property. *Ahlers*, 485 U.S. at 208, 108 S.Ct. at 969. However, the exclusivity of the opportunity to purchase stock is irrelevant. Even if specified creditors and outside investors were given the opportunity to purchase stock for new value as well, old equity would still be given something of value which may be described as "property." A stock purchase option is property whether or not other people are also given such an option. *See Kham & Nate's Shoes*, 908 F.2d at 1360.

As stated earlier, whether a particular plan gives old equity a property interest "on account of" its old ownership interests in violation of the absolute priority rule or for another, permissible reason is a factual question. The answer depends upon whether the requirements of the new value exception are met. We believe that this same analysis applies whether a plan gives old equity an exclusive or non-exclusive right of participation in a new value transaction. What matters instead is whether the proposed transaction meets the criterion "necessary to the success of the reorganization". In other words, if an exclusive participation plan satisfies that requirement, then it allows the partners the sole right to participate in a new value transaction not because of illegitimate collusion between old equity and the plan proponent but because such participation is necessary for a successful reorganization and in the best interests of all concerned. Of course, any exclusive participation plan must also fulfill the new value doctrine's four other requirements as well.

In sum, where the strictures of the new value exception are met, there is simply no violation of the absolute priority rule, whether the plan provides for exclusive or nonexclusive participation, because old equity will not retain or receive property "on account of" its old ownership interests in violation of section 1129(b)(2)(B)(ii).

B. *Congress' Failure to List the New Value Exception as a Specific Doctrine Permitted under the "Fair and Equitable" Principle Does Not Demonstrate an Intent to Eliminate It.*

While the absolute priority rule clearly does not *prohibit* confirmation of a new value exception plan in a cramdown, this does not necessarily mean that the "fair and equitable" provisions of the Code should be interpreted as *permitting* confirmation of such a plan. Bancorp argues that Congress' failure expressly to provide for the continuation of the new value exception in the provision setting forth the requirements of the "fair and equitable" principle must be interpreted as an implicit statement that it did not intend the doctrine to survive the adoption of the Code. Recognizing that the Code does not unambiguously allow for new capital contribution plans, Bonner argues that such plans are consistent with the "fair and equitable" principle and that despite the absence of an express provision, Congress intended to maintain the new value exception.

Bonner relies upon "the normal rule of statutory construction ... that if Congress intends for legislation to change the interpretation of a judicially created concept, it makes that intent specific." * * * This rule is followed with particular care in construing the Bankruptcy Code. *Midlantic*, 474 U.S. at 501, 106 S.Ct. at 759. When Congress amends the bankruptcy laws, it does not start from scratch. * * * The Bankruptcy Code should not be read to abandon past bankruptcy practice absent a clear indication that Congress intended to do so. * * *

At oral argument Bancorp suggested that the new value exception was mentioned once in *dicta* by the Supreme Court in *Case v. Los*

Angeles Lumber Products and thereafter never heard from again. Consequently, Bancorp argues that Congress would not have known of the principle when it enacted the Code. *Cf. United States v. Ron Pair Enterp., Inc.*, 489 U.S. 235, 246, 109 S.Ct. 1026, 1033, 103 L.Ed.2d. 290 (1989)(practice of denying post-petition interest to holders of non-consensual liens was an exception to an exception practiced only by a few courts so Congress would not have known of it). We disagree.

There is simply no question that the new value exception was an established pre-Code Bankruptcy practice of which Congress would have had (and did have) knowledge. * * * First, several Supreme Court cases had mentioned the principle, albeit the last time in 1946. * * * Second, several appellate court cases recognized the new value doctrine after 1946. Finally, a proposal to broaden the new value exception was put before Congress during the drafting of the Code. While the proposal was rejected, that action demonstrates that Congress knew of the doctrine when it enacted the Code.

Once it has been shown that Congress was aware of a pre-Code practice, the remaining inquiry under *Dewsnup* and *Davenport* is whether it has made clear its intent to change that practice. Bancorp argues that the codification of the formerly judicially-defined concept of "fair and equitable" without a reference to the new value exception show Congress' clear intent to eliminate the doctrine. * * * However, section 1129(b)(2) explicitly defines the term "fair and equitable" as merely *including* the general requirements listed in the Code and expressly leaves room for additional factors to be considered in applying the principle in other particular circumstances. *See* 11 U.S.C. § 102(3)(defining "includes" as "not limiting"). There is nothing in the language of the Code that suggests that courts cannot continue to apply the requirements of the new value exception in determining whether a plan that affords old equity a property interest in exchange for a capital contribution is "fair and equitable." * * * In any event, the text of section 1129(b)(2) does not evidence the clear intent necessary to support a conclusion that Congress decided to eliminate the new value doctrine; silence is not a sufficient basis from which we may infer such a purpose. * * *

Where the text of the Code does not unambiguously abrogate pre-Code practice, courts should presume that Congress intended it to continue unless the legislative history dictates a contrary result. *See Dewsnup*, 502 U.S. 410, 112 S.Ct. at 779. It does not do so here. If anything, the legislative history of the Code supports the continued existence of the new value doctrine. It contains statements by sponsors of the Code that although section 1129(b)(2) lists several specific factors interpreting "fair and equitable", others were omitted to avoid statutory complexity and because courts would independently find that they were fundamental to "fair and equitable treatment." *See* 124 Cong.Rec. 32407 (Sept. 28, 1978)(Statement of Rep. Don Edwards); 124 Cong.Rec. 34006 (Oct. 5, 1978)(statement of Senator Dennis DeConcini). This legislative history is evidence that Congress enacted the Code with knowledge that other, judicially-created standards governing the application of the "fair and equitable" principle existed and that it failed to include such standards for reasons other than an intent to eliminate them.

As stated earlier, in enacting the Code Congress rejected a proposal by the Bankruptcy Commission to expand the new value exception significantly. *See* Victor Brudney, *The Bankruptcy Commission's Proposed Modifications of the Absolute Priority Rule,* 48 Am.Bankr.L.J. 305, 335–36 (1974). That proposal would have eliminated the "money or money's worth" requirement set forth in *Case v. Los Angeles Lumber* and permitted new "important" contributions, including contributions of management, to suffice. *Report of the Commission on the Bankruptcy Laws of the United States,* H.R.Doc. No. 93–137, 93d Cong., 1st Sess., pt.I, 258–59; pt. II, §§ 7–303(7), 7–310 (1973). * * * Congress' rejection of the Bankruptcy Commission's proposal shows only that it did not want to broaden the exception; it does not indicate rejection of the exception itself. * * * Indeed, "the Commission's proposal presupposed the existence of the new value exception, and Congress's rejection of the modification could just as easily be construed as an endorsement of the status quo." *Snyder,* 967 F.2d at 1130.

In sum, neither the text nor the legislative history of section 1129(b)(2) justifies the conclusion that the new value exception was eliminated. *See Bryson,* 961 F.2d at 504 n. 13. Congress' failure to include explicitly the well-established requirements of the new value exception in section 1129(b)(2) is of no assistance to Bancorp. Given that there is no evidence of a clear intent on the part of Congress to eliminate the new value exception in either the statutory text or the legislative history, under *Dewsnup* and *Davenport* pre-Code practice continues to apply.

C. *Congress' Overhaul of the Reorganization Process Does Not Justify a Conclusion that the New Value Exception was Abolished.*

Bancorp contends that where the Code totally revamps an area of bankruptcy law, pre-Code practice may appropriately be ignored. Bancorp relies on the *Union Bank v. Wolas,* 502 U.S. 151, 112 S.Ct. 527, 116 L.Ed.2d 514 (1992), in support of this proposition. In *Wolas* the Court unanimously found that the text of the Code sharply limited the pre-Code practice at issue. Under the Bankruptcy Act a trustee could avoid a debtor's payments on a long-term debt if they were made in the ninety days prior to bankruptcy. However, he could not avoid such payments made on current expenses. In contrast, section 547(c)(2) of the Code states that a trustee cannot avoid payments made during the prescribed period if they were in the "ordinary course of [debtor's] business or financial affairs." The Court found that the plain meaning of this Code section circumscribed the trustee's pre–Code avoidance powers with respect to long term debt. 502 U.S. at ___, 112 S.Ct. at 530. While the *Wolas* Court relied in part upon the major changes made to the statutory framework by the enactment of the Code, it did so only as a *confirmation* of its earlier conclusion that the plain text of the Code provision altered pre-Code practice. 502 U.S. at ___, ___, 112 S.Ct. at 530, 532. Here, and as shown above, the language of the text at issue, section 1129(b)(2), does not by its terms affect the new value exception in any respect.

Bancorp next argues that the changes made to the reorganization process were more drastic than those at issue in *Wolas* and therefore pre-Code practice should be discarded. As Bancorp notes, under the Bankruptcy Act there were two reorganization chapters, X (publicly held companies) and XI (privately held companies), which varied in certain important respects.[34] On the one hand, Congress' combining them into a single reorganization chapter was a significant Code innovation. *See A.V.B.I.,* 143 B.R. at 747. On the other hand, the new Chapter 11 shifted bargaining power away from creditors and in favor of debtors. Consequently, it made plan confirmation easier. While it might be, as Bancorp argues, that the new value exception is not as necessary under the current regime, *see also In re Outlook/Century, Ltd.,* 127 B.R. 650, 657 (Bankr.N.D.Cal.1991), we believe that the structural changes to the reorganization process made by the Code are in harmony with the pro-confirmation principle underlying the new value exception. Accordingly, these changes cannot carry Bancorp's argument that the new value doctrine is no longer viable.

Specifically, Bancorp recounts that under the Act voting on the confirmation of a plan was by individual creditors rather than by classes of creditors, as is the case under the Code. It contends that the new value exception was designed merely to prevent one dissenting creditor from preventing confirmation. * * * However, there is no significant difference between the problem that a holdout class poses for confirmation and that posed by a holdout creditor. *Woodscape Ltd. Partnership (In re Woodscape Ltd. Partnership),* 134 B.R. 165, 168, 171 (Bankr.D.Md. 1991). While Bancorp assumes that the new value exception was intended to solve a no longer existent individual holdout problem, it could just as logically be argued that the new value exception was intended to prevent confirmation holdouts, individual or class, from derailing an otherwise "fair and equitable" plan. *See In re Pullman Construction Indus.,* 107 B.R. 909, 944–45 (Bankr.N.D.Ill.1989). From this perspective, the rationale for the new value exception is as applicable today as it ever was, and there is no reason for us to view it as defunct.

Bancorp also contends that the Code meant to give creditors, not the bankruptcy court, the power to decide when to waive the absolute priority rule. *See Kham & Nate's Shoes No. 2 v. First Bank,* 908 F.2d 1351, 1360 (7th Cir.1990)(creditors effectively own bankrupt firms and they should decide whether old equity should participate). It is true that 11 U.S.C. section 1126(c) allows creditors to consent to confirmation

---

34. For example, Chapter X had an absolute priority rule; Chapter XI did not. Trustees were mandatory in Chapter X cases; the debtor retained control under Chapter XI.

of a plan that does not comply with the absolute priority rule. However, that section permits creditors to waive a priority *they* possess. The new value exception allows bankruptcy courts to afford a priority to *others* over the creditors. There is simply no logical analysis that would allow us to concluded that by permitting creditors to waive their own priority Congress demonstrated the intent to deprive bankruptcy courts of *their* power to afford investors of new capital a priority over an impaired class of creditors. Moreover, the very purpose of the Code's cramdown provision, section 1129(b), which had no direct equivalent under the Act, is to allow the court, and not the creditors, to decide whether a "fair and equitable" plan should be confirmed over creditor objections. While creditor autonomy is certainly an important aspect of the reorganization process, the argument that the new value exception impedes that autonomy is really a complaint against the practice of confirmation by cramdown. That grievance cannot be addressed here.

Finally, Bancorp argues that the Code's creation of the entity of the debtor-in-possession to run the business in lieu of a trustee would cause self dealing by insiders if the new value exception were still allowed. *See A.V.B.I.*, 143 B.R. at 743. However, the very purpose of the Code's creation of the debtor-in-possession was to increase the power of those in control of the debtor during the reorganization process. Bankruptcy law is very formalistic in that it treats the debtor, the debtor-in-possession, and old equity as legally distinct entities when in reality they may all be one and the same. * * * The risk of self-dealing among these entities at the expense of creditors is a risk created by the Code itself. The stringent requirements of the new value exception are designed to mitigate that risk. The enactment in the Code of changes that aggravate the self-dealing problem constitutes good reason for courts to make certain that a proposed new value plan strictly adheres to the requirements of the exception. The modifications to the reorganization process are not, however, cause for us to ignore several decades of bankruptcy practice in determining Congress' intent with respect to the new value exception.

Despite all of the differences between the Act and the Code, the primary rationale for the new value exception has not been eliminated by any statutory alteration to the confirmation process. The new value exception is based on "practical necessity", on the recognition that new money frequently could not be obtained for the reorganized debtor in the absence of that doctrine. *See Mason v. Paradise Irrigation Dist.*, 326 U.S. 536, 542, 66 S.Ct. 290, 292 (1946); *Kansas City Terminal Ry. Co. v. Central Union Trust Co.*, 271 U.S. 445, 455, 46 S.Ct. 549, 551 (1926). That practical necessity remains just as pertinent under the Code. Where the main justification for a long-term judicially sanctioned practice has not dissipated, either through a change in conditions or by way of legislative amendment, there is simply no reason to disregard the practice absent a clear legislative intent to abolish it. Bancorp's structural-change arguments simply do not convince us that pre-Code practice should be ignored in this case.

D. The New Value Exception is Consistent with the Underlying Policies of Chapter 11.

In interpreting statutory language we are not confined to the specific provision at issue but may look to the structure of the law as a whole and to its object and policy. * * * The new value exception, properly applied, serves both goals. By permitting prior stockholders to contribute new money in exchange for participation in the reorganized company, the debtor is given an additional source of capital. The new contribution increases the amount available for the estate to use both in its reorganization and in funding the plan and paying creditors. Without the inducement of participation in the reorganized debtor, the new money may be unavailable. All parties involved, including the creditors, benefit from an increase in the assets of the estate.

" 'Prior owners are a source of capital different in kind from new investors in that they have an ongoing role in the reorganization and a prior investment in the company.' " *Prudential Ins. Co. v. F.A.B. Indus. (In re F.A.B. Indus.)*, 147 B.R. 763, 769 n. 13 (C.D.Cal.1992) (quoting Nimmer, *supra* note 23, at 1050), *appeal docketed*, No. 93–55055 (9th Cir. Jan. 13, 1993). Moreover, in many situations the new value exception allows control and management of the company to remain with the original owners, who arguably can best reestablish a profitable business. Old owners may have valuable expertise and experience that outside investors lack. * * * Some studies demonstrate that reorganizations have been more successful when former management was allowed to use its expertise in running the business. Harvey Miller, *Commentary on Absolute Priority*, 1991 Annual Survey of American Law 49, 50.

It has been argued that the new value exception allows old equity to repurchase the business at a bargain price, while superior creditors go unpaid, and that this result is contrary to the Chapter 11 policy of protecting creditor interests. *See, e.g., A.V.B.I.*, 143 B.R. at 747. We believe that this argument is incorrect in two respects. First, while the protection of creditors' interests is an important purpose under Chapter 11, the Supreme Court has made clear that successful debtor reorganization and maximization of the value of the estate are the primary purposes.[37] Chapter 11 is designed to avoid liquidations under Chapter 7, since liquidations may have a negative impact on jobs, suppliers of the business, and the economy as a whole. * * * The ability of stockholders to remain in possession and control of operations, rehabilitate the business, and retain ownership through the new value exception encourages debtors to attempt Chapter 11 reorganization instead of simply liquidating their assets and starting over.

Second, we believe that if the new value exception's requirements are properly applied, creditors' interests will generally be benefited as

---

37. From one perspective, the debate over the survival of the new value exception is a division between those who perceive the paramount objective of Chapter 11 to be successful reorganization of the debtor and those who believe it should be protection of creditors' interests.

well. The strictures of the new value doctrine provide creditors with significant safeguards against collusion between the proponent of the reorganization plan and the old equity owners.[38] Although the new value exception has been criticized as a subversion of the absolute priority rule, its requirements actually enhance the rule. As we noted earlier, they constitute guidelines by which a court can ensure that old equity will *not* acquire an interest in the reorganized debtor or other property *on account of* its old ownership interests. In fact, the new value exception puts limits on the power of old equity to gain an interest in the reorganized business beyond that provided in the explicit language of the Code. For example, there is nothing in the text of the Code that prevents stockholders from obtaining property in the reorganized debtor in exchange for contributions of labor; such a transaction would not give old equity any property "on account of" its prior ownership interests. Yet the requirements of the new value exception prohibit this type of transaction. * * *

As long as courts carefully apply the new value exception, it will not operate as a mechanism by which old equity can escape the requirements of the absolute priority rule. If a plan meets all the requirements of the new exception, it may be confirmed in a cramdown, assuming all other conditions for confirmation are present. Within the confines of the Code, bankruptcy courts are courts of equity. *Ahlers*, 485 U.S. at 206, 108 S.Ct. at 968. Properly applied, the new value exception allows bankruptcy courts to fulfill their assigned role of balancing the interests of debtors, creditors, old owners, and the public, guided by the overriding goal of ensuring the success of the reorganization. * * *

Thus, our conclusion that nothing in the Bankruptcy Code forbids the confirmation of plans that comply with the new value doctrine is entirely consistent with Congressional bankruptcy policy. Because our reading of the statute will not produce results demonstrably at odds with the intentions of its drafters, we must enforce the Code according to its terms. *United States v. Ron Pair Enterp., Inc.*, 489 U.S. 235, 242, 109 S.Ct. 1026, 1030, 103 L.Ed.2d 290 (1989). Therefore, Bonner's Plan is not unconfirmable simply because it provides for a new value transaction.

V. The New Value Exception and the Bancorp's Motion for Relief From the Automatic Stay

As noted above, the precise issue posed by Bancorp's motion for relief from stay is not whether Bonner's plan will ultimately be confirmed under section 1129 but whether there is a reasonable possibility that it can be confirmed within a reasonable time. That is all that Bonner need show to defeat Bancorp's section 362(d)(2) motion. * * * It

---

38. If old equity contributes a substantial amount of new capital to the business undergoing reorganization, then the risk of a later failure falls more heavily on stockholders than creditors. *See Nimmer, supra* note 23, at 1050–52, 1072–73.

need not put forth evidence of the type it would be required to produce in a confirmation hearing.

Bancorp correctly argues that if Bonner's Plan cannot possibly satisfy all of the requirements of the new value exception it cannot be confirmed as a matter of law and relief from the stay must be granted. While it is true that in certain cases an appellate court can determine the feasibility of confirmation as a matter of law, *see id.*, because of the lack of a sufficient factual record we cannot do so here. The bankruptcy court never held a hearing on the feasibility of the confirmation of Bonner's plan and the district court failed to reach the issue as well. On this record we cannot say as matter of law that Bonner's proposed Plan cannot satisfy all of the requirements of the new value exception. A remand to the bankruptcy court is required to determine the feasibility of confirmation and whether, despite the survival of the new value exception, Bancorp's motion for relief from the stay of the foreclosure sale of Bonner Mall should be granted.

VI. Conclusion

Viewed properly, "the new value exception" may be seen as a rule of construction, or a rule that serves to define the meaning of the absolute priority rule and determine when it has been satisfied. As such it is as pertinent today as it was under pre-Code bankruptcy practice. The arguments that Bancorp advances do not persuade us that Congress would have had any reason to disregard a beneficial rule of construction that assists courts in implementing an important bankruptcy doctrine at the very time it was incorporating that doctrine into the Bankruptcy Code.

Nothing in the text of the Code prohibits the confirmation of plans that properly employ the new value doctrine. Nor does the legislative history demonstrate that Congress intended to abrogate this judicially created, pre-Code legal principle. Therefore, we concluded that the new value "exception", with its stringent requirements, survives. We recognize that, if applied carelessly, the doctrine has the potential to subvert the interests of creditors and allow debtors and old equity to abuse the reorganization process. The proper answer to these concerns is vigilance on the part of bankruptcy courts in ensuring that all of the requirements of the new value exception are met in every case. Here, it is unclear whether Bonner's plan can meet all of the requirements of the doctrine and achieve confirmation. Nevertheless, it may well be within the realm of potentially confirmable plans and thereby survive Bancorp's motion for relief from the automatic stay. The bankruptcy court must make that determination initially.

The judgment of the district court is **AFFIRMED** and the case is **REMANDED** to the bankruptcy court for further proceedings consistent with this opinion.

KHAM & NATE'S SHOES NO. 2, INC. v. FIRST BANK
United States Court of Appeals, Seventh Circuit, 1990.
908 F.2d 1351.

EASTERBROOK, CIRCUIT JUDGE.

Kham & Nate's Shoes No. 2, Inc., ran four retail shoe stores in Chicago. It has been in bankruptcy since 1984, operating as a debtor in possession. First Bank of Whiting, one of Kham & Nate's creditors, appeals from the order confirming its plan of reorganization. This order not only reduces the Bank's secured claim to unsecured status but also allows Khamolaw Beard and Nathaniel Parker, the debtor's principals, to retain their equity interests despite the firm's inability to pay its creditors in full. The bankruptcy judge subordinated the Bank's claims after finding that it behaved "inequitably", and he allowed Beard and Parker to retain their interests on the theory that their guarantees of new loans to be made as part of the reorganization are "new value".

I

The Bank first extended credit to the Debtor in July 1981. This $50,000 loan was renewed in December 1981 and repaid in part in July 1982. The balance was rolled over until late 1983, when with interest it came to $42,000. In September 1983 Bank issued several letters of credit in favor of Debtor's customers. Debtor furnished a note to support these letters of credit; the Bank's security interest was limited to the goods the suppliers furnished. In late 1983 Debtor, experiencing serious cash-flow problems, asked for additional capital, which Bank agreed to provide if the loan could be made secure. That was hard to do, for Debtor had lost money the previous two years and owed more than $440,000 to tax collectors; any new loan from Bank would stand behind the back tax liabilities. The parties discussed two ways to make Bank secure: a guarantee by the Small Business Administration, and a bankruptcy petition followed by an order giving a post-petition loan superpriority.

While waiting for the SBA to act on its application, Debtor filed its petition under Chapter 11 of the Bankruptcy Code in January 1984. Judge Toles granted its application for an order under 11 U.S.C. § 364(c)(1) giving a loan from Bank priority even over the administrative expenses of the bankruptcy. Debtor and Bank then signed their loan agreement, which opens a $300,000 line of credit. The contract provides for cancellation on five days' notice and adds for good measure that "nothing provided herein shall constitute a waiver of the right of the Bank to terminate financing at any time".

The parties signed the contract on January 23, 1984, and Debtor quickly took about $75,000. Suppliers began to draw on the letters of credit. On February 29 Bank mailed Debtor a letter stating that it would make no additional advances after March 7. Although the note underlying the line of credit required payment on demand, Bank did not make the demand. It continued honoring draws on the letters of credit. Debtor's ultimate indebtedness to Bank was approximately $164,000: $42,000 outstanding on the loan made in 1981, $47,000 on the letters of credit, and $75,000 on the line of credit. Debtor paid $10,000 against the line of credit in April 1985 but has made no further payments. Debtor did not ask the court to order Bank to make further advances or to grant super-priority to another creditor to facilitate loans from another source.

There matters stood until the spring of 1988, when Debtor proposed its fourth plan of reorganization. Although the previous three plans had called for Bank to be paid in full, the fourth plan proposed to treat Bank's claims as general unsecured debts. This fourth plan also proposed to allow the shareholders to keep their stock, in exchange for guaranteeing new loans to Debtor.

Bankruptcy Judge Coar held an evidentiary hearing and concluded that Bank had behaved inequitably in terminating the line of credit and inducing Debtor's suppliers to draw on the letters of credit. These draws, the judge concluded, converted Bank from an unsecured lender (the position it held before the bankruptcy) to a super-secured lender under Judge Toles' financing order. Judge Coar first vacated the financing order and then subordinated Bank's debt, on the authority of 11 U.S.C. § 510(c). Finally, Judge Coar confirmed the plan of reorganization, including the provision allowing the stockholders of Debtor to retain their interests. He found that their guarantees were "new value" equivalent to the worth of the interests they would retain, which the judge thought small. The district judge affirmed, 104 B.R. 909 (N.D.Ill. 1989).

* * *

IV

A plan of reorganization may be confirmed only if each class of impaired creditors votes to accept it. There is one exception to the requirement of approval: 11 U.S.C. § 1129(b)(1), provides that a "fair and equitable" plan may be crammed down the throats of objecting creditors. The Code says that a plan treats unsecured creditors fairly and equitably if "the holder of any claim or interest that is junior to the claims of such class will not receive or retain under the plan on account of such junior claim or interest any property." 11 U.S.C. § 1129(b)(2)(B)(ii). This is the "absolute priority rule". An objection to the plan may be overridden only if every class lower in priority is wiped out. Priority is "absolute" in the sense that every cent of each class comes ahead of the first dollar of any junior class. See Walter J. Blum & Stanley A. Kaplan, *The Absolute Priority Doctrine in Corporate Reorganizations,* 41 U.Chi.L.Rev. 651 (1974).

Judge Coar approved a "cram-down" plan in this case. Unsecured creditors (including Bank) will not be paid in full. Bank objected to the plan, and the court overrode its objection after finding that the plan would be "fair and equitable". Yet the court did not extinguish the interests of every class junior to the unsecured creditors. Instead it allowed the stockholders to retain their interests, reasoning that by guaranteeing a $435,000 loan to be made as part of the plan, Beard and Parker contributed "new value" justifying the retention of their stock. The size of the new debt made the risk of the guarantees "substantial", the court found. The risk also exceeded the value of the retained stock, because "given the history of Debtor and the various risks associated with its business", the stock would have only "minimal" value. Beard and Parker thus would contribute more than they would receive, so the court allowed them to keep their stock.

There is something unreal about this calculation. If the stock is worth less than the guarantees, why are Beard and Parker doing it? If the value of the stock is "minimal", why does Bank object to letting Beard and Parker keep it? Is *everyone* acting inconsistently with self-interest, as the court's findings imply? And why, if the business is likely to fail, making the value of the stock "minimal", could the court confirm the plan of reorganization? Confirmation depends on a conclusion that the reorganized firm is likely to succeed, and not relapse into "liquidation, or the need for further financial reorganization". 11 U.S.C. § 1129(a)(11). If, as the bankruptcy court found, the plan complies with this requirement, then the equity interest in the firm *must* be worth something—as Beard, Parker, and Bank all appear to believe.

Stock is "property" for purposes of § 1129(b)(2)(B)(ii) even if the firm has a negative net worth, *Norwest Bank Worthington v. Ahlers,* 485 U.S. 197, 208, 108 S.Ct. 963, 969, 99 L.Ed.2d 169 (1988). An option to purchase stock also is "property". The bankruptcy judge gave Beard and Parker a no-cost option to buy stock, which they could exercise if they concluded that the shares were worth more than the risk created by the guarantees. Whether we characterize the stock or the option to buy it as the "property", the transaction seems to run afoul of § 1129(b)(2)(B)(ii) for it means that although a class of unsecured creditors is not paid in full, a junior class (the stockholders) keeps some "property".

Only the "new value exception" to the absolute priority rule could support this outcome. Dicta in cases predating the 1978 Code said that investors who put up new capital may retain interests equal to or lower in value than that new contribution. These interests are not so much "retained" as purchased for the new value (the "option" characterization of the transaction). Some firms depend for success on the entrepreneurial skills or special knowledge of managers who are also shareholders. If these persons' interests are wiped out, they may leave the firm and reduce its value. If they may contribute new value and retain an interest, this may tie them to the firm and so improve its prospects.

In principle, then, the exchange of stock for new value may make sense. When it does, the creditors should be willing to go along. Creditors effectively own bankrupt firms. They may find it worthwhile, as owners, to sell equity claims to the managers; they may even find it worthwhile to give the equity away in order to induce managers to stay on and work hard. Because the Code allows creditors to consent to a plan that impairs their interests, voluntary transactions of this kind are possible. Only collective action problems could frustrate beneficial arrangements. If there are many creditors, one may hold out, seeking to engross a greater share of the gains. But the Code deals with holdups by allowing half of a class by number (two-thirds by value) to consent to a lower class's retention of an interest. 11 U.S.C. § 1126(c). Creditors not acting in good faith do not count toward the one-third required to block approval, § 1126(e). When there is value to be gained by allowing a lower class to kick in new value and keep its interest, the creditors should be willing to go along. *Ahlers,* 485 U.S. at 207, 108 S.Ct. at 968. A "new value exception" means a power in the *judge* to "sell" stock to the managers even when the creditors believe that this transaction will *not* augment the value of the firm. To understand whether the Code gives the judge this power (and, if it does, the limits of the power), it is necessary to examine the genesis of the doctrine.

The Bankruptcy Act of 1898 required plans of reorganization to be "fair and equitable" but did not define that phrase. It also allowed creditors to consent to plans that impaired their interests, but the consent had to be unanimous. The absolute priority rule came into being as a cross between the interpretation of "fair and equitable" and a rule of contract law. *Northern Pacific Ry. v. Boyd,* 228 U.S. 482, 33 S.Ct. 554, 57 L.Ed. 931 (1913). Because contracts give creditors priority over shareholders, a plan of reorganization had to do the same. But under the 1898 Act bankruptcy also was a branch of equity, so it is not surprising that equitable modifications of the doctrine developed. One of these was the "new value exception" to the absolute priority doctrine. So far as the Supreme Court is concerned, however, the development has been 100% dicta.

Kansas City Terminal Ry. v. Central Union Trust Co., 271 U.S. 445, 46 S.Ct. 549, 70 L.Ed. 1028 (1926), is the genesis of the exception. The Court conceived the absolute priority rule as barring any retention of interest by a shareholder if any layer of creditors is excluded. It used this rule to veto a decision by the secured creditor to allow the shareholder a stake when junior creditors were cut out and objected. Yet the senior creditor, which as a practical matter owned 100% of the firm, must have had a reason to suffer the continued existence of the shareholder. The plan in *Kansas City Ry.* was identical in principle to selling the firm to the secured creditor at auction, and the secured creditor giving some stock to the manager and former shareholder. Only the fact that both steps were rolled into one plan of reorganization gave the junior creditor an opportunity to say no (as a practical matter to hold out for some portion of the gains). The Court said in dicta that this right to object did not give the junior creditor as potent a power as it might, because the judge could modify the strict priority equitably if the shareholder agreed to contribute new value.

Case v. Los Angeles Lumber Products Co., 308 U.S. 106, 60 S.Ct. 1, 84 L.Ed. 110 (1939), came next. The bankruptcy judge took the hint in *Kansas City Ry.* and allowed shareholders to retain an interest in exchange for their promise to contribute value in the form of continuity of management, plus financial standing and influence in the community that would enable the debtor to raise new money. It allowed the shareholders to retain their interests even though the class of senior creditors objected (because unanimity could not be achieved)—a dramatic step from the suggestion in *Kansas City Ry.* that new value plus the *consent* of the creditor whose claim exceeded the value of the firm would suffice. The Supreme Court reversed, holding that new value must mean "money or money's worth", 308 U.S. at 121–22, 60 S.Ct. at 10–11. It did not remark on the difference between consent and objection from the creditors, and it did not really need to given its conclusion that nonmonetary value is insufficient.

Cases in the lower courts proceeded to apply the dicta in *Case* and *Kansas City Ry.* without noticing the difference between consent and objection by the creditors. But see *SEC v. Canandaigua Enterprises Corp.,* 339 F.2d 14, 21 (2d Cir.1964)(Friendly, J.), questioning the doctrine on this basis; Henry J. Friendly, *Some Comments on the Corporate Reorganization Act,* 48 Harv.L.Rev. 39, 77–78 (1934). Perhaps this distinction was not an essential one in the administration of a common law doctrine, especially not when (a) the unanimity rule made the lack of consent the norm, and (b) bankruptcy was a branch of equity.

Everything changed with the adoption of the Code in 1978. The definition of "fair and equitable" is no longer a matter of common law; § 1129(b)(2) defines it expressly. Holdouts that spoiled reorganizations and created much of the motive for having judges "sell" stock to the manager-shareholders no longer are of much concern, now that § 1126(c) allows the majority of each class (two-thirds by value) to give consent. And bankruptcy judges no longer have equitable powers to modify contracts to achieve "fair" distributions. Bankruptcy judges enforce entitlements created under state law. *Butner v. United States,* 440 U.S. 48, 99 S.Ct. 914, 59 L.Ed.2d 136 (1979); *Levit v. Ingersoll Rand Financial Corp.,* 874 F.2d 1186, 1197–98 (7th Cir.1989); *In re Iowa R.Co.,* 840 F.2d 535 (7th Cir.1988). "[W]hatever equitable powers remain in the bankruptcy courts must and can only be exercised within the confines of the Bankruptcy Code." *Ahlers,* 485 U.S. at 206, 108 S.Ct. at 968.

Whether the "new value exception" to the absolute priority rule survived the codification of that rule in 1978 is a question open in this circuit. *In re Stegall,* 865 F.2d 140, 142 (7th Cir.1989). The language of the Code strongly suggests that it did not, and we are to take this language seriously even when it alters pre-Code practices. *Pennsylvania Department of Welfare v. Davenport,* 495 U.S. 552, 110 S.Ct. 2126, 2130–31, 109 L.Ed.2d 588 (1990); *United States v. Ron Pair Enterprises, Inc.,* 489 U.S. 235, 109 S.Ct. 1026, 1030–33, 103 L.Ed.2d 290 (1989); *Levit,* 874 F.2d at 1196–97. See also Douglas G. Baird & Thomas H. Jackson,

Bargaining After the Fall and the Contours of the Absolute Priority Rule, 55 U.Chi.L.Rev. 738, 746–47 & n. 23, 756–60 (1988). The legislative history reinforces the implication of the text. The Bankruptcy Commission proposed a modification of the absolute priority rule, and its proposal was not warmly received. See, e.g., Victor Brudney, *Bankruptcy Commission's Proposed "Modifications" of the Absolute Priority Rule,* 48 Am.Bankr.L.J. 305 (1974). Congress moved in the other direction, enacting the rule in an uncompromising form: "The general principle of the subsection permits confirmation notwithstanding non-acceptance by an impaired class if that class and all below it in priority are treated according to the absolute priority rule. The dissenting class must be paid in full before any junior class may share under the plan." H.R.Rep. No. 95–595, 95th Cong., 1st Sess. 413 (1977), U.S.Code Cong. & Admin.News 1978, pp. 5787, 6369. Neither the report nor any part of the text of the Code suggests a single exception to this blanket rule.

Bank asks us to hold that the new value exception vanished in 1978. We stop short of the precipice, as the Supreme Court did in *Ahlers,* 485 U.S. at 203–04 n. 3, 108 S.Ct. at 967–68 n. 3, for two reasons: first, the consideration for the shares is insufficient even if the new value exception retains vitality; second, although Bank vigorously argues the merits of the new value exception in this court, it did not make this argument in the bankruptcy court. Despite Bank's failure to preserve its argument, the history and limits of the rule before 1978 are pertinent to our analysis because, as the Court held in *Ahlers,* 485 U.S. at 205–06, 108 S.Ct. at 968–69, at a minimum the Code forbids any expansion of the exception beyond the limits recognized in *Case.*

Case rejected the argument that continuity of management plus financial standing that would attract new investment is "new value". According to the Court, only an infusion of capital in "money or money's worth" suffices. *Ahlers* reinforces the message, holding that a promise of future labor, coupled with the managers' experience and expertise, also is not new value. It remarked that the promises of the managers in *Case* "[n]o doubt * * * had 'value' and would have been of some benefit to any reorganized enterprise. But ultimately, as the Court said * * *, '[t]hey reflect merely vague hopes or possibilities.' The same is true of respondents' pledge of future labor and management skills." 485 U.S. at 204, 108 S.Ct. at 967 (citations omitted). The Court observed, *ibid.,* again quoting from *Case,* that the promise was "intangible, inalienable, and, in all likelihood, unenforceable. It 'has no place in the asset column of the balance sheet of the new [entity].'"

Guarantees are no different. They are intangible, inalienable, and unenforceable by the firm. Beard and Parker may revoke their guarantees or render them valueless by disposing of their assets; although a lender may be able to protest the revocation, the debtor cannot compel the guarantor to maintain the pledge in force. Guarantees have "no place in the asset column" of a balance sheet. We do not know whether these guarantees have the slightest value, for the record does not reveal whether Parker and Beard have substantial unencumbered assets that the guarantees would put at risk. If Beard and Parker were organizing a new firm in Illinois, they could not issue stock to themselves in exchange for guarantees of loans. Illinois requires the consideration for shares to be money or other property, or "labor or services actually performed for the corporation", Ill.Rev.Stat. ch. 32 ¶ 6.30. So Beard and Parker could subscribe for shares against a promise of labor, but the firm could not issue the shares until the labor had been performed. A guarantee does not fit into any of the statutory categories, and there is no reason why it should. One who pays out on a guarantee becomes the firm's creditor, a priority higher than that of stockholder. A guarantor who has *not* paid has no claim against the firm. Promises inadequate to support the issuance of shares under state law are also inadequate to support the issuance of shares by a bankruptcy judge over the protest of the creditors, the real owners of the firm.

Debtor relies on *In re Potter Material Service, Inc.,* 781 F.2d 99 (7th Cir.1986), but it does not support the bankruptcy judge's decision. The new value in *Potter* was a combination of $34,800 cash plus a guarantee of a $600,000 loan. If Beard and Parker had contributed substantial cash, we would have a case like *Potter.* They didn't, and we don't. To the extent *Potter* implies that a guarantee alone is "new value", it did not survive *Ahlers. Potter* observed that the guarantor took an economic risk, 781 F.2d at 103. *Ahlers* holds that *detriment* to the shareholder does not amount to "value" to the firm; there must be an infusion of new capital. See John D. Ayer, *Rethinking Absolute Priority after Ahlers,* 87 Mich.L.Rev. 963 (1989). A guarantee may be costly to the guarantor, but it is not a balance-sheet asset, and it therefore may not be treated as new value. The plan of reorganization should not have been confirmed over Bank's objection.

Vacated and Remanded.

Notes and Questions

1. Who is right, Judge Reinhardt or Judge Easterbrook? Under the plan proposed in *Bonner Mall* it appears that the bank may receive a secured claim on the entire value of the mall, $3.2 million. On its unsecured claim of $3.4 million, the bank would receive 300,000 shares of preferred stock with an estimated value of $300,000, stock that could possibly be converted into 300,000 shares of common stock. In addition, certain of the creditors including the bank, would receive a mortgage on a piece of property that might be worth $2 million or, maybe, zero. The old shareholders provide certain working capital in return for 2 million shares of the new corporation.

Under what circumstances would it be clear that the plan is unfair to the bank? What circumstances would make it seem clearly fair? If the value of the mall will soon rise to $5,000,000, the plan seems unfair to bank. True? On the other hand, if that is true, bank could have protected itself by making the 1111(b) election. Not so?

2. If the mall is worth $3.2 million and has no prospect of ever being worth more in the foreseeable future, bank gets everything it could possibly hope for. True?

3. Perhaps one should look at the absolute priority rule as a form of bargaining leverage granted to the secured creditor vis-a-vis the debtor. If that is so, bank could hold out (by threat of a veto of any plan) until it got the highest possible offer from the existing holders. True? On the other hand, it might blackmail the holders. True?

4. The Ninth Circuit suggests that the debate over the new value exception is an artifact of an *a priori* conclusion about the purpose of Chapter 11. Those who like the new value find Chapter 11's paramount purpose to successful reorganization. Those who oppose new value see the protection of creditors' interests as paramount. What do you think?

Problem 9-10

The Action Auto reorganization plan calls for new investment by a group of investors that includes some of the prior owners of the company. Could that plan be confirmed over the objection of Class 12 creditors? Could it be confirmed over the objection of Class 7 if all other classes vote for the plan?

Problem 9-11

Debtor partnership owes $10 million to Bank, secured by a mortgage on Debtor's hotel, which is valued at $7 million. It owes Hershel Finance $2 million which is unsecured. Debtor also owes $300,000 to twelve unsecured trade creditors. It proposes a plan with five classes: (1) $7 million to Bank secured by a lien on the hotel and to be paid in annual payments over six years at 9 percent interest; (2) Hershel's claim to be paid in full over three years with interest at 10 percent; (3) Bank's deficiency claim to receive $.05 per dollar paid with interest in six years; (4) all other unsecured claims to receive $.90 per dollar three months after confirmation; (5) former owners retain their ownership in return for a new investment of $50,000 each.

a. Assume that only Bank votes no on the plan. Five of the trade creditors do not vote. All other creditors vote yes. What are Bank's best arguments to prevent confirmation? Should it make an 1111(b) election?

b. Assume that the hotel is worth $10 million. Debtor adjusts the treatment of the Bank debt accordingly and proves the feasibility of making all the scheduled payments. How can Debtor modify the remainder of the plan to achieve confirmation if we assume that Bank and two unsecured creditors vote no, while Hershel and three unsecured creditors vote yes? Can the modified plan be confirmed if it is further revised to eliminate the contribution of new money by the former owners?

Problem 9-12

In Problem 9-6 above (page 560), assume that Bank One and Bank Two will accept a plan that treats them in a fair and equitable manner, but all other creditors will vote no to any plan. Assume that the value of the company as a reorganized, going business is $1.5 million, while its liquidation value is $800,000. Draft a confirmable plan.

§ 7. DISCLOSURE, VOTING AND PRE–PACKAGED PLANS

One of the prices that a debtor pays for entering the gates to bankruptcy is to make disclosure to its creditors of a large variety of facts and information that are normally private. The purpose of this disclosure is several fold. First, it may be useful to enable a trustee or one of the creditors to pursue and avoid payments that have been made to other creditors, to insiders, or to other friends of the debtor. Second, this information enables the creditors to shape their behavior pending the proposal of a plan of reorganization or liquidation. For example, a secured creditor who is contemplating the possibility of having the stay lifted might be interested in knowing the nature of free assets that would be available and would welcome information that would enable him to determine the probability of a successful reorganization. Finally, and most important for our purposes, the disclosures enable the creditor to bargain over a plan and ultimately to decide whether to vote for or against such a plan.

The first disclosures in a Chapter 11 are under Rule 1007; the debtor in a Chapter 11 is required to file with the petition or shortly thereafter not only a list of its creditors but also a general schedule of assets and liabilities, current income and expenditures, and in some cases a "statement of financial affairs." Next the debtor must submit to examination as provided in section 343 at the meeting of creditors that is provided for under 341(a). The courts have been quite insistent upon the appearance of the debtor at this meeting and upon the debtor's submission to examination under oath. A third important source of information is the Rule 2004 examinations. Bankruptcy Rule 2004 authorizes the broadest possible kind of deposition examination: "on motion of any party in interest, the court may order the examination of any entity."

Finally, one should understand that the largest creditors in a sizeable Chapter 11 case will come to the table with a great deal of information that they have acquired privately both before and after the Chapter 11 filing. Large secured creditors will have received substantial documentation about the debtor's financial affairs at the time they made their loans, and if they have done their job, will have received updates as the debtor slid toward Chapter 11. The large creditors, particularly those sitting on secured and unsecured committees during the bankruptcy, will also have received direct information from the debtor in possession about the value of various assets, their sale and use, and the revenues and expenditures of the business.

In some settings, and for some creditors, a disclosure statement at the time of the plan is almost superfluous. Some creditors will have collected a huge body of information, both prepetition and postpetition, from voluntary disclosures, from the documents filed with the petition, from Rule 2004 hearings, and from informal negotiations over proposed plans. On the other hand, smaller creditors in large cases and most creditors in small cases with few assets may be completely in the dark. Presumably the small creditors in the large cases hope to stand in line with their larger brethren and get the same handout. They hope to be protected by an active creditors' committee formed of larger creditors who share their own interests. Where the creditors' committee is not active, that is no solution. Nor is it a reliable solution where the small creditors' interests diverge from those of the large creditors.

So one comes to section 1125, postpetition disclosure and solicitation. That section explicitly recognizes a substantial difference in the knowledge and need for information of the various parties. Its operative section requires that the potential voter receive "adequate information".

Subsection (c) explicitly recognizes the difference in the need for information of the various claimants. Although it requires that the same disclosure statement be transmitted to each member of a particular class, it authorizes different disclosure statements "differing in amount, detail, or kind of information, as between classes."

Rules 3016 and 3017 implement the provisions of section 1125. Rule 3017 contemplates a hearing 25 days or more after the disclosure statement is prepared and parties are given notice. Even if no one objects or otherwise asks for a hearing, a disclosure statement hearing must be held. An objection to the disclosure statement will provide an additional occasion for dissatisfied creditors to argue for better treatment and to litigate over the debtor's failure to give it, albeit in the guise of complaining about the form of disclosure.

Potentially more troublesome than defining the rules concerning the debtor in possession's obligations for disclosure and solicitation is defining the rules with respect to the opposing creditors' obligations. Surely creditors can negotiate with a debtor in possession and with one another, and can solicit votes in opposition to the debtor in possession's proposal. After all, that is the whole point of a vote, and the Act should encourage such behavior to keep the debtor in possession, who has the upper hand and who possesses most of the knowledge, from taking advantage of others. Frequently the solicitation of a no vote will be accompanied by intimations, if not explicit suggestions, about other and more favorable plans to be proposed by the creditor who is soliciting the no vote. Can a creditor who has not shown his plan to the light of day skulk around like the seller of fake watches and show scraps of his proposed plan to various creditors in an effort to get them to vote no? We hope the answer is yes, but the courts have just begun to wrestle with this problem. To understand the problem and to formulate your own views on these questions, consider the following case.

CENTURY GLOVE, INC. v. FIRST AMERICAN BANK OF NEW YORK

United States Court of Appeals, Third Circuit, 1988.
860 F.2d 94.

* * *

I.

Century Glove filed its petition seeking reorganization in bankruptcy on November 14, 1985. On August 1, 1986, Century Glove filed its reorganization plan, along with a draft of the disclosure statement to be presented along with the plan. Arguing that Century Glove's largest claimed assets are speculative lawsuits (including one against FAB), FAB presented a copy of an alternative plan to the unsecured creditors' committee. FAB advised that it would seek court approval to present its plan as soon as possible. The committee ultimately rejected the plan in favor of that of the debtor. On December 2, 1986, the bankruptcy court approved Century Glove's disclosure statement. A copy of the plan, the statement, and a sample ballot were then sent to Century Glove's creditors entitled to vote on the plan's acceptance.

Between December 12 and December 17, 1986, an attorney for FAB, John M. Bloxom, telephoned attorneys representing several of Century Glove's creditors. Among these creditors were Latham Four Partnerships ("Latham Four") and Bankers Trust New York Corporation ("BTNY"). Bloxom sought to find out what these creditors thought of the proposed reorganization, and to convince them to vote against the plan. He said that, while there was no other plan approved for presentation, and thus no other plan "on the table," FAB had drafted a plan and had tried to file it. The creditors' attorneys then asked for a copy of the plan, which FAB provided. The copies were marked "draft" and covering letters stated that they were submitted to the creditors for their comments. The draft did not contain certain information necessary for a proper disclosure statement, such as who would manage Century Glove after reorganization.

With a copy of its draft plan, FAB also sent to Latham Four a copy of a letter written to the unsecured creditors' committee by its counsel. In the letter, dated August 26, 1986, counsel questioned the committee's endorsement of the Century Glove plan, arguing that the lawsuits which Century Glove claims as assets are too speculative. As stated, the committee endorsed the plan anyway. Upset with this decision, one of its members sent a copy of the letter to a former officer of Century Glove. The officer then sent a copy, unsolicited, to FAB. Uncertain whether the letter was protected by an attorney-client privilege, FAB asked the committee member whether he had disclosed the letter voluntarily. He said that he had, and furnished a second copy directly to FAB. FAB attached this letter to a motion before the bankruptcy court seeking to have the committee replaced. The bankruptcy court later held the letter a privileged communication.

BTNY had made a preliminary decision on September 12, 1986, to reject Century Glove's plan. It reaffirmed this decision on December 15, when it received a copy of the plan and disclosure. Counsel for BTNY spoke with Bloxom the next day, December 16, 1986, and Bloxom mailed a letter confirming the call, but by mistake Bloxom did not send a draft of the alternate plan until December 17. On that day, counsel for BTNY prepared its ballot rejecting Century Glove's plan, and informed Bloxom of its vote.

After receiving the several rejections, Century Glove petitioned the bankruptcy court to designate, or invalidate, the votes of FAB, Latham Four and BTNY. Century Glove argued that FAB had acted in bad faith in procuring these rejections.

II.

The bankruptcy court held that FAB had violated 11 U.S.C. § 1125(b), which allows solicitation of acceptance or rejections only after an approved disclosure statement has been provided the creditor. Though a statement had been filed and provided, the bankruptcy court stated that:

> solicitations * * * must be limited by the contents of the plan, the disclosure statement, and any other court-approved solicitation material. The solicitee may not be given information outside of these approved documents.

The bankruptcy court found that FAB violated the section by providing additional materials such as copies of its draft plan. 74 B.R. 952.

The bankruptcy court also concluded that FAB had violated "the spirit of § 1121(b), since FAB was apparently seeking approval of a plan which was not yet filed and which it could not file * * *."[2] This "impropriety" was "heightened" by the absence from the FAB plan of such information as "who will manage the debtor." The bankruptcy court also found "improper" the disclosure by FAB of the August 26, 1986 letter to the creditors' committee. The court found that FAB's "machinations" in procuring a second copy of the letter showed that it was "obviously wary" that the letter might be privileged.

The bankruptcy court held invalid Latham Four's vote. It allowed the vote of BTNY, however, finding that the creditor had proved it had not relied on FAB's statements in deciding to reject Century Glove's plan. The court declined to bar FAB from participating further in the reorganization, finding such a sanction "too harsh," but instead, ordered FAB to pay for "all costs incurred by [Century Glove] in prosecuting" its motions. The amount of these damages was not specified. Both parties appealed the decision to the district court.

In a decision dated January 5, 1988, the district court affirmed the bankruptcy court rulings allowing BTNY's vote, but reversed the desig-

---

2. The parties do not dispute that 11 U.S.C. § 1121(b), which provides the debtor the exclusive right to file a plan for a limited period of time, applied at all times relevant to this action.

nation of Latham Four and the imposition of money sanctions against FAB. 81 B.R. 274. The district court disagreed that § 1125(b) requires approval for all materials accompanying a solicitation, and found such a reading in conflict with the bankruptcy code's policy of fostering free negotiation among creditors. The district court held that merely supplying additional information does not constitute "bad faith" or a violation of the bankruptcy rules. Therefore, the court concluded, the bankruptcy court had erred in finding that FAB had improperly solicited rejections of the Century Glove plan.

The district court next considered whether FAB had improperly sought acceptance of its own plan. The court found that, in order to facilitate negotiations, communications between creditors should not easily be read as solicitations. Because Bloxom did not make a "specific request for an official vote," In re Snyder, 51 B.R. 432, 437 (Bankr. D.Utah 1985), FAB's action "may only be fairly characterized as part of FAB's negotiations." Because FAB did not unlawfully solicit rejections, and did not solicit acceptances, the designation and sanction orders of the bankruptcy court were reversed. Century Glove appeals to this court.

III.

* * *

A.

The bankruptcy court held that FAB had "clearly violated" 11 U.S.C. § 1125(b), which bars the solicitation of acceptances or rejections until a creditor has received "adequate information" approved by the court. Ultimately, the bankruptcy court ordered FAB to pay the debtor's costs as a sanction for that violation. The bankruptcy court also considered whether certain votes should be designated under 11 U.S.C. § 1126(e). That section allows the bankruptcy court to hold invalid any vote that was not made or solicited "in good faith or in accordance with the provisions of this title." Although the bankruptcy court relied on its finding of liability under § 1125(b) in deciding whether to designate votes, we find the costs and designation decisions separate.

Section 1125(b) bars certain solicitation activities, regardless of the intent of the actor. Whether that provision is violated is not a matter left to the discretion of the bankruptcy court, but is a matter of fact and law. Section 1126(e), on the other hand, is not simply a remedy for § 1125(b) violations. It grants the bankruptcy court discretion to sanction any conduct that taints the voting process, whether it violates a specific provision or is in "bad faith." Thus, the bankruptcy court also considered several "improprieties" unrelated to the § 1125(b) decision in deciding whether the designate votes. Further, § 1126(e) grants a limited discretion: the bankruptcy court may designate a vote or not. The section does not give the court discretion to impose other remedies, such as the payment of costs. Thus, determining whether the bankruptcy court acted properly in imposing costs does not determine whether it acted properly in designating (or not) certain votes. We therefore find the bankruptcy court's order imposing costs and designating one vote separate decisions. We review each for finality.

* * *

23. We therefore hold that the district court's decision reversing the designation of Latham Four's vote and permitting the votes of the other creditors is not subject to review at this time. However, the decision holding that FAB did not violate 11 U.S.C. § 1125(b) and reversing the imposition of costs does present a separate and final order. We will review the merits of that decision.

IV.

Century Glove argues that the district court erred in holding FAB did not improperly solicit rejections of Century Glove's reorganization plan. Since a district court sits in an appellate capacity over bankruptcy decisions, our review of the district court's decision is plenary. *Universal Minerals, Inc. v. C.A. Hughes & Co.,* 669 F.2d 98, 101–02 (3d Cir.1981). We should apply the same standard of the review the district court should have applied. The bankruptcy court based its finding that FAB had violated 11 U.S.C. § 1125(b) primarily on its determination that a solicitee may not be provided with materials not approved by the court. The district court disagreed with this reading of the law. As a question of the proper interpretation of the bankruptcy code, we have plenary review. However, we can reverse the factual findings of the bankruptcy court only if, applying the proper law, they are clearly erroneous. Bankruptcy Rule 8013.

There is no question that, at the time of FAB's solicitations, the solicitees had received a summary of the plan and a court-approved statement disclosing adequate information. Also, the bankruptcy court's factual conclusion that FAB was seeking rejections of Century Glove's plan is not clearly erroneous, and so must be assumed. Century Glove argues that FAB also was required to get court approval before it could disclose additional materials in seeking rejections.

Century Glove's interpretation of the section cannot stand. Century Glove argues, and the bankruptcy court assumed, that only approved statements may be communicated to creditors. The statute, however, never limits the facts which a creditor may receive, but only the *time* when a creditor may be solicited. Congress was concerned not that creditors' votes were based on misinformation, but that they were based on no information at all. *See* H.R. 95–595, at pp. 225–25, 95th Cong., 2d Sess., 124 Cong.Rec. ___, *reprinted in,* 1978 U.S.C.C.A.A.N. 5963, 6185 (House Report). Rather than limiting the information available to a creditor, § 1125 seeks to guarantee a minimum amount of information to the creditor asked for its vote. *See* S.R. 95–989, at pp. 121, 95th Cong., 2d Sess., 124 Cong.Rec. ___, *reprinted in,* 1978 U.S.C.C.A.A.N. 5787, 5907 ("A plan is necessarily predicated on knowledge of the assets and liabilities being dealt with and on factually supported expectations as to the future course of the business * * *.")(Senate Report). The provision sets a floor, not a ceiling. Thus, we find that § 1125 does not on its face empower the bankruptcy court to require that all communications between creditors be approved by the court.

As the district court pointed out, allowing a bankruptcy court to regulate communications between creditors conflicts with the language of the statute. A creditor may receive information from sources other than the disclosure statement. Section 1125 itself defines "typical investor" of a particular class in part, as one having "such ability to obtain such information from sources other than the disclosure required by this section * * *." 11 U.S.C. § 1125(a)(2)(C). In enacting the bankruptcy code, Congress contemplated that the creditors would be in active negotiations with the debtor over the plan. *See infra,* part V. The necessity of "adequate information" was intended to help creditors in their negotiations. *See In re Gulph Woods Corp.,* 83 B.R. 339 (Bankr.E.D.Pa.1988). Allowing the bankruptcy court to regulate communications between creditors under the guise of "adequate information" undercuts the very purpose of the statutory requirement.

Lastly, Century Glove's reading of § 1125 creates procedural difficulties. Century Glove provides this court no means to distinguish predictably between mere interpretations of the approved information, and additional information requiring separate approvals. Therefore, to be safe, the creditor must seek prior court approval for every communication with another creditor (or refrain from communication), whether soliciting a rejection or an acceptance. Congress can hardly have intended such a result. It would multiply hearings, hence expense and delay, at a time when efficiency is greatly needed. We also note that, as expressed in the House Report, Congress evidently contemplated a single hearing on the adequacy of the disclosure statement. *See* House Report, 1978 U.S.C.C.A.A.N. at 6186.

Century Glove argues that two additional instances show that FAB violated § 1125(b). First, it claims that FAB's draft plan contained material misrepresentations, mostly omissions. Second, it claims that FAB improperly disclosed to Latham Four a letter the bankruptcy court later found privileged. The bankruptcy court found both "improper" in support of its finding under § 1125(b), and Century Glove argues that the bankruptcy court's decision can be affirmed on these grounds. The problem with the argument is that it rests on an erroneous interpretation of the law. Once adequate information has been provided a creditor, § 1125(b) does not limit communication between creditors. It is not an anti-fraud device. Thus, the bankruptcy court erred in holding that FAB had violated § 1125(b) by communicating with other materials. The district court therefore properly reversed the bankruptcy court on this issue.

V.

Though FAB was not limited in its solicitation of rejections, § 1125 did prevent FAB from soliciting acceptances of its own plan. The bankruptcy court held that, "since FAB was apparently seeking approval of a plan which was not yet filed," FAB violated § 1125. The court also found that FAB's actions violated the spirit of § 1121, which provides the debtor with a limited, exclusive right to present a plan. Reversing, the district court held that solicitations barred by § 1125(b) include only the "specific request for an official vote," and not discussions of and negotiations over a plan leading up to its presentation. *In re Snyder,* 51 B.R. 432, 437 (Bankr.D.Utah 1985). Because Bloxom explained that he was sending the draft only for discussion purposes, the district court found that the transmittal "may only be fairly characterized as part of FAB's negotiations." We exercise plenary review over the proper interpretation of the legal term "solicitation."

We agree with the district court that "solicitation" must be read narrowly. A broad reading of § 1125 can seriously inhibit free creditor negotiations. All parties agree that FAB is not barred from honestly negotiating with other creditors about its unfiled plan. "Solicitations with respect to a plan do not involve mere requests for opinions." Senate Report, 1978 U.S.C.C.A.A.N. at 5907. The purpose of negotiations between creditors is to reach a compromise over the terms of a tentative plan. The purpose of compromise is to win acceptance for the plan. We find no principled, predictable difference between negotiation and solicitation of future acceptances. We therefore reject any definition of solicitation which might cause creditors to limit their negotiations.

A narrow definition of "solicitation" does not offend the language or policy of 11 U.S.C. § 1121(b). The section provides only that the debtor temporarily has the exclusive right to *file* a plan (and thus have it voted on). It does not state that the debtor has a right to have its plan *considered* exclusively. A right of exclusive consideration is not warranted in the policy of the section. Congress believed that debtors often delay confirmation of a plan, while creditors want quick confirmation. Therefore, *unlimited* exclusivity gave a debtor "undue bargaining leverage," because it could use the threat of delay to force unfair concessions. House Report, 1978 U.S.C.C.A.A.N. at 6191. On the other hand, Congress evidently felt that creditors might not seek the plan fairest to the debtor. Therefore, Congress allowed a *limited* period of exclusivity, giving the debtor "adequate time to negotiate a settlement, without unduly delaying creditors." *Id.* Section 1121 allows a debtor the threat of limited delay to offset the creditors' voting power of approval. FAB did nothing to reduce Century's threat of limited delay, and so did not offend the balance of bargaining powers created by § 1121 or the "spirit" of the law.

On the contrary, Century Glove's reading of § 1121(b) would in fact give the debtor powers not contemplated by Congress. The ability of a creditor to compare the debtor's proposals against other possibilities is a powerful tool by which to judge the reasonableness of the proposals. A broad exclusivity provision, holding that only the debtor's plan may be "on the table," takes this tool from creditors. Other creditors will not have comparisons with which to judge the proposals of the debtor's plan, to the benefit of the debtor proposing a reorganization plan. The history of § 1121 gives no indication that Congress intended to benefit the debtor in this way. The legislative history counsels a narrow reading of the section, one which FAB's actions do not violate.

We recognize that § 1125(b) bars the untimely solicitation of an "acceptance or rejection," indicating that the same definition applies to both. A narrow definition might allow a debtor to send materials seeking to prepare support for the plan, "for the consideration of the creditors," without adequate information approved by the court. Though such preparatory materials may undermine the purpose of adequate disclosure, the potential harm is limited in several ways. First, a creditor still must receive adequate information before casting a final vote, giving the creditor a chance to reconsider its preliminary decision. The harm is further limited by free and open negotiations between creditors. Last, because they are not "solicitations," pre-disclosure communications may still be subject to the stricter limitations of the securities laws. 11 U.S.C. § 1125(e). Where, as here, the creditors are counselled and already have received disclosure about the debtor's business, there seems little need for additional procedural formalities. *See e.g., In re Northwest Recreational Activities, Inc.,* 4 B.R. 43 (Bankr.N.D.Ga.1980)(negotiations between debtor and creditor precede § 1125(b) approvals).

Therefore, we hold that a party does not solicit acceptances when it presents a draft plan for the consideration of another creditor, but does not request that creditor's vote. Applying this definition, FAB did not solicit acceptances of its plan. Century Glove does not dispute that FAB never asked for a vote, and clearly stated that the plan was not yet available for approval. Bloxom communicated with lawyers for the creditors, and there is no suggestion by Century that these lawyers did not understand the limitations. Also as Century argues, FAB never sent its plan to Hartford Insurance because Hartford firmly opposed Century's plan. Contrary to Century's conclusion, though, this fact argues that FAB sent copies of its plan because it was interested in obtaining rejections, not acceptances. (An opponent of Century's plan would be an ideal person to solicit for acceptances.) These undisputed facts require a finding that FAB did not "solicit" acceptances within the meaning of § 1125(b).

VI.

We hold that the district court correctly determined that Century Glove failed to show that FAB violated 11 U.S.C. § 1125 by soliciting acceptances or improperly soliciting rejections. We therefore will affirm the district court's order reversing the imposition of costs against FAB. We do not decide, however, whether the circumstances merit designation of the votes of any creditors.

Problem 9–13

Bob Cratchett Inc., a medium-sized business, declared bankruptcy on October 13, 1989. In 1985, Nickleby Bank, together with seven other banks, lent Cratchett $2 million secured by an office building and property. Shortly before bankruptcy, when Cratchett had fallen two months behind in loan payments, the bank creditors formed a steering committee to investigate Cratchett's financial affairs. A complete report had been presented to all bank creditors.

On January 23, 1990 the debtor sought court approval of a disclosure statement. The statement included the following information: history of the debtor and events leading to bankruptcy, description of available assets and their value, anticipated future operations of the company, brief synopsis of the current financial condition, a liquidation analysis prepared by the company's Chief Financial Officer, identification of future management, proposed Chapter 11 plan, and an estimate of all fees. The proposed plan provided for continued loan installments for a portion of the bank debt and the conversion of the remaining portion into preferred stock. Trade creditors received 35 percent of their claims. Professional fees were paid in full.

What objections to the disclosure statement could the bank creditors raise? The trade creditors?

Problem 9–14

Boz Corporation, operating under the name Kopperfield Korners, is the largest convenience store chain in the world. In 1987, Boz was acquired through a leveraged buyout transaction. The Corporation borrowed approximately $4.0 billion in secured term loans and debt securities to fund the purchase. By late 1989 Boz realized that the large debt load capital foreclosed expenditures necessary.

On April 9, 1990, Boz proposed an exchange agreement which involved the issue of new securities in exchange for the debt and securities previously issued. Kopperfield Korners Japan and T.T. Company (the Purchasers) agreed to acquire 75 percent of the new securities.

In response to the exchange offer, the holders of Boz's old securities formed a Committee to seek to maximize the value they would obtain in any restructuring. The Committee conducted a due diligence review of Boz which included forecasts, valuation analysis, and the preparation of a counterproposal. During the review and negotiations, Boz's financial condition continued to deteriorate. By June 1990, Boz had ceased to make interest payments on its debt securities.

Eventually Boz and the Committee agreed on a restructuring plan. On August 2, 1990 Boz mailed a prospectus reflecting the agreed upon security exchange terms. The Committee's approval of the proposal was conditional on Boz's submission of materials to the SEC relating to acceptances of a prepackaged plan of reorganization. While soliciting acceptances of its exchange offer, Boz and the Purchaser prepared a reorganization plan which was filed confidentially with the SEC. The SEC filing included information concerning the proposed solicitation of acceptances of the Plan. The Purchaser participated in the Plan preparation but warned Boz that if a bankruptcy petition was filed it would review the circumstances and reconsider its participation in the restructuring.

In September 1990, Boz revised the previously released prospectus to incorporate the reorganization plan and solicitation of acceptances into the exchange offers. On October 22, the exchange offers and solicitation period for plan acceptances expired. Boz had failed to receive the requisite number of tender offers to consummate the exchange offers but did receive enough acceptances to present the reorganization plan to the court. On October 23, the Purchaser and Boz entered into a stock purchase agreement which allowed Boz to file the reorganization plan with the Bankruptcy Court.

Boz's bankruptcy petition was filed on October 24, 1990. The court began the confirmation hearing less than two months later. The issue was the validity of an acceptance vote of a pre-filing plan. Several investors, dissatisfied with the voting process, protested the confirmation. Consider the validity of the pre-packaged and accepted plan. Read the provisions of section 1126(b) and Rule 3018. The following information may be relevant:

a. Report filed with the court indicated that the plan had been accepted by the following percentage and amount:

Class	% Number	% Amount
Old Sr. Notes	87	97
Old Sr. Subord. Notes	70	96
Old Sr. Subord. Disct. Notes	81	99
Old Subord. Debentures	80	82
Old Jr. Subord. Debent.	80	91
Preferred Shares	95.5	

b. The tender of a bond without a vote was deemed to be a vote in favor of the plan.

c. The soliciting dealers received a fee for each tender that was received.

d. Boz considered the vote of record holders in tabulating the votes. No effort was made to determine if the record holder had authority to vote for the plan. Record holders often act as agents or "bailees" for the true owners.

Questions

1. What kind of cases are well suited to so called "pre-packaged plans"?

2. What kind of disclosures should be required and what are the trade-offs? (At least one of the positive trade-offs is that a pre-packaged plan presumably gets in and out of bankruptcy in a short period of time and without the grotesque dead weight loss that attends long-lasting Chapter 11 proceedings.)

Another important question regarding pre-confirmation creditor behavior involves the extent to which trading in claims is permissible. In the following case, a third party (Japonica Partners) attempted to gain control of the debtor (Allegheny International) by buying enough claims to allow it to block confirmation of Allegheny's plan, and then win confirmation of its own plan. As is obvious from the opinion, the judge was thoroughly offended by Japonica's behavior. Apparently he thought that Japonica had hoodwinked him, along with the rest of the parties involved in the case. Bear in mind that all of the parties involved are highly sophisticated, each spent many thousands of dollars on attorneys and financial advisors.

IN RE ALLEGHENY INTERNATIONAL, INC.

United States Bankruptcy Court, Western District of Pennsylvania, 1990.
118 B.R. 282.

Memorandum Opinion

JOSEPH L. COSETTI, CHIEF JUDGE.

The matter presently before the court is the debtor's motion to confirm its plan of reorganization and the objections of various parties to confirmation. The court confirms the plan of reorganization, subject to the conditions and limitations set forth below. Intertwined with the motion to confirm is the Debtor's Motion Under Bankruptcy Code Section 1126(e) to Designate and Disqualify Votes of Claims and Interests Directed by Japonica Partners and Others Acting in Concert (the "debtor's motion to designate"). Also pending are Japonica's Motion Under Bankruptcy Code Section 1126(e) to Designate and Disqualify Votes of Claims and Interests Not Solicited or Procured in Good Faith ("Japonica's motion to designate") and the Motion of the Official Committee of Equity Security Holders of Allegheny International, Inc. to Disqualify All Votes on the Debtor's Stock Plan Pursuant to Bankruptcy Code Section 1126(e)(the "Equity Committee's motion to designate").

In addition, the group of 16 banks who were prepetition secured lenders to the debtor have brought an adversary action at Adversary No. 90–260 seeking equitable relief against Japonica Partners, L.P. ("Japonica") and its affiliates.

The debtor's motion to designate is granted; the votes of which are the subject of that motion are disqualified. Japonica's motion to designate and the Equity Committee's motion to designate are denied, but based on those facts certain limitations, discussed below, are imposed on certain of the secured lenders and the debtor's insiders, as well as Donaldson, Lufkin and Jenrette ("DLJ") and its affiliates. With respect to the action against Japonica by the bank group, Japonica and its affiliates are enjoined, as set forth below.

The instant matters are core proceedings, involving confirmation of a plan of reorganization, 28 U.S.C. § 157(b)(2)(L), and "other proceedings affecting * * * the adjustment of the debtor-creditor or the equity security holder relationship * * *." 28 U.S.C. § 157(b)(2)(O). This court has jurisdiction over the parties and subject matter pursuant to 28 U.S.C. § 1334.

This opinion shall constitute findings of fact and conclusions of law, pursuant to Bankruptcy Rule 7052.

For the motions to designate, we take up the saga, beginning on December 29, 1989, when the debtor filed the instant plan of reorganization. The court conducted several days of hearings on the disclosure statement in January 1990. The court approved the debtor's disclosure statement on February 5, 1990, setting the last day to ballot on the debtor's plan as March 30, 1990, at 5:00 P.M.

However, on January 24, 1990, near the conclusion of the hearings on the debtor's disclosure statement, Japonica filed its plan of reorganization (the "Japonica plan") and disclosure statement which mirrored and utilized in large part the debtor's material and organization. The court was urged by Japonica not to approve the debtor's disclosure statement until Japonica's disclosure statement could be approved and a joint ballot distributed. Japonica requested an extraordinary reduction in the time the rules provided for confirmation. The court feared additional delay and denied the request. The court set separate schedules for confirmation of the plans and promised Japonica an opportunity for creditors to vote on the Japonica plan before any order of confirmation would be issued.

The Japonica plan offered cash equivalent to $6.42 per share with holdbacks, as compared to the debtor's proposed stock plan which offered $7.00 per share. Under the Japonica plan, Japonica would acquire control of the debtor. Although Japonica had indicated its interest in acquiring control of the debtor as early as July 1989, Japonica held no interest as a creditor or equity holder of the debtor until immediately prior to the filing of its proposed plan and disclosure statement. To qualify as a party in interest authorized to file a plan, Japonica purchased public subordinated debentures of the debtor with a face value of $10,000 for $2,712. At that time, the court was unaware that the purchase of claims would be the tactic used by Japonica to gain control.

A. Acquisition of Claims by Japonica

On February 23, 1990, Japonica began purchasing claims of the secured bank lenders, Class 2.AI.2. This occurred after the debtor's disclosure statement was approved and the debtor's plan balloting had commenced. This was also after Japonica had proposed a plan and disclosure statement and had become a proponent of a plan. The purchase of the following claims gave Japonica control of approximately 27% of the claims in Class 2.AI.2:

NAME OF BANK	DATE SOLD	FACE AMOUNT	PRICE PAID	% OF FACE AMOUNT
Canadian Imperial Bank of Commerce ("CIBC")	2/23/90	$12,614,800	$10,121,543.25	80.24%
Israel Discount Bank of New York	2/23/90	2,803,289	2,247,005.25	80.16%
The Northern Trust Company	2/26/90	5,606,578	4,498,462.50	80.24%

NAME OF BANK	DATE SOLD	FACE AMOUNT	PRICE PAID	% OF FACE AMOUNT
Harris Trust and Savings Bank	2/26/90	11,213,154	8,966,925.00	79.97%
NCNB National Bank of North Carolina	3/13/90	8,409,868	6,747,237.00	80.23%
First National Bank of Boston	3/23/90	9,811,511	8,339,784.35	85%

Debtor's Exhibit D-1. On or about March 26, 1990, Japonica purchased the claim of Continental Bank, N.A. ("Continental"), with a face amount of $12,614,800, for $11,284,060, or 95% of the face amount. Following the purchase of the claim of Continental, Japonica held 33.87% of the claims in Class 2.AI.2, enabling Japonica to block an affirmative vote by that class on the debtor's plan of reorganization. 11 U.S.C. § 1126(c). After achieving its blocking position, Japonica purchased the claim of Bank of Hawaii, with a face amount of $2,242,630, for $1,838,956.60, or 82% of the face amount. Under the terms of the assignments by the aforementioned banks, Japonica caused the votes of the claims it purchased to be voted against the debtor's plan.

In addition to purchasing the claims for cash, Japonica agreed to indemnify the assigning banks for all expenses and liability arising from certain lawsuits against the members of Class 2.AI.2. At least some of the assigning banks would not sell their claims unless Japonica agreed to assume such liability. For example, CIBC would not have sold its claim at any price unless Japonica agreed to assume the expenses and liability arising from those lawsuits. The most notable of those lawsuits is an adversary action in this court, at Adversary No. 88–186, in which the Official Committee of Unsecured Creditors of Allegheny International, Inc. (the "Creditors' Committee") has sued the secured bank lenders under theories of preference, fraudulent conveyance, equitable subordination, and lender liability.

Japonica also purchased claims from senior unsecured creditors in Class 4.AI.2. Japonica purchased the claims of Swiss Volksbank and certain other holders of Swiss Franc notes, with a face amount of $21,793,590, for $14,383,769.40, or 66% of the face amount. Japonica caused the votes of these claims to be voted against the debtor's plan. Although Japonica purchased less than 1/3 of the claims in Class 4.AI.2, its negative votes were sufficient to defeat the debtor's plan in that class because of the large number of claims in Class 4.AI.2 that did not vote. It should be noted that Swiss Volksbank was a member of the Creditors' Committee and the Creditors' Committee had recommended a favorable vote on the debtor's plan. It should also be noted that the Creditors' Committee, on behalf of all these unsecured creditors, is a plaintiff in the bank litigation. Unsecured creditors, such as the holders of the Swiss Franc notes, have interests adverse to the interests of the secured bank lenders and would benefit from a favorable result in the litigation. Therefore, Japonica has purchased claims which constitute a blocking position in two classes whose interests are diametrically opposed in the bank litigation.

B. The Debtor's Motion to Designate

Section 1126(e) of the Bankruptcy Code, 11 U.S.C. § 1126(e), empowers the court to "designate" (i.e., disqualify) the ballot of "any entity whose acceptance or rejection * * * was not in good faith or was not solicited or procured in good faith * * *." However, the Bankruptcy Code does not define "good faith." There are few precedents, none controlling, concerning 11 U.S.C. § 1126(e); therefore, we look to the plain language of the section and section 203 of the Bankruptcy Act, the precursor of section 1126(e), as well as the cases interpreting section 203 of the Act.

Section 203 of the Bankruptcy Act provided that "[i]f the acceptance or failure to accept a [Chapter X] plan by the holder of any claim or stock is not in good faith, in light of or irrespective of the time of acquisition thereof, the judge may * * * direct that such claim or stock be disqualified for the purpose of determining the requisite majority for the acceptance." In *Young v. Higbee Co.*, 324 U.S. 204, 211, 65 S.Ct. 594, 598, 89 L.Ed. 890 (1945), the Supreme Court declared that "the history of [section 203] makes clear that it was intended to apply to those stockholders whose selfish purpose was to obstruct a fair and feasible reorganization * * *." The history of section 203, which the court discussed in a footnote, remains relevant:

> A year before the House Committee on the Judiciary held its extensive hearings on the Chandler Act a Circuit Court of Appeals held that a creditor could not be denied the privilege of voting on a reorganization plan under Sec. 77B, although he bought the votes for the purpose of preventing confirmation unless certain demands of his should be met. *Texas Hotel [Securities] Corporation v. Waco Development Co.*, 5 Cir., 87 F.2d 395 [1936]. The hearings make clear the purpose of the Committee to pass legislation which would bar creditors from a vote who were prompted by such a purpose. To this end they adopted the 'good faith' provisions of Sec. 203. Its purpose was to prevent creditors from participating who 'by the use of obstructive tactics and hold-up techniques exact for themselves undue advantages from the other stockholders who are cooperating.' Bad faith was to be attributed to claimants who opposed a plan for a time until they were 'bought off'; those who 'refused to vote in favor of a plan unless * * * given some particular preferential advantage.' * * *

Id. at 211 n. 10, 65 S.Ct. at 598 n. 10.

From the preceding paragraph, it is clear that section 203 of the Bankruptcy Act was enacted, inter alia, in response to *Texas Hotel Securities Corp. v. Waco Development Co.*, 87 F.2d 395 (5th Cir.1936), cert. denied sub nom., *Waco Development Co. v. Rupe.*, 300 U.S. 679, 57

S.Ct. 671, 81 L.Ed. 883 (1937). That case is strongly analogous to the case at bar. Because of the strong similarity, and because section 203 is the precursor of section 1126(e), it is appropriate to examine that decision.

In 1928, Waco Development Company ("Waco") deeded a vacant lot to Texas Hotel Securities Corporation ("THSC"), an entity run by Conrad Hilton. THSC built and furnished a hotel on the lot with money raised from the issuance of mortgage notes. The hotel, but not the furniture, was then deeded back to Waco which assumed the mortgage notes. THSC then leased the hotel and made further improvements to the hotel not required by the lease. THSC ultimately defaulted on the lease. In a Texas state court proceeding, the lease was canceled and the furnishings and the value of the improvements were forfeited to Waco.

Waco subsequently sought to reorganize under section 77B of the Bankruptcy Act. THSC acquired claims against Waco for the avowed purpose of controlling the plan of reorganization so that THSC could ostensibly recover losses associated with the cancellation and forfeiture and regain management of the hotel. In this connection, Hilton voted against the plan of reorganization, which had provided that the hotel would be leased to another entity.

The Court of Appeals for the Fifth Circuit held that Hilton's negative vote, which resulted in failure to confirm, was not improper or unlawful. However, William O. Douglas, who was then a commissioner of the Securities and Exchange Commission, saw Hilton's actions as "extort[ing] tribute from other creditors and stockholders as the price of their assent to a plan."

In the case at bar, Japonica, by acquiring a blocking position, has defeated the debtor's plan and can defeat any other plan and thereby obstruct a "fair and feasible reorganization." Japonica, like Hilton in the *Waco* case, bought a blocking position after the debtor proposed its plan of reorganization. In *Waco,* Hilton's objective was to force Waco to reestablish Hilton's interest in the hotel. In the instant case, Japonica's interest is to take over and control the debtor. Section 1126(e) and its predecessor were intended to enable the court to disqualify the votes of parties who engage in such conduct.

In a subsequent case interpreting section 203 of the Bankruptcy Act, the Circuit Court of Appeals for the Second Circuit held that the purchase of claims for the purpose of securing approval or rejection of a plan of reorganization is not per se bad faith:

> The mere fact that a purchase of creditors' interest is for * * * securing the approval or rejection of a plan does not of itself amount to 'bad faith.' When that purchase is in aid of an interest other than an interest as a creditor, such purchases may amount to 'bad faith' under section 203 of the Bankruptcy Act.

In re P–R Holding Corp., 147 F.2d 895, 897 (2d Cir.1945). Bankruptcy courts interpreting section 1126(e) have quoted this language with approval. *In re Gilbert,* 104 B.R. 206 (Bankr.W.D.Mo.1989); *In re MacLeod Co., Inc.,* 63 B.R. 654 (Bankr.S.D.Ohio 1986). Although Lederman testified that he voted against the plan for economic reasons, the court does not find the economic reasons offered by Japonica creditable. We find that Japonica acted "in aid of an interest other than an interest as a creditor * * *." *In re P-R Holding,* 147 F.2d at 897. The overriding fact that causes this court to reach this conclusion is that Japonica chose to buy claims which gave it unique control over the debtor and the process. With one minor exception, Japonica purchased its claims—and became a creditor—after the debtor's disclosure statement was approved. Japonica knew what it was getting into when it purchased its claims. Japonica is a voluntary claimant. If Japonica was unsatisfied by the proposed distribution, it had the option of not becoming a creditor. Japonica could have proposed its plan without buying these claims.

1. *The Court Finds that Japonica Acted in Bad Faith*

Japonica's actions with respect to the purchase of claims were in bad faith. Notwithstanding Japonica's allegedly longstanding interest in the debtor, Japonica filed its plan of reorganization at the eleventh hour.[7] Notwithstanding Japonica's allegedly longstanding interest in the debtor, Japonica did not purchase significant claims until the voting period on the debtor's plan. Japonica was also at this time a proponent of a plan. The particular claims that Japonica purchased, and the manner in which they were purchased, can be used to determine their intent. Japonica purchased a clear blocking position in Class 2.AI.2, the secured bank lenders. Because that class was the most senior class, a negative vote in that class made confirmation extremely difficult, if not impossible. Japonica paid approximately 80% of the face amount for the first five claims in Class 2.AI.2. As Japonica approached ownership of 33% in amount of this class, it paid 85% of the face amount for the next claim, that of First National Bank of Boston. It then purchased the claim of Continental Bank for *95% of the face amount.* This gave Japonica 33.87% of the amount of Class 2.AI.2 claims. Thereafter, Japonica purchased one more bank claim, but only for 82% of the face amount. If Japonica purchased bank claims solely for economic purposes, it would not have paid 95% of the face amount and then returned to an 82% purchase. Instead, it purchased almost exactly the amount required to block the plan of reorganization.

Lederman was a bankruptcy lawyer who clearly understood the significance of 33 1/3% of a class. The court finds from these facts Japonica's purpose was control and was in bad faith. Japonica recited to the court that it wanted to provide cash to creditors. Japonica's plan proposes to pay cash to creditors, but with a portion held back pending

---

7. Bankruptcy Rule 3016 provides that "[a] party in interest, other than the debtor, who is authorized to file a plan under § 1121(c) * * * may file a plan *at any time before the conclusion of the hearing on the disclosure statement * * *.*" (emphasis added). Japonica filed its plan of reorganization on January 24, 1990—the last day of the hearing on the debtor's disclosure statement.

resolution of unresolved claims. Because the court believed this recitation, the court granted additional time to Japonica for its plan. However, the court was misled. Japonica's purpose was control and so we find.

Similarly, Japonica purchased only enough claims in Class 4.AI.2 to block an affirmative vote by that class. That class follows Class 2.AI.2 in priority. Thus, Japonica purchased a blocking position in the two highest classes which were impaired, ensuring that the debtor could not confirm its plan of reorganization. Again, we note that the two classes in which Japonica purchased claims have directly opposite interests with respect to the bank litigation. The court is hard pressed to characterize Japonica's actions as merely furthering their own economic interests.

Votes must be designated when the court determines that the "creditor has cast his vote with an 'ulterior purpose' aimed at gaining some advantage to which he would not otherwise be entitled in his position." *In re Gilbert,* 104 B.R. at 216; * * *

In *In re MacLeod,* 63 B.R. at 656, the bankruptcy court designated the votes of dissenting creditors who were competitors because the court concluded that those votes were cast for the "ulterior purpose of destroying or injuring debtor in its business so that the interests of the competing business * * * could be furthered." Although the debtor and Japonica are not engaged in competing businesses, the court finds *In re MacLeod* analogous to the case sub judice. Japonica and the debtor were proponents of competing plans of reorganization. Japonica's stated purpose was to take over the debtor. To do so, it was necessary for Japonica to block confirmation of the debtor's plan of reorganization. Thus, the court concludes that Japonica's actions were for an ulterior motive.

Under chapter 11, creditors and interest holders vote for or against a plan of reorganization, after adequate disclosure, if such vote is in their best economic interests. If, as in the instant case, an outsider to the process can purchase a blocking position, those creditors and interest holders are disenfranchised. If competing plans of reorganization are pending, the court must consider the preferences of the creditors and interest holders. If a plan proponent, such as Japonica, can purchase a blocking position, the votes of the other creditors and interest holders are rendered meaningless. Moreover, Japonica, who chose to become a creditor, should not have veto control over the reorganization process. The court does not believe that such a result was intended by Congress. Therefore, for all of the reasons stated above, the court designates the votes of Japonica pursuant to 11 U.S.C. § 1126(e) in Class 2.AI.2 and Class 4.AI.2.

C. *The Alleged Milligan Conspiracy*

Prior to voting on the debtor's plan of reorganization, various creditors expressed concern about the liquidity and stability of the stock they would receive under the debtor's plan. Those creditors, particularly the secured lenders, emphasized the need for an orderly sale mechanism for creditors who did not wish to hold the stock long term. They feared that large blocks of stock would be sold soon after the plan was consummated and as a result of these big sales, the market would be flooded and the price of the stock would be depressed. The unsecured creditors also feared the banks could cause a control transaction to occur, defeating the purpose of the reorganization plan and making the warrants worthless.

From depositions it appears that in late January 1990, Charles O'Hanlon, a representative of Mellon Bank, N.A., the agent for the consortium of 26 banks that comprised the secured lenders, met in Florida with representatives of the debtor, including James D. Milligan, the chief executive officer of Sunbeam and the chairman, chief executive officer, and chief executive officer-designate of the reorganized AI, to discuss, inter alia, the concerns of the secured lenders about the liquidity of the stock and request a mechanism for sale of the stock by those banks that would want to sell. At that meeting, O'Hanlon asked Milligan and Samuel H. Iapalucci, the vice president and chief financial officer, to help locate prospective purchasers of the reorganization stock. O'Hanlon and Milligan both agreed that neither Milligan nor the debtor should actually be involved in the sale or purchase of the stock. However, an officer of Standard Chartered Bank testified that John Elwood, the director of reorganization for the debtor, advised him of the possibility of a buyer of the when-issued shares. An officer of National Westminster Bank testified about a similar conversation with Anthony Munson, the treasurer of the debtor.

Although the exact chronology is unclear from the record, Milligan had discussions with various potential investors familiar to him, including Melvyn Klein, Daniel Lufkin, and the Belzberg Brothers of Canada, concerning purchase of the reorganization securities. O'Hanlon and Gerald Shapiro, chairperson of the Creditors' Committee, had agreed that "DLJ" would be acceptable. At some time, Milligan advised Lawrence M. v. D. Schloss of DLJ that he had spoken with representatives of GKH Partners, who had indicated interest in purchasing the reorganization securities upon their issuance.

On March 7, 1990, at a meeting in Lufkin's office in New York City, Milligan told Lufkin that the aforementioned investors, and others, had "a desire to own equity in whatever company I ran, and that creditors had expressed a desire to sell equity, and they had selected or intended to indicate that DLJ could act as an agent on behalf of would-be purchasers * * *." Iapalucci was also present at that meeting; he explained the plan, including the "poison pill" or change of control provision. That provision provides that no entity or entities acting in concert could acquire more than 30% of the when-issued stock without the offer being made to all shareholders. The next day, Milligan, Iapalucci, representatives of DLJ, and representatives of GKH met at DLJ's offices. Shortly after that meeting, as part of their due diligence, representatives of DLJ and GKH toured various facilities of the debtor. Milligan participated in those tours.

On or about March 16, 1990, DLJ advised those secured lenders who had not sold their claims that a "group of investors has proposed buying when-issued stock from the individual AI Secured Banks. The proposed purchase price is $6.25 per share." Thereafter, Schloss advised the bank group's financial advisor, Houlihan Lokey Howard & Zukin ("Houlihan Lokey") of the outline of the plan to purchase the when-issued stock. Houlihan Lokey then notified all of the banks, and provided DLJ with the names and addresses of the contact people for each of the members of the bank group.

DLJ acted as the agent for those investors. The identities of those investors were undisclosed at the time of the offer. The DLJ offer was made to every member of Class 2.AI.2 who had not assigned its claim to Japonica. DLJ, acting on behalf of its investors, negotiated individually with each bank that was interested in selling its when-issued shares, ultimately entering into Stock Purchase Agreements with the [several] banks.

* * *

Neither Milligan nor any other representative of the debtor were involved in the negotiations.

* * *

The stock purchase agreements did not require the banks to vote in favor of the debtor's plan. In fact, some of the banks required a specific provision to that effect in their stock purchase agreements. However, the stock purchase agreements required the banks to use their "best efforts" to effectuate such agreements. Three banks which did not enter into stock purchase agreements voted in favor of the debtor's plan.

Prior to March 16, 1990, the debtor had arranged a meeting with Swiss Volksbank. That meeting was requested by Swiss Volksbank, and was intended as a discussion of the company and the plan of reorganization. On the morning of March 19, 1990, the following people met with representatives of Swiss Volksbank: Oliver Travers, the chairman and chief executive officer of the debtor; Munson; Robert Martin of Smith Barney Harris & Upham, the debtor's financial advisor; and M. Weston Chapman of DLJ. At that meeting, counsel for Swiss Volksbank indicated to Chapman that the Swiss noteholders were interested in selling their stock; they did not want to hold stock in a reorganized company. None of those parties offered to purchase any of the reorganization stock of the Swiss noteholders, although Chapman raised that possibility at another meeting later that day. Swiss Volksbank stated that they had received an offer from Japonica, so that time was of the essence. DLJ and the Swiss Volksbank did not enter into a stock purchase agreement, but it appears that they began the process. As stated above, Japonica ultimately purchased a significant portion of the Swiss Franc notes.

As of March 30, 1990, when the voting on the debtor's plan concluded, the court had not approved Japonica's disclosure statement. Therefore, creditors and interest holders could only vote for, or against, the debtor's plan. The court approved the Japonica disclosure statement on May 3, 1990.

1. *Votes in Favor of the Plan Will Not Be Designated*

The motions to designate which Japonica and the Equity committee have filed seek to designate all votes filed in favor of the debtor's plan. Japonica and the Equity committee assert that the transactions involving DLJ, Milligan, and the secured lenders were not disclosed, in violation of 11 U.S.C. § 1125. Japonica and the Equity Committee contend that the other creditors would not have voted for the debtor's plan if they had known about the alleged "Milligan conspiracy." They assert that the purpose of the transaction was to take control of the debtor and entrench Milligan and certain debtor executives as the management. Japonica and the Equity Committee further assert that such control of the debtor was to be obtained without paying a premium to other creditors. Japonica and the Equity Committee also assert that the debtor has discriminated against certain creditors and the equity holders as a result of the attempted transaction with DLJ. Japonica and the Equity Committee further assert that the debtor's plan was proposed in bad faith, in contravention of 11 U.S.C. § 1123. In this connection, the parties agree that many of the issues raised in these two motions overlap with objections to confirmation.

Although the court will not designate all votes on the debtor's plan of reorganization, as requested by Japonica and the Equity Committee, certain activities and matters which the court finds objectionable will be dealt with in the context of confirmation. Section 1126(e) provides that the court may designate the votes of "any entity whose acceptance or rejection * * * was not in good faith, or was not solicited or procured in good faith * * *." Even if the court should hold that the attempted transaction between DLJ and the banks was not in good faith, the court cannot disqualify the votes of the other remaining claimants who knew nothing about the transaction. The remedy under 11 U.S.C. § 1126(e) is to disqualify acceptances or rejections that have been improperly solicited. *Trans World Airlines, Inc. v. Texaco, Inc. (In re Texaco, Inc.),* 81 B.R. 813 (Bankr.S.D.N.Y.1988). Simply stated, the court should designate the votes of only those creditors or interest holders who were engaged in wrongdoing. There is no authority for designating the votes of innocent creditors or interest holders.

Nor do we find sufficient grounds for designating the votes of the banks that accepted the various offers. Although we are concerned by the conduct of DLJ and the secured banks, we cannot conclude that the banks voted "in aid of an interest other than an interest as a creditor * * *." *In re P–R Holding,* 147 F.2d at 897. Unlike Japonica, the banks have been parties to this case since that fateful Saturday afternoon in February 1988. Similarly, we cannot conclude that the banks acted for an improper or ulterior motive. *In re Pine Hill Collieries Co.,* 46 F.Supp. 669 (E.D.Pa.1942). The banks voted for the debtor's plan because they thought it to be in their best interest. The banks favored the debtor's plan even without the possibility of selling their shares. Notwithstanding their concerns about the liquidity of the reorganization shares, the banks intended to vote for the debtor's plan of reorganization. Although some of the aforementioned testimony may have been self-serving, it is consistent with the representations made in court over the last several months. An earlier, similar, permutation of the present plan of reorganization was a joint submission of the debtor and the bank group, although the plan of reorganization sub judice was not filed jointly with the bank group. The court finds that the attempted transaction between DLJ and the banks did not cause the banks to change their intended votes for the debtor's plan. Moreover, three banks that did not enter into agreements with DLJ voted in favor of the debtor's plan and their votes would be sufficient to carry the class.

It must also be emphasized that the contemplated purchase price for the when-issued shares, $6.25, was not a premium. It fell within the range of estimates that previously had been made of the value of the when-issued shares, and is consistent with the court's determination of value, discussed below. It should be noted that Japonica later purchased the claims of Class 4.AI.2 at a price equivalent to $7 per share.

However, because it appears to the court that the transactions with DLJ may have permitted DLJ or others to take control of the debtor, the court treats these matters as objections to confirmation. The court does not view those events as a "Milligan conspiracy," although it finds the process inept and ill-timed and lacking disclosure.

All of the parties know that this reorganization has been a fragile process. Consensus has been virtually unattainable. The court questions the thought given to these activities which could upset the delicate process. The third involvement of DLJ is incredible, in light of this court's oft-stated disgust with their earlier failed efforts.

Nevertheless, the court denies the motions of Japonica and the Equity Committee to designate all other votes in favor of the debtor's plan. Later in the context of confirmation, the court will resolve the matters it finds inequitable.

II. THE COMPLAINT OF THE BANKS FOR EQUITABLE RELIEF AND TO RESTRAIN JAPONICA AND ITS AFFILIATES

On April 14, 1989 Japonica announced a tender offer for all claims in Class 7.AI.1, the subordinated debt, and for certain of the claims in Class 5.CH.1, Chemetron general unsecured claims. This tender offer was held open until May 16, 1990. Through the tender offer, Japonica acquired approximately 62% of the claims in Class 7.AI.1 and 36% of the debentures in Class 5.CH.1.

On May 3, 1990 the court approved Japonica's disclosure statement. The court notes that on that date Japonica's tender offer was still outstanding. Therefore, from the approval of its disclosure statement on May 3, 1990, until the expiration of the tender offer, May 16, 1990,

Japonica was soliciting claims outside its plan while it was a proponent both before and after it had an approved disclosure statement.

The court further notes that on June 7, 1990 Japonica purchased the claims of several insurance companies in Class 4.AI.2, senior unsecured claims. Those creditors had voted against Japonica's plan. Thereafter, on June 8, 1990, the final day for voting on Japonica's plan, those insurance companies moved for leave to change their vote. Japonica purchased those claims for $7.00 per share—more than the $6.42 per share which was offered by the Japonica plan.

The results of the balloting on Japonica's plan were filed with the court on June 21, 1990. Three classes of creditors and one class of interest holders did not accept the Japonica plan. The Japonica plan voting results appear as follows:

Class	% of the Voters	% of the Dollars
2.AI.2	36	38
4.AI.2	87	17
5.AI	84	80
5.CH.1	92	66
7.AI.1	88	95
8.AI.1	92	N/A
8.AI.2	74	N/A
9.AI.1	47	N/A

It should be noted again at this point that Japonica's plan was allowed to go forward for voting by creditors because it promised a cash payout to the creditors. Although the court believed the debtor's plan could be confirmed, creditors had consistently expressed strong interest in receiving cash rather than stock. Therefore, the court indulged Japonica and allowed it to go forward with its plan. The Japonica cash plan failed to win the approval of three classes of creditors and cannot be confirmed.

* * *

On June 12, 1990, a group of 16 banks commenced an adversary action, at Adversary No. 90–260, against Japonica and its affiliates. That action seeks, inter alia, the following equitable relief: enjoining Japonica from interfering with the management or exercising control over the business or property of the debtor; requiring that all distributions to Japonica be held as security for the performance of certain obligations under the certificate of reorganization of the reorganized debtor and enjoining Japonica from exercising control over the reorganized debtor; prohibiting Japonica from designating directors of the reorganized debtor; limiting the distribution to Japonica to the lesser of the amount they paid to purchase the claims or the distribution provided in their plan; or, equitably subordinating the claims purchased by Japonica to all other claims.

* * *

In a factually related matter, the debtor's motion to designate, the court found that Japonica entered upon a course of conduct designed to gain control of the debtor. The facts in this proceeding reinforce the court's finding of bad faith conduct of Japonica to further manipulate the bankruptcy process by the strategic purchase of claims. The court intends to issue an injunction related to the issues of control and governance.

A. Public Tender Offer of the Subordinated Debentures While Japonica Was a Proponent of a Plan

Japonica, a proponent of a plan, chose an "end run" around the bankruptcy process by purchasing through its public tender offer approximately 62% of a class. Before the Japonica disclosure statement was approved, Japonica launched a public tender offer for all claims in Class 7.AI.1 and for certain of the claims in Class 5.CH.1. The tender offer expired during the voting period for the Japonica plan. Pursuant to its tender offer, Japonica acquired approximately 62% of Class 7.AI.1 and 36% of the debentures in Class 5.CH.1.

Japonica did not receive this court's approval for its tender offer. As a plan proponent, Japonica could not have solicited acceptances until a disclosure statement had been approved. 11 U.S.C. § 1125(b). Japonica's action caused discriminatory treatment among members of the same class, in violation of 11 U.S.C. § 1123(a)(4). Those who accepted the Japonica tender offer received immediate cash. Those creditors who did not would receive their distribution at a later undetermined date, pursuant to the "official" Japonica plan. Those creditors would receive potentially more cash, but subject to an undesired holdback.

During this period, Japonica had incompatible and inconsistent roles. Japonica made an offer to purchase the claims of Class 7.AI.1. Japonica was also a plan proponent with an offer to that class. The court finds that Japonica acted in bad faith by offering to provide a settlement to a class of claimholders in the absence of a confirmed plan. By doing so, Japonica did not comply with the letter or the spirit of the Bankruptcy Code.

It is beyond dispute that a debtor may not pay creditors outside of a plan of reorganization. Other courts have held that such attempts were an impermissible circumvention of the Bankruptcy Code.

In a prior opinion in this case, this court declared that the assignment of claims "allows a third party to do something which the debtor cannot" before confirmation of a plan because of the constraints of sections 1125 and 1129. *In re Allegheny International, Inc.*, 100 B.R. 241, 243 (Bankr.W.D.Pa.1988). Although the court was critical of the process, the court allowed the trading in claims because the purchasers of claims there were speculators who were using their own resources. Under the special facts of this case, the court cannot apply the same distinction to Japonica. The earlier purchasers of claims were not proponents of a plan—Japonica is!

Japonica's strategic purchases of claims in strategic classes to advance the position of the proponent is not acceptable and constitutes at least bad faith, if not an unlawful act, in the pursuit of confirmation of its plan. 11 U.S.C. § 1129(a)(3).

As the above cited opinion indicated, the result would have been different if the claims purchasers had inside knowledge. Referring to the 1983 Advisory Committee Note to Rule 3001(e), the court stated that, "[w]e recognize that the cases cited therein involved breaches of fiduciary duty. A breach of fiduciary duty implies inside knowledge." *Id.* at 243. As already discussed, Japonica had vast knowledge of the most intimate details of this company unmatched by any other creditor. Japonica possessed all the knowledge of an insider.

Most important, if Japonica had made a substantially similar tender offer to this class as part of its own plan, the plan would not meet the fair and equitable test of senior classes which might reject the plan. Nor would such a plan provision meet the "best interests of creditors test" of 11 U.S.C. § 1129(a)(7)(A) if a single senior creditor objected. By providing that class with immediate cash, the plan would not be fair and equitable to other classes with higher priority who are burdened by a holdback provision. The control tactic of this tender offer itself was extremely inequitable. It placed unfair choices upon the debenture holders. It constitutes bad faith. The class of debenture holders had already voted overwhelmingly for the debtor's plan. During the Japonica disclosure hearing in open court, Fidata Trust Company New York ("Fidata"), the indenture trustee, indicated strong opposition to the Japonica plan. Fidata objected to the lower distribution compared to the debtor's plan and the holdback provisions of the Japonica plan. Further, they objected to the distribution of immediate cash to shareholders who were junior to them. It is almost certain that the "fair and equitable" standard on cram down and the best interest of creditors test by a single creditor would be raised at confirmation.

Further, although the tender offer provided the immediate possibility of cash, the total amount of debentures to be purchased, if any, was not disclosed or committed. These creditors had to speculate if Japonica would only purchase a blocking position. Would there be more delay? The tender offer, if included in the plan, would not be adequate disclosure under 11 U.S.C. § 1125. The debenture class was forced to face a real dilemma—cash now, but in indefinite amounts, or more delay related to confirmation of the Japonica plan. The debenture holders were coerced into selling their claims. This constitutes bad faith.

B. Purchase of Senior Claims in Class 4.AI.2 and 5.CH.1 by a Proponent

Prior to the close of balloting on June 8, 1990, the insurance companies held approximately 35% of the amount of the claims in Class 4.AI.2 and rejected the Japonica plan. These negative votes precluded the confirmation of the Japonica plan. The Japonica plan offered claimants in Class 4.AI.2 87% of their pre-petition claims. When the holdback provisions are considered, the distribution could be reduced to 70%.

Pursuant to assignment agreements dated June 8, 1990 between the insurance companies and Japonica, Japonica purchased the claims of the insurance companies in Class 4.AI.2 for 93.2% of their pre-petition claim. This price was in excess of 6% more than the highest amount to be distributed under the Japonica plan and in excess of 23% more if the holdbacks are considered. Japonica paid more directly to purchase the claims than offered by their plan. This was a naked attempt to purchase votes.

The insurance companies pursuant to the assignment agreement were required to move for leave to change or withdraw their ballots. The court denied this motion.

On June 8, 1990, after purchasing these claims, Japonica also proposed a modification of their plan as it affects Class 4.AI.2, ostensibly to provide the entire class with the same benefit! This modification proposes to pay 94.86% of the pre-petition debt. Recall that earlier in this case, in March of 1990, during the balloting period on the debtor's plan, Japonica had purchased $31 million of the 7 3/4 Swiss Franc Notes for 66% of the pre-petition claims. These claimants are in the same class. The modification that Japonica proposes will pay back to Japonica a handsome profit on the claims that it purchased. Japonica has provided no explanation that new capital will be made available from third parties. Japonica intends to use the debtor's existing cash, assets, and debt to fund this modification. This is *chutzpah* with a vengeance. It is also bad faith.

These facts are close to those in *In re P–R Holding Corp.*, 147 F.2d at 897. In that case, two non-creditors purchased claims to ensure the success of a plan of reorganization beneficial to them. The court held that the purchase of claims "in aid of an interest other than an interest as a creditor * * * may amount to 'bad faith' * * *. [C]ertainly there is 'bad faith' when those purchases result in a discrimination in favor of the creditors selling their interests." *See also In re Featherworks Corp.*, 36 B.R. 460, 463 (E.D.N.Y.1984)("The other creditors, all of whom had already voted, were not similarly afforded a chance to convert their claims to immediate cash * * *. [T]he court does not believe that the law countenances vote trafficking and assertedly otherwise innocent self-dealing *after the votes have been cast."*)

The conduct here is even more offensive than in *P–R Holding*. Here, the sellers were members of the Creditors' Committee and they owed a fiduciary duty to other class members. The purchasers in *P–R Holding* offered to forego the benefits of the claims which they had wrongfully acquired and thereby increase the distributions to others. Here, after having committed a wrongful act, Japonica proposes to pay themselves handsomely under an outrageous view of equity. We find bad faith.

C. *Japonica Partners as a Proponent of a Plan Sought
and Received Inside Information and Should be
Treated as a Fiduciary and an Insider*

Japonica argues that they are not insiders, as that is defined in 11 U.S.C. § 101(30). It is clear to this court that Congress intended that an insider includes "one who has a sufficiently close relationship with the debtor that his conduct is made subject to closer scrutiny than those dealing at arms length with the debtor." S.Rep. No. 989, 95th Cong., 2d Sess. 25 (1978); H.R.Rep. No. 595, 95th Cong., 1st Sess. 312 (1979), U.S.Code Cong. & Admin.News 1978, pp. 5787, 5810, 6269 (legislative history to 11 U.S.C. § 101(30)).

The rules of construction for the Bankruptcy Code specifically state that the terms "includes" and "including" "are not limiting." 11 U.S.C. § 102(3). The use of the term "insider" at 11 U.S.C. § 101(30) provides an illustrative, rather than an exhaustive list of the persons or entities which may qualify as insiders of the debtor.

As a proponent, Japonica sought an order of court to conduct "due diligence" which it needed to obtain bank financing to implement its plan. Japonica had complained that the debtor was not cooperative and that the additional data was required to confirm the public information which Japonica already possessed. This due diligence would be accomplished over a period of time as short as seven days.

A very different story was developed at trial. The testimony of F. Ann Ross–Ray, Esq., was clear, definite and compelling. Over a three-month period, from March 16, 1990 to approximately June 11, 1990, Lederman, Paul B. Kazarian, and William Webber, along with their associates, requested and received the full cooperation of the debtor in obtaining information. It is clear that they received a great volume of information that was not available to other creditors, shareholders, and the general public. This delivery of information was voluminous and thorough. This type of information is available only to insiders. At first Japonica dealt only with Ross–Ray; later they grew bolder and went directly to employees to obtain information they desired.

It is true, as Japonica argues, that they did not have actual control or legal decision making power. However, it is also true that they attempted to influence, in not very subtle ways, decisions made by the debtor. This was especially so when they regarded the decisions as important to their possible future administration. For example, they became deeply involved in the debtor's insurance coverage and the disposal of certain assets.

The testimony of Lewis U. Davis, Jr., Esq., was also clear and convincing. The debtor desired to prevent a loss of value to the enterprise and to provide for an orderly transition in the event that Japonica obtained control under Japonica's plan or under the debtor's plan. The debtor cooperated far beyond the requirement of the March 15, 1990 Order.

Davis testified that on or about June 11, 1990, after the insurance claims had been purchased, Lederman, in the name of Japonica, demanded that a principal of Japonica, Paul B. Kazarian, be named chairman of the board of directors of the debtor, and that Lederman, the other principal, be appointed general counsel and chief administrative officer. Lederman further demanded that Milligan be made to resign so that he could be replaced by Webber, Japonica's designee. Japonica caused to be issued press releases announcing that it now controlled the debtor. Under the pretext of performing due diligence, it is clear that Japonica exploited its special access to information, personnel and the premises of the debtor to attempt to assert its influence and control. Japonica's actual behavior was a breach of this court's order and of bankruptcy principles. In addition, it was disquieting, rude, overbearing and disruptive of employee-management relations.

Japonica sought and received inside information as a proponent of a plan. This court finds as a matter of fact that Japonica is an insider and a fiduciary for purpose of this reorganization.

* * *

The following incident is also illustrative of Japonica's new-found arrogance. At a telephone conference on June 21, 1990, after the close of balloting, Japonica refused to make the results of the balloting available to creditors, even though Japonica had promised to do so and even though Japonica had been receiving the daily results from the entity tabulating the ballots. At the confirmation hearing on June 28, 1990, dramatically at 10:00 A.M. the courtroom door opened and the results were revealed. This behavior illustrates the arrogance with which Japonica and their attorneys have treated the court, and it lends credence to the testimony of Davis and Ross–Ray.

The court finds that Japonica has engaged in a pervasive pattern of bad faith designed to control the debtor and manipulate the bankruptcy process. Its actions are a clear violation of the purposes of chapter 11. All of the above actions of Japonica provide this court with ample grounds to impose restraints and sanctions.

D. *The Purpose of Chapter 11 Versus Control Profit*

A noted commentator suggests that the ultimate intent of bankruptcy is to maximize results for all creditors:

> The basic problem that bankruptcy law is designed to handle, both as a normative matter and as a positive matter, is that the system of individual creditor remedies may be bad for the creditors as a group when there are not enough assets to go around. Because creditors have conflicting rights, there is a tendency in their debt-collection efforts to make a bad situation worse. Bankruptcy law responds to this problem.

* * *

Bankruptcy provides a way to make these diverse individuals act as one, by imposing a *collective* and *compulsory* proceeding on them.

* * *

This is the historically recognized purpose of bankruptcy law and perhaps is none too controversial in itself.

T. Jackson, *The Logic and Limits of Bankruptcy Law,* 10–13 (1986). The purpose of reorganization is to offer an opportunity to maximize results for all creditors and interest holders. Japonica's actions and statements make abundantly clear that it is "control" and "control profit" that they seek. This control profit will not be shared through a reorganization plan with all creditors and all interest holders. A control profit will be shared by only Japonica and their affiliates. Japonica intends to use its newly acquired control to extract economic profit for itself, not to maximize the results for all creditors.

Trading in claims to achieve profits on a specific claim may not be destructive of the reorganization process (a) when both buyer and seller are informed; (b) when the purchaser is willing to hold the claim until distribution; and, (c) when the original claimant does not wish to hold the claim or needs immediate cash. However, the technical provisions of the Code, such as the automatic stay, are designed to achieve the purposes of the reorganization process and to maximize results for all creditors. These provisions are not designed to create delay and pressure claimants to sell. Delay reduces the value of claims. Japonica has deliberately created delay which has improved their ability to buy claims.

The confirmation process enables creditors to modify themselves. The purpose is to increase the pool of value for all creditors and shareholders. Here, Japonica clearly attempts to deprive creditors of the control premium by a manipulation of the reorganization process through the strategic purchase of claims. Acquiring claims with the clear purpose of achieving control of the debtor, thereby earning a control profit, does not maximize the result for all creditors. Such action manipulates the process.

E. *The Control Provision*

As a result of the negotiations with various constituents prior to the filing of the debtors' plan, the debtor included a provision in the Certificate of Incorporation of Sunbeam/Oster Companies, Inc., that would ensure that any premiums paid to acquire control of the debtor would be shared with all stockholders. Many creditors feared that banks would use their position as the largest stockholder to control the reorganized debtor.

The Control Transaction provision, contained in Article Sixth of the Certificate of Incorporation, states that in the event of a Control Transaction any time during the period ending two years after the effective date, any holder of common stock of the corporation may "put" his or her shares to the "Controlling Person" (i.e., demand that the Controlling Person purchase those shares) prior to or within forty-five days after certain notice requirements are met.

A Controlling Person means "any person who has or has the right to acquire, or any group of persons acting in concert for purposes of voting their shares that has or has the right to acquire, voting power over shares of Common Stock of the Corporation that would entitle the holders thereof to cast at least 30% of the votes that all Holders of Common Stock would be entitled to cast in an election of directors * * *." *Id.* The definition of Controlling Person excludes inter alia any person who received common stock pursuant to the plan "unless either (x) such person acquires additional shares of Common Stock for the actual purpose of exercising control over the Corporation, or (y) in any event, such person acquires beneficial ownership *in excess of 45% of the Common Stock of* the Corporation." *Id.* (emphasis added).

We find that in the event that such shares are "put" to the Controlling Person, the Controlling Person is required to pay to such holder an amount equal to the highest per share price paid in acquiring any share of common stock beneficially owned (after the Effective Date and before the end of the forty-five day period) by the Controlling Person. Thus, any premium price paid for control must also be shared with other stockholders. The consideration to be paid to such holders of common stock who "put" their shares to the Controlling Person shall be in cash or the same form as was previously paid in order to acquire shares of common stock which are beneficially owned by the Controlling Person. The Control Transaction provision further provides that, to the extent shares of common stock beneficially owned by the Controlling Person were acquired as a result of distributions under the plan, such shares will be deemed to have been acquired with cash.

Japonica's objections to these provisions, as a matter of law, have little merit. First, Japonica complains that the warrants to be issued to holders pursuant to the plan are counted for purposes of determining whether a person meets the threshold requirement for being deemed a "Controlling Person." Then Japonica objects that neither the exclusion for shares issued pursuant to the plan of reorganization nor the definition of Control Transaction contains an exception for shares purchased on the exercise of the warrants issued pursuant to the plan. Japonica believes that the exercise of warrants issued for purchase of common stock could give rise to an obligation to allow all other shareholders in the corporation to "put" their shares to a Controlling Person. This is not an accurate interpretation of the Control Transaction provision.

This provision provides that at all times the warrants are to be counted for the purposes of determining whether a person is a Controlling Person. However, once the warrants have been exercised, they do not exist and the new stock is counted in the place of the previous warrants. For example, if a stock and warrant holder is determined to own 29% of the company, 9% of which is in the form of warrants and later such person exercises all 9% of those warrants to purchase shares of common stock, such shares of common stock would be counted in the place of the warrants and that person would continue to be viewed as owning 29% of the company.

Japonica also objects that "[t]he Control Transaction provisions may result in different treatment for creditors in the same class," in violation of 11 U.S.C. § 1123(a)(4). There is nothing in the Control Transaction provision that will result in different treatment to creditors within the same class. Japonica uses the example of a creditor in Class 7.AI.1 who holds significant claims in that class as well as claims in other classes, so that the creditor holds warrants and stock sufficient to meet the threshold for causing such person to be deemed to be a Controlling Person. It should be noted that at the time of the hearing on the debtor's disclosure statement in January 1990, and at the end of balloting, there was no creditor that would have received, under the provision in which shares and warrants were to be counted, beneficial ownership in excess of 45% of the common stock of the corporation. Since that time, Japonica has voluntarily purchased claims in various classes which are to receive stock and warrants.

Japonica also objects, at ¶¶ 23–24 of their supplemental objections, to the effect that the Control Transaction provision would have on holders of claims in Class 2.AI.2, the Allegheny Secured Bank Claims. Evidently at the time this objection was raised, Japonica knew that when it completed its plan to purchase claims, it would have acquired a significant amount of claims in Class 7.AI.1 which, after distribution, would be counted with Japonica's holdings at Class 2.AI.2 and Class 4.AI.2, the Allegheny Senior Unsecured Claims. It is clear that Japonica understood and correctly feared the effect that the Control Transaction provision would have on their attempt to control the debtor by this means. The court and other creditors did not appreciate Japonica's concern because they did not know of Japonica's intent. These objections raised by Japonica to the Control Transaction provision are not well-founded.

Actually, Japonica objected to the debtor's plan before it had purchased enough claims to trigger the Control Transaction provision. It appears that its intent to breach that provision may have been long formed. From written and oral objections at the hearing on the debtor's disclosure statement, it is clear that Japonica knew of the intent of these provisions in advance of their claims purchases and accepted the risk that these control provisions could be applied to them.

Japonica has indicated it will not observe the control provisions of the debtor's plan. The banks ask that those provisions be enforced. This court believes it is appropriate to enforce the control provision for at least three reasons. First, because the court believes that the provisions are enforceable under both Pennsylvania and Delaware law; second, because they are separately enforceable as part of the debtor's plan of reorganization which has been approved by the requisite classes; and, third and most important, Japonica's inequitable and bad faith behavior, found above, requires that the intent and substance of these control provisions be enforced as a sanction upon Japonica.

The court intends to mold an injunction to carry out the intent of these control transaction provisions on Japonica by at least denying Japonica's right to vote their shares, unless forty-five days from the date of this confirmation order, Japonica indicates the ability and the agreement to accept the "puts."

F. Section 105 and the Inherent Powers of a Bankruptcy Court Provide the Necessary Power to Grant Orders for Appropriate Relief

* * *

The court's equity powers are codified at section 105 of the Bankruptcy Code, 11 U.S.C. § 105. That section empowers the court to "issue any order, process, or judgment necessary or appropriate to carry out the provisions of" the Bankruptcy Code and is an extremely broad grant of authority to do what is necessary to aid its jurisdiction over a bankruptcy case. 2 *Collier on Bankruptcy* ¶ 105.02 (15th ed. 1981).

* * *

Equitable relief under section 105 also is appropriate to prevent "end runs" on the bankruptcy process. For example, the "power to enjoin assures that a creditor may not do indirectly that which he is forbidden to do directly." *In re Otero Mills, Inc.*, 21 B.R. 777, 778 (Bankr.D.N.M.1982), *aff'd*, 25 B.R. 1018 (D.N.M.1982). Japonica has done indirectly what they could not do directly.

Japonica has interfered with management and attempted to seize control of the debtor. Japonica has abused and manipulated the bankruptcy process. Japonica has unilaterally resorted to out-of-court measures to impose its will upon the debtor and creditors in a manner not permitted by the Code. Japonica's actions are a grave threat to the prospect of prompt and successful reorganization.

This court is compelled by the facts and by the purpose of bankruptcy reorganization and the law to grant equitable relief in the instant case. Historically, in response to this kind of conduct, bankruptcy courts have granted a wide range of relief. However, in the use of this broad power, this court will exercise only such power as will accomplish the objective of the reorganization consistent with the intended provisions of the plan and disclosure statement and on the basis on which the plan was accepted.

Shares to be distributed to Japonica or their affiliates shall be held in trust by the debtor and shall not be entitled to vote on any matter while in trust or owned by Japonica. Japonica, however, may enjoy the other benefits of ownership, such as dividends and proceeds from sale. If, within 45 days from the date of this order, and subject to approval by this court, Japonica establishes with the debtor that it has the ability to respond to puts from all other shareholders and warrant holders at $7.00

per share and $1.53 per warrant, then the debtor and Japonica are to facilitate the purchase transaction and an orderly change in control. If, within 45 days, Japonica does not agree, or does not establish its ability to accept the put of shares and warrants, then the trust of its shares shall continue for three years. Japonica may choose to continue to own the shares or may set in motion with the cooperation of the reorganized debtor and the consent of this court an orderly sale of such shares to parties who consent to the Control Transaction provision.

The remedies this court has selected do not deny at this time the bargain Japonica may have achieved on its trading in claims. The remedies are designed to deny control and the control profit through the denial of the voting power of those shares.

* * *

D. The Equity Committee's and Japonica's Objection to Confirmation Based on the Actions of Milligan and DLJ

In the analysis of the Japonica and Equity motions to designate which the court denied above, the court promised a further look at the same events as an objection to confirmation. The facts are not in dispute. The purposes and intent of the parties are in dispute. The objectors argued that these purchases were an attempt to entrench the management of Milligan and to ensure control. The defendants argue that this was an attempt to provide liquidity and to provide stability for future shareholders. In any case, Milligan is an insider and it was not appropriate for insiders to participate in these arrangements without disclosure to other creditors. The court is sympathetic to the desire by various potential shareholders for stability and order in the market. The court is not supportive of entrenching any particular management or conversely permitting a control profit not to be widely shared.

The Control Transaction provision, which comes into effect when a Controlling Person owns 30% of the shares, attempts to deal with the problem. That provision is no longer adequate for that purpose. Because the court intends to impose a nonvoting limitation on the Japonica shares, a much smaller number of shares could control the reorganized company. Japonica is estimated to control approximately 50%. Thus, 30% would equate to approximately 60% of the remaining stock.

As part of the confirmation process and as a response to Milligan's involvement and the possibility that control was the objective of DLJ and their affiliates, the triggering 30% control provision is reduced to 15% for as long as the Japonica shares do not have the right to vote.

A plan of reorganization which distributes shares is inherently forward looking. The debtor's plan utilizes a distribution of shares. The debtor's projected sales and profit turnaround is an inherent part of this plan. In this fact situation, these shares carry the hope of future improvement. Warrants even more than shares carry this hope of improvement. A control change could prevent these benefits from being fully realized by shareholders, and also by warrant holders. The debtor is directed to place at least a three-year period of life on the warrants.

Because of the limited number of bank claimants and the large amount of their debt ($186 million), the control provisions in the charter were initially designed to prevent the banks from effecting a change in control and benefitting uniquely.

Even though it now applies principally to Japonica, the court deems it appropriate to continue to achieve this result as part of the confirmation process. As a sanction for the involvement of Milligan and DLJ in this process, the bank agreements entered into with DLJ and others for the purpose of selling issued shares at $6.25 are avoided.

The debtor may develop a procedure to lock up these blocks of stock and to create a facility permitting the orderly sale of shares to the general investing public. The court will retain jurisdiction to insure that these developments are consistent with the plan. A change in control not related to the performance of the debtor is to be discouraged. The new Board of Directors is to be specifically enjoined from permitting such a change without protecting the minority shareholders' and warrant holders' interests.

Japonica will be denied the right to vote its shares for at least three years. Japonica will be enjoined from selling its shares to parties who do not agree in advance to abide by the control provisions. Japonica's voluntary divestiture below 45% or below 30% will not expiate its bad faith activities. Japonica's shares will remain with the debtor in trust for as long as the Japonica shares cannot be voted. The control provision is lowered to 15%. The DLJ/bank contracts to purchase when issued shares at $6.25 are avoided as inconsistent with the control provision and because they were not properly disclosed.

* * *

V. Conclusion

The court believes that the preceding discussion addresses all substantial objections to confirmation. Other matters are addressed in the Order of Confirmation. The court finds that the debtor's plan of reorganization fully satisfies the requirements of 11 U.S.C. § 1129.

[The Confirmation Order is omitted.]

Notes and Questions

1. All of the parties involved in Allegheny were so unhappy with Judge Cosetti's rulings that they settled. The debtor agreed to modifications of its plan resulting in Japonica's gaining control of the debtor, and the creditors receiving cash recovery at the highest price per share estimated by the debtor. See Minkel & Baker, Claims and Control in Chapter 11 Cases: A Call for Neutrality, 13 Cardozo L.Rev. 35 (1991).

2. Judge Cosetti is concerned that allowing trading in claims allows a third party to do something a debtor cannot do: pay cash to a creditor who

wants out of the case. Some commentators have voiced a similar concern: "If the debtor were to offer a group of creditors a cash recovery prior to a plan, it would have to comply with section 1125, so that claims sellers would need a disclosure statement so they could judge whether or not to accept the cash offer. Why should a nondebtor claims purchaser not have to comply with these provisions?" Fortgang & Mayer, Trading Claims and Taking Control of Corporations in Chapter 11, 12 Cardozo L.Rev. 1, 44–45 (1990). Can you think of an answer to Fortgang and Mayer's question?

3. The court found that Japonica had violated section 1123(a)(4) with its public tender offer (see part II.A of the opinion), in that creditors who accepted the offer received immediate cash for their claims, while those who did not might receive more cash for their claims at a later, undetermined date. Consequently, the two types of creditors (acceptors and non-acceptors) who held claims in the same class were treated differently, in violation of section 1123(a)(4). There is a fair argument that Japonica's actions did not violate section 1123(a)(4). To see what it is, read the section carefully.

4. The court in *Allegheny* used pre-Code case law to develop its standard for "good faith" as contemplated by Code section 1126(e) (allowing designation of votes not in good faith). The court did not mention that under the Bankruptcy Act of 1898, every plan was required to satisfy the absolute priority rule. Recall that under the Code, there is no such requirement unless the cramdown provisions of section 1129(b) are invoked. Consequently, when a party's votes were designated under the Act of 1898, the party was still assured the protection of the absolute priority rule, while under the Code, dissenters whose votes are designated will not receive such protection (since, presumably, cramdown will be unnecessary when the dissenters' votes are designated). What considerations should figure into a decision as to whether a party has acted with good enough faith to satisfy section 1126(e)?

5. Minkel and Baker maintain: "[T]ransfer of a claim results in a substitution of holders and nothing more. Holders of other claims and equity interests merely have a new face to negotiate with. They may find the new face more aggressive or less pleasant, but beauty is in the eye of the beholder. The underlying rights and priorities of the parties have not changed." Minkel & Baker, *Claims and Control in Chapter 11 Cases: A Call for Neutrality*, 13 Cardozo L.Rev. 35 (1991). Is it that simple, or is there something to Judge Cosetti's concern that "[i]f a plan proponent, such as Japonica, can purchase a blocking position, the votes of the other creditors and interest holders are rendered meaningless"? *Allegheny*, 118 B.R. at 290.

§ 8. POST CONFIRMATION

Once the plan has been confirmed, what happens? In the best of all possible worlds the debtor steps forth from the bankruptcy court free of debt (or bent only slightly under its weight) enters into business, prospers and lives happily ever after. In the worst of all possible worlds, the debtor stumbles at its first step and fails ever to complete any significant portion of the payments under the plan.

The latter case suggests a variety of questions. First, one might wonder whether the plan can be modified. According to section 1127, the plan can be modified not only before confirmation but also afterwards. Section 1127(b), (c) and (d) provide for such modification, require notification of the various parties and allow certain short cut presumptions about acceptance or rejection of any modified plan.

Second, one might ask about the extent to which the bankruptcy court retains jurisdiction for the purpose of requiring debtor compliance with the plan. Although the Code obviously contemplates certain jurisdiction after the plan (otherwise there would be no possibility of modification of a plan that had been confirmed), the extent to which the bankruptcy court's jurisdiction can be invoked to enforce the plan is unclear.

Traditionally, courts have viewed confirmation as just one step in the administration of a reorganization case. Confirmation of the plan did not interfere with the ability of the court to make sure that the plan was carried out. Under the old Bankruptcy Act, the case terminated with the entry of a final decree. A case brought under the Code will terminate when the court orders it closed, and that time, according to Rule 3022, is also the time of the final decree. As long as a case is open are there any limits on the court's jurisdiction? Section 1142 states that the debtor shall "comply with any order of the court," and then specifies that the court may direct the debtor to carry out other activities such as the transfer of property. Therefore one may read section 1142 as a specific delegation of jurisdiction to the bankruptcy court for the purpose of ordering the debtor to comply with the plan. Conceivably section 1142 should be regarded as the delegation of jurisdiction to the court to supervise and carry out the plan.

However, it is better practice for the court explicitly to reserve jurisdiction. Chapter 11 post-confirmation generally follows Chapter X practice. In Chapter X cases, courts held that the debtor should not be indefinitely kept "under the judicial wing" after confirmation and substantial consummation. Therefore it may be important to put a term on the plan which gives the court jurisdiction to supervise and carry out the plan. If jurisdiction is not reserved and the debtor defaults, the creditor will probably have to pursue its claim outside the bankruptcy courts. Hopper, *Confirmation of a Plan Under Chapter 11 of the Bankruptcy Code and the Effect of Confirmation on Creditor's Rights*, 15 Ind.L.Rev. 501, 521–22 (1982).

If the court reserves jurisdiction to order the carrying out of the plan, can the debtor be sued in state court? Note that the stay in section 362(c)(2) continues until a discharge is granted or denied. Under section 1141(d)(1)(A), the debt is discharged at confirmation. Thus on confirmation the stay of state court action presumably would no longer apply, unless section 1142 is deemed to be an appropriation of the field.

Section 1141 spells out the "effect of confirmation." The provisions of a confirmed plan bind the debtor and creditor and virtually all of the other interested parties, whether or not those parties are impaired and whether or not they have accepted the plan. Confirmation of the plan vests all property of the estate in the debtor, and presumably that includes property that is not specifically dealt with in the plan. Section 1141(c) specifies that property dealt with by the plan is free and clear of all claims and interests of creditors, but it does not discuss the interest of creditors in property passing to the debtor but not dealt with in the plan. Because section 1141(d) generally discharges the debtor from any debt which arose before the confirmation, no creditor whose claim was so discharged would have a claim on any asset that passed out of the estate to the debtor, unless he had some form of lien that had not been avoided. Can a creditor with a security interest in an asset not dealt with under the plan, now come and seize that asset?

Finally, section 1144 authorizes revocation of an order of confirmation anytime within 180 days after the confirmation, but only after hearing and only if "such order was procured by fraud."

§ 9. BANKRUPTCY AND THE WEALTHY INDIVIDUAL DEBTOR

Almost all of the cases that we study in this book involve corporate or partnership business enterprises. In several places we confront individual debtors who file bankruptcy even though they have substantial assets and, in some cases, high earning potential. Certainly James Taylor had high earning potential when he filed in Chapter 11.

In some cases these debtors seek to keep assets from their creditors. In other cases they need only the fresh start. Some of these debtors are operating businesses and thus are clearly qualified for Chapter 11 as well as Chapter 7. Prior to the Supreme Court's recent decision in *Toibb v. Radloff,* 501 U.S. 157, 111 S.Ct. 2197, 115 L.Ed.2d 145 (1991), there was a question whether an individual not engaged in business qualified for Chapter 11. Reading the plain language to allow such a person to use Chapter 11, the Supreme Court held an individual who was not engaged in business qualified for Chapter 11 treatment.

The interesting question is not whether such persons qualify for Chapter 11 treatment, but why they would choose Chapter 11 over Chapter 7 and what benefits would be thought to accrue to an individual debtor in Chapter 11 compared with the benefits that might accrue in Chapter 7. Note that the rules on exempting property from the creditors' grasp in section 522 do not favor one chapter over the other. If there were generous exemptions in the state whose law applies, the debtor could use those directly in a Chapter 7 or indirectly (as a floor on the best interest test) in Chapter 11. The most obvious motivation for using Chapter 11 instead of a Chapter 7 is to maintain control of the business and other assets. Since there will always be an independent trustee in Chapter 7, but rarely such a trustee in Chapter 11, the debtor may prefer a Chapter 11 where he can be the debtor in possession and, within limits, keep his own secrets and run his own affairs. In many circumstances this surely is a powerful reason to choose Chapter 11 over Chapter 7.

It is unlikely that section 707(b)(designed to catch high income debtors) will reach most of these people. That is because their debts will not be "primarily consumer debts," but rather will arise out of bad investment decisions or poor business judgment. A case that well illustrates the problem is *In re Cooley,* 87 B.R. 432 (Bankr.S.D.Tex.1988). Dr. Cooley was an internationally renowned heart surgeon whose annual gross revenue was several millions of dollars. Presumably he got into trouble not because his consumer debts were too high, but because his investments in the Houston real estate market and elsewhere went sour. John Connally, a former Texas governor and United States cabinet member, suffered the same fate as Dr. Cooley.

To the extent such persons wish to insulate assets from the seizure by their creditors they can be expected to engage in the kind of activity discussed in Chapter 10, namely to transform non-exempt assets into exempt assets. In some cases that transformation requires one to move to a state where there will be more generous exemptions. It is claimed that the largest recent bankruptcy in Kansas City, Missouri (Kroh Bros.) was stimulated by one of the brother's change of residence from the Missouri side of the line to the Kansas side of the line. This signaled the creditors that Mr. Kroh was readying himself for bankruptcy.

It is possible that a debtor with considerable assets can manipulate the Chapter 11 in such a way as to maintain a substantially larger share of those assets than would otherwise be possible. In such a case, one would expect to see exactly the same kind of conflicts between the debtor in possession on the one hand and the creditors on the other that one sees in the more conventional business bankruptcies. One would expect the same kind of disputes about the value of assets, the earning potential of the business, etc.

Finally, of course, one might favor a Chapter 11 over a Chapter 7 in order to continue the operation of the business and continue to draw the salary one might earn from one's own business pending its liquidation.

In an article entitled *Creditors' Strategies in Individual Bankruptcy Cases Under Chapter 11,*[1] the authors make the following comment on the use of Chapter 11 as opposed to Chapters 7 or 13 by an individual debtor:

> Chapter 11 has advantages for a properly positioned individual debtor. In Chapter 11, unlike Chapter 7, the debtor maintains control of the bankruptcy estate's assets as debtor-in-possession. The debtor receives his discharge in Chapter 11 at plan confirmation; in Chapter 13 the discharge is granted only upon completion of

---

   1. D.B. Tatge and D.D. Meier, *Creditors' Strategies in Individual Bankruptcy Cases Under Chapter 11,* 95 Commercial L.J. 255, 256–257 (Fall 1990).

payments under the plan. Under Chapter 11, a debtor can modify both the interest rate and maturity of a long-term residential mortgage obligation; under Chapter 13, such a modification is prohibited. However, Chapter 13 permits the curing of defaults on a residential mortgage during the term of the Chapter 13 plan.

In Chapter 11, the debtor's post-petition earnings from services are not property of the estate. Accordingly, creditors have no *statutory* basis to ask the court to control or limit the debtor's expenditures of such earnings post-petition. In some cases this may enable a high-income debtor to maintain a lavish lifestyle not usually associated with bankruptcy. In contrast, creditors in a Chapter 13 can require a debtor to use all of his disposable income (from post-petition earnings) to fund his plan. The debtor will generally have a longer period to propose and confirm a plan in Chapter 11; the debtor's exclusive right to propose a plan ("exclusivity") normally lasts 120 days. In Chapter 13, the plan must be filed within fifteen days of the petition. In Chapter 11 there is no five year limitation on plan length, as there is in Chapter 13, and taxes may be paid off in six years, as opposed to five. Most of the foregoing advantages to individual debtors in Chapter 11 constitute opposite and equal disadvantages to the affected creditors.

Chapter 11 also poses disadvantages to individual debtors, the most obvious being high administrative costs. Significant costs may be incurred in preparing the debtor's plan and the supporting disclosure statement, attending the necessary hearings, and in administering the voting on the plan. Litigation may also be protracted in Chapter 11, increasing administrative costs. However, to the extent that the debtor's primary source of income is from personal services, which income is not property of the estate, the creditors bear these administrative costs. The long time spent in Chapter 11 perpetuates the stigma of bankruptcy, to the extent that any stigma still exists, and to some extent extends the court's oversight of the debtor's personal and business transactions.

Prior to 1994 a principal obstacle to the use of Chapter 13 was the low limits on debt—$100,000 unsecured and $350,000 secured. In 1994, Congress raised the limits to $250,000 of noncontingent unsecured debt and $750,000 of noncontingent secured debt. These changes will make Chapter 13 a viable alternative for many who otherwise would have had to file under Chapter 11. Of course, there are many other reasons that favor one of the chapters over the others. It is too soon to tell whether this offer of Chapter 13 will be accepted by significant numbers of persons who are newly eligible for Chapter 13.

Questions

1. Do you understand each of the arguments the authors make to explain the virtues of Chapter 11 as compared with the other Chapters? For example, why does it matter that there will be a trustee appointed in a Chapter 7 case?

2. Analyze the strategies that are suggested for creditors. Can you suggest any others?

3. Assume that your debtor, formerly a successful lawyer practicing in New York City, files in Chapter 11. The debtor owns a home with a value in excess of $2,000,000 in southern Connecticut. Will a court lift the stay and authorize your client, the mortgagee, to foreclose and sell the home on the ground that the debtor has no equity and the asset is not needed for the reorganization? See section 362(b)(2).

If the property is owned jointly and only the husband files, will that stop the foreclosure of the mortgage? (Assume alternatively that the wife signed or did not sign the mortgage.) Consider section 363(h) and the possible application of community property law.

Even the most aggressive creditor will concede some income to the debtor to enable the debtor to continue his life. Creditors have made a variety of interesting arguments to capture a portion of the debtor's postpetition earnings. The arguments about what part of the sole proprietorship's income must be included into the bankruptcy estate—and ultimately given to the creditors—rests upon an interpretation of sections 541(a)(6) and (a)(7). The former section excludes proceeds, products, offspring and rent, that are property of the estate "such as are earnings from services performed by an individual debtor after the commencement of the case." The following case summarizes the learning on this question and adopts a novel (and questionable) interpretation of section 541(a)(6).

IN RE HERBERMAN

United States Bankruptcy Court, Western District of Texas, 1990.
122 B.R. 273.

Order Granting Motion to Compel Debtors to Deliver Property to the Estate

LEIF M. CLARK, BANKRUPTCY JUDGE.

This decision addresses the issue whether income accruing to an individual debtor during the course of a chapter 11 bankruptcy from his operation of a service oriented sole proprietorship is property of the estate. The creditors assert that all income accruing to the debtor postpetition and pre-confirmation is property of the estate. The debtor maintains that all income from services provided by the individual debtor is excluded from the estate by Section 541(a)(6) of the Bankruptcy Code.

BACKGROUND

The debtor, Dr. Herberman, filed his Chapter 11 petition July 3, 1989. Although he is a long standing resident of El Paso, Texas, he chose to file in Austin, Texas. On January 1, 1990, Dr. Herberman's creditors prevailed on a motion for change of venue and the case was transferred to El Paso. The motion for turnover of property of the estate under consideration was filed by a group of Dr. Herberman's former business associates, specifically these are, James Duvall, Crown

Point Corporation, James Peterson, Pinecliff Corporation, Ira Batt, Nell Sergent, Paul Sergent, Irene Batt, Albert Cox and Maureen Cox (the "Cox Group").

Dr. Herberman is an established, well-respected urologist. He has practiced in the El Paso community for over 20 years. The two other urologists who testified at the hearing on this matter stated that they were familiar with Dr. Herberman's work and that he was held in high esteem in the El Paso medical community. He is Board Certified in his specialty and has been chosen to be a Fellow of the American College of Surgeons.

Dr. Herberman's medical practice is profitable. During the past five years he has reported the following income figures:

1985:	$127,000
1986:	$479,000
1987:	$430,000
1988:	$547,554
1989:	$698,631

Dr. Herberman operates as the only physician in a sole proprietorship. He has both a surgery and an office practice, with the latter serving to support the former. The debtor's practice is based on volume, including volume surgeries. He advertises heavily in both English and Spanish. On his office days, he is limited to spending only a few minutes with each patient. His surgeries are scheduled (often back to back) at various hospitals in the El Paso area. To make the operation flow, Dr. Herberman employs ten other individuals. These employees schedule patient appointments, take background information, channel patients into examination rooms, submit insurance forms, assure collections and schedule surgeries. The assistance of these employees is essential to the financial performance of Dr. Herberman's practice. In short, he could not generate the revenues he does without the volume, and he could not handle the volume without his staff.

Dr. Herberman's offices are relatively large, with parking for upwards of at least a dozen cars. His practice does not involve a significant need for sophisticated or expensive office equipment, drugs, or supplies, though he of course does have examining tables and medical "tools." He also has the usual complement of routine office equipment and furniture.

Discussion

The debtor asserts that all income from his practice is excluded from the estate as his personal service earnings, relying on Section 541(a)(6) and a bankruptcy decision out of the Southern District of Texas (also involving a physician). *See* 11 U.S.C. § 541(a)(6)(" * * * except such as are earnings from services performed by an individual debtor after the commencement of the case"); *In re Cooley,* 87 B.R. 432 (Bankr.S.D.Tex. 1988).

The creditors maintain that all of debtor's income become property of the estate under Section 541(a)(7), and that only the court-approved "salary" of the debtor is then excluded by operation of Section 541(a)(6).

The case law on this issue is limited. In the opinion of this court, the two reported seminal cases on point,[1] while logical and well written, are not faithful to the essential statutory framework laid out in the Bankruptcy Code. We commence with a discussion of these two decisions.

A. *Prior case authority*

1. In re FitzSimmons

In *FitzSimmons,* the bankruptcy court had permitted an attorney who operated his practice as a sole proprietorship to pay himself a salary of $3,500 per month out of the funds of his law practice, but required him to remit to a trustee at the end of each month all funds generated by the law practice in excess of $15,000. *In re FitzSimmons,* 725 F.2d 1208, 1209 (9th Cir.1984). The Bankruptcy Appellate Panel reversed the bankruptcy court's order "insofar as it holds that post-bankruptcy earning from services performed by an individual debtor are property of the estate in a Chapter 11 case." *In re Fitzsimmons,* 20 B.R. 237, 240 (Bankr.9th Cir.1982). On appeal, the Ninth Circuit held that, pursuant to Section 541(a)(6), all the earnings generated by services "personally" performed by an individual debtor are excluded from becoming property of the estate, reversing the bankruptcy court's "salary" approach. *Fitzsimmons,* 725 F.2d at 1211. The court reasoned that the creditors of a sole proprietorship should be entitled to enjoy the profits of the business just as surely as they are visited with its losses during bankruptcy, but that the earnings generated by the *individual debtor* (as distinguished from the sole proprietorship) are excluded by operation of Section 541(a)(6). The circuit court went on to note that the debtor's personal services did not include "the business' invested capital, accounts receivable, good will, employment contracts with the firm's staff, client relationships, fee agreements, or the like." *Id.*

2. In re Cooley

In *Cooley* the bankruptcy court for the Southern District of Texas was confronted with a Chapter 11 debtor who was also a world renowned heart surgeon. *In re Cooley,* 87 B.R. 432 (Bankr.S.D.Tex.1988). The debtor, Dr. Denton Cooley, operated his practice as a sole proprietorship but employed four associate surgeons who accounted for a substantial amount of his revenues. One of Dr. Cooley's major creditors moved to limit the operation of Dr. Cooley's business.[2]

The court agreed with *Fitzsimmons* that all of Dr. Cooley's earnings post-petition and pre-confirmation were properly excluded from the

---

1. *In re FitzSimmons,* 725 F.2d 1208 (9th Cir.1984); and, *In re Cooley,* 87 B.R. 432 (Bankr.S.D.Tex.1988).

2. It is worthy of some small note that counsel for the debtor here advanced the position of the creditor in the *Cooley* case.

bankruptcy estate, but disagreed with the Ninth Circuit's engrafting of the word "personal" into Section 541(a)(6):

> To the extent that [*Fitzsimmons*] requires a valuation of an individual's personal or "hands-on" services, I cannot concur. The earnings exception does not by its language direct that I conduct a valuation hearing to ascertain that portion of the postpetition income stream of a sole proprietorship attributable to the personal services of an individual debtor * * *. Instead, I hold that * * * the burden of proof rests upon the creditor as movant to show that the purported individual debtor's earnings are in actuality "[p]roceeds, product, offspring, rents [or] profits" derived from those assets or other property interests which have previously accrued to the estate by operation of Section 541.

In re Cooley, 87 B.R. at 441. In essence, the *Cooley* court read the exclusionary language of Section 541(a)(6) to insulate all earnings by an individual debtor *vel non*, while the balance of that subsection could be used to "pare off" assets which could be shown to spring from sources other than the individual debtor's earnings. It would be up to creditors to both raise the issue and prove up the "attribution." The court observed that this approach, in addition to being what it believed to be a more faithful reading of the plain meaning of the statute, also furthered two other policies. First, it furthered the individual debtor's fresh start. Second, it guarded against potential conflict with the Thirteenth Amendment's prohibition on involuntary servitude. *Id.*

3. *Problems with Cooley and FitzSimmons*

In the view of this court, the statutory construction adopted by both *Cooley* and *Fitzsimmons* reads past the plain meaning of Section 541(a)(6), and similarly overlooks the plain thrust of Section 541(a)(7). In addition, the approach of these cases results in the construction of a special set of rules of interpretation for chapter 11 cases involving individuals (including sole proprietorships), when a much simpler, more harmonious (and hence preferable) rule that would apply equally to all chapter 11 debtors, regardless of legal form, is available. The approach of *Cooley* and *Fitzsimmons* also improperly glosses over the important interplay of the individual debtor's dual role as income generator and "trustee" (i.e., debtor-in-possession). We look first at Section 541(a)(6).

a. *Section 541(a)(6)*

Section 541(a)(6) states that "[p]roceeds, product, offspring, rents, or profits of or from property of the estate * * * " are property of the estate. 11 U.S.C. § 541(a)(6). For example, rents generated by an apartment complex owned by the estate are property of the estate by virtue of this subsection. So are the sales income of the "mom and pop" grocery store, the oil and gas income of a multinational oil company, or the proceeds from the sale of a farmer's alfalfa crop.

The subsection backs out of the estate "*such* [proceeds, product, offspring, rents and profits] as are earnings from services performed by an individual debtor after the commencement of the case." 11 U.S.C. § 541(a)(6). Thus, if an individual debtor, by his services performed post-petition, has *earned* (not generated) some portion of the proceeds, profits, rents, etc., of or from the estate's property, then that portion will not be included as property of the estate.

The precondition to getting to this "backout" exception for personal service earnings is that the monies in question be "of or from property of the estate." In other words, contrary to *Cooley,* this backout language simply does not apply if the monies in question are not in the first instance proceeds, etc. "of or from property of the estate."[3] This is the clear import of the plain language of the statute. Section 541(a)(6) is one of seven subsections which define under what, if any, circumstances various interests become property of a bankruptcy estate. The role of Subsection (a)(6) is restricted to a discussion of proceeds, etc. "of or from property of the estate." The exception clause is contained *within* this provision, and commences "except *such* as are earnings from services performed * * * " The word "such" can only refer to the "proceeds, [etc.] of or from property of the estate" referenced in the first part of the subsection. Earnings from services which are *not* proceeds, etc. of or from property of the estate in the first place are not governed by the exception clause in subsection (a)(6).

Thus, a doctor's billings, a lawyer's billings, a dentist's billings—indeed the billings of virtually any service-oriented enterprise fall *outside* the plain language of Section 541(a)(6). These are earnings by the debtor, to be sure, but they are not "proceeds, product, offspring, profits, or rents of or from property of the estate." Therefore, the "earnings exception" does not apply to them and they are not excluded from the estate by that exception, contrary to *Cooley* and *Fitzsimmons.*

So, Section 541(a)(6) is not the general exclusion for post-petition wages and salary for which it is so often cited. Its role is narrower. If that subsection does not govern personal service income in the service enterprise cases, however, then what does? We turn to the more general provisions of subsection (a)(7) for guidance.

b. *Section 541(a)(7)*

Section 541(a)(7) states that property of the estate includes "[a]ny interest in property that *the estate* acquires after the commencement of the case." 11 U.S.C. § 541(a)(7)(emphasis added). To understand and appreciate the full sweep of this relatively straightforward provision, especially in the chapter 11 context, it is important to evaluate the concept of a bankruptcy *estate.*

Upon a voluntary chapter 11 filing, a bankruptcy "estate," is called into existence by the debtor. 11 U.S.C. §§ 301, 541, 1101. An estate is a separate legal identity, created on (and by) the filing of a bankruptcy

---

3. *Cooley* made the backout exception the general rule, and the "proceeds, [etc.] of or from property of the estate" the exception. The facial structure of the statute does not support this approach.

petition, and continuing until confirmation, conversion, or dismissal of the case. 11 U.S.C. §§ 541(a), 1112. As such, an estate is more than just its property. It is an active legal *enterprise,* comprised of that property, to be sure, but also operating under the aegis of the Bankruptcy Code. It can sue or be sued. It can buy and sell property. 11 U.S.C. § 363. It can operate a business. 11 U.S.C. § 1108. It has a defined lifetime, at the conclusion of which assets are appropriately disposed of, in accordance with applicable provisions of the Bankruptcy Code. 11 U.S.C. § 1141. A chapter 11 estate has an operating officer, who also serves as trustee for the estate. In the usual case, that operating officer/trustee is the debtor itself, as "debtor-in-possession." 11 U.S.C. §§ 1101, 1107.

Until confirmation, conversion or dismissal, this trustee is permitted to "operate the debtor's business." 11 U.S.C. § 1108. In chapter 11, the debtor, during this financial reorganization effort, both commands (as trustee) and works for (in the pursuit of the debtor's business) the bankruptcy estate. The debtor thus continues in business, operated by the debtor-in-possession (or a trustee, if one has been appointed) and the enterprise thus generates income postpetition.

There can be no "part" of a debtor that is not "in bankruptcy" during the pendency of a chapter 11 proceeding. For example, when an aircraft manufacturer builds a plane, then leases it out and generates lease income, or sells it outright, everything generated belongs to the estate—the cash sale price, the profit, the excess income from leasing—everything. When a supermarket sells groceries, or an insurance agent sells insurance, or a hospital sells hospital care, or fundamentalist ministry sells "time-shares" in its theme park, no one could seriously question that all the revenues generated become property of the estate. When Texaco filed bankruptcy, there was no part of Texaco which could be identified as a matter of fact or law as operating "outside the bankruptcy." All of its employees, from its chairman of the board to its roustabouts and service station operators, were working for the bankruptcy estate during the pendency of the reorganization. All aspects of Texaco's operations were protected by the automatic stay, but all aspects were also accountable to the bankruptcy process.

All the earnings of an enterprise during bankruptcy, regardless of source, must of necessity be "an interest in property" acquired by the estate after the commencement of the case, because the debtor's business is operated by the debtor-in-possession, the trustee of the estate.[4] All post-petition earnings of the enterprise logically fall neatly into Section 541(a)(7) as "interest[s] in property acquired by the estate during the pendency of the bankruptcy." 11 U.S.C. § 541(a)(7).

---

4. It is not difficult to see why such a provision was needed. Were the income generated *not* property of the estate, it could be distributed, transferred, converted, or otherwise dissipated with virtual impunity, a statutory framework that could only invite serious abuse, regardless whether the debtor were an individual, a corporation, or a partnership.

This obvious conclusion causes no difficulty to anyone when the earnings in question are generated by a corporation in bankruptcy (e.g., Texaco), yet apparently offends the sensibilities of courts when it is an individual in bankruptcy doing the earning. It should not, though. Certainly nothing in subsection (a)(7) itself suggests that the rule should be any different, merely because the form of the enterprise operated by the estate is a sole proprietorship.[6] There are other provisions which adequately address the question of an individual debtor's compensation during the pendency of the chapter 11 case. *See* 11 U.S.C. § 503(b)(1)(A); *see also* discussion *infra*.

Section 541 simply achieves the relatively basic congressional aim of casting a broad jurisdictional net over the interests in property that should justifiably be subject to the bankruptcy process. *See United States v. Whiting Pools, Inc.*, 462 U.S. 198, 203–05, 103 S.Ct. 2309, 2312–13, 76 L.Ed.2d 515 (1983). Subsection (a)(7) applies with equal force to all chapters, without distinction. 11 U.S.C. § 103. It also draws no distinction among the forms of enterprises involved, be they corporate, partnership, or sole proprietorships.

This court shares the *Cooley* court's reluctance to engraft exceptions onto Section 541, especially when the statute seems to work just fine without such judicial modifications. *See In re Cooley*, 87 B.R. at 439. Section 541(a)(7) thus brings all the earnings of the enterprise between the filing and the confirmation, conversion or dismissal of a chapter 11 case into the bankruptcy estate—even if the enterprise doing the earning is a sole proprietorship, and even if the income is generated by the debtor's personal services in a service-oriented enterprise such as the practice of medicine, law, or dentistry.[7]

c. *The individual debtor's dual role*

Both *Cooley* and *Fitzsimmons* fail to take into account the significance of the relationship between the debtor and the estate created by a chapter 11 filing, a factor which affects (or should affect) the way one views this issue. Both cases appear to give short shrift to the fiduciary obligations imposed by Section 1107.

As earlier noted, the estate enterprise has an operating officer, a "trustee" with a fiduciary obligation owed to the estate's beneficiaries, its unsecured creditors. In a chapter 11 case, it is the debtor-in-possession who assumes this obligation (unless a trustee is appointed under Section 1104). *In re Q.P.S., Inc.*, 99 B.R. at 845; 11 U.S.C.

---

6. In fact, the analysis should apply with equal force to the individual chapter 11 debtor *not* doing business as a sole proprietor, though there is less justification for chapter 11 relief in the first place, except to conduct an orderly self-controlled liquidation.

7. The debtor has argued correctly that, but for the debtor's efforts, none of the dollars would be generated, even though it may take the assistance of staff people to make the income generation possible. The court accepts this truism, but notes that,

§ 1107.[8] The debtor first submits all of his property to the newly-created estate, then assumes the role of trustee over the management and utilization of those assets. He also makes executive decisions for the operation and administration of the estate. For example, he decides what causes of action to pursue or to settle, what avoidance actions to initiate or refrain from initiating, what claims to contest or not to contest, and what property will or will not be assembled into the estate.

In short, the debtor-in-possession enjoys considerable power and benefits in his role as trustee over his own assets. On top of it all, both the debtor and the estate are protected by the automatic stay during the pendency of the reorganization. 11 U.S.C. § 362(a).

By the same token, the debtor-in-possession in chapter 11 assumes the substantial duties and responsibilities of a trustee. *In re Q.P.S., Inc.*, 99 B.R. at 845; 11 U.S.C. § 1107. For example, the debtor-in-possession must account for all of the estate's property. In the operation of the debtor's business, he is also accountable to the estate's beneficiaries, his creditors, and may be "removed from office," as it were, and be replaced by a trustee if he fails to responsibly discharge that responsibility. 11 U.S.C. §§ 1104(a), 1107. The court may also, on motion of a party, dismiss or convert the case if the debtor is suffering continuing losses without prospect for reorganization. 11 U.S.C. § 1112(b)(1). The debtor-in-possession also reviews claims, and has an obligation to object to those claims which should not be allowed by the terms of the Bankruptcy Code. That duty extends to administrative claims asserted under Section 503 as well as to unsecured claims under Section 502.

The debtor-in-possession, as trustee, operates the debtor's business. 11 U.S.C. § 1108. In that capacity, the debtor-in-possession may hire (or retain) personnel to operate that business. During the interval between filing the petition and plan confirmation all persons working on behalf of the debtor-in-possession are in fact employees of the estate for as long as the entity is in bankruptcy. The bankruptcy court has the authority to regulate the employment and compensation of persons who are employed by a bankruptcy estate. *In re Amarex, Inc.*, 853 F.2d 1526 (10th Cir.1988); *In re Sweetwater*, 57 B.R. 354 (D.Utah 1985). Section 503(b)(1)(A) contemplates the allowance of actual, necessary costs and expenses of preserving the estate, "including wages, salaries or commissions for services rendered after the commencement of the case." 11 U.S.C. § 503(b)(1)(A). The debtor-in-possession, as trustee, is responsible for assuring that the estate incurs only actual, necessary costs and expenses, and has a duty to object to claims which exceed this standard. *See* 11 U.S.C. § 1107(a).

---

under the analysis adopted here, it is an irrelevant truism.

8. (a) Subject * * * to such limitations or conditions as the court prescribes, a debtor in possession shall have all the rights * * * and powers, and shall perform all the functions and duties * * * of a trustee serving in a case under this chapter.

11 U.S.C. § 1107(a).

When the enterprise which files is a sole proprietorship, the foregoing observations take on a special significance, because the person filling the fiduciary role of debtor-in-possession is also *working for* the debtor-in-possession conducting the debtor's business. As a general rule, a fiduciary's engaging in self-dealing or appropriating estate benefits for personal gain is not permissible. In the chapter 11 context, the debtor as debtor-in-possession must reconcile this duty with his self-interested role as the entrepreneur operating the business of the enterprise. As trustee, the debtor-in-possession has an obligation to the estate's beneficiaries to keep operating costs down while maximizing dividends. As an employee, of course, the debtor's self-interest in making money is usually paramount. Given a conflict between the two roles, the higher duty of the debtor as trustee/fiduciary must take precedence over the more self-interested concerns of the debtor as employee. Regardless of the entrepreneurial considerations which obtained prior to bankruptcy, once bankruptcy is filed, a whole new set of rules must apply—rules derived from the vested interests of third parties (creditors) and the fiduciary duties imposed upon the debtor *qua* debtor-in-possession. The fiduciary duties which the debtor assumed by filing chapter 11 must result in *self-imposed* limitations on self-compensation. The inherent self-dealing and appropriation of estate opportunity for personal gain are otherwise antithetical to the debtor's discharge of his fiduciary obligations as debtor-in-possession.

Were the debtor a corporation wholly owned by an individual who also served as the corporation's principal employee, we would not question a creditor's challenging the wages which that person was drawing out of the debtor corporation. That the enterprise which files bankruptcy happens to be a sole proprietorship rather than a corporation should not make a difference. If anything, the creditor has even greater justification for being concerned in the case of a sole proprietorship because of the inherent danger of self-dealing and appropriation of estate opportunity for personal gain.[14]

The dual role of debtor as trustee and debtor as employee in the sole proprietorship chapter 11 lends further support to the statutory analysis adopted by this court. In the pursuit of his fiduciary duties, the doctor, lawyer, dentist or other service professional who files chapter 11 bankruptcy will curtail withdrawing anything more than a reasonable "salary" from the estate in compensation for his services as "employee" during the pendency of the chapter 11—or will justifiably be forced to by his creditors.

Any interpretation of the statute which fails to take this dual role of the individual chapter 11 debtor into account not only underestimates

---

14. The *Cooley* and *Fitzsimmons* approaches actually exacerbate this problem, because they invite individuals to use chapter 11 to shelter their income *and* obtain a discharge *and* control the case administration *and* avoid the scrutiny of an independent chapter 7 trustee. The approach adopted by this court, by contrast, encourages responsibility and self-restraint on the part of the debtor-in-possession and discourages abuse.

the fiduciary role of the debtor-in-possession but also undercuts the integrity of the bankruptcy process. The approach adopted by this court preserves the integrity of the process by imposing on the individual debtor the same expectations as are placed on corporate and partnership debtors in chapter 11. In so doing, it also spares us from having to invent special judicial exceptions to the plain language of the statute for individual debtor cases. That is certainly a desirable outcome.

d. The debtor's "salary"

The conclusion we reach here about an individual debtor's income generated post-petition and preconfirmation being part of property of the estate does *not*, of course, mean that the individual debtor is expected to work for the estate for free. The debtor justifiably expects to be paid for services rendered to the estate. Indeed, the Bankruptcy Code contemplates that the estate will incur expenses in its operations, including the wage and salary expenses associated with the estate's income production. 11 U.S.C. §§ 1108, 503(b)(1)(A). To the extent that compensating the debtor for contributing to the income production process is itself "in the ordinary course of the business of the debtor," that compensation is permitted.

In fact, the legislative history to Sections 503 and 541 anticipated that, in the case of a sole proprietorship, the debtor would draw a salary, subject to Section 503(b)(1)(A). *See* H.R.Rep. No. 595, 95th Cong., 1st Sess. 355 (1977), U.S.Code Cong. & Admin.News 1978, 5787, 5963, 6310 (wages, salaries and commissions for services rendered after the commencement of the case are presumed to be actual, necessary costs and expenses of preserving the estate).

The legislative history also confirms that, once those wages are paid out to an individual debtor out of property of the estate, they are no longer "property of the estate:"

> Postpetition payments to an individual debtor for services rendered to the estate are administrative expenses, and are *not* property of the estate *when received by the debtor*. This situation would most likely arise when the individual was a sole proprietor and was employed by the estate to run the business after the commencement of the case. An individual debtor in possession would be so employed, for example.

H.R.Rep. No. 595, 95th Cong., 1st Sess. 355 (1977), U.S.Code Cong. & Admin.News 1978, 6311 (emphasis added). This is where the "backout exception" in Section 541(a)(6) comes into play. The source of postpetition payments to the debtor *qua* employee of the estate for services rendered is monies generated by the enterprise's activities, which are in turn *property of the estate* by virtue of Section 541(a)(7). The debtor's "salary" thus comes out of "proceeds * * * of or from property of the estate," triggering the precondition which *now* permits us to use the backout exception for personal service income in Section 541(a)(6): "except such [proceeds] as are earnings from services performed by an individual debtor after the commencement of the case." 11 U.S.C. § 541(a)(6).

We have thus come full circle, and arrived at a coherent, harmonious interpretation of the applicable statutes without having to invent special rules for individuals who file chapter 11. That result is in turn consistent with the clearly expressed congressional intent that Chapter 11 be a form of general relief, affording the benefits of reorganization to a wide spectrum of enterprises from sole proprietorships to publicly traded multinational corporations. *See* H.R.Rep. No. 595, 95th Cong., 1st Sess. 205–09 (1977), U.S.Code Cong. & Admin.News 1978, 6165–6171. In this court's view, that is far preferable to forays into judicial amendment of the Bankruptcy Code.

B. *Objections to proposed analysis*

1. *The involuntary servitude shibboleth*

The debtor has argued that the interpretation espoused in this opinion effectively places the debtor into involuntary (or at least indentured) servitude. The argument overlooks that this bankruptcy was itself a voluntarily initiated proceeding which carries with it certain burdens.

The involuntary servitude argument, in short, is little more than a shibboleth. The debtor always has the keys to the shackles. Economic necessity may discourage him from freeing himself, but is hardly the equivalent a law or force compelling performance or continuance of service in violation of the Constitution.

2. *Noncompliance by debtor*

The debtor has indicated that, if this ruling holds, he will simply "go across the street," as it were, and set up shop in competition with the estate. While there is no law which could prevent the debtor from exercising this option, there are severe consequences which might discourage it. By going into competition with his own estate, the debtor will have breached his fiduciary obligations to the estate, endangering if not in fact abandoning his entitlement to relief under chapter 11. A motion to convert or to appoint a chapter 11 trustee would no doubt be immediately and summarily granted under such circumstances. A debtor in possession simply cannot ignore his fiduciary obligations by putting his own interests before those of his beneficiaries, the creditors. He simply cannot lightly appropriate estate opportunities, or engage in self-dealing activities without in the process risking loss of all the benefits of chapter 11. *In re Q.P.S., Inc.* 99 B.R. at 845. To boot, a debtor who made so foolhardy a choice would no doubt buy himself a massive lawsuit premised on his breach of his fiduciary obligations. Such a choice might even endanger his discharge. *See* 11 U.S.C. § 727(a)(2)(B).

None of these consequences lead this court to conclude that its interpretation is anything but the right result. A debtor has a variety of options available and each has its consequences. If the debtor does not want to work for his creditors, he can choose another chapter. If the debtor elects to "thumb his nose" at his creditors by going into competition with his own estate, he can do so and brook the lawsuit that will surely follow as one of the consequences of such brazen arrogance. These are all acceptable outcomes, so far as this court is concerned. If anything, they support the interpretation of the statute which this opinion espouses.

3. Impact on "fresh start"

The debtor asserts, following *Cooley,* that dedicating any portion of the income generated by the individual debtor to the estate undercuts the debtor's "fresh start." The Bankruptcy Code does not explicitly grant a fresh start to debtors, though its structure is such that it certainly promotes it. However, in a chapter 11 case, most of the benefits of the fresh start are deferred to confirmation. The discharge is only entered upon confirmation of the plan. 11 U.S.C. § 1141. The automatic stay certainly protects the debtor (as well as the estate and its assets) from collection activity for the period preceding confirmation, but the fresh start for the chapter 11 debtor does not begin to take effect until the automatic stay is extended by the permanent injunction of Section 524.

Obviously, certain features of the fresh start "kick in" prior to confirmation. Exempt property, for example, is determined within thirty days of the first meeting of creditors, absent an objection. 11 U.S.C. § 522(*l*); Bankr.R. 4003(b). In general, however, the fresh start policy, so paramount in chapter 7, is subordinated in chapter 11 to the more specific goal of reorganization. Thus, the debtor is still (in the voluntary case) wedded to the bankruptcy process by virtue of his role as debtor-in-possession. The debtor-in-possession *operates the debtor's business,* a concept completely antithetical to the notion that the debtor is "starting afresh" free of creditor claims. 11 U.S.C. § 1108. A creditors' committee may well scrutinize the operation of that business in chapter 11, and may even decide to put someone else in charge via a motion to appoint a trustee, to seek to convert the case to chapter 7 liquidation, or to propose their own plan. Until confirmation of a plan, it is premature to speak of a debtor's fresh start.

The ruling of the court on this issue thus does not undermine the debtor's fresh start, because in chapter 11 it is largely deferred until after confirmation. If anything, the ruling prevents the debtor from grabbing a "head start" by collecting unrestricted income while under the protection of chapter 11 and the automatic stay.

4. Inconsistency with Chapter 13

Not raised by any party, but suggested by a recent case out of Indiana, is the statutory argument that our interpretation is inconsistent with Section 1306. Chapter 13, by special provision, makes postpetition wages property of the estate. 11 U.S.C. § 1306. Goes the argument, were our interpretation correct, there would be no need for this special provision because Section 541(a)(7) would already incorporate postpetition earnings into the estate.

That is not true, though. First (and most obviously), our interpretation of Section 541(a)(7) only picks up as property of the estate income generated by *the estate.* Debtors in chapter 13 cases are, by definition, *wage earners,* i.e., they are not working for the estate—they are working for third parties. Section 541(a)(7) does not apply to these wages and, but for the operation of Section 1306, such wages would not be included in the chapter 13 estate.

Even if wages *were* picked up by Section 541(a)(7), they would cease to be included in property of the estate *upon confirmation.* Section 1306, by contrast, extends the concept of "property of the estate" to wages earned by the debtor *until the case is closed, dismissed or converted* to another chapter, a point far *beyond* confirmation in chapter 13. Thus, contrary to *Fitzsimmons,* Section 541(a)(7) would be inadequate to meet the special needs of chapter 13, which requires that wages be committed for an extended period of time (three years or longer) but which also requires that confirmation take place relatively early in the case. *See In re Mack,* 46 B.R. 652 (Bankr.E.D.Pa.1985); *In re Denn,* 37 B.R. 33 (Bankr.D.Minn.1983).

In chapter 11, the estate ceases to exist on confirmation, and property is re-vested in the debtor. 11 U.S.C. § 1141. Effective upon confirmation, all the income generated by the debtor thus ceases to be property of the estate. In chapter 13, the concept of property has been considerably expanded by Section 1306 to include post-confirmation wages extending for years after confirmation. That special provision does not undercut our interpretation of Section 541(a)(6) and (7).

Also worth noting is that Section 1306 makes earnings from services performed by the debtor property of the estate up to the point the case is closed, dismissed, or *converted* to another chapter. 11 U.S.C. § 1306(a)(2). The *Fitzsimmons* court relied on this provision to argue that Congress knew how to include income from personal services as property of the estate, adding that there is no similar provision in other chapters or in Section 541 itself. Implicit in this argument is the notion that, because there is an express provision for postpetition income in Section 1306, there is an implied exclusion in the other chapters. Goes the argument, the earnings in chapter 13 case[s] that are property of the estate cease to be property of the estate when the case is converted to another chapter, such as chapter 11. Therefore, such earnings would not be property of the estate in chapter 11.

This argument reads too much into Section 1306(a)(2), which merely defines the end point for the chapter 13 estate (upon closing, dismissal, or *conversion* of the case to a *different* chapter). Congress did *not* say anything about whether the wages which were property of the estate in chapter 13 would or would not be property of the estate in any *other* chapter. What most clearly demonstrates this is that, even though

Section 1306(a)(2) specifically terminates the chapter 13 estate's interest in earnings upon conversion to *chapter 12,* chapter 12 itself *also* includes earnings from services performed by the individual debtor after the commencement of the case for a period of years. 11 U.S.C. § 1207(a)(2). Section 1306 places no limit on the chapter 12 definitions of estate property. There is no reason to read it to place a limit on chapter 11 estate property either.

5. *Valuation*

The debtor's next contention is that this court's interpretation of property of the estate imposes an impossible valuation problem on both the parties and the court. In fact, however, the valuation question is easier to resolve under this court's interpretation than under the *Cooley* and *Fitzsimmons* approaches. Both of these courts assumed that we must start our inquiry by asking what monies are attributable to "personal services" (*Fitzsimmons*) or to "earnings of the individual" (*Cooley*). These approaches require the court to devise tests for isolating these funds from the balance of the estate's income.[18]

Under our interpretation, this sort of question is not even asked. Our analysis follows a two step process. First, we ask "what monies are generated by the estate?" Second, we ask "what funds should be paid over to the debtor in compensation for his or her services to the estate?" We are no longer constrained to anguish over whether monies are generated by personal goodwill as opposed to enterprise goodwill, as did the *Fitzsimmons* and *Cooley* courts. Our task is, by comparison, relatively simple. We merely decide how much to pay the debtor for services performed. That analysis is controlled by Section 503(b)(1)(A), which advises, in essence, that actual and necessary costs may be allowed as an off-the-top administrative expense. 11 U.S.C. § 503(b)(1)(A). It is a task upon which courts have embarked before in corporate and partnership cases. The approach need be very little different in the individual debtor case.[19]

There are two approaches that might be taken to determine what expenses are actual and necessary. One assumes that all wages are *prima facie* actual and necessary. The other assumes that wages should conform to a standard of "reasonableness," defined by a community in

---

18. In the view of this court, those tests are cumbersome and unpredictable, because they require a court to seek out sources for the revenue other than the professional. In fact, that inquiry is highly artificial and yields odd results. For example, all would agree that the receptionist needs a desk, but how much revenue does the desk yield? What proportion of the total revenues are attributable to the desk? The inquiry borders on the ludicrous, yet is little different from asking the same sorts of questions about the receptionist himself, or the radiologist, or the associate in a multi-doctor practice (such as was the situation in *Cooley*).

19. In fact, the approach is easiest in the case in which the debtor is *not* a sole proprietor, for there, the debtor is *not* working for the estate, but for some third party. In that case, *all* of the debtor's income is insulated from "property of the estate" because it is not the debtor's business being operated by the estate. Section 541(a)(7) is thus not implicated.

turn determined by the court. This latter approach posits that, if an expense is unreasonable, it is certainly not necessary (even though it might be actual). Under this latter approach, the court would hear testimony concerning ranges of compensation for similar performance and from this testimony would decide on the level of compensation. That is the approach adopted in this case.

After consideration of the testimony taken at the hearing[20] the court concludes that Dr. Herberman should receive 75% of the total income generated by the practice (after paying expenses of the practice such as utilities, staff salaries, and the like) as his compensation during the pendency of the case. These monies are excluded from the estate when received by the debtor (as they have been here) by virtue of Section 541(a)(6). The balance of earnings are property of the estate for which Dr. Herberman, as debtor-in-possession, must account.

However, since this decision is a departure from established precedent, the court also finds that that portion of the balance of earnings generated between the date of filing and the date the motion under consideration was filed should not become property of this particular estate. Under the state of the case law as of the filing of this case, Dr. Herberman had no reason to anticipate this ruling, and hence no reason to segregate or account for those receipts.

The income produced by the practice after the date the motion was filed is property of the estate. The Cox Group's motion should have put Dr. Herberman on notice that his right to keep all the income from the practice as his own was then in question. He could at that point have reasonably anticipated at least the possibility of an adverse ruling that could result in a disgorgement order.

CONCLUSION

For the foregoing reasons, all of the debtor's income during the period between filing and confirmation became property of the estate under Section 541 of the Bankruptcy Code. By the same token, Dr. Herberman was entitled to receive compensation for the services he rendered to the estate during this period. Dr. Herberman shall segregate and account for the income which, per this decision, is property of the estate. The debtor's plan of reorganization must in turn take these funds into account in terms of satisfying the requirements of Section 1129(a)(7).

So ORDERED.

---

20. This included testimony from three of the nine urologists in El Paso regarding their levels of compensation, the likelihood that anyone would buy another urologist's practice in El Paso, the "open hospital" policy in El Paso, the kinds of hours one must work to generate the levels of income achieved, the relationship between one's surgery practice and one's office practice, the role of other staff, equipment, and facilities in the generation of income, and the repute in which Dr. Herberman is held in the community as a surgeon of some note. The court also considered documentary evidence regarding what a new doctor might be expected to earn.

Questions

1. Explain to someone in Dr. Herberman's shoes (or John Connally's, or Dr. Cooley's, or James Taylor's) all of the reasons why one might select Chapter 11 instead of Chapter 7.

2. Should the Congress add a section similar to 1325(b)(1)(B) to Chapter 11?

3. At the time the loan is made, can a creditor do anything to insure that his debtor will not go through bankruptcy and come out on the other side with a high income, but free of his debts?

Chapter Ten

CHAPTERS 7 & 13

§ 1. INTRODUCTION

In a corporate liquidation, discharge from one's debts is meaningless. Indeed, the Bankruptcy Code provides for no discharge in such circumstances because, by hypothesis, the liquidated corporate bankrupt will be a shell with no need for a discharge. In consumer bankruptcy on the other hand, the discharge is everything. Whether the consumer is proposing an actual liquidation under Chapter 7, a liquidation in disguise under Chapter 13 or a plan with extensive payments under Chapter 13, the critical motivation for going into bankruptcy is almost certainly to achieve a "fresh start."

Because exemptions have now become relatively generous and because the typical consumer bankrupt has few assets, consumer bankruptcies are less likely to produce the kinds of conflicts among creditors that one sees in Chapter 11 or in corporate liquidations. The presence of significant assets in those cases moves the various creditors to assert their claims with vigor. In the typical consumer bankruptcy the unsecured creditors wind up with only a few cents on the dollar; the most imaginative use of the avoidance power is likely to be the trustee's claim that the purchase money security interest against the debtor's automobile is unperfected.

Where, as frequently occurs, a creditor's claim exceeds the value of his collateral or where any remaining equity could be exempted under section 522, the trustee will have little motivation to recover the property for the estate. Under such circumstances, he is likely to abandon the property pursuant to section 554. Section 554 does not specify to whom property is abandoned but the legislative history indicates that in general it may be abandoned to any party with a possessory interest in it. H.R.Rep. No. 595, 95th Cong., 1st Sess. 377, *reprinted in* 1978 U.S.Code Cong. & Ad.News 5963, 6333; S.Rep. No. 989, 95th Cong., 2d Sess. 92 *reprinted in* 1978 U.S.Code Cong. & Ad.News 5787, 5878. However, if the property is abandoned under subsection (c)—scheduled but not administered—it is deemed abandoned to the debtor. Id. While the automatic stay of section 362 continues to prohibit creditor actions with respect to the abandoned property, the scope of permissible creditor actions following bankruptcy is not clear.

The most intricate legal question in consumer liquidation, however, is likely to involve interpretation of the exceptions from discharge (section 523) or to relate somehow to the questions of reaffirmation (section 524) or the debtor's exercise of his exemption rights (section 522). A few particularly heinous acts may deprive the debtor of any right to discharge whatsoever. A more common and related event is a case in which a particular creditor asserts not that the debtor should be denied a discharge entirely but that that creditor's particular debt should not be discharged for one reason or another. Section 523 identifies nine separate forms of debt that are not to be discharged in a Chapter 7 liquidation.

Taxes entitled to priority under section 507 are excepted from discharge by subsection (a)(1). Examples of such taxes include withholding taxes, customs duties or property taxes due within the year prior to bankruptcy, excise or income taxes arising within three years prior to bankruptcy or employer payroll taxes of less than $2000 on wages earned within ninety days prior to bankruptcy.

The debtor is also denied discharge under section 523 from a tax liability in instances where the debtor filed a fraudulent return, filed a late return within two years prior to bankruptcy, failed to file a return or otherwise willfully attempted to evade or defeat the tax. Alimony, maintenance or support owed directly to a spouse or child is excepted from discharge by subsection (a)(5). Educational loans such as a Guaranteed Student Loan are excepted from discharge by subsection (a)(8) unless the loan first became due more than seven years prior to bankruptcy or the debtor can show exception imposes an "undue hardship" on the debtor or the debtor's dependents. Fines are made nondischargeable by subsection (a)(7), while debts incurred as a result of an intentional tort (a "willful and malicious injury") are excepted from discharge by subsection (a)(6).

In addition, consumer debts incurred through fraud, false representations or false pretenses other than a statement about the debtor's financial condition are excepted from discharge by subsection (a)(2); if the debt was incurred through the intentional use of a false written financial statement, discharge is denied if the creditor "reasonably relied" on the statement. Fraudulent intent may be shown by a number of objective factors such as the length of time between incurrence of the debt and bankruptcy, a sharp change in the debtor's buying habits and the like. Subsection 523(a)(2) provides that debts incurred pursuant to certain sudden spending binges by the debtor, shortly before going into bankruptcy, will be presumptively nondischargeable.

To protect debtors against abusive use of this section, section 523(d) imposes sanctions upon a creditor who unsuccessfully attempts to gain an exception from discharge for his debt on the basis of subsection (a)(2), and is not substantially justified in doing so. In that instance a creditor must pay the debtor's court costs and reasonable attorney's fees unless special circumstances would make such an award unjust. In a similar vein, the debtor who has violated his fiduciary duty in incurring a debt is denied discharge of that debt by subsection (a)(4).

Certain exceptions from discharge are made to prevent manipulation of the bankruptcy laws. Failure to include a debt on the schedule makes it nondischargeable. (Subsection (a)(3).) Debts previously denied discharge are also excepted from discharge by subsection (a)(9).

Clearly some debts enjoy a higher status than others, at least in Chapter 7. The student should examine the provisions of section 523(a) and ask why certain debts are not discharged but carried over, thus impeding the fresh start. What is the policy that justifies the exception from discharge of liability for "willful and malicious injury" by the debtor? Is it the same policy that justifies the exception to discharge of alimony or maintenance payable to a former spouse or for child support? How does one explain the exception for student loans that is contained in section 523(a)(8)? To some extent this hierarchy can be explained by looking to elemental ideas of fairness; to some extent these distinctions can be justified on the ground that certain liabilities are designed to punish a defendant. Perhaps the exception for willful and malicious injury springs from tort's roots in criminal law.

A creditor's failure to raise the issue of nondischargeability prior to the conclusion of the case may be barred from later raising it—depending upon the nature of the debt. If the debt is of the kind specified in section 523(a)(2), (4), or (6)(debts incurred through the use of fraud or false representations, through the violation of fiduciary duty or as a result of an intentional tort), the debt is discharged. If, however, the debt falls under one of the other exceptions in section 523, the creditor may still raise the matter in state court notwithstanding closure of the debtor's bankruptcy estate.

In view of consumer bankruptcy's deep concern with the policy of a fresh start, it is not surprising that the drafters have dealt with the question of reaffirmation, the act by which an otherwise dischargeable debt remains binding notwithstanding the discharge. Similarly, it is not surprising to find a provision such as section 525 that prohibits certain parties from engaging in discriminatory treatment against those who have taken bankruptcy. Apart from an occasional interpretative question under sections 523 and 522, consumer bankruptcies under Chapter 7 have presented few interesting legal questions.

The interesting policy question, both under Chapter 7 and under Chapter 13, is the extent to which society should make a fresh start available to individual debtors. Since the enactment of the Bankruptcy Reform Act of 1978, the number of consumer bankruptcies has increased radically. Some of this increase is directly responsible to pent up demand among those who were advised to wait until the Bankruptcy

Code's enactment; other parts of it are attributable to the economic conditions, and to the recent Supreme Court decision allowing attorneys to advertise, but some part is attributable to the fact that the Bankruptcy Code is more generous to consumer debtors than the prior law. As we will see, for the first time there are federal exemptions and these (together with liberalized state exemptions stimulated by the federal exemptions) alone make bankruptcy more palatable.

The cases under Chapter 13 still present important questions concerning its appropriate use as a quasi-liquidation device, concerning the appropriate scope of discrimination among various creditors by the debtor in formulating the plan and concerning certain procedural limitations on the operation of the plan.

Because of the unforeseen turn taken by Chapter 13 cases, the consumer credit lobby has pushed for its amendment. In 1981 the Senate held hearings on a bill that would have made various changes in the Bankruptcy Code. The Technical Amendments Act, S–2000, contained a provision that would have required certain individuals to go into Chapter 13. Section 109 of the bill stated: "An individual may be a debtor under Chapter 7 only if such individual cannot pay a reasonable part of his debts out of his anticipated future income." If the court was to determine that a debtor could make substantial payments towards reducing his debt, he would be required to seek relief under Chapter 13. The bill would also have modified the exemptions under Chapter 13 to make them more nearly consistent with the more restrictive exemptions found in Chapter 7.

The rationale of the bill's proponents was simple. In their view the issue was not one of industry versus consumer, but one of consumer versus debtor. They argued that the cost of those debtors who refused or were unable to repay their loans must be borne by the consumers seeking credit. This cost would become manifest as an increased financing cost for all consumers and an increased difficulty in obtaining credit. To enable as much credit to be extended at as low a cost as possible, the creditors would have required that all consumers who filed bankruptcy pay back as much of their debts as they could. Supporting this position, members of the consumer credit lobby cited evidence compiled by Dr. Johnson of the Purdue Management School which indicated that about 40 percent of the debtors who filed petitions under Chapter 7 could actually repay a substantial amount of their debts.

In addition, supporters of the bill noted that the Bankruptcy Code did not take into account how the credit industry worked. They pointed out that while the decision to extend credit was based on the borrower's expected ability to repay those debts out of future earnings, the Bankruptcy Code focused entirely on the liquidation value of the debtor's assets. Senator DeConcini observed that his constituents were amazed to learn that a debtor's future earnings were not considered under Chapter 7.

Despite widespread support for the bill in the Senate, the bill was not adopted by the House. Based on the testimony before the Senate Judiciary Committee, opponents disagreed with the empirical conclusions of the Johnson study and also apparently saw three main problems with the bill. They felt that it would burden the courts and prove to be unmanageable. Moreover, they argued it conflicted with the basic policies underlying the Code.

First, opponents of the bill argued that its passage would result in an increase in the amount of litigation. Even supporters of the bill admitted that at first there might be an increase in litigation. However, they argued that once debtors and creditors saw how the courts would handle the petitions that the number of cases would diminish because debtors who could make substantial repayments would stop filing under Chapter 7.

Second, the bill's opponents claimed that the bill would be unworkable. They argued that it would be impossible to make accurate predictions of a debtor's earnings or expenses. (The fact that the bill allowed a debtor who was denied relief under Chapter 7 to re-petition if his circumstances changed did not appease them. They saw it as adding still more cases to the courts' dockets.) Moreover, with regard to the question of expenses, they noted that the bill would provide a very arbitrary standard. The court would be forced to deal with the difficult issue, what is a reasonable budget. It would be forced to answer: Can a debtor eat steak every night? Once a week? May a debtor drive his car to work, or must he take the bus? Could he go to a Broadway play? A half-price movie?

Proponents of the bill argued that such decisions would not pose an unmanageable problem. Indeed, they pointed out that the decisions which would have to be made to determine whether a debtor could afford to pay back a substantial part of his debt would be no different than the decisions that are now made in Chapter 13 cases in determining whether a debtor's plan was feasible.

Finally, the opponents of the bill objected to it on policy grounds, contending that it would conflict with the fresh start principle. Some likened the proposal to a form of peonage that was abolished by the Thirteenth Amendment. They argued that the bill would foster an increase in improvident lending.

In conclusion, the presence of this bill indicates the disquiet over the present state of consumer bankruptcies under the Code. While this bill was defeated, other attempts may be made to modify the law. Despite its failure, the bill gives an insight into some of the issues that arise in bankruptcy cases under Chapters 7 and 13. Some watered down parts of the creditor's bill became law in 1984 as subtitle A to Title III of the 1984 Act.

CHAPTER 13 CONSUMER PLANS

On its face Chapter 13 bears little resemblance to Chapter XIII; in practice the dissimilarity is even more pronounced. In most jurisdictions few consumers found it in their interest to use Chapter XIII. Now there is a heavy case load of Chapter 13 plans in nearly every jurisdiction. Partly this increased use is attributable to Congress's conscious change of the law to allow cramdowns and to make Chapter 13 more palatable to the consumer debtor than Chapter XIII had been. Partly the growth in the use of Chapter 13 arises from factors apparently unforeseen by the drafters of the new Bankruptcy Code. For a variety of reasons which will become obvious, it is now in the interest of many debtors, who are essentially seeking a liquidation and who have no intention or ability to pay a large percentage of their obligations, to use Chapter 13 in lieu of Chapter 7.

The qualifications for treatment under Chapter 13 are different from those under Chapter 7 but are relatively simple. First a debtor under Chapter 13 must be an "individual with regular income" as defined in section 101(24). Section 109(e) permits only individuals that owe noncontingent, liquidated, unsecured debts of less than $250,000 and noncontingent liquidated secured debts of less than $750,000 to be debtors under Chapter 13. Because of these relatively high amounts, and because there is no specific requirement that the debtor be only a consumer, small unincorporated businesses may now use Chapter 13. There are occasional interpretative problems lurking in the questions when does one have "regular income" and how does one evaluate "liquidated" debt in order to determine whether the $250,000 and $750,000 numbers have been met, but by and large there are few issues concerning the basic applicability of Chapter 13.

Unlike Chapter 7, there is no provision for involuntary petitions under Chapter 13. Thus creditors are not capable of throwing a debtor into Chapter 13 although they can do so under Chapter 7. From time to time creditor groups have suggested that they should have the power to force certain debtors into Chapter 13 and presumably to require them to pay substantial amounts of their obligations in lieu of permitting liquidation under Chapter 7.

CHAPTER 7 COMPARED

In theory Chapter 13 gives the individual debtor a number of advantages over Chapter 7. In practice those advantages are more limited than it may seem at first. An apparently significant advantage is that Chapter 13 debtors may retain their assets and pay creditors out of postpetition earnings. Conversely, Chapter 7 debtors liquidate their assets and pay their creditors out of liquidated funds. Considering the entire universe of Chapter 7 and Chapter 13, one distinguishing the two on that ground would doubtless be mistaken. Many Chapter 7 cases are "no asset" cases, at least in the sense that there are no assets after exemptions are accounted for that are not subject to security interests. In such cases no assets are "turned over" to the trustee for liquidation. The Chapter 7 debtor retains the exempt assets and holds assets subject to security interests at least if he can negotiate deferred payments with his secured creditors.

To put the point a slightly different way, Chapter 13 gives debtors bargaining power, particularly with their secured creditors, that they do not enjoy in a Chapter 7. Assume, for example, that a debtor has defaulted on her car loan and on her mortgage and that the two secured creditors are threatening, one to repossess the car and the other to foreclose on the home. If the debtor files in Chapter 7 the debts, but not the security claim, will be discharged, and the debtor will have to undertake negotiation with the two creditors to keep them from asserting their security interests against the two assets. If the secured creditors refuse to renegotiate their loans, the debtor will have to give up the assets to them if she cannot pay off the accelerated loans in full.

Conversely, in Chapter 13 the debtor can "deaccelerate" the loans, pay the arrearage on the home mortgage over the three year life of the plan and continue current monthly payments on her home mortgage outside of the plan. If the debtor can make such payments, the secured creditor is helpless to oppose it, for the court will undo the acceleration even over the creditor's objection.

In the auto loan case, the debtor will be permitted to write the loan down to the present value of the car as a secured loan, pay that secured loan over the three to five year life of the plan and then pay off the remaining, unsecured portion at a fraction of its face value. Within the limits that we will discuss below, this plan too can be imposed upon a non-consenting creditor.

Thus, to say that a Chapter 13 allows the individual debtor to "keep" assets that would be put up for auction in Chapter 7 is to overstate the case. Even in Chapter 7 there will be negotiation with various creditors, and even there (because of the exemption laws) the debtor will keep many assets free of any creditor's claim. However, these negotiations are facilitated by the rules in Chapter 13, that in effect authorize debtors to procure a unilateral loan from their existing creditors for a three to five year period simply by proposing a plan.

Second, Chapter 13 appeals to debtors who have large debts that would not be discharged in Chapter 7. As it was originally written, the discharge in Chapter 13 was much broader than discharge in Chapter 7; sometimes the Chapter 13 discharge was called the "superdischarge." Initially, all prepetition debts except those for alimony, maintenance and child support were discharged in Chapter 13. Thus, for example, liability for an intentional tort that would have been excepted from the discharge in Chapter 7 was dischargeable in Chapter 13. The same was true for student loans and the liabilities arising out of fraud.

By periodic amendment since 1978, Congress has reduced the difference between discharge in the two chapters. In addition to liabilities for alimony and child support, liabilities arising out of drunk driving accidents, student loans, and apparently criminal restitution and criminal fines are now excepted from discharge in section 1328 of Chapter 13. Since Congress both struck and amended section 1328(a)(3) in 1994, we are uncertain about the status of criminal fines and criminal restitution. One section of the 1994 amendment purports to repeal 1328(h), the section that had excepted "criminal restitution." Another provision of the 1994 amendment purports to amend that section to add "or a criminal fine" to the provision. Lord only knows what Congress intended.

Third, a debtor in Chapter 7 is taking a higher, though modest, risk that discharge will be denied in toto. In Chapter 7, discharge can be denied on any one of ten different grounds. These provisions are not applicable to the debtor in Chapter 13.

Fourth, Chapter 13 stays suit against certain co-debtors; a Chapter 7 filing would leave the creditor free to sue the co-signer. This provision frees the debtor from worrying that his co-signing associates will use extra legal coercion when they discover that he has filed in bankruptcy and that *they* must pay *his* debt.

Fifth, debtors who cannot file in Chapter 7 because they have received a discharge in bankruptcy within 6 years, can use Chapter 13. Receiving a discharge under any of the bankruptcy chapters bars a debtor from filing in Chapter 7 for six years. Chapter 13 debtors are not subject to any similar limitation. They can file successive Chapter 13 petitions, limited in time only by the provision requiring the debtor to wait 180 days after certain dismissals.

Finally, Chapter 13 may offer some balm to one who feels it is reprehensible to fail to pay one's debts. The rising rate of consumer bankruptcies has suggested to some that the moral obligation once felt by many debtors has disappeared, yet some debtors feel a moral as well as a legal obligation to pay their debts. For them a Chapter 13 plan that entails payment of all or substantially all of their debt over a period of time is more acceptable than a Chapter 7 discharge. Moreover, some people believe that creditors who would not lend to a recent Chapter 7 debtor may be more willing to lend money to a recent Chapter 13 graduate.

§ 2. CHAPTER 7 LIQUIDATION

After one reading of sections 701 through 728, a student is likely to get a completely distorted view of the actual consumer liquidation process. Section 702 provides rules to permit the creditors to elect a trustee and section 701 states that the United States trustee "shall appoint" an interim trustee from a panel of private trustees. Thus in every Chapter 7 there will be a trustee who has the duties set out in section 704. One reading section 705 might conclude there will always be a creditors' committee as well. The student may have visions of a court room filled with milling creditors, each with his counsel shouting and pushing at their first meeting provided in section 341, waiting for a chance to examine the debtor under section 343, and present at the discharge hearing under section 524(d).

All of that would be wrong. In the typical consumer bankruptcy there is likely to be a single representative in court on the first meeting; the debtor and his lawyer will probably step aside with the gentleman, obviously well known to the U.S. trustee, who is the ad interim trustee. After a quick but searching set of questions from this trustee (and perhaps from a lawyer there who represents high volume consumer lenders such as credit card issuers), the first meeting is over. Even the debtor may not come to the court for his discharge, nor will it be attended by his creditors. In fact, one suspects that in many consumer bankruptcies the creditors are completely passive. Section 362 keeps them from any straightforward attempts to collect their debts and the low probability of any return from the typical "no asset" consumer bankruptcy makes it uneconomical for them to go to court to quarrel with the debtor, or with the other creditors over scraps that may be left over upon the liquidation.

Even though the great majority of Chapter 7 debtors have few assets, there are many Chapter 7 debtors, both corporate and individual, that have significant assets to be divided among their creditors. It is not uncommon for a corporate debtor who has filed initially in Chapter 11 to convert to Chapter 7 for liquidation. Although most individuals with considerable assets file Chapter 11 and so retain control of the bankruptcy and avoid the appointment of a trustee, some of those will also find themselves in Chapter 7 where there will be substantial assets to distribute.

At this point the student should examine section 726 and visualize the typical consumer debtor in Chapter 7. Although there are exceptions, that person is not likely to be a lawyer, a doctor or an airline pilot. He is more likely to be someone laid off from a blue collar job. He may own a car but he is unlikely to own any real estate; his worldly acquisitions are likely to consist of little more than some miscellaneous pieces of household goods and perhaps the right to a pension. Inevitably, his automobile will be subject to a security interest and thus will not be available for the general creditor. When one reaches section 726 on distribution of the property of the estate, there will be little or nothing to be distributed in the classic consumer bankruptcy.

Thus, to think of Chapter 7 as a process whereby the trustee collects the debtor's assets and distributes them is fundamentally wrong. A real distribution is but an occasional byproduct of an unusual Chapter 7 case. More commonly the debtor goes into bankruptcy, is discharged and spends any excess assets in the bankruptcy process itself for the employment of counsel and payment of fees. In short, consumer bankruptcy is properly regarded as a "discharge" process rather than as a "liquidation and distribution" process. With the growth of the new Chapter 13, that has become even more the case under the Bankruptcy Reform Act of 1978 than was formerly true. A casual reading of the published opinions would suggest that Chapter 13 draws off a substantial number of consumers with significant assets; therefore even more than formerly, Chapter 7 consumer cases are likely to be "no asset" cases.

Because the typical Chapter 7 consumer case is a no asset case, the interesting legal issues are likely to revolve around the questions concerning exceptions to discharge under section 523, reaffirmations of debts under section 524, redemption of assets under section 722 and discrimination against those who have received discharges under section 525. Of course they will also present interesting and difficult interpretive issues under section 522 on exemptions.

IN RE KREPS

United States Court of Appeals, Seventh Circuit, 1983.
700 F.2d 372.

SWYGERT, SENIOR CIRCUIT JUDGE. This is an appeal from a judgment of the district court, affirming an order by the Bankruptcy Court granting a discharge in favor of the debtors, Orrin C. Kreps, Jr. and his wife, over the objections of the First National Bank of Lansing ("First National"). There are two issues on this appeal. First, did the Bankruptcy Court apply the correct legal standard? Second, were the Bankruptcy Court's fact findings clearly erroneous? This appeal represents our first opportunity to interpret section 523(a)(2)(B)(iii) of the Bankruptcy Act of 1978, 11 U.S.C. Section 523(a)(2)(B)(iii)(Supp. III 1979), an issue explicitly reserved in Matter of Garman, 625 F.2d 755, 759 n. 6 (7th Cir.1980), cert. denied, sub nom. Garman v. Northern Trust Co., 450 U.S. 910, 101 S.Ct. 1347, 67 L.Ed.2d 333 (1981). We reverse.

I.

Many of the relevant facts are not disputed. Kreps and First National had a close business relationship. Gilbert J. Rynberk, Jr., First National's president, dealt personally with Kreps for fifteen years prior to the time of the loan at issue in these proceedings. First National had made a number of short-term loans to Kreps and, when requested, First National had routinely renewed these loans. These loans were related to Kreps' home construction business.

On August 17, 1978 Kreps received a $32,000 personal loan from First National. The loan was a ninety-day signature-only unsecured note. Possible uses of the money and Kreps' assets were discussed. It is conceded that Kreps indicated that the money might be used for a Wisconsin land deal; Kreps, however, did not use the money for that purpose. Kreps sought and received a renewal of the loan in November 1978.

In February 1979 Kreps again sought renewal of the loan. Following discussions with Kreps, Rynberk prepared a list of Kreps' assets which Kreps signed. It is undisputed that this statement contained materially false information. The statement indicated that Kreps owned two lots and a house when, in fact, he owned only the house and the lot on which the house stood. It was false in other aspects which First National does not argue were material. First National renewed the loan, and shortly thereafter Kreps filed a petition for bankruptcy.

II.

The Bankruptcy Court found that the February 1979 written statement was materially false concerning Kreps' financial condition and that it was made with an intent to deceive. The Bankruptcy Court, however, also found that First National had not reasonably relied upon the statement. The relevant aspects of the decision are:

> There is a question about the purpose of giving the statement of assets. Kreps talked about the long time he had done business with plaintiff and about their simple loan procedure in the past and said he assumed the statement was needed for the file in case a bank examiner came in or something of that sort. Rynberk's testimony was to the effect that the statement was needed to assure the bank that there were assets available if the loan was not repaid. However, it seems possible Rynberk may have said something about a bank examiner. When asked if he did, he answered "no, not that I recall" which was something less than positive.
>
> The evidence does not convince the Court that Rynberk for the bank relied upon the statement of assets when renewing the loan. The court believes the renewal was induced by the bank's excellent loan experience with Kreps for more than 15 years.

Unpublished Order Bankruptcy No. 79–60904 (November 21, 1980) at 4.

In response to First National's motion for a new trial, the Bankruptcy Court said:

> The evidence clearly shows that the bankrupt had obtained loans from the plaintiff for many years and that the plaintiff's president (Rynberk) had personally handled the debtor's loans for 15 years. There was no evidence presented at trial that financial statements or security were required by the plaintiff in past dealings with the defendant. The financial statement involved here was not given until the loan was renewed for the second time.
>
> The plaintiff's brief charges that the court erred as a matter of law in holding that the plaintiff did not rely upon the financial statement when renewing the note. The court's determination that there was no reliance is a finding of fact and not a matter of law, as the brief would have one believe. The execution of a financial statement does not establish that a creditor relies on the statement when a loan is granted. The party alleging reliance must make an affirmation showing of such reliance. *In re* Little, 65 F.2d 777 (2d Cir.1933); Matter of Lind, 6 B.R. 374 (Bankr.S.D.Tex.1980); *In re* Ketter, 5 Bankr.Ct.Dec. 1043 (E.D.Wis.1979); *In re* Day, 11 F.Supp. 400 (D.Mass.1935).

Rynberk, who personally handled the loan transaction for the plaintiff, testified that he relied on the financial statement on the second renewal of the loan. Now, if the court was bound by the testimony of loan officers about reliance, trials would end at that point and lending institutions would win 100% of the cases because in the court's considerable experience with such cases it has never heard a loan officer testify that he did not rely upon a financial statement and does not expect to hear one do so. Looking at the evidence as a whole, the court believes Rynberk was induced to allow the loan renewal by reason of his bank's loan experience with the debtor dating back 15 years. The court is not convinced that Rynberk would not have approved the renewal if the financial statement had not been given. The plaintiff had the burden of proof in regard to the reliance issue and the court finds it failed to meet this burden. *See* 3 Collier on Bankruptcy, Sec. 523.09(4)(15th Ed.1980).

What has been said about loan officers in trials always testifying that they relied on financial statements is not intended to imply that they intentionally gave false testimony. There seems to be something in the makeup of human beings which enables them, by the processes of hindsight, self-deception, rationalization, forgetfulness and whatever else comes into play, to convince themselves that events of the past were different than what actually took place back at the time when they had only the benefit of foresight. In the field of psychology, these processes are known by the following terms: selective perception, selective retention and selective forgetfulness.

Unpublished Order Bankruptcy No. 79–60904 (March 25, 1981) at 1–2.

III.

Section 523(a)(2) differs in language from its predecessor, section 17(a)(2) of the Bankruptcy Code, 11 U.S.C. Section 35(a)(2)(1976). Section 17(a)(2) provided in relevant part that a discharge in bankruptcy shall not release

> liabilities for * * * obtaining [a] * * * renewal of credit *in reliance* upon a materially false statement in writing respecting his financial condition made * * * with intent to deceive * * *.

Cases interpreting section 17(a)(2) developed two judicial glosses. First, because direct proof of actual reliance is difficult, actual reliance may be proven by circumstantial evidence of reliance. *See* Matter of Garman, *supra*, 625 F.2d at 759. Second actual reliance must be reasonable, Carini v. Matera, 592 F.2d 378, 381 (7th Cir.1979)(*per curiam*). In *Matter of Garman*, we discussed the meaning of "reasonable". We held that this second aspect of the section 17(a)(2) reliance test is not meant as an invitation to "second guess a creditor's decision to make a loan or to set loan policy for the creditor." 625 F.2d at 761. Further section 17(a)(2) was not intended to empower the court to "undertake a subjective evaluation and judgment of a creditor's lending policies and practices." *Id.* at 759. *Garman* reversed the Bankruptcy

Court's finding that the creditor's reliance upon net worth, rather than income, was unreasonable.

Congress clearly indicated that section 523(a)(2)(B)(iii) is merely a codification of the cases construing section 17(a)(2). "[T]he creditor must not only have relied on a false statement in writing, the reliance must have been reasonable. This codifies case law construing [section 17(a)(2)]." H.R.Rep. No. 595, 95th Cong., 1st Sess. 364 (1977); S.Rep. No. 989, 95th Cong., 2d Sess. 77–79 (1978), U.S. Code Cong. & Admin. News 1978, pp. 5787, 5864, 6320.

First National's assertion that the Bankruptcy Court applied an erroneous rule of law because the Bankruptcy Court misapplied *Garman's* "reasonable reliance" holding is incorrect. The Bankruptcy Court here did not determine whether First National's reliance was reasonable. Such a determination was unnecessary because the Bankruptcy Court found that First National had not actually relied upon the false statement.

After a review of the evidence, however, we are convinced that the Bankruptcy Court's finding of non-reliance was clearly erroneous. The burden of proving each element, including reasonable reliance, lies on the creditor. *See In re* Taylor, 514 F.2d 1370, 1373 (9th Cir.1975). First National satisfied its burden of proving actual reliance. Rynberk, the responsible bank officer, asserted that the bank would not have renewed the loan on the second occasion but for the letter furnished by the debtor. It is uncontested that First National never before sought any financial information when Kreps sought a renewal. Such increased vigilance is important circumstantial evidence of actual reliance. The debtor's ambiguous and uncorroborated assertion that the statement was given merely to satisfy a bank examiner should be given little weight when the testimony is studied in detail.

Although the Bankruptcy Court made no explicit finding as to the reasonableness of First National's reliance, our review of the evidence indicates that a remand for entry of judgment in favor of the creditor is proper. In *Garman* the Bankruptcy Court had made no finding of fact concerning the debtor's intent. 625 F.2d at 764. Nevertheless, as in *Garman,* under the circumstances of this case, we conclude that further litigation concerning the reasonableness of the bank's reliance is unnecessary. The evidence indicates that First National, faced with a second renewal request, wished assurance that its long-time customer had sufficient resources to pay the obligation. This assurance took the form of a listing of assets and a promise, as provided in the last paragraph of the letter, * * * that "if the loan is not paid * * * [the debtor] agree[s] to secure the loan with an Assignment of Beneficial Interest in [our home]." No evidence in the record indicates that the bank's reliance upon the letter was unreasonable.

Accordingly, the judgment of the district court is reversed and the cause is remanded for the entry of a judgment in favor of the First National Bank of Lansing.

Problem 10–1

1. Could the creditor in *Kreps* have ignored the bankruptcy proceeding and sued on the debt in state court after the bankruptcy proceeding? See section 523(c)(1). Why do you suppose that Congress insisted that certain creditors assert nondischargeability in the bankruptcy court but allowed others to sue in state court on a debt they allege was not discharged?

2. If fraud was committed in procuring of a loan of $100,000, and the loan was later rewritten with the addition of $20,000 in a transaction where no fraud was committed, what part of the debt is not dischargeable?

3. What of the case in which there was no fraud in the original $100,000 loan, but fraud was committed in a rewrite of the loan that raised it to $120,000?

IN RE TOUCHARD

United States Bankruptcy Court, District of Utah, 1990.
121 B.R. 397.

Findings of Fact, Conclusions of Law, and Order

JUDITH A. BOULDEN, BANKRUPTCY JUDGE.

This adversary proceeding came on for trial upon the complaint of Household Bank, N.A. (Household) against Angela Marie Touchard (Touchard), the debtor in this chapter 7 case. Household's complaint sought judgment in the sum of $11,146.30 together with interest, costs, and attorney's fees, on a credit card debt owed Household by Touchard, and that the debt be determined nondischargeable pursuant to 11 U.S.C. § 523(a)(2)(A).[1]

The court has reviewed the documentary evidence, the testimony, demeanor, and credibility of the witness, heard and considered the arguments of counsel, and made an independent review of the applicable law. Based upon the foregoing, the court enters the following Findings of Fact, Conclusions of Law, and Order.

FINDINGS OF FACT

1. On September 19, 1989, Touchard filed a petition for relief under chapter 7 of the Bankruptcy Code. Household is a national banking association and an unsecured creditor of Touchard.

2. Household's complaint was timely filed.

3. Touchard was a nominally self-employed, twenty-one-year-old high school graduate at the time she made the credit card purchases complained of and was a student when she filed this bankruptcy.

4. Touchard testified that she arranged an unsecured loan from a family friend to finance a housecleaning business that Touchard intended to initiate. No specific date was established for the receipt of the

---

[1]. Subsequent citations are to Title 11 of the United States Code unless otherwise noted.

funds. The anticipated loan was to be, at maximum, $15,000. Touchard anticipated her salary from the business was to be between $2,400 and $2,800 gross per month. The repayment terms of the loan were ambiguous. Touchard also anticipated the receipt of $2,000 to $3,000 from her father to be used to finance the housecleaning venture. Touchard asserted that she intended to pay the amounts owing to Household from the revenue generated from her new business. Touchard produced no corroborating evidence of either loan.

5. On August 24, 1989, Touchard filed a police report claiming that her apartment was burglarized and that over $15,000 in personal property, including recently purchased cleaning supplies to be used in the housecleaning business, was taken. The circumstances of the burglary are not convincing and the court discounts the accuracy of Touchard's testimony regarding this incident.

6. Allegedly, as a result of the theft of the cleaning supplies, the family friend and Touchard's father both declined to advance the funds previously promised, and as a result, Touchard could not generate sufficient income to pay Household.

7. Based upon the circumstances of the case, the demeanor of the witness, and the lack of corroborative evidence, the court finds Touchard's testimony relating to the loans and the theft not credible.

8. Prior to filing bankruptcy, a judgment for $65,000 had been entered against Touchard. In May of 1989, subsequent to entry of the judgment, Touchard discussed with an attorney the effect of filing a petition in bankruptcy and the potential dischargeability of the $65,000 judgment.

9. At the time Touchard incurred the debt which is the subject of this litigation, she was unable to pay her debts as they became due. In addition to the $65,000 judgment, Touchard was also obligated to pay a judgment for approximately $17,000 to the Taft Carbide Federal Credit Union for the use of a Visa share loan, an obligation of $1,893 to Dillard's Department Store, $4,500 to Lomas Bank, U.S.A., for the use of a bank card, $3,200 to Discover Card, and obligations arising from the use of other house credit cards.

10. In 1986, Household's predecessor in interest issued Touchard a Visa charge card, account no. 4668007013593850, providing an annual percentage rate of 17.90% on any outstanding balance.

11. Touchard made purchases on the Visa account regularly from the time the account was opened. Her initial credit limit of $1,000 was eventually increased to $2,500 in early 1989. Touchard did not exceed her credit limit prior to July of 1989. Between March 7, 1988, and July 3, 1989, Touchard's Visa charges averaged approximately $714 per month. She regularly paid at least the minimum payment on the account.

12. The last payment received by Household from Touchard was in the amount of forty-three dollars on July 3, 1989, representing the

minimum payment due for the June 8, 1989, statement. Her balance as of the July 9, 1989, billing date was $2,202.06. The balance on the account listed in Touchard's bankruptcy schedule of liabilities was $11,147.00, which amount remains unpaid.

13. Between June 28, 1989, and August 8, 1989, Touchard made purchases on the Visa account totalling $8,912.56, thereby exceeding her credit limit of $2,500 and bringing her account balance to $11,146.30.

14. The purchases made on July 1, 1989, placed Touchard over her $2,500 credit limit. The amount of purchases made in excess of the credit limit after July 1, 1989, totaled $8,646.30.

15. Between June 28, 1989 and July 26, 1989, Touchard made 242 charges.[2] Of those charges, only seventeen were for amounts over fifty dollars.

16. The charges were made primarily at department and specialty stores such as Dillard's Department Store, Macy's, K–Mart, Foot Locker, Mervyn's, and Merle Norman. Touchard testified that between thirty to forty percent of the purchases made were for supplies and goods relating to her housecleaning business, with the balance for personal items. The documentary evidence is inconclusive.

17. Touchard filed her petition for bankruptcy more than forty days after her last purchase made with Household's Visa card.

18. The testimony of Touchard relating to her intention to repay the numerous charges for personal as well as business items from the funds to be derived from the loan from her family friend and her father is not credible.

19. Household retained counsel to institute and prosecute this adversary proceeding. The terms of the Visa application provide the following: "Cardholder agrees to pay if delinquency collection procedures are instituted, reasonable cost of collection, including attorney fees of 25% of the principal, finance charge and court cost if suit is filed, or other cost of collection incurred by bank in the enforcement hereof, whether or not suit is brought." No evidence regarding the amount of

---

2. Notwithstanding the 242 charges admitted to by Touchard at trial, the court counts 239 charges on the Visa billing statements admitted into evidence. At the highest use of her card, between July 7, 1989 and July 16, 1989, she made an average of 19.8 charges per day.

Date	No. of Charges
6/28/89	2
6/29/89	2
7/01/89	5
7/02/89	2
7/04/89	1
7/05/89	5
7/06/89	9
7/07/89	21
7/08/89	6
7/09/89	17
7/10/89	16
7/11/89	15
7/12/89	20
7/13/89	6
7/14/89	17
7/15/89	54
7/16/89	26
7/17/89	6
7/18/89	3
7/20/89	2
7/22/89	2
7/23/89	1
7/26/89	1

attorney's fees and costs incurred therein has been presented to the court.

CONCLUSIONS OF LAW

From the foregoing Findings of Fact, the court enters the following Conclusions of Law:

1. This adversary proceeding is a core proceeding over which this court has jurisdiction pursuant to 28 U.S.C. § 157(b)(2)(I). A final order may be entered by this court subject to review under 28 U.S.C. § 158.

2. Venue is proper under 28 U.S.C. § 1409(a).

3. Household has the burden of proof in objecting to Touchard's discharge and must prove the elements of nondischargeability for false pretenses and false representation by clear and convincing evidence. Bankruptcy Rule 4005; *Driggs v. Black (In re Black)*, 787 F.2d 503, 505 (10th Cir.1986).

4. Pursuant to section 523(a)(2)(A), any "purchase of goods on credit by a debtor who does not intend to pay therefor, constitutes false representation." 3 *Collier on Bankruptcy* ¶ 523.08 at 523–50 (15th ed. 1988).

5. In order to except Touchard's obligation from discharge, Household must prove by clear and convincing evidence that "the debtor made a [materially] false representation or willful representation; the representation was made with the intent to deceive the creditor; the creditor relied on the representation; the creditor's reliance was reasonable; and the creditor sustained a loss as a result of the debtor's representation." *First Bank of Colo. Springs v. Mullet (In re Mullet)*, 817 F.2d 677, 680 (10th Cir.1987).

6. In ascertaining whether Touchard made a materially false representation or willful misrepresentation, this court adopts the "implied representation" doctrine relating to credit card purchases. Under that doctrine, "credit card purchases include an implied representation that the cardholder has the ability and intention to pay for the charge incurred." *May Co. v. Chech (In re Chech)*, 96 B.R. 781, 783 (Bankr. N.D.Ohio 1988). Touchard's implied representation that she had the current ability to repay the charges incurred was false.

7. Household has proved by clear and convincing evidence that Touchard made a materially false representation, upon which it reasonably relied, and that Household suffered a loss as a result.

8. The court now examines whether Touchard had the required intent to deceive. This court refers to factors other courts in this circuit have used in determining Touchard's intent:

> (1) The length of time between making the charges and filing bankruptcy, particularly if the charges were made outside the section 523(a)(2)(C) presumption of dischargeability periods;

> (2) the number of charges made and whether multiple charges were made on the same day;

(3) the amount of charges made and whether charges were less than the applicable floor limit;

(4) whether the charges were above the credit limit on the account;

(5) a sharp change in the buying habits of the debtor;

(6) whether or not an attorney had been consulted concerning the filing of bankruptcy before the charges were made;

(7) whether the purchases were made for luxuries or necessities;

(8) the financial condition of the debtor at the time the charges were made;

(9) whether or not the debtor was employed, and if unemployed, the debtor's prospects for employment; and

(10) the financial sophistication of the debtor.

See *May Dep't Stores Co. v. Kurtz (In re Kurtz),* 110 B.R. 528, 529–30 (Bankr.D.Colo.1990); *United Bank v. Favinger (In re Favinger),* 1988 W.L. 174692 (Bankr.D.Colo.1988). Of the ten factors recited, all but perhaps the last factor are applicable in this case.

9. Touchard completed making the credit charges over forty days prior to filing for bankruptcy. This enabled all of the purchases to remain outside the forty-day period (which establishes a presumption of nondischargeability) pursuant to section 523(a)(2)(C).

10. Touchard made numerous charges after exceeding her credit limit, many of the charges being made in the same store on the same day for under fifty dollars. Touchard offered no reasonable explanation for this behavior. This pattern of spending diverged remarkably from her previous spending habits.

11. At the time she made the purchases, Touchard had graduated from high school, was nominally self-employed, and had overly optimistic plans of starting a housecleaning business. Furthermore, she was deeply in debt.

12. Touchard first contacted an attorney and was informed of the dischargeability of debts in bankruptcy in May of 1989. Touchard's testimony reveals that more than three months prior to incurring the charges discussed herein, she had at least considered bankruptcy and had consulted an attorney regarding an appeal of a substantial judgment outstanding against her.

13. The majority of Touchard's purchases were for clothing and other personal purposes. Only between thirty to forty percent of the purchases were for purposes relating to her prospective housecleaning business.

14. Cumulatively, the above factors show a clear and convincing intent to defraud. Although the intent to deceive may be inferred from the circumstances in a credit card case, this court need not rely solely on

circumstantial evidence. This court finds Touchard's intent to defraud based on her demeanor and credibility as well.

15. Section 523(a)(2)(A) "includes only those frauds involving moral turpitude or intentional wrong, and does not extend to fraud implied in law which may arise in the absence of bad faith or immorality." *In re Black,* 787 F.2d at 505. Touchard's fraud involved intentional wrong.

16. Based upon all the evidence, including the credibility of the witness, this court concludes that Touchard intended to deceive Household and that she incurred the debt to Household by false representation in the abusive use of her Visa credit card.

17. Household asserts that the entire account balance of $11,146.30 plus interest should be adjudged nondischargeable.

18. The last payment in the amount of forty-three dollars, representing the minimum payment due for the June 8, 1989, statement, was received by Household on July 3, 1989. The balance on the Visa account as of the July 9, 1989, statement was $2,202.06. There is no evidence to support a finding that Touchard did not intend to pay for purchases made before the date Touchard sent the minimum forty-three dollar payment and before she exceeded her credit limit of $2,500.

19. The charges made on July 1, 1989, placed Touchard over her credit limit of $2,500. Although there is no evidence that Touchard received independent written notification from Household that she had exceeded her credit limit, it is reasonable to infer from Touchard's pattern of purchases and from prior Visa billing statements that she knew or should have known her credit limit had been exceeded.

20. "If a creditor can prove by clear and convincing evidence that the debtor obtained credit through fraud, the court should declare the debt nondischargeable in an amount which it can reasonably estimate as obtained by the fraud." *John Deere Co. v. Gerlach (In re Gerlach),* 897 F.2d 1048, 1052 (10th Cir.1990). Therefore, the amount of the debt nondischargeable is $8,646.30; the amount of purchases in excess of Touchard's $2,500 credit limit.

21. Household seeks, in addition to judgment for the account balance, judgment for attorney's fees and cost incurred in this nondischargeability action.

22. Touchard is liable for attorney's fees and costs incurred by Household in initiating and prosecuting this adversary proceeding under the terms of her Visa application to the extent those fees are found to be reasonable by this court.

THEREFORE, it is hereby

ORDERED, that Household is entitled to judgment against Touchard in the amount of $8,646.30 together with interest at the rate of 17.9 percent per annum until the filing of this petition, and at the judgment rate henceforth until paid, and, it is further

ORDERED, that the debt owed by Touchard to Household as set forth above is not dischargeable pursuant to 11 U.S.C. § 523(a)(2)(A), and, it is further

ORDERED, that reasonable attorney's fees as allowed by the court upon subsequent motion are likewise nondischargeable, and, it is further

ORDERED, that Household submit a judgment in accord herewith.

Problem 10–2

1. Othello, an automobile dealer, sold two automobiles covered by Desdemona Bank's perfected security interest "out of trust"—that is, in violation of his floor planning arrangement—to a third party and failed to remit the proceeds as he was required to do by the security agreement. Approximately a week later Othello filed a Chapter 7 petition. Can Desdemona Bank prevent its claim against Othello from being discharged? If so, on what ground? Must the Bank take any action to prevent discharge of its debt?

2. Assume that Othello is a surgeon practicing in Cincinnati, Ohio. Othello had been "going naked," that is, practicing without insurance. After the spouse of a disappointed patient recovered a judgment against him of $1,500,000, he filed a petition in Chapter 7. His schedules show an annual income of approximately $450,000 and apart from the malpractice judgment, only nominal debts. Your firm represents the judgment creditor and your senior partner has asked whether this is an appropriate case for dismissal under 707(b), and, if so, how such a dismissal is to be procured.

3. Your client is sole proprietor of a pizza parlor in Peoria, Illinois; she filed a petition in Chapter 7 on September 1, 1991. She has struggled with the pizza parlor for many years prior to declaring bankruptcy and at the time of the bankruptcy she owed various tax liabilities. Which of the following liabilities will not be discharged?

   a. Sales tax owed to the state of Illinois for sales in the calendar year 1987.

   b. State withholding tax on employees' salaries for 1987 that was not withheld or paid.

   c. Income tax for the calendar year 1986. Assume that your client filed a return on April 15, 1987 for the 1986 tax year, but that return did not disclose all of the tax later found to be due. The Internal Revenue Service discovered this in an audit in 1990 and made a demand for its payment in July, 1990.

4. In January, 1991, Romeo and Juliet (husband and wife), both lawyers, come to you for counseling concerning a potential bankruptcy. Both of them graduated from law school in 1983. At that time Juliet owed $40,000 in student loans and Romeo owed $70,000. With the birth of their second child Juliet ceased practice in 1987. Recently Romeo lost his job with a large firm when the firm split up. Juliet still owes $30,000 of her student loans and Romeo owes $65,000 of his. During 1986 and a portion of 1987, Romeo procured the agreement of the lender of his student loan to reduce the amount of his payments. The two of them ask whether their student

loan liability can be discharged in a Chapter 7 or Chapter 13. What do you advise?

One of your clients suggests the possibility of paying off at least a portion of their student loans by drawing against their credit cards. He suggests that the credit card debt could then be discharged in a later bankruptcy. What do you think?

5. Another of your potential bankruptcy clients has come to you as a result of a $200,000 judgment that he recently suffered because of an auto accident. Only $100,000 is covered by insurance. Although he was not prosecuted for drunken or impaired driving nor was he given a Breathalyzer, the accident report shows that your client had been drinking at the time of the accident and suggests that he may have been drunk.

He has been told that the liability will be discharged either in a Chapter 7 or Chapter 13 despite the drunk driving exception to discharge since he was never charged, nor was there a formal finding that he was driving while drunk or impaired. What do you think? (Assume for the purpose of this problem there is now no possibility that he will suffer a criminal or civil sanction because of drunken or impaired driving.)

6. Assume now that your client with the judgment for $200,000 has taken bankruptcy in Chapter 7. The time for the discharge hearing is coming and the judgment creditor has not filed a proof of claim. Can and should you file a claim on the judgment creditor's behalf? See sections 501, 523(a)(10).

Note: *Discharge from Criminal Restitution Liability*

Twice in the last decade the Supreme Court has faced the question whether a debtor who has committed welfare fraud can be discharged from her criminal restitution liability. In the first case, *Kelly v. Robinson*, 479 U.S. 36, 107 S.Ct. 353, 93 L.Ed.2d 216 (1986), the Court of Appeals for the Second Circuit held that liability to be dischargeable in a Chapter 7 case. The Supreme Court reversed. Four years later the same argument was made in a Chapter 13 case, *Pennsylvania Department of Public Welfare v. Davenport*, 495 U.S. 552 110 S.Ct. 2126, 109 L.Ed.2d 588 (1990), and the Supreme Court there found that the criminal restitution liability was discharged. It rested both of its decisions on the fact that 523(a)(7) excepted from a Chapter 7 discharge liability for a "fine, penalty, or forfeiture payable to and for the benefit of a governmental unit," but the Chapter 13 did not have a similar exception from discharge. In response to the *Davenport* case, Congress amended section 1328(a)(3) in 1990 to reverse the outcome. As we indicated above, Congress purported both to repeal 1328(a)(3) and to amend it in 1994. One of these acts—presumably the repeal—must have been a mistake.

THE DISCHARGE, STATE RESTRICTIONS ON THE DISCHARGE, SECTIONS 524 AND 525

Section 524 states that a discharge voids any judgment and, under section 524(a)(2) and (3), operates as an injunction against the commencement or continuation of an action "to collect, recover or offset any

* * * debt as a personal liability of the debtor, * * *." Nevertheless, the acts which produced the bankruptcy and the debts discharged in it may have ancillary consequences under state law.

Section 525 may be considered to be an extension of the policies embodied in section 362 and in the injunction under section 524(a) against the attempt to collect a discharged debt. As it was originally written by the Bankruptcy Commission in 1973, the precursor to section 525 would have prohibited almost all forms of discrimination against someone because that person had been in bankruptcy. That proposal was too much for the Congress to stomach. Instead Congress enacted the far more limited rule now seen in section 525. The idea that a lender or other party should not discriminate against someone because that person has been in bankruptcy is, of course, contrary to the selfish interest of any creditor. Such a creditor might properly conclude that one who has tasted the juicy fruit of the bankruptcy tree is more likely to return to it than someone who has never tasted the fruit.

Section 525(a) is a codification of a limited principle expressed by the Supreme Court in *Perez v. Campbell*, 402 U.S. 637, 91 S.Ct. 1704, 29 L.Ed.2d 233 (1971). That case involved an Arizona statute that withdrew the driver's license of anyone who suffered a judgment arising out of a vehicular accident and who had not paid the judgment within a certain period of time. The statute applied whether the debtor had taken bankruptcy or not. In *Perez v. Campbell* the Supreme Court of the United States held that the Arizona law was an impermissible restriction on the federal exercise of the bankruptcy power. Section 525(a) is shaped by and based upon that decision.

One should note that section 525 is necessarily interrelated with several other sections. First, an act of discrimination under section 525 might also be claimed to be a violation of the injunction under section 524 or (if the case is still open) the stay under section 362. It is possible the acts prohibited by section 525 will be permitted under section 365 to one who opposes a debtor's assumption.

To see the relationship among these sections, consider a 1988 case from the Court of Appeals for the Third Circuit. In *Brown v. Pennsylvania State Employees Credit Union*, 851 F.2d 81 (3d Cir.1988), the Credit Union sent a letter to a member who had just filed a bankruptcy petition. The letter read in part as follows:

> It is the Credit Union's policy to deny future services to members when any portion of the debt is discharge in bankruptcy. However, if the obligation is reaffirmed with court approval, you would remain eligible for services as though the bankruptcy had not occurred.

Is this a not so subtle attempt to collect the debt in violation of the stay? Clearly the Credit Union would have had the right to refuse to deal with the debtor in the future (if it did not violate section 525 by so doing), but the letter goes beyond that; it invites a reaffirmation, in effect, a collection of the debt. Ignoring the similarity between a reaffirmation and the coerced payment of an outstanding obligation, the Court of

Appeals affirmed a finding that the Credit Union did not act with the purpose of collecting the debt. It discusses the interrelationship of sections 362, 524, and 525 as follows:

> We hold that PSECU did not violate § 362 or § 524 of the bankruptcy code merely by informing Brown of its policy. Nothing in the bankruptcy code requires this creditor to do business with this debtor. To require dealings would impermissibly extend the scope of the code's anti-discrimination provisions, and Brown fails to make out a case warranting an extension on the particular facts of this case. Because PSECU may refuse Brown services, we agree with the bankruptcy court that PSECU may inform Brown of its policy. In refusing to impose sanctions on PSECU, this court agrees with other courts of appeals which have considered the issue, and our decision does not infringe on the policies of the bankruptcy code.
>
> The limited scope of the anti-discrimination provisions of the code demonstrates the PSECU may lawfully refuse to deal with Brown on account of her discharged debt. Section 525 bars only governmental agencies and employers from discriminating against a debtor on account of a previous bankruptcy filing. * * * Congress rejected a general anti-discrimination policy. * * * Brown has conceded, as both lower courts found, that § 525 does not bar PSECU from enforcing its policy. Yet, any refusal of future services by a present creditor has some coercive impact. If we hold that the impact itself is sufficient to violate the bankruptcy injunctions of § 362 and § 524, then a creditor—whether or not a governmental unit or employer—may be prevented from denying future services because of a prior discharged debt. The debtor could do indirectly what she cannot accomplish directly through the anti-discrimination provision. We cannot find that Congress intended this result.

One sympathetic to the debtor can easily think of half a dozen ways in which the Court could have come to the opposite conclusion under sections 362, 524, or even 525. The case is quite striking in its hostility to these sections and in its willingness to read them narrowly and contrary to the debtor's apparent interest.

In one of Congress' few recent acts of generosity toward student borrowers, it added section 525(c) in the 1994 amendments. That subsection prohibits discrimination against student loan borrowers because they have been bankrupt or insolvent or failed to pay a debt that was discharged. This subsection is different from 525(a) and (b). Section 525(c) deals with the behavior of a lender in making a new credit decision, a decision that would inevitably be influenced by a debtor's earlier bankruptcy or insolvency. In effect, the Congress is telling the creditor that it must disregard the very information that may be most relevant to its credit decision. Given the direct clash between the obvious self interest of a creditor and the apparent commands of 525(c), we expect to see some interesting cases growing out of 525(c).

It is not happenstance that most of the Court of Appeals cases identified in this chapter go against the debtor. As one rises through the district court to the Court of Appeals, one finds less and less sympathy for the fresh start and for the claims of the debtor. The original growth of cases decided by bankruptcy judges shortly after the new Code became effective in 1978 has been trimmed by later decisions of all of the Courts of Appeals.

FLORIDA BOARD OF BAR EXAMINERS v. G.W.L.

Supreme Court of Florida, 1978.
364 So.2d 454.

ENGLAND, CHIEF JUSTICE, and OVERTON, JUSTICE. The petitioner, G.W.L., applied for admission to The Florida Bar and received a passing score on the bar examination. The Florida Board of Bar Examiners, acting as our agent for the admission process, undertook an investigation into his character, fitness, and general qualifications to practice law in the state. The Board refused to recommend G.W.L. for admission to the Bar, and he now petitions this Court for admission. We allowed argument because this petition raises a matter of general importance in the admission process, specifically the effect of a bankruptcy petition on a Bar applicant's fitness to practice law. We agree with the recommendation of the Board and decline to admit the petitioner on the facts and circumstances in the record in this case, but this affirmance is without prejudice and the petitioner may seek a further hearing to offer additional evidence of his present good moral character.

To understand the ramifications of our decision today, it is necessary to recount the events surrounding the petitioner's discharge in bankruptcy. In doing so, it must be with the recognition that it is not the act of filing for bankruptcy but the circumstances surrounding this particular bankruptcy application that demonstrate a lack of good moral character and justify the Board's decision.

G.W.L. completed his secondary education in the northeast and attended an eastern university from September, 1969, until June, 1973. During that period he received approximately $1,900 in 3 1/2% interest student loans from the university, which amount was to be repaid within ten years after the termination of his status as a full-time student.

In September, 1973, the petitioner entered law school. To finance his legal education, he borrowed approximately $2,500 per year from a bank under a government-sponsored 7% interest student loan program. Similar ten-year repayment terms were agreed upon. When he received his Juris Doctor degree in May, 1976, G.W.L.'s financial obligations totaled $9,893. Initial payments were scheduled to begin nine months after graduation with the bulk of the payments not due for three years. There were no exceptional financial problems or identified misfortunes, and the obligations appeared normal for any student attending undergraduate and graduate educational programs on student loans.

For some months prior to his graduation, G.W.L. attempted unsuccessfully to find legal employment locally. On May 19, 1976, he simultaneously filed with the Board a late student registration and an application to take the bar examination in Florida. He also arranged several job interviews in southwest Florida where his parents reside. His initial efforts to secure employment in Florida, however, proved fruitless. On May 20, 1976, three days prior to his graduation from law school, the petitioner executed a voluntary petition for bankruptcy which he filed in the appropriate United States District Court on May 26, 1976. With the exception of one debt in the amount of $8.01, none of the debts listed in his petition were due at the time of filing.

In June, 1976, G.W.L. concluded his personal participation in the bankruptcy proceedings and moved to Florida. He made informal arrangements with the court-appointed trustee to defer action on his petition for discharge for six months, allegedly with the understanding that if he could find a job and begin repaying his creditors he would voluntarily withdraw the bankruptcy petition. Nevertheless, the petition was granted on December 20, 1976, and by order of the bankruptcy court the petitioner was adjudged bankrupt and released from all his debts. Coincidentally, G.W.L. secured employment as a law clerk in a law office in Florida on December 20, 1976, at a wage of $70 per week.

G.W.L. passed the July, 1976, Florida bar examination and the customary background investigation was undertaken. During the course of the investigation, the Board discovered the bankruptcy petition and undertook a more extensive investigation of his activities in connection with that action. By letter of December 6, 1976, the Board notified the petitioner that it wished to inquire into the circumstances surrounding the filing of his voluntary petition for bankruptcy and requested that he appear before the Board in regard to that matter. An informal hearing was held on January 14, 1977, at which G.W.L. appeared, answered questions, and offered his explanation of the matter.

On January 19, the Board notified G.W.L. that it had decided to defer final consideration of his application to permit further investigation. Immediately following the hearing G.W.L. made arrangements for repayment of the debts discharged by the bankruptcy order of December 20, 1976. On February 20, specifications were drawn and served on the petitioner, advising him of the Board's intent to base its findings and conclusions on the testimony elicited at the informal hearing and informing him of his right to a formal hearing at which he would be entitled to be represented by counsel, to present evidence, to question witnesses, and, if necessary, to use the Board's subpoena power to secure the attendance of witnesses. The petitioner responded to the specifications by letter dated March 8, 1977, in which he expressly declined a formal hearing and agreed to a determination of his application on the basis of facts then before the Board. The letter also advised the Board that he had secured employment as a law clerk and had voluntarily resurrected his discharged debts.

Within thirty days after receiving the letter, the Board recommended against petitioner's admission to the practice of law. After rejecting a request for reconsideration, the Board notified G.W.L. of its action by letter dated September 14, 1977. On November 14, the petitioner filed his petition for admission with this Court. The Board submitted a response to the petition on December 16, 1977, and we heard arguments on the matter in chambers on February 6, 1978.

The critical inquiry in this case is whether the manner in which the petitioner voluntarily secured a discharge of his debts in bankruptcy justifies a finding of a lack of good moral character sufficient to make him unfit to practice law in Florida. The Board found that his activities proved him unfit to practice law, based on the following indicia:

(1) The petitioner had worked each summer during undergraduate school and two of the three summers during law school. At the time he prepared his bankruptcy petition, he had not fully tested the Florida job market either as to law-related employment or other jobs commensurate with skills he had earlier developed.

(2) The petitioner explained to the Board that his decision to consider practice in Florida was made after April, 1976, when his car broke down and was sold. This explanation was contradicted by evidence that he considered entering the practice of law in Florida at least as early as February, 1976, when he wrote to the Board for bar admission forms. His parents had lived in Florida for some years before that date.

(3) The petitioner suggested that his motivation for bankruptcy was in part pressure from creditors, particularly in the form of certain "dunning" letters that he allegedly received from bank lenders and from the newspaper with which he had advertised the sale of his car. His debt to the newspaper in the amount of $8.01 was incurred in April, 1976, one month before his bankruptcy petition was filed. The petitioner could not produce copies of the dunning correspondence to which he referred, indicating that he had destroyed those received from lending institutions. The Board found his claim of being driven to bankruptcy by "pressure" from his $8 one-month-old debt or his unmatured student loan obligations unbelievable.

The petitioner argues for admission essentially on two grounds, one legal and the other factual. First, he asserts that bankruptcy is a statutory right, available to all persons in this country not only for the benefit of the bankrupt but also for the benefit of the general public. Therefore, he claims that a bar applicant's exercise of the statutory right cannot be said to reflect adversely on the character or fitness of the applicant. Second, he asserts that his decision to act before his significant debts became due was neither a fraud on his creditors nor otherwise morally reprehensible. Although the petitioner concedes that it would have demonstrated a lack of requisite character and fitness to have contracted for the debts with the concurrent intention to file for bankruptcy and avoid their repayment, he argues that neither the Board's charges nor the record shows that he had any such preconceived intent.

The Board's position on the petitioner's admission application rests on the premise that while the filing of a petition in bankruptcy is lawful and does not of itself demonstrate a lack of fitness, conduct that is not unlawful may nevertheless fall short of the standards of moral character which must be met before one is qualified for admission to the bar. The Board recommends that this Court follow the view of the Oregon Supreme Court that: "Legality is beside the point. The issue is applicant's sense of ethics." Application of Alpert, 269 Or. 508, 514, 525 P.2d 1042, 1045 (1974). It insists that its rejection of the petitioner's application was based on the circumstances surrounding his filing the bankruptcy petition rather than on the election to file itself. As factual support for its conclusion, the Board points out that the petitioner formed his intent to obtain a discharge before graduating from law school, long before the major debts were due, and apparently because (according to his testimony) he "found it an unfortunate but practical way of getting out of this awful situation of having no money and an awful lot of debts * * *."

The Court, under its constitutional authority to "regulate the admission of persons to the practice of law," has the authority to require proficiency in the law and good moral character before it admits an applicant to practice before the courts of this state. The sole purpose of these requirements is to protect the public. The petitioner in the instant case had demonstrated his proficiency by passing the required bar examination. The issue before us is whether he has established his good moral character, taking into consideration the facts and circumstances under which he sought bankruptcy.

The term "good moral character" has no absolute definition. *See Konigsberg v. State Bar of California,* 353 U.S. 252, 77 S.Ct. 722, 1 L.Ed.2d 810 (1957). One definition would require that only conduct or acts which historically constitute an act of moral turpitude justify a finding of a lack of good moral character. This Court in *State ex rel. Tullidge v. Hollingsworth,* 108 Fla. 607, 611, 146 So. 660, 661 (1933), defined moral turpitude as follows: "Moral turpitude involves the idea of inherent baseness or depravity in the private social relations or duties owed by man to man or by man to society * * *." Recently we expressed the view that issuing a worthless check without the intent to defraud was not an offense of moral turpitude but it was unethical conduct for a member of the bar. *The Florida Bar v. Davis,* 361 So.2d 159 (Fla.1978). Such conduct was the subject of bar discipline in the *Davis* case, and the lawyer was suspended for twelve months.

In our view, a finding of a lack of "good moral character" should not be restricted to those acts that reflect moral turpitude. A more appropriate definition of the phrase requires an inclusion of acts and conduct which would cause a reasonable man to have substantial doubts about an individual's honesty, fairness, and respect for the rights of others and for the laws of the state and nation. *See Konigsberg, supra.*

As we noted in *Florida Board of Bar Examiners re Eimers*, 358 So.2d 7 (Fla.1978), the nature of the practice of law provides the unscrupulous attorney with frequent opportunities to defraud the client or obstruct the judicial process. It is our constitutional responsibility to protect the public by taking necessary action to ensure that the individuals who are admitted to practice law will be honest and fair and will not thwart the administration of justice. In our view, a definition of good moral character which limits an adverse finding to those acts which constitute an offense evincing moral turpitude is inadequate because, as we have held in bar disciplinary matters, it would not sufficiently protect the public interest. *The Florida Bar v. Davis, supra.* The inquiry into good moral character which emphasizes honesty, fairness, and respect for the rights of others and for the laws of this state and nation is a proper and suitable standard for those who desire to be an integral part of the administration of justice in the courts of this state. We recognize, as we did in *Eimers, supra,* that the standard of conduct required of an applicant for admission to the bar must have a rational connection to the applicant's fitness to practice law, and the standard must be applied with that limitation in mind or the term "good moral character" could become "a dangerous instrument of the right to practice law."

We must now determine two issues. First, are the facts in this case such that a reasonable man would have substantial doubts about the petitioner's honesty, fairness, and respect for the rights of others and for the laws of the state and nation? Second, is the conduct involved in this case rationally connected to the petitioner's fitness to practice law?

In our view, both questions must be answered in the affirmative. We find that the Board had ample record evidence from which it could conclude that the principal motive of the petitioner in filing his petition for bankruptcy was to defeat creditors who had substantially funded seven years of educational training. Whether that motive was present as the debts were incurred or was formed toward the end of his law school training, the Board could fairly conclude from the petitioner's own testimony and prior behavior that he exercised his legal right to be freed of debt by bankruptcy well before the first installments on his debt became due, with absolutely no regard for his moral responsibility to his creditors. The petitioner's admittedly legal but unjustifiably precipitous action, initiated before he had obtained the results of the July bar examination, exhausted the job market, or given his creditors an opportunity to adjust repayment schedules, indicates a lack of the moral values upon which we have a right to insist for members of the legal profession in Florida. The petitioner's course of conduct in these personal affairs raises serious questions concerning the propriety of his being a counselor to others in their legal affairs, and is rationally connected to his fitness to practice law.

The fundamental purposes of the federal bankruptcy act are to facilitate the rehabilitation of the bankrupt debtor and to provide a means for equitable distribution of the bankruptcy assets among his or her creditors. At an early date in the history of the act, it was construed to "relieve the honest debtor from the weight of indebtedness which has become oppressive, and to permit him to have a fresh start in business or commercial life, freed from the obligation and responsibilities which may have resulted from business misfortunes." Wetmore v. Markoe, 196 U.S. 68, 77, 25 S.Ct. 172, 176, 49 L.Ed. 390, 394 (1904). Although the discharge bars the underlying legal remedy for collecting a debt, the underlying moral obligation to repay the debt remains and in fact constitutes sufficient consideration to make a subsequent reaffirmation legally enforceable. Kesler v. Department of Public Safety, 369 U.S. 153, 170, 82 S.Ct. 807, 817, 7 L.Ed.2d 641, 653 (1962); Silva v. Robinson, 115 Fla. 830, 156 So. 280 (1934).

The record before us reflects that the petitioner suffered no unusual misfortune or financial catastrophe prior to his filing the bankruptcy petition. His position was no different than that of other students who used student loans to obtain and complete their education. Although he did not have employment at the time of his graduation and for six months thereafter, the student loans were not yet due and for the most part would not be due for at least a year. In our view, his filing of the bankruptcy petition showed a disregard not only for the rights of his creditors but also for future student loan applicants. The filing of the bankruptcy petition was not illegal, but in our view it was done in such a morally reprehensible fashion that it directly affects his fitness to practice law.

To foreclose any misconstruction of this decision, we must emphasize that this ruling should not be interpreted to approve any general principle concerning bankruptcies nor to hold that the securing of a discharge in bankruptcy is an act inherently requiring the denial of admission to the bar. We further do not wish this decision to be construed to hold that any comparable exercise of a clear legal right will necessarily imperil bar admission.

In making our final determination in this case, we cannot ignore the fact that the action of this individual was not unusual conduct in his graduation year. In 1976 there were 8,461 bankruptcy petitions filed by college graduates in order to eliminate legal responsibility for student loans. The number was sufficient to move Congress to amend the bankruptcy act to limit the circumstances under which an adjudication of bankruptcy will operate to discharge federally insured student loan obligations. 20 U.S.C.A. Section 1087-3(1978). *See* State v. Wilkes, 41 N.Y.2d 655, 394 N.Y.S.2d 849, 363 N.E.2d 555 (1977). Student loan bankruptcies have resulted in litigation elsewhere. E.g., Girardier v. Webster College, 563 F.2d 1267 (8th Cir.1977); Handsome v. Rutgers University, 445 F.Supp. 1362 (D.N.J.1978). A concurring judge in the *Girardier* case expressed his view on the "fresh start" purpose of the bankruptcy act as it pertains to student loan bankruptcies thusly:

"[A]ppellants have obtained far more than the fresh start contemplated by the Bankruptcy Act—they have obtained a head start because each has secured something of value that cannot be lost or taken away and which will give each appellant a continuing, lifelong economic benefit * * *." 563 F.2d at 1278.

We find the conduct of the petitioner in the instant case, although not illegal at the time, morally reprehensible. While we recognize that a significant segment of his generation behaved similarly, in our minds his conduct was clearly wrong. There may be justification for the assertion that the moralities of this exercise of a clear legal right were not fully considered or understood by the young people who undertook these student loan bankruptcies. Many have now found their future professional careers tarnished or jeopardized. In bar discipline or admission matters, we customarily take into account the youth and inexperience of attorneys in considering the appropriate action and we believe we should do so in this instance.

G.W.L. waived his opportunity for a formal hearing on his moral fitness for bar admission. Therefore, he did not present other evidence of good moral character to the Board to offset the lack of good moral character indicated by his conduct leading up to the bankruptcy discharge. At a future hearing, the petitioner may be able to present evidence of good moral character to offset the circumstances now in the record.

Taking all of these factors into account, we now approve the finding of the Board of Bar Examiners, without prejudice to G.W.L. to apply for a formal hearing before the Board to present evidence of his present good moral character.

It is so ordered.

SUNDBERG and ALDERMA, JJ., concur.

(Dissenting and concurring opinions omitted.)

Questions

1. Because GWL's case was decided in 1978 before the effective date of the Code, there is no discussion of section 525. More surprisingly there is no discussion of *Perez v. Campbell*. Would the case come out the same way today?

2. Assume that one who has declared bankruptcy seeks (1) a license to run a horse-racing track or (2) a charter to operate a state bank. May the pertinent state or federal agencies deny such a license or charter without violating 525(a) solely because of the debtor's prior bankruptcy? May they use the applicant's bankruptcy as one of the reasons for such denial?

DUFFEY v. DOLLISON
United States Court of Appeals, Sixth Circuit, 1984.
734 F.2d 265.

ENGEL, CIRCUIT JUDGE.

The precise issue presented by this appeal is whether Ohio's Motor Vehicle Financial Responsibility Act, Ohio Revised Code §§ 4509.01–.99 (Baldwin 1975), as it has been applied to the Duffeys, conflicts with section 525 of the Bankruptcy Act of 1978, 11 U.S.C. § 525 (1982), thereby violating the Supremacy Clause of the United States Constitution. U.S. Const. art. VI, cl. 2.

Motor vehicle financial responsibility laws, which require motorists to maintain some type of automobile insurance or otherwise to furnish proof of financial responsibility, have been enacted in nearly all states. Some states compel all drivers to furnish proof that they are adequately insured as a precondition to the issuance of driver's or automobile licenses. *E.g.,* Mich.Comp.Laws Ann. §§ 500.3101–.3179 (1983). Other states, such as Ohio, have enacted less comprehensive laws which require proof of financial responsibility only when a driver has failed, within a reasonable time, to satisfy a judgment for damages arising from an automobile accident or has been convicted of certain serious traffic offenses. The public benefit from such laws has long been recognized. *See Kesler v. Department of Public Safety,* 369 U.S. 153, 158–68, 82 S.Ct. 807, 811–16, 7 L.Ed.2d 641 (1962). The Supreme Court has established that states may constitutionally require all motorists to carry liability insurance or post security before they are issued driver's licenses. *Bell v. Burson,* 402 U.S. 535, 539, 91 S.Ct. 1586, 1589, 29 L.Ed.2d 90 (1971).

The validity of the Ohio statute is a matter of great concern to those interested in keeping irresponsible drivers off the highways as well as to those individuals who, voluntarily or involuntarily, go into bankruptcy. While we have been furnished no Ohio statistics, the general pervasiveness of the problem is well illustrated by the stipulated findings in *Henry v. Heyison,* 4 B.R. 437 (E.D.Pa.1980). There, the court noted that in one year, 12,000 drivers in Pennsylvania had their driver's licenses suspended as the result of unsatisfied motor vehicle tort judgments. *Id.* at 439 n. 4. Of those 12,000 drivers, 300 had reported that their motor vehicle tort judgments were discharged in bankruptcy proceedings. *Id.*

This appeal is particularly important because several bankruptcy courts that have considered whether the Ohio Motor Vehicle Financial Responsibility Act unconstitutionally conflicts with federal bankruptcy laws have reached opposite conclusions. *Compare In re Cerny,* 17 B.R. 221, 224 (Bankr.N.D.Ohio 1982)("[T]he [Ohio] statute is being applied nondiscriminatorily and is therefore consistent with 11 U.S.C. § 525.") *with In re Shamblin,* 18 B.R. 800, 803 (Bankr.S.D.Ohio 1982)("Ohio's [statute] is discriminatory and in violation of § 525 of the Bankruptcy Code.") *and In re Duffey,* 13 B.R. 785, 788 (Bankr.S.D.Ohio 1981) (Ohio's financial responsibility law and policy discriminates against bankrupts and hence violates section 525 of the Bankruptcy Code). A fourth bankruptcy court in Ohio, under circumstances quite different from those involved here, found that the Ohio statute does not invariably conflict with the Bankruptcy Act. *In re Hinders,* 22 B.R. 810 (Bankr. S.D.Ohio 1982). Our decision here does not address the facts of *Hin-*

ders, nor does it pass upon the merits of that case or the law expressed in it.

Finally, the present controversy is significant because it involves a potential conflict between important state and federal interests: state concern for public safety and federal concern for establishing uniform bankruptcy laws. Clearly if these competing interests are incompatible, the Supremacy Clause dictates that we resolve the conflict in favor of federal law. Good policy and good sense, however, suggest the desirability of accommodating both interests if this can reasonably be achieved.

I.

The facts here are stipulated. On June 18, 1979, a judgment of $912.76, arising from an auto accident, was entered against George Duffey in the Municipal Court of Franklin County, Ohio. This judgment was not satisfied within 30 days and, consequently, Mr. Duffey's operator's license and vehicle registration were suspended on July 28, 1980, by the Registrar of Motor Vehicles, Dean Dollison, pursuant to Ohio Revised Code section 4509.37. On May 23, 1980, a judgment of $1,131.90, arising from an auto accident, was entered against Shari Duffey in the Franklin County Municipal Court. This judgment also was not satisfied within 30 days, resulting in the suspension of Mrs. Duffey's driving privileges on October 28, 1980.

The Duffeys, on January 27, 1981, filed a voluntary joint bankruptcy petition under Chapter 7 of the Bankruptcy Act. A copy of their bankruptcy petition, which listed the unsatisfied accident-related judgments in the schedule of debts, was sent by the Duffeys to Registrar Dollison with the request that he reinstate their driving privileges. Dollison, while recognizing that the judgment debts were subject to discharge and that the Duffeys could not be required to satisfy or reaffirm the debt as a condition to reobtaining their licenses, nevertheless refused to vacate the order of suspension until the Duffeys had filed evidence of financial responsibility as required under Ohio Revised Code section 4509.40.

On February 24, 1981, the Duffeys brought suit in bankruptcy court in the Southern District of Ohio for reinstatement of their driving privileges. In that action the Duffeys argued that Ohio's requirement of proof of financial responsibility, as it applies to individuals whose unsatisfied tort judgments have been stayed or discharged by bankruptcy, unconstitutionally conflicts with the federal bankruptcy provision prohibiting the discriminatory treatment of bankrupts, 11 U.S.C. § 525 (1982). The bankruptcy judge agreed that the challenged provisions of the Ohio Motor Vehicle Financial Responsibility Act conflict with the Bankruptcy Act and ordered the Registrar to reinstate the Duffeys' driving privileges. The Registrar appealed this decision to the United States District Court for the Southern District of Ohio. In a carefully considered opinion, United States District Judge John D. Holschuh reversed the decision of the bankruptcy court and held that Ohio's financial responsibility requirement does not violate section 525 of the

Bankruptcy Act because the state statute applies equally to bankrupts and nonbankrupts. We affirm.

II.

The Supreme Court, in *Perez v. Campbell,* 402 U.S. 637, 91 S.Ct. 1704, 29 L.Ed.2d 233 (1971), stated that "[d]eciding whether a state statute is in conflict with a federal statute and hence invalid under the Supremacy Clause is essentially a two-step process of first ascertaining the construction of the two statutes and then determining the constitutional question whether they are in conflict." *Id.* at 644, 91 S.Ct. at 1708. In making this decision a reviewing court must "determine whether a challenged state statute 'stands as an obstacle to the accomplishment and execution of the full purposes and objectives of Congress.'" *Id.* at 649, 91 S.Ct. at 1711 (quoting *Hines v. Davidowitz,* 312 U.S. 52, 67, 61 S.Ct. 399, 404, 85 L.Ed. 581 (1941)). Applying the *Perez* approach, we therefore first ascertain the construction of the Ohio Motor Vehicle Financial Responsibility Act and section 525 of the Bankruptcy Act, and then determine whether the statutes conflict.

A.

The Ohio Motor Vehicle Financial Responsibility Act provides that "[w]henever any person fails within thirty days to satisfy a judgment rendered within this state, upon written request of the judgment creditor or his attorney," the court must forward a certified copy of the judgment to the registrar of motor vehicles. Ohio Rev.Code Ann. § 4509.35 (Baldwin 1975). Upon receipt of a certified copy of the unsatisfied judgment, the registrar shall "suspend the license and registration and nonresident's operating privilege of any person against whom such judgment was rendered, except as provided in sections 4509.01 to 4509.78 of the Revised Code." Ohio Rev.Code Ann. § 4509.37 (Baldwin 1975). Driving privileges must remain suspended for seven years; however, "[t]he registrar shall vacate the order of suspension *upon proof that such judgment is stayed,* or satisfied in full * * * *and upon such person's filing with the registrar of motor vehicles evidence of financial responsibility* in accordance with section 4509.45 of the Revised Code." Ohio Rev.Code Ann. § 4509.40 (Baldwin 1975)(emphasis added). Proof of financial responsibility must be maintained for three years and may be given by filing a certificate of insurance, a surety bond, a certificate of deposit, or a certificate of self-insurance. Ohio Rev.Code Ann. § 4509.45 (Baldwin 1975).

The Ohio Supreme Court has not authoritatively construed the Motor Vehicle Financial Responsibility Act. Consequently, we look to lower court decisions in Ohio construing the statute, and to the language of the Act itself. It has been observed that the purpose of the Act is to "provide sanctions which would encourage owners and operators of motor vehicles on Ohio highways to obtain liability insurance sufficient in amount to protect others who might be injured through the negligent operation of a motor vehicle." *Iszczukiewicz v. Universal Underwriters Insurance Co.,* 182 F.Supp. 733, 735 (N.D.Ohio 1960). Following the

United States Supreme Court's decision in *Perez v. Campbell,* 402 U.S. 637, 91 S.Ct. 1704, 29 L.Ed.2d 233 (1971), the former version of Ohio's Motor Vehicle Financial Responsibility Act was declared unconstitutional to the extent that it required payment of a tort judgment as a condition to restoration of driving privileges, even though the underlying judgment was stayed, or discharged in bankruptcy. *Weaver v. O'Grady,* 350 F.Supp. 403, 407 (S.D.Ohio 1972). The Act as it is now written cures that defect. Ohio Rev.Code Ann. § 4509.40 (Baldwin 1975). However, bankruptcy does not relieve the judgment debtor of the requirement of posting proof of future financial responsibility. *House v. O'Grady,* 35 Ohio Misc. 20, 299 N.E.2d 706 (Ct.C.P.Franklin County 1973).

The Ohio Act has as its object the protection of the public from financially irresponsible motorists who have proved unwilling or unable to satisfy a judgment arising from an automobile accident. The statute embodies a "one-bite" approach to achieving this purpose by permitting motorists the privilege of driving without any proof of financial responsibility until they incur an accident-related judgment and fail to satisfy it within 30 days.

Section 525 has yet to be authoritatively construed by the United States Supreme Court. However, the legislative history indicates that section 525, "codifies the result of *Perez v. Campbell,* 402 U.S. 637, 91 S.Ct. 1704, 29 L.Ed.2d 233 (1971), which held that a State would frustrate the Congressional policy of a fresh start for a debtor if it were permitted to refuse to renew a drivers license because a tort judgment resulting from an automobile accident had been unpaid as a result of a discharge in bankruptcy." S.Rep. No. 989, 95th Cong., 2d Sess. 81, *reprinted in* 1978 U.S.Code Cong. & Ad.News 5787, 5867. Therefore when construing section 525, it is helpful to examine the *Perez* holding.

In *Perez,* the petitioners filed a voluntary bankruptcy petition two days before judgment was entered against them for personal injuries and property damages which arose from an automobile collision. The judgment was discharged in bankruptcy by order of the district court. Nevertheless, the State of Arizona suspended the Perezes' driving privileges pursuant to a statute which provided for such suspension when an accident-related judgment went unsatisfied for 60 days. In order to regain their privileges, the Perezes were required to satisfy the judgment and give proof of future financial responsibility. Unlike the Ohio Act, the Arizona statute required satisfaction of the judgment even though it was discharged in bankruptcy or its collection stayed. *Id.* at 638–42, 91 S.Ct. at 1705–1707.

In considering whether the Arizona law unconstitutionally conflicted with the Bankruptcy Act, the Court noted that "the validity of [the] limited requirement that some drivers post evidence of financial responsibility for the future in order to regain driving privileges is not questioned here." *Id.* at 642, 91 S.Ct. at 1707. The only issue the Court examined was whether a State may enact a statute "providing that a discharge in bankruptcy of [an] automobile accident tort judgment shall have no effect on the judgment debtor's obligation to repay the judgment creditor, at least insofar as such repayment may be enforced by the withholding of driving privileges by the State." *Id.* at 643, 91 S.Ct. at 1708. The majority determined that the statute jeopardized the "fresh start" objectives of the Bankruptcy Act by providing creditors leverage for collection of judgments which had been discharged in bankruptcy. *Id.* at 646–48, 91 S.Ct. at 1710–10. In the majority's view, one of the primary purposes of the Bankruptcy Act "is to give debtors 'a new opportunity in life and a clear field for future effort, unhampered by the pressure and discouragement of preexisting debt.'" *Id.* at 648, 91 S.Ct. at 1710 (quoting *Local Loan Co. v. Hunt,* 292 U.S. 234, 244, 54 S.Ct. 695, 699, 78 L.Ed. 1230 (1934)). Because the Arizona law obstructed these objectives, it was found to be invalid under the Supremacy Clause. *Id.,* 402 U.S. at 656, 91 S.Ct. at 1714.

Thus the *Perez* decision, which section 525 of the Bankruptcy Act codifies, specifically left open the issue we now consider: whether bankrupts who have discharged an accident-related judgment can be required, as a condition to the restoration of driving privileges suspended prior to the bankruptcy, to post evidence of financial responsibility. The legislative history indicates that section 525 was intended by Congress to incorporate further refinements of the *Perez* doctrine:

> [T]he enumeration of various forms of discrimination against former bankrupts is not intended to permit other forms of discrimination. The courts have been developing the *Perez* rule. This section permits further development to prohibit actions by governmental or quasi-governmental organizations that perform licensing functions, such as a State bar association or a medical society, or by other organizations that can seriously affect the debtors' livelihood or fresh start * * *.

S.Rep. No. 989, *supra,* at 81, 1978 U.S.Code & Ad.News at 5867. It appears that section 525 is intended to ensure that bankrupts are not deprived of a "fresh start" because of governmental discrimination against them, based "solely" on the bankruptcy. Senate Report 989 specifies that "the effect of * * * section [525], and of further interpretations of the *Perez* rule, is to strengthen the anti-reaffirmation policy found in section 524(b). Discrimination based solely on nonpayment could encourage reaffirmations, contrary to the expressed policy." *Id.* The House further noted regarding Section 525:

> [T]he purpose of the section is to prevent an automatic reaction against an individual for availing himself of the protection of the bankruptcy laws. Most bankruptcies are caused by circumstances beyond the debtor's control. To penalize a debtor by discriminatory treatment as a result is unfair and undoes the beneficial effects of the bankruptcy laws. However, in those cases where the causes of a bankruptcy are intimately connected with the license, grant, or employment in question, an examination into the circumstances surrounding the bankruptcy will permit governmental units to pur-

sue appropriate regulatory policies and take appropriate action without running afoul of bankruptcy policy.

H.R.Rep. No. 595, 95th Cong., 1st Sess. 165 *reprinted in* 1978 U.S.Code Cong. & Ad.News 5963, 6126 (footnote omitted). Therefore, we agree with the district court's conclusion that "the primary purpose of section 525 of the Bankruptcy Code is to prevent the government either from denying privileges to individuals solely as a reaction to their filing bankruptcy or from conditioning the grant of privileges on the bankrupt's reaffirmation of certain debts." *Duffey v. Dollison,* No. C–2–81–1154, slip op. at 8 (S.D.Ohio Aug. 13, 1982). It is thus necessary to determine whether the Ohio Financial Responsibility Act impedes the accomplishment of, or frustrates, these Congressional objectives. *Perez v. Campbell,* 402 U.S. 637, 649, 91 S.Ct. 1704, 1711, 29 L.Ed.2d 233 (1971).

III.

In considering whether a state statute impermissibly conflicts with a federal law, a court "must be guided by respect for the separate spheres of governmental authority preserved in our federalist system." *Alessi v. Raybestos–Manhattan, Inc.,* 451 U.S. 504, 522, 101 S.Ct. 1895, 1905, 68 L.Ed.2d 402 (1981). "[P]re-emption of state law by federal statute or regulation is not favored 'in the absence of persuasive reasons—either that the nature of the regulated subject matter permits no other conclusion, or that the Congress has unmistakably so ordained.'" *Chicago & North Western Transportation Co. v. Kalo Brick & Tile Co.,* 450 U.S. 311, 317, 101 S.Ct. 1124, 1130, 67 L.Ed.2d 258 (1981)(quoting *Florida Lime & Avocado Growers, Inc. v. Paul,* 373 U.S. 132, 142, 83 S.Ct. 1210, 1217, 10 L.Ed.2d 248 (1963)).

The Duffeys contend that Ohio law requires them to post proof of financial responsibility "solely" because they have not paid a debt that is dischargeable in bankruptcy. Therefore in the Duffeys' view, the Ohio Act violates section 525 of the Bankruptcy Act because section 525 specifically prohibits states from using the failure to pay a debt as the basis for denying a driver's license.

We agree with the district court that the Duffeys misinterpret both section 525 and the Ohio Act. Of course, the former Ohio statute, by requiring payment of the judgment notwithstanding bankruptcy, would indeed violate section 525; as the legislative history of section 525 indicates, this would be "the *Perez* situation." S.Rep. No. 989, 95th Cong., 2d Sess. 81, *reprinted in* 1978 U.S.Code Cong. & Ad.News 5787, 5867. However, since the present Ohio Act provides that a judgment stayed or discharged in bankruptcy need not be satisfied by the judgment debtor as a condition to the restoration of driving privileges, it clearly is consistent with the immediate holding in *Perez:* the Act neither provides creditors "leverage for the collection of damages," nor under the facts here does it coerce bankrupts into reaffirming discharged debts. *Perez v. Campbell,* 402 U.S. 637, 646–47, 91 S.Ct. 1704, 1710–10, 29 L.Ed.2d 233 (1971).

We recognize that the portion of the Ohio Act which suspends motorists' driving privileges for failure to satisfy a judgment is not triggered unless a judgment creditor requests in writing that a certified copy of the unsatisfied judgment be forwarded to the Registrar. Ohio Rev.Code Ann. § 4509.35 (Baldwin 1975). It is conceivable that under certain circumstances not present here, a creditor might attempt to use this ability to initiate license suspension proceedings to coerce a debtor into reaffirming all or part of a judgment that is stayed by the Bankruptcy Act.

However under the facts of this case, the Duffeys could not have been coerced into reaffirming the stayed judgments because the judgments had been certified to the Registrar and the requirement of furnishing proof of financial responsibility had been fixed *before* the Duffeys filed in bankruptcy. Once the judgment were certified, the Duffeys could not have regained their driving privileges without furnishing proof of financial responsibility even by paying the judgments. Thus, at that juncture, the judgment creditors could do nothing further to benefit or inconvenience the Duffeys; there was no leverage which could have induced the Duffeys to reaffirm their debts. As applied here the Ohio Act, which depends on judgment creditors to initiate license suspension proceedings, employs a reasonable method for relieving the state of the burden of policing every accident-related judgment. Ohio simply has chosen in civil cases to place the responsibility for reporting unsatisfied tort judgments on the party in the best position to know whether a judgment has been satisfied, and with the greatest incentive to notify the Registrar of nonpayment.

The Duffeys would have us hold that the Ohio Motor Vehicle Financial Responsibility Act violates section 525 because the Act fails to treat a bankrupt as though he or she had never incurred a dischargeable, accident-related tort judgment. Under such an interpretation, once a judgment is discharged or stayed, states would be absolutely prohibited from imposing or continuing any burden, whether a reaffirmation of liability or the imposition of financial responsibility requirements. We believe that this reads more into section 525 than Congress intended.

As the district court correctly noted:

> [N]either the language of the statute nor its legislative history indicates that section 525 was intended by Congress to erase all traces of a discharged debt and thereby foreclose the imposition of any future responsibility requirements. To the contrary, the legislative history of section 525 contemplates both the consideration of the circumstances surrounding bankruptcy and the valid imposition of future financial responsibility requirements.

Duffey v. Dollison, No. C-2-81-1154, slip op. at 10 (S.D.Ohio Aug. 13, 1982). This conclusion is amply supported by the legislative history. Senate Report 989 specifically observes that section 525 "does not prohibit consideration of other factors, *such as future financial responsibility or ability,* and does not prohibit imposition of requirements such as net capital rules, if applied nondiscriminatorily." S.Rep. No. 989, *supra*, at 81, 1978 U.S.Code Cong. & Ad.News at 5867 (emphasis added). House Report No. 595 makes this point even more emphatically:

> [T]he prohibition [of section 525] *does not extend so far as to prohibit examination of the factors surrounding bankruptcy, the imposition of financial responsibility rules if they are not imposed only on former bankrupts,* or the examination of prospective financial condition or managerial ability * * *. [I]n those cases where the causes of a bankruptcy are intimately connected with the license, grant, or employment in question, an examination into the circumstances surrounding the bankruptcy will permit governmental units to pursue appropriate regulatory policies and take appropriate action without running afoul of bankruptcy policy.

H.R.Rep. No. 595, 95th Cong. 1st Sess. 165 *reprinted in* 1978 U.S.Code Cong. & Ad.News 5963, 6126 (emphasis added). Thus, Congress has evinced a clear intent to permit the imposition of financial responsibility requirements, so long as they are not discriminatorily applied to bankrupts.

The Ohio Financial Responsibility Act in no way discriminates against bankrupts, or penalizes them for filing in bankruptcy. The Act provides that "any person" who fails to satisfy an accident-related judgment within 30 days shall have his or her driving privileges suspended by the Registrar. Ohio Rev.Code Ann. §§ 4509.35, .37 (Baldwin 1975). The statute applies without exception to *any* person who fails to satisfy a judgment for whatever reason, whether because of unwillingness, inadvertence, or inability to pay. Once a judgment has been certified to the Registrar for nonpayment, the debtor's obligation to furnish proof of financial responsibility becomes fixed. Thereafter, neither payment of the debt, reaffirmation, nor bankruptcy can relieve the debtor of this requirement. Judgment debtors such as the Duffeys who seek relief under the bankruptcy laws are therefore treated no differently from any other judgment debtor. Indeed it is this lack of discrimination to which the Duffeys take exception. By arguing that bankrupts who have proved to be irresponsible drivers should be excused from the requirement of posting proof of financial responsibility, the Duffeys in effect ask this court "to go beyond the fresh start policy of *Perez* and * * * give a debtor a head start over persons who are able to satisfy their unpaid judgment debts without resort to a discharge in bankruptcy." *In re Cerny,* 17 B.R. 221, 224 (Bankr.N.D.Ohio 1982). We do not believe that section 525 was intended by Congress to afford debtors in bankruptcy such preferential treatment.

We therefore hold that Ohio's "one-bite" approach to the imposition of financial responsibility requirements, as applied to the Duffeys, violates neither the *Perez* holding nor its statutory codification, section 525 of the Bankruptcy Act. As Judge Holschuh persuasively reasoned,

> [i]t is undisputed that Ohio may require all motorists to carry liability insurance or post security before they are issued operator's

licenses. *Bell v. Burson,* 402 U.S. 535, 91 S.Ct. 1586, 29 L.Ed.2d 90 (1971). If the State may legitimately establish such a prerequisite to the grant of driving privileges, a less stringent requirement should *a fortiori* be valid. The challenged Ohio statutes afford individuals the opportunity of driving without any showing of financial responsibility until they incur a judgment which they are unable to pay. This "one-bite" approach undoubtedly makes it possible for many individuals who otherwise could not afford insurance to obtain driving privileges. [The Duffeys] argue that because Ohio has used this more lenient approach, it is forbidden to suspend their driving privileges, despite the fact that they have demonstrated irresponsibility as a driver coupled with an inability to satisfy a resulting judgment. [This] argument, however, ignores the potential consequences to the victims of an accident caused by an individual who is an irresponsible driver.

Duffey v. Dollison, C-2-81-1154, slip op. at 12 (S.D.Ohio Aug. 13, 1982).

Our ruling here is a relatively narrow one. We uphold the Ohio Act where the requirement to furnish proof of financial responsibility has become fixed, through certification to the Registrar, prior to bankruptcy. Where the obligation has thus become fixed, neither payment of the judgment, nor arrangement with the creditor, nor bankruptcy can relieve the debtor of the requirement of furnishing proof of financial responsibility. In this respect the Ohio Act does not have the effect of discriminating between those who are bankrupt and those who are not. It cannot induce the bankrupt to reaffirm a discharged debt, or to pay thereafter, for neither action can affect the legal requirement to post proof of financial responsibility.

The judgment of the district court is AFFIRMED.

Note

To prohibit all private discrimination against a person because that person has been in bankruptcy would be Orwellian, would it not? In 1984 Congress amended section 525 to forbid a private employer from implementing discriminatory employment practices against a debtor solely because he has taken bankruptcy or has been insolvent before or during a bankruptcy proceeding. Is there not at least enough immoral odor attached to a bankrupt that a creditor should be free to decline to lend to such a person in the future for that reason alone?

Several courts as well as the Congress have addressed the question since the enactment of the Code. In 1980, Bankruptcy Judge Wooten ruled that the private suppliers of a debtor could not discriminate against him for filing for relief in bankruptcy. He granted an injunction against the creditors to require them "to cease and desist from refusing to deal with Blackwelder [the debtor]" and further required them "to deal with" the debtor on a cash basis. *In re Blackwelder Furniture Co., Inc.,* 7 B.R. 328, 341 (Bankr. W.D.N.C.1980). But in 1981 another bankruptcy court held that "the debtor's application to compel Radio Station WRKL to accept the debtor's advertising on a cash in advance basis is denied." *In re Coachlight Dinner*

Theatre of Nanuet, Inc., 8 B.R. 657, 660 (Bankr.S.D.N.Y.1981). Moreover, Congress itself has noted that section 525 "is not so broad as a comparable section proposed by the Bankruptcy Commission, S. 236, 94th Cong., 1st Sess. section 4–508 (1975), which would have extended the prohibition to any discrimination, even by private parties." Senate Report 95–989 (1978) p. 81, House Report 95–595 (1977) p. 367. However, Congress' addition of section 525(c)(that appears to prohibit creditors' discrimination against a potential debtor who is asking for a student loan) takes a step back toward the more generous position of the Bankruptcy Commission. Not so?

Problem 10–3

You are a lawyer practicing law in Gainesville, Florida. Last year you conducted a successful criminal defense of Iago who was charged with selling two pounds of cocaine. Your defense involved several appearances on motions and a two week trial. At the conclusion of the trial you charged Iago your standard fee of $150 an hour, a total in this case of $27,500. Of that amount you had received $5,000 in advance.

Two months after the conclusion of the trial Iago went into bankruptcy where he listed you as an unsecured creditor to the tune of $22,500. (The trustee was so ingracious that he asked the return of the $5,000 retainer on the ground that it constituted a voidable preference.) It is now one year hence and Iago has returned for more legal services. Would any of the following scenarios violate sections 524, 523, or 525?

1. Even though he offered to pay cash in advance for your services, you tell Iago to get out of your office and never to return.

2. Provided he pays the $22,500 owed from the prior case, you agree to represent Iago.

3. After he freely offers to pay the $22,500 without any prodding by you and in fact pays $10,000 of it, you agree to represent Iago.

REDEMPTION AND REAFFIRMATION, THE CONSUMER BANKRUPT AND HIS AUTOMOBILE, SECTION 722 AND 524(c)

Prior to 1978, it was common for consumer bankrupts who owned automobiles to retain their cars by reaffirming the full amount of the indebtedness secured by these cars. Of course debtors reaffirmed many other debts as well. Then, as now, contract doctrine held that there is a sufficient moral obligation to constitute consideration for a reaffirmed debt despite that debt's discharge. Thus courts have normally found reaffirmations to be binding contracts despite the apparent lack of consideration on the part of the creditor. Because an automobile often depreciates more rapidly than the debt that it secures declines, debtors in such circumstances often reaffirmed debts whose principal balances exceeded the fair market value of their automobiles. Doubtless, debtors in a variety of other circumstances were coerced into reaffirming under threat of refusal to lend money in the future or out of concern for other extra-judicial consequences.

The Kennedy Commission's bankruptcy proposal prohibited reaffirmations entirely. In response to consumer creditors' complaints, that section was modified by Congress and was replaced by provisions now found in section 524(c). That section is so filled with restrictions and pitfalls that a cynic might suggest it was put there in the hope and belief that it would prove unworkable and thus ultimately have the same consequence as though reaffirmations had been prohibited altogether.

Of equal importance to the typical automobile reaffirmation case is section 722. That section permits the debtor to purchase his automobile or similar personal assets for the lesser of the principal amount outstanding on the secured debt or the fair market value of the asset. Often the value of the automobile will be less than the amount of the principal and thus the debtor in bankruptcy will enjoy a right not available under section 9–506 of the Uniform Commercial Code (which would require payment of the entire debt not just the lesser of the amount of the debt or the value of the collateral). The case that follows discloses a small fly in that ointment: under Chapter 7 the debtor must pay cash to redeem his collateral under section 722. His alternatives are to proceed under Chapter 13 or to procure the creditor's agreement to a reaffirmation under section 524(c). The case that follows discloses the interplay between sections 722 and 524. How would the case have come out had it been under Chapter 13?

IN RE BELL

United States Court of Appeals, Sixth Circuit, 1983.
700 F.2d 1053.

KRUPANSKY, CIRCUIT JUDGE. This action joins the legal issue of whether redemption of secured collateral in a Chapter 7 bankruptcy proceeding may be achieved through installment payments.

Debtors, Thomas and Louis Bell (Bells), were parties to a purchase money security agreement with General Motors Acceptance Corporation (GMAC) covering a 1978 Chevrolet Van. The agreement contemplated that the Bells would pay the balance of the purchase price, approximately $6,000 together with financing charges, in equal monthly installments. At the time debtors filed a joint petition in bankruptcy on March 28, 1980, under Chapter 7 of the Bankruptcy Reform Act of 1978 (Bankruptcy Act), 11 U.S.C. Section 701 *et seq.*, the fair market value of the Van exceeded the outstanding balance on the agreement by approximately $1,000, the debtors had tendered all monthly installments on their obligation to GMAC and had otherwise not defaulted upon any term of the contract. The Van became property of the estate subsequent to which the debtors exempted their equity and the trustee abandoned the estate's interest. GMAC filed a complaint to reclaim the Van and debtors counterclaimed seeking authorization from the bankruptcy court to retain possession of the Van upon continued payment of monthly installments. The Bankruptcy Court permitted installment redemption.

In re Bell, 8 B.R. 549 (Bankr.E.D.Mich.1981), and the District Court reversed, *In re* Bell, 15 B.R. 859, 8 B.C.D. 127 (E.D.Mich.1981).

The Bankruptcy Reform Act of 1978 authorizes a Chapter 7 debtor to redeem certain secured property:

> An individual debtor may, whether or not the debtor has waived the right to redeem under this section, redeem tangible personal property intended primarily for personal, family, or household use, from a lien securing a dischargeable consumer debt, if such property is exempt under section 522 of this title or has been abandoned under section 554 of this title, by paying the holder of such lien the amount of the allowed secured claim of such holder that is secured by such item.

11 U.S.C. Section 722. This provision generally permits a debtor to redeem tangible secured personal property by paying the creditor the approximate fair market value of said property, or the amount of the claim, whichever is less. *See In re* Zimmerman, 4 B.R. 739 (Bankr.S.D.Calif.1980); *In re* Hart, 8 B.R. 1020 (N.D.N.Y.1981). However, Section 722 is facially silent as to the mechanics of redemption and, particularly, on whether the redemption may be accomplished through installment payments. The weight of authority has denied installment redemption * * *.

The bankruptcy redemption provision, Section 722, is a legislative derivative of the redemption provision of 9–506, Uniform Commercial Code. The official comment to 9–506 provides:

> "Tendering fulfillment" obviously means more than a new promise to perform the existing promise; it requires payment in full of all monetary obligations then due and performance in full of all other obligations then matured.

The legislative history of Section 722 does not reflect a Congressional intent which contemplated anything other than an intent to incorporate the fundamental requirement of "lump sum" redemption as suggested in the underlying UCC provision upon which Section 722 was predicated * * *.

More importantly, the redemption remedy of Section 722 must be construed *in pari materia* with the reaffirmation provision, 11 U.S.C. Section 524(c), which pertinently provides:

> (c) An agreement between a holder of a claim and the debtor, the consideration for which, in whole or in part, is based on a debt that is dischargeable in a case under this title is enforceable only to any extent enforceable under applicable non-bankruptcy law, whether or not discharge of such debt is waived, only if—

* * *

> (4) In a case concerning an individual, to the extent such debt is a consumer debt that is not secured by real property of the debtor, the court approves such agreements as—

* * *

(B)(i) entered into in good faith; and (ii) in settlement of litigation under section 523 of this title, or providing for redemption under section 722 of this title.

Section 524(c) authorizes a Chapter 7 debtor to seek renegotiation of the terms of the security agreement with the creditor thereby creating an alternative method pursuant to which a debtor may attempt to retain possession of secured collateral. Such an alternative, obviously attractive to the debtor financially unable to redeem the secured collateral through a lump-sum payment, is the equitable complement to Section 722. * * * Simply, a debtor incapable or unwilling to tender a lump-sum redemption and redeem the secured collateral for its fair market value may reaffirm with the creditor; contrawise, a debtor confronted with a creditor unwilling to execute a renegotiation may retain the secured collateral by redeeming it for its fair market value, which value may be substantially less than the contractual indebtedness. However, Section 524(c) facially contemplates that the creditor, for whatever reason, may reject any and all tendered reaffirmation offers; Section 524(c) envisions execution of an "agreement" which, by definition, is a voluntary undertaking * * *. Accordingly, if a debtor is authorized by the bankruptcy court to redeem by installments over the objection of the creditor, such practice would render the voluntary framework of Section 524(c) an exercise in legislative futility * * *. Phrased differently:

> Of course, if Section 722 payments could be made by installment, no debtor would ever have reason to reaffirm under Section 524(c)(4)(B)(ii), since, by right, he could obtain under Section 722 the same end—continuing possession of his property—under the same terms—payment by installment—for what would often be a significantly lower price. Thus, installment payments under Section 722 would render useless Congress' carefully laid scheme for voluntary agreement under Section 524—clearly indicating that Congress had no intention to allow such payments under Section 722.

In re Hart, *supra,* 8 B.R. at 1022.

Further, authorization of installment redemption would interpose into Chapter 7 a procedure which Chapter 7 is ill-equipped to implement. A Chapter 7 proceeding, whereby the debtor is discharged through liquidation, may conclude prior to the expiration of the installment payment period. A default by the debtor subsequent to discharge—possibly predicated upon a waste of the collateral, inability to meet the monthly installments or lack of motivation to continue payments on a rapidly depreciating collateral such as a vehicle—would burden the creditor with the expense and effort of reapplying to the bankruptcy court for relief * * *. A bankruptcy court's inability to effectively monitor the installment program and to expeditiously and meaningfully enforce the installment redemption raises serious issues of adequate creditor protection * * *.

A Chapter 7 debtor may assume the anomalous position of being financially unable to redeem the secured collateral by a lump-sum payment and concurrently incapable of persuading a creditor to reaffirm. However, a debtor's inability to exercise the Section 722 option of redemption, in the absence of installment redemption, cannot serve as a basis for the bankruptcy court to abdicate its judicial function of statutory interpretation and resort to legislation by judicial decree * * *. As has been aptly observed:

> Congress was well aware that the typical debtor might well find lump sum redemption unavailable and therefore provided a mechanism for achieving an installment redemption, to wit, by consensual agreement. That this mechanism may well be imperfect cannot be gainsaid; * * * it may well be short circuited by the recalcitrant creditor who refuses to come to terms. But those deficiencies are more properly directed to Congressional review, and consequently, provide a poor excuse for judicial legislation.

In re Schweitzer, *supra,* 19 B.R. at 864 (footnote omitted). While a bankruptcy court is invested with equity jurisprudence, application of that jurisdiction must comport to and remain compatible with the prevailing legislative intent * * *. A bankruptcy court's imposition of installment redemption clearly contravenes the overall statutory scheme and destroys the delicate balance between Section 722 and Section 524(c), and therefore finds no sanction in principles of equity.

Debtors posit that preclusion of installment redemption will precipitate situations wherein a Chapter 7 debtor will possess no viable method of retaining a possession of secured collateral. However, a debtor may avoid such an untenuous position by initially filing a petition for bankruptcy under Chapter 13 or converting an existing Chapter 7 proceeding to a Chapter 13 proceeding. Chapter 13 is designed to provide a debtor with a fresh start through rehabilitation, unlike Chapter 7 which provides a fresh start through liquidation. As such, Chapter 13 authorizes redemption by installment over an objection by the creditor (a "cramdown"), the very result sought in the action at bar. 11 U.S.C. Section 1325(a)(5) * * *. In sum, construction of Chapter 7 and 13 *in pari materia* discloses that within the overall statutory scheme a debtor desirous of retaining possession of secured collateral is accorded that election by filing a Chapter 13 petition.

Lastly, the debtors maintain that no default had occurred under the terms of the security agreement and that, upon the trustee's abandonment of the Van under 11 U.S.C. Section 554, the debtors reacquired the collateral since they held the primary possessory interest. Debtors posit that they enjoyed the same rights after abandonment as before the filing of the bankruptcy petition including the right to continue monthly installments so long as no default, as defined by the security agreement, intervened. Under this theory, the right to continued possession of the secured collateral emanates from the security agreement rather than under a Section 722 redemption. However, it has been recognized that a return of abandoned property to the party with the primary possessory interest (usually the debtor) merely provides that debtor with time to enforce his right to redeem the property under Section 722 or to seek a reaffirmation of the agreement under Section 524(c). The automatic stay of 11 U.S.C. Section 362(a)(5) continues in effect, and prevents repossession by the creditor until the case is closed, dismissed, or discharge is granted or denied pursuant to 11 U.S.C. Section 362(c)(2). Analyzing the relationship between Section 362(a)(5)(debtors protection of the automatic stay) and Section 554 (abandonment), the Court in *In re Cruseturner* has summarized:

> Accordingly, Section 362(a)(5) grants the debtor time to enforce rights in his property given him under Sections 722 and 524(c).
>
> The effect of Section 362(a)(5) is to provide the debtor with separate protection of his property. This enables him to exercise his right to redeem either by acquiring refinancing or by otherwise gathering the necessary funds, or to negotiate a reaffirmation. Unless earlier relief is requested by the creditor, the creditor may not repossess property, despite any abandonment by the trustee, until one of the three acts specified in Section 362(c)(2) occurs * * *. The application of Section 362 to exempt property and abandoned property is co-extensive with the redemption right given in Section 722, for this right extends to exempt property as well as to non-exempt property which may be abandoned by the trustee. Likewise, the stay will cover property which may be the subject of reaffirmation agreements.

8 B.R. at 592.

Further, a serious issue exists as to whether the debtors held the primary possessory interest in the Van upon abandonment. The security agreement authorized GMAC to immediately repossess the Van upon the filing of a bankruptcy petition (bankruptcy clause). While this bankruptcy clause was initially inoperative under 11 U.S.C. Section 541(c)(1), and the Van had become property of the estate under 11 U.S.C. Section 544 irrespective of such clause, the Section 541(c) prohibition against such a bankruptcy clause has been held inoperable once the asset has been abandoned from the estate. *See: In re* Schweitzer, *supra,* 19 B.R. at 865 *et seq.* Accordingly, the bankruptcy clause became effective upon abandonment, the debtors were in default of the security agreement and therefore no longer entitled to the primary possessory interest in the Van.

Further, a discharge of the debtor's personal liability on the security agreement through bankruptcy constructively vitiated Paragraph 6 of the security agreement which provides that "buyer shall be liable for a deficiency." Negation of the creditor's right to seek personal liability precipitated a default so as to empower GMAC with the primary possessory right to the Van.

In sum, this Court concludes that redemption and reaffirmation constituted the exclusive methods pursuant to which the Bells could retain possession of the secured collateral. The sole method of redemption available to a Chapter 7 debtor under Section 722 is a lump-sum redemption. Accordingly, the judgment of the district court is AFFIRMED.

Notes and Questions

1. How could the debtor have achieved his goal notwithstanding the court's opinion?

2. If the debtor does not personally appear at his discharge hearing to receive instructions on the reaffirmation in section 524(d)(or if no hearing is held because the local judge has done away with them), what is the consequence? Is there neither a discharge nor a reaffirmation?

3. The outcome of *In re Bell* may be important. Had the debtor's arguments been accepted, GMAC would have been forced to accept a continuing lien on the van without any corresponding personal obligation on the Bells to pay the remaining installments. (The discharge would relieve the Bells of any personal liability on the debt.) Conceivably the Bells could put the van to very hard use for a while and, when the van became worthless, inform GMAC that they would no longer make installment payments and GMAC was free to come and repossess the vehicle.

Unlike Chapter 11 or Chapter 13 cases in which discharge is granted only after payments under the plan have been completed, discharge in a Chapter 7 case such as the Bells would occur prior to the conclusion of the installment payments. The ill-treated creditor might consider requesting the court to revoke the discharge pursuant to section 727(d) but that section is predominantly concerned with fraud by the debtor occurring in the process of obtaining a discharge and not with reprehensible behavior by the debtor following discharge. What other remedies might a creditor pursue in this situation?

4. As part of the consumer creditor amendments in 1984, section 521(2) was added to the Code. This section requires that a debtor "file with the clerk a statement of his intention with respect to the retention or surrender of [secured and other property] and state the debtor's intention to redeem such property, or that the debtor intends to reaffirm debt secured by such property * * * " Section 521 forces the debtor to make a decision about reaffirmation, redemption and such, and prevents the debtor from holding the creditor in limbo for an indefinite period. What is the sanction for failing to choose?

Problem 10–4

You are counsel for GMAC and have worked out an arrangement with Lear's counsel for Lear to reaffirm his entire $25,000 debt for the purchase of a used Cadillac. It appears that the retail value of the car might be as high as $25,000, but it is more likely around $19,000 and the wholesale value between $16,500 and $17,500. At the reaffirmation hearing the court proposes to deny the reaffirmation on the ground that Lear is reaffirming for an amount greater than the fair market value of the automobile. The court concludes that it is not in the "best interest of the debtor" for him to reaffirm for it may impose an undue hardship upon him. (Assume that Lear is unmarried and has no dependents).

1. How would you respond?

2. Assume that the agreement was filed on March 1. On May 20, before the debt has been discharged, Lear informs the court that he wishes to rescind the agreement. May Lear do so?

3. What is the proper measure of fair market value? Is it:

a. What Lear would have to spend to replace the car?

b. What the creditor would realize on its sale?

c. The subjective value attached to the car by Lear?

d. Other?

§ 3. CHAPTER 13

A. *Eligibility*

Section 109(e) states who is eligible for Chapter 13 relief:

Only an individual with regular income that owes, on the date of the filing of the petition, noncontingent, liquidated, unsecured debts of less than $250,000 and noncontingent, liquidated, secured debts of less than $750,000, or an individual with regular income and such individual's spouse, except a stockbroker or a commodity broker, that owe, on the date of the filing of the petition, noncontingent, liquidated, unsecured debts that aggregate less than $250,000 and noncontingent, liquidated, secured debts of less than $750,000 may be a debtor under chapter 13 of this title.

Determining eligibility is occasionally tricky. The bankruptcy judge must first determine whether the debtor is "an individual," who has "regular income," and whether debtor's "noncontingent" and "liquidated" debts exceed the statutory limits. Moreover, the judge must determine which debts are "secured" and "unsecured," whether claims means the same thing as debts, and a host of additional eligibility questions. Section 101(29) defines "individual with regular income."

Often at issue, however, is the question *when* the debtor must have "regular income." If the debtor has the same job at the time the plan is filed at the first meeting of the creditors and when the plan is confirmed, surely the debtor meets the "regular income" requirement. But what of the debtor who has a job at the time of filing, but not at confirmation or vice versa? Confirmation typically occurs several months after the filing and that is the time when the courts normally measure this requirement. Since it is then that the plan's feasibility is determined, it makes sense to require that the debtor have regular income at confirmation. If the debtor does not have regular income then, it is hard to see how a feasible plan can be proposed. In effect denial of a plan on the ground that the debtor is not eligible for want of regular income may be no different from a denial on the ground the plan is not feasible.

Unsecured debts cannot exceed $250,000 and secured debts cannot exceed $750,000. In either case, however, only debts that are "noncontingent" and "liquidated" are included in this limitation. For this reason, debtors wishing to file in Chapter 13 who have large debts sometimes argue that a particular debt is contingent or unliquidated and therefore not to be counted against the $250,000 or $750,000.

A debt is contingent "[i]f the debtor's legal duty to pay, i.e., his liability, does not come into existence until triggered by the occurrence of a future event that was reasonably within the presumed contemplation of the parties at the time the original relationship between the parties was created." Simply because a debt is disputed, however, does not mean that it is contingent or unliquidated. In *In re Michaelsen*, buyers advanced $98,000 on contracts to purchase unimproved land from the debtor. They claimed that the debtor had breached the contract because the land was encumbered. The debtor argued the advance was a "deposit" for the homes to be built on the property and not a "debt" under section 109(e). Concluding that misappropriation of the money was a breach of the contract, the court found that a "claim for breach of contract * * * is not contingent, although it may be disputed." In contrast a liquidated debt must be certain both as to "amount and liability."

Initially one determines eligibility from the dollar amount of debt shown on the debtor's statement. If before confirmation the court finds that debts exceed the section 109(e) limitations, the debtor is ineligible and the case must be dismissed or converted. Some courts hold that the case must be dismissed even if this discovery is first made after confirmation. Other courts hold that section 109(e) is not jurisdictional and that a confirmed plan should not be dismissed on the basis of ineligibility. We agree with the latter cases. After the debtor, the trustee and the court have travelled the Chapter 13 road all the way to confirmation of a plan, we see little to be gained in allowing a disgruntled creditor who belatedly raises his head to attack the court's jurisdiction. Only modest injury is likely to be done to any given creditor by allowing even an ineligible case to be heard under Chapter 13, better to force those who wish to speak up early in the transaction or forever hold their peace.

After the filing of the petition, a Chapter 11 case is likely to amble on for months or even years at a leisurely pace without the filing of a plan, and, of course, without any payment to creditors. That is not true in Chapter 13. Rule 3015 authorizes the filing of a plan with a petition and requires that a plan be filed within 15 days after the petition unless the court grants a greater time. Under section 1326, the debtor "shall commence making the payments proposed by a plan within 30 days after the plan is filed." Thus, in many Chapter 13's the debtor's first payment will be due only a month after the petition has been filed.

Whether there is to be payment to a particular creditor under a Chapter 13 plan and whether a particular debt is to be discharged is interrelated in a complex way with the debtor's listing of the creditor in its statement and with the creditor's filing of a claim under Rule 3002. This relationship becomes particularly complex when one begins to consider secured creditors with unavoidable security interests and creditors such as the Internal Revenue Service, who may have sizable claims for past income taxes but in undetermined amount.

Consider first the case in which the debtor fails to list the creditor in his Chapter 13 statement. Because of that, the clerk will not send notice to the creditor. If the creditor does not procure notice of the debtor's bankruptcy in some other way, its debt will not be discharged irrespective of the plan and notwithstanding the statement in 1328 that confirmation of the plan and payment of the debts in it entitle the debtor to "a discharge of all debts provided for by the plan * * *."

In 1984 the Court of Appeals for the Tenth Circuit affirmed a finding that the comparable provision of Chapter 11 (section 1141) did not discharge the debt of a creditor who was omitted from the schedules and had never received notice. Reliable Electric Co. v. Olson Construction Co., 726 F.2d 620 (10th Cir.1984). The court found that it would be a violation of the due process clause of the United States Constitution to hold otherwise. Moreover, it reached that conclusion despite the fact that the creditor's lawyer had received informal notice that the debtor was in Chapter 11 proceedings.

One might wonder, how can a creditor who does not file a proof claim (and for whom one is not filed by someone else) be "provided for by the plan" and so subject to discharge under section 1328(a)? First, of course, it is possible that the debtor or trustee will list the creditor's claim at a lower value than the creditor believes is proper. But more likely the plan could provide for the creditor's claim generically without any specific reference to a particular creditor's claim.

Where it could be shown that the debtor had evidence of the amount of the claim yet failed to file a proof of claim under Rule 3004, a different outcome might be appropriate. In that case it would seem proper for the court to read the "provided for" language in section 1328 narrowly and to find that a plan by a debtor who declines to file a proof of claim for a debt that he knows he owes, does not "provide for" the debt.

CONFIRMATION HEARING; FORM OF CREDITOR OBJECTIONS

Except for the ministerial event of granting the discharge after the payments have been made under the plan, the concluding formal event in a Chapter 13 is the "confirmation hearing". Section 1324 directs the court to hold a hearing and provides that any party in interest may object to confirmation at that time. If there are objections to the plan, presumably there will be testimony during the confirmation hearing concerning those objections and argument concerning their legal validity. If there is no objection, we suspect that the hearing will be perfunctory and that numerous hearings might "occur" in a minute's time in a single court room.

Rules 3020 and 9014 govern the making of objections to the confirmation of a plan. Once a creditor receives notice of the confirmation, it is the creditor's responsibility to serve the debtor, the trustee and any committee with its objection. Under Rule 9014 the case then follows the usual rules for contested matters to make certain that everyone knows the basis for the objection and that the debtors and others have an opportunity to respond. It is here that the law under sections 1322 and 1325 is made.

If there is no objection to the plan, Rule 3020(b)(2) authorizes the court to "determine that the plan has been proposed in good faith and not by any means forbidden by law without receiving evidence." Does one infer from that statement that the court must hear evidence on other issues on 1322 and 1325 such as feasibility, for example? Since by hypothesis we are speaking of cases where there is no objection, one would expect this issue to be seldom raised, even if the courts were doing things completely forbidden by the statute. For that reason and possibly for others, there is little case law on this question. Indeed, some courts seem to say that no hearing is necessary where there is no objection to the plan. At least one judge has stated that the court has an independent duty to determine that each plan meets the requirements of section 1325 and that such a duty can be fulfilled only by holding a hearing. As we indicated above, we suspect the practice varies greatly from jurisdiction to jurisdiction. In courts that are overflowing with Chapter 13 cases, and particularly in those where there is an efficient and reliable Chapter 13 trustee in whom the judge has confidence, we doubt the courts often make an independent evaluation of the merits of the confirmability of a plan under section 1325 where the trustee is satisfied and where there are no creditor objections. In such cases we see no reason why valuable judicial time should be taken up with such administrative detail.

THE CHAPTER 13 TRUSTEE
APPOINTMENT, DUTIES, AND PAYMENT

Under 28 U.S.C. § 586, a federal official, the United States trustee, may "appoint one or more individuals to serve as standing trustee" in Chapter 12 and 13 cases if the number of cases warrant such appointment. In the few federal districts where there is no United States trustee, this section does not apply. Because it contemplates the possibility that there will be such a small number of Chapter 12 or Chapter 13 cases in some districts that there will be no need for a standing trustee, the possibility also exists that there will be no standing trustee even when there is a United States trustee.

In most districts a standing trustee handles all Chapter 13 cases. The trustee's obligations have not been a source of controversy. They are spelled out in section 1302(b). The trustee has a broad mandate and one suspects that the trustee's role is what the trustee makes it. Not only is the trustee instructed to "advise and assist the debtor", but also to insure that the debtor commences making payments and to appear and be heard at critical points when the plan is under consideration. In a sense the trustee is at once a collection agency, a debt counsellor and adviser concerning the intricacies of bankruptcy practice and the idiosyncracies of the local judges and rules.

PAYMENT TO TRUSTEE

While the trustee's general powers have been noncontroversial, how and what trustees are to be paid has been an issue of considerable controversy. Section 28 U.S.C. 586(e) governs payment for Chapter 12 and 13 trustees. If one stands back from the intricacies of 586(e), one sees the general rule, namely, that the trustee's salary and other expenses are to be borne by the debtors (but really by the creditors, not so?) in the form of a percentage levy on the amounts paid through the Chapter 13 and Chapter 12 process. In general the trustee collects 10 percent of the amounts paid through a Chapter 13 plan and a scaled percentage (from 10 down to 3 percent) in Chapter 12 cases.

These fees go into three pockets. First they pay the trustee's salary. That salary is set by the Attorney General in consultation with the United States trustee; it may not exceed the salary for step 1 in GS–16. Second, the percentage fee pays the "actual, necessary expenses incurred" by the standing trustee. These fees would pay office rent, secretarial and other clerical help, computer costs, and any other appropriate expenses. The third beneficiary of the fee is the "United States Trustee System Fund", a fund to pay for the United States trustee portion of the system and for that trustee's office.

Section 1326(c) provides that the trustee, not the debtor, makes the payments under the plan to particular creditors:

> (c) Except as otherwise provided in the plan or in the order confirming the plan, the trustee shall make payments to creditors under the plan.

In the typical case the debtor might pay $1,000 per month to the trustee, the trustee will subtract his $100 and pay the remaining $900 to various creditors. When the system operates in that fashion, there is little difficulty—at least from the trustee's point of view. The trustee takes his 10 percent off the top and distributes the rest.

EASTLAND MORTGAGE CO. v. HART

United States Court of Appeals, Tenth Circuit, 1991.
923 F.2d 1410.

Before MOORE, TACHA and BRORBY, CIRCUIT JUDGES.

Per Curiam.

The issue in this bankruptcy case is whether a home mortgage protected by 11 U.S.C. § 1322(b)(2) can be bifurcated into secured and unsecured portions based on the fair market value of the property under a threshold application of the provisions of 11 U.S.C. § 506(a) to an undersecured mortgage. The district court found that the attempt to do so was a modification of the mortgage and, as such, was improper. We hold that the bifurcation was a recognition of the legal status of the creditor's interest in the debtors' property and not a modification of the mortgage. We reverse.

Danny L. Hart and Joanne E. Hart, debtors in the chapter 13 bankruptcy action from which this appeal arose, took out a loan secured by a mortgage held by the Federal National Mortgage Association and serviced by appellee Eastland Mortgage Company, a creditor in the bankruptcy action. The mortgage described the security for the loan to be the real property to which the Harts' mobile home is attached,

> TOGETHER WITH all the improvements now or hereafter erected on the property, and all easements, rights, appurtenances, rents, royalties, mineral, oil and gas rights and profits, water rights and stock and all fixtures now or hereafter a part of the property. All replacements and additions shall also be covered by this Security Instrument. All of the foregoing is referred to in this Security Instrument as the "Property."

In re Hart, No. 88–6229–TS, Order Concerning Debtors' Motion to Amend Plan at 5 (Bankr.W.D.Okla. Mar. 24, 1988)(hereafter, the "bankruptcy court order"). At the time the Harts submitted their chapter 13 wage earner plan to the bankruptcy court for approval, a $55,000 balance remained on Eastland's note. However, the fair market value of the property described in the mortgage was stipulated to be $30,000. One part of the Harts' chapter 13 plan, approved by the bankruptcy court without objection, referred to the mortgage as a $55,000 secured indebtedness, while other parts of the plan referred to the mortgage as a $30,000 secured and $25,000 unsecured indebtedness. When the Harts filed a motion to amend the plan, correcting what they referred to as a "scrivener's error" so that the plan consistently listed $30,000 of the debt as secured and $25,000 as unsecured, Eastland objected.

The bankruptcy court granted the Harts' motion to amend and approved the plan over Eastland's objections. Eastland appealed to the district court, and that court reversed, holding modification of the mortgage to be inappropriate, given the protection of residential mortgages granted by 11 U.S.C. § 1322(b)(2). *In re Hart,* No. CIV–89–797–T, Order (August 28, 1989)(hereafter, the "district court order"). The Harts appealed to this court.

* * *

Chapter 13 of the Bankruptcy Code of 1978, 11 U.S.C. §§ 1301–30 (1988)

> provides for the adjustments of the debts of an individual with regular income, through extensions and composition plans, usually extending no more than three years, § 1322(c) of the Code, funded out of the Chapter 13 petitioner's future income (which is submitted to the court for the payment of the debts as provided for by the plan,

§ 1322(a) of the Code). The adjustments and extensions so allowed, however, are subject to provisions that protect the interests of creditors, including, inter alia, their secured interests.

Grubbs v. Houston First Am. Sav. Ass'n, 730 F.2d 236, 237 (5th Cir. 1984)(en banc).

Two sections of the Code are particularly important in this case. The first is 11 U.S.C. § 1322(b)(2). Section 1322 sets forth the required contents of a chapter 13 debtor's plan for rehabilitation. Subsection (b)(2) provides that the plan may: "modify the rights of holders of secured claims * * * or of holders of unsecured claims, or leave unaffected the rights of holders of any class of claims."

The original draft of the Code, prepared by the Commission on the Bankruptcy Laws of the United States, recommended permitting modification of secured indebtedness on personal property. *Grubbs,* 730 F.2d at 243–44; *In re Neal,* 10 B.R. 535, 538 (Bankr.S.D.Ohio 1981); *see also* H.R.Rep. No. 595, 95th Cong., 1st Sess., *reprinted in* 1978 U.S.Code Cong. & Ad.News 5963; S.Rep. No. 989, 95th Cong., 2d Sess., *reprinted in* 1978 U.S.Code Cong. & Ad.News 5787. The House version of the Code, H.R. 8200, 95th Cong., 1st Sess. (1977), expanded this capability for modification of secured interests to include both real and personal property. *Grubbs,* 730 F.2d at 243; *In re Neal,* 10 B.R. at 538–39. The Senate version, S. 2266, 95th Cong., 2d Sess. (1978), restricted the House version's broad right to modification by adding the underlined phrase of the following passage, "(2) modify the rights of holders of secured claims (*other than claims wholly secured by mortgages on real property*) or of holders of unsecured claims." *Grubbs,* 730 F.2d at 245 & n. 14; *In re Neal,* 10 B.R. at 539. The final version of the Code reflected the efforts of a compromise committee. "There was no explanation as to the rationale for the change of the word 'wholly' to the word 'only.'" *Id.* The change in the order of the words in the clause also remains unexplained.

In *Grubbs,* the Fifth Circuit found that Congress intended to protect the home mortgage industry:

> With regard to § 1322(b)(2), the Senate receded from its position that no "modification" was to be permitted of *any* mortgage secured by real estate; it instead agreed to a provision that modification was to be barred *only* as to a claim "secured only by a security interest in real property *that is the debtor's principal residence.*" This limited bar was apparently in response to perceptions, or to suggestions advanced in the legislative hearings [by advocates for secured creditors], that, home-mortgagor [sic] lenders, performing a valuable social service through their loans, needed special protection against modification thereof (*i.e.,* reducing installment payments, secured valuations, etc.).

730 F.2d at 246 (emphasis in original);

* * * At least one court has concluded that the benefit of section 1322(b)(2) was intended to apply only to lending institutions dealing solely in real estate loans, such as banks and savings and loan associations, as opposed to finance companies who regularly take other forms of security, such as motor vehicles and household furnishings. *United Companies Fin. Corp. v. Brantley,* 6 B.R. 178, 189 (Bankr.N.D.Fla.1980); *cf. In re Glenn,* 760 F.2d at 1434 (application of section 1322(b)(2) often arises in the context of consumer debts for personal property secured by the debtor's home or in the context of financing for business ventures secured by the debtor's home).

The other section of the Code bearing on this case is 11 U.S.C. § 506(a):

* * *

"Section 506 * * * governs the definition and treatment of secured claims * * *. Subsection (a) of § 506 provides that a claim is secured only to the extent of the value of the property on which the lien is fixed; the remainder of that claim is considered unsecured." *United States v. Ron Pair Enters., Inc.,* 489 U.S. 235, 238–39, 109 S.Ct. 1026, 1029, 103 L.Ed.2d 290 (1989); *see also Dewsnup v. Timm (In re Dewsnup),* 908 F.2d 588, 590 (10th Cir.1990)(citing *Ron Pair Enters.*)(11 U.S.C. § 506(a) and (d) govern the definition and treatment of secured claims); H.R.Rep. No. 595, 95th Cong., 1st Sess. 356, *reprinted in* 1978 U.S.Code Cong. & Admin.News 5963, 6312–13.

The dispositive issue in this case is whether Eastland's undersecured loan may be bifurcated into two *claims* by applying the general principles of section 506(a) to the mortgage and then protecting only the secured claim by the provisions of section 1322(b)(2). We believe it can.

Eastland claims that this court does not have jurisdiction to examine this issue. Eastland notes that the bankruptcy court did not reach this issue because it found that rents, royalties, profits and stock were "collateral other than the debtor's principal residence, and thus the claim was not protected by section 1322(b)(2)," bankruptcy court order at 5–6, and that the Harts did not "cross-appeal" the issue in the district court. The Harts counter that they noted the issue in their "appellee's statement" to the district court and that such notice is sufficient to confer district court jurisdiction over the issue, pursuant to Fed. R.Bankr.P. 8010(a)(2).

We hold that we do have jurisdiction to rule on this issue for two reasons. First, in this circuit, "[a]n appellee may defend the judgment won below on any ground supported by the record without filing a cross appeal." *Robinson v. Robinson (In re Robinson),* 921 F.2d 252 (10th Cir.1990)(citing *Koch v. City of Hutchinson,* 847 F.2d 1436, 1441 n. 14 (10th Cir.)(en banc), *cert. denied,* 488 U.S. 909, 109 S.Ct. 262, 102 L.Ed.2d 250 (1988)).

And second, although the record on appeal does not include the Harts' appellee's statement, they evidently did bring the issue to the district court's attention because the district court order states: "Debtors contend that even if Eastland's claim is within the scope of 1322(b)(2), debtors can still bifurcate the claim into secured and unsecured claims and modify the unsecured portion pursuant to 11 U.S.C. § 506(a)." District court order at 3.

The district court did not consider this issue, on the grounds that "the issue is not before this Court on appeal." *Id.* at 4. However, the district court could have addressed the issue had it concluded that it was dispositive. *See Pizza of Haw., Inc. v. Shakey's, Inc. (In re Pizza of Haw., Inc.),* 761 F.2d 1374, 1377 (9th Cir.1985)(district court has the discretion to consider any issue presented by the lower court record, even if not addressed in the bankruptcy court). As also noted above, this court has the same scope of review over bankruptcy court decisions as does the district court. Thus, the issue of threshold bifurcation of the Harts' mortgage prior to application of section 1322(b)(2) protection from modification is properly before us.

Threshold bifurcation of undersecured mortgages has been recognized recently by both the Third and the Ninth Circuits. In *Hougland v. Lomas & Nettleton Co. (In re Hougland),* 886 F.2d 1182 (9th Cir.1989), the Ninth Circuit held that:

> [I]t is clear that section 506(a) applies to Chapter 13 proceedings. *See* § 103(a). There is, therefore, no reason to believe that the phrases "secured claim" and "unsecured claim" in section 1322(b)(2) have any meaning other than those given to them by section 506(a).
>
> * * *
>
> Congress quite plainly has provided for the separation of undersecured claims into two components—a secured component and an unsecured component. It has then provided for their treatment in Chapter 13 proceedings. The secured portion has special protection when residential real estate lending is involved. The unsecured portion does not.

Id. at 1183, 1185. *Accord Wilson v. Commonwealth Mortgage Corp.,* 895 F.2d 123, 127, 128 (3d Cir.1990)("[W]e hold today that section 1322(b)(2) does not preclude the modification of any 'unsecured' portion of an undersecured [mortgage debt]."); *Gaglia v. First Fed. Savs. & Loan Ass'n,* 889 F.2d 1304, 1311 (3d Cir.1989)("Whether the plan complies with § 1322(b)(2) depends on the extent to which the claim is secured, an issue that is determined by reference to § 506."); *In re Lewis,* 875 F.2d 53, 56 (3d Cir.1989)(in a chapter 13 proceeding, a claim secured only by a security interest in the debtor's residence may be voided to the extent it is not an allowed secured claim as defined by section 506). *See also* 5 Collier on Bankruptcy ¶ 1322.06[1][a] at 1322–15 (L. King, 15th ed. 1979 & Supp. Dec. 1989).

While no other circuit courts have ruled on this issue, district courts and bankruptcy courts from other circuits reflect a split of authority.

Courts within the Fourth, Sixth, and Seventh Circuits have favored protection of only the secured portion of a home mortgage under section 1322(b)(2), applying section 506(a) and then submitting only the secured portion of the claim to the protection of section 1322(b)(2). *See McNair v. Chrysler First Fin. Servs. Corp. (In re McNair),* 115 B.R. 520, 523 (Bankr.E.D.Va.1990); *In re Demoff,* 109 B.R. 902, 915 (Bankr.N.D.Ind. 1989); *In re Hill,* 96 B.R. 809, 813–14 (Bankr.S.D.Ohio 1989); *In re Frost,* 96 B.R. 804, 807 (Bankr.S.D.Ohio 1989).

To the contrary, bankruptcy courts in the Fifth, Eighth, and Eleventh Circuits have held that such bifurcation is inappropriate. The bankruptcy courts in these circuits rely on some or all of four rationales: (1) the legislative history mandates protection of the home mortgage lender, and bifurcation impermissibly dilutes that protection; (2) as a matter of statutory construction, the requirements of a specific section, in this case section 1322(b)(2), control those of a general section, in this case section 506(a); (3) as a matter of statutory construction, the courts should look to the definition of "claim" from section 101(4), which includes both secured and unsecured claims, rather than the definition of "secured claim" from section 506(a); and (4) analysis of the legislative history should look back to Chapter XIII of the now-repealed Bankruptcy Act, predecessor to the Code, for guidance in the definition of secured claims. *See In re Chavez,* 117 B.R. 733, 736–37 (Bankr.S.D.Fla.1990); *In re Sauber,* 115 B.R. 197, 199 (Bankr.D.Minn.1990); *In re Schum,* 112 B.R. 159, 162 & n. 3 (Bankr.N.D.Tex.1990); *In re Kaczmarczyk,* 107 B.R. 200, 202–03 (Bankr.D.Neb.1989); *In re Russell,* 93 B.R. 703, 705 (D.N.D. 1988); *In re Catlin,* 81 B.R. 522, 524 (Bankr.D.Minn.1987). We are not persuaded that application of any of these four rationales, taken individually or cumulatively, results in a correct reading of the Code as currently enacted.

The position of the Third and Ninth Circuits and the other courts which have adopted threshold bifurcation under section 506(a) prior to submission of the secured claim portion of a mortgage to the protection of section 1322(b)(2) reflects the plain meaning of section 1322(b)(2), which states:

> Subject to subsections (a) and (c) of this section, the plan may—
>
> * * *
>
> modify the rights of holders of secured claims, other than a claim secured only by a security interest in real property that is the debtor's principal residence, or of holders of unsecured claims, or leave unaffected the rights of holders of any class of claims.

In interpreting any statute, we " 'begin with the language employed by Congress and the assumption that the ordinary meaning of that language accurately expresses the legislative purpose.' " *Justice v. Valley Nat. Bank,* 849 F.2d 1078, 1084 (8th Cir.1988)(quoting *Park 'N Fly, Inc. v. Dollar Park & Fly, Inc.,* 469 U.S. 189, 194, 105 S.Ct. 658, 661, 83 L.Ed.2d 582 (1985)). "The plain meaning of legislation should be conclusive, except in the 'rare cases [in which] the literal application of a statute will produce a result demonstrably at odds with the intention of its drafters.'" *Ron Pair Enters.,* 489 U.S. at 242, 109 S.Ct. at 1031 (quoting *Griffin v. Oceanic Contractors, Inc.,* 458 U.S. 564, 571, 102 S.Ct. 3245, 3250, 73 L.Ed.2d 973 (1982)). In addition, using a literal reading of 11 U.S.C. § 1322(b)(2) is less speculative and less quasi-legislative than attempting to ferret its meaning from its legislative history, which, as we have seen, is not clear enough with respect to this issue to show a "demonstrably" different congressional intent than that indicated by the plain meaning of the statute itself.

We join the Third and Ninth Circuits in holding that an undersecured mortgage is, for the purposes of the bankruptcy code, two *claims,* and only the secured *claim* is protected by section 1322(b)(2). More importantly, we recognize that while bifurcation, in the literal sense, may be a modification of the *mortgage* represented in the secured and unsecured claims, bifurcation is not, of itself, a "modification" of the secured claim made impermissible by section 1322(b)(2). Indeed, the act of bifurcation recognizes, but does not affect, the secured claim.

We find nothing in the plain language of section 1322(b)(2) which instructs us to go beyond the Code's statutory definition of the term "secured claims" to protect the unsecured portion of an undersecured home mortgage. We note that the Harts' plan provided for the secured claim to be paid in full without adjustment in the interest rate or repayment schedule stated in the loan documents. Under this plan, payment of only the secured portion of the debt is not a modification of the creditor's rights under the mortgage, and thus is allowed under 11 U.S.C. § 1322(b)(2).

Tangentially, the Harts argue that their mortgage is secured by more than "only an interest in real property that is [their] principal residence," thereby removing the mortgage from the protection of section 1322(b)(2) and freeing them to subject it to section 506(a) bifurcation. Both the bankruptcy court and the district court confined their analysis to this approach in analyzing the bifurcation issue. The bankruptcy court concluded that:

> While such items as "rents, royalties * * * profits * * * and stock" may be related to realty, clearly they are not realty and certainly are not considered a part of a mortgagor's principal residence. Although Eastland argues none of those items are present in this case at this time, the drafters of the mortgage form certainly placed the mortgagee in a position to claim such items as its collateral if they arise in the future. Thus, Eastland cannot now be heard to say its claim is limited to only Debtors' principal residence.

Bankruptcy court order at 5. Through this analysis, the bankruptcy court removed the mortgage from the protection of section 1322(b)(2) and allowed application of the bifurcation provisions of section 506(a).

The district court reversed. It stated that, "Eastland does not seriously contend that rents and profits are real property. Therefore * * * the language of the clause covers items other than real property."

District court order at 2. However, the district court concluded that Eastland's mortgage was totally protected by section 1322(b)(2) because the non-realty items did not presently exist and therefore could not be construed as security for the mortgage, citing the definition of a secured claim found in 11 U.S.C. § 506 and *In re Foster,* 61 B.R. at 495 (additional security must have actual independent value; land bank stock's value is illusory). District court order at 2–3. The district court concluded that because a mortgage does not exist on items which do not exist, nothing other than the Harts' real property secured the loan, and Eastland's mortgage was totally protected by section 1322(b)(2).

The Harts argue that, in finding that the additional items of collateral had no value, the district court made a finding of fact unsupported by the record. They argue, citing Fed.R.Bankr.P. 8013, that the district court had no jurisdiction to make such findings of fact. We agree.

The Third Circuit clarified the federal appeals court's role in reviewing district court decisions in bankruptcy cases:

> As an appellate court twice removed from the primary tribunal, we review both the factual and the legal determinations of the district court for error. The district court does not sit as a finder of facts in evaluating them as a court of review, and therefore its evaluation of the evidence is not shielded by the "clearly erroneous" standard of Fed.R.Civ.P. 52(a), which applies only to a *trial* court sitting as a fact finder. We are in as good a position as the district court to review the findings of the bankruptcy court, so we review the bankruptcy court's findings by the standards the district court should employ, to determine whether the district court erred in its review. To the extent the parties challenge the choice, interpretation, or application of legal precepts, we always employ the fullest scope of review: we examine the decision of the court from which the appeal is taken for error, and the legal determinations of the district court as a reviewing tribunal are not shielded by any presumption of correctness.

Universal Minerals, Inc. v. C.A. Hughes & Co., 669 F.2d 98, 101–02 (3d Cir.1981)(emphasis in original).

While the district court "is free to draw inferences from undisputed facts," *Adams v. United States (In re Breit),* 460 F.Supp. 873, 875 (E.D.Va.1978), it "may not accept the findings of the bankruptcy court and then go on to make additional findings having the effect of contradicting the conclusions of the bankruptcy court." *In re Neis,* 723 F.2d 584 at 589 (7th Cir.1983). "Merely because a reviewing Court on the same evidence may have reached a different result will not justify setting a finding aside." *Machinery Rental, Inc. v. Herpel (In re Multiponics, Inc.),* 622 F.2d 709, 723 (5th Cir.1980)(citing *United States v. National Ass'n of Real Estate [Bds.],* 339 U.S. 485, 495–96, 70 S.Ct. 711, 717–18, 94 L.Ed. 1007 (1950)).

In this case, the district court went beyond the factual findings of the bankruptcy court to find that the rents and profits listed as security on the Harts' mortgage are illusory, apparently based on undocumented, albeit uncontested, statements in Eastland's brief to the district court. The district court then went on to use this finding of fact to reverse the legal conclusion of the bankruptcy court. This use of a finding of fact by the district court in a bankruptcy appeal, unsupported by the record, is reversible error.

The order of the District Court for the Western District of Oklahoma is REVERSED and this matter is REMANDED to the Bankruptcy Court for the Western District of Oklahoma for further proceedings consistent with this opinion.

BRORBY, CIRCUIT JUDGE, dissenting.

As I would affirm the decision of the district court, I must dissent.

The principal issue we must decide is the apparent tension between two separate provisions of the Bankruptcy Code. 11 U.S.C. § 506(a) provides that a claim is secured only to the extent of the value of the property on which the lien is fixed. The balance of the debt is unsecured. On the other hand, 11 U.S.C. § 1322(b)(2) provides that a plan may modify the rights of holders of secured claims "other than a claim secured only by a security interest in real property that is the debtor's principal residence * * *." *Id.*

The majority's conclusion is that § 1322(b)(2) applies only after the secured debt has been reduced to the fair market value of the property. In other words, § 1322(b)(2) "kicks in" only to prevent any further modification of this secured claim. The problem with this approach is that it renders § 1322(b)(2) essentially meaningless.

The majority accurately describes the split in authority on this issue and cites numerous bankruptcy court decisions in the Fifth, Eighth and Eleventh Circuits that have disagreed with the majority's approach. I am persuaded by these decisions. I believe these cases correctly analyze the problem and reach the better solution.

Notes and Questions

1. In 1994, Congress added sections 1322(c)(1) and (2). Section 1322(c)(2) reads in full as follows:

> A case in which the last payment on the original payment schedule for a claim secured only by a security interest in real property that is the debtor's principal residence is due before the date on which the final payment under the plan is due, the plan may provide for the payment of the claim as modified pursuant to section 1325(a)(5) of this title.

Is the quoted amendment to 1322(c) a congressional endorsement of the decision in *Eastland Mortgage*? By indorsing the treatment in 1325(a)(5)(an "allowed secured claim"), is Congress authorizing the division of a loan secured by one's principal residence into a secured and unsecured portion? Yet Congress purports to deal only with the limited number of cases where the remaining maturity on the mortgage is five years or less. Because it failed otherwise to touch 1322(b)(2) one could argue for the opposite inference. (That is, for the inference that when the mortgage has more than five years to run, the court is without authority to divide the obligation into secured and unsecured portions and to write down the latter.)

2. If one assumes that the debtor is trying to modify the mortgage with a remaining term in excess of five years, there are several problems in addition to those posed by 1322(b)(2).

Assume a case like *Hart*, but one in which the debtor proposes to modify a mortgage for its remaining 20 year life. The debtor will divide the mortgage in two, pay a 10 percent dividend on the unsecured portion of the mortgage (a $2,000 dividend on a $20,000 liability) and pay the remaining $30,000 over the remaining life of the mortgage. The creditor, of course, will make the argument under sections 506 and 1322(b)(2) that was rejected in *Hart*. If you represent the debtor, how do you respond to the two following arguments?

a. Debtor's proposal violates section 1322(c) which limits plans to five years. By modifying the remaining mortgage the debtor is in effect proposing a planned payment that lasts 20 years.

b. To the extent that the term of the unsecured portion of the mortgage debt exceeds five years, it is not dischargeable under section 1328(a) because of section 1328(a)(1) that excludes from discharge debts provided for under section 1322(b)(5). In this case the debt is one "on which the last payment is due after the date on which the final payment of the plan is due * * *". As such, it is covered by section 1322(b)(5) and accordingly is not dischargeable under the terms of 1322(a)(1).

Problem 10–5

1. Cordelia is proposing a Chapter 13 plan. She proposes to pay her mortgage arrearages within the plan and through the trustee. However, Cordelia wishes to make the current mortgage payments directly to the mortgagee. The trustee of Cordelia's bankruptcy protests that the direct payments would still be payments "under the plan." Thus, the trustee would be entitled to a percentage fee based on those payments. Is the trustee entitled to a fee associated with the payments? Does it make a difference that the claim is "fully secured"?

2. Suppose instead, that Cordelia's mortgage note requires monthly payments of $289.00. At the petition date, Cordelia was two months in arrears. Cordelia proposes to pay the arrearages, without interest, in 36 payments of $16.06. The regular monthly payments will be continued throughout the plan and all administrative expenses will be paid. Any creditor objections?

Note: Johnson v. Home State Bank, Herein of "Chapter 19" and "Chapter 20" Cases

In *Johnson v. Home State Bank* the Johnsons, who were Kansas farmers, first went through Chapter 7 and were discharged from their personal liability on the mortgage at issue under the case. The mortgage secured debts of approximately $470,000. After the Chapter 7 proceeding, the mortgagee foreclosed on its mortgage claim (now a non recourse claim because of the debtor's Chapter 7 discharge) and received an in rem judgment of about $200,000 for the bank.

On the eve of the foreclosure sale, the Johnsons filed in Chapter 13. The bankruptcy court confirmed the Chapter 13 plan and allowed the debtors to pay off the $200,000 non recourse liability in the plan. The District Court and the Court of Appeals held the debtor could not undertake such a "Chapter 20", but the Supreme Court agreed with the bankruptcy judge and found for the debtors.

The Bank claimed that a mortgage liability on which the personal liability had been discharged no longer constituted a "claim"—at least for the purpose of inclusion in a subsequent Chapter 13. The Bank also argued that the debtor was behaving in bad faith and that the plan was not feasible. Relying mostly on the plain language of the statute, the Supreme Court found that the Bank's non recourse mortgage was a "claim" and could be included in a Chapter 13 plan. Do you understand why the Johnsons proceeded as they did? Can you foresee circumstances in which it would be in your interest as a lawyer to propose similar combinations of Chapters 7 and 13 or Chapters 7 and 12?

CO–DEBTOR STAY

Normally the stay protects only the debtor and property of the estate. If a second party not in bankruptcy is also liable on the debt, the stay does not normally prohibit a creditor from pursuing that person. Section 1301 is an exception to that rule. It extends the stay to certain co-debtors liable on consumer debt.

Section 1301 has not been the subject of much litigation but it has posed a few issues for the courts. Here we discuss two of those: (1) what is a consumer debt, (2) when may the stay be lifted because the co-obligor, and not the debtor in bankruptcy, "received the consideration" for the claim held by the creditor?

Section 101(8) defines consumer debt as "debt incurred by an individual primarily for a personal, family, or household purpose." Because the state of the debt is identified by the use to which the debtor puts the commodity, it is that use, not the nature of the commodity that determines whether the debt is a consumer or business debt. For example, the purchase of a single lawnmower for use at one's house would give rise to a consumer debt, but the purchase of five lawnmowers for use in a lawnmowing service would give rise to a business debt. That is so, even though the commodities purchased were identical. One court made the point as follows: "Where the debtor's entry into a credit transaction is motivated by a desire for business profit, the debt created thereby cannot be classified as consumer debt." If the creditor can establish that its debt was not "primarily" for a personal, family or household purpose, but was in fact for business, the stay does not apply.

For that reason we are likely to see a continuing trickle of litigation on the question what is and what is not a consumer debt.

The second and ultimately more troublesome question is presented by creditors who seek to have the stay lifted under 1301(c)(1). It directs the court to lift the stay to the extent that the non-debtor co-obligor "received the consideration for the claim held by such creditor." Assume, for example, husband and wife purchased a car that was used exclusively by wife. Husband goes into bankruptcy and wife asserts the protection of 1301. If the court finds that the wife's exclusive use of the car was "the consideration" for the purchase price, the stay must be lifted. In effect, this provision distinguishes the cases where the person outside of bankruptcy is truly the guarantor from cases where the one outside of bankruptcy is the principal obligor and the one inside bankruptcy is the guarantor.

Where the one outside of bankruptcy is the sole beneficiary of the loan, all courts agree that the stay must be lifted. Where both the debtor and the co-obligor receive some benefit from the transaction, it is less clear how the court should proceed. In such a case one could say that neither party is merely the guarantor, that each are truly debtors; therefore, the stay should be lifted. On the other hand, (c)(1) speaks of such individual receiving "the" consideration. One could read that wording to mean the stay should be lifted only in the case in which all of the consideration goes to the non-debtor co-obligor.

Finally, note a second important basis for lifting the stay under 1301. Section 1301(c)(2) requires that the stay be lifted "to the extent that the plan filed by the debtor proposes not to pay such claims." If the debtor proposes the payment of 50 percent of the co-signed claim, presumably the other 50 percent can be collected from the co-debtor prior to the conclusion of the Chapter 13 upon a lifting of the stay.

PRIORITIES AND PAYMENT

Priority rules under Chapter 13 are essentially the same as those under the other chapters. In Chapter 13, as in the other chapters, the value and amount of the secured creditor's claim is determined under 506; here, as elsewhere, the perfected secured creditor gets the benefit of its security. The best interest test means that the secured creditor must be paid under the plan the present value of its collateral. If that is done, the debtor may keep and use the collateral.

Section 1326(b)(1) requires that administrative expenses be paid in full "before or at the time of each payment to creditors." Presumably this means that administrative expenses incurred prior to the first payment under the plan must be paid in full as part of the payment before any payment may be made under the plan to creditors. This treatment is generally consistent with 1129(a)(9)(A) that requires payment in cash of administrative expenses on the effective date of the plan.

Other priority claims must be paid in full in deferred cash payments under 1322(a)(2). Under 1322 the holder of a particular claim can agree to accept less than full payment. Note, too, that the requirement is merely for "full payment", not for payment of present value equal to the total claimed. If, for example, the debtor's unpaid income tax liability under 507(a)(7) for the three years prior to the filing of the petition was $10,000, that amount could be paid over the life of the plan (payments totaling $10,000) even though the present value of those payments would be substantially less than $10,000.

Finally, the unsecured creditors are to be paid over the life of the plan. As we will see, the unsecured creditor's principal protection is the best interest test, namely, the right to receive payments with a present value equal to the liquidation value of their interest in the debtor's estate if the debtor were liquidated.

Whether a debtor in Chapter 13 can use other means to prefer one unsecured creditor over another is the same question as that faced above with respect to Chapter 11. By adopting the rules of section 1122 from Chapter 11, section 1322(b)(1) authorizes separate classes. It specifically provides that the debtor may not "discriminate unfairly against any class so designated." And 1325 requires that any plan be proposed "in good faith." Theoretically, all of this leaves us in the same position as we found ourselves in Chapter 11; in fact, debtors have proposed and courts have approved many forms of discrimination between classes of unsecured creditors.

SECURED CREDITORS

In Chapter 13, as elsewhere in bankruptcy, section 506 determines who is a secured creditor. One is secured only to the extent that the value of that person's collateral and irrespective of the face amount of the claim. Thus a mortgage on property worth $200,000 securing an outstanding debt of $300,000 represents a $200,000 secured claim and a $100,000 unsecured claim. In Chapter 13 as in Chapter 11 and Chapter 7 the claims will be split and the parts treated separately.

For the most part there are no surprises for secured creditors here. Chapter 13 differs from Chapter 11 in that there are no votes in and no absolute priority rule; thus a "cramdown" can be imposed on creditors without the necessity of a vote and without the protection of the absolute priority (section 1129(b)(2)). But the basic protection for a secured creditor in Chapter 13 is the same as that in Chapter 11, namely, the best interest test. With respect to secured creditors the test is stated in 1325(a)(5). In effect, the best interest test in this setting assures that the secured creditor will get the value of its collateral either through secured payments with a present value equal to the collateral or by the debtor's surrender of the property to secured creditor.

Although there is no provision in Chapter 13 for a vote, note that 1325(a)(5)(A) provides for secured creditors' "acceptance" and, in that circumstance, the secured creditor need not be given payment with a present value equal to its collateral.

In addition to the fact that secured and unsecured creditors have no vote under Chapter 13 and thus cannot use that practical and strategic power, Chapter 13 differs in one other important way from Chapter 11. There is no Chapter 13 analog to 1111(b). Recall that 1111(b) in effect allows a secured creditor to continue its security interest in the asset to the full amount of its claim, both secured and unsecured. In the words of 1111(b), it treats the entire claim as "secured". There is no such right in Chapter 13.

GENERAL CREDITOR, DISCRIMINATION AND THE FLOOR

Litigation concerning general creditor priority and treatment in a Chapter 13 plan takes two forms. First, an unsecured creditor sometimes argues that the total payment to it is less than it deserves under the best interest test. That argument is based on section 1325(a)(4). Second, unsecured creditors sometimes object to their treatment on the ground that they are the object of "unfair discrimination" and thus that the plan violates section 1322(b)(1).

For reasons that are sometimes obvious and sometimes not, a debtor often proposes a large payment to certain unsecured creditors and a modest payment to others. When each of the creditors would have a claim with the same priority against the debtor's assets and thus realize the same percentage of its claim in a Chapter 7 case, a creditor who is receiving the worse of it in Chapter 13 argues alternatively that the plan cannot be approved because of 1322(b)("unfairly discriminates"), or because of 1325(a)(3)(not proposed in good faith, or proposed "by * * * [a means] forbidden by law").

Unlike Chapter 11 where the issue of discrimination between classes of unsecured creditors is occasionally discussed but is rarely a central issue, there are many Chapter 13 cases where discrimination between classes is a fighting issue. It is through these Chapter 13 cases that one can appreciate the uncertainty in the law about the debtor's right to discriminate not only in Chapter 13, but also in Chapter 11.

One should appreciate that every classification is likely to result in some discrimination in favor of one creditor and against another. Because section 1325(b) requires that the debtor give up all of his or her disposable income in most cases, there is no "extra money" that will go to creditor A which does not come from creditor B. Put another way, modification of a debtor's plan is likely to be a zero sum game in which gains that go to one creditor because of classification or for other reasons, come out of the pockets of other creditors. (Plus one for creditor A is minus one for creditor B and the sum is zero.) That being the case, Congress must have intended that a certain level of discrimination is to be expected and is acceptable.

Chapter 13 explicitly provides for two forms of discrimination between unsecured creditors. First, section 1322(b)(1) authorizes the designation of classes as provided in section 1122. Section 1122 in turn authorizes the establishing of a separate class of claims "consisting only of every unsecured claim that is less than or reduced to an amount that the court approves as reasonable and necessary for administrative convenience." In Chapter 11 this provision is used to dispose of small claims by paying them in full, even in circumstances where other unsecured creditors with larger claims will receive much less than full payment. Presumably a Chapter 13 plan that fully paid every claim under $50 but paid only 60 percent of claims over $50 would be permissible under 1322(b)(1).

In the 1984 amendments to 1322(b), Congress endorsed a second specific form of discrimination. After 1984, the section provides that "such plan may treat claims for a consumer debt of the debtor if an individual is liable on such consumer debt with the debtor differently than other unsecured claim". If, for example, a friend who is not in bankruptcy has co-signed a loan, section 1322(b)(1) in effect authorizes the debtor to pay that debt in full, even while the debtor is paying far less than that to all other unsecured creditors. This subsection is a recognition of the debtor's desire to payoff co-signed debt and is, we suppose, a legislative bow to the pitiful state of consumer guarantors, mostly parents, spouses, and friends. One reading the cases should be careful to distinguish between the post–1984 and the pre–1984 decisions. Many of the pre–1984 cases that raised the discrimination question are guarantee cases that would now be covered explicitly by (b)(1).

DETERMINING THE AMOUNT OF PAYMENTS TO BE MADE UNDER THE PLAN

There are at least three legal principles in Chapter 13 that a creditor can claim to be a floor on the amount that may be paid. By far the most significant of these is a rule well known to students of other chapters, the best interest rule. That rule, found in 1325(a)(4), says essentially that each creditor must receive property with a present value under the plan at least equal to the amount that that creditor would receive if the debtor's assets were liquidated under Chapter 7. Thus, if the debtor has $10,000 of non-exempt assets that would go to his creditors in Chapter 7, payments under his plan must have a present value of $10,000 for the same creditors under Chapter 13. The rule is stated in full in 1325(a)(4):

> the value, as of the effective date of the plan, of property to be distributed under the plan on account of each allowed unsecured claim is not less than the amount that would be paid on such claim if the estate of the debtor were liquidated under chapter 7 of this title on such date[.]

One can regard the rule as an algebraic equation in which the value of the property that would be distributed in Chapter 7 is on one side; the amount on the other side is the present value of the payments to be made under the plan.

From this test springs a large headache, not only for the trustee and lawyers, but also for the courts, namely, how does one compute present value. It ultimately boils down to a determination of the proper "discount", or interest charge attributable to future payments. The question is easy to pose, but hard to answer. What set of payments over three years, for example, is precisely equal to $1,000 in hand today? The answer to that question will depend upon the creditworthiness of the debtor, upon the credit market and on the attendant alternative investments that might be available to one who had the $1,000 in hand. Where the payment is made in property other than dollars, it would depend even upon an estimation of the value of the property. The best interest test is the most important legally and the most thorny factually. It is the mainline defense of a creditor who believes that it is being underpaid.

The second legal principle that sometimes forms a floor on the debtor's permissible payments is the requirement in 1325(b)(1)(B) that the debtor give up all of his or her "disposable income" for three years if there are objecting creditors. To see how this rule might apply to require greater payments than the best interest rule would, consider a debtor with no unencumbered assets, but with $100,000 of unsecured debt and a yearly income of $70,000. Because there are no assets and because future income need not be paid out in Chapter 7, but is kept entirely by the debtor, such a debtor could meet the best interest tests in 1325(a)(4) with a plan that paid nothing to unsecured creditors. Nevertheless, such a debtor might have substantial disposable income, and thus might be required under 1325(b)(1)(B) to make substantial payments over the three year period.

The disposable income requirement was added in 1984 at the urging of creditors who put forward the examples of just the kind suggested, where there were few assets but relatively large incomes. We suspect that the rule has bite in many cases, but that those cases are fewer than the cases where the best interest rule sets the floor.

Yet less important is a third legal requirement sometimes put forward by creditors. This is the requirement in 1325(a)(3) that the plan be proposed in "good faith." In the early days of Chapter 13 many creditors argued, some successfully, that plans which paid only small amounts were not made in good faith and thus could not be confirmed even though they complied with the best interest test. For the most part those cases have gone against the creditor and the courts are now willing to approve even relatively small payouts (provided the plans meet the other tests) as being in good faith.

REQUIREMENTS FOR A CONFIRMABLE PLAN

To determine what must be in a plan, the student should consider sections 1322 and 1325 in particular. Note the requirement in 1322(a)(1) that the future earnings of the debtor go to the trustee for disbursement. Although Chapter 13 contains an expansive discharge, sections such as 1322(a)(2), requiring "full payment" of priority claims for a confirmable plan, substantially reduce the apparent generosity of that discharge. We have already considered 1322(b)(2) and we have noted in 1322(c) that the plan not be longer than three years unless the court approves a longer period, but in no event longer than five years.

Section 1325 contains many provisions that are now familiar to those who have studied the comparable section in Chapter 11, section 1129. For example, 1325(a)(4) is the familiar best interest test; the creditor must receive as much here as he would have received in a Chapter 7 liquidation. Section 1325(b) may be regarded as a poor man's absolute priority rule. Added to the Code as part of the 1984 creditor amendments, this provision allows the court to order a debtor to make available to creditors the debtor's entire "projected disposable income," over a three year period. Operating correctly, this section will keep debtors who have substantial income from keeping all of that income and at the same time enjoying the expansive discharge in Chapter 13.

Section 1325 also contains more mysterious provisions such as that in (a)(3) that the plan be proposed "in good faith." How that rule fits together with the disposable income rule in 1325(b) is a matter of some debate. Needless to say, what is and what is not a good faith plan will cause a never ending debate.

FIDELITY & CASUALTY COMPANY OF NEW YORK v. WARREN

United States Bankruptcy Appellate Panel, Ninth Circuit, 1988.
89 B.R. 87.

Opinion

Before VOLINN, MEYERS and JONES, BANKRUPTCY JUDGES.

VOLINN, BANKRUPTCY JUDGE:

The bankruptcy court confirmed the debtor's Chapter 13 plan without conducting an evidentiary hearing concerning debtor's good faith. Appellant, which holds a default judgment for alleged embezzlement by the debtor, contends that the court should have required or permitted further inquiry on the good faith issue.

ISSUES ON APPEAL

The questions presented are whether there is a relationship between the good faith and best effort requirements of 11 U.S.C. § 1325, and the appropriate scope of inquiry attendant to a finding concerning good faith in filing a Chapter 13 plan. Specifically, the issues are:

1. Does fulfillment of the "best effort" requirement of 11 U.S.C. § 1325(b)(1)(B) satisfy the "good faith" requirement of 11 U.S.C. § 1325(a)(3)?

2. When a creditor with a debt that is potentially nondischargeable under Chapter 7 objects to confirmation of a minimal repayment plan, thereby seeking to preclude discharge of his debt by virtue of 11 U.S.C.

§ 1328(a), commonly known as the "super-discharge," must the court conduct or permit a hearing on the issue of good faith?

3. What is the nature and standard of proof required of a debtor at a Chapter 13 confirmation hearing where there is an issue as to good faith?

FACTS

Appellee debtor Austin Warren ("Warren") worked for Bob Warren Pontiac, Inc. The employer collected $40,594.88 during 1981 under an employee fidelity bond issued by appellant Fidelity & Casualty Company of New York ("Fidelity") for losses due to alleged embezzlement by Warren. Fidelity, as subrogee, later sued Warren, obtaining a default judgment in 1984 of $40,970, for the amounts it paid to Warren's former employer, plus interest, and costs of $113.

After Fidelity attempted to collect through garnishment on its judgment, Warren filed a Chapter 7 petition on May 31, 1985. When Fidelity filed an adversary proceeding to determine the dischargeability of the debt, Warren converted his case to Chapter 13.

In his Chapter 13 case, Warren scheduled $3,500 in priority debts and $44,736.37 in other unsecured debts, including $40,970 to appellant Fidelity; there were no secured debts. His property schedules indicated that he neither owned any real property nor any nonexempt personal property. His amended plan provided for full payment of administrative expenses, including $900 in attorneys' fees, and $3,500 in priority tax claims; he proposed to pay over 36 months about two percent or $1,000 on the unsecured, nonpriority claims, including that of Fidelity. Appellant filed an objection to the plan contending *inter alia* that it was not filed in good faith.

The parties stipulate that the debtor has applied all his disposable income to the plan. We assume, *arguendo*, that Warren's payment of $1,000 over a period of three years towards satisfaction of some $44,000 in debts fulfills the "best effort" requirement of 11 U.S.C. § 1325(b).

A three year plan was confirmed over Fidelity's objections. The factual and legal issues raised here, including that of good faith, were asserted by Fidelity before the bankruptcy court. No testimony was taken on the issue of good faith, or otherwise. It appears that the debtor did not attend the confirmation hearing. All that occurred at the hearing was a brief colloquy between counsel and the court which was concluded by the court stating it would confirm the plan. The order confirming the plan is a preprinted form which states ultimate conclusory findings and does not specifically address the issues raised by Fidelity.

CONTENTIONS

Appellant contends that more than "best effort" is required when both a nominal repayment plan and a predominant nondischargeable debt are present; that improper motivation and insincerity of the debtor demonstrating lack of good faith should be inferred, thereby preventing confirmation of a plan unless the debtor produces evidence of other mitigating factors.

Appellee debtor takes the position that the debtor's intentions are matters of fact reviewable only under the clearly erroneous standard and, therefore, the "basis of the court's ruling that the facts justified confirmation is not appealable." Appellee's Brief at 4. He argues further that the cases cited by appellant do not support any theory that bad faith is conclusively shown when a nominal repayment plan and a nondischargeable debt are present. Finally, he urges that sufficient evidence of good faith is shown in the record.

While conceding that best effort alone does not satisfy the good faith requirement, appellee states:

> Not only has this debtor devoted substantially all of his income to the plan, it was extended past three years in order to pay more to the unsecured creditors and his income and expenses [sic] do not show that he can live more modestly than he is doing at present. These are *all* indications of good faith.

Appellee's Brief at 7. The foregoing statement, focused on best effort, exemplifies what was presented to the trial court.

* * *

DISCUSSION

I. Good Faith Defined

"Good faith" under 11 U.S.C. § 1325(a)(3) is neither defined by statute, nor explained in legislative history. *Goeb v. Heid (In re Goeb),* 675 F.2d 1386, 1389–90 (9th Cir.1982).

Nevertheless, the former Bankruptcy Act employed the term and concept of good faith as a confirmation standard not only in Chapter XIII (former 11 U.S.C. § 1051 and Rule 13–213(a)), but also in Chapters X, XI and XII. Cases thereunder were numerous and varied considerably depending on the circumstances before the court. Variable treatment of the term "good faith" has been continued under the present chapters of the Bankruptcy Code, including Chapter 13, as will be demonstrated by the cases discussed below. *See, e.g.,* 5 *Collier on Bankruptcy* ¶¶ 1129.02[3] (Chapter 11), 1325.04 (Chapter 13)(L.P. King 15th ed. 1988).

The court pursuant to 11 U.S.C. § 1325(a)(3) has an independent duty to make a considered assessment of the debtor's good faith. *In re Hale,* 65 B.R. 893, 897 (Bankr.S.D.Ga.1986); *In re Meltzer,* 11 B.R. 624, 626 (Bankr.E.D.N.Y.1981). The latter court explained:

> The determination with which the bankruptcy court is entrusted under § 1325(a)(3) is not a ministerial one. Like any judicial determination which a bankruptcy court is called on to make during the course of a proceeding, it calls for the exercise of the Court's informed and independent judgment.

Meltzer, 11 B.R. at 626. The court's duty has been characterized as follows:

> It should be noted here that Chapter 13 provides that the bankruptcy judge shall preside over confirmation proceedings. If confirmation depended entirely upon arithmetical computations or the absence of illegal activity in the case, there would be no need for a judge. Confirmation of a Chapter 13 plan requires the exercise of judicial discretion and assessment of evidence by a bankruptcy judge. The good faith requirement is one of the central, perhaps the most important confirmation finding to be made by the court in any Chapter 13 case. Each case must be judged on its own facts.

Georgia R.R. Bank & Trust Co. v. Kull (In re Kull), 12 B.R. 654, 658 (S.D.Ga.1981), *aff'd sub nom. Kitchens v. Georgia R.R. Bank & Trust Co. (In re Kitchens),* 702 F.2d 885 (11th Cir.1983); *accord In re Chaffin,* 836 F.2d 215, 216 (5th Cir.1988)("[t]he court has the authority and duty to examine a plan even when no creditor has objected * * *.").

Even though good faith in Chapter 13 has not been precisely defined, guidelines have been developed for bankruptcy courts to follow:

> Given the nature of bankruptcy courts and the absence of congressional intent to specially define "good faith," we believe that the proper inquiry is whether the Goebs acted equitably in proposing their Chapter 13 plan. *A bankruptcy court must inquire* whether the debtor has misrepresented facts in his plan, unfairly manipulated the Bankruptcy Code, or otherwise proposed his Chapter 13 plan in an inequitable manner. Though it may consider the substantiality of the proposed repayment, the court must make its good-faith determination in the light of *all* militating factors.

Goeb, 675 F.2d at 1390 (emphasis added).

II. Procedure

The procedural framework for a confirmation hearing on a plan is found in Bankruptcy Rule 3020, which is applicable to Chapters 9, 11, and 13. B.R. 3020 advisory committee's note. Rules 3020(b)(1), (2) deal respectively with objections to confirmation and the hearing. Objections to confirmation are required to be filed and served on the trustee and the debtor. This was done by appellant.

Rule 3020(b)(1) states that an objection to confirmation is governed by Bankruptcy Rule 9014 which in turn activates a number of the Part VII rules (including Bankruptcy Rule 7052, based on Federal Rule of Civil Procedure 52) relating to adversary proceedings. Rule 3020(b)(2), at the time of the confirmation hearing in November, 1986, provided:

> If no objection is timely filed, the court may find, without receiving evidence, that the plan has been proposed in good faith and not by any means forbidden by law.

Appellant appeared at the confirmation hearing to pursue its objections, one of which was addressed to the issue of good faith. The debtor was not present. Counsel for the parties engaged in brief colloquy which was focused on how much the debtor would pay under the plan. The record is devoid of any consideration other than this factor and fails to show that the debtor presented any meaningful testimony relative to his good faith despite appellant being ready to proceed on this issue.

Rule 3020(b)(2) states that without objection the court "may" find that the plan was filed in good faith without receiving evidence. It has been indicated in a Chapter 13 case that the permissive "may" allows the court, even without objection, to require that evidence as to good faith be presented. *In re Cash,* 51 B.R. 927, 930–31 (Bankr.N.D.Ala. 1985); *accord Hale,* 65 B.R. at 893 & n. 1, 897. Where there is an objection, more than bare presentation of the plan and provision for payment thereunder is requisite.

III. Legislative History

A.

Chapter 13 was designed and enacted as a vehicle for voluntary repayment with future income through composition and/or extension of debts. *In re Iacovoni,* 2 B.R. 256, 263 (Bankr.D.Utah 1980)(citing Commission on the Bankruptcy Laws of the U.S., H.R.Doc. No. 137, 93d Cong., 1st Sess., pts. I & II at 159–60 (1973) *reprinted in* 2 App. *Collier on Bankruptcy,* pt. I (L.P. King 15th ed. 1988)). The Commission Report, which provided a foundation for the Code, based its recommendations for Chapter 13 on the Commissioners' conclusion that many debtors prefer to pay their debts rather than suffer the stigma and loss of credit standing attendant to bankruptcy. *Id.* (Commission Report at 157).

With reference to the broader discharge recommended in Chapter 13 as opposed to Chapter 7, the Commission noted:

> If the debtor wants to pay his debts pursuant to a plan, and if creditors are willing to go along, he should be allowed to do so. The fact that a discharge would not be available in a liquidation case should furnish a greater incentive for the debtor to perform under the plan.

Id. (Commission Report at 175).

The Commission's concept of Chapter 13 was substantially adopted by Congress as illustrated in the Senate and House Reports. *See Iacovoni,* 2 B.R. at 264. From the perspective of the House of Representatives, Chapter 13 was designed to accomplish the following:

> The purpose of Chapter 13 is to enable an individual, under court supervision and protection, to develop and perform under a plan for the repayment of his debts over an extended period. * * *

> The benefit to the debtor of developing a plan of repayment under Chapter 13, rather than opting for liquidation under Chapter 7, is that it permits the debtor to protect his assets. In a liquidation case, the debtor must surrender his nonexempt assets for liquidation

and sale by the trustee. Under Chapter 13, the debtor may retain his property by agreeing to repay his creditors. Chapter 13 also protects a debtor's credit standing far better than a straight bankruptcy, because he is viewed by the credit industry as a better risk. In addition, it satisfies many debtors' desire to avoid the stigma attached to straight bankruptcy and to retain the pride attendant on being able to meet one's obligations. The benefit to creditors is self-evident: their losses will be significantly less than if their debtors opt for straight bankruptcy.

H.Rep. No. 595, 95th Cong., 1st Sess. 118 (1977), *reprinted in* 1978 U.S.Code Cong. & Admin.News 5787, 6079, *and in* 2 App. *Collier on Bankruptcy, supra,* pt. II; *see also Iacovoni,* 2 B.R. at 265 (" 'partial repayment' of unsecured debts under Chapter 13 is preferable to almost certain nonpayment of those debts in 'straight bankruptcy' where 'both the debtor and his creditors are the losers.' ")(citing and quoting H.R. Debates, 123 Cong.Rec. H11690–92, H11696–710 IV–12 (daily ed. Oct. 27, 1977)).

Thus, Chapter 13 was designed with an emphasis on debt repayment. The legislative reports quoted above indicate that "the special benefits bestowed upon a Chapter 13 debtor are premised upon his willingness to repay at least some portion of his debts * * *." *Bank of Am. Nat. Trust & Savings Ass'n v. Slade (In re Slade),* 15 B.R. 910, 912 (9th Cir.BAP 1981).

B.

Although legislative history emphasizes debt repayment to creditors as a basic policy goal of Chapter 13, it is now established that nominal payment by the debtor to creditors does not necessarily constitute bad faith. *E.g., Kitchens,* 702 F.2d at 888 (citing *In re Estus,* 695 F.2d 311 (8th Cir.1982); *Deans v. O'Donnell,* 692 F.2d 968, 969–71 (4th Cir.1982); *Barnes v. Whelan,* 689 F.2d 193 (D.C.Cir.1982); *In re Goeb,* 675 F.2d at 1388–89; *In re Rimgale,* 669 F.2d 426 (7th Cir.1982)). Conversely, ability to pay based upon the debtor's budget should not be the sole focus of examination. *Goeb,* 675 F.2d at 1390–91. As emphasized by the court in *Goeb,* "bankruptcy courts cannot substitute a glance at the amount to be paid under the plan for a review of the totality of the circumstances." *Id.* at 1391.

While it is not practical to provide a list of all relevant considerations, *e.g., Goeb* at 1390 & n. 10, a number of specific factors have been adopted as guidelines for determining good faith on a case-by-case basis:

> 1) The amount of the proposed payments and the amounts of the debtor's surplus;
>
> 2) The debtor's employment history, ability to earn, and likelihood of future increases in income;
>
> 3) The probable or expected duration of the plan;

4) The accuracy of the plan's statements of the debts, expenses and percentage of repayment of unsecured debt, and whether any inaccuracies are an attempt to mislead the court;

5) The extent of preferential treatment between classes of creditors;

6) The extent to which secured claims are modified;

7) The type of debt sought to be discharged, and whether any such debt is nondischargeable in Chapter 7;

8) The existence of special circumstances such as inordinate medical expenses;

9) The frequency with which the debtor has sought relief under the Bankruptcy Reform Act;

10) The motivation and sincerity of the debtor in seeking Chapter 13 relief; and

11) The burden which the plan's administration would place upon the trustee.

In re Brock, 47 B.R. 167, 169 (Bankr.S.D.Cal.1985)(quoting *Estus,* 695 F.2d at 317); *accord Kitchens,* 702 F.2d at 888–89.

Despite the specific lack of definition of the term "good faith," Congressional statements of policy may be considered in determining what factors should be evaluated when reviewing a particular plan. Thus, "[a] good faith test * * * should examine the intentions of the debtor and the legal effect of the confirmation of a Chapter 13 plan in light of the spirit and purposes of Chapter 13." *Chinichian v. Campolongo (In re Chinichian),* 784 F.2d 1440, 1444 (9th Cir.1986).

In the foregoing context, the debtor has the burden to establish good faith, which has been characterized as "especially heavy" when a "superdischarge" is sought. *In re Wall,* 52 B.R. 613, 616 (Bankr.M.D.Fla. 1985).

III. Good Faith Versus Best Effort

A.

In 1984, Section 1325(b) of the Bankruptcy Code was amended to require in the event of objections, at least, that the debtor's disposable income be dedicated to payment under the Chapter 13 plan. This has given rise to some contention that the amendment, because of its specificity, has displaced the need or requirement that the debtor's motives or prebankruptcy conduct be examined under the good faith standard of Section 1325(a)(3). See Bell, *The Effect of the Disposable Income Test of Section 1325(b)(1)(B) upon the Good Faith Inquiry of Section 1325(a)(3),* 5 Bankr.Dev.J. 267 (1987), for an extensive discussion of this subject.

While 11 U.S.C. § 1328(c) permits the discharge in Chapter 13 of debts which are nondischargeable in Chapter 7, application of the good faith standard under Section 1325(a)(3) may nevertheless preclude the

Section 1328 discharge. Conversely, a nondischargeable debt does not per se prevent discharge. *E.g., Street v. Lawson (In re Street),* 55 B.R. 763, 764–65 (9th Cir.BAP 1985); *Slade,* 15 B.R. at 911–12.

In light of the spirit and purposes of Chapter 13, courts should not grant, without due consideration, a discharge under Chapter 13 which might not be available under Chapter 7. As noted by the Ninth Circuit, relative to a plan which proposed to discharge a debt for embezzlement:

> The facts presented to this court suggest that Gregory's plan might have been vulnerable to challenge on the absence of good faith ground. Bankruptcy courts have held that although the use of Chapter 13 to obtain the discharge of debts nondischargeable under Chapter 7 by itself is not sufficient to prove bad faith, it is a factor to be considered with others. *See, e.g., In re Meltzer,* 11 B.R. 624, 627 (Bankr.E.D.N.Y.1981)(good faith consistently found to be absent "where all the facts lead inexorably to the conclusion that the petition has been filed to avoid, at minimal, cost, a[n otherwise] nondischargeable debt") * * *.

Lawrence Tractor Co. v. Gregory (In re Gregory), 705 F.2d 1118, 1121 n. 4 (9th Cir.1983).

B.

In *Goeb,* the bankruptcy court had considered a plan that provided more than would have been paid in a Chapter 7 liquidation by paying secured and priority creditors in full and a one percent dividend to unsecured creditors. The court below denied confirmation based on the impression that the debtors filed under Chapter 13 in order to defer payment of back taxes, without intending to substantially repay unsecured creditors. 675 F.2d at 1387, 1391. While commenting that nominal payments may be indicia of unfair manipulation of Chapter 13, the court, on appeal, reversed and remanded the case for further consideration as to good faith. *Id.* at 1391.

In *Slade,* which considered a nominal repayment plan where the predominant liability involved a default judgment for embezzlement, this court affirmed a finding of good faith substantially because the debtors were devoting their best efforts to the plan. 15 B.R. at 912.

Finally, in *Street,* which involved, as here, conversion from Chapter 7 to 13, the court acknowledged that seeking to discharge an otherwise nondischargeable debt is one factor reflecting negatively upon good faith. 55 B.R. at 765. Because the debtor's schedules were incomplete, the court reversed and remanded so that further information could be provided and considered. *Id.* at 764, 765–66.

While the results and tenor of the decisions in *Slade, Goeb,* and *Street* might be read to lead incrementally toward virtual displacement of Chapter 7 by Chapter 13, we are of the view that such a result is intended neither by the courts nor Congress. *Goeb, Slade* and *Street* do not hold that the requirement of good faith may be satisfied solely by consideration of best efforts criteria. *Slade* and *Street* do not preclude, and indeed warrant, further inquiry as to good faith when a nominal repayment plan is attended by a nondischargeable debt.

C.

The Code in 11 U.S.C. § 1325(a)(3), initially mandates "good faith." Once past this threshold, the debtor may proceed to confirmation unless the trustee or a creditor objects, in which case § 1325(b)(1)(B) requires distribution of disposable income to the greatest extent available. Thus, good faith is a discrete and paramount test. *See Hale,* 65 B.R. at 895–96.

There are numerous cases where best effort was undisputed, but where good faith was questioned by the court. For example, confirmation was denied on bad faith grounds when the court was convinced that the debtor intended that the plan substantially reduce a jury verdict for criminal conduct to an amount deemed appropriate by the debtor and held that this abused the spirit of the Code. *In re Kourtakis,* 75 B.R. 183, 188 (Bankr.E.D.Mich.1987). In *Brock,* the court found that the motivation of a debtor, who attempted to discharge a debt arising from embezzlement, was not to repay the creditor, but to escape the consequences of the judgment and, therefore, the plan was not within the spirit and purpose of the Code. 47 B.R. at 169–70. *Accord Hale,* 65 B.R. at 895–97. In *Hale,* the court found good faith lacking in a case, involving an attempt to obtain a Chapter 13 discharge of student loans.

In *Meltzer,* the court found that the plan, proposing to discharge unpaid parking violations excepted from discharge in debtor's earlier Chapter 7 case, was "a disguised Chapter 7, drafted so as to avoid the restrictions and limitations that Congress has imposed on that remedy." 11 B.R. at 628.

The debtor's prebankruptcy past is not immune from inclusion in the totality of circumstances examination attendant to review under the good faith standard. *See Neufeld v. Freeman,* 794 F.2d 149, 152–53 (4th Cir.1986); *accord Memphis Bank & Trust Co. v. Whitman,* 692 F.2d 427, 432 (6th Cir.1982); *In re Easley,* 72 B.R. 948, 953–54 (Bankr.M.D.Tenn. 1987).

Conclusion

The super discharge of Chapter 13 was provided by Congress as an incentive for the debtor to commit to a repayment plan under Chapter 13, as an alternative to providing creditors nothing under Chapter 7. Given a proper case, the court need not, and should not, neutralize that incentive by confirming Chapter 13 plans that are in essence veiled Chapter 7 cases.

Logic requires there be an articulated standard distinguishing entitlement to dischargeability under Chapter 13 vis-a-vis Chapter 7. To put it otherwise, there must be criteria which preclude by-pass of nondischargeability under Chapter 7 simply by detouring or converting to Chapter 13. Where there is an absence of any significant factual element distinguishing the circumstances of a Chapter 13 petition with a substantial nondischargeable debt from those attendant to a Chapter 7 petition, the debtor should not be permitted to nullify major provisions of 11 U.S.C. § 523 merely by paying an insignificant portion of the nondischargeable debt. Congress in Chapter 7 does not allow "best effort" to discharge certain debts. Neither should best effort alone discharge them in Chapter 13. Good faith requires more.

We hold that the good faith requirement under 11 U.S.C. § 1325(a)(3) is separate and distinct from the best effort requirement of 11 U.S.C. § 1325(b)(1)(B). The court should conduct more than a ministerial review related to payments in order that it may make an informed and independent judgment concerning whether a plan was proposed in good faith. Although the trial court's finding of good faith in the context of a Chapter 13 plan normally should not be overturned, the procedural history of this case indicates that no actual inquiry into the totality of the circumstances was made by the court below. When factors of minimal repayments and a nondischargeable debt are present, particular scrutiny by the court is required and the debtor has the burden of producing more than simply evidence of best effort.

We reverse and remand for further proceedings consistent herewith.

Problem 10–6

Macbeth lists the following debts.

Unsecured	
Student Loan	$14,250.00
Employee Credit Union Loan	2,350.00
Other Unsecured Loan	34,000.00
Delinquent Child Support	2,500.00
Delinquent Divorce Property Settlement (Car Payment)	5,400.00
Secured	
Furniture Loan	1,500.00
Mortgage	60,000.00
Tax Lien	5,400.00

Macbeth is $5,000 behind on his mortgage payments. He is in default on all of his other obligations as well. Most of the defaults at this point are de minimis, however. Macbeth is a purchasing manager at the Ford Motor Company. His salary there is $47,000. He has annual child support obligations of $6,000 and he has an obligation to pay off the debt on his former wife's automobile of $5,400. The balance sheet indicates he is currently in arrears $2,500 on his child support, and he has defaulted on his ex-wife's car payments.

He would like to propose a plan under which he would pay his mortgage outside of the plan (these payments are $1000 per month), continue to pay on the furniture loan and pay off the taxes, and pay 10 percent on the remaining obligations over three years and then discharge them.

1. What difficulties do you see with his proposal?

2. If he were to consider a Chapter 7 filing instead of a Chapter 13, how would that change things for him? (Assume that the house is worth approximately $80,000.) He has a $10,000 debt secured by his own automobile that is worth $7,500.

3. A secured creditor who holds a second mortgage of $3,000 on Macbeth's house recently filed a late proof of claim. Can that debtor participate in the Chapter 13 plan? Would the debtor participate in a Chapter 7 distribution? If not, would the creditor's lien continue? (Assume that Macbeth failed to list the second mortgage in the papers he filed with the court.)

4. Assume that Macbeth failed to list a small loan of $7500. Will this debt be discharged in the Chapter 13 or in a Chapter 7 if the creditor does not find out about the bankruptcy until the discharge?

§ 4. EXEMPTIONS

INTRODUCTION

The Supreme Court of Texas has defined an exemption as "a right given by law to a debtor to retain a portion of his property free from the claims of his creditors." Pickens v. Pickens, 125 Tex. 410, 414, 83 S.W.2d 951, 954 (1935). Initially one should understand that the "right" is qualified. In general, mortgages and other security interests are not subject to the exemptions. Thus a creditor holding a mortgage or other consensual security interest on an article of exempt property may normally enforce that lien notwithstanding the exemption law. Many exemption statutes permit enforcement of certain other kinds of claims even against exempt property. For example, many states permit exempt property to be levied upon in satisfaction of tax liabilities.

Most, but not all American exemption law can be found in the statutes of the various states. Additional exemption laws are to be found in various federal statutes (e.g., the Social Security law which exempts Social Security payments from the reach of creditors). Most important of all, section 522 of the Bankruptcy Code contains a set of federal exemptions to be applied in bankruptcy.

The American exemption law grew out of English law that initially allowed a debtor to preserve his clothing from his creditors. Later English law allowed debtors to exempt other articles such as tools of the trade. Early American exemption statutes contained correspondingly restrictive rules and granted debtors only limited exemption rights. As a general proposition, the exemption laws become more generous as one proceeds south and west from New England. Arguably some of the expansive exemption laws in the southwestern states grew out of a populist dislike for "Eastern" creditors. See Vukowich, *Debtors Exemption Rights,* 62 Geo.L.J. 779 (1974). During the depression of the 1930's many states liberalized their exemption laws. The Bankruptcy Reform

Act of 1978 has itself stimulated a recent wave of modification of the state statutes.

To give the student the flavor of a typical exemption law we set out the law from three states below. The Ohio statute set out below was enacted in 1980 in response to the Bankruptcy Reform Act. It represents the ideas of a modern legislature about the appropriate exemption rules. Conversely, in Vermont's statute one can easily see the vestiges of an earlier era in its exemption of church pews and oxen. In Texas a man and wife can exempt property far beyond what an Englishman, New Englander (or a creditor?) would have considered appropriate.

Problem 10–7

Anthony and Cleopatra, husband and wife, filed for bankruptcy in February of 1983. They list the following assets:

Personal clothing

Diamond wedding ring worth $2,000

Other various inexpensive jewelry with a total estimated value of $500.

A house valued at $40,000 subject to a $20,000 mortgage.

Home furnishings and appliances worth approximately $4,000.

Checking and savings account deposits totaling $2,500.

Both are retired. They derive income from social security and veteran's benefits and from private pension payments. Compare their exemption status under the Ohio, Texas and Vermont statutes.

STATE EXEMPTION STATUTES

OHIO

§ 2329.66 Exempted interests and rights

(A) Every person who is domiciled in this state may hold property exempt from execution, garnishment, attachment, or sale to satisfy a judgment or order, as follows:

(1) The person's interest, not to exceed five thousand dollars, in one parcel or item of real or personal property that the person or a dependent of the person uses as a residence;

(2) The person's interest, not to exceed one thousand dollars, in one motor vehicle;

(3) The person's interest, not to exceed two hundred dollars in any particular item, in wearing apparel, beds, and bedding, and the person's interest, not to exceed three hundred dollars in each item, in one cooking unit and one refrigerator or other food preservation unit;

(4)(a) The person's interest, not to exceed four hundred dollars, in cash on hand, money due and payable, money to become due within ninety days, tax refunds, and money on deposit with a bank, savings and loan association, credit union, public utility, landlord, or other person.

This division applies only in bankruptcy proceedings. This exemption may include the portion of personal earnings that is not exempt under division (A)(13) of this section.

(b) Subject to division (A)(4)(d) of this section, the person's interest, not to exceed two hundred dollars in any particular item, in household furnishings, household goods, appliances, books, animals, crops, musical instruments, firearms, and hunting and fishing equipment, that are held primarily for the personal, family, or household use of the person.

(c) Subject to division (A)(4)(d) of this section, the person's interest in one or more items of jewelry, not to exceed four hundred dollars in one item of jewelry and not to exceed two hundred dollars in every other item of jewelry.

(d) Divisions (A)(4)(b) and (4)(c) of this section do not include items of personal property listed in division (A)(3) of this section.

If the person does not claim an exemption under division (A)(1) of this section, the total exemption claimed under division (A)(4)(b) of this section shall be added to the total exemption claimed under division (A)(4)(c) of this section and the total shall not exceed two thousand dollars. If the person claims an exemption under division (A)(1) of this section, the total exemption claimed under division (A)(4)(b) of this section shall be added to the total exemption claimed under division (A)(4)(c) of this section and the total shall not exceed one thousand five hundred dollars.

(5) The person's interest, not to exceed an aggregate of seven hundred fifty dollars, in all implements, professional books, or tools of his profession, trade, or business, including agriculture;

(6)(a) The person's interest in a beneficiary fund set apart, appropriated, or paid by a benevolent association or society, as exempted by section 2329.63 of the Revised Code;

(b) The person's interest in contracts of life or endowment insurance or annuities, as exempted by section 3911.10 of the Revised Code;

(c) The person's interest in a policy of group insurance or the proceeds of such a policy, as exempted by section 3917.05 of the Revised Code;

(d) The person's interest in money, benefits, charity, relief, or aid to be paid, provided, or rendered by a fraternal benefit society, as exempted by section 3921.18 of the Revised Code;

(e) The person's interest in the portion of benefits under policies of sickness and accident insurance and in lump sum payments for dismemberment and other losses insured under such policies, as exempted by section 3923.19 of the Revised Code.

(7) The person's professionally prescribed or medically necessary health aids;

(8) The person's interest in a burial lot, including, but not limited to, exemptions under section 517.09 or 1721.07 of the Revised Code;

(9) The person's interest in:

(a) Moneys paid or payable for living maintenance or rights, as exempted by section 3304.19 of the Revised Code;

(b) Worker's compensation, as exempted by section 4123.67 of the Revised Code;

(c) Unemployment compensation benefits, as exempted by section 4141.32 of the Revised Code;

(d) Aid to dependent children payments, as exempted by section 5107.12 of the Revised Code;

(e) General assistance payments, as exempted by section 5113.03 of the Revised Code.

(10)(a) Except in cases in which the person was convicted of or pleaded guilty to a violation of section 2921.41 of the Revised Code and in which an order for the withholding of restitution from such payments was issued under division (C)(2)(b) of that section, and only to the extent provided in the order, and except as provided in section 3113.21 of the Revised Code, the person's right to a pension, benefit, annuity, or retirement allowance and to accumulated contributions, as exempted by section 145.56, 146.13, 742.47, 3307.71, 3309.66, or 5505.22 of the Revised Code, and the person's right to benefits from the policemen and firemen's death benefit fund;

(b) Except as provided in section 3113.21 of the Revised Code, the person's right to receive a payment under any pension, annuity, or similar plan or contract, not including a payment from a stock bonus or profit sharing plan or a payment included in division (A)(6)(b) or (10)(a) of this section, on account of illness, disability, death, age, or length of service, to the extent reasonably necessary for the support of the person and any of his dependents, except if all the following apply:

(i) The plan or contract was established by or under the auspices of an insider that employed the person at the time his rights under the plan or contract arose;

(ii) The payment is on account of age or length of service;

(iii) The plan or contract is not qualified under the "Internal Revenue Code of 1986," 100 Stat. 2085, 26 U.S.C. 1, as amended.

(c) Except for any portion of the assets that were deposited for the purpose of evading the payment of any debt, the person's right in the assets held in, or to receive any payment under, any individual retirement account, individual retirement annuity, or Keogh or "H.R. 10" plan that provides benefits by reason of illness, disability, death, or age, to the extent reasonably necessary for the support of the person and any of his dependents.

(11) The person's right to receive spousal support, child support, an allowance, or other maintenance to the extent reasonably necessary for the support of the person and any of his dependents;

(12) The person's right to receive, or moneys received during the preceding twelve calendar months from any of the following:

(a) An award of reparations under sections 2743.51 to 2743.72 of the Revised Code, to the extent exempted by division (D) of section 2743.66 of the Revised Code;

(b) A payment on account of the wrongful death of an individual of whom the person was a dependent on the date of the individual's death, to the extent reasonably necessary for the support of the person and any of his dependents;

(c) A payment, not to exceed five thousand dollars, on account of personal bodily injury, not including pain and suffering or compensation for actual pecuniary loss, of the person or an individual for whom the person is a dependent;

(d) A payment in compensation for loss of future earnings of the person or an individual of whom the person is or was a dependent, to the extent reasonably necessary for the support of the debtor and any of his dependents.

(13) Except as provided in section 3113.21 of the Revised Code, personal earnings of the person owed to him for services rendered within thirty days before the issuing of an attachment or other process, the rendition of a judgment, or the making of an order, under which the attempt may be made to subject such earnings to the payment of a debt, damage, fine, or amercement, in an amount equal to the greater of the following amounts:

(a) If paid weekly, thirty times the current federal minimum hourly wage; if paid biweekly, sixty times the current federal minimum hourly wage; if paid semimonthly, sixty-five times the current federal minimum hourly wage; or if paid monthly, one hundred thirty times the current federal minimum hourly wage which is in effect at the time the earnings are payable, as prescribed by the "Fair Labor Standards Act of 1938," 52 Stat. 1060, 29 U.S.C. 206(a)(1), as amended;

(b) Seventy-five per cent of the disposable earnings owed to the person.

(14) The person's right in specific partnership property, as exempted by division (B)(3) of section 1775.24 of the Revised Code;

(15) A seal and official register of a notary public, as exempted by section 147.04 of the Revised Code;

(16) Any other property that is specifically exempted from execution, attachment, garnishment, or sale by federal statutes other than the "Bankruptcy Reform Act of 1978," 92 Stat. 2549, 11 U.S.C. 101, as amended;

(17) The person's interest, not to exceed four hundred dollars, in any property, except that this division applies only in bankruptcy proceedings.

(B) As used in this section:

(1) "Disposable earnings" means net earnings after the garnishee has made deductions required by law, excluding the deductions ordered pursuant to section 3113.21 of the Revised Code.

§ 2329.661 Certain claims not exempted

(A) Division (A)(1) of section 2329.66 of the Revised Code does not:

(1) Extend to a judgment rendered on a mortgage executed, or security interest given on real or personal property by a debtor or to a claim for less than four hundred dollars for manual work or labor;

(2) Impair the lien, by mortgage or otherwise, of the vendor for the purchase money of real or personal property that the debtor or a dependent of the debtor uses as a residence, the lien of a mechanic or other person, under a statute of this state, for materials furnished or labor performed in the erection of a dwelling house on real property, or a lien for the payment of taxes due on real property;

(3) Affect or invalidate any mortgage on any real property, or any lien created by such a mortgage.

(B) No promise, agreement, or contract shall be made or entered into that would waive the exemption laws of this state, and every promise, agreement, or contract insofar as it seeks to waive the exemption laws of this state is void.

(C) Section 2329.66 of the Revised Code does not affect or invalidate any sale, contract of sale, conditional sale, security interest, or pledge of any personal property, or any lien created thereby.

§ 2329.662 Federal exemption not authorized

Pursuant to the "Bankruptcy Reform Act of 1978," 92 Stat. 2549, 11 U.S.C. 522(b)(1), this state specifically does not authorize debtors who are domiciled in this state to exempt the property specified in the "Bankruptcy Reform Act of 1978," 92 Stat. 2549, 11 U.S.C. 522(d).

VERMONT

§ 2740. Goods and chattels; exemptions from attachment and execution

The goods or chattels of a debtor may be taken and sold on execution, except the following articles, which shall be exempt from attachment and execution, unless turned out to the officer to be taken on the attachment or execution, by the debtor:

(1) the debtor's interest, not to exceed $2,500.00 in aggregate value, in a motor vehicle or motor vehicles;

(2) the debtor's interest, not to exceed $5,000.00 in aggregate value, in professional or trade books or tools of the profession or trade of the debtor or a dependent of the debtor;

(3) a wedding ring;

(4) the debtor's interest, not to exceed $500.00 in aggregate value, in other jewelry held primarily for the personal, family or household use of the debtor or a dependent of the debtor;

(5) the debtor's interest, not to exceed $2,500.00 in aggregate value, in household furnishings, goods or appliances, books, wearing apparel, animals, crops or musical instruments that are held primarily for the personal, family or household use of the debtor or a dependent of the debtor;

(6) growing crops, not to exceed $5,000.00 in aggregate value;

(7) the debtor's aggregate interest in any property, not to exceed $400.00 in value, plus up to $7,000.00 of any unused amount of the exemptions provided under subdivisions (1), (2), (4), (5) and (6) of this section;

(8) one cooking stove, appliances needed for heating, one refrigerator, one freezer, one water heater, sewing machines;

(9) ten cords of firewood, five tons of coals or 500 gallons of oil;

(10) 500 gallons of bottled gas;

(11) one cow, two goats, 10 sheep, 10 chickens, and feed sufficient to keep the cow, goats, sheep or chickens through one winter;

(12) three swarms of bees and their hives with their produce in honey;

(13) one yoke of oxen or steers or two horses kept and used for team work;

(14) two harnesses, two halters, two chains, one plow, and one ox yoke;

(15) the debtor's interest, not to exceed $700.00 in value, in bank deposits or deposit accounts of the debtor;

(16) the debtor's interest, not to exceed $10,000.00 in aggregate value, in self-directed retirement accounts of the debtor;

(17) professionally prescribed health aids for the debtor of a dependent of the debtor;

(18) any unmatured life insurance contract owned by the debtor, other than a credit life insurance contract;

(19) property traceable to or the debtor's right to receive, to the extent reasonably necessary for the support of the debtor and any dependents of the debtor:

(A) Social Security benefits;

(B) veteran's benefits;

(C) disability or illness benefits;

(D) alimony, support or separate maintenance;

(E) compensation awarded under a crime victim's reparation law;

(F) compensation for personal bodily injury, pain and suffering or actual pecuniary loss of the debtor or an individual on whom the debtor is dependent;

(G) compensation for the wrongful death of an individual on whom the debtor was dependent;

(H) payment under a life insurance contract that insured the life of an individual on whom the debtor was dependent on the date of that individual's death;

(I) compensation for loss of future earnings of the debtor or an individual on whom the debtor was or is dependent;

(J) payments under a pension, annuity, profit-sharing, stock bonus, or similar plan or contract on account of death, disability, illness, or retirement from or termination of employment.—Amended 1987, No. 233 (Adj.Sess.).

TEXAS

§ 41.001. Interests in Land Exempt From Seizure

(a) A homestead and one or more lots used for a place of burial of the dead are exempt from seizure for the claims of creditors except for encumbrances properly fixed on homestead property.

(b) Encumbrances may be properly fixed on homestead property for:

(1) purchase money;

(2) taxes on the property; or

(3) work and material used in constructing improvements on the property if contracted for in writing before the material is furnished or the labor is performed and in a manner required for the conveyance of a homestead, with joinder of both spouses if the homestead claimant is married.

(c) The homestead claimant's proceeds of a sale of a homestead are not subject to seizure for a creditor's claim for six months after the date of sale.

§ 41.002. Definition of Homestead

(a) If used for the purposes of an urban home or as a place to exercise a calling or business in the same urban area, the homestead of a family or a single, adult person, not otherwise entitled to a homestead, shall consist of not more than one acre of land which may be in one or more lots, together with any improvements thereon.

(b) If used for the purposes of a rural home, the homestead shall consist of:

(1) for a family, not more than 200 acres, which may be in one or more parcels, with the improvements thereon; or

(2) for a single, adult person, not otherwise entitled to a homestead, not more than 100 acres, which may be in one or more parcels, with the improvements thereon.

(c) A homestead is considered to be rural if, at the time the designation is made, the property is not served by municipal utilities and fire and police protection.

(d) The definition of a homestead as provided in this section applies to all homesteads in this state whenever created.

§ 41.003. Temporary Renting of a Homestead

Temporary renting of a homestead does not change its homestead character if the homestead claimant has not acquired another homestead.

§ 41.004. Abandonment of a Homestead

If a homestead claimant is married, a homestead cannot be abandoned without the consent of the claimant's spouse.

§ 41.005. Voluntary Designation of Homestead

(a) If a rural homestead of a family is part of one or more parcels containing a total of more than 200 acres, the head of the family and, if married, that person's spouse may voluntarily designate not more than 200 acres of the property as the homestead. If a rural homestead of a single adult person, not otherwise entitled to a homestead, is part of one or more parcels containing a total of more than 100 acres, the person may voluntarily designate not more than 100 acres of the property as the homestead.

(b) If an urban homestead of a family, or an urban homestead of a single adult person not otherwise entitled to a homestead, is part of one or more lots containing a total of more than one acre, the head of the family and, if married, that person's spouse or the single adult person, as applicable, may voluntarily designate not more than one acre of the property as the homestead.

(c) To designate property as a homestead, a person or persons, as applicable, must make the designation in an instrument that is signed and acknowledged or proved in the manner required for the recording of other instruments. The person or persons must file the designation with the county clerk of the county in which all or part of the property is located. The clerk shall record the designation in the county deed records. The designation must contain:

(1) a description sufficient to identify the property designated;

(2) a statement by the person or persons who executed the instrument that the property is designated as the homestead of the person's family or as the homestead of a single adult person not otherwise entitled to a homestead;

(3) the name of the original grantee of the property; and

(4) for a rural homestead, the number of acres designated and, if there is more than one survey, the number of acres in each.

(d) A person or persons, as applicable, may change the boundaries of a homestead designated under this section by executing and recording an instrument in the manner required for a voluntary designation. A change under this subsection does not impair rights acquired by a party before the change.

(e) If a person or persons, as applicable, have not made a voluntary designation of a homestead under this section as of the time a writ of execution is issued against the person, any designation of the person's or persons' homestead must be made in accordance with Subchapter B.

(f) An instrument that made a voluntary designation of a homestead in accordance with prior law and that is on file with the county clerk on September 1, 1987, is considered a voluntary designation of a homestead under this section.

§ 41.006. Certain Sales of Homestead

(a) Except as provided by Subsection (c), any sale or purported sale in whole or in part of a homestead at a fixed purchase price that is less than the appraised fair market value of the property at the time of the sale or purported sale, and in connection with which the buyer of the property executes a lease of the property to the seller at lease payments that exceed the fair rental value of the property, is considered to be a loan with all payments made from the seller to the buyer in excess of the sales price considered to be interest subject to Title 79, Revised Statutes (Article 5069–1.01 et seq., Vernon's Texas Civil Statutes).

(b) The taking of any deed in connection with a transaction described by this section is a deceptive trade practice under Subchapter E, Chapter 17, Business & Commerce Code, and the deed is void and no lien attaches to the homestead property as a result of the purported sale.

(c) This section does not apply to the sale of a family homestead to a parent, stepparent, grandparent, child, stepchild, brother, half brother, sister, half sister, or grandchild of an adult member of the family.

§ 42.001 Personal Property Exemption

(a) Personal property, as described in Section 42.002, is exempt from garnishment, attachment, execution, or other seizure if:

(1) the property is provided for a family and has an aggregate fair market value of not more than $60,000, exclusive of the amount of any liens, security interests, or other charges encumbering the property; or

(2) the property is owned by a single adult, who is not a member of a family, and has an aggregate fair market value of not more than $30,000, exclusive of the amount of any liens, security interests, or other charges encumbering the property.

(b) The following personal property is exempt from seizure and is not included in the aggregate limitations prescribed by Subsection (a):

(1) current wages for personal services, except for the enforcement of court-ordered child support payments;

(2) professionally prescribed health aids of a debtor or a dependent of a debtor.

(c) This section does not prevent seizure by a secured creditor with a contractual landlord's lien or other security in the property to be seized.

(d) Unpaid commissions for personal services not to exceed 25 percent of the aggregate limitations prescribed by Subsection (a) are exempt from seizure and are included in the aggregate.

§ 42.002 Personal Property

(a) The following personal property is exempt under Section 42.001(a):

(1) home furnishings, including family heirlooms;

(2) provisions for consumption;

(3) vehicles and implements;

(4) tools, equipment, books, and apparatus, including boats and motor vehicles used in a trade or profession;

(5) wearing apparel;

(6) jewelry not to exceed 25 percent of the aggregate limitations prescribed by Section 42.001(a);

(7) two firearms;

(8) athletic and sporting equipment, including bicycles;

(9) a two-wheeled, three-wheeled, or four-wheeled motor vehicle for each member of a family or single adult who holds a driver's license or who does not hold a driver's license but who relies on another person to operate the vehicle for the benefit of the nonlicensed person;

(10) for their consumption:

(A) two horses, mules, or donkeys and a saddle, blanket, and bridle for each;

(B) 12 head of cattle;

(C) 60 head of other types of livestock; and

(D) 120 fowl;

(11) and the present value of any life insurance policy to the extent that a member of the family of the insured or a dependent of a single insured adult claiming the exemption is a beneficiary of the policy; and

(b) Personal property, unless precluded from being encumbered by other law, may be encumbered by a security interest under Section 9.203, Business & Commerce Code, or Sections 41 and 42, Certificate of Title Act (Article 6687–1, Vernon's Texas Civil Statutes), or by a lien fixed by other law.

§ 42.003 Designation of Exempt Property

(a) If the number or amount of a type of personal property owned by a debtor exceeds the exemption allowed by Section 42.002 and the debtor can be found in the county where the property is located, the officer making a levy on the property shall ask the debtor to designate the personal property to be levied on. If the debtor cannot be found in the county or the debtor fails to make a designation within a reasonable time after the officer's request, the officer shall make the designation.

(b) If the aggregate value of a debtor's personal property exceeds the amount exempt from seizure under Section 42.001(a), the debtor may designate the portion of the property to be levied on. If, after a court's request, the debtor fails to make a designation within a reasonable time or if for any reason a creditor contests that the property is exempt, the court shall make the designation.

EXEMPTIONS IN BANKRUPTCY

As a general rule under the Bankruptcy Act of 1898 the debtor in bankruptcy asserted his own state exemptions. By asserting the exemptions, the debtor could keep the assets from the estate and hold them from the reach of the trustee. Obviously this procedure resulted in widely varying outcomes in bankruptcy before federal courts in different states. Some thought that result to be anomalous. In response to this anomaly, the early drafts of the Bankruptcy Reform Act of 1978 contained a set of federal exemptions that would have applied to all bankruptcy proceedings wherever situated.

In Congress the bankruptcy commission's exemption proposal underwent two fundamental changes. First, Congress provided the debtor with the option to choose state or federal exemption rules. This change appears to have been in response to concerns of states in the West and Southwest (most notably California and Texas) that their more generous exemptions would be lost, and also to the fear that the exemption of property held as tenants by the entirety would otherwise be lost in states recognizing that property interest. See e.g., Proposed Bankruptcy Act Revision: Hearings on H.R. 31 and H.R. 32. Before the Subcomm. on Civil and Constitutional Rights of the House Committee on the Judiciary, 94th Cong.2d Sess. 1256 (Statement of Robert Ward) and 1278–1282 (Statement of Hon. Joe Lee) (1976). Second, Congress authorized the various states to "opt out" of the option. Section 522 authorizes a state to require all of its residents to take only the state exemptions and to prohibit them from asserting the federal exemptions contained in section 522(d). At this writing well over half of the states have opted out. In those states, persons filing bankruptcy may not use the federal exemptions in section 522(d).

With the inclusion of these two fundamental changes in section 522 and with the subsequent opting out of many states, we have come almost all the way around the circle. In those states a debtor is in essentially the same position as he would have been under the Bankruptcy Act of 1898. However, in many of those states the Act of 1978 has caused significant change. In many of the opt-out states the legislatures have amended and liberalized the local exemptions as a quid pro quo for depriving their debtors of the federal exemptions. Note that some of the states that have not opted out are among the largest and most populous states. Among those allowing the debtor to choose state or federal bankruptcy exemptions are California, New York, Pennsylvania, Texas, and Michigan.

Although most of the legal issues associated with exemptions under the Bankruptcy Code arise out of section 522, a few originate in section 541—the section that identifies the property of the estate. Under section 541, property that may ultimately be regarded as exempt is deemed to be part of the estate and subject to bankruptcy jurisdiction until the debtor exercises his right of exemption. Section 541(b), (c), and (d) specifically exclude certain property from the estate. The effect of such an exclusion is tantamount to that property's exemption from the claims of creditors. Upon conclusion of the bankruptcy, the creditors' claims will be discharged and pending the outcome of the bankruptcy, section 362 is likely to inhibit any creditor action against the property.

The student should now turn to section 522 and study its various sections. Section (b) describes the debtor's option (assuming that his state has not opted out). Section 522(c) states the obvious, namely that exempt assets cannot be reached to satisfy dischargeable debts. It states by implication something else that is less obvious, namely that nondischargeable tax claims, nondischargeable alimony and most unavoided liens may be collected out of exempt property. (Quaere: What result if state law would allow property to be held exempt from alimony claims?)

Section 522(d) is the new departure; it is the statement of a separate set of federal bankruptcy exemptions. It was apparently taken from the Uniform Act on exemptions and it may be regarded as a model of modern exemption laws. The student will have occasion to return to this section, to deal with the interpretive difficulties that are presented by it and that are illustrative of the interpretative difficulties presented by all exemption lists of the kind set out there. The student should pay particular attention to the kinds of property that are covered by section 522(d). On the one hand, section 522(c)(1)–(9) covers a variety of tangible property, real and personal, such as an automobile or a residence. On the other hand, section 522(d)(10) and (11) list intangible benefits such as social security, unemployment compensation and other claims.

In 1994 the Congress amended all of the dollar amounts in 522(d). For example, it raised the amount of the debtor's exemption in a residence from $7,500 to $15,000. In addition the 1994 amendments provided for automatic three year adjustment of the dollar amounts by the Judicial Conference of the United States. These adjustments are to "reflect" the change in the Consumer Price Index.

Section 522(e) protects the debtor's exemption rights, whether state or federal, by making any waiver of exemptions or avoiding powers unenforceable. Section 522(f) avoids certain judicial liens and a limited class of security interests that would otherwise be effective. It is a compromise provision between the position of certain consumer advocates (who believe a secured creditor should never have a non-purchase money security interest in items such as household goods) and the position of secured creditors (who regarded security interest in household goods indistinguishable from any other). The negative implication of section 522(f) bolsters the direct inference that may be drawn from section 522(c)(2)—namely that a security interest remains effective notwithstanding the exemptions unless voided by some other provision. Subsections (g), (h) and (i) have to do with property that has been transferred and may be recovered by the estate. A final important subsection is (m) that deals with the common case of husband and wife who have filed jointly.

The issues here may be divided into two general categories. First are issues that could be presented equally in a bankruptcy court or in a state court proceeding in which a creditor is attempting to seize the assets of a debtor. These are the interpretation of the exemption statutes, whether those be section 522(d) or state law. They include questions about the status of the exemption after exempt property has been sold and proceeds are held by the debtor and about the general treatment of exemptions when both a husband and a wife claim them.

Second are issues peculiar to bankruptcy. These include issues about the avoidance of liens under section 522(f) and about the election under section 522(b) and the integration of state and federal exemptions in such case. All of the cases that follow are bankruptcy cases; however the student should understand that many of the same issues could have been and often are raised in state proceedings.

EXEMPTIONS, LIENS, AND SECURITY INTERESTS

As we have indicated above, the debtor has the power to "waive" his exemption by granting a security interest or a mortgage to his creditor. However, section 522(e) provides that a waiver "in favor of a creditor that holds an unsecured claim" is unenforceable. Moreover, section 522(f) provides that certain, otherwise valid and fully perfected security interests, may be avoided.

In general section 522(f) deals with nonpurchase money, nonpossessory security interests in household furnishings, tools of the trade, health aids and the like. The provision is aimed squarely at the blanket security interest that was often taken by a small loan company. In such cases the small loan company never intended to repossess and resell such assets. It fully recognized that their market value would be less than the cost of repossession and resale. Nevertheless the small loan company took security interests in such assets because it knew the debtor would pay his debt rather than give them up. He would do so out of a personal or sentimental attachment to such items or because he would have found it more expensive to buy replacements elsewhere than to pay up.

One may regard section 522(f) as the hunting dog exception; it is a section which prohibits security interest (as long as it is not purchase money) in the debtor's hunting dog. The dog may well have a negative market value but the debtor might be so firmly attached to his dog that he would be willing to pay a large debt in order to keep him. The same could be said of the debtor's favorite but greasy arm chair or of his artificial leg. Automobiles were apparently not intended to be included (automobiles do have market value), but they—together with a variety of other items—have presented a series of interpretive difficulties in applying section 522(f). We address some of those below.

Until the Supreme Court resolved the issue in 1991 in Farrey v. Sanderfoot, 500 U.S. 291, 111 S.Ct. 1825, 114 L.Ed.2d 337 (1991), husbands sometimes attempted to use section 522(f)(1) as a way to escape liens they had granted to their ex-wives to secure obligations arising out of divorce settlements. Assume that husband and wife own a home jointly and that as part of the divorce settlement husband agrees to purchase wife's half. Assume further that the divorce decree provides that the wife will have a lien on the home until full payment has been made. Ex-husband then goes into bankruptcy and claims the home is exempt and asserts the right to avoid the judicial lien under the terms of section 522(f)(1).

In *Farrey*, the Supreme Court rejected the husband's claim. Surely the Court is correct. The classic judicial lien is a non-purchase money, non-reliance lien achieved by an unsecured creditor who did not bargain for the lien at the time of his loan. The divorce case is much more like a purchase money loan in which the wife strikes a bargain with the husband and takes contemporaneous security in the form of a lien on the house to secure the husband's obligation to pay. In effect, the wife's lien is a lien taken in reliance upon a concurrent promise, not after-thought security procured on a loan that was originally unsecured. Section 522(f)(1)(A) in the 1994 amendment codifies and elaborates upon the Supreme Court decision in *Farrey*.

Sections (g), (h), and (i) allow the debtor to assert exemptions with respect to certain property that has been transferred out of the estate by a voidable transfer and that could be brought back by the trustee or by the debtor. One must read those sections carefully to see which transfers might qualify and which might not.

Problem 10–8

Iago, a well-to-do client who has fallen on bad times comes to you to confirm some advice that he has received from a bankruptcy lawyer. He is contemplating personal bankruptcy as a result of various individual investments that have gone sour. The bankruptcy lawyer whom he has tentatively hired to represent him in the bankruptcy has suggested two possibilities:

(1) That he purchase a $2,000,000 homestead at once with the prospect that he go into bankruptcy sometime in the next year.

(2) That he purchase a paid-up insurance policy with a similar cash surrender value.

Would these moves be successful in Texas?

What if they were done in a jurisdiction that exempted homesteads and cash surrender values of insurance with no direct limitation as to dollar amount and time of purchase?

Problem 10–9

You represent a bank that does a great deal of consumer secured lending. Over the past year the bank has been challenged under section 522(f) in a variety of cases, and would like your opinion about several of them:

1. Debtor Falstaff was a leader of a rock band (Big F and the Red Devils). He borrowed $20,000 from the bank to finance a tour for his band. He gave the bank a security interest in his musical instruments. The instruments were nearly new and were appraised by an expert at $40,000. They included a variety of speakers and amplification equipment, several electric guitars, other musical instruments and a synthesizer. The bandleader is now threatening bankruptcy. Assume that the state exemption law has an explicit exemption without dollar limit for "tools of the trade." What will be the outcome under section 522(f) if the bandleader elects the state exemptions? The federal exemptions?

2. Bank made a loan on a relatively new used car belonging to Desdemona. The car had a fair market value of $15,000 and the bank loaned $9,200 to her. It took and properly perfected its security interest. Now Desdemona is in bankruptcy and her lawyer claims the security interest on her automobile can be avoided under section 522(f). He points out that Ms. D is a real estate saleswoman and that she uses the car regularly in her business to commute to and from work, and to view properties and to show properties to prospective customers. What result?

3. In the third case Bank took a purchase money security interest in a 1992 Cadillac belonging to Starveling. It loaned $16,000 of which $15,000 is still outstanding. The car is now worth $13,000. Through some slip up, Bank failed to perfect its security interest. However, the security agreement was validly executed and is valid against the debtor.

    a. Starveling has asserted the right to invalidate the bank's security interest and to take the automobile under the provisions of section 522(g) and (h). May he do that?

b. The trustee in bankruptcy has asserted the right to avoid Bank's security interest and to take the automobile for the estate. May he do that?

c. How would the answers to a) and b) change if the bank's security interest was not a purchase money security interest?

4. Bank has taken a nonpurchase money nonpossessory security interest in the household furnishings of debtor Desdemona. Ms. D. now in Chapter 7, proposes to avoid bank security interest under section 522(f). May she do so in any of the following circumstances?

a. Assume these events took place in Louisiana and that Louisiana has opted out of section 522. The state exemption laws in Louisiana do not exempt household furnishings, household goods or other items identified in section 522(f)(2).

b. Suppose these events took place in Georgia or Tennessee, states which have also opted out of section 522, and that the outstanding balance on the loan is greater than the value of Desdemona's household furnishings. The exemption statutes in these states do not merely specify the sorts of possessions that may be exempted or provide generally that the "debtor's property" is exempt. Rather they state that only the "debtor's interest" (in Georgia) or the "debtor's equity interest" (in Tennessee) is exempt. Bank argues that since Desdemona has no equity in the encumbered asset, she cannot exercise any exemption under state law and, consequently, should not be allowed to avoid the security interest now under section 522(f). Will this argument be successful? (Consider the fact that the Georgia exemption statute is very similar to the correlative federal exemption.)

EXEMPTION OF RETIREMENT BENEFITS, A SPECIAL CASE

It comes as some surprise that the exemption status of retirement plan assets and benefit payments is quite uncertain under the bankruptcy law. Retirement plans take many forms and are affected by various federal and state laws—including the provisions of ERISA and the Federal Tax Code. Difficulties in determining exemption status arise from the lack of clarity and from the complexity of the laws involved. This confusion probably stems from Congress' ambivalence: should a creditor have maximum access to the bankrupt's assets or should a person be assured a comfortable retirement?

The three most common retirement programs are corporate pension plans, self employed retirement plans (referred to as Keogh or HR 10 plans) and Individual Retirement Arrangements ("IRAs"). If a corporate pension plan is a "qualified" plan under ERISA and federal tax law (ERISA designates the IRS as the primary determinant of qualified status), certain benefits (including the deductibility of contributions by the employer and exclusion from income by the employee) accrue to the employer and the employee. To qualify under sections 401–408 of the Tax Code, a plan must meet requirements intended to prevent the plan from discriminating in favor of executives or other employees and to prevent the use of plan funds for other than the benefit of employees. The plan must also meet certain vesting, funding, participation and payment requirements.

Keogh plans allow self employed individuals to take tax deductions for contributions they make to pension or profit sharing plans for their or their employees' benefit. Under a Keogh plan, benefits cannot be paid to the self employed individual until he reaches age 59 ½ without incurring a 10 percent tax penalty.

Individual Retirement Arrangements allow certain individuals to take tax deductions for contributions made to an Individual Retirement Account (IRA).

In considering the exemption status of retirement plan interests certain questions arise. These include:

1. Should the debtor's interest be included within the bankruptcy estate under section 541 of the Bankruptcy Code?

2. If the debtor's interest is included within the estate, to what extent does section 522(d) exempt plan assets or benefits?

3. If the debtor's interest is included within the estate and the state and other federal exemption option is taken, to what extent are plan assets exempted a) under applicable state law; b) under other federal law?

Beginning in the early 1980s and continuing until the *Patterson* decision by the Supreme Court in 1992, the bankruptcy, district, and circuit courts were in disagreement about the exemption of ERISA qualified plans of one who was in bankruptcy. Some courts read section 541(c)(2) to exclude them entirely. Other courts found 541(c)(2) to be irrelevant. Because some of the debtors were relatively wealthy physicians and business executives, and because some of their creditors were divorced spouses or former patients who had suffered injuries arising from the doctor's malpractice, the equities were often with the creditors and not with the debtor.

PATTERSON v. SHUMATE
Supreme Court of the United States, 1992.
504 U.S. 753, 112 S.Ct. 2242, 119 L.Ed.2d 519.

Judges: BLACKMUN, J., delivered the opinion for a unanimous Court. SCALIA, J., filed a concurring opinion.

JUSTICE BLACKMUN delivered the opinion of the Court.

The Bankruptcy Code excludes from the bankruptcy estate property of the debtor that is subject to a restriction on transfer enforceable under "applicable nonbankruptcy law." 11 U.S.C. § 541(c)(2). We must decide in this case whether an anti-alienation provision contained in an ERISA-qualified pension plan constitutes a restriction on transfer enforceable under "applicable nonbankruptcy law," and whether, accordingly, a debtor may exclude his interest in such a plan from the property of the bankruptcy estate.

I

Respondent Joseph B. Shumate, Jr., was employed for over 30 years by Coleman Furniture Corporation, where he ultimately attained the position of president and chairman of the board of directors. Shumate and approximately 400 other employees were participants in the Coleman Furniture Corporation Pension Plan (Plan). The Plan satisfied all applicable requirements of the Employee Retirement Income Security Act of 1974 (ERISA) and qualified for favorable tax treatment under the Internal Revenue Code. In particular, Article 16.1 of the Plan contained the anti-alienation provision required for qualification under § 206(d)(1) of ERISA, 29 U.S.C. § 1056(d)(1)("Each pension plan shall provide that benefits provided under the plan may not be assigned or alienated"). Shumate's interest in the plan was valued at $250,000.

In 1982, Coleman Furniture filed a petition for bankruptcy under Chapter 11 of the Bankruptcy Code. The case was converted to a Chapter 7 proceeding and a trustee, Roy V. Creasy, was appointed. Shumate himself encountered financial difficulties and filed a petition for bankruptcy in 1984. His case, too, was converted to a Chapter 7 proceeding, and petitioner John R. Patterson was appointed trustee.

Creasy terminated and liquidated the Plan, providing full distributions to all participants except Shumate. Patterson then filed an adversary proceeding against Creasy in the Bankruptcy Court for the Western District of Virginia to recover Shumate's interest in the Plan for the benefit of Shumate's bankruptcy estate. Shumate in turn asked the United States District Court for the Western District of Virginia, which already had jurisdiction over a related proceeding, to compel Creasy to pay Shumate's interest in the Plan directly to him. The bankruptcy proceeding subsequently was consolidated with the district court action.

The District Court rejected Shumate's contention that his interest in the Plan should be excluded from his bankruptcy estate. The court held that § 541(c)(2)'s reference to "nonbankruptcy law" embraced only state law, not federal law such as ERISA. Creasy v. Coleman Furniture Corp., 83 B.R. 404, 406 (1988). Applying Virginia law, the court held that Shumate's interest in the Plan did not qualify for protection as a spendthrift trust. The District Court also rejected Shumate's alternative argument that even if his interest in the Plan could not be excluded from the bankruptcy estate under § 541(c)(2), he was entitled to an exemption under 11 U.S.C. § 522(b)(2)(A), which allows a debtor to exempt from property of the estate "any property that is exempt under Federal law." Id., at 409–410. The District Court ordered Creasy to pay Shumate's interest in the Plan over to his bankruptcy estate.

The Court of Appeals for the Fourth Circuit reversed. 943 F.2d 362 (1991). The court relied on its earlier decision in Anderson v. Raine (In re Moore), 907 F.2d 1476 (1990), in which another Fourth Circuit panel was described as holding, subsequent to the District Court's decision in the instant case, that "ERISA-qualified plans, which by definition have a non-alienation provision, constitute 'applicable nonbankruptcy law' and contain enforceable restrictions on the transfer of pension interests." 943 F.2d, at 365. Thus, the Court of Appeals held that Shumate's interest in the Plan should be excluded from the bankruptcy estate under § 541(c)(2). The court then declined to consider Shumate's alternative argument that his interest in the Plan qualified for exemption under § 522(b).

We granted certiorari, 502 U.S. 1057, 112 S.Ct. 932, 117 L.Ed.2d 104 (1992), to resolve the conflict among the Courts of Appeals as to whether an anti-alienation provision in an ERISA-qualified pension plan constitutes a restriction on transfer enforceable under "applicable nonbankruptcy law" for purposes of the § 541(c)(2) exclusion of property from the debtor's bankruptcy estate.

II

A

In our view, the plain language of the Bankruptcy Code and ERISA is our determinant. See Toibb v. Radloff, 501 U.S. 157, ___, 111 S.Ct. 2197, ___, 115 L.Ed.2d 145 (1991). Section 541(c)(2) provides the following exclusion from the otherwise broad definition of "property of the estate" contained in § 541(a)(1) of the Code:

> "A restriction on the transfer of a beneficial interest of the debtor in a trust that is enforceable under applicable nonbankruptcy law is enforceable in a case under this title" (emphasis added).

The natural reading of the provision entitles a debtor to exclude from property of the estate any interest in a plan or trust that contains a transfer restriction enforceable under any relevant nonbankruptcy law. Nothing in § 541 suggests that the phrase "applicable nonbankruptcy law" refers, as petitioner contends, exclusively to state law. The text contains no limitation on "applicable nonbankruptcy law" relating to the source of the law.

Reading the term "applicable nonbankruptcy law" in § 541(c)(2) to include federal as well as state law comports with other references in the Bankruptcy Code to sources of law. The Code reveals, significantly, that Congress, when it desired to do so, knew how to restrict the scope of applicable law to "state law" and did so with some frequency. See, e.g., 11 U.S.C. § 109(c)(2)(entity may be a debtor under Chapter 9 if authorized "by State law"); 11 U.S.C. § 522(b)(1)(election of exemptions controlled by "the State law that is applicable to the debtor"); 11 U.S.C. § 523(a)(5)(a debt for alimony, maintenance, or support determined "in accordance with State or territorial law" is not dischargeable); 11 U.S.C. § 903(1)("a State law prescribing a method of composition of indebtedness" of municipalities is not binding on nonconsenting creditors); see also 11 U.S.C. §§ 362(b)(12) and 1145(a). Congress' decision to use the broader phrase "applicable nonbankruptcy law" in § 541(c)(2) strongly suggests that it did not intend to restrict the provision in the manner that petitioner contends.

The text of § 541(c)(2) does not support petitioner's contention that "applicable nonbankruptcy law" is limited to state law. Plainly read, the provision encompasses any relevant nonbankruptcy law, including federal law such as ERISA. We must enforce the statute according to its terms. See United States v. Ron Pair Enterprises, Inc., 489 U.S. 235, 241, 109 S.Ct. 1026, 1030, 103 L.Ed.2d 290 (1989).

B

Having concluded that "applicable nonbankruptcy law" is not limited to state law, we next determine whether the anti-alienation provision contained in the ERISA-qualified plan at issue here satisfies the literal terms of § 541(c)(2).

Section 206(d)(1) of ERISA, which states that "each pension plan shall provide that benefits provided under the plan may not be assigned or alienated," 29 U.S.C. § 1056(d)(1), clearly imposes a "restriction on the transfer" of a debtor's "beneficial interest" in the trust. The coordinate section of the Internal Revenue Code, 26 U.S.C. § 401(a)(13), states as a general rule that "[a] trust shall not constitute a qualified trust under this section unless the plan of which such trust is a part provides that benefits provided under the plan may not be assigned or alienated," and thus contains similar restrictions. See also 26 CFR 1.401(a)–13(b)(1)(1991).

Coleman Furniture's pension plan complied with these requirements. Article 16.1 of the Plan specifically stated: "No benefit, right or interest" of any participant "shall be subject to alienation, sale, transfer, assignment, pledge, encumbrance or charge, seizure, attachment or other legal, equitable or other process."

Moreover, these transfer restrictions are "enforceable," as required by § 541(c)(2). Plan trustees or fiduciaries are required under ERISA to discharge their duties "in accordance with the documents and instruments governing the plan." 29 U.S.C. § 1104(a)(1)(D). A plan participant, beneficiary, or fiduciary, or the Secretary of Labor may file a civil action to "enjoin any act or practice" which violates ERISA or the terms of the plan. 29 U.S.C. §§ 1132(a)(3) and (5). Indeed, this Court itself vigorously has enforced ERISA's prohibition on the assignment or alienation of pension benefits, declining to recognize any implied exceptions to the broad statutory bar. See Guidry v. Sheet Metal Workers Pension Fund, 493 U.S. 365, 110 S.Ct. 680, 107 L.Ed.2d 782 (1990).

The anti-alienation provision required for ERISA qualification and contained in the Plan at issue in this case thus constitutes an enforceable transfer restriction for purposes of § 541(c)(2)'s exclusion of property from the bankruptcy estate.

III

Petitioner raises several challenges to this conclusion. Given the clarity of the statutory text, however, he bears an "exceptionally heavy" burden of persuading us that Congress intended to limit the § 541(c)(2) exclusion to restrictions on transfer that are enforceable only under state spendthrift trust law. Union Bank v. Wolas, 502 U.S. 151, ___, 112 S.Ct. 527, ___, 116 L.Ed.2d 514 (1991).

A

Petitioner first contends that contemporaneous legislative materials demonstrate that § 541(c)(2)'s exclusion of property from the bankruptcy estate should not extend to a debtor's interest in an ERISA-qualified pension plan. Although courts "appropriately may refer to a statute's legislative history to resolve statutory ambiguity," Toibb v. Radloff, 501 U.S. at ___, 111 S.Ct. at ___, the clarity of the statutory language at issue in this case obviates the need for any such inquiry. See ibid.; United States v. Ron Pair Enterprises, Inc., 489 U.S. at 241, 109 S.Ct. at 1030; Davis v. Michigan Dept. of Treasury, 489 U.S. 803, 809 n. 3, 109 S.Ct. 1500, 1511 n. 3, 103 L.Ed.2d 891 (1989).[4]

Even were we to consider the legislative materials to which petitioner refers, however, we could discern no "clearly expressed legislative intention" contrary to the result reached above. See Consumer Product Safety Comm'n v. GTE Sylvania, Inc., 447 U.S. 102, 108, 100 S.Ct. 2051, 2056, 64 L.Ed.2d 766 (1980). In his brief, petitioner quotes from House and Senate reports accompanying the Bankruptcy Reform Act of 1978 that purportedly reflect "unmistakable" congressional intent to limit § 541(c)(2)'s exclusion to pension plans that qualify under state law as spendthrift trusts. Those reports contain only the briefest of discussions addressing § 541(c)(2). The House Report states: "Paragraph (2) of subsection (c) ... preserves restrictions on transfer of a spendthrift trust to the extent that the restriction is enforceable under applicable nonbankruptcy law." H.R.Rep. No. 95–595, p. 369 (1977); see also S.Rep. No. 95–989, p. 83 (1978)(§ 541(c)(2) "preserves restrictions on a transfer of a spendthrift trust"). A general introductory section to the House Report contains the additional statement that the new law "continues over the exclusion from property of the estate of the debtor's interest in a spendthrift trust to the extent the trust is protected from creditors under applicable State law." H.R.Rep. No. 95–595, p. 176. These meager excerpts reflect at best congressional intent to include state spendthrift trust law within the meaning of "applicable nonbankruptcy law." By no means do they provide a sufficient basis for concluding, in derogation of the statute's clear language, that Congress intended to exclude other state and federal law from the provision's scope.

B

Petitioner next contends that our construction of § 541(c)(2), pursuant to which a debtor may exclude his interest in an ERISA-qualified

---

4. Those Courts of Appeals that have limited "applicable nonbankruptcy law" to state spendthrift trust law by ignoring the plain language of § 541(c)(2) and relying on isolated excerpts from the legislative history thus have misconceived the appropriate analytical task. See, e.g., Daniel v. Security Pacific Nat. Bank (In re Daniel), 771 F.2d at 1359–1360; Lichstrahl v. Bankers Trust (In re Lichstrahl), 750 F.2d at 1490; Samore v. Graham (In re Graham), 726 F.2d at 1271–1272; Goff v. Taylor (In re Goff), 706 F.2d at 581–582.

pension plan from the bankruptcy estate, renders § 522(d)(10)(E) of the Bankruptcy Code superfluous. Under § 522(d)(10)(E), a debtor who elects the federal exemptions set forth in § 522(d) may exempt from the bankruptcy estate his right to receive "a payment under a stock bonus, pension, profitsharing, annuity, or similar plan or contract ..., to the extent reasonably necessary for the support of the debtor and any dependent of the debtor." If a debtor's interest in a pension plan could be excluded in full from the bankruptcy estate, the argument goes, then there would have been no reason for Congress to create a limited exemption for such interests elsewhere in the statute.

Petitioner's surplusage argument fails, however, for the reason that § 522(d)(10)(E) exempts from the bankruptcy estate a much broader category of interests than § 541(c)(2) excludes. For example, pension plans established by governmental entities and churches need not comply with Subchapter I of ERISA, including the anti-alienation requirement of § 206(d)(1). See 29 U.S.C. §§ 1003(b)(1) and (2); 26 CFR 1.401(a)-13(a) (1991). So, too, pension plans that qualify for preferential tax treatment under 26 U.S.C. § 408 (individual retirement accounts) are specifically excepted from ERISA's anti-alienation requirement. See 29 U.S.C. § 1051(6). Although a debtor's interest in these plans could not be excluded under § 541(c)(2) because the plans lack transfer restrictions enforceable under "applicable nonbankruptcy law," that interest[5] nevertheless could be exempted under § 522(d)(10)(E).[6] Once petitioner concedes that § 522(d)(10)(E)'s exemption applies to more than ERISA-qualified plans containing anti-alienation provisions, his argument that our reading of § 541(c)(2) renders the exemption provision superfluous must collapse.

C

Finally, petitioner contends that our holding frustrates the Bankruptcy Code's policy of ensuring a broad inclusion of assets in the bankruptcy estate. See 11 U.S.C. § 541(a)(1)(estate comprised of "all legal and equitable interests of the debtor in property as of the commencement of the case"). As an initial matter, we think that petitioner mistakes an admittedly broad definition of includable property for a "policy" underlying the Code as a whole. In any event, to the extent

---

5. We express no opinion on the separate question whether § 522(d)(10)(E) applies only to distributions from a pension plan that a debtor has an immediate and present right to receive, or to the entire undistributed corpus of a pension trust. See, e.g., In re Harline, 950 F.2d, at 675; Velis v. Kardanis, 949 F.2d, at 81–82. See also Arnopol, Including Retirement Benefits in a Debtor's Bankruptcy Estate: A Proposal for Harmonizing ERISA and the Bankruptcy Code, 56 Mo.L.Rev. 491, 535–536 (1991).

6. Even those courts that would have limited § 541(c)(2) to state law acknowledge the breadth of the § 522(d)(10)(E) exemption. See In re Goff, 706 F.2d, at 587 (noting that § 522(d)(10)(E) "reaches a broad array of employment benefits, and exempts both qualified and unqualified pension plans")(footnote omitted); In re Graham, 726 F.2d, at 1272 (observing that "the § 522(d)(10)(E) exemption would apply to non-ERISA plans as well as to qualified ERISA plans"). See also Arnopol, 56 Mo. L.Rev., at 525–526, 552–553; Seiden, Chapter 7 Cases: Do ERISA and the Bankruptcy Code Conflict as to Whether a Debtor's Interest in or Rights Under a Qualified Plan Can be Used to Pay Claims?, 61 Am. Bankr.L.J. 301, 318 (1987).

that policy considerations are even relevant where the language of the statute is so clear, we believe that our construction of § 541(c)(2) is preferable to the one petitioner urges upon us.

First, our decision today ensures that the treatment of pension benefits will not vary based on the beneficiary's bankruptcy status. See Butner v. United States, 440 U.S. 48, 55, 99 S.Ct. 914, 918, 59 L.Ed.2d 136 (1979) (observing that "uniform treatment of property interests" prevents "a party from 'receiving a windfall merely by reason of the happenstance of bankruptcy,' " quoting Lewis v. Manufacturers National Bank, 364 U.S. 603, 609, 81 S.Ct. 347, 350, 5 L.Ed.2d 323 (1961)). We previously have declined to recognize any exceptions to ERISA's anti-alienation provision outside the bankruptcy context. See Guidry v. Sheet Metal Workers Pension Fund, 493 U.S. 365, 110 S.Ct. 680, 107 L.Ed.2d 782 (1990)(labor union may not impose constructive trust on pension benefits of union official who breached fiduciary duties and embezzled funds). Declining to recognize any exceptions to that provision within the bankruptcy context minimizes the possibility that creditors will engage in strategic manipulation of the bankruptcy laws in order to gain access to otherwise inaccessible funds. See Seiden, Chapter 7 Cases: Do ERISA and the Bankruptcy Code Conflict as to Whether a Debtor's Interest in or Rights Under a Qualified Plan Can be Used to Pay Claims?, 61 Am.Bankr.L.J. 301, 317 (1987)(noting inconsistency if "a creditor could not reach a debtor-participant's plan right or interest in a garnishment or other collection action outside of a bankruptcy case but indirectly could reach the plan right or interest by filing a petition ... to place the debtor in bankruptcy involuntarily").

Our holding also gives full and appropriate effect to ERISA's goal of protecting pension benefits. See 29 U.S.C. §§ 1001(b) and (c). This Court has described that goal as one of ensuring that "if a worker has been promised a defined pension benefit upon retirement—and if he has fulfilled whatever conditions are required to obtain a vested benefit—he actually will receive it." Nachman Corp. v. Pension Benefit Guaranty Corp., 446 U.S. 359, 375, 100 S.Ct. 1723, 1733, 64 L.Ed.2d 354 (1980). In furtherance of these principles, we recently declined in *Guidry*, notwithstanding strong equitable considerations to the contrary, to recognize an implied exception to ERISA's anti-alienation provision that would have allowed a labor union to impose a constructive trust on the pension benefits of a corrupt union official. We explained:

> "Section 206(d) reflects a considered congressional policy choice, a decision to safeguard a stream of income for pensioners (and their dependents, who may be and perhaps usually are, blameless), even if that decision prevents others from securing relief for the wrongs done them. If exceptions to this policy are to be made, it is for Congress to undertake that task." 493 U.S., at 376, 110 S.Ct., at 1733.

These considerations apply with equal, if not greater, force in the present context.

Finally, our holding furthers another important policy underlying ERISA: uniform national treatment of pension benefits. See Fort Halifax Packing Co. v. Coyne, 482 U.S. 1, 9, 107 S.Ct. 2211, 2216, 96 L.Ed.2d 1 (1987). Construing "applicable nonbankruptcy law" to include federal law ensures that the security of a debtor's pension benefits will be governed by ERISA, not left to the vagaries of state spendthrift trust law.

IV

In light of our conclusion that a debtor's interest in an ERISA-qualified pension plan may be excluded from the property of the bankruptcy estate pursuant to § 541(c)(2), we need not reach respondent's alternative argument that his interest in the Plan qualifies for exemption under § 522(b)(2)(A).

The judgment of the Court of Appeals is affirmed.

It is so ordered.

JUSTICE SCALIA, concurring.

The Court's opinion today, which I join, prompts several observations.

When the phrase "applicable nonbankruptcy law" is considered in isolation, the phenomenon that three Courts of Appeals could have thought it a synonym for "state law" is mystifying. When the phrase is considered together with the rest of the Bankruptcy Code (in which Congress chose to refer to state law as, logically enough, "state law"), the phenomenon calls into question whether our legal culture has so far departed from attention to text, or is so lacking in agreed-upon methodology for creating and interpreting text, that it no longer makes sense to talk of "a government of laws, not of men."

Speaking of agreed-upon methodology: It is good that the Court's analysis today proceeds on the assumption that use of the phrases "state law" and "applicable nonbankruptcy law" in other provisions of the Bankruptcy Code is highly relevant to whether "applicable nonbankruptcy law" means "state law" in § 541(c)(2), since consistency of usage within the same statute is to be presumed. This application of a normal and obvious principle of statutory construction would not merit comment, except that we explicitly rejected it, in favor of a one-subsection-at-a-time approach, when interpreting another provision of this very statute earlier this Term. See Dewsnup v. Timm, 502 U.S. 410, ___, 112 S.Ct. 773, ___, 116 L.Ed.2d 903 (1992)(Scalia, J., dissenting). "We express no opinion," our decision said, "as to whether the words [at issue] have different meaning in other provisions of the Bankruptcy Code." I trust that in our search for a neutral and rational interpretive methodology we have now come to rest, so that the symbol of our profession may remain the scales, not the see-saw.

Notes and Questions

1. Justice Scalia is getting cranky in his old age, not so?

2. Assume that a plastic surgeon, who has done thousands of breast implants between 1980 and 1992 comes to you in July of 1992. He anticipates many malpractice suits from those operations. He currently has $1,000,000 in his ERISA Keogh plan; a financial advisor has suggested that he liquidate his Keogh plan and put the money in an individual retirement account because such accounts are exempt under the state law where he practices. What do you advise?

THE INTERSECTION OF FRAUDULENT CONVEYANCE AND EXEMPTION RULES

SMILEY v. FIRST NATIONAL BANK OF BELLEVILLE

United States Court of Appeals, Seventh Circuit, 1989.
864 F.2d 562.

WILL, SENIOR DISTRICT JUDGE.

Plaintiffs, creditors of defendants C. Ritchey Smiley and his wife Marie W. Smiley, filed involuntary Chapter 7 bankruptcy proceedings against the Smileys and subsequently objected to their discharge. The bankruptcy court discharged Marie Smiley but refused to discharge Mr. Smiley. The district court affirmed and Mr. Smiley appealed. We affirm.

I. FACTUAL BACKGROUND.

Defendant Smiley was a businessman in O'Fallon, Illinois who owned a real estate development company, an insurance agency, a travel agency and one-half of another real estate company called Remax. As a result of the high interest rates and general decline in the real estate market in 1983 and 1984, Mr. Smiley's businesses fell on hard times. Defendant's wife, Marie Smiley, had wanted for some period of time to leave the O'Fallon area to be closer to one of her daughters in either Kansas or Texas. Because of the declining business conditions and because he wanted to escape any embarrassment to his wife and mother from his business failures, Mr. Smiley shared his wife's desire to leave.

In July of 1984, the Smileys were visiting their daughter in Kansas and looked at homes there. In September of 1984, the Smileys' search became more serious, and on November 7, 1984, the Smileys' daughter signed on their behalf a contract to purchase a house in Prairie Village, Kansas. The closing on the purchase took place on November 15. The purchase price of approximately $380,000 was financed by taking out a second mortgage on the Smileys' O'Fallon residence (which raised it from $52,000 to $210,000), by taking out a $200,000 loan from Citizens Bank & Trust of Shawnee, Kansas secured by Mr. Smiley's interest in a promissory note from Yong B. and Anne Kim ("the Kim Note") and by taking out a $36,500 loan against one of Mr. Smiley's life insurance policies.

Mr. Smiley carried out a set of transactions in preparation for the purchase of the Kansas home and for resolving his financial difficulties. On October 30, 1984, the Smileys deeded their property in O'Fallon to their daughter's corporation, Lynk, Inc., for two alleged purposes: to make it easier to finance their Kansas home and to prevent any one creditor from obtaining a preference. In early November, the title to the O'Fallon house was returned to the Smileys. Mr. Smiley, along with his attorney, Mr. Bold, met with all of his creditors on October 31, 1984 to discuss Mr. Smiley's financial problems. Mr. Smiley said that he would like to keep his home and estimated that the creditors should receive about forty cents on the dollar if they agreed to a voluntary work out.

At the next creditors' meeting on November 16, which took place after the purchase of the Kansas home, Mr. Bold presented the Smileys' plan of liquidation. Three of the assets discussed were those which made the purchase of the Kansas house possible: the life insurance, the Kim Note and the O'Fallon home. Mr. Smiley represented that the life insurance policy had a cash surrender value of between $4,000 and $7,000, although its actual cash surrender value was $36,000, and indicated that its entire value (minus enough to pay premiums for one year) was available to the creditors. He proposed to sell or borrow against the Smileys' one-third interest in the Kim Note and make one half of its proceeds available to the creditors. Finally, the creditors were informed that the Smileys wanted to keep their home, which was subject to a $52,000 mortgage (the O'Fallon residence). The creditors rejected the November 16 proposal and suggested that Mr. Smiley make a new one.

Neither Mr. Smiley nor Mr. Bold told the creditors at the November 16 meeting about the purchase of the Kansas home or about the various means of financing its purchase. When questioned at the bankruptcy hearing about the nondisclosures, Mr. Smiley stated that the purchase did not affect the Smileys' assets and that he understood that Mr. Bold would send an explanation to Mr. Lowery (the attorney for the creditors). The three assets discussed above are part of a total of $2,288,857 in assets subject to $2,614,262 in liabilities, as reflected in the bankruptcy schedules eventually filed by the Smileys.

After the November 16 meeting, the Smileys moved to the Kansas house bringing with them some of their personal property. The Smileys moved the rest of their personal property within one week. Within a few days, the creditors discovered the remortgage of the O'Fallon property and filed an involuntary bankruptcy petition on November 21.

The Smileys did not contest the petition, but filed bankruptcy schedules on February 1, 1985 claiming that the entire value of the Kansas home, as well as their personal property, car and insurance policies, were exempt pursuant to Kansas exemption law. Kans.Stat. Ann. §§ 40–711, 60–2301, 60–2304 (1987). The bankruptcy trustee objected to the Kansas exemptions, and the bankruptcy court determined that 11 U.S.C. § 522(b)(2)(A)(1982) required the Smileys to claim their exemptions based on Illinois and not Kansas law, because of the short length of their residence in Kansas. The Illinois homestead exemption is limited to $7500. Ill.Rev.Stat. ch. 110, para. 12–901 (1984).

As a result, the creditors were returned to a similar position than the one they were in before the purchase of the Kansas house with regard to the Smileys' assets. The only loss they experienced because of the Smileys' attempt to obtain the Kansas exemptions was a $20,000 loss on the sale of the Kansas house purchased by the Smileys for approximately $380,000 and sold by the bankruptcy trustee for approximately $360,000.

The bankruptcy court pointed out in its decision that the denial of discharge under Section 727(a)(2)(A) requires not only proof of a transfer of non-exempt to exempt property, but also proof of actual intent to hinder, delay or defraud a creditor. The court also concluded that proof that the creditors were actually hindered, delayed or defrauded is not required. The Smileys' behavior after their creditors began to discuss repayment was not, according to the court, satisfactorily explained, and the court resolved that Mr. Smiley intended to conceal assets from the Smileys' creditors in violation of Section 727. Because of Mrs. Smiley's lack of knowledge of Mr. Smiley's business affairs, the court discharged her. On appeal, the district court affirmed the bankruptcy court's decision denying discharge of Mr. Smiley.

II. Discussion.

The bankruptcy court's denial of discharge relied on 11 U.S.C. § 727(a)(2)(A)(1982) which provides in part:

(a) The court shall grant the debtor a discharge, unless—

* * *

(2) the debtor, with intent to hinder, delay, or defraud a creditor or an officer of the estate charged with custody of property under this title, has transferred, removed, destroyed, mutilated, or concealed, or has permitted to be transferred, removed, destroyed, mutilated, or concealed—

(A) property of the debtor, within one year before the date of the filing of the petition; * * *

There is no dispute that the conversions of assets were authorized by the debtor, Mr. Smiley, or that they were carried out within a year before the date that the involuntary petition was filed. The only two elements at issue are: (1) whether Mr. Smiley's property was "transferred, removed, destroyed, mutilated, or concealed" within the meaning of the statute and (2) whether Mr. Smiley intended "to hinder, delay, or defraud" his creditors.

Whether property of the debtor was transferred, removed, destroyed, mutilated, or concealed.

The bankruptcy court concluded, without discussion, that the Smileys had by their actions transferred, removed, destroyed, mutilated, or concealed property. (Slip op. at 9). The reference to Mr. Smiley's "intent to conceal assets * * *," *id.* at 13, is part of the court's discussion of intent "to hinder, delay, or defraud" and therefore does not indicate how the Smileys' acts should be classified. Mr. Smiley argues that no transfer or concealment occurred, because his attempt to exchange non-exempt for exempt property failed. Brief of Appellant–Defendant at 38–43. In support of this argument, Mr. Smiley cites *Liller Bldg. Co. v. Reynolds,* 247 F. 90 (4th Cir.1917) and *In re Adeeb,* 787 F.2d 1339 (9th Cir.1986).

In *Liller,* the debtor attempted to shield personal assets by placing them in corporate form. The court determined that the corporate assets were not exempt but that because the assets were never beyond the reach of the creditors or outside the jurisdiction of the bankruptcy court, they were never transferred within the meaning of the bankruptcy statute. Mr. Smiley urges us to apply the *Liller* court's reasoning to his case and conclude that he made no transfers, since his failure to qualify for the Kansas exemptions meant that those assets were never effectively removed from the reach of the creditors or the jurisdiction of the bankruptcy court. However, we find that the narrow definition for "transfer" relied upon by the *Liller* court can no longer be the law since the Bankruptcy Reform Act took effect. Under that Act, "transfer" is defined as "every mode, direct or indirect, absolute or conditional, voluntary or involuntary, of disposing of or parting with property or with an interest in property, including retention of title as a security interest and foreclosure of the debtor's equity of redemption * * * " 11 U.S.C. § 101(50)(1982).

The Senate Report referring to this definitional section provides:

[a] transfer is a disposition of an interest in property. The definition of transfer is as broad as possible. Many of the potentially limiting words in current law are deleted, and the language is simplified. Under this definition, any transfer of an interest in property is a transfer, including a transfer of possession, custody, or control even if there is not transfer of title, because possession, custody, and control are interests in property. A deposit in a bank account or similar account is a transfer. (citation omitted)

The $158,000 additional mortgage on the O'Fallon residence, the pledging of the Kim Note to secure a $200,000 loan and the borrowing of an additional $36,500 on his life insurance constitute transfers under the present statutory definition, whether the Smileys were ultimately successful in getting the assets classified as exempt or not. * * * The decision about whether a person's property is exempt is separate from and subsequent to the question of whether any transfers were made. That conclusion is consistent with the holding of the *Adeeb* court.

In *Adeeb,* the debtor transferred assets for no consideration to friends and then, on the advice of a bankruptcy attorney, reversed almost all of the transfers before his creditors filed an involuntary bankruptcy petition. The court held that a debtor "may not be denied discharge of his debts if he reveals the transfers to his creditors, recovers substantially all of the property *before he files his bankruptcy petition,* and is otherwise qualified for a discharge." 787 F.2d at 1345 (emphasis added).

The debtor in *Adeeb* had made a mistake which he corrected before filing for bankruptcy so that his creditors would not be prejudiced. In the present case, Mr. Smiley made no attempt to undo all his transfers either before or after the bankruptcy petition was filed. The only asset which he retransferred before the bankruptcy petition was filed was the title to the O'Fallon residence, subject to the additional mortgage. The transfers previously discussed are sufficient for purposes of section 727. The policy behind the *Adeeb* decision—to "encourage[ ]debtors to reveal transfers and to attempt to recover property previously transferred," *id.* at 1345, is not applicable here where property was recovered only as a result of the action of the bankruptcy trustee and court.

Whether Mr. Smiley intended to hinder, delay, or defraud his creditors.

A debtor may retain as personal property assets which are exempted from the bankruptcy estate under the state or local law of the debtor's domicile. Conversions of assets from non-exempt to exempt forms within the year preceding a petition for bankruptcy are not necessarily fraudulent to creditors. * * * The House and Senate Reports regarding the 1978 revision of the Bankruptcy Code provide:

> As under current law, the debtor will be permitted to convert nonexempt property into exempt property before filing a bankruptcy petition. The practice is not fraudulent as to creditors, and permits the debtor to make full use of the exemptions to which he is entitled under the law.

* * * To deny discharge, a court must find proof of the debtor's actual intent to defraud, but that finding may be inferred from the circumstances of the debtor's conduct. A bankruptcy court's finding that a debtor acted with intent to hinder, delay, or defraud is a factual determination that may be reversed only if it is clearly erroneous.

Courts have come to different conclusions about what constitutes an intent to hinder, delay, or defraud under 11 U.S.C. § 727(a)(2). Some courts have denied discharge upon a finding that at least part of the debtor's motivation for obtaining exempt property was to keep assets away from creditors. *See, e.g., In re Schwingle,* 15 B.R. 291, 294–95 (W.D.Wis.1981); *In re Ford,* 53 B.R. 444, 450 (W.D.Va.1984)(upholding denial of discharge because the bankruptcy court "concluded that the primary motivation for the conversion was [the debtor's] intention to remove the real estate from the creditor's reach ..."), *aff'd sub nom. Ford v. Poston,* 773 F.2d 52 (4th Cir.1985).

One commentator has pointed out that a debtor's desire to acquire a particular asset could theoretically be distinguished from his or her intent to shield assets, but that practically debtors have mixed motives for acquiring exempt assets (to buy a new house, for instance, and to shield assets from creditors). * * * However, a rule which denies discharge where a debtor's motive is to shield assets rewards debtors for ignorance of the law and penalizes knowledgeable debtors for taking advantage of their full rights under the law. A second group of courts has relied on the policy behind bankruptcy exemptions of protecting debtors from destitution in resolving that the bankruptcy courts should set a limit on the amount of assets which debtors may shield prior to bankruptcy.[1]

A third group of courts disregards both the actual amount claimed as exempt and any evidence that the debtor is motivated by a desire to shield assets. Those courts deny discharge only where the debtor has committed some act extrinsic to the conversion which hinders, delays or defrauds. * * * We agree with the foregoing decisions that we should not prohibit a debtor's full use of exemptions within the limits of the law.

We, therefore, find it irrelevant that Mr. Smiley stood to gain a large amount of money from his creditors had his Kansas exemptions been upheld. In addition, his knowledge of Kansas exemption law is irrelevant, since we do not find bankruptcy planning necessarily to be a fraud on creditors. We look, however, for extrinsic signs of fraud. Such signs include:

> (1) that the debtor obtained credit in order to purchase exempt property; (2) that the conversion occurred after the entry of a large judgment against the debtor; (3) that the debtor had engaged in a pattern of sharp dealing prior to bankruptcy; * * * and [(4)] that the conversion rendered the debtor insolvent.

4 *Collier on Bankruptcy,* ¶ 727.02[3] at 19–20 (15th ed. 1986) (footnotes omitted).

Although the bankruptcy court found that Mr. Smiley's course of conduct was evidence of fraud, he did not exhibit sharp dealing such as that shown by the debtor in the case of *In re Reed,* 700 F.2d 986 (5th Cir.1983). The *Reed* court wrote, that "Reed's whole pattern of conduct evinces that intent [to defraud]." * * * After obtaining an agreement from his creditors to postpone collection of his debts, Reed borrowed money to augment his antique collection. He set up a separate bank account opened without the knowledge of his creditors in which he deposited his business receipts. He repaid from that account the money he had borrowed to buy the antiques. In addition to the antiques, Reed accumulated other personal assets and then sold all of them for less than fair market value. He transferred the proceeds to exempt property by applying them towards the mortgages on his house. Reed's entire course of conduct evidenced that he intended not only to take advantage of his exemption rights, but that he intended to deceive his creditors into

---

1. In the case of *In re Reed,* 11 B.R. 683, 688 (Bankr.N.D.Tex.1981), the Texas bankruptcy court wrote,

> From the legislative history and from further comments in the cited paragraph in Colliers [3 *Colliers on Bankruptcy* ¶ 522.08[4] at 40–41 (15th ed. 1987)] it appears that the basis for that law which permits the conversion of non-exempt property to exempt property * * * is that that result is necessary in order to furnish the "fresh start" and to provide the debtor with minimum exemptions * * *. There can be scant support for that position in Texas, however, where the homestead exemption reaches to infinity.

Accord, Norwest Bank Nebraska, N.A. v. Tveten, 848 F.2d 871, 876 (8th Cir.1988); *In re Collins,* 19 B.R. 874, 877 (Bankr. M.D.Fla.1982); *In re Zouhar,* 10 B.R. 154, 157 (Bankr.D.N.M.1981).

thinking that there would be assets available to them when, in fact, Reed was converting every one of his assets to an exempt form.

Even though Mr. Smiley's conduct is distinguishable from the pattern of sharp dealing shown by Mr. Reed, it is similar to Mr. Reed's conduct in one important respect. The unlimited homestead exemption in states such as Texas and Kansas provides an incentive for debtors such as Mr. Smiley and Mr. Reed to keep their creditors in the dark about their conversion activities. Both Mr. Smiley and Mr. Reed made efforts to hide the conversion of assets from their creditors. Mr. Smiley purchased the Kansas property without revealing the transaction to his creditors although he met with them the day after the closing. However, a finding of fraud requires more than a failure to volunteer information. * * *

At the time of the November 16, 1984 meeting with his creditors, however, Mr. Smiley not only failed to volunteer information, but he misrepresented the value of his assets. He told his creditors that his assets included the full value of the O'Fallon house, the Kim Note and the life insurance policies, even though those assets had already been very substantially encumbered in order to purchase the Kansas home. In addition, Mr. Smiley told the creditors that the life insurance policy had a much lower cash surrender value than it actually had. In the *Reed* case, the debtor's actions and representations deceived his creditors and kept them from seeking payment. Similarly, in this case, Mr. Smiley's statements that his assets, in their unencumbered form, were available to his creditors kept them from filing an involuntary petition until they discovered by their own effort the additional mortgage on the O'Fallon property.

Since Mr. Smiley was trying to take advantage of legal exemptions, it is not clear that he intended to *defraud* his creditors. Nevertheless, it is at least a reasonable inference to draw from his behavior that he intended to hinder and delay them. He had every incentive to keep the creditors from filing bankruptcy until he could establish Kansas residency so that he could take advantage of the Kansas exemptions. Mr. Smiley's discharge must be denied pursuant to Section 727 because it is clear that he intended to hinder or delay his creditors, even if he had no intent to defraud them. * * *

When Mr. Smiley filed his statement of financial assets as required by 11 U.S.C. § 521 (1982), he made a full disclosure and claimed exemptions under Kansas law. However, this disclosure did not reverse the transfers or show that Mr. Smiley meant to reverse the effect of his earlier misrepresentations. It is laudable that Mr. Smiley ultimately did not try to conceal assets on his bankruptcy schedules, but he was simply attempting to take advantage of the Kansas exemptions. The disclosure does not alter the reasonable conclusion of the bankruptcy judge that Mr. Smiley on November 16 had acted with the intent to hinder or delay discovery of his impaired assets.

Mr. Smiley's creditors were ultimately harmed by his misrepresentation at most to the extent of $20,000, but proof of harm is not a required element of a cause of action under Section 727. * * * All of the cited cases, except for *Adeeb* and *Harris*, are cases where the misrepresentations which led to denial of discharge were made under oath on a petition for discharge. But where there is a material misrepresentation the degree of dishonesty is not measured. * * * In addition, a fair reading of the statute makes it clear that so long as there is an *intent* to hinder, delay, or defraud, in combination with an act such as a transfer, then a debtor should be denied the privilege of discharge. The statute does not provide that the creditors must have, in fact, been hindered, delayed or defrauded.

III. Conclusion.

On or before November 15, 1984, the day he closed the purchase of a new residence in Kansas, Mr. Smiley increased the mortgage on his Illinois residence by $158,000, pledged his interest in the Kim Note to secure a personal loan of $200,000 and borrowed an additional $36,500 on his life insurance. All of the foregoing proceeds were used to purchase the Kansas residence.

Under the current provisions of 11 U.S.C. § 727, each of these constituted a transfer since they involved "disposing of or parting with * * * an interest in property * * * " That conclusion is consistent with the Congressional intent to make the definition of transfer "as broad as possible."

On November 16, 1984, Mr. Smiley and his counsel met with creditors. At no time during that meeting was there any disclosure of the additional mortgage of $158,000 on the O'Fallon, Illinois residence, the pledging of the Kim Note as collateral for the $200,000 personal note or the additional loan on the life insurance policy. Nor was it disclosed that, on the previous day, the proceeds from these transactions had been used to purchase a residence in Kansas which he believed would be exempt from his creditors' claims. On the contrary, Mr. Smiley misrepresented the value of the three assets and their availability to satisfy his creditors' claims.

The bankruptcy court found and the district court affirmed that Mr. Smiley's actions were motivated by an intent to hinder, delay, or defraud his creditors by concealing or transferring assets. That finding is clearly correct. What Mr. Smiley was obviously doing, while he sought to qualify for the Kansas exemption, was delaying his creditors from filing an involuntary petition, which they did when they discovered the second mortgage on the O'Fallon property.

Since there were both transfers and an intent to hinder, delay, or defraud his creditors, the district court's affirmance of the bankruptcy court's denial of Mr. Smiley's discharge was clearly correct under Section 727 and is affirmed. (citations omitted)

Notes and Questions

1. Reconsider Problem 10–8 on page 747 *infra* in view of the *Smiley* case.

2. What kind of evidence, other than that provided in *Smiley* would show an intention to "hinder, delay, and defraud"? (Is the mere coincidence of the transfer and the filing of bankruptcy sufficient?)

3. Assume that the trustee calls the debtor's lawyer as a witness and asks whether the lawyer met with the debtor shortly before the transfer and, if so, whether the lawyer advised transferring assets into exempt property. Can the lawyer refuse to answer either or both questions on the grounds of privilege?

*

Index

References are to Chapters and Sections

ADEQUATE PROTECTION
Equity cushion, 4–4.
Lifting of automatic stay, 4–4.
Value of collateral, 4–5.

ADMINISTRATIVE EXPENSES
See, also, Priority of Creditors.
In general, 8–2.
Environmental claims, 8–4.
Postpetition priority, 5–5.
Postpetition trade creditors, 5–1, 5–4.

ADMINISTRATIVE POWERS
In general, 5–1.
Adequate protection 4–4, 4–5.
Automatic stay, 4–1, 4–2, 4–3, 4–4.
Obtaining postpetition credit, 5–5.
Paying creditors and suppliers, 5–4.
Sales out of ordinary course, 5–2.
Use of cash collateral, 5–3.

ASSETS
See, also, Exemptions.
Protection, see Automatic Stay.
Sale by debtor, 5–2.
Seizure, 1–2.

ASSIGNMENT
For the benefit of creditors, 1–4.
Wage assignment, 1–4.

AUTOMATIC STAY
Adequate protection, 4–4.
Application to co-debtors under Chapter 13, 10–3.
Exceptions, 4–1, 4–2.
Lifting, 4–4.
Parties affected, 4–3.
Reach, 4–2.
Roadmap to Bankruptcy Code section 362, 4–1.
Scope, 4–1.

AVOIDANCE POWERS
In general, 7–1.
Fraudulent conveyances, 7–6.
Postpetition transactions, 7–7.
Preferences, 7–3.
Rejection of executory contracts, 6–2.
Setoff, 7–4.
Subordination, 7–5.

AVOIDANCE POWERS—Cont'd
Trustee as lien creditor, 7–2.

BANKRUPTCY CODE
See, also, Chapter . . .
In general, 2–3.
Goals of, 2–1.
History, 2–2.
Interpretation, 2–5.
Number of filings, 2–2.
Purposes, 2–1.

BANKRUPTCY COURT
Jurisdiction, 3–1.
Jury trials, 3–3.
Venue, 3–2.

CASH COLLATERAL, 5–3.

CHAPTER 3 (Bankruptcy Code)
See, also, Administrative Powers.
In general, 2–3.

CHAPTER 5 (Bankruptcy Code)
See, also, Avoidance Powers; Exemptions.
In general, 2–3.

CHAPTER 7 (Bankruptcy Code)
In general, 2–3 and Chapter 10.
Compared to Chapter 13, 10–1.
Discharge, 10–1, 10–2.
Life of typical case, 2–6.
Liquidation, 10–2.
Proof of claim, 8–1.
Reaffirmation, 10–2.
Redemption, 10–2.
Value of claim, 8–2.

CHAPTER 9 (Bankruptcy Code)
In general, 2–3.

CHAPTER 11 (Bankruptcy Code)
See, also, Administrative Powers; Plan of Reorganization Under Chapter 11.
In general, 2–3, 9–1.
Claim recognition, 8–1.
Compared to Chapter 7 for individual debtors, 9–9.
Creditors' committees, 2–4.
Debtor in possession, 5–1, 9–1.

767

References are to Chapters and Sections

CHAPTER 11 (Bankruptcy Code)—Cont'd
Disclosure statement, 9–7.
Individual debtors, 9–9.
Life of typical case, 2–6.
Procedure, 8–1.
Rejection of collective bargaining agreements, 6–4.
Valuation under, 4–5.

CHAPTER 13 (Bankruptcy Code)
In general, 2–3 and Chapter 10.
Co-debtor stay, 10–3.
Compared to Chapter 7, 10–1.
Confirmation of plan, 10–3.
Consumer plans, 10–1.
Creditor objections to plan, 10–3.
Discrimination between creditor classes, 10–3.
Eligibility, 10–3.
Exemptions, 10–4.
Life of typical case, 2–6.
Modification of secured claim, 10–3.
Proof of claim, 8–1.
Trustee appointment, duties, payment, 10–3.

CLAIMS
See, also, Priority of Creditors.
Allowance, 8–1.
Classification, 9–4.
Definition, under Bankruptcy Code, 2–5.
Discharge, 8–1.
Distribution, 8–6.
Environmental, 8–4.
Impaired, 9–3.
Origination, 8–5.
Secured, 8–2.
Subordination, 7–5.
Tort, 8–4, 8–5.
Unamortized original issue discount, 8–3.
Unsecured, 8–3.
Valuation, 8–5, 8–6.

CODEBTORS
See, also, Entireties; Partnerships.
Stay under Chapter 13, 10–3.

COLLATERAL
Cross-collateralization, 5–5.
Value of, 4–5.

COLLECTIVE BARGAINING AGREEMENTS, 6–4.

CONFIRMATION OF PLANS
See Chapter 13; Plan of Reorganization Under Chapter 11.

CONSUMER DEBT
See, also, Chapter 7; Chapter 13; Exemptions.
Consumer plans under Chapter 13, 10–1.
Discharge, 10–1.
Fair Debt Collection Practices Act, 1–8.
Formal collection of, 1–8.
Liquidation under Chapter 7, 10–2.

CONSUMER DEBT—Cont'd
Reaffirmation, 10–1.

CRAMDOWN
In general, 9–1, 9–5.
Under Chapter 13, 10–3.

CREDITORS' COMMITTEE
In general, 2–4.
Action by, 6–4.

CREDITORS' RIGHTS
See, also, Consumer Debt; Exemptions; Secured Claim, Formal collection of; Unsecured Claim, Formal collection of.
Debtor liability, 1–2.
Informal debt collection, 1–7, 1–8.
Setoff, 7–4.

DEBTOR IN POSSESSION
See, also, Administrative Powers.
In general, 2–4, 9–1.
Administrative powers, 5–1.
Cash Collateral, 5–4.
Chapter 11 transformation, 5–1.
Postpetition credit, 5–5.

DEFAULT, 1–3.

DISCHARGE
Exemptions, 10–1, 10–2, 10–4.
Reaffirmation, 10–1, 10–2.

DISCRIMINATION
Against former bankrupts, 10–2.
Between classes of creditors under Chapter 13, 10–3.

ENTIRETIES
In general, 1–2.
Creditors' rights, 1–2.

EXECUTORY CONTRACTS
In general, 6–1.
Assignability, 6–1.
Characterization, 6–2.
Collective bargaining agreements, 6–4.
Franchising agreements, 6–3.
Leases, 6–3.
Personal service contracts, 6–2.

EXEMPTIONS
In general, 1–2, 10–1, 10–4.
Avoidance of liens, 10–4.
Federal exemption law, 10–4.
Federal-state exemption election, 10–4.
Intersection of exemption rules and fraudulent conveyances, 10–4.
Limits, generally 1–2.
Pension plans, 10–4.
Retirement benefits, 10–4.
Spendthrift trusts, 1–2, 10–4.
State exemption law, 10–4.

FRAUDULENT CONVEYANCES
In general, 7–6.

INDEX

References are to Chapters and Sections

FRAUDULENT CONVEYANCES—Cont'd
Intercompany guarantee agreements, 7–6.
Intersection of fraudulent conveyances and exemption rules, 10–4.
Leveraged buyouts, 7–6.
Mercantile fraudulent conveyances, 7–6.
Proof of intent, 7–6.
Sufficiency of consideration, 7–6.

HISTORY AND PURPOSES OF BANKRUPTCY LEGISLATION, 2–1, 2–2.

JUDGES
Bankruptcy judge, 2–4.

JURISDICTION
Bankruptcy court jurisdiction, 3–1.
Enforcement of reorganization plan, 9–8.
Jury trials in bankruptcy cases, 3–3.

LEASES
Assignability, 6–1, 6–3.
Assumption, rejection of, 6–1, 6–2, 6–3.
Balancing interests, 6–3.
Distinguished from security interests, 6–2.

LENDER LIABILITY, 1–7.

LEVERAGED BUYOUTS, 7–6.

LIABILITY OF DEBTORS
Joint, 1–2.
Nature of, 1–2.
Partnership, 1–2.
Several, 1–2.

LIENS
Definitions, 2–5.
Equitable lien, 7–2.
Judicial lien, 1–4.
Preference protection, 7–3.
Statutory lien, 1–4.

LIFTING OF AUTOMATIC STAY
See Automatic Stay.

LIQUIDATION
Prior to confirmation of plan, 5–2.
Under Chapter 7, 10–2.

PARTNERSHIPS
In general, 1–2.
Automatic stay, application to, 4–3.
Uniform Partnership Act, 1–2.
Venue problems, 3–2.

PERFECTION OF SECURITY INTERESTS, 7–2.

PLAN OF REORGANIZATION UNDER CHAPTER 11
See, also, Administrative Powers; Chapter 11.
In general, 9–1.
Best interest test, 9–5.
Classification of claims, 9–4.
Competing plans, 9–2.
Confirmation, 9–1, 9–5, 9–7.

PLAN OF REORGANIZATION UNDER CHAPTER 11—Cont'd
Cramdown, 9–1, 9–5.
Disclosure statement, 9–7.
Example, 9–1.
Exclusivity period, 9–2.
"Fair and equitable" requirement, 9–5.
Feasibility, 9–5.
Impairment of claims, 9–3.
Modification, 9–8.
Negotiation, 9–1.
New value, 9–6.
Plan of reorganization under Chapter 13, See Chapter 13.
Post-confirmation, 9–8.
Postpetition, 9–2.
Pre-packaged plan, 9–7.
Rejection, 9–5.
Sale of assets prior to confirmation, 5–2.
Solicitation of acceptance/rejection, 9–7.
Voting, 8–1, 8–5, 9–3, 9–7.

POSTPETITION TRANSACTIONS
Avoidance, 7–7.
Obtaining Credit, 5–5.
Priority, 5–1, 5–5.
Under Chapter 11, 9–2.

PREFERENCES
See also, Avoidance Powers; Priority of Creditors; Timing of Transfers; Voidable Preferences.
In general, 7–3.

PRESENT VALUE, 9–4.

PRIORITY OF CREDITORS
In general, 1–6.
Administrative expenses, 5–1, 5–4, 5–5, 8–2.
Breached executory contracts, 6–1.
Cross-collateralization, 5–5.
Environmental claims, 8–4.
Favored creditors under Chapter 11, 9–4.
New value exception, 9–6.
Postpetition, 5–1, 5–5.
Secured creditors, 8–2.
Subordination, 7–5.
Super-priority, 5–5.
Unsecured claims, 8–3.
Voidable preferences, 7–3.

PROPERTY OF THE ESTATE, 4–2.

REAFFIRMATION, 10–1, 10–2.

REDEMPTION, 10–2.

REMEDIES
See Creditors' Rights.

REORGANIZATION PLAN
See Plan of Reorganization Under Chapter 11.

RETIREMENT BENEFITS
See Exemptions.

SECURED CLAIM
    See, also, Priority of Creditors.
    In general, 1–5.
Adequate protection, 4–4.
Claim priority, 8–2.
Election to be treated as fully secured, 9–5.
Formal collection of, 1–5.
Modification under Chapter 13, 10–3.

SECURITY INTEREST
    In general, 1–5.
As voidable preference, 7–3.
Distinguished from lease, 6–2.

SETOFF, 7–4.

SHAREHOLDERS
Absolute priority rule, 9–6.
Leveraged buyouts, 7–6.
New value, 9–6.

STAY
See Automatic Stay.

SUBORDINATION
    In general, 1–5, 7–5.
Consensual subordination, 7–5.
Court ordered equitable subordination, 7–5.

TIMING OF TRANSFERS
Judicial liens, 7–3.
Security transactions, 7–3.
Substantially contemporaneous transactions, 7–3.

TORT CLAIMS, 8–4, 8–5.

TRUSTEE
    In general, 2–4.
Chapter 7, appointment, 10–2.
Chapter 13, appointment, duties, payment, 10–3.
Duties, 2–4.
Lien creditor and purchaser, trustee as, 7–2.
U.S. trustee, 2–4.

UNSECURED CLAIM
    In general, 8–3.
Cross-collateralization, 5–5.
Formal collection of, 1–4.

VALUE OF CREDITORS' INTERESTS
Adequate protection of, 4–4.
Claim value, 8–2, 8–5, 8–6.
Collateral value, 4–5, 8–2.
Methods of valuation, 4–5, 8–6.
Present value, 9–4.

VENUE
Bankruptcy court, 3–2.
Cases, 3–2.
Proceedings, 3–2.
Transfer, 3–2.

VOIDABLE PREFERENCES
    See also, Avoidance Powers.
    In general, 7–3.
Payments for the benefit of insiders, 7–3.
Timing of transfers, 7–3.

†